International Organizations and the Law of the Sea

Documentary Yearbook 1995

Issued by
The Netherlands Institute for the Law of the Sea (NILOS)

Volume 11, 1995

MARTINUS NIJHOFF PUBLISHERS
THE HAGUE / LONDON / BOSTON

Library of Congress Catalog Card Number: 88-440074

British Library Cataloguing in Publication Data
International Organizations and the Law of the Sea : Documentary Yearbook. -Vol. 1 (1985)
1. International Law–Periodicals
I. Netherlands Institute for the Law of the Sea
341.4'5'05 JX4411

ISBN 90-411-0435-6
ISSN 0920-7767

Published by Kluwer Law International,
P.O. Box 85889, 2508 CN The Hague, The Netherlands.

Sold and distributed in the U.S.A. and Canada
by Kluwer Law International,
675 Massachusetts Avenue, Cambridge, MA 02139, U.S.A.

In all other countries, sold and distributed
by Kluwer Law International, Distribution Centre,
P.O. Box 322, 3300 AH Dordrecht, The Netherlands.

Printed on acid-free paper

Kluwer Law International incorporates the publishing programmes of
Graham & Trotman Ltd, Kluwer Law and Taxation Publishers,
and Martinus Nijhoff Publishers.

Printed in the Netherlands

TABLE OF CONTENTS

ADDRESSES

United Nations Publications
Sales Section, 2 United Nations Plaza
Room DC2-853, Dept. 410
New York, N.Y. 10017, USA
Fax: 1-212-963 3489

United Nations Publications
Sales Office and Bookshop
CH-1211 Geneva 10, Switzerland
Fax: 41-22-740 0931

UN Sales publ US: http://www.un.org/Pubs/sales.htm
ICJ: http://www.icj-cij.org

Division for Ocean Affairs
& the Law of the Sea (DOALOS)
Office of Legal Affairs
United Nations
New York, N.Y. 10017, USA
Fax: 1-212-963 5847

Oceans & Coastal Areas
Programme Activity Centre
UNEP
P.O. Box 30552
Nairobi, Kenya
Fax: 254-2-226 890/215 787

DOALOS: http://www.un.org/Depts/los/los_docs.htm

UNCTAD
United Nations Sales Section
Palais des Nations
CH-1211 Geneva 10, Switzerland
Fax: 41-22-907 0043

FAO
Via delle Termi di Caracalla
00100 Rome, Italy
Fax: 39-6-514 6172/579 73152

UNCTAD: http://www.unicc.org/unctad/en/pressref/bublead.htm
FAO: http://www.fao.org/CATALOG/GIPHOME.htm

IAEA
Wagramerstrasse 5
P.O. Box 100
A-1400 Vienna, Austria
Fax: 43-1-234 564

ILO
Publications Division
International Labour Office
CH-1211 Geneva 22, Switzerland
Fax: 41-22-798 8685

IAEA: http://www.iaea.or.at/worldatom/publications/
ILO: http://www.unicc.org/ilo/public/english/180publn/index.htm

IMO
4 Albert Embankment
London SE1 7SR, United Kingdom
Fax: 44-71-587 3210

IOC/UNESCO
7, Place de Fontenoy
75700 Paris, France
Fax: 33-1-405 69316

IMO: http://www.imo.org/imo/pubs/pubstart.htm
IOC/UNESCO: http://www.unesco.org/general/eng/publish/index.htm

WMO
Publications Unit
41, Giuseppe-Motta
Case postale No 2300
CH-1211 Geneva 2, Switzerland
Fax: 41-22-734 2326
http://www.wmo.ch/web/catalogue/NEW%20HTML/frame/frame.html

EDITORS' NOTE

This Volume 11 of *International Organizations and the Law of the Sea - Documentary Yearbook* was again prepared on the basis of experience gained in producing previous volumes and taking into account various comments and suggestions made by members of our Advisory Board and by reviewers.[1] The Volume covers the documents, both legal and non-legal, of the United Nations family of international organizations which are structured along two main categories. In particular, documents of the UN General Assembly, Meeting of States Parties to the 1982 UN Convention on the Law of the Sea (LOS Convention), UN International Sea-Bed Authority, UN Conference on Straddling Fish Stocks and Highly Migratory Fish Stocks, Follow-Up to the UN Global Conference on the Sustainable Development of Small Island Developing States (SIDS), UN ECOSOC, UN ECE, UNEP and UNCTAD are included first. They are followed by the documents of specialized agencies and other autonomous organizations within the UN system that include FAO, IAEA, IMO and UNESCO/IOC. The numerous regional programmes and organizations, a number of which reports annually to the UN General Assembly (UNGA), are covered by documents of the respective global organizations.

The major General Assembly's documents remain the annual Law of the Sea Resolution (50/23) and the Report of the Secretary-General giving an excellent overview of all developments in the context of the new oceans regime. The 1995 Law of the Sea Report was prepared, as every year, by the Division for Ocean Affairs and the Law of the Sea (DOALOS) of the UN Office of Legal Affairs (OLA). The DOALOS operates (since 1 March 1992) in continuation of the UN Office for Ocean Affairs and the Law of the Sea (OALOS). It was headed in 1995 by its distinguished Director Dr. Jean-Pierre Lévy (France), who was succeeded since 1 February 1996 by Dr. Moritaka Hayashi (Japan), as followed since 20 October 1996 by Dr. Ismail Steiner (Tanzania). The DOALOS/OLA is charged with a general mandate to contribute to the better understanding and widespread acceptance of the LOS Convention at national, regional and international levels. The numerous DOALOS publications continue to be only listed in the *Yearbook*, but the reader will find (through the Index of Keywords) a detailed record of DOALOS activities in the abovementioned Report and some other relevant documents.

As a result of deposition of the 60th ratification (by Guyana) during the 48th session of the General Assembly in 1993, the LOS Convention entered into force on 16 November 1994. Prior thereto, further rounds of the UN Secretary-General's Informal Consultations led successfully to the adoption at the resumed 48th session of the General Assembly (by a vote of 121:0:7) of the Resolution 48/263 of 28 July 1994. The UNGA Resolution's Annex contains an Agreement Relating

1 For reviews of Vol. 1 - 1985 (1987) of the *Yearbook*, see E. Decaux, 115 *Journal du Droit International* 282-283 (1988/1); M.I. Glassner, *Political Geography Quarterly* of 8 February 1989; L.A. Kimball, 12 *Marine Policy* 415-416 (1988/4); A.V. Lowe, 3 *International Journal of Estuarine & Coastal Law (IJECL)* (presently, *International Journal of Marine & Coastal Law [IJMCL])* 280-281 (1988/3); Swan Sik Ko, 35 *Netherlands International Law Review* 100-101 (1988/1); R. Wolfrum, 30 *German Yearbook of International Law (GYIL)* 463-464 (1987); also noted in 33 *Annuaire Français de Droit International (AFDI)* 1077 (1987). For reviews of Vol. 2 - 1986 (1988) of the *Yearbook*, see D. Freestone, 4 *IJECL* 310-311 (1989/3); *Lloyd's Maritime Commercial Law Quarterly* (1989). For review of Vol. 3 - 1987 (1989) of the *Yearbook*, see D. Freestone, 6 IJECL 151-153 (1991/2). For joint reviews of Vols 1-5, see B. Boczek, "Basic Sources of Law of the Sea Documentation," 15 *Marine Policy* 455-459 (1991/6), and of Vols 5-6, see E.D. Brown, 17 *Marine Policy* 67 (1993/1), and D. Freestone, 10 *IJMCL* 143-144 (1995). For reviews of Vol.8, see D. Köning, 38 *GYIL* 467 (1995); 40 *AFDI* 1208 (1994). For reviews of Vol.9, see J. Thomas, 3 *OGLTR* 136-7 (1996), and J. Morris, 3 *Int.ML* 110-1 (1996).

to the Implementation of Part XI of the United Nations Convention on the Law of the Sea, with the entry into force of the two instruments having been closely intertwined.[2]

The entry into force of the LOS Convention and the provisional application of the Part XI Agreement as followed by the Agreement's entry into force on 28 July 1996 marked, according to Dr. Moritaka Hayashi, the beginning of a new phase in the functions of the UN Secretary-General with regard to the two instruments.[3] A detailed set of (mostly long-term) mandates for the Secretary-General and, through him, particularly the DOALOS/OLA, include the increased reporting responsibilities, the unprecedented (and distinct from the usual depositary functions) responsibilities pertaining to deposit of charts and geographical coordinates concerning national maritime zones, as well as responsibilities relating to the Commission on the Limits of the Continental Shelf (CLCS), conducting special studies, dispute settlement (including in the context of the ITLOS' establishment), and provision of advice and assistance to states. Other mandates comprise functions relating to other agreements, normal depositary functions, and a number of short-term responsibilities of the UN Secretary-General. By mid-1996, the LOS Convention was in a crucial phase of its evolution because of the rapid move toward universalization of its States Parties; the building of the key institutions (ISBA, ITLOS, CLCS) under the Convention; the consolidation and further strengthening of its regime through the adoption of complementary instruments; and the emerging consensus on the role of the UNGA as the global ocean forum.[4] The ITLOS was inaugurated in Hamburg on 18 October 1996, when the 21 Judges took their oath of office and signed solemn declarations in the presence of the UN Secretary-General Boutros-Ghali, the Secretary-General of ISBA Assembly, Dr. Satya N. Nandan, and other high dignitaries.[5] The first ITLOS President became Dr. Thomas A. Mensah (Ghana) and Vice-President - Dr. Rüdiger Wolfrum (Germany), while the Tribunals Registrar is Mr. Kumar Chitty (Sri Lanka).[6]

The General Assembly's Resolutions reflect the major - new and continuing - issues on the UN agenda, such as Declaring 1998 International Year of the Ocean, zones of peace (Indian Ocean, South Atlantic, Africa), biological diversity, climate change, naval armaments and disarmament, large-scale driftnet (gillnet) fishing, transit of land-locked countries, Universal Congress on the Panama Canal, and actions in the follow-up to the United Nations Conference on Environment and Development (UNCED) that was held on 3-14 June 1992 in Rio de Janeiro, Brazil, and that was assessed by the 1997 Special Session of UNGA on the Overall Review and Appraisal of Agenda 21. These issues find further reflection in documents of relevant organizations, covered by this Volume, in the context of their respective mandates. In follow-up to Chapter 17 of the UNCED Agenda 21,

---

2 See *UN/DOALOS Law of the Sea Bulletin*, Special Issue IV, 16 November 1994, and for status of the Convention and the Part XI Agreement as at 30 May 1997, see *id.* No. 34 (1997). Cf. D.H. Anderson, "Legal Implications of the Entry Into Force of the UN Convention on the Law of the Sea," 44 *International & Comparative Law Quarterly (ICLQ)* 313-326 (1995); Anderson, "Resolution and Agreement Relating to the Implementation of Part XI of the UN Convention on the Law of the Sea: A General Assessment", 55 *ZaöRV* 275-289 (1995); J.P. Lévy, "Les Nations Unies et la Convention sur le droit de la mer," 28 *Revue belge de droit international* 11-35 (1995); M. Hayashi, "Prospects for Universal Acceptance of the Part XI Agreement," 7 *Georgetown International Environmental Law Review (GIELR)* 687-695 (1995); Hayashi, "The 1994 Agreement for the Universalization of the Law of the Sea Convention," 27 *Ocean Development & International Law (ODIL)* 31-39 (1996).

3 M. Hayashi, "The Role of the Secretary-General Under the LOS Convention and the Part XI Agreement," 10 *IJMCL* 157-164 (1995).

4 See M. Hayashi, "The Law of the Sea: The Year in Review," in *A Return to Abundant Seas: Management of Fisheries and the Ocean Environment, Proceedings of the 30th LSI Annual Conference, Al-Ain, Abu Dhabi, 19-22 May 1996* (in press).

5 See *ITLOS Press Release, ITLOS/Press/2*, 18 October 1996.

6 See *Id., ITLOS/Press/1*, 5 October 1996, and *ITLOS/Press/3*, 23 October 1996, respectively. Cf. "International Tribunal Starts Work", 27 *Environmental Policy and Law* 2-4 (1997).

the two major UN Conferences initiated in 1993 were those on the Sustainable Development of SIDS and on Straddling/Highly Migratory Fish Stocks which were meanwhile concluded in 1994 and 1995 respectively. The significance of issues dealt with by the latter UN Conference is reflected by two additional Resolutions (50/549 and 50/552) on unauthorized fishing in zones of national jurisdiction and on fisheries bycatch and discards. At its 6th session, this Conference adopted (without a vote) on 4 August 1995 the text of the Agreement for the Implementation of the Provisions of the UN Convention on the Law of the Sea relating to the Conservation and Management of Straddling Fish Stocks and Highly Migratory Fish Stocks.[7]

The United Nations section contained in this Volume also covers various ocean-related documents submitted individually by states, by means of their Letters to the Secretary-General, on the *Estai* incident occurred on 9 March 1995 in the NAFO Regulatory Area (Spain), the navigational rights and freedoms (Russia and Turkey), and territorial and maritime limits (Turkey and Greece). The *Estai* incident has been a subject of the *Spain v. Canada Fisheries Jurisdiction* case which is presently pending (in the phase of jurisdiction) before the International Court of Justice,[8] whereas the Russian/Turkish[9] and Greco/Turkish[10] exchanges reflect the two ongoing disputes which have been subjected to bilateral negotiations between the respective states. The Russian/Turkish controversy over the Turkish Straits (Strait of Istanbul, Strait of Canakkale and Sea of Marmara) has also been reflected in the debates of the respective IMO bodies which are covered by this Volume. Other reproduced documents of the General Assembly provide the reader with an access to important decisions taken in 1995 by the ASEAN, the Movement of the Non-Aligned Countries, the Group of 77 and the South Pacific Forum. The reproduced ECOSOC documents of 1995 include the Report on Studies and Activities Carried Out During the Period 1993-1994 in regard to a Project for a Europe-Africa Permanent Link Through the Strait of Gibraltar, and the Report of the Meeting held by the Working Group on Maritime Cooperation of the ECOSOC Commission on Narcotic Drugs in 1994-1995.

Four of the individual organizations which are covered by our *Yearbook* are primarily responsible for implementation of the new oceans regime under the Law of the Sea Convention, i.e. UNEP - for environmental protection in general, UNESCO/IOC - for marine scientific research, FAO - for fisheries, and IMO - for shipping and marine pollution. The UNEP Governing Council, the FAO Committee on Fisheries and the IMO Assembly held all their regular biennial sessions in 1995, devoting special attention to their actions in follow-up to the UNCED, as further reported upon at their ses-

---

7 For Agreement's status as at 30 May 1997, see *UN/DOALOS Law of the Sea Bulletin* No. 34 (1997). Cf. M. Hayashi, "The 1995 Agreement on Straddling and Highly Migratory Fish Stocks," 8 *EC-ACP Bulletin* 4-7 (1995 No.4); D.H. Anderson, "The Straddling Stocks Agreement of 1995 - an Initial Assessment," 45 *ICLQ* 463-475 (1996); M. Hayashi, "The 1995 Agreement on Straddling Fish Stocks and Higly Migratory Fish Stocks: Significance for the Law of the Sea Convention," 29 *Ocean and Coastal Management* 51-69 (1996); Hayashi, "Enforcement by Non-Flag States on the High Seas Under the 1995 Agreement on Straddling and Highly Migratory Fish Stocks", 9 *GIELR* 1-36 (1996); A. Tahindro, "Conservation and Management of Straddling Fish Stocks and Highly Migratory Fish Stocks," 28 *ODIL* 1-58 (1997); B. Kwiatkowska, "Expansion of Protective Jurisdiction: Future Challenges", in *Lessons from the Past - Blueprints for the Future, Proceeedings of the 25th Anniversary Conference of the Canadian Council of International Law, Château Laurier, Ottawa, 16-18 October 1997* (in press).

8 ICJ Reports 1995, 87, and 1996, 58; *ICJ Communiqué* No.96/18, 10 May 1996. Cf. Kwiatkowska, *supra* note 7.

9 See G. Plant, "Navigation Regime in the Turkish Straits for Merchant Ships in Peacetime", 20 *Marine Policy* 15-27 (1995); "New and Amended TSS and Routeing Systems", *IMO News* 19-22 (1997, Nos 2/3).

10 See B. Kwiatkowska, "The International Court of Justice and the Law of the Sea - Some Reflections", 11 *IJMCL* 500, 530 (1996).

sions in 1997. The same applies to the IOC which in 1995 held its biennial session of the Assembly (alternating with sessions of the Executive Council). Two additional UN organizations covered by the *Yearbook* have dealt continuously with other important aspects of ocean affairs within their broader mandates, i.e. IAEA - radioactive marine pollution, and UNCTAD - ports and shipping.

It is due to limited space that, as in the previous Volumes, the most important documents are reproduced in whole or in part, while other relevant documents are only listed. The listed documents include, as appropriate, the ocean-related conventions adopted under the auspices of international organizations which may be found in other accessible collections of legal documents, e.g., *International Legal Materials*, *Law of the Sea Bulletin* and other publications issued by the UN DOALOS/OLA, or *International Journal of Marine and Coastal Law*. For the convenience of readers who would wish to order documents only partly reproduced or listed in the *Yearbook*, the addresses of international organizations concerned are added after the Table of Contents. Moreover, an Index of Keywords is included with a view to facilitate access by the reader to the complex and often interrelated matters dealt with by various organizations as well as to the information concerning individual states, regions and international instruments.

Like previous volumes, this Volume 11 would not have been published without the kind, and in most cases continuous, assistance of number of individuals. The editors wish to express their gratitude to the following persons for their help in obtaining documents:

UN - Mrs. Alice ter Horst of the Netherlands Ministry of Foreign Affairs, The Hague;
UNCTAD - Mr. R. Vogel, Deputy Director of the Shipping Division, Geneva;
FAO - Dr. William Edeson, Legal Adviser, Rome;
IAEA - Dr. Odette Jankowitsch, Senior Legal Officer, and the staff of the Division of Publications, Vienna;
IMO - Ms. Michele Fore of the Documents Section, London.

The editors remain grateful to the members of the Advisory Board for their continuing support and also to the reviewers for all valuable suggestions related to this *Yearbook*. Special thanks are due to Mrs. Annebeth Rosenboom and other staff members of Kluwer Law International (which presently incorporates Martinus Nijhoff Publishers), for their cooperation in the publication of the *Yearbook* in general and this Volume in particular.

Professor Barbara Kwiatkowska
Deputy Director NILOS

Professor Alfred H.A. Soons
Director NILOS

Utrecht, 18 November 1997

NILOS, Faculty of Law,
Utrecht University
Achter Sint Pieter 200,
3512 HT Utrecht - NL,
Fax: 31-30-2537 073

UNITED NATIONS
(UN)

DOCUMENTS REPRODUCED IN WHOLE OR IN PART:

GENERAL ASSEMBLY (UNGA)

Reports & Notes of the UN Secretary-General

Letters to the United Nations Addressed to the Secretary-General

FOLLOW-UP TO UN GLOBAL CONFERENCE ON THE SUSTAINABLE DEVELOPMENT OF SMALL ISLAND DEVELOPING STATES

Report of the UN Secretary-General

Resolution of the UNGA

ECONOMIC AND SOCIAL COUNCIL (ECOSOC)

Resolutions and Decisions of the Substantive Session of the ECOSOC, Geneva, 26 June-28 July 1995

ECONOMIC COMMISSION FOR EUROPE (ECE)

DOCUMENTS NOT REPRODUCED:

DIVISION FOR OCEAN AFFAIRS AND THE LAW OF THE SEA, OFFICE OF LEGAL AFFAIRS (DOALOS/OLA)

70. Doc. no.: UN Sales No.E.95.V.10
Date: 1995
Title: The Law of the Sea - Current Developments in State Practice No.IV

71. Doc. no.: UN Sales No.E.95.V.11
Date: 1995
Title: The Law of the Sea - A Select Bibliography 1994

72. Doc. no.: UN Sales No/E.95.V.21
Date: 1995
Title: The Law of the Sea - Conservation and Utilization of the Living Resources of the Exclusive Economic Zone: Legislative History of Articles 61 and 62 of the UN Convention on the Law of the Sea

1. LAW OF THE SEA - REPORT OF THE UN SECRETARY-GENERAL

Doc. no.: A/50/713 & Corr. 1 — 1 November 1995 & 6 February 1996

CONTENTS

INTRODUCTION

1. The present report is submitted to the General Assembly in response to its resolution 49/28 of 6 December 1994, in which the Secretary-General was requested to report to the Assembly annually, as from its fiftieth session, on developments pertaining to the implementation of the United Nations Convention on the Law of the Sea and on other developments relating to ocean affairs and the law of the sea, as well as on the implementation of that resolution.

2. The General Assembly suggested that such an annual comprehensive report could also serve as a basis for his reports to all States parties to the Convention, which is called for under article 319 (2) (a) of the Convention. The Secretary-General intends to prepare such a report to States parties in early 1996 on the basis of the present report, taking into account the consideration of the item "Law of the sea" at the current session of the General Assembly.

3. The following reports submitted by the Secretary-General to the General Assembly at the current session are also relevant to the present subject: "United Nations Conference on Straddling Fish Stocks and Highly Migratory Fish Stocks" (A/50/550); "Unauthorized fishing in zones of national jurisdiction and its impact on the living marine resources of the world's oceans and seas" (A/50/549); "Large-scale pelagic drift-net fishing and its impact on the living marine resources of the world's oceans and seas" (A/50/553); and "Fisheries by-catch and discards and their impact on the sustainable use of the world's living marine resources", prepared by the Food and Agriculture Organization of the United Nations (FAO) (A/50/552). All four reports will be considered by the General Assembly under a sub-item together with the item "Law of the sea", in accordance with its decision.

4. The present report is divided into two main chapters: chapter I is devoted to developments pertaining to the implementation of the Convention and chapter II to other developments relating to ocean affairs and the law of the sea. The third element in the General Assembly's requests, i.e., the implementation of resolution 49/28, is reflected in both chapters as appropriate.

5. The international community has now entered an important transitional era for the law of the sea and international cooperation in ocean affairs. Following upon more than a decade of slowly accumulating practice in the application of the new legal regime, the present period is one which calls for a new focus on rapid adjustment, consolidation and strengthening of international law and policy on ocean issues.

6. There have been 21 ratifications or accessions since the requirement for entry into force of the Convention was met in November 1993; the 1994 Agreement relating to the implementation of Part XI of the Convention has successfully facilitated a wider acceptance of the Convention; and through the adoption of the 1995 Agreement on straddling fish stocks and highly migratory fish stocks, there is new, concrete evidence of the determination of the international community to strengthen the international legal order for the oceans wherever and whenever there are urgent and compelling needs that can be resolved only through the elaboration of new or additional rules. New international policy also is emerging on the sustainable development of marine and coastal areas and resources, stimulated by the United Nations Conference on Environment and Development (UNCED), by the entry into force of the Convention on the Law of the Sea and of other conventions which contribute to its objectives, by the adoption of new global programmes on major aspects of ocean affairs, and new or revised strategies by international organizations, including the development and financial institutions.

7. Virtually every intergovernmental forum with an interest in oceans and coastal areas and necessarily having a particular focus derived from its main objectives, is currently making a major effort to adopt integrated approaches and establish cross-sectoral relationships. The very nature of ocean affairs argues for such an approach, as recognized also by the Convention in its preamble, and consequently by the General Assembly, for the purpose of considering its item on the law of the sea. Any uncertainty as regards the choice of forum for the consideration of an issue, or duplication in the number of forums considering essentially the same issue, and any uncertainty as to the way in which issues are to be interrelated and integrated, can create new problems for international cooperation and coordination in ocean affairs. It could also cause impediments for the harmonized development of international law relating to the oceans.

8. The oversight role of the General Assembly, as reflected in its resolution 49/28, with respect to the implementation of the Convention and the conduct of international cooperation in support of its objects and purposes can be expected to assume yet greater importance over the present period, and beyond. In the view of the Secretary-General, it is timely for Member States to consider further how best to fulfil this oversight role, bearing in mind the need for regular and comprehensive review of the implementation of the Convention, which entails frequently also consideration of the implementation of important related conventions and instruments, as well as for identification of issues of particular importance for the maintenance of the legal order for the oceans, for peace and security, and for the conservation and sustainable development of its resources.

I. DEVELOPMENTS RELATING TO THE IMPLEMENTATION OF THE CONVENTION

A. The Convention and the implementing agreements

1. Status of the Convention

9. The United Nations Convention on the Law of the Sea 1/ entered into force on 16 November 1994. Since then, by 15 October 1995, 13 more States (Austria, Bolivia, Cook Islands, Croatia, Greece, India, Italy, Lebanon, Samoa, Sierra Leone, Singapore, Slovenia and Tonga) deposited their instruments of ratification, accession or succession, bringing the total number of States parties to 81. 2/

2. Status of the Agreement relating to the implementation of Part XI of the Convention

10. On 28 July 1995, the Agreement relating to the Implementation of Part XI of the United Nations Convention on the Law of the Sea of 10 December 1982, 3/ which was signed by 79 States, was closed for signature. On that date, 16 States 4/ became bound by the Agreement under the simplified procedure set out in article 5. Eleven States, which had been parties to the Convention before the adoption of the Agreement, notified the depositary in writing that they were not availing themselves of the simplified procedure. 5/ Some others, which had also notified that they were not availing themselves of the procedure under article 5, proceeded with the ratification of the Agreement. 6/

11. According to article 6, the Agreement will enter into force 30 days after the date on which 40 States have established their consent to be bound, provided that such States include at least seven of the States referred to in paragraph 1 (a) of resolution II of the Third United Nations Conference on the Law of the Sea and that at least five of those States are developed States. Although 41 States 7/ have consented to be bound by the Agreement, the requirements of article 6 have not been met for the Agreement to enter into force.

12. However, pending its entry into force, the Agreement is being applied provisionally by 124 States as of 15 October 1995 in accordance with article 7 and section 1, paragraph 12, of the annex. Among the States entitled to apply the Agreement provisionally by virtue either of their consent to the adoption of the Agreement in the General Assembly or of their signature, 14 States have notified the Secretary-General that they do not wish to apply it provisionally. 8/ For these States, their consent to be bound by the Agreement is subject to ratification.

3. Adoption of the Agreement for the implementation of the Convention provisions relating to straddling fish stocks and highly migratory fish stocks

13. The United Nations Conference on Straddling Fish Stocks and Highly Migratory Fish Stocks on 4 August 1995 adopted the Agreement for the Implementation of the Provisions of the United Nations Convention on the Law of the Sea of 10 December 1982 relating to the Conservation and Management of Straddling Fish Stocks and Highly Migratory Fish Stocks (see paras. 170-172 below). 9/

B. Meetings of States Parties to the Convention

14. The Convention provides, in article 319, paragraph 2 (e), that the Secretary-General shall "convene necessary meetings of States Parties in accordance with [the] Convention". Initially, on the recommendation of the Preparatory Commission for the International Seabed Authority and for the International Tribunal for the Law of the Sea, the Secretary-General convened a Meeting of States Parties to the Convention immediately following entry into force of the Convention, on 21 and 22 November 1994, to discuss the organization of the International Tribunal for the Law of the Sea, and in particular, the deferment of the first election of its members. 10/ In convening the Meeting, in addition to States parties, invitations were also addressed to other States and the entities referred to in article 305, paragraph 1 (c), (d), (e) and (f), of the Convention to participate as observers, subject to a decision to be taken by States parties at the beginning of their meeting.

15. In accordance with paragraph 10 of resolution I of the Third United Nations Conference on the Law of the Sea, the Meeting had before it the report of the Preparatory Commission, containing recommendations regarding practical arrangements for the Tribunal. 11/

16. The Meeting, having elected Mr. Satya N. Nandan (Fiji) as its President, took, on the recommendations of the Preparatory Commission, 12/ *inter alia*, the following decisions:

(a) The first election of the members of the Tribunal would be deferred until 1 August 1996, and this would be a one-time deferment;

(b) The nominations for members would open on 16 May 1995 and would close on 17 June 1996. A State in the process of becoming a party to the Convention might nominate candidates. Such nominations would remain provisional and would not be included in the list of candidates to be circulated by the Secretary-General unless the State concerned had deposited its instrument of ratification or accession before 1 July 1996;

(c) The list of candidates would be circulated on 5 July 1996.

17. In the first year after the entry into force of the Convention, a second Meeting of States Parties was necessary in order to deal, *inter alia*, with organizational matters relating to the establishment of the Tribunal, which included the practical arrangements therefor. Accordingly, the Secretary-

General convened the second Meeting of States Parties from 15 to 19 May 1995. 13/ In addition to the entities other than States parties that had earlier been invited, relevant international organizations and non-governmental organizations were also invited to participate as observers.

18. The Meeting considered and agreed on the structure and composition of the Bureau. It also considered the draft rules of procedure submitted by the Secretariat and adopted a revision thereof as its rules of procedure. 14/ A rule relating to decisions having financial implications was left to be developed.

19. On organizational matters, the Meeting discussed and agreed on several criteria regarding the establishment of the Tribunal, its initial functions and related matters, and the Meeting took, inter alia, the following decisions:

(a) The members of the Tribunal would hold their first organizational session on 1 October 1996;

(b) The President of the Tribunal would reside at its seat and all other members would attend meetings of the Tribunal as and when required;

(c) The overall remuneration of the members would consist of an annual allowance, a special allowance for each day that they are engaged in the business of the Tribunal and a subsistence allowance for each day that they attend meetings;

(d) The official languages of the Tribunal would be English and French. A party to a dispute might use another language for written and oral pleadings and related documentation, but the translation and interpretation into one of the official languages should be at that party's expense;

(e) When a language other than the Tribunal's official languages chosen by a party was an official language of the United Nations, the decision of the Tribunal should be translated into that official language at no cost to the parties;

(f) Subject to availability of funds, and provided that it would not result in an increase in the budget, consideration would be given in the future to the translation of final decisions of the Tribunal into the other official languages of the United Nations at the request of any of the States parties.

20. The Meeting also decided that the principle of cost-effectiveness would apply to all aspects of the Tribunal's work.

21. With respect to the question of the budget and the source of the budget or its funding, the Meeting requested the Secretariat to prepare a draft initial budget. The criteria agreed upon, as referred to above, would be used for purposes of organization and for assessing budgetary implications during the initial financial period (1 August 1996-31 December 1997). The States parties intend to adopt the budget at a Meeting to be held from 4 to 8 March 1996, which would be preceded by a Meeting to be held from 27 November to 1 December 1995, to review the draft budget with the participation of financial experts of delegations. The Meeting also noted that there would be a need for transition from the services of the Secretariat to the Registry of the Tribunal.

C. Actions taken by States

1. Maritime limits

22. According to information obtained by the Secretary-General as at 15 October 1995, the outer limits of the claims by 146 coastal States to the various maritime zones, measured from baselines, are as shown below. No

information is available on the legislation of five other coastal States: Bosnia and Herzegovina, Eritrea, Georgia, Slovenia and Yugoslavia.

(a) Territorial sea		Number of States
12 miles 15/		121
Less than 12 miles		9
More than 12 miles		15
(200 miles	10)	
(20-50 miles	5)	
(b) Contiguous zone		
24 miles		47
Less than 24 miles		8
More than 24 miles		1
(c) Exclusive economic zone		
200 miles		86
Up to a line of delimitation, by determination of coordinates or without limits		10
(In addition, 15 States claim a fishery zone of 200 miles and 4 States claim a fishery zone of less than 200 miles.)		
(d) Continental shelf		
200-metre isobath plus exploitability criterion		37
Outer edge of continental margin, or 200 miles		25
200 miles		7
Others		13

In addition, 16 States have claimed archipelagic State status, although not all have specified archipelagic baselines.

2. National legislation

23. Following the previous reporting year, the trend in State practice to adopt or modify legislation in order to comply with the provisions of the Convention has continued to slow down during the past year. The entry into force of the Convention has thus far apparently not prompted States parties to amend their legislation that does not conform to the Convention.

24. Four European States - Croatia, Finland, Germany and Ukraine - transmitted to the Secretariat their new legislation on maritime areas under their jurisdiction. Croatia adopted a comprehensive Maritime Code on 27 September 1994, 16/ comprising 13 parts and 1,056 articles. It defines the baselines from which the territorial sea is measured, establishes a 12-mile territorial sea and provides for the possible establishment of an exclusive economic zone up to the outer limits permitted by international law. It also contains the regime of the continental shelf, which extends up to the delimitation line with neighbouring States, and deals with shipping and navigation, including the regime of ports.

25. Finland, by an Act dated 30 July 1995, 17/ has amended the Act of 18 August 1956 defining the limits of the territorial waters, which are divided into internal waters and external waters or the territorial sea. The external

limits of the territorial sea were extended from 4 to 12 miles, with the exception of the Gulf of Finland where the limit is 3 miles.

26. By a proclamation dated 11 November 1994, Germany extended the outer limit of the territorial sea from 3 to 12 miles both in the North Sea and in the Baltic Sea. Further, by a proclamation dated 25 November 1994, Germany established an exclusive economic zone in the North Sea and in the Baltic Sea. 18/ The limits of the German territorial sea and exclusive economic zone in the North Sea and in the Baltic Sea are indicated on Maritime Boundaries Charts Nos. 2920 and 2921, which have been deposited with the Secretary-General in accordance with articles 16, paragraph 2, and 75, paragraph 2, of the Convention on the Law of the Sea (see para. 39 below).

27. The task force established under the 1992 Paris Declaration on the Coordinated Extension of Jurisdiction in the North Sea 19/ presented its report on 7 February 1995. One of the main objectives of the task force was to promote the further establishment of exclusive economic zones in the North Sea in order to improve enforcement of international rules relating to pollution from ships. France, Germany, Norway and Sweden have already established an exclusive economic zone. Among the four other North Sea States, draft legislation has been completed in the Netherlands and Denmark. A first draft has been elaborated by Belgium. The United Kingdom of Great Britain and Northern Ireland adopted a merchant shipping (prevention of pollution) Act in 1994 and an Order-in-Council is being drafted to control pollution from ships within the limits of a zone permitted under the exclusive economic zone provisions.

28. Ukraine adopted on 16 May 1995 an Act 20/ establishing an exclusive economic zone which extends up to 200 miles. The Act comprises 32 articles, dealing with delimitation, sovereign rights over the living and non-living resources, jurisdiction with regard to artificial islands, installations and structures, the protection of the marine environment and the conduct of marine scientific research. It also establishes the supremacy of the Convention over the Act in case of conflict.

29. In Asia, Thailand communicated to the press, in September 1995, the establishment of a contiguous zone of 24 miles from the baselines from which the territorial sea is measured. 21/

30. Three protests were filed by Germany on behalf of the European Union. The first protest, 22/ dated 23 December 1994, relates to the straight baselines claims by Thailand in Area 4 considered to be "excessively long". The second protest, dated 14 December 1994, concerns the regulations adopted by Costa Rica subjecting to prior authorization the entry into and the passage through its territorial sea of foreign fishing vessels. 23/ The third protest, dated 14 December 1994, concerns the Act of 1993 on the Marine Areas of the Islamic Republic of Iran in the Persian Gulf and in the Oman Sea. 24/ The European Union considered that several baseline segments were "excessively long". The protest dealt also with the rules defining the innocent passage in relation to the defence and security of the Islamic Republic of Iran, the prior authorization of warships, submarines, nuclear-powered ships and vessels or any other floating objects or vessels carrying nuclear or other dangerous or noxious substances, harmful to the environment. The protest underscored that the Act was not in conformity with articles 5, 7, 19, 56, 58 and 78 of the Convention. 25/

31. A regional review of the maritime legislation of 146 coastal States reveals the impact of the Convention on their legislative activity:

(a) For Africa, at the time of the adoption of the Convention or shortly thereafter, 12 States 26/ adopted new legislation regarding their maritime zones. Cape Verde adopted a new law in 1992 in order to correct that of 1977, in which archipelagic baselines were not drawn in conformity with the Convention. Nine States still claim territorial seas extending beyond the

12-mile limit permitted under international law. They are: Angola with 20 miles; Nigeria and Togo with 30 miles; Cameroon with 50 miles; and Benin, Congo, Liberia, Sierra Leone and Somalia with 200 miles. Of those States, Benin, Congo and Liberia are not parties to the Convention.

(b) For Asia, it is convenient to view the practice of 49 States in their subregional contexts: (i) 16 of the 18 East and South Asian States claim a 12-mile territorial sea. Singapore claims 3 miles and the Philippines a rectangular zone. All these States, with the exception of Brunei Darussalam, Cambodia and China, had enacted their legislation before the adoption of the Convention. With the exception of China, Japan, the Republic of Korea and Singapore, which claim a 200-mile fishing zone, the 14 remaining States of this subregion have established an exclusive economic zone of 200 miles; (ii) Fifteen of the 16 States of the South Pacific have established a 12-mile territorial sea. Only Palau has set its claim to 3 miles. Ten of these States adopted their laws in the 1970s. All States claim a 200-mile zone, with three of them claiming a fishing zone (Nauru, Palau and Papua New Guinea); (iii) Four Gulf States have changed their maritime area jurisdiction very recently: Qatar in 1992; Bahrain, the Islamic Republic of Iran and United Arab Emirates in 1993. Oman adopted a territorial sea of 12 miles and an exclusive economic zone of 200 miles in 1981; (iv) Among the East Mediterranean States, the Syrian Arab Republic has a 35-mile territorial sea claim. Jordan and Turkey have territorial seas of 3 and 6 miles respectively.

(c) For Latin America and the Caribbean, among the 13 island States of the Caribbean Sea, only the Bahamas and the Dominican Republic have set claims to a territorial sea of less than 12 miles. Among the 18 Central and South American States, 5 which are not parties to the Convention claim a 200-mile territorial sea: Ecuador, El Salvador, Nicaragua, Panama and Peru. Argentina, Brazil and Chile have recently rolled back their territorial sea limits to 12 miles. Uruguay, having become a party to the Convention, has set its claims to the extent permitted by the Convention.

(d) For Europe and North America, 26 States claim a 12-mile territorial sea. Only three States still claim a territorial sea under 12 miles: Denmark (3 miles), Norway (4 miles) and Greece (6 miles). Fourteen States have proclaimed an exclusive economic zone. Eight claim fishing zones: Belgium, Canada, Denmark, Finland, Ireland, Malta, Netherlands and the United Kingdom. Eight States have established a contiguous zone, five extending up to 24 miles.

3. Other developments

32. In its resolution 49/82 of 15 December 1994 on the implementation of the Declaration of the Indian Ocean as a Zone of Peace, the General Assembly noted that the entry into force of the Convention "enhances prospects for mutually accommodative measures of cooperation on a regional as well as global basis, including the freedom of the high seas, in conformity with the Convention".

33. At the Ministerial Meeting of the Coordinating Bureau of the Movement of Non-Aligned Countries (25-27 April 1995), the Ministers welcomed the entry into force of the Convention and the establishment of the International Seabed Authority in Jamaica. They believed that the Convention and its agreements represented significant achievements of the international community through multilateral efforts in creating a legal order for the seas and oceans which would, inter alia, facilitate international communication, promote the peaceful uses of the seas and oceans, the equitable and efficient utilization of their resources, the conservation of their living resources, as well as the protection and preservation of the marine environment. The Ministers expressed the hope that the Agreement relating to the implementation of Part XI of the Convention would be implemented in all of its aspects, including the agreement to set up the Authority without introducing new conditionalities that worked against the interests of the developing countries. 27/

34. The twenty-sixth South Pacific Forum (3-15 September 1995) "urged all Forum member countries to become parties to the 1982 United Nations Convention on the Law of the Sea at the earliest opportunity". 28/

35. In the Declaration adopted on 29 September 1995 at their nineteenth annual meeting, the Ministers for Foreign Affairs of the Group of 77 welcomed the entry into force of the Convention and invited countries that had not done so to accede to it. 29/

D. Actions taken by the Secretary-General

1. Establishment of a system for the deposit, recording and publicity of charts and geographical coordinates

(a) Due publicity obligations with respect to charts and geographical coordinates

36. Under articles 16 (2) (limits of the territorial sea), 47 (9) (archipelagic baselines), 75 (2) (exclusive economic zone) and 84 (2) (delimitation of the continental shelf) of the Convention, "due publicity" is to be given by the coastal State to charts or lists of geographical coordinates and a copy of each such chart or list is to be deposited with the Secretary-General. Similarly, under article 76 (9) (definition of the continental shelf), the coastal State is to deposit with the Secretary-General charts and relevant information, including geodetic data, permanently describing the outer limits of its continental shelf so that the Secretary-General may give "due publicity" thereto.

37. The General Assembly, conscious of these provisions, requested in its resolution 49/28, paragraph 15, the Secretary-General to carry out a number of functions consequent upon the entry into force of the Convention, inter alia, by:

> "(f) Establishing appropriate facilities, as required by the Convention, for the deposit by States of maps, charts and geographic coordinates concerning national maritime zones and establishing a system for their recording and publicity ..."

38. In order to carry out the functions entrusted to the Secretary-General under the Convention, and pursuant to the above request by the General Assembly, the Division for Ocean Affairs and the Law of the Sea of the Office of Legal Affairs, as the responsible substantive unit of the Secretariat, has established facilities for the deposit of charts and lists of geographical coordinates, including geodetic data, and adopted a system for their recording and publicity.

39. The Division, in order to give equal treatment to all States, will endeavour to be of service to States parties by publishing the charts and geographical coordinates received by the Secretary-General in a systematic and uniform manner. For administrative purposes, States parties have been invited by the Secretary-General to submit the charts concerned in triplicate together with relevant legislation, including lists of geographical coordinates, in electronic format whenever possible.

40. With respect to the recording system, the Division has already devised an internal computerized "data record". As for publicity, the Division has started to prepare a "Maritime Zone Notification" (MZN) for the purpose of informing States parties of the deposit of charts and geographical coordinates. The first MZN, dated 8 March 1995, concerned the deposit by Germany of the charts and geographical coordinates of its territorial sea and exclusive economic zone. Moreover, the MZN, together with the lists of geographical coordinates and charts deposited, is reproduced in a Law of the Sea Information Circular (LOSIC) and the charts and the text of the relevant legislation are published in the Law of the Sea Bulletin. 30/

(b) Other due publicity obligations

41. Consequent upon the entry into force of the Convention, the Division has taken due note of other "due publicity" obligations which must be complied with by States parties. Firstly, coastal States, pursuant to article 21 (3), shall give "due publicity" to all laws and regulations they may adopt on innocent passage through the territorial sea. Secondly, States bordering straits, pursuant to article 42 (3), shall give "due publicity", to all laws and regulations they may adopt relating to transit passage through straits used for international navigation. Lastly, pursuant to articles 22 (4), 41 (6) and 53 (10), coastal States, States bordering straits and archipelagic States shall give "due publicity" to the charts indicating the designation, prescription or substitution of sea lanes and traffic separation schemes in the territorial sea and in straits used for international navigation as well as of air routes above archipelagic sea lanes used for international overflight.

42. The Division has taken initiatives in bringing to the attention of States parties its willingness to assist them with their obligations of such "due publicity". Accordingly, by notes verbales addressed to the States parties concerned, the Division has invited them to submit to the Legal Counsel a copy of the laws and regulations relating to transit passage through straits used for international navigation and to innocent passage through the territorial sea, as well as the charts indicating established sea lanes, traffic separation schemes and air routes above archipelagic sea lanes. Three States have so far responded to the invitation.

2. Preparation of the lists of conciliators, arbitrators and special arbitrators

43. The Convention confers on the Secretary-General a number of functions relating to the procedures for the settlement of disputes. In addition to the major task of preparing for the establishment of the International Tribunal for the Law of the Sea (see paras. 55-58 below), the Secretary-General is required to draw up and maintain lists of conciliators and arbitrators for the conciliation and arbitration procedures as set out in Annexes V and VII, respectively, to the Convention. Accordingly, the Secretary-General addressed a note verbale to all States to nominate conciliators and arbitrators in accordance with Annex V, article 2, and Annex VII, article 2. Every State party is entitled to nominate four conciliators and four arbitrators. The persons nominated as arbitrators should, in addition to the requirements of fairness, competence and integrity, be experienced in maritime affairs. Although only States parties to the Convention are entitled to nominate conciliators and arbitrators, the Secretary-General, bearing in mind the desire to achieve universal participation in the Convention and also the decisions taken by the Meeting of States Parties regarding the nomination of candidates for the Tribunal (see para. 16 above), invited all States to submit nominations, it being understood that inclusion in the list would be on the condition that the nominating States become a State party to the Convention. As at 15 October 1995, only one State party has submitted nominations for conciliators and arbitrators.

44. Annex VIII, article 2, to the Convention mandates four international organizations to draw up lists of experts in the fields of fisheries, protection and preservation of the marine environment, marine scientific research, and navigation, including pollution from vessels and by dumping, respectively. The Secretary-General has drawn the attention of the four designated organizations, i.e., FAO, the United Nations Environment Programme (UNEP), the Intergovernmental Oceanographic Commission (IOC) of the United Nations Educational, Scientific and Cultural Organization (UNESCO) and the International Maritime Organization (IMO), to the provisions of that annex and requested them to take appropriate action in this regard. The Secretary-General also requested the above organizations to send a copy of the list to him, when established, and

any subsequent changes which might be made to such list. So far FAO has received nominations from five States parties, and both IMO and IOC from 11 States parties. 31/

3. Development of a centralized system of integrated legislative databases

45. The Division for Ocean Affairs and the Law of the Sea has continued to develop a computer-generated information system on national legislation relating to the law of the sea. 32/ In this connection, an extensive review of national legislative acts from more than 140 States, as made available throughout the years to the United Nations, has been completed and a comprehensive inventory of those acts has been established. Thus, necessary prerequisites for further expansion, updating and verification of data stored in the system have been fulfilled. Projected improvements will further strengthen the Division's capacity in monitoring the practice of States. The system may also be a useful tool for assisting States at the preparatory stage of their legislative process. The pilot version of the computerized system is operational in the Division and ready to respond to various queries by interested permanent and observer missions, United Nations agencies as well as other international organizations.

46. Pursuant to the General Assembly's call, in resolution 49/28, for the development of "a centralized system with integrated databases for providing coordinated information and advice, inter alia, on legislation and marine policy", the Division established contacts with relevant organizations and has established initial working relationship with FAO.

47. Those contacts were made in order to avoid duplication in the compilation of legislation which falls under the competence of the United Nations as well as to explore existing projects and to improve the existing flow of information. In particular, the Division's computerized projects could be efficiently complemented, inter alia, by FAO's databases concerning fisheries legislation and agreements, which are being developed. Steps have been taken to advance future cooperation, including electronic transmission of data between the Division and FAO, with a view to acquiring experience for the establishment of similar links with other agencies and organizations. Through such links, a substantial increase in Division capabilities to respond to requests for information and assistance to States is expected in view of the implementation of the Convention and the recently adopted Agreement relating to the conservation and management of straddling fish stocks and highly migratory fish stocks. The cooperative arrangements, however, involve complex technical problems and therefore need to be carefully elaborated.

E. Preparations for the establishment of the institutions created by the Convention

1. International Seabed Authority

48. The International Seabed Authority, established by the Convention with its seat in Jamaica, is the organization through which its members shall organize and control activities of exploration for, and exploitation of, the resources of the seabed and ocean floor and subsoil thereof, beyond the limits of national jurisdiction (the Area). The membership comprises States parties to the Convention and States non-parties which have consented to apply the Agreement provisionally (see para. 12 above).

49. Pursuant to article 308 (3) of the Convention, the Assembly of the Authority met on the date of entry into force of the Convention, i.e., 16 November 1994. The meeting, primarily of a ceremonial nature, was held at Kingston, Jamaica, from 16 to 18 November 1994. In 1995, the Assembly held two

more meetings at Kingston, from 27 February to 17 March 1995 and from 7 to 18 August 1995, respectively.

50. During those meetings, it carried out a number of functions, advancing the organizational work substantially. 33/ The Assembly elected Mr. Hasjim Djalal (Indonesia) as President of its first session. The Assembly also elected four Vice-Presidents and appointed a 9-member Credentials Committee. Following the outcome of deliberations in a 10-member Working Group on the Draft Rules of Procedure appointed by it, the Assembly adopted the rules of procedure. 34/

51. The Assembly received the final report of the Preparatory Commission 35/ consisting of 13 volumes, which represent a comprehensive documentation of the work of the Preparatory Commission.

52. One of the earliest tasks of the Assembly was to elect the 36 members of the Council, comprising four groups representing - in essence, four sets of interests, i.e., consumers/importers of the minerals that could be supplied from the deep seabed sources, investors in deep seabed mining, producers/exporters of such minerals from land-based sources and developing States representing special interests, as well as a group of 18 members elected according to the principle of ensuring an equitable geographical distribution of seats in the Council as a whole. 36/ Although substantial progress was made within each group and among the various groups, including among the five regions, and in spite of efforts by the President of the Assembly, the bureau and individual delegations, the Council could not be composed by the end of the first session of the Assembly. Informal inter-sessional consultations by the President of the Assembly on this subject are scheduled to be held in New York from 6 to 8 December 1995.

53. In the absence of the Council and of the Secretary-General, who is to be elected by the Assembly from among the candidates proposed by the Council, the Assembly decided upon certain administrative and budgetary arrangements for the Authority on an interim basis. It requested the Secretary-General of the United Nations to submit to the General Assembly at its fiftieth session, on behalf of the Authority, a draft budget covering the administrative expenses of the Authority for 1996. The Secretary-General has already responded to that request. 37/ It also requested that the staff and facilities previously available to the United Nations Kingston Office for the Law of the Sea be continued as the interim secretariat of the Authority as of 1 October 1995, and authorized the Secretary-General of the United Nations to administer the interim secretariat until the entry on duty of the Secretary-General of the Authority. This decision of the Assembly is being implemented.

54. The Assembly decided to request the holding to two meetings of the Authority in 1996: the first meeting to take place beginning on 11 March 1996 for up to three weeks, if necessary, principally for the purpose of electing the members of the Council and the Secretary-General of the Authority and establishing the Finance Committee; the second meeting to take place beginning on 5 August 1996 for up to two weeks, primarily for the Finance Committee, the Council and the Assembly to consider and decide on the budget and to establish the Legal and Technical Commission. During these meetings, the Assembly and the Council, as far as practicable, shall also consider other items on their agendas.

2. International Tribunal for the Law of the Sea

55. The establishment of the Tribunal, as set out in its statute, is to commence with the election of members within six months of the date of entry into force of the Convention. That date, however, has been deferred as explained in paragraph 16 above by the decision of the Meeting of States Parties. The Meeting also established several criteria relevant to the establishment and organization of the Tribunal (see paras. 19-20 above).

56. In accordance with the decision of the Meeting of States Parties, nominations for the members of the Tribunal was opened on 16 May 1995 and all States were invited to submit nominations with the proviso that nominations by a State not party to the Convention shall not be included in the list of candidates to be circulated by the Secretary-General on 5 July 1996 unless the State concerned has deposited its instrument of ratification or accession before 1 July 1996. The nominations will be closed on 17 June 1996. 38/

57. In response to the decision of the Meeting of States Parties and as endorsed by the General Assembly, 39/ Mr. Gritakumar Chitty of the Division for Ocean Affairs and the Law of the Sea, Office of Legal Affairs, has been designated as the officer charged with making preparations of a practical nature for the organization of the Tribunal, including the establishment of a library, with the necessary secretariat support. 40/

58. The Legal Counsel, on the invitation of the German Government, visited Bonn and Hamburg in June 1995 and held consultations with both the federal and the Hamburg authorities on a series of issues regarding the practical arrangements for the establishment of the Tribunal.

3. Commission on the Limits of the Continental Shelf

59. With the entry into force of the Convention, another new institution, the Commission on the Limits of the Continental Shelf, must be established, in accordance with article 76 and Annex II, within 18 months, i.e., before 16 May 1996. The members of the Commission are to be elected at a Meeting of States Parties convened by the Secretary-General. The Commission consists of 21 members who shall be experts in the field of geology, geophysics or hydrography, elected by States parties from among their nationals, having due regard to the need to ensure geographical representation, and who shall serve in their personal capacities.

60. The functions of the Commission shall be: (a) to consider the data and other material submitted by coastal States concerning the outer limits of the continental shelf in areas where those limits extend beyond 200 miles, and to make recommendations in accordance with article 76 and the statement of understanding adopted by the Third United Nations Conference on the Law of the Sea concerning a specific method to be used in establishing the outer edge of the continental margin; and (b) to provide scientific and technical advice, if requested by the coastal State concerned, during the preparation of such data.

61. In an effort to ensure that the Commission upon its establishment has sufficient material and information and to facilitate an efficient commencement of its work, and without prejudice to the decisions of the Commission in this regard, the Division for Ocean Affairs and the Law of the Sea, as the secretariat of the Commission, has attempted to identify some of the issues that will have to be addressed by the Commission when it begins its examination of the submissions of coastal States. This was done with the assistance of a representative group of experts, which was convened at United Nations Headquarters from 11 to 14 September 1995. 41/

62. Since the issue of the definition of the continental shelf had already been addressed by the Division in 1993 by convening a group of experts and publishing a study, 42/ the recent meeting of the group of experts focused its attention principally on the functions and scientific and technical needs of the Commission and on the possible format of the coastal State's submission regarding the limits of its continental shelf.

F. Actions taken by relevant international organizations and bodies

63. The General Assembly, in its resolution 49/28, paragraph 18, invited the competent international organizations to assess the implications of the entry into force of the Convention in their respective fields of competence and to identify any additional measures that might need to be taken as a consequence of its entry into force with a view to ensuring a uniform, consistent and coordinated approach to the implementation of its provisions. The Assembly considered that this activity was also important for the implementation of Agenda 21, paragraphs 17.116 and 17.117. 43/

64. The results of these assessments by the competent international organizations 44/ will be very important for the preparation of the comprehensive report for the fifty-first session of the General Assembly, which the Secretary-General was requested to prepare in paragraph 19 of resolution 49/28, on the impact of the entry into force of the Convention on related existing or proposed instruments and programmes. As one of the initial steps to implement this and other related requests of the General Assembly, the Division has established a list of focal points for law of the sea matters in those organizations. Cooperation in these areas will be greatly expedited by this system of designated focal points.

65. A number of organizations and convention secretariats have initiated reviews in response to resolution 49/28; several, including the United Nations Commission on Narcotic Drugs (see A/49/631, para. 178), had already anticipated the need to revisit the Convention in order to clarify certain relationships consequent upon its entry into force. At the same time, in view of the entry into force of the Convention, the Division is frequently consulted on specific questions arising from the interrelationships among maritime instruments and the need to promote consistency in further legal development. A number of current activities under related treaties and instruments, involving particular questions of conformity and consistency with the Convention, are described in the following section.

1. International Maritime Organization

66. The IMO Council has considered the significance of the entry into force of the Convention and the specific measures undertaken by the Secretary-General to maintain appropriate cooperation between the IMO secretariat and the Division for Ocean Affairs and the Law of the Sea, including cooperation to assess the implications of the entry into force of the Convention for the various competent international organizations, in accordance with the requests made in General Assembly resolution 49/28. 45/ Since in many areas the Convention recognizes IMO as the "competent international organization" and IMO standards are regarded as "generally accepted international standards", the entry into force is also of particular significance for States parties to the Convention which are not members of IMO or parties to IMO conventions.

67. The Council stressed IMO's role as the "competent international organization" for the United Nations system, and therefore for the Convention, in the field of shipping and the effect of shipping on the marine environment. 46/ But since effective fulfilment of IMO's role will require a clear identification of the relevant provisions of the Convention and their relationship to IMO instruments, programmes and activities, the IMO secretariat will prepare a detailed study on the Convention in relation to IMO instruments, programmes and activities. 47/ This will also ensure that the governing bodies of IMO, its committees and subsidiary bodies are all fully aware of the organization's competence in respect of the Convention and of the legal framework within which that competence has to be exercised.

68. The work of IMO has provided many concrete examples of the close relationships between the Convention and the many, more specialized legal instruments in the maritime field. Concern to ensure that proposals are in line with the Convention provisions has been evident on many occasions, and specific questions have been frequently referred to the Legal Committee in accordance with IMO procedures. 48/ In a number of instances, IMO committees and meetings of the 1972 Convention on the Prevention of Marine Pollution by Dumping Wastes and Other Matter (London Convention) have directed the IMO secretariat to consult the Division for Ocean Affairs and the Law of the Sea.

69. The Council foresees no need to institute new or additional procedures for dealing with law of the sea issues, and is confident that wide dissemination of the forthcoming IMO study will ensure the necessary awareness of these issues in the relevant IMO committees and bodies. At the same time, however, the Council has stressed that IMO must be kept aware of developments and trends in the practice of States and other international organizations in order to fulfil its role as a "competent international organization"; it consequently called upon the Secretary-General of IMO to follow closely all relevant developments in the General Assembly of the United Nations and in the meetings of States parties to the Convention and to report periodically to the Council.

2. World Meteorological Organization

70. In response to a request made by the Executive Council of the World Meteorological Organization (WMO) in 1994 as a consequence of the pending entry into force of the Convention, the WMO Secretary-General has brought to the attention of WMO members the necessary information on the legal status of observations from voluntary observing ships and related observations. 49/ This was considered necessary in order to assist States in national discussions relating to the maintenance of marine observation networks. The information circulated included the earlier consensus in the WMO Congress (1979 and 1983) to the effect that activities carried out under World Weather Watch and the Integrated Global Ocean Services System (IGOSS) were routine observations and data collection, and were not covered by the consent regime for marine scientific research in Part XIII of the Convention.

71. The letter circulated in 1994 thus affirmed the indispensable nature of routine meteorological and oceanographic observations, including those from the exclusive economic zone, for services in support of safety of life and property at sea; and also affirmed that these observations formed part of agreed, long-standing operations systems and were freely exchanged among countries for the general benefit. The Secretary-General of WMO has also advised that since these observations are generally made voluntarily by ships engaged in normal trading activities, the ship personnel should have the necessary assurances of the continuing legality and importance of their work.

3. Intergovernmental Oceanographic Commission

72. In recent years, IOC has expended considerable effort in assessing the impact of the Convention on the functions and activities of the Commission and has expedited this work as a consequence of the entry into force of the Convention. In 1994, the Executive Council authorized the IOC Secretary to take immediate action to fulfil the short-term responsibilities, such as those under Annex VIII to the Convention. The IOC Assembly (June 1995) discussed "IOC and UNCLOS" at length, on the basis of an extensive report prepared by a working group. 50/ The report analysed IOC's role as the competent international organization to promote and facilitate international cooperation in marine science under the relevant Convention provisions, offered guidelines for cooperative arrangements with the International Seabed Authority and other organizations, identified priority areas for IOC's attention and suggested such future activities as preparation of detailed guidance on the application of the

consent regime for marine scientific research, further to Draft Standard Form A, suggested in the publication of the Division for Ocean Affairs and the Law of the Sea on the subject. 51/

73. Particular note was taken of the need to conclude agreements with the International Seabed Authority and the Division for Ocean Affairs and the Law of the Sea regarding the discharge of its responsibilities. The IOC Assembly established an open-ended inter-sessional working group on the "IOC role in relation to UNCLOS" to complete the review of the Convention and to suggest actions to be taken by IOC, taking into account the competence of the bodies established under the Convention and that of other existing bodies of the United Nations system. The terms of reference of the group require that it take special account of the rights and duties of coastal States relating to the general principles of prior consent for the implementation of activities in the exclusive economic zone and on the continental shelf. 52/

74. IOC's main contribution to the effective implementation of the Convention lies in its programme areas dealing with ocean mapping, marine environmental research and monitoring, ocean observing systems, education, training and mutual assistance, and research programmes on living and non-living resources. To help fulfil its role with respect to the Commission on the Limits of the Continental Shelf, as set forth in article 3 (2) of Annex II to the Convention, and to promote understanding of the scientific aspects of the implementation of article 76, IOC organized an ad hoc expert consultation within the framework of its programme on Ocean Science in relation to Non-Living Resources (OSNLR). 53/

75. The IOC programme, as reformulated for 1996-1997, 54/ will be specifically recognized as being implemented within the framework of Agenda 21, the relevant conventions, including the Convention on the Law of the Sea, and the Programme of Action for the Sustainable Development of Small Island Developing States. 55/ Four main objectives have now been set: to reduce the scientific uncertainties regarding oceans and coastal areas; to strengthen data exchange and ocean service; to foster capacity-building in developing countries and stimulate international and regional cooperation for marine research and systematic ocean observations.

4. International Labour Organization

76. The secretariat of the International Labour Organization (ILO) has asserted the Organization's competence under the United Nations Convention on the Law of the Sea in the field of maritime labour and safety, as deriving from its Constitution in relation to the application of international labour Conventions and Recommendations, which cover such topics as occupational health and safety, working conditions, labour inspections, human rights and economic and social policy generally. A number of them are important for preventing accidents at sea and protecting the marine environment, 56/ and some specifically address the situation of seafarers, fishermen and other fish workers. ILO consequently cooperated with IMO on the amendments to the 1978 International Convention on Standards, Certification and Watchkeeping for Seafarers (STCW), as it had earlier with IMO and FAO on the 1993 Protocol to the Torremolinos Convention for the Safety of Fishing Vessels.

77. As regards future instruments and consistency with the Convention on the Law of the Sea, ILO advises that the draft revised texts for five of its maritime instruments, approved by a Tripartite Meeting on Maritime Labour Standards (December 1994) for adoption by an International Labour Conference, include references to the entry into force of the Convention and generally take account of the relevant provisions.

5. United Nations Environment Programme

78. UNEP places great emphasis on the importance of the entry into force of the Convention and on its nature as a comprehensive, enforceable environmental convention and a strategic instrument for promoting an integrated approach to the sustainable development of marine and coastal areas. 57/ The UNEP Governing Council, furthermore, has included the entry into force of the Convention in the group of "major international events" having important implications for the Programme; 58/ this group also includes "An Agenda for Peace", 59/ and "An Agenda for Development". 60/ Attention was drawn not only to the impacts of the provisions of Part XII of the Convention, but also to such other provisions as article 43 (pollution in international straits), articles 61-68 and 116-120 (living resources in the exclusive economic zone and on the high seas), and article 145 (pollution from activities in the international seabed area). The broad range of responsibilities that States parties to the Convention assume was stressed, including the obligation to take legal action in the case of breaches of relevant national and international legal requirements. 61/

79. The UNEP Regional Seas Programme is an important avenue for the implementation of the Convention, and the Oceans and Coastal Areas Programme Activity Centre is designated as the focal point for ensuring UNEP's role as a competent international organization under the Convention. Note should therefore be taken of the decision to integrate programmes on freshwater and marine water bodies in the Centre. This integration of aquatic issues is also reflected in the International Waters component of the Global Environment Facility and in the draft global programme of action to protect the marine environment from land-based activities to be adopted at an intergovernmental conference in November 1995 (see paras. 196-197 below). The Governing Council has also noted the importance of the entry into force of the Convention for the future global programme. 62/

80. The scope of and the tasks undertaken by the UNEP regional seas programmes (now encompassing 13 conventions and action plans involving over 140 countries and territories) are limited only by the desires of its constituent Governments, and a focus on designing, implementing and enforcing legislation, as a cooperative regional undertaking, would promise greater cost-effectiveness and efficiency, as well as facilitate the fulfilment of obligations under the Convention on the Law of the Sea and/or the regional convention or action plan.

81. UNEP's support for the development of national legislation and institutions and training in environmental law, policy and administration will also be undertaken in the context of the implementation of the Programme of Action for the Sustainable Development of Small Island Developing States, 63/ again with a distinct law of the sea component.

6. Food and Agriculture Organization of the United Nations

82. In its resolutions on large-scale pelagic drift-net fishing, on the United Nations Conference on Straddling Fish Stocks and Highly Migratory Fish Stocks, on fisheries by-catch and discards, and on unauthorized fishing in zones of national jurisdiction, the General Assembly has specifically noted the competence of FAO in these questions as they relate to the implementation of the Convention. In recent years, therefore, the Division for Ocean Affairs and Law of the Sea has developed special working procedures with FAO, *inter alia*, on the collection, review and analysis of information from various sources. Following the adoption of the 1995 Agreement for the implementation of the Convention provisions relating to the conservation and management of straddling fish stocks and highly migratory fish stocks, which includes important monitoring and reporting activities, and taking account also of the adoption of the 1995 Code of Conduct for Responsible Fisheries, these practices will be further refined, in order also to avoid duplication of effort and to maximize the value of the work involved.

7. United Nations regional commissions

83. The Economic Commission for Europe (ECE), which carries out important activities in the field of environmental law, has drawn attention to the regional conventions for which it is responsible, many of which are also important for the effective implementation of the Convention on the Law of the Sea. Particular note should be taken of the 1979 Convention on Long-range Transboundary Air Pollution and the 1991 Espoo Convention on Environmental Impact Assessment in a Transboundary Context as the means of implementing, regionally, the relevant provisions of the Convention on the Law of the Sea. The Espoo Convention covers activities, such as ports and offshore installations, which may have a significant impact on the marine environment and requires a comprehensive impact assessment at an early planning stage of activities to be carried out under the jurisdiction of one party and are likely to have a significant transboundary impact within an area, including the territorial sea, under the jurisdiction of another party.

84. The Economic Commission for Latin America and the Caribbean (ECLAC) has been restructured and reprogrammed, 64/ *inter alia*, to integrate a sustainable development strategy and to create subprogrammes for the Caribbean and for Mexico and Central America. This is now considered to offer better opportunities for conducting coastal and marine activities. ECLAC has established a "task team" within the Natural Resources and Energy Unit of the new Environment and Development Division to develop some activities in the marine sector, including those directed at supporting member States' negotiations within the context of the International Seabed Authority on land-based mineral production, environmental aspects of seabed mining and scientific research. Developments with respect to the Convention on the Law of the Sea would also be duly incorporated in the programme of the Commission.

85. The Economic and Social Commission for Asia and the Pacific (ESCAP) has a well-established Marine Affairs Programme. Its main emphasis is on the development of regional marine mineral resources, especially within the context of integrated coastal area management. Activities also involve promoting coordination among three subregional intergovernmental organizations: the Committee for Coastal and Offshore Geoscience Programmes in East and South-East Asia, the South Pacific Applied Geoscience Commission, and the Indian Ocean Marine Affairs Conference, all of which take a strong interest in the effective implementation of the Convention.

86. The Economic Commission for Africa (ECA) has also emphasized the importance of the ratification of the Convention on the Law of the Sea and its implementation, particularly in the ECA Strategy and Action Programme for Integrated Development and Management of Marine/Ocean Affairs in Africa. 65/

G. Legal developments under related treaties and instruments

1. IMO conventions: main developments

87. Steady progress has been made by Governments in ratifying or acceding to the various IMO conventions. There now remain only 5 out of 40 conventions that are not yet in force. 66/ Main developments are as follows:

- The 1990 International Convention on Oil Pollution Preparedness, Response and Cooperation (OPRC) entered into force on 13 May 1995;

- The 1992 Protocols to the 1969 International Convention on Civil Liability for Pollution Damage (CLC) and the 1971 International Convention on the Establishment of an International Fund for Compensation for Oil Pollution Damage (FUND) will enter into force on 30 May 1996;

- The 1989 International Convention on Salvage will enter into force on 14 July 1996;
- Amendments have been adopted to the 1973 International Convention for the Prevention of Pollution from Ships, as modified by the Protocol of 1978 relating thereto (MARPOL 73/78) to improve the implementation of its annexes I, II, III and V, and particularly in respect of inspections by port States; they will enter into force on 3 March 1996;
- A diplomatic conference scheduled for late 1996 will consider the adoption of a new annex to MARPOL containing mandatory measures to prevent air pollution from ships;
- Amendments to chapter V of the 1974 International Convention for the Safety of Life at Sea (SOLAS), to introduce mandatory ships' routeing systems, will enter into force on 1 January 1997 under the "tacit acceptance" procedure. Consequential amendments to the General Provisions on Ships' Routeing would also take effect at that time;
- Comprehensive amendments to STCW were adopted by a Conference of STCW Parties in July 1995. They are expected to enter into force on 1 February 1997 under the "tacit acceptance" procedure;
- A concurrent conference adopted the 1995 International Convention on Standards of Training, Certification and Watchkeeping for Fishing Vessel Personnel (STCW-F). This new Convention, containing the first mandatory safety standards and applying to crews of fishing vessels generally 24 metres or more in length, will enter into force 12 months after being accepted by 15 States;
- A Conference of Contracting Governments (November 1995) will adopt amendments to SOLAS aimed at enhancing the safety of ro-ro (roll-on, roll-off) passenger ships. The 1995 amendments to STCW and the draft STCW Code also include measures to improve the safety of these ships;
- A diplomatic conference in April 1996 will consider the adoption of the draft convention for liability and compensation in connection with the carriage of hazardous and noxious substances by sea (HNS Convention) and the draft protocol to revise the 1976 Convention on the Limitation of Liability for Maritime Claims 67/ (see also para. 113 below);
- The International Safety Management Code (ISM Code) is expected to become mandatory on 1 July 1998;
- Still under consideration is the possible revision of the 1952 International Convention for the Unification of Certain Rules relating to Arrest of Seagoing Ships, in the light of developments as reflected in the 1993 International Convention on Maritime Liens and Mortgages;
- The feasibility of a new convention on offshore mobile craft (based on a revised draft by the Comité maritime international) will be taken up in 1996. The question of a more comprehensive instrument on offshore structures has been generally considered by IMO bodies to lie outside the organization's competence. 68/

2. Navigational rules and the law of the sea

88. In the current reporting period, IMO bodies have considered several fundamental issues of importance to the interpretation and application of the Convention on the Law of the Sea: restrictions on navigational rights in the

form of mandatory ship routeing and reporting, with commensurate benefits, however, for the protection of the marine environment and maritime safety; legal as well as practical problems as concerns the regime of transit passage through international straits; and the adverse impacts of naval blockades and alien smuggling by ship (see paras. 145, 161-164).

(a) Mandatory ships' routeing

89. Mandatory measures with respect to ships' routeing and ship reporting have been dealt with extensively in previous reports of the Secretary-General in view of their considerable importance for the navigational rights and duties under the Convention and in particular the implementation of its article 211 (6).

90. The newly amended regulation V/8 of SOLAS provides that ships' routeing systems may be made mandatory for "all ships, certain categories of ships or ships carrying certain cargoes" when adopted and implemented in accordance with IMO guidelines and criteria. 69/ Prior to this development, only the observance of traffic separation schemes was mandatory, and the observance of ships' routeing systems only recommendatory. The new regulation V/8 therefore will make such systems mandatory at the request of Governments, provided that the proposal is approved by IMO.

91. Nothing in this SOLAS amendment is to prejudice rights and duties under "international law or the legal regime of international straits"; furthermore the regulation specifically provides that all adopted ships' routeing systems and actions taken to enforce compliance shall be consistent with the relevant provisions of the Convention on the Law of the Sea.

92. The connection between the introduction of mandatory routeing systems and the new SOLAS provision on mandatory ship reporting to vessel traffic systems should also be noted (see A/49/631, para. 116). Both provisions reflect important progress in the task undertaken at IMO to provide port and coastal States with the regulatory framework necessary to prevent accidents in their jurisdictional waters.

93. The guidelines and criteria referred to in the new SOLAS regulation are the General Provisions on Ships' Routeing, originally adopted in 1985, and now amended to take account of the introduction of mandatory ships' routeing systems. 70/ With respect to systems which would extend beyond the territorial sea or lie in an international strait, the General Provisions enumerate the various elements which are to be considered and on which consultations are required with IMO: possible alternative routeing measures, the traffic pattern, navigational hazards, navigational aids, state of hydrographic surveys, marine environmental considerations, the extent of the proposed application to ships and their cargoes, and the delineation and charting of the proposed system.

94. In respect of routeing systems intended primarily for environmental protection, IMO would have to consider whether the proposal could reasonably be expected to significantly prevent or reduce the risk of pollution or other damage, and whether the proposed size of an area to be protected, particularly "areas to be avoided", would unreasonably limit navigation. According to the amended General Provisions, IMO will not adopt a proposed routeing system until it is satisfied that it does not impose unnecessary constraints on shipping; in particular, an area to be avoided will not be adopted if it would impede the passage of ships through an international strait.

95. The question of imposing routeing restrictions on the carriage of radioactive material has also been raised at IMO in the context of follow-up to matters complementary to the INF Code (transport of irradiated nuclear fuel, plutonium and high-level radioactive waste by sea). 71/ The matter was referred to the Legal Committee, where it was recognized that in order to minimize the risks involved in such transport, coastal States had the right to make specific routeing proposals to IMO. It was also agreed that continued consideration of

the subject in the technical bodies of IMO, particularly the Maritime Safety Committee and its Subcommittee on the Safety of Navigation, should take account of the relevant provisions of the Convention. Various countries continue to express their dissatisfaction with the rate of progress in controlling transport of these substances, pointing particularly at the need to set criteria for restricting or excluding entry into certain sea areas, to explore compulsory salvage and to prepare a mechanism of consultation between exporting and importing States and interested coastal States. The view has also been expressed that a general exclusion from certain areas would be an excessive measure, in conflict with the Convention, in particular articles 22, 23, 58 and 211. 72/

96. It may be noted that the 26th South Pacific Forum (September 1995) reiterated its policy of having the highest international safety and security standards for such shipments, conducted in a manner which addresses all possible contingencies, and in full consultation with Forum countries. 73/ The Forum has also adopted the Waigani Convention on 16 September 1995, banning the importation of all hazardous and radioactive wastes from outside the Convention area to Pacific island developing States parties, and ensuring that any transboundary movements of hazardous wastes within the Convention area are completed in a controlled and environmentally sound manner.

97. An important basic aspect of ships' routeing is the status of hydrographic surveying and nautical charting, on which there are serious deficiencies worldwide. IMO and the International Hydrographic Organization (IHO) have joined in pressing this point also in the context of any future consideration of UNCED follow-up. 74/

(b) Navigation and the regime for international straits

98. Particular questions as to the conformity of national rules and regulations on navigation with international rules and regulations arose last year with respect to the Turkish Regulations for Traffic Order in the Area of Straits and the Sea of Marmara and the 1994 IMO Rules and Recommendations on Navigation through the Strait of Istanbul, the Strait of Çanakkale and the Sea of Marmara (see A/49/631, paras. 118-122).

99. The Maritime Safety Committee has suggested that if, in the light of experience gained in the implementation of the IMO Rules and Recommendations, the need emerges for action to be taken on technical issues related to navigation in these areas, IMO is the right forum to take such action, and its mechanism for the purpose is the standing Working Group on Ships' Routeing. 75/ The IMO Rules and Recommendations were implemented only recently, on 24 November 1994, so that it is still too early to determine what the actual deficiencies in their implementation might be. It may be noted that the changed legal context brought about by the recent amendments to SOLAS Chapter V regarding mandatory ships' routeing and reporting systems and the corresponding amendments to the General Provisions on Ships' Routeing may contribute to future action to strengthen or modify the existing IMO Rules and Recommendations and consequently the national regulations.

100. Several delegations have made statements for the record, including comments on article 38 (2) of the Convention, both asserting and denying that the regime of transit passage applies in the Black Sea Straits. 76/

3. ILO conventions and recommendations

101. Draft texts (Proposed Conclusions) have been approved for adoption by a future International Labour Conference. They would revise substantially a number of existing maritime labour instruments to improve the conditions of work for seafarers, and would apply also to commercial maritime fishing and to

offshore units, to the extent that competent State authorities deemed practicable. 77/

102. The Proposed Conclusions concern:

- The 1926 Labour Inspection (Seamen) Recommendation (No. 28), calling for both a convention and a recommendation on ship inspection, with emphasis on living and working conditions;

- The 1958 Wages, Hours of Work and Manning (Sea) Convention (Revised) (No. 109) and 1958 Recommendation (No. 109), calling for a Convention on hours of work and manning which would establish international limits on maximum working hours or minimum rest periods, and a Recommendation which would be a comprehensive instrument primarily on seafarers' wages;

- The 1920 Placing of Seamen Convention (No. 9), which would be revised to become both a Convention and a Recommendation, which would, inter alia, regulate private employment services for seafarers;

- Extension of the 1976 Merchant Shipping (Minimum Standards) Convention (No. 147) through the addition of several more recent maritime labour Conventions to the appendix to that Convention. This Convention, with 53 parties, is an important aspect of port State control of ships. It refers in turn to the other ILO instruments on accident prevention, officers' certificates of competency, ship construction standards for crew, etc.

103. The drafting of the Proposed Conclusions has been proposed, in consultation with the Division for Ocean Affairs and Law of the Sea, to overcome potential problems arising from the difference in the scope of application of ILO instruments to vessels: ILO provisions normally apply to vessels registered in the territory of an ILO member State, whereas article 94 of the Convention on the Law of the Sea provides that a State's duties relate to ships flying its flag. Thus, jurisdiction could be split in the cases of bareboat charters and suspended registrations, leading to practical problems over real rights (e.g., liens to cover wage claims) and non-real rights (e.g., crew safety matters). The proposed addition would permit identification of the State that would have responsibility as regards a particular ship for a particular purpose.

4. Developments in environmental law

104. International legal and related efforts in the field of environment continue to see rapid development, constituting a substantial framework of legal, administrative, economic, financial and technical measures to prevent, control and reduce the adverse impact of human activities on terrestrial and aquatic ecosystems. The United Nations Convention on the Law of the Sea is a major component in this large and growing family of international legal instruments. Many of these instruments contribute, directly and indirectly, to the protection of the marine and coastal environment and to sustainable resource development, and thus to the attainment of the objectives of the Convention. Its effective implementation in these areas is in fact equally dependent on the effective implementation of these conventions as well as on the consistent and uniform application of the provisions of the Convention by parties to those conventions. In the light of the entry into force of the Convention, various Conferences of Parties and other competent bodies have taken up various aspects of their relationship with the Convention.

105. Many international organizations are seeking to strengthen greatly their technical cooperation programmes and advisory services in support of effective implementation of environmental and other treaties, as well as of UNCED-related activities. Donor organizations, in their policies and guidelines, have also

begun to take account of specific needs associated with ensuring the effective implementation of treaty obligations and other international commitments and to help Governments integrate regional and global objectives into their national environment and development policies. The World Bank has specifically stated that it will not finance projects that contravene any international environmental agreement to which the member country concerned is a party, and that for certain projects, especially those financed through the Global Environment Facility, ratification of the relevant convention can be a prerequisite to receiving financing. 78/ It includes the Convention on the Law of the Sea in its list of key agreements.

(a) The London Convention

106. The 1972 London Convention on the Prevention of Marine Pollution by Dumping of Wastes and Other Matter is undergoing a substantial amendment process. A diplomatic conference in 1996 is expected to adopt a protocol extensively amending the Convention. The entry into force of the Convention on the Law of the Sea is therefore of considerable, and immediate, interest.

107. The 1994 Consultative Meeting of Contracting Parties noted that States parties to the Convention on the Law of the Sea would be legally bound to adopt laws and regulations and take other measures to prevent, reduce and control pollution by dumping. These must be no less effective than the global rules and standards referred to in article 210 of the Convention. These global rules and standards were considered to be those of the London Convention 1972 (see A/49/631, paras. 84-85).

108. At the request of the Consultative Meeting, the Secretary-General of IMO has written to States parties to the Convention on the Law of the Sea that are not parties to the London Convention, drawing attention to their obligations relating to the prevention of marine pollution by dumping of wastes and other matter at sea; to the objectives of, and the achievements made under the London Convention; and to the assistance which can be provided through cooperation with the contracting parties to that Convention. In the communication, the States parties to the Convention on the Law of the Sea were urged to become parties to the London Convention and to participate in the current process of its review and amendment, considering that the outcome of that work will have far-reaching implications for the future development of relevant global rules and standards. 79/

109. The amendment process has entailed extensive discussions on the future scope of the London Convention, including its extension to internal waters, artificial reefs, abandoned cables and offshore oil and gas operations. The issue of the scope of the Convention and the discussions of contracting parties are indicative of important trends in the development of international environmental law, including the emphasis on the application of the precautionary and polluter-pays principles and the widening of the objectives to include elimination as well as prevention, reduction and control of pollution. The broadening of definitions to cover all the environmentally adverse effects of human activities is also apparent in the discussions of the Amendment Group as the concept of "degradation of the marine environment" has effectively replaced "marine pollution" in many contexts (see also ibid., paras. 74-76).

(b) Marine biodiversity and the Convention on Biological Diversity

110. The subject of coastal and marine biodiversity was one of the priority items identified by the First Conference of Parties to the Convention on Biological Diversity (December 1994), which also recognized the relevance of obligations under the Convention on the Law of the Sea to its implementation. 80/ Its Subsidiary Body on Scientific, Technical and Technological Advice (SBSTTA) has since also reiterated that national legislation on biodiversity should be in conformity with the Convention on the Law of the Sea, the agreement to be concluded on straddling fish stocks and

highly migratory fish stocks, the FAO Code of Conduct for Responsible Fisheries, and IMO Guidelines dealing with harmful organisms transported in ships' ballast water.

111. SBSTTA has prepared an extensive recommendation for the Second Conference of Parties (November 1995), and for the Commission on Sustainable Development in 1996, on coastal and marine biodiversity (see paras. 201-202 below). 81/

(c) Responsibility and liability

112. Article 235, paragraph 3, of the Convention calls on States to cooperate in the further development of international law relating to responsibility and liability for environmental damage, including the development of criteria and procedures for payment of compensation, and the settlement of related disputes. Developments at IMO have considerably advanced the implementation of this provision as concerns pollution from ships. In addition to the entry into force of the 1992 Protocols concerning civil liability for oil pollution, 82/ the IMO Legal Committee has now concluded its work on the draft HNS Convention and the draft protocol to revise the Convention on the Limitation of Liability for Maritime Claims. A diplomatic conference will be convened early in 1996.

113. The draft HNS Convention covers in principle all kinds of hazardous and noxious substances defined by reference to lists of substances contained in other IMO instruments. The scope of application of the draft HNS Convention includes damage by contamination of the environment caused in the exclusive economic zone of contracting States. The HNS Convention is based on a two-tier system in one instrument, with shipowner liability supplemented by a fund financed through contributions from cargo interests. Decisions on the inclusion or exclusion of radioactive materials and coal from the draft HNS Convention, and on the notion of linkage between the HNS Convention and general limitation treaties, will have to be decided at the diplomatic conference. Many Governments are giving high priority to the adoption of this instrument, since without a global HNS Convention it is feared that regional regimes might develop, with consequent difficulties for the international shipping industry.

114. In 1996, the Legal Committee will take up the question, referred to it by the Marine Environment Protection Committee, as to whether it is feasible and desirable to establish an international regime on compensation for pollution from ships' bunkers. Such compensation is not covered by the 1969 Civil Liability Convention or by the draft HNS Convention. The question of compulsory insurance is also already on the agenda of the Legal Committee. 83/

(d) Regional environmental agreements

115. There are two new regional seas programmes: the North-West Pacific, with four participating States; and the South Asian Seas, with five participating States. Two existing programmes have expanded their membership: the East Asian Seas, with five additional States; and the South-East Pacific, with four additional States from the Central American region. There are now eight regional conventions in force, and the convention for the Eastern Africa region lacks only one ratification or accession for its entry into force. Of the 25 protocols to these regional conventions, five are not yet in force: two in the East Africa region, the protocol on protected areas in the Caribbean, and the dumping protocol for the Black Sea. 84/

116. In June 1995, amendments were adopted to the 1976 Barcelona Convention for the Protection of the Mediterranean Sea against Pollution and its Dumping Protocol, which incorporate the relevant advances made in international environmental law in the intervening years. The Conference of Plenipotentiaries also adopted the Protocol concerning Specially Protected Areas and Biological Diversity in the Mediterranean. 85/ Like the Caribbean protocol, it will require a follow-up meeting to adopt the technical annexes.

117. The 1995 Amendments change the title of the Barcelona Convention to the Convention for the Protection of the Marine Environment and the Coastal Region of the Mediterranean. It thus becomes the first marine environmental instrument fully to integrate land and sea issues, recognizing that the main impacts on the marine environment come from land-based activities. The amendments delete the specific exclusion of internal waters made in the 1976 Convention and allow each party to extend the application of the Convention to coastal areas within its own territory, according to its own definition. 86/

118. The 1995 Amendments to the Barcelona Convention refer only to the "relevant provisions" of the Convention on the Law of the Sea and provide that nothing in the Barcelona Convention and its Protocols "shall prejudice the rights and positions of any State" concerning the latter Convention. In fact, most parties to the Barcelona Convention are already parties to the Convention on the Law of the Sea. The new Protocol on protected areas contains a similar provision, with particularity as concerns the extent of marine areas and their delimitation, navigational rights on the high seas and in international straits, and the right of innocent passage. Designated "specially protected areas of Mediterranean importance" may lie partly or wholly on the high seas.

II. OTHER DEVELOPMENTS RELATING TO THE LAW OF THE SEA AND OCEAN AFFAIRS

A. Maritime disputes and conflicts

1. Settlement of disputes

(a) Bahrain and Qatar

119. On 1 July 1994, the International Court of Justice delivered a judgment on jurisdiction and admissibility in the Case concerning Maritime Delimitation and Territorial Questions between Qatar and Bahrain, ruling that Qatar and Bahrain had entered into international agreements by which they had undertaken to submit to the Court the whole of the dispute between them and fixing 30 November 1994 as the time-limit for submission (see A/49/631, para. 45).

120. On 30 November 1994, Qatar filed in the Registry a document entitled "Act to comply with paragraphs (3) and (4) of operative paragraph 41 of the Judgment of the Court dated 1 July 1994". In the document, Qatar referred to "the absence of an agreement between the Parties to act jointly" and stated that it was thereby submitting the whole of the dispute between Qatar and Bahrain. In Qatar's view, the following subjects fell within the Court's jurisdiction:

> "1. The Hawar Islands, including the island of Janan;
>
> "2. Fasht al Dibal and Qit'at Jaradah;
>
> "3. The archipelagic baselines;
>
> "4. Zubarah;
>
> "5. The areas for fishing for pearls and for fishing for swimming fish and any other matters connected with maritime boundaries."

121. Further to its application, Qatar requested the Court to adjudge and declare that Bahrain had no sovereignty or other territorial right over the island of Janan or over Zubarah, and that any claim by Bahrain concerning archipelagic baselines and areas for fishing for pearls and swimming fish would be irrelevant for the purpose of maritime delimitation in the case under consideration.

122. On 30 November 1994, Bahrain submitted to the Court a "Report" on the attempt by the parties to implement the judgment of 1 July 1994. In that Report, Bahrain understood the 1994 Judgment as confirming that the submission to the Court of "the whole of the dispute" must be "consensual in character, that is, a matter of agreement between the Parties". On 5 December 1994, Bahrain further submitted observations on Qatar's "Act", stating that the Act, even when considered in the light of the Judgment, could not create that jurisdiction or effect a valid submission in the absence of Bahrain's consent.

123. On 15 February 1995, the Court delivered a judgment on jurisdiction and admissibility, finding, by 10 votes to 5, that it had jurisdiction to adjudicate upon the dispute submitted to it between Qatar and Bahrain; and further that the application of Qatar as formulated on 30 November 1994 was admissible. 87/

124. Subsequently, by an Order of 28 April 1995, the Court fixed 29 February 1996 as the time-limit for the filing by each of the parties of a Memorial on the merits.

(b) Australia and Portugal

125. On 22 February 1991, Portugal filed in the Registry of the International Court of Justice an application instituting proceedings against Australia in a dispute concerning "certain activities of Australia with respect to East Timor" (see A/46/724, para. 40). It claimed that Australia, by negotiating with Indonesia an "agreement relating to the exploration and exploitation of the continental shelf in the area of the 'Timor Gap'", signed on 11 December 1989, and by the ratification and the initiation of the performance of that agreement and subsequent related measures, as well as by the exclusion of any negotiation on those matters with Portugal, had caused "particularly serious legal and moral damage to the people of East Timor and to Portugal, which will become material damage also if the exploitation of hydrocarbon resources begins".

126. In its application Portugal requested the Court, inter alia, to adjudge and declare that Australia had: (a) infringed the right of the people of East Timor to self-determination, to territorial integrity and unity and its permanent sovereignty over its natural wealth and resources, and was in breach of the obligation not to disregard but to respect that right, that integrity and that sovereignty; and (b) infringed the powers of Portugal as the administering Power of the Territory of East Timor.

127. In its counter-Memorial, Australia raised questions concerning the jurisdiction of the Court and the admissibility of the application.

128. In its judgment of 30 June 1995, the Court found that it could not exercise the jurisdiction conferred upon it by the declarations made by the parties to adjudicate upon the dispute. On Australia's principal objection to the effect that Portugal's application would require the Court to determine the rights and obligations of Indonesia, the Court concluded, inter alia, that Australia's behaviour could not be assessed without first entering into the question why Indonesia could not lawfully have concluded the 1989 Treaty, while Portugal allegedly could have done so; the very subject-matter of the Court's decision would necessarily be a determination whether, having regard to the circumstances in which Indonesia had entered and remained in East Timor, it could or could not have acquired the power to enter into treaties on behalf of East Timor relating to the resources of its continental shelf. The Court stated that it could not make such a determination in the absence of the consent of Indonesia. 88/

(c) Canada and Spain

129. On 28 March 1995, Spain filed in the Registry of the International Court of Justice an application instituting proceedings against Canada with respect to a dispute relating to the Canadian Coastal Fisheries Protection Act, as amended on 12 May 1994, and to the implementing regulations of that Act, as well as to

certain measures taken on the basis of that legislation, more particularly the boarding on the high seas, on 9 March 1995, of a fishing boat, the Estai, sailing under the Spanish flag (see also paras. 182-183 below).

130. The application indicated, inter alia, that by the amended Act an attempt had been made to impose on all persons on board foreign ships a broad prohibition on fishing in the North-West Atlantic Fisheries Organization (NAFO) Regulatory Area, that is, on the high seas, outside Canada's exclusive economic zone; that the Act expressly permitted the use of force against foreign fishing boats on the high seas; that the implementing regulations of 25 May 1994 provided, in particular, for "the use of force by fishery protection vessels against the foreign fishing boats covered by those rules ... which infringe their mandates in the zone of the high seas within the scope of those regulations"; and that the implementing regulations of 3 March 1995 expressly permitted such conduct as regards Spanish and Portuguese ships on the high seas.

131. The application alleged the violation of various principles and norms of international law and stated that there was a dispute between Spain and Canada which, going beyond the framework of fishing, seriously affected the very principle of the freedom of the high seas and, moreover, implied a serious infringement of the sovereign rights of Spain.

132. Spain requested the Court to declare: (a) that the legislation of Canada, in so far as it claimed to exercise a jurisdiction over ships flying a foreign flag on the high seas, was not opposable to Spain; (b) that Canada was bound to refrain from any repetition of the acts complained of, and to offer to Spain the reparation that was due; and (c) consequently, that the boarding on the high seas, on 9 March 1995, of the ship Estai flying the flag of Spain and the measures of coercion and the exercise of jurisdiction over that ship and over its captain constituted a concrete violation of the aforementioned principles and norms of international law.

133. As a basis of the Court's jurisdiction, the application referred to the declarations of Spain and of Canada made in accordance with Article 36, paragraph 2, of the Statute of the Court.

134. In a letter of 21 April 1995, Canada contested jurisdiction, stating that the Court lacked jurisdiction to deal with the application by reason of paragraph 2 (d) of the declaration, dated 10 May 1994, whereby Canada had accepted the compulsory jurisdiction of the Court. In that regard, the Spanish application had specified, inter alia, that the exclusion of the jurisdiction of the Court in relation to disputes which might arise from management and conservation measures taken by Canada with respect to vessels fishing in the NAFO Regulatory Area and the enforcement of such measures, under paragraph 2 (d) of the Canadian declaration, did not even partially affect the current dispute, because its application did not refer exactly to the disputes concerning those measures, but rather to their origin, to the Canadian legislation which constituted their frame of reference. 89/

135. By an Order of 2 May 1995, the President declared that the written proceedings should first address the question of the jurisdiction of the Court to entertain the dispute, and fixed 28 September 1995 as the time-limit for the filing of a Memorial by Spain, and 29 February 1996 as the time-limit for the filing of a counter-Memorial by Canada. 90/

(d) Kuwait, Saudi Arabia and the Islamic Republic of Iran offshore boundaries

136. In an effort to settle outstanding issues on the final demarcation of the Kuwait-Saudi offshore borders, high-level meetings were held in Saudi Arabia for three days in mid-July 1995 between the Kuwaiti Minister for Foreign Affairs and the Saudi Minister of Defence. The two countries reportedly agreed on several specific points with regard to their common sea boundary, leaving it to technical experts from each side to follow up on the agreed points at later

meetings. The outstanding border issue between the two countries relates to the demarcation of the offshore boundary of the partitioned neutral zone up to the Persian Gulf median line separating Saudi Arabia's and Kuwait's maritime zone from those of the Islamic Republic of Iran. Meanwhile, it was reported on 18 July that Kuwait was to start negotiations shortly with the Islamic Republic of Iran on the demarcation of the territorial border between those two countries. The settlement of the Kuwait-Saudi Arabia border would clear one obstacle to an agreement on maritime boundary between Kuwait and the Islamic Republic of Iran. 91/

2. Other developments

(a) Israel's naval activities in Lebanese territorial waters

137. Early in 1995, Lebanon submitted to the IMO Secretariat a complaint with respect to Israel's naval blockade of South Lebanon. Subsequently, Lebanon complained to the Maritime Safety Committee, the Legal Committee and the Council that Israel's activities within the territorial waters of South Lebanon, which included the inspection and detention of national and foreign ships as well as the use of gunfire against fishing boats, amounted to a naval blockade and constituted a threat to the freedom and security of international maritime navigation, and that the actions were in "flagrant violation of international law, the 1982 United Nations Convention on the Law of the Sea and the Conventions on fishing and maritime ports" and a violation of the spirit and letter of the IMO Convention.

138. Israel informed the Maritime Safety Committee that enhanced security activities, which involved making enquiries, identification and the occasional delaying of vessels off the coast of Lebanon in areas near the approaches to Israel had been carried out solely because the Lebanese Government was unable to effectively guarantee that those waters would not serve as a passage for hostile terrorist attacks on Israel. As long as such dangerous circumstances prevailed, it was the obligation and duty of Israel to act in accordance with the right of self-defence in international law, and to maintain those limited and necessary measures so as to guarantee the safety and security of Israel against terror. Furthermore, Israel did not consider IMO to be the proper forum for the consideration of those security issues. The various IMO forums which had been addressed took note of the statements made as well as those of other delegations. 92/

(b) Situation in the South China Sea

139. Disputes relating to sovereignty and jurisdiction over some sea and seabed areas in the South China Sea have continued as sources of tension among countries in the region. 93/ In February 1995, the Philippines expressed concern over reports that China had built certain structures in the region, namely on the Panganiban Reef (Mischief Reef) in the Kalayaan island group, an action that the Philippines maintained was inconsistent with international law and the spirit and intent of the 1992 Manila ASEAN Declaration on the South China Sea by the Association of South-East Asian Nations (ASEAN). 94/

140. At their meeting in July 1995, the ASEAN Foreign Ministers expressed their concern over recent events and called on all claimants to refrain from taking actions which could destabilize the region, including possibly undermining the freedom of navigation and aviation in the affected areas. They reiterated the significance of promoting confidence-building measures and mutually beneficial cooperative ventures in the ongoing Informal Workshop Series on Managing Potential Conflicts in the South China Sea initiated by Indonesia. 95/

141. Despite the continued tension, there were signs that the countries involved were moving towards a peaceful, negotiated solution, based on the principles of

international law, and particularly the Convention on the Law of the Sea. For example, China and the Philippines have reportedly agreed on a mutual code of conduct that would allow for freedom of navigation through the South China Sea chain of islands and to settle the issues "in a peaceful and friendly manner" in accordance with the recognized principles of international law, including the Convention on the Law of the Sea." 96/

(c) Situation in the Caspian Sea

142. The situation in the Caspian Sea has also continued to be a source of possible tension owing to conflicting claims over its status (see A/49/631, para. 56). It was reported that at a May 1995 meeting of the five littoral States, the participants failed to resolve their differences over the legal status of the Caspian. Azerbaijan and Kazakstan maintained that the Caspian should be classified under maritime law as an enclosed sea. The Russian Federation and the Islamic Republic of Iran, on the other hand, maintained that the Caspian was a lake and its resources should be shared on the basis of common ownership. Declaring the Caspian an enclosed sea would give coastal States the rights to develop subsoil reserves in sectors drawn in accordance with the provisions of the Convention on the Law of the Sea, particularly those relating to the exclusive economic zone. 97/

(d) Dispute over Persian Gulf islands

143. The dispute between the United Arab Emirates and the Islamic Republic of Iran concerning sovereignty over the islands of Abu Musa, Greater Tunb and Lesser Tunb has remained unresolved. The United Arab Emirates reportedly announced in late 1994 its desire to refer the dispute to the International Court of Justice owing to Iran's "intransigence and its strong unwillingness to end its occupation of the three islands". The Islamic Republic of Iran, on the other hand, maintains that "cordial and bilateral dialogue" is the only way to settle the dispute. 98/ The Gulf Cooperation Council, at a meeting held in Manamah from 19 to 21 December 1994, also called on the Islamic Republic of Iran to submit the matter to the International Court of Justice, noting in a declaration "the Islamic Republic of Iran's failure to demonstrate any serious desire to discuss the ending of occupation (of the three islands)". 99/

B. Peace and security

144. One of the objectives laid down in the preamble to the Convention is the establishment of a legal order for the seas and oceans which will promote their peaceful uses. The comprehensive framework established by the Convention for the regulation of all ocean space promotes the peaceful uses of the seas and oceans and therefore constitutes an important contribution to the strengthening of peace, security, cooperation and friendly relations among all nations. The Convention can thus be viewed as an important contribution to "An Agenda for Peace" and a particularly useful tool for preventive diplomacy.

145. In the area of peace-keeping, naval forces are being employed in pursuit of the collective interest of the international community for, *inter alia*, humanitarian relief, peace-keeping measures or enforcement operations designed to make economic sanctions effective. The impact of enforcement measures on merchant shipping was brought to the attention of IMO last year by the International Chamber of Shipping (ICS) in connection with shipping to and from ports in Jordan, Montenegro, Haiti and certain ports in Liberia and Angola. ICS proposed to IMO's Facilitation Committee the development of recommendations for the guidance of naval forces enforcing United Nations blockades in order to facilitate legitimate maritime traffic in such circumstances. 100/ The majority of the Committee members supported the proposal in principle. Realizing the political and legal implications involved, however, the Committee instructed the secretariat to seek the advice of the Security Council's Sanctions Committee. 101/ The IMO Council, in its consideration in June 1995 of the

Facilitation Committee's proposed action, decided that the Committee should only deal with the issue if a request to that effect was received from the relevant Sanctions Committee and that, therefore, no further action should be taken at the time. 102/

146. The broadening of the concept of security, particularly to include food, resource and environmental security, as well as security against organized transnational crime and certain other crimes, has distinct maritime components, such as control over natural resource exploitation, illicit drug trafficking by sea, terrorism, smuggling of aliens, and piracy and armed robbery.

147. It has been suggested that maritime cooperation on ocean resources surveillance would be a particularly promising confidence-building measure which may be valuable in minimizing the risk of conflict in North-East and South-East Asia. 103/ That type of surveillance has precedents in the Asia-Pacific region, including both multilateral (e.g., fisheries surveillance cooperation in the South Pacific Forum) and bilateral (e.g., Australia/Indonesia Timor Gap surveillance and Malaysia/Indonesia pollution monitoring) measures. In the case of the Timor Gap, agreement on joint surveillance activities between Australia and Indonesia was not only an integral part of the agreement to establish the Zone of Cooperation in the Timor Sea, but it has also served as a catalyst for more general arrangements for coordinating surveillance operations between the two countries in the broader area of the Timor and Arafura seas.

148. Cooperation in ocean resources surveillance and development also has precedents in other regions of the world. For example, in the area of the South-West Atlantic, Argentina and the United Kingdom are cooperating through the South Atlantic Fisheries Commission in the conservation of fish stocks (see paras. 190-192 below) and have now, pursuant to a joint declaration signed on 27 September 1995, extended this cooperation to the exploration for and exploitation of hydrocarbons in the South-West Atlantic. 104/

149. Another valuable confidence-building measure which has been suggested for North-East and South-East Asia is the establishment of regional incidents-at-sea agreements which not only would include provisions of time-tested bilateral incidents-at-sea agreements but would also address particular non-military maritime security concerns. 105/ A regional incidents-at-sea agreement and a text on search and rescue have been negotiated under the Middle East peace process and are expected to be adopted at the end of the year.

150. The conviction that the establishment of internationally recognized nuclear-weapon-free zones on the basis of arrangements freely arrived at among the States of the region concerned enhances global and regional peace and security was reaffirmed by the 1995 Review and Extension Conference of the Treaty on the Non-Proliferation of Nuclear Weapons. 106/

151. In addition to the two existing nuclear-weapon-free zones, in Latin America and the Caribbean and in the South Pacific, a treaty establishing a similar zone in Africa was adopted by the OAU Council of Ministers of the Organization of African Unity (OAU) in 1995 and subsequently endorsed by the OAU Assembly of Heads of State and Government. 107/ One of the objectives laid down in the preamble to the Treaty on an African Nuclear-Weapon-Free Zone is that of keeping Africa free of environmental pollution by radioactive wastes and other radioactive matter. The Treaty and its three protocols apply to the territory, which is defined as "the land territory, internal waters, territorial seas and archipelagic waters and the airspace above them as well as the seabed and subsoil beneath", within the zone. The rights, or the exercise of the rights, of any State under international law with regard to freedom of the seas remain unaffected by the Treaty. Each party is left to decide for itself whether to allow visits by foreign ships to its ports, transit of its airspace by foreign aircraft and navigation by foreign ships in its territorial sea or archipelagic waters in a manner not covered by the rights of innocent passage, archipelagic sea lane passage or transit passage of straits. The Treaty prohibits the

testing of nuclear explosive devices and it also prohibits the dumping of radioactive wastes.

152. The decision of France to resume testing in the Pacific has been criticized, inter alia, by the Permanent Mechanism for Consultation and Policy Coordination (Rio Group), 108/ the South Pacific Forum, 109/ the South Pacific States Members of the United Nations, 110/ and the Movement of Non-Aligned Countries, 111/ as well as by the many Governments which have referred to the issue in the current session of the General Assembly. On 22 September 1995, the International Court of Justice dismissed New Zealand's request for an examination of the situation in accordance with the Court's 1974 judgment in the Nuclear Tests Case (New Zealand v. France) on the basis that it did not fall within the provisions of paragraph 63 of that judgment. The basis of that judgment was France's undertaking not to conduct any further atmospheric nuclear tests and therefore only a resumption of nuclear tests in the atmosphere would have affected it. 112/

C. Crimes at sea

153. The alarming rate of expansion of organized transnational crime, its global reach, its evasion of national controls and the lack of effective international cooperation in preventing and combating it threatens the security and stability of all States and makes effective national measures and global action imperative. Transnational criminals are engaged in trafficking in arms, drugs, hazardous substances, endangered species and even human beings, leaving behind a trail of crime, corruption and human and environmental damage. 113/

154. Efforts by the international community are intensifying in the search for ways and means of strengthening and improving national capabilities and international cooperation against crime at sea and of laying the foundations for concerted and effective global action against such crime and the prevention of its further expansion.

1. Illicit traffic in narcotic drugs and psychotropic substances

155. The legal framework governing international cooperation in the suppression of illicit traffic in narcotic drugs and psychotropic substances by sea is provided for in article 108 of the 1982 United Nations Convention on the Law of the Sea and article 17 of the 1988 United Nations Convention against Illicit Traffic in Narcotic Drugs and Psychotropic Substances. 114/ Article 108, paragraph 1, obligates all States to cooperate in the suppression of illicit traffic in narcotic drugs and psychotropic substances engaged in by ships on the high seas "contrary to international conventions", and article 17, paragraph 1, requires all States to cooperate to the fullest extent possible to suppress illicit traffic by sea "in conformity with the international law of the sea". As of 11 October 1995, 49 States parties to the 1982 Convention are also parties to the 1988 Convention.

156. However, international cooperation has not been effective enough to counter illicit traffic in narcotic drugs and psychotropic substances by sea. According to the Working Group on Maritime Cooperation of the Commission on Narcotic Drugs 115/ and the replies from 51 countries to a questionnaire on the status of international cooperation in the implementation of article 17, 116/ the barriers to international cooperation include the inability of some States to exercise effective jurisdiction over vessels flying their flag outside the territorial sea, and accordingly their inability to reply to requests by other States to board such vessels, as well as the inability of States to exercise criminal jurisdiction over offenders other than their nationals on board vessels beyond the territorial sea. Furthermore, maritime law-enforcement capability was often weak, and domestic legal restrictions in some States regarding the use of naval

vessels in drug law-enforcement operations further limited the interception capabilities of several coastal States. The Working Group considered that it was necessary to endeavour to strengthen the existing international legal framework, to encourage universal ratification of the 1982 and 1988 Conventions and to promote bilateral and multilateral agreements.

157. The Working Group on Maritime Cooperation, established in 1994 with the mandate to develop a comprehensive set of principles and specific recommendations to enhance on a global basis the implementation of article 17 (A/49/631, paras. 178-180), concluded its work at its second meeting in February 1995 with the adoption of, inter alia, the following recommendations: 117/

- States should maintain a register containing information on vessels flying their flag, designate an authority or authorities to receive or respond to requests made pursuant to article 17, and improve and streamline channels for direct communication between competent authorities;

- States should take the necessary measures to ensure that they exercise effective jurisdiction over ships flying their flags in accordance with the principles of the international law of the sea, and exercise jurisdiction over drug-trafficking offences involving vessels without nationality or those assimilated to them in accordance with international law;

- States should reach agreement on the general minimum safeguards applicable in cases involving the boarding of suspected vessels and on the measures that might be taken by the intervening State in relation to a suspicious vessel, such as stopping, boarding, inspection and search.

158. The recommendations are prefaced by a general recommendation that observance of the principles of international law, in particular those concerning the full respect of sovereignty and territorial integrity and the principles of the international law of the sea regime, should govern international cooperation in the fight against illicit traffic by sea of narcotic drugs and psychotropic substances.

159. The Working Group pointed out that the technique of controlled delivery usually produces better law enforcement results than does intervention at sea. It recommended that, where operational circumstances permit, preference should be given to the surveillance of vessels and the increased use of controlled delivery in order to target the crime syndicates involved, rather than to boarding operations.

160. The Working Group's report on the meeting and the recommendations adopted were endorsed by the Commission on Narcotic Drugs. 118/ The Secretary-General hailed the recommendations and principles as representing "a milestone in efforts to contain the problem of illicit drug shipments that traverse international waters". 119/

2. Smuggling of aliens

161. There has been a resurgence of incidents involving the smuggling of aliens by ship. Aliens are being smuggled in the holds of ships, in containers and on board fishing vessels, many of which are not registered. Often the mode of transportation is changed several times between the country of origin and the country of destination. Reports demonstrate that this organized transnational crime constitutes serious threat to the safety of life at sea.

162. The Facilitation Committee of IMO has emphasized that from the humanitarian, operational and administrative points of view, it is high time to solve the problems related to stowaways and that an international agreement on the treatment of stowaways would be of benefit to national immigration authorities as well as to the shipping industry. There is currently no international agreement as to where and how stowaways would be disembarked, or as to how their return or repatriation should be organized. The resolution of stowaway cases is difficult because of different national legislation in each of the several potential countries involved: the country of embarkation, the country of disembarkation, the flag State of the vessel, the country of apparent, claimed or actual nationality of the stowaway, and the countries of transit during repatriation. 120/

163. The Facilitation Committee has established a working group with the mandate to develop a resolution for adoption at the twentieth session of the IMO Assembly in 1997 on the need to deal in a practical way with the ever increasing problem of stowaways, to reduce the problem for shipping and to ensure proper treatment of stowaways. It was agreed that such an Assembly resolution might be further implemented by means of a memorandum of understanding between national Administrations, given the need for involvement of immigration as well as maritime authorities. 121/

164. The Economic and Social Council, in its resolution 1995/10 of 24 July 1995, on criminal justice action to combat the organized smuggling of illegal migrants across national boundaries adopted on 24 July 1995, urged States to share information, to coordinate law enforcement activities between national authorities in cooperation with competent international bodies and carriers engaged in international transport, and otherwise to cooperate, if their law permitted, in order to trace and arrest those who organized the smuggling of illegal migrants and to prevent the illegal transport by smugglers of third-country nationals through their territory.

3. Piracy and armed robbery at sea

165. As of 31 August 1995, the total number of acts of piracy and armed robbery against ships reported to IMO since 1991 was 568, and 51 of those acts took place between January and August 1995. 122/ The Maritime Safety Committee at its sixty-fifth session, 123/ noting with concern that the piracy and armed robbery trend, which in the middle of 1994 had been downwards, had now reversed, in particular in South-East Asia and South America, invited all Governments concerned and the industry to intensify their efforts to eliminate such unlawful activities in all areas concerned. The International Chamber of Commerce (International Maritime Bureau) issued a warning to shipping on the increase in the number of attacks against ships which had occurred in Indonesian waters during the last quarter of 1994, particularly on container and bulk carrier vessels. 124/ In view of the upward trend in attacks, the Committee decided that the IMO secretariat should issue monthly reports on all incidents of piracy and armed robbery against ships reported to the organization and, in addition, on a quarterly basis, composite reports accompanied by an analysis of the situation.

D. Conservation and management of living marine resources

1. World fisheries situation

166. In a report entitled "The state of world fisheries and aquaculture", prepared for the Ministerial Meeting on Fisheries (Rome, 14-15 March 1995), held in conjunction with the twenty-first session of the FAO Committee on Fisheries, FAO reported that total world fish production had reached 101.3 million tonnes in 1993, up from 97 million tonnes in 1991, owing to input almost entirely from aquaculture. 125/ In order to maintain a consumption rate of about 13 kilograms

per person per year to the year 2010 in the face of population growth, 91 million tonnes of food fish per year would be required. Such an increase was considered feasible if aquaculture production could be doubled in the next 15 years and if significant improvements could be achieved in the conservation and management of world marine fisheries, through stock rebuilding and more rational harvesting practices, and with the application of food technology to improve utilization of by-catches and small pelagic fish yields for direct human consumption. 126/

167. The report noted also that more than 69 per cent of the world's marine stocks were either fully exploited, overfished, depleted or in the process of rebuilding from overfishing and therefore in need of urgent corrective conservation and management measures, 127/ and that such conservation and management measures should include reduction of overcapacity and fishing efforts. 128/

168. At its twenty-first session, the Committee on Fisheries also agreed that an improvement in fisheries conservation and management was essential for long-term sustainable fisheries development and that international cooperation was essential for effective fisheries management, calling in particular for the strengthening of regional fishery bodies as means of achieving such cooperation. 129/ Following an exchange of views on the problem of fleet overcapacity, over-investment, excessive manpower in the fishing sector and the difficulty in finding a solution to the problem as well as the possible negative effects of increased overcapacity in the industrial sector on artisanal fisheries, the Committee urged FAO to study further the effects of subsidies to industrial fisheries on competition and trade, in particular with regard to the impacts on fish exports from developing countries. 130/ Moreover, the Committee supported the view that discards should be minimized and that post-harvested losses should be reduced. 131/

169. The Ministerial Meeting on Fisheries adopted the Rome Consensus on World Fisheries, in which it urged Governments and international organizations to take prompt action, inter alia, to: reduce fishing to sustainable levels in areas and on stocks currently heavily exploited or overfished; adopt policies, apply measures and develop techniques to reduce by-catches, fish discards, and post-harvest losses; review the capacity of fishing fleets in relation to sustainable yields of fishery resources and where necessary reduce these fleets; continue and, when possible, increase technical, financial and other assistance to developing countries, in particular to least developed countries, to support their efforts in fisheries conservation and management, and in aquaculture development; and effectively implement the relevant rules of international law on fisheries and related matters which are reflected in the provisions of the United Nations Convention on the Law of the Sea. 132/

2. Agreement for the Implementation of the Provisions of the United Nations Convention on the Law of the Sea of 10 December 1982 relating to the Conservation and Management of Straddling Fish Stocks and Highly Migratory Fish Stocks

170. The United Nations Conference on Straddling Fish Stocks and Highly Migratory Fish Stocks concluded its work on 4 August 1995 by adopting without a vote the Agreement for the Implementation of the Provisions of the United Nations Convention on the Law of the Sea of 10 December 1992 relating to the Conservation and Management of Straddling Fish Stocks and Highly Migratory Fish Stocks. The Agreement is to be opened for signature on 4 December 1995. It is aimed at facilitating the implementation of the relevant provisions of the United Nations Convention on the Law of the Sea relating to the conservation and management of straddling fish stocks and highly migratory fish stocks as well as strengthening the cooperation of States for that purpose.

171. The Secretary-General has submitted to the General Assembly a report on the Conference, together with the text of the Agreement (A/50/550).

172. In the Declaration adopted on 29 September 1995 at their nineteenth annual meeting, the Ministers for Foreign Affairs of the Group of 77 noted the successful conclusion of the Conference as "an essential contribution towards conservation and sustainable use of marine living resources" and in particular expressed satisfaction at the recognition in the Agreement of the special requirements of developing States. 133/

3. Code of Conduct for Responsible Fisheries

173. On the basis of the substantial comments and detailed suggestions received at the FAO 1994 Technical Consultations (A/49/631, paras. 148-149), the FAO secretariat submitted a revised draft of the Code of Conduct for Responsible Fisheries to the twenty-first session of the Committee on Fisheries in March 1995. The Committee stressed the importance of the Code of Conduct as "an instrument which can support the implementation of the United Nations Convention on the Law of the Sea and UNCED". 134/

174. In June 1995, the Council established an open-ended Technical Committee to continue elaboration of the Code. The Technical Committee met in June and September 1995 and completed the final text of the draft Code taking into account the outcome of the United Nations Conference on Straddling Fish Stocks and Highly Migratory Fish Stocks. The draft Code has been submitted to the one hundred and ninth session of the FAO Council, which is to transmit it to the twenty-eighth session of the FAO Conference in October 1995 for adoption.

175. The draft Code sets out principles and international standards of behaviour for responsible fisheries practices with a view to ensuring the effective conservation, management and development of living aquatic resources, with due respect for the ecosystem and biodiversity. It recognizes the nutritional, economic, social, environmental and cultural importance of fisheries, as well as the interests of all those concerned with the fishery sector. The Code is voluntary and global in scope. However, certain parts of it are based on relevant rules of international law, including those contained in the Convention on the Law of the Sea. The Code is to be interpreted and applied, inter alia, in conformity with those rules and in a manner consistent with the Agreement on the conservation and management of straddling fish stocks and highly migratory fish stocks. The Agreement to Promote Compliance with International Conservation and Management Measures by Fishing Vessels on the High Seas forms an integral part of the Code.

4. Protection of marine mammals

176. At its forty-seventh annual meeting (Dublin, Ireland, 29 May-2 June 1995), the International Whaling Commission (IWC) adopted several decisions regarding the management of marine mammals following its 1994 ban on commercial whaling around Antarctica (A/49/631, paras. 150-155).

177. With respect to the question of whale killing methods, which was considered within a workshop of the Technical Committee, IWC agreed to revise the action plan on whale killing methods and decided to continue to review the effectiveness of secondary killing methods with a view to reducing time to death in whales and encouraged the application of the most effective methods. 135/ The Commission also decided to reconsider the question of introducing a schedule amendment on the electric lance at its 1996 meeting with a view to reaching a decision and urged the contracting parties, in the meantime, to suspend the use of this gear as a method of killing whales. 136/

178. With respect to the management of small cetaceans in areas under national jurisdiction, IWC took note of the opposition of several contracting parties, members of the Organization of Eastern Caribbean States, to its competence in the management of small cetaceans and related research in their territorial seas and exclusive economic zones, "which their Governments consider to be their sovereign right". 137/

179. With respect to the commercial whaling of mink whales in the North-Eastern Atlantic, IWC, noting that the Scientific Committee had agreed that there was currently no valid abundance estimate for mink whales in the region, called on Norway to halt immediately all whaling activities under its jurisdiction. The Commission also indicated that, notwithstanding the objection of Norway, commercial whaling should not be taking place while the moratorium remained in force. 138/ In addition, IWC recommended that whaling for research scientific purposes under special permit be undertaken by non-lethal methods and scientific research involving the killing of cetaceans be permitted only in exceptional circumstances. 139/

5. Regional developments

(a) Atlantic Ocean

180. The International Commission for the Conservation of Atlantic Tunas (ICCAT) at its ninth special meeting (Madrid, 28 November-2 December 1994) adopted several recommendations with a view to: maintaining the current levels of bluefin tuna catch in the Eastern Atlantic Ocean, the Mediterranean and the Western Atlantic Ocean; and reducing the levels of southern albacore catch in the South Atlantic and Atlantic swordfish catch in the North and South Atlantic.

181. In addition, ICCAT adopted resolutions on: the greater enforcement responsibility of contracting parties to ensure that their nationals and fishing vessels complied with General Assembly resolution 46/215 of 20 December 1991 on large-scale pelagic drift-net fishing; prohibition of large pelagic long-line fishing in the Mediterranean Sea in June and July; request to contracting parties to report fishing activities violating ICCAT conservation management measures and to collect information aboard fishing vessels of non-contracting parties fishing in the ICCAT Convention Area upon the consent of the vessel master to board; and request to port State contracting parties to inspect such vessels and request to contracting parties to discourage their nationals from associating with activities of non-contracting parties which would undermine ICCAT conservation and management measures. 140/

(b) North Atlantic

182. After a dispute involving the arrest of a Spanish vessel and the application by Spain of an aspect of the case to the International Court of Justice (see paras. 129-135 above), on 16 April 1995, Canada and the European Union reached an agreement establishing the terms and conditions of fishing on the Grand Banks within the regulatory area of NAFO. 141/ The agreement, which included enhanced control and enforcement measures, provided for the deployment of observers and satellite tracking devices on board fishing vessels operating in the area. Canada and the European Union would also jointly propose to NAFO that these measures be adopted by all NAFO members for 1995 and beyond. 142/ Under the agreement, the two parties would implement immediately on a provisional basis such control and enforcement as increase of the inspection presence, improved hail system, dockside inspection, effort plans and catch reporting, list of major infringements including established procedures for inspection of major infringements, follow-up of apparent infringements and pilot project for observers and satellite tracking.

183. At its September 1995 meeting, NAFO adopted the above package of control measures as applicable to all its members as from 1 January 1996. 143/

(c) North-East Atlantic

184. The European Commission and Morocco agreed on 13 October 1994 to end their four-year agreement a year early on 30 April 1995, after failing to break a talks deadlock at a mid-term review. Earlier negotiations having produced no results, on 28 August 1995 the European Union (EU) began a new round of talks with Morocco for the renewal of the 1992 agreement, which granted fishing rights to EU fishing vessels, mainly Spanish vessels, in areas under the national jurisdiction of Morocco. 144/

185. Morocco indicated that, in order to protect dwindling fish stocks and guarantee local fishermen future work, it planned to halve the number of European Union fishing vessels operating within its exclusive economic zone and cut their catch quotas by 30 to 65 per cent for different species, including sardines, tuna, squid and shrimp. The European Union, in return, proposed a maximum cut of 25 per cent, which Morocco found unacceptable given the fact that Moroccan authorities believed that there had been over-exploitation of fishery resources, particularly of squid. 145/

186. On 13 October 1995, Morocco and the European Union announced that they had reached a general understanding on catch quotas within the Moroccan exclusive economic zone. The compromise entailed a reduction of the European Union fish efforts by 40 per cent and included the obligation of landing part of the catches in Moroccan ports. Under the new agreement, however, the European Union was expected to pay the same amount of financial compensation to Morocco as established in the previous agreement although its level of fishing effort was greatly reduced by the new agreement. 146/

(d) Mediterranean

187. A diplomatic conference on fisheries management in the Mediterranean was held in Crete from 12 to 14 December 1994 on the initiative of the European Commission. The "Solemn Declaration on the Conservation and Management of the Fishery Resources of the Mediterranean", adopted at the end of the conference, encouraged effective regional cooperation among the parties concerned, including all coastal States and all States whose vessels fished in the Mediterranean. Such cooperation, covering the resources, the environment and the application of legal principles, would be aimed at implementing a system of conservation and management, harmonized at the Mediterranean level, on the basis of the best available scientific advice and the most beneficial existing practices, with the purpose of ensuring effective protection of the fishery resources in the Mediterranean as well as their rational exploitation under the most favourable circumstances. 147/

(e) South Pacific

188. The South Pacific Forum, at its meeting in September 1995, welcomed and noted the significance of the adoption of the Agreement relating to the conservation and management of straddling fish stocks and highly migratory fish stocks and urged all interested States to become parties to the Agreement as soon as possible. In the light of the outcome of the United Nations Conference on Straddling Fish Stocks and Highly Migratory Fish Stocks, the Forum considered that comprehensive regional fisheries management arrangements, and a structure consistent with the Conference outcome to administer them, should be developed as a matter of urgency. The Forum registered its view that those management arrangements must be based on a precautionary approach to ensure the sustainable exploitation of the region's valuable tuna resources. 148/

189. The first meeting of the Commission for the Conservation of Southern Bluefin Tunas, established by the Convention for the Conservation of Southern Bluefin Tunas, was held at Wellington, New Zealand, in May 1994 (see A/48/527, para. 127). The meeting noted that the stock of southern bluefin tunas remained severely depleted, with the parental stock at its lowest level ever. However,

there were indications that the major catch cutbacks in 1988 and 1989 should now, or next year, begin to benefit the parent stocks and reverse the decline. Also, improvements in recruitment and current fishing mortality, if maintained during the 1990s, could ensure the stock recovery. The Commission intended to hold a series of scientific meetings to develop better methods of data collection and to address various sources of uncertainty in the stock assessment. The urgent problem of incidental take of seabirds by long-line fishery would also be addressed. 149/

(f) South Atlantic

190. At the tenth meeting of the South Atlantic Fisheries Commission (London, 5-6 June 1995), the Argentinian and United Kingdom delegations welcomed the report of the Scientific Subcommittee of the Fisheries Commission and agreed that they attached fundamental importance and the greatest priority to conserving various species in the fisheries, most notably illex and blue whiting, on the basis of the best available scientific advice. 150/

191. The Commission took note of the recommendation of the Subcommittee that additional research on blue whiting was urgently needed, and agreed that the planning of the blue whiting research would be the subject of consultation between the relevant institutions of the member States. The Commission expressed its satisfaction for the existing cooperation between the institutions and scientists of member States and encouraged them to develop their consultations further. 151/

192. The Commission noted with concern the illegal activities of fishing vessels in the South-West Atlantic and agreed to continue cooperation, including an intensified exchange of information, to curtail such activities. 152/

E. Marine environmental protection and sustainable resource development: major policy and programme initiatives

193. International policy in the area of marine environmental protection has been progressively strengthened and refined through the adoption of major policy instruments. The United Nations Convention on the Law of the Sea is as much a strategic policy document as it is a treaty instrument. 153/ The adoption of Agenda 21, the entry into force of the Convention, the adoption of the Agreement on straddling fish stocks and highly migratory fish stocks, the forthcoming global plan of action on the protection of the marine environment from land-based activities (November 1995), and review of the implementation of chapter 17 of Agenda 21 by the Commission on Sustainable Development in 1996, will have a cumulative impact on the development of international policy in this area.

194. Implementation of the Convention on the Law of the Sea requires a very wide spectrum of activities, most of which are still at a relatively early stage of development. There is also a particular need to consider questions of sound management, including its scientific basis, and to clarify just how best to develop, through international cooperation, the approach of integrated marine and coastal management, targeting particular areas. There is clearly an inadequate level of implementation of existing conventions and of international rules, regulations and standards, as reflected in the insufficient adaptation of national legislation and procedures, the inefficiency of enforcement and the increasing gap between developed and developing countries in their capacity for implementation. Furthermore, lack of investment in ocean potential, lack of awareness of both the potentials and the impacts, lack of human and financial resources have all complicated the process of implementation of the Convention and related instruments and the promotion of international cooperation in ocean affairs.

195. Preparation of the necessary documentation on the implementation of chapter 17 of Agenda 21, for the review to be conducted by the Commission on

Sustainable Development, has been delegated to the Administrative Committee on Coordination Subcommittee on Oceans and Coastal Areas, with the primary objective of facilitating the preparation of inputs by the Secretary-General and the United Nations system to the Commission.

1. Protection of the marine environment from land-based activities

196. A global programme of action for the protection of the marine environment from land-based activities is expected to be completed and adopted at an intergovernmental conference in Washington, D.C. in November 1995. 154/ Like the Programme of Action for the Sustainable Development of Small Island Developing States, the programme on land-based activities will provide a new framework for the coordination of the efforts of the various international organizations having relevant mandates and activities. Also, these two global programmes will complement each other in important ways.

197. The primary emphasis of the new programme will be on promoting and facilitating national and regional measures, particularly through integrated coastal area management approaches, supported by global mechanisms. In terms of particular contaminants, the global programme will emphasize sewage and industrial waste-waters and persistent organic pollutants. In terms of global measures, the programme concentrates on institutional aspects, calling for a clearing-house and a regular international forum for review. With respect to persistent organic pollutants, proposals were advanced for the global programme to initiate, directly, an intergovernmental process to consider and negotiate a global, legally binding instrument. However, much of this legal development may focus more within the broad field of chemical safety.

198. UNEP Governing Council decision 18/32 of 25 May 1995, on persistent organic pollutants, 155/ anticipates that a decision on an appropriate legal mechanism on persistent organic pollutants will be taken up by the UNEP Governing Council and the World Health Assembly by 1997, based on the results of the ECE process, the outcome of the Washington Conference and the recommendations of the Intergovernmental Forum on Chemical Safety.

199. Account should be taken of the important advances made by parties to the Barcelona Convention on the subject of land-based activities (see paras. 116-118 above): expansion of the scope of the Convention; the joining in a single provision of land-based sources with atmospheric sources of marine pollution; and the inclusion of underground watercourses and run-off in indirect sources to better integrate coastal area management with water resources management. These same approaches are to be adopted in the new global programme on land-based activities

2. Science and ocean policy

200. It has been emphasized in many forums, including UNCED in its Agenda 21, chapter 17, that international decision-making on ocean issues generally should be made in a holistic way, and be based on "good science". An initiative has been taken by the Government of the United Kingdom to convene an International Workshop on Environmental Science, Comprehensiveness and Consistency in Global Decisions on Ocean Issues (November 1995). The workshop will assess the extent to which international organizations have suitable access to good science, and the effectiveness of current arrangements where global actions are required. This exploration of the way in which international decisions on ocean issues make use of scientific advice is expected to lead to a determination as to whether an intergovernmental panel on the oceans, under the auspices of the relevant United Nations agencies, should be established. 156/

201. The Group of Experts on the Scientific Aspects of Marine Environmental Protection (GESAMP) has long been a model for inter-agency cooperation in a complex area spanning many agency mandates, and the principal instrument for joint assessments of the state of the marine environment. 157/ As such, GESAMP makes an important contribution to the overall United Nations mandate for the system-wide Earthwatch, involving the inter-agency coordination of observation, assessment and reporting activities in the United Nations system. The sponsoring organizations of GESAMP are currently investigating how best to achieve a new assessment by the year 2000, in order that it can also serve as a major element in the decadal State of the World Environment report, which UNEP must prepare for 2002. The GESAMP agencies also anticipate some important differences from previous assessments, particularly in the need to provide Governments with more forward-looking reports that try to anticipate and give early warning of coming problems.

202. The General Assembly has proclaimed 1998 to be the International Year of the Ocean. 158/ This initiative is expected to generate important cooperative efforts in the United Nations system 159/ and stimulate greater global awareness of the oceans and greater cooperation for the effective protection and management of marine and coastal areas and resources. The Government of Portugal has been particularly supportive of this Expo '98 initiative; for example, Expo '98 in Lisbon will be devoted entirely to ocean issues, looking to the future and the "urgency of implementing rational and scientific strategies that will ensure the ecological balance of the planet". 160/ The United Nations and UNESCO will together lead a joint United Nations system participation in this world exposition.

3. Marine and coastal biodiversity

203. It has been recognized for some time that the regime set forth in the Convention on Biological Diversity, even as supplemented by certain provisions in the Convention on the Law of the Sea, does not provide a coherent and comprehensive regime appropriate to the particularities of marine life-forms. The issue of marine and coastal biodiversity therefore became one of the first priorities for consideration by the parties to the Biodiversity Convention, and thus for its Subsidiary Body on Scientific, Technical and Technological Advice (SBSTTA) at its first meeting in September 1995. 161/ The main features of the initial advice prepared by the SBSTTA concern the importance of integrated marine and coastal area management as the most suitable framework in which to address human impacts on biodiversity, and the special problems created by fisheries, aquaculture and the introduction of alien organisms. An ad hoc panel of experts will now proceed to identify particular needs, such as gaps in knowledge of the distribution and abundance of marine and coastal biodiversity and the linkages with watershed management.

204. From the scope of the work undertaken by SBSTTA at its first meeting, it may be concluded that it will be necessary to establish a close connection with the institutional process established for the implementation of the global programme of action for protection of the marine environment from land-based activities. The connection would be particularly important with regard to the promotion of integrated coastal area management approaches at the national and regional levels and the development of clearing-houses or linkages for information exchange. Having decided to establish a clearing-house, the parties to the Convention are now studying the feasibility of developing an institutional capacity that can provide brokerage services and assist national capacity-building, as well as provide information and data exchange.

4. Integrated coastal area management

205. Agenda 21 and virtually every other related global and regional policy instrument all point to the adoption of integrated coastal area management

(ICAM) approaches as offering the best results for environmentally sustainable development over the longer term. While all such policy instruments share certain basic themes and objectives, the particular objectives in each context can lead to different perceptions as to how an integrated management approach can be applied to programming and activities within the United Nations system, and how the ICAM process would be initiated and maintained in concrete, geographically specific situations.

206. Thus, international organizations face a particular problem in responding effectively to this important challenge, both individually and collectively. A highly significant step for the general effectiveness of United Nations system cooperation and coordination in ocean affairs has been taken by the Administrative Committee on Coordination Subcommittee on Oceans and Coastal Areas in its decision to pursue the development of a comprehensive programme framework to embrace the development of appropriate strategies as well as planning and implementation of concrete ICAM-related activities. Recommendations on this programme initiative will be put before the Commission on Sustainable Development in 1996.

207. Numerous workshops and other meetings on the subject of ICAM have been held in recent years. An important recent development has been the proposed project on environment and development in coastal regions and in small islands, which would bring together all relevant IOC and UNESCO programmes, integrating the environmental and social sciences, and giving added value to them. 162/ At IMO also, there is a strong interest in using an ICAM approach to improve the situation as regards the operation of waste reception facilities for ships, waste management issues within the ambit of the London Convention and the development and maintenance of ports and harbours in the interests of maritime trade.

5. Waste reception facilities and other port-related problems

208. IMO is attempting to deal in a more integrated fashion with ship/port interface (SPI) questions, e.g., the establishment and operation of reception facilities, including funding mechanisms, risk analysis in port planning and port operations, and emergency preparedness and response. An SPI Working Group has been established to provide a necessary focal point within the organization and to facilitate consideration of the complex demands of international maritime trade. Coordination of activities in the port sector will in any event require close contact between IMO, ILO and the United Nations Conference on Trade and Development (UNCTAD). The International Hydrographic Organization (IHO) also has expressed a strong interest in the subject, citing the effects on port development and operation of problems created by absent or inadequate hydrographic capability and lack of coordination between port and hydrographic authorities. 163/

209. The implementation of the obligation contained in MARPOL to provide port reception facilities for ships' wastes faces mounting problems of both a technical and a financial nature. IMO and UNCTAD have joined in a search for solutions, and now consider that the most feasible approach would be to focus on individual ports, with some aspects handled at the national, regional or even global level. There is wide agreement that shipowners should pay for waste reception services, but it may be necessary to impose a mandatory scheme to avoid unfair competition between ports. This could be done by amending MARPOL to incorporate an International Code of Reception Facilities with provisions on the calculation of a fee to finance the running of reception facilities.

6. Technical cooperation and capacity-building

210. A number of organizations have modified and reoriented technical cooperation programmes substantially, many, including particularly the IMO

Integrated Technical Cooperation Programme, in order to promote and facilitate the effective implementation of conventions and the adoption of national legislation and regulations. This entails a considerable effort to harmonize objectives and efforts under numerous instruments, and to do so to the extent feasible within a comprehensive and integrated approach to marine and coastal area management.

211. A new IOC strategy for capacity-building in marine sciences, services and observations has been elaborated "in response to UNCLOS and UNCED", which calls for closer partnerships with other relevant programmes, including the TRAIN-SEA-COAST Programme (see paras. 251-256 below).

212. The establishment of a technical cooperation programme is a feature of the current revision of the London Convention; the process has also focused attention on IMO's responsibilities with respect to that Convention, considering that it does not deal directly with shipping, but deals with important aspects of marine environmental protection, particularly waste management. The London Convention is primarily responsible for IMO's involvement in the area of marine protection from land-based activities, including integrated coastal zone and marine pollution risk management. As has been pointed out by the IMO Secretary-General, the development of a technical cooperation and assistance programme under the London Convention, with clearing-house functions, will call for additional financial means. 164/

F. Maritime safety and pollution prevention

1. General issues

213. IMO continues to focus attention on the effects of two decades of difficult economic conditions in the shipping industry: a combination of older vessels and poorer maintenance has obvious safety implications. Major structural changes in the industry have brought declines in the fleets of the traditional flags while newer shipping nations have emerged.

214. Until recently the indications were that IMO's efforts to improve safety and reduce pollution were paying off. The rate of serious casualties was falling and the amount of oil and other pollutants entering the sea from ships was decreasing quite dramatically. But recently there has been a disturbing rise in accidents. Future projections show growing cargo volumes and higher percentages of dangerous and processed goods, as well as yet greater movement in the recruitment of seafarers from developing countries. The projected shortfall in the numbers of ships' officers and ratings as against the projected increase in the number of ships in the maritime trade, and the already high average age of these ships, poses a great challenge for maximizing the benefits of modern technological innovations and upgrading safety standards and training standards for seafarers.

215. IMO is greatly concerned that measures to date may not be enough to cope with problems that may become worse in the next few years. Major changes in approach may have to be made, including changes in the overall approach to maritime safety.

2. Vessel safety

216. Improvements in ro-ro (roll-on, roll-off) passenger ferry safety have been treated as a matter of urgency at IMO, so that in a very short time, amendments to SOLAS were prepared for adoption in November 1995. The economic impacts will be considerable: the amendments apply also to the existing ro-ro fleet, requiring many ships to undergo extensive conversions.

217. The safety of bulk carriers is a special question, as casualty statistics demonstrate: 15 total losses occurred in 1994 with a total loss of 141 seamen. 165/ A substantial review of the situation is now under way at IMO. 166/ Loading and unloading operations, as well as stowage and securing, have been the subject of new amendments to chapter VI of SOLAS (to enter into force on 1 January 1996). It may also be noted that port State control action has been stepped up: as of 1 July 1996, an expanded inspection will be carried out once a year on all bulk carriers older than 12 years, calling at ports of European Union member States. 167/

218. The nineteenth IMO Assembly is expected to adopt a new resolution on the safety of ships carrying solid bulk cargoes that will give high priority to the development of a set of comprehensive requirements and recommendations covering, inter alia, survivability standards, design and construction standards, operational standards and management and training. In the meantime, Governments, classification societies, shipowners and masters, and terminal operators are called on to take immediate action along the lines recommended in an annex to the resolution. 168/

219. With respect to the safety of small fishing vessels and training of their personnel, IMO considers entry into force of the 1993 Torremolinos Protocol (relating to the 1977 International Convention for the Safety of Fishing Vessels) a matter of urgency.

3. Flag State and port State control

220. The IMO Subcommittee on Flag State Implementation is charged generally with the task of monitoring the overall effectiveness of IMO conventions and instruments and proposing concrete measures over a wide spectrum. Currently, it is finalizing work on a draft code of international standards and recommended practices in maritime accident investigations, preparing basic guidance on the infrastructure, personnel and capabilities necessary for a flag State to carry out its treaty obligations, and analysing deficiency data to determine which flag States are in urgent need of assistance.

221. The Subcommittee is also responsible for reviewing the overall situation as regards port State control and is now amalgamating all IMO provisions on the subject, including those in the 1995 Amendments to STCW (see para. 87 above).

222. Regional systems of port State control continue to be strengthened. Caribbean countries are now actively considering maritime transport issues at the regional level, including such diverse issues as management of ship wastes from tourism. The Association of Caribbean States is stressing implementation of crucial international maritime conventions within an agreed harmonized framework and has decided to examine the feasibility of broadening participation in the draft Caribbean agreement on port State control to include all Caribbean countries and territories. 169/

223. Regional systems have also had the effect of widening the ratification and improving the implementation of ILO standards as well as IMO standards. ILO also emphasizes that port State control, while only an adjunct to flag State control, is none the less effective in placing greater pressure on flag States and shipowners to improve maritime labour conditions.

G. Other uses of the seas

1. Right of access of land-locked States

224. Practical needs and problems of land-locked and transit developing countries were discussed extensively at the two Meetings of Governmental Experts from Land-locked and Transit Developing Countries and Representatives of Donor

Countries and Financial and Development Institutions, held in May 1993 170/ and in June 1995, 171/ respectively, pursuant to General Assembly resolutions 46/212 of 20 December 1991 and 48/169 of 20 December 1993, as well as at a Symposium for Land-locked and Transit Developing Countries (New York, 14-16 June 1995). 172/

225. As a result of those deliberations, a Global Framework for Transit Transport Cooperation between Land-locked and Transit Developing Countries and the Donor Community was adopted by the Second Meeting of Governmental Experts and subsequently endorsed by the Trade and Development Board of UNCTAD at its autumn session (11-20 September 1995). 173/ The document pointed out, inter alia, that the use of international agreements had long been a successful instrument in promoting an efficient and reliable transit transport system and recommended that land-locked and transit developing countries should consider further enhancing efforts to adhere to those agreements. It also recommended that the Governments of port States consider taking the necessary administrative action to accede to and implement relevant international conventions related to port safety and pollution control and to port facilities and services for transit traffic.

226. On 19 December 1994, the General Assembly adopted resolution 49/102, on transit environment in the land-locked States in Central Asia and their transit developing neighbours, in which the Assembly recognized the importance of the access to the sea by those States for their overall socio-economic development and invited the Secretary-General of UNCTAD, in consultation with the Governments concerned and in cooperation with relevant United Nations bodies, to elaborate a programme for improving the efficiency of the current transit environment in the newly independent and developing land-locked States in Central Asia and their transit developing neighbours and to make a comprehensive analysis and study of the transit system for Central Asian countries, paying particular attention to the development of all new, appropriate and feasible alternative transit routes and corridors, including the shortest ones.

227. In another development concerning a land-locked country, the Foreign Ministers of Greece and the former Yugoslav Republic of Macedonia on 14 September 1995 signed a wide-ranging interim accord on their mutual relations. 174/ The two parties agreed that, having regard to the fact that one party was a land-locked State, they should be guided by the applicable provisions of the United Nations Convention on the Law of the Sea as far as practicable both in practice and when concluding bilateral agreements in various areas of mutual interest. They also agreed to promote, on a reciprocal basis, road, rail, maritime and air transport and communication links, using the best available technologies, and to facilitate the transit of their goods between them and through their territories and ports.

2. Archaeological and historical objects found at sea

228. With the advance in technology, which now permits the recovery of objects of archaeological or historical value sunk almost at any depth, growing attention is being paid to the legal issues relating to their removal and their protection. The United Nations Convention on the Law of the Sea deals with some aspects of the questions only in general terms, in articles 149 and 303 as well as article 33, which is referred to in article 303.

229. In 1993, the Executive Board of UNESCO adopted a resolution by which it requested the Director-General to undertake a study of the feasibility of a new instrument for the protection of the underwater cultural heritage. The UNESCO secretariat study, issued in March 1995, concluded that "it would be feasible to elaborate a legal instrument for this seriously threatened part of humanity's heritage". 175/ The secretariat further believed that the draft of a convention on the subject prepared by the Cultural Heritage Committee of the International

Law Association in 1994, which had been presented to UNESCO by the Association, was a useful basis for the development of the future instrument. 176/

230. Having considered the secretariat study, the Executive Board, in a decision of 1 June 1995, considered that the jurisdictional aspects of the proposal, in particular its possible implications for the provisions about national jurisdiction contained in the United Nations Convention on the Law of the Sea, required further examination, and recommended that the Director-General convene a group of experts to discuss all aspects of the proposal, with emphasis on jurisdictional matters. The meeting of the experts group, originally scheduled for September 1995, has been postponed to the first half of 1996.

231. In the meantime, upon invitation by the UNESCO secretariat, the Division for Ocean Affairs and the Law of the Sea prepared comments on archaeological and historical objects under the Convention for submission to the UNESCO General Conference in October 1995. The paper explained the background of the questions involved and analysed the legislative history of the above-mentioned articles of the Convention.

3. The offshore industry

(a) Removal and disposal of installations and structures

232. Articles 60, paragraph 3, and 80 of the Convention on the Law of the Sea require installations or structures to be removed essentially "to ensure safety of navigation". Entire removal is not specified; rather, appropriate publicity is required concerning any installations or structures which are not entirely removed. The Convention recognizes the need for the competent international organization to establish international standards, which must be taken into account by States when removing an installation or structure. Such guidelines and standards were established by the IMO Assembly in 1989. 177/ The Convention makes no reference to the ultimate fate of decommissioned installations or structures or their components, by disposal at sea (dumping) or otherwise. Other relevant provisions are article 208, paragraph 1, dealing with pollution of the marine environment from seabed activities within national jurisdiction, and article 210 on dumping.

233. Questions of the removal and disposal of offshore structures have been closely followed at the regional level, particularly in Europe, by the Oslo and Helsinki Commissions, and in South-East Asia. ESCAP recently held a training seminar with information and advice on legal aspects provided by the Division for Ocean Affairs and the Law of the Sea.

234. Practice in regional cooperation has not been uniform. In some cases the requirement for removal is stricter than what is required by the 1982 Convention and by the 1989 IMO Guidelines and Standards. In some cases disposal at sea is not an option; for example, the 1992 Convention on the Protection of the Marine Environment of the Baltic Sea requires entire removal and disposal on land. A number of offshore structures in the North Sea/North-East Atlantic are nearing the end of their lifetime, so that a similar approach is being contemplated in this region also. At the Fourth International Conference on the Protection of the North Sea (June 1995), the majority of ministers agreed that more environmentally acceptable and controllable land-based solutions were preferable and that decommissioned offshore installations should either be reused or disposed of on land. 178/ The Oslo and Paris Commissions (June 1995) adopted a moratorium on the disposal at sea of decommissioned offshore installations, with effect from 4 August 1995, and also agreed that the revised London Convention should require disposal on land. 179/

(b) Pollution from offshore activities

235. Having reviewed existing regulatory measures relating to discharge, emissions and safety of offshore operations, IMO has found no compelling need at this time for further development of globally applicable environmental regulations. 180/

236. Existing global regulations include the provisions on offshore units in the International Convention on Oil Pollution Preparedness, Response and Cooperation (OPRC). Article 3 (b) (ii) of MARPOL 73/78 and regulation 21 of annex I thereto exempt from MARPOL's coverage discharges arising from the exploration, exploitation and associated offshore processing of seabed mineral resources and discharges associated with production water, displacement water (associated with separation storage) and platform drainage, namely those oily waters arising from exploration and exploitation of mineral resources.

237. Most harmonized regulations have been developed at the regional level, and IMO has actively encouraged the strengthening and expansion of a regional approach in this area. There are currently four regional agreements, covering the Kuwait region, the North-East Atlantic, the Baltic Sea and the Mediterranean Sea. The Fourth International Conference on the Protection of the North Sea called on the industry to develop and implement effective environmental management systems, utilizing the best techniques and methods to deal with those cases where there are no alternatives to the use of oil-based muds. The Oslo and Paris Commissions were requested to investigate pollution from produced water, to consider banning by 1997 the discharge of oil-contaminated cuttings into the sea, to assess possible needs for cleaning up contaminated seabeds and to adopt a Harmonized Mandatory Control System for the use and discharge of chemicals offshore.

238. Article III (1) (c) of the London Convention, on the definition of dumping, excludes from the scope of the Convention the disposal of material associated with offshore operations for seabed mineral resources. Proposals have been made to delete the subparagraph to allow possible regulation of these activities under the Convention, noting that the discharge of many substances from offshore installations is currently prohibited or controlled by virtue of their inclusion in annexes I or II to the Convention. 181/

H. Marine science and technology

239. Significant advances have occurred in marine science and technology despite the fact that in recent years funds for research and development have been relatively scarce. Scientific and technological developments are influenced by, and in turn influence, man's evolving relationship with the oceans.

240. In the field of marine biology, new discoveries of marine creatures dwelling on or in seabed ooze, often miles deep, thriving in pitch darkness under enormous pressure, have led experts radically to revise upwards their rough estimates of the number of species of all types of marine life from 200,000 to between 10 million and 100 million, which is the same as the range projected by the possible total number of terrestrial species. 182/ The newly recognized creatures are considered important because of their possible commercial value as well as because of their role in maintaining the earth's ecological balance. The potential commercial value of the new organisms lies in their great genetic diversity. The aim is to use their exotic genes to develop new drugs, catalysts and agents that can break down wastes.

241. Hydrothermal vents, which occur at an average depth of about 7,300 ft, with temperatures reaching up to 750° F, are perhaps the most extreme deep seabed habitat for marine organisms. The new discoveries have been made in numerous oceanographic research trips. For example, a team of scientists, in a research trip in summer 1994 to a site of volcanic eruption in Juan de Fuca ridge, off

America's north-western coast, made striking observations of vast bacterial "mats" emerging from undersea vents with the fresh magma. They are primitive, heat-loving bacteria that thrive on hydrogen sulphide and live in nearly boiling hot water. 183/ Another team of scientists drilling deep beneath the seabed has encountered evidence that scores of microbial life forms flourish deep within the planet. The scientists' findings are complemented by those of another team drilling independently deep beneath land. 184/

242. Growing attention is being paid to investigations on the commercial uses of exotic undersea and deep earth species. For example, a company based in San Diego, California, is looking for bacterial enzyme adapted to high temperature and intense pressures that might be industrially useful. 185/ The on-land drilling programme mentioned above has isolated more than 5,000 microbes from the deep earth and is making them available to scientists in government and industry. Some of the microbes are already being scanned for antibiotics and agents that might help fight diseases. 186/ Japanese biologists have begun a major effort to retrieve microbes from the deep, and perhaps to make new drugs and tools for genetic engineering. 187/ One of their projects involves building a plant that can reproduce on land the extreme pressures and temperatures found in the sea's depths. The aim is to have a repository for breeding unique bacteria and organisms brought to land.

243. The scientific and commercial value of deep seabed genetic resources has raised questions regarding the legal status of these resources and activities involving them. The Convention on the Law of the Sea does not specifically refer to such resources, since their potential use was not known to the negotiators. It has been suggested that if found in areas beyond the national jurisdiction of any State these resources fall within the high seas legal regime and are freely accessible to all States subject to the rights and obligations of other States. While the term "living resources" in the Convention might be broad enough to include free living and symbiotic micro-organisms, the collection and subsequent use of microbial genetic resources is not necessarily analogous to traditional methods of harvesting marine living resources. They are studied as part of marine scientific research and may be passed to industry for biotechnological applications. It has therefore been suggested that a fundamental consideration in discussions would be the legal status and nature of marine scientific research involving these resources.

244. SBSTTA recommended in its report to the forthcoming meeting of the Conference of the Parties to the Convention on Biological Diversity that it intended to address questions related to bio-prospecting on the deep seabed, including access to its genetic resources, at its forthcoming meeting. 188/ It is to be noted that the recommendation did not enjoy the full support of SBSTTA. One delegation expressed the view that the issue of bio-prospecting on the deep seabed was beyond the scope of that Convention. 189/

245. In the field of marine geology, research efforts have focused on obtaining a better understanding of the formation of the earth's crust. Research in deep-sea volcanic activities can shed light on the evolution of the earth's crust as well as on the fate of the earth's climate. The trip to the site of volcanic eruption in Juan de Fuca ridge (see para. 241) was part of a series of trips that have given scientists their first look at what happens when the earth's crust is created at the underwater ridges in association with volcanic eruptions. Also, for the first time ever, scientists will drill into the vent of a deep-sea volcano. 190/

246. Offshore oil and gas development spurred a number of efforts in marine geological and geochemical research. This year, one interesting scientific finding was that although the reservoir in Eugene Island in the Gulf of Mexico from which oil was being pumped was formed at the time of the Pleistocene era less than 2 million years ago, oil now being recovered from the reservoir has a chemical signature characteristic of the Jurassic period, which ended more than 150 million years ago. The implication, researchers believe, is that highly

pressurized oil from lower levels of "stacked" reservoirs is frequently breaking through geological barriers and "burping" upward, eventually reaching the reservoir from which oil is being pumped. Others, while acknowledging that oil is almost certainly flowing into certain reservoirs from somewhere, are doubtful of the "stacked" reservoir idea as well as about the extent of replenishment in the reservoir being exploited. 191/

I. Capacity-building in the law of the sea and ocean affairs

1. Fellowships

247. The Division for Ocean Affairs and the Law of the Sea has continued its activities under the Hamilton Shirley Amerasinghe fellowship programme. The fellowship is aimed at providing training and assistance to chosen fellows in order to acquire additional knowledge of the law of the sea and its wider application. The fellows pursue postgraduate-level research and training in the field of the law of the sea, its implementation and related marine affairs at a participating university of their choice. They are in addition given the opportunity to carry out an internship programme with the Division for up to three months. 192/

248. For the 1995/96 school year, the United Kingdom has made a special contribution to fund a fellowship under this programme. 193/ The Advisory Panel welcomed the contribution. While extending its appreciation to the United Kingdom Government, the Panel expressed the hope that this could become a tradition as a continuing commitment on the part of the United Kingdom Government and urged other countries to consider making similar contributions.

249. The United Kingdom contribution has made it possible to award two fellowships in 1994, to be implemented in 1995/96. The Advisory Panel recommended Mr. Maurice Kengne Kamgue, a diplomatic officer from Cameroon, for the ninth annual award and Mr. Frank Elizabeth, a State Counsel of Seychelles, for the special award under the United Kingdom contribution. 194/

250. The Advisory Panel noted that as in the previous years, the candidates were all of a very high calibre and recommended that efforts be made to acquire additional funding for fellowships from philanthropic and other institutions and to encourage universities to award fellowships to all finalists in the programme. Along those lines on the basis of the Panel's endorsement, selected candidates would be designated as "Finalists" in consideration for the award and that they should be encouraged to use this information in applying directly to universities for fellowship consideration.

2. The TRAIN-SEA-COAST Programme

251. Under the TRAIN-SEA-COAST Programme launched in 1994 (see A/49/631, paras. 234-243) in cooperation with the Science, Technology and Private Sector Division of the United Nations Development Programme (UNDP), the first Course Developers Workshop was convened in Stony Brook, Long Island, United States of America, from 23 January to 3 February 1995. At the Workshop, 19 professionals from participating TRAIN-SEA-COAST centres and three from United Nations agencies (IMO, United Nations Institute for Training and Research, and Universal Postal Union) were trained in the preparation of advanced, high quality course material to TRAIN-SEA-COAST standards in the form of standardized training packages. Additionally, as members of the TRAIN-SEA-COAST network, the participants discussed an extensive menu of courses and agreed, at the network level, on their particular course development tasks.

252. Following the Workshop, the participants returned to their respective institutions to establish their Course Development Units (CDUs). Most of the CDUs are now fully established. Others face some constraints owing primarily to

funding limitations, availability of personnel on a full-time basis, and commitments made prior to their joining the TRAIN-SEA-COAST Programme. Despite these limitations, the majority of CDUs, having the equipment and the team in place, have started the preparation of courses.

253. After the training of course developers, activities in the central unit (the Division for Ocean Affairs and the Law of the Sea) focused on: building-up of an information and assistance programme; setting up of a programme strategy; and network consolidation. The first includes a communication system through monthly contact sheets to follow the stage of development of standardized training packages and formal progress reports through which the central unit provides regular quality control of the training packages under preparation.

254. The programme strategy consists of the following key elements: a closer involvement with United Nations agencies and with TRAIN-X sister programmes; assessment of the training component of approved field projects of Global Environment Facility and UNDP; fund-raising and marketing of the programme; and network expansion.

255. Consultations have been undertaken with sister programmes on possible modes of cooperation and assistance between the programmes. Similar consultations were undertaken with IOC of UNESCO on possible modes of cooperation with the TRAIN-SEA-COAST Programme. Consultations with other United Nations agencies are also under way.

256. Network expansion activities focus on identification and assessment of potential new TRAIN-SEA-COAST CDUs and the organization and implementation of a Second Course Developers Workshop tentatively scheduled for the first semester of 1996.

Notes

1/ Official Records of the Third United Nations Conference on the Law of the Sea, vol. XVII (United Nations publication, Sales No. E.84.V.3), document A/CONF.62/122.

2/ These States are as follows: Angola, Antigua and Barbuda, Australia, Austria, Bahamas, Bahrain, Barbados, Belize, Bolivia, Bosnia and Herzegovina, Botswana, Brazil, Cameroon, Cape Verde, Comoros, Cook Islands, Costa Rica, Côte d'Ivoire, Croatia, Cuba, Cyprus, Djibouti, Dominica, Egypt, Fiji, Gambia, Germany, Ghana, Greece, Grenada, Guinea, Guinea-Bissau, Guyana, Honduras, Iceland, India, Indonesia, Italy, Iraq, Jamaica, Kenya, Kuwait, Lebanon, Mali, Malta, Marshall Islands, Mauritius, Mexico, Micronesia (Federated States of), Namibia, Nigeria, Oman, Paraguay, Philippines, Saint Kitts and Nevis, Saint Lucia, Saint Vincent and the Grenadines, Samoa, Sao Tome and Principe, Senegal, Seychelles, Sierra Leone, Singapore, Slovenia, Somalia, Sri Lanka, Sudan, the former Yugoslav Republic of Macedonia, Togo, Tonga, Trinidad and Tobago, Tunisia, Uganda, United Republic of Tanzania, Uruguay, Viet Nam, Yemen, Yugoslavia, Zaire, Zambia and Zimbabwe.

3/ General Assembly resolution 48/263, annex.

4/ These States are: Bahamas, Barbados, Côte d'Ivoire, Grenada, Guinea, Iceland, Jamaica, Namibia, Nigeria, Sri Lanka, Togo, Trinidad and Tobago, Uganda, Yugoslavia, Zambia and Zimbabwe.

5/ These States are: Brazil, Cameroon, Cape Verde, Egypt, Indonesia, Malta, Philippines, Sudan, Tunisia, United Republic of Tanzania and Uruguay.

6/ These States are: Cyprus, Fiji, Micronesia (Federated States of), Paraguay, Senegal and Seychelles.

7/ These States are: Australia, Austria, Bahamas, Barbados, Belize, Bolivia, Cook Islands, Côte d'Ivoire, Croatia, Cyprus, Fiji, Germany, Greece, Grenada, Guinea, Iceland, India, Italy, Jamaica, Kenya, Lebanon, Mauritius, Micronesia (Federated States of), Namibia, Nigeria, Paraguay, Samoa, Senegal, Seychelles, Sierra Leone, Singapore, Slovenia, Sri Lanka, the former Yugoslav Republic of Macedonia, Togo, Tonga, Trinidad and Tobago, Uganda, Yugoslavia, Zambia and Zimbabwe.

8/ These States are: Brazil, Bulgaria, Denmark, Iran (Islamic Republic of), Ireland, Jordan, Mexico, Morocco, Portugal, Romania, Saudi Arabia, Spain, Sweden and Uruguay.

9/ A/CONF.164/37.

10/ The report of the first Meeting of States Parties is contained in document SPLOS/3.

11/ The report was subsequently issued as LOS/PCN/152, vols. I-IV.

12/ The recommendations are contained in the statement by the Chairman (LOS/PCN/L.115/Rev.1, para. 43).

13/ The report of the second Meeting of States Parties is contained in document SPLOS/4.

14/ SPLOS/2/Rev.3.

15/ "Miles" throughout this document refers to "nautical miles".

16/ The text of the Code is available only in Croatian.

17/ Act amending an Act on the Border of the Territorial Waters of Finland (981/95), entered into force on 2 August 1995. Text to be reproduced in Law of the Sea Bulletin, No. 29 (1995).

18/ Ibid., No. 27 (1995), pp. 55-61.

19/ Ibid., No. 23 (1993), p. 65.

20/ To be reproduced in ibid., No. 30, to be published in 1996.

21/ Information confirmed by a representative of the Permanent Mission of Thailand to the United Nations.

22/ Law of the Sea Bulletin, No. 28 (1995), p. 31.

23/ Ibid., pp. 31-32.

24/ The text of the Act is reproduced in ibid., No. 24 (1993), pp. 10-15.

25/ The acceding States, i.e., Austria, Finland and Sweden, also endorsed the protest.

26/ These States were: Cape Verde, Comoros, Equatorial Guinea, Ghana, Guinea, Guinea-Bissau, Madagascar, Mauritania, Namibia, Senegal, United Republic of Tanzania and Zaire.

27/ A/49/920-S/1995/489, annex I, para. 28.

28/ A/50/475, annex, para. 14.

29/ A/50/518, annex, para. 33.

30/ Starting with No. 27, the Bulletin has become a sales publication of the United Nations, whereas LOSIC is not a sales item. LOSIC is a new periodical publication of the Division with the objective of communicating to all States and entities, in particular States not yet parties to the Convention, information on actions taken by States parties in implementing the Convention as well as on activities undertaken by the Division pursuant thereto. Thus far, LOSIC Nos. 1 and 2 have been issued.

31/ The lists prepared by these organizations are included in Law of the Sea Information Circular No. 2.

32/ For wider and speedy dissemination of more general information on the law of the sea, the Division has, as the first unit in the Organization, started to post information on the United Nations Gopher, a part of the Internet. At its address, "gopher.un.org", the menu pick of "Law of the Sea" provides the user with many documents, e.g., the current status and the full text of the United Nations Convention on the Law of the Sea, the 1994 Agreement on Part XI of the Convention and the 1995 Agreement on fish stocks. Information on the International Tribunal for the Law of the Sea, the International Seabed Authority as well as selected documents and press releases concerning them are also available.

The Division now has its own Home Page within the United Nations Home Page. Located at "http://un.org/Depts/DOALOS", it has a content similar to that of the Gopher but also includes graphics and will be capable of being made "interactive" so that remote users may query it and receive customized outputs meeting their individual needs.

33/ For further details of the work of the Assembly during these meetings, see ISBA/A/L.1/Rev.1 and Corr.1, and ISBA/A/L.7/Rev.1.

34/ ISBA/A/WP.3.

35/ LOS/PCN/153.

36/ For further details about the composition of the Council, see article 161 (1) of the Convention and section 3, para. 15, of the annex to the Agreement.

37/ See A/C.5/50/28.

38/ Twenty-two nominations were received by the Secretariat by 15 October 1995.

39/ General Assembly resolution 49/28, para. 11.

40/ SPLOS/4, para. 14.

41/ It should be noted that the convening of such a meeting by the Division was part of its continuing efforts to promote the uniform and consistent development of States practice in a manner consistent with the provisions of the Convention, and in pursuing a series of special studies which are intended to provide assistance to States in their application of some highly technical provisions of the Convention. In the past, four such studies were prepared with the assistance of the groups of experts: (1) The Law of the Sea. Baselines: An Examination of the Relevant Provisions of the United Nations Convention on the Law of the Sea (United Nations publication, Sales No. E.788.V.5); (2) The Law of the Sea. Marine Scientific Research: A Guide to the Implementation of the Relevant Provisions of the United Nations Convention on the Law of the Sea (United Nations publication, Sales No. E.91.V.3); (3) The Law of the Sea. The Regime for High Seas Fisheries: Status and Prospects (United Nations publication, Sales No. E.92.V.12); and (4) The Law of the Sea. Definition of the Continental Shelf: An Examination of the Relevant Provisions of the United Nations Convention on the Law of the Sea (United Nations publication, Sales No. E.93.V.16).

42/ See note 41 above.

43/ Paragraph 17.116 sets forth the objectives of chapter 17, programme area F, on strengthening international cooperation, and paragraph 117 calls on the General Assembly to provide for regular intergovernmental consideration "of general marine and coastal issues, including environment and development matters ..."

44/ In view of the need to have a common understanding in the United Nations system as to which organizations should be considered "competent international organizations" for the purposes of the Convention, an agreed listing has been prepared by the Division for Ocean Affairs and the Law of the Sea and will be published in a forthcoming issue of the Law of the Sea Bulletin.

45/ See IMO documents C 74/22(b)/1, paras. 4, 5 and 9; C 74/27(c), paras. 225 to 228; C 74/SR.4; and A 19/27.

46/ See article 59 of the Convention on the International Maritime Organization.

47/ The study will involve updating and expansion of a study done in 1986 on the implications of the Convention for IMO, to include also current programmes of work and the IMO's long-term plan.

48/ E.g., mandatory ship reporting by the Maritime Safety Committee in 1993. See A/48/527, paras. 52-56.

49/ See WMO document EC-XLVI, para. 6.4.2, and WMO circular letter of 12 August 1994.

50/ "Report of the ad hoc Working Group on IOC Responsibilities and Actions in relation to UNCLOS", IOC document IOC/INF-990.

51/ Marine Scientific Research: A guide to the Implementation of the Relevant Provisions of the United Nations Convention on the Law of the Sea (United Nations publication, Sales No. E.91.V.3).

52/ See IOC-XVIII/3 prov., Pt.3; and IOC resolution XVIII-4 on IOC and UNCLOS.

53/ See IOC document IOC/INF-991.

54/ See IOC document IOC-XVIII/2, annex 7.

55/ Report of the Global Conference on the Sustainable Development of Small Island Developing States, Bridgetown, Barbados, 26 April-6 May 1994 (United Nations publication, Sales No. E.94.I.8 and corrigendum), chap. I, resolution 1, annex II.

56/ Recent ILO instruments of particular relevance to the protection of the marine environment include the Chemicals Convention 1990 (No. 170) and Recommendation (No. 177), the Prevention of Major Industrial Accidents Convention 1993 (No. 174) and Recommendation (No. 180).

57/ Oceans Day Message by the UNEP Executive Director, 8 June 1995.

58/ See Official Records of the General Assembly, Fiftieth Session, Supplement No. 25 (A/50/25), annex, decision 18/16.

59/ See A/47/277-S/24111.

60/ See A/48/689, A/48/935 and A/49/665.

61/ See UNEP document UNEP/GC.18/26.

62/ See Governing Council decision 18/31 on the protection of the marine environment from land-based activities, and the related decision 18/32 on persistent organic pollutants; Official Records of the General Assembly, Fiftieth Session, Supplement No. 25 (A/50/25), annex.

63/ See note 55 above.

64/ See ECLAC resolution 541 (XXV) on restructuring and resolution 544 (XXV) on environment and development.

65/ See ECA document NRD/MAR/1/94.

66/ See IMO document C 74/4 and addendum.

67/ The texts of the draft convention and the draft protocol are contained in IMO documents LEG/CONF.10/6 (a) and (b).

68/ See IMO document LEG 72/9, paras. 111-115.

69/ Adopted by resolution MSC.46(65); see IMO document MSC 65/25/Add.1, annex 2. The regulation does not apply to warships, naval auxiliary or other government vessels, although they are encouraged to participate in ships' routeing systems.

70/ IMO document MSC 65/25/Add.1, annex 3 - subject to final adoption by the 19th IMO Assembly (November 1995).

71/ The International Atomic Energy Agency (IAEA) plans to start revising the emergency response planning provisions in late 1996 and to initiate research into the severity of accidents at sea under all relevant accident scenarios, in particular fire accidents in relation to IAEA packaging performance standards.

72/ See IMO documents LEG 72/9, paras. 116-121, and MSC 65/25, paras. 24.1-24.8.

73/ A/50/475, annex.

74/ See IMO document on the implementation of Agenda 21 (MEPC 36/INF.2), in relation to Agenda 21, para. 17.30 (a) (vii).

75/ IMO document MSC 65/25, paras. 19.5-19.7. This Working Group is also cited in IMO's report on the implementation of Agenda 21 (MEPC 37/INF.2) as the IMO machinery responsible for the implementation of para. 17.30 (a) (ii) as concerns ships' routeing, and as being adequate for current needs.

76/ See statements by the Russian Federation, Greece, Cyprus, Bulgaria, Turkey and Romania in IMO document MSC 65/25/Add.2, annexes 34 to 39, and by the United States of America in Add.2/Corr.1. The Russian Federation, in its submission, reported that 80 ships flying its flag had been stopped in the area between July and December 1994.

77/ See Report of the Tripartite Meeting on Maritime Labour Standards (December 1994) ILO document GB.262/3; the revisions are contained in documents TMMLS/1994/I-IV.

78/ See Mainstreaming the Environment: The World Bank Group and the Environment since the Rio Earth Summit: Fiscal 1995 (The World Bank, Washington, D.C.), pp. 54-61.

79/ The IMO letter to States parties to the Convention on the Law of the Sea, dated 16 June 1995, has also been circulated in Law of the Sea Information Circular No. 2.

80/ UNEP document UNEP/CBD/COP/1/4.

81/ See the report of the first SBSTTA meeting (UNEP document UNEP/CBD/COP/2/5), particularly recommendation I/8 and the annex on integrated marine and coastal area management.

82/ The 1992 Protocols to the CLC and FUND Conventions more than double the amount of compensation, extend the scope of application of the treaties to the exclusive economic zones of Contracting States, and introduce a more expeditious system of amending the limitation amounts by the IMO Legal Committee.

83/ See IMO document LEG 72/9, paras. 124-127.

84/ See Status of regional agreements negotiated in the framework of the Regional Seas Programme (UNEP publication), revision 4, December 1994.

85/ The Final Act of the Conference is contained in UNEP document UNEP (OCA): MED IG.6/7.

86/ The area of application of the 1995 Protocol includes "the seabed and its subsoil; the waters, the seabed and its subsoil on the landward side of the baseline ... extending ... up to the freshwater limit; the terrestrical coastal areas designated by each of the Parties, including wetlands".

87/ Maritime Delimitation and Territorial Questions between Qatar and Bahrain, Jurisdiction and Admissibility, Judgment, I.C.J Reports 1995, p. 6.

88/ Communication from the Registry of the International Court of Justice, 2 August 1995.

89/ International Court of Justice, Fisheries Jurisdiction (Spain v. Canada). Application Instituting Proceedings, filed in the Registry of the Court on 28 March 1995.

90/ Ibid., Order of 2 May 1995.

91/ Middle East Economic Survey, 24 July 1995.

92/ The written statements by the delegations of Lebanon and of Israel to the Maritime Safety Committee, as well as the written statements made on the issue by the delegations of the Syrian Arab Republic, Morocco and the League of Arab States are reproduced in annexes 41 to 45 to the report of the Committee (IMO document MSC 65/25/Add.2). For the discussions on the issue in the Maritime Safety Committee, the Legal Committee and the Council, see IMO documents MSC 65/25, paras. 24.41-24.44; LEG 72/9, paras. 132-136; and C 74/SR.7, pp. 11-12, respectively.

93/ For background, see A/47/623, paras. 33-36, and A/49/631, para. 55.

94/ Asahi Shimbun (Tokyo), 26 and 29 March, 5 April 1995.

95/ A/49/953-S/1995/652, annex, para. 9.

96/ Agence France-Presse, 11 August 1995.

97/ Reuter European Business Report, 30 June 1995.

98/ Middle East Economic Survey, 19 December 1994.

99/ See A/49/815-S/1994/1446.

100/ IMO document FAL 23/8/4.

101/ IMO document FAL 23/19, paras. 8.1-8.4.

102/ IMO document C 74/SR.3, pp. 5-7.

103/ See "Risk reduction and maritime security in Asia and the Pacific", paper, presented to the Seventh Regional Disarmament Meeting in the Asia-Pacific Region, Katmandu, 13-15 February 1995. Disarmament: A periodic review by the United Nations, vol. XVIII, No. 2 (1995), p. 78.

104/ The text of the joint declaration, entitled "Cooperation over offshore activities in the South-West Atlantic", was transmitted to the Secretariat by the Permanent Mission of the United Kingdom of Great Britain and Northern Ireland to the United Nations.

105/ See "Concluding statement of the Seventh Regional Meeting". Disarmament: A periodic review by the United Nations, vol. XVIII, No. 21 (1995), p. 190.

106/ NPT/CONF.1995/32/DEC.2.

107/ See A/50/426.

108/ A/50/425-S/1995/787, para. 20.

109/ A/50/225 and A/50/475, appendix III.

110/ A/50/224.

111/ A/50/317-S/1995/627.

112/ United Nations Department of Public Information press release ICJ/541 of 22 September 1995. France has not signed any of the Protocols to the South Pacific Nuclear Free Zone Treaty (Treaty of Rarotonga), but the President of France declared on 23 October 1995 that France would sign all the protocols in the first half of 1996 as soon as it had completed the last of its nuclear testing. See also A/50/665-S/1995/877.

113/ A/50/373, para. 7.

114/ E/CONF.82/15 and Corr.2.

115/ E/CN.7/1995/13, chap. II, paras. 13, 20 and 22.

116/ See UNDCP/1994/MAR.2 and Add.1, and UNDCP/1994/MAR.WP.1.

117/ E/CN.7/1995/13, pp. 2-7.

118/ Official Records of the Economic and Social Council, 1995, Supplement No. 9 (E/1995/29), chap. XII.A, resolution 8 (XXXVIII).

119/ Official Records of the General Assembly, Fiftieth Session, Supplement No. 1 (A/50/1), para. 374.

120/ Joint submission by the United Kingdom and the International Chamber of Shipping, IMO document FAL 23/10/1.

121/ IMO document FAL 23/19, sect. 10.

122/ See IMO documents MSC 65/16/Add.1 (regional analysis of reports on piracy and armed robbery received by the IMO secretariat in the period between the end of September 1994 and the end of December 1994); MSC 65/16/Add.2 (information provided by the Government of Bangladesh); MSC/Circ.679 (reports of incidents received between 31 December 1994 and 31 March 1995); MSC/Circ.698 (reports of incidents received between 31 March and 30 June 1995); and MSC/Circ.701 and 703 (monthly reports for July and August 1995, respectively).

123/ See IMO document MSC 65/25, sect. 16.

124/ IMO document 65/16/1.

125/ The State of World Fisheries (Rome, FAO, 1995), p. 3.

126/ Ibid., p. 5.

127/ Ibid., p. 8.

128/ Ibid., p. 12.

129/ Report of the twenty-first session of the Committee on Fisheries, Rome, 10-13 March 1995, FAO Fisheries Report No. 524, paras. 17-18.

130/ Ibid., para. 19.

131/ Ibid., para. 21.

132/ Text transmitted by FAO to the United Nations Secretariat on 28 March 1995.

133/ A/50/518, annex, para. 33.

134/ Report of the twenty-first session of the Committee on Fisheries (see note 129 above), para. 11.

135/ International Whaling Commission, Chairman's draft report of the forty-seventh annual meeting, 29 May-2 June 1995, p. 46.

136/ Ibid., resolution on methods of killing whales, ibid., p. 48.

137/ Ibid., resolution on small cetaceans, p. 50.

138/ Ibid., resolution on North-Eastern Atlantic mink whales, p. 51.

139/ Ibid., resolution on whaling under special permit in sanctuaries, and resolution on whaling under special permit, pp. 54-56.

140/ ICCAT Newsletter, vol. 25, 1 May 1995.

141/ Law of the Sea Bulletin, No. 28 (1995), p. 34.

142/ Government of Canada, news release, 2 May 1995.

143/ Ibid., 15 September 1995.

144/ Le Monde (Paris), 30 April 1995.

145/ IPS Daily Journal, vol. 3, No. 75 (25 April 1995); Le Monde (Paris), April 1995.

146/ Le Monde (Paris), 15 and 16 October 1995.

147/ Communication of the European Communities addressed to the Secretary-General, 14 February 1995.

148/ A/50/475, annex, paras. 9 and 11.

149/ Review of the State of World Fishery Resources: Marine Fisheries, FAO Fisheries Circular No. 884 (Rome, FAO, 1995), p. 62.

150/ A/AC.109/2027, para. 20 (1) and (4).

151/ Ibid., para. 20 (4) and (5).

152/ Ibid., para. 20 (7).

153/ Thus, General Assembly resolution 49/28 points to the "strategic importance of the Convention as a framework for national, regional and global action in the marine sector, as recognized also ... in chapter 17 of Agenda 21" (preamble).

154/ The report of the final preparatory meeting (Reykjavik, March 1995) is contained in UNEP document UNEP/ICL/IG/1/L.6.

155/ Official Records of the General Assembly, Fiftieth Session, Supplement No. 25 (A/50/25), annex.

156/ The Workshop originated in a recommendation of the British Government Panel on Sustainable Development (January 1995).

157/ The last GESAMP "State of the Marine Environment", published in 1989, took five years to complete.

158/ General Assembly resolution 49/131.

159/ Organized through the Intersecretariat Committee for Scientific Programmes Relating to Oceanography, for which IOC provides the secretariat.

160/ Letter dated 9 May 1995 from the Prime Minister of Portugal to the Secretary-General.

161/ UNEP document UNEP/CBP/COP/2/5.

162/ See IOC resolution XVIII-7.

163/ IMO document MSC 65.17/1.

164/ IMO document A 19/7.

165/ IMO document MSC 65/25, p. 8.

166/ IMO document MSC 65/INF.15.

167/ See IMO document MSC 65/25, para. 5.6.

168/ IMO document MSC 65/25/Add.1, annex 10.

169/ See A/50/407, annex I.

170/ See TD/B/LDC/AC.1/3.

171/ TD/B/LDC/AC.1/6.

172/ A/50/341, annex, paras. 3-6.

173/ A/56/341, para. 3; see also TD/B/42(1)/11-TD/B/LDC/AC.1/7.

174/ S/1995/74, annex I.

175/ UNESCO document 146 EX/27, para. 38.

176/ Ibid., para. 20.

177/ Text reproduced in Law of the Sea: Annual Review of Ocean Affairs, Law and Policy, Main Documents, 1989 (United Nations publication, Sales No. E.93.V.5), p. 395.

178/ The North Sea Declaration, reproduced in IMO document MEPC 37/INF.14, para. 54.

179/ See IMO document LC 18/3.

180/ See IMO document MEPC 37/INF.2, annex, pp. 1-15.

181/ See IMO document LC 17/14, paras. 5.28-5.29.

182/ The New York Times, 17 October 1995. It should be noted that the estimate is not universally accepted; some experts are of the opinion that the deep sea total is unlikely to exceed a half million species.

183/ The Economist, 3 September 1994.

184/ The New York Times, 4 October 1994.

185/ The Economist, 3 September 1994.

186/ The New York Times, 4 October 1994.

187/ Ibid., 18 October 1994.

188/ UNEP document UNEP/CBD/COP/2/5, recommendation I/8.

189/ Ibid., para. 75.

190/ The New York Times, 9 August 1994.

191/ Ibid., 26 September 1995.

192/ The fellowship award is given by the Legal Counsel, on the recommendations of an Advisory Panel of prominent personalities in law of the sea and international affairs under the chairmanship of Professor John Norton Moore, Director of the Center for Oceans Law and Policy, University of Virginia School of Law. Nine awards have been made since 1986.

193/ In making this donation, the United Kingdom requested that the candidate should be chosen from a developing country and should pursue a one year LL.M. programme or carry out advanced study and research at the graduate level at a university in the United Kingdom followed by an internship period with the Division for Ocean Affairs and the Law of the Sea.

194/ Mr. Kamgue is expected to carry out his fellowship and research and study at the Graduate Institute of International Studies, Geneva, and Mr. Elizabeth has already commenced his advanced research and study at Cambridge University Research Centre for International Law.

CORRIGENDUM

1. Paragraph 98

At the end of the paragraph, before the parentheses, insert the following sentence

Turkey maintained that its national regulations were in full conformity with the IMO rules and regulations, which it considered to be more stringent, and invoked the Basel Convention in respect to the transboundary movement of wastes.

2. Paragraph 99

The second and third sentences should read

The IMO Rules and Recommendations were implemented only recently, on 24 November 1994, so that it is still too early to establish that there have been any major difficulties in their implementation. It may be noted that the changed legal context brought about by the recent amendments to SOLAS Chapter V regarding mandatory ships' routeing and reporting systems and the corresponding amendments to the General Provisions on Ships' Routeing may contribute to the further development of the IMO Rules and Recommendations in the future.

3. Paragraph 100

The paragraph should read

100. Several delegations made statements for the record on various aspects of the question, including those asserting and denying the applicability of the regime of transit passage through the Straits concerned. 76/

4. Endnote 75, line 1

For IMO document MSC 65/25, paras. 19.5-19.7 read IMO document MSC 65/25, paras. 19.16 and 19.17.

5. Endnote 76

At the end of the note, add the following sentence

Turkey questioned the allegation and the figures cited, and stated that delays were inevitable for safety as stipulated in IMO Rules 1.2 and 1.3 and that such traffic management rules were a necessary precaution to ensure the safety of all maritime traffic and to ensure safe and orderly traffic flow (see IMO document MSC 65/25/Add.2, annex 38).

2. STRENGTHENING OF SECURITY AND COOPERATION IN THE MEDITERRANEAN REGION - REPORT OF THE UN SECRETARY-GENERAL*

Doc. no.: A/50/300 21 July 1995

CONTENTS

Page

I. INTRODUCTION

1. In its resolution 49/81 of 15 December 1994, the General Assembly encouraged all States of the Mediterranean region to promote genuine openness and transparency in all military matters, particularly by participating in the United Nations system for the standardized reporting of military expenditures as well as by providing accurate data and information to the Register of Conventional Arms. It also invited those States to address, through various forms of cooperation, problems and threats posed to the region, such as terrorism and criminal acts, as well as illegal drug production, consumption and trafficking. The Assembly requested the Secretary-General to submit a report on means to strengthen security and cooperation in the Mediterranean region.

---

* A/50/150.

2. With a view to facilitating the preparation of such a report, the Secretary-General addressed notes verbale to all Member States requesting their views on the matter.

3. As at 11 July 1995, five Governments have replied to the notes verbale of the Secretary-General and their responses are reproduced in section III below. Any replies or notifications received subsequently will be published as addenda to the present report.

II. CONSIDERATION OF THE QUESTION OF THE STRENGTHENING OF SECURITY AND COOPERATION IN THE MEDITERRANEAN REGION DURING THE FORTY-NINTH SESSION OF THE GENERAL ASSEMBLY

4. The First Committee held a general debate on all disarmament and international security items allocated to it, including item 68 on the strengthening of security and cooperation in the Mediterranean region; the report on its consideration of the item is contained in document A/49/705.

5. During the general debate, several Member States, including Algeria, Cyprus, the Libyan Arab Jamahiriya, Malta and Tunisia, addressed issues related to security and cooperation in the Mediterranean region. While pointing out the different sources of instability and calling for initiatives and action, all sought to encourage efforts that would make the Mediterranean region a centre of peace, security, development and economic prosperity.

6. The draft resolution on the item (A/C.1/49/L.47/Rev.2) was introduced by Algeria on behalf of the sponsors, which included almost all the coastal States of the Mediterranean. The sponsors were Albania, Algeria, Andorra, Bosnia and Herzegovina, Croatia, Cyprus, Egypt, France, Greece, Italy, the Libyan Arab Jamahiriya, Malta, Mauritania, Monaco, Morocco, Portugal, San Marino, Spain and Tunisia.

7. In introducing the revised draft resolution on behalf of its sponsors, the representative of Algeria pointed out that the increase in the number of sponsors compared with the previous year was a perfect illustration of the state of mind in most Mediterranean countries and of their willingness to work together to strengthen cooperation and security in the Mediterranean basin.

8. The representative of Algeria pointed out that the draft resolution differed from previous resolutions in that it dealt with a broader range of questions relating to security and cooperation in the Mediterranean. He added that, having taken into account the prevalent dynamics of peace in the region, the sponsors wanted to express their sincere desire to give fresh impetus to their multifaceted relations so as to bolster the climate of confidence and security that was essential if the Mediterranean was to be a lake of peace and cooperation (see A/C.1/49/PV.21).

9. While the General Assembly would bear in mind all the initiatives taken by the Mediterranean countries, it would also reaffirm their primary role. The Assembly would recognize the indivisible character of security in the Mediterranean and the determination of the Mediterranean countries to intensify the process of dialogue and consultations, with a view to resolving the problems existing in the region, eliminating the causes of tension and fostering closer European-Mediterranean cooperation.

10. In the operative part of the draft resolution, the provisions that encouraged riparian States to continue their efforts to remove all obstacles to the promotion of confidence-building and disarmament measures in order to establish a climate of peace, security, stability and prosperity in the Mediterranean region had been strengthened.

11. In view of the new dynamic motivating most of the coastal States of the Mediterranean region, the sponsors were confident that the resolution enjoyed the support of all the members of the First Committee and called for it to be adopted without a vote. The General Assembly adopted the draft resolution without a vote as resolution 49/81.

III. REPLIES RECEIVED FROM GOVERNMENTS

BELARUS

[Original: English]

[6 July 1995]

The pertinent ministerial bodies of Belarus support the efforts envisaged in General Assembly resolution 49/81 and aimed at developing various forms of international cooperation in crime prevention and elimination and has undertaken appropriate measures to that end. Thus, in January 1993, an Agreement was signed on cooperation between the Ministry of the Interior of Belarus and the Ministry of the Interior of Italy in the field of transfer of illicit drugs and psychotropic substances along the "Balkan road" and for computerized data exchange. A meeting between the Ministers of the Interior of Belarus and Italy, held at Rome in May 1993 during the international conference on European drug transfer, resulted in the signing of an inter-ministerial agreement on cooperation in combating the transfer of illicit drugs and psychotropic substances and organized crime.

COLOMBIA

[Original: Spanish]

[20 April 1995]

1. Colombia believes that the evolution of international relations requires that a new, realistic approach be taken to the problems of global security. Such an approach must be based on an integrated concept encompassing both the principles governing relations among States and those concerning respect for human life.

2. Colombia supports the Declaration on the Strengthening of International Security and the Declaration on Principles of International Law concerning Friendly Relations and Cooperation among States in accordance with the Charter of the United Nations, as well as activities to strengthen security in the various regions and cooperation on matters of common interest to the States of a given region.

3. Colombia therefore supports the determination of the Mediterranean countries to strengthen their security, eliminate causes of tension, promote confidence-building measures and work for international cooperation, particularly in the economic, social, humanitarian and environmental spheres.

FRANCE*

[Original: French]

[31 May 1995]

1. The European Union recalls its common replies contained in documents A/48/514/Add.1 and A/49/333. The Union reiterates the principal elements set forth in those documents and wishes to add the following comments.

2. The European Union is convinced that current security and cooperation problems in the Mediterranean region demand a multi-disciplinary approach. Moreover, the complexity of the issues necessitates a comprehensive and concerted initiative allowing each specific problem to be addressed separately.

3. The European Union is of the view that relations among the Mediterranean countries should be such as to guarantee the prosperity and stability of the countries concerned and gradually make the region an area for exchanges and dialogue. But that can come about only through political dialogue, sustained and balanced socio-economic development, the eradication of poverty and broader understanding among the various cultures.

4. For the Mediterranean to become a common area of peace and stability the following fundamental principles must be respected: equality and sovereignty, non-interference, respect for territorial sovereignty, renunciation of the use of force, the peaceful settlement of disputes and the establishment of good-neighbourliness as well as of confidence-building and security measures. The establishment of this common area will also necessitate a joint effort to combat terrorism, organized crime and drug trafficking, as well as the attainment of disarmament and non-proliferation objectives in compliance with the principles of international law and the resolutions of the United Nations, taking into account proposals for regional demilitarization.

5. The European Union has encouraged several initiatives aimed at promoting dialogue and cooperation between the two shores of the Mediterranean, not only in the context of the Union's foreign policy but also in other forums and organizations to which the members of the Union belong. In the field of security, the Western European Union, the defence component of the European Union, has, since 1992, provided a framework for dialogue with the southern littoral States in pursuance of two objectives: contributing to stability in the region through direct contacts for the exchange of information and views on issues involving mutual security and other interests; and complementing, in the area of security, their political and economic relations with the European Union. This dialogue (in which five North African countries are already participating and which could be extended to others in the future) reflects a global concept of security and is designed to bring about greater mutual awareness and understanding, thereby diminishing the possibility of mistaken perceptions of threats.

6. The members of the European Union are also participating in other Mediterranean-focused initiatives to promote dialogue. In the framework of the Organization for Security and Cooperation in Europe (OSCE), the Budapest Summit in December 1994 gave new impetus to relations with non-participating Mediterranean countries by offering the latter new opportunities to cooperate in the work of the organization on issues likely to affect the region as a whole. Further, experience gained in the context of the Conference on Security and Cooperation in Europe (CSCE)/OSCE could prove useful as a possible complement to the cultural and religious aspects of different local societies in the establishment of a more open dialogue in the region. In addition, the Mediterranean Forum began its work in June 1994 in an informal meeting of the

---

* On behalf of the States members of the European Union.

Ministers for Foreign Affairs of the 10 countries on the two shores of the Mediterranean, followed by a further meeting in April 1995. At this most recent meeting, the Forum objective of promoting political, economic and regional cultural cooperation was reaffirmed. The Mediterranean Forum has also demonstrated its usefulness by making a significant contribution to other forums, such as the initiative on a Euro-Mediterranean partnership. In the framework of the Atlantic alliance, preliminary contacts have been made with the littoral States of the southern Mediterranean with a view to establishing a dialogue on security issues that would promote an atmosphere of greater understanding and, thereby, regional stability.

7. In the sphere of disarmament and non-proliferation, the European Union welcomes the decision taken at the Review and Extension Conference of the Parties to the Treaty on the Non-Proliferation of Nuclear Weapons on the unlimited extension of the Treaty and the fact that the decision was adopted without a vote. The Union invites all the States of the region to honour their commitments as signatories to agreements on arms control and disarmament and invites all Mediterranean States that have not yet done so to accede to the non-proliferation Treaty. This invitation also extends to chemical weapons, so that the Convention on the Prohibition of the Development, Production, Stockpiling and Use of Chemical Weapons and on Their Destruction can, as soon as possible, obtain the requisite number of new ratifications for its entry into force. The Union also supports efforts under way to provide the Convention on the Prohibition of the Development, Production and Stockpiling of Bacteriological (Biological) and Toxin Weapons and on Their Destruction with a verification protocol, and encourages all States of the Mediterranean region to comply with the confidence-building measures agreed at the Third Review Conference of the latter Convention.

8. The European Union is convinced that improved transparency in military matters will promote stability in the Mediterranean region. The Union calls upon all the States of the region to submit to the United Nations Register of Conventional Arms not only information on transfers of conventional weapons, including the "not applicable" responses which make a significant contribution to the success of the Register, but also to expand such information to include military holdings and procurement through national production, as stipulated in paragraph 10 of General Assembly resolution 46/36 L of 9 December 1991. The Union also strongly encourages all the States of the Mediterranean region to participate in the United Nations system for the standardized reporting of military expenditures.

9. The creation of a zone of peace, stability and prosperity in the Mediterranean is clearly motivated by a determination to resolve the serious issues facing the littoral countries. The problem of terrorism was emphasized in the preparatory phase of the Barcelona Euro-Mediterranean conference, and the importance of efforts to combat drug trafficking was recalled in paragraph 7 of the Essen Declaration on Mediterranean Policy of the European Council.

10. The strengthening of cooperation among the countries of the region on questions relating to terrorism would, inter alia, include increased exchanges of information, improved training for the services responsible for the prevention and elimination of terrorism, and assessment of the various components of terrorism.

11. Similarly, with respect to drug trafficking, the European Union advocates close cooperation of police and customs services based on exchanges of information; on greater awareness of the need to make use of advanced technology to detect suspicious shipments; on the establishment of coordinated and effective control of maritime traffic in the framework of international conventions and the strengthening of legal measures against drug trafficking; and on respect for the relevant international commitments.

12. The European Union is convinced that it is incumbent upon it as well as its Mediterranean partners to act together to turn the Mediterranean basin into, more than at present, an area for exchanges and dialogue in order to guarantee peace, stability and well-being for its peoples. In this spirit and in accordance with the strategies defined in the meetings of the European Council at Lisbon (June 1992), Corfu (June 1994) and Essen (December 1994), the European Union is resolved to define, in a spirit of partnership, a lasting framework for relations with the countries of the Mediterranean.

13. In furtherance of this aim, a Euro-Mediterranean ministerial conference will be held at Barcelona on 27 and 28 November 1995 at which the European Union and its partners in the western and eastern Mediterranean will jointly define their future relations. Participation in the conference will include the States members of the European Union as well as the Mediterranean countries institutionally associated with the European Union, Morocco, Algeria, Tunisia, Egypt, Israel, the Syrian Arab Republic, Jordan, Lebanon, Turkey, Malta and Cyprus, and the Palestinian Authority.

14. The aim of the conference is not to provide a specific forum for the settlement of any given conflict. Thus it will not interfere with ongoing regional initiatives such as the Middle East peace process. In Essen, the European Council very clearly specified that the aim of the conference was to initiate a permanent and regular dialogue. Thus, the Euro-Mediterranean conference could provide the foundation for a process of cooperation among the Mediterranean littoral States. In addition, it could serve as a mechanism for political dialogue among the participating States in order to define common principles and interests with respect to both their internal stability (State subject to the rule of law, human rights) and external stability (fundamental principles of good-neighbourliness among States, including general security questions). The Barcelona Euro-Mediterranean conference should, in particular, establish as an objective the promotion of political, economic and social initiatives intended to promote the harmonization of societies on the two shores of the Mediterranean basin, thus transcending the traditional dichotomy between development aid and mass migration.

LEBANON

[Original: Arabic]

[17 May 1995]

1. The Government of Lebanon agrees with paragraph 6 of General Assembly resolution 49/81 encouraging States to make known the details of their military expenditures and their levels of armament. It considers that this policy should cover all the States of the region, including Israel, and should also provide for an inventory of the nuclear and chemical weapons that Israel has introduced into the region in spite of the promises given by Israeli officials not to take the initiative in this matter. Paragraph 6 of the resolution is restricted to conventional weapons, but Lebanon considers there is no justification for this and that there should be an attempt to construct a comprehensive list of the arsenals of States.

2. Lebanon agrees with the provisions of paragraph 8 of the resolution relating to the dangers to which the peoples of the region are exposed from terrorist activities, provided there is a precise definition of what is meant by the word "terrorism", provided that such a definition includes an affirmation of the right of peoples to use military means to defend their sovereignty and in response to the occupation of their territory, and provided that it is clear that the definition of the word "terrorism" does not include the resistance operations in the South.

3. Lebanon agrees with the provisions of paragraph 8 concerning the necessity of cooperation to address the dangers arising from drug production, trafficking

and consumption and thinks that attention should be drawn to the efforts of the countries of the region, including Lebanon, and to the results achieved by Lebanon in restricting the illegal activities, which had become worse during the war years.

4. Lebanon agrees with the provisions of paragraph 8 concerning the necessity of preserving fundamental freedoms and a democratic basis and protecting them from anything that might weaken or endanger them, provided that it is clear that occupation is one of these dangers and that its continuation threatens freedoms and democratic civilian life in Lebanon and other countries that have been exposed to aggression and occupation. It is also necessary to stress that non-compliance with United Nations resolutions, including Security Council resolution 425 (1978) of 19 March 1978, is a violation of fundamental rights and a weakening of the principles on which democratic societies are based.

5. Furthermore, the continued detention of Lebanese citizens in the Khiam prison camp without any legal justification constitutes an impediment to cooperation and security in the region, and it must be ended in order to facilitate cooperation for security in the Middle East region.

RUSSIAN FEDERATION

[Original: Russian]

[15 June 1995]

1. The strengthening of security and cooperation in the Mediterranean region is, in the view of the Russian Federation, one of the priority tasks of the international community.

2. The Russian Federation is closely bound to the Mediterranean region by historical, geopolitical, economic and cultural ties. It is with great satisfaction that we note the promising developments in the situation in the Mediterranean. Despite occasional disruptions, the Middle East peace process remains on a generally positive track, the dialogue between Europe and North Africa is being revitalized and economic cooperation among coastal States is growing. At the same time, however, favourable trends are alternating with a number of factors that are disturbing or threatening peace and stability. These include the acute crisis in the Balkans, the smouldering Cypriot problem, unresolved differences between Turkey and Greece, the periodic flare-up of tension in the Middle East, the uncertain situation regarding the Libyan Arab Jamahiriya, illegal migration, the growth of religious violence, which feeds on the alarming disparities between rich and poor in individual countries, and on lagging economic development in various States.

3. In order to strengthen security in the Mediterranean region and prevent any further erosion of stability there, a comprehensive approach is necessary, which would include parallel steps to eliminate hot spots, reduce military presence and develop regional cooperation on the basis of greater economic integration. In this connection, the elaboration and promotion of measures to build confidence among the countries of the Mediterranean are also of considerable importance. The Russian Federation continues to be in favour of a greater role for the United Nations in the mobilization of multilateral efforts to resolve common military, political, economic and humanitarian problems. In view of the timeliness of disarmament issues for the region, it might be appropriate to expand the debate on problems of disarmament in the Mediterranean region in the First Committee of the General Assembly.

4. An important political as well as geographic consideration is, in our view, the close interdependence of the Black Sea and Mediterranean Sea basins and the common interests of the States situated in this area in the settlement of regional problems. We believe that greater attention should be paid to the

creation of mechanisms for integrating the region of the Black and Mediterranean seas.

5. The Russian Federation welcomes the process of intensification of ties between the countries of the Mediterranean region and States outside the region, which is in keeping with new realities and is gathering force. One aspect of this process is the establishment of a Mediterranean forum, in whose activities we would be prepared to participate as an observer. In our view, the United Nations could make a vital contribution to the stability of this process.

6. The 1991 proposal to convene a conference on security and cooperation in the Mediterranean region should be developed and expanded. The "product" of such a conference might, in the initial stage, include voluntary commitments in the area of confidence-building measures, the creation of political mechanisms for monitoring the non-proliferation of weapons of mass destruction, the elaboration of rules and procedures covering the military and political aspects of security and environmental cooperation.

3. PROGRESS IN THE IMPLEMENTATION OF SPECIFIC ACTIONS RELATED TO THE PARTICULAR NEEDS AND PROBLEMS OF LAND-LOCKED DEVELOPING COUNTRIES - NOTE BY THE UN SECRETARY-GENERAL

Doc. no.: A/50/341 22 September 1995

1. In paragraph 17 of its resolution 48/169 of 21 December 1993, the General Assembly welcomed the report of the Secretary-General of the United Nations Conference on Trade and Development on specific action related to the particular needs and problems of land-locked developing countries (A/48/487, annex) and requested him to prepare another report, taking into account the provisions of that resolution, for submission to the General Assembly at its fiftieth session.

2. Pursuant to that request, the Secretary-General has the honour to transmit to the Assembly the report of the Secretary-General of the United Nations Conference on Trade and Development (see annex).

3. Furthermore, the report of the Second Meeting of Governmental Experts from Land-locked and Transit Developing Countries and Representatives of Donor Countries and Financial and Development Institutions, called for in paragraph 10 of the same resolution, is also before the General Assembly in document TD/B/42(1)/11-TD/B/LDC/AC.1/7. Annexed to that report is the Global Framework for Transit Transport Cooperation between Land-locked and Transit Developing Countries and the Donor Community, which, inter alia, outlines a wide range of recommendations for further appropriate action to improve transit transport systems.

Annex

SPECIFIC ACTION RELATED TO THE PARTICULAR NEEDS AND PROBLEMS OF LAND-LOCKED DEVELOPING COUNTRIES

Progress report by the UNCTAD secretariat*

CONTENTS

* Previously issued as document TD/B/42(1)/14.

INTRODUCTION

1. In paragraph 17 of its resolution 48/169, the General Assembly welcomed the reports of the Secretary-General of the United Nations and of the Secretary-General of UNCTAD on specific action related to the specific needs and problems of land-locked developing countries (A/48/487) and requested the latter to prepare another report, taking into account the provisions of the above resolution, for submission to the General Assembly at its fiftieth session. In accordance with Conference resolution 137(VI), the report is being submitted to the General Assembly through the Trade and Development Board.

I. ACTIVITIES OF THE UNITED NATIONS CONFERENCE ON TRADE AND DEVELOPMENT (UNCTAD)

A. Evaluation of the transit systems of land-locked and transit developing countries

2. In paragraph 10 of its resolution 48/169, the General Assembly requests the Secretary-General of UNCTAD to make an evaluation of the transit systems of the land-locked and transit developing countries. The purpose of this evaluation was to serve as a basis for the review of the progress in the development of the transit systems which was undertaken by the Second Meeting of Governmental Experts from Land-locked and Transit Developing Countries and Representatives of Donor Countries and Financial Development Institutions called for by the General Assembly in the same paragraph of the resolution. The results of this evaluation are outlined in the documentation for the above meeting contained in annex III of the report of the meeting which is before the Board for consideration and will be submitted to the General Assembly at its fiftieth session (TD/B/42(1)/11-TD/B/LDC/AC.1/7).

B. Symposium for land-locked and transit developing countries

3. In paragraph 12 of General Assembly resolution 48/169, the Secretary-General of UNCTAD is invited to organize, in collaboration with the Administrator of the United Nations Development Programme (UNDP) and the executive heads of the regional commissions, a symposium for land-locked and transit developing countries to address specific regional problems in improving transit transport systems. The preparations for this symposium, which took place from 14 to 16 June 1995 in New York, involved the following key activities.

4. The UNCTAD secretariat fielded several experts in Africa and Asia who carried out comprehensive analyses of the specific actions being taken at the national and subregional levels to develop and improve the transit transport systems and made recommendations for future work. These regional studies were supplemented by the ongoing work of the UNCTAD's secretariat related to the particular needs and problems of land-locked and transit developing countries, as well as by contributions from the regional commissions, UNDP, the World Bank and the regional development banks. Summaries of these contributions, as well as those of replies received from individual land-locked and transit developing countries and relevant international and intergovernmental organizations are given in section II below. These summaries were submitted to the Symposium in document UNCTAD/LLDC/SYMP/2 and Add.1. 1/

5. The 32 land-locked and transit developing countries that participated in the Symposium 2/ agreed on a range of proposals for the development of a global framework for transit transport cooperation. These proposals covered the key areas in the transit transport sector, namely, rail and road transit traffic, port facilities and services, inland waterways, airfreight and communications. Proposals for donor support to the sector were also elaborated. The conclusions and recommendations for appropriate action in the above areas which were agreed upon by the Symposium were further discussed with the development partners in the intergovernmental meeting of experts referred to in paragraph 2 above, which finally adopted the Global Framework for Transit Cooperation between the Land-locked and Transit Developing Countries and the Donor Community. This Framework, which is annexed to the report of the meeting, represented a major breakthrough towards the establishment of triangular arrangements for an efficient and self sustainable transit transport cooperation.

C. Other UNCTAD activities

6. As part of its technical cooperation activities on behalf of land-locked and transit developing countries, UNCTAD continued to implement three

subregional transit transport technical assistance projects in West/Central, East/Central and southern Africa. Because of the financial problems of the funding agencies, these activities, however, mainly focused on the assessment of the results that had been achieved during the previous years of the projects. This assessment was used as a basis for the terminal reviews of the projects that were undertaken in the second half of 1994.

7. The beneficiary countries of the above projects highly commended the work of the projects and their positive impact on the improvement of the transit transport systems and urged donor institutions to seriously consider providing resources for the reactivation of the activities of the projects. The UNCTAD secretariat was requested to play a catalyst role in mobilizing this support. Since then, contacts with various funding agencies have been established in this regard, and detailed future work programmes have been elaborated. The intergovernmental meeting of experts with donors underscored the importance of reviving these projects and it is expected that this endorsement will lead to a favourable response to the current efforts by the UNCTAD secretariat to mobilize resources that are required to set a new technical assistance programme in motion.

II. CONTRIBUTIONS BY INDIVIDUAL COUNTRIES AND BY INTERNATIONAL AND INTERGOVERNMENTAL ORGANIZATIONS

A. Summaries of replies received from individual countries

Argentina

8. In addition to the Paraguay-Parana waterway transport agreement of 30 June 1992 between Argentina, Bolivia, Brazil, Paraguay and Uruguay, the transit transport of Bolivia and Paraguay with Argentina is governed by the following agreements:

(a) With Bolivia:

(i) Border traffic agreement (17 September 1937);

(ii) Agreement establishing a mixed commission for border traffic (18 July 1970);

(iii) Santa Cruz-Trinidad railway agreement (31 December 1970);

(b) With Paraguay:

(i) Border waterway transport agreement (31 July 1972);

(ii) Land transport agreement (30 October 1992).

Burkina Faso

9. Burkina Faso cooperates with the neighbouring transit countries in the framework of bilateral and subregional transit agreements and arrangements. The Heads of State of the Economic Community of West African States (ECOWAS) signed two conventions designed to regulate transit operations, namely the "Convention sur le transport routier inter États" (TIE) (Inter-State Road Transport Convention) and the "Convention sur le transit routier inter-États" (TRIE) (Inter-State Road Transit Convention). At the national level, Burkina Faso is undertaking measures to improve transit systems, including the reduction of road tolls and other controls. At the bilateral level, it has supported coordinated efforts to reduce transit times and costs and to improve the statistical database regarding intercountry transit operations.

Central African Republic

10. The six Heads of States members of the Central African Customs and Economic Union (UDEAC) agreed in 1994 to take measures to improve the current transit system in the subregion. The Central African Republic took the initiative to set up specific working groups to make recommendations regarding new arrangements to improve customs procedures and practices, the organization of the international road transport system, the transit bond guarantee system and the conditions of the vehicles involved in the transit operations.

Congo

11. The rehabilitation of the transit system is the priority area in the National Transport Plan of the Congo. The Ministry of Transport and Civil Aviation has taken a number of measures to facilitate the procedures for the movement of transit cargo from the Central African Republic. This initiative is part of the support programme for the subregion, which is sponsored by the European Union and the World Bank.

Djibouti

12. The Djibouti Government is making efforts to develop its container terminal into a regional maritime facility for handling transit goods. In December 1993, the Government signed a convention in Addis Ababa to this effect. This convention outlines a number of facilitating measures, including tariff reduction for transit cargo. There are, however, still problems related to the poor implementation of agreed measures. Furthermore, the rail and road facilities leading to the port are inadequate. There is, therefore, a need for efficient multimodal transport systems that effectively link the port to the neighbouring countries.

Ghana

13. Ghana, as a transit country, has adopted a number of policy measures and initiated some actions to assist neighbouring land-locked countries. These include, ongoing internal consultations to simplify customs documentation and administrative procedures; the review of customs administrative charges on transit cargo; the allocation of adequate land to Mali and Burkina Faso for the development of facilities at the Tema Harbour; the development of an inland waterways transport facility as well as the construction and rehabilitation of relevant road linkages. Action is also being initiated to create a free port regime for the port of Tema that would facilitate the flow of transit traffic to the land-locked countries, and to develop an electronic data interchange (EDI) system. An open-door policy has been pursued, aiming at liberalizing most of Ghana's economic activities, including transport and communication services. Financial constraints on the implementation of most of the transport plans, cumbersome customs procedures and the absence of an institutional framework to monitor the implementation of bilateral agreements are the main obstacles to the development of the transit system.

Lao People's Democratic Republic

14. The Australian-funded "friendship bridge" over the Mekong, which was opened in early 1994, is the first one to connect Thailand and the Lao People's Democratic Republic. Moreover, a series of meetings between the two countries are being conducted to enhance bilateral cooperation with respect to all forms of transport links. A memorandum on cooperation in communications for 1994 was signed between the Lao People's Democratic Republic and Viet Nam, which describes priority road connections between the two countries, in particular

those allowing the Lao People's Democratic Republic to use the facilities in ports in Viet Nam. In January 1994, an agreement was also signed in Kunming between China, Myanmar, the Lao People's Democratic Republic and Thailand that will provide for two-way navigation on part of the Mekong river.

Malawi

15. The Government of Malawi continues to participate, under regional arrangements like the Preferential Trade Area for Eastern and Southern African States (PTA) and the Southern African Development Community (SADC), in transit traffic facilitation as well as entering into bilateral agreements. Malawi is committed to cooperating with its transit neighbours in removing problems related to poor formulation and weak monitoring of implementation and settlement of disputes with respect to such aspects as transit routes by rail, road and inland-waterways, customs documentation and procedures, bonding guarantee systems, storage facilities for goods in transit, road maintenance regimes, road user charges and procedures for clearing and forwarding. More specifically, Malawi has initiated action on a number of issues, such as the restructuring of the railways in an effort to move to a more aggressive market-oriented management, plans for the establishment of a road fund to be used specifically for the maintenance of the roads, the implementation of PTA-harmonized transit charges, carrier licences, and harmonized axle-load limits, and 24 hour-a-day service at the borders. Furthermore, with the assistance of the United States Agency for International Development (USAID), a national transport policy framework has been drafted, which aims at developing a coordinated transport system, in a market-oriented approach, and a sound base for the various carriers to provide reliable, efficient and economic services to the people. However, Malawi recognizes that there is an acute shortage of trained human resources in the country to meet the requirements of transit operations at all levels. Human resource development programmes are therefore a priority in the development of transport.

16. On the whole, Malawi feels that most of the recommendations of the Meeting of the Governmental Experts from Land-locked and Transit Developing Countries and Representatives of Donor Countries and Financial and Development Institutions held in May 1993 in New York are yet to be implemented. It is regrettable that some transit countries have not shown the appropriate willingness in that respect. Some countries have instituted stringent policies governing transit traffic to the detriment of the economies of land-locked countries. Lack of cooperative efforts on the part of some neighbouring transit countries and lack of commitment to the implementation of bilateral or regional agreements reached in the relevant institutional forums continue to be major impediments in the improvement of transit systems.

Mali

17. The Malian economy is heavily constrained by the high transit costs which it incurs on the movement of its import and export cargoes. These transport costs are estimated at 8 per cent of the gross domestic product (GDP) and represent about 30 per cent of the total import costs. Mali has signed a number of bilateral and multilateral agreements with its neighbouring countries, including the TIE and TRIE Conventions (see para. 9 above). These agreements allow for the use of port facilities under the management of Malian agencies. Côte d'Ivoire and Senegal provide the port facilities for Malian cargo and special arrangements have been agreed upon with these transit countries with regard to customs documentation and procedures and other related facilities. It is important to note that, in response to General Assembly resolution 48/169, Côte d'Ivoire suspended the traditional payment of a special fee for the certificate that is required to accompany vehicles transporting transit goods to Mali (Lettre de voiture). Furthermore, Mali established a national committee for the follow-up of the activities of the now terminated UNDP/UNCTAD subregional transit transport project. Mali also drew up an investment

programme for the transport sector for the period of 1994-1998, for which donor financing is being sought.

Mongolia

18. Transit transport operations in Mongolia are governed by bilateral cooperation agreements with China, Kazakstan and the Russian Federation. Mongolia initiated measures to enhance railway capacity. The Mongolia railway system, which covers 1,800 kilometres, plays an important role in the movement of transit cargo. Cargo to and from the Russian Federation and Europe is transported via a broad-gauge line with no interruption along the routes; however, cargo to and from China and Asian countries needs transshipment. Mongolia is, therefore, taking measures to improve the transshipment facilities at the borders.

19. The implementation of the proposed project of Tumen River Economic Development Area, in which Mongolia is participating, will enable Mongolia to use a new port on the Pacific Ocean via China. Furthermore, the planned construction of more than 3,000 kilometres of railway from the eastern frontier of Mongolia to the city of Biisk in the Russian Federation under the same project is expected to reduce the transit time considerably. A number of projects for upgrading transit roads are also under implementation. This includes a highway connecting the western region of the country with the Russian Federation and China.

Senegal

20. Senegal provides transit facilities for Mali's transit traffic. In order to facilitate the transit services for Malian goods, a bilateral treaty was signed with Mali related to international rail/road transit which will soon be ratified. At the subregional level, Senegal also signed the TRIE Convention within the framework of ECOWAS. It also holds regular consultations with its neighbouring countries with a view to streamlining transit formalities and procedures.

Swaziland

21. A multilateral agreement which has been concluded within the framework of the Southern African Customs Union has considerably facilitated the transit of goods through South Africa, and the conclusion of an agreement with Mozambique is seriously being considered. Transit and international road routes and rail facilities in Swaziland are reasonably maintained and operated. Development of the transport sector is, however, being affected by scarce trained human resources and inefficient institutional capacities. A fairly adequate transit system exists in South Africa. However, the transit facilities in Mozambique are poor and not reliable. The corridor connecting Swaziland to the seaports in Mozambique, which offers the potential for significant reduction in transit costs, is underutilized at present. Technical assistance is required to facilitate discussions on various transit transport issues between Mozambique and Swaziland.

Uganda

22. Uganda's transit network includes the northern and central corridor transit axes. Mechanisms, such as the Joint Consultation Committees at the bilateral level between Uganda and each of the transit/land-locked countries, are in place to ensure that the relevant rules are implemented. Poor road infrastructure is no longer a problem for transit traffic through Uganda. There is need, however, to harmonize the regulations pertaining to inland waterways transport systems, especially for Lake Victoria. The Uganda Railways Corporation has adequate

locomotives and general purpose wagons. Nevertheless, arrangements are under way to alleviate the situation relating to the lack of tankers and container wagons.

23. Issues pertaining to faster transit of goods across borders are being addressed through, inter alia, the creation of a modern customs facility at Malaba and the installation of the Advanced Cargo Information System (ACIS). The Government intends to set up an inland dry port in Uganda, with a view to minimizing the delays associated with customs and clearance procedures.

24. Transport infrastructure rehabilitation and maintenance for the transit network is one of the major priorities in the public investment programme in Uganda. Furthermore, the Government has reduced its intervention in transit transport operations as part of its policy to liberalize trade and transport.

Zambia

25. With regard to policies and actions to improve intraregional transit trade, Zambia supports the simplification and harmonization of customs and administrative documentation, including the implementation of the Road Customs Transit Document (RCTD), which is designed to facilitate and expedite road traffic operations. Zambia also attaches great importance to action by PTA and SADC member States in the following areas: rehabilitation and maintenance of the transport infrastructure, the establishment of dry ports to speed up transit time, the implementation of the regional bond guarantee scheme, gradual relaxation of visa requirements, accession to the harmonized commodity description and coding system, lifting of export and import duties on transit traffic and the development of bonded warehouses.

B. Summaries of replies received from international organizations

Economic Commission for Africa (ECA) 3/

26. Land-locked countries have benefited from specific action in the area of transport and communications to ease the flow of transit traffic at regional or subregional levels. Under the ongoing project related to the Second United Nations Transport and Communications Decade in Africa, ECA is required to coordinate and facilitate the consolidation and establishment of a network of transport corridors through appropriate mix of transport modes, including those that serve the interests of land-locked countries. A survey of transit costs for transit transport is to be conducted on a subregional basis and various seminars in the field of road transport have been convened to help these countries in identifying the main problems associated with road deterioration and poor maintenance of truck and transit roads, as well as in strengthening human resources capabilities within the transport and communications sector. ECA has also prepared studies and technical publications on subjects such as the development of inland container terminals, the evaluation of railway transport services and the development of freight forwarding, which are being used by transit countries in the management and planning of their transit transport operations.

27. ECA is also carrying out activities which benefit land-locked countries in such fields as statistics and data processing, food and agriculture, industry and human settlements, marine affairs, water and energy resources.

Economic Commission for Europe (ECE) 4/

28. ECE plays an important role in trade and transport facilitation. Its work in this area involves the development of legal instruments governing international transport of goods and passages of vehicles.

29. With regard to the international transport of goods, ECE has played a key role in putting in place various international conventions and agreements that regulate rail traffic and international road traffic. A range of procedures for temporary importation, transport of dangerous goods and for border controls of goods have also been developed. The border controls of goods is regulated by the International Convention on the Harmonization of Frontier Controls of Goods. The Convention covers areas such as customs procedures and other controls, medico-sanitary inspections, veterinary inspection and phyto-sanitary inspection.

30. The facilitation of the passage of road vehicles is governed by international conventions which are supplemented by bilateral agreements. The regulatory measures of this legal regime cover road permits and quotas, temporary importation of vehicles, international motor vehicle insurance and taxation of road vehicles in international traffic.

31. International transport operations in Europe are regulated by two European Agreements on Road Traffic and on Road Signs and Signals. In addition to these agreements, a large number of multilateral agreements facilitate international road transport in Europe and are concerned, inter alia, with transport documents, liability of road carriers, and civil liability for damages caused during the carriage of dangerous goods. Furthermore, three multilateral infrastructure agreements have been negotiated between the European Governments to facilitate cooperation and coordination among them with regard to the development of homogeneous transport infrastructure. These legal transport systems in Europe constitute useful models, which can be adapted in developing countries.

Economic Commission for Latin America and the Caribbean (ECLAC) 5/

32. ECLAC supports South America's two land-locked countries - Bolivia and Paraguay - in their efforts to improve transport and customs transit facilities across neighbouring countries for access to seaports. ECLAC's assistance in this area is carried out at both the multilateral and the bilateral level. Bolivia in particular has been the recipient of such assistance. ECLAC recently collaborated with UNCTAD in preparing a proposal to install the rail component (RailTracker) of ACIS to handle traffic between Arica (Chile) and La Paz. Bolivia and Chile are currently seeking financing for this project. In the other two cases, ECLAC helped Bolivia to formulate and negotiate separate agreements with Chile and Peru to facilitate transit operations to and from certain ports on the Pacific Ocean. These operations are carried out within the framework of the integrated transit system (SIT), whereby goods imported to Bolivia through Chile or Peru can automatically be transshipped to the railways for onward movement without additional customs procedures.

Economic and Social Commission for Asia and the Pacific (ESCAP) 6/

33. There are all together 12 land-locked countries in the ESCAP region, namely: Afghanistan, Armenia, Azerbaijan, Bhutan, Kazakstan, Kyrgyzstan, Lao People's Democratic Republic, Mongolia, Nepal, Tajikistan, Turkmenistan, and Uzbekistan. The efforts of the ESCAP secretariat to assist the land-locked and transit countries of the region have been mainly focused on land transport, transit arrangements, environment and natural resource management, technical development and trade promotion. In order to enhance further the trade of its member countries within and outside the region, the ESCAP secretariat promotes regional and subregional cooperation for the development of land transport infrastructure in Asia, including land-locked countries. In this regard, the proposed project on Asian Land-locked Transport Infrastructure Development (ALTID) is expected to make a major contribution to the development of transport infrastructure in the region.

34. Resolution 48/11 adopted by the Commission recommended the accession of all its members to major international conventions in the field of transport facilitation. Regarding facilitation of rail freight traffic, the ALTID project will focus not only on the southern route linking Europe and South-East Asia but also on the northern route providing a Europe-Asia transport alternative with a competitive edge over the existing sea transport routes. It is planned that this railway line will be operational by 1997.

35. A number of land-locked and transit countries of the region are signatory to several international conventions on transit traffic such as the Convention and Statute on Freedom of Transit and the Convention on Transit Trade of Land-locked States. Bilateral transit agreements also exist between some of the land-locked countries of the region and their transit neighbours. The development of a regional transit treaty that could be used as a model by all countries could further improve the transit system. In this connection, the ESCAP secretariat is exploring the possibility of assisting interested countries in developing such an agreement.

36. ESCAP activities also focus on problems confronting the land-locked countries regarding the development of food processing, in particular deficiencies in the storage and transport systems. Technical assistance for trade promotion of the land-locked countries has traditionally been accorded priority attention in the secretariat's mandate relating to international trade.

International Telecommunication Union (ITU)

37. ITU is aware of the communication needs of the land-locked developing countries, particularly their national and external telecommunication needs for overall development in general and for the enhancement and management of transport systems in particular. In Africa, the Pan African Telecommunication Network (PANAFTEL) was developed to facilitate intra-African communication and trade and any telecommunication links between land-locked countries and their neighbours with access to the sea. The network provided very useful services in managing and controlling these systems. Telecommunication facilities of all sorts are therefore of great value to land-locked countries.

United Nations Development Programme (UNDP) 7/

38. The transit transport systems of the land-locked developing countries can only be effectively improved with the cooperation of transit countries. Any proposed changes in transit systems must, therefore, take into consideration the interest of both the land-locked and the transit countries concerned. UNDP's support to land-locked and transit countries is at the country or regional level, with capacity-building as the overriding strategic objective of such support. Most national projects and programmes financed by UNDP in the land-locked countries directly or indirectly take into account the particular geographical difficulties of these countries.

World Bank 8/

39. Since the World Bank is already active in many of the land-locked developing countries, it has the potential to play an important role in successfully contributing to the development of the transport systems of these countries, particularly with regard to the facilitation of access to import and export markets. The Bank's basic operational goals of poverty alleviation and food security are dependent on improving the reliability of transit operations. While the Bank has no policy specifically addressing the problems of land-locked countries, most relevant issues are covered in broader policies related to transport and trade facilitation, and fall within the broader approach encouraging a broader commercial orientation and promoting competitiveness in transport services. The Bank has undertaken a number of regional studies aimed

at gaining a better understanding of the magnitude of the problems in land-locked developing countries and enhancing efforts to facilitate regional trade development. On the operational level, it has approved several projects in Africa which put special emphasis on linking up land-locked developing countries with their transit neighbours.

C. Summaries of replies received from intergovernmental organizations

African Development Bank 9/

40. The Bank has not yet elaborated any specific policy with respect to land-locked and transit countries. However, given that 15 out of the Bank's 51 regional member countries are land-locked countries, the Bank has, since its establishment, provided support to the land-locked and transit countries, by financing projects and studies related to transport infrastructure. Particular reference should be made to the Bank's support to the United Nations Transport and Communications Decade in Africa and to the establishment of a reform programme for UDEAC. With regard to the future, the Bank will provide special support to private, public and semi-public transport companies whose activities promote the process of economic integration in the region.

Asian Development Bank

41. In the formulation of transport and communications projects, the problems of land-locked developing countries members of the Bank have always been taken into account. In Nepal and Mongolia, the Bank has supported the air transport sector. The Bank also assisted Mongolia in strengthening its international telecommunications links. Through a regional technical assistance for six countries of the greater Mekong subregion, the Bank has identified priority projects to improve transportation among these countries.

42. The Bank's future assistance strategy is to continue its past emphasis on regional cooperation among the member States. Furthermore, the Bank supports the establishment of an effective legal and regulatory framework to govern the development and improvement of transport and communications infrastructure. Future bank assistance to land-locked countries will also include the support for the development of harmonized systems of procedures for handling transit cargo.

Economic Community of West African States (ECOWAS)

43. One of the main objectives of ECOWAS is to put in place an integrated, coordinated, efficient and responsive transit system within the Community that should meet the long-term needs for socio-economic development of the subregion. The weak implementation and reinforcement of agreed protocols, however, is a major impediment in improving transit systems. For example, it has been observed that agreed customs procedures related to the Protocol on Inter-State Road Transit (ISRT) are not followed and, as a result, there are increased delays in the movement of cargo. With respect to the guarantee mechanism for inter-State road transit of goods established by the Community, which is aimed at reducing costs and solving the problems related to the escort for vehicles in transit, the executive secretariat of ECOWAS has mounted a campaign directed at national administrations and economic operators, with a view to achieving effective application by all member States of the mechanism. As for the single road transport document valid for movement across several countries, the poor coordination of multiple enforcement measures and the frequent violations of the provisions of the agreement by transport operators are still major constraints in the effective implementation of the document.

International Civil Aviation Organization (ICAO)

44. The UNDP/ICAO regional project for Asia and the Pacific (RAS/93/032), scheduled to be implemented in 1996, will benefit the land-locked countries of the region. Although there is considerable scope for the development of air freight in these countries, there are still a range of difficulties hindering the full development of an efficient air freight system. These include: unsuitable, old, or uneconomical aircraft utilized for air freight; absence of bilateral air transport agreements; inefficient ground facilities; underdeveloped organization and management capabilities for marketing and air freight activities; large imbalance between volume of imports and exports; and lack of coordination and cooperation between neighbouring countries with respect to air freighting.

Ministerial Conference of West and Central African States
on Maritime Transport (MINCONMAR)

45. MINCONMAR's maritime policy gives special attention to the particular needs of the land-locked member countries, particularly with respect to transit matters. An ad hoc commission was set up in October 1979 to study the constraints of land-locked countries. Recommendations have been made by the ad hoc commission regarding, inter alia, the issue of preferential freight rates for land-locked countries, the participation of these countries in port activities and the establishment of institutional bodies such as "shippers councils" and the simplification of the administrative and customs procedures. However, inadequate support by the donor community has made the implementation of the above initiatives difficult. In this regard it is also noted that the UNDP/UNCTAD transit transport project, which was heavily involved in improving the transit systems in the subregion, has had to be discontinued for lack of donor support.

Permanent Secretariat of the Transit Transport Coordination
Authority of the Northern Corridor

46. The Authority's policy with regard to infrastructure includes the enforcement of axle-load limits for transit vehicles; more extensive use of rail for transit traffic; the establishment of inland container depots; and the improvement of road safety on transit routes. So far as the non-physical aspects of transit transport are concerned, efforts are being made to reduce transit costs and transit time by the formulation and follow-up of a number of measures with regard to customs formalities for containers, harmonization of working hours and joint controls at transit adjacent customs posts. Improvement of the efficiency of the Road Customs Transit Document (RCTD) is also sought. Furthermore, the abolition of other administrative and statutory impediments to the free flow of transit traffic - such as high transit taxes, police escorts, and reduced permissible transit time - are among the major objectives of the work of the Coordination Authority. The Authority has also initiated measures to develop and improve lake traffic operations, and the training for the various groups of operators involved in transit transport.

Preferential Trade Area for Eastern and Southern African States

47. The original objective of integrating the socio-economic fabric of the PTA through transport and communications continues to be of high priority in the 1990s and beyond, as enunciated in the PTA Trade and Development Strategy adopted by the Tenth Summit of the PTA Authority in January 1992. Between 1982 and 1992, substantial progress has been achieved in rehabilitating and upgrading transport and communication infrastructures that had become unserviceable.

48. Poor road conditions are primarily responsible for high operating costs. However, the efficiency of the industry could be substantially improved by:

improving the availability of vehicles and spare parts, improving access to commercial credit, and reducing government regulations and restrictions on market entry. In most countries members of the PTA, priority is traditionally given to the construction of new roads rather than the maintenance of existing ones. A large part of the network can be saved at a reasonable cost if timely periodic maintenance is undertaken.

49. The PTA programmes on insurance, the use of the single Road Customs Transit Document (RCTD), the enforcement of standards for axle-load limits, the harmonization of road user charges, and the liberalization of the commercial trucking industry have significantly reduced transit related costs and facilitated the movement across frontiers of vehicles and persons.

50. The strategy for the revival of railways focuses on institutional and policy reforms, which include, among others, granting by Governments of managerial and commercial autonomy to railways. In the PTA railways strategy for the 1990s and beyond priority is given to the development of railways as the main mode of transport. With respect to multimodal transport, priority is being accorded to investments in appropriate technology that will facilitate the development of containerization. The potential to improve inland waterways transport faces a host of difficulties which make it expensive and inefficient. This is due to lack of policy coordination among bordering countries for the development of waterways. Following a recommendation by the PTA secretariat, four permanent technical committees were established to propose and implement joint regional transport programmes including those related to inland waterways development.

D. Conclusions

51. The replies summarized in this document came from individual countries, United Nations regional commissions and specialized agencies as well as from intergovernmental organizations. Although a much larger number of replies would have been desirable in order to draw firm conclusions, these replies do make general observations that are relevant to the basic issues and problems of transit transport.

52. The replies clearly underline the fact that rail and road services are particularly relevant for transit transport operations. Although physical infrastructure development remains a priority concern for many countries, the removal of non-physical barriers to the smooth movement of transit cargoes is assuming significant importance in the formulation of transit transport policies. This relates largely to the simplification and harmonization of customs and administrative procedures in ports and along the transit transport corridors, as well as to the simplification of other controls for the movement of cargo. Furthermore, railways are now being required to operate more on the basis of commercial criteria. Inter-railway cooperation arrangements are also being increasingly promoted. Investments in road transport infrastructure are directed more towards maintenance than to construction of new roads. Road users are having to make a greater contribution towards the cost of construction and maintenance of roads through the introduction of road user charges.

53. Inter-State cooperation is considered essential for efficient transit transport operations. Bilateral agreements have been the most common instruments for such cooperation. In addition, in Africa, regional agreements within the context of regional integration schemes such as ECOWAS, PTA and UDEAC have been a major vehicle for promoting cooperative arrangements. The need to ratify international conventions related to transit transport has been recognized, but few countries in Africa, Asia and Latin America have become parties thereto. The scope and content of regional agreements in the framework of ECOWAS and PTA have encompassed broad issues in transit transport, including commitments relating to common road standards, permissible axle-load limits, international customs transit regimes and institutional arrangements.

54. On the whole, the implementation of agreed regional standards and practices has been unsatisfactory because of the lack of adequate mechanisms to monitor and enforce the agreed rules and practices. The Northern Corridor Transit Agreement, which sets out the terms and conditions for the use of the transit corridor from Mombasa, Kenya, to the land-locked countries of Uganda, Rwanda and Burundi is, perhaps, the most successfully implemented agreement. The agreement created a small secretariat which has been active in reviewing problems arising from implementation of the Northern Corridor Transit Agreement and assisting member States to resolve them. Technical assistance from UNCTAD and other international agencies is generally viewed as a critical support measure to improve the efficiency of transit transport operations. The replies from agencies have underlined the continued importance of such assistance.

Notes

1/ For the list of the key documents before the Symposium, see annex III to the report of the intergovernmental meeting.

2/ Afghanistan, Benin, Bolivia, Brazil, Bhutan, Cameroon, China, Congo, Eritrea, Ethiopia, Guinea, India, Iran (Islamic Republic of), Kazakstan, Kenya, Kyrgyzstan, Lao People's Democratic Republic, Lesotho, Malawi, Mali, Mongolia, Namibia, Nepal, Niger, Nigeria, Pakistan, Paraguay, Rwanda, Thailand, Togo, Uganda and Uzbekistan.

3/ For the full text, see UNCTAD/LDC/Misc.30.

4/ For the full text, see UNCTAD/LDC/Misc.34.

5/ For the full text, see UNCTAD/LDC/Misc.28.

6/ For the full text, see UNCTAD/LDC/Misc.27.

7/ For the full text, see UNCTAD/LDC/Misc.35.

8/ For the full text, see UNCTAD/LDC/Misc.31.

9/ For the full text, see UNCTAD/LDC/Misc.33.

4. PROPOSALS ON THE FORMAT, SCOPE AND ORGANIZATIONAL ASPECTS OF THE 1997 SPECIAL SESSION OF THE GENERAL ASSEMBLY ON THE OVERALL REVIEW AND APPRAISAL OF AGENDA 21 - REPORT OF THE UN SECRETARY-GENERAL*

Doc. no.: A/50/453 20 September 1995

SUMMARY

Under Agenda 21, the General Assembly was entrusted with the task of regularly reviewing implementation of the commitments it contained. In its resolution 47/190, the Assembly decided to convene, not later than in 1997, a special session for the purpose of an overall review and appraisal of Agenda 21, and requested the Secretary-General to prepare a report on the modalities for the organization and scope of such a special session. In accordance with that mandate, the present report contains proposals concerning the scope of the discussions, including priorities for future action and the institutional framework, and organizational matters. The report presents proposals on the documentation to be prepared for the session and also on the session's possible outcome. As to organizational matters, the report covers the possible timing of, level of representation at and participation of major groups in the special session. The report suggests guidelines for conducting the preparatory process for the session, including the role to be played by the Commission on Sustainable Development at its fifth session.

CONTENTS

* A/50/150.

I. INTRODUCTION

A. Mandate

1. In its resolution 47/190 of 22 December 1992, the General Assembly endorsed the Rio Declaration on Environment and Development, Agenda 21 and the Non-legally Binding Authoritative Statement of Principles for a Global Consensus on the Management, Conservation and Sustainable Development of All Types of Forests, as adopted at the United Nations Conference on Environment and Development (UNCED) on 14 June 1992.

2. In the same resolution, the General Assembly, on the recommendation of the Conference, decided to convene, not later than 1997, a special session for the purpose of an overall review and appraisal of Agenda 21, and requested the Secretary-General to submit to it at its forty-ninth session a report containing recommendations for its consideration on the format, scope and organizational aspects of such a special session.

3. Taking into account the fact that a number of intergovernmental processes that had been recommended in Agenda 21 were currently taking place or had only recently been concluded, the Secretary-General proposed, in a note to the Assembly at its forty-ninth session (A/49/463), that it postpone discussion of the format, scope and organizational aspects of the special session of the General Assembly in 1997 to a later stage; the Assembly took note of the proposal in its decision 49/437.

B. Background: United Nations Conference on Environment and Development and related processes

4. UNCED represented a milestone in promoting international cooperation and action on sustainable development, and had a profound effect on the work of the organizations and bodies of the United Nations system. UNCED recommendations also identified specific actions to be undertaken in order to achieve sustainable development at national and regional levels.

5. Since UNCED, a large number of intergovernmental processes that had been recommended in Agenda 21 have completed their work. The United Nations Convention to Combat Desertification in those Countries Experiencing Serious Drought and/or Desertification, particularly in Africa was opened for signatures in October 1994. The Global Conference on the Sustainable Development of Small Island Developing States (Bridgetown, Barbados, 25 April-6 May 1994), adopted the Declaration of Barbados and the Programme of Action for the Sustainable Development of Small Island Developing States. The United Nations Conference on

Straddling Fish Stocks and Highly Migratory Fish Stocks concluded its proceedings with the adoption of the Agreement for the Implementation of the Provisions of the United Nations Convention on the Law of the Sea of 10 December 1982 relating to the Conservation and Management of Straddling Fish Stocks and Highly Migratory Fish Stocks. During this period, the Global Environment Facility, managed jointly by the World Bank, the United Nations Development Programme (UNDP) and the United Nations Environment Programme (UNEP), has been replenished and restructured in order to enable universal participation in its decision-making. The United Nations Framework Convention on Climate Change and the Convention on Biological Diversity, which were opened for signatures during UNCED, have both entered into force and have already held their first meetings of Conferences of the Parties. The outcomes of these processes, together with Agenda 21 and the Rio Declaration on Environment and Development, are commonly referred to as the Rio commitments and will have to be considered by the General Assembly at its special session if it is to obtain a full picture of the results achieved.

6. Furthermore, a number of major international conferences held since UNCED, such as the World Conference on Human Rights, the International Conference on Population and Development, the World Summit for Social Development, and the Fourth World Conference on Women, as well as the forthcoming Second United Nations Conference on Human Settlements (Habitat II), are also closely related to the implementation of Agenda 21, since they add substantially to the international understanding and consensus on various critical elements of sustainable development; the comprehensive review of Agenda 21 also needs to take into account the outcomes of these conferences as well.

7. At its substantive session of 1995, the Economic and Social Council decided on the modalities of a comprehensive and coordinated follow-up to major international conferences in the economic, social and related fields. In his report to the Council (E/1995/86), the Secretary-General presented his views on how this coordinated approach could be furthered, including the establishment of the relevant monitoring mechanisms, with a view to promoting programme harmonization and policy integration at both the country level and the inter-agency level, as well as at the intergovernmental level. The Council decided that, within the framework of its coordination segment, it would carry out a review each year of cross-cutting themes common to major international conferences, and/or would contribute to an overall review of the implementation of the programme of action of a United Nations conference.

8. The finalization of the discussions on an agenda for development, which will integrate many of the above-mentioned initiatives, will also have a major impact on the special session.

9. In considering preparations for such an overall review and post-1997 arrangements, special focus needs to be given to the outcome of the 1995 substantive session of the Economic and Social Council. In the first instance, the Council, in selecting themes for its coordination segment, may wish to choose a theme that would maximize its contribution to the 1997 review of Agenda 21. Such a theme could focus on one major cross-sectoral issue or on a sectoral issue for which greater attention is required.

10. To fulfil the mandate of UNCED and other conferences, institutional arrangements have been established. The intergovernmental follow-up of UNCED has remained within the framework of the United Nations system and is the special responsibility of the General Assembly, as the supreme policy-making forum providing overall guidance to Governments, the United Nations system and relevant treaty bodies. In addition to the General Assembly, the Economic and Social Council has been provided with the responsibility of providing system-wide coordination, and of overseeing implementation of Agenda 21 and making recommendations in that regard.

II. SCOPE OF THE DISCUSSIONS

A. Priorities

11. The overall review of the implementation of Agenda 21 by the General Assembly at its special session will need to determine the critical areas of sustainability for the years to come. The concept of sustainable development encompasses economic, social, environmental and institutional dimensions. The identification of the critical areas of sustainability will have to be based on a comprehensive review of the progress achieved in the implementation of the Rio commitments at all levels, taking into account relevant conclusions of subsequent global conferences. The objective should be to maintain the political momentum and give a clear sense of direction for future actions to be taken by Governments, intergovernmental bodies and major groups aimed at reaching sustainable development. The Assembly will have to identify priorities at the special session, including priorities for the institutional follow-up to UNCED and the role of the United Nations system, in particular the Commission on Sustainable Development.

12. In identifying the critical constraints to the implementation of the Rio commitments at the local, country, regional and international levels and the means for Governments, international organizations and major groups to overcome them, the Assembly may wish to consider strengthening its substantive activities as well as adopting supportive measures necessary for the achievement of sustainable development goals, such as the provision of financial resources, transfer of environmentally sound technologies and creation of institutional mechanisms.

13. Further, in the light of paragraphs 7 to 9 above, the recommendations of the Assembly could include the identification of possible themes for future consideration by the Council or its subsidiary bodies, particularly the Commission on Sustainable Development, with a view to ensuring a harmonized and non-duplicative approach to the issues involved.

14. Public awareness and the promotion of sustainable development values through, inter alia, educational systems, remain major tasks necessary for the successful implementation of the Rio commitments. The Assembly may wish to explore further means of enhancing this process.

15. The Assembly may also wish to place a special emphasis on the issue of sustainable consumption and production patterns as an umbrella concept that facilitates the integration of environmental and economic questions. If the Assembly decides to do so, those provisions will have to be consequently reflected in the work programme of the Commission.

16. The Commission on Sustainable Development has approved a work programme on indicators on sustainable development; its implementation is under way. The Commission has encouraged Governments to develop or conduct studies on the development of indicators of sustainable development in accordance with specific national conditions. Their elaboration will have a significant impact on the process of monitoring progress achieved since UNCED. The Commission provides the necessary platform for the preparation of such indicators; at the special session, the Assembly could provide the necessary stimulus for their broad application.

B. Institutional framework

17. On the recommendation of Agenda 21 and in order to ensure the effective follow-up of the Conference, as well as to enhance international cooperation, rationalize the intergovernmental decision-making capacity for the integration of environment and development issues and examine the progress in the implementation of Agenda 21 at the national, regional and international levels, the Economic and Social Council established the Commission on Sustainable

Development as a subsidiary body. Since its first session, the Commission has developed certain innovative characteristics:

(a) The Commission has managed to maintain a high political profile. The high-level segment of the Commission is attended by large numbers of ministers and high-level decision makers from all over the world. Attendance is not limited solely to ministers of environment; ministers for development, agriculture, forestry and finance also participate. The Assembly may wish to further encourage this type of participation as a means of fully integrating a whole spectrum of different aspects of sustainable development;

(b) The Commission has incorporated into its work, on an unprecedented scale, the representatives of major groups involved in the promotion of sustainable development. Major groups are consulted on a variety of issues in the course of the inter-sessional period, and the dialogue between them and member States during Commission sessions has also been steadily reinforced. The secretariat of the Commission collects and analyses information on major groups' involvement in Agenda 21 implementation;

(c) Commission activities are not limited to its annual sessions. The Commission provides a framework for a larger process of inter-sessional meetings, the outcomes of which it subsequently reviews and analyses. It has also established two ad hoc working groups that hold sessions prior to the meetings of the Commission in order to prepare its discussions on specific agenda items. Duration of those ad hoc working group meetings, as well as subjects to be discussed, are determined by the Commission at its consecutive sessions and remain flexible but harmonized with its programme of work. These year-round activities are coordinated by the Bureau of the Commission, which meets regularly in order to take the best advantage of the above-mentioned events while preparing for the main session of the Commission. Efforts have been made to make this process transparent and to make information on meetings and their outcomes widely available;

(d) Monitoring of the implementation of UNCED commitments by the Commission has involved the whole United Nations system. Various organizations and bodies have participated in the preparations for and the proceedings of the Commission. Task managers from the organizations of the United Nations system have been nominated to ensure an effective and coordinated follow-up in the sectoral and cross-sectoral issues identified by Agenda 21. The coordination of those activities has been entrusted by the Administrative Committee on Coordination to the Inter-Agency Committee for Sustainable Development (IACSD);

(e) The Commission has also developed a capacity for monitoring at all levels the implementation of the Rio commitments. Its particularly innovative role in the monitoring of progress achieved and major obstacles encountered at the national level, through voluntary reporting by member States. The Commission has been able to analyse a number of the reports presented to date. The Commission also serves as a platform for the exchange of information on national policies and practices introduced as a result of UNCED;

(f) Interaction between intergovernmental bodies active in the area of sustainable development is increasing. For example, the Council of the Food and Agriculture Organization of the United Nations (FAO) considered the issues related to land management that were also on the agenda of the third session of the Commission; a ministerial meeting on forestry was convened by FAO prior to the Commission's third session; and the UNEP Governing Council, after the fourth session of the Commission, made a decision in which it emphasized the need for UNEP to continue to provide effective support to the work of the Commission, inter alia, through the provision of scientific, technical and policy information and advice on environment. Some other intergovernmental bodies also committed themselves to substantively contributing to the work of the Commission.

18. The General Assembly may wish to:

(a) Build further on the above-mentioned characteristics of the Commission, while deciding on the desirable focus of its future activities;

(b) Provide guidance concerning the priorities for the further work of the Commission, particularly as reflected in its multi-year thematic work programme;

(c) Consider ways and means of enhancing policy coherence and further strengthening coordination between the Commission and other appropriate intergovernmental bodies;

(d) Give further support to the system of task managers as an effective mechanism for meeting the demands related to the functioning of IACSD while implementing Agenda 21 in respective thematic areas.

19. In accordance with its resolution 47/191, at the special session the Assembly is also expected to review the organizational modalities for the Commission. The Assembly could thus reflect on aspects of the existing structure of the Commission, such as the organization of its high-level segment and general debate, the participation of major groups, side events and the functioning of its Bureau.

20. The review of the institutional framework established for the implementation of the Rio commitments should also examine innovations and changes that have taken place since UNCED in the policies, programmes and structures of the organizations and bodies of the United Nations system, as well as in the activities of non-United Nations institutions.

21. The General Assembly is also expected to decide on the next review timetable for assessing further progress in achieving sustainable development goals in the period after the special session.

III. DOCUMENTATION

22. The General Assembly may wish to request the Secretary-General to prepare a comprehensive report on the overall assessment of the progress achieved since UNCED in the implementation of Agenda 21, the Rio Declaration on Environment and Development and related conference outcomes, as well as on recommendations for future actions and priorities, including those concerning institutional matters, in particular the role of the Commission on Sustainable Development.

23. Such a comprehensive report would draw upon concise reports that will be prepared for the fifth session of the Commission and would contain an assessment of progress achieved in specific sectoral and cross-sectoral areas, as well as recommendations for future action. The Commission would thus be able to undertake the review process and analyse progress achieved with a view to preparing for the special session. The above-mentioned concise reports will also serve as background documentation for the Assembly's deliberations; the modalities for their preparation will be a subject for discussion by IACSD.

24. On the basis of national reports received so far and expected for forthcoming sessions of the Commission, and in close cooperation with the Governments concerned, the Commission secretariat intends to prepare country profiles aimed at a concise presentation of progress made and constraints encountered in implementing Agenda 21. These country profiles will be presented to the Commission at its 1997 session to allow for the review of the progress achieved at the national level.

IV. OUTCOME OF THE SPECIAL SESSION

25. The General Assembly may wish to reflect on the possible outcome of the 1997 review exercise. One option would be to prepare a substantive document in the form of a political declaration assessing progress achieved and setting priorities for future action on how to best reach sustainable development goals. Such a declaration could build on the review of progress achieved in the implementation of the Rio commitments as well as the achievements of recently held major United Nations conferences and an agenda for development. It should also take into consideration the institutional aspects of future monitoring of Agenda 21 implementation by the appropriate United Nations bodies.

V. ORGANIZATIONAL ASPECTS OF THE SPECIAL SESSION

26. Eighteen special sessions of the General Assembly have been organized to discuss topics of special importance to the international community. The last (eighteenth) special session was held from 23 April to 1 May 1990 to discuss the theme "Economic cooperation, in particular the revitalization of the economic growth and development of the developing countries". Previous special sessions of the General Assembly did not establish any fixed pattern as far as duration or level of representation are concerned.

27. Drawing on experience from previous special sessions of the General Assembly, the organization of UNCED and other major conferences organized in recent years under the auspices of the United Nations, including the International Conference on Population and Development and the World Summit for Social Development, the Secretary-General has suggested that the session be held for a period of five working days, a time-frame that will accommodate the statements of the representatives of all Member States and will allow for interaction with United Nations agencies and the representatives of major groups.

28. If the need arises, the General Assembly could allocate some time for a preconsultation in the week(s) preceding the session.

29. Bearing in mind the provisions of its resolution 47/190, the Assembly may decide that the special session should be a self-standing event and that it should take place before its fifty-second session. Alternatively, at its current session, the Assembly may consider the possibility of building the review exercise into its fifty-second session, to be held in 1997.

30. Should the Assembly decide on the former alternative, having considered the calendar of conferences for 1997 and the fact that the preparations for the session are to be undertaken by the Commission on Sustainable Development at its fifth session, the proposed time-frame for the special session is the third or fourth week in June 1997, i.e., 16 to 20 June or 23 to 27 June, with the understanding that the fifth session of the Commission on Sustainable Development will be held either early in 1997 or back to back with the special session, so that the Commission can act as a preparatory committee for the special session.

31. Whatever the specific arrangements for the Assembly's review, it is essential to ensure that its outcome contributes to maintaining the political momentum and visibility of the sustainable development agenda as well as to the broader discussion currently under way of the reform of the United Nations in the economic, social and related fields and to discussions on the agenda for development and the coordinated follow-up of other major United Nations conferences.

VI. LEVEL OF REPRESENTATION

32. UNCED brought together an unprecedented number of heads of State and Government, delegates, representatives of non-governmental organizations, and the mass media, a sign of the tremendous importance given to the issues discussed at the Conference.

33. The General Assembly may envisage a level of representation at the special session that will maintain the high political momentum reached during UNCED, which was attended by 118 heads of State and Government.

VII. PARTICIPATION OF MAJOR GROUPS

34. Chapter 23 of Agenda 21 on strengthening the role of major groups defines very clearly the critical role of genuine involvement of all social groups in the effective implementation of the objectives, policies and mechanisms that were agreed by Governments in all programme areas of Agenda 21. UNCED itself brought together an unprecedented number of participants representing major groups, especially non-governmental organizations, which have also been involved in follow-up at both the national and international levels. The continuing concern remains the broadening of the spectrum of the representation of major groups, as well as transparency in the procedures of their selection for the various coordination and consultation mechanisms, in this case in relation to the preparations for and proceedings of the special session. Funding the participation of representatives of major groups in such processes remains by far the most acute problem.

35. It has also been widely recognized that, in preparing for UNCED and subsequently monitoring progress in the implementation of its commitments through the Commission on Sustainable Development, the international community has largely benefited from the intellectual input of major groups and from an interactive dialogue with them. However, the rules of procedure of the General Assembly do not allow the active participation of representatives of major groups in its deliberations. The General Assembly may wish to consider some options for the involvement of major groups during its special session. For example, the Assembly may wish to suspend its deliberations for the duration of one or two meetings in order to enter into an informal dialogue with the representatives of major groups, or to legislate that for the special session under consideration the rules for participation be amended to allow for participation along the lines of participation at UNCED.

36. A number of parallel events enabling the broadening of the scope of the dialogue by involving the representatives of the major groups could be considered. In addition, before or during the deliberations of the session, the organization of various forums of major groups could be also encouraged. The Assembly may wish to encourage major groups to participate in preparations for the session and review the implementation of Agenda 21 in the areas of their particular concern, assessing their role in that implementation.

37. It is therefore suggested that the special session integrate in its core debate, as well as accompanying proceedings, the widest possible representation of major groups and sectors of civil society. The Assembly may consider encouraging Governments to include the representatives of major groups in their national preparatory processes, as well as in their delegations to the session.

VIII. PREPARATORY PROCESS

38. At the special session, the General Assembly must accomplish a considerable amount of work: it must review Agenda 21 and the realization of commitments included therein and define the future role of the Commission on Sustainable Development, providing guidance to its future programme of work. It is also expected that the Assembly will give new and reinforced political impetus to

further work on achieving sustainable development at all levels. This task will require careful and time-consuming preparation, which should begin at the current session of the Assembly. The Assembly may wish to give more specific policy guidance on the work to be accomplished before the special session. Since Agenda 21 underlines that preparations for the special session should be conducted at a high level, the Commission on Sustainable Development, above all its ministerial segment, should also be involved in determining the methods of reviewing commitments and identifying priorities for the future.

39. The Commission on Sustainable Development, when adopting its multi-year thematic programme of work, decided to undertake at its fifth session in 1997 an overall review of the progress achieved with a view to preparing for the special session. The General Assembly may wish to clearly determine the role to be played by the Commission at its fifth session as well as the tasks to be accomplished at the special session itself. For example, on the basis of analyses made during its previous sessions, the Commission could undertake an in-depth evaluation of progress achieved and could identify major concerns and gaps in implementing sustainable development goals. On the other hand, at the special session, the Assembly could look more specifically at the priorities for the future and institutional follow-up. In order to reach agreement on the final document, the Assembly may wish to establish an ad hoc committee of the whole.

40. The Assembly may also wish to consider proposing the organization of meetings under the auspices of the regional commissions to assess progress made at the regional level, according to the provisions of Agenda 21. If the input from such meetings are to be integrated into the overall review, they will have to be organized as early as possible in 1996.

5. UNAUTHORIZED FISHING IN ZONES OF NATIONAL JURISDICTION AND ITS IMPACT ON THE LIVING MARINE RESOURCES OF THE WORLD'S OCEANS AND SEAS - REPORT OF THE UN SECRETARY-GENERAL

Doc. no.: A/50/549 12 October 1995

CONTENTS

I. INTRODUCTION

1. The General Assembly, at its forty-ninth session, in its resolution 49/116 of 19 December 1994, took up for the first time the question of unauthorized fishing in zones of national jurisdiction and its impact on the living marine resources of the world's oceans and seas.

2. In that resolution, the General Assembly, recalling Agenda 21, 1/ adopted by the United Nations Conference on Environment and Development, in particular its chapter 17, concerning the sustainable development and conservation of the marine living resources of areas under national jurisdiction, as well as the Programme of Action for the Sustainable Development of Small Island Developing States, 2/ adopted by the Global Conference on the Sustainable Development of Small Island Developing States, in particular its chapter IV, concerning the sustainable development and conservation of the coastal and marine resources of areas under national jurisdiction, expressed deep concern at the detrimental impact of unauthorized fishing in zones under national jurisdiction and called upon States to take the responsibility, consistent with their obligations under

international law as reflected in the United Nations Convention on the Law of the Sea, of taking measures to ensure that no fishing vessels entitled to fly their national flag fished in zones under the national jurisdiction of other States unless duly authorized by the competent authorities of the coastal State or States concerned, and stated that such authorized fishing operations be carried out in accordance with the conditions set out in the authorization.

3. The General Assembly also called upon development assistance organizations to make it a high priority to support efforts by the developing coastal States, in particular the least developed countries and the small island developing States, to improve the monitoring and control of fishing activities and the enforcement of fishing regulations. The Assembly further requested the Secretary-General to bring the resolution to the attention of all members of the international community, relevant intergovernmental organizations, the organizations and bodies of the United Nations system, regional and subregional fisheries bodies and relevant non-governmental organizations, and to submit to the General Assembly at its fiftieth session a report on the steps taken and on problems encountered in the implementation of the resolution, and thereafter as might be determined by the Assembly.

4. Accordingly, the Secretary-General sent a note verbale to all members of the international community, drawing their attention to resolution 49/116. Letters were also addressed to relevant intergovernmental organizations, the organizations and bodies of the United Nations system, regional and subregional fisheries bodies and relevant non-governmental organizations. The Secretary-General has received a number of responses and submissions from States, intergovernmental organizations, organizations and bodies of the United Nations system, regional and subregional fisheries organizations and non-governmental organizations. He wishes to express his appreciation for all the contributions, and in particular for the detailed report submitted by the Food and Agriculture Organization of the United Nations (FAO).

5. The present report, which takes into account such contributions, is submitted to the General Assembly in response to the request contained in resolution 49/116.

II. INFORMATION PROVIDED BY STATES

6. In its response to the Secretary-General dated 28 May 1995, the Federated States of Micronesia stated that it had no law concerning unauthorized fishing in zones of national jurisdiction of other States.

7. In its reply of 9 June 1995 to the Secretary-General, Guyana indicated that Guyanese vessels were cautioned against fishing illegally in waters of other States where it was difficult to prevent such fishing, e.g., in Suriname. In addition, Guyana had been negotiating for vessels to be permitted to fish in that country's waters. While regulations to ensure compliance had not been enacted by the Government, Guyana was anticipating the assistance of FAO to redraft and produce comprehensive fisheries regulations.

8. In its submission of 22 June 1995 to the Secretary-General, Qatar informed him that the granting of fishing licences was regulated by Law No. 4 (1984) and Executive Order No. 2 (1985) dealing with the exploitation and protection of the living marine resources of Qatar. Those licences were issued only to fishing vessels owned by nationals of the State of Qatar in order to allow them to operate fisheries within its territorial waters. Consequently, foreign fishing vessels were prohibited from fishing without first obtaining a licence from the Fishery Resources Department, which had not to date issued any such licences to foreign-owned vessels.

9. In its response of 25 June 1995 to the Secretary-General, Morocco stated that its legislation in force did not envisage penalties against the fishing

vessels flying its flag which would fish in zones not under the jurisdiction of Morocco. However, the draft maritime code under consideration provides appropriate measures so that no such vessels would be able to operate in zones under national jurisdiction of other States or under the management regime of subregional or regional organizations unless duly authorized.

10. In its reply to the Secretary-General dated 29 June 1995, Venezuela transmitted the text of the Presidential Decree of 26 November 1992, which prohibited commercial fishing activities within the 3-nautical-mile coastal belt and in areas under a regime of special administration as well as in all coastal waters. Moreover, commercial fishing in waters under national sovereignty or under national jurisdiction without due permit or licence issued by the Ministry of Agriculture and Livestock or fishing activities in areas not covered by the authorization was also prohibited.

11. In its submission of 11 July 1995 to the Secretary-General, Mexico provided the following information:

> "The principal legal instruments governing fishing activity in Mexico are the Fisheries Act and its Regulations, which have been in force since July 1992. Both the Act and its Regulations set out measures intended to prevent fishing vessels registered in Mexico and flying the Mexican flag from engaging in unauthorized fishing on the high seas or in waters under foreign jurisdiction. They also contain provisions aimed at ensuring that such vessels, wherever they fish, comply with measures established by coastal States for the management of living marine resources.
>
> Article 2 of the Fisheries Act establishes that the foregoing applies also to vessels of Mexican registry and flying the Mexican flag that engage in fishing on the high seas or in waters under foreign jurisdiction by virtue of concessions, permits, authorizations or any other similar legal document issued by a foreign Government to Mexico or to its nationals.
>
> Furthermore, article 15, subsection I, of this Act states that 'the Secretariat (Secretariat for the Environment, Natural Resources and Fisheries (SEMARNAP)) may, on a non-transferable basis, authorize only individuals or corporate entities of Mexican nationality having vessels registered in Mexico and flying the Mexican flag to engage in fishing on the high seas or in waters under the jurisdiction of another State'.
>
> In order to obtain such authorization, pursuant to article 40 of the Fisheries Act, the following requirements must be met:
>
> - SEMARNAP must be provided with information regarding the vessel and its fishing gear, technical and economic capacity and crew;
>
> - International navigation and fishery regulations, especially those established by foreign Governments in waters under their jurisdiction, must be observed and strictly complied with; and
>
> - Where Governments allow individuals to obtain commercial fishing licences or permits directly, the parties concerned shall, at the request of SEMARNAP, verify that the catches are taken under the authorization of such licences or permits.
>
> The Fisheries Act and its Regulations also specify the penalties in cash and in kind to which Mexican vessels that violate these provisions are liable."

12. In its response of 13 July 1995 to the Secretary-General, Maldives stated that General Assembly resolution 49/116 on unauthorized fishing in zones of national jurisdiction and its impact on the living marine resources of the world's oceans and seas was extremely important for the Maldives owing to its

geographical location and its dependence on fisheries and the marine environment. Maldives itself did not have any vessels fishing in zones of national jurisdiction of other States or on the high seas. In addition, it relied "very heavily" on fisheries and was concerned about poaching in its exclusive economic zone. In the past nine months 15 trawlers from four different countries had been apprehended while poaching in the Maldives exclusive economic zone. Such trawlers were dealt with under the Maldives Fisheries Law.

13. In its reply of 18 July 1995 to the Secretary-General, Oman submitted the following information regarding the measures taken by Omani authorities with respect to the issue of unauthorized fishing in areas under national jurisdiction:

> "1. A Fisheries and Protection of Marine Resources Act was promulgated by Sultan's Decree No. 81/53, as amended, and an implementing regulation on the operation of the Act was issued under Ministerial Decision No. 94/4. The Act regulates fishing and provides for the protection and development of fisheries, and it defines offences and establishes penalties for those who violate its provisions. The Act stipulates in part:
>
> (a) That the necessary licences must be obtained, namely:
>
> (i) Licences to engage in fishing as a regular occupation;
>
> (ii) A fishing-boat licence;
>
> (iii) A licence to deal in marine living resources;
>
> (iv) Licences for sports fishing;
>
> (b) That the appropriate sanitary measure must be taken with a view to protecting and developing marine living resources, including:
>
> (i) The immediate return to the sea of undersized fish;
>
> (ii) A prohibition on the taking of sea turtles;
>
> (iii) A prohibition on the taking of certain fish during their breeding season;
>
> (iv) A ban on fishing with certain types of nets and certain equipment;
>
> (v) A ban on the dumping of fish remains;
>
> (vi) A ban on the dumping of waste from factories and of chemicals, oil and other substances harmful to marine living resources;
>
> (c) That fishing must be regulated:
>
> (i) So that mechanized fishing methods and dredgers may not be used without permission from the competent authorities;
>
> (ii) So that the configuration of fishing boats and their accessory equipment may not be modified or altered without the agreement of the competent authorities.
>
> "2. Monitoring for the purpose of protecting fishing resources is being stepped up by:
>
> Increased activity by inspectors monitoring vessels under contract for fishing with national companies so as to ensure that,

following coordination with the competent authorities, they adhere to sanitary methods in their fishing operations;

Constant monitoring by inspectors in order to require fishermen to use sanitary methods in fishing operations, in processing and handling fish and in exporting fish by land, sea and air in accordance with the law in force in Oman.

"3. Penalties are being increased and are enforced against those who violate the provisions of the Act.

"4. No foreign vessel is permitted to fish in the exclusive economic zone of Oman without obtaining a licence from the competent authorities and agreeing to abide by the provisions of the Act.

"5. Oman currently issues licences to fishing boats to operate within its exclusive economic zone, whether they are foreign vessels leased to Omani companies or Omani fishing boats operating in the commercial sector or the traditional sector."

14. In its submission to the Secretary-General dated 19 July 1995, Turkey indicated that vessels flying the Turkish flag were periodically warned by the relevant Turkish authorities not to fish in zones under the national jurisdiction of other States. In case of non-compliance with the warnings of the Turkish authorities, the fishing licence of the party responsible for the violation would be cancelled.

15. In its report to the Secretary-General dated 1 August 1995, China provided the following information:

"When China first began to engage in fishing on the high seas, the Chinese Ministry of Agriculture required Chinese fishing vessels to comply strictly with all applicable measures of international law and practice and refrain from entering the exclusive economic zone of any other State for the purpose of engaging in unauthorized fishing.

"On 9 November 1994 the Chinese Ministry of Agriculture issued ministerial order No. 4, which stipulated that fishing vessels operating in waters beyond China's national jurisdiction must comply strictly with international laws and practices, the relevant resolutions of the United Nations and fisheries agreements which China had concluded with other States, and that such vessels should not enter the exclusive economic zone of any other country to engage in unauthorized fishing. Violators of this order would, in accordance with Chinese domestic laws and regulations, be subject to such penalties as the issuing of a formal reprimand, imposition of a fine, confiscation of the catch and suspension or revocation of fishing permits."

16. In its reply of 10 August 1995 to the Secretary-General, Thailand made the following submission:

"...

"The Government of Thailand has taken several measures in relation to the above-mentioned resolution. These include the adoption of measures to control the number of fishing vessels operating beyond its national jurisdiction and of the fishing gears; the registration of new fishing vessels; and requiring permission to be sought in advance from the authorities concerned (Department of Fisheries). The relevant national legislation, the Fisheries Act of B.E. 2490 (1947), has also been amended with a view to imposing the responsibility on the vessel owners for their violation of other countries' national jurisdiction. The Government is now contemplating amending the Fisheries Act to impose the responsibility on the vessel masters. Negotiating with its neighbouring countries on the delimitation of the maritime boundaries and on resources management constitutes another measure in this regard.

"However, the Government of Thailand is of the opinion that in order to reach a just and lasting solution to this problem the letter and spirit of the 1982 United Nations Convention on the Law of the Sea, particularly article 62, must be observed and fully implemented without unreasonable requirements on the part of the coastal States."

17. In its submission to the Secretary-General dated 11 September 1995, Finland indicated that Finnish fishing vessels could practise fishing only in the area of the Baltic Sea. The fishing regulations of the Baltic Sea and the internal fishing arrangements of the European Union with their control systems would prevent unauthorized fishing as referred to in General Assembly resolution 49/116. There had therefore been no need for further measures to be taken in regard to the matter.

III. INFORMATION PROVIDED BY INTERNATIONAL ORGANIZATIONS

A. Intergovernmental organizations

18. In its response to the Secretary-General dated 3 July 1995, FAO submitted the following report:

"...

"Generalized concerns about unauthorized fishing

"FAO members do not report specifically to the organization about illegal fishing activity. However, in the course of meetings of FAO bodies and through other channels, concerns about, and reports of, illegal fishing activity are made known publicly by national authorities.

"At an Organisation for Economic Cooperation and Development (OECD) workshop on enforcement measures, held in Paris on 21 and 22 September 1993, the participant from Norway reported that in the Barents Sea, where the Russian Federation and Norway are the coastal States with a joint responsibility for the management of the most important species, there was strong evidence of cheating and overfishing by fishermen and there was a need to improve the systems of control and enforcement in that area.

"A technical consultation on sustainable fisheries development in the area of the FAO Western Central Atlantic Fishery Commission (WECAFC), held at Caraballada, Venezuela, from 18 to 22 October 1993, agreed that the conflict between industrial and artisanal fisheries continued to be a problem in the region, given the difficulties of coming up with equitable solutions. Positive changes were also reported, however, in countries such as Colombia and Venezuela, where progress had been made in the establishment of coastal areas for the exclusive use of artisanal fishermen and regulatory measures had been introduced to protect coastal fishery resources.

"At the FAO Indo-Pacific Fishery Commission (IPFC) 3/ Symposium held at Bangkok from 23 to 26 November 1993, it was reported that Thailand had lost access to about 777,000 square kilometres of fishing grounds as a direct result of the adoption of exclusive economic zones, resulting in a reduction in marine landings of some 200,000 metres each year. 4/ As a result, many Thai fishing vessels and fishermen were arrested every year for alleged intrusions into neighbouring waters. During the 1981-1992 period, 1,503 Thai fishing vessels were arrested by other countries

(Malaysia 598, Viet Nam 444, Myanmar 303, India 61, Indonesia 55, Cambodia 36, and Bangladesh 6).

"In spite of the introduction by many countries of regulations to control trawling through bans on trawls in certain areas off the coast, it has been noted by many countries (and as Malaysia reported to the IPFC 1993 symposium in Bangkok) that zoning of trawler operations has failed to prevent conflicts between the trawlers and traditional fishermen. A major reason for this has been the failure of the trawlers to abide by the regulations - encroaching into forbidden waters when enforcement vessels are not present, and the fact that many vessels not licensed to trawl use trawling gear covertly.

"A number of delegations at the ninth session of the FAO Fishery Committee for the Eastern Central Atlantic (CECAF) Subcommittee on Management of Resources within the Limits of National Jurisdiction, held at Agadir, Morocco, from 5 to 9 December 1994, recognized the increasing importance of monitoring, control and surveillance (MCS) of foreign fishing operations in the fisheries management process. It was recognized that the navy and air force played key roles in certain countries in administering the patrol vessels and aircraft.

"The FAO Indian Ocean Fisheries Commission (IOFC) Committee for the Development and Management of the Fishery Resources of the Gulfs held its eighth session from 17 to 29 December 1994 at Muscat, Oman, and expressed concern at the prevalence of illegal fishing and the need to develop a common approach to such activity. It was noted that shrimp trawlers of certain countries, in order to continue landing species for which a closed season was in force, sometimes landed at ports of nearby countries. The serious concerns of the Islamic Republic of Iran with regard to the need to protect the marine resources were fully endorsed.

"The FAO Indo-Pacific Tuna Development and Management Programme (IPTP) 5/ reports frequent incidents where foreign flag drift-netters and longliners are arrested in coastal States' waters, but a number of fishermen are understood to find it difficult to read charts and are unsure of their location. A number of drift-netters fish along the Arabian Sea coast as far down, possibly, as Somalia, and some have been arrested for unauthorized fishing by the Oman authorities.

"Because of the highly migratory nature of tuna and tuna-like species, the management measures adopted by the International Commission for the Conservation of Atlantic Tunas (ICCAT) 6/ do not discriminate between exclusive economic zones and high seas. ICCAT has had a continuous problem regarding non-contracting parties whose vessels carry out fishing activities that are not in compliance with the Commission's regulatory measures. This problem is mostly related to high seas fisheries, but such fishing activities also take place in the exclusive economic zones of some of the coastal States.

"The October 1994 Global Fisheries Enforcement Workshop, hosted by the Government of the United States of America, concluded, inter alia, that unauthorized fishing in the exclusive economic zones of coastal States was common in most areas of the world and that the incidence of such fishing was not declining. Renewed international attention was focusing on unauthorized fishing and the role of MCS systems, both within exclusive economic zones and on the high seas, as an essential element for the achievement of long-term sustainable fisheries conservation and management. 7/

"Unauthorized fishing in the exclusive economic zones of small island developing States

"Small island developing States face particular problems with respect to the monitoring of unauthorized fishing 8/ within their exclusive economic zones. This is because the exclusive economic zones of these States normally harbour pelagic and other resources of high commercial value, their exclusive economic zones are very large relative to their land areas and the States individually have limited resources to monitor fishing activities within their exclusive economic zones.

"Recognizing their individual vulnerability to unauthorized fishing and their individual lack of capacity to address the problem, regional groupings of small island developing States in the Caribbean (Organization of East Caribbean States (OECS) and the Caribbean Community (CARICOM)), the Indian Ocean (West Indian Ocean Tuna Organization (WIOTO)) and the South Pacific (South Pacific Forum Fisheries Agency (FFA)) are cooperating in a variety of ways to monitor, control and discourage unauthorized fishing within their respective regions. Initiatives being pursued include regional MCS programmes, the establishment of regional registers of fishing vessels, the requirement for all catches to be transshipped in ports and the establishment of comprehensive observer programmes.

"Unauthorized fishing in the exclusive economic zones of small island developing States in the Caribbean region is problematic. It has been reported by OECS that unauthorized fishing in the exclusive economic zones of OECS member States is common. Recently, poachers have been targeting both pelagic and high-value inshore (reef and bank demersal) resources which are already fully or over-exploited. The OECS MCS programme is geared to reducing unauthorized fishing in the region. 9/

"Information concerning the incidence of unauthorized fishing in the exclusive economic zones of small island developing States in the Indian Ocean is not readily available. However, there are indications that a problem of unauthorized fishing of some considerable magnitude exists. This situation was confirmed by the representative of Maldives in November 1993 when he told a symposium convened under the auspices of IPFC that 'illegal foreign fishing in the outer reaches of the Maldives' exclusive economic zone by industrial fleets operating in the Indian Ocean is increasing, creating problems due to the country's limited enforcement capacity'. 10/

"South Pacific States have identified unauthorized fishing in their region by Asian distant-water fishing nation fleets as being a major obstacle to rational fisheries conservation and management (e.g., Kiribati and Papua New Guinea). 11/ Moreover, in December 1994, at the Multilateral High-level Conference on South Pacific Tuna Fisheries, it was pointed out that 'there is ample evidence that foreign fishermen have systematically contravened coastal State regulations for many years and that, because of the high cost of surveillance, it has been very easy for them to escape detection'. 12/ In response to this situation regional MCS cooperation in the South Pacific has reached an advanced level, and the Treaty on Cooperation in Fisheries Surveillance and Law Enforcement, commonly known as the Niue Treaty, signed in July 1992 by the FFA member States, gives effect to this cooperation.

"Efforts to improve the monitoring, control and surveillance of fishing activities and the enforcement of fishing regulations

"Since 1980 FAO has provided developing countries with dedicated policy, legal and technical advice, and training 13/ relating to fisheries MCS. 14/ In the mid-to-late 1970s two considerations figured significantly in FAO's assessment of the need for such technical assistance. These considerations were the (a) deliberations of the Third

United Nations Conference on the Law of the Sea, and (b) recognition of the central importance of MCS to effective fisheries conservation and management.

"The Third United Nations Conference on the Law of the Sea (1973-1982) led to the adoption of a new international legal regime for the management of the world's oceans, the 1982 United Nations Convention on the Law of the Sea (1982 Convention). 15/ Shortly after the commencement of the Conference, the international community agreed that in order to secure enhanced fisheries conservation and management, States would need to be given additional jurisdiction over fisheries resources adjacent to their coasts. This recognition had major implications for MCS policy and operations in that coastal States would be required, in future, to monitor and enforce fisheries conservation and management measures, no longer within a narrow territorial sea of 12 miles but rather over a much greater area in an exclusive economic zone extending up to 200 nautical miles from the coast.

"In 1979 the FAO Conference considered international fisheries developments and in particular the impact of the Law of the Sea Conference on national fisheries conservation and management, and in resolution 4/79, adopted by the Conference on 27 November 1979, invited 'the Director-General to continue and intensify efforts to mobilize the financial, technical and other forms of assistance required to implement the Programme of Assistance in the Development and Management of Fisheries in Exclusive Economic Zones'. 16/ It was that resolution that gave the impetus to establish a specific programme for the conservation and management of fisheries resources in exclusive economic zones, to be known as the FAO Exclusive Economic Zone Programme. 17/

"In addition to international developments related to the elaboration of the 1982 Convention, FAO continued to stress, in fisheries policy and technical advice provided to its developing members, that the implementation of conservation and management measures in exclusive economic zones would be unlikely to bring sustained long-term benefits in the absence of sound, reliable and cost-effective MCS systems. That was necessary to ensure that fisheries conservation and management measures adopted were observed and implemented.

"In concert with, and in support of, the provision of MCS technical assistance, FAO also provided developing countries with management and legal advice to: (a) bring national fisheries legislation in line with the provisions of the 1982 Convention; (b) harmonize legislation of regional groupings; (c) enhance national capacity in the legislative and fisheries law area; and (d) ensure that there was an unambiguous and appropriate legal base in support of the adoption and implementation of fisheries conservation and management arrangements.

"At its tenth session, held at in Mombasa, Kenya, from 7 to 11 November 1994, IOFC noted with appreciation the efforts by FAO to assist members of its Committee for the Management of Indian Ocean Tuna in the south-west Indian Ocean to strengthen their national capabilities in fisheries monitoring, control and surveillance. The Commission expressed its support for the proposal to organize once again a workshop on fishery monitoring, control and surveillance in the south-west Indian Ocean, which would be held in that region, in order to assist the members concerned with this important aspect of fisheries management.

"At the ninth session of the CECAF Subcommittee on Management of Resources within the Limits of National Jurisdiction, held at Agadir, Morocco, from 5 to 9 December 1994, several countries expressed interest in improving the performance of inspectors and observers involved in MCS and it was noted that the FAO project for improvement of the legal framework for fisheries cooperation, management and development of coastal States

(GCP/RAF/302/EEC) would probably organize a seminar/workshop on the topic in response to this interest.

"At the twenty-first session of the FAO Committee on Fisheries (COFI), held in Rome from 10 to 13 March 1995, several members asked for support in efforts to improve MCS in view of its importance for fishery management.

"Technical assistance provided by FAO (undertaken between 1980 and 1995 in many regions of the world) falls essentially into two categories: (a) national reviews of current MCS situations and, based on the particular needs of and conditions in States, the elaboration of policy options for enhancing such systems; and (b) regional capacity-building and institutional strengthening programmes. For policy reasons regarding its maintenance of neutrality vis-à-vis all members, FAO has not been involved in providing operational MCS assistance, though operational-level training can be organized if appropriate funding is identified.

"Prominent among national requests for assistance have been the evaluation of existing MCS arrangements, advice concerning the adoption of appropriate MCS arrangements or means to strengthen existing arrangements, assessment of institutional arrangements and the evaluation of training needs. At the national level, requests for MCS assistance were often related to actual or perceived problems with the legal and illegal operation of foreign fishing fleets in the exclusive economic zones of the requesting States. 18/

"A majority of the regional MCS technical assistance provided by FAO has been delivered through the organization's regional fishery bodies or programmes. This assistance, both of a policy development and systems nature, has been delivered primarily in workshop mode where important common MCS issues have been addressed and evaluated. 19/

"FAO regards the provision of MCS technical assistance to national fisheries administrations and/or regional fisheries organizations as an essential component of capacity-building and institutional strengthening so that in the longer run developing States will be better placed to conserve and manage their fisheries resources more effectively. However, capacity-building is a slow process, often requiring many years of consistent and costly application before policies and programmes are established firmly and the benefits of assistance provided become apparent. 20/

"It is being increasingly realized that the best prospects for strengthening the MCS capacity of developing States lies in regional cooperation. Indeed, given the scarcity of resources with which to support national MCS programmes and the variable results achieved from these programmes, developing States with common fisheries and fishing interests have demonstrated that significant progress towards enhancing fisheries conservation and management can be made through regional MCS initiatives. Developing States are therefore being urged to assess and address MCS both in terms of national programmes and through regional, cooperative networks.

"Conclusion

"Requests for MCS technical assistance by FAO's developing members are expected to remain high as a consequence of a number of factors, including:

(a) Continued over-exploitation of the resources in many countries, which will indirectly encourage some States' fleets to fish in waters of neighbouring countries;

(b) Increased realization by States that MCS is an integral and essential component of fisheries conservation and management and that prospects for achieving conservation and management objectives and sustainable development will be limited in the absence of effective MCS;

(c) Recognition that fisheries falling under national jurisdiction will become subject to greater international scrutiny with respect to the nature and effectiveness of conservation and management measures adopted and implemented. In this connection the international community will expect States to take concrete steps towards implementing the goals and objectives of sustainable development as set out in the Rio Declaration on Environment and Development and Agenda 21;

(d) Acknowledgement that fishing in areas under national jurisdiction and on the high seas carries with it substantial flag State responsibilities that must be fulfilled through States having greater control over the operation of their fleets. To this end States may need to adopt measures associated with the implementation of the Agreement to Promote Compliance with International Conservation and Management Measures by Fishing Vessels on the High Seas, concluded in 1993 under FAO auspices, and the outcomes of international negotiations, and in particular those parts relating to MCS, for the FAO Code of Conduct for Responsible Fisheries and the United Nations Conference on Straddling Fish Stocks and Highly Migratory Fish Stocks."

19. In its response of 23 May to the Secretary-General, the Council of Europe indicated that as the provisions of General Assembly resolution 49/116 concerned the sustainable use and conservation of marine living resources, they would be particularly taken into account in the activities contributing to the implementation of the Bern Convention of 19 September 1979 on the Conservation of European Wildlife and Natural Habitats.

20. In its reply of 3 July 1995 to the Secretary-General, the Banco Centroamericano de Intergración Económica reported that it had no further information to add with regard to the implementation of General Assembly resolution 49/116.

B. Regional and subregional fisheries organizations and arrangements

21. In its reply to the Secretary-General dated 26 May 1995, the Latin America Organization for the Development of Fisheries (OLDEPESCA) stressed that owing to the adverse impact of unauthorized fishing in zones under national jurisdiction, it was imperative for States, in the exercise of their sovereign rights and in accordance with international law, to adopt measures which ensured that no fishing vessels flying their flags would be able to fish in zones under the jurisdiction of other States unless duly authorized by the competent authorities of those States. Such authorized fishing operations should be carried out in accordance with the conditions set out in the authorization. OLDEPESCA also supported the relevant provisions of resolution 49/116 requesting development assistance organizations to make it a high priority to grant financial and technical assistance to the least developed countries with a view to improving the monitoring and control of fishing activities and the enforcement of fishing regulations. Such a recommendation should be encouraged in view of the fact that the majority of the world's catch was harvested in zones under the national jurisdiction of developing coastal States, thereby affecting their economies and the benefit they could derive from their resources, including their food security.

22. In its response of 26 June 1995 to the Secretary-General, the Northwest Atlantic Fisheries Organization (NAFO) submitted the following information:

"...

"The Northwest Atlantic Fisheries Organization has established and maintains the Scheme of Joint International Inspection and Surveillance in the NAFO Regulatory Area. The Scheme incorporates national and international elements of inspection in the north-west Atlantic Ocean. The contracting parties of NAFO have been always cooperating closely with the coastal States of the convention area to ensure the objectives of the NAFO Convention which could be consonant to some extent with the objectives of resolution 49/116.

"..."

23. In its reply to the Secretary-General dated 28 June 1995, the International Commission for the Conservation of Atlantic Tunas (ICCAT) made the following submission:

"...

"Because of the highly migratory nature of tuna and tuna-like species, the management measures adopted by the Commission do not include any discriminatory provisions as regards exclusive economic zones or high seas. In November 1993, ICCAT adopted a Declaration requesting the United Nations Conference on Straddling Fish Stocks and Highly Migratory Fish Stocks, inter alia, to consider urgently the necessity of managing the stocks of highly migratory species throughout their entire migratory range. ICCAT has had a continuous problem regarding non-contracting parties whose vessels carry out fishing activities that are not in compliance with the Commission's regulatory measures. This problem is mostly related to high seas fisheries, but such fishing activities also take place in the exclusive economic zones of some of the coastal States. Again, the statistics available and the reports of such fishing activities do not distinguish between exclusive economic zones and high seas. Hence, it would be difficult to separate such issues between these two zones.

"In order to reduce such fishing activities by non-contracting parties, which undermine the effectiveness of ICCAT regulatory measures, the Commission has taken various actions, such as diplomatic démarches, frequent requests to such non-contracting parties to implement the ICCAT regulatory measures, etc. The Commission has also adopted a Bluefin Tuna Statistical Document Programme, whereby all the bluefin tuna imported into an ICCAT contracting party must be accompanied by a statistical document. ICCAT has also adopted various resolutions, including on the possibility of taking trade measures, sighting reports, and friendly visits to the non-contracting parties' vessels fishing in the ICCAT convention area, and vessel tracking.

"As indicated above, most of these measures are applicable, regardless of the exclusive economic zone or the high seas nature of the fishery.

" "

24. The Commission for the Conservation of Antarctic Marine Living Resources (CCAMLR), in a communication addressed to the Secretary-General dated 29 June 1995, indicated that other than fully supporting the aims and principles of the resolution, it had no additional comments to make.

25. In a note to the Secretary-General dated 20 June 1995, the North Atlantic Salmon Conservation Organization (NASCO) informed the Secretary-General that NASCO was not aware of any activities within the convention area which would be inconsistent with General Assembly resolution 49/116.

26. In its submission of 24 June 1995 to the Secretary-General, the Asia Pacific Fisheries Commission (APFIC) reported that, according to the information it had received from its member States:

(a) Malaysia did not have any distant-water fishing fleet that could probably violate resolution 49/116. However, Malaysia faced problems of encroachment by fishing vessels from neighbouring countries. In spite of the high fines and mandatory confiscation of fishing vessels and fishing gear imposed upon conviction under the Malaysian Fisheries Act 1985, the number of foreign fishing vessels arrested in Malaysian fisheries waters had increased. Unauthorized foreign fishing had created various problems, especially in the management of the fisheries resources in areas under national jurisdiction. Management strategies implemented might not meet the objective of sustainable development of fisheries resources if those foreign fishing vessels would keep on encroaching into Malaysian waters and would keep on poaching its fisheries resources. One of the actions taken by Malaysia to overcome the problem of foreign fishing in areas under its national jurisdiction was the introduction of the monitoring, control and surveillance programme in fisheries management. The programme would provide effective methods towards getting required data from the collection of biological data to stock evolution, design of control, monitoring of the performance of the fisheries resources and taking the necessary enforcement actions to ensure that only authorized fishing vessels conducted fishing activities within designated areas in the Malaysian exclusive economic zone;

(b) Pakistan had no high seas fishing fleet of its own. Some trawlers and longliners were operating in Pakistan's exclusive economic zone under licensing arrangements and therefore there arose no question of poaching in the exclusive economic zone of other States by Pakistani flag vessels;

(c) Sri Lanka had noticed during the last few years an increasing number of incidents where Sri Lankan fishing boats had drifted into the exclusive economic zones of neighbouring countries, especially to India and Maldives, owing to a lack of knowledge of boundaries. There also had been cases where during innocent passage Sri Lankan fishing boats had been apprehended and legal action instituted by India and Maldives. One of the methods of resolving these problems was to have bilateral talks with the neighbouring countries, such as Maldives. This had been already initiated with Maldives and was intended to obtain fishing permits for Sri Lankan fishermen to fish in the exclusive economic zone of that country. In addition, it was reported that a large number of Indian fishing boats had crossed over into the Sri Lankan exclusive economic zone in the Palk Bay area to catch shrimp. Therefore, one of the major constraints was the lack of facilities for monitoring and surveillance. Assistance from developed countries was requested to strengthen monitoring and surveillance capability;

(d) Hong Kong drew attention to a number of practical difficulties in following up reports concerning unauthorized fishing or fishing in an unapproved manner in foreign waters by boats based in Hong Kong, despite its willingness to cooperate with the authorities concerned. As most of the fishing done by the fleet based in Hong Kong was in waters beyond Hong Kong jurisdiction, the authorities would consider it more appropriate for the countries concerned to take appropriate action to control fishing in their own waters, in view of the fact that it would be difficult to control the activities of boats based in Hong Kong once they had left local waters.

27. In its report to the Secretary-General dated 4 July 1995, the North-East Atlantic Fisheries Commission (NEAFC) indicated that General Assembly resolution 49/116 was of less concern to NEAFC as a body, since its major focus appeared to be on the duties of flag States in respect of vessels fishing in zones under national jurisdiction of other States. NEAFC was not a flag State, nor did its jurisdiction extend to areas under contracting parties' national jurisdiction without the agreement of the contracting party concerned. However, Norway, as a contracting party, had informed NEAFC that Norway's responsibility as a flag State was taken care of by bilateral agreements with other coastal States. Any unauthorized fishing in zones of national jurisdiction was prevented by implementation of a licence system. Under such a system, when Norwegian vessels planned to fish in the European Union's zones, an application to issue a licence would be sent by the Norwegian authorities to the European Union and the response accordingly received would be dispatched to the vessel concerned. In this way Norwegian authorities sought to make sure that only duly authorized fishing was conducted in other States' national zones by Norwegian vessels.

C. <u>Organizations and bodies of the United Nations</u>

28. In its response of 25 April 1995 to the Secretary-General, the Economic Commission for Europe (ECE) indicated that it was involved in the issues addressed by General Assembly resolution 49/116. However, it had brought the resolution to the attention of its regional advisers to be taken into account when advising ECE member States on integrated coastal management or similar issues relevant for ECE island States.

29. In its reply of 12 May 1995 to the Secretary-General, the Economic and Social Commission for Asia and the Pacific (ESCAP) stated that it was not involved in any activities related to living marine resources and therefore had no submission to make with regard to General Assembly resolution 49/116.

30. In its submission to the Secretary-General dated 31 May 1995, the United Nations Conference on Trade and Development (UNCTAD) indicated that the subject of General Assembly resolution 49/116 was outside its mandate and did not therefore call for any comments.

31. In its report of 5 June 1995 to the Secretary-General, the United Nations Development Programme (UNDP) provided the following information:

> "... UNDP, through its support of developing countries, is both directly and indirectly involved in controlling unauthorized fishing.
>
> "Clearly the TRAIN-SEA-COAST programme, which is run together with the Division [for Ocean Affairs and the Law of the Sea, Office of Legal Affairs], will be training a cadre of developing-country personnel capable of increased efficiency in their monitoring, control and surveillance activities.
>
> "UNDP is a steering committee member of a biannual fisheries development donor consultation. At the last consultation, which took place in Paris in April 1994, some of the donors were considering making the existence of a fisheries management regime, including monitoring, control and surveillance, a prerequisite for assistance to the fisheries of any given country.
>
> "In May 1994, UNDP chaired a workshop on donor collaboration at the Global Conference on the Sustainable Development of Small Island Developing States in Barbados. UNDP's Sustainable Development Network is working on a sub-network called SIDSNET, and UNDP's Technical Cooperation among Developing Countries (TCDC) Unit is working on a Small Island Developing States (SIDS) technical assistance programme.
>
> "Perhaps our most direct involvement will be a project which we are currently considering with FAO. The FAO Council has developed a code of conduct for responsible fisheries, which is about to be approved by the FAO Council and Assembly. UNDP is working with FAO on a possible technical assistance proposal to help countries implement the code of conduct, which by definition calls for many of the same actions as are covered by General Assembly resolution 49/116."

32. In its response to the Secretary-General dated 23 June 1995, the United Nations Economic Commission for Latin America and the Caribbean (ECLAC) stated that it did not have any specific information to submit for the reporting period.

IV. INFORMATION PROVIDED BY NON-GOVERNMENTAL ORGANIZATIONS

33. In its submission of 30 June 1995 to the Secretary-General, the Hellenic Marine Environment Protection Association (HELMEPA) indicated that the issue of unauthorized fishing in zones of national jurisdiction, with its impact on the

living marine resources of the planet, was of concern to HELMEPA. However, the Association's membership, consisting of 538 ocean-going Greek vessels, did not include fishing vessels or fishermen. Therefore, HELMEPA neither was in a position to collect and provide information on the problems encountered in the implementation of General Assembly resolution 49/116 nor had the opportunity to support its objectives in the appropriate forums.

Notes

1/ Report of the United Nations Conference on Environment and Development, Rio de Janeiro, 3-14 June 1992 (United Nations publication, Sales No. E.93.I.8 and corrigenda), vol. I: Resolutions Adopted by the Conference, resolution 1, annex II.

2/ Report of the Global Conference on the Sustainable Development of Small Island Developing States, Bridgetown, 25 April-6 May 1994 (United Nations publication, Sales No. E.94.I.18 and corrigenda), chap. I, resolution 1, annex II.

3/ Now called the Asia-Pacific Fishery Commission.

4/ B. Phasuk, "Fishing effort regulations in the coastal fisheries of Thailand", in Socio-economic issues in coastal fisheries management: Proceedings of the IPFC Symposium held in conjunction with the twenty-fourth session of the Indo-Pacific Fishery Commission, Bangkok, Thailand, 23-26 November 1993 (FAO, Bangkok, RAPA publication 1994/8) pp. 111-122.

5/ E-mail communication dated 17 May 1995.

6/ Fax communication dated 5 June 1995.

7/ As discussed in "The state of world fisheries and aquaculture" (FAO, Rome, 1995), prepared for and discussed at the FAO Twenty-First Session of the Committee on Fisheries (COFI), held in Rome from 10 to 15 March 1995, as well as the FAO Ministerial Meeting on Fisheries, held in Rome from 14 to 15 March 1995.

8/ Unauthorized fishing is only one aspect of the problem faced by small island developing States with respect to the operation of some distant-water fishing nation fleets within their exclusive economic zones. Equally problematic and significant from a fisheries conservation and management point of view is the widespread non-reporting and under-reporting of fish catches.

9/ D. V. Robin and P. A. Murray, "Profile of fisheries enforcement in the Organization of Eastern Caribbean States subregion". Paper presented at the Global Fisheries Enforcement Workshop, Washington, D.C., 25-27 October 1994.

10/ FAO, Indo-Pacific Fishery Commission: Socio-economic issues in coastal fisheries management (FAO, Bangkok, RAPA publication 1994/8), p. 5.

11/ See papers presented by the representatives of Kiribati and Papua New Guinea at the Global Fisheries Enforcement Workshop, Washington, D.C., 25-27 October 1994.

12/ South Pacific Forum Fisheries Agency, Record of the proceedings of the multilateral High-level Conference on South Pacific Tuna Fisheries (FFA, Honiara, 1995), p. 9.

13/ For a summary of this technical assistance, see David J. Doulman, "Technical assistance in fisheries monitoring, control and surveillance. A historical perspective of FAO's role", FAO Fisheries Circular No. 882 (FAO, Rome, 1994). This section of the FAO report draws substantially on information contained in that circular.

14/ For a recent review of MCS systems and procedures, see P. Flewwelling, "An introduction to monitoring, control and surveillance systems for captures fisheries", FAO Fisheries Technical Paper No. 338 (FAO, Rome, 1995).

15/ Official Records of the Third United Nations Conference on the Law of the Sea, vol. XVII (United Nations publication, Sales No. E.84.V.3), document A/CONF.62/122. The Convention entered into force on 16 November 1994.

16/ FAO, Report of the Conference of FAO, (twentieth session, Rome, 10-28 November 1979 (FAO, Rome, 1979), pp. 28-32.

17/ The objectives of the programme were: (a) to strengthen the capabilities of coastal countries and groupings of countries to manage and develop their fisheries; (b) to promote the rational management and the full use by developing countries of fishery resources in their exclusive economic zones; and (c) to strengthen the efforts of developing countries to secure a greater share of, and higher benefits from, living marine resources as part of initiatives to establish a new international economic order.

18/ While the operation of foreign fleets in the exclusive economic zones is of significance because of sovereignty considerations, States need to be encouraged to recognize that fishing activities by national and joint-venture fleets must also be subject to effective MCS if fisheries conservation and management objectives are to be achieved and sustainable resource utilization assured. Indeed, it is often these fleets that present the most severe threats to fisheries conservation and management because they tend to operate closer inshore where resources in the exclusive economic zones are subject to the most intense fishing effort and are less likely to be penalized in the event of violation.

19/ There has in fact been little emphasis on operation-level training because such training tends to be somewhat sensitive and longer-term. However, such training has been undertaken as part of FAO's regional initiatives in the region of the Association of South-East Asian Nations (ASEAN).

20/ The challenges associated with strengthening MCS capacity in developing States are part of the broader requirement associated with strengthening fisheries administration generally. Until such administration is improved the capacity of developing States to "absorb" MCS technical assistance will be constrained.

6. FISHERIES BY-CATCH AND DISCARDS AND THEIR IMPACT ON THE SUSTAINABLE USE OF THE WORLD'S LIVING MARINE RESOURCES - NOTE BY THE UN SECRETARY-GENERAL

Doc. no.: A/50/552 12 October 1995

1. At its forty-ninth session, the General Assembly, in its resolution 49/118 of 19 December 1994, recognized that in relevant provisions of the United Nations Convention on the Law of the Sea 1/ States are called upon to take into consideration, when establishing conservation and management measures for target fisheries, the effects on associated or dependent species, taking into account the best scientific evidence available. It recalled that the United Nations Conference on Environment and Development (UNCED) and the International Conference on Responsible Fishing had agreed to promote the development and use of selective fishing gears and practices that minimized waste in the catch of target fish species and minimized by-catch of non-target fish and non-fish species. The Assembly also invited relevant subregional and regional fisheries management organizations and arrangements as well as the Food and Agriculture Organization of the United Nations (FAO) to review, within their respective competencies, the impact of fisheries by-catch and discards on the sustainable use of living marine resources. FAO was also invited to formulate fisheries by-catch and discard provisions in its Code of Conduct for Responsible Fishing, taking into account work being done elsewhere.

2. In response to that resolution, FAO has submitted for the attention of the General Assembly the report which is annexed to the present note.

Notes

1/ Official Records of the Third United Nations Conference on the Law of the Sea, vol. XVII (United Nations publication, Sales No. E.84.V.3), document A/CONF.62/122.

ANNEX

Report of the Food and Agriculture Organization of the United Nations on fisheries by-catch and discards and their impact on the sustainable use of the world's living marine resources

I. ASSESSMENT OF FISHERIES BY-CATCH AND DISCARDS

1. FAO promotes national and international action for the rational management and development of world fisheries. It does this not only through the regular

programme of activities at its headquarters, but also through the field and regional offices and regular consultation with regional (FAO and non-FAO) fishery bodies, the fishing industry and other institutions. a/

2. The definition of "by-catch" is all "species captured other than target species". b/ "Discards" may constitute a small-to-significant fraction of the identified by-catch, depending on the nature of the fisheries and local customs.

3. Since the creation of FAO in 1945, the fishery scientists working outside and within the framework of FAO fishery activities have been aware, in the context of fishery management, of the importance of gear selectivity in minimizing the by-catch of undersized fish of target species, non-target fish species and non-fish species. Indeed several FAO regional bodies have introduced regulatory measures for gear, c/ including the regulations concerning the use of minimum mesh size in gears used for the catch of certain target species.

4. Fishery managers and conservation/environmental groups have been concerned that by-catch, and discards, may be contributing to biological overfishing and altering the structure of marine ecosystems.

5. The recent global assessment of fisheries by-catch and discards estimated an annual discard range of between 17.9 and 39.5 million tonnes, with a mean estimate of 27 million tonnes. No estimate could however be given of the mortality level of "escapees" from fishing gear during operations. Although many of the discards include non-target or low-value species, undersized fish of target species are also discarded. The combined effect of this practice may threaten the maintenance of biodiversity and the long-term sustainability of fisheries.

6. The discard range may be an underestimate in that recreational fishery discards are not included; the database for some areas of the world is incomplete, and discard rates are not included for marine mammals, seabirds, turtles and, for many areas, invertebrates.

7. Although discards in tropical industrial shrimp-trawl fisheries are generally high, in many of the world's artisanal fisheries a variable share of the shrimp by-catch may be species retained for human consumption or for other purposes. Further, discard rates and numbers may misrepresent the impacts because for a number of species some fraction of the discard survives. Without good estimates of the biomass discarded, the survival rate, other fish-related losses and the landed catch of a particular species, it will be impossible to assess overall impacts of fishing.

8. In general, since the 1992 United Nations Conference on Environment and Development (UNCED), fisheries conservation and management practice has emphasized an ecosystem approach, taking full account, inter alia, of the need to exploit fisheries in a precautionary manner. The ecosystem approach differs significantly from past approaches to fisheries conservation and management, whereby the primary concern was the impact of fishing on the target species, with lesser concern for impacts on non-target fish and animal populations.

9. The ecosystem approach to fisheries management necessitates further significant extension of fisheries research beyond an emphasis on target-species and single-species approaches to stock assessment and to the determination of optimal exploitation. A new research emphasis and a significant additional capacity, including that for the development of new methods, are required to make such research effective so as to lead to meaningful advice on fisheries management in the ecosystem context. Additional research and data collection are particularly needed to assess the biological impact of by-catch. The status of the stocks of non-target species and their biologically allowable mortality are now frequently not determined, regardless of being necessary information for rational fisheries management.

10. Some of the impacts of discarding may include: (a) foregone catch as a result of mortalities imposed on recruits to the target fishery; (b) foregone catch resulting from mortalities imposed on target fisheries by fisheries targeting other species; (c) reduction of fishing time resulting from by-catch quotas; (d) costs of purchasing gear adapted to comply with discarding measures; (e) loss of catch and time when a gear type is outlawed and no efficient alternative gear type is available or can be deployed owing to vessel or other restrictions; and (f) loss of catch owing to capture of immature fish being subtracted from the total allowable catch (TAC). There may well be an impact of an economic nature owing to the introduction of required observer programmes and sorting costs. Much more work is needed to assess adequately the true economic cost of discards on fishers and the benefits and costs of potential solutions to society as a whole. In some cases, mortalities associated with discards may decrease key predator or competitor populations and enhance system productivity. Furthermore discarding practices may permit fisheries to remain cost-effective.

11. There is a growing global recognition that the world's fishing effort already exceeds what is necessary to harvest sustainable yields of marine fish. d/ The single action that will provide the greatest improvements to the by-catch and discard problem in certain fisheries will be the reduction of these effort levels. Without such control, other solutions to the by-catch and discard problem will be less effective and real success in efforts to better manage the ocean's resources will be more difficult to attain.

12. In the Rome Consensus on World Fisheries, adopted by the Ministerial Meeting on Fisheries, held in Rome on 14 and 15 March 1995, it is stated that improved fisheries conservation and management, along with better protection from harmful sea- and land-based activities, are crucial to maintaining world fish resources and aquatic ecosystems. The Ministerial Meeting urged that Governments and international organizations take prompt action, inter alia, to adopt policies, apply measures and develop techniques to reduce by-catches, fish discards and post-harvest losses.

13. On a number of occasions FAO and other agencies have organized activities to address the question of the utilization of by-catch so as to contribute towards food security. This was addressed at a consultation organized in 1981, e/ and has been addressed at a Technical Cooperation among Developing Countries (TCDC) workshop on the utilization of by-catch from shrimp trawlers, organized by the Government of Madagascar, the Special Unit for Technical Cooperation among Developing Countries of the United Nations Development Programme (UNDP) and FAO, at Nosy Bé, Madagascar, from 6 to 8 June 1995. Although shrimp fisheries account for the largest share of discards in global fisheries, it should also be noted that much of the shrimp produced in tropical waters is harvested by artisanal traps, and other species caught along with shrimp are rarely discarded, but rather consumed in the fishing villages. f/

II. UNITED NATIONS CONFERENCE ON STRADDLING FISH STOCKS AND HIGHLY MIGRATORY FISH STOCKS

14. Data and related information concerning high seas fisheries are poor and incomplete, and as a result conservation and management of high seas resources is weak. Consistent with the 1982 United Nations Convention on the Law of the Sea, the United Nations Conference on Straddling Fish Stocks and Highly Migratory Fish Stocks, convened in 1993 as a consequence of the 1992 United Nations Conference on Environment and Development, seeks to improve and strengthen the conservation and management of these two types of stocks and to ensure that, as a foundation for conservation and management, data and the timeliness for the provision of data are greatly enhanced.

15. The revised Draft Agreement for the Implementation of the Provisions of the United Nations Convention on the Law of the Sea of 10 December 1982 relating to the Conservation and Management of Straddling Fish Stocks and Highly Migratory Fish Stocks g/ (the Draft Agreement), prepared by the Chairman of the

Conference, takes a strong ecosystem approach to high seas fisheries conservation and management and requires that high seas fishing activity be assessed in terms of the "impacts of fishing, other human activities and environmental factors on target species and species belonging to the same ecosystem or dependent upon or associated with the target species" (art. 5 (d)), to "adopt, where necessary, conservation and management measures for species belonging to the same ecosystem or dependent on or associated with the target species, with a view to maintaining or restoring populations of such species above levels at which their reproduction may become seriously threatened" (art. 5 (e)) and to "promote the development and require the use of selective, environmentally safe and cost-effective fishing gear and techniques in order to minimize pollution, waste, discards, catch by lost or abandoned gear, catch of non-target species (both fish and non-fish species) (hereinafter referred to as non-target species) and impacts on associated or dependent species, in particular endangered species" (art. 5 (f)). As part of this ecosystem approach to fisheries conservation and management high seas fishers are obligated to report comprehensively, through appropriate subregional or regional fisheries management organizations or arrangements, on all target and non-target (by-catch) species taken in the course of fishing operations. Comprehensive data must be provided on target and non-target species caught and retained, as well as other species that are discarded. h/ The requirements and standards to be established for high seas catch reporting represent a significant departure from conventional fisheries catch/effort reporting whereby retained target species data are normally the only data reported.

16. If fully implemented through effective flag State control, the Draft Agreement i/ will facilitate the collection and reporting of reliable catch and related data not only for target species, but also for by-catch and discarded fish and animal species. The availability of these data will enable assessments to be made to more accurately determine the effects of fishing both on target species and more broadly on the ecosystem as a whole. However, to obtain a complete and comprehensive evaluation of the impact of fishing on the ecosystem, similar requirements for fisheries falling under zones of national jurisdiction will also be required.

III. DRAFT CODE OF CONDUCT FOR RESPONSIBLE FISHERIES

17. According to instructions of FAO governing bodies, the draft Code of Conduct for Responsible Fisheries j/ has been formulated to be consistent with the 1982 United Nations Convention on the Law of the Sea, taking into account the 1992 Declaration of Cancún, the 1992 Rio Declaration and the provisions of Agenda 21 of UNCED, the Strategy endorsed by the 1984 FAO World Conference on Fisheries Management and Development and other relevant instruments. It will also take into account the outcome of the United Nations Conference on Straddling Fish Stocks and Highly Migratory Fish Stocks.

18. Certain articles of the draft Code of Conduct address matters of concern, pertaining to by-catch and discards, in follow-up to General Assembly resolution 49/118 of 19 December 1994. It should be emphasized that the draft Code is currently open for revision.

19. Article 6.2.2 of the draft Code of Conduct is concerned with objectives within the overall issue of fisheries management, and the relevant text (subject to revision) notes that "States and fisheries management organizations or arrangements should ensure that long-term management objectives are set to provide a high probability that, inter alia, waste, by-catch and discards in fisheries are progressively reduced and avoided as far as practical."

20. Another subsection which may be amended in the final wording pending progress at the United Nations Conference on Straddling Fish Stocks and Highly Migratory Fish Stocks is article 6.6.10, which states:

"In order to protect juveniles or spawners, avoid waste and reduce the catch which is not sought or retained by the fishers, fisheries management authorities should implement technical measures such as minimum landing size limits, mesh or gear regulations, closed areas, including marine reserves, or closed seasons where necessary. Regulations governing multi-species fisheries should be designed to ensure minimum discarding."

21. Article 7.4.5 is concerned with fishing practices within the overall issue of fishing operations, and the relevant text notes that "States, with relevant groups from industry, should encourage the development and implementation of technologies and operational methods that reduce discards. At the same time they should discourage, as appropriate, the use of fishing gear and practices that lead to the discarding of catch and should promote the use of fishing gears and practices that increase survival rates of escaping fish."

22. Article 7.5.1 is concerned with fishing gear selectivity, also within the overall issue of fishing operations, and the text notes that "States should require that fishing gear, methods and practices are sufficiently selective so as to minimize the catch of non-target species, waste, discards and threats to endangered species, and that the intent of related regulations is not circumvented by technical devices. In this regard, fishers should cooperate in the development of selective gears and methods. States should ensure that information on new developments and requirements is made available to all fishers."

23. With regard to protection of the marine environment, article 7.7.1 reads: "States should introduce and enforce laws or regulations based on the International Convention for the Prevention of Pollution from Ships, 1973, as amended by the Protocol of 1978 (MARPOL 73/78)."

24. Article 10.1.8 of the draft Code of Conduct is concerned with responsible fish utilization within the overall context of post-harvest practices and trade, and the text notes that "States should encourage those involved in fish processing, distribution and marketing to reduce post-harvest losses and waste, and improve the utilization of by-catch to the extent that it is consistent with responsible fisheries management practices."

25. Article 11.10 is concerned with fisheries research, and states that "States should carry out studies on the selectivity of fishing gears to target species and on the behaviour of target and the non-target species to the fishing gear with a view to minimizing non-utilized catches and safeguarding the biodiversity of ecosystems as an aid for management decisions."

IV. CONCLUSION

26. A major strategy to reduce the level of by-catch would be improvement in the selectivity of fishing gear and fishing methods. While there has been an increase in activity to develop selective gears and techniques, much of the research has been carried out in the higher latitudes and is not readily transferable to multi-species tropical fisheries, where the tropical shrimp trawls still produce high rates of by-catch.

27. The strategy to reduce the negative impact of by-catch would include: (a) a specific emphasis on reducing by-catch of stocks reduced below their optimum levels, (b) a better disposal of by-catch or utilization of by-catch for human consumption, and other purposes benefiting people, especially if the stocks remain above optimal levels. This strategy necessitates the determination of the status of stocks, individuals of which constitute the by-catch, and the biologically allowable mortality for these stocks, requiring an additional research capacity for these tasks; certainly, until this is carried out, a precautionary approach to fisheries management may need to be applied.

28. FAO estimates that a significant reduction in discards by the year 2000 of around 60 per cent could be achieved by: (a) a concentrated effort to improve the selectivity of fishing gear; (b) the development of international standards for research, and an additional research designed specifically to address problems resulting from by-catch; (c) greater interaction between research staff, industry and fisheries managers; and (d) the application of appropriate technology through fisheries regulations. To achieve this goal, FAO and national research institutes will need to strengthen and widen the scope of current programmes on gear selectivity. k/

29. As a consequence of a decision of the FAO Council (108th session, 5-14 June 1995), an open-ended Technical Committee has been set up to review and agree on the form and content of the Code of Conduct for Responsible Fisheries and any follow-up action, including further provisions with regard to by-catch and discards if necessary, which may be required to finalize the Code prior to its submission to the Twenty-eighth Session of the FAO Conference (Rome, 20 October-2 November 1995) for approval and adoption. Since the United Nations Conference on Straddling Fish Stocks and Highly Migratory Fish Stocks should conclude its work in August 1995, the relevant part of the draft text could then be reconciled with the language agreed upon at the Conference.

Notes

a/ FAO has consulted with its own regional fishery bodies (the General Fisheries Council for the Mediterranean, the Fishery Committee for the Eastern Central Atlantic, the Indian Ocean Fisheries Commission, the Asia-Pacific Fisheries Commission and the Western Central Atlantic Fisheries Commission) in compiling the present report.

b/ D. L. Alversen, M. H. Freeberg, J. G. Pope and S. A. Murawski, "A global assessment of fisheries by-catch and discards", FAO Fisheries Technical Paper No. 339 (Rome, 1994).

c/ Mesh size and other regulatory measures to reduce by-catch have been examined by FAO and its regional bodies over many years. For example, the FAO Fishery Committee for the Eastern Central Atlantic (CECAF) at its third session in 1972 recommended the introduction of a provisional minimum mesh size of 70mm for use by vessels fishing for hake or sea bream in the CECAF area.

d/ Summarized in the FAO report entitled "The state of world fisheries and aquaculture" (Rome, 1995), prepared for and discussed at the FAO Twenty-first Session of the Committee on Fisheries (COFI) held in Rome from 10 to 15 March 1995, as well as the FAO Ministerial Meeting on Fisheries held in Rome on 14 and 15 March 1995.

e/ "Fish by-catch, bonus from the sea", Report of a Technical Consultation on Shrimp By-catch Utilization, Georgetown, Guyana, 27-30 October 1981 (Ottawa, Canada, International Development Research Centre).

f/ F. Teutscher, "By-catch in tropical shrimp fisheries", prepared for the TCDC workshop on the utilization of by-catch from shrimp trawlers, Nosy Bé, Madagascar, 6-8 June 1995.

g/ A/CONF.164/22/Rev.1.

h/ See A/CONF.164/22/Rev.1, annex 1, "Standard requirements for collection and sharing of data".

i/ The Conference subsequently adopted, on 4 August 1995, the Agreement for the Implementation of the Provisions of the United Nations Convention on the Law of the Sea of 10 December 1982 relating to the Conservation and Management of Straddling Fish Stocks and Highly Migratory Fish Stocks (A/CONF.164/37). The Agreement incorporated the draft provisions quoted here with no substantive changes.

j/ FAO document CL 108/20, prepared for the 108th Session of the Council of FAO, Rome, 5-14 June 1995.

k/ See "The state of world fisheries and aquaculture", op. cit., p. 21.

7. LARGE-SCALE PELAGIC DRIFTNET FISHING AND ITS IMPACT ON THE LIVING MARINE RESOURCES OF THE WORLD'S OCEANS AND SEAS - REPORT OF THE SECRETARY-GENERAL

Doc. no.: A/50/553 12 October 1995

CONTENTS

I. INTRODUCTION

1. The General Assembly, at its forty-ninth session, in its decision 49/436 of 19 December 1994, took note with appreciation of the report of the Secretary-General (A/49/469) and, while acknowledging the substantial progress achieved since 1992 in support of the objectives of resolution 46/215 of 20 December 1991, 1/ expressed serious concern over reports of continuing conduct and activities inconsistent with the terms of that resolution. It therefore urged the international community to take greater enforcement responsibility to ensure full compliance with resolution 46/215, and requested the Secretary-General to take into account decision 49/436 in preparing his report on further developments relating to the implementation of that resolution.

2. In accordance with decision 49/436, the Secretary-General sent a note verbale to all members of the international community, drawing their attention to resolution 46/215. Letters were also addressed to intergovernmental and non-governmental organizations and well-established scientific institutions with expertise in the area of living marine resources.

3. The Secretary-General has received a number of responses and submissions from States, intergovernmental and non-governmental organizations and scientific organizations. He wishes to express his appreciation for all the contributions.

4. The present report, which takes into account such contributions, is submitted to the General Assembly in response to the request contained in decision 49/436.

II. ACTIVITIES OF INTERGOVERNMENTAL ORGANIZATIONS

5. The Commission for the Conservation of Antarctic Marine Living Resources (CCAMLR) replied to the Secretary-General on 15 May 1995, recalling that the matter of large-scale drift-net fishing had been discussed at the annual meeting of CCAMLR in 1990, resulting in the adoption of resolution 7/IX, 2/ which declared that, in accordance with General Assembly resolution 44/225, there would be no expansion of large-scale pelagic drift-net fishing into the high seas of the convention area. Since the adoption of resolution 7/IX, no cases of activities or conduct inconsistent with the terms of that resolution had been reported to the Commission within the CCAMLR convention area.

6. In its response to the Secretary-General dated 18 May 1995, the South Pacific Forum Fisheries Agency (FFA) indicated that since its last submission to

the Secretary-General on the issue in July 1994, no incident of fishing with long drift-nets had been drawn to the attention of the Agency.

7. The Council of Europe informed the Secretary-General on 23 May 1995 that in view of the fact that decision 49/436 dealt with the sustainable use and conservation of marine living resources, it would be particularly taken into account in the activities aimed at the implementation of the Bern Convention of 19 September 1979 on the Conservation of European Wildlife and Natural Habitats.

8. In its report to the Secretary-General dated 22 June 1995, the Food and Agriculture Organization of the United Nations (FAO) submitted the following information:

> "16. On the basis of information available to FAO the incidence of large-scale pelagic drift-net fishing, in contravention of United Nations General Assembly resolution 46/215 and subsequent resolutions, has declined further in the 1994/95 period. This situation might be attributed principally to: (i) the United Nations moratorium being successfully implemented in accordance with the relevant United Nations General Assembly resolutions, and (ii) enhanced flag State control on the part of States and entities which previously sanctioned the use of this type of gear.
>
> "17. The major area for large-scale pelagic drift-net fishing is the Mediterranean Sea, with vessels predominantly being of Italian flag or origin. These vessels are operating in contravention of both the United Nations international moratorium on large-scale pelagic drift-net fishing and European Community (EC) law. Given the fragility and biological importance of the Mediterranean Sea, the continued use of this gear in this area is viewed by many as a matter of considerable international concern."

9. The United Nations Economic Commission for Latin America and the Caribbean (ECLAC), in its submission to the Secretary-General of 23 June 1995, indicated that it had no specific information to submit for the reporting period with respect to information requested in General Assembly decision 49/436 concerning the implementation of resolution 46/215.

III. REVIEW BY REGION

A. General

1. Information provided by States

10. In its reply of 24 May 1995, Colombia informed the Secretary-General that Colombia was of the view that large-scale pelagic drift-net fishing had a great impact on the living marine resources of the world's oceans and seas, and therefore it supported the relevant provisions of resolution 46/215. In addition, no Colombian fishing vessel was engaged in high seas drift-net fishing in the world's oceans and seas.

11. In its reply to the Secretary-General dated 19 June 1995, the United States of America made the following submission:

> "...
>
> "As a principal co-sponsor of General Assembly resolution 46/215, as well as resolution 44/225 (1989) and 45/197 (1990), and supporter of decisions 47/443 (1992), 48/445 (1993) and 49/436 (1994), the United States takes a particular interest in the effective and full implementation of a global moratorium on all large-scale pelagic drift-net fishing on the high seas in the light of the adverse impacts such fishing has upon the world's living marine resources.

"The United States firmly believes that the best available scientific evidence demonstrates the wastefulness and potential ecosystem-scale negative impacts of large-scale pelagic drift-net fishing on the high seas. The United States believes it was appropriate that the General Assembly, in recognition of the unacceptable impacts of large-scale pelagic drift-net fishing on the high seas, and by its resolution 46/215, called upon all members of the international community to ensure that a global moratorium on all large-scale pelagic drift-net fishing on the high seas be fully implemented by 31 December 1992.

"The United States attaches great importance to compliance with resolution 46/215, has taken measures individually and collectively to prevent large-scale pelagic drift-net fishing on the high seas and has called upon all members of the international community to implement and comply with the resolution. The United States has urged all members of the international community, intergovernmental organizations, non-governmental organizations and scientific institutions with expertise in relation to living marine resources to report to the Secretary-General any activity or conduct inconsistent with the terms of resolution 46/215.

"Since 1990, it has been unlawful for any United States national or fishing vessel to engage in large-scale drift-net fishing in any area under the fisheries jurisdiction of the United States or beyond the exclusive economic zone of any nation.

"The Driftnet Act Amendments of 1990, and more recently the High Seas Driftnet Fisheries Enforcement Act, enacted in November 1992, made it the stated policy of the United States to, among other things, implement resolution 46/215 and secure a permanent ban on the use of destructive fishing practices, in particular large-scale drift-nets, by persons or vessels fishing beyond the exclusive economic zone of any nation. Additionally, the Act provides for the denial of port privileges for any large-scale drift-net fishing vessel and sanctions for any nation whose nationals or vessels conduct large-scale drift-net fishing beyond the exclusive economic zone of any nation, including a prohibition on the importation into the United States of fish and fish products and sport fishing equipment.

"On 8 March 1993, the United States announced plans to promote observance of the global moratorium on large-scale pelagic drift-net fishing on the high seas, including steps the United States intends to take in the event United States enforcement authorities have reasonable grounds to believe that any foreign flag vessel encountered on the high seas is conducting, or has conducted, large-scale pelagic drift-net fishing operations inconsistent with resolution 46/215. United States enforcement officials will follow established procedures for determining flag-State identity or registration and will take law-enforcement actions in conjunction with the flag State and consistent with the 1982 United Nations Convention on the Law of the Sea. Under customary international law and United States law, a vessel considered stateless and found to be conducting large-scale pelagic drift-net fishing operations on the high seas would be subject to penalty in the United States.

"Since submission of its report to the Secretary-General in July 1994, the United States has taken a number of steps to implement the General Assembly's resolutions and decisions on large-scale pelagic drift-net fishing on the high seas.

"To monitor compliance with the drift-net moratorium in 1994, the United States Coast Guard and the United States National Marine Fisheries Service continued to carry out enforcement and surveillance activities in the North Pacific in areas of former large-scale drift-net fishing. United States Coast Guard cutters logged 146 vessel days at sea and Coast Guard aircraft flew 223 hours in the 1994 drift-net monitoring programme. No large-scale high seas drift-net activity was sighted by United States enforcement patrols in 1994.

"All United States Coast Guard operations were coordinated with enforcement officials of Japan, Canada and the Russian Federation. In addition, direct lines of communication have been established between the Coast Guard and the Russian Federation Border Guard to facilitate sharing of information.

"...

"In two European fisheries, questions have been raised regarding the use of large-scale drift-nets on the high seas. Environmental groups charged last year that fishermen of several European Union (EU) member nations continued to conduct large-scale high seas drift-net fishing.

"The countries concerned have been conducting diligent enforcement in the fishery, and the United States expects that these efforts, in addition to the framework established by international law, EU regulations, and EU member State regulations, are sufficient to ensure full compliance with resolution 46/215.

"Under a Memorandum of Understanding between the United States Departments of Transportation, Commerce and Defense, signed 11 October 1993, the United States is utilizing the surveillance capabilities of the Department of Defense for locating and identifying vessels violating resolution 46/215. Formal procedures for communicating vessel locations to the Department of Commerce and the United States Coast Guard, as well as concerned Governments, have been established.

"The United States continues to attach extreme importance to compliance with resolution 46/215 and encourages all members of the international community to take measures to prohibit their nationals and vessels from undertaking any activity contrary to the terms of resolution 46/215, and to impose appropriate penalties against any that may undertake such activities."

12. In its response of 29 June 1995 to the Secretary-General, New Zealand expressed the view that the Secretary-General's annual report to the General Assembly was a significant tool of accountability which it strongly supported. It also remained opposed to large-scale pelagic drift-net fishing and attached great importance to the full implementation of the global moratorium in accordance with resolution 46/215. New Zealand was aware of reports in some areas and wished to express its deep concern about such reports and to urge all countries to direct their fishing industries to comply fully with the global moratorium. It therefore welcomed the decision by the General Assembly at its forty-ninth session to urge authorities of members of the international community to take greater enforcement responsibility to ensure full compliance with resolution 46/215 and to impose appropriate sanctions, consistent with international law, against acts contrary to the terms of the resolution.

2. Information provided by international organizations

13. In its above-mentioned report to the Secretary-General (see para. 8), FAO made the following submission:

"4. The Government of Japan, the Government of the Republic of Korea and the fisheries administration in Taiwan, Province of China, have all introduced policies and measures aimed at implementing fully General Assembly resolution 46/215 and subsequent resolutions. There have been no reports that vessels of these flags have been engaged in large-scale pelagic drift-net fishing in 1994/95.

"5. In 1994 it had been reported that French and Italian vessels with large-scale pelagic drift-net gear in excess of 2.5 kilometres continued to operate in the North-East Atlantic Ocean and in the Mediterranean Sea, respectively. The Italian fleet exceeds 600 vessels and targets swordfish stocks on a seasonal basis. Both fleets have reportedly been operating in contravention of General Assembly resolution 46/215 and subsequent resolutions and EC Council regulation 345/92. However, France has agreed to enforce EC Council regulation 345/92, which limits the length of drift-nets to 2.5 kilometres per vessel, thereby abiding by EC law and the United Nations international moratorium.

"6. Conflict among EC fishermen over the use of large-scale pelagic drift-nets in 1994 was reported in the Bay of Biscay. Spanish fishermen, who are forced by national law to use pole-and-line gear when targeting albacore tuna in the Bay of Biscay, maintained that Irish and French vessels were using drift-nets in excess of 2.5 kilometres. In some instances Spanish fishermen were reported to have boarded Irish vessels and cut their nets, while a French vessel was escorted to a port in Galicia.

"7. With the exception of the Mediterranean Sea and the Bay of Biscay in the North-East Atlantic Ocean, there have been no reports of fishing with large-scale drift-nets in the 1994/95 period."

14. In its submission of 29 June 1995 to the Secretary-General, the Secretariat of the Asia Pacific Fishery Commission (APFIC) reported that:

(a) Malaysia did not have any large-scale pelagic drift-net fishing that would fall under the ambit of General Assembly resolution 46/215. However, Malaysia had imposed a ban on the use of any drift-net or gill with a mesh size of less than 25.4 centimetres (10 inches) in waters under its own jurisdiction;

(b) Pakistan indicated that there was no large-scale drift-net fishing in Pakistan. The small-scale artisanal fishermen did use the pelagic gill net in coastal waters off Pakistan, which did not pose any threat to non-target species such as dolphins and whales;

(c) The Philippines had indicated that its fishing authorities had recommended to the Philippine Government to accede to Protocol II of the Convention for the Prohibition of Fishing with Long Drift-nets in the South Pacific since the Philippines' gill nets were not forbidden by the Convention in view of the fact that they ranged from 300 to 800 metres and operated only in coastal waters for the harvesting of pelagic and demersal species using boats of less than 3 gross tons. Likewise, the Philippine Government ought to prohibit transshipment of large-scale drift-net catches within areas under national jurisdiction;

(d) Hong Kong was not aware of any boats based in Hong Kong using large-scale pelagic drift-net fishing. In addition, the method was not used in Hong Kong territorial waters by foreign vessels.

3. Information provided by non-governmental organizations

15. In its submission of 25 April 1995 to the Secretary-General, the Cousteau Society submitted the following statement:

"The Cousteau Society completely supports and reaffirms the importance of General Assembly decision 49/436, and completely supports and reaffirms the importance of a global moratorium on all large-scale pelagic drift-net fishing, as referred to in paragraphs 3 (c) and 4 of resolution 46/215.

"Captain Cousteau has repeatedly spoken out about the destructive nature of drift-net fishing on fish stocks, and indeed worked actively to support the moratorium. Obviously, destructive fishing practices continue, but this does not mean that the higher goal of a full-scale moratorium should not be continuously sought, especially in view of the interests and rights of future generations."

16. In its reply of 30 June 1995, the Hellenic Marine Environment Protection Association (HELMEPA) informed the Secretary-General that although the issue of large-scale pelagic drift-net fishing and its impact on the living marine resources of the world's oceans and seas was of concern to HELMEPA, the Association's membership did not include fishing vessels or fishermen. The Association was therefore not in a position to collect and provide information on the problems encountered in the implementation of resolution 46/215, nor had it had the opportunity to support its objectives in the appropriate forums.

17. In its response to the Secretary-General dated 30 June 1995, Greenpeace International stated that despite the European Council Regulation (EEC) No. 345/92 amending Council Regulation (EEC) No. 3094/86, which banned pelagic drift-nets longer than 2.5 kilometres, the European Union still had probably the largest large-scale, high seas drift-net fleet in the world and continued to act in contravention of General Assembly resolution 46/215 and subsequent General Assembly decisions with respect to drift-net fishing.

18. In its reply to the Secretary-General dated 13 July 1995, the Federation of Japan Tuna Fisheries Cooperative Associations made the following submission:

"...

"We are convinced that the United Nations should reconsider its course of action with regard to [General Assembly resolution 46/215] because:

(1) The resolution has lacked as its basis concrete scientific evidences to prove that drift-net fishing destroys the marine environment and damages the ecosystem;

(2) The decision-making process has bypassed the due considerations of scientific evidence; and therefore

(3) The process has failed to bring about a real consensus among the concerned parties.

"We understand that at regional levels through observer programmes and other kinds of scientific surveys, strenuous efforts had been made to collect data to study the impacts of drift-net fisheries on the related resources and to work out measures to remedy its ecological problems. However, despite such efforts, the United Nations General Assembly had neglected them altogether and without thorough scientific debates and without leaving the matter to the competent agency for further study, political and quick solutions were sought and the banning resolution was adopted.

"The resolution therefore inevitably has inherent problems and adoption of such resolution has left a stain upon the reputation of the United Nations.

"From the viewpoint of sustainable use of food resources, we would like to firmly request that the United Nations should take up this matter again totally from scratch and assign to the FAO, which is a specialized agency established under the United Nations to cope with issues of food security, duties of close examinations of accumulated data at this stage."

B. Atlantic Ocean

1. Information provided by States

19. In its reply of 9 June 1995, Guyana informed the Secretary-General that no illegal drift-net fishing had been reported in Guyanese waters and that no high seas drift-net fishing had been permitted by its authorities.

20. In its submission of 24 July 1995, the Netherlands reported to the Secretary-General that, in conformity with European Community regulation 345/92, Netherlands law prohibited the use and possession of drift-nets with a length of over 2.5 kilometres. Observance of this rule was enforced by the Fisheries Inspection Service and no infringements had ever been reported.

21. In its response to the Secretary-General dated 21 July 1995, Venezuela reported that under its legislation the use of drift-nets was prohibited for all vessels, either national or foreign, of length equal or exceeding 14 metres in zones under national jurisdiction and on the high seas. Any commercialization of fishery products harvested with the above-mentioned gear was also prohibited, even if the catches were made on the high seas by foreign fishing vessels. In addition, violations would be prosecuted in conformity with the Fisheries Law and its regulations, without prejudice to the revocation of fishing permits and the application of other applicable administrative sanctions.

2. Information provided by international organizations

22. In its submission of 30 May 1995, the International Commission for the Conservation of Atlantic Tunas (ICCAT) informed the Secretary-General that a resolution on large-scale pelagic drift-net fishing had been adopted by ICCAT at its ninth special meeting (Madrid, November-December 1994). In that resolution, ICCAT had called upon its member States, inter alia, to take greater enforcement responsibility to ensure that their nationals and fishing vessels complied with General Assembly resolution 46/215 and to impose the appropriate sanctions against their nationals and fishing vessels that would act contrary to the terms of that resolution. In addition, in its above-mentioned report to the Secretary-General (see para. 8) FAO indicated that ICCAT had advised it that, although the Commission was still in the process of collecting data for the 1994/95 period, there had been no reports of catches made by large-scale pelagic drift-nets in the Commission area.

23. In its reply of 20 June 1995 to the Secretary-General, the North Atlantic Salmon Conservation Organization (NASCO) indicated that it was not aware of any activities within the convention area which would be inconsistent with General Assembly decision 49/436.

24. In its response of 26 June 1995, the North Atlantic Fisheries Organization (NAFO) informed the Secretary-General that NAFO contracting parties had unanimously concurred with United Nations resolutions and decisions on the subject and that there had not been any large-scale pelagic drift-net fishing activity within the convention area during these years.

25. According to the FAO report to the Secretary-General, the Fishery Committee for the Eastern Central Atlantic (CECAF) had indicated that there were no reports of catches of large-scale pelagic drift-net fishing in the CECAF area during 1994/95.

26. In its submission to the Secretary-General dated 4 July 1995, the International Council for the Exploration of the Sea (ICES) reported that member States had informed it that they were unaware of any activities by their nationals in the ICES area which might be inconsistent with General Assembly resolution 46/215.

27. In its reply of 4 July 1995 to the Secretary-General, the North-East Atlantic Fisheries Commission (NEAFC) indicated that General Assembly decision 49/436 was of direct relevance to NEAFC in so far as it related to fishing on the high seas, although article 1.2 of the NEAFC Convention stated that the Convention did not apply to highly migratory species within the mandate of other international agreements such as ICCAT. None the less, NEAFC was not aware of any drift-net fishing being conducted in NEAFC's international waters. In addition, Norway, as a contracting party, had informed NEAFC that Norwegian vessels did not carry out large-scale pelagic drift-net fishing on the high seas. A very limited drift-net fishery for mackerel took place each spring in Norwegian coastal waters without by-catch problems. The short seasonal drift-net mackerel fishery was not considered to be of a scale or to involve wasteful fishing methods that would be inconsistent with the General Assembly resolutions and decisions on the issue.

3. Information provided by non-governmental organizations

28. In its above-mentioned report to the Secretary-General (see para. 17), Greenpeace International made the following submission:

"In 1994, just before the so-called 'tuna war' started in the North-East Atlantic, illegal French, Irish and United Kingdom drift-netters were detected both by Spanish fishermen and Spanish fisheries control boats. Conflicts arose between Spanish fishermen (which use traditional gears in the albacore fishery) and drift-net fishermen from other countries; a French drift-net vessel was seized by several Spanish live-bait and pole-and-line boats.

"It is common knowledge that nets of 2.5 kilometres in length are not economically viable, neither in the Mediterranean swordfish fishery, nor in the North-East Atlantic albacore fishery. Therefore, in Greenpeace's view, illegal large-scale drift-net fishing is bound to continue in the North-East Atlantic if high seas drift-net fishing is not altogether banned and effective enforcement action taken. Furthermore, because of the incompatibility between drift-nets and other more selective gears in the same fishing areas, conflicts among fleets are expected again this year.

"EU authorities are well aware of the non-implementation of the EU Regulation and the United Nations moratorium. The European Commission stated in its communication to the European Union Council of Ministers on 8 April 1994 that:

> 'The allowing of nets up to 2.5 kilometres long has to be seriously questioned. First of all, it is a cardinal factor in fraud. Secondly, it is an avenue through which the use of drift-nets can be expanded.'

"This year, in reaction to the violent conflicts provoked by large-scale illegal drift-netting in the North-East Atlantic last year, the EU member States involved and the European Commission are deploying no less than seven patrol vessels in the area. The proportion of patrol vessels, concentrated in the area where the smallest portion of the EU drift-net fleet operates (less than 90 drift-net vessels), shows the tremendous difficulty involved in enforcing the 2.5 kilometre length limit imposed by the EU Regulation.

"It remains to be seen whether this unprecedented and costly level of control will result in the effective enforcement of the EU Regulation throughout the season. Greenpeace has repeatedly warned that attempting to regulate drift-nets through means of a length limit was impossible for a fleet of over 700 vessels operating in both the North-East Atlantic and the Mediterranean Sea.

"..."

C. Baltic Sea

29. In its submission to the Secretary-General dated 11 September 1995, Finland indicated that General Assembly resolution 46/215 on large-scale pelagic drift-net fishing had not caused any measures to be taken in Finland since drift-nets used for salmon fishing in the Baltic Sea were smaller than those used in the oceans and no other fish were caught in this type of salmon fishing.

D. Indian Ocean and South China Sea

1. Information provided by States

30. In its report to the Secretary-General dated 21 June 1995, Sri Lanka made the following submission:

> "There is no large-scale pelagic drift-net fishing in the high seas by Sri Lankan fishermen. Permits are granted by Sri Lanka to fishing boats of foreign origin to land fish in Sri Lankan ports caught in the high seas using long lines only.
>
> "Sri Lanka is committed to conservation and sustainable development of fisheries. Accordingly, a new Fisheries and Aquatic Resources Bill has been formulated for which the approval of the Cabinet of Ministers has been obtained. It will be submitted to Parliament in due course. There are provisions in this Bill for licensing of all major fishing activities and a separate section on conservation of fisheries. Once the Bill becomes law, strict enforcement of the legislation would be undertaken. Even the provisions of the present Fisheries Ordinance on conservation are enforced.
>
> "..."

31. In its reply of 10 August 1995 to the Secretary-General, Thailand made the following submission:

> "At the outset, it should be mentioned that the drift-nets being used by the Thai fisheries are of a different type from those referred to in decision 49/436. However, the Department of Fisheries has conducted a study to evaluate the impact of drift-nets of 2.5 and 9.5 kilometres and found that no endangered species (sea turtles, dugongs and dolphins) could be found to have been caught. The drift-nets used by the Thai fishers thus have caused no impact on the living marine resources or marine ecosystem as required by the decision."

2. Information provided by international organizations

32. According to the above-mentioned report of FAO (see para. 8) to the Secretary-General, the Indo-Pacific Tuna Development and Management Programme (IPTP) had indicated that in the Indian Ocean there had been no reports of fishing with large-scale pelagic drift-nets since Taiwan, Province of China, had taken measures to prevent the use of this type of gear by its flag vessels.

E. The Mediterranean

1. Information provided by States

33. In its response to the Secretary-General dated 13 June 1995, Cyprus stated that no drift-net fishing from Cyprus flag vessels took place in the Mediterranean, either inside or outside the territorial sea limits of Cyprus. In addition, it stressed that the relevant legislation allowed the Department of Fisheries to deny fishing permits to drift-net fishing operations.

34. In its report dated 25 June 1995, Morocco informed the Secretary-General that drift-nets had been authorized only for artisanal coastal fishery without modern technical capability operating in areas under Moroccan jurisdiction. This type of fishing was limited to the Moroccan Mediterranean coastal area and did not bear any similarity with large-scale pelagic drift-nets, the use of which had been consistently denounced by Morocco. Furthermore, Morocco had established technical regulations restricting the use and scope of this small-scale drift-net fishing. Foreign fishing fleets authorized to operate in areas under national jurisdiction were forbidden to practice drift-net fishing.

2. Information provided by international organizations

35. In its report to the Secretary-General, FAO indicated that the General Fisheries Council for the Mediterranean (GFCM) had advised that there had been no complaints from members concerning fishing with large-scale pelagic drift-nets in the 1994/95 period. Some GFCM members had made a substantial effort to reduce this type of fishing in the region.

3. Information provided by non-governmental organizations

36. In its above-mentioned report to the Secretary-General, Greenpeace International indicated that:

> "Large scale high-seas drift-net fishing is continuing in 1995. The Italian swordfish drift-net fleet, consisting (as it has for the past several years) of more than 600 vessels, continues to operate in contravention of European Union regulations, using an average net length of 12.5 kilometres per vessel. Illegal Italian drift-netters currently moor in Italian harbours, carrying on board large-scale illegal nets with total impunity.
>
> "On 4 May 1995, a sperm-whale calf appeared on Posilippo beach (Naples, Italy) with the tail cut. This is a common practice among fishermen to release cetaceans from drift-nets. On 6 May 1995, three sperm whales were discovered entangled in a piece of drift-net 30 nautical miles from South Sardinia.
>
> "On 5 May 1995, the Spanish Army arrested an illegal Italian drift-netter while operating in Spanish territorial waters. An unknown number of other illegal boats were detected in the vicinity, fishing in international waters. According to Spanish fishermen, since May 1995, sights of illegal Italian drift-netters have been frequent in the international waters of the western Mediterranean, both in the Balearic Sea and between the Balearic Islands and the Spanish mainland.
>
> "In a recent survey, in June 1995, the Greenpeace vessel MV Greenpeace has detected dozens of large-scale drift-nets in the eastern Mediterranean. Encounters with three vessels in particular showed that they were using nets that measured at least between 7 and 10 kilometres in length. The drift-net vessel Diomede I had set its net, estimated at 7 kilometres in length, in a cargo shipping traffic lane. The net had already been cut by a propeller of a passing ship when the MV Greenpeace arrived.
>
> "On 27 June, in the western Mediterranean, an illegal Italian drift-netter was found selling swordfish in Minorca harbour, Spain. Spanish authorities measured the net, which was 4.5 kilometres long, and confiscated 2 kilometres of net from the vessel. Before the authorities could take further legal action, the vessel escaped from the harbour. This is the second time the Spanish authorities have found an illegal Italian drift-netter in Spanish waters this year.

"Greek fishermen have regularly contacted Greenpeace to report the presence of Italian drift-net vessels fishing in the Ionian Sea. As in recent years, it appears that the fishing area of the illegal Italian fleet continues to cover almost all international waters of the Mediterranean, although a small reduction of the fleet has been noticed in the waters off Spain (probably as a result of environmentalists' protests as well as repeated arrests by the Spanish Navy).

"But this does not necessarily indicate that the fleet is decreasing. Greenpeace has been informed about contacts between interested parties to export Italian drift-nets to Tunisia. Rumours also mention Malta, Albania and Croatia. Italian drift-net vessels may also be reflagging to some of those countries.

"Morocco is developing a pelagic drift-net fishery and Moroccan fishermen have been buying drift-nets from Spanish suppliers. This new fishery is being developed in the absence of studies on its potential environmental impact. There is no assessment of the swordfish population, the main target species. Even though swordfish is a major commercial species, no appropriate management measures have been put in place. Data on fleet size, net lengths, fishing areas and incidental catches are not publicly available, if they exist at all.

"..."

F. Pacific Ocean

1. Information provided by States

37. In a note dated 18 May 1995 addressed to the Secretary-General, Fiji made the following submission:

"Fiji has provision and has undertaken the following measures at the national level which are consistent with the above-mentioned resolution. Fiji has signed and ratified the Wellington Convention for the Prohibition of Fishing with Long Drift-nets in the South Pacific Region. The Wellington Convention entered into force on 17 May 1991.

"In its national laws, there is a legislative provision which provides for administrative and operational flexibility to address the problem of the continued use of drift-nets. In particular, your attention is drawn to subsection 1 (d) of section 22 of the Marine Space Acts (chapter 158A of the Laws of Fiji), which states that: 'The Minister may prescribe the classes of licences, whether by reference to the size of the vessel, size of catch, method of fishing, species of catch or otherwise.' Under section 15 of the aforementioned legislation, the Minister responsible for fisheries may suspend or cancel a licence to fish granted to a foreign fishing vessel where there has been a determination that such vessel has contravened any regulations which have prescribed, inter alia, methods of fishing.

"Having regard to the foregoing, Fiji believes that it has an appropriate legal regime which, when fully utilized, will contribute to the effective implementation of the desire of the international community to halt the practice of drift-net fishing.

"..."

38. In its report to the Secretary-General dated 18 May 1995, the Federated States of Micronesia indicated that section III (4)(c) of Title 24 (Marine resources) of the Code of the Federated States of Micronesia provided that a permit application might be denied in the case "where the [Micronesian Maritime] Authority determines that the permit would authorize fishing with or by means of

the use of drift-net or gill net or other substantially similar method of catching fish". In addition, the Federated States of Micronesia is party to both the Tarawa Declaration, outlawing drift-netting in the South Pacific Forum region, and the Wellington Convention.

39. In its above-mentioned report to the Secretary-General (see para. 11), the United States of America gave the following information:

> "In December 1994, the United States and the People's Republic of China extended for two years a Memorandum of Understanding designed to ensure effective cooperation and implementation of resolution 46/215. Under the terms of the agreement, originally signed on 3 December 1993, enforcement officials of either country may board and inspect vessels flying the United States or People's Republic of China flag in the North Pacific Ocean found using or equipped to use large-scale high seas pelagic drift-nets inconsistent with the provisions of resolution 46/215.
>
> "The agreement also provides for enforcement officials of either country to ride on board high seas drift-net fishery enforcement vessels of the other country. The United States Coast Guard will carry People's Republic of China ship riders on two high seas fishery enforcement patrols this year in areas of former large-scale high seas drift-net fishing activity. During one of these patrols, the United States Coast Guard and the Russian Federal Border Service will conduct a coordinated high seas drift-net fishing surveillance operation.
>
> "The United States Coast Guard's high seas enforcement plan for 1995 will include over 110 days of cutter patrols and an estimated 215 hours of airborne surveillance from United States Coast Guard air patrols based in Alaska and Hawaii. These flights will be coordinated with similar enforcement efforts by Canada to provide maximum patrol-area coverage."

40. In its above-mentioned submission to the Secretary-General (see para. 12), New Zealand indicated that there had been no drift-net activity within the areas under its jurisdiction over the past 12 months. It reiterated also its call for all countries eligible to do so to support fully the Convention for the Prohibition of Fishing with Long Drift-nets in the South Pacific and its two Protocols.

41. In its reply of 1 June 1995, the Cook Islands informed the Secretary-General that its Government had taken measures to prevent large-scale pelagic drift-net fishing operations on the high seas by ratifying the Convention for the Prohibition of Fishing with Long Drift-nets in the South Pacific (Wellington Convention) on 24 January 1990. Since the entry into force of the Wellington Convention, there had been no reports of activity in the Cook Islands exclusive economic zone or adjacent high seas involving the use of large-scale drift-nets. In addition, the Cook Islands enacted in 1989 the Marine Resources Act which, under section 15, banned any fishing vessel from being used or assisting any drift-net fishing in the Cook Islands or the fishing waters thereof. The Act also made it an offence for any Cook Islands national to engage or assist in any drift-net fishing activities. Where any fishing vessel was used in contravention of the Act, the owner, charterer and master each committed an offence and would be liable upon conviction to a fine not exceeding $NZ 250,000. Fishing activity in the exclusive economic zone of the Cook Islands was monitored by the Cook Islands Ministry of Marine Resources. Regular inspections were carried out by patrol boats from Australia, New Zealand and the Cook Islands and air patrols were undertaken by naval aircraft from Australia, New Zealand and France. Dockside inspections of foreign fishing vessels were carried out at ports of unloading in the region such as Pago Pago, American Samoa, and any irregularities were reported to the Ministry of Marine Resources. Beginning in 1996, the monitoring of fishing vessels operating in the region would be significantly enhanced through the introduction of a regional vessel monitoring system, which would provide an accurate picture of fishing vessel activity on a near real-time basis.

42. In its submission of 1 August 1995 to the Secretary-General, China provided the following information:

"...

"Following the adoption of General Assembly resolution 44/225 on 22 December 1989, the Ministry of Agriculture of the People's Republic of China officially issued the text of that resolution on 10 November 1990 and called upon local government authorities and fisheries enterprises to follow its provisions strictly. The Ministry further decided that it would no longer approve applications for the development of large-scale pelagic drift-net fishing operations on the high seas. At the same time, the Ministry required the six vessels that had already obtained permission to use drift-nets for fishing on the high seas to suspend their use of large-scale pelagic drift-nets, in accordance with General Assembly resolution 44/225.

"On 13 February 1993, the Ministry of Agriculture of China issued a regulation prohibiting the use of large-scale drift-nets on the high seas and notified local Chinese government authorities and fisheries enterprises of that regulation. The regulation reiterated the Chinese Government's ban on the use of large-scale drift-nets in fishing operations on the high seas by all vessels of Chinese registry. Vessels violating that regulation would be subject to the following penalties:

(1) Determination of the administrative responsibility to be borne by the head of the unit operating the vessel;

(2) Confiscation of the catch, the fishing gear used and the income derived from the violation, and the imposition of a fine; and

(3) Suspension or revocation of the credentials of the offending vessel's crew.

"...

"In May of 1993, two vessels registered in China for long-line fishing (the Yinyu No. 601 and Yinyu No. 602) were discovered to have large-scale drift-nets on board without permission and to be engaging in drift-net fishing operations in the waters of the North Pacific in violation of General Assembly resolution 46/215 and the relevant Chinese Government regulations. During the same month the Dayuanyu No. 206 illegally flew the Chinese national flag in the waters of the North Pacific, despite having had its registry revoked by China, and carried large-scale drift-net equipment on board. The Ministry of Agriculture of China has imposed penalties on all three vessels in accordance with the provisions of Chinese domestic laws and regulations.

"...

"On 3 December 1993, for the purpose of effective cooperation and implementation of General Assembly resolution 46/215, representatives of the Government of the People's Republic of China and the Government of the United States of America signed the Memorandum of Understanding Between the Government of the People's Republic of China and the Government of the United States of America on Effective Cooperation and Implementation of United Nations General Assembly Resolution 46/215 of December 20, 1991. That Memorandum entered into force on the date of signature. No fishing vessels were found to be in violation of relevant United Nations resolutions during the period that the Memorandum was in force. In December 1994, in order to further strengthen this international cooperation, the Governments of China and the United States of America decided to extend the period of validity of the Memorandum to 31 December 1996. Officials of China and the United States have already begun conducting cooperative joint boardings and inspections of vessels in the waters of the North Pacific."

2. Information provided by international organizations

43. In its above-mentioned report to the Secretary-General (para. 6), the South Pacific Forum Fisheries Agency (FFA) drew attention to the fact that the Convention for the Prohibition of Fishing with Long Drift-nets in the South Pacific had entered into force on 17 May 1991. It had been signed by 14 FFA member countries, the most recent being Fiji in August 1993. Seven other countries and the New Zealand Protectorate of Tokelau had ratified the Convention. The United States had signed and ratified Protocol I to the Convention, while Chile had signed and ratified Protocol II.

44. In its reply to the Secretary-General dated 26 May 1995, the North Pacific Anadromous Fish Commission (NPAFC) submitted the following information:

> "The Convention for the Conservation of Anadromous Stocks in the North Pacific Ocean was signed at Moscow on 11 February 1992 by Canada, Japan, the Russian Federation and the United States and came into force on 16 February 1993. The Convention prohibits directed fishing for anadromous fish (Pacific salmon and steelhead trout) on the high seas of the North Pacific Ocean and also includes measures to minimize the amount of anadromous fish taken in other fisheries. The parties to the Convention are allowed to take action individually or collectively to prevent unauthorized fishing activities by others, and to prevent trafficking in illegally harvested anadromous fish. Each party has the authority to board, inspect and detail fishing vessels found operating in violation of the Convention. Thus, though the Convention was not elaborated to implement General Assembly resolution 46/215 or to prohibit large-scale pelagic drift-net fishing itself as described in the resolution, this Convention has eventually contributed to the implementation of the resolution, by prohibiting directed fishing for anadromous fish on the high seas area of the North Pacific Ocean, where fishing had been mainly conducted by using drift-nets.
>
> "The Convention established the North Pacific Anadromous Fish Commission in order to promote the conservation of anadromous stocks in the North Pacific Ocean and its adjacent seas and serve as a forum for the cooperation and coordination of enforcement activities, and scientific research.
>
> "The Commission reviewed the enforcement activities by each party at its 1993 and 1994 annual meetings.
>
> "...
>
> "In 1994 there was one drift-net vessel encountered that had gill nets visible on the deck. The vessel could not be identified and efforts to apprehend the vessel were unsuccessful.
>
> "All parties to the Convention will implement their enforcement plans during the current year.
>
> "At the second annual meeting - 1994, the view was expressed that success in achieving the goals of the Convention related to the cooperative enforcement activities of the parties.
>
> "..."

45. In its report to the Secretary-General, FAO indicated that the Inter-American Tropical Tuna Commission had advised that there was no evidence

that large-scale pelagic drift-net fishing had occurred in the Eastern Pacific Ocean in 1994/95.

Notes

1/ In resolution 46/215 the General Assembly called, inter alia, for full implementation of a global moratorium on all large-scale pelagic drift-net fishing on the high seas.

2/ See A/46/615, para. 15.

8. ZONE OF PEACE AND COOPERATION OF THE SOUTH ATLANTIC - REPORT OF THE UN SECRETARY-GENERAL

Doc. no.: A/50/671 24 October 1995

CONTENTS

I. INTRODUCTION

1. At its forty-ninth session, the General Assembly adopted resolution 49/26 of 2 December 1994 on a zone of peace and cooperation of the South Atlantic in which, inter alia, it took note of the report of the Secretary-General. 1/ It welcomed with satisfaction the holding of the third meeting of the States members of the zone, held at Brasilia on 21 and 22 September 1994, and took note

of the Final Declaration, the Declaration on the Denuclearization of the South Atlantic, the Declaration on the Marine Environment, the Declaration on Business Cooperation in the South Atlantic and the decision on the establishment of the Permanent Committee of the zone of peace and cooperation of the South Atlantic, adopted at the meeting. 2/

2. In the same resolution, the General Assembly affirmed the importance of the South Atlantic to global maritime and commercial transactions and its determination to preserve the region for all activities protected by customary international law, as reflected in the United Nations Convention on the Law of the Sea. 3/

3. The General Assembly called upon all States to cooperate in the promotion of the objectives established in the declaration of the zone of peace and cooperation of the South Atlantic and to refrain from any action inconsistent with those objectives and with the Charter and relevant resolutions of the United Nations, particularly action which might create or aggravate situations of tension and potential conflict in the region. It also requested the relevant organizations, organs and bodies of the United Nations system to render appropriate assistance which States of the zone might seek in their joint efforts to implement the objectives of the zone. The Assembly requested the Secretary-General to keep the implementation of resolution 41/11 of 27 October 1986 and subsequent resolutions on the matter under review and to submit a report to the General Assembly at its fiftieth session, taking into account, inter alia, the views expressed by Member States.

4. Pursuant to the above resolution, the Secretary-General addressed a note verbale on 4 May 1995 to the Governments of the States Members of the United Nations, requesting their views on the implementation of the declaration on the zone of peace and cooperation of the South Atlantic. On the same day, letters were also dispatched to the relevant organizations and bodies of the United Nations requesting them to convey their contributions for the preparation of the report of the Secretary-General by 1 August 1995.

5. As of 11 October 1995, five Governments had replied to the Secretary-General. Those replies are reproduced in section II of the present report. Any further replies and notifications that may be received at a later date will be published as addenda to the present report.

6. By the same date, communications had been received from five of the organizations and United Nations bodies addressed, and are set out in section III of the present report.

II. REPLIES RECEIVED FROM GOVERNMENTS

A. Argentina

[Original: Spanish]

[1 August 1995]

1. The Argentine Republic once again affirms its full support for the principles and purposes of the zone of peace and cooperation of the South Atlantic declared in General Assembly resolution 41/11 of 27 October 1986.

2. In this connection, it wishes to underline the special importance which the promotion of democracy and political pluralism and the protection of human rights and fundamental freedoms have for the strengthening of the zone, without which a truly effective zone of peace would be very difficult to envisage.

3. The commitment of the Argentine Republic to the consolidation of a lasting peace in the region has been tangibly demonstrated by its participation in the United Nations Angola Verification Mission (UNAVEM), even at the cost of loss of life.

4. As regards the peaceful uses of nuclear energy and international cooperation, the Argentine Republic believes it is important to strengthen and promote the development of international law relating to the physical protection of nuclear materials.

5. As the Foreign Minister of Argentina stated at the Review and Extension Conference of the Parties to the Treaty on the Non-Proliferation of Nuclear Weapons, held in April-May 1995:

> The transport of materials such as plutonium or highly enriched uranium raised major questions regarding contamination, which require the closest possible attention of the international community.
>
> The recent transit of radioactive waste through the waters of the South Atlantic has placed Argentina in a difficult situation because of the clear ecological risks it may face, given the particular characteristics inherent in navigation in the southern seas. We believe that the international community should go on record in favour of the efforts being made to strengthen existing instruments in the area of physical protection of nuclear materials and management of radioactive waste, in order to make those instruments truly useful in the event of an ecological emergency.

6. The Argentine Government has repeatedly expressed its concern about the protection of the environment of the south-west Atlantic, in particular about the dangers caused by the passage of ships transporting highly radioactive substances.

7. The United Nations Convention on the Law of the Sea confers on coastal States the authority to exercise jurisdiction in their exclusive economic zone, inter alia, for the protection and preservation of the marine environment, and they thus have the power to enact and enforce norms aimed at avoiding contamination of their waters. Argentina has exercised and will continue to exercise that authority in accordance with international law.

8. Argentina acts responsibly in all matters relating to the protection and preservation of resources. However, without international cooperation, Argentina's efforts to preserve and protect the environment in the south-west Atlantic could prove to be insufficient.

9. While the Argentine Republic respects freedom of navigation as governed by international instruments, it believes that such freedom should be regulated in the case of ships transporting highly radioactive substances. The Government is determined to call upon the relevant international organizations to enforce and strengthen international rules and standards for preventing, reducing and controlling contamination, and to develop rules regulating the passage of ships transporting highly radioactive substances, to ensure, in particular, that the packing of such substances meets the requirements of the International Maritime Organization (IMO) and the International Atomic Energy Agency (IAEA) concerning safety in packing.

10. Finally, the Argentine Republic wishes once again to state that the colonial situation of the Malvinas, South Georgia and South Sandwich Islands persists in the South Atlantic, affecting its territorial integrity. The increasing normalization of relations between Argentina and the United Kingdom of Great Britain and Northern Ireland, the ongoing cooperation efforts and the expressly manifest will to regain sovereignty by peaceful means and in accordance with the principles of international law, of which the Secretary-General and the United Nations General Assembly have been informed, in addition to the constitutional commitment to respect the way of life of the inhabitants of the Malvinas Islands, have not achieved a solution to the sovereignty dispute, which is greatly desired in the South Atlantic region.

B. Brazil

[Original: English]

[14 August 1995]

1. The Government of Brazil reiterates its commitment to the purposes and objectives of the zone of peace and cooperation of the South Atlantic (ZPCSA), as expressed in resolution 41/11, in subsequent resolutions of the General Assembly and in the decisions and declarations adopted by its Member States.

2. Brazil hosted the third meeting of the States members of the ZPCSA, held at Brasilia on 21 and 22 September 1994. The Final Declaration of that meeting, Declarations on the Denuclearization of the South Atlantic, on the Marine Environment and on Business Cooperation, and a decision on the inter-sessional follow-up mechanism have been circulated in a document submitted to the General Assembly at its forty-ninth session. 4/

3. Recent developments in the context of the South Atlantic, such as the integration of a democratic South Africa in the ZPCSA and progress in subregional integration agreements, offer new opportunities for enhancing the links among countries sharing the African and South American coasts of the South Atlantic. Further joint efforts are to be expected in order to address challenges in areas such as the easing of tension, preservation of the environment, non-proliferation of weapons of mass destruction and cooperation for development, and in multilateral issues.

4. The Government of Brazil looks forward to participating in the next meetings of the member States of the zone and welcomes the offers made by the Governments of South Africa, Argentina and Benin to host future meetings.

C. Malawi

[Original: English]

[9 August 1995]

The Government of Malawi is committed to the promotion of international peace and security, and questions of peace and security are central to its domestic and foreign policies. The Government therefore endorses the objectives of the resolution. In addition, it supports measures which are aimed at the conservation and sustainable utilization of natural resources.

D. South Africa

[Original: English]

[11 October 1995]

1. South Africa welcomes the objectives of General Assembly resolution 49/26 of 2 December 1994. Bringing the countries of the South Atlantic rim together in closer understanding and cooperation and by bridging a military-free and nuclear-free ocean to increase political, economic and cultural links between eastern South America and West African countries, can be warmly subscribed to.

2. In this regard the South African Government wishes to underline recent developments in relations between South Africa and the States members of the zone of peace and cooperation of the South Atlantic, which developments have contributed not only to a lessening of tension in the South Atlantic but also to prospects for increasingly close economic and other contacts.

3. It is clear that the emergence of a democratic non-racial Government of National Unity in South Africa, preceded by the independence of Namibia and the reintegration of Walvis Bay into that territory, has not only afforded South Africa the advantage of becoming the twenty-fourth member State of the zone, but also provided a more propitious environment for furthering the objectives of the zone.

4. The Government of South Africa remains committed to the principles and objectives of the Declaration of the third meeting of the States members of the zone of peace and cooperation of the South Atlantic, held in Brazil on 21 and 22 September 1994, and reaffirms its belief in the zone as a veritable instrument for promoting international peace and security as well as development cooperation.

5. As a mark of its commitment, South Africa will be hosting the fourth ministerial meeting of the zone in Cape Town, South Africa, early in 1996.

6. South Africa recognizes the intraregional opportunities for the expansion of trade, investment, cultural, tourism, sporting and other links and wishes to cooperate in these fields in a positive and constructive manner.

7. The zone provides a very important opportunity and framework for promoting the common interests and aspirations of those African and South American States which share the South Atlantic. Such an instrument could also provide impetus and substance to South-South dialogue and cooperation in general.

8. Global developments that have brought an end to the cold war and realigned balances of power, particularly also in the South Atlantic, afford member States a safer environment in which to pursue more relevant and substantive economic, social, environmental and other regional issues, and as a grouping vis-à-vis the rest of the world.

9. These new opportunities should be sought and vigorously pursued. As it will be chairing the next meeting, South Africa will hope to make a meaningful input in this regard.

10. It remains necessary, at the same time, not to become complacent about the many problems that do beset the region and individual Member States. Poverty and deprivation, human rights and asymmetrical development that would benefit all, and not just some, must continue to receive earnest attention. The region is capable of looking to itself for solutions and the necessary political will must be found to establish that beyond dispute.

E. United Kingdom of Great Britain and Northern Ireland

[Original: English]

[9 August 1995]

The Government of the United Kingdom of Great Britain and Northern Ireland welcomes the objectives of General Assembly resolution 49/26 of 2 December 1994, which are to promote peace and cooperation in the South Atlantic. In this regard, the British Government wishes to draw the Secretary-General's attention to developments in Anglo-Argentine relations which have contributed to the lessening of tension in the south-west Atlantic. In particular, cooperation continues in the forum of the South Atlantic Fisheries Commission (contributing to the conservation of stocks), and in the field of military confidence-building measures under the Interim Reciprocal Information and Consultation System. Discussions continue to try to find areas for cooperation over oil exploration around the Falkland Islands (Malvinas), and to enable the removal of land mines left on the Islands following the conflict of 1982.

III. REPLIES RECEIVED FROM ORGANIZATIONS AND BODIES OF THE UNITED NATIONS SYSTEM

A. Department of Public Information

1. The adoption of General Assembly resolution 49/26 was highlighted by the Department's daily news programmes for broadcasting organizations, including the Radio Bulletin Board, and received emphasis in its press release service on 2 December 1994. United Nations information centres and services, particularly those located in the region, publicized the action taken by the General Assembly through their newsletters.

2. From the beginning of December 1994 to the end of June 1995, questions relating to the purposes and objectives of the zone, with particular emphasis on the interrelationship of peace, security and sustainable development, have been the subject of 612 radio magazine and documentary programmes produced altogether in 11 languages and distributed to about 800 broadcasting organizations. During the same period, 506 press releases in English and French on issues pertaining to the resolution, including press coverage of the World Summit for Social Development and of meetings of intergovernmental bodies at Headquarters, have been produced and distributed. A great number of those press releases, as well as relevant background notes, have been transmitted by electronic mail and by pouch to United Nations offices around the world, and through publicly accessible databases and networks such as the Internet.

3. Through newsletters, group briefings, adaptation of information materials produced at Headquarters and other forms of dissemination of information, all United Nations information centres have drawn attention to the efforts of the international community with regard to the establishment of a zone of peace and cooperation of the South Atlantic and its objectives. These activities related to the Vienna Declaration and Programme of Action 5/ adopted by the World Conference on Human Rights on 25 June 1993 to promote human rights, the progress towards the full entry into force of the Treaty for the Prohibition of Nuclear Weapons in Latin America and the Caribbean (Treaty of Tlatelolco), 6/ the implementation of the Declaration on the Denuclearization of Africa, 7/ the United Nations Convention on the Law of the Sea and its importance to the South Atlantic, the Rio Declaration on Environment and Development and Agenda 21, 8/ and the activities of the Organization on achieving a lasting peace and on rendering humanitarian assistance to Angola and Liberia. Within the region addressed by the resolution, special efforts with regard to the objectives of the resolution have been undertaken by the information service in Santiago and the information centres in Accra, Buenos Aires, Dakar, Lagos, Mexico City, Rio de Janeiro, Washington and Windhoek.

4. Nine productions of the United Nations Television series "UN in Action" for broadcasting by over 100 television stations, and six productions of its programme "World Chronicle" for broadcasting by television stations in North America, have been directed to issues with relevance to the resolution. Issues before the World Summit for Social Development were the theme of a 30-minute programme which was aired by major television organizations.

B. Economic Commission for Europe

1. Although the major part of the zone falls outside the geographical scope of the region of the Economic Commission for Europe (ECE), the Commission is offering its cooperation, if needed, in the field of the environment, in which it has developed a number of environmental conventions that could serve as a model for other regional groupings.

2. ECE would like to draw particular attention to the Secretary-General's note to the Economic and Social Council 9/ on a Europe-Africa permanent link through the Strait of Gibraltar and corresponding Council resolution 1993/60 of 30 July 1993. A similar note has been prepared for the forthcoming session of

the Council, outlining the work done on the bridge or tunnel options during the period 1993-1994. ECE has been following this issue since 1982.

C. Economic Commission for Latin America and the Caribbean

1. The activities of the Economic Commission for Latin America and the Caribbean (ECLAC) focused on implementing the recommendations of the meetings of experts on the law of the sea of the States members of the zone, in the framework of the results of the United Nations Conference on Environment and Development.

2. Since there have been no further meetings of its kind since 1991, the ECLAC contribution to the goals of General Assembly resolutions on the subject has been essentially through the transmission of pertinent documentation of its activities in relevant areas such as the United Nations Convention on the Law of the Sea, the Convention on Biological Diversity 10/ and the Basel Convention on the Control of the Transboundary Movement of Hazardous Wastes and their Disposal, 1989. 11/ ECLAC has been sending these documents to Headquarters for submission to the Coordinator of the zone.

3. ECLAC believes that stronger cooperation on environmental affairs in the zone is essential and would like to be informed about technical forums to be convened in the future, as well as about other possible existing channels for information exchange with the newly established Permanent Committee on the Zone of Peace and Cooperation of the South Atlantic. Two specific areas deserve inclusion in cooperation efforts between experts of States members of the zone. The first is the need for cooperation between Africa and Latin America in the control of the illegal traffic of hazardous products and wastes and, in this connection, in the fostering of closer links between the Bamako Convention on the Ban of the Import into Africa and the Control of Transboundary Movement and Management of Hazardous Wastes within Africa, 12/ and the Latin American and Caribbean arrangements. The establishment of regional centres for training and transfer of technology in the field could be another interesting area of cooperation. The second area relates to the need for the preparation of guidelines on the conservation and sustainable use of marine biological diversity. ECLAC convened a meeting in October 1994 to analyse some aspects referring to coastal management in marine and coastal areas of high biodiversity in the Atlantic.

D. United Nations Educational, Scientific and Cultural Organization

1. The United Nations Educational, Scientific and Cultural Organization (UNESCO) and its Intergovernmental Oceanographic Commission (IOC) are working in the South Atlantic through the regional subsidiary body of IOC for the central eastern Atlantic (IOCEA), through Integrated Management of Coastal Systems (COMAR) in Africa and South America, through a subregional programme for the upper south-west Atlantic of Argentina, Brazil and Uruguay, and through the initiation of a programme for the Benguela Current system, including Namibia and South Africa, and possibly other partners in Africa.

2. In this context, South-South cooperation is encouraged. Several activities are carried out jointly with the United Nations Division for Ocean Affairs and the Law of the Sea. IOC has proposed a training centre in West Africa as part of the United Nations/United Nations Development Programme Train-Sea-Coast Programme.

E. World Meteorological Organization

1. Three countries bounding the South Atlantic (Argentina, Brazil and South Africa) accepted international responsibility, under the new WMO marine

Broadcast Systems for the Global Maritime Distress and Safety System of IMO, for the broadcast of meteorological forecasts and warning, via satellite, in support of maritime safety, to specified zones in the South Atlantic. These broadcast services are now operational. The same three countries also accepted provisional responsibility for providing meteorological support services, under the WMO Marine Pollution Emergency Response Support System (MPRESS), for the same zones, for operations in response to marine pollution emergencies on the high seas. Formal trials of the MPRESS are now under way.

2. Following a joint initiative of the WMO/IOC Data Buoy Cooperation Panel and WMO/IOC/United Nations Environment Programme (UNEP)/International Council of Scientific Unions (ICSU) Global Climate Observing System (GCOS), a cooperative international South Atlantic Buoy Programme (ISABP) was formally established in October 1994. The programme groups 12 institutions from six countries with interests in the South Atlantic (Argentina, Brazil, Germany, South Africa, the United Kingdom, and the United States of America), with the objective of maintaining operationally an agreed network of drifting buoys in the South Atlantic, measuring various meteorological and surface oceanographic variables, in support of major programmes of WMO such as the World Weather Watch (WWW) and those implemented jointly with IOC, such as GCOS, the Global Ocean Observing System (GOOS) and the World Climate Research Programme (WCRP). All data from these buoys are distributed globally through the Global Telecommunication System (GTS) of WMO. Technical coordination for ISABP is provided by the South African Weather Bureau.

3. Under the IOC/WMO Integrated Global Ocean Services System (IGOSS), the Argentine navy maintains a specialized oceanographic centre for the collection, processing, archival and delivery, as required, of sub-surface oceanographic data (primarily temperature and salinity) for the South Atlantic.

Notes

1/ A/49/524.

2/ A/49/467, annexes I-V.

3/ Official Records of the Third United Nations Conference on the Law of the Sea, vol. XVII (United Nations publication, Sales No. E.84.V.3), document A/CONF.62/122.

4/ A/49/467.

5/ A/CONF.157/24 (Part I), chap. III.

6/ United Nations, Treaty Series, vol. 634, No. 9068.

7/ Official Records of the General Assembly, Twentieth Session, Annexes, agenda item 105, document A/5975.

8/ See Report of the United Nations Conference on Environment and Development, Rio de Janeiro, 3-14 June 1992, vol. I, Resolutions adopted by the Conference (United Nations publication, Sales No. E.93.I.8 and corrigenda), resolution 1, annex I.

9/ E/1993/80.

10/ See United Nations Environment Programme, Convention on Biological Diversity (Environmental Law and Institutions Programme Activity Centre), June 1992.

11/ International Legal Material, vol. 28, p. 687.

12/ Ibid., vol. 30, 1991 and vol. 31, 1992.

9. FALKLAND ISLANDS (MALVINAS) - WORKING PAPER PREPARED BY THE UN SECRETARIAT

Doc. no.: A/AC.109/2027 & Corr. 1 22 June & 10 July 1995

CONTENTS

FALKLAND ISLANDS (MALVINAS) 1/

I. GENERAL

1. The Falkland Islands (Malvinas), which is administered by the United Kingdom of Great Britain and Northern Ireland, comprises two large islands known as East and West Falkland, as well as some 200 smaller islands, and has a total area of about 12,173 square kilometres. The Territory is situated in the South Atlantic, about 770 kilometres north-east of Cape Horn and about 480 kilometres east of the South American mainland. South Georgia, located about 1,300 kilometres south-east of the Falkland Islands (Malvinas) group, and the South Sandwich Islands, about 750 kilometres east-south-east of South Georgia, are administered from the Falkland Islands (Malvinas) as a separate Territory; the Governor of the Falkland Islands (Malvinas) acts as Commissioner for South Georgia and the South Sandwich Islands.

2. According to the 1991 census, the population of the Territory was 2,121, excluding military personnel and contract workers, but including some expatriate staff in permanent posts. Of the total, 1,643 lived in Stanley, the capital, and its environs and the remainder on farms and in small settlements varying in size from around 30 people to several farms run by only one family. Most settlement communities have fewer than 10 people. In 1980, according to the census of that year, of the 1,813 permanent inhabitants, 1,360 were born in the Territory and about 300 in the United Kingdom.

II. CONSTITUTION AND GOVERNMENT

3. The Constitution of the Falkland Islands (Malvinas), which came into effect on 18 April 1985, vests executive power in a Governor, who is the personal representative of the British monarch, assisted by an Executive Council consisting of the Chief Executive and the Financial Secretary and three members of the Legislative Council chosen by the eight elected members from among themselves. The Chief Executive and Financial Secretary are ex officio members of both councils and have no vote. One of the principal features of the Constitution is the reference in the preamble to the islanders' right to self-determination in conformity with the provisions of the Charter of the United Nations. (For further details, see the 1985 working paper prepared by the Secretariat (A/AC.109/835 and Corr.1, paras. 4-39).)

4. The Territory is divided into two constituencies for electoral purposes: the Stanley Constituency, which comprises the capital and its environs, and the Camp Constituency, made up of the rest of the Territory. There are four elected members for each constituency. All Commonwealth citizens 18 years or older who satisfy the residency requirements are allowed to vote. Elections must be held at intervals not longer than just over four years. The last general election was held in October 1993.

III. POLITICAL DEVELOPMENTS

5. In a letter dated 23 August 1994 and addressed to the Secretary-General, the Permanent Representative of Argentina to the United Nations transmitted the text of a protest note dated 22 August 1994 from the Government of the Argentine Republic to the Government of the United Kingdom of Great Britain and Northern Ireland regarding "the unilateral measure" taken by the United Kingdom of Great Britain and Northern Ireland "extending its alleged maritime jurisdiction" in the waters adjacent to the Falkland Islands (Malvinas). The Permanent Representative of Argentina requested that the note and its annex be circulated as a document of the General Assembly under item 45 of the provisional agenda of the forty-ninth session entitled "Question of the Falkland Islands (Malvinas)", and of the Security Council, and drawn to the attention of the Special Committee on the Situation with regard to the Implementation of the Declaration on the Granting of Independence to Colonial Countries and Peoples (A/49/334-S/1994/988).

6. The text of the note was as follows:

"The Ministry of Foreign Affairs, International Trade and Worship presents its compliments to the Embassy of the United Kingdom of Great Britain and Northern Ireland and refers to the unilateral British decision to extend its alleged jurisdiction over the maritime space west of and adjacent to the area described in the annex to the Joint Statement of 28 November 1990.

"The Argentine Government registers its most serious protest and rejection of that measure which involves maritime spaces adjacent to Argentine national territory, and does not accept the attempt to extend the dispute over sovereignty to an undisputed area.

"In the maritime space in which the United Kingdom seeks to extend its alleged jurisdiction, the Argentine Republic has exercised, exercises and will continue to exercise sovereign rights, particularly in respect of the administration and control of fisheries.

"The British action implies a departure from the Joint Statement and the bilateral understandings reached from 1990 until now regarding the South-West Atlantic.

"Furthermore, the action of the United Kingdom disregards the General Assembly resolutions which call on the parties to the dispute to find a solution to the controversy regarding sovereignty over the Malvinas, South Georgia and South Sandwich islands by means of negotiations and which call upon the two parties 'to refrain from taking decisions that would imply introducing unilateral modifications in the situation' (General Assembly resolution 31/49 of 1976).

"The Argentine Government reserves the right to raise the question of the serious situation deriving from the measure adopted by the British Government in the competent international forums, particularly the General Assembly of the United Nations.

"Without prejudice thereto, and in exercise of its jurisdiction over the said area, the Argentine Government will continue to administer and exploit the living marine resources in that zone, and to monitor and control the activities carried out therein, for the better conservation of the resources.

"Furthermore, the Argentine Government considers that unilateral decisions of this nature interfere with the maintenance and possible deepening of the bilateral understandings on fisheries, with negative consequences for the conservation of the living marine resources in the South-West Atlantic.

"Consequently, the Argentine Government urges the British Government to refrain from putting the measure into effect and from any unilateral act in the area in question so as to permit the continuation of the fruitful cooperation achieved thus far."

7. In a letter dated 26 August 1994 and addressed to the Secretary-General, the Permanent Representative of the United Kingdom of Great Britain and Northern Ireland to the United Nations transmitted the text of the note of the same date from his Government in response to the note from the Government of the Argentine Republic. The Permanent Representative of the United Kingdom of Great Britain and Northern Ireland requested that the letter and its annex be circulated as a document of the General Assembly, under item 45 of the provisional agenda, and of the Security Council (A/49/341-S/1994/1005).

8. The text of the note was as follows:

"The British Embassy presents its compliments to the Ministry of Foreign Affairs, International Trade and Worship, and with reference to the latter's note of 22 August 1994 (A/49/334, annex) has the honour, on instructions, to state the following in response.

"The United Kingdom has no doubts about its sovereignty over the Falkland Islands and its consequential right to extend maritime jurisdiction around the Territory in accordance with the rules of international law. Accordingly, the Embassy is instructed to reject the protest contained in the Ministry's note.

"The Embassy does not accept the statement in the Ministry's note that 'the Argentine Republic has exercised, exercises and will continue to exercise sovereign rights, particularly in the matter of administration and control of fishing activities' in the area lying to the west of and adjacent to the area described in the annex to the Joint Statement of 28 November 1990. The United Kingdom does not recognize Argentine jurisdiction over the area, which lies within 200 miles of the Falkland Islands and more than 200 miles from Argentine baselines.

"In regard to the reference in the Ministry's note to resolutions of the General Assembly of the United Nations about the Falkland Islands, the position of the British Government on these resolutions is well known and remains unchanged.

"The United Kingdom has taken action to include certain waters which are within 200 miles of Falkland Islands baselines into the Falkland Islands outer conservation zone to prevent the continuation of uncontrolled fishing taking place in that area to the prejudice of the stocks of fish and, in particular, of illex squid. Argentina's well-known concerns about uncontrolled fishing in the South-West Atlantic are shared by the United Kingdom.

"The United Kingdom remains interested in cooperating with Argentina on measures to ensure the effective conservation of the living marine resources in the South-West Atlantic."

9. In August 1994, the National Congress of Argentina revised the text of the country's Constitution and included, inter alia, a transitory provision which reaffirmed Argentina's rights to the Falkland Islands (Malvinas) and stated that, in recovering those rights, respect for international law and the way of life of the population of the Islands should be paramount. 2/

10. In response to the above action, the Embassy of the United Kingdom of Great Britain and Northern Ireland in Buenos Aires presented a note dated 30 August 1994 to the Ministry of Foreign Affairs, International Trade and Worship of Argentina. The text of the note was as follows:

"Her Britannic Majesty's Embassy presents its compliments to the Ministry of Foreign Affairs, International Trade and Worship - Malvinas and South Atlantic Division - and has the honour to inform the Ministry that the Government of the United Kingdom of Great Britain and Northern Ireland have become aware of the decision of the Argentine Constituent Assembly to approve a revised Constitution which includes a clause purporting to claim sovereignty over the Falkland Islands, South Georgia and the South Sandwich Islands and their surrounding maritime areas.

"The United Kingdom has no doubt about its sovereignty over, and maritime jurisdiction and rights in respect of, the Falkland Islands, South Georgia and the South Sandwich Islands. Consequently, the Embassy are instructed to reject the Argentine claim in the revised Constitution to sovereignty over these territories and wish to protest formally at the renewed assertion of this claim.

"As regards the reference in the revised Constitution to the inhabitants of the Falkland Islands, the Government of the United Kingdom recall the manifested strongly held wish of the Falkland Islanders to remain British." 3/

11. A poll conducted in November 1994 on the islands by the internationally recognized public opinion organization MORI and paid for by Argentine businessmen has shown that the overwhelming majority of islanders were opposed to any negotiation with Argentina over sovereignty and to any idea of accepting payment in return for a transfer of sovereignty to Argentina. 4/

12. In his Christmas message to the people of the Falkland Islands (Malvinas), the Prime Minister of the United Kingdom of Great Britain and Northern Ireland, inter alia, confirmed that the policy of his Government in defending the rights of the islanders was both "just and essential" and that the Government would "not be diverted from that course"; that the islanders had "the right to be governed under the flag of their own choice" and the Government would "continue to uphold that right"; that the recent opinion poll conducted in the islands "made clear the very strong feelings" that the islanders had on this subject and that the Government's feelings were "no less firm". 5/

13. In his article on the Falkland Islands (Malvinas) published in December 1994, the Secretary of State for Foreign and Commonwealth Affairs, Mr. Douglas Hurd, concluded that the question of sovereignty of the Falkland Islands was in effect settled. In his view, the islanders would not accept Argentine rule, and no one would in practice force it on them. As regards the contacts between the islanders and Argentina, Mr. Hurd believed that was a matter that the islanders would have to work out for themselves and that the British Government would not lean on them to enter into contacts that they suspected or disliked. In conclusion, Mr. Hurd wrote that, because of what had happened in 1982, the British commitment to the Falkland Islands had from time to time to be restated. 6/

14. On 3 January 1995, the Government of Argentina issued the following statement: 7/

"Today being the one hundred sixty-second anniversary of the illegitimate British occupation of the Malvinas Islands, the Argentine people and Government once again reaffirm Argentina's sovereign rights over the Malvinas Islands, the South Georgia Islands, the South Sandwich Islands and the surrounding seas.

"The Argentine Government reiterates that it remains determined to resume exercising its sovereign rights through negotiations leading to a just and final solution of this territorial dispute and stresses that it proposes to continue moving ahead in the dialogue with the United Kingdom in order to build strong relationship of mutual trust and cooperation in the South-West Atlantic.

"At the same time, the Argentine Government reiterates its willingness to engage in dialogue and cooperation with the inhabitants of the Malvinas Islands and to safeguard their interests and well-being. This position is upheld by the new Constitutional text which, in its first transitory provision, establishes recovery of these territories and full exercise of sovereignty, while respecting the inhabitants' way of life and in accordance with the principles of international law, as a permanent and absolute objective of the Argentine people."

15. On 22 March 1995, during the debate on the Falkland Islands in the House of Commons, the Minister of State, Foreign and Commonwealth Office, summarized his Government's policy towards the Falkland Islands as follows: once the Argentines accepted that the islanders were British and had their own right to self-determination, relations [with Argentina] could be built on a normal basis; the islanders were not a transitory population, they had been there without interruption since 1833 and had chosen throughout all that time to remain under the British flag; assertions that the Falklands would become Argentine were highly objectionable to his Government and the islanders and they rejected them and would continue to do so at every opportunity; his Government cooperated with Argentina in many areas and agreements had been signed on visa abolition, cultural cooperation, investment protection and promotion, antinarcotics and air services; his Government had no doubt about the sovereignty of the Falklands and the right of self-determination involved respecting the wishes of the people of the Falklands; his Government was committed to the defence of the islands, and, finally, his Government was actively helping the islanders to benefit from prospective oil and gas resources. 8/

IV. MINE CLEARING

16. As noted in the previous working paper prepared by the Secretariat (A/AC.109/1198, para. 35), the Argentine Government offered the United Kingdom to clear the mines laid in the Falkland Islands (Malvinas) during the conflict of 1982. In July 1994, the Argentine Government and the Government of the United Kingdom of Great Britain and Northern Ireland presented notes to the Government of the United States of America, requesting its cooperation to carry forward the bidding process on the projects of mine clearing and to take necessary steps in order to guarantee the effective removal of mines. The Government of the United States responded positively to this request in August of that year by specifying modalities of the bidding process. As of the time of preparation of the present paper, a regular exchange between the Argentine Government and that of the United States has been taking place in order to arrange the details of the operation and its financing.

V. ECONOMIC CONDITIONS

A. General

17. Detailed information on developments in the economy of the Falkland Islands (Malvinas) is provided in the previous working paper prepared by the Secretariat (A/AC.109/1198, paras. 38-42).

B. Agriculture, land tenure and livestock

18. Detailed information on developments in the field of agriculture, land tenure and livestock is provided in the previous working paper (A/AC.109/1198, paras. 43-46).

C. Fisheries

19. Detailed information under this section is provided in the previous working paper (A/AC.109/1198, paras. 47-55).

20. The tenth meeting of the South Atlantic Fisheries Commission took place in London on 5 and 6 June 1995. The text of the joint communiqué is reproduced below:

"1. The Tenth Meeting of the South Atlantic Fisheries Commission took place in London on 5 and 6 June 1995. The British delegation was led by the head of the South Atlantic and Antarctic Department, Mr. Tony Longrigg, and the Argentine delegation by the head of the Malvinas and South Atlantic Department, Minister Luis Mendiola.

"2. The British and Argentine delegations agreed that there applied to this meeting and its consequences the formula on sovereignty over the Falkland Islands, South Georgia and the South Sandwich Islands and the surrounding maritime areas agreed by the British and Argentine Governments in paragraph 2 of the Joint Statement issued in Madrid on 19 October 1989.

"3. The South Atlantic Fisheries Commission welcomed the report of the Scientific Subcommittee on its fifth meeting which was held in London on 1 and 2 June 1995.

"4. The delegations agreed that they attached fundamental importance and the greatest priority to conserving the various species in the fisheries, most notably illex and blue whiting, on the basis of the best available scientific advice. They welcomed the cooperation between INIDEP and Imperial College and encouraged the scientists to maintain and develop their consultations further. They recommended to their Governments that the early warning system should be improved so that the scientists could provide a joint assessment without delay. They agreed that INIDEP and Imperial College should discuss this with a view to making recommendations on this issue to the next meeting of the South Atlantic Fisheries Commission.

"5. The delegations welcomed the positive experience of the joint research cruises carried out in 1993, 1994 and 1995. They confirmed that preparations would be made for a joint blue whiting cruise in the second half of 1995 and for a joint illex pre-recruit survey in February 1996. The Commission noted the recommendation of the Scientific Subcommittee that additional research on blue whiting was urgently needed, and agreed that the planning of the blue whiting cruise would be the subject of early consultation between INIDEP and Imperial College.

"6. Both delegations welcomed the procedures under the rapid communications system, which they agreed was working well.

"7. The Commission noted with concern illegal activities of fishing vessels in the South-West Atlantic and agreed to continue cooperation, including an intensified exchange of information, to curtail such activities.

"8. The delegations discussed the conservation of migratory and straddling stocks and species related to them in international waters - in accordance with paragraph 4 (d) of the Joint Statement of 28 November 1990 - and the work of the United Nations Conference on Straddling Fish Stocks and Highly Migratory Fish Stocks. They agreed to discuss the issue further at the next meeting of the South Atlantic Fisheries Commission.

"9. The Commission noted that 'the Subcommittee encouraged scientists from the delegations to submit joint publications to international scientific journals based on some of the joint scientific work carried out'. The two delegations agreed that the formula on sovereignty referred to in paragraph 2 above would apply to all such joint publications.

"10. The Commission agreed to meet again in Buenos Aires in November 1995.

"11. The meeting took place in a warm and friendly atmosphere." 9/

21. The Territory's fishing sector is based on the sale of licences to vessels fishing for squid and other species in the Falkland Islands conservation zones. A zone, with a radius of 150 miles, was established by the administering Power with effect from 1 February 1987 and involves a licensing regime under which the number of fishing vessels and therefore the total catch is limited. On 26 December 1990 a further Falklands Outer Conservation Zone, extending to 200 miles, was established. In August 1994, the administering Power extended the Outer Conservation Zone to its full 200-mile limit, to the west of and adjacent to the area described in the annex to the joint statement of 28 November 1990. Argentina protested this action (see paras. 5 and 6 above), and the United Kingdom rejected that protest (see paras. 7 and 8 above).

22. In November 1994, a total of 220 applications for 1995 season fishing licences were received by the Fisheries Department of the Falkland Islands (Malvinas). Of that number 49 were applications for long-term licences. These applications were assessed against the points system, which is part of the policy adopted recently by the Fisheries Department. The objective of the policy is to give emphasis to the participation by the Territory's residents in fishing activities within the Falklands conservation zones and the creation of a fishing industry within the islands' private sector. 10/

23. Among the countries licensed to fish in the islands' waters during 1995 are Belize, Chile, France, Honduras, Italy, Japan, the Republic of Korea, Panama, Poland, Portugal and Spain.

24. In order to preserve the illex squid stocks to the south of the 45th parallel, the United Kingdom decided to close the illex fishing season as early as 20 May 1995; Argentina did so as early as 4 June 1995. Both countries employed again the mechanism of "early warning" agreed upon at the seventh meeting of the South Atlantic Fisheries Commission.

D. Industry and tourism

25. Detailed information on industrial developments and tourism sector is provided in the previous working paper (A/AC.109/1198, paras. 56-59).

E. Oil

26. Detailed information on developments in the field of oil exploration is provided in the previous working paper (A/AC.109/1198, paras. 60-64).

27. In early October 1994, the British press reported that British Gas and the recently privatized Argentine petroleum company YPF had expressed interest in forming a joint venture to search for oil in the islands' waters. According to the information provided to the Secretariat by the Permanent Mission of Argentina to the United Nations, the Argentine Government warned the oil companies interested in the area through "letters of discomfort", about the administrative and legal consequences of their activities in the disputed areas, should they not have the proper authorization of the Argentine Government.

28. In response to above press reports, on 15 October 1994, the Falkland Islands (Malvinas) Government published the following press release: 11/

> "The Falkland Islands Government welcomes the reported interest of British Gas/YPF in the development of any oil reserves which may be discovered around the Falkland Islands. So far the Falkland Islands Government has received no approach from the proposed consortium."

29. By publishing on 22 October 1994 a special supplement to Penguin News entitled "Oil and the Falklands" the territorial Government launched a programme of public relations and dissemination of information on oil matters directed to the islands' inhabitants before enacting the Offshore Minerals Bill (1994). The bill was scheduled for discussion by the Legislative Council in late October 1994.

30. On 27 October 1994, the Legislative Council passed the bill, which provided the basic legal framework for the exploration for oil around the Falkland Islands (Malvinas) and for exploiting oil if the search was successful. In its essentials, the bill allows the Government to grant licences to explore and exploit offshore and gives the Government powers over the operation; provides for health and safety regulations in the offshore industry; deals with underwater pipelines and procedures for the decommission of equipment; and provides for environmental impact control by the Government. 12/

31. In early February 1995, representatives of the United Kingdom and Argentina held a two-day meeting in Buenos Aires to study the possibility of cooperating in oil exploitation in the South Atlantic. The delegations released a declaration at the end of the meeting stressing the "reasonably positive" nature of the dialogue. 13/

F. Energy, transport and communications

32. Detailed information under this section is provided in the previous working paper (A/AC.109/1198, paras. 65-70).

33. According to the information provided to the Secretariat by the Permanent Mission of Argentina to the United Nations, its Government considers that the re-establishment of communications between the mainland and the Falkland Islands (Malvinas) would contribute to a better understanding among the inhabitants of the whole region, as well as in a very meaningful way, to the development of the trade and the economy. It is also trying, in the interests of the islanders, to facilitate as much as possible the establishment of sea and air links between the Islands and the Argentine mainland or neighbouring countries.

G. Banking

34. The Standard Chartered Bank of the United Kingdom opened a branch at Stanley in 1983. Both United Kingdom and local coinage are used, together with local currency notes of £20, £10 and £5 values.

35. According to the local press reports, two banks in the United Kingdom expressed interest in operating in the Territory. 14/

H. Public finance and international trade

36. Detailed information under this section is provided in the previous working paper (A/AC.109/1198, paras. 72-77).

37. According to the information provided to the Secretariat by the Permanent Mission of Argentina to the United Nations, its Government favours the

re-establishment and normalization of trade between the Falkland Islands (Malvinas) and the Argentine mainland.

VI. SOCIAL AND EDUCATIONAL CONDITIONS

38. Detailed information under this section is provided in the previous working paper (A/AC.109/1198, paras. 78-97).

VII. PARTICIPATION IN INTERNATIONAL ORGANIZATIONS AND ARRANGEMENTS

39. The Government of the Falkland Islands (Malvinas) participates in activities of the Commonwealth. It also takes part in the work of multilateral organizations concerned with exploitation and preservation of marine resources in the South Atlantic.

40. In January 1995, for the first time in its history, the Government of the Falkland Islands (Malvinas) hosted a Commonwealth Parliamentary Association Seminar which was attended by representatives of the United Kingdom and its dependent territories as well as nations of the Mediterranean region. Among the participants were representatives of the Falkland Islands (Malvinas), Malta, the Isle of Man, Guernsey, Gibraltar, Jersey and St. Helena. 15/

VIII. CONSIDERATION BY OTHER INTERGOVERNMENTAL ORGANIZATIONS

Organization of American States

41. At its twenty-fifth regular session, held at Montrouis, Haiti, from 6 to 9 June 1995, the General Assembly of the Organization of American States, taking into account the fact that, on numerous occasions, it had declared that the question of the Malvinas Islands constituted a question of permanent hemispheric interest and recalling its resolution AG/Res.928 (XVIII-0/88), adopted by consensus, requesting Argentina and the United Kingdom to resume negotiations in order to find, as soon as possible, a peaceful solution to the sovereignty dispute, expressed its satisfaction at the reaffirmation by the Government of Argentina of its willingness to continue to explore all possible avenues for a peaceful solution of the controversy, particularly its positive consideration regarding the inhabitants of the Malvinas Islands. The Assembly decided to continue to examine the question at its future sessions until it was definitively solved.

IX. FUTURE STATUS OF THE TERRITORY

A. Special Committee on the Situation with regard to the Implementation of the Declaration on the Granting of Independence to Colonial Countries and Peoples

42. The Special Committee considered the question of the Falkland Islands (Malvinas) at its 1431st and 1433rd meetings on 11 and 12 July 1994, when it had before it a working paper on developments concerning the Territory prepared by the Secretariat (A/AC.109/1198).

43. The Special Committee granted requests for hearing petitioners and, at its 1433rd meeting, heard statements by four petitioners (A/AC.109/PV.1433).

44. The representative of Venezuela introduced, on behalf also of Chile and Cuba, draft resolution A/AC.109/L.1819.

45. Following statements by the representatives of Tunisia and Papua New Guinea, the Committee adopted draft resolution A/AC.109/L.1819 without a vote. Statements in explanation of position were made by the representatives of Fiji and Sierra Leone (A/AC.109/PV.1433). The representative of Cuba made a statement (A/AC.109/PV.1433).

46. At the same meeting, the Minister for Foreign Affairs of Argentina made a statement (A/AC.109/PV.1433), in which he said that the Malvinas Islands constituted part of the territory of Argentina, and their recovery was a constant and unforsakable cause for the entire Argentine people and that his Government would continue to carry out diplomatic efforts in all forums until such time as the restitution of those territories had been achieved (for the full text of the statement see A/AC.109/PV.1433).

47. On 21 July 1994, the text of the resolution (A/AC.109/2003) was transmitted to the Permanent Representatives of the United Kingdom of Great Britain and Northern Ireland and of Argentina to the United Nations for the attention of their respective Governments.

B. General Assembly

Position of the Government of Argentina

48. During the general debate of the forty-ninth session of the General Assembly, the President of the Argentine Republic, in the course of his statement on 27 September 1994 (A/49/PV.6), reaffirmed the position of his Government that Argentina had well-founded and unequivocal sovereign rights over the Malvinas and over South Georgia and the South Sandwich Islands. He emphasized that in 1994 that claim took on special meaning, since the Argentine people, through their representatives in the National Congress, had reformed the supreme law of the country, giving constitutional status to the question of the islands by including, in the new text of the Constitution, a transitory provision that reaffirmed their rights and stated that, in recovering those rights, respect for international law and the way of life of the population of the islands should be paramount.

Position of the United Kingdom of Great Britain and Northern Ireland

49. Speaking during the general debate at the forty-ninth session of the General Assembly (A/49/PV.8) and in response to the remarks of the President of Argentina, the Secretary of State for Foreign and Commonwealth Affairs of the United Kingdom of Great Britain and Northern Ireland reiterated that his Government was quite clear about British sovereignty over the Falkland Islands and the other British dependencies in the South Atlantic and so it was concerned at the recent incorporation into the Constitution of Argentina of the new clause to which the President of the Argentine Republic had referred. Noting the difference with Argentina over that issue, he stated at the same time that his Government had joined a dialogue with the Argentine Government on fisheries and petroleum development and looked forward to resuming discussions in the near future with the Argentine authorities on a new agreement on fishing and on the development of possible hydrocarbon resources in the South Atlantic continental shelf.

Contributions by other member States

50. During the debate in the Special Political and Decolonization Committee (Fourth Committee) of the General Assembly, the representative of Brazil made a statement on behalf of the Rio Group (A/C.4/49/SR.5), in which he said, inter alia, that, in the Latin American region, the members of the Rio Group were confident that the improved relations between Argentina and the United Kingdom would permit a peaceful solution to the long-standing dispute over the Malvinas, South Georgia and the South Sandwich Islands. Speaking in exercise of

the right of reply (A/C.4/49/SR.5), the representative of the United Kingdom and Northern Ireland said that the representative of Brazil, speaking on behalf of the Rio Group earlier in the meeting, had expressed the wish for a solution to be found to the sovereignty dispute over the Falklands, South Georgia and the South Sandwich Islands. The position of the United Kingdom Government on those matters was well known. It had been most recently set out by the Foreign Secretary in his speech to the General Assembly on 28 September 1994 (A/49/PV.8).

51. On 3 November 1994, at its 50th meeting, the General Assembly, taking into account its decision 48/408 of 16 November 1993, decided to defer consideration of the question of the Falkland Islands (Malvinas) and to include it in the provisional agenda of its fiftieth session (A/49/PV.50).

Notes

1/ The information contained in the present paper is based on official documents of the Governments of Argentina and the United Kingdom of Great Britain and Northern Ireland, information provided by the Permanent Missions of the two States to the United Nations and published reports.

2/ See A/49/PV.6.

3/ Text of the note by the British Embassy in Buenos Aires (photocopy), 30 August 1994.

4/ Penguin News (Stanley), 17 and 24 December 1994.

5/ Text of the Falklands Christmas Message (photocopy), 30 December 1994.

6/ Falkland Islands Newsletter (London), December 1994, pp. 2-3.

7/ Text of press communiqué (photocopy), 3 January 1995.

8/ United Kingdom, House of Commons, Official Report, Parliamentary Debates (Hansard), 22 March 1995, pp. 280-284.

9/ Tenth meeting of the South Atlantic Fisheries Commission: London, 5-6 June 1995 (photocopy).

10/ Penguin News, 19 November 1994.

11/ Penguin News, 15 October 1994.

12/ Penguin News, 22 and 29 October 1994.

13/ Foreign Broadcast Information Service, FBIS-LAT-95-024, 6 February 1995.

14/ Penguin News, 18 February 1995.

15/ Penguin News, 21 January 1995.

Corrigendum

Paragraph 50, sixth line

For long-standing dispute read long-standing sovereignty dispute

-----

10. LETTER DATED 31 MARCH 1995 FROM THE PERMANENT REPRESENTATIVE OF SPAIN TO THE UNITED NATIONS ADDRESSED TO THE SECRETARY-GENERAL*

Doc. no.: A/50/98-S/1995/252 31 March 1995

On instructions from my Government, I have the honour to inform you that in recent weeks situations of tension have occurred on the high seas in the north-west Atlantic between fishing vessels flying the Spanish flag and Canadian patrol boats, and that these have involved the use of force on the part of the latter.

In particular, I wish to refer to the fact that on 9 March 1995 the fishing vessel Estai, flying the Spanish flag, was arrested in international waters by Canadian patrol boats using armed force. Both the fishing boat and the crew were taken to the port of St. John's, where they were detained until their subsequent release on bail. It should be emphasized that when paying the bail, the owner of the detained vessel made an explicit statement of non-recognition of the jurisdiction of the Canadian courts.

Subsequent to these incidents, various acts of harassment by Canadian patrol boats of Spanish fishing vessels operating on the high seas have taken place, including a serious incident on 26 March in which the nets of the Spanish fishing vessel Pescamar 1 were deliberately cut by a Canadian patrol boat.

These actions, which constitute a flagrant violation by Canada of international law and of the Charter of the United Nations, have caused serious harm to Spanish citizens and in some cases have endangered their lives and physical integrity, a situation to which the Spanish Government has reacted by immediately making the relevant protests through the diplomatic channel, while fully reserving its rights and its claim to the corresponding compensation for the damage and injury sustained.

As an additional means of defending its nationals, the Spanish Government has decided to send two units of the Spanish Navy to the area where the incidents took place to protect Spanish vessels engaging in their activities under the protection of the principle of freedom of the high seas and in conformity with the applicable regulations established by the competent international organizations.

In addition, as part of the Spanish Government's firm intention to resolve international disputes by peaceful means in accordance with the provisions of

* A/50/50.

the Charter of the United Nations, on 28 March 1995 Spain filed the relevant complaint against Canada with the International Court of Justice, seeking its ruling and the restoration of the rights violated.

I should be grateful if you would have this letter circulated as a document of the General Assembly, under items 39 and 98 (c) of the preliminary list, and of the Security Council.

(Signed) Juan A. YAÑEZ-BARNUEVO

11. LETTER DATED 9 JUNE 1995 FROM THE PERMANENT REPRESENTATIVE OF GREECE TO THE UNITED NATIONS ADDRESSED TO THE SECRETARY-GENERAL*

Doc. no.: A/50/216-S/1995/476 12 June 1995

Upon instructions of my Government and referring to the resolution adopted yesterday, 8 June 1995, by the Turkish National Assembly through which it transfers to the Turkish Government its competences, including those that will be deemed necessary, from a military point of view, for the maintenance and the defence of the vital interests of Turkey if Greece implements the Convention on the Law of the Sea, which the Greek Parliament ratified last week, I would like to bring the following to your attention.

It is beyond any doubt that the above-mentioned resolution constitutes a direct violation of article 2, paragraph 4, of the Charter of the United Nations, which stipulates that "all Members shall refrain in their international relations from the threat or use of force against the territorial integrity or political independence of any State", as well as of many similar provisions of international treaties and conventions. What Turkey is in fact attempting to do is to intimidate Greece into forfeiting a right acknowledged to all signatory parties, by article 3 of the 1982 Convention on the Law of the Sea, and already exercised by a large number of States.

It is not the first time that Turkey flagrantly violates international law. It should be noted however that this time the contempt of international lawderives from the legislative body of a country which, having already been charged with past and recent violations of international law, is seeking closer political and economic cooperation with the democratic countries of the European Union.

The Greek Government attaches a particular importance to the Turkish threat, all the more so since the latter emanates from a neighbouring and allied country and is not, obviously, intended to prevent the commitment of an illegal act, but, on the contrary, to prevent the implementation of rules and rights deriving from international law.

The argument contained in the said resolution, namely that the legal status of the Aegean Sea has been defined by the Treaty of Lausanne of 1923 and that an eventual decision of the Greek side to extend its national territorial waters to 12 miles would reverse this status, is totally unfounded, since the rights of the coastal countries are defined by the international law of the sea, both conventional and customary.

---

* A/50/50/Rev.1.

Moreover, the Turkish allegation regarding the obstruction of the freedom of navigation in the Aegean Sea is also unfounded, since Greece has always made clear that it does not intend to deprive ships of other nations of their right of innocent passage, in conformity with international law.

In the same context, it should be noted that Turkey, contrary to the provisions of the Montreaux Convention of 1936 on the Status of the Straits, has recently adopted domestic legislation, imposing serious restrictions on the freedom of navigation through the straits.

The fact that the Turkish National Assembly has decided to transfer to the Turkish Government its above-mentioned competences confirms very clearly the well-known Turkish claims against the Greek islands of the Aegean and the sovereign rights of Greece regarding its national territorial waters and airspace.

It should be underlined that the said resolution of the Turkish National Assembly is only one of a series of recent Turkish provocative acts that lead to the conclusion that Turkey is seeking the deterioration of Greek-Turkish relations, thus creating dangerous implications for peace and stability in the region.

In the light of the above, a comparison of the difference in mentality between the two countries is inevitable, since Turkey's target seems to be the deterioration of the political climate in the Balkans, while Greece is undertaking serious and difficult initiatives in an effort to restore peace in the same area.

In concluding, I would like to reiterate the official position of the Greek Government that Greece intends to exercise its right to extend its territorial waters up to 12 miles, in accordance with international law, when this is considered appropriate.

I would like to request that this letter be circulated as a document of the General Assembly under items 39, 75 and 81 of the preliminary list, and of the Security Council.

(Signed) Christos G. ZACHARAKIS
Permanent Representative

12. LETTER DATED 21 JUNE 1995 FROM THE PERMANENT REPRESENTATIVE OF TURKEY TO THE UNITED NATIONS ADDRESSED TO THE SECRETARY-GENERAL*

Doc. no.: A/50/256-S/1995/505 23 June 1995

With reference to the letter of the Permanent Representative of Greece circulated as a document of the General Assembly and of the Security Council (A/50/216-S/1995/476), I have the honour, upon instructions of my Government, to bring to your attention a potentially serious situation with respect to the issue of territorial sea in the Aegean and to represent Turkey's position in this regard.

The Greek Parliament has recently ratified the 1982 Law of the Sea Convention. The statements of Greek government officials, as reported in the Greek press, and confirmed by the aforementioned letter, indicate that Greece intends to extend the breadth of its territorial sea in the Aegean from the present 6 miles to 12 miles. As stated by Greek officials, this decision will be taken at the appropriate time in accordance with the Greek "national strategy".

The issue of the maritime jurisdiction areas in the Aegean and the breadth of the territorial sea in this context is a serious matter that requires careful consideration. The elements involved should be considered in their proper context based on facts and be put under objective analysis. It is regrettable that the Greek letter at reference represents an attempt to distort and misrepresent the well-known position of Turkey on this issue and the underlying legitimate reasons, in connection with the recent declaration adopted by the Turkish Grand National Assembly.

The purpose of this letter is to set the record straight in this regard.

Turkey and Greece have a number of bilateral disputes concerning the Aegean Sea. These differences essentially involve the status quo in the Aegean as determined by the relevant international treaties and instruments, particularly the 1923 Lausanne peace treaty.

Turkey attaches vital importance to the maintenance of the status quo in the Aegean with respect to maritime jurisdiction areas. In this context, the breadth of the territorial sea is the cardinal element of the delicate balance of rights and interests of the two neighbouring countries in the Aegean.

---

* A/50/50/Rev.1.

Turkey and Greece both have basic rights and legitimate interests in the Aegean involving their security, economy, navigation and other traditional uses of the high seas. The two countries have commonly used the Aegean for these purposes in accordance with international law. This has been one of the fundamental elements of the Aegean status quo.

The Greek perception laying claim to the whole of the Aegean Sea and its consistent attempts to alter the status in total disregard of Turkey's rights and interests lie at the heart of the bilateral disputes in the Aegean.

The Aegean is a narrow, semi-enclosed sea with the most peculiar geographical features. The special circumstances are unusual and exceptional. With its complex and singular structure, the Aegean is a unique sea. In view of this, the issue of the territorial sea may not be considered in isolation from the unique features of the Aegean.

Under the present 6-mile territorial sea limit of both countries, Greece, owing to the existence of numerous islands, possesses approximately 43.5 per cent of the Aegean. Turkey's share is 7.5 per cent. The remaining half of the Aegean is high seas, which is freely used by Turkey and the international community in accordance with international law.

Any extension of the Greek territorial sea beyond 6 miles will transform the Aegean virtually into a Greek lake. Greek sovereignty would be extended over the present high seas, the international airspace as well the continental shelf, which remains a disputed area yet to be delimited between Turkey and Greece.

Thus Turkey, with a long coastline in the Aegean measured in thousands of miles, will be locked out of this sea. The Turkish coasts will be encircled by Greek territorial waters and Turkey will be virtually cut off from the high seas.

The consequences of the extension of the Greek territorial sea, in essence, are not limited to the internationally recognized navigational rights and freedoms as has been presented by Greece.

As a result, almost all the Aegean Sea, with its seabed, superjacent waters and airspace, will automatically fall under Greek sovereignty and jurisdiction.

The Greek letter in reference conveniently remains silent on this score and instead refers to the right of "innocent passage" under international law, as if what is involved here solely concerned the right of navigation.

Greece cites article 3 of the 1982 Law of the Sea Convention as the basis of its right to extend its territorial sea. This argument has no valid basis.

In the first place, Turkey is not a party to the said Convention. Secondly, it may be worthwhile to recall that Turkey has consistently maintained its objection to a 12-mile limit for the breadth of the territorial sea in the context of semi-enclosed seas where special circumstances prevail. Therefore, it is obvious that the 12-mile limit could not be opposable to Turkey as a rule that acquired the character of customary law, in the special case of the Aegean. Thirdly, the 12-mile limit envisaged in article 3 is neither compulsory nor a limit to be applied automatically. It is a maximum permissible breadth that may be applied, as the circumstances permit, within the limitation imposed by the general principle of international law as embodied in article 300 of the Convention, namely the obligation to exercise rights in a manner that would not constitute an abuse of right.

In this context, it is worth recalling the recent statement made by Greek European Affairs Minister, George Mangakis, in connection with the ratification of the Law of the Sea Convention. The Athens News Agency bulletin of

1 June 1995 quoted Minister Mangakis as stating that "the Convention was truly of national importance, as it provided the country (Greece) with a weapon in the defence of its rights and national interests". The statement speaks for itself. This is incontestable proof of how Greece perceives the issue of territorial sea.

It was against this background that the Grand National Assembly of Turkey adopted the declaration in question. It was an expression of the legitimate concerns of Turkey in the face of Greek designs on the Aegean.

The Greek letter contains certain inappropriate references in depicting the respective policies and practices of Turkey and Greece. These assertions call for a brief and factual reply.

First, it is alleged that there have been other occasions of violation of international law by Turkey. It is an irony that Greece raises the issue of respect for international law. The Greek attitude and its reluctance in cooperation against terrorism; the illegal Greek claim for 10-mile airspace beyond its 6-mile territorial sea, which is not recognized by the international community; and the militarization of certain islands in the Aegean contrary to its contractual obligations under international treaties that placed these islands under demilitarized status are outstanding examples of the ostensible Greek claim for respect for international law and legality.

It is also claimed that Greece has a peaceful posture in the Balkans in contrast to the alleged policy orientation of Turkey aimed at the deterioration of the political climate in the Balkan region.

The Greek contribution to peace and stability in the Balkans is manifested by the Greek stand in the ongoing Bosnian tragedy; by the imposition of the illegal embargo against the Republic of Macedonia; and by its hostile policy towards its two neighbours, Albania and Macedonia.

The letter of the Greek Permanent Representative repeats once again the unfounded allegation that Turkey has claims against the Greek islands. This is simply not true. Turkey harbours no designs or territorial ambitions against Greece or any of its neighbours.

Turkey is fully committed to the peaceful settlement of the whole range of disputes through dialogue and negotiations in a spirit of mutual understanding and accommodation. The two neighbours have a vast community of interests in defusing tensions and creating conditions that would ensure the development of friendship. Turkey still awaits a positive response of Greece to its repeated calls for charting such a new course in bilateral relations. This will not only serve the best interests of the two nations, but will also contribute to peace and stability in the region.

Greece, however, seems determined to pursue a different course. It is the declared intention of Greece to retain the threat of unilateral extension of territorial sea in the Aegean as a permanent and perpetual policy instrument in its relations with Turkey.

Turkey will not acquiesce in unilateral acts designed to upset the status quo in relation to maritime jurisdiction areas in the Aegean. Turkey is determined to protect fully its legitimate rights and interests in the face of a <u>fait accompli</u> in the Aegean. Turkey will be obliged to take all necessary measures, as required by the circumstances, for this purpose in the case of such a development.

It is our sincere hope that our neighbour Greece will refrain from pursuing an adventurous policy and realize the long-term benefits of achieving a lasting settlement of bilateral disputes and friendship and cooperation between Turkey and Greece.

I would like to request that this letter be circulated as a document of the General Assembly under items 39, 75 and 81 of the preliminary list, and of the Security Council.

(Signed) İnal BATU
Permanent Representative

13. LETTER DATED 29 JUNE 1995 FROM THE PERMANENT REPRESENTATIVE OF GREECE TO THE UNITED NATIONS ADDRESSED TO THE SECRETARY-GENERAL*

Doc. no.: A/50/264-S/1995/526 29 June 1995

I do not deem it necessary to detain you with a detailed answer to the letter addressed to you by the Permanent Representative of Turkey (A/50/256-S/1995/505) in reply to mine dated 9 June 1995 (A/50/216-S/1995/476), for the simple reason that Mr. Batu's letter fully confirms the point that I brought to your attention with regard to the recent resolution adopted by the Turkish National Assembly, namely, that Turkey has once more violated the fundamental principle enshrined in the Charter of the United Nations that calls for restraint from the threat or use of force in international relations, and to which Turkey has subscribed, thus assuming the obligation to uphold it as a State Member of the Organization.

This persistent Turkish practice is openly and defiantly admitted by the Permanent Representative of Turkey, who maintains in his letter that there are bilateral differences between Greece and Turkey on the issue of the Aegean Sea, while making it very clear, at the same time, in unequivocal and threatening terms, that his country is determined to protect its rights and interests through all possible means.

I leave it to your judgement and to that of the other Members of the United Nations, to appreciate Turkey's commitment to international law and order and to respect of its own signature.

As regards the assurances given by Mr. Batu that Turkey does not harbour any designs or territorial ambitions against Greece or any of its neighbours and without going into any historic retrospection that would give ample and eloquent proof of Turkey's traditional performance in the broader area of the Balkans and the Middle East, suffice it to recall the notorious contemporary case of the military invasion and ongoing occupation of Cyprus.

I would like to request that this letter be circulated as a document of the General Assembly under items 39, 75 and 81 of the preliminary list, and of the Security Council.

(Signed) Christos G. ZACHARAKIS
Permanent Representative

---

* A/50/50/Rev.1.

14. LETTER DATED 12 JULY 1995 FROM THE PERMANENT REPRESENTATIVE OF TURKEY TO THE UNITED NATIONS ADDRESSED TO THE SECRETARY-GENERAL*

Doc. no.: A/50/279-S/1995/568 12 July 1995

With reference to the letter addressed to you by the Permanent Representative of Greece, dated 29 June 1995 (A/50/264-S/1995/526), I must take strong exception regarding its tone and content.

To begin with, the letter of Mr. Zacharakis aims once again at distorting facts and fails to address the main issues in focus and in that respect stands to be out of context.

Unfortunately, it appears that Greece still continues to stand by its past irredentist aspirations. Since the foundation of the nation State of Greece some 160 years ago, on five occasions it has tripled the size of its territory, mostly against Turkey. Two other attempts by Greece at expansion towards the east were repulsed, in Anatolia in the 1920s and in the eastern Mediterranean region in the 1970s.

On the other hand, in the course of these 160 years, Turkey has not acquired an inch of Greek territory.

The foreign policy of the Republic of Turkey has been one of moderation. Turkey has had no territorial ambitions beyond its national borders. Unlike Hellenism, which, as a national ideology, has no limits, the Turkish national pact aims to preserve the existing Turkish borders. Turkey continues to respect fully the territorial integrity of all its neighbours, including Greece.

As for the Cyprus issue, the Turkish intervention in 1974 was based on an international treaty and therefore was totally legitimate. Mr. Zacharakis should also recognize the responsibility of his country in the current state of affairs in Cyprus, by perpetrating a coup d'état in 1974 with the aim of annexing Cyprus to Greece.

The Greek allegation that Turkey poses a threat to Greece is by all measures a misrepresentation. Such an allegation is used by Greece as a pretext for its expansionist goals and hostile attitude towards Turkey. It is Greece that has territorial ambitions in areas beyond its territories, not only in the Aegean, but also in the eastern Mediterranean, Thrace, Macedonia and Epirus.

---

* A/50/50/Rev.1.

The new military defence doctrine of Greece, which is based on the concept of establishing a single Hellenic space, is an expansionist and offensive military posture based on race. Such a posture presents a major threat to peace and stability in our region. Furthermore, Greece's alignment with the terrorist organizations that harbour futile aspirations against Turkey's territorial integrity and political unity is common knowledge. We find the current and unqualified support given by Greece to terrorism, which is internationally recognized as the main threat to humanity, most deplorable.

I should like to confirm that Turkey is determined not to compromise its basic legal rights and interests in the Aegean in the face of Greek designs.

But looking to the future, I should like to reaffirm our readiness to engage in a process of meaningful dialogue to achieve mutually acceptable, just and equitable solutions to all our differences through result-oriented negotiations. We continue to believe that the betterment of Turkish-Greek relations is in the best interests of both nations and is essential for the promotion of much-needed stability in our region.

I should like to request that this letter be circulated as a document of the General Assembly, under items 39, 75 and 81 of the preliminary list, and of the Security Council.

(Signed) İnal BATU
Permanent Representative

15. LETTER DATED 20 JULY 1995 FROM THE CHARGÉ D'AFFAIRES A.I. OF THE PERMANENT MISSION OF GREECE TO THE UNITED NATIONS ADDRESSED TO THE SECRETARY-GENERAL**

Doc. no.: A/50/303*-S/1995/603* 24 July 1995

My Government had wished not to carry on the correspondence on the issue of the recent Turkish threats against my country, which were brought to your attention by Ambassador Christos Zacharakis in his letters dated 21 and 29 June 1995 (A/50/256-S/1995/505 and A/50/264-S/1995/526). However, I am compelled to come back to this matter, hopefully for the last time, since some points contained in the letter dated 12 July 1995 addressed to you by the Permanent Representative of Turkey (A/50/279-S/1995/568) cannot be ignored.

Once again, Turkey does not even attempt to conceal the threatening and expansionist views which it harbours against my country, in blatant violation of international law and the Charter of the United Nations. Furthermore, it continues to stand by its persistent practice of distorting historical facts and the fundamental principles of Greek foreign policy. In this context, Turkey misrepresents the struggle for freedom of the Greek people who, like other Balkan nations, were subjugated under Ottoman rule for more than four centuries, as Greek expansionist policy at its expense.

As regards the fallacious and slanderous allegations contained in the letter, concerning my country's stance on the issue of terrorism, I will not limit myself to a flat and categorical contradiction, taking also into account the fact that no probative evidence whatsoever substantiating the charges has ever been produced. I would like to add, on this point, that Turkey should first make sure that it has cleared up the shambles in its own back yard by restoring democratic freedoms for the whole of its population before it attempts to find scapegoats and to export the internal problems created by its own policies. This would serve not only the goal of stability in the area, but also the interests of Turkey, which takes satisfaction in picturing itself as a model of a secular State that nourishes the ambition to promote its relations with the European Union.

Finally, as regards Turkey's "readiness to engage in a process of dialogue" with Greece, I would like to point out that such a dialogue can only be meaningful and worthy of its name if all parties to it refrain from threats,

* Reissued for technical reasons.
** A/50/50/Rev.1.

unfounded allegations and provocative violations of fundamental principles of international law. Unfortunately, Turkey's behaviour gives ample proof that its "readiness for dialogue" is not an exercise in honesty and good intentions, but rather in propaganda.

I would like to request that this letter be circulated as a document of the General Assembly, under items 39, 75 and 81 of the preliminary list, and of the Security Council.

(Signed) Vassilis KASKARELIS
Deputy Permanent Representative
Chargé d'affaires a.i.

16. LETTER DATED 18 MAY 1995 FROM THE PERMANENT REPRESENTATIVE OF INDONESIA ADDRESSED TO THE SECRETARY-GENERAL* (COMMUNIQUÉ OF MINISTERIAL MEETING OF THE COORDINATING BUREAU OF THE NON-ALIGNED COUNTRIES, BANDUNG, INDONESIA, 25-27 APRIL 1995)

Doc. no.: A/49/920-S/1995/489 16 June 1995

In my capacity as Chairman of the Coordinating Bureau of the Non-Aligned Movement, I have the honour to transmit herewith the communiqué of the Ministerial Meeting of the Coordinating Bureau of the Movement of Non-Aligned Countries, held at Bandung, Indonesia, from 25 to 27 April 1995 (see annexes).*

I should be grateful if you would have the text of the present letter and its annex circulated as an official document of the forty-ninth session of the General Assembly, under agenda items 12, 18, 24, 25, 33, 34, 35, 38, 39, 40, 42, 43, 44, 48, 51, 52, 55, 56, 57, 58, 60, 62, 63, 64, 65, 68, 69, 70, 71, 72, 74, 79, 87, 88, 89, 92, 93, 94, 95, 97, 98, 99, 100, 101, 142, 154, 156 and 158, and of the Security Council.

(Signed) Nugroho WISNUMURTI
Ambassador
Permanent Representative

COMMUNIQUÉ

Ministerial Meeting of the Coordinating Bureau of the Non-Aligned Countries
Bandung, Indonesia, 25 - 27 April 1995

1. The Coordinating Bureau of the Non-Aligned Countries met at the Ministerial level in Bandung, Indonesia, from 25 to 27 April 1995 to prepare for the Eleventh Summit Conference of the Movement which is scheduled to be held in Cartagena, Colombia, during 18-20 October 1995.

2. The Meeting was chaired by H.E. Mr. Ali Alatas, Minister for Foreign Affairs of Indonesia. Other officers of the Bureau who were elected are as follows :

* The text of the annexes is being circulated in the languages of submission only.

Vice-Chairmen	:	
Africa	**1.**	**Burkina Faso**
	2.	**Congo**
	3.	**Sierra Leone**
	4.	**South Africa**
	5.	**Sudan.**
Asia	**1.**	**Islamic Republic of Iran**
	2.	**Democratic People's Republic of Korea**
	3.	**Palestine**
	4.	**Syrian Arab Republic.**
Latin America and the Caribbean	**1.**	**Chile**
	2.	**Colombia**
	3.	**Cuba**
	4.	**Suriname.**
Europe		**Malta**
Rapporteur General	:	**Egypt**

3. Representatives of the following countries which are members of the Non-Aligned Movement participated in the Meeting : Afghanistan, Algeria, Angola, Bangladesh, Belize, Benin, Bhutan, Bolivia, Botswana, Brunei Darussalam, Burkina Faso, Burundi, Cambodia, Cameroon, Cape Verde, Central African Republic, Chad, Chile, Colombia, Comoros, Congo, Côte d'Ivoire, Cuba, Cyprus, Ecuador, Egypt, Eritrea, Ethiopia, Gambia, Ghana, Guatemala, Guinea, Guinea-Bissau, Guyana, Honduras, India, Indonesia, Iran, Iraq, Jordan, Kenya, Democratic People's Republic of Korea, Kuwait, Lao People's Democratic Republic, Lebanon, Lesotho, Liberia, Libya, Madagascar, Malawi, Malaysia, Maldives, Mali, Malta, Mauritania, Mauritius, Mongolia, Morocco, Mozambique, Myanmar, Namibia, Nepal, Nicaragua, Niger, Nigeria, Oman, Pakistan, Palestine, Panama, Papua New Guinea, Peru, Philippines, Qatar, Rwanda, Sao Tome and Principe, Saudi Arabia, Senegal, Sierra Leone, Singapore, South Africa, Sri Lanka, Sudan, Suriname, Swaziland, Syria, Tanzania, Thailand, Togo, Tunisia, Uganda, United Arab Emirates, Uzbekistan, Venezuela, Viet Nam, Yemen, Zambia, Zimbabwe.

4. Representatives of the following countries, organizations and national liberation movements attended the Meeting as observers : Azerbaijan, Brazil, China, Costa Rica, Croatia, El Salvador, Kyrgyztan, Mexico, United Nations, Organization of the Islamic Conference (OIC).

5. Guest delegations from the following countries and organizations were also present at the Meeting : Australia, Austria, Bosnia and Herzegovina, Bulgaria, Canada, Czech Republic, Finland, Germany, Holy See, Hungary, Italy, Netherlands, New Zealand, Norway, Poland, Romania, Russian Federation, Slovak Republic, Slovenia, Spain, Sweden, Switzerland, Food and Agriculture Organization of the United Nations (FAO), International Committee of the Red Cross (ICRC), United Nations Committee on the Exercise of the Inalienable Rights of the Palestinian People, United Nations Development Program (UNDP), United Nations Industrial Development Organization (UNIDO), United Nations Children's Fund (UNICEF), World Food Program (WFP), World Health Organization (WHO), United Nations Educational Scientific and Cultural Organization (UNESCO), Indian Institute for Non Aligned Studies, United Nations High Commisioner for Refugees (UNHCR), Asian-African Legal Consultative Committee (AALCC), South Centre.

6. The Meeting was inaugurated by His Excellency Mr. Soeharto, President of the Republic of Indonesia and Chairman of the Non-Aligned Movement on the occasion of the ceremony commemorating the Fortieth Anniversary of the Asian-African Conference which was held on 24 April 1995. His inspiring keynote address was acclaimed as a valuable contribution to the deliberations and the successful outcome of the Meeting, and the text of which was unanimously adopted as an official document. (see annex II).

7. The Ministers warmly welcomed the State of Eritrea as a member of the Movement and the Russian Federation as a guest. The Ministers called upon the Coordinating Bureau in New York to continue its work, through its Working Group on Methodology, concerning the criteria, duration and rights of guest states in the Movement.

8. To finalize the preparations for the Ministerial Meeting, the Coordinating Bureau at Ambassadorial/Senior Officials level met on 21-22 April 1995, in Bandung, and was chaired by H.E. Mr. Nana S. Sutresna, Ambassador-at-Large, Head Executive Assistant to the NAM Chairman.

9. The Ministers observed the Fortieth Anniversary of the Asian-African Conference by participating in the commemoration on 24 April 1995, in Bandung, and reiterated their deep conviction in the continuing validity of the objectives enunciated in the Final Communique of the 1955 Conference. They stressed in particular the importance and enduring relevance of the Ten Principles embodied in the Declaration on the Promotion of World Peace and Cooperation. They further expressed their belief that the Commemoration has provided an opportunity to strengthen the Non-Aligned Movement, to further enhance its role and to reinforce unity and solidarity among its members.

[...]

28. The Ministers welcomed the entry into force of the Law of the Sea Convention of 1982 and the establishment of the International Seabed Authority in Jamaica. They expressed their hope that more countries will ratify the Convention and its implementing agreements. The Ministers believed that the Convention and the agreements represent significant achievements of the international community through multilateral efforts in creating a legal order for the seas and oceans which will, inter alia, facilitate international communication, promote the peaceful uses of the seas and oceans, the equitable and efficient utilization of their resources, the conservation of their living resources, as well as the protection and preservation of the marine environment. The Ministers expressed the hope that agreement relating to Part XI of the UN Convention on the Law of the Sea of 1982 will be implemented in all of its aspects including the agreement to set up International Seabed Authority without introducing new conditionalities that work against the interests of the developing countries.

[...]

57. The Ministers emphasized the need to resolve all sovereignty and jurisdictional disputes concerning South China Sea by peaceful means without resort to force and urged all parties to exercise restraint with a view to creating a positive climate for the eventual resolution of all contentious issues. They expressed concern over recent developments that may lead to a deterioration of peace and stability in the region. In this context the Ministers supported the principles contained in the 1992 ASEAN Declaration on the South China Sea and stressed the need for the full implementation of such principles by all the parties concerned. They expressed the hope that all concerned will refrain from further actions that may undermine peace, stability, trust and confidence in the region. To this end, the Ministers welcomed the Indonesian initiative in sponsoring the workshops on managing the potential conflicts in the South China Sea and other measures launched by the countries in the region and China to enhance cooperation and to ensure the peaceful settlement of all outstanding questions.

58. The Ministers expressed their concern over the fact that the Korean Peninsula is still divided in spite of the desire and aspirations of the Korean people and reaffirm their support for the efforts of the Korean people to reunite their homeland based on the principles set forth in the North-South Joint Statement of 4 July 1972 as well as the Agreement concluded in February 1992. They noted the importance of guaranteeing a durable peace and security in the Korean Peninsula for the sake of the common prosperity of the Korean people as well as the peace and security of North-East Asia and the rest of the world. The Ministers

expressed the hope that the nuclear issue in the Korean Peninsula, given its political and military nature, should be resolved by peaceful means through dialogue and negotiations among all the parties concerned and full implementation of the Agreed Framework between the Democratic People's Republic of Korea and the United States of America and other agreed relevant documents, taking into account the need for continued cooperation with the IAEA.

59. The Ministers noted with satisfaction further positive developments of dialogue and cooperation for peace and security in Southeast Asia as demonstrated at the ASEAN Regional Forum held in Bangkok on 25 July 1994. The ARF endorsed the purposes and principles of ASEAN's Treaty of Amity and Cooperation in South East Asia as a code of conduct in governing relations among states in the region and a unique diplomatic instrument for regional confidence - building, preventive diplomacy and political and security cooperation.

60. The Ministers viewed as positive the developments occurring in Haiti since their last meeting and the establishment of the Central American Social Integration System as the first sub-regional follow up to the Copenhagen Summit. They took note with satisfaction of the latest agreements reached between the Government of Guatemala and the National Revolutionary Unit of Guatemala (URNG), and expressed the hope that the Final Peace Accord would be signed during the current year. They expressed their appreciation of the UN's valuable contribution in the Guatemalan peace process and the successful completion of its mission in El Salvador. They also expressed their hope that Guatemala and Belize will resume and successfully conclude their negotiations at the earliest possible date in order to find a final solution to the dispute. They expressed further the hope that other disputes in the region could be resolved through peaceful means by the parties concerned in accordance with the Ten Bandung Principles of 1955.

61. The Ministers once again called upon the Government of the United States to put to an end to the economic, commercial and financial embargo imposed on Cuba for over three decades and for the speedy and effective implementation of relevant General Assembly resolutions, which have been adopted by an increasing majority. They further reaffirmed the view that differences between both countries should be resolved through dialogue and negotiations. The Ministers also expressed their concern regarding new draft legislation before the United States Congress that would tighten the embargo against Cuba and expand its extra-territorial nature, and reiterated their solidarity with the Republic of Cuba.

[...]

67. The Ministers reviewed the developments that occurred in the Mediterranean region since the Jakarta Summit and recalled the Ministerial Meetings of the Mediterranean Non-Aligned Countries held in Valletta in 1984, in Brioni in 1987 and in Algiers in 1989. They reaffirmed their determination to pursue their initiatives aimed at promoting comprehensive and equitable cooperation in the region. The Ministers expressed their support to the initiatives of the Mediterranean countries in their efforts to adopt effective measures to promote confidence-and-security-building and stability in their region by the elimination of all causes of tension and the consequent threat to peace and security.

68. In this context, the Ministers reiterated their full support to the efforts aimed at the reactivation of the Group 5+5 which constitutes a concrete and important contribution to a comprehensive approach for Mediterranean co-operation and security. They also reiterated their support to the proposal to convene a CSCM. The Ministers also welcomed the ongoing informal dialogue taking place within the Mediterranean Forum, initiated by H.E. President Mohamed Hosni Mubarak of Egypt and the OSCE. They further welcomed the proposal of H.M. King Hassan II of Morocco at the CSCE Ministerial Meeting in Rome in December 1993, to host a Ministerial Meeting on security and co-operation in the Mediterranean. They also welcomed the initiative by Malta to set up a Council of the Mediterranean. The Ministers took note of the convening, in November 1995, of the IPU Second Conference on Security and Co-operation in the Mediterranean to be held in Malta and the Euro-Med Conference to be held in Barcelona.

69. The Ministers stressed that respect for the right of self-determination, elimination of foreign occupation and foreign bases, non-intervention and non-interference in the internal affairs and respect for sovereignty of states are prerequisites for the establishment of peace and security in the region.

70. The Ministers took note of the efforts of the Non-Aligned Mediterranean countries to strengthen further their co-operation in facing terrorist activities which pose a serious threat to peace, security and stability in the region and therefore to the improvement of the current political, economic and social situation.

[...]

94. The Ministers reviewed the situation since the UNCED Conference in Rio in June 1992 and while reaffirming their commitment to advancing the outcomes of the Conference through the spirit of partnership, they also expressed their disappointment with the lack of implementation of the provisions particularly regarding transfer of environmentally sound technology on a concessional basis and the failure to provide new and additional financial resources for the implementation of programs and projects of Agenda 21. Moreover, while they recognized the progress in restructuring and replenishment of the Global Environmental Facility (GEF) and the coming into effect of the GEF Trust Fund on March 16, 1995, they noted that these resources fell far short of the agreed requirements for the implementation of Agenda 21. They, therefore, called on the international community, particularly the developed countries, to fulfill their commitments in this regard and to enable the developing countries to fulfill theirs.

95. The Ministers expressed their concern for the unsafe maritime transportation and dumping of nuclear wastes as well as for the risks and dangers this transportation and dumping presents especially to sea coastal areas and fisheries and any other areas, particularly those under state sovereignty and jurisdiction. The Ministers agreed that it is necessary to strengthen current international regulations on this matter through enhancing transparency and controls as well as participation by affected States, in the framework of the Basel Convention and of competent international fora, such as the International Atomic Energy Agency and the International Maritime Organization. They also recognized the need for strengthening existing laws and regulations regarding management of toxic and hazardous wastes and called for further development of relevant international laws and regulations. In this context the Ministers reiterated their support for the decision of the Second Conference of the Basel Convention which decided inter alia the prohibition by the end of 1997 of all transboundary movement of hazardous wastes destined for recovery and/or recycling from OECD to non OECD countries, and urged for its strict implementation.

96. The Ministers, in noting the fundamental role played by science and technology in advancing economic growth and sustainable development, stressed the importance of access to technology including environmentally sound technology and that its transfer to the developing countries should be on a preferential and concessional basis. They also firmly believed that such transfer should not be solely left in the hands of the private sector or based on market prices and that the national capacities of the developing countries should be substantially supported by the international community.

[...]

17. LETTER DATED 3 AUGUST 1995 FROM THE PERMANENT REPRESENTATIVE OF BRUNEI DARUSSALAM TO THE UNITED NATIONS ADDRESSED TO THE SECRETARY-GENERAL (JOINT COMMUNIQUE OF THE 28TH ASEAN MINISTERIAL MEETING, BANDAR SERI BEGAWAN, BRUNEI DARUSSALAM, 29-30 JULI 1995)

Doc. no.: A/49/953-S/1995/652 4 August 1995

On behalf of the Permanent Representatives to the United Nations of the States members of the Association of South-East Asian Nations (ASEAN), I have the honour to transmit to you herewith the text of the joint communiqué of the twenty-eighth ASEAN ministerial meeting, which was held in Brunei Darussalam on 29 and 30 July 1995.

I should be grateful if you would have the text of the present letter and its annex circulated as a document of the General Assembly under agenda items 38, 57, 62, 70, 88 (a) and 92, and of the Security Council.

(Signed) Pengiran ABDUL MOMIN
Permanent Representative

Annex

Joint Communiqué of the Twenty-Eighth ASEAN Ministerial Meeting held at Bandar Seri Begawan, Brunei Darussalam, on 29 and 30 July 1995

1. The Twenty-Eighth ASEAN Ministerial Meeting was held in Bandar Seri Begawan from 29 to 30 July 1995.

2. The Foreign Ministers welcomed Viet Nam as the seventh member of ASEAN. They also welcomed the accession of Cambodia to the Treaty of Amity and Cooperation in South-East Asia. Cambodia was also granted observer status. They believed that these events marked a historic step towards building a South-East Asian community and looked forward to the future when all South-East Asian nations become members of ASEAN. The Ministers called for increased cooperation with Cambodia and Laos to assist them in preparing for their eventual membership in ASEAN.

3. The Foreign Ministers welcomed the decision by Myanmar to accede to the Treaty of Amity and Cooperation in South-East Asia.

Political and security cooperation

4. Considering the important role of ASEAN in maintaining peace, stability, and prosperity in this region as well as in enhancing cooperation in the wider Asia-Pacific, the Foreign Ministers reaffirmed their commitment to working closely with others, particularly ASEAN's Dialogue and Consultative Partners, and Observers. In reviewing the developments of the ASEAN Regional Forum (ARF) since its inauguration in Bangkok last year, the Ministers expressed satisfaction with the progress made thus far. In this regard, they reaffirmed that the ASEAN Concept Paper on the ARF has contributed significantly towards moving the ARF process forward at a pace comfortable to all participants. They re-emphasized ASEAN's role as the primary driving force of the ARF which is a high-level consultative forum to facilitate open dialogue and discussions on political and security issues of common interest and concern in the Asia-Pacific region. They also stressed the importance of building confidence among ARF participants so as to develop a more predictable and constructive pattern of behaviour. This, they felt, would ensure lasting peace, stability, and prosperity for the region and its people. They looked forward to a successful second ARF meeting.

5. The Foreign Ministers expressed satisfaction with the progress made by ASEAN in the dialogue and consultation process on political and security issues which now included the ASEAN China Senior Officials Consultation (ASEAN-China SOM) and the ASEAN-European Union Senior Officials Meeting (ASEAN-EU SOM). The Ministers also expressed their appreciation to Canada for the initiative of hosting the ASEAN-Canada consultation in May 1995, in order for ASEAN's view to be made known to the G-7 Meeting in Halifax. The Ministers also expressed their satisfaction over the results of these consultations. The Ministers agreed that such meetings served to strengthen ASEAN's cooperative relations with various countries and partners.

6. The Foreign Ministers noted with satisfaction the progress made in the implementation of ASEAN's "Programme of action on ZOPFAN". The Ministers also noted the positive progress in solving the legal and technical aspects of the draft Treaty on South-East Asia Nuclear Weapons Free Zone (SEANWFZ). They further noted similar progress in deciding on the most appropriate instrument by which countries outside the region would be able to associate themselves with the Treaty of Amity and Cooperation in South-East Asia. The Foreign Ministers agreed that the association of non-South-East Asian countries to the Treaty of Amity and Cooperation would enhance peace and stability of the region.

7. The Foreign Ministers commended the good cooperative relations developed between ASEAN and non-governmental bodies such as the ASEAN Institute of Strategic and International Studies (ASEAN-ISIS) and the Council for Security and Cooperation in the Asia Pacific (CSCAP). They agreed that these bodies had provided useful ideas and proposals for political and security cooperation in the region.

International and regional issues

8. The Foreign Ministers exchanged views on the current regional and international situation. The Ministers noted with satisfaction the continuing positive developments in ASEAN and the wider Asia-Pacific. In this regard, they stressed the importance of a stable relationship among the major Powers. The Ministers also expressed the hope that countries in the region would continue to work together to maintain security and stability to ensure rapid economic growth and progress.

9. The Foreign Ministers expressed their concern over recent events in the South China Sea. They encouraged all parties concerned to reaffirm their commitment to the principles contained in the 1992 ASEAN Declaration of the South China Sea, which urges all claimants to resolve their differences by peaceful means and to exercise self-restraint. They also called on them to

refrain from taking actions that could destabilize the region, including possibly undermining the freedom of navigation and aviation in the affected areas. They also encouraged the claimants to address the issue in various bilateral and multilateral forums. In this regard, they reiterated the significance of promoting confidence-building measures (CBMs) and mutually beneficial cooperative ventures in the ongoing Informal Workshop Series on Managing Potential Conflicts in the South China Sea initiated by Indonesia.

10. The Foreign Ministers discussed the situation in the Korean Peninsula. They welcomed the positive outcome of the talks held in Kuala Lumpur between the United States and the Democratic People's Republic of Korea (DPRK) and expressed the hope that this would lead to the full implementation of the Agreed Framework reached in Geneva. The Ministers reiterated their belief that resuming the dialogue between the DPRK and the Republic of Korea was extremely important for peace and security in the Korean Peninsula. They expressed the hope that these developments would contribute to the improvement of the situation.

11. The Foreign Ministers expressed grave concern over the current situation in Bosnia and Herzegovina and issued a statement on the subject.

12. The Foreign Ministers welcomed the progress made in the Middle East peace process, in particular the implementation of the PLO-Israeli Declaration of Principles on Interim Self-Government Arrangements of 1993. The Ministers stressed the importance of continuing the discussions between the Palestinians and Israelis to reach an agreement on the details of the withdrawal of Israeli soldiers from the West Bank. They also welcomed the peace treaty between Jordan and Israel and the ongoing discussions between Syria and Israel and believed that these would contribute to a comprehensive settlement to the Middle East problem.

13. The Foreign Ministers noted with satisfaction the successful outcome of the Ministerial Meeting of the Coordinating Bureau of the Non-Aligned Movement (NAM) held in Bandung from 25 to 27 April 1995. They supported in particular the NAM Ministers' pledge to do their utmost to strengthen South-South cooperation with a view to achieving economic security and collective self-reliance. The Ministers also noted with satisfaction the commemoration of the Fortieth Anniversary of the Asian-African Conference held in Bandung on 24 April 1995 and reiterated their conviction that the objectives enunciated in the Final Communiqué of the Conference continue to be valid.

14. The Foreign Ministers emphasized the importance of the Nuclear Non-Proliferation Treaty (NPT) in promoting international peace and security. Bearing in mind the objectives of general and complete disarmament, the Foreign Ministers noted the outcome of the recent 1995 Review and Extension Conference of the Parties to the NPT and attached particular importance to the establishment of internationally recognized nuclear-weapon-free zones by the year 2000. In this regard, the Foreign Ministers deplored the resumption or planned resumption of nuclear tests in the Asia-Pacific in view of the commitment of all State Parties to the NPT to exert utmost restraint on nuclear-weapons testing and to conclude the Comprehensive Test Ban Treaty in 1996. They also called on all nuclear-weapon States to desist from testing nuclear devices.

15. In view of the United Nations important role and contribution to development in the last 50 years, the Foreign Ministers emphasized the need for ensuring that the United Nations remain at the centre of efforts to enhance international economic cooperation for development. They attached great importance to the elaboration of an Agenda for Development as the basis for restoring the centrality of development in the work of the United Nations and in addressing the needs and priorities of developing countries. Towards this end, and in order to reinforce the development role of the United Nations, the Ministers expressed support for the position of the Non-Aligned Movement and the Group of 77. The United Nations organizations which promote and enhance international economic cooperation for sustained economic growth and sustainable

development on a global basis including UNCTAD and UNIDO, should be strengthened. The Ministers strongly felt that the mandate of the United Nations in the field of development should be clearly emphasized in all attempts to reform, revitalize and strengthen the world Organization, especially in conjunction with the observance of its fiftieth foundation anniversary this year.

16. The Foreign Ministers noted with appreciation all efforts that have been undertaken by the international community within the framework of the Comprehensive Plan of Action (CPA) of 1989. The Foreign Ministers expressed serious concern over recent developments which affected the implementation and successful conclusion of the CPA. They urged all resettlement countries to weigh carefully the implications of adopted proposed legislation which has already generated false hopes of resettlement directly from the camps in the first asylum countries. They reiterated their commitment to the objectives of the CPA which remained the most realistic option to resolve the problem of Indo-Chinese refugees. They called on all parties to the CPA to remain fully committed to the implementation of the relevant Memoranda of Understanding and the decisions of the Fifth and Sixth Steering Committee Meetings with the view to bringing it to a conclusion by the target date of the end of 1995. They called upon the donor community to continue to provide adequate resources to the UNHCR to complete its operations.

Fifth ASEAN Summit

17. The Foreign Ministers looked forward to the Fifth Meeting of the ASEAN Heads of Government to be held in Thailand on 14-15 December 1995. The heads of Government will review developments and progress in ASEAN since the last Summit in Singapore in 1992. The Fifth Summit will chart ASEAN's future direction towards intensifying political, economic and functional cooperation to make ASEAN an even more cohesive and dynamic regional grouping. The Foreign Ministers also requested Thailand as the host country to invite the heads of Government of Cambodia, Laos and Myanmar to a meeting with the ASEAN Heads of Government during the Summit.

Asia-Europe Meeting (ASEM)

18. The Foreign Ministers noted that the leaders of Asia and Europe welcomed the holding of the Asia-Europe Meeting (ASEM) scheduled for early 1996 in Thailand. They agreed that the Meeting would serve as a means of establishing strong links between Asia and Europe at the highest level.

International economic issues

19. The Foreign Ministers welcomed the ratification of the Final Act of the Uruguay Round by all member countries. They noted Viet Nam's application for WTO membership and expressed the hope that Viet Nam would soon be admitted. They urged the timely access of major trading countries and economies to the WTO and called on all signatories to implement their Uruguay Round commitments in a faithful and timely manner. They requested members to reaffirm their commitment to the principle of free trade by liberalizing their markets further and continuing with their efforts in bringing down trade barriers in accordance with their commitments and the provisions of the Uruguay Round agreements. Recognizing that trade would become more competitive as a result of the Uruguay Round, the Ministers emphasized the need for member countries to keep pace with world market developments by conducting improvements in production, quality control, product innovation, distribution, financing and technology.

20. The Foreign Ministers expressed satisfaction with the appointment of Singapore as the Chairman of the General Council of the WTO, and Thailand as the Chairman of the Committee of Agriculture of the WTO, and that the First WTO Ministerial Conference will be held in Singapore. They noted that these are manifestations of the international recognition of the important role played by ASEAN in promoting global trade liberalization.

21. The Foreign Ministers requested the International Monetary Fund to monitor international currency movements more closely in order to avoid a financial crisis similar to that of Mexico's. They cautioned that the continuing imbalances in the international currency markets might seriously affect financial flows to the region and might have adverse consequences for countries with large foreign debt obligations. The Foreign Ministers agreed on the need for enhanced cooperation between the Bretton Woods institutions and the WTO to further strengthen the global economic system.

22. The Foreign Ministers reiterated their stand, as underlined by the ASEAN Labour Ministers during their informal meeting at Chiang Mai in April 1995, to oppose any attempt to link labour standards with international trade and to use labour standards to interfere in the internal affairs of developing countries. They welcomed the recent position adopted by the ILO Governing Body's Working Party to suspend any further discussion of the link between international trade and social standards. The Foreign Ministers renewed their call on the ILO to undertake a thorough review of labour standards, some of which are not relevant to the economic and labour environment of the developing countries on the road to industrialization.

23. The ASEAN Foreign Ministers noted the decisions of the Halifax Summit. Whilst recognizing that the prevention of financial crisis is the preferred course of action, the Foreign Ministers welcomed the Summit's decision to create an emergency fund to defuse future Mexico-type financial crises. The Foreign Ministers welcomed the Summit's call for a comprehensive approach by lending institutions to help the poorest countries with large debt burdens. At the same time, the Foreign Ministers expressed concern that no stronger actions were taken for coordinating macroeconomic policies among the G-7 countries to manage the sharp currency fluctuations in the world's foreign exchange markets.

<u>ASEAN Free Trade Area</u>

24. The Foreign Ministers noted with satisfaction the significant progress made in the implementation of AFTA. They expressed their full support for the reduction of the time-frame in the implementation of AFTA from 15 to 10 years ending in 2003 and noted that member countries will begin to implement the new tariff reduction schedules by 1 January 1996. The Ministers also took note of the inclusion of the products in the Temporary Exclusion List which is currently being worked by member countries with the list for the first instalment being finalized by the Seventh AFTA Council in September 1995.

25. The Ministers also called upon member countries to accelerate harmonization of customs procedures, tariff nomenclature and standards and to intensify their efforts to remove non-tariff barriers in order to further accelerate growth in intra-ASEAN trade. The Ministers noted with satisfaction the decision to include unprocessed agriculture products in the CEPT Scheme and called upon member countries to intensify their efforts to realize it, taking into account the level of development of the respective countries. They however expressed the hope that member countries should make all efforts in ensuring that the Temporary Exclusion List and the Sensitive List are kept to a minimum. The Ministers also noted with satisfaction the establishment of the AFTA Unit and the National AFTA Units in the respective member countries which will facilitate greater private sector participation in the AFTA process.

26. They welcomed the initiation of consultations between ASEAN and Australia and New Zealand to discuss possible linkages between AFTA and the Australia-New Zealand Closer Economic Relations Trade Agreement (ANZCERTA) with a view to enhancing economic interaction between the two regions.

<u>Other areas of economic cooperation</u>

27. In view of the increasing competitiveness of the world's economy and the rapid globalization of trade, the Foreign Ministers supported efforts of the Economic Ministers to expand economic cooperation in other areas such as

services, intellectual property and investment. The Foreign Ministers welcomed the decision of the ASEAN Economic Ministers to look into new activities and/or schemes to accelerate industrial cooperation in the region with emphasis on technology-based industries and physical infrastructure investments. In this regard, they noted that a Framework Agreement on Cooperation in Services and ASEAN Framework on Intellectual Property Cooperation are being formulated. The Foreign Ministers agreed that ASEAN cooperation in services would entail commitments on an ASEAN preferential basis aimed at realizing a free trade area in services in the long run. They also supported efforts to explore the possibility of setting up an ASEAN patent and trademark system.

28. The Foreign Ministers welcomed the initiatives taken by the ASEAN Ministers on Agriculture and Forestry to sign the MOU on ASEAN Cooperation and Joint Approaches in Agriculture and Forest Products Promotion Scheme in August 1994. The MOU aims at sustaining the expansion of ASEAN agriculture and forest products and at enhancing collaboration between the public and private sectors.

East Asia Economic Caucus (EAEC)

29. The Foreign Ministers reaffirmed their commitment to an early realization of the EAEC. They recognized the usefulness of more focused discussions on specific economic and development issues, particularly on matters that will contribute to greater development of the East Asia region.

Asia Pacific Economic Cooperation (APEC)

30. The Foreign Ministers noted that APEC had made significant progress towards its long-term goal of free and open trade and investment in the Asia-Pacific regions as embodied in the Bogor Declaration. The Ministers emphasized the need for APEC to proceed in a manner consistent with the principles of the GATT/WTO. Noting the importance of the Kuching consensus and the considerable progress made by APEC since that consensus, the Foreign Ministers reaffirmed that ASEAN should continue to play a central role in APEC. The Foreign Ministers underscored the importance of economic and technical cooperation in the Bogor Declaration and in this context welcomed Japan's initiative on "Partners for Progress". The Foreign Ministers expressed the hope that the APEC Economic Leaders Meeting in Osaka and the Seventh APEC Ministerial Meeting to be hosted by Japan in November 1995 would carry forward the APEC process.

Functional cooperation

31. The Foreign Ministers agreed that, as part of the efforts to achieve greater social and economic progress in the region and to enable ASEAN to face the challenges of the twenty-first century, ASEAN functional cooperation should be further strengthened and intensified.

32. The Foreign Ministers noted with satisfaction that cooperation in science and technology, environment, culture and information, social development, and drugs and narcotics control had further intensified and increased in focus with the completion of Plans of Action for each of the five functional areas and the implementation of a number of initial activities. They also expressed satisfaction at the progress made in the preparation of the ASEAN Regional Programme on Prevention and Control of HIV/AIDS.

33. The Foreign Ministers welcomed the decision of the ASEAN Ministerial Meeting on the Management of Transboundary Pollution to adopt the ASEAN Cooperation Plan on Transboundary Pollution with a view to managing the increasing periodicity and worsening impact of transboundary pollution in the region.

EXTERNAL RELATIONS

Cooperation with Dialogue Partners

34. The Foreign Ministers noted that the Dialogue Process has acquired greater importance in promoting a better understanding of issues brought about by rapid changes in the world environment. The Ministers expressed the hope that although the Dialogues shall continue to serve as a forum for discussing divergent interests, it could place more emphasis on shared interests and objectives in addressing global challenges. The Ministers recognized that the inaugural ASEAN-EU SOM, held in Singapore from 2 to 4 May 1995, marked an important step in this direction and paved the way for the deepening of mutual understanding and economic cooperation between the European Union and ASEAN.

35. The Foreign Ministers recognized the growing significance of economic cooperation with the Dialogue Partners. They reiterated their request for the Dialogue Partners to be more forthcoming in their response to ASEAN's concerns on trade, investment and market access issues. The Ministers expressed appreciation for the assistance provided by the Dialogue Partners in the implementation of various development projects. They noted that development cooperation projects are increasingly directed at promoting economic and commercial objectives.

Cooperation with Non-Dialogue Partners

36. The Foreign Ministers noted that ASEAN cooperation with India in the fields of trade, investment, science and technology and tourism has made progress. Modalities for implementing ASEAN-Pakistan Sectoral Relations have been initiated. The Ministers noted the outcome of the First ASEAN-China Joint Science and Technology Meeting held in Brunei Darussalam in March 1995. The Foreign Ministers noted the progress in ASEAN-Russia relations and welcomed efforts being made to identify areas of mutual interest in order to enhance relations. The Foreign Ministers expressed satisfaction with the expansion of ASEAN's relations with other regional organizations and noted the efforts undertaken by the ASEAN secretariat in this regard. The Foreign Ministers also noted that the ASEAN secretariat is undertaking a review of the criteria and priorities for ASEAN's external relations.

18. LETTER DATED 18 SEPTEMBER 1995 FROM THE CHARGE D'AFFAIRES A.I. OF THE PERMANENT MISSION OF PAPUA NEW GUINEA TO THE UNITED NATIONS ADDRESSED TO THE SECRETARY-GENERAL(COMMUNIQUE OF THE 26TH SOUTH PACIFIC FORUM, MADANG, PAPUA NEW GUINEA, 3-15 SEPTEMBER 1995)

Doc. no.: A/50/475 26 September 1995

In my capacity as Chairman of the South Pacific Forum countries, represented at the United Nations, I am pleased to forward herewith the official communiqué signed by all Heads of Government of the South Pacific Forum at Madang, Papua New Guinea, on 15 September 1995.

I request that this communiqué be widely disseminated to the general membership of the United Nations as a document of the General Assembly during this historic fiftieth session, under agenda items 29, 39, 47, 65, 70, 90, 94, 95, 96, 97, 100 and 112.

(Signed) Max H. RAI
Deputy Permanent Representative
Chargé d'affaires a.i.

ANNEX

Communiqué of the Twenty-sixth South Pacific Forum, held at Madang, Papua New Guinea, from 3 to 15 September 1995

1. The Twenty-sixth South Pacific Forum was held at Madang from 13 to 15 September 1995, and was attended by Heads of State and Government, or their representatives, of Australia, the Cook Islands, the Federated States of Micronesia, Fiji, Kiribati, Nauru, New Zealand, Niue, Palau, Papua New Guinea, the Marshall Islands, Samoa, Solomon Islands, Tonga, Tuvalu and Vanuatu.

2. The Forum thanked the people and the Government of Papua New Guinea for the generous hospitality provided to all delegations to the Forum. It welcomed Palau by acclamation as its sixteenth member, and invited Palau to accede to the Forum Secretariat Agreement. The Forum also extended warm congratulations and good wishes to the Government and people of Papua New Guinea on the occasion of the twentieth anniversary of the country's independence. The Forum expressed its deep appreciation to the outgoing Chairman for his excellent leadership.

Securing development beyond 2000

3. The Forum's considerations focused on the theme "Securing development beyond 2000", and leaders adopted a Plan of Action (appendix I) for

implementation, following valuable informal discussions at their retreat. The Plan of Action gives close consideration to a wide range of strategies, recognizing that security involves strengthening national and regional relations, especially capacities to sustain development in the medium and long term, as well as regional stability.

Vision statement

4. The leaders adopted the South Pacific Forum Vision Statement (appendix II), presented by the Chair of the Forum and Prime Minister of Papua New Guinea, setting out a vision for enhancing regional cooperation over the next quarter century. The Forum believed this statement sets out clear visionary but achievable goals, based on its members' many shared interests and building on the Forum's tradition of close regional consultation, which would significantly strengthen the region's capacity to adapt to a rapidly changing international and regional environment.

Nuclear testing

5. Forum leaders issued a statement (appendix III) expressing their extreme outrage at the resumption of French nuclear testing in the Pacific. They again demanded that France desist from any further tests. The outrage of Forum member countries was so much the greater because of the intransigence of France, together with the People's Republic of China, in persisting with their nuclear tests in the face of the strong views of the Pacific region. The Forum endorsed the Lakatoro Declaration by the Melanesian Spearhead Group, and the Declaration by the South Pacific Environment Ministers Meeting, held in August 1995.

Development

6. The Forum welcomed progress in the issues to which leaders had committed themselves at the 1994 Brisbane Forum.

Regional air services

7. Leaders noted the positive developments which had taken place in aviation in the region since the 1994 Forum, especially the steps taken to stem the substantial losses being incurred by some airlines. They endorsed the outcome of the Joint Meeting of Aviation Authorities and Operators, and the recommendations of ministers responsible for aviation meeting at the South Pacific Regional Civil Aviation Council. Leaders considered that these recommendations provided an appropriate framework within which Governments and airlines could work together, both at a national level and regionally, to improve further the performance of the aviation industry in supporting national economic development and social needs in the South Pacific. They noted concerns that raising capital for equipment purchases would be a crucial problem, and supported representations, especially by the recently formed regional subgrouping of Nauru, Tuvalu, Kiribati and the Marshall Islands, being made to the Asian Development Bank to change its policies to allow it to finance aircraft purchases, as it already financed other transportation infrastructure development.

8. Leaders agreed to convene a meeting of regional ministers of civil aviation, aviation authorities, airline representatives and other related experts at Rarotonga in early 1996 to advance through cooperative initiatives the further development of civil aviation services throughout the Forum region. Leaders expressed their appreciation for the report on rationalization of air services in the South Pacific, and of the work of the Association of South Pacific Airlines for its positive support in developing that framework.

Fisheries

9. The Forum welcomed and noted the significance of the adoption at New York on 4 August 1995 of the Agreement for the Implementation of the Provisions of

the United National Convention on the Law of the Sea of 10 December 1982 relating to the Conservation and Management of Straddling Fish Stocks and Highly Migratory Fish Stocks, and urged all interested States to become parties to the Agreement as soon as possible.

10. The Forum expressed its appreciation for the outstanding work of the United Nations Conference Chairman, Mr. Sarya N. Nandan (Fiji), in bringing the Conference to a successful conclusion with the adoption by consensus of the Agreement. The Forum also expressed its appreciation to the Forum Fisheries Agency for its work in coordinating and formulating the regional input to the United Nations Conference discussions.

11. In the light of the outcome of the United Conference on Straddling Fish Stocks and Highly Migratory Fish Stocks, the Forum considered that comprehensive regional fisheries management arrangements, and a structure consistent with the Conference outcome to administer them, should be developed as a matter of urgency. The Forum registered its view that those management arrangements must be based on a precautionary approach to ensure the sustainable exploitation of the regions's valuable tuna resources.

12. Forum leaders noted significant progress in the implementation of regional fisheries commitments over the last year, including the conclusion of the Federated States of Micronesia Arrangement for Regional Fisheries Access; the region's significant contribution to the United Nations Conference on Straddling Fish Stocks and Highly Migratory Fish Stocks; work to develop comprehensive regional fisheries management arrangements; progress in the pursuit of multilateral fisheries access arrangements; and progress in the development of the regional Vessel Monitoring System.

13. The Forum supported continued efforts to conclude additional multilateral fishing agreements with Distant Water Fishing Nations, ensuring that in doing so no member country would be made worse off than it was under its existing bilateral fishing agreements.

<u>Law of the sea</u>

14. The Forum urged all Forum member countries to become parties to the 1982 United Nations Convention on the Law of the Sea at the earliest opportunity.

<u>Forestry</u>

15. Forum members endorsed the draft code of conduct on logging and committed themselves to implementation of its provisions as part of their national codes.

<u>Shipping</u>

16. The Forum accepted the recommendations of the Regional Shipping Council regarding the future management and operations of the Pacific Forum Line.

<u>Tourism</u>

17. The Forum noted that the South Pacific lay at the centre of one of the most rapidly growing tourism networks in the world. Leaders agreed, therefore, to direct their respective tourism authorities to explore options for increasing joint promotions, both within and beyond the region. In particular, they will examine transport needs, including national facilities and international links, as well as needs - and openings for investment - in relation to accommodation.

<u>Economic policy issues</u>

18. The Forum supported a number of national policy measures and regionally based activities which would contribute to the aim of securing development beyond 2000. These included:

(a) Securing the potential benefits of globalization by enhancing competitiveness through promoting price stability (low inflation); avoiding artificial distortions to the prices of domestic resources (land, labour, capital); reducing trade taxes and import duties, which adversely affect export competitiveness; and removing implicit and explicit barriers to foreign direct investment;

(b) Adopting and implementing the investment principles agreed to by members of Asia Pacific Economic Cooperation (APEC), as a signal to potential investors of the region's serious intentions to promote and encourage foreign direct investment;

(c) Working towards implementation of trade reform measures as required by GATT/World Trade Organization, including by replacing non-tariff barriers with tariffs, and setting a time-frame for minimizing tariff levels;

(d) Promoting trade both within and outside the region by harmonizing and standardizing administrative procedures in the areas of customs and quarantine, labelling and packaging, phytosanitary and other sanitary requirements, export/import controls, exchange controls and technical standards;

(e) Improving public sector efficiency and cost-effectiveness by rationalization of public services; attention to policy coherence and commitment to the principle of good governance; and strengthening cooperative relationships between government ministries and agencies;

(f) Improving aid management and regional cooperation by endorsing the proposed regional strategy;

(g) Recognizing the valuable contribution of the agricultural sector to domestic food security, export development, incomes and employment and the need for positive measures in support of agricultural development, including minimizing price distortions and promoting agricultural research and information dissemination, for both marketable and subsistence crops;

(h) Enhancing development by the adoption and maintenance of appropriate and sustainable fiscal policy settings;

(i) Placing greater emphasis on population management strategies as a fundamental way of accelerating development;

(j) Ensuring that development strategies place appropriate emphasis on the promotion of outer island and remote community development.

19. The Forum noted that a continuing concern for the countries of the region was that flows of economic assistance, bilaterally and multilaterally, were reaching a ceiling, with many donors reducing assistance or diverting it to economies outside the region. It urged the donor community not to forget he needs of the Pacific region. In this context the Forum appreciated the continuing increase in Japanese assistance. At the same time, it also urged Japan to give favourable consideration to rendering assistance to a wider range of regional organizations, especially of the South Pacific Regional Environment Programme (SPREP) programmes which were of central importance to the sustainable development prospects of Pacific island countries.

Forum finance ministers meeting

20. Forum leaders welcomed the outcome of the Forum finance ministers meeting in 1995. They agreed that finance ministers should meet again at Port Moresby in December 1995 to develop further that outcome.

Representative office, Tokyo

21. The Forum expressed its appreciation to the Government of Japan for providing funding assistance for the recently completed feasibility study on the establishment of the South Pacific Economic Exchange Support Centre in Tokyo to promote trade, investment and tourism between Japan and the Forum island countries, and strongly reaffirmed its commitment to the Centre. It looked forward to a positive decision on support for the Centre from Japan in the context of its 1996 budget. The Forum agreed also to approach similarly other Governments and international organizations for assistance in mounting regional promotions, including permanent South Pacific trade commissions, in East Asia, Europe and North America.

Social issues

Participation in international conferences

22. The Forum noted with satisfaction the significant contribution made by Pacific Island countries to the outcome of the recent international conferences on population and development, social development and women. It encouraged regional efforts to integrate population and environment concerns. The Forum also lent formal support for the World Food Summit to be convened by the Food and Agriculture Organization of the United Nations in November 1996.

Pacific children and the Convention on the Rights of the Child

23. The Forum restated its support for the welfare of Pacific children and encouraged Pacific island countries which had not yet done so to become parties to the Convention on the Rights of the Child. The Forum noted the Pacific Culture of Peace Festival for Children which had been hosted by the Cook Islands and sponsored by UNESCO, sharing the sentiments expressed in the children's appeal to world leaders on children's rights, peace and the environment.

Environmental issues

Climate change

24. The Forum reaffirmed the importance of climate change to the region, recognizing the threat posed to Forum island countries. It welcomed the outcome of the Conference of the Parties to the United Nations Framework Convention on Climate Change, held at Berlin from 28 March to 7 April 1995, the early commencement of negotiations aimed at strengthening the Convention and the inclusion of the draft protocol of the Alliance of Small Island States for consideration in the negotiating process. The Forum stressed the priority that should be given to programmes in support of the objectives of the Framework Convention, including reduction of greenhouse gas emissions, enhancement of sinks, energy efficiency, renewable energy sources, and research assisting countries to meet their obligations under the Convention.

Global Environment Facility

25. The Forum endorsed the draft Pacific Strategy for accessing Funds of the Global Environment Facility (GEF). It called on GEF in particular to support activities that would enable countries to implement the Framework Convention and plan for adaptation to climate change. The Forum commended a preliminary portfolio of projects to GEF for its support.

Barbados Programme of Action

26. The Forum called on all members, development partners, the United Nation system and regional organizations to participate actively in the regional consultative mechanism, including through the provision of necessary information to SPREP and the Pacific Operations Centre of the Economic and Social Commission

for Asia and the Pacific, and to work in cooperation with the mechanism's advisory committee.

Biodiversity

27. The Forum reiterated the importance of the Biodiversity Convention. It called on all members to become parties to the Convention and to participate to the fullest possible extent in the meetings of the contracting parties to the Convention. The Forum supported international action to develop a framework on biosafety and to consider the need for, and modalities of, a protocol on biosafety taking into account the specific needs and circumstances of small island developing States. The Forum commended the work programme on marine biodiversity as being in the strong interest of Forum members.

28. The Forum recorded its support for the initiative taken under the Convention on International Trade in Endangered Species to facilitate the involvement in and accession to the Convention of small island States, and urged members to consider accession. Leaders commended the successful SPREP campaign for the Year of the Sea Turtle (1995). It called upon members to extend the moratoria established on commercial takes of sea turtles, and support conservation projects building on the awareness created by the Year of the Sea Turtle campaign.

International Coral Reef Initiative

29. The Forum encouraged member Governments to endorse the call to action of the International Coral Reef Initiative and to develop national efforts to develop the framework for action of that Initiative.

Coastal Protection Action Plan

30. The Forum agreed to give serious consideration to the Action Plan on Coastal Protection.

Ocean issues

31. The Forum reiterated the importance of the oceans to its members and expressed its support for efforts to protect the oceans from land-based and other sources of pollution. The Forum noted that an intergovernmental conference to be held in Washington, D.C., in October 1995 is to consider a global programme of action for the protection of the marine environment from land-based activities.

Hazardous and radioactive wastes

32. The Forum adopted the Convention to Ban the Importation into Forum Island Countries of Hazardous and Radioactive Wastes and to Control the Transboundary Movement and Management of Hazardous Wastes within the South Pacific Region (Waigani Convention) for signature on 16 September 1995. The Convention was an important milestone in banning the importation of all hazardous and radioactive wastes from outside the Convention area to Pacific island developing States parties, and ensuring that any transboundary movements of hazardous wastes within the Convention area were completed in a controlled and environmentally sound manner. The Forum thanked the working group of officials and the secretariat for the intensive work put into completing the Convention since the 1994 Forum. The Forum urged all members to sign and ratify the Convention expeditiously to bring it into effect as soon as possible, in accordance with their national processes.

33. The Forum recalled in this context its continuing opposition to dumping of radioactive waste at sea and called for universal adherence to the prohibition of this practice by the London Convention of 1972. It reiterated its support for the London Convention and the need for its effective enforcement.

34. The Forum expressed the region's continuing concerns about the Johnson Atoll Chemical Agent Destruction System, reiterating its consistent past position that the facility should be permanently closed when the current programme of chemical weapons and agent destruction was completed.

Political and security issues

New Caledonia

35. The Forum noted that, while implementation of the Matignon Accords had continued smoothly and generally positively in the past 12 months, the territory's long-term political and constitutional future remained uncertain. The Forum felt that, as the count-down to the 1998 referendum began in earnest, regional monitoring of the situation should be stepped up. This included reactivating, in cooperation with the French authorities, the Forum's Ministerial Committee on New Caledonia. The Forum reiterated its view that the 1998 referendum should closely follow accepted United Nations principles and practices.

36. The Forum reaffirmed its support for continuing contacts with New Caledonia as a constructive contribution towards the Matignon process. It noted the particular role of the Kanak Training Fund in this, and the Fund's continuing successful operation.

Law enforcement cooperation

37. The Forum commended the continued progress in implementation of the Honiara Declaration on Law Enforcement, and the developing Secretariat programme in the area. It expressed appreciation for the cooperation in this programme of specialist regional law enforcement agencies. The Forum noted in particular the process of modernizing extradition laws in the region, in cooperation with the Commonwealth Secretariat and the Pacific Islands Law Officers Meeting, on the basis of a set of principles agreed by officials.

Other nuclear issues

38. The Forum expressed continuing concern about shipments of plutonium and radioactive wastes through the region. It noted with appreciation the cooperation of Japan in responding to the Forum's concerns by the provision of information on, and consultation about, the shipments. It reiterated, however, the expectation that such shipments should be carried out in accordance with the highest international safety and security standards, in a manner which satisfactorily addressed all possible contingencies, and in full consultation with Forum countries.

39. The Forum welcomed the indefinite extension of the Treaty on the Non-Proliferation of Nuclear Weapons at the Review and Extension Conference of the Parties in May 1995, as achieving a long standing Forum objective. It urged all non-signatories to the Treaty to accept the Treaty as soon as possible. It also urged the nuclear Powers to focus on meeting without delay their obligation under the Treaty to negotiate in good faith towards complete nuclear disarmament.

40. The Forum noted that an advisory opinion would soon be delivered by the International Court of Justice on the legality of nuclear weapons.

41. The Forum noted developments on civil nuclear liability and called on the Standing Committee on Nuclear Liability of the International Atomic Energy Agency to conclude promptly a civil nuclear liability regime by the tenth anniversary of the Chernobyl accident.

42. The Forum expressed its support for the establishment of a credible civil nuclear liability regime including adequate compensation for the victims of transboundary damage in accordance with the principles of the Rio Declaration by

incorporating a dedicated transboundary fund of sufficient size. The Forum also believed that such a regime must be capable of attracting widespread adherence from both nuclear and non-nuclear-power generating States throughout the world. The Forum noted that, consistent with the Convention for the Protection of the Natural Resources and Environment of the South Pacific Region, it was important that such a regime incorporate environmental damage within its scope.

Rehabilitation of former nuclear-weapon-test sites

43. The Forum welcomed the increased attention to problems of safety and contamination related to the discontinuation of nuclear operations formerly associated with nuclear-weapon programmes. The Forum called upon all Governments and international organizations that had expertise in the field of clean-up and disposal of radioactive contaminants to give appropriate assistance for remedial purposes when requested by affected countries. The Forum noted that, although some efforts had already been made in this regard, there was still considerable work to be done. The Forum also noted the existence of a special responsibility towards those peoples of the former United Nations Trust Territory administered by the United States, the Marshall Islands, who had been adversely affected as a result of nuclear-weapon tests conducted during the period of the Trusteeship. This responsibility included safe resettlement of displaced human populations and the restoration to economic productivity of affected areas.

Relations with the United Nations

44. The Forum expressed its deep appreciation to the United Nations General Assembly for granting it observer status. It also expressed its appreciation to the Forum secretariat and the South Pacific Applied Geoscience Commission group of Forum country missions in New York for the commendable cooperation they had developed to give substance to the observer role. The Forum, acknowledging the growing importance of the United Nations in this, its fiftieth anniversary year, encouraged Forum members not also members of the United Nations, and other regional organizations to make use of the channel for the region into the United Nations provided by observer status.

45. The Forum reconfirmed its unanimous support, declared at the 1994 Brisbane Forum, for the candidature of Australia for the United Nations Security Council for the two-year term 1997-1998, at elections to be held in October 1996.

46. The Forum asked its members to consider the candidacy of Japan for a seat on the Security Council for the two-year term 1997-1998. In view of the mutual support arrangement between Australia and Sweden, the Forum also asked its members to consider the candidacy of Sweden for the seat of the Western European and Other States on the Security Council for the same period.

Relations with the Association of South-East Asian Nations (ASEAN)

47. The Forum was encouraged by the developing contacts between the Forum and ASEAN secretariats, which were important in strengthening the overall relationship between the two regions. It reiterated the importance of strengthening these links and noted that the Secretary-General would be exploring with his ASEAN counterpart the possibility of a ministerial meeting with ASEAN in 1996 on the margins of the United Nations General Assembly.

Relations with Arab Petroleum Exporting Countries (APEC)

48. The Forum recognized the importance of APEC and noted that its status as an observer was a valuable basis for strengthening its relations with that organization. It considered that the Forum secretariat had a key role to play in keeping Forum island countries informed about APEC activities and processes of relevance to them.

Forum country initiatives

Assembly of Pacific island communities

49. The Forum noted the Melanesian Spearhead Group proposal for an assembly of Pacific island communities and encouraged the Pacific island countries and territories to consider the proposal further.

Institutional matters

Post-Forum dialogue

50. The Forum welcomed the Republic of Korea as a post-Forum dialogue partner, to participate for the first time in the dialogue at Port Moresby, on 17 and 18 September. This reflected the growing importance of the dialogue, and the interest which Forum countries had in strengthening relations with the Republic of Korea, an increasingly significant economic and political presence in the region.

Forum secretariat-wide review

51. The Forum endorsed the key recommendations of the Forum secretariat-wide review regarding the strengthening of the policy role of the secretariat, enhancing regional coordination and review through the South Pacific Organizations Coordinating Committee mechanism, and assisting member countries to develop their own capacity for economic and sectoral policy development, implementation and evaluation. The Forum also supported a rationalization of the divisional structure appropriate to servicing this redefined mandate.

Name change

52. The Forum noted that, with the admission of Palau, there was merit in considering renaming the organization.

PIBA/PINA

53. The Forum noted that officials had discussed the useful work done by the Pacific Islands Broadcasting Association (PIBA) and the Pacific Islands News Association (PINA) and that PIBA and PINA had been encouraged to develop their work programmes, working closely with the Forum secretariat.

Reports of regional organizations

54. The Forum received and adopted the annual report of the Secretary-General of the Forum secretariat. It also received with appreciation the annual reports of the following:

(a) Director of the Forum Fisheries Agency;

(b) Director of the South Pacific Applied Geoscience Commission;

(c) Vice-Chancellor of the University of the South Pacific;

(d) Director of the South Pacific Regional Environment Programme;

(e) Director of the Tourism Council of the South Pacific.

Date and venue of next meeting

55. The Forum reaffirmed its appreciation and acceptance of the kind offer of the Republic of the Marshall Islands to host the Twenty-seventh South Pacific Forum. The date for the Forum would be finalized by the Republic of the Marshall Islands in consultation with the Secretariat.

APPENDIX I

Securing development beyond 2000

Plan of action adopted by the Twenty-sixth South Pacific Forum

1. The Twenty-sixth South Pacific Forum, which met at Madang from 13 to 15 September 1995, gave close consideration to a wide range of strategies for securing development beyond the year 2000. In doing so, it recognized that security involves strengthening national and regional relations, especially capacities to sustain development in the medium and long terms, as well as regional stability.

2. Specific measure to which the Forum has agreed to give prompt attention are listed below. They include the endorsement of a logging code of conduct, measures to cooperate in promoting trade, transport and tourism and an examination of how the Forum might enhance regional support arrangements. Other measures may be added by agreement as those listed are put into effect, further consideration is given to related issues, and additional strategies are devised for strengthening cooperation in securing development beyond 2000.

Increasing economic cooperation

3. Forum members are conscious of the changes in international economic relations consequent on the formation of the World Trade Organization and likely to follow from the agreement by members of the Asia Pacific Economic Cooperation Forum to lower tariffs in the wider Asia-Pacific region. They are also aware of the increasing opportunities for mutually beneficial interaction arising from development in Forum member countries, and keen to cooperate in putting them to mutual advantage. They have, therefore, agreed to review existing patterns of trade, investment and other aspects of regional economic relations with a view to broadening, deepening and diversifying regional economic cooperation.

4. Issues to which they believe that particular attention should be given include strategies for increasing national and regional competitiveness by cooperating in reducing both tariff and non-tariff barriers to trade in the region, drawing on experience with other regional and subregional arrangements and consistent with the principles of the World Trade Organization. The implications of - and for - taxation regimes, exchange rates, transport arrangements and labour costs should be carefully examined. Niche markets should be identified and developed. Quarantine requirements should be clarified in purpose, scope and application and, as far as possible, standardized.

5. Opportunities for enhancing regional cooperation in respect of standards, product identification and consumer protection should be explored, particularly in so far as national institutions might help to achieve economies of scale by performing regional roles.

6. The South Pacific Forum secretariat will identify practical options, and submit them for consideration by the Forum Officials Committee, which will recommend a plan of action to enhance regional economic cooperation for discussion at the Twenty-seventh South Pacific Forum.

7. Individual Forum members will seek funding, from domestic and/or other sources, to assist in promoting regional economic cooperation, including shop-front facilities to publicize products exported from and investment possibilities in other Forum member countries.

8. Forum members will approach other Governments and international organizations for assistance in mounting regional promotions, including

permanent South Pacific trade commissions, in East Asia, Europe and North America.

9. Aware of the difficulties often involved in travelling or moving goods within the region, Forum members have agreed that their ministers responsible for transport, including shipping and civil aviation, should meet in order to discuss common problems and to identify areas where enhanced cooperation might provide solutions. The formation of strategic alliances between services providers is an option which they believe is especially worthy of close attention.

10. Particular issues and options which they believe that relevant authorities should consider carefully include the economies that might be achieved by sharing aircraft; the manner in which travel and trade might be facilitated by coordinating airline and shipping schedules; the designation of additional regional and subregional hubs; and the advantages of jointly promoting links into, within and out of the region.

11. The need for additional facilities, including accommodation, at prospective stopovers and destinations will also be examined.

12. The South Pacific lies at the centre of one of the most rapidly growing tourism networks in the world. The region has much to offer to potential visitors in search of natural beauty, cultural spectacle and diversity, and recreation, including rest, sport and adventure.

13. Individual countries have priorities of their own, especially in trying to balance the kinds and numbers of tourists they seek with maintaining cultural integrity and environmental conservation. Together, they can offer a great deal to visitors from within the region or beyond, including distinctive cultural experiences.

14. Forum members have, therefore, agreed to direct their respective tourism authorities to explore options for increasing joint promotions, both within and beyond the region. In particular, they will examine transport needs, including national facilities and international links, as well as needs - and openings for investment - in relation to accommodation.

15. Their overall aim will be to encourage everyone concerned with the industry's future to take a long-term view; to ensure that visitors are made welcome by local communities (which should benefit from their presence) and to see that tourists get genuine value for the money they spend. Issues like seasonality should also be addressed.

16. Expert bodies like the Tourism Council of the South Pacific and the Pacific Area Travel Association will be invited to give advice.

17. The Forum agrees that the various measures outlined in this Plan for promoting regional cooperation in trade, transport and tourism should be implemented without delay.

18. The Forum agreed that its Chairman convene or ensure meetings are convened of relevant Ministers during the next 12 months to implement this Plan, and that the Twenty-seventh South Pacific Forum should review progress made in securing development beyond 2000 through enhancing regional economic cooperation.

<u>Logging code of conduct</u>

19. Forum members endorsed the draft regional code of conduct on logging and committed themselves to implementation of its provisions as part of their national codes.

Regional support arrangements

20. Having considered possible threats and existing arrangements, Forum members have agreed that the most serious threats that the region seems likely to have to face in the future are not military in nature but may include challenges to national integrity and independence, environmental damage and national disasters. The Forum, therefore, agreed to examine a comprehensive approach towards security and to broaden and deepen cooperation accordingly.

21. The Forum Officials Committee has, therefore, been directed to report back to the Twenty-seventh South Pacific Forum with detailed proposals for arrangements designed to ensure that the region can consult promptly in response to legitimate requests, and provide such assistance as may be agreed in a timely, efficient and cost-effective manner.

22. The arrangements must be consistent with - and supportive of - other arrangements for regional cooperation, while avoiding waste and duplication.

23. Issues to be addressed in the report of the Committee will include a mechanism providing for consultations between regular, annual Forum meetings; procedures for facilitating cooperation through appropriate preparations in respect of training logistics, and control of agreed operations; as well as the legal safeguards required.

APPENDIX II

South Pacific Forum Vision Statement

Issued at Madang, Papua New Guinea, on 14 September 1995

The leaders who have participated in the 26th meeting of the South Pacific Forum, the paramount regional intergovernmental organization in the South Pacific, have a vision for enhancing regional cooperation for the next 25 years in which:

Forum members cooperate on the basis of equality, friendship and mutual respect - with due regard for what each can afford - in efforts to maintain security, improve living standards and ensure sustainable development throughout the region;

Opportunities for cooperation with other Governments, non-governmental organizations and international organizations, including other bodies in the Asia-Pacific region, are actively pursued and developed;

Resources, including fisheries, forestry, minerals, water and land, are developed with proper regard for conservation, the legacy of past generations and the future;

Unity in securing shared interests contributes to the national, regional and global good;

Material progress is matched by improvement in the quality of people's lives, including human development, equality between women and men, and protection of children;

Vulnerability to the effects of natural disasters, environmental damage and other threats will be overcome;

Indigenous and other values, traditions and customs of the region are respected and promoted through cultural, sporting and other exchanges;

Self-determination will be exercised in the remaining dependent territories, and unwelcome activities by external Powers, including nuclear testing, will cease;

International economic cooperation, through trade, investment and other exchanges, strengthens subsistence and commercial agriculture, industry development and competition, leading to growth - with equity, broadly-based participation and capacity-building for self-reliance;

Openness, accountability and other principles of good government are embodied in the practices, policies and plans of regional institutions; and

National, subregional and regional efforts to achieve the Forum's vision receive the support they require from the Forum secretariat and other regional organizations.

APPENDIX III

Forum leaders' statement on nuclear testing

Leaders express their extreme outrage at the resumption of French nuclear testing in the Pacific. Forum leaders again demand that France desist from any further tests in the region and call on other countries also to seek to persuade France to cease testing.

The Forum also notes that the painful memories resulting from nuclear testing conducted in the region a half-century ago still haunt many people in the region.

Should France continue its testing in the Pacific, the Forum will review France's status as a post-Forum dialogue partner.

The outrage of Forum members countries is so much the greater because of the intransigence of France, together with the People's Republic of China, in persisting with their nuclear tests in the face of not only the strong views of the Pacific region, but also the appeal of the ASEAN regional forum, and the world-wide sentiment against testing.

The decisions by the Governments of France and the People's Republic of China to continue testing are completely contrary to the undertaking on 11 May 1995 at the Review and Extension Conference of the Parties to the Treaty on the Non-Proliferation of Nuclear Weapons to exercise "utmost restraint" in nuclear testing pending the completion of negotiations on a comprehensive test-ban treaty that would ban nuclear tests for all time.

The conclusion of a comprehensive test-ban treaty is an objective of the highest importance for the international community. Leaders therefore welcome the recent announcements of the United States of America and France to support a truly comprehensive test-ban treaty. They call on all members of the international community, and especially the nuclear weapon States, to spare no effort to ensure the conclusion of a comprehensive test-ban treaty no later than 1996.

In the spirit of this renewed emphasis on global disarmament, leaders call on France to sign and ratify the protocols of the South Pacific Nuclear Free Zone Treaty. They urge the United States and the United Kingdom of Great Britain and Northern Ireland to do likewise, noting that the People's Republic of China and the Russian Federation have already signed the protocols.

The decision of the Government of Vanuatu to sign the South Pacific Nuclear Free Zone Treaty at the Forum is warmly welcomed.

The Forum will continue to oppose nuclear testing at every opportunity, including at the United Nations General Assembly.

Leaders commend the efforts commenced by the Forum delegation to Paris in June. They thank the Forum Regional Action Committee for its work in supporting the activities of Forum Governments and endorse the report of its activities presented to the Forum.

Leaders welcome New Zealand's action to resume its 1973 International Court of Justice case against French nuclear testing and its environmental effects in the Pacific and commend the action of Forum members seeking to intervene in the proceedings to support New Zealand's request to the Court.

Leaders reiterate the call by the Melanesian Spearhead Group leaders through the Lakatoro Declaration and by the South Pacific Environment Ministers Meeting in August 1995 for France to close its nuclear testing facilities in the Pacific, except as required for environmental monitoring; to accept full and exclusive responsibility for any adverse impacts from French testing on the Pacific environment and people; and to provide access to the international community to all the scientific data it holds to the testing sites themselves to make possible an independent and comprehensive assessment of the risks involved.

Finally, Forum leaders express their sincere appreciation to people from the region and around the world who have offered their support and their voice to the campaign against nuclear testing. They renew their undertaking to take all possible steps to stop nuclear testing and the proliferation of nuclear weapons.

19. LETTER DATED 2 OCTOBER 1995 FROM THE PERMANENT REPRESENTATIVE OF THE PHILIPPINESTO THE UNITED NATIONS ADDRESSED TO THE SECRETARY-GENERAL (MINISTERIAL DECLARATION OF THE GROUP OF 77 ADOPTED ON 29 SEPTEMBER 1995)

Doc. no.: A/50/518 6 October 1995

I have the honour to transmit herewith the Ministerial Declaration of the Group of 77 adopted on the occasion of the nineteenth annual meeting of Ministers for Foreign Affairs of the Group of 77, held at United Nations Headquarters in New York on 29 September 1995 (see annex).

On behalf of the Group of 77, I would highly appreciate if you would arrange for the present letter and its annex to be circulated as an official document of the General Assembly under agenda items 12, 20, 23, 24, 39, 52, 94, 95, 96, 97, 100, 101, 102, 161 and 163.

(Signed) Felipe MABILANGAN
Permanent Representative of the
Philippines to the United Nations
Chairman of the Group of 77
New York

ANNEX

Ministerial Declaration of the Group of 77 adopted on 29 September 1995

1. The Nineteenth Annual Meeting of the Ministers for Foreign Affairs of the Group of 77 was held in New York on 29 September 1995.

2. The Ministers expressed the view that the occasion of the 50th Anniversary of the United Nations provided a historic opportunity for all Member States of the United Nations to work towards fulfilling the purposes and principles of the Charter with renewed vigor and effectiveness in order to ensure a better life for all peoples, the eradication of poverty as well as reducing inequalities and gaps in living standards among nations and promoting development. They were convinced this remained the critical challenge for mankind as it entered the 21st century. Towards this end, the Ministers emphasized that in a world characterized by deepening interdependence and the globalization and the liberalization of the world economy, which presents both opportunities and challenges in terms of positive growth impulses and negative shocks, peace and security cannot be ensured in the absence of sustained economic growth and development, particularly in developing countries.

3. In reviewing developments in the world economic situation, the Ministers noted that there exist some positive trends in the world economy but continued to express concern at the slow and unbalanced growth of the global economy. They also expressed concern at the continuing adverse external economic environment for development characterized by increased protectionist tendencies in and unilateral actions by the developed countries, the worsening terms of trade of developing countries, stagnation and decline in ODA flows, restrictions on access to technologies critical to development, the inadequate allocation of resources of international financial institutions and volatile financial flows to developing countries linked, among others, to instability in global capital markets and fluctuations in exchange rates. Moreover, they noted with concern that the income gap between the developed and developing countries continued to widen. They stressed the need for these trends to be reversed decisively.

4. The Ministers stressed that international cooperation for development should be aimed at creating an international economic environment which supports and facilitates the national efforts of developing countries aimed at renewing sustained economic growth and development. Essential to this was the need for continuous macroeconomic policy coordination at the international level to foster the sustained growth of the world economy and for international economic decision-making processes to be transparent and involve fully the developing countries. At the same time, they stressed the critical need for developed countries and developing countries to engage in a comprehensive and constructive dialogue on all key development issues and to foster a genuine partnership for development. The early fulfillment of agreed international commitments and targets on development, which, in turn, required the provision of adequate resources, was deemed necessary. They reiterated that without adequate resources the development commitments agreed at the various international conferences and meetings on development would remain unfulfilled.

[...]

25. The Ministers stressed the need for prompt and full implementation of the commitments and recommendations of the United Nations Conference on Environment and Development (UNCED), which have more relevance today than ever before. In this regard, they stressed that such implementation should not contradict the right of developing countries to benefit fully from the utilization of their resources vital for sustained economic growth and development. They also urgently called on the international community, particularly the developed countries, to fulfill all their commitments contained in Agenda 21.

26. They expressed their profound regret that the developed countries have failed to fulfill the commitments they made at UNCED and renewed their call on developed countries to fulfill their commitments to provide adequate, predictable, new and additional financial and other resources towards this end. They also reaffirmed the important role that the Bretton Woods and other international financial institutions should play in this regard. They also stressed that developed countries should take concrete measures for the transfer of environmentally sound technologies to developing countries on favourable terms, including on concessional and preferential terms.

27. They emphasized the importance of implementing the recommendation of the International Conference on Population and Development into action at all levels, and that such implementation would require new and additional resources.

28. The Ministers reiterated the importance of convening a Global Conference on Migration and Development bearing in mind the recommendations of the General Assembly, and reaffirmed the need for international cooperation and concerted responses to the plight and predicament of migrant workers and their families. Towards this end, they encouraged all

countries to become party to the UN Convention on the Protection of Migrant Workers and Their Families.

29. The Ministers stressed that in order for developing countries to implement the decisions under the Convention on Biological Diversity, priority should be given to the access and transfer of appropriate biotechnologies, and to a more constructive and cooperative approach by developed countries with developing country partners for the equitable sharing of benefits from the use of biological resources. In this context, they consider the need to examine ways and means for the effective protection, compensation and use of traditional forest related knowledge, innovations and practices of forest dwellers, indigenous people and other local communities, as well as fair and equitable sharing of benefits arising from such knowledge, innovations and practices. The Ministers also supported the idea to enhance the scope of the debate with regard to this issue in different fields. The Ministers also welcomed the generous offer of the Government of Indonesia to host the COP-2 of the Convention on Biodiversity in November 1995 and urged member states to participate actively in the Conference.

30. The Ministers underscored their determination to adhere to the principles and fulfill the commitments contained in the Declaration of the World Summit for Social Development and emphasized the importance of implementing the Programme of Action aimed at eradication of poverty, enhancement of productive employment and reduction of unemployment, and to foster social integration.

31. The Ministers welcomed the convening of the First Conference of the Parties on the Framework Convention on Climate Change and the decisions agreed and noted that it was a first step in the process which must lead to concrete initiatives aimed at the full implementation of the Convention. They urged Annex 1 parties to fulfil their obligations under the Convention, particularly the provision of new and additional resources and the transfer of environmentally sound technologies on preferential and concessional basis.

32. The Ministers urged all Member States of the UN to accelerate the process of signature and ratification of the International Convention to Combat Desertification in Those Countries Experiencing Serious Drought and/or Desertification, particularly in Africa, with a view to expediting the entry into force and full and effective implementation of the Convention and its regional annexes. There is a need for the international community to provide substantial financial resources and other forms of active support for the efforts of all affected developing country parties, particularly those in Africa, and the least developed countries, to combat desertification and mitigate the effects of drought.

33. The Ministers welcomed the entry into force of the UN Convention of the Law of the Sea and invited countries that have not done so to accede to it. They looked forward to the successful outcome of the forthcoming Meeting of the States Parties to the Convention, including the establishment of the International Tribunal for the Law of the Sea. The Ministers noted the recent successful conclusion of the United Nations Conference on Straddling Fish Stocks and Highly Migratory Fish Stocks as an essential contribution towards conservation and sustainable use of marine living resources, and in particular expressed satisfaction at the recognition in the Agreement adopted by the Conference of the special requirements of developing States in relation to the conservation, management and development of fisheries for those stocks.

[...]

20. LETTER DATED 13 NOVEMBER 1995 FROM THE PERMANENT REPRESENTATIVE OF THE RUSSIAN FEDERATION TO THE UNITED NATIONS ADDRESSED TO THE SECRETARY-GENERAL (NAVIGATION IN THE BLACK SEA STRAITS)

Doc. no.: A/50/754 14 November 1995

I have the honour to submit the text of a document related to the issue of transit and navigation in the Black Sea Straits (see annex).

I should be grateful if you would have this letter and its annex circulated as a document of the General Assembly under agenda item 39.

(Signed) S. LAVROV

Annex

[Original: Russian]

Navigation in the Black Sea Straits

Ensuring the safety of navigation in the Black Sea Straits is becoming, in the current circumstances, a matter of increasing urgency, since it is a major condition for avoiding accidents and incidents involving ships and preventing the related threat of pollution or other damage to the Straits and the adjacent coastal areas.

In this regard, we can only welcome the improvements in the organization and technical capacity of the Turkish coastal services and the adoption of rules that would help ensure such safety and facilitate international navigation through the Straits.

At the same time, the Maritime Traffic Regulations for the Turkish Straits and the Marmara Region, which were adopted by the Turkish Government and entered into force on 1 July 1994, go beyond the solution of technical problems related to ensuring safe navigation and do not conform to the provisions of the Convention regarding the regime of the Straits, adopted in Montreux in 1936, and other universally recognized norms of maritime law.

A number of articles of the Regulations provide for the introduction of procedures regulating passage through the Straits and of substantial restrictions, including the complete prohibition of such passage, for certain categories of vessels depending on their length, draught, cargo and so forth. Maritime traffic in the Straits may even be halted without sufficiently valid reasons. In some cases, the use of paid services, such as towing, has been made obligatory. The Regulations require vessels to provide information that is not stipulated in the Montreux Convention. The wording relating to transit is ambiguous, which gives room for arbitrary interpretation and the application of measures with respect to a vessel in transit through the Straits that should not be applied to it.

Irrespective of the various ways in which they may be interpreted, the Regulations, in accordance with articles 1 and 2 (d), are applicable to military vessels, in spite of the fact that customs and health inspections, penalties and other similar measures are incompatible with the international legal status of military vessels, which possess immunity.

At the same time, the Montreux Convention provides that "merchant vessels shall enjoy complete freedom of transit and navigation through the Straits, by day and by night, under any flag and with any kind of cargo, without any formalities", except for the sanitary control of merchant vessels entering the Straits and payment for optional services, such as pilotage and towage, rendered at the request of the agent or master of any such vessel.

In the light of the foregoing, one can only conclude that the basic provisions of the Montreux Convention have not been duly reflected in the Regulations in spite of the fact that all Parties to the Convention, including Turkey, assumed the obligation to exercise the principle of freedom of transit and navigation by sea in the Straits in accordance with the provisions of the Convention (art. 1). Further, no account has been taken of the universally recognized norms of ordinary maritime law, which do not permit the creation of obstacles or the halting of transit through straits used by international shipping.

The above-mentioned position has been supported by such a competent intergovernmental organization as the International Maritime Organization (IMO). In May 1994, the IMO Maritime Safety Committee considered draft international rules on navigation in the Straits submitted by the Turkish side and in many respects repeating the Regulations. The Committee rejected the Turkish proposals, which sought to establish Turkish control over navigation in the Straits, and adopted the rules and recommendations based on the strict observance of the principle of the freedom of navigation through this international waterway. In particular, the Committee stressed that Turkey's national norms should conform fully with the rules and recommendations, which will enter into force in November 1995. In October 1994, the IMO Legal Committee reaffirmed this appeal to Turkey.

The document of the Black Sea Economic Cooperation Working Group on Transport, adopted in June 1994 in Istanbul, also provides that documents adopted by a littoral State should respect the special regime of the Straits established by the Montreux Convention and should be in full conformity with IMO decisions.

One might have expected that Turkey would take steps to implement the IMO decisions. Unfortunately, in the year and a half that has elapsed since May 1994, Turkey has not deemed it necessary to do this. Turkey has also not responded to proposals to settle disputes through bilateral consultations. Instead, Turkish representatives limit themselves to the groundless assertion that, since the issuance in November 1994 of the instruction on the application of the Regulations, there are no longer any discrepancies between the Regulations and the IMO rules. However, although the instruction is more flexible, it is, unlike the Regulations, an administrative - and not a legislative - document, and not only can it not rescind the Regulations but it can itself at any time be made tougher or rescinded by a simple order of an administrative official.

In practice, Turkey's attempt to amend, on a unilateral basis, the regime of navigation in the Straits has already resulted in considerable economic loss as a consequence of the unjustified detention of vessels prior to their entry into the Straits, first and foremost for countries of the Black Sea littoral. As regards the Russian Federation, between 1 July 1994 and 30 September 1995, there have been 249 cases of detention of Russian vessels, which led to the loss of 1492 hours of operating time and the direct loss of more than $670,000, not considering lost profit, lost contracts and lateness penalties.

Turkey's attempt to introduce unilaterally its own rules for transit through the Straits can create an extremely dangerous precedent for international shipping in other geographical regions.

The United Nations General Assembly, as the body that coordinates and monitors the use of the world's oceans and seas in accordance with the provisions of the United Nations Convention on the Law of the Sea, should not disregard acts that contradict universally recognized principles and norms of international law. Strict adherence to the principle of the conscientious implementation of international obligations will, undoubtedly, help bring about an improvement in the situation regarding the Black Sea Straits and will speed up efforts to find a constructive solution to the problem of ensuring the safety of navigation in the Straits.

21. LETTER DATED 7 DECEMBER 1995 FROM THE PERMANENT REPRESENTATIVE OF TURKEY TO THE UNITED NATIONS ADDRESSED TO THE SECRETARY-GENERAL (NAVIGATION THROUGH THE TURKISH STRAITS)

Doc. no.: A/50/809 | 8 December 1995

I have the honour to submit the text of a document related to navigation through the Turkish Straits.

I should be grateful if the text of the present letter and its annex could be circulated as a document of the fiftieth session of the General Assembly under agenda item 39.

(Signed) Hüseyin E. ÇELEM
Ambassador
Permanent Representative

ANNEX

Navigation through the Turkish Straits

1. The Turkish Straits, composed of the Sea of Marmara and the straits of Istanbul and of Çanakkale, are unique in many respects. These Straits, with a very narrow and winding shape, are one of the most hazardous, crowded, difficult and potentially dangerous waterways from the point of view of navigation in the world. Furthermore, they also bear unique physical, geographical, hydrological and oceanographic, and legal characteristics and complicated navigational conditions.

2. The Strait of Istanbul, which runs straight through the city of 12 million inhabitants, is approximately 31 kilometres long and 700 metres wide at its narrowest point. As it has several sharp turns, the ships are bound to alter course at least 12 times at these bends.

3. The Strait of Çanakkale is about 70 kilometres long, with a general width ranging from 1.3 to 2 kilometres. A very sharp course alteration is needed at its narrowest point.

4. The Sea of Marmara, between the Istanbul and the Çanakkale straits, is an internal body of water of Turkey, with a densely populated coastline, through which every transiting vessel has to pass.

5. The Turkish Straits are among the most crowded sea lanes in the world. Navigation in the Straits is highly congested by merchant traffic, coasters, fishing vessels and local traffic. This dense traffic includes the transport of noxious, dangerous and hazardous cargoes (011, liquified natural gas (LNG), liquefied petroleum gas (LPG), chemicals, other explosive and environmentally hazardous substances).

6. Approximately 50,000 vessels and more than 150 foreign warships transit the Straits per year. The number of local crossings by intra-city ferries and other shuttle boats is approximately 1,000 per day. This figure does not include the movement of transiting ships, leisure craft and fishing vessels. One and one half million people are daily on the move by way of sea crossing from one side to another in Istanbul.

7. Owing to many physical constraints, the Straits already present a bottleneck for maritime traffic. The risks and dangers associated with tanker navigation, maritime accidents and environmental catastrophes are further aggravated by the increase in density of traffic, tanker size and cargo capacity, as well as the nature of the cargo.

8. The Turkish Straits are among the very few straits which fall outside Part III of the United Nations Convention on the Law of the Sea, to which Turkey is not a party. As stipulated in article 35 (c) of the said Convention, passage through the Turkish Straits is regulated by a long-standing international agreement, namely the 1936 Montreux Convention regarding the Regime of Straits. The mode of passage which has been in effect in the Turkish Straits is clearly different from the transit passage regime which has been developed throughout the Convention on the Law of the Sea.

9. Turkey is committed to the principle of freedom of navigation through the international straits. The essence of the freedom of navigation is that it should be exercised and implemented in safe conditions both for the navigators and for the inhabitants of the coasts bordering the Straits. Therefore, it is the right and indeed the responsibility of Turkey, as the only bordering country, to protect the public and the environment as well as to ensure the safety of navigation and the efficiency of traffic flow in the Straits. In line with this, since 1936 Turkey has on a number of occasions put into effect rules for regulating the traffic in the Straits, the most recent one prior to 1994 being the 1982 Istanbul Port Regulations.

10. With these considerations in mind, a set of regulations for maritime traffic in the Strait of Istanbul, the Sea of Marmara and the Strait of Çanakkale was promulgated on 11 January 1994 and entered into force on 1 July 1994.

11. All actions taken by Turkey have been completely in line with the Montreux Convention as well as the principles of general international law. The Montreux Convention, which affirms the freedom of navigation through the Turkish Straits, at the same time highlights Turkey's full sovereignty over the Straits area. The purpose of the new regulations is to ensure, to the extent possible, the safety of navigation while providing security to the inhabitants in and around the Straits area as well as the environment at the current dense level of maritime traffic.

12. Turkey, fully cognizant of its responsibilities, has submitted traffic separation schemes (TSS) in the Turkish Straits to the International Maritime Organization (IMO). The relevant bodies of IMO, the Subcommittee on Safety of Navigation and the Maritime Safety Committee (MSC), have fully discussed and adopted the TSS and a set of associated special rules and recommendations having relevance to the safe navigation of large vessels in the straits of Istanbul and Çanakkale, for the purposes of the TSS.

13. The special rules and recommendations adopted by MSC at its sixty-third session in May 1994 have a specific purpose and scope related to large vessels.

The TSS and these associated rules and recommendations became effective on 24 November 1994. Both the TSS and the rules and recommendations were adopted by the nineteenth IMO Assembly, which took place between 13 and 24 November 1995.

14. IMO rules and recommendations are limited in scope. They are functional and pertain to specific situations with respect to the implementation of the TSS in the straits of Istanbul and Çanakkale.

15. On the other hand, the Regulations, which fall within national jurisdiction and therefore were not submitted to IMO, are comprehensive in scope and contain detailed provisions covering all aspects of traffic management in the whole area of the Straits, as well as rules to be applied to all vessels irrespective of their size.

16. In our times, it is not possible to consider, in the international law of the sea, the notion of "freedom of passage" independently from the notion of "safe navigation".

17. In addition, it is a fundamental principle of international law that the status of the maritime waters within a strait is in no way to be affected by the very fact that these waters are used for international navigation. The status of the Turkish Straits is such that they are internal waters. Turkey, taking into consideration the principles of freedom of passage and safety of navigation, as well as the spirit of the Montreux Convention, has enacted the Regulations for an orderly traffic management in the Turkish Straits.

18. Therefore, the Turkish Regulations are fully in line with applicable international law and freedom of navigation. The Regulations uphold the 1936 Montreux Convention and in no way infringe upon its provisions. They are not aimed at restricting or impairing the right of navigation in the Turkish Straits.

19. Had no regulations been adopted for passage through the Turkish Straits, accidents that could have happened not only would have endangered the densely populated urban areas and the environment, but also would have resulted in closure to traffic of the Straits for extended periods. That in turn would have impaired freedom of passage through the Straits.

20. Based on factual evidence, the record of implementation contains ample evidence to prove this.

21. Between 1 July 1994 and November 1995, 58,948 vessels passed through the Straits of Istanbul. One hundred sixty-four of them were large vessels, 15 per cent carrying dangerous cargo.

22. There has been a sharp and steady increase in the number of vessels using the Straits. In 1994, the daily average number of ships using the Straits was 77. This figure reached 90 vessels per day in 1994 and 132 vessels per day in the first 10 months of 1995. In October 1995, 4,166 vessels belonging to 57 countries used the Strait of Istanbul. The daily average was 134 vessels. Six hundred eleven of these were large vessels, 383 of which carried dangerous cargo, 207 being loaded tankers.

23. Despite the sharp and steady increase in the number and tonnage of vessels using the Straits, casualty rates have declined considerably recently, from 27 major accidents in 1993 to 17 in 1994. Eleven of them occurred prior to the new Regulations. In 1995, only four accidents took place in the Strait of Istanbul.

24. As for the issue of delays, the safe passage of a large vessel could be ensured by temporarily suspending the TSS and two-way traffic and instituting one-way traffic arrangements. This could only be accomplished by requiring waiting periods at the entrance to the Straits. In many instances, the vessels

of the complaining States had to await the safe passage of vessels flying their own flag.

25. Having given this factual background on issues related to the Turkish Straits, I would now like to refer to the letter of Ambassador Lavrov of the Russian Federation, which was circulated as a document of the General Assembly (A/50/754) on 14 November 1995.

26. From the very beginning, the Russian side has attributed ill intentions to the Turkish side. These attributions are totally unfounded, all the more so in the light of the record of implementation. The Russian side appears, in words, to have a certain consideration for Turkey's concerns on issues of safety, yet acts with well-known political and economic motives, in total disregard of these legitimate concerns.

27. The letter presents a totally distorted view of the Maritime Traffic Regulations introduced by Turkey on 1 July 1994. By using very condensed and vague language, it intends to mislead those who are not very familiar with the issues involved.

28. Information requested for large vessels is simply necessary for scheduling the passage of such vessels in an orderly manner. In addition, the relevant provision of the 1989 Basel Convention on the Control of Transboundary Movements of Hazardous Wastes and their Disposal has in fact been reflected in the Regulations. Furthermore, provisions of such international conventions as the Convention on the International Regulations for Preventing Collisions at Sea and the International Convention for the Safety of Life at Sea (SOLAS) have also been duly and adequately reflected in the Regulations.

29. There are no categorical restrictions in the Regulations for any type of vessel that is capable of passing safely through the Straits. But, for example, vessels not under command or restricted in their ability to manoeuvre could hardly be exempt in the Straits from the rules which are internationally deemed as necessary for the safety of navigation in other bodies of sea. Also, passage of vessels with an air draught above a certain height is physically constrained owing to the presence of two bridges in Istanbul.

30. Suspension of traffic exceptionally for brief periods such as for compulsory cases, and on reasonable grounds, is a necessity. As an example, a need may arise for laying sewage pipelines by the Municipality. In fact, the last time, a similar task was carried out by using a Russian vessel.

31. Vessels with air draught of between 54 and 58 metres will need to be escorted by tugboats to ensure that such vessels remain on course while passing under the two bridges, since the heights of the bridges are not uniform over their arches. Even a slight deviation of such a vessel would cause a collision. For the same reason and as is also stipulated in item 5 of the IMO rules, a vessel under tow may only pass through the Straits when being towed by a suitable tugboat of sufficient strength.

32. The basic information requested on the vessel and its cargo is required only for the purposes of managing the traffic flow efficiently and taking any measures that may be needed, such as suspending two-way traffic and regulating one-way traffic. Furthermore, items 1 and 2 of the IMO rules strongly recommend participation in this reporting system. In addition, in article 2 of the Montreux Convention communication to the coastal State of information concerning name, nationality, tonnage, destination and last port of call is also provided for.

33. Any misunderstanding as to whether the definition of "vessels" includes warships has been sufficiently addressed in a note given to the Russian Federation and other interested parties who made such a request. Thus, the issue of which articles of the Regulations pertain to military vessels has been clarified. Hence, the terms of the Montreux Convention are totally upheld.

Also, the principle of sovereign immunity and the precepts of international law concerning vessels of war are naturally unaffected. However, in the interest of safety of navigation, call point reports are highly appreciated.

34. The eighth and ninth paragraphs of the document (ibid., annex) are also replete with errors and distortions.

35. No "Turkish proposals" were declined in the May 1994 meeting of the IMO Maritime Safety Committee. The Russian side insists on confusing an explanatory note which had been presented by Turkey, with the draft rules and recommendations that were actually discussed and adopted by the MSC. In fact, the Turkish delegation actively contributed to the preparation of these rules, which in no way contradict or restrict the regulations.

36. The reference to the Black Sea Economic Cooperation Working Group on Transit is not relevant since the Regulations do not contradict the 1936 Montreux Convention.

37. In conclusion, the only constructive approach to the solution of the problem of ensuring the safety of navigation in the Straits is to abide by the rules and regulations in effect. Indeed, the traffic in the Straits is too dense and the risks involved are too high to allow for an "à-la-carte" usage. Moreover, not only the coastal State but also each of the user States has a vested interest in a managed passage in conformity with recent developments of international law and practice.

38. Turkey is and has always been receptive to suggestions for bilateral review of any complaints concerning the implementation of the Regulations. However, Turkey would be rather reluctant to enter into a debate with parties that choose to adopt confrontational approaches on this issue in international forums.

39. With these considerations in mind, I should also emphasize that the General Assembly of the United Nations is not the right forum to handle this purely technical issue.

22. UNGA RESOLUTION ON LAW OF THE SEA

Doc. no.: A/Res.50/23 5 December 1995

The General Assembly,

Emphasizing the universal character of the United Nations Convention on the Law of the Sea, 59/ its fundamental importance for the maintenance and strengthening of international peace and security, as well as for the sustainable use and development of the seas and oceans and their resources,

Considering that, in its resolution 2749 (XXV) of 17 December 1970, it proclaimed that the seabed and ocean floor, and the subsoil thereof, beyond the limits of national jurisdiction (hereinafter referred to as "the Area"), as well as the resources of the Area, are the common heritage of mankind, and considering also that the Convention, together with the Agreement relating to the Implementation of Part XI of the United Nations Convention on the Law of the Sea of 10 December 1982, 60/ provides the regime to be applied to the Area and its resources,

Recalling its resolution 49/28 of 6 December 1994, on the law of the sea, adopted consequent to the entry into force of the Convention on 16 November 1994,

Aware of the importance of the effective implementation of the Convention and its uniform and consistent application, as well as the growing need to promote and facilitate international cooperation on the law of the sea and ocean affairs at the global, regional and subregional levels,

Conscious of the strategic importance of the Convention as a framework for national, regional and global action in the marine sector, as recognized also by the United Nations Conference on Environment and Development in chapter 17 of Agenda 21, 61/

Recognizing the impact on States of the entry into force of the Convention and the increasing need, particularly of developing States, for advice and assistance in its implementation in order to benefit thereunder,

Noting the responsibilities of the Secretary-General and competent international organizations under the Convention, in particular pursuant to its entry into force and as required by resolution 49/28,

---

59/ Official Records of the Third United Nations Conference on the Law of the Sea, vol. XVII (United Nations publication, Sales No. E.84.V.3), document A/CONF.62/122.

60/ Resolution 48/263, annex.

61/ Report of the United Nations Conference on Environment and Development, Rio de Janeiro, 3-14 June 1992 (A/CONF.151/26/Rev.1 (Vol. I and Vol. I/Corr.1, Vol. II, Vol. III and Vol. III/Corr.1)) (United Nations publication, Sales No. E.93.1.8 and corrigenda), Vol. I: Resolutions Adopted by the Conference, resolution 1, annex II.

Reaffirming the importance of the annual consideration and review by the General Assembly of the overall developments pertaining to the implementation of the Convention, as well as of other developments relating to the law of the sea and ocean affairs,

Noting the decisions taken by States parties to the Convention to convene meetings of States parties to deal with the initial budget and organizational and other related matters of the International Tribunal for the Law of the Sea in preparation for its establishment and the election of its members, 62/ as well as to prepare for and organize the election of the members of the Commission on the Limits of the Continental Shelf,

Noting also that the Assembly of the International Seabed Authority has concluded its first session and has scheduled two meetings of the Authority for 1996, from 11 March for up to three weeks, if necessary, and from 5 August for up to two weeks, in Kingston, Jamaica, 63/

Noting further that the Assembly of the Authority requested arrangements for the interim secretariat of the Authority, authorizing the Secretary-General to administer the interim secretariat until the Secretary-General of the Authority is able to assume effectively the responsibility of the Authority's secretariat, 64/

Recalling that the Agreement relating to the Implementation of Part XI of the United Nations Convention on the Law of the Sea of 10 December 1982 provides that the institutions established by the Convention shall be cost-effective, 65/ and recalling also that the meeting of States parties to the Convention decided that this principle would apply to all aspects of the work of the Tribunal, 66/

Emphasizing the importance of making adequate provisions for the efficient functioning of the institutions established by the Convention,

1. Calls upon all States that have not done so to become parties to the United Nations Convention on the Law of the Sea and to ratify, confirm formally or accede to the Agreement relating to the Implementation of Part XI of the United Nations Convention on the Law of the Sea of 10 December 1982 in order to achieve the goal of universal participation;

2. Calls upon States to harmonize their national legislation with the provisions of the Convention and to ensure the consistent application of those provisions;

3. Reaffirms the unified character of the Convention;

4. Recalls its decision to fund the budget for the administrative expenses of the Authority initially from the regular budget of the United Nations, in accordance with the provisions of the Agreement; 67/

5. Approves the provision by the Secretary-General of such services as may be required for the two meetings of the International Seabed Authority to be held in 1996, from 11 to 22 March and from 5 to 16 August;

6. Approves also the request of the Assembly of the Authority to continue the staff and facilities previously available to the Kingston Office for the Law of the Sea as the interim secretariat of the Authority, and authorizes the Secretary-General to administer the interim secretariat until the Secretary-General of the Authority is able to assume effectively the responsibility of the Authority's secretariat;

7. Requests the Secretary-General to convene the meetings of States parties to the Convention from 4 to 8 March, from 6 to 10 May and from 29 July to 2 August 1996;

62/ SPLOS/4, para. 38.

63/ ISBA/A/L.7/Rev.1, para. 35.

64/ ISBA/A/L.5 and ISBA/A/L.7/Rev.1, para. 33.

65/ Resolution 48/263, annex: annex to the Agreement, sect. 1, para. 2.

66/ SPLOS/4, para. 25 (e).

67/ Resolution 48/263, para. 8; ibid., annex: annex to the Agreement, sect. 1, para. 14.

8. Notes with appreciation the progress made in practical arrangements for the establishment of the International Tribunal for the Law of the Sea, and in preparations for the establishment of the Commission on the Limits of the Continental Shelf;

9. Expresses its appreciation to the Secretary-General for the annual comprehensive report on the law of the sea 68/ and the activities of the Division for Ocean Affairs and the Law of the Sea of the Office of Legal Affairs, in accordance with the provisions of the Convention and the mandate set forth in resolution 49/28;

10. Reaffirms the importance of ensuring the uniform and consistent application of the Convention and a coordinated approach to its effective implementation, and of strengthening technical cooperation and financial assistance for this purpose, stresses once again the continuing importance of the Secretary-General's efforts to these ends, and reiterates its invitation to the competent international organizations and other international bodies to support these objectives;

11. Requests the Secretary-General to ensure that the institutional capacity of the Organization adequately responds to the needs of States and competent international organizations by providing advice and assistance, taking into account the special needs of developing countries;

12. Invites Member States and others in a position to do so to contribute to the further development of the fellowship programme on the law of the sea and training and educational activities on the law of the sea and ocean affairs established by the Assembly in its resolution 35/116 of 10 December 1980, and advisory services in support of effective implementation of the Convention;

13. Requests the Secretary-General to report to the Assembly at its fifty-first session on the implementation of the present resolution, in connection with his annual comprehensive report on the law of the sea;

14. Decides to include in the provisional agenda of its fifty-first session the item entitled "Law of the sea".

RECORDED VOTE ON RESOLUTION 50/23:

In favour: Algeria, Andorra, Angola, Antigua and Barbuda, Argentina, Armenia, Australia, Austria, Bahrain, Bangladesh, Barbados, Belarus, Belgium, Belize, Benin, Bolivia, Botswana, Brazil, Brunei Darussalam, Bulgaria, Burkina Faso, Cambodia, Cameroon, Canada, Cape Verde, Chad, Chile, China, Costa Rica, Cote d'Ivoire, Cuba, Cyprus, Czech Republic, Denmark, Djibouti, Egypt, El Salvador, Eritrea, Ethiopia, Federated States of Micronesia, Fiji, Finland, France, Georgia, Germany, Ghana, Greece, Grenada, Guatemala, Guinea, Guinea-Bissau, Guyana, Haiti, Honduras, Hungary, Iceland, India, Indonesia, Iran, Ireland, Israel, Italy, Jamaica, Japan, Jordan, Kazakstan, Kenya, Kuwait, Lao People's Democratic Republic, Latvia, Lebanon, Libya, Liechtenstein, Lithuania, Luxembourg, Madagascar, Malawi, Malaysia, Maldives, Mali, Malta, Marshall Islands, Mauritania, Mauritius, Mexico, Monaco, Morocco, Myanmar, Namibia, Netherlands, New Zealand, Nigeria, Oman, Pakistan, Panama, Papua New Guinea, Paraguay, Philippines, Poland, Portugal, Qatar, Republic of Korea, Republic of Moldova, Romania, Russian Federation, Samoa, Saudi Arabia, Seychelles, Singapore, Slovakia, South Africa, Spain, Sri Lanka, Sudan, Suriname, Swaziland, Sweden, The former Yugoslav Republic of Macedonia, Thailand, Togo, Trinidad and Tobago, Tunisia, United Arab Emirates, Ukraine, United Kingdom, United States, United Republic of Tanzania, Uruguay, Viet Nam, Yemen, Zambia, Zimbabwe.

Against: Turkey.

Abstaining: Ecuador, Peru, Venezuela.

68/ A/50/713.

Absent: **Afghanistan, Albania, Azerbaijan, Bahamas, Bhutan*, Bosnia and Herzegovina, Burundi, Colombia, Congo, Croatia, Dominica, Democratic Peoples Republic of Korea, Equatorial Guinea, Estonia*, Gabon, Gambia, Kyrgyzstan, Lesotho, Mongolia, Mozambique, Nepal, Nicaragua, Niger, Norway*, Palau, Rwanda, Saint Kitts and Nevis, Saint Lucia, Saint Vincent and the Grenadines, San Marino, Senegal, Sierra Leone, Slovenia, Solomon Islands, Syria, Tajikistan, Turkmenistan, Uganda, Uzbekistan, Vanuatu, Zaire.**

* **Later advised the Secretariat that it had intended to abstain.**

23. UNGA RESOLUTION ON UNIVERSAL CONGRESS ON THE PANAMA CANAL

Doc. no.: A/Res.50/12 7 November 1995

The General Assembly,

Recalling its resolutions 49/28 of 6 December 1994 on the law of the sea, 49/99 of 19 December 1994 on international trade and development and 49/131 of 19 December 1994 on the declaration of 1998 as International Year of the Ocean, and resolutions 2.5 of 16 November 1993, 26/ adopted by the General Conference of the United Nations Educational, Scientific and Cultural Organization at its twenty-seventh session, and 1994/48 of the Economic and Social Council of 29 July 1994, both on the International Year of the Ocean,

Bearing in mind that on 7 September 1977 Mr. Jimmy Carter, President of the United States of America, and General Omar Torrijos, Head of Government of the Republic of Panama, signed in Washington the Treaty concerning the Permanent Neutrality and Operation of the Panama Canal 27/ and the Panama Canal Treaty, 28/ known as the Torrijos-Carter treaties, which stipulate that, at noon on 31 December 1999, the Canal, including all improvements, is to come under the control of the Republic of Panama, which shall assume total responsibility for its management, operation and maintenance,

Emphasizing the significance of the Washington Declaration, signed on 7 September 1977 by the heads of State, heads of Government and representatives of the American republics, which recognizes "the importance for the hemisphere, for trade and for world shipping of the agreements designed to ensure the accessibility and continued neutrality of the Panama Canal",

Welcoming the plans of the Government of Panama to hold a Universal Congress on the Panama Canal in Panama City in September 1997, with the participation of Governments, international bodies, public and private academic institutions, maritime users and international shipping companies, to examine jointly the role which the Panama Canal should play in the twenty-first century,

Underlining the fact that the International Congress for Study of the Interocean Canal (Congrès international d'études du canal interocéanique) was convened by the Société de géographie de Paris, met from 15 to 29 May 1879 in the French capital, under the presidency of Count Ferdinand de Lesseps, builder of the Suez Canal, and culminated in the resolution that the canal should be built along the route traced between the Gulf of Limón on the Atlantic Ocean and the Bay of Panama on the Pacific Ocean,

---

26/ See United Nations Educational, Scientific and Cultural Organization, Records of the General Conference, Twenty-seventh Session, Paris, 15 October to 16 November 1993, Vol. I, Resolutions, sect. III.2.

27/ United Nations, Treaty Series, vol. 1161, No. 18342.

28/ Ibid., vol. 1280, No. 21086.

Cognizant of the fact that, in keeping with the spirit of a new global alliance for sustainable development, it is necessary to formulate a balanced, integrated approach to environmental, trade and development issues,

Convinced, therefore, that the Universal Congress on the Panama Canal will promote international cooperation towards ensuring an orderly, sustainable development of the uses and resources of the Atlantic and Pacific Oceans and the rational exploitation and development of the Canal watershed and coastal areas, bearing in mind that Panama's coastline on the two oceans stretches for 2,988.3 kilometres in all, of which 1,700.6 kilometres are on the Pacific Ocean and 1,287.7 are on the Caribbean Sea,

Noting with appreciation the progress of the Tripartite Commission, consisting of the Republic of Panama, the United States of America and Japan, in the plans for the construction in the Isthmus of Panama of a sea-level canal or the enlargement of the present lock canal,

Reaffirming its resolution 31/142 of 17 December 1976, on the one hundred and fiftieth anniversary of the Amphictyonic Congress of Panama, in which it recalled that Simón Bolívar, the Liberator, referred on several occasions to the need for a possible opening of a canal in Panama, which "will shorten distances throughout the world, strengthen commercial ties" between the continents and promote the exchange of products "from the four corners of the globe",

Noting with satisfaction that by its resolution 49/131, 1998 was proclaimed International Year of the Ocean, during which year the Lisbon World Exposition is to be held,

Emphasizing that the Universal Congress on the Panama Canal has among its priority aims the promotion of international cooperation with a view to achieving an orderly, sustainable development of the uses and resources of the Atlantic and Pacific Oceans,

1. Supports the initiative of the Government of Panama in convening the Universal Congress on the Panama Canal, with the participation of Governments, international bodies, public and private academic institutions, maritime users and international shipping companies, to examine jointly the role which the Panama Canal should play in the twenty-first century;

2. Requests Member States to assist generously in this undertaking;

3. Urges the competent organs, programmes and specialized agencies of the United Nations system, in particular, the United Nations Development Programme, the United Nations Environment Programme and the International Maritime Organization, to study the possibility of providing assistance from within existing resources for the organization of the Universal Congress on the Panama Canal;

4. Emphasizes the importance of the Universal Congress on the Panama Canal and expresses the hope that its results will contribute to the growth of world trade and to sustained economic growth and sustainable development throughout the world;

5. Requests the Secretary-General to submit to the General Assembly at its fifty-first session a report on the implementation of the present resolution;

6. Decides to include in the provisional agenda of its fifty-first session the item entitled "Universal Congress on the Panama Canal".

24. UNGA RESOLUTION ON ZONE OF PEACE AND COOPERATION OF THE SOUTH ATLANTIC

Doc. no.: A/Res.50/18 27 November 1995

The General Assembly,

Recalling its resolution 41/11 of 27 October 1986, in which it solemnly declared the Atlantic Ocean, in the region between Africa and South America, the "Zone of peace and cooperation of the South Atlantic",

Recalling also its subsequent resolutions on the matter, including resolution 45/36 of 27 November 1990, in which it reaffirmed the determination of the States of the zone to enhance and accelerate their cooperation in the political, economic, scientific, cultural and other spheres,

Reaffirming that the questions of peace and security and those of development are interrelated and inseparable, and that cooperation for peace and development among States of the region will promote the objectives of the zone of peace and cooperation of the South Atlantic,

Aware of the importance that the States of the zone attach to the region's environment, and recognizing the threat that pollution from any source poses to the marine and coastal environment, its ecological balance and its resources,

1. Reaffirms the importance of the purposes and objectives of the zone of peace and cooperation of the South Atlantic as a basis for the promotion of cooperation among the countries of the region;

2. Calls upon all States to cooperate in the promotion of the objectives established in the declaration of the zone of peace and cooperation of the South Atlantic and to refrain from any action inconsistent with those objectives and with the Charter of the United Nations and relevant resolutions of the Organization, particularly action which may create or aggravate situations of tension and potential conflict in the region;

3. Takes note of the report of the Secretary-General of 24 October 1995, 38/ submitted in accordance with its resolution 49/26 of 2 December 1994;

4. Recalls the agreement reached at the third meeting of the States members of the zone, held at Brasilia in 1994, to encourage democracy and political pluralism and, in accordance with the Vienna Declaration and Programme of Action adopted by the World Conference on Human Rights on 25 June 1993, 39/ to promote and defend all human rights and fundamental freedoms and to cooperate towards the achievement of those goals;

38/ A/50/671.

39/ A/CONF.157/24 (Part I), chap. III.

5. Welcomes the progress towards the full entry into force of the Treaty for the Prohibition of Nuclear Weapons in Latin America and the Caribbean (Treaty of Tlatelolco), 40/ and the conclusion of a treaty on a nuclear-weapon-free zone in Africa;

6. Expresses its appreciation for the efforts of the international community, in accordance with Security Council resolution 976 (1995) of 8 February 1995, aimed at contributing to an effective and lasting peace in Angola on the basis of the "Acordos de Bicesse" 41/ and the Lusaka Protocol; 42/

7. Also welcomes recent positive developments in the situation of Liberia, including progress towards peace and national reconciliation in accordance with the Abuja Agreement 43/ to supplement the Cotonou 44/ and Akosombo 45/ Agreements as subsequently clarified by the Accra Agreement; 46/

8. Commends the efforts of Member States and humanitarian organizations to render humanitarian assistance to Angola and Liberia, and urges them to continue to provide and to increase such assistance;

9. Affirms the importance of the South Atlantic to global maritime and commercial transactions and its determination to preserve the region for all activities protected by international law, as reflected in the United Nations Convention on the Law of the Sea; 47/

10. Further welcomes the offer by South Africa to host at Cape Town, on 1 and 2 April 1996, the fourth meeting of the States members of the zone;

11. Requests the relevant organizations, organs and bodies of the United Nations system to render all appropriate assistance which States of the zone may seek in their joint efforts to implement the declaration of the zone of peace and cooperation of the South Atlantic;

12. Requests the Secretary-General to keep the implementation of resolution 41/11 and subsequent resolutions on the matter under review and to submit a report to the General Assembly at its fifty-first session, taking into account, inter alia, the views expressed by Member States;

13. Decides to include in the provisional agenda of its fifty-first session the item entitled "Zone of peace and cooperation of the South Atlantic".

RECORDED VOTE ON 50/18

In favour: Algeria, Andorra, Angola, Argentina, Armenia, Australia, Austria, Azerbaijan, Barbados, Belarus, Belgium, Benin, Bhutan, Bolivia, Botswana, Brazil, Brunei Darussalam, Bulgaria, Burkina Faso, Cambodia, Cameroon, Canada, Chad, Chile, China, Colombia, Cote d'Ivoire, Croatia, Cuba, Cyprus, Czech Republic, Democratic People's Republic of Korea, Denmark, Djibouti, Ecuador, Equatorial Guinea, Estonia, Ethiopia, Federated States of Micronesia, Finland, France, Gabon, Gambia, Georgia, Germany, Ghana, Greece, Guinea, Guinea-Bissau, Guyana, Honduras, Hungary, Iceland, India, Indonesia, Iran, Ireland, Italy, Jamaica, Japan, Jordan, Kazakstan, Kenya, Lebanon, Libya, Liechtenstein, Lithuania, Luxembourg, Madagascar, Malawi, Malaysia, Maldives, Mali, Malta, Marshall Islands, Mauritius, Mexico, Mongolia, Mozambique, Myanmar, Namibia, Netherlands, New Zealand, Nicaragua, Nigeria, Norway, Oman, Pakistan, Panama, Papua New Guinea, Paraguay, Peru, Philippines, Poland, Portugal, Qatar, Republic of Korea, Russian Federation, Saint Lucia, San Marino,

---

40/ United Nations, Treaty Series, vol. 634, No. 9068.

41/ S/22609, annex.

42/ S/1994/1441, annex.

43/ S/1995/742, annex.

44/ S/26272, annex.

45/ S/1994/1174, annex.

46/ S/1995/7, annex.

47/ Official Records of the Third United Nations Conference on the Law of the Sea, vol. XVII (United Nations publication, Sales No. E.84.V.3), document A/CONF.62/122.

Saudi Arabia, Senegal, Singapore, Slovakia, South Africa, Spain, Sri Lanka, Suriname, Swaziland, Sweden, Thailand, The former Yugoslav Republic of Macedonia, Togo, Trinidad and Tobago, Tunisia, Turkey, Uganda, Ukraine, United Arab Emirates, United Kingdom, Uruguay, Viet Nam, Zaire, Zambia.

Against: None.

25. UNGA RESOLUTION ON QUESTION OF NEW CALEDONIA

Doc. no.: A/Res.50/37 6 December 1995

The General Assembly,

Having considered the question of New Caledonia,

Having examined the chapter of the report of the Special Committee on the Situation with regard to the Implementation of the Declaration on the Granting of Independence to Colonial Countries and Peoples relating to New Caledonia, 92/

Reaffirming the right of peoples to self-determination as enshrined in the Charter of the United Nations,

Recalling its resolutions 1514 (XV) of 14 December 1960 and 1541 (XV) of 15 December 1960,

Noting the importance of the positive measures being pursued in New Caledonia by the French authorities, in cooperation with all sectors of the population, to promote political, economic and social development in the Territory, including measures in the area of environmental protection and action with respect to drug abuse and trafficking, in order to provide a framework for its peaceful progress to self-determination,

Noting also, in this context, the importance of equitable economic and social development, as well as continued dialogue among the parties involved in New Caledonia in the preparation of the act of self-determination of New Caledonia,

Welcoming the strengthening of the process of review of the Matignon Accords 93/ through the increased frequency of coordination meetings,

Noting with satisfaction the intensification of contacts between New Caledonia and neighbouring countries of the South Pacific region,

1. Urges all the parties involved, in the interest of all the people of New Caledonia and building on the positive outcome of the mid-term review of the Matignon Accords, to maintain their dialogue in a spirit of harmony;

92/ A/50/23 (Part V), chap. IX.

93/ See A/AC.109/1000, paras. 9-14.

2. Invites all the parties involved to continue promoting a framework for the peaceful progress of the Territory towards an act of self-determination in which all options are open and which would safeguard the rights of all New Caledonians according to the letter and the spirit of the Matignon Accords, which are based on the principle that it is for the populations of New Caledonia to choose how to control their destiny;

3. Welcomes measures that have been taken to strengthen and diversify the New Caledonian economy in all fields, and encourages further such measures in accordance with the spirit of the Matignon Accords;

4. Also welcomes the importance attached by the parties to the Matignon Accords to greater progress in housing, employment, training, education and health care in New Caledonia;

5. Acknowledges the contribution of the Melanesian Cultural Centre to the protection of the indigenous culture of New Caledonia;

6. Notes the positive initiatives aimed at protecting New Caledonia's natural environment, notably the "Zonéco" operation designed to map and evaluate marine resources within the economic zone of New Caledonia;

7. Acknowledges the close links between New Caledonia and the peoples of the South Pacific and the positive actions being taken by the French and provincial authorities to facilitate the further development of those links, including the development of closer relations with the member countries of the South Pacific Forum;

8. Welcomes, in particular, in this regard, continuing high-level visits to New Caledonia by delegations from countries of the Pacific region and high-level visits by delegations from New Caledonia to member countries of the South Pacific Forum;

9. Requests the Special Committee on the Situation with regard to the Implementation of the Declaration on the Granting of Independence to Colonial Countries and Peoples to continue the examination of this question at its next session and to report thereon to the General Assembly at its fifty-first session.

26. UNGA RESOLUTION ON QUESTIONS OF AMERICAN SAMOA, ANGUILLA, BERMUDA, THE BRITISH VIRGIN ISLANDS, THE CAYMAN ISLANDS, GUAM, MONTSERRAT, PITCAIRN, ST.HELENA, TOKELAU, THE TURKS AND CAICOS ISLANDS AND THE UNITED STATES VIRGIN ISLANDS

Doc. no.: A/Res.50/38 6 December 1995

The General Assembly,

Having considered the questions of the Non-Self-Governing Territories of American Samoa, Anguilla, Bermuda, the British Virgin Islands, the Cayman Islands, Guam, Montserrat, Pitcairn, St. Helena, Tokelau, the Turks and Caicos Islands and the United States Virgin Islands, hereinafter "the Territories",

Having examined the relevant chapter of the report of the Special Committee on the Situation with regard to the Implementation of the Declaration on the Granting of Independence to Colonial Countries and Peoples, 94/

Recognizing that 1995 is the fiftieth anniversary of the United Nations and that decolonization is one of the proudest achievements of the Organization,

Recalling its resolution 1514 (XV) of 14 December 1960, containing the Declaration on the Granting of Independence to Colonial Countries and Peoples, and all resolutions and decisions of the United Nations relating to those Territories, including, in particular, the resolutions adopted by the General Assembly at its forty-ninth session on the individual Territories covered by the present resolution,

Recognizing that the specific characteristics and the sentiments of the people of the Territories require flexible, practical and innovative approaches to the options of self-determination, without any prejudice to territorial size, geographical location, size of population or natural resources,

Recalling its resolution 1541 (XV) of 15 December 1960, containing the principles that should guide Member States in determining whether or not an obligation exists to transmit the information called for under Article 73 e of the Charter of the United Nations,

Conscious of the need to ensure the full and speedy implementation of the Declaration in respect of the Territories, in view of the target set by the United Nations to eradicate colonialism by the year 2000,

Noting with appreciation the continuing exemplary cooperation of New Zealand, as administering Power, in the work of the Special Committee, and welcoming its statement that it will abide by the wishes of the population of Tokelau in determining their future political status,

Welcoming the stated position of the Government of the United Kingdom of Great Britain and Northern Ireland that it continues to take seriously its obligations under the Charter of the United Nations to develop self-government in the dependent Territories and, in cooperation with the locally elected Governments, to

---

94/ A/50/23 (Part VI), chap. X.

ensure that their constitutional frameworks continue to meet the wishes of the people, and the emphasis that it is ultimately for the peoples of the Territories to decide their future status,

Aware of the special circumstances of the geographical location and economic conditions of each Territory, and bearing in mind the necessity of promoting economic stability and diversifying and strengthening further the economies of the respective Territories as a matter of priority,

Conscious of the particular vulnerability of the small Territories to natural disasters and environmental degradation,

Aware of the usefulness, both to the Territories and to the Special Committee of the participation of appointed and elected representatives of the Territories in the work of the Special Committee,

Expressing its conviction that referendums and other forms of popular consultation on the future status of the Non-Self-Governing Territories are an appropriate means of ascertaining the wishes of the peoples in those Territories with regard to their future political status,

Mindful that United Nations visiting missions provide one effective means of ascertaining the situation in the Territories, and considering that the possibility of sending further visiting missions to the Territories at an appropriate time and in consultation with the administering Powers should be kept under review,

Mindful also that some Territories have not had any United Nations visiting mission for a long period of time,

Noting with appreciation the contribution to the development of some Territories by specialized agencies and other organizations of the United Nations system, in particular the United Nations Development Programme, as well as regional institutions such as the Caribbean Development Bank,

1. Approves the chapter of the report of the Special Committee on the Situation with regard to the Implementation of the Declaration on the Granting of Independence to Colonial Countries and Peoples relating to the Non-Self-Governing Territories of American Samoa, Anguilla, Bermuda, the British Virgin Islands, the Cayman Islands, Guam, Montserrat, Pitcairn, St. Helena, Tokelau, the Turks and Caicos Islands and the United States Virgin Islands, hereinafter "the Territories"; 95/

2. Reaffirms the inalienable right of the people of the Territories to self-determination, including independence, in conformity with the Charter of the United Nations and General Assembly resolution 1514 (XV), containing the Declaration on the Granting of Independence to Colonial Countries and Peoples;

3. Reaffirms also that it is ultimately for the people of the Territories themselves to determine freely their future political status in accordance with the relevant provisions of the Charter, the Declaration and the relevant resolutions of the General Assembly, and in that connection calls upon the administering Powers, in cooperation with the territorial Governments, to facilitate programmes of political education in the Territories in order to foster an awareness among the people of the possibilities open to them in the exercise of their right to self-determination, in conformity with the legitimate political status options clearly defined in resolution 1541 (XV);

4. Requests the administering Powers to ascertain expeditiously, by means of popular consultations, the wishes and aspirations of the peoples of Non-Self-Governing Territories regarding their future political status so that the Special Committee can review the status of the Territories in accordance with the expressed wishes of the peoples of the Territories;

5. Also requests the administering Powers to facilitate the dispatch of the United Nations visiting missions to the Non-Self-Governing Territories regarding their future political status so that the Special Committee can review the status of the Territories in accordance with the expressed wishes of the peoples of the Territory;

6. Reaffirms the responsibility of the administering Powers under the Charter to promote the economic and social development and to preserve the cultural identity of the Territories, and recommends that priority continue to be given, in consultation, with the territorial Governments concerned, to the strengthening and diversification of their respective economies;

95/ A/50/23 (Part VI), chap. X.

7. Requests the administering Powers to take all necessary measures to protect and conserve the environment of the Territories under their administration against any environmental degradation, and requests the specialized agencies concerned to continue to monitor environmental conditions in those Territories;

8. Calls upon the administering Powers to continue to take all necessary measures, in cooperation with the respective territorial Governments, to counter problems related to drug trafficking, money laundering and other offences;

9. Stresses that the achievement of the declared goal of eradication of colonialism by the year 2000 requires full and constructive cooperation by all parties concerned, and appeals to the administering Powers to continue to give their full support to the Special Committee;

10. Urges Member States to contribute to the efforts of the United Nations to usher in the twenty-first century in a world free of colonialism, and calls upon them to continue to give their full support to the Special Committee in its endeavours towards that noble goal;

11. Invites the specialized agencies and other organizations of the United Nations system to initiate or to continue to take all necessary measures to accelerate progress in the social and economic life of the Territories;

12. Requests the Special Committee to continue the examination of the question of the small Territories and to recommend to the General Assembly the most suitable steps to be taken to enable the populations of those Territories to exercise their right to self-determination, and to report thereon to the Assembly at its fifty-first session.

B

1. American Samoa

The General Assembly,

Referring to resolution A above,

Noting the fact that a large number of American Samoans have emigrated to the United States of America and are residing there,

Noting also the constitutional developments in the Territory,

Noting further that the Territory, similar to isolated communities with limited funds, continues to experience lack of adequate medical facilities and other infrastructural requirements,

Recalling the dispatch in 1981 of a United Nations visiting mission to the Territory,

1. Requests the administering Power to carry out, at the earliest possible date, a democratic exercise to ascertain the wishes of the people of American Samoa regarding the future status of the Territory;

2. Calls upon the administering Power to continue to assist the territorial Government in the economic and social development of the Territory and the development of manpower resources.

2. Anguilla

The General Assembly,

Referring to resolution A above,

Noting that general elections were held in March 1994,

Conscious of the commitment of both the Government of Anguilla and the administering Power to a new and closer policy of dialogue and partnership through the Country Policy Plan for 1993-1997,

Aware that the exploitation of deep-sea resources would help reduce the risk of depleting the Territory's own fishing resources as a result of overfishing,

Noting the need for continued cooperation between the administering Power and the territorial Government in tackling the problems of drug trafficking and money laundering,

Recalling the dispatch in 1984 of a United Nations visiting mission to the Territory,

1. Requests the administering Power to carry out, at the earliest possible date, an exercise to ascertain the wishes of the people of Anguilla regarding the future status of the Territory;

2. Requests all countries, organizations and United Nations agencies with deep-sea fishing experience to assist the Territory in improving its capacity in exploiting deep-sea fishing.

3. Bermuda

The General Assembly,

Referring to resolution A above,

Noting the results of the independence referendum held on 16 August 1995,

Conscious of the different viewpoints of the political parties of the Territory on the future status of the Territory,

Noting the measures taken by the Government to combat racism and the plan to set up a Commission for Unity and Racial Equality,

Noting also the closure of the Canadian base in 1994 and the announced plans of the United Kingdom of Great Britain and Northern Ireland and the United States of America to close their respective air and naval bases in Bermuda in 1995,

Calls upon the administering Power to continue its programmes of socio-economic development.

4. British Virgin Islands

The General Assembly,

Referring to resolution A above,

Noting the completion of the constitutional review in the Territory and the coming into force of the amended Constitution, and noting also the results of the general elections held on 20 February 1995,

Noting further the results of the constitutional review of 1993-1994, which made it clear that a prerequisite to independence must be a constitutionally expressed wish by the people as a result of a referendum,

Taking note of the statement by the Chief Minister of the British Virgin Islands that the Territory was ready for constitutional and political advancement towards full internal self-government and that the administering Power should assist through gradual transfer of power to elected territorial representatives,

Noting that the Territory is emerging as one of the world's leading off-shore financial centres,

Noting also the need for continued cooperation between the administering Power and the territorial Government in countering drug trafficking and money laundering,

1. Requests the administering Power to continue the process for facilitating the expression of the will of the people regarding the future status of the Territory;

2. Also requests the administering Power, specialized agencies and other organizations of the United Nations system and all financial institutions to continue to provide assistance to the Territory for socio-economic development and development of human resources, bearing in mind the vulnerability of the Territory to external factors.

5. Cayman Islands

The General Assembly,

Referring to resolution A above,

Noting the constitutional review of 1992-1993, according to which the population expressed the sentiment that the existing relations with the United Kingdom of Great Britain and Northern Ireland should be maintained and that the current status of the Territory should not be altered,

Noting also the actions taken by the territorial Government to implement its localization programme to promote increased participation of the local population in the decision-making process in the Cayman Islands,

Noting with concern the vulnerability of the Territory to drug trafficking and related activities, as well as the measures taken by the authorities to deal with those problems,

Noting that the Territory has emerged as one of the world's leading off-shore financial centres,

Recalling the dispatch in 1977 of a United Nations visiting mission to the Territory,

1. Requests the administering Power to continue to provide the territorial Government with all required expertise to enable it to achieve its socio-economic aims;

2. Also requests the administering Power, in consultation with the territorial Government, to continue to facilitate the expansion of the current programme of securing employment for the local population, in particular at the decision-making level;

3. Requests the specialized agencies and other organizations of the United Nations system to continue and increase their programmes of assistance to the Territory with a view to strengthening, developing and diversifying its economy;

4. Calls upon the administering Power and the territorial Government to continue to cooperate to counter problems related to money laundering, smuggling of funds and other related crimes, as well as drug trafficking.

6. Guam

The General Assembly,

Referring to resolution A above,

Noting the results of the general elections held in November 1994,

Recalling that, in a referendum held in Guam in 1987, the people of Guam endorsed a draft Commonwealth Act that would establish a new framework for relations between the Territory and the administering Power, providing internal self-government for Guam and recognition of the right of the people of Guam to self-determination for the Territory,

Aware of the continued negotiations between the administering Power and the territorial Government on the draft Guam Commonwealth Act and on the future status of the Territory, with particular emphasis on the question of the evolution of the relationship between the United States of America and Guam,

Recalling the statement by the Special Representative of the United States of America on 12 December 1993 that the Administration hoped to have comments on the Commonwealth Bill before Congress by the end of 1994,

Cognizant that the administering Power continues to implement its programme of transferring surplus federal land to the Government of Guam,

Noting that the people of the Territory have called for reform in the programme of the administering Power with respect to the thorough and expeditious transfer of land property to the people of Guam,

Conscious that immigration into Guam has resulted in the indigenous Chamorros becoming a minority in their homeland,

Aware of the potential for diversifying and developing the economy of Guam through commercial fishing and agriculture and other viable activities,

Recalling the dispatch in 1979 of a United Nations visiting mission to the Territory,

1. Calls upon the administering Power and the territorial Government to expedite the early conclusion of the negotiations on the draft Guam Commonwealth Act and on the future status of the Territory;

2. Requests the administering Power to continue to assist the elected territorial Government in achieving its political, economic and social goals;

3. Also requests the administering Power, in cooperation with the territorial Government, to continue the transfer of land to the people of the Territory and to take the necessary steps to safeguard their property rights;

4. Further requests the administering Power to continue to recognize and respect the political rights and the cultural and ethnic identity of the Chamorro people and to take all necessary measures to respond to the concerns of the territorial Government with regard to the immigration issue;

5. Requests the administering Power to continue to support appropriate measures by the territorial Government aimed at promoting growth in commercial fishing and agriculture and other viable activities.

7. Montserrat

The General Assembly,

Referring to resolution A above,

Noting the functioning of a democratic process in Montserrat,

Taking note of the reported statement of the Chief Minister that his preference was for independence within a political union with the Organization of Eastern Caribbean States and that self-reliance was more of a priority than independence,

Recalling that a United Nations visiting mission to the Territory took place in 1982,

1. Requests the administering Power to conduct an appropriate exercise, at the earliest possible date, to ascertain the will of the people regarding the future status of the Territory;

2. Requests the specialized agencies and other organizations of the United Nations system, as well as regional and other multilateral financial institutions, to continue their assistance to the Territory in the strengthening, development and diversification of the economy of Montserrat in accordance with its medium- and long-term development plans.

8. Pitcairn

The General Assembly,

Referring to resolution A above,

Taking into account the unique nature of the Territory in terms of population and area,

Expressing its satisfaction with the continued economic and social advancement of the Territory, as well as with the improvement of its communications with the outside world and its management plan to address conservation issues,

Requests the administering Power to continue its assistance for improvement of the economic, social, educational and other conditions of the population of the Territory.

9. St. Helena

The General Assembly,

Referring to resolution A above,

Aware of the request by the Legislative Council of St. Helena that the administering Power conduct a constitutional review in the Territory,

Taking into account the unique character of the Territory, its population and its natural resources,

Aware of the efforts of the administering Power and the territorial authorities to improve the socio-economic conditions of the population of St. Helena, in particular in the sphere of food production,

1. Requests the administering Power to conduct the constitutional review in the Territory, taking into account the wishes of its population;

2. Requests the administering Power and relevant regional and international organizations to continue to support the efforts of the territorial Government to address the socio-economic development of the Territory.

10. Tokelau

The General Assembly,

Referring to resolution A above,

Having heard the statements of the representatives of New Zealand, the administering Power, and the Special Representative of Tokelau, who conveyed a message from the Council of Faipule (joint chairmen of the General Fono (Council)) to the Committee,

Recalling the solemn declaration on the future status of Tokelau delivered by the Ulu o Tokelau (highest authority of Tokelau) on 30 July 1994, that an act of self-determination in Tokelau is now under active consideration, together with the constitution of a self-governing Tokelau, and that the present preference of Tokelau is for a status of free association with New Zealand,

Noting the emphasis placed in the solemn declaration on the terms of Tokelau's intended free association relationship with New Zealand, including the expectation that the form of help Tokelau could continue to expect from New Zealand in promoting the well-being of its people, besides its external interests, would be clearly established in the framework of that relationship,

Noting also the Territory's concentrated focus in 1995 on strengthening its national institutions and creating a structure of government to meet modern needs, preparatory to the exercise by the people of Tokelau of their right to self-determination,

Acknowledging the endeavours of Tokelau to be self-reliant to the greatest extent possible,

Noting with appreciation the continuing exemplary cooperation of the administering Power with regard to the work of the Special Committee on the Situation with regard to the Implementation of the Declaration on the Granting of Independence to Colonial Countries and Peoples relating to Tokelau and its readiness to permit access by United Nations visiting missions to the Territory,

Recalling the dispatch in 1994 of a United Nations visiting mission to Tokelau,

1. Notes, on the basis of statements made by representatives of the administering Power and Tokelau subsequent to the 1994 United Nations visiting mission, that Tokelau is working towards an act of self-determination that would result in Tokelau assuming a status in accordance with the options on future status for Non-Self-Governing Territories contained in principle VI of the annex to General Assembly resolution 1541 (XV) of 15 December 1960;

2. Also notes the expressed wishes of the people of the Territory indicating a strong preference for a status of free association with New Zealand;

3. Further notes the readiness of the people of Tokelau to assume full governmental responsibility and to conduct their own affairs within the framework of a constitution, which is currently being developed;

4. Welcomes the assurances of the Government of New Zealand that it will meet its obligations to the United Nations with respect to Tokelau and abide by the freely expressed wishes of the people of Tokelau with regard to their future status;

5. Invites the administering Power and United Nations agencies to continue their assistance to the social and economic development of Tokelau.

11. Turks and Caicos Islands

The General Assembly,

Referring to resolution A above,

Noting recent changes to the Constitution of the Territory and the intention of the territorial Government to continue to campaign for further constitutional changes,

Noting also that general elections took place in the Territory on 31 January 1995,

Noting further the policy of the authorities of maintaining a balance between creating a more liberal investment environment and preserving access by the population to economic benefits,

Noting the increase in aid, in particular financial assistance, granted to the territorial Government by the Government of the United Kingdom of Great Britain and Northern Ireland,

1. Requests the administering Power to conduct, at the earliest possible date, an appropriate exercise to ascertain the will of the people regarding the future status of the Territory;

2. Calls upon the administering Power and the relevant regional and international organizations to continue to support the efforts of the territorial Government to address the socio-economic development of the Territory.

12. United States Virgin Islands

The General Assembly,

Referring to resolution A above,

Noting that general elections were held in November 1994,

Noting that a majority of those who voted in the referendum on the political status of the Territory on 11 October 1993 supported the existing territorial status arrangement with the United States of America,

Noting further the continuing interest of the territorial Government in seeking associate membership in the Organization of Eastern Caribbean States and observer status in the Caribbean Community,

Noting the necessity of further diversifying the Territory's economy,

Noting also that the question of Water Island is still under consideration,

Noting further that in 1993 the territorial Government purchased the assets of the West Indian Company, which had significant property and development interests in the Charlotte Amalie Harbour,

Recalling the dispatch in 1977 of a United Nations visiting mission to the Territory,

1. Requests the administering Power to continue to assist the elected territorial Government in achieving its political, economic and social goals;

2. Also requests the administering Power to facilitate the participation of the Territory, as appropriate, in various organizations, in particular the Organization of Eastern Caribbean States and the Caribbean Community;

3. Welcomes the negotiations between the administering Power and the territorial Government on the question of Water Island.

RECORDED VOTE ON RESOLUTION 50/38:

In favour: Afghanistan, Albania, Algeria, Andorra, Antigua and Barbuda, Armenia, Australia, Austria, Azerbaijan, Bahamas, Bahrain, Bangladesh, Barbados, Belarus, Belize, Benin, Bolivia, Bosnia and Herzegovina, Botswana, Brazil, Brunei Darussalam, Bulgaria, Burkina Faso, Burundi, Cameroon, Canada, Cape Verde, Chad, Chile, China, Colombia, Cote d'Ivoire, Croatia, Cuba, Cyprus, Czech Republic, Denmark, Djibouti, Dominica, Democratic People's Republic of Korea, Ecuador, Egypt, El Salvador, Estonia, Ethiopia, Federated States of Micronesia, Fiji, Finland, Gabon, Germany, Ghana, Greece, Grenada, Guinea, Guinea-Bissau, Guyana, Haiti, Honduras, Hungary, Iceland, India, Indonesia, Iran, Ireland, Italy, Jamaica, Japan, Jordan, Kazakstan, Kenya, Kuwait, Lao People's Democratic Republic, Latvia, Lebanon, Lesotho, Libya, Liechtenstein, Lithuania, Luxembourg, Madagascar, Malawi, Malaysia, Maldives, Mali, Malta, Marshall Islands, Mauritania, Mauritius, Mexico, Mongolia, Morocco, Myanmar, Nepal, Netherlands, New Zealand, Nicaragua, Niger, Nigeria, Norway, Oman, Pakistan, Panama, Papua New Guinea, Paraguay, Peru, Philippines, Poland, Portugal, Qatar, Republic of Korea, Republic of Moldova, Romania, Russian Federation, Saint Lucia, Samoa, Saudi Arabia, Senegal, Sierra Leone, Singapore, Slovakia, Slovenia, Solomon Islands, South Africa, Spain, Sri Lanka, Sudan, Suriname, Swaziland, Sweden, Syria, The former Yugoslav Republic of Macedonia, Thailand, Togo, Trinidad and Tobago, Tunisia, Turkey, United Arab Emirates, Uganda, Ukraine, United Republic of Tanzania, Uruguay, Vanuatu, Venezuela, Viet Nam, Zambia, Zimbabwe.

Against: Georgia, Israel, United Kingdom, United States.

Abstaining: Argentina, Belgium, France.

Absent: Angola, Bhutan, Cambodia, Congo, Costa Rica, Equatorial Guinea, Eritrea, Gambia, Guatemala, Kyrgyzstan, Monaco, Mozambique, Namibia, Palau, Rwanda, Saint Kitts and Nevis, Saint Vincent and the Grenadines, San Marino, Seychelles, Tajikistan, Turkmenistan, Uzbekistan, Yemen, Zaire.

27. UNGA RESOLUTION ON AMENDMENT OF THE TREATY BANNING NUCLEAR WEAPON TESTS IN THE ATMOSPHERE, IN OUTER SPACE AND UNDER WATER

Doc. no.: A/Res.50/64 12 December 1995

The General Assembly,

Recalling its resolutions 46/28 of 6 December 1991, in which it noted the convening of the Amendment Conference of the States Parties to the Treaty Banning Nuclear Weapon Tests in the Atmosphere, in Outer Space and under Water from 7 to 18 January 1991, 48/69 of 16 December 1993, in which it noted the convening of a special meeting of the States parties to that Treaty on 10 August 1993, and 49/69 of 15 December 1994, in which it noted with satisfaction the commencement of multilateral negotiations for a comprehensive nuclear-test-ban treaty in the Conference on Disarmament on 1 February 1994,

Reiterating its conviction that a comprehensive nuclear-test-ban treaty is the highest-priority measure for the cessation of the nuclear-arms race and for the achievement of the objective of nuclear disarmament,

Recalling the central role of the United Nations in the field of nuclear disarmament and in particular in the cessation of all nuclear-test explosions, as well as the persistent efforts of non-governmental organizations in the achievement of a comprehensive nuclear-test-ban treaty,

Convinced that the Amendment Conference will facilitate the attainment of the objectives set forth in the Treaty and thus serve to strengthen it,

Recalling its recommendation that arrangements be made to ensure that intensive efforts continue, under the auspices of the Amendment Conference, until a comprehensive nuclear-test-ban treaty is achieved, and its call that all parties participate in, and contribute effectively to the success of, the Amendment Conference,

1. Urges all States that have not already done so to adhere to the Treaty Banning Nuclear Weapon Tests in the Atmosphere, in Outer Space and under Water 4/ at the earliest possible date;

2. Urges all States parties to the Treaty to contribute to the conclusion of a comprehensive nuclear-test-ban treaty as soon as possible and no later than 1996 and to its expeditious entry into force;

3. Requests the President of the Amendment Conference to conduct consultations to those ends;

4. Decides to include in the provisional agenda of its fifty-first session the item entitled "Amendment of the Treaty Banning Nuclear Weapon Tests in the Atmosphere, in Outer Space and under Water".

4/ United Nations, Treaty Series, vol. 480, No. 6964.

RECORDED VOTE ON RESOLUTION 50/64:

In favour: Afghanistan, Algeria, Angola, Antigua and Barbuda, Bahamas, Bahrain, Bangladesh, Barbados, Belize, Benin, Bhutan, Bolivia, Botswana, Brazil, Brunei Darussalam, Burkina Faso, Burundi, Cambodia, Cameroon, Cape Verde, Chad, Chile, Colombia, Congo, Costa Rica, Cote d'Ivoire, Cuba, Cyprus, Democratic People's Republic of Korea, Djibouti, Ecuador, Egypt, El Salvador, Equatorial Guinea, Ethiopia, Federated States of Micronesia, Fiji, Gabon, Ghana, Guatemala, Guinea, Guinea-Bissau, Guyana, Haiti, Honduras, India, Indonesia, Iran, Jamaica, Jordan, Kazakstan, Kenya, Kuwait, Lao People's Democratic Republic, Lebanon, Lesotho, Libya, Madagascar, Malawi, Malaysia, Maldives, Mali, Mauritania, Mauritius, Mexico, Mongolia, Morocco, Mozambique, Myanmar, Namibia, Nepal, Nicaragua, Niger, Nigeria, Oman, Pakistan, Panama, Papua New Guinea, Paraguay, Peru, Philippines, Qatar, Rwanda, Samoa, Saudi Arabia, Senegal, Sierra Leone, Singapore, Solomon Islands, South Africa, Sri Lanka, Sudan, Suriname, Swaziland, Syria, Thailand, Togo, Trinidad and Tobago, Tunisia, Uganda, United Arab Emirates, United Republic of Tanzania, Uruguay, Vanuatu, Venezuela, Viet Nam, Yemen, Zaire, Zambia, Zimbabwe.

Against: Israel, Russian Federation, United Kingdom, United States.

Abstaining: Albania, Andorra, Argentina, Armenia, Australia, Austria, Azerbaijan, Belarus, Belgium, Bulgaria, Canada, Croatia, Czech Republic, Denmark, Estonia, Finland, Georgia, Germany, Greece, Hungary, Iceland, Ireland, Italy, Japan, Latvia, Liechtenstein, Lithuania, Luxembourg, Malta, Marshall Islands, Netherlands, New Zealand, Norway, Poland, Portugal, Republic of Korea, Republic of Moldova, Romania, Slovakia, Slovenia, Spain, Sweden, The former Yugoslav Republic of Macedonia, Turkey, Ukraine.

Absent: Bosnia and Herzegovina, China, Dominica, Eritrea, France, Gambia, Grenada, Kyrgyzstan, Monaco, Palau, Saint Kitts and Nevis, Saint Lucia, Saint Vincent and the Grenadines, San Marino, Seychelles, Tajikistan, Turkmenistan, Uzbekistan.

28. UNGA RESOLUTION ON COMPREHENSIVE NUCLEAR-TEST-BAN TREATY

Doc. no.: A/Res.50/65 12 December 1995

The General Assembly,

Recalling its resolutions 48/70 of 16 December 1993 and 49/70 of 15 December 1994, in which the entire international community supported the multilateral negotiations on a comprehensive nuclear-test-ban treaty,

Reaffirming that a comprehensive nuclear-test ban is one of the highest priority objectives of the international community in the field of disarmament and non-proliferation,

Convinced that the most effective way to achieve an end to nuclear testing is through the conclusion of a universal and internationally and effectively verifiable comprehensive nuclear-test-ban treaty that will attract the adherence of all States and will contribute to the prevention of the proliferation of nuclear weapons in all its aspects, to the process of nuclear disarmament and therefore to the enhancement of international peace and security,

Noting the aspirations expressed by the parties to the 1963 Treaty Banning Nuclear Weapon Tests in the Atmosphere, in Outer Space and under Water 5/ to seek to achieve the discontinuance of all test explosions of nuclear weapons for all time, which are recalled in the preamble to the 1968 Treaty on the Non-Proliferation of Nuclear Weapons, 6/

Welcoming the further elaboration of the rolling text in the Ad Hoc Committee on a Nuclear Test Ban of the Conference on Disarmament, as reflected in the report of the Conference and its appendix, 7/ and the decision of the Conference to continue its work in inter-sessional meetings,

1. Welcomes the continuing efforts in the multilateral negotiation on a comprehensive nuclear-test-ban treaty in the Ad Hoc Committee on a Nuclear Test Ban of the Conference on Disarmament, the significant contributions to the rolling text made by States participating in those negotiations and progress in key areas;

2. Calls upon all States participating in the Conference on Disarmament, in particular the nuclear-weapon States, to conclude, as a task of the highest priority, a universal and multilaterally and effectively verifiable comprehensive nuclear-test-ban treaty which contributes to nuclear disarmament and the prevention of the proliferation of nuclear weapons in all its aspects, so as to enable its signature by the outset of the fifty-first session of the General Assembly;

5/ United Nations, Treaty Series, vol. 480, No. 6964.

6/ Ibid., vol. 729, No. 10485.

7/ Official Records of the General Assembly, Fiftieth Session, Supplement No. 27, chap. III, sect. A.

3. Also calls upon participants in the Conference on Disarmament to advance work on the basis of the rolling text during the inter-sessional negotiating period so as to proceed to the final phase of the negotiation at the beginning of 1996;

4. Further calls upon the Conference on Disarmament to re-establish the Ad Hoc Committee at the commencement of its 1996 session, and to renew its mandate in order to complete the final text of the treaty as soon as possible in 1996;

5. Urges all States to support the multilateral negotiations in the Conference on Disarmament for a comprehensive nuclear-test-ban treaty and their prompt conclusion;

6. Declares its readiness to resume consideration of this item, as necessary, before its fifty-first session in order to endorse the text of a comprehensive nuclear-test-ban treaty;

7. Requests the Secretary-General to ensure the provision to the Conference on Disarmament of adequate administrative, substantive and conference support services for these negotiations;

8. Decides to include in the provisional agenda of its fifty-first session an item entitled "Implementation of the comprehensive nuclear-test-ban treaty".

29. UNGA RESOLUTION ON GENERAL AND COMPLETE DISARMAMENT (A: NUCLEAR TESTING; E: PROHIBITION OF THE DUMPING OF RADIOACTIVE WASTES)

Doc. no.: A/Res.50/70 12 December 1995

The General Assembly,

Welcoming the easing of international tension and the strengthening of trust between States that have prevailed following the end of the cold war,

Reaffirming that the cessation of all nuclear testing will contribute to the non-proliferation of nuclear weapons in all its aspects, to the process of nuclear disarmament leading to the ultimate objective of the complete elimination of nuclear weapons and therefore to the further enhancement of international peace and security,

Convinced that the cessation of all nuclear testing will provide a favourable climate for the conclusion of negotiations on a comprehensive nuclear-test-ban treaty,

Considering that nuclear testing is not consistent with undertakings by the nuclear-weapon States at the 1995 Review and Extension Conference of the Parties to the Treaty on the Non-Proliferation of Nuclear Weapons,

Deeply concerned about the potential negative effects of underground nuclear testing on health and the environment,

Sharing alarm expressed internationally, regionally and nationally at recent nuclear tests,

1. Commends those nuclear-weapon States observing nuclear testing moratoria, and urges them to continue those moratoria pending the entry into force of a comprehensive nuclear-test-ban treaty;

2. Strongly deplores all current nuclear testing;

3. Strongly urges the immediate cessation of all nuclear testing.

[...]

E

Prohibition of the dumping of radioactive wastes

The General Assembly,

Bearing in mind resolutions CM/Res.1153 (XLVIII) of 1988 37/ and CM/Res.1225 (L) of 1989, 38/ adopted by the Council of Ministers of the Organization of African Unity, concerning the dumping of nuclear and industrial wastes in Africa,

Welcoming resolution GC(XXXIV)/Res/530 establishing a Code of Practice on the International Transboundary Movement of Radioactive Waste, adopted on 21 September 1990 by the General Conference of the International Atomic Energy Agency at its thirty-fourth regular session, 39/

Welcoming also resolution GC(XXXVIII)/Res/6, adopted on 23 September 1994 by the General Conference of the International Atomic Energy Agency at its thirty-eighth regular session, 40/ inviting the Board of Governors and the Director-General of the Agency to commence preparations for a convention on the safety of radioactive waste management,

Considering its resolution 2602 C (XXIV) of 16 December 1969, in which it requested the Conference of the Committee on Disarmament, 41/ inter alia, to consider effective methods of control against the use of radiological methods of warfare,

Recalling resolution CM/Res.1356 (LIV) of 1991, adopted by the Council of Ministers of the Organization of African Unity, 42/ on the Bamako Convention on the Ban on the Import of Hazardous Wastes into Africa and on the Control of Their Transboundary Movements within Africa,

Aware of the potential hazards underlying any use of radioactive wastes that would constitute radiological warfare and its implications for regional and international security, in particular for the security of developing countries,

Recalling its resolutions 43/75 Q of 7 December 1988, 44/116 R of 15 December 1989, 45/58 K of 4 December 1990, 46/36 K of 6 December 1991, 47/52 D of 9 December 1992, 48/75 D of 16 December 1993 and 49/75 A of 15 December 1994,

Desirous of promoting the implementation of paragraph 76 of the Final Document of the Tenth Special Session of the General Assembly, 43/ the first special session devoted to disarmament,

1. Takes note of the part of the report of the Conference on Disarmament relating to a future convention on the prohibition of radiological weapons; 44/

2. Expresses grave concern regarding any use of nuclear wastes that would constitute radiological warfare and have grave implications for the national security of all States;

37/ A/43/398, annex I.

38/ See A/44/603, annex I.

39/ See International Atomic Energy Agency, Resolutions and Other Decisions of the General Conference, Thirty-fourth Regular Session, 17-21 September 1990 (GC(XXXIV)/RESOLUTIONS(1990)).

40/ Ibid., Thirty-eighth Regular Session, 19-23 September 1994 (GC(XXXVIII)/RES/DEC/(1994)).

41/ The Conference of the Committee on Disarmament became the Committee on Disarmament as from the tenth special session of the General Assembly. The Committee on Disarmament was redesignated the Conference on Disarmament as from 7 February 1984.

42/ See A/49/390, annex I.

43/ Resolution S-10/2.

44/ See Official Records of the General Assembly, Fiftieth Session, Supplement No. 27 (A/50/27).

3. Calls upon all States to take appropriate measures with a view to preventing any dumping of nuclear or radioactive wastes that would infringe upon the sovereignty of States;

4. Requests the Conference on Disarmament to take into account, in the negotiations for a convention on the prohibition of radiological weapons, radioactive wastes as part of the scope of such a convention;

5. Also requests the Conference on Disarmament to intensify efforts towards an early conclusion of such a convention and to include in its report to the General Assembly at its fifty-first session the progress recorded in the negotiations on this subject;

6. Takes note of resolution CM/Res.1356 (LIV) of 1991, adopted by the Council of Ministers of the Organization of African Unity, on the Bamako Convention on the Ban on the Import of Hazardous Wastes into Africa and on the Control of Their Transboundary Movements within Africa;

7. Expresses the hope that the effective implementation of the International Atomic Energy Agency Code of Practice on the International Transboundary Movement of Radioactive Waste will enhance the protection of all States from the dumping of radioactive wastes on their territories;

8. Welcomes current efforts of the International Atomic Energy Agency in the preparation of a draft convention on the safe management of radioactive waste;

9. Decides to include in the provisional agenda of its fifty-first session the item entitled "Prohibition of the dumping of radioactive wastes".

[...]

RECORDED VOTE ON RESOLUTION 50/70 A:

In favour: Algeria, Argentina, Australia, Austria, Bahamas, Bangladesh, Barbados, Belarus, Belgium, Belize, Bhutan, Botswana, Brazil, Brunei Darussalam, Canada, Chile, Colombia, Costa Rica, Cuba, Denmark, Ecuador, Eritrea, Ethiopia, Federated States of Micronesia, Fiji, Finland, Ghana, Guatemala, Guyana, Iceland, India, Indonesia, Ireland, Italy, Jamaica, Japan, Kazakstan, Kyrgyzstan, Lesotho, Liechtenstein, Luxembourg, Malawi, Malaysia, Maldives, Malta, Marshall Islands, Mauritius, Mexico, Mongolia, Mozambique, Myanmar, Nepal, Netherlands, New Zealand, Nicaragua, Nigeria, Norway, Palau, Panama, Papua New Guinea, Paraguay, Peru, Philippines, Portugal, Republic of Korea, Rwanda, Samoa, Sierra Leone, Singapore, Solomon Islands, South Africa, Sri Lanka, Suriname, Swaziland, Sweden, Thailand, Trinidad and Tobago, Uganda, Ukraine, United Republic of Tanzania, Uruguay, Venezuela, Viet Nam, Zambia, Zimbabwe.

Against: Benin, Cameroon, Chad, China, Congo, Côte d'Ivoire, Djibouti, Equatorial Guinea, France, Gabon, Madagascar, Mali, Mauritania, Monaco, Niger, Senegal, Togo, United Kingdom.

Abstaining: Afghanistan, Albania, Andorra, Angola, Armenia, Bulgaria, Burundi, Cambodia, Croatia, Cyprus, Czech Republic, Democratic People's Republic of Korea, El Salvador, Estonia, Georgia, Germany, Greece, Guinea, Guinea-Bissau, Hungary, Israel, Kenya, Latvia, Lebanon, Libya, Lithuania, Morocco, Namibia, Pakistan, Poland, Republic of Moldova, Romania, Russian Federation, Slovakia, Slovenia, Spain, Sudan, Syria, The former Yugoslav Republic of Macedonia, Tunisia, Turkey, United States, Zaire.

Absent: Antigua and Barbuda, Azerbaijan, Bahrain, Bolivia, Bosnia and Herzegovina, Burkina Faso, Cape Verde, Dominica, Egypt, Gambia, Grenada, Haiti, Honduras, Iran*, Jordan, Kuwait, Lao People's Democratic Republic, Oman, Qatar, Saint Kitts and Nevis, Saint Lucia, Saint Vincent and the Grenadines, San Marino, Saudi Arabia, Seychelles, Tajikistan, Turkmenistan**, United Arab Emirates, Uzbekistan, Vanuatu, Yemen.

[...]

* Later advised the Secretariat that it had intended to vote against.
** Later advised the Secretariat that it had intended to abstain.

30. UNGA RESOLUTION ON STRENGTHENING OF SECURITY AND COOPERATION IN THE MEDITERRANEAN REGION

Doc. no.: A/Res.50/75 12 December 1995

The General Assembly,

Recalling its previous resolutions on the subject, including resolution 49/81 of 15 December 1994,

Reaffirming the primary role of the Mediterranean countries in strengthening and promoting peace, security and cooperation in the Mediterranean region,

Bearing in mind all the previous declarations and commitments, as well as all the initiatives taken by the riparian countries at the recent summits, ministerial meetings and various forums concerning the question of the Mediterranean region,

Recognizing the efforts made so far and the determination of the Mediterranean countries to intensify the process of dialogue and consultations with a view to resolving the problems existing in the Mediterranean region and to eliminate the causes of tension and the consequent threat to peace and security,

Recognizing also the indivisible character of security in the Mediterranean and that the enhancement of cooperation among Mediterranean countries with a view to promoting the economic and social development of all peoples of the region will contribute significantly to stability, peace and security in the region,

Recognizing further that prospects for closer Euro-Mediterranean cooperation in all spheres can be enhanced by positive developments world wide, in particular in Europe, in the Maghreb and in the Middle East,

Noting with satisfaction the positive developments in the Middle East peace process that will lead to achieving a comprehensive, just and lasting peace in the region and therefore to promoting confidence-building measures and a good-neighbourly spirit among the countries of the area,

Expressing satisfaction at the growing awareness of the need for more joint efforts by all Mediterranean countries so as to strengthen economic, social, cultural and environmental cooperation in the region,

Reaffirming the responsibility of all States to contribute to the stability and prosperity of the Mediterranean region and their commitment to respect the purposes and principles of the Charter of the United Nations, as well as the provisions of the Declaration on Principles of International Law concerning Friendly Relations and Cooperation among States in accordance with the Charter of the United Nations, 101/

Expressing its concern at the persistent tension and continuing military activities in parts of the Mediterranean that hinder efforts to strengthen security and cooperation in the region,

Taking note of the report of the Secretary-General on this item, 102/

1. Reaffirms that security in the Mediterranean is closely linked to European security as well as to international peace and security;

2. Expresses its satisfaction at the continuing efforts by Mediterranean countries to contribute actively to the elimination of all causes of tension in the region and to the promotion of just and lasting solutions to the persistent problems of the region through peaceful means, thus ensuring the withdrawal of foreign forces of occupation and respecting the sovereignty, independence and territorial integrity of all countries of the Mediterranean and the right of peoples to self-determination, and therefore calls for full adherence to the principles of non-interference, non-intervention, non-use of force or threat of use of force and the inadmissibility of the acquisition of territory by force, in accordance with the Charter and the relevant resolutions of the United Nations;

3. Commends the efforts by the Mediterranean countries in meeting common challenges through coordinated overall responses, based on a spirit of multilateral partnership, towards the general objective of turning the Mediterranean basin into an area of dialogue, exchanges and cooperation, guaranteeing peace, stability and prosperity;

4. Recognizes that the elimination of the economic and social disparities in levels of development as well as other obstacles in the Mediterranean area will contribute to enhancing peace, security and cooperation among Mediterranean countries through the existing forums;

5. Calls upon all States of the Mediterranean region that have not yet done so to adhere to all the multilaterally negotiated legal instruments related to the field of disarmament, thus creating the necessary conditions for strengthening peace and cooperation in the region;

6. Encourages all States of the region to favour the necessary conditions for strengthening the confidence-building measures among them by promoting genuine openness and transparency on all military matters, by participating, inter alia, in the United Nations system for the standardized reporting of military expenditures as well as by providing accurate data and information to the United Nations Register of Conventional Arms;

7. Encourages the Mediterranean countries to strengthen further their cooperation in combating terrorism, which poses a serious threat to peace, security and stability in the region and therefore to the improvement of the current political, economic and social situation;

8. Invites all States of the region to address, through various forms of cooperation, problems and threats posed to the region, such as terrorism, international crime and illicit arms transfers, as well as illicit drug production, consumption and trafficking, which jeopardize the friendly relations among States, hinder the development of international cooperation and result in the destruction of human rights, fundamental freedoms and the democratic basis of pluralistic society;

9. Encourages the continued widespread support among the Mediterranean countries for the convening of a conference on security and cooperation in the Mediterranean, as well as the ongoing regional consultations to create the appropriate conditions for its convening;

10. Requests the Secretary-General to submit a report on means to strengthen security and cooperation in the Mediterranean region;

11. Decides to include in the provisional agenda of its fifty-first session the item entitled "Strengthening of security and cooperation in the Mediterranean region".

101/ Resolution 2625 (XXV), annex.

102/ A/50/300.

31. UNGA RESOLUTION ON IMPLEMENTATION OF THE DECLARATION OF THE INDIAN OCEAN AS A ZONE OF PEACE

Doc. no.: A/Res.50/76 12 December 1995

The General Assembly,

Recalling the Declaration of the Indian Ocean as a Zone of Peace, contained in its resolution 2832 (XXVI) of 16 December 1971, and recalling also its resolution 49/82 of 15 December 1994 and other relevant resolutions,

Recalling also the report of the Meeting of the Littoral and Hinterland States of the Indian Ocean held in July 1979, 103/

Having considered the conclusions and recommendations reached by the Ad Hoc Committee on the Indian Ocean during its sessions in 1995, 104/

Emphasizing the need to foster consensual approaches, in particular given the prevailing international climate, which is conducive to the pursuit of such endeavours,

Noting the initiatives taken by countries in the region to promote cooperation, in particular economic cooperation, in the Indian Ocean area and the possible contribution of such initiatives to overall objectives of a zone of peace,

Convinced that the participation of all the permanent members of the Security Council and the major maritime users of the Indian Ocean in the work of the Ad Hoc Committee is important and would assist the progress of mutually beneficial dialogue to develop conditions of peace, security and stability in the Indian Ocean region,

1. Takes note of the report of the Ad Hoc Committee on the Indian Ocean; 105/

2. Considers that greater efforts and more time are required to develop a focused discussion on practical measures to ensure conditions of peace, security and stability in the Indian Ocean region;

3. Reiterates its conviction that the participation of all permanent members of the Security Council and the major maritime users of the Indian Ocean in the work of the Ad Hoc Committee is

---

103/ Official Records of the General Assembly, Thirty-fourth Session, Supplement No. 45 and corrigendum (A/34/45 and Corr.1).

104/ See Official Records of the General Assembly, Fiftieth Session, Supplement No. 29 (A/50/29).

105/ Ibid.

important and would greatly facilitate development of a mutually beneficial dialogue to advance peace, security and stability in the Indian Ocean region;

4. Requests the Chairman of the Ad Hoc Committee to pursue his dialogue on the work of the Committee with the permanent members of the Security Council and major maritime users of the Indian Ocean and to apprise the Ad Hoc Committee of his consultations and other relevant developments at a meeting to be held in 1996 for that specific purpose, to take place before the 1997 regular session of the Committee;

5. Requests the Ad Hoc Committee to submit to the General Assembly at its fifty-first session a report on the consultations held;

6. Requests the Secretary-General to continue to render all necessary assistance to the Ad Hoc Committee, including the provision of summary records;

7. Decides to include in the provisional agenda of its fifty-first session, the item entitled "Implementation of the Declaration of the Indian Ocean as a Zone of Peace".

RECORDED VOTE ON RESOLUTION 50/76:

In favour: Afghanistan, Algeria, Angola, Antigua and Barbuda, Argentina, Australia, Azerbaijan, Bahamas, Bahrain, Bangladesh, Barbados, Belarus, Belize, Benin, Bhutan, Bolivia, Botswana, Brazil, Brunei Darussalam, Burkina Faso, Burundi, Cambodia, Cameroon, Cape Verde, Chad, Chile, China, Colombia, Congo, Costa Rica, Cote d'Ivoire, Cuba, Cyprus, Djibouti, Democratic Republic of Korea, Ecuador, Egypt, El Salvador, Equatorial Guinea, Eritrea, Ethiopia, Federated States of Micronesia, Fiji, Gabon, Ghana, Guatemala, Guinea, Guinea-Bissau, Guyana, Haiti, Honduras, India, Indonesia, Iran, Jamaica, Japan, Jordan, Kazakstan, Kenya, Kuwait, Kyrgyzstan, Lao People's Democratic Republic, Lebanon, Lesotho, Libya, Madagascar, Malawi, Malaysia, Maldives, Mali, Marshall Islands, Mauritania, Mauritius, Mexico, Mongolia, Morocco, Mozambique, Myanmar, Namibia, Nepal, New Zealand, Nicaragua, Niger, Nigeria, Oman, Pakistan, Panama, Papua New Guinea, Paraguay, Peru, Philippines, Qatar, Republic of Korea, Russian Federation, Rwanda, Samoa, Saudi Arabia, Senegal, Sierra Leone, Singapore, Solomon Islands, South Africa, Sri Lanka, Sudan, Suriname, Swaziland, Syria, Thailand, Togo, Trinidad and Tobago, Tunisia, United Arab Emirates, Uganda, Ukraine, United Republic of Tanzania, Uruguay, Vanuatu, Venezuela, Viet Nam, Yemen, Zaire, Zambia, Zimbabwe.

Against: France, United Kingdom, United States.

Abstaining: Albania, Andorra, Armenia, Austria, Belgium, Bosnia and Herzegovina, Bulgaria, Canada, Croatia, Czech Republic, Denmark, Estonia, Finland, Georgia, Germany, Greece, Hungary, Iceland, Ireland, Israel, Italy, Latvia, Liechtenstein, Lithuania, Luxembourg, Malta, Netherlands, Norway, Poland, Portugal, Republic of Moldova, Romania, Slovakia, Slovenia, Spain, Sweden, The former Yugoslav Republic of Macedonia, Turkey, Uzbekistan.

Absent: Dominica, Gambia, Grenada, Monaco, Palau, Saint Kitts and Nevis, Saint Lucia, Saint Vincent and the Grenadines, San Marino, Seychelles, Tajikistan, Turkmenistan.

32. UNGA RESOLUTION ON SPECIFIC ACTIONS RELATED TO THE PARTICULAR NEEDS AND PROBLEMS OF LAND-LOCKED DEVELOPING COUNTRIES

Doc. no.: A/Res.50/97 20 December 1995

The General Assembly,

Recalling the provisions of its resolutions 44/214 of 22 December 1989, 46/212 of 22 December 1991 and 48/169 of 21 December 1993,

Recognizing that the lack of territorial access to the sea, aggravated by remoteness and isolation from world markets, and prohibitive transit costs and risks impose serious constraints on the overall socio-economic development efforts of the land-locked developing countries,

Recognizing also that 16 of the land-locked developing countries are also classified by the United Nations as least developed countries and that their geographical situation is an added constraint on their overall ability to cope with the challenges of development,

Recognizing further that most transit countries are themselves developing countries facing serious economic problems, including the lack of adequate infrastructure in the transport sector,

Recalling that measures to deal with the transit problems of land-locked developing countries require closer and even more effective cooperation and collaboration between those countries and their transit neighbours,

Welcoming the entry into force on 16 November 1994 of the United Nations Convention on the Law of the Sea, 33/

Recognizing the important role played by bilateral cooperative arrangements and regional and subregional cooperation and integration in alleviating the transit problems of the land-locked developing countries and improving the transit transport systems in land-locked and transit developing countries,

Recognizing also the importance of continuing the activities of the regional commissions to improve the transit transport infrastructure in the land-locked and transit developing countries,

Noting the importance of strengthening the existing international support measures with a view to addressing further the problems of land-locked developing countries,

1. Reaffirms the right of access of land-locked developing countries to and from the sea and freedom of transit through the territory of transit States by all means of transport, in accordance with international law;

33/ Official Records of the Third United Nations Conference on the Law of the Sea, vol. XVII (United Nations publication, Sales No. E.84.V.3), document A/CONF.62/122.

2. Also reaffirms that transit developing countries, in the exercise of their full sovereignty over their territory, have the right to take all measures necessary to ensure that the rights and facilities provided for land-locked developing countries should in no way infringe upon their legitimate interests;

3. Calls upon both the land-locked developing countries and their transit neighbours, in the spirit of South-South cooperation, including bilateral cooperation, to implement measures to strengthen further their cooperative and collaborative efforts in dealing with their transit problems;

4. Appeals once again to all States, international organizations and financial institutions to implement, as a matter of urgency and priority, the specific actions related to the particular needs and problems of land-locked developing countries envisaged in the previous resolutions adopted by the General Assembly and the United Nations Conference on Trade and Development and in the International Development Strategy for the Fourth United Nations Development Decade 34/ and the Declaration on International Economic Cooperation, in particular the Revitalization of Economic Growth and Development of the Developing Countries, adopted at the eighteenth special session of the General Assembly and contained in the annex to its resolution S-18/3 of 1 May 1990, as well as the relevant provisions of the Programme of Action for the Least Developed Countries for the 1990s 35/ and the outcomes of recent major United Nations conferences relevant to land-locked developing countries;

5. Invites the land-locked developing countries and their transit neighbours to intensify further their cooperative arrangements for the development of transit infrastructures, institutions and services to facilitate the faster movement of goods in transit, with financial and technical assistance from donors and financial institutions;

6. Emphasizes that assistance for the improvement of transit transport facilities and services should be integrated into the overall economic development strategies of the land-locked and transit developing countries and that donor assistance should consequently take into account the requirements for the long-term restructuring of the economies of the land-locked developing countries;

7. Invites donor countries and multilateral financial and development institutions to provide land-locked and transit developing countries with appropriate financial and technical assistance in the form of grants or concessional loans for the construction, maintenance and improvement of their transport, storage and other transit-related facilities, including alternative routes and improved communications;

8. Invites the United Nations Development Programme further to promote, as appropriate, subregional, regional and interregional projects and programmes and to expand its support in the transport and communications sectors to the land-locked and transit developing countries and its technical cooperation for development geared towards promoting national and collective self-reliance among them;

9. Takes note of the report of the Second Meeting of Governmental Experts from Land-locked and Transit Developing Countries and Representatives of Donor Countries and Financial and Development Institutions, held in New York from 19 to 22 June 1995, 36/ and endorses the Global Framework for Transit Transport Cooperation between Land-locked and Transit Developing Countries and the Donor Community contained therein;

10. Requests the Secretary-General of the United Nations Conference on Trade and Development, in collaboration with the donor countries and institutions, in particular the United Nations Development Programme, the regional commissions and relevant subregional institutions, to organize, within existing resources, specific consultative groups, when requested by the land-locked and transit developing countries concerned, to identify priority areas for action at the national and subregional level and draw up action programmes for the period 1996-1997;

11. Requests the Secretary-General to convene in 1997, within the overall level of resources for the biennium 1996-1997, another meeting of governmental experts from land-locked and transit developing countries and representatives of donor countries and financial and development institutions, including relevant

---

34/ Resolution 45/199, annex.

35/ Report of the Second United Nations Conference on the Least Developed Countries, Paris, 3-14 September 1990 (A/CONF.147/18), part one.

36/ TD/B/42(1)-TD/B/LDC/AC.1/7.

regional and subregional economic organizations and commissions, to review progress in the development of transit systems in the land-locked and transit developing countries, taking into account, inter alia, the results of the consultative group meetings referred to in paragraph 10 of the present resolution, with a view to exploring the possibility of formulating specific action-oriented measures and the ongoing study undertaken by the United Nations Conference on Trade and Development on the implications of the globalization and liberalization of the world economy for the development prospects of land-locked developing countries;

12. Requests the Secretary-General of the United Nations Conference on Trade and Development to seek voluntary contributions to ensure participation of representatives from land-locked and transit developing countries in the meeting of governmental experts from land-locked and transit developing countries and representatives of donor countries and financial and development institutions referred to in paragraph 11 of the present resolution;

13. Notes with appreciation the contribution of the United Nations Conference on Trade and Development in formulating international measures to deal with the special problems of the land-locked developing countries, and urges the Conference, inter alia, to keep under constant review the evolution of transit transport infrastructure facilities, institutions and services, monitor the implementation of agreed measures, collaborate in all relevant initiatives, including those of the private sector and non-governmental organizations, and serve as a focal point on cross-regional issues of interest to land-locked developing countries;

14. Invites the Secretary-General of the United Nations, in consultation with the Secretary-General of the United Nations Conference on Trade and Development, to take appropriate measures for the effective implementation of the activities called for in the present resolution and of existing measures in support of land-locked developing countries, within the context of the ninth session of the Conference;

15. Welcomes the note by the Secretary-General and the progress report of the secretariat of the United Nations Conference on Trade and Development on specific actions related to the particular needs and problems of land-locked developing countries, 37/ and requests the Secretary-General of the United Nations, together with the Secretary-General of the United Nations Conference on Trade and Development, to prepare a report on the implementation of the present resolution and submit it to the Trade and Development Board and to the General Assembly at its fifty-second session.

37/ A/50/341.

33. UNGA RESOLUTION ON CONVENTION BIOLOGICAL DIVERSITY

Doc. no.: A/Res.50/111 20 December 1995

The General Assembly,

Reaffirming its resolutions 49/117 on the Convention on Biological Diversity and 49/119 on the International Day for Biological Diversity of 19 December 1994,

Recalling the Convention on Biological Diversity, 113/

Recalling also Agenda 21, 114/ particularly its chapter 15 on the conservation of biological diversity, and related chapters,

Recalling further the recommendations made at the third session of the Commission on Sustainable Development on the review of chapter 15 of Agenda 21 on the conservation of biological diversity, 115/

Deeply concerned by the continuing loss of the world's biological diversity and, on the basis of the provisions of the Convention, reiterating the commitment to the conservation of biological diversity, and the sustainable use of its components, as well as the fair and equitable sharing of benefits arising from the use of genetic resources,

1. Welcomes the results of the first meeting of the Conference of the Parties to the Convention on Biological Diversity, held at Nassau, the Bahamas, from 28 November to 9 December 1994, as reflected in the report of the Executive Secretary of the Convention, 116/ submitted in accordance with paragraph 4 of General Assembly resolution 49/117;

2. Takes note that the Conference of the Parties to the Convention on Biological Diversity has decided to accept the offer of the Government of Canada to host the secretariat of the Convention, and expresses its appreciation for the support offered by the Canadian authorities to ensure the effective functioning of the secretariat;

113/ See United Nations Environment Programme, Convention on Biological Diversity (Environmental Law and Institution Programme Activity Centre), June 1992.

114/ Report of the United Nations Conference on Environment and Development, Rio de Janeiro, 3-14 June 1992, vol. I, Resolutions Adopted by the Conference (United Nations publication, Sales No. E.93.I.8 and corrigendum), resolution 1, annex II.

115/ See Official Records of the Economic and Social Council, 1995, Supplement No. 12 (E/1995/32), chap. I, para. 230 (i).

116/ A/50/218.

3. Takes note of the results of the first meeting of the Subsidiary Body on Scientific, Technical and Technological Advice, held at the headquarters of the United Nations Educational, Scientific and Cultural Organization in Paris from 4 to 8 September 1995, including its medium-term programme of work for 1996-1997 and its contribution to the Open-ended Ad Hoc Intergovernmental Panel on Forests of the Commission on Sustainable Development;

4. Calls upon those States that have not yet ratified the Convention to expedite their internal procedures of ratification, acceptance or approval;

5. Invites the Executive Secretary of the Convention on Biological Diversity to report, through the Economic and Social Council, to the General Assembly at its fifty-first session on the results of the second meeting of the Conference of the Parties to the Convention, held at Jakarta, Indonesia, from 6 to 17 November 1995, and also invites the Secretary to make the reports of the Conference of the Parties to the Convention available to the Commission on Sustainable Development.

34. UNGA RESOLUTION ON SPECIAL SESSION FOR THE PURPOSE OF AN OVERALL REVIEW AND APPRAISAL OF THE IMPLEMENTATION OF AGENDA 21

Doc. no.: A/Res.50/113 20 December 1995

The General Assembly,

Recalling its resolution 47/190 of 22 December 1992, in which it decided to convene, not later than 1997, a special session for the purpose of an overall review and appraisal of the implementation of Agenda 21, 125/

Having considered the report of the Secretary-General containing proposals on the format, scope and organizational aspects of such a special session, 126/

1. Decides to convene the special session envisaged in resolution 47/190 for a duration of one week during the month of June 1997 at the highest possible level of participation;

2. Encourages participants at the high-level meeting of the Commission on Sustainable Development to be held during its fourth session, in 1996, to address, inter alia, matters related to the special session of the General Assembly decided on above;

3. Invites the Commission to devote its Ad Hoc Open-ended Inter-Sessional Working Group meeting, to be held in February 1997, to assisting the Commission in undertaking the review for the special session;

4. Welcomes the decision of the Commission to devote its fifth session, in 1997, to preparations for the special session, and decides that that session of the Commission will be open-ended in its deliberations, allowing for the full participation of all States;

5. Invites the Commission to make available to the Assembly at the special session all relevant reports prepared under the aegis of the Commission, along with the recommendations of the Commission thereon;

6. Welcomes the decisions of the Governing Council of the United Nations Environment Programme, in which the Council emphasized the need for the Programme, in accordance with its mandate in the implementation of Agenda 21, to continue to provide effective support to the work of the Commission on Sustainable Development, and in which the Council decided to hold its nineteenth session early in 1997 with a view to making a contribution to the special session;

125/ Report of the United Nations Conference on Environment and Development, Rio de Janeiro, 3-14 June 1992, vol. I, Resolutions Adopted by the Conference (United Nations publication, Sales No. E.93.I.8 and corrigenda), resolution 1, annex II.

126/ A/50/453.

7. Invites Governments as well as relevant regional and subregional organizations to consider undertaking reviews of progress achieved since the United Nations Conference on Environment and Development at the national, subregional, regional and interregional levels with a view to contributing to the preparations for the special session;

8. Welcomes the preparation of hemispheric, regional and subregional conferences on sustainable development, and in that context invites the Governments concerned to contribute to the special session the outcomes of such conferences;

9. Also invites all other relevant organizations and bodies of the United Nations system, including the United Nations Conference on Trade and Development, the specialized agencies and other multilateral organizations, including the multilateral financial institutions and the World Trade Organization, to contribute to the special session, and requests the Inter-Agency Committee on Sustainable Development, in close coordination with the Commission on Sustainable Development, to ensure an effective and coordinated system-wide response to the preparation of the special session;

10. Further invites the conferences of parties or other regulatory bodies of the United Nations Framework Convention on Climate Change, the Convention on Biological Diversity and the United Nations Convention to Combat Desertification in Those Countries Experiencing Serious Drought and/or Desertification, Particularly in Africa, as well as the regulatory bodies of other relevant instruments, as appropriate, and the Global Environment Facility, to provide their inputs to the special session;

11. Recognizes the important role played by major groups, including non-governmental organizations, at the United Nations Conference on Environment and Development and in the implementation of its recommendations, and recognizes the need for their active involvement in preparations for the special session, as well as the need to ensure appropriate arrangements for their contribution during the special session;

12. Invites Governments to assist the developing countries, in particular the least developed among them, in participating fully and effectively in the special session and its preparatory process, and in that regard invites them to make appropriate contributions to the Trust Fund to Support the Work of the Commission on Sustainable Development;

13. Requests the Secretary-General to prepare, for the consideration of the Commission on Sustainable Development at its fifth session, a comprehensive report containing an overall assessment of the progress achieved since the United Nations Conference on Environment and Development in the implementation of Agenda 21 at all levels, 127/ and in the implementation of related outcomes, as well as recommendations for future actions and priorities, and requests that the report include:

(a) Concise reports containing an assessment of the progress achieved in specific sectoral and cross-sectoral areas;

(b) Country profiles providing a concise presentation of progress made and constraints encountered in implementing Agenda 21 at the national level, compiled on the basis of national information received and in close cooperation with the Governments concerned;

(c) Major and emerging trends and issues within the framework of Agenda 21 and related outcomes of the Conference in the area of sustainable development, including the environmental impact of activities that are gravely hazardous to the environment, taking into account the views of States;

(d) Recommendations on the future role of the Commission in the follow-up to the outcome of the Conference and related outcomes, building on experience gained since 1992;

14. Requests the Secretary-General to mount a public information programme to raise global awareness of both the special session to review the implementation of Agenda 21 and the work undertaken by the United Nations in the follow-up to the Conference;

15. Decides that the preparations for the special session and the special session itself shall be kept within the agreed appropriation level for the 1996-1997 biennium;

127/ Report of the United Nations Conference on Environment and Development, Rio de Janeiro, 3-14 June 1992, vol. I, Resolutions Adopted by the Conference (United Nations publication, Sales No. E.93.I.8 and corrigenda), resolution 1, annex II.

16. Decides to include a sub-item entitled "Special session for the purpose of an overall review and appraisal of the implementation of Agenda 21" in the provisional agenda of its fifty-first session, and requests the Secretary-General to submit to it at that session a progress report on the state of preparations for the 1997 special session.

35. UNGA RESOLUTION ON PROTECTION OF GLOBAL CLIMATE FOR PRESENT AND FUTURE GENERATIONS OF MANKIND

Doc. no.: A/Res.50/115 20 December 1995

The General Assembly,

Recalling its resolutions 45/212 of 21 December 1990, 46/169 of 19 December 1991, 47/195 of 22 December 1992, 48/189 of 21 December 1993 and 49/120 of 19 December 1994,

Noting with satisfaction that a large number of States and one regional economic integration organization have ratified the United Nations Framework Convention on Climate Change 131/ and calling upon other States to take appropriate action to that end,

Noting that, in accordance with paragraphs 1 and 2 of General Assembly resolution 48/189, the first session of the Conference of the Parties to the United Nations Framework Convention on Climate Change was convened from 28 March to 7 April 1995 in Berlin, and that it was attended by one hundred and sixteen of the then one hundred and eighteen Parties to the Convention, as well as by a large number of governmental, intergovernmental and non-governmental observers,

Expressing its deep appreciation to the Government of Germany for the generous manner in which it hosted the first session of the Conference of the Parties,

Looking forward to the ongoing work of the Conference of the Parties and its subsidiary bodies in addressing climate change within the framework of the United Nations Framework Convention on Climate Change and to the successful conclusion of the Berlin Mandate 132/ process at the third session of the Conference of the Parties,

Noting the important scientific contribution of the World Meteorological Organization/United Nations Environment Programme Intergovernmental Panel on Climate Change to the Convention process and looking forward to the completion of its second assessment report,

Recognizing the contribution to the Convention process of the interim secretariat of the Convention, within the framework of the Department for Policy Coordination and Sustainable Development of the Secretariat, as well as the support provided to that secretariat by the World Meteorological Organization, the United Nations Environment Programme, the United Nations Conference on Trade and Development, the United Nations Development Programme and bilateral contributors,

---

131/ A/AC.237/18 (Part II)/Add.1 and Corr.1, annex I.

132/ FCCC/CP/1995/7/Add.1, decision 1/CP.1.

Taking note of the advice of the Secretary-General on an institutional linkage for the secretariat of the Convention with the United Nations, including the procedures indicated therein for the application of the Financial Regulations and the Staff Regulations and Staff Rules of the United Nations and for the appointment and accountability of the head of that secretariat, 133/

Taking note also of the decision of the Conference of the Parties, 134/ on the basis of the advice of the Secretary-General, that the Convention secretariat shall be institutionally linked to the United Nations, while not being fully integrated into the work programme and management structure of any particular department or programme,

Taking note further of the financial procedures for the Conference of the Parties to the United Nations Framework Convention on Climate Change, its subsidiary bodies and its permanent secretariat adopted at its first session, 135/ whereby, inter alia, the Secretary-General is asked to establish trust funds for the purposes of the Convention, to be managed by the head of the Convention secretariat in accordance with duly delegated authority,

Taking note further of the decision of the Conference of the Parties 136/ whereby the General Assembly is requested, bearing in mind the institutional linkage of the Convention secretariat to the United Nations and the large number of States that are Parties to the Convention, to decide to finance from the regular programme budget of the United Nations the conference-servicing costs arising from sessions of the Conference of the Parties and its subsidiary bodies for the duration of the institutional linkage mentioned above,

Having considered the report of the Secretary-General on the implementation of General Assembly resolution 49/120, with particular reference to the implications arising from the report of the Conference of the Parties on its first session, 137/

1. Takes note with appreciation of:

(a) The report of the Intergovernmental Negotiating Committee on a Framework Convention on Climate Change on its eleventh session; 138/

(b) The final report prepared on behalf of the Committee, by its Chairman, on the completion of the Committee's work; 139/

(c) The report of the Conference of the Parties to the Convention on its first session 140/ and its presentation on behalf of the President of the Conference;

2. Endorses the institutional linkage between the Convention secretariat and the United Nations, as advised by the Secretary-General and adopted by the Conference of the Parties; 141/

3. Requests the Secretary-General to review the functioning of this institutional linkage not later than 31 December 1999, in consultation with the Conference of the Parties, with a view to making such modifications as may be considered desirable by both parties and to report thereon to the General Assembly;

133/ See A/AC.237/79/Add.1; FCCC/CP/1995/5/Add.4; and A/50/716, para. 49.

134/ FCCC/CP/1995/7/Add.1, decision 14/CP.1.

135/ FCCC/CP/1995/7/Add.1, decision 15/CP.1, annex I.

136/ FCCC/CP/1995/7/Add.1, decision 14/CP.1.

137/ A/50/716.

138/ A/AC.237/91 and Add.1.

139/ A/50/536.

140/ FCCC/CP/1995/7 and Add.1.

141/ FCCC/CP/1995/7/Add.1, decision 14/CP.1.

4. Notes that the Conference of the Parties has decided to accept the offer of the Government of Germany to host the Convention secretariat 142/ and expresses its appreciation for the support offered by the future host Government for the relocation and effective functioning of the Convention secretariat;

5. Notes with appreciation contributions made to the extrabudgetary funds established under paragraphs 10 and 20 of General Assembly resolution 45/212, and maintained in accordance with Assembly resolution 47/195;

6. Urges Member States that are Parties to the Convention to pay promptly and in full for each of the years 1996 and 1997, in accordance with the indicative scale adopted by consensus by the Conference of the Parties, 143/ the contributions required for the trust fund for the core budget of the Convention envisaged in paragraph 13 of its financial procedures, so as to ensure continuity in the cash flow required to finance the ongoing work of the Conference of the Parties, the subsidiary bodies and the Convention secretariat;

7. Calls upon Member States that are Parties to the Convention to also contribute generously to the trust fund for participation in the Convention process envisaged in paragraph 15 of its financial procedures, as well as to the trust funds envisaged for supplementary activities under the Convention; 144/

8. Decides to include in the calendar of conferences and meetings for 1996-1997 the sessions of the Conference of the Parties and its subsidiary bodies envisaged for that biennium entailing twelve weeks of conference-servicing facilities;

9. Requests the Secretary-General to make the necessary arrangements to include in the calendar of conferences and meetings for the biennium 1998-1999 those sessions of the Conference of the Parties and its subsidiary bodies that the Conference may need to convene in that period;

10. Takes note of the transitional arrangement for administrative support to the Convention secretariat, outlined in the report of the Secretary-General on the implementation of General Assembly resolution 49/120, with particular reference to the implications arising from the report of the Conference of the Parties, on its first session, 145/ which should facilitate the establishment and relocation of the Convention secretariat and assist it in addressing any initial financial and personnel problems that may be encountered within this context, also takes note of the financing arrangements contained in operative paragraphs 8 and 9 above, and requests the Secretary-General to review these arrangements towards the end of the biennium 1996-1997 and to report upon the results of this review to the Assembly at its fifty-second session;

11. Notes that the Secretary-General intends:

(a) To transfer the end-1995 balance in the trust fund for the negotiating process established under paragraph 20 of General Assembly resolution 45/212 into the trust fund for the core budget of the Convention envisaged in paragraph 13 of its financial procedures;

(b) To transfer the end-1995 balance in the special voluntary fund for participation in the negotiating process established under paragraph 10 of the same resolution into the trust fund for participation in the Convention process envisaged in paragraph 15 of the aforementioned financial procedures;

12. Requests the Secretary-General to report to the General Assembly at its fifty-first session on the implementation of the present resolution;

13. Decides to include in the provisional agenda of its fifty-first session the item entitled "Protection of global climate for present and future generations of mankind".

142/ Ibid., decision 16/CP.1.

143/ FCCC/CP/1995/7/Add.1, decision 15/CP.1, annex II.

144/ Ibid., decision 15/CP.1, annex I, and decision 18/CP.1.

145/ A/50/716, paras. 36-38.

36. UNGA DECISION ON QUESTION OF THE FALKLAND ISLANDS (MALVINAS)

Doc. no.: A/Dec.50/406 31 October 1995

At its 45th plenary meeting, on 31 October 1995, the General Assembly decided to defer consideration of the item entitled "Question of the Falkland Islands (Malvinas)" and to include it in the provisional agenda of its fifty-first session.

37. UNGA DECISION ON QUESTION OF GIBRALTAR

Doc. no.: A/Dec.50/415 | 6 December 1995

At its 82nd plenary meeting, on 6 December 1995, the General Assembly, on the recommendation of the Special Political and Decolonization Committee (Fourth Committee), 152/ adopted the following text as representing the consensus of the members of the Assembly:

"The General Assembly, recalling its decision 49/420 of 9 December 1994 and recalling at the same time that the statement agreed to by the Governments of Spain and the United Kingdom at Brussels on 27 November 1984 153/ stipulates, inter alia, the following:

> 'The establishment of a negotiating process aimed at overcoming all the differences between them over Gibraltar and at promoting cooperation on a mutually beneficial basis on economic, cultural, touristic, aviation, military and environmental matters. Both sides accept that the issues of sovereignty will be discussed in that process. The British Government will fully maintain its commitment to honour the wishes of the people of Gibraltar as set out in the preamble of the 1969 Constitution'.

takes note of the fact that, as part of that process, the Ministers for Foreign Affairs of Spain and of the United Kingdom hold annual meetings alternately in each capital, the most recent of which took place in London on 20 December 1994, and urges both Governments to continue their negotiations with the object of reaching a definitive solution to the problem of Gibraltar in the light of relevant resolutions of the General Assembly and in the spirit of the Charter of the United Nations."

152/ A/50/602, para. 30.

153/ A/39/732, annex.

38. RULES OF PROCEDURE FOR MEETINGS OF STATES PARTIES TO THE 1982 UN CONVENTION ON THE LAW OF THE SEA

Doc. no.: SPLOS/2/Rev.3 26 July 1995

CONTENTS

RULES OF PROCEDURE FOR MEETINGS OF STATES PARTIES

Introductory note

On 28 July 1994 the General Assembly of the United Nations adopted the Agreement relating to the implementation of Part XI of the United Nations Convention on the Law of the Sea, and the Agreement has been provisionally applied since 16 November 1994.

According to the Agreement, its provisions and Part XI of the Convention are to be interpreted and applied together as a single instrument; these rules and references in these rules to the Convention are to be interpreted and applied accordingly.

I. MEETINGS

Rule 1

Use of terms

For the purposes of these rules:

"Convention" means the United Nations Convention on the Law of the Sea;

"Statute" means the Statute of the International Tribunal for the Law of the Sea, contained in Annex VI of the Convention;

"States Parties" means Parties to the Convention as referred to in article 1, paragraph 2, of the Convention;

"Meeting of States Parties" or "Meeting" means a Meeting of States Parties convened in accordance with the relevant provisions of the Convention. Such Meeting may be adjourned and may be resumed as required and shall terminate when the next Meeting of States Parties convenes;

"President" means the President of the Meeting of States Parties;

"Secretary-General" means the Secretary-General of the United Nations;

"Secretariat" means the Secretariat of the United Nations. 1/

"International Tribunal" means the International Tribunal for the Law of the Sea;

"Registrar" means the Registrar of the International Tribunal for the Law of the Sea;

"Commission" means the Commission on the Limits of the Continental Shelf.

Rule 2

Application

These rules shall apply to any Meeting of States Parties convened in accordance with the relevant provisions of the Convention. These rules may also apply, subject to the provisions of article 312 of the Convention, to any amendment conference convened in accordance with that article, if the conference so decides.

Rule 3

Convening of Meetings of States Parties

1. Meetings of States Parties in accordance with article 319, paragraph 2 (e) of the Convention shall be convened by the Secretary-General, when he considers this necessary, or in accordance with paragraph 2 below.

2. Any State Party may request the Secretary-General to convene such a Meeting. The Secretary-General shall immediately inform the other States

---

1/ It is understood that the United Nations Secretariat will provide services to Meetings of States Parties in accordance with the relevant General Assembly resolutions.

Parties of the request and inquire whether they concur in it. If within thirty days of the date of communication by the Secretary-General a majority of the States Parties concur in the request, a Meeting shall be convened by the Secretary-General and it shall be held no earlier than thirty days and no later than ninety days after the receipt of such concurrence, unless a Meeting is already scheduled to be held within six months of the request.

Rule 4

Convening of Meetings for elections and for purposes of organization

1. Meetings shall be convened every three years for the election of the Members of the International Tribunal in accordance with the provisions of article 4 of the Statute.

2. Meetings shall be convened every five years for the election of the members of the Commission in accordance with the provisions of Annex II, article 2, of the Convention.

3. Meetings shall be convened as necessary in order to deal with the matters referred to in articles 18 and 19 of the Statute and other matters concerning the organization of the International Tribunal or the Commission, when so required.

4. A Meeting of States Parties shall also be convened:

(a) On the date of an election fixed by the President of the International Tribunal in accordance with article 6, paragraph 1, of the Statute following the occurrence of a vacancy in the membership of the International Tribunal;

(b) On the date of an election to fill a vacancy in the membership of the Commission, fixed by the Secretary-General after consultation with the States Parties.

Rule 5

Notification

1. The Secretary-General shall notify all States Parties of the dates, the venue and the purpose of such Meeting at least sixty days in advance of the Meeting.

2. Copies of the notice convening each Meeting of States Parties shall be sent by the Secretariat to the observers referred to in rule 18.

II. AGENDA

Rule 6

Provisional agenda

1. The Secretary-General shall prepare the provisional agenda for each Meeting.

2. The provisional agenda for each Meeting shall be communicated by the Secretariat to the States Parties and to observers at least forty-five days before the opening of the Meeting, together with any supporting documents, if necessary.

3. The provisional agenda for the Meeting shall, inter alia, include, as appropriate:

(a) Items the inclusion of which has been decided at a previous Meeting;

(b) Items relating to the organization of the Meeting, when so required, including matters pertaining to the budgetary aspects;

(c) Elections to fill vacancies in the membership of the International Tribunal or of the Commission;

(d) Any report of the International Tribunal on its work;

(e) Any item proposed by the International Tribunal;

(f) Items relating to the organization of the International Tribunal, when so required, including matters pertaining to the budget for the current or next financial period and the report on the accounts for the previous financial period.

Rule 7

Supplementary items

Supplementary items, proposed for inclusion in the agenda at least thirty days before the date fixed for the opening of the Meeting, shall be placed in a supplementary list, which shall be communicated to the States Parties and to observers at least twenty days before the opening of the Meeting.

Rule 8

Additional items

Additional items of an important and urgent character, proposed for inclusion in the agenda less than thirty days before the opening of the Meeting or during a Meeting, may be placed on the agenda if the States Parties so decide by a majority of the States Parties present and voting.

Rule 9

Adoption of the agenda

At each Meeting, the provisional agenda and any supplementary list shall be submitted to the Meeting of States Parties for approval by a majority of States Parties present and voting, as soon as possible after the opening of the Meeting.

Rule 10

Amendment and deletion of items

Items on the agenda may be amended or deleted by a majority of the States Parties present and voting.

Rule 11

Modifications of the allocation of expenses

No proposal for a modification of the allocation of expenses of the International Tribunal for the time being in force shall be placed on the agenda unless it has been communicated to the States Parties at least sixty days before the opening of the Meeting.

III. REPRESENTATION AND CREDENTIALS

Rule 12

Representation

1. Each State Party shall be represented by accredited representatives and such alternate representatives and advisers as may be required.

2. Observers shall be represented by accredited or designated representatives, as the case may be, and by such alternate representatives and advisers as may be required.

3. The representative may designate an alternate representative or an adviser to act in his capacity.

Rule 13

Submission of credentials

1. The credentials of representatives and the names of alternate representatives and advisers shall be submitted to the Secretariat, if possible not later than twenty-four hours after the opening of the Meeting. Any changes in the composition of the delegations shall also be submitted to the Secretariat.

2. The credentials shall be issued either by the Head of State or Government or by the Minister for Foreign Affairs or any person authorized by either of them, or, in the case of the entities referred to in article 305, paragraph 1 (f), of the Convention, by another competent authority.

Rule 14

Credentials Committee

A Credentials Committee shall be appointed at the beginning of each Meeting. It shall consist of nine States Parties, which shall be appointed by the Meeting on the proposal of the President. The Committee shall elect its own officers. It shall examine the credentials of representatives of States Parties and report to the Meeting without delay.

Rule 15

Provisional participation

Pending a decision of the Meeting of States Parties upon their credentials, representatives shall be entitled to participate provisionally in the Meeting.

Rule 16

Objection to a delegation

If an objection is raised against the representation of a delegation, such objection shall be considered by the Credentials Committee forthwith. The report thereon shall be submitted to the Meeting of States Parties without delay for its decision.

Rule 17

Accreditation of observers

The names of accredited or designated representatives of observers shall be submitted to the Secretariat.

IV. PARTICIPATION OF OBSERVERS

Rule 18

Observers

1. Observers at the Third United Nations Conference on the Law of the Sea who have signed the Final Act and who are not referred to in article 305, paragraph 1 (c), (d), (e) or (f), of the Convention may participate as observers in Meetings of States Parties.

2. The following, if they are not Parties to the Convention, may participate as observers in Meetings:

(a) States that have signed the Convention;

(b) International organizations referred to in Annex IX of the Convention;

(c) Entities referred to in article 305, paragraph 1, subparagraphs (c), (d) and (e), of the Convention;

(d) Signatories to the Final Act of the Third United Nations Conference on the Law of the Sea.

3. The International Seabed Authority may participate as an observer.

4. The specialized agencies of the United Nations system, the International Atomic Energy Agency and other intergovernmental organizations that are invited to the Meeting may also participate as observers.

5. Non-governmental organizations recognized by the Economic and Social Council whose fields of competence are relevant to the law of the sea and other non-governmental organizations invited by the Meeting of States Parties which have demonstrated their interest in matters under the consideration of the Meeting may also participate as observers.

6. Representatives of observers referred to in paragraphs 1, 2 and 3 of this rule may participate, subject to the provisions of these rules, in the deliberations of the Meeting but shall not be entitled to participate in the taking of decisions.

7. Written statements submitted by observers shall be distributed to the Meeting by the Secretariat.

8. Observers referred to in paragraphs 4 and 5 of this rule may designate representatives to sit at public meetings of the Meetings of States Parties and,

upon invitation by the President and subject to the approval by the Meeting, may make oral statements and submit written statements on questions within the scope of their activities.

V. OFFICERS

Rule 19

Election of officers

The Meeting of States Parties shall elect from among the representatives of States Parties participating in the Meeting the following officers: a President and four Vice-Presidents, one from each region, excluding the region of the President. Their terms of office shall continue until the next Meeting elects its officers.

Rule 20

General powers of the President

1. In addition to exercising the powers conferred upon him elsewhere by these rules, the President shall preside at plenary meetings, declare the opening and closing of each meeting, direct the discussions at such meetings, accord the right to speak, put questions to the vote and announce decisions. The President shall rule on points of order and, subject to these rules of procedure, have complete control over the proceedings and over the maintenance of order thereat. The President may propose to the Meeting of States Parties the limitation of time to be allowed to speakers, the limitation of the number of times each representative may speak on any question, the closure of the list of speakers, the adjournment or closure of the debate and the suspension or the adjournment of the meeting.

2. The President, in the exercise of his functions, remains under the authority of the Meeting of States Parties.

Rule 21

Acting President

1. If the President is absent from a meeting or any part thereof, he shall designate one of the Vice-Presidents to take his place.

2. A Vice-President acting as President shall have the same powers and duties as the President.

Rule 22

Replacement of the President

If the President is unable to perform his functions, a new President shall be elected.

Rule 23

Voting rights of the President

The President, or a Vice-President acting as President, shall not vote but shall designate another member of his delegation to vote in his place.

VI. BUREAU

Rule 24

Composition and functions

The President and Vice-Presidents shall constitute the Bureau, which shall meet as necessary during the Meeting to review the progress of work and to make recommendations for furthering such progress. It shall also meet at such other times as the President deems necessary or upon the request of any other of its members. The Bureau shall assist the President in the general conduct of work which falls within the competence of the President. The Chairmen of any subsidiary bodies may be invited to attend meetings of the Bureau.

VII. SECRETARIAT

Rule 25

Duties of the Secretary-General

1. The Secretary-General shall act at the Meetings of States Parties in his capacity as Secretary-General of the United Nations. The Secretary-General may designate a member of the Secretariat to participate on his behalf.

2. The Secretary-General shall be responsible for making the arrangements related to Meetings of States Parties and shall provide and direct the staff required by such Meetings and meetings of any subsidiary bodies as may be established.

Rule 26

Duties of the Secretariat

The Secretariat shall receive, translate, reproduce and distribute documents, reports, resolutions and decisions of the Meeting of States Parties and any subsidiary bodies that may be established; interpret speeches made at meetings, prepare and circulate the records of the Meeting, have the custody and proper preservation of the documents in the archives of the United Nations, distribute all documents of the Meeting to the States Parties and observer States; and, generally, perform all other work which the Meeting of States Parties may require and provide copies of relevant documents for the archives of the Tribunal.

VIII. LANGUAGES

Rule 27

Languages

Arabic, Chinese, English, French, Russian and Spanish shall be the languages of the Meeting of States Parties and any subsidiary bodies that may be established.

Rule 28

Interpretation

1. Speeches made in a language of the Meeting of States Parties shall be interpreted into the other such languages.

2. Any representative may make a speech in a language other than a language of the Meeting of States Parties. In that case the representative shall provide for interpretation into one of the languages of Meetings. Interpretation into the other languages of the Meeting of States Parties by the interpreters of the Secretariat may be based on the interpretation given in the first such language.

Rule 29

Languages of official documents

Official documents shall be published in the languages of the Meeting of States Parties.

IX. RECORDS

Rule 30

Sound recordings of meetings

The Secretariat shall make and keep sound recordings of plenary meetings, and of meetings of any subsidiary bodies when so decided.

X. PUBLIC AND PRIVATE MEETINGS

Rule 31

General principles

1. Plenary meetings shall be held in public unless the Meeting of States Parties decides otherwise.

2. As a general rule, meetings of any subsidiary bodies shall be held in private.

3. All decisions of the Meeting of States Parties taken at a private meeting shall be announced at an early public meeting. At the close of a private meeting of any subsidiary body, the President may issue a communiqué through the Secretariat.

XI. MINUTE OF SILENT PRAYER OR MEDITATION

Rule 32

Invitation to silent prayer or meditation

Immediately after the opening of the first plenary meeting and immediately preceding the closing of the final plenary meeting, the President shall invite the representatives to observe one minute of silence dedicated to prayer or meditation.

XII. CONDUCT OF BUSINESS

Rule 33

Quorum

1. The President may declare a meeting open and permit the debate to proceed when representatives of at least one third of the States Parties participating in the Meeting are present.

2. The presence of representatives of a majority of the States Parties so participating shall be required for any decision to be taken, provided that for a decision on any matter of substance the presence of representatives of two thirds of the States Parties so participating shall be required.

Rule 34

Speeches

No representative may address the Meeting of States Parties without having previously obtained the permission of the President. Subject to rules 41 and 44, the President shall call upon speakers in the order in which they signify their desire to speak. The Secretariat shall be in charge of drawing up a list of such speakers. The President may call a speaker to order if the remarks of the speakers are not relevant to the subject under discussion.

Rule 35

Precedence

The Chairman of any subsidiary body may be accorded precedence for the purpose of explaining the conclusions arrived at by that body.

Rule 36

Statement by the Secretary-General of the United Nations

The Secretary-General of the United Nations, or a member of the Secretariat designated by him as his representative, may at any time make either oral or written statements to the Meeting of States Parties concerning any question under consideration by it.

Rule 37

Statements by the President and the Registrar of the International Tribunal and the Secretary-General of the International Seabed Authority

The President and the Registrar of the Tribunal and the Secretary-General of the International Seabed Authority shall be invited to Meetings of States Parties and may make written or oral statements concerning any question under consideration by the Meeting and provide information on those institutions as appropriate.

Rule 38

Statement by the Registrar

The Registrar, or a member of the Registry designated by him as his representative, may at any time make either oral or written statements to the Meeting of States Parties concerning any question relating to the administrative or financial implications of the proposed action for the International Tribunal.

Rule 39

Points of order

During the discussion of any matter, a representative of a State Party may rise to a point of order, and the point of order shall be immediately decided by the President in accordance with these rules of procedure. A representative of a State Party may appeal against the ruling of the President. The appeal shall be immediately put to the vote, and the President's ruling shall stand unless overruled by a majority of the States Parties present and voting. A representative rising to a point of order may not speak on the substance of the matter under discussion.

Rule 40

Time-limit on speeches

The Meeting of States Parties may limit the time to be allowed to each speaker and the number of times each representative of a State Party may speak on any question. Before a decision is taken, two representatives of States Parties may speak in favour of, and two against, a proposal to set such limits. When the debate is limited and a representative exceeds the allotted time, the President shall call that representative to order without delay.

Rule 41

Closing of list of speakers and right of reply

During the course of a debate, the President may announce the list of speakers and, with the consent of the Meeting of States Parties, declare the list closed. The President may, however, accord the right of reply to any representative if a speech delivered after he has declared the list closed makes this desirable.

Rule 42

Adjournment of debate

During the discussion of any matter, a representative of a State Party may move the adjournment of the debate on the question under discussion. In addition to the proposer of the motion, two representatives of States Parties may speak in favour of, and two against, the motion, after which the motion shall be immediately put to the vote. The President may limit the time to be allowed to speakers under this rule.

Rule 43

Closure of debate

A representative of a State Party may at any time move the closure of the debate on the question under discussion, whether or not any other representative has signified his wish to speak. Permission to speak on the motion shall be accorded only to two representatives of States Parties opposing the closure, after which the motion shall be immediately put to the vote. If the Meeting of States Parties is in favour of the closure, the President shall declare the closure of the debate. The President may limit the time to be allowed to speakers under this rule.

Rule 44

Suspension or adjournment of the meeting

During the discussion of any matter, a representative of a State Party may move the suspension or the adjournment of the meeting. Such motions shall not be debated, but shall be immediately put to the vote. The President may limit the time to be allowed to the speaker moving the suspension or adjournment of the meeting.

Rule 45

Order of procedural motions

Subject to rule 39, the following motions shall have precedence in the following order over all other proposals or motions before the Meeting of States Parties:

(a) To suspend the meeting;

(b) To adjourn the meeting;

(c) To adjourn the debate on the question under discussion;

(d) To close the debate on the question under discussion.

Rule 46

Proposals and amendments

Proposals and amendments shall normally be submitted in writing to the Secretariat, which shall circulate copies to the delegations. As a general rule, no proposal shall be discussed or put to the vote at any meeting unless copies of it have been circulated to all delegations in the languages of the Meeting of States Parties not later than the day preceding the meeting. The President may, however, permit the discussion and consideration of amendments, or of motions as to procedure, even though such amendments and motions have not been circulated or have only been circulated the same day.

Rule 47

Decisions on competence

Subject to rule 45, any motion calling for a decision on the competence of the Meeting of States Parties to adopt a proposal submitted to it shall be put to the vote before a decision is taken on the proposal in question.

Rule 48

Withdrawal of motions

A motion may be withdrawn by its proposer at any time before voting on it has commenced, provided that the motion has not been amended. A motion thus withdrawn may be reintroduced by any representative of a State Party.

Rule 49

Reconsideration of proposals

When a proposal has been adopted or rejected, it may not be reconsidered at the same meeting unless the Meeting of States Parties, by a two-thirds majority of the States Parties present and voting, so decides. Permission to speak on a motion to reconsider shall be accorded only to two representatives of States Parties opposing the motion, after which it shall be immediately put to the vote.

Rule 50

Consideration of financial implications

Before the Meeting of States Parties takes a decision having financial implications, it shall receive and consider a report on such implications from the Secretariat or, from the Registrar for decisions having financial or administrative implications relating to the Tribunal.

XIII. DECISION-MAKING

Rule 51

Voting rights

Each State Party shall have one vote. Participation in decision-making by the entities referred to in article 305, paragraph 1 (f), of the Convention shall be in accordance with Annex IX of the Convention.

Rule 52

General agreement

1. The Meeting of States Parties should conduct its work on the basis of general agreement.

2. It may proceed to a vote in accordance with rule 53 only after all efforts at achieving general agreement have been exhausted.

Rule 53

Decisions on questions of substance

Subject to rule 52, decisions on matters of substance shall be taken by a two-thirds majority of the States Parties present and voting, provided that such majority includes a majority of the States Parties participating in the Meeting. 2/

2/ This rule is without prejudice to the rules relating to financial and budgetary matters, which are being developed.

Rule 54

Decisions on questions of procedure

1. Except as otherwise provided in these rules, decisions on all matters of procedure shall be taken by a majority of the States Parties present and voting.

2. If the question arises whether a matter is one of procedure or of substance, the President shall rule on the question. An appeal against this ruling shall immediately be put to the vote and the President's ruling shall stand unless the appeal is approved by a majority of the States Parties present and voting.

Rule 55

Decisions on amendments to proposals relating to questions of substance

Decisions on amendments to proposals relating to questions of substance, and on parts of such proposals put to the vote separately, shall be made by a two-thirds majority of the States Parties present and voting, provided that such majority includes a majority of the States Parties participating in the Meeting.

Rule 56

Meaning of "States Parties present and voting" and "States Parties participating in the Meeting"

1. For the purposes of these rules, the phrase "States Parties present and voting" means States Parties present and casting an affirmative or negative vote; States Parties which abstain from voting shall be considered as not voting.

2. Subject to the provisions of rules 12 to 16 and without prejudice to the powers and functions of the Credentials Committee, the term "States Parties participating in the Meeting" in relation to any particular Meeting means any State Party whose representatives have registered with the Secretariat as participating in that Meeting and which has not subsequently notified the Secretariat of its withdrawal from that Meeting or part of it. The Secretariat shall keep a register for this purpose.

Rule 57

Method of voting

1. The Meeting of States Parties shall, in the absence of mechanical means for voting, vote by show of hands or by standing, but a representative of any State Party may request a roll-call. The roll-call shall be taken in the English alphabetical order of the names of the States Parties participating in the Meeting, beginning with the State Party whose name is drawn by lot by the President. The name of each State Party shall be called in any roll-call, and one of its representatives shall reply "yes", "no" or "abstention". The result of the voting shall be inserted in the record in the English alphabetical order of the names of the States Parties.

2. When the Meeting of States Parties votes by mechanical means, a non-recorded vote shall replace a vote by show of hands or by standing and a recorded vote shall replace a roll-call vote. A representative of a State Party may request a recorded vote. In the case of a recorded vote, the Meeting shall, unless a representative of a State Party requests otherwise, dispense with the procedure of calling out the names of the States Parties; nevertheless, the

result of the voting shall be inserted in the record in the same manner as that of a roll-call vote.

Rule 58

Conduct during voting

After the President has announced the commencement of voting, no representative of a State Party may interrupt the voting, except that representatives of States Parties may interrupt on a point of order in connection with the actual conduct of the voting.

Rule 59

Explanation of vote

Representatives of States Parties may make brief statements consisting solely of explanations of their votes before the voting has commenced or after the voting has been completed. The President may limit the time to be allowed for such statements. The representative of a State Party sponsoring a proposal or motion shall not speak in explanation of vote thereon, except if it has been amended.

Rule 60

Division of proposals and amendments

A representative of a State Party may move that parts of a proposal or of an amendment be voted on separately. If objection is made to the request for division, the motion for division shall be voted upon. Permission to speak on the motion for division shall be given only to two speakers in favour and two speakers against. If the motion for division is carried, those parts of the proposal or of the amendment which are approved shall then be put to the vote as a whole. If all operative parts of the proposal or of the amendment have been rejected, the proposal or the amendment shall be considered to have been rejected as a whole.

Rule 61

Order of voting on amendments

When an amendment is moved to a proposal, the amendment shall be voted on first. When two or more amendments are moved to a proposal, the Meeting shall first vote on the amendment furthest removed in substance from the original proposal and then on the amendment next furthest removed therefrom, and so on until all the amendments have been put to the vote. Where, however, the adoption of one amendment necessarily implies the rejection of another amendment, the latter amendment shall not be put to the vote. If one or more amendments are adopted, the amended proposal shall then be voted upon. A motion is considered an amendment to a proposal if it merely adds to, deletes from or revises part of the proposal.

Rule 62

Order of voting on proposals

If two or more proposals relate to the same question, the Meeting of States Parties shall, unless it decides otherwise, vote on the proposals in the order

in which they have been submitted. The Meeting may, after each vote on a proposal, decide whether to vote on the next proposal.

Rule 63

Election of officers

All elections of officers of the Meeting of States Parties shall be held by secret ballot unless otherwise decided by the Meeting.

Rule 64

Restricted balloting for one elective place

1. When only one person or State Party is to be elected and no candidate obtains in the first ballot the votes of a majority of the States Parties present and voting, a second ballot restricted to the two candidates obtaining the largest number of votes shall be taken. If in the second ballot the votes are equally divided, the President shall decide between the candidates by drawing lots.

2. In the case of a tie in the first ballot among more than two candidates obtaining the largest number of votes, a second ballot shall be held. If on that ballot a tie remains among more than two candidates, the number shall be reduced to two by lot and the balloting, restricted to them, shall continue in accordance with the preceding paragraph.

3. These provisions shall not prejudice the application of rules 69 to 71.

Rule 65

Restricted balloting for two or more elective places

When two or more elective places are to be filled at one time under the same conditions, those candidates, not exceeding the number of such places, obtaining in the first ballot the majority required shall be elected. If the number of candidates obtaining such a majority is less than the number of persons or States Parties to be elected, there shall be additional ballots to fill the remaining places, the voting being restricted to the candidates obtaining the greatest number of votes in the previous ballot to a number not more than twice the places remaining to be filled; provided that, after the third inconclusive ballot, votes may be cast for any eligible person or State Party. If three such unrestricted ballots are inconclusive, the next three ballots shall be restricted to the candidates who obtained the greatest number of votes in the third of the unrestricted ballots, to a number not more than twice the places remaining to be filled, and the following three ballots thereafter shall be unrestricted, and so on until all the places have been filled. These provisions shall not prejudice the application of rules 69 to 71.

Rule 66

Equally divided votes

If a vote is equally divided on matters other than elections, a second vote shall be taken at a subsequent meeting which shall be held within forty-eight hours of the first vote; and it shall be expressly mentioned in the agenda that a second vote will be taken on the matter in question. If that vote also results in equality, the proposal shall be regarded as rejected.

XIV. SUBSIDIARY BODIES

Rule 67

Establishment

1. The Meeting of States Parties may establish such subsidiary bodies as it deems necessary for the exercise of its functions.

2. The composition and competence of each subsidiary body will be determined by the Meeting of States Parties.

Rule 68

Rules of procedure of subsidiary bodies

Unless otherwise decided by the Meeting of States Parties, these rules apply, mutatis mutandis, to the proceedings of subsidiary bodies, except that:

(a) The Chairman of a subsidiary body may exercise the right to vote;

(b) The presence of representatives of a majority of the members of any subsidiary body shall be required for any decision to be taken.

XV. ELECTIONS TO THE INTERNATIONAL TRIBUNAL FOR THE LAW OF THE SEA

Rule 69

Election of the Members of the International Tribunal

The elections of the Members of the International Tribunal shall take place in accordance with the Statute.

XVI. ELECTIONS TO THE COMMISSION ON THE LIMITS OF THE CONTINENTAL SHELF

Rule 70

Elections of the members of the Commission

The elections of the members of the Commission shall take place in accordance with article 76 and Annex II of the Convention.

Rule 71

By-elections

If the office of a member of the Commission becomes vacant, the Meeting of States Parties shall, in accordance with rule 70, elect a member for the remainder of the predecessor's term.

XVII. ADMINISTRATIVE AND BUDGETARY QUESTIONS RELATING TO THE INTERNATIONAL TRIBUNAL

Rule 72

Regulations for financial administration

The Meeting of States Parties shall establish regulations for the financial administration of the International Tribunal.

Rule 73

Proposed periodic budget

The Meeting of States Parties shall consider and approve the proposed periodic budget of the International Tribunal submitted by the Tribunal.

Rule 74

Contributions

The Meeting of States Parties shall, in accordance with article 19 of the Statute, decide on the terms and the manner in which States Parties and the International Seabed Authority shall contribute to the expenses of the International Tribunal.

XVIII. AMENDMENTS

Rule 75

Method of amendment

These rules of procedure may be amended by a decision of the Meeting of States Parties taken by a two-thirds majority of the States Parties present and voting, provided it includes a majority of States Parties participating in the meeting, after the Bureau has reported on the proposed amendment.

39. REPORT OF THE MEETING OF STATES PARTIES TO THE 1982 UN CONVENTION ON THE LAW OF THE SEA, NEW YORK, 15-19 MAY 1995 - PREPARED BY THE SECRETARIAT

Doc. no.: SPLOS/4 & Corr.1 26 July & 17 November1995

CONTENTS

I. INTRODUCTION

A. Convening of the Meeting

1. The Meeting of the States Parties to the 1982 United Nations Convention on the Law of the Sea (hereinafter referred to as the "Convention") was convened in accordance with article 319, paragraph 2 (e), of the Convention and the decision taken at its previous Meeting. 1/ Pursuant thereto, and in accordance with the provisional rules of procedure adopted by the Meeting of States Parties, invitations to participate in the Meeting had been addressed by the Secretary-General of the United Nations to all States Parties to the Convention. Invitations to participate as observers were addressed to other States, and to entities referred to in article 305, paragraphs (c), (d), (e) and (f) of the Convention, observers at the Preparatory Commission for the International Seabed Authority and for the International Tribunal for the Law of the Sea and to the specialized agencies of the United Nations, the International Atomic Energy Agency (IAEA) and several non-governmental organizations.

B. Opening of the Meeting

2. The Meeting was held in New York from 15 to 19 May 1995 to deal with organizational matters relating to the International Tribunal for the Law of the Sea.

3. The Meeting was opened by the President, Mr. Satya N. Nandan (Fiji).

C. Attendance

4. On the basis of delegations that attended and/or those that had submitted credentials or notifications, the following attendance was recorded: (a) 46 States Parties; (b) 55 States observers; (c) 4 observers from specialized agencies and United Nations bodies; (d) 1 entity referred to in annex IX of the Convention; (e) 3 intergovernmental organizations; and (f) 2 non-governmental organizations. The Credentials Committee, in accordance with the rules of procedure for the Meeting of States Parties, will review the credentials at the next Meeting and report to the plenary.

D. Documentation

5. In addition to the documentation available at the previous Meeting, the documents before the Meeting were: report of the Meeting of States Parties (SPLOS/3); informal proposals for the organization of work (note from the President) (SPLOS/CRP.1); agenda for the Meeting of States Parties, as adopted by the previous Meeting (SPLOS/1/Rev.1); provisional rules of procedure of the

Meeting of States Parties, as revised (SPLOS/2/Rev.1) and report of the Preparatory Commission for the International Seabed Authority and for the International Tribunal for the Law of the Sea regarding practical arrangements for the establishment of the Tribunal, in four volumes (LOS/PCN/152, vols. I-IV). Also available was the draft budget for the first financial period of the International Tribunal for the Law of the Sea - Preliminary Estimates (LOS/PCN/142).

II. CONDUCT OF BUSINESS

A. Organization of work

6. The President of the Meeting welcomed participants. Referring to the agenda for the Meeting (SPLOS/1/Rev.1), he noted that at the previous Meeting the consideration of agenda items 1-3 and 8 had been completed; agenda items 5, 6 and 9 had been deferred for later consideration; agenda item 4 had been partially considered; and he had made proposals regarding agenda item 7, on the organization of work, in conference room paper SPLOS/CRP.1.

7. The President explained his proposals for the organization of work as contained in conference room paper SPLOS/CRP.1. He proposed that as a first order of business the Meeting should consider the provisional rules of procedure and adopt them. He called upon the regional groups to consult among themselves and for each group to nominate one Vice-President, with the exception of the Asian Group, since the current President was from that region. He indicated that he would consult with delegations in the appointment of a Credentials Committee and would propose a slate of candidates for that purpose. The Meeting approved the proposals.

8. Attention was drawn by the President to the report of the Preparatory Commission and its recommendations, noting that consideration of the report constituted the most substantive part of the work of the Meeting. While the Preparatory Commission had made recommendations on some items, others had been referred directly to the Meeting of States Parties. It was decided that the report would be taken up later following consideration of other items.

9. It was noted that the administrative arrangements for the Tribunal during the start-up phase were important and needed to be resolved during the Meeting. The Meeting agreed to defer consideration of the question of the composition of the Tribunal until it was clearer as to which States would be parties to the Convention at the time of the election of the judges.

10. The Meeting decided to deal first with the rules of procedure and then to take up a second group of items on the agenda during the current Meeting, while consideration of the other items were deferred to the next Meeting.

11. The Meeting accepted the President's proposal that the negotiations be conducted at informal open-ended meetings of the whole. To the extent necessary, informal consultations, also open-ended, would be carried out. He indicated that he would report back to the plenary on the progress of work and with proposals on the pending matters.

B. Statement by the Legal Counsel

12. The President called upon the Legal Counsel of the United Nations to make a statement. The Legal Counsel presented the revised draft rules of procedure for the Meeting (SPLOS/2/Rev.1), prepared at its request by the Secretariat. He noted that the revised rules were adapted to make them suitable for all or any purposes for which a Meeting of States Parties may be convened. The revision fully reflected the decisions taken at the previous Meeting, which amended and adopted certain rules, with consequential changes resulting from those amendments.

13. The Legal Counsel also presented the Meeting with the comprehensive record of the work of the Preparatory Commission in pursuance of its mandate to make recommendations on practical arrangements for the establishment of the International Tribunal for the Law of the Sea. He informed the Meeting that the records were being issued as a composite publication in four volumes. 2/ These documents would also serve for the archives of the Tribunal.

14. He further informed the meeting that in accordance with paragraph 11 of General Assembly resolution 49/28 of 6 December 1994, Mr. Gritakumar Chitty had been designated as the staff member charged with making preparations of a practical nature for the organization of the Tribunal, including the establishment of a library, with the necessary Secretariat support. He noted that Mr. Chitty had previously served as Secretary of Special Commission 4 of the Preparatory Commission for the International Seabed Authority and for the International Tribunal for the Law of the Sea, and prior to that he had served as Secretary of the plenary meetings of the Third United Nations Conference on the Law of the Sea, dealing with the subject of settlement of disputes.

15. The Legal Counsel also informed the Meeting of his proposed visit to Bonn and Hamburg on 29 and 30 June 1995 at the invitation of the Government of Germany, during which he would hold consultations on matters related to arrangements of a practical nature for the establishment of the Tribunal, with the authorities in both Bonn and Hamburg.

16. The President thanked the Legal Counsel and expressed the appreciation of the Meeting for the presentation of the revised provisional rules of procedure and also for the presentation of the composite documentation of the Preparatory Commission contained in four volumes. The Meeting also took note of the designation of the officer charged with making arrangements of a practical nature for the establishment of the Tribunal and also noted that the necessary Secretariat support for the fulfilment of these functions would be provided. The Meeting also took note of the Legal Counsel's impending consultations in Bonn and Hamburg.

C. Credentials Committee

17. The President after consultations proposed the following nine States as members of the Credentials Committee: Cameroon, Croatia, Germany, Malta, Marshall Islands, Philippines, Senegal, Trinidad and Tobago and Uruguay.

18. The Meeting approved the election of the members of the Credentials Committee and decided that the Committee would take up the credentials report at its next Meeting of States Parties. For this purpose it was decided that the Meeting of States Parties convened on 21 and 22 November 1994, the current Meeting (15-19 May 1995) and the meeting to be convened from 27 November to 1 December 1995 be treated as continuing, *inter alia*, for the purposes of credentials. Attention was drawn to the fact that the credentials presented by delegations should cover attendance at these three meetings.

D. Election of officials

19. The meeting elected Australia as a Vice-President upon the nomination by the Western European and Others Group.

20. The meeting decided to defer consideration of the election of the other officials pending agreement within the regional groups.

E. Rules of procedure

21. The meeting further considered the draft provisional rules of procedure contained in document SPLOS/2/Rev.1. A revision thereto was issued in document

SPLOS/2/Rev.2, dated 18 May 1995, on the basis of the deliberations of the Meeting at its first meeting.

22. The revised rules were considered and it was noted that some rules, particularly the rule relating to decisions having financial implications, were still to be developed. Subject to this, as recorded in the footnote to rule 52, the revised draft rules (SPLOS/2/Rev.2) were adopted, taking into account the changes referred to below.

(a) Rule 2. The title of that rule ("Purposes") was amended to read "Application";

(b) In rule 2, last sentence:

(i) After the words "that article", the words "and to any other Meeting of States Parties" were deleted;

(ii) After the word "conference", the words "or Meeting" were deleted;

(c) Rule 3 was revised to read as follows:

"<u>Rule 3</u>

"1. Meetings of States Parties in accordance with article 319, paragraph 2 (e), of the Convention shall be convened by the Secretary-General, when he considers this necessary or in accordance with paragraph 2 below.

"2. Any State Party may request the Secretary-General to convene such a Meeting. The Secretary-General shall immediately inform the other States Parties of the request and inquire whether they concur in it. If within thirty days of the date of communication by the Secretary-General a majority of the States Parties concur in the request, a Meeting shall be convened by the Secretary-General and it shall be held no earlier than thirty days and no later than ninety days after the receipt of such concurrence, unless a Meeting is already scheduled to be held within six months of the request."

The rule would be given a title.

(d) Rule 3 <u>bis</u> would become rule 4 and the rest of the rules would be renumbered accordingly;

(e) A rule would be included to provide for the President and the Registrar of the Tribunal and the Secretary-General of the Authority to be invited to Meetings and to provide information on those institutions as appropriate.

23. The new introductory note to the revised rules (SPLOS/2/Rev.2) refers to the Agreement relating to the Implementation of part XI of the Convention: It is to be noted that the delegation of Mexico was against any reference being made to the Agreement relating to the Implementation of part XI of the Convention either in the context of the definition of the term "Convention" under draft rule 1 or in the context of the introductory note in document SPLOS/2/Rev.2. However, the delegation of Mexico did not oppose, as a compromise, a reference to the Agreement being made in the introductory note to document SPLOS/2/Rev.2. However, the delegation of Mexico requested that its view be recorded that the Agreement should not influence decisions that the States Parties might take about the Tribunal in the light of the fact that the Tribunal was essentially regulated by annex VI to the Convention, its own Statute, rather than part XI.

24. The Secretariat was requested to scrutinize the provisional rules of procedure and thereby ensure consistency in the terminology and cross-referencing as well as making any editorial changes as may be necessary. The Secretariat was also requested to re-issue the document as soon as practicable.

III. OTHER ACTION AND DECISIONS TAKEN BY THE MEETING

A. Organizational matters

25. The Meeting considered the requirements of the Tribunal and agreed on the approach to be taken as regards its establishment, its initial functions and related matters. For purposes of organization and for assessing budgetary implications during the initial financial period, 1 August 1996 to 31 December 1997, the following conclusions and decisions were reached:

(a) Members of the Tribunal:

(i) The members of the Tribunal would hold their first organizational session on 1 October 1996;

(ii) The members of the Tribunal would meet for up to 12 weeks during the period of the budget in order to take the necessary decisions for the internal organization of the Tribunal. Provision would also need to be made for preparatory work by members of the Tribunal;

(iii) The President of the Tribunal would reside at the seat of the Tribunal. All other members of the Tribunal would attend meetings of the Tribunal as and when required;

(iv) The overall remuneration of the members of the Tribunal would consist of three elements: an annual allowance; a special allowance for each day that they were engaged on the business of the Tribunal; and a subsistence allowance for each day that they attend meetings at the seat of the Tribunal or elsewhere. The overall remuneration for the members of the Tribunal should not exceed that of a judge of the International Court of Justice;

(b) Languages. The decisions taken regarding the official and working languages of the Tribunal and the use of other languages are as follows:

(i) The official languages of the Tribunal were English and French. Decisions of the Tribunal should be given in the two official languages and the Tribunal should determine which of the two texts was considered as authoritative;

(ii) A party to a dispute before the Tribunal might use another language for its written and oral pleadings and related documentation: the translation and interpretation into one of the official languages of the Tribunal should be at that party's expense;

(iii) When a language other than one of the official languages of the Tribunal was chosen by the parties to the dispute, and that language was an official language of the United Nations, the decision of the Tribunal should, at the request of any party, be translated into that official language of the United Nations at no cost to the parties;

(iv) Subject to availability of funds, and provided that it would not result in an increase in the budget of the Tribunal, consideration would be given in the future to the translation of final decisions of the Tribunal into the other official languages of the United Nations at the request of any of the States Parties. For that purpose, any contributions from any source would be welcomed. There should be established a voluntary fund to receive such contributions;

(c) <u>Registry</u>. The Meeting considered that arrangements would be needed for the phasing-in of the staff of the Registry and for the transitional phase before the Registry was in place;

(d) <u>Funding</u>. The Meeting also decided that the funding of the budget would be considered and decided together with the budget;

(e) <u>Cost-effectiveness</u>. The Meeting further decided that the principles of cost-effectiveness would apply to all aspects of the work of the Tribunal.

26. The Meeting decided that the Secretariat would be requested to submit the draft budget by 1 September 1995. The draft would be the subject of deliberations at the next Meeting.

B. <u>Preparation of the initial budget</u>

27. The President drew attention to the question of the budget of the Tribunal and the source of the budget or its funding. It was noted that various working papers and draft budgets had been prepared, on the basis of various options, for the consideration and deliberations of the Preparatory Commission. The Meeting having considered the requirements of the Tribunal, agreed on the approach to be taken regarding its establishment, its initial functions and related matters. The President therefore proposed, on the basis of those indications and assumptions, to request the Secretariat to prepare a draft budget. That would permit the Meeting to deliberate on it more concretely and to give an indication of the total budget required for the initial period of the Tribunal. The Meeting concurred with the President's proposal.

28. The approach and assumptions relevant to preparing the draft budget were circulated informally and approved by the Meeting. <u>3</u>/ They are as follows:

(a) The States Parties intend to adopt the budget for the Tribunal covering an initial period (1 August 1996 to 31 December 1997) at a Meeting to be held in March 1996. This will be preceded by a short Meeting of States Parties, with financial experts, to be held from 27 November to 1 December 1995, to review a draft of the budget;

(b) In preparation for these meetings, the States Parties request the Secretariat to prepare and circulate, by 1 September 1995 at the latest, a draft budget. The estimates are to be based on the indications, assumptions and decisions concerning the members, the languages, the Registry, the funding and the application of the principle of cost-effectiveness as referred to in paragraphs 28 and 29 above.

C. <u>Initial funding or financing</u>

29. While the Meeting was conscious of the provisions of the statute of the Tribunal, it decided to revert to the matter at a later stage. The Meeting noted that there would be a need for transition from the services of the Secretariat to the Registry of the Tribunal.

D. <u>Decisions and recommendations to the General Assembly</u>

30. The Meeting agreed that a timetable for the future meetings should be submitted to the General Assembly with the recommendations of the Meeting. The Secretariat was called upon, in its annual report on the law of the sea, to summarize the deliberations of the Meeting so that the Assembly might be aware of what has been dealt with and take cognizance of matters that might be of interest to the Assembly.

E. Access to the Tribunal

31. The question of access to the Tribunal by States other than States Parties was considered. It was understood that the terms and conditions for access would take into consideration the provisions of Security Council resolution 9 (1946) in relation to access to the International Court of Justice, since that resolution provided a useful precedent, and since the Meeting concurred with the main elements of that resolution.

F. Draft protocol on privileges and immunities

32. It was agreed that the draft protocol on privileges and immunities would be taken up at a later meeting. The document presented by the Preparatory Commission (LOS/PCN/152, vol. I), together with its recommendations, would be examined and a decision would be made as to what would be the forum for its adoption.

G. United Nations laissez-passer and the participation by the Tribunal in the United Nations Joint Staff Pension Fund and the common system of the United Nations

33. It was understood that the use of the United Nations laissez-passer and the participation of the Tribunal in the United Nations Joint Staff Pension Fund (UNJSPF) and the United Nations common system would be dependent upon the relationship arrangement to be made between the Tribunal and the United Nations and that this would require further examination at a later stage.

H. Administrative arrangements

34. Consistent with the specifications for the preparation of the initial budget, determinations were also made by the Meeting with regard to the administrative arrangements for the Tribunal. It was suggested that the date on which the judges take up office should be a date in September 1996. Following the election of the 21 judges, which will take place on 1 August 1996, the President of the Tribunal will, as required by the Convention, be resident at the seat. The other judges would be on call. During the initial period following the election, they will have to convene in order to undertake internal organizational matters of the Tribunal, including the adoption of the rules of procedure (see para. 25 (a) above).

35. The Meeting noted that there would be a need for transition from the services of the Secretariat of the United Nations to the Registry of the Tribunal. The preliminary budget proposal called for above would be required to take those matters more fully into account in the context of the financial obligations (see para. 25 (c) above).

IV. SITE AND PERMANENT HEADQUARTERS OF THE TRIBUNAL

36. At the invitation of the President, the delegation of Germany, as the host country, reported on the status of progress in the preparations based on the presentations previously made to the Preparatory Commission and reflected in its records. Attention was drawn to the records of the Preparatory Commission as contained in document LOS/PCN/152, volume I, pages 20, 21 and 155 to 159. It was reported that the planning for the building and its equipment would be developed on the basis of the notifications previously provided in the reports by the German delegation to the Preparatory Commission. The Meeting was further informed that the equipment and furnishings, which would be provided by the host country, would include equipment for heating, lighting, telephones, telefax, interpreters booths and sanitary and electronic installations. The Meeting was also informed that the tenders for contract to carry out the construction would

be issued in July 1995 and that construction would begin by the start of 1996 and the buildings should be ready for use at the end of 1998. In the meantime, the German Government would provide the Tribunal with suitable temporary buildings and interim equipment for its initial internal deliberations as well as for the commencement of its judicial work. The details for the requirements of these would be the matter of discussion between the Legal Counsel of the United Nations and the German authorities during his visit at the end of June 1995.

V. OTHER MATTERS

Convening of the next Meeting

37. The Meeting decided that it would reconvene in New York for a period of one week between 27 November and 1 December 1995. It would consider the preliminary budget to be prepared by the Secretariat and the other pending items on its agenda (SPLOS/1/Rev.1). In view of the consideration of financial matters of that report, delegations were advised to include financial experts on their delegations for that purpose.

38. The following schedule of meetings was agreed upon for the Meetings of States Parties:

(a) Meeting of States Parties (including financial experts) to review a draft initial budget of the Tribunal to be prepared by the Secretariat and to consider pending items on its agenda, 27 November-1 December 1995;

(b) Meeting of States Parties to consider and adopt the draft initial budget of the Tribunal, 4-8 March 1996;

(c) Meeting of States Parties to consider organizational matters of the Tribunal and to elect the members of the Commission on the Continental Shelf, 29 April-10 May 1996;

(d) Meeting of States Parties for the election of the judges of the Tribunal, 29 July-2 August 1996.

Notes

1/ Meeting convened ad hoc on 21 and 22 November 1994. Refer document SPLOS/3, para. 17.

2/ LOS/PCN/152, vols. I-IV. This would constitute the report of the Preparatory Commission under paragraph 10 of resolution I containing recommendations regarding practical arrangements for the establishment of the International Tribunal for the Law of the Sea.

3/ The terms of the informal proposal circulated by the President and subsequently approved by the Meeting are reflected in paragraphs 28 and 31 of the present report.

<u>Corrigendum</u>

<u>Page 9, paragraph 28 (b</u>)

The end of the paragraph <u>should read</u>

in paragraphs 25 and 27 above.

-----

40. DRAFT INITIAL BUDGET FOR THE INTERNATIONAL TRIBUNAL FOR THE LAW OF THE SEA COVERING THE PERIOD AUGUST 1996-DECEMBER 1997 - PREPARED BY THE SECRETARIAT

Doc. no.: SPLOS/WP.1 31 August 1995

CONTENTS

I. INTRODUCTION

1. The International Tribunal for the Law of the Sea 1/ was created by the 1982 United Nations Convention on the Law of the Sea. 2/ The Statute of the Tribunal (annex VI to the Convention) sets out its method of functioning and its composition as a body of 21 independent Members (judges). The Preparatory Commission for the International Seabed Authority and for the International Tribunal for the Law of the Sea was charged with making the necessary arrangements for the commencement of the functions of the Tribunal, inter alia, preparing a report containing recommendations regarding practical arrangements for the establishment of the Tribunal, to be submitted to the Meeting of States Parties to the Convention. 3/ The Preparatory Commission set up a Special Commission 4, to which it delegated this responsibility. 4/ The Secretariat was mandated to prepare the necessary working papers for the Special Commission. Accordingly the Secretariat formulated, among others, the working papers on the administrative arrangements, structure and financial implications of establishing the Tribunal. 5/ This was supplemented with alternatives as to the number of official working languages. 6/ Subsequently the Preparatory Commission stipulated that the future Tribunal should be cost-effective and should reflect the level of activity that could be reasonably expected in the early years. The Secretariat responded with a proposal for phasing in the establishment of the Tribunal during the formative period. 7/ It also presented a paper on issues concerning the initial financing and budget of the Tribunal. 8/ These were intended to cover the start-up and first years of functioning of the Tribunal. Based on the review of those papers by the Special Commission, at its request the Secretariat formulated a revised working paper setting out the estimated financial implications of alternative approaches to the phasing-in of the Tribunal and also a report on the alternatives as to the means of initial financing. 9/

2. The above-mentioned working papers and their revisions covered the first functional phase of the Tribunal. However, it was recognized that as a completely new institution, the Tribunal would have to go through a preliminary organizational stage before it could reach the first functional phase. 10/ The administrative arrangements and financial implications of this preliminary organizational phase - the start-up period of the Tribunal's activities - were addressed in an additional working paper (LOS/PCN/142) dated 1 August 1994 which was intended to facilitate consideration of the requisite budgetary arrangements in view of the then imminent entry into force of the Convention on 16 November 1994.

3. The Meeting of States Parties to the United Nations Convention on the Law of the Sea was first convened on 21 and 22 November 1994. The Meeting decided to postpone the election of judges of the Tribunal to 1 August 1996, and took other decisions as well. 11/ The next Meeting was held in New York from 15 to 19 May 1995, and had before it all the above-mentioned documents. 12/ The

Meeting considered the requirement for administrative and budgetary arrangements. It agreed on the approach to be followed and took several decisions concerning the establishment of the Tribunal, its initial functions and related matters. 13/

4. The approach and assumptions relevant to preparing the draft budget were laid out in some detail. 14/ The Meeting of States Parties emphasized once more that the principle of cost-effectiveness would apply to all aspects of the work of the Tribunal. The Meeting requested the Secretariat to prepare a draft budget for the initial period August 1996-December 1997 on the basis of these indications and assumptions. It was also decided that a Meeting of States Parties would be held from 27 November to 1 December 1995, with the participation of financial experts, to review the draft budget. Thereafter the adoption of the initial budget for the Tribunal would take place at a Meeting of States Parties to be held in March 1996.

5. The present paper has been prepared by the Secretariat in response to the request referred to above.

II. WORK PROGRAMME OF THE TRIBUNAL DURING THE INITIAL PERIOD

6. The initial budgetary period would comprise the preliminary organizational phase or the "start-up" period of the Tribunal's activities. The period would commence following the election of the 21 Members of the Tribunal 15/ on 1 August 1996 at the Meeting of States Parties to be convened for the purpose. 16/, 17/ The financial implications of convening and servicing the Meetings of States Parties are not included in these budgetary estimates. 18/ It is understood that initially all the Members of the Tribunal would be actively engaged in the review and the adoption of the rules and internal organization of the Tribunal. 19/ During this initial period, the full complement of 21 judges would be expected to participate in executive sessions for a total of up to 12 weeks of meetings. 20/ It is assumed that the organizational meetings would be periodic and not continuous, 21/ and that there would be three organizational meetings of limited duration (four weeks each). Provision would also need to be made for preparatory work by Members of the Tribunal, 22/ which it is assumed would be for an equal time period of 12 weeks.

7. The Tribunal as a whole will first convene on 1 October 1996 to hold its first organizational session of four weeks' duration. 23/ At that organizational meeting, two weeks could be set aside for preliminary organization, election of the President and Vice-President, setting-up of chambers and committees, etc., and other practical internal arrangements. This could be followed by the inauguration of the Tribunal with a formal swearing-in ceremony for the judges, who could thereafter resume in executive session for the remaining two weeks. They would then disperse and resume in executive session early in the next year (1997). During the intervening period, the President, supported by an Acting Registrar and a nucleus Registry, would continue the organizational work. They would carry out the follow-up activity to the first executive session and would prepare for the subsequent one. The next executive session, also assumed to be of four weeks' duration, could be held early in the following year. 24/ This would be followed by one further session of four weeks' duration later in the year. 25/

8. Once the preliminary organizational phase is completed, it is assumed that the Tribunal would be in a position to enter the first functional phase, by January 1998. There was extensive discussion in Special Commission 4 about the expected level of activity of the Tribunal in the first functional phase and the consequent requirement for Members to participate actively, as well as for staffing of the Registry. It was the understanding of the Special Commission that at the outset the workload of the Tribunal would be light and that initially there might not be a need for the full complement of Members to be active participants. 26/ Thus, alternative schemes and phasing-in approaches were discussed. 27/

9. For the purpose of determining the level of activity in the first functional phase and the consequential level of services, it is assumed that the annual workload of the Tribunal would comprise five to six contentious cases 28/ and four to six applications such as those for provisional measures or the prompt release of vessels and crews. This assumption is also consistent with the deliberations in Special Commission 4 as reflected in LOS/PCN/SCN.4/WP.16/Add.6, paragraph 18. 29/

10. Thereafter the requisite level of staff and services to fulfil the requirements of the first functional phase and the appropriate arrangements would be determined by the Tribunal and its Registry.

11. The Registry is the administrative organ of the Tribunal. It will provide legal, procedural, administrative and any technical support required for the Tribunal. It will also have responsibility for the financial and accounting administration, and for documentation, archiving and library services. The organization of the Registry and the appointment of staff is to be approved by the Tribunal on the recommendation of the Registrar.

12. It is assumed that in the first functional phase, an appropriate structure for the Registry would require three main functional divisions, as follows: (a) Legal Division; (b) Documentation/Archives/Linguistic Services Division; and (c) Division for Administration and General Services.

A. Judiciary

13. During the preliminary organizational phase, which is anticipated to span 15 months from when they first convene, the judges would organize the work, elect officials from among themselves, make the necessary administrative arrangements and appoint an Acting Registrar. Pending arrangements for and approval of long-term financial and budgetary arrangements, arrangements would be made for start-up of operations with a small nucleus of staff to service the meetings of the judges and to organize the Registry. Pending the establishment of terms, conditions and other arrangements, and the adoption of administrative and financial rules and a long-term budget, an Acting Registrar would be charged with carrying out the functions. The judges would also have to adopt the Rules of the Tribunal, formulate the terms and conditions of service for the officials and staff of the Registry, organize the procedures and arrangements, including those for dealing with cases and internal procedures, for budget, accounts, administration, personnel, etc., elect a Registrar and appoint a deputy.

14. For the purpose of the deliberations of the judges, the whole range of working papers and documents required by the Tribunal for their use, review and adoption have been incorporated as addenda to the report of the Preparatory Commission to the Meeting of States Parties (LOS/PCN/152). The original working papers and the revisions by the Secretariat after review by Special Commission 4, which provide a history of developments, would also be available, as would the other documentation of the Special Commission. 30/ Consequently it is assumed that during the preliminary organizational phase there would be a very limited need for new documentation; it is also not anticipated that a volume of new documentation would emanate from the executive sessions of the judges. Limited requirements as to interpretation and translation are also anticipated in view of the fact that documentation is available in all six languages and in the light of the decision of the Meeting of States Parties that the Tribunal shall function in only two official working languages. 31/

B. Registry

15. During this period the Registry would also have to carry out its internal administrative organization and recruitment, while giving effect to the personnel, budgetary and accounting arrangements that are adopted. At the end

of the organizational phase, the organizational arrangements for the first functional phase would need to be made.

III. APPROACH AND ASSUMPTIONS RELEVANT TO PREPARING THE DRAFT BUDGET FOR THE INITIAL PERIOD

A. <u>Members of the Tribunal and their remuneration</u>

16. According to SPLOS/4, <u>32</u>/ the overall remuneration of the Members of the Tribunal will consist of three elements: an annual allowance, a special allowance for each day that they are engaged on the business of the Tribunal, and a subsistence allowance for each day that they attend meetings at the seat of the Tribunal; the overall remuneration for the Members of the Tribunal shall not exceed the level of remuneration of a Judge of the International Court of Justice.

17. The Judges of the International Court of Justice currently receive a net salary of $145,000 per annum (see A/C.5/48/66). Therefore, the overall remuneration for the Members of the International Tribunal for the Law of the Sea would not exceed $145,000.

18. As regards subsistence allowance payable for each day that a judge attends meetings at the seat of the Tribunal, it is assumed in the present paper, consistent with the previous working papers <u>33</u>/ and LOS/PCN/142, paragraph 24, that where active engagement and presence at the seat of the Tribunal is required for a prolonged period, the maximum subsistence allowance would be for 250 days in any calendar year. For the purpose of the estimates in the present paper, the current level of daily subsistence allowance for Hamburg under United Nations practice has been used. <u>34</u>/ The maximum amount of subsistence allowance for any calendar year would therefore be computed at approximately $45,000.

19. Following the discussion in Special Commission 4 and the Meeting of States Parties as to the level of remuneration of the Members of the Tribunal on the basis of equivalencies with remuneration levels of Judges of the International Court of Justice and taking into account the requirements of the Statute, <u>35</u>/ for the purpose of the estimates in the present paper, it is assumed that the annual allowance would be $50,000. Thus, the maximum special allowance for any calendar year would also be $50,000. <u>36</u>/

20. When the remuneration levels of Judges of the International Court of Justice change, adjustment will be made to the overall remuneration of Members of the Tribunal.

21. According to SPLOS/4, paragraph 25 (a) (iii), during the initial period, August 1996-December 1997, other than the President, the 20 Members of the Tribunal would not be required to reside at the seat of the Tribunal. They would thus receive the annual allowance of $50,000, the special allowance for each day that he/she is engaged on the business of the Tribunal and a subsistence allowance for each day that he/she attends meetings at the seat of the Tribunal. The President of the Tribunal will reside at the seat of the Tribunal and would be entitled to an annual overall remuneration of $145,000. In addition, he will receive a special annual allowance, <u>37</u>/ which for the purpose of the estimates in the present paper is assumed to be $15,000.

22. The Members of the Tribunal will meet for up to 12 weeks during the initial period, August 1996-December 1997. <u>38</u>/ Thus, other than the President of the Tribunal, each of the 20 Members of the Tribunal would receive the special allowance for 12 weeks as well as subsistence allowance for 12 weeks during the period.

23. In the same subparagraph, SPLOS/4 indicates that provision would also need to be made for preparatory work by Members of the Tribunal. For the purpose of these estimates and the computations in annex I to the present paper, it is

assumed that such preparatory work would require 12 weeks. It is also assumed that in carrying out such preparatory work all 20 Members (the President being resident at the seat) would meet at the seat of the Tribunal for only half of the 12 weeks, i.e., 6 weeks. These assumptions mean that on account of preparatory work, other than the President of the Tribunal, each of the 20 Members of the Tribunal would receive the special allowance for 12 weeks and subsistence allowance for 6 weeks.

24. Annex I to the present paper provides the calculations of annual and special allowances as well as subsistence allowance of Members of the Tribunal for the period August 1996-December 1997.

B. Staff of the Registry and their remuneration

25. In the development of the Registry the evolutionary approach will apply, and in this respect the initial period between August 1996 and December 1997 can be considered to represent the transitional phase from the start-up of the Registry in August 1996. The transition itself is assumed to respond to demand, and would involve three stages. The first stage is the start-up of the Registry in August 1996 for eight months up to March 1997, with a small nucleus of staff to service the executive sessions of the judges and to serve to organize the Registry. Consequently, the number and level of the staff at start-up would be those presented in annex II to the present paper. The period from April 1997 to October 1997 will comprise the second stage of seven months, with a slightly larger contingent of staff. In order for the Tribunal to be ready to receive applications or cases and to perform its judicial functions, the Registry would have to have the contingent of staff required on board by November 1997 (see annexes III and IV). Assumptions as regards the level and functions of posts in the first functional phase involved closely follow the equivalent functions performed by staff of the International Court of Justice and the staffing structure of that Court. The review of Special Commission 4 included a review of those requirements as well. Annex V to the present paper provides the data on the number and level of the staff of the Registry of the Tribunal at various times between August 1996 and December 1997, reflecting the transitional stages explained above.

26. A completely new and independent body, which is also unique sui generis, when embarking on the start-up of its functions, is likely to require a certain amount of prior preparation. Such preparation would involve a number of administrative as well as substantive aspects:

(a) As regards facilities, inter alia, the Registry office facilities, those of the judges and meetings facilities, and the other utilities need to be in place and in working order. Requisite furniture and equipment also need to be in place. For the preparatory period itself, it is assumed that the temporary building facilities provided by the host country would include rental office furniture;

(b) The basic system of communications, including mail and courier service, local and long-distance telephone, facsimile services, access to relevant information networks and databases, need to be operational;

(c) Substantive materials, inter alia, drafts of basic rules, regulations and procedures regarding administrative, financial and personnel matters, in order even to recruit the first batch of staff in August 1996, need to be on hand;

(d) Essential elements of the Headquarters Agreement need to be concluded, or provisional application thereof agreed upon, in connection with the start-up of operations, pending the adoption of the Agreement between the host country and the Tribunal;

(e) Hiring arrangements have to be organized.

In view of these needs of a preparatory nature, in the present paper assumptions have been made for post requirements for an Administrative Officer (P-5) and a Substantive Legal Officer and a Computer Systems Officer (two P-3) as well as three assistants in the General Service category, for a preparatory period from April to July 1996 (following the adoption of the draft initial budget of the Tribunal at the Meeting of States Parties to be held in March 1996).

27. In the present paper it is assumed that the staff of the Registry would be remunerated according to the practice of the United Nations common system of organizations, 39/ information relating to the application of which is provided in the notes to table 1.

C. Other items of recurrent expenditure

28. Estimates of other objects of expenditure in the present paper are based on the budgetary experience of units of the United Nations which have comparable number, category and level of staff, and are consistent with those presented in LOS/PCN/142. The budgetary experience of the International Court of Justice in the initial period has been drawn upon, in particular. Adjustments have been made bearing in mind the intrinsic uncertainties as well as the special needs of the Tribunal as a unique sui generis institution and as an institution commencing functioning with an evolutionary approach. Such adjustments involve, in particular, such objects of expenditure as temporary assistance for meetings, general temporary assistance, temporary posts, official travel of staff (which includes travel of the Members of the Tribunal to attend meetings of the Tribunal in Hamburg or elsewhere) and communications. With regard to communications, attention has been given to the requirements of facsimile services and of accesses to networks and legal databases as used in an international court. 40/ Attention is drawn to the fact that SPLOS/4 indicates the need for preparatory work by the Members of the Tribunal. It is expected that Members would do some preparatory work at home which might require accesses to computer networks as well as facsimile services and groupware and networking facilities among the Members themselves and between the Members and the Registry officials. These matters also have implications for acquisition of computer and related equipment which are factored in under "Non-recurrent expenditures" in the present paper. As regards supplies and materials no provision has been made for acquisition of library holdings. This would require prior evaluation of availability from other sources and an assessment and the level of requirements.

D. Non-recurrent expenditures

29. Estimates of non-recurrent expenditures, including those pertaining to office equipment and furniture, data-processing equipment, transportation equipment, etc., are based on the budgetary experience of the United Nations, and are consistent with those presented in LOS/PCN/142 (see also para. 28).

E. Currency

30. The current cost estimations have been made in United States dollars. However, in determining the currency in which the Tribunal would operate, the Meeting of States Parties would have to determine whether the currency to be used would be that of the host country, as is the practice in the case of the United Nations.

F. Estimates

31. The preliminary estimates of the administrative expenses of the Tribunal for the period from 1 August 1996 to 31 December 1997 are presented in table 1. It is to be noted that these estimates do not include estimates for the receipt of applications or cases and deliberations thereon during this period (see footnote (b) of table 1).

IV. FUNDING OF THE BUDGET FOR THE INITIAL PERIOD

32. The Convention states that the expenses of the Tribunal shall be borne by the States Parties and the International Seabed Authority and also by other users of the Tribunal, which includes States that are not States Parties. 41/

33. There is no clear guidance in the Convention with regard to the manner in which the financing of the Tribunal would be apportioned between States Parties and the Authority. 42/ It is to be added that, according to SPLOS/4, paragraph 28, "the funding of the budget would be considered and decided (by the Meeting of States Parties) together with the budget".

34. It is to be noted that the administrative expenses of the Tribunal covering the period from August 1996 to December 1997, as estimated in table 1, do not include the costs that would be required in preparing for the start-up of operations during the period from April to July 1996. Such costs are estimated at $191,500, and consist of staff costs ($156,000) and costs of preparatory missions ($35,500). The Meeting of States Parties would also have to decide how these resources would be provided.

Notes

1/ Hereinafter referred to as "the Tribunal".

2/ Hereinafter referred to as "the Convention".

3/ See para. 10 of Resolution I of the Third United Nations Conference on the Law of the Sea. The Meeting of States Parties for election of the Members (judges) of the Tribunal is to be convened in accordance with annex VI, article 4 (4) of the Convention.

4/ The documentation of Special Commission 4 is contained in LOS/PCN/152, vols. I-IV.

5/ LOS/PCN/SCN.4/WP.8 (LOS/PCN/152(Vol. II), at p. 260).

6/ LOS/PCN/SCN.4/WP.8/Add.1 (LOS/PCN/152(Vol. II), at p. 278).

7/ LOS/PCN/SCN.4/WP.8/Add.2 (LOS/PCN/152(Vol. II), at p. 280).

8/ LOS/PCN/SCN.4/WP.11 (LOS/PCN/152(Vol. II), at p. 329).

9/ LOS/PCN/SCN.4/WP.16/Add.6 and 7 respectively, (LOS/PCN/152(Vol. I), at pp. 150 and 188, respectively). See also Chairman's summary of discussions contained in LOS/PCN/SCN.4/L.14 and Add.1 in relation to the former and LOS/PCN/SCN.4/L.18 in relation to the latter (LOS/PCN/152(Vol. III), at pp. 281, 294 and 339, respectively).

10/ See para. 1 above; see also LOS/PCN/SCN.4/WP.8/Add.2, para. 13.

11/ See SPLOS/3.

12/ See notes 5 to 9 above.

13/ See SPLOS/4, in particular, parts IIIA-C.

14/ SPLOS/4, paras. 25-29.

15/ The Convention specifies the number in annex VI, article 2(1).

16/ SPLOS/3, para. 16 (a).

17/ SPLOS/4, para. 37.

18/ The financial implications of the Meeting of States Parties, including the conference-servicing implications, are not reflected in the present paper, as separate estimates would be required for them. The responsibility for the convening and servicing of the Meetings of States Parties was conferred upon the Secretary-General of the United Nations as a result of the adoption of the Convention and resolutions of the General Assembly.

19/ SPLOS/4, para. 25(a)(ii).

20/ Ibid.

21/ This would follow the pattern of meetings and arrangements made initially by the International Tribunal for the former Yugoslavia.

22/ SPLOS/4, para. 25(a)(ii).

23/ SPLOS/4, para. 25(a)(i).

24/ Possibly in February/March 1997.

25/ Possibly in August/September 1997.

26/ LOS/PCN/SCN.4/WP.16/Add.7, para. 4.

27/ For details about the schemes and approaches, see LOS/PCN/SCN.4/WP.16/Add.6, para. 18.

28/ The same level of activity with regard to contentious cases at the International Court of Justice in 1990.

29/ It follows on the assumption in LOS/PCN/SCN.4/WP.8, para. 44.

30/ For the list of working papers, see LOS/PCN/142, annex IV. The working papers themselves are contained in LOS/PCN/152, vols. I-IV.

31/ SPLOS/4, para. 28(2)(II)(i).

32/ See SPLOS/4, para. 25(a)(iv).

33/ See notes 5 to 7 above.

34/ $219 for the first 60 days and approximately $164 thereafter (see ICSC/CIRC/DSA/240, p. 15).

35/ See Convention, annex VI, article 18.

36/ According to the Convention, annex VI, article 18 (1), in any year the total sum payable to any Member of the Tribunal as special allowance shall not exceed the amount of the annual allowance. Special allowance would be paid to a Member on a pro rata basis for those days that he/she is engaged in the business of the Tribunal, the maximum of which would only be 250 working days in a year, following standard United Nations practice.

37/ See annex VI, article 18(2).

38/ See SPLOS/4, para. 25(a)(ii).

39/ See also LOS/PCN/142, para. 25.

40/ Based on suggestions contained in communications from delegations.

41/ Convention, annex VI, article 19.

42/ LOS/PCN/SCN.4/WP.16/Add.7, para. 10.

Annex I

ANNUAL ALLOWANCE, AS WELL AS SPECIAL ALLOWANCE AND SUBSISTENCE ALLOWANCE FOR RELEVANT DAYS FOR THE MEMBERS OF THE TRIBUNAL DURING THE PERIOD FROM AUGUST 1996 TO DECEMBER 1997

(Thousands of United States dollars)

Number of Members	Annual allowance per Member (12 months)	Annual allowance for Members for the 17-month period	President's special allowance (12 months)	President's special allowance for the 17-month period	Special allowance per Member (12 months)	Special allowance for Members for the 17-month period	Subsistence allowance per Member per day	Subsistence allowance for Members for the 17-month period	Overall remuneration of Members for the 17-month period
President - 1	50.0	70.8	15.0	21.3	50.0	70.8	$219 a/ $164 b/	45.0 c/	
Other Members - 20	50.0	1 416.7	-	-	50.0	461.5 d/	$219 a/ $164 b/	367.9 + 184.0 e/	
Total Members - 21		1 487.5		21.3		532.3		596.9	2 638.1

a/ Daily subsistence allowance rate applicable for the first 60 days.

b/ Daily subsistence allowance rate applicable after the first 60 days.

c/ See paras. 18 and 21 above.

d/ For 12 weeks of meetings plus 12 weeks of preparatory work, within the 17-month period, on a pro-rata basis of a 52-week calendar year.

e/ See para. 23 above.

Annex II

POST REQUIREMENTS OF THE REGISTRY AT THE START-UP OF OPERATIONS a/

D-2	D-1	P-5	P-4	P-3	P-2/1	Total Profes-sional and above	General Service (Prin-cipal level)	General Service (Other level)	Total General Service	Grand total
1	1	1	1	1	2	7	0	14	14	21

a/ See LOS/PCN/142.

Annex III

REGISTRY STAFFING LEVELS AND DESIGNATIONS AT THE END OF THE ORGANIZATIONAL PHASE AND AT THE BEGINNING OF THE FIRST FUNCTIONAL PHASE a/

Level	Functions	Number of posts
ASG	Registrar	1
D-2	Deputy Registrar	1
D-1	Principal Legal Secretary (Secretary, Rules Committee)	1
P-5	Executive Officer (Accounts/Budget/Administration) (Secretary, Budgetary and Administrative Committee)	1
	Senior Secretary (Secretary, Public Relations)	1
	Senior Secretary	1
P-4	Accountant/Establishment Officer	1
	Head, Documents Dept./Librarian (Secretary, Library and Archives Committee)	1
	First Secretary (Secretary, Staff Appeals Board)	1
	First Secretaries	0
	Special Assistant	0
	Revisers/Translators	2
	Information Officer	1
	Head of Office Secretarial Services	0
P-3	Secretaries	1
	Special Assistant	1
	Revisers/Translators	0
	Head of Archives	1
	Head of Administration/Personnel	0
	Coordinator, General Services	0
	Librarian	1
P-2/P-1	Associate Secretary	0
	Judiciary Secretaries/Researchers	1
	Associate Librarian	0
	Associate Administrative/Budget Officer	1
	Head of Office Secretarial Services	1
	Head of Printing	1
	Associate Archives Officer	1
General Service	Principal level	5
	Other levels	28
	Security Officers	2
	Total	56

Post requirements

ASG	D-2	D-1	P-5	P-4	P-3	P-2/1	Total Profes-sional and above	General Service (Prin-cipal level)	General Service (Other level)	Total General Service	Grand total
1	1	1	3	6	4	5	21	5	30	35	56

a/ See LOS/PCN/SCN.4/WP.8/Add.2, LOS/PCN/SCN.4/WP.16/Add.6, LOS/PCN/SCN.4/L.14 and LOS/PCN/142.

Annex IV

REGISTRY STAFF DISTRIBUTION BASED ON FUNCTIONS AND DIVISIONS AT THE END OF THE ORGANIZATIONAL PHASE AND AT THE BEGINNING

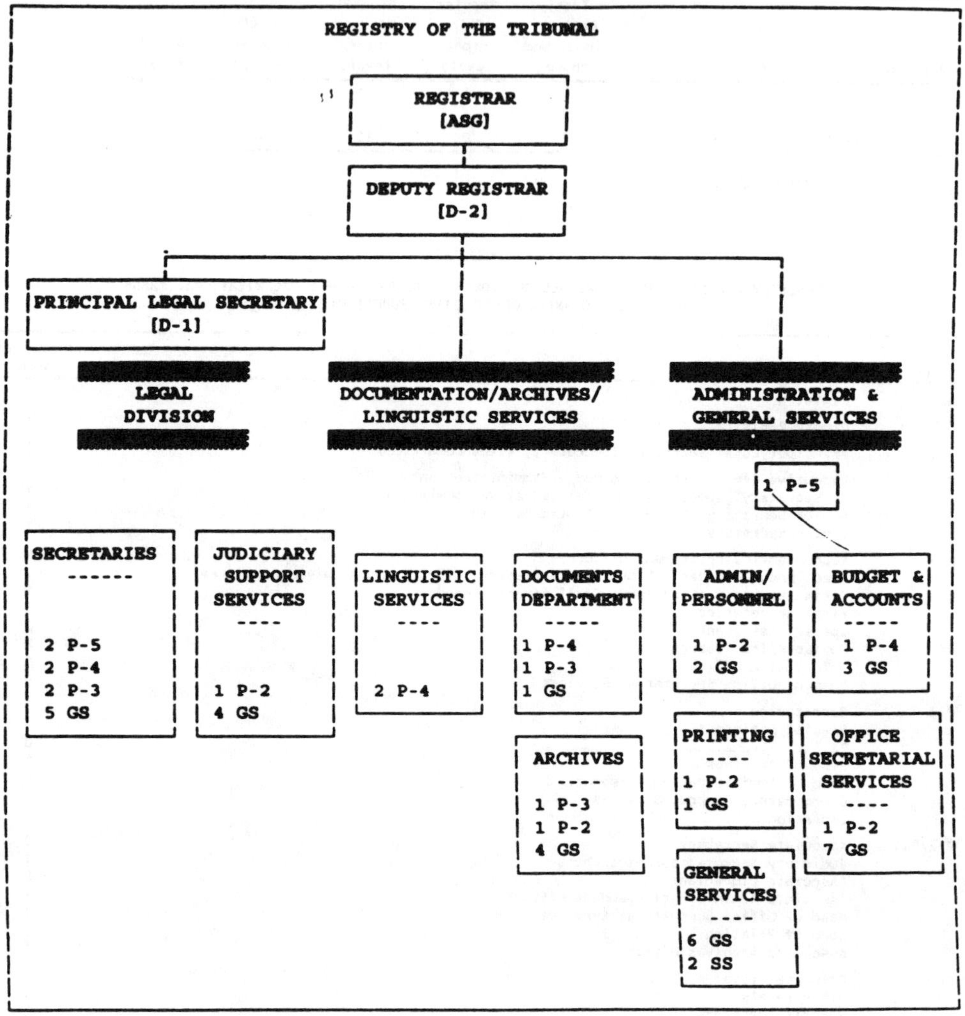

a/ See LOS/PCN/SCN.4/WP.8/Add.2, LOS/PCN/SCN.4/WP.16/Add.6, LOS/PCN/SCN.4/L.14 and LOS/PCN/142.

Annex V

POST REQUIREMENTS OF THE REGISTRY DURING THE PERIOD FROM AUGUST 1996 TO DECEMBER 1997, UNDER THE TRANSITION APPROACH

ASG	D-2	D-1	P-5	P-4	P-3	P-2/1	Total Professional and above	General Service (Principal level)	General Service (Other levels)	Total General Service	Grand total
						August 1996-March 1997					
	1	1	1	1	1	2	7		14	14	21
						April-October 1997					
1	1	1	2	3	2	3	13	2	16	18	31
						November-December 1997					
1	1	1	3	6	4	5	21	5	30	35	56

Table

ADMINISTRATIVE EXPENSES OF THE TRIBUNAL a/, b/ COVERING THE PERIOD AUGUST 1996-DECEMBER 1997 (17 MONTHS)

(Preliminary estimates) c/

(Thousands of United States dollars)

Objects of expenditure	Expenses
A. Recurrent expenditures	
Established posts	2 355.1 d/
Temporary assistance for meetings	116.9
General temporary assistance	107.0
Overtime	24.5
Temporary posts	128.2
Common staff costs	853.5 d/, e/
Representation allowance	3.1 d/
Official travel	150.0
External printing and binding	37.8
Annual and special allowances of Members	2 638.1
Rental and maintenance of premises	(143.4) f/
Rental and maintenance of furniture and equipment	141.4
Communications	53.9
Hospitality	4.2
Miscellaneous services	2.9
Supplies and materials	46.6
B. Non-recurrent expenditures	
Purchase of furniture and equipment	173.0
Total	6 835.7

(Footnotes on following page)

(Footnotes to table)

---

a/ These estimates are preliminary and indicative, based on previous documentation (LOS/PCN/SCN.4/WP.8 and addenda, LOS/PCN/SCN.4/WP.16/Add.6 and LOS/PCN/142), from which the relevant items have been extrapolated. The relevant administrative and budgetary departments have yet to do the same.

b/ If any applications or cases are submitted during this period, the financial implications of court proceedings will have to be estimated separately and appropriate budgetary arrangements provided.

c/ Does not include costs of preparatory missions for preparing facilities and staff costs during the preparatory period, April-July 1996.

d/ The remuneration of the staff is composed of various elements which, for budgetary purposes, are usually combined under three objects of expenditure, namely, costs of posts, common staff costs and representation allowance. Following the standard practice of the United Nations, estimates for these three objects of expenditure are based on Standard Salary Costs prepared by the Data Analysis and Systems Control Unit of the Programme Planning and Budget Division, Office of Programme Planning, Budget and Accounts, Department of Administration and Management. Standard Salary Costs provides data on annual total net salary (equal to net base salary plus post adjustment), common staff costs and representation allowance, by category/level, by duty station and by calendar year. In the table, the figures for "Established posts" stand for total net salary. Also, in the absence of data applicable to United Nations staff in Hamburg, Germany, the data for The Hague duty station have been used. There are periodic revisions of Standard Salary Costs, for the purpose of the table, the latest available revision, version 48/01, has been used.

e/ Includes initial travel of the Members of the Tribunal.

f/ Not included in total. In the event that no rental is involved, maintenance costs may be required. Assumes only utility payments and for services in the light of the fact that the host country is providing permanent facilities and other temporary facilities pending completion of the permanent facility.

41. ELECTION OF THE MEMBERS OF THE COMMISSION ON THE LIMITS OF THE CONTINENTAL SHELF - INFORMATION NOTE BY THE UN SECRETARIAT

Doc. no.: SPLOS/CRP.2 2 October 1995

1. In accordance with article 76 of the United Nations Convention on the Law of the Sea, the Commission on the Limits of the Continental Shelf shall be established in conformity with the provisions of annex II of the Convention. The Commission must be established within 18 months after the date of entry into force of the Convention, i.e., before 16 May 1996 (article 2, paragraph 2, of annex II of the Convention). The members of the Commission are to be elected at a Meeting of States Parties convened by the Secretary-General at United Nations Headquarters. The Commission shall consist of 21 members who shall be experts in the field of geology, geophysics or hydrography, elected by States Parties from among their nationals, having due regard to the need to ensure equitable geographical representation, who shall serve in their personal capacities.

2. The functions of the Commission shall be:

(a) To consider the data and other material submitted by coastal States concerning the outer limits of the continental shelf in areas where those limits extend beyond 200 nautical miles, and to make recommendations in accordance with article 76 and the Statement of Understanding adopted on 29 August 1980 by the Third United Nations Conference on the Law of the Sea;

(b) To provide scientific and technical advice, if requested by the coastal State concerned during the preparation of the data referred to in subparagraph (a).

3. It should be recalled that the Ad Hoc Meeting of States Parties held in New York from 21 to 22 November 1994 decided on a precise schedule for the nomination and election of the members of the International Tribunal for the Law of the Sea (SPLOS/3, para. 16). The Secretary-General suggests that a similar decision be taken by States Parties for the election of the Commission on the Limits of the Continental Shelf. Accordingly, the following schedule is proposed:

(a) The first election of the 21 members of the Commission would be held at the Meeting of States Parties which is scheduled to be convened at the United Nations Headquarters from 29 April to 10 May 1996. No decision has been taken concerning the precise date of election. Therefore, for purposes of computing the time-limits for notifications and invitations, the earliest possible date for election within the planned meeting, namely 29 April 1996, has been used;

(b) The nominations would open on 15 December 1995. A State in the process of becoming a party to the Convention might nominate candidates. Such nominations would remain provisional and would not be included in the list to be circulated by the Secretary-General in accordance with annex II, article 2, paragraph 2, of the Convention, unless the State concerned had deposited its instrument of ratification or accession before 29 March 1996;

(c) The nominations would close on 15 March 1996;

(d) The list of candidates would be circulated by the Secretary-General on 8 April 1996.

4. It should be noted that the Convention provides that not less than three members shall be elected from each geographical region (annex II, article 2, paragraph 3, of the Convention).

5. Finally, the State Party which nominates a member of the Commission shall defray the expenses of that member while in performance of Commission duties. However, the coastal State concerned shall defray the expenses incurred in respect of the advice referred to in article 3, paragraph 1 (b), of annex II of the Convention. The secretariat of the Commission shall be provided by the Secretary-General of the United Nations.

42. RULES OF PROCEDURE OF THE ASSEMBLY OF THE INTERNATIONAL SEABED AUTHORITY (ADOPTED AT ITS 15TH MEETING, ON 17 MARCH 1995)

Doc. no.: ISBA/A/6 7 July 1995

CONTENTS

Introductory note

On 28 July 1994 the General Assembly of the United Nations adopted the Agreement relating to the implementation of Part XI of the United Nations Convention on the Law of the Sea, and the Agreement has been provisionally applied since 16 November 1994.

According to the Agreement, its provisions and Part XI of the Convention are to be interpreted and applied together as a single instrument; the present rules and references in these rules to the Convention are to be interpreted and applied accordingly.

I. SESSIONS

Regular sessions

Rule 1

Regular annual sessions

The Assembly shall meet in regular annual sessions unless it decides otherwise.

Rule 2

Date and duration

The date of commencement and the duration of each such session shall be decided by the previous session of the Assembly.

Rule 3

Notification of members

The Secretary-General shall notify the members of the Assembly at least sixty days in advance of the opening of a regular session.

Special sessions

Rule 4

Convening of special sessions

1. The Assembly may convene special sessions and shall fix the date of commencement and the duration of each such session.

2. At the request of the Council or of a majority of the members of the Authority, the Secretary-General shall convene a special session of the Assembly and it shall meet no earlier than thirty days and no later than ninety days after the receipt of such a request unless the request has stipulated otherwise.

3. Any member of the Authority may request the Secretary-General to convene a special session of the Assembly. The Secretary-General shall immediately inform the other members of the Authority of the request and inquire whether they concur in it. If within thirty days of the date of communication by the Secretary-General a majority of the members of the Assembly concur in the request, a special session of the Assembly shall be convened by the Secretary-General and it shall meet no earlier than thirty days and no later than ninety days after the receipt of such concurrence.

Rule 5

Notification of members

The Secretary-General shall notify the members of the Assembly at least thirty days in advance of the opening of a special session.

Regular and special sessions

Rule 6

Place of meeting

The Assembly shall meet at the seat of the Authority unless it decides otherwise.

Rule 7

Notification to observers

Copies of the notice convening each session of the Assembly shall be addressed to observers referred to in rule 82.

Rule 8

Temporary adjournment of session

The Assembly may decide at any session to adjourn temporarily and resume its meetings at a later date. A regular session shall not normally be adjourned beyond the end of the year.

II. AGENDA

Regular sessions

Rule 9

Provisional agenda

The provisional agenda for a regular session shall be drawn up by the Secretary-General and communicated to the members of the Assembly and to observers referred to in rule 82 at least sixty days before the opening of the session.

Rule 10

Drawing up of the provisional agenda

The provisional agenda of a regular session shall include:

(a) The report of the Secretary-General on the work of the Authority;

(b) Reports from the Council and the Enterprise, 1/ and special reports requested from the Council or any other organs;

(c) Items the inclusion of which has been ordered by the Assembly at a previous session;

(d) Items proposed by the Council;

(e) Items proposed by any member of the Assembly;

(f) Items pertaining to the budget for the next financial period and the report on the accounts for the last financial period;

(g) Items which the Secretary-General deems it necessary to put before the Assembly.

Rule 11

Supplementary items

Any member of the Assembly, the Council or the Secretary-General may, at least thirty days before the date fixed for the opening of a regular session, request the inclusion of supplementary items in the agenda. Such items shall be placed on a supplementary list, which shall be communicated to the members of the Assembly and to observers referred to in rule 82 at least twenty days before the opening of the session.

1/ See footnote 2.

Rule 12

Additional items

Additional items of an important and urgent character, proposed for inclusion in the agenda less than thirty days before the opening of a regular session or during a regular session, may be placed on the agenda if the Assembly so decides by a majority of the members of the Assembly present and voting. No additional item may, unless the Assembly decides otherwise by a two-thirds majority of the members of the Assembly present and voting, be considered until seven days have elapsed since it was placed on the agenda.

Special sessions

Rule 13

Communication of the provisional agenda

The provisional agenda of a special session shall be communicated to the members of the Assembly and to observers referred to in rule 82 at least fourteen days before the opening of the session.

Rule 14

Provisional agenda

The provisional agenda for a special session shall consist only of those items proposed for consideration in the request for the holding of the session.

Rule 15

Supplementary items

Any member of the Assembly, the Council or the Secretary-General may, at least seven days before the date fixed for the opening of a special session, request the inclusion of supplementary items in the agenda. Such items shall be placed on a supplementary list, which shall be communicated to the members of the Assembly and to observers referred to in rule 82 as soon as possible.

Rule 16

Additional items

During a special session, items on the supplementary list and additional items may be added to the agenda by a two-thirds majority of the members of the Assembly present and voting.

Regular and special sessions

Rule 17

Explanatory memorandum

Any item proposed for inclusion in the agenda shall be accompanied by an explanatory memorandum and, if possible, by basic documents or by a draft resolution.

Rule 18

Adoption of the agenda

At each session, the provisional agenda and the supplementary list shall be submitted to the Assembly for approval as soon as possible after the opening of the session.

Rule 19

Amendment and deletion of items

Items on the agenda may be amended or deleted by the Assembly by a majority of the members of the Assembly present and voting.

Rule 20

Debate on inclusion of items

Debate on the inclusion of an item in the agenda shall be limited to three representatives of the members of the Assembly in favour of, and three against, the inclusion. The President may limit the time to be allowed to speakers under this rule.

Rule 21

Modification of the allocation of expenses

No proposal for a modification of the allocation of expenses for the time being in force shall be placed on the agenda unless it has been communicated to the members of the Assembly at least ninety days before the opening of the session.

III. REPRESENTATION

Rule 22

Representation

1. Each member of the Assembly shall be represented by an accredited representative and such alternate representatives and advisers as may be required.

2. Observers referred to in rule 82 shall be represented by accredited or designated representatives, as the case may be, and by such alternate representatives and advisers as may be required.

3. The representative may designate an alternate representative or an adviser to act in his capacity.

IV. CREDENTIALS

Rule 23

Submission of credentials

The credentials of representatives and the names of alternate representatives and advisers shall be submitted to the Secretary-General if possible not later than twenty-four hours after the opening of the session. The credentials shall be issued either by the Head of the State or Government, by the Minister for Foreign Affairs or person authorized by him or, in the case of entities referred to in article 305, paragraph 1 (f) of the United Nations Convention on the Law of the Sea, by another competent authority.

Rule 24

Credentials Committee

A Credentials Committee shall be appointed at the beginning of each session. It shall consist of nine members of the Assembly, who shall be appointed by the Assembly on the proposal of the President. The Committee shall elect its own officers. It shall examine the credentials of representatives of members and report to the Assembly without delay.

Rule 25

Provisional admission to a session

Pending a decision of the Assembly upon their credentials, representatives shall be entitled to participate provisionally in the Assembly.

Rule 26

Objection to the representation

If an objection is raised against a representative, such objection shall be considered by the Credentials Committee forthwith. The report thereon shall be submitted to the Assembly without delay for its decision.

V. PRESIDENT AND VICE-PRESIDENTS

Rule 27

Temporary President

At the opening of each regular session of the Assembly, the President of the previous session or, in his absence, the head of the delegation from which the President of the previous session was elected shall preside until the Assembly has elected a President for the session.

Rule 28

Elections

At the beginning of each regular session the Assembly shall elect its President and four Vice-Presidents in such a way as to ensure the representative character of the Bureau. They shall hold office until a new President and other officers are elected at the next regular session.

Rule 29

Acting President

If the President finds it necessary to be absent during a meeting or any part thereof, he shall designate one of the Vice-Presidents to take his place.

Rule 30

Powers of the Acting President

A Vice-President acting as President shall have the same powers and duties as the President.

Rule 31

Replacement of the President

If the President is unable to perform his functions, a new President shall be elected for the unexpired term.

Rule 32

General powers of the President

In addition to exercising the powers conferred upon him elsewhere by these rules, or by the United Nations Convention on the Law of the Sea, the President shall declare the opening and closing of each plenary meeting of the session, direct the discussions in plenary meeting, ensure observance of these rules, accord the right to speak, put questions and announce decisions. He shall rule on points of order and, subject to these rules, shall have complete control of the proceedings at any meeting and over the maintenance of order thereat. The President may, in the course of the discussion of an item, propose to the Assembly the limitation of the time to be allowed to speakers, the limitation of the number of times each representative may speak, the closure of the list of speakers or the closure of the debate. He may also propose the suspension or the adjournment of the meeting or the adjournment of the debate on the item under discussion.

Rule 33

Limitation of the powers of the President

The President, in the exercise of his functions, remains under the authority of the Assembly.

Rule 34

Voting of the President and Acting President

The President, or a Vice-President acting as President, shall not vote but shall designate another member of his delegation to vote in his place.

VI. BUREAU

Rule 35

The President and Vice-Presidents shall constitute the Bureau which shall meet periodically throughout each session to review the progress of the Assembly and its subsidiary organs and to make recommendations for furthering such progress. It shall also meet at such other times as the President deems necessary or upon the request of any other of its members. The Bureau shall assist the President in the general conduct of the work of the Assembly which falls within the competence of the President. The Chairmen of the subsidiary organs of the Assembly may be invited to attend meetings of the Bureau.

VII. SECRETARIAT

Rule 36

Duties of the Secretary-General

1. The Secretary-General shall act in that capacity in all meetings of the Assembly and its subsidiary organs. He may designate a member of the Secretariat to act in his place at these meetings. He shall discharge such other responsibilities as are assigned to him by the Assembly in the conduct of its business.

2. The Secretary-General shall provide and direct the staff required by the Assembly and its subsidiary organs.

Rule 37

Duties of the Secretariat

The Secretariat shall receive, translate, reproduce and distribute documents, reports and resolutions of the Assembly and its subsidiary organs; interpret speeches made at the meetings; prepare and circulate, if so decided by the Assembly in accordance with rule 42, the records of the session; have the custody and proper preservation of the documents in the archives of the Authority; distribute all documents of the Assembly to the members of the Authority and observers referred to in rule 82; and, generally, perform all other work which the Assembly may require.

Rule 38

Report of the Secretary-General on the work of the Authority

The Secretary-General shall make an annual report, and such supplementary reports as are necessary, to the Assembly at its regular session on the work of the Authority. He shall communicate the annual report to the members of the Authority and observers referred to in rule 82 at least forty-five days before the opening of the regular session.

VIII. LANGUAGES

Rule 39

Languages

Arabic, Chinese, English, French, Russian and Spanish shall be the languages of the Assembly and its subsidiary organs.

Rule 40

Interpretation

1. Speeches made in a language of the Assembly shall be interpreted into the other such languages.

2. Any representative may make a speech in a language other than a language of the Assembly. In that case he shall himself provide for interpretation into one of the languages of the Assembly. Interpretation into the other languages of the Assembly by the interpreters of the Secretariat may be based on the interpretation given in the first such language.

Rule 41

Languages of resolutions and other documents

All resolutions and other documents shall be published in the languages of the Assembly.

IX. RECORDS

Rule 42

Records and sound recordings of meetings

1. The Assembly may keep summary records of plenary meetings if it so decides. As a general rule, such records shall be circulated as soon as possible, simultaneously in all languages of the Assembly, to all representatives, who shall inform the Secretariat within five working days after the circulation of the summary record of any changes they wish to have made.

2. The Secretariat shall make and retain sound recordings of meetings of the Assembly, and of its subsidiary organs when they so decide.

X. PUBLIC AND PRIVATE MEETINGS OF THE ASSEMBLY AND ITS SUBSIDIARY ORGANS

Rule 43

Public and private meetings

1. The meetings of the Assembly shall be held in public unless the Assembly decides that exceptional circumstances require that the meeting be held in private.

2. As a general rule, meetings of subsidiary organs shall be held in private.

3. All decisions of the Assembly taken at a private meeting shall be announced at an early public meeting of the Assembly. At the close of a private meeting of a subsidiary organ, the Chairman may issue a communiqué through the Secretary-General.

XI. MINUTE OF SILENT PRAYER OR MEDITATION

Rule 44

Invitation to silent prayer or meditation

Immediately after the opening of the first plenary meeting and immediately preceding the closing of the final plenary meeting of each session of the Assembly, the President shall invite the representatives to observe one minute of silence dedicated to prayer or meditation.

XII. PLENARY MEETINGS

Conduct of business

Rule 45

Quorum

The President may declare a meeting open and permit the debate to proceed when at least a majority of the members of the Assembly are present.

Rule 46

Speeches

No representative may address the Assembly without having previously obtained the permission of the President. The President shall call upon speakers in the order in which they signify their desire to speak. The President may call a speaker to order if his remarks are not relevant to the subject under discussion.

Rule 47

Precedence

The Chairman of a subsidiary organ may be accorded precedence for the purpose of explaining the conclusions arrived at by that organ.

Rule 48

Statement by the Secretariat

The Secretary-General or a member of the Secretariat designated by him as his representative may at any time make either oral or written statements to the Assembly concerning any question under consideration by it.

Rule 49

Points of order

During the discussion of any matter, a representative of a member of the Assembly may rise to a point of order, and the point of order shall be immediately decided by the President in accordance with these rules of procedure. A representative of a member of the Assembly may appeal against the ruling of the President. The appeal shall be immediately put to the vote, and the President's ruling shall stand unless overruled by a majority of the members of the Assembly present and voting. A representative rising to a point of order may not speak on the substance of the matter under discussion.

Rule 50

Time-limit on speeches

The Assembly may limit the time to be allowed to each speaker and the number of times each representative may speak on any question. Before a decision is taken, two representatives of members of the Assembly may speak in favour of, and two against, a proposal to set such limits. When the debate is limited and a representative exceeds his allotted time, the President shall call him to order without delay.

Rule 51

Closing of list of speakers, right of reply

During the course of the debate, the President may announce the list of speakers and, with the consent of the Assembly, declare the list closed. He may, however, accord the right of reply to any representative if a speech delivered after he has declared the list closed makes this desirable.

Rule 52

Adjournment of debate

During the discussion of any matter, a representative of a member of the Assembly may move the adjournment of the debate on the item under discussion. In addition to the proposer of the motion, two representatives of members of the Assembly may speak in favour of, and two against, the motion, after which the motion shall be immediately put to the vote. The President may limit the time to be allowed to speakers under this rule.

Rule 53

Closure of debate

A representative of a member of the Assembly may at any time move the closure of the debate on the question under discussion, whether or not any other representative has signified his wish to speak. Permission to speak on the motion shall be accorded only to two representatives of members of the Assembly opposing the closure, after which the motion shall be immediately put to the vote. If the Assembly is in favour of the closure, the President shall declare the closure of the debate. The President may limit the time to be allowed to speakers under this rule.

Rule 54

Suspension or adjournment of the meeting

During the discussion of any matter, a representative of a member of the Assembly may move the suspension or the adjournment of the meeting. Such motions shall not be debated, but shall be immediately put to the vote. The President may limit the time to be allowed to the speaker moving the suspension or adjournment of the meeting.

Rule 55

Order of procedural motions

Subject to rule 49, the following motions shall have precedence in the following order over all other proposals or motions before the meeting:

(a) To suspend the meeting;

(b) To adjourn the meeting;

(c) To adjourn the debate on the item under discussion;

(d) To close the debate on the item under discussion.

Rule 56

Proposals and amendments

Proposals and amendments shall normally be submitted in writing to the Secretary-General, who shall circulate copies to the delegations. As a general rule, no proposal shall be discussed or put to the vote at any meeting of the Assembly unless copies of it have been circulated to all delegations in the languages of the Assembly not later than the day preceding the meeting. The President may, however, permit the discussion and consideration of amendments, or of motions as to procedure, even though such amendments and motions have not been circulated or have only been circulated the same day.

Rule 57

Decisions on competence

Subject to rule 55, any motion calling for a decision on the competence of the Assembly to adopt a proposal submitted to it shall be put to the vote before a vote is taken on the proposal in question.

Rule 58

Withdrawal of motions

A motion may be withdrawn by its proposer at any time before voting on it has commenced, provided that the motion has not been amended. A motion thus withdrawn may be reintroduced by any member.

Rule 59

Reconsideration of proposals

When a proposal has been adopted or rejected, it may not be reconsidered at the same session unless the Assembly, by a two-thirds majority of the members of the Assembly present and voting, so decides. Permission to speak on a motion to reconsider shall be accorded only to two representatives of members of the Assembly opposing the motion, after which it shall be immediately put to the vote.

XIII. DECISION-MAKING

Rule 60

Voting rights

Each member of the Assembly shall have one vote. Participation in decision-making by entities referred to in article 305, paragraph 1 (f), of the United Nations Convention on the Law of the Sea shall be in accordance with Annex IX of the Convention.

Rule 61

Decision-making

1. As a general rule, decision-making in the Assembly should be by consensus.

2. If all efforts to reach a decision by consensus have been exhausted, decisions by voting in the Assembly on questions of procedure shall be taken by

a majority of members present and voting, and decisions on questions of substance shall be taken by a two-thirds majority of members present and voting, as provided for in article 159, paragraph 8, of the Convention.

3. Decisions of the Assembly on any matter for which the Council also has competence or on any administrative, budgetary or financial matter shall be based on the recommendations of the Council. If the Assembly does not accept the recommendation of the Council on any matter, it shall return the matter to the Council for further consideration. The Council shall reconsider the matter in the light of the views expressed by the Assembly.

4. Decisions by the Assembly having financial or budgetary implications shall be based on the recommendations of the Finance Committee.

Rule 62

Decisions on amendments to proposals relating to questions of substance

Decisions of the Assembly on amendments to proposals relating to questions of substance, and on parts of such proposals put to the vote separately, shall be made by a two-thirds majority of the members of the Assembly present and voting, provided that such majority includes a majority of the members participating in the session.

Rule 63

Use of terms

1. For the purpose of these rules, the phrase "members of the Assembly present and voting" means members of the Assembly present and casting an affirmative or negative vote. Members of the Assembly who abstain from voting shall be considered as not voting.

2. Subject to the provisions of rules 23 to 26 and without prejudice to the powers and functions of the Credentials Committee, the term "members of the Assembly participating" in relation to any particular session of the Assembly means any member of the Assembly whose representatives have registered with the Secretariat as participating in that session and which has not subsequently notified the Secretariat of its withdrawal from that session or part of it. The Secretariat shall keep a register for this purpose.

Rule 64

Deferment of voting on questions of substance coming up for voting for the first time

When a question of substance comes up for voting for the first time, the President may, and shall, if requested by at least one fifth of the members of the Assembly, defer the issue of taking a vote on that question for a period not exceeding five calendar days. This rule may be applied only once to any question, and shall not be applied so as to defer the question beyond the end of the session.

Rule 65

Deferment of voting upon request for an advisory opinion

Upon a written request addressed to the President and sponsored by at least one fourth of the members of the Assembly for an advisory opinion on the conformity with the United Nations Convention on the Law of the Sea of a proposal before the Assembly on any matter, the Assembly shall request the Seabed Disputes Chamber of the International Tribunal for the Law of the Sea to give an advisory opinion thereon and shall defer voting on that proposal pending receipt of the advisory opinion by the Chamber. If the advisory opinion is not received before the final week of the session in which it is requested, the Assembly shall decide when it will meet to vote upon the deferred proposal.

Rule 66

Method of voting

1. The Assembly shall, in the absence of mechanical means for voting, vote by show of hands or by standing but a representative of any member of the Assembly may request a roll-call. The roll-call shall be taken in the English alphabetical order of the names of the members of the Assembly participating in that session, beginning with the member whose name is drawn by lot by the President. The name of each member of the Assembly shall be called in any roll-call, and one of its representatives shall reply "yes", "no" or "abstention". The result of the voting shall be inserted in the record in the English alphabetical order of the names of the members.

2. When the Assembly votes by mechanical means, a non-recorded vote shall replace a vote by show of hands or by standing and a recorded vote shall replace a roll-call vote. A representative of any member of the Assembly may request a recorded vote. In the case of a recorded vote, the Assembly shall, unless a representative of a member of the Assembly requests otherwise, dispense with the procedure of calling out the names of the members; nevertheless, the result of the voting shall be inserted in the record in the same manner as that of a roll-call vote.

Rule 67

Conduct during voting

After the President has announced the commencement of voting, no representative of a member of the Assembly may interrupt the voting, except that representatives of members of the Assembly may interrupt on a point of order in connection with the actual conduct of voting.

Rule 68

Explanation of vote

Representatives of members of the Assembly may make brief statements consisting solely of explanations of their votes before the voting has commenced or after the voting has been completed. The President may limit the time to be allowed for such statements. The representative of a member of the Assembly sponsoring a proposal or motion shall not speak in explanation of vote thereon, except if it has been amended.

Rule 69

Division of proposals and amendments

A representative of a member of the Assembly may move that parts of a proposal or of an amendment should be voted on separately. If objection is made to the request for division, the motion for division shall be voted upon. Permission to speak on the motion for division shall be given only to two speakers in favour and two speakers against. If the motion for division is carried, those parts of the proposal or of the amendment which are approved shall then be put to the vote as a whole. If all operative parts of the proposal or of the amendment have been rejected, the proposal or the amendment shall be considered to have been rejected as a whole.

Rule 70

Order of voting on amendments

When an amendment is moved to a proposal, the amendment shall be voted on first. When two or more amendments are moved to a proposal, the Assembly shall first vote on the amendment furthest removed in substance from the original proposal and then on the amendment next furthest removed therefrom, and so on until all the amendments have been put to the vote. Where, however, the adoption of one amendment necessarily implies the rejection of another amendment, the latter amendment shall not be put to the vote. If one or more amendments are adopted, the amended proposal shall then be voted upon. A motion is considered an amendment to a proposal if it merely adds to, deletes from or revises part of the proposal.

Rule 71

Order of voting on proposals

If two or more proposals relate to the same question, the Assembly shall, unless it decides otherwise, vote on the proposals in the order in which they have been submitted. The Assembly may, after each vote on a proposal, decide whether to vote on the next proposal.

Rule 72

Elections

All elections shall be held by secret ballot.

Rule 73

Restricted balloting for one elective place

1. When one person or a member of the Assembly is to be elected and no candidate obtains in the first ballot the votes of a majority of the members of the Assembly present and voting, a second ballot restricted to the two candidates obtaining the largest number of votes shall be taken. If in the second ballot the votes are equally divided, the President shall decide between the candidates by drawing lots.

2. In the case of a tie in the first ballot among more than two candidates obtaining the largest number of votes, a second ballot shall be held. If on that ballot a tie remains among more than two candidates, the number shall be reduced to two by lot and the balloting, restricted to them, shall continue in accordance with the preceding paragraph.

3. If a two-thirds majority is required, the balloting shall be continued until one candidate secures two thirds of the votes cast; provided that, after the third inconclusive ballot, votes may be cast for any eligible person or member. If three such unrestricted ballots are inconclusive, the next three ballots shall be restricted to the two candidates who obtained the greatest number of votes in the third of the unrestricted ballots, and the following three ballots thereafter shall be unrestricted, and so on until a person or member of the Assembly is elected.

4. The above provisions of this rule shall not prejudice the application of rules 83, 84 and 96.

Rule 74

Restricted balloting for two or more elective places

When two or more elective places are to be filled at one time under the same conditions, those candidates, not exceeding the number of such places, obtaining in the first ballot the majority required shall be elected. If the number of candidates obtaining such a majority is less than the number of persons or members of the Assembly to be elected, there shall be additional ballots to fill the remaining places, the voting being restricted to the candidates obtaining the greatest number of votes in the previous ballot to a number not more than twice the places remaining to be filled; provided that, after the third inconclusive ballot, votes may be cast for any eligible person or member of the Assembly. If three such unrestricted ballots are inconclusive, the next three ballots shall be restricted to the candidates who obtained the greatest number of votes in the third of the unrestricted ballots, to a number not more than twice the places remaining to be filled, and the following three ballots thereafter shall be unrestricted, and so on until all the places have been filled. The above provisions of this rule shall not prejudice the application of rules 83, 84 and 96.

Rule 75

Equally divided votes on matters other than elections

If a vote is equally divided on matters other than elections, a second vote shall be taken at a subsequent meeting which shall be held within 48 hours of the first vote; and it shall be expressly mentioned in the agenda that a second vote will be taken on the matter in question. If this vote also results in equality, the proposal shall be regarded as rejected.

XIV. SUBSIDIARY ORGANS

Rule 76

Establishment

The Assembly may establish such subsidiary organs as it finds necessary for the exercise of its functions.

Rule 77

Composition

In the composition of subsidiary organs due account shall be taken of the principle of equitable geographical distribution and of special interests and the need for members qualified and competent in the relevant technical questions dealt with by such organs.

Rule 78

Statements by non-members of a subsidiary organ

Any member of the Assembly that is not a member of a subsidiary organ shall have the right to explain its views to that organ when a matter particularly affecting it is under consideration.

Rule 79

Officers, conduct of business and voting

The rules relating to officers, conduct of business and voting of the Assembly apply, mutatis mutandis, to the proceedings of subsidiary organs except that the Chairman of a subsidiary organ may exercise the right to vote.

XV. SUSPENSION OF RIGHTS

Rule 80

Suspension of the exercise of voting rights

A member of the Assembly which is in arrears in the payment of its financial contributions to the Authority shall have no vote if the amount of its arrears equals or exceeds the amount of the contributions due from it for the preceding two full years. The Assembly may, nevertheless, permit such a member of the Assembly to vote if it is satisfied that the failure to pay is due to conditions beyond the control of the member.

Rule 81

Suspension of the exercise of rights and privileges of membership

1. A member of the Authority which has grossly and persistently violated the provisions of Part XI of the United Nations Convention on the Law of the Sea may be suspended from the exercise of the rights and privileges of membership by the Assembly upon the recommendation of the Council.

2. No action may be taken under paragraph 1 until the Seabed Disputes Chamber of the International Tribunal for the Law of the Sea has found that a member of the Authority has grossly and persistently violated the provisions of Part XI of the Convention.

XVI. OBSERVERS

Rule 82

1. The following may participate as observers in the Assembly:

(a) States and entities referred to in article 305 of the United Nations Convention on the Law of the Sea which are not members of the Authority;

(b) National liberation movements which in their respective regions are recognized by the Organization of African Unity or by the League of Arab States;

(c) Observers to the Third United Nations Conference on the Law of the Sea who have signed the Final Act and who are not referred to in article 305, paragraph 1 (c), (d), (e) and (f), of the United Nations Convention on the Law of the Sea;

(d) The United Nations, its specialized agencies, the International Atomic Energy Agency and other intergovernmental organizations invited by the Assembly;

(e) Non-governmental organizations with which the Secretary-General has entered into arrangements in accordance with article 169, paragraph 1, of the United Nations Convention on the Law of the Sea, and other non-governmental organizations invited by the Assembly which have demonstrated their interest in matters under the consideration by the Assembly.

2. Observers referred to in paragraph 1 (a), (b) and (c) of this rule may participate subject to the provisions of these rules in the deliberations of the Assembly and its subsidiary organs but shall not be entitled to participate in the taking of decisions.

3. Observers referred to in paragraph 1 (d) of this rule may participate in the deliberations of the Assembly upon the invitation of the President on questions within the scope of their competence.

4. Written statements submitted by observers referred to in paragraph 1 (d) of this rule shall be distributed by the Secretariat to the members of the Assembly.

5. Observers referred to in paragraph 1 (e) of this rule may sit at public meetings of the Assembly, and upon the invitation of the President and subject to the approval by the Assembly may make oral statements on questions within the scope of their activities.

6. Written statements submitted by observers referred to in paragraph 1 (e) of this rule within the scope of their activities which are relevant to the work of the Assembly should be made available by the Secretariat in the quantities and in the languages in which the statements are submitted.

XVII. ELECTIONS TO ORGANS

Members of the Council

Rule 83

Nominations

1. Before electing the members of the Council, the Assembly shall establish lists of countries fulfilling the criteria for membership in the groups of States referred to in rule 84 (a) to (d). If a State fulfils the criteria for membership in more than one group it will be included in the lists of all relevant groups but it may only be proposed by one group for election to the Council and it shall represent only that group in voting in the Council.

2. Each group of States referred to in rule 84 (a) to (d) shall be represented in the Council by those members nominated by that group. Each group shall nominate only as many candidates as the number of seats required to be filled by that group. When the number of potential candidates in each of the groups referred to in rule 84 (a) to (e) exceeds the number of seats available in each of those respective groups, as a general rule, the principle of rotation shall apply. States members of each of those groups shall determine how this principle shall apply in those groups.

Rule 84

Elections

The Council shall consist of 36 members of the Authority elected by the Assembly in the following order:

(a) Four members from among those States Parties which, during the last five years for which statistics are available, have either consumed more than 2 per cent in value terms of total world consumption or have had net imports of more than 2 per cent in value terms of total world imports of the commodities produced from the categories of minerals to be derived from the Area, provided that the four members shall include one State from the Eastern European region having the largest economy in that region in terms of gross domestic product and the State, on the date of entry into force of the Convention, having the largest economy in terms of gross domestic product, if such States wish to be represented in this group;

(b) Four members from among the eight States Parties which have made the largest investments in preparation for and in the conduct of activities in the Area, either directly or through their nationals;

(c) Four members from among States Parties which, on the basis of production in areas under their jurisdiction, are major net exporters of the categories of minerals to be derived from the Area, including at least two developing States whose exports of such minerals have a substantial bearing upon their economies;

(d) Six members from among developing States Parties, representing special interests. The special interests to be represented shall include those of States with large populations, States which are land-locked or geographically disadvantaged, island States, States which are major importers of the categories of minerals to be derived from the Area, States which are potential producers of such minerals and least developed States;

(e) Eighteen members elected according to the principle of ensuring an equitable geographical distribution of seats in the Council as a whole, provided that each geographical region shall have at least one member elected under this subparagraph. For this purpose, the geographical regions shall be Africa, Asia, Eastern Europe, Latin America and the Caribbean and Western Europe and Others.

Rule 85

Terms of office

Each member of the Council shall be elected for four years. At the first election, however, the term of one half of the members of each group referred to in rule 84 shall be for two years. Determination of the members whose terms are to expire at the end of two years shall, as a general rule, be left to the agreement of each group. If no agreement can be reached, the members whose terms are to expire at the end of two years shall be chosen by lot to be drawn by the President of the Assembly immediately after the first election.

Rule 86

Eligibility for re-election

Members of the Council shall be eligible for re-election, but due regard should be paid to the desirability of rotation of membership. Members of the Council which were elected upon the nomination by one of the groups referred to in rule 84 (a) to (d) but which fulfil the criteria for membership in other groups, may be re-elected to the Council upon the nomination by one of those groups.

Rule 87

By-elections

Should a member cease to belong to the Council before its term of office expires, a by-election shall be held separately at the next session of the Assembly to elect a member for the unexpired term.

The Secretary-General of the Authority

Rule 88

Election of the Secretary-General

The Secretary-General shall be elected for four years by the Assembly from among the candidates proposed by the Council and may be re-elected.

The Enterprise 2/

Rule 89

Elections

1. The Assembly shall elect, upon the recommendation of the Council, the fifteen members of the Governing Board of the Enterprise.

2. In the election of the members of the Board, due regard shall be paid to the principle of equitable geographical distribution. In submitting nominations of candidates for election to the Board, members of the Authority shall bear in mind the need to nominate candidates of the highest standard of competence, with qualifications in relevant fields, so as to ensure the viability and success of the Enterprise.

Rule 90

Terms of office

1. Members of the Board shall be elected for four years and may be re-elected; due regard shall be paid to the principle of rotation of membership.

2. Members of the Board shall continue in office until their successors are elected.

Rule 91

By-elections

If the office of a member of the Board becomes vacant, the Assembly shall, in accordance with rule 89, elect a new member for the remainder of his predecessor's term.

2/ According to the Agreement relating to the implementation of Part XI of the United Nations Convention on the Law of the Sea, the Secretariat of the Authority shall perform the functions of the Enterprise until it begins to operate independently of the Secretariat. Upon the approval of a plan of work for exploitation for an entity other than the Enterprise, or upon receipt by the Council of an application for a joint-venture operation with the Enterprise, the Council shall take up the issue of the functioning of the Enterprise independently of the Secretariat of the Authority. If joint-venture operations with the Enterprise accord with sound commercial principles, the Council shall issue a directive pursuant to article 170, paragraph 2, of the Convention providing for such independent functioning.

Rule 92

The Director-General of the Enterprise

The Assembly shall, upon the recommendation of the Council and the nomination of the Governing Board, elect the Director-General of the Enterprise, who shall not be a member of the Board. The Director-General shall hold office for a fixed term, not exceeding five years, and may be re-elected for further terms.

XVIII. ADMINISTRATIVE AND BUDGETARY QUESTIONS

Rule 93

Proposed annual budget

The Assembly shall consider and approve the proposed annual budget of the Authority submitted by the Council taking into account the recommendations of the Finance Committee.

Rule 94

Financial implications of resolutions

No resolution involving expenditure shall be recommended for approval by the Assembly unless it is accompanied by an estimate of expenditures prepared by the Secretary-General and any recommendations of the Finance Committee.

Rule 95 3/

Contributions

The Assembly shall assess the contributions of members of the Authority to the administrative budget of the Authority in accordance with an agreed scale of assessment based upon the scale used for the regular budget of the United Nations until the Authority shall have sufficient income from other sources to meet its administrative expenses.

XIX. FINANCE COMMITTEE

Rule 96

Finance Committee

1. The Assembly shall elect 15 members of the Finance Committee from the candidates nominated by the States Parties by taking into due account the need for equitable geographical distribution and the representation of special interests. Members of the Finance Committee shall have appropriate qualifications relevant to financial matters.

3/ According to the Agreement relating to the implementation of Part XI of the United Nations Convention on the Law of the Sea, the administrative expenses of the Authority shall be met through the budget of the United Nations until the end of the year following the year during which that Agreement enters into force.

2. Candidates for the election to the Finance Committee shall be nominated by the States Parties. They shall be of the highest standards of competence and integrity.

3. No two members of the Finance Committee shall be nationals of the same State Party.

4. Each group of States referred to in rule 84 (a) to (d) shall be represented on the Finance Committee by at least one member. Until the Authority has sufficient funds other than assessed contributions to meet its administrative expenses, the membership of the Finance Committee shall include representatives of the five largest financial contributors to the administrative budget of the Authority. Thereafter, the election of one member from each group shall be on the basis of nomination by the members of the respective group, without prejudice to the possibility of further members being elected from each group.

5. Members of the Finance Committee shall hold office for a term of five years. They shall be eligible for re-election for a further term.

6. In the event of the death, incapacity or resignation of a member of the Finance Committee prior to the expiration of the term of office, the Assembly shall elect for the remainder of the term a member from the same geographical region or group of States.

XX. AMENDMENTS

Rule 97

Method of amendment

These rules of procedure may be amended by a decision of the Assembly, taken by a simple majority of the members of the Assembly present and voting, after a committee has considered the proposed amendment.

43. STATEMENT OF THE PRESIDENT OF THE ASSEMBLY ON THE WORK OF THE ASSEMBLY DURING THE SECOND PART OF ITS FIRST SESSION, 27 FEBRUARY - 17 MARCH 1995

Doc. no.: ISBA/A/L.1/Rev.1 22 March 1995

1. The second part of the first session of the Assembly of the International Seabed Authority was convened at Kingston, Jamaica, from 27 February to 17 March 1995. The first part, which was primarily of a ceremonial nature, had also been held at Kingston from 16 to 18 November 1994 to commemorate the establishment of the International Seabed Authority, which coincided with the entry into force of the United Nations Convention on the Law of the Sea. The third part of the first session is scheduled to be held at Kingston from 7 to 18 August 1995.

Opening of the session

2. Mr. Hans Corell, Under-Secretary-General for Legal Affairs and Legal Counsel of the United Nations, acting as the Temporary President of the Assembly, opened the second part of the first session. During the initial meeting (6th meeting of the plenary), the Assembly decided to commence its work under the draft rules of procedure recommended by the Preparatory Commission for the International Seabed Authority and for the International Tribunal for the Law of the Sea until such time as it adopted its own rules of procedure. The Assembly also amended the provisional agenda (ISBA/A/1) by changing the order of items 2, 3 and 4, as follows:

2. Election of the President.

3. Adoption of the agenda.

4. Adoption of the rules of procedure.

Election of the President

3. At the 7th meeting of the plenary, the Assembly elected by acclamation Mr. Hasjim Djalal (Indonesia) as President of its first session and also adopted its agenda (ISBA/A/4).

Election of Vice-Presidents, appointment of a Working Group on the Draft Rules of Procedure and appointment of the Credentials Committee

4. The Assembly elected by acclamation four Vice-Presidents: Algeria, Canada, Mexico and the Russian Federation. It also appointed 10 members of the Working Group on the Draft Rules of Procedure: Egypt (Chairman), Brazil, Germany, Indonesia, Jamaica, Poland, Republic of Korea, Russian Federation, Senegal and United Kingdom of Great Britain and Northern Ireland. It further appointed a 9-member Credentials Committee, consisting of Austria (Chairman), Cameroon, China, Costa Rica, Japan, Nigeria, Poland, United States of America and Uruguay.

Working Group on the Draft Rules of Procedure

5. The Preparatory Commission for the International Seabed Authority and for the International Tribunal for the Law of the Sea had recommended to the Assembly for its consideration draft rules of procedure (LOS/PCN/WP.20/Rev.3). In addition, and in the light of the adoption by the United Nations General Assembly on 28 July 1994 of the Agreement relating to the implementation of Part XI of the United Nations Convention on the Law of the Sea (General Assembly resolution 48/263), the Secretariat prepared document ISBA/A/WP.1 containing suggestions for revising the draft rules of procedure of the Assembly issued by the Preparatory Commission taking into account the provisions of the Agreement. At the request of the Assembly, the Secretariat then prepared a working paper by merging the two documents, and the new document (ISBA/A/WP.2) was then considered by the Working Group. Following discussions, the Working Group submitted to the Assembly an updated version of the draft rules of procedure (ISBA/A/WP.3). The Assembly subsequently discussed the document at the 14th and 15th plenary meetings, and adopted the draft rules of procedure, together with a draft rsolution (ISBA/A/L.2).

The Credentials Committee

6. The Credentials Committee held one meeting, on 14 March 1995, at which it had before it a memorandum prepared by the Secretariat dated 14 March 1995 on the status of credentials of representatives participating in the second part of the first session of the Assembly of the International Seabed Authority. Having examined the credentials of the representatives, the Committee recommended in its report (ISBA/A/5) a draft resolution accepting the credentials of the representatives concerned. At the 14th plenary meeting, on 16 March 1995, the Assembly approved the report of the Credentials Committee (ISBA/A/5).

Election of the members of the Council

7. The Assembly decided, in accordance with section 3, paragraph 10, of the Annex to the Agreement, that countries fulfilling the criteria for membership in each group of States referred to in section 3, paragraph 15 (a) to (d), of the Annex to the Agreement would nominate their candidates for election to the Council of the Authority and would also determine how the principle of rotation would apply in case the number of potential candidates in any of the groups exceeded the number of seats available in that group. The Assembly also decided that regional groups would nominate their candidates for the Council according to the principle of ensuring an equitable geographical distribution of seats in the Council as a whole, pursuant to section 3, paragraph 15 (e), of the Annex to the Agreement, bearing in mind the candidates to be nominated under paragraph 15 (a) to (d).

8. In view of the complexity of determining the criteria for membership in the various groups of States in the Council, as specified in section 3, paragraph 15, of the Annex to the Agreement, and in order to facilitate the determination of States falling under various groups, the Secretariat, at the

request of a number of delegations, had circulated an informal working paper, dated 9 November 1994, entitled "Indicative list of States which would fulfil the criteria for membership in the various groups of States in the Council of the International Seabed Authority in accordance with paragraph 15 of section 3 of the Annex to the Agreement relating to the implementation of Part XI of the United Nations Convention on the Law of the Sea of 10 December 1982". During the inter-sessional period and thereafter, the Secretariat received from delegations suggestions for corrections with regard to the contents of the informal paper. On the basis of such inputs, the Secretariat prepared an updated version of the informal paper, and circulated it on 27 February 1995. In view of difficulties in ascertaining appropriate statistical and other data, it is understood that the updated version should be regarded as a guide only, not as establishing absolute or definitive criteria, and shall not prejudice the rights of delegations to submit or use other data.

9. The Assembly decided that for the purpose of nominating their candidates and determining how the principle of rotation would apply, States which considered themselves as fulfilling the criteria for membership in each group of States referred to in section 3, paragraph 15 (a) to (d), of the Annex to the Agreement should meet among themselves.

10. Accordingly, the various groups of States met. The meetings of the group of States referred to in paragraph 15 (a), "States Parties which, during the last five years for which statistics are available, have either consumed more than 2 per cent in value terms of total world consumption or have had net imports of more than 2 per cent in value terms of total world imports of the commodities produced from the categories of minerals to be derived from the Area", known as Group A, were attended by Belgium, Brazil, China, France, Germany, Italy, Japan, the Republic of Korea, the Russian Federation, the United Kingdom and the United States (Coordinator). The Group met to discuss the nomination of four States meeting the criteria contained in that paragraph for election to the Council.

11. The Group decided not to recommend a list of States meeting the criteria of paragraph 15 (a). Members of the Group held different views on the interpretation of the criteria. Some expressed the view that the criteria required that a consuming or importing State must meet the 2 per cent threshold for the value of each of the four minerals (manganese, copper, cobalt and nickel). Others expressed the view that the criteria required that States meet the threshold for the combined value of all four minerals. Without prejudice to the resolution of this question in regard to future elections, the Group decided to take a flexible and inclusive approach to its deliberations.

12. The Group took note of the fact that the United States, the United Kingdom, the Russian Federation, Japan, Germany, Belgium and Italy informed the President of the Assembly of their interest in being nominated for election to the Council. Belgium, Italy and Germany decided to withdraw their requests to be nominated by the Group on the understanding that, without prejudice to the interests of other States meeting the criteria in paragraph 15 (a), the application of the principle of rotation in future elections would provide opportunities for their election to the Council as representatives of the Group.

13. The United States indicated its readiness to be elected to a two-year term, while Japan and the United Kingdom wished to be elected to a four-year term. The Russian Federation expressed its desire to be elected to a four-year term, but indicated its readiness to consider being elected to a two-year term on certain conditions, namely:

(a) That in its decision the Assembly will affirm, at the time of election, that paragraph 15 (a) requires the inclusion of one State from the Eastern European region having the largest economy in that region in terms of gross domestic product and of the State, on the date of entry into force of the Convention, having the largest economy in terms of gross domestic product, should those States seek re-election to the Council under that paragraph;

(b) That the principle of rotation would apply to Japan and the United Kingdom after four years;

(c) That the desire of the Russian Federation to be elected to a four-year term was the only obstacle to the election of the Council by the Assembly.

14. After the initial meetings of the group of States referred to in paragraph 15 (b), "States Parties which have made the largest investments in preparation for and in the conduct of activities in the Area, either directly or through their nationals", known as Group B, the coordinator of the Group, Canada, informed the President that after considering information provided by delegations with respect to investments by their States in preparation for and in the conduct of activities in the Area, the delegations unanimously agreed that the following States constituted the eight largest investors for the purposes of paragraph 15 (b): China, France, Germany (Coordinator), India, Japan, Netherlands, Russian Federation and United States.

15. The Group of the eight largest investors proceeded to discuss the nomination of the four candidates to represent the Group in the Council. Five States - China, France, Germany, India and the Netherlands - declared their intention to represent the Group in the Council. In consultations between the interested States as well as between them and the coordinator, it was not possible to reach agreement on which four States should be nominated. It was also not possible to decide which of the candidates would be nominated to serve on the Council for a two-year term or for a four-year term. Also unresolved was the question of the application of the principle of rotation.

16. The meetings of the group of States referred to in paragraph 15 (c), "States Parties which, on the basis of production in areas under their jurisdiction, are major net exporters of the categories of minerals to be derived from the Area", known as Group C, were attended by Australia (Coordinator), Brazil, Canada, Chile, China, Cuba, France, Gabon, India, Indonesia, Mauritania, Mexico, Namibia, the Philippines, Poland, the Russian Federation, South Africa, the United States and Zambia.

17. Six countries from this Group - Australia, Chile, Gabon, Indonesia, Poland and Zambia - presented their candidatures for the four seats available in this Group. Although some delegations have indicated a willingness to be flexible at the current stage - particularly in the light of the fact that other issues still need to be resolved - there has been no final agreement on the four candidates.

18. It was also agreed that the principle of rotation should apply to future elections of candidates for the Group, and that this should be interpreted as meaning that there is a general expectation that members of this Group will move on and off the Council. This would not preclude the possibility of individual countries making informal arrangements between themselves, such as reciprocal support arrangements. Nor would it preclude countries having consecutive terms on the Council, if this was agreed by the Group.

19. It was further agreed that at the current stage it was not appropriate to make a definitive list of countries eligible for election to the Group. However, some delegations suggested that this was something which should be considered in the future. Reference was made to an informal understanding reached at the Third United Nations Conference on the Law of the Sea that the Group should reflect an equal balance between developing and developed countries. Other delegations stated that they were not aware of that understanding. The issue of which candidates would be nominated for a two-year term and which would be nominated for a four-year term was not discussed.

20. The meetings of the group of States referred to in paragraph 15 (d), "developing States Parties, representing special interests. The special interests to be represented shall include those of States with large populations, States which are land-locked or geographically disadvantaged,

island States, States which are major importers of the categories of minerals to be derived from the Area, States which are potential producers of such minerals and least developed States", known as Group D, were attended by Argentina, Bangladesh, Brazil, Burkina Faso, Cameroon, China, Costa Rica, Cuba, Egypt, Fiji, Gabon, India, Indonesia (Coordinator), Jamaica, Kuwait, Malaysia, Malta, Marshall Islands, Mauritania, Mexico, Mozambique, Myanmar, Nigeria, Oman, Paraguay, Philippines, Republic of Korea, Sudan, Trinidad and Tobago, United Arab Emirates, Viet Nam and Zambia. Twelve States - Argentina, Bangladesh, Brazil, Cameroon, Egypt, Jamaica, Kuwait, Nigeria, Oman, Paraguay, Philippines and Sudan - declared their intention to seek nomination to the Council within this Group, and other States also expressed their interest in being nominated in either Group D or Group E, which would consist of 18 members elected according to the principle of ensuring an equitable geographical distribution of seats in the Council as a whole. In view of the discussions taking place in other groups, no definitive list of candidates for this Group has been drawn up.

21. The President conducted intensive consultations with the Chairmen of the regional groups to ascertain their views as to what constitutes "an equitable geographical distribution of seats in the Council as a whole". He requested the respective Chairmen to seek the views of the members of their regional groups. All regional groups considered this issue, and varying opinions and points of view were expressed. Reference was made to the distribution of seats in various other international organizations, and examples were offered of how seats in such organizations were distributed among the regional groups.

22. The President, after several lengthy discussions, proposed a formula for allocating the seats in the Council in respect of each regional group. His proposal took into account the concept of proportionality and the need to maintain a balance in the representation in the Council.

23. The President also made the following suggestions:

(a) The distribution of seats among the geographical regions for this election of the members of the Council shall be without prejudice to the distribution of seats among the geographical regions for the next election of the members of the Council, which will have to take into account the new membership of the Authority at that time;

(b) Representation in the present Council by a member of a particular group of States referred to in section 3, paragraph 15 (a) to (d), of the Annex to the Agreement, shall, whether or not the principle of rotation is applied in that Group, be without prejudice to its representing other groups of States in the future; at the same time, the representation by members in the present Council of the various groups of States does not preclude the rights of other States to represent these groups in the future;

(c) The general balance of seats established in the present Council between developing and developed countries shall be maintained in the future.

24. The President's proposal regarding the allocation of seats in the Council was discussed extensively in meetings of regional groups. No unanimous decision emerged from the discussions of the proposal, and it was not yet possible to reach consensus on this issue. It is expected that the matter will be further discussed and, it is to be hoped, resolved during the third part of the first session of the International Seabed Authority, to be held at Kingston from 7 to 18 August 1995.

44. STATEMENT OF THE PRESIDENT ON THE WORK OF THE ASSEMBLY DURING THE THIRD PART OF ITS FIRST SESSION, 7 - 18 AUGUST 1995

Doc. no.: ISBA/A/L.7/Rev.1 11 October 1995

1. The third part of the first session of the Assembly of the International Seabed Authority was held at Kingston, Jamaica, from 7 to 18 August 1995.

2. At the opening meeting (the 16th meeting of the Plenary), I reported on the inter-sessional consultations I had undertaken in May in New York on the outstanding issues relating to the composition of the Council, in particular those pertaining to Groups A, B, C and D. My report on these inter-sessional consultations can be found in document ISBA/A/L.3 of 9 August 1995 and ISBA/A/L.3/Corr.1 of 15 August 1995.

3. In presenting my report, I reiterated that there was an urgent need to resolve the problems relating to the composition of the Council, and I requested the regional groups and other interested parties to engage in serious consultations and negotiations in order to achieve the necessary solutions as quickly as possible. I also reminded the Assembly that there were several other items on its agenda that needed to be dealt with. Among these were: election of the members of the Finance Committee; presentation of the final report of the Preparatory Commission; discussion of those sections of the final report on matters relating to the Authority that the Assembly may decide to consider, including the draft Agreement between the International Seabed Authority and the Government of Jamaica regarding the Headquarters of the International Seabed Authority; the draft Protocol on Privileges and Immunities of the International Seabed Authority and the Draft Agreement concerning the Relationship between the United Nations and the International Seabed Authority; appointment of the Secretary-General of the Authority, as soon as the list of candidates for the election of the Secretary-General is recommended to the Assembly by the Council; follow-up of the decisions taken by the Preparatory Commission on the implementation of resolution II; transfer of the property and records of the Preparatory Commission to the Authority; provisional budget and financial organization; follow-up of the training programme; organization of the secretariat of the International Seabed Authority; date of the second session of the Assembly; and any other matters.

Election of the members of the Council

4. During the last few days I have held numerous consultations with the Chairmen of the regional groups as well as other interested parties. During these meetings I stressed that it was important, especially for the reputation of the Authority, that the Council be established as soon as possible. I wish

to thank all the delegations who worked very hard in an attempt to bring the negotiations to a successful conclusion.

5. During my consultations with Groups A, B, C and D, the following developments occurred. The members of Group A reaffirmed the candidacy of Japan, the United Kingdom of Great Britain and Northern Ireland, the Russian Federation and the United States of America for the Council. It was also pointed out that Japan and the United Kingdom had agreed to four-year terms and the United States to a two-year term. The position of the Russian Federation on the matter is set out in paragraphs 4 to 6 of the statement of the President at the opening meeting of the third part of the first session (ISBA/A/L.3). At the same time some delegations expressed the view that the decision on the length of terms should be taken subject to agreed arrangements in Group B. However the principle of rotation in Group A was still unresolved.

6. As regards Group B, I felt that despite intensive consultations the deliberations had not moved forward sufficiently and it appeared that the Group needed more time to settle their arrangements.

7. The situation in Group C is very promising since, through the tremendous efforts on the part of all concerned, the Group was successful in reaching an understanding. They agreed on the selection of four candidates - Chile and Australia for two-year terms and Indonesia and Zambia for four-year terms. There was a further understanding that Indonesia and Zambia would serve only for two years and then relinquish their seats to Gabon and Poland, without prejudice to the right of any other Group members, including Indonesia and Zambia, to contest any seats as they became vacant.

8. As for Group D, I continued to urge its members to identify the six candidates for the seats available to that Group and to reach agreement on who will represent the special interests stipulated in the Convention and in the Agreement on the implementation of Part XI of the Convention.

9. As regards Group E, it was felt that the selection of members to be elected for two or four years and the distribution of seats among the respective geographical groups were possible. I was gratified to note that the Group had taken a somewhat flexible position on these issues.

10. Since it was not possible during this session to make sufficient progress to elect the Council, I have consulted with the Chairmen of the regional groups and the bureau regarding the holding of informal inter-sessional consultations. There was no objection to holding such consultations in New York from 6 to 8 December 1995 following the signing ceremony of the Agreement on straddling fish stocks and highly migratory fish stocks and the discussion of the law of the sea item in the General Assembly. It was pointed out that it was important to have a clear perception of the purpose of the negotiations, that there was a need to accommodate the views of others and that there must be a firm commitment to making the consultations as meaningful as possible so as to assist the Assembly at its next session in establishing the Council and the Finance Committee and appointing the Secretary-General.

<u>Other matters considered by the Assembly</u>

11. The Assembly held preliminary discussions on the question of the priorities of the Authority during its initial phase of work; on decisions to be made in relation to the recommendations of the Preparatory Commission for the International Seabed Authority and for the International Tribunal for the Law of the Sea; and on follow-up of the Commission's decisions concerning the registered pioneer investors, including the training to be provided by them.

12. It was suggested that two themes be considered by the Assembly, one being the issue of transparency in the relationship between the Council and the wider membership of the Assembly, and the other being the development of principles

regarding environmental protection. It was felt that consideration of those issues need not prejudge the Council's competence in these matters.

13. The Assembly also held a discussion on the training programme relating to seabed mining. The Secretariat informed the Assembly that it had received a number of reports from registered pioneer investors regarding the discharge of their obligations, including the provision of training to persons designated by the Preparatory Commission or by the Assembly.

Discussion on the establishment of the Finance Committee

14. During the discussions on this subject, the view was expressed that informal consultations to be conducted by the President with the Chairmen of the regional groups were the best way forward to resolve the issue regarding the establishment of the Finance Committee. It was felt that a formal debate in Plenary might distract from the central issue of establishing the Council. Another view expressed was that it would be appropriate to hold a discussion on the Finance Committee in the Plenary while the President conducted consultations with the Chairmen of the regional groups.

15. Following this preliminary exchange of views I held some consultations with the Chairmen of the regional groups, but no substantial progress was achieved. In view of the special qualifications for membership of the Finance Committee, I should like to invite delegations to take into account the need for the candidates they propose to possess the qualifications stipulated in the Agreement and the rules of procedure and be prepared to undertake all the functions required of them.

Discussion on the Headquarters Agreement

16. The Assembly considered the draft Headquarters Agreement prepared by the Preparatory Commission at its 21st meeting, and felt that it was basically acceptable and could be used as a starting-point for negotiations with the Government of Jamaica. It approved the setting up of a small, open-ended ad hoc Working Group to identify issues that should be taken into account by the Authority or the Secretary-General in such negotiations.

17. It was agreed that the President of the Assembly should appoint a coordinator for the Working Group. The Assembly decided that the Ad Hoc Working Group would deal also with the Protocol on the Privileges and Immunities of the Authority, but that priority would be given to the examination of the Headquarters Agreement. The Assembly authorized the Secretary-General, after his appointment, to negotiate, as a matter of priority, the Headquarters Agreement with the Government of Jamaica and to submit the final draft of that Agreement to the Assembly for adoption.

18. The Vice-President of the Assembly from Mexico was appointed Coordinator of the Working Group, which held two meetings on Wednesday, 16 August, and Thursday, 17 August 1995. During these meetings the Working Group examined the draft Headquarters Agreement prepared by the Preparatory Commission.

Report of the Credentials Committee

19. During the third part of the first session of the Assembly, the Credentials Committee held two meetings, on 8 and 16 August 1995. The first meeting was devoted to the organization of the Committee's work. In view of the fact that Mr. Helmut Tuerk could not attend the third part of the first session of the Assembly, the Committee decided to elect Mr. Alexander Grubmayer (Austria) as its new Chairman.

20. After examining the credentials of delegations, the Credentials Committee presented its report (ISBA/A/7).

Discussions on the participation of the Federal Republic of Yugoslavia (Serbia and Montenegro)

21. The Chairman of the Credentials Committee informed the Assembly that the Federal Republic of Yugoslavia (Serbia and Montenegro) had submitted credentials stating that its Permanent Representative to the United Nations in New York and the Minister Counsellor at the Permanent Mission had been authorized to represent the State at the third part of the first session of the International Seabed Authority. During discussions in the Credentials Committee, it had been pointed out that since the Federal Republic of Yugoslavia (Serbia and Montenegro) could not continue automatically the membership of the former Socialist Federal Republic of Yugoslavia in treaty organs, it should not be allowed to participate in the session.

22. Since the Credentials Committee had decided that it did not have the authority to take a decision on the matter, a draft decision on the participation of the Federal Republic of Yugoslavia (Serbia and Montenegro) was submitted by the delegations of Croatia, Egypt, Kuwait, Malaysia, Oman, Qatar, Senegal, Tunisia, United Arab Emirates and the United States of America. The draft decision (ISBA/A/L.4) called upon the Assembly to decide that the Federal Republic of Yugoslavia should not participate at its first session. Prior to the adoption of the decision, some delegations said that they would not participate in the voting because they felt it unnecessary for the Assembly to take a decision on the matter. The Assembly then adopted the decision at its 23rd meeting without a vote.

Presentation of the final report of the Preparatory Commission

23. At the 22nd meeting of the Plenary, the Rapporteur-General of the Preparatory Commission (Ambassador Kenneth Rattray of Jamaica) presented its final report (LOS/PCN/153) on behalf of the Chairman of the Preparatory Commission. The report was prepared in accordance with paragraph 11 of resolution I of the Third United Nations Conference on the Law of the Sea. As required by paragraph 11 of resolution I, the report excludes the recommendations of the Preparatory Commission regarding the practical arrangements for the establishment of the International Tribunal for the Law of the Sea.

24. The report consists of 13 volumes, which represent a comprehensive documentation of the work of the Preparatory Commission during its sessions from 1983 to 1994. The report is structured on the basis of the institutional framework of the Preparatory Commission, which consisted of: the Plenary, including the General Committee; Special Commission 1; Special Commission 2; Special Commission 3; and Special Commission 4. For the purpose of the present report the Assembly is not concerned with Special Commission 4, whose area of responsibility related only to the Tribunal.

25. I wish to express my sincere gratitude and also that of the Authority to Ambassador Rattray for his comprehensive statement (ISBA/A/L.6) presenting the final report of the Preparatory Commission.

Future administrative and budgetary arrangements for the Authority

26. According to section 1, paragraph 14, of the annex to the Agreement on the implementation of Part XI of the Convention, until the end of the year following the year during which the Agreement enters into force, the administrative

expenses of the Authority shall be met through the budget of the United Nations. Within the biennial cycle of the budget of the United Nations, budgetary provisions have thus been made for the expenses of the Authority, up to the end of 1995, amounting to $776,000, under a newly created budget section, section 33, entitled "International Seabed Authority".

27. The budget of the Authority for 1996 was to have been prepared by the Secretary-General of the Authority. However, in the absence of the Secretary-General of the Authority and in the context of the submission and review of the proposed programme budget of the United Nations for the biennium 1996-1997, the Secretariat of the United Nations has proposed, solely as a stopgap measure, "to retain [under sect. 33] the 1994-1995 appropriation in the resource base for 1996-1997 [i.e., $776,000], pending submission of the budget of the Authority, as agreed by its Assembly, to the General Assembly at its fiftieth session". 1/

28. This is a contingency measure proposed only because a budget submission containing a detailed analysis and estimation of resource requirements prepared by the Secretary-General of the Authority does not exist. It should be noted that the proposed amount cannot fully cover the expenses of the Authority in 1996. It should be noted further that it will be impossible to have any budget submission prepared by the Secretary-General of the Authority before March 1996, at the earliest, which would be too late for it to be considered by the General Assembly at its fiftieth session.

29. It is thus imperative that a proper budget submission be made in advance of the fiftieth session of the General Assembly. In view of the fact that the expenses of the Authority are being met through the budget of the United Nations and that the Secretary-General of the United Nations has been filling the lacunae until the Secretary-General of the Authority is appointed, I proposed that the Assembly take a decision to entrust the task of preparing the budget of the Authority for 1996 to the Secretary-General of the United Nations and submitted a draft decision to that effect (ISBA/A/L.5).

30. With regard to the secretariat arrangements for the Authority before the Secretary-General enters on duty, certain provisions are absolutely essential to cover the gap between 1 October 1995 and the time the secretariat of the Authority is initiated by the Secretary-General of the Authority himself. This is especially urgent given that the Kingston Office for the Law of the Sea, which has been providing secretariat services to the Preparatory Commission and, since November 1994, to the Authority, is scheduled to be abolished on 30 September 1995. In view of this situation I also proposed in the draft decision that the Assembly request the continued use of the facilities and staff of the Kingston Office for the Law of the Sea as the interim secretariat of the Authority from 1 October 1995 until the time the Secretary-General of the Authority enters on duty, and also that it authorize the Secretary-General of the United Nations to administer the interim secretariat.

31. I also suggested that for the purpose of bridging the gap between 1 October 1995 and the entry on duty of the Secretary-General of the Authority, the interim secretariat should make the necessary arrangements so that the existing agreements with the Government of Jamaica, e.g., the Headquarters Agreement and the Protocol on Privileges and Immunities, are extended. The interim secretariat would also initiate some of the preparatory work so that the preliminary organizational matters can be dealt with efficiently in the start-up phase. As you may recall, the recommendations of the Preparatory Commission regarding the programme of work for the start-up phase are contained in document LOS/PCN/143.

32. The costs of the meetings of the Assembly next year will constitute one important factor to be borne in mind in drawing up the budget for the Authority in 1996. Another important factor will be the cost of providing, through the facilities and staff of the Kingston Office for the Law of the Sea, interim secretariat services for the Authority. I therefore suggested that the Assembly

should draw the attention of the Secretary-General of the United Nations to these factors, so as to provide him with guidance in drawing up that budget.

33. During the discussion on these proposals it was clarified that although the actual amount required to cover these expenses could not be accurately calculated at this time, the draft budget to be proposed would be based on the same assumptions and requirements as provided for in the initial budget approved by the General Assembly of the United Nations last year. The Assembly then approved these proposals by adopting the draft decision submitted by the President (ISBA/A/L.5).

Future meetings

34. I suggest that during the first week of the next session, the Assembly should concentrate on the election of the Council, the establishment of the Finance Committee and the appointment of the Secretary-General. The next priority should be the adoption of the rules of procedure of the Council.

35. On the basis of the decision adopted by the Assembly (ISBA/A/L.5), I have requested the Secretariat to provide for two meetings of the Authority in 1996, as follows:

(a) The first meeting to take place from 11 March 1996 for up to three weeks, if necessary, principally for the purpose of electing the Council and the Secretary-General and establishing the Finance Committee;

(b) The second meeting to take place for up to two weeks from 5 August 1996, primarily for the Finance Committee, the Council and Assembly to consider and decide on the budget and to establish the Legal and Technical Commission.

36. During these meetings, the Assembly and the Council, as far as practicable, shall also consider the other items on their agendas.

37. I take it that the Assembly takes note of the above statement and agrees to transmit it to the General Assembly of the United Nations for necessary action.

38. I wish to invite delegations to consider during the inter-sessional period the composition of the bureau for the next session.

* * *

39. Since this meeting brings to an end the first session of the Assembly, I should like to take the opportunity to express my sincere gratitude especially to the Vice-Presidents of the Assembly, the Chairmen of the regional groups, the coordinators of the interested groups and all delegations that have participated in the meetings of the Assembly of the International Seabed Authority. I should also like to thank all the members of the Secretariat who have facilitated our work.

40. Finally, I should be grateful if the Jamaican delegation would transmit my deep appreciation and that of all members of the Assembly to the Government and people of Jamaica for their very kind hospitality.

Notes

1/ Official Records of the General Assembly, Fiftieth Session, Supplement No. 6 (A/50/6/Rev.1), vol. II, part XIII, para. 33.4.

45. LETTER DATED 25 AUGUST 1995 FROM THE CHARGE D'AFFAIRES A.I. OF THE PERMANENT MISSION OF YUGOSLAVIA TO THE UNITED NATIONS ADDRESSED TO THE SECRETARY-GENERAL*
(STATEMENT DATED 25 AUGUST 1995 FROM THE FEDERAL FOREIGN OFFICE FOLLOWING THE DECISION TO PREVENT THE FEDERAL REPUBLIC OF YUGOSLAVIA FROM PARTICIPATION IN THE WORK OF THE ISBA ASSEMBLY)

Doc. no.: A/50/385 29 August 1995

I have the honour to transmit herewith the statement of the Federal Ministry of Foreign Affairs following the decision to prevent the Federal Republic of Yugoslavia from participating in the work of the first session of the Assembly of the International Seabed Authority (see annex).

I should be grateful if you would have the present letter and its annex circulated as an official document of the General Assembly under item 39 of the provisional agenda.

(Signed) Dragomir DJOKIC
Ambassador
Chargé d'affaires a.i.

ANNEX

Statement dated 25 August 1995 from the Federal Ministry of Foreign Affairs following the decision to prevent the Federal Republic of Yugoslavia from participating in the work of the Assembly of the International Seabed Authority

Following the decision of the Assembly of the International Seabed Authority to prevent the Federal Republic of Yugoslavia from participating in the first session of the Assembly, the Federal Ministry protests most strongly and points out that the decision represents a flagrant violation of the norms of international law. The decision to prevent the Federal Republic of Yugoslavia from participating has no legal basis in the United Nations Convention on the Law of the Sea of 1982 or in any other rule of international law and is in outright contravention of the opinion of the Legal Counsel of the United Nations that "the status of Yugoslavia as a party to the treaties is not affected by the adoption of General Assembly resolution 47/1".

---

* A/50/150.

Proceeding from the principled and consistent position that the adoption and implementation of the United Nations Convention on the Law of the Sea is an important contribution to the promotion of international cooperation in this field, Yugoslavia has ratified the Convention and, as a State party, has implemented and supported the provisions of the Convention in good faith. The Federal Republic of Yugoslavia has also acceded to the Agreement relating to the implementation of Part XI of the United Nations Convention on the Law of the Sea and fulfilled all the conditions for equitable participation in the work of the International Seabed Authority, its organs and, in particular, its Assembly.

The decision to prevent the Federal Republic of Yugoslavia from participating in the work of the Assembly, taken under the pressure of a small group of countries, is contrary to the basic principles on which the International Seabed Authority was established and organized. Participation of all State parties in the work of the Assembly is an essential precondition for the normal and legal functioning of the International Seabed Authority.

The Federal Ministry of Foreign Affairs wishes in particular to point out that this legally ungrounded and politically motivated decision constitutes a dangerous precedent at the very beginning of the work of the International Seabed Authority and that it threatens its role and reputation as a universal and independent forum of international cooperation in this field.

46. PROPOSED UN PROGRAMME BUDGET FOR THE BIENNIUM 1996-1997; PART XIII, SECTION 33; INTERNATIONAL SEABED AUTHORITY*

Doc. no.: A/50/6 (Sec. 33) 12 May 1995

Contents

Table 33.1 **Summary by object of expenditure**
(Thousands of United States dollars)

Object of expenditure	*1992-1993 expenditures*	*1994-1995 appropriations*	*Resource growth*		*Total before recosting*	*Recosting*	*1996-1997 estimates*
			Amount	*Percentage*			
Grants and contributions	—	776.0	—	—	776.0	—	776.0
Total	**—**	**776.0**	**—**	**—**	**776.0**	**—**	**776.0**

33.1 By its resolution 48/263 of 28 July 1994, the General Assembly decided to fund the administrative expenses of the International Seabed Authority until the end of the year following the year during which the Agreement relating to the implementation of Part XI of the United Nations Convention on the Law of the Sea of 10 December 1982 enters into force.

33.2 Under the provisions of the Agreement, the maximum period during which the administrative expenses of the Authority would be met by the United Nations would thus be until the end of 1999. It is not anticipated that the Agreement will enter into force in 1995. Consequently, the administrative expenses of the Authority will need to be met from the regular budget of the United Nations in 1996.

33.3 As indicated in paragraph 7 of the statement of programme budget implications submitted in connection with the adoption of resolution 48/263 (A/C.5/48/80), the Secretary-General intends to transmit to the General Assembly on an annual basis the budget of the Authority as agreed by its Assembly. It remains his view that such expenses should be treated outside the procedures related to the outline and to the contingency fund.

33.4 The programme budget for 1994-1995 includes an appropriation of $776,000 for the initial administrative expenses of the Authority in 1995. It is proposed to retain the 1994-1995 appropriation in the resource base for 1996-1997, pending submission of the budget of the Authority, as agreed by its Assembly, to the General Assembly at its fiftieth session.

---

* The present document contains section 33 of the proposed programme budget for the biennium 1996-1997. The complete proposed programme budget will subsequently be issued in final printed form as *Official Records of the General Assembly, Fiftieth Session, Supplement No.6* (A/50/6/Rev.1).

47. REVISED ESTIMATES FOR THE INTERNATIONAL SEABED AUTHORITY FOR 1996 - 7TH REPORT OF THE UN ADVISORY COMMITTEE ON ADMINISTRATIVE AND BUDGETARY QUESTIONS

Doc. no.: A/50/7/Add.6 6 December 1995

1. The Advisory Committee on Administrative and Budgetary Questions has considered the report of the Secretary-General relating to the revised estimates for the International Seabed Authority for 1996 (A/C.5/50/28). During its consideration of the report, the Advisory Committee met with representatives of the Secretary-General, who provided additional information.

2. As recalled in paragraph 2 of the Secretary-General's report, by its resolution 48/263 of 17 August 1994, the Assembly decided to fund the administrative expenses of the Authority until the end of the year following the year during which the agreement relating to the implementation of Part XI of the United Nations Convention on the Law of the Sea entered into force.

3. The Advisory Committee notes from paragraph 4 of the Secretary-General's report that, as the agreement has not yet entered into force, the administrative expenses of the Authority in 1996 are still to be met through the budget of the United Nations.

4. The Advisory Committee also notes that the Council responsible for proposing candidates for the position of the Secretary-General of the Authority has not yet been established, and thus the election of the Secretary-General of the Authority has not taken place.

5. With regard to the entry into force of the agreement, the Advisory Committee recalls article 6 of the annex to General Assembly resolution 48/263, which states that the Agreement shall enter into force 30 days after the date on which 40 States have established their consent to be bound, provided that such States include at least 7 pioneer investors and that at least 5 of those States are developed States. In this connection, the Advisory Committee was informed that, as of 27 November 1995, 41 States had ratified the agreement, out of which 3 States were pioneer investors (2 of which are developed States).

6. The Advisory Committee recalls and reiterates its comment in paragraph 4 of its report (A/49/7/Add.3) that, even though the procedures for review and approval of the budget by the Finance Committee, the Council and then the Assembly of the Seabed Authority are specific and involve action by Governments, as long as the budget of the International Seabed Authority is to be financed by the regular budget of the United Nations, the approval of the funding must be in accordance with Article 17 of the Charter of the United Nations, i.e., the budget of the Authority would have to be approved by the General Assembly after review by the Advisory Committee.

7. In paragraph 25 of his report, the Secretary-General indicates that the total budget of the Authority in 1996 amounts to $2,656,800; consisting of $1,318,900 for conference-servicing expenses and $1,337,900 for expenses of the secretariat.

8. As indicated in paragraph 26 of the Secretary-General's report, the estimated amount of $1,318,900 for conference-servicing expenses will be met from the resources to be appropriated under section 26 E of the proposed programme budget for the biennium 1996-1997. The Advisory Committee was informed that the meeting time may in fact be overstated by one week and that, depending on the length of the sessions, it may be possible to reduce the cost of conference services. A breakdown of the cost estimates based on the five- and four-week sessions is annexed hereto. The Advisory Committee expects that any savings will be reflected in the relevant performance report on the programme budget for 1996-1997.

9. Upon inquiry, the Advisory Committee was informed that the number of official languages per session of the Finance Committee in table 1 of the Secretary-General's report would be six and not one.

10. As indicated in paragraph 46 of the Secretary-General's report, the proposed programme budget for the biennium 1996-1997 retained the 1994-1995 appropriation of $776,000 as a resource base for 1996-1997, pending the submission of the budget of the Authority to the General Assembly at its fiftieth session. The Secretary-General is therefore requesting an additional appropriation of $561,900 under section 33.

11. The Advisory Committee notes from paragraphs 13 and 20 of his report that the Secretary-General has, when indicating the services to be performed by the interim secretariat, mentioned "administrative" as well as "substantive" services. Upon inquiry, the Advisory Committee was informed that the present estimates (see para. 7 above) related to the administrative expenses on staff and conference services of the Authority and not to its operational activities. In this connection, the Advisory Committee recommends that, in future, the budget presentation should be clarified so that it is consistent with General Assembly resolution 48/263.

12. The Advisory Committee notes from paragraph 28 of the Secretary-General's report that staff resources for the period from 1 January to 31 March 1996 are estimated at 14 posts (1 P-5, 2 P-2 and 11 local staff), the same number and level as those of the Kingston Office for the Law of the Sea. The Advisory Committee understands that this interim Secretariat will be assisted in a number of ways by the United Nations Secretariat in setting up an administrative structure. On the assumption that the Secretary-General of the Authority is elected in March 1996, the staff resources for the period from 1 April to 31 May 1996 are estimated at 16 posts (1 Under-Secretary-General, 2 P-5 and 13 local staff). For the period after 31 May 1996, the budget estimates provide for 23 posts (1 Under-Secretary-General, 1 D-2, 2 P-5, 2 P-2 and 17 local staff). In view of the functions to be performed, it is the opinion of the Advisory Committee that the number of local staff posts appears to be high. The Committee recommends that 14 local staff be approved for the period after 31 May 1996; the consequential reduction would be $29,700. The Advisory Committee was informed that United Nations standards were applied to the costing of posts.

13. Paragraph 31 of the Secretary-General's report makes provision of $54,400 under general temporary assistance. The Advisory Committee notes that the services to be supported under this estimate include additional secretaries, administrative assistants, research assistants, data and information assistants, library assistants and messengers. In this connection, the Advisory Committee recalls what it stated in its first report on the proposed programme budget for the biennium 1996-1997 1/ that, as a rule, general temporary assistance should be used for additional staff during peak workload period and for the replacement of staff on prolonged sick leave or maternity. The Advisory Committee trusts

that the use of resources for general temporary assistance will be limited to purposes for which it was intended. Should there be a need for additional staff, they should be justified through specific requests.

14. Provision of $20,000 is made in paragraph 32 of the Secretary-General's report under consultants. Upon inquiry, the Advisory Committee was informed that, if the Secretary-General of the Authority is elected in March 1996, consultants will be necessary to assist the small interim secretariat in Kingston to prepare the budget of the Authority.

15. In paragraph 39 of the annex to the Secretary-General's report, provision is made of $18,000 under local transportation. In view of the fact that this item has appeared in a number of budget presentations, the Secretary-General is requested to come up with a policy on the issue. It is the view of the Advisory Committee, for example, that staff being assisted with transport should also make a contribution.

16. Taking into account its comments above, the Advisory Committee recommends approval of an additional appropriation of $532,200 under section 33 of the proposed programme budget for 1996-1997.

<u>Notes</u>

<u>1</u>/ <u>Official Records of the General Assembly, Fiftieth Session, Supplement No. 7</u> (A/50/7), para. 68.

Annex

CONFERENCE-SERVICING ESTIMATES

	March 1996 (3 weeks)	August 1996 (2 weeks)	Total
A. Cost-estimates (for 5 weeks) (as per A/C.5/50/28)			
Pre-session documentation (ACEFRS)	33 000	67 200	100 500
Meeting servicing (ACEFRS)	573 300	451 800	1 025 100 a/
In-session documentation (ACEFRS)	35 500	89 000	124 500
Post-session documentation (ACEFRS)	34 000	34 800	68 800
Total	676 100	642 800	1 318 900

	March 1996 (2 weeks)	August 1996 (2 weeks)	Total
B. Cost estimates (for 4 weeks)			
Pre-session documentation (ACEFRS)	33 300	67 200	100 500
Meeting servicing (ACEFRS)	451 800	451 800	903 600 a/
In-session documentation (ACEFRS)	35 500	89 000	124 500
Post-session documentation (ACEFRS)	34 000	34 800	68 800
Total	554 600	642 800	1 197 400
C. Documentation (total number of pages) b/			
Pre-session	30	180	
In-session	120	240	
Post-session	60	90	

---

a/ Savings of approximately $121,500 would come from daily subsistence allowance and salaries of conference-servicing staff brought to the meeting site.

b/ There will be no change in documentation requirements even though the first session is shortened to a two-week period.

48. UNITED NATIONS CONFERENCE ON STRADDLING FISH STOCKS AND HIGHLY MIGRATORY FISH STOCKS - REPORT OF THE SECRETARY-GENERAL

Doc. no.: A/50/550 12 October 1995

CONTENTS

I. INTRODUCTION

1. The United Nations Conference on Straddling Fish Stocks and Highly Migratory Fish Stocks was convened pursuant to paragraph 1 of General Assembly resolution 47/192 of 22 December 1992, in accordance with the mandate agreed upon at the United Nations Conference on Environment and Development.

2. The United Nations Conference on Environment and Development, held at Rio de Janeiro from 3 to 14 June 1992, adopted Agenda 21, 1/ paragraph 17.49 of which reads as follows:

"States should take effective action, including bilateral and multilateral cooperation, where appropriate at the subregional, regional and global levels, to ensure that high seas fisheries are managed in accordance with the provisions of the United Nations Convention on the Law of the Sea. In particular, they should:

"...

"(e) Convene, as soon as possible, an intergovernmental conference under United Nations auspices, taking into account relevant activities at the subregional, regional and global levels, with a view to promoting effective implementation of the provisions of the United Nations Convention on the Law of the Sea on straddling fish stocks and highly migratory fish stocks. The conference, drawing, inter alia, on scientific and technical studies by the Food and Agriculture Organization of the United Nations (FAO) should identify and assess existing problems related to the conservation and management of such fish stocks, and consider means of improving cooperation on fisheries among States, and formulate appropriate recommendations. The work and the results of the conference should be fully consistent with the provisions of the United Nations Convention on the Law of the Sea, in particular the rights and obligations of coastal States and States fishing on the high seas."

3. The General Assembly, in its resolution 47/192, recalled Agenda 21, in particular chapter 17, programme area C, relating to the sustainable use and conservation of marine living resources of the high seas, and decided that the Conference, in accordance with the mandate quoted above, should take into account relevant activities at the subregional, regional and global levels, with a view to promoting effective implementation of the provisions of the United Nations Convention on the Law of the Sea on straddling fish stocks and highly migratory fish stocks. The Assembly further decided that the Conference, drawing, inter alia, on scientific and technical studies by the Food and Agriculture Organization of the United Nations, should: (a) identify and assess existing problems related to the conservation and management of such fish stocks; (b) consider means of improving fisheries cooperation among States; and (c) formulate appropriate recommendations.

4. The General Assembly also reaffirmed that the work and results of the Conference should be fully consistent with the provisions of the United Nations Convention on the Law of the Sea, in particular the rights and obligations of coastal States and States fishing on the high seas, and that States should give full effect to the high seas fisheries provisions of the Convention with regard to fisheries populations whose ranges lie both within and beyond exclusive economic zones (straddling fish stocks) and highly migratory fish stocks.

5. By the same resolution, the General Assembly invited relevant specialized agencies and other appropriate organs, organizations and programmes of the United Nations system, as well as regional and subregional fisheries organizations, to contribute relevant scientific and technical studies and reports. It also invited relevant non-governmental organizations from developed and developing countries to contribute to the Conference within the areas of their competence and expertise.

6. Subsequently, in its resolutions 48/194 and 49/121, adopted on 21 December 1993 and 19 December 1994 respectively, the General Assembly renewed the mandate of the Conference and requested the Secretary-General to submit to the General Assembly the final report on the work of the Conference. The present report is submitted in response to the request contained in those resolutions.

II. SESSIONS OF THE CONFERENCE

7. Pursuant to General Assembly resolutions 47/192, 48/194 and 49/121, the sessions of the United Nations Conference on Straddling Fish Stocks and Highly Migratory Fish Stocks were held at United Nations Headquarters in New York as follows: 2/

- First session: 19 to 23 April 1993;
- Second session: 12 to 30 July 1993;
- Third session: 14 to 31 March 1994;
- Fourth session: 15 to 26 August 1994;
- Fifth session: 27 March to 12 April 1995;
- Sixth session: 24 July to 4 August 1995. 3/

III. PARTICIPATION IN THE CONFERENCE

8. Pursuant to paragraph 4 of General Assembly resolution 47/192, the following were invited to the Conference:

(a) States Members of the United Nations or members of the specialized agencies and the International Atomic Energy Agency;

(b) Representatives of organizations that have received a standing invitation from the Assembly to participate, in the capacity of observers, in the sessions and work of all international conferences convened under its auspices;

(c) Associate members of regional commissions;

(d) Representatives of the national liberation movements recognized by the Organization of African Unity in its region;

(e) Specialized agencies and the International Atomic Energy Agency, as well as other organs, organizations and programmes of the United Nations system;

(f) Relevant intergovernmental organizations that had been invited to participate in the work of the Preparatory Committee for the United Nations Conference on Environment and Development;

(g) Regional and subregional fisheries organizations;

(h) Relevant non-governmental organizations.

9. The representatives of the following States participated in the sessions of the Conference: Albania, Algeria, Angola, Antigua and Barbuda, Argentina, Australia, Austria, Bahamas, Bahrain, Bangladesh, Barbados, Belarus, Belgium, Belize, Benin, Brazil, Bulgaria, Burundi, Cameroon, Canada, Cape Verde, Chile, China, Colombia, Congo, Cook Islands, Costa Rica, Côte d'Ivoire, Cuba, Cyprus, Democratic People's Republic of Korea, Denmark, Djibouti, Ecuador, Egypt, El Salvador, Eritrea, Estonia, Fiji, Finland, France, Gabon, Gambia, Germany, Ghana, Greece, Grenada, Guatemala, Guinea, Guinea-Bissau, Guyana, Honduras, Hungary, Iceland, India, Indonesia, Iran (Islamic Republic of), Ireland, Israel, Italy, Jamaica, Japan, Kazakstan, Kenya, Kiribati, Latvia, Lebanon, Lesotho, Libyan Arab Jamahiriya, Liechtenstein, Lithuania, Luxembourg, Madagascar, Malaysia, Maldives, Mali, Malta, Marshall Islands, Mauritania, Mauritius, Mexico, Micronesia (Federated States of), Morocco, Myanmar, Namibia, Netherlands, New Zealand, Nicaragua, Niger, Nigeria, Niue, Norway, Pakistan, Palau, Panama, Papua New Guinea, Peru, Philippines, Poland, Portugal, Qatar, Republic of Korea, Romania, Russian Federation, Saint Lucia, Samoa, Saudi Arabia, Senegal, Seychelles, Sierra Leone, Singapore, Solomon Islands, South

Africa, Spain, Sri Lanka, Suriname, Sweden, Switzerland, Syrian Arab Republic, Thailand, Togo, Tonga, Trinidad and Tobago, Tunisia, Turkey, Tuvalu, Uganda, Ukraine, United Arab Emirates, United Kingdom of Great Britain and Northern Ireland, United Republic of Tanzania, United States of America, Uruguay, Vanuatu, Venezuela, Viet Nam, Zambia and Zimbabwe.

10. The representative of the European Community 4/ participated in the sessions without the right to vote.

11. The following associate members of a regional commission were represented as observers at the sessions: Montserrat and United States Virgin Islands.

12. The following national liberation movement was represented as observer at the first session: Pan Africanist Congress of Azania.

13. The following specialized agencies were represented as observers at the sessions: Food and Agriculture Organization of the United Nations (FAO), United Nations Educational, Scientific and Cultural Organization (UNESCO) and World Bank.

14. The Intergovernmental Oceanographic Commission of UNESCO (IOC), the United Nations Development Programme (UNDP) and the United Nations Environment Programme (UNEP) were also present as observers at the sessions.

15. The following intergovernmental organizations were represented as observers at the sessions: Asian-African Legal Consultative Committee, Commission on the Indian Ocean, Inter-American Tropical Tuna Commission, International Commission for the Conservation of Atlantic Tunas, International Council for the Exploration of the Sea, International Maritime Satellite Organization, International Whaling Commission, Latin American Organization for the Development of Fisheries, Ministerial Conference on Fisheries Cooperation among African States bordering the Atlantic Ocean, North Atlantic Salmon Conservation Organization, Northwest Atlantic Fisheries Organization, Organization of African Unity, Organisation for Economic Cooperation and Development, South Pacific Commission, South Pacific Permanent Commission, and South Pacific Forum Fisheries Agency.

16. The following non-governmental organizations were represented as observers at the sessions: Alaska Marine Conservation Council, Alaska Public Interest Research Group, American Oceans Campaign, American Society of International Law, Association Algérienne pour la Protection de la Nature et de l'Environnement, Association Tunisienne pour la Protection de la Nature et de l'Environnement, Association of the Bar of the City of New York, Atlantic Salmon Federation, Bering Sea Fisherman's Association, Both Ends, Canadian Oceans Caucus, Center for Development of International Law, Center for Marine Conservation, Centre de Recherches pour le Développement des Technologies Intermédiares de Pêche, Comité Catholique contre la Faim et pour le Développement, Confederación de Trabajadores Portuarios, Gente de Mar y Pesqueros de Chile, Confederación Nacional de Pescadores Artesanales de Chile, Coordinadora de Tripulantes Pesqueros Industriales del Cono Sur de América Latina, Council on Ocean Law, Earth Council, Earth Island Institute, Earthtrust, Environmental Defense Fund, Federación Nacional de Cooperativas Pesqueras del Ecuador, Federation of Japan Tuna Fisheries Cooperative Associations, Fish, Food and Allied Workers, Fisheries Council of Canada, Four Directions Council, Friends of the Earth International, Friends World Committee for Consultations (Quaker United Nations Office), Fundación Hernandiana, Global Education Associates, Greenpeace International, Groupement d'Intérêt Économique, International Coalition of Fisheries Associations, International Coastal and Ocean Organization, International Collective in Support of Fishworkers, International Confederation of Free Trade Unions, International Institute for Sustainable Development, International Law Association, International Ocean Institute, International Union for the Conservation of Nature and Natural Resources (IUCN), Japan Fisheries Association, Kandune Self-Help Water Project, Marine Environmental

Research Institute, Namibian Food and Allied Workers Union, National Audubon Society, National Wildlife Federation, Nationwide Coalition of Fisherfolks for Aquatic Reform, Natural Resources Defense Council, Netherlands National Committee for IUCN, Newfoundland and Labrador Environmental Association, Newfoundland Inshore Fisheries Association, Ocean Trust, Oceans Institute of Canada, Overseas Fishery Cooperation Foundation, Pamalakaya (National United Movement of Fisherfolk - Philippines), Red Mexicana de Acción frente al Libre Comercio, Réserve Internationale Maritime en Mediterranée Occidentale, Samoan Association of Non-governmental Organizations, Sindicato de Obreros Marítimos Unidos, SONAR (Save Our Northwest Atlantic Resources), Trickle-Up Program, United Nations Association in Canada, United Nations Association-United Kingdom, United Nations Environment and Development-United Kingdom Committee, Wildlife Conservation Society, Women and Fisheries Network, World Wide Fund for Nature, World Wide Fund Suisse.

17. Pursuant to paragraph 9 of General Assembly resolution 47/192, a voluntary fund was established in the Secretariat for the purpose of assisting developing countries, especially those most concerned by the subject-matter of the Conference, in particular the least developed among them, to participate in the Conference. Contributions to the Fund were made by the Governments of Canada, Japan, Norway and the Republic of Korea.

IV. OFFICERS AND COMMITTEES

18. At its first meeting, the Conference elected Mr. Satya N. Nandan (Fiji) as its Chairman.

19. The Conference also elected the representatives of Chile, Italy and Mauritania as Vice-Chairmen.

20. The Conference appointed the representatives of the following States as members of the Credentials Committee: Antigua and Barbuda, Argentina, Burundi, China, Kenya, New Zealand, Papua New Guinea, Russian Federation and United States of America. At its first meeting, on 28 July 1993, the Credentials Committee elected Mr. Alberto Luis Daverede (Argentina) as its Chairman.

21. At the first and second sessions, Mr. Carl-August Fleischhauer, Under-Secretary-General for Legal Affairs, the Legal Counsel, and thereafter Mr. Hans Corell, served as Secretary-General of the Conference, representing the Secretary-General of the United Nations. For the first four sessions, Mr. Dolliver L. Nelson, and thereafter Mr. Moritaka Hayashi, served as Secretary of the Conference.

22. In accordance with paragraph 11 of General Assembly resolution 47/192, FAO provided an officer, Mr. David J. Doulman, to serve as Scientific and Technical Adviser to the Conference.

V. DOCUMENTATION OF THE CONFERENCE

23. The Conference documentation 5/ included, inter alia, the following:

(a) Rules of procedure; 6/

(b) Proposals and other communications submitted by delegations; 7/

(c) Reports and studies submitted by the Secretariat, FAO and IOC; 8/

(d) Reports and comments submitted by intergovernmental organizations, regional and subregional fisheries organizations and arrangements; 9/

(e) Statements by the Chairman of the Conference; 10/

(f) A guide to the issues before the Conference, the negotiating texts and the draft agreement prepared by the Chairman of the Conference. 11/

VI. WORK OF THE CONFERENCE

24. The Conference adopted its agenda and the rules of procedure at its first session.

25. At the second session, the Conference devoted the first three days to general debate, following which the Chairman outlined the key issues on which there was general agreement. 12/

26. At the same session, the Conference proceeded to examine the issues relating to straddling fish stocks and highly migratory fish stocks as contained in the document entitled "A guide to the issues before the Conference prepared by the Chairman" (A/CONF.164/10).

27. At the end of the second session, the Chairman prepared a negotiating text (A/CONF.164/13), which the Conference considered at the third session.

28. Also at the third session, the Conference established two open-ended working groups to consider the information papers, prepared by FAO at the request of the Conference, on the precautionary approach to fisheries management and on management reference points. Mr. Andrés Couve (Chile) and Mr. Andrew Rosenberg (United States of America) served as chairmen of the working groups. The results of the work of the two working groups are contained in documents A/CONF.164/WP.1 and WP.2. At the end of the third session, the Chairman submitted a revision of his negotiating text (A/CONF.164/13/Rev.1), which reflected the work of the working groups.

29. At the fourth session, the Chairman prepared a new revision to his negotiating text in the form of a binding instrument, entitled "Draft Agreement for the Implementation of the Provisions of the United Nations Convention on the Law of the Sea of 10 December 1982 relating to the Conservation and Management of Straddling Fish Stocks and Highly Migratory Fish Stocks" (A/CONF.164/22). At the end of the fifth session, the Chairman prepared a revised text of the draft Agreement (A/CONF.164/22/Rev.1).

30. At the sixth session, the Conference considered the revised text of the draft Agreement and suggested drafting changes and editorial improvements (A/CONF.164/CRP.7). Following the deliberations of the Conference, the Chairman proposed for adoption a "Draft Agreement for the Implementation of the Provisions of the United Nations Convention on the Law of the Sea of 10 December 1982 relating to the Conservation and Management of Straddling Fish Stocks and Highly Migratory Fish Stocks" (A/CONF.164/33).

31. On 4 August 1995, the Conference adopted without a vote the Agreement for the Implementation of the Provisions of the United Nations Convention on the Law of the Sea of 10 December 1982 relating to the Conservation and Management of Straddling Fish Stocks and Highly Migratory Fish Stocks, as well as resolutions I and II (A/CONF.164/32, annex). At the same meeting, the Conference approved the draft Final Act (A/CONF.164/32). 13/ In doing so, the Conference discharged the mandate given to it by the General Assembly in its resolution 47/192. The Conference requested the Secretariat to prepare the final text of the Agreement, incorporating necessary editing and drafting changes and ensuring concordance among the six language versions. 14/ The final text of the Agreement and of the two resolutions are contained respectively in annexes I and II to the present report.

32. The Conference decided to resume its sixth session on 4 December 1995 for a ceremony of signature of the Agreement and the Final Act.

Notes

1/ Report of the United Nations Conference on Environment and Development, Rio de Janeiro, 3-14 June 1992 (United Nations publication, Sales No. E.96.I.8 and corrigenda), vol. I: Resolutions adopted by the Conference, resolution 1, annex II.

2/ The reports on each of the sessions are contained in A/CONF.164/9 (first (organizational) session), A/CONF.164/16 and Corr.1 (second session), A/CONF.164/20 (third session), A/CONF.164/25 (fourth session), A/CONF.164/29 (fifth session) and A/CONF.164/36 (sixth session).

3/ See paragraph 32 below.

4/ Rule 2 of the rules of procedure of the Conference (A/CONF.164/6) provides that:

> "The representative of the European Economic Community shall participate in the Conference in matters within its competence without the right to vote. Such representation shall in no case entail an increase of the representation to which the States members of the European Economic Community would otherwise be entitled."

In adopting the above rule the Conference recorded the following understanding:

> "This rule is agreed upon in view of the fact that, with regard to the conservation and management of the sea fishing resources, States members of the European Economic Community have transferred competence to the Community, and in no way does it constitute a precedent for other United Nations forums where a similar transfer of competence does not occur. (See Declaration of the European Economic Community upon signing the United Nations Convention on the Law of the Sea. Multilateral Treaties Deposited with the Secretary-General (United Nations Publication, Sales No. E.95.V.5), chap. XXI.6.)" (A/CONF.164/6, note 1)

The Secretariat was informed during the third session of the Conference that the European Economic Community had changed its name to "European Community".

5/ For a complete listing of the Conference documentation, see A/CONF.164/INF/16.

6/ A/CONF.164/6.

7/ A/CONF.164/L.1 to L.50.

8/ Report of the Technical Consultation on High Seas Fishing and the papers presented at the Technical Consultation on High Seas Fishing (FAO) (A/CONF.164/INF/2); information on activities of the Intergovernmental Oceanographic Commission relevant to the United Nations Conference on Straddling Fish Stocks and Highly Migratory Fish Stocks (A/CONF.164/INF/3); some high seas fisheries aspects relating to straddling fish stocks and highly migratory fish stocks (FAO) (A/CONF.164/INF/4 and Corr.1); background paper prepared by the Secretariat (A/CONF.164/INF/5); the precautionary approach to fisheries with reference to straddling fish stocks and highly migratory fish stocks (FAO) (A/CONF.164/INF/8); and reference points for fisheries management: their potential application to straddling and highly migratory resources (FAO) (A/CONF.164/INF/9).

9/ Report of the first session of the International Conference on the Conservation and Management of the Marine Living Resources in the High Seas of the Okhotsk Sea (submitted by the delegation of the Russian Federation) (A/CONF.164/INF/6); ad hoc consultation on the role of regional fishery agencies in relation to high seas fishing statistics (A/CONF.164/INF/10); comments by the

Coordinating Working Party on Fishery Statistics on annex I to the Draft Agreement for the Implementation of the Provisions of the United Nations Convention on the Law of the Sea of 10 December 1982 relating to the Conservation and Management of Straddling Fish Stocks and Highly Migratory Fish Stocks (A/CONF.164/INF/13).

10/ A/CONF.164/7, 8, 11, 12, 15, 17, 19, 21, 24, 26, 28, 30 and 35.

11/ A guide to the issues before the Conference (A/CONF.164/10); negotiating text (A/CONF.164/13); revised negotiating text (A/CONF.164/13/Rev.1); draft Agreement for the Implementation of the Provisions of the United Nations Convention on the Law of the Sea of 10 December 1982 relating to the Conservation and Management of Straddling Fish Stocks and Highly Migratory Fish Stocks (A/CONF.164/22); revised Draft Agreement (A/CONF.164/22/Rev.1); and Draft Agreement (A/CONF.164/33).

12/ See A/48/479, para. 10.

13/ The final text of the Final Act was issued as document A/CONF.164/38.

14/ The final edited text of the Agreement was issued as document A/CONF.164/37.

ANNEX I

AGREEMENT FOR THE IMPLEMENTATION OF THE PROVISIONS OF THE UNITED NATIONS CONVENTION ON THE LAW OF THE SEA OF 10 DECEMBER 1982 RELATING TO THE CONSERVATION AND MANAGEMENT OF STRADDLING FISH STOCKS AND HIGHLY MIGRATORY FISH STOCKS*

The States Parties to this Agreement,

Recalling the relevant provisions of the United Nations Convention on the Law of the Sea of 10 December 1982,

Determined to ensure the long-term conservation and sustainable use of straddling fish stocks and highly migratory fish stocks,

Resolved to improve cooperation between States to that end,

Calling for more effective enforcement by flag States, port States and coastal States of the conservation and management measures adopted for such stocks,

Seeking to address in particular the problems identified in chapter 17, programme area C, of Agenda 21 adopted by the United Nations Conference on Environment and Development, namely, that the management of high seas fisheries is inadequate in many areas and that some resources are overutilized; noting that there are problems of unregulated fishing, over-capitalization, excessive fleet size, vessel reflagging to escape controls, insufficiently selective gear, unreliable databases and lack of sufficient cooperation between States,

Committing themselves to responsible fisheries,

Conscious of the need to avoid adverse impacts on the marine environment, preserve biodiversity, maintain the integrity of marine ecosystems and minimize the risk of long-term or irreversible effects of fishing operations,

---

* Issued as document A/CONF.164/37.

Recognizing the need for specific assistance, including financial, scientific and technological assistance, in order that developing States can participate effectively in the conservation, management and sustainable use of straddling fish stocks and highly migratory fish stocks,

Convinced that an agreement for the implementation of the relevant provisions of the Convention would best serve these purposes and contribute to the maintenance of international peace and security,

Affirming that matters not regulated by the Convention or by this Agreement continue to be governed by the rules and principles of general international law,

Have agreed as follows:

PART I

GENERAL PROVISIONS

Article 1

Use of terms and scope

1. For the purposes of this Agreement:

(a) "Convention" means the United Nations Convention on the Law of the Sea of 10 December 1982;

(b) "conservation and management measures" means measures to conserve and manage one or more species of living marine resources that are adopted and applied consistent with the relevant rules of international law as reflected in the Convention and this Agreement;

(c) "fish" includes molluscs and crustaceans except those belonging to sedentary species as defined in article 77 of the Convention; and

(d) "arrangement" means a cooperative mechanism established in accordance with the Convention and this Agreement by two or more States for the purpose, *inter alia*, of establishing conservation and management measures in a subregion or region for one or more straddling fish stocks or highly migratory fish stocks.

2. (a) "States Parties" means States which have consented to be bound by this Agreement and for which the Agreement is in force.

(b) This Agreement applies *mutatis mutandis*:

(i) to any entity referred to in article 305, paragraph 1 (c), (d) and (e), of the Convention and

(ii) subject to article 47, to any entity referred to as an "international organization" in Annex IX, article 1, of the Convention

which becomes a Party to this Agreement, and to that extent "States Parties" refers to those entities.

3. This Agreement applies *mutatis mutandis* to other fishing entities whose vessels fish on the high seas.

Article 2

Objective

The objective of this Agreement is to ensure the long-term conservation and sustainable use of straddling fish stocks and highly migratory fish stocks through effective implementation of the relevant provisions of the Convention.

Article 3

Application

1. Unless otherwise provided, this Agreement applies to the conservation and management of straddling fish stocks and highly migratory fish stocks beyond areas under national jurisdiction, except that articles 6 and 7 apply also to the conservation and management of such stocks within areas under national jurisdiction, subject to the different legal regimes that apply within areas under national jurisdiction and in areas beyond national jurisdiction as provided for in the Convention.

2. In the exercise of its sovereign rights for the purpose of exploring and exploiting, conserving and managing straddling fish stocks and highly migratory fish stocks within areas under national jurisdiction, the coastal State shall apply mutatis mutandis the general principles enumerated in article 5.

3. States shall give due consideration to the respective capacities of developing States to apply articles 5, 6 and 7 within areas under national jurisdiction and their need for assistance as provided for in this Agreement. To this end, Part VII applies mutatis mutandis in respect of areas under national jurisdiction.

Article 4

Relationship between this Agreement and the Convention

Nothing in this Agreement shall prejudice the rights, jurisdiction and duties of States under the Convention. This Agreement shall be interpreted and applied in the context of and in a manner consistent with the Convention.

PART II

CONSERVATION AND MANAGEMENT OF STRADDLING FISH STOCKS AND HIGHLY MIGRATORY FISH STOCKS

Article 5

General principles

In order to conserve and manage straddling fish stocks and highly migratory fish stocks, coastal States and States fishing on the high seas shall, in giving effect to their duty to cooperate in accordance with the Convention:

(a) adopt measures to ensure long-term sustainability of straddling fish stocks and highly migratory fish stocks and promote the objective of their optimum utilization;

(b) ensure that such measures are based on the best scientific evidence available and are designed to maintain or restore stocks at levels capable of producing maximum sustainable yield, as qualified by relevant environmental and economic factors, including the special requirements of developing States, and taking into account fishing patterns, the interdependence of stocks and any generally recommended international minimum standards, whether subregional, regional or global;

(c) apply the precautionary approach in accordance with article 6;

(d) assess the impacts of fishing, other human activities and environmental factors on target stocks and species belonging to the same ecosystem or associated with or dependent upon the target stocks;

(e) adopt, where necessary, conservation and management measures for species belonging to the same ecosystem or associated with or dependent upon the target stocks, with a view to maintaining or restoring populations of such species above levels at which their reproduction may become seriously threatened;

(f) minimize pollution, waste, discards, catch by lost or abandoned gear, catch of non-target species, both fish and non-fish species, (hereinafter referred to as non-target species) and impacts on associated or dependent species, in particular endangered species, through measures including, to the extent practicable, the development and use of selective, environmentally safe and cost-effective fishing gear and techniques;

(g) protect biodiversity in the marine environment;

(h) take measures to prevent or eliminate overfishing and excess fishing capacity and to ensure that levels of fishing effort do not exceed those commensurate with the sustainable use of fishery resources;

(i) take into account the interests of artisanal and subsistence fishers;

(j) collect and share, in a timely manner, complete and accurate data concerning fishing activities on, inter alia, vessel position, catch of target and non-target species and fishing effort, as set out in Annex I, as well as information from national and international research programmes;

(k) promote and conduct scientific research and develop appropriate technologies in support of fishery conservation and management; and

(l) implement and enforce conservation and management measures through effective monitoring, control and surveillance.

Article 6

Application of the precautionary approach

1. States shall apply the precautionary approach widely to conservation, management and exploitation of straddling fish stocks and highly migratory fish stocks in order to protect the living marine resources and preserve the marine environment.

2. States shall be more cautious when information is uncertain, unreliable or inadequate. The absence of adequate scientific information shall not be used as a reason for postponing or failing to take conservation and management measures.

3. In implementing the precautionary approach, States shall:

(a) improve decision-making for fishery resource conservation and management by obtaining and sharing the best scientific information available and implementing improved techniques for dealing with risk and uncertainty;

(b) apply the guidelines set out in Annex II and determine, on the basis of the best scientific information available, stock-specific reference points and the action to be taken if they are exceeded;

(c) take into account, inter alia, uncertainties relating to the size and productivity of the stocks, reference points, stock condition in relation to such reference points, levels and distribution of fishing mortality and the impact of fishing activities on non-target and associated or dependent species, as well as existing and predicted oceanic, environmental and socio-economic conditions; and

(d) develop data collection and research programmes to assess the impact of fishing on non-target and associated or dependent species and their environment, and adopt plans which are necessary to ensure the conservation of such species and to protect habitats of special concern.

4. States shall take measures to ensure that, when reference points are approached, they will not be exceeded. In the event that they are exceeded, States shall, without delay, take the action determined under paragraph 3 (b) to restore the stocks.

5. Where the status of target stocks or non-target or associated or dependent species is of concern, States shall subject such stocks and species to enhanced monitoring in order to review their status and the efficacy of conservation and management measures. They shall revise those measures regularly in the light of new information.

6. For new or exploratory fisheries, States shall adopt as soon as possible cautious conservation and management measures, including, inter alia, catch limits and effort limits. Such measures shall remain in force until there are sufficient data to allow assessment of the impact of the fisheries on the long-term sustainability of the stocks, whereupon conservation and management measures based on that assessment shall be implemented. The latter measures shall, if appropriate, allow for the gradual development of the fisheries.

7. If a natural phenomenon has a significant adverse impact on the status of straddling fish stocks or highly migratory fish stocks, States shall adopt conservation and management measures on an emergency basis to ensure that fishing activity does not exacerbate such adverse impact. States shall also adopt such measures on an emergency basis where fishing activity presents a serious threat to the sustainability of such stocks. Measures taken on an emergency basis shall be temporary and shall be based on the best scientific evidence available.

Article 7

Compatibility of conservation and management measures

1. Without prejudice to the sovereign rights of coastal States for the purpose of exploring and exploiting, conserving and managing the living marine resources within areas under national jurisdiction as provided for in the Convention, and the right of all States for their nationals to engage in fishing on the high seas in accordance with the Convention:

(a) with respect to straddling fish stocks, the relevant coastal States and the States whose nationals fish for such stocks in the adjacent high seas area shall seek, either directly or through the appropriate mechanisms for cooperation provided for in Part III, to agree upon the measures necessary for the conservation of these stocks in the adjacent high seas area;

(b) with respect to highly migratory fish stocks, the relevant coastal States and other States whose nationals fish for such stocks in the region shall cooperate, either directly or through the appropriate mechanisms for cooperation provided for in Part III, with a view to ensuring conservation and promoting the objective of optimum utilization of such stocks throughout the region, both within and beyond the areas under national jurisdiction.

2. Conservation and management measures established for the high seas and those adopted for areas under national jurisdiction shall be compatible in order to ensure conservation and management of the straddling fish stocks and highly migratory fish stocks in their entirety. To this end, coastal States and States fishing on the high seas have a duty to cooperate for the purpose of achieving compatible measures in respect of such stocks. In determining compatible conservation and management measures, States shall:

(a) take into account the conservation and management measures adopted and applied in accordance with article 61 of the Convention in respect of the same stocks by coastal States within areas under national jurisdiction and ensure that measures established in respect of such stocks for the high seas do not undermine the effectiveness of such measures;

(b) take into account previously agreed measures established and applied for the high seas in accordance with the Convention in respect of the same stocks by relevant coastal States and States fishing on the high seas;

(c) take into account previously agreed measures established and applied in accordance with the Convention in respect of the same stocks by a subregional or regional fisheries management organization or arrangement;

(d) take into account the biological unity and other biological characteristics of the stocks and the relationships between the distribution of the stocks, the fisheries and the geographical particularities of the region concerned, including the extent to which the stocks occur and are fished in areas under national jurisdiction;

(e) take into account the respective dependence of the coastal States and the States fishing on the high seas on the stocks concerned; and

(f) ensure that such measures do not result in harmful impact on the living marine resources as a whole.

3. In giving effect to their duty to cooperate, States shall make every effort to agree on compatible conservation and management measures within a reasonable period of time.

4. If no agreement can be reached within a reasonable period of time, any of the States concerned may invoke the procedures for the settlement of disputes provided for in Part VIII.

5. Pending agreement on compatible conservation and management measures, the States concerned, in a spirit of understanding and cooperation, shall make every effort to enter into provisional arrangements of a practical nature. In the event that they are unable to agree on such arrangements, any of the States concerned may, for the purpose of obtaining provisional measures, submit the dispute to a court or tribunal in accordance with the procedures for the settlement of disputes provided for in Part VIII.

6. Provisional arrangements or measures entered into or prescribed pursuant to paragraph 5 shall take into account the provisions of this Part, shall have due regard to the rights and obligations of all States concerned, shall not jeopardize or hamper the reaching of final agreement on compatible conservation and management measures and shall be without prejudice to the final outcome of any dispute settlement procedure.

7. Coastal States shall regularly inform States fishing on the high seas in the subregion or region, either directly or through appropriate subregional or regional fisheries management organizations or arrangements, or through other appropriate means, of the measures they have adopted for straddling fish stocks and highly migratory fish stocks within areas under their national jurisdiction.

8. States fishing on the high seas shall regularly inform other interested States, either directly or through appropriate subregional or regional fisheries management organizations or arrangements, or through other appropriate means, of the measures they have adopted for regulating the activities of vessels flying their flag which fish for such stocks on the high seas.

PART III

MECHANISMS FOR INTERNATIONAL COOPERATION CONCERNING STRADDLING FISH STOCKS AND HIGHLY MIGRATORY FISH STOCKS

Article 8

Cooperation for conservation and management

1. Coastal States and States fishing on the high seas shall, in accordance with the Convention, pursue cooperation in relation to straddling fish stocks and highly migratory fish stocks either directly or through appropriate subregional or regional fisheries management organizations or arrangements, taking into account the specific characteristics of the subregion or region, to ensure effective conservation and management of such stocks.

2. States shall enter into consultations in good faith and without delay, particularly where there is evidence that the straddling fish stocks and highly migratory fish stocks concerned may be under threat of over-exploitation or where a new fishery is being developed for such stocks. To this end, consultations may be initiated at the request of any interested State with a view to establishing appropriate arrangements to ensure conservation and management of the stocks. Pending agreement on such arrangements, States shall observe the provisions of this Agreement and shall act in good faith and with due regard to the rights, interests and duties of other States.

3. Where a subregional or regional fisheries management organization or arrangement has the competence to establish conservation and management measures for particular straddling fish stocks or highly migratory fish stocks, States fishing for the stocks on the high seas and relevant coastal States shall give effect to their duty to cooperate by becoming members of such organization or participants in such arrangement, or by agreeing to apply the conservation and management measures established by such organization or arrangement. States having a real interest in the fisheries concerned may become members of such organization or participants in such arrangement. The terms of participation in such organization or arrangement shall not preclude such States from membership or participation; nor shall they be applied in a manner which discriminates against any State or group of States having a real interest in the fisheries concerned.

4. Only those States which are members of such an organization or participants in such an arrangement, or which agree to apply the conservation and management measures established by such organization or arrangement, shall have access to the fishery resources to which those measures apply.

5. Where there is no subregional or regional fisheries management organization or arrangement to establish conservation and management measures for a particular straddling fish stock or highly migratory fish stock, relevant coastal States and States fishing on the high seas for such stock in the subregion or region shall cooperate to establish such an organization or enter

into other appropriate arrangements to ensure conservation and management of such stock and shall participate in the work of the organization or arrangement.

6. Any State intending to propose that action be taken by an intergovernmental organization having competence with respect to living resources should, where such action would have a significant effect on conservation and management measures already established by a competent subregional or regional fisheries management organization or arrangement, consult through that organization or arrangement with its members or participants. To the extent practicable, such consultation should take place prior to the submission of the proposal to the intergovernmental organization.

Article 9

Subregional and regional fisheries management organizations and arrangements

1. In establishing subregional or regional fisheries management organizations or in entering into subregional or regional fisheries management arrangements for straddling fish stocks and highly migratory fish stocks, States shall agree, *inter alia*, on:

(a) the stocks to which conservation and management measures apply, taking into account the biological characteristics of the stocks concerned and the nature of the fisheries involved;

(b) the area of application, taking into account article 7, paragraph 1, and the characteristics of the subregion or region, including socio-economic, geographical and environmental factors;

(c) the relationship between the work of the new organization or arrangement and the role, objectives and operations of any relevant existing fisheries management organizations or arrangements; and

(d) the mechanisms by which the organization or arrangement will obtain scientific advice and review the status of the stocks, including, where appropriate, the establishment of a scientific advisory body.

2. States cooperating in the formation of a subregional or regional fisheries management organization or arrangement shall inform other States which they are aware have a real interest in the work of the proposed organization or arrangement of such cooperation.

Article 10

Functions of subregional and regional fisheries management organizations and arrangements

In fulfilling their obligation to cooperate through subregional or regional fisheries management organizations or arrangements, States shall:

(a) agree on and comply with conservation and management measures to ensure the long-term sustainability of straddling fish stocks and highly migratory fish stocks;

(b) agree, as appropriate, on participatory rights such as allocations of allowable catch or levels of fishing effort;

(c) adopt and apply any generally recommended international minimum standards for the responsible conduct of fishing operations;

(d) obtain and evaluate scientific advice, review the status of the stocks and assess the impact of fishing on non-target and associated or dependent species;

(e) agree on standards for collection, reporting, verification and exchange of data on fisheries for the stocks;

(f) compile and disseminate accurate and complete statistical data, as described in Annex I, to ensure that the best scientific evidence is available, while maintaining confidentiality where appropriate;

(g) promote and conduct scientific assessments of the stocks and relevant research and disseminate the results thereof;

(h) establish appropriate cooperative mechanisms for effective monitoring, control, surveillance and enforcement;

(i) agree on means by which the fishing interests of new members of the organization or new participants in the arrangement will be accommodated;

(j) agree on decision-making procedures which facilitate the adoption of conservation and management measures in a timely and effective manner;

(k) promote the peaceful settlement of disputes in accordance with Part VIII;

(l) ensure the full cooperation of their relevant national agencies and industries in implementing the recommendations and decisions of the organization or arrangement; and

(m) give due publicity to the conservation and management measures established by the organization or arrangement.

Article 11

New members or participants

In determining the nature and extent of participatory rights for new members of a subregional or regional fisheries management organization, or for new participants in a subregional or regional fisheries management arrangement, States shall take into account, inter alia:

(a) the status of the straddling fish stocks and highly migratory fish stocks and the existing level of fishing effort in the fishery;

(b) the respective interests, fishing patterns and fishing practices of new and existing members or participants;

(c) the respective contributions of new and existing members or participants to conservation and management of the stocks, to the collection and provision of accurate data and to the conduct of scientific research on the stocks;

(d) the needs of coastal fishing communities which are dependent mainly on fishing for the stocks;

(e) the needs of coastal States whose economies are overwhelmingly dependent on the exploitation of living marine resources; and

(f) the interests of developing States from the subregion or region in whose areas of national jurisdiction the stocks also occur.

Article 12

Transparency in activities of subregional and regional fisheries management organizations and arrangements

1. States shall provide for transparency in the decision-making process and other activities of subregional and regional fisheries management organizations and arrangements.

2. Representatives from other intergovernmental organizations and representatives from non-governmental organizations concerned with straddling fish stocks and highly migratory fish stocks shall be afforded the opportunity to take part in meetings of subregional and regional fisheries management organizations and arrangements as observers or otherwise, as appropriate, in accordance with the procedures of the organization or arrangement concerned. Such procedures shall not be unduly restrictive in this respect. Such intergovernmental organizations and non-governmental organizations shall have timely access to the records and reports of such organizations and arrangements, subject to the procedural rules on access to them.

Article 13

Strengthening of existing organizations and arrangements

States shall cooperate to strengthen existing subregional and regional fisheries management organizations and arrangements in order to improve their effectiveness in establishing and implementing conservation and management measures for straddling fish stocks and highly migratory fish stocks.

Article 14

Collection and provision of information and cooperation in scientific research

1. States shall ensure that fishing vessels flying their flag provide such information as may be necessary in order to fulfil their obligations under this Agreement. To this end, States shall in accordance with Annex I:

(a) collect and exchange scientific, technical and statistical data with respect to fisheries for straddling fish stocks and highly migratory fish stocks;

(b) ensure that data are collected in sufficient detail to facilitate effective stock assessment and are provided in a timely manner to fulfil the requirements of subregional or regional fisheries management organizations or arrangements; and

(c) take appropriate measures to verify the accuracy of such data.

2. States shall cooperate, either directly or through subregional or regional fisheries management organizations or arrangements:

(a) to agree on the specification of data and the format in which they are to be provided to such organizations or arrangements, taking into account the nature of the stocks and the fisheries for those stocks; and

(b) to develop and share analytical techniques and stock assessment methodologies to improve measures for the conservation and management of straddling fish stocks and highly migratory fish stocks.

3. Consistent with Part XIII of the Convention, States shall cooperate, either directly or through competent international organizations, to strengthen

scientific research capacity in the field of fisheries and promote scientific research related to the conservation and management of straddling fish stocks and highly migratory fish stocks for the benefit of all. To this end, a State or the competent international organization conducting such research beyond areas under national jurisdiction shall actively promote the publication and dissemination to any interested States of the results of that research and information relating to its objectives and methods and, to the extent practicable, shall facilitate the participation of scientists from those States in such research.

Article 15

Enclosed and semi-enclosed seas

In implementing this Agreement in an enclosed or semi-enclosed sea, States shall take into account the natural characteristics of that sea and shall also act in a manner consistent with Part IX of the Convention and other relevant provisions thereof.

Article 16

Areas of high seas surrounded entirely by an area under the national jurisdiction of a single State

1. States fishing for straddling fish stocks and highly migratory fish stocks in an area of the high seas surrounded entirely by an area under the national jurisdiction of a single State and the latter State shall cooperate to establish conservation and management measures in respect of those stocks in the high seas area. Having regard to the natural characteristics of the area, States shall pay special attention to the establishment of compatible conservation and management measures for such stocks pursuant to article 7. Measures taken in respect of the high seas shall take into account the rights, duties and interests of the coastal State under the Convention, shall be based on the best scientific evidence available and shall also take into account any conservation and management measures adopted and applied in respect of the same stocks in accordance with article 61 of the Convention by the coastal State in the area under national jurisdiction. States shall also agree on measures for monitoring, control, surveillance and enforcement to ensure compliance with the conservation and management measures in respect of the high seas.

2. Pursuant to article 8, States shall act in good faith and make every effort to agree without delay on conservation and management measures to be applied in the carrying out of fishing operations in the area referred to in paragraph 1. If, within a reasonable period of time, the fishing States concerned and the coastal State are unable to agree on such measures, they shall, having regard to paragraph 1, apply article 7, paragraphs 4, 5 and 6, relating to provisional arrangements or measures. Pending the establishment of such provisional arrangements or measures, the States concerned shall take measures in respect of vessels flying their flag in order that they not engage in fisheries which could undermine the stocks concerned.

PART IV

NON-MEMBERS AND NON-PARTICIPANTS

Article 17

Non-members of organizations and non-participants in arrangements

1. A State which is not a member of a subregional or regional fisheries management organization or is not a participant in a subregional or regional fisheries management arrangement, and which does not otherwise agree to apply the conservation and management measures established by such organization or arrangement, is not discharged from the obligation to cooperate, in accordance with the Convention and this Agreement, in the conservation and management of the relevant straddling fish stocks and highly migratory fish stocks.

2. Such State shall not authorize vessels flying its flag to engage in fishing operations for the straddling fish stocks or highly migratory fish stocks which are subject to the conservation and management measures established by such organization or arrangement.

3. States which are members of a subregional or regional fisheries management organization or participants in a subregional or regional fisheries management arrangement shall, individually or jointly, request the fishing entities referred to in article 1, paragraph 3, which have fishing vessels in the relevant area to cooperate fully with such organization or arrangement in implementing the conservation and management measures it has established, with a view to having such measures applied de facto as extensively as possible to fishing activities in the relevant area. Such fishing entities shall enjoy benefits from participation in the fishery commensurate with their commitment to comply with conservation and management measures in respect of the stocks.

4. States which are members of such organization or participants in such arrangement shall exchange information with respect to the activities of fishing vessels flying the flags of States which are neither members of the organization nor participants in the arrangement and which are engaged in fishing operations for the relevant stocks. They shall take measures consistent with this Agreement and international law to deter activities of such vessels which undermine the effectiveness of subregional or regional conservation and management measures.

PART V

DUTIES OF THE FLAG STATE

Article 18

Duties of the flag State

1. A State whose vessels fish on the high seas shall take such measures as may be necessary to ensure that vessels flying its flag comply with subregional and regional conservation and management measures and that such vessels do not engage in any activity which undermines the effectiveness of such measures.

2. A State shall authorize the use of vessels flying its flag for fishing on the high seas only where it is able to exercise effectively its responsibilities in respect of such vessels under the Convention and this Agreement.

3. Measures to be taken by a State in respect of vessels flying its flag shall include:

(a) control of such vessels on the high seas by means of fishing licences, authorizations or permits, in accordance with any applicable procedures agreed at the subregional, regional or global level;

(b) establishment of regulations:

(i) to apply terms and conditions to the licence, authorization or permit sufficient to fulfil any subregional, regional or global obligations of the flag State;

(ii) to prohibit fishing on the high seas by vessels which are not duly licensed or authorized to fish, or fishing on the high seas by vessels otherwise than in accordance with the terms and conditions of a licence, authorization or permit;

(iii) to require vessels fishing on the high seas to carry the licence, authorization or permit on board at all times and to produce it on demand for inspection by a duly authorized person; and

(iv) to ensure that vessels flying its flag do not conduct unauthorized fishing within areas under the national jurisdiction of other States;

(c) establishment of a national record of fishing vessels authorized to fish on the high seas and provision of access to the information contained in that record on request by directly interested States, taking into account any national laws of the flag State regarding the release of such information;

(d) requirements for marking of fishing vessels and fishing gear for identification in accordance with uniform and internationally recognizable vessel and gear marking systems, such as the Food and Agriculture Organization of the United Nations Standard Specifications for the Marking and Identification of Fishing Vessels;

(e) requirements for recording and timely reporting of vessel position, catch of target and non-target species, fishing effort and other relevant fisheries data in accordance with subregional, regional and global standards for collection of such data;

(f) requirements for verifying the catch of target and non-target species through such means as observer programmes, inspection schemes, unloading reports, supervision of transshipment and monitoring of landed catches and market statistics;

(g) monitoring, control and surveillance of such vessels, their fishing operations and related activities by, inter alia:

(i) the implementation of national inspection schemes and subregional and regional schemes for cooperation in enforcement pursuant to articles 21 and 22, including requirements for such vessels to permit access by duly authorized inspectors from other States;

(ii) the implementation of national observer programmes and subregional and regional observer programmes in which the flag State is a participant, including requirements for such vessels to permit access by observers from other States to carry out the functions agreed under the programmes; and

(iii) the development and implementation of vessel monitoring systems, including, as appropriate, satellite transmitter systems, in accordance with any national programmes and those which have been subregionally, regionally or globally agreed among the States concerned;

(h) regulation of transshipment on the high seas to ensure that the effectiveness of conservation and management measures is not undermined; and

(i) regulation of fishing activities to ensure compliance with subregional, regional or global measures, including those aimed at minimizing catches of non-target species.

4. Where there is a subregionally, regionally or globally-agreed system of monitoring, control and surveillance in effect, States shall ensure that the measures they impose on vessels flying their flag are compatible with that system.

PART VI

COMPLIANCE AND ENFORCEMENT

Article 19

Compliance and enforcement by the flag State

1. A State shall ensure compliance by vessels flying its flag with subregional and regional conservation and management measures for straddling fish stocks and highly migratory fish stocks. To this end, that State shall:

(a) enforce such measures irrespective of where violations occur;

(b) investigate immediately and fully any alleged violation of subregional or regional conservation and management measures, which may include the physical inspection of the vessels concerned, and report promptly to the State alleging the violation and the relevant subregional or regional organization or arrangement on the progress and outcome of the investigation;

(c) require any vessel flying its flag to give information to the investigating authority regarding vessel position, catches, fishing gear, fishing operations and related activities in the area of an alleged violation;

(d) if satisfied that sufficient evidence is available in respect of an alleged violation, refer the case to its authorities with a view to instituting proceedings without delay in accordance with its laws and, where appropriate, detain the vessel concerned; and

(e) ensure that, where it has been established, in accordance with its laws, a vessel has been involved in the commission of a serious violation of such measures, the vessel does not engage in fishing operations on the high seas until such time as all outstanding sanctions imposed by the flag State in respect of the violation have been complied with.

2. All investigations and judicial proceedings shall be carried out expeditiously. Sanctions applicable in respect of violations shall be adequate in severity to be effective in securing compliance and to discourage violations wherever they occur and shall deprive offenders of the benefits accruing from their illegal activities. Measures applicable in respect of masters and other officers of fishing vessels shall include provisions which may permit, inter alia, refusal, withdrawal or suspension of authorizations to serve as masters or officers on such vessels.

Article 20

International cooperation in enforcement

1. States shall cooperate, either directly or through subregional or regional fisheries management organizations or arrangements, to ensure compliance with and enforcement of subregional and regional conservation and management measures for straddling fish stocks and highly migratory fish stocks.

2. A flag State conducting an investigation of an alleged violation of conservation and management measures for straddling fish stocks or highly migratory fish stocks may request the assistance of any other State whose cooperation may be useful in the conduct of that investigation. All States shall endeavour to meet reasonable requests made by a flag State in connection with such investigations.

3. A flag State may undertake such investigations directly, in cooperation with other interested States or through the relevant subregional or regional fisheries management organization or arrangement. Information on the progress and outcome of the investigations shall be provided to all States having an interest in, or affected by, the alleged violation.

4. States shall assist each other in identifying vessels reported to have engaged in activities undermining the effectiveness of subregional, regional or global conservation and management measures.

5. States shall, to the extent permitted by national laws and regulations, establish arrangements for making available to prosecuting authorities in other States evidence relating to alleged violations of such measures.

6. Where there are reasonable grounds for believing that a vessel on the high seas has been engaged in unauthorized fishing within an area under the jurisdiction of a coastal State, the flag State of that vessel, at the request of the coastal State concerned, shall immediately and fully investigate the matter. The flag State shall cooperate with the coastal State in taking appropriate enforcement action in such cases and may authorize the relevant authorities of the coastal State to board and inspect the vessel on the high seas. This paragraph is without prejudice to article 111 of the Convention.

7. States Parties which are members of a subregional or regional fisheries management organization or participants in a subregional or regional fisheries management arrangement may take action in accordance with international law, including through recourse to subregional or regional procedures established for this purpose, to deter vessels which have engaged in activities which undermine the effectiveness of or otherwise violate the conservation and management measures established by that organization or arrangement from fishing on the high seas in the subregion or region until such time as appropriate action is taken by the flag State.

Article 21

Subregional and regional cooperation in enforcement

1. In any high seas area covered by a subregional or regional fisheries management organization or arrangement, a State Party which is a member of such organization or a participant in such arrangement may, through its duly authorized inspectors, board and inspect, in accordance with paragraph 2, fishing vessels flying the flag of another State Party to this Agreement, whether or not such State Party is also a member of the organization or a participant in the arrangement, for the purpose of ensuring compliance with conservation and management measures for straddling fish stocks and highly migratory fish stocks established by that organization or arrangement.

2. States shall establish, through subregional or regional fisheries management organizations or arrangements, procedures for boarding and inspection pursuant to paragraph 1, as well as procedures to implement other provisions of this article. Such procedures shall be consistent with this article and the basic procedures set out in article 22 and shall not discriminate against non-members of the organization or non-participants in the arrangement. Boarding and inspection as well as any subsequent enforcement action shall be conducted in accordance with such procedures. States shall give due publicity to procedures established pursuant to this paragraph.

3. If, within two years of the adoption of this Agreement, any organization or arrangement has not established such procedures, boarding and inspection pursuant to paragraph 1, as well as any subsequent enforcement action, shall, pending the establishment of such procedures, be conducted in accordance with this article and the basic procedures set out in article 22.

4. Prior to taking action under this article, inspecting States shall, either directly or through the relevant subregional or regional fisheries management organization or arrangement, inform all States whose vessels fish on the high seas in the subregion or region of the form of identification issued to their duly authorized inspectors. The vessels used for boarding and inspection shall be clearly marked and identifiable as being on government service. At the time of becoming a Party to this Agreement, a State shall designate an appropriate authority to receive notifications pursuant to this article and shall give due publicity of such designation through the relevant subregional or regional fisheries management organization or arrangement.

5. Where, following a boarding and inspection, there are clear grounds for believing that a vessel has engaged in any activity contrary to the conservation and management measures referred to in paragraph 1, the inspecting State shall, where appropriate, secure evidence and shall promptly notify the flag State of the alleged violation.

6. The flag State shall respond to the notification referred to in paragraph 5 within three working days of its receipt, or such other period as may be prescribed in procedures established in accordance with paragraph 2, and shall either:

(a) fulfil, without delay, its obligations under article 19 to investigate and, if evidence so warrants, take enforcement action with respect to the vessel, in which case it shall promptly inform the inspecting State of the results of the investigation and of any enforcement action taken; or

(b) authorize the inspecting State to investigate.

7. Where the flag State authorizes the inspecting State to investigate an alleged violation, the inspecting State shall, without delay, communicate the results of that investigation to the flag State. The flag State shall, if evidence so warrants, fulfil its obligations to take enforcement action with respect to the vessel. Alternatively, the flag State may authorize the inspecting State to take such enforcement action as the flag State may specify with respect to the vessel, consistent with the rights and obligations of the flag State under this Agreement.

8. Where, following boarding and inspection, there are clear grounds for believing that a vessel has committed a serious violation, and the flag State has either failed to respond or failed to take action as required under paragraphs 6 or 7, the inspectors may remain on board and secure evidence and may require the master to assist in further investigation including, where appropriate, by bringing the vessel without delay to the nearest appropriate port, or to such other port as may be specified in procedures established in accordance with paragraph 2. The inspecting State shall immediately inform the flag State of the name of the port to which the vessel is to proceed. The

inspecting State and the flag State and, as appropriate, the port State shall take all necessary steps to ensure the well-being of the crew regardless of their nationality.

9. The inspecting State shall inform the flag State and the relevant organization or the participants in the relevant arrangement of the results of any further investigation.

10. The inspecting State shall require its inspectors to observe generally accepted international regulations, procedures and practices relating to the safety of the vessel and the crew, minimize interference with fishing operations and, to the extent practicable, avoid action which would adversely affect the quality of the catch on board. The inspecting State shall ensure that boarding and inspection is not conducted in a manner that would constitute harassment of any fishing vessel.

11. For the purposes of this article, a serious violation means:

(a) fishing without a valid licence, authorization or permit issued by the flag State in accordance with article 18, paragraph 3 (a);

(b) failing to maintain accurate records of catch and catch-related data, as required by the relevant subregional or regional fisheries management organization or arrangement, or serious misreporting of catch, contrary to the catch reporting requirements of such organization or arrangement;

(c) fishing in a closed area, fishing during a closed season or fishing without, or after attainment of, a quota established by the relevant subregional or regional fisheries management organization or arrangement;

(d) directed fishing for a stock which is subject to a moratorium or for which fishing is prohibited;

(e) using prohibited fishing gear;

(f) falsifying or concealing the markings, identity or registration of a fishing vessel;

(g) concealing, tampering with or disposing of evidence relating to an investigation;

(h) multiple violations which together constitute a serious disregard of conservation and management measures; or

(i) such other violations as may be specified in procedures established by the relevant subregional or regional fisheries management organization or arrangement.

12. Notwithstanding the other provisions of this article, the flag State may, at any time, take action to fulfil its obligations under article 19 with respect to an alleged violation. Where the vessel is under the direction of the inspecting State, the inspecting State shall, at the request of the flag State, release the vessel to the flag State along with full information on the progress and outcome of its investigation.

13. This article is without prejudice to the right of the flag State to take any measures, including proceedings to impose penalties, according to its laws.

14. This article applies mutatis mutandis to boarding and inspection by a State Party which is a member of a subregional or regional fisheries management organization or a participant in a subregional or regional fisheries management arrangement and which has clear grounds for believing that a fishing vessel flying the flag of another State Party has engaged in any activity contrary to

relevant conservation and management measures referred to in paragraph 1 in the high seas area covered by such organization or arrangement, and such vessel has subsequently, during the same fishing trip, entered into an area under the national jurisdiction of the inspecting State.

15. Where a subregional or regional fisheries management organization or arrangement has established an alternative mechanism which effectively discharges the obligation under this Agreement of its members or participants to ensure compliance with the conservation and management measures established by the organization or arrangement, members of such organization or participants in such arrangement may agree to limit the application of paragraph 1 as between themselves in respect of the conservation and management measures which have been established in the relevant high seas area.

16. Action taken by States other than the flag State in respect of vessels having engaged in activities contrary to subregional or regional conservation and management measures shall be proportionate to the seriousness of the violation.

17. Where there are reasonable grounds for suspecting that a fishing vessel on the high seas is without nationality, a State may board and inspect the vessel. Where evidence so warrants, the State may take such action as may be appropriate in accordance with international law.

18. States shall be liable for damage or loss attributable to them arising from action taken pursuant to this article when such action is unlawful or exceeds that reasonably required in the light of available information to implement the provisions of this article.

Article 22

Basic procedures for boarding and inspection pursuant to article 21

1. The inspecting State shall ensure that its duly authorized inspectors:

(a) present credentials to the master of the vessel and produce a copy of the text of the relevant conservation and management measures or rules and regulations in force in the high seas area in question pursuant to those measures;

(b) initiate notice to the flag State at the time of the boarding and inspection;

(c) do not interfere with the master's ability to communicate with the authorities of the flag State during the boarding and inspection;

(d) provide a copy of a report on the boarding and inspection to the master and to the authorities of the flag State, noting therein any objection or statement which the master wishes to have included in the report;

(e) promptly leave the vessel following completion of the inspection if they find no evidence of a serious violation; and

(f) avoid the use of force except when and to the degree necessary to ensure the safety of the inspectors and where the inspectors are obstructed in the execution of their duties. The degree of force used shall not exceed that reasonably required in the circumstances.

2. The duly authorized inspectors of an inspecting State shall have the authority to inspect the vessel, its licence, gear, equipment, records, facilities, fish and fish products and any relevant documents necessary to verify compliance with the relevant conservation and management measures.

3. The flag State shall ensure that vessel masters:

(a) accept and facilitate prompt and safe boarding by the inspectors;

(b) cooperate with and assist in the inspection of the vessel conducted pursuant to these procedures;

(c) do not obstruct, intimidate or interfere with the inspectors in the performance of their duties;

(d) allow the inspectors to communicate with the authorities of the flag State and the inspecting State during the boarding and inspection;

(e) provide reasonable facilities, including, where appropriate, food and accommodation, to the inspectors; and

(f) facilitate safe disembarkation by the inspectors.

4. In the event that the master of a vessel refuses to accept boarding and inspection in accordance with this article and article 21, the flag State shall, except in circumstances where, in accordance with generally accepted international regulations, procedures and practices relating to safety at sea, it is necessary to delay the boarding and inspection, direct the master of the vessel to submit immediately to boarding and inspection and, if the master does not comply with such direction, shall suspend the vessel's authorization to fish and order the vessel to return immediately to port. The flag State shall advise the inspecting State of the action it has taken when the circumstances referred to in this paragraph arise.

Article 23

Measures taken by a port State

1. A port State has the right and the duty to take measures, in accordance with international law, to promote the effectiveness of subregional, regional and global conservation and management measures. When taking such measures a port State shall not discriminate in form or in fact against the vessels of any State.

2. A port State may, inter alia, inspect documents, fishing gear and catch on board fishing vessels, when such vessels are voluntarily in its ports or at its offshore terminals.

3. States may adopt regulations empowering the relevant national authorities to prohibit landings and transshipments where it has been established that the catch has been taken in a manner which undermines the effectiveness of subregional, regional or global conservation and management measures on the high seas.

4. Nothing in this article affects the exercise by States of their sovereignty over ports in their territory in accordance with international law.

PART VII

REQUIREMENTS OF DEVELOPING STATES

Article 24

Recognition of the special requirements of developing States

1. States shall give full recognition to the special requirements of developing States in relation to conservation and management of straddling fish

stocks and highly migratory fish stocks and development of fisheries for such stocks. To this end, States shall, either directly or through the United Nations Development Programme, the Food and Agriculture Organization of the United Nations and other specialized agencies, the Global Environment Facility, the Commission on Sustainable Development and other appropriate international and regional organizations and bodies, provide assistance to developing States.

2. In giving effect to the duty to cooperate in the establishment of conservation and management measures for straddling fish stocks and highly migratory fish stocks, States shall take into account the special requirements of developing States, in particular:

(a) the vulnerability of developing States which are dependent on the exploitation of living marine resources, including for meeting the nutritional requirements of their populations or parts thereof;

(b) the need to avoid adverse impacts on, and ensure access to fisheries by, subsistence, small-scale and artisanal fishers and women fishworkers, as well as indigenous people in developing States, particularly small island developing States; and

(c) the need to ensure that such measures do not result in transferring, directly or indirectly, a disproportionate burden of conservation action onto developing States.

Article 25

Forms of cooperation with developing States

1. States shall cooperate, either directly or through subregional, regional or global organizations:

(a) to enhance the ability of developing States, in particular the least-developed among them and small island developing States, to conserve and manage straddling fish stocks and highly migratory fish stocks and to develop their own fisheries for such stocks;

(b) to assist developing States, in particular the least-developed among them and small island developing States, to enable them to participate in high seas fisheries for such stocks, including facilitating access to such fisheries subject to articles 5 and 11; and

(c) to facilitate the participation of developing States in subregional and regional fisheries management organizations and arrangements.

2. Cooperation with developing States for the purposes set out in this article shall include the provision of financial assistance, assistance relating to human resources development, technical assistance, transfer of technology, including through joint venture arrangements, and advisory and consultative services.

3. Such assistance shall, inter alia, be directed specifically towards:

(a) improved conservation and management of straddling fish stocks and highly migratory fish stocks through collection, reporting, verification, exchange and analysis of fisheries data and related information;

(b) stock assessment and scientific research; and

(c) monitoring, control, surveillance, compliance and enforcement, including training and capacity-building at the local level, development and funding of national and regional observer programmes and access to technology and equipment.

Article 26

Special assistance in the implementation of this Agreement

1. States shall cooperate to establish special funds to assist developing States in the implementation of this Agreement, including assisting developing States to meet the costs involved in any proceedings for the settlement of disputes to which they may be parties.

2. States and international organizations should assist developing States in establishing new subregional or regional fisheries management organizations or arrangements, or in strengthening existing organizations or arrangements, for the conservation and management of straddling fish stocks and highly migratory fish stocks.

PART VIII

PEACEFUL SETTLEMENT OF DISPUTES

Article 27

Obligation to settle disputes by peaceful means

States have the obligation to settle their disputes by negotiation, inquiry, mediation, conciliation, arbitration, judicial settlement, resort to regional agencies or arrangements, or other peaceful means of their own choice.

Article 28

Prevention of disputes

States shall cooperate in order to prevent disputes. To this end, States shall agree on efficient and expeditious decision-making procedures within subregional and regional fisheries management organizations and arrangements and shall strengthen existing decision-making procedures as necessary.

Article 29

Disputes of a technical nature

Where a dispute concerns a matter of a technical nature, the States concerned may refer the dispute to an ad hoc expert panel established by them. The panel shall confer with the States concerned and shall endeavour to resolve the dispute expeditiously without recourse to binding procedures for the settlement of disputes.

Article 30

Procedures for the settlement of disputes

1. The provisions relating to the settlement of disputes set out in Part XV of the Convention apply mutatis mutandis to any dispute between States Parties to this Agreement concerning the interpretation or application of this Agreement, whether or not they are also Parties to the Convention.

2. The provisions relating to the settlement of disputes set out in Part XV of the Convention apply mutatis mutandis to any dispute between States Parties to this Agreement concerning the interpretation or application of a subregional, regional or global fisheries agreement relating to straddling fish stocks or

highly migratory fish stocks to which they are parties, including any dispute concerning the conservation and management of such stocks, whether or not they are also Parties to the Convention.

3. Any procedure accepted by a State Party to this Agreement and the Convention pursuant to article 287 of the Convention shall apply to the settlement of disputes under this Part, unless that State Party, when signing, ratifying or acceding to this Agreement, or at any time thereafter, has accepted another procedure pursuant to article 287 for the settlement of disputes under this Part.

4. A State Party to this Agreement which is not a Party to the Convention, when signing, ratifying or acceding to this Agreement, or at any time thereafter, shall be free to choose, by means of a written declaration, one or more of the means set out in article 287, paragraph 1, of the Convention for the settlement of disputes under this Part. Article 287 shall apply to such a declaration, as well as to any dispute to which such State is a party which is not covered by a declaration in force. For the purposes of conciliation and arbitration in accordance with Annexes V, VII and VIII to the Convention, such State shall be entitled to nominate conciliators, arbitrators and experts to be included in the lists referred to in Annex V, article 2, Annex VII, article 2, and Annex VIII, article 2, for the settlement of disputes under this Part.

5. Any court or tribunal to which a dispute has been submitted under this Part shall apply the relevant provisions of the Convention, of this Agreement and of any relevant subregional, regional or global fisheries agreement, as well as generally accepted standards for the conservation and management of living marine resources and other rules of international law not incompatible with the Convention, with a view to ensuring the conservation of the straddling fish stocks and highly migratory fish stocks concerned.

Article 31

Provisional measures

1. Pending the settlement of a dispute in accordance with this Part, the parties to the dispute shall make every effort to enter into provisional arrangements of a practical nature.

2. Without prejudice to article 290 of the Convention, the court or tribunal to which the dispute has been submitted under this Part may prescribe any provisional measures which it considers appropriate under the circumstances to preserve the respective rights of the parties to the dispute or to prevent damage to the stocks in question, as well as in the circumstances referred to in article 7, paragraph 5, and article 16, paragraph 2.

3. A State Party to this Agreement which is not a Party to the Convention may declare that, notwithstanding article 290, paragraph 5, of the Convention, the International Tribunal for the Law of the Sea shall not be entitled to prescribe, modify or revoke provisional measures without the agreement of such State.

Article 32

Limitations on applicability of procedures for the settlement of disputes

Article 297, paragraph 3, of the Convention applies also to this Agreement.

PART IX

NON-PARTIES TO THIS AGREEMENT

Article 33

Non-parties to this Agreement

1. States Parties shall encourage non-parties to this Agreement to become parties thereto and to adopt laws and regulations consistent with its provisions.

2. States Parties shall take measures consistent with this Agreement and international law to deter the activities of vessels flying the flag of non-parties which undermine the effective implementation of this Agreement.

PART X

GOOD FAITH AND ABUSE OF RIGHTS

Article 34

Good faith and abuse of rights

States Parties shall fulfil in good faith the obligations assumed under this Agreement and shall exercise the rights recognized in this Agreement in a manner which would not constitute an abuse of right.

PART XI

RESPONSIBILITY AND LIABILITY

Article 35

Responsibility and liability

States Parties are liable in accordance with international law for damage or loss attributable to them in regard to this Agreement.

PART XII

REVIEW CONFERENCE

Article 36

Review conference

1. Four years after the date of entry into force of this Agreement, the Secretary-General of the United Nations shall convene a conference with a view to assessing the effectiveness of this Agreement in securing the conservation and management of straddling fish stocks and highly migratory fish stocks. The Secretary-General shall invite to the conference all States Parties and those States and entities which are entitled to become parties to this Agreement as well as those intergovernmental and non-governmental organizations entitled to participate as observers.

2. The conference shall review and assess the adequacy of the provisions of this Agreement and, if necessary, propose means of strengthening the substance and methods of implementation of those provisions in order better to address any continuing problems in the conservation and management of straddling fish stocks and highly migratory fish stocks.

PART XIII

FINAL PROVISIONS

Article 37

Signature

This Agreement shall be open for signature by all States and the other entities referred to in article 1, paragraph 2(b), and shall remain open for signature at United Nations Headquarters for twelve months from the fourth of December 1995.

Article 38

Ratification

This Agreement is subject to ratification by States and the other entities referred to in article 1, paragraph 2(b). The instruments of ratification shall be deposited with the Secretary-General of the United Nations.

Article 39

Accession

This Agreement shall remain open for accession by States and the other entities referred to in article 1, paragraph 2(b). The instruments of accession shall be deposited with the Secretary-General of the United Nations.

Article 40

Entry into force

1. This Agreement shall enter into force 30 days after the date of deposit of the thirtieth instrument of ratification or accession.

2. For each State or entity which ratifies the Agreement or accedes thereto after the deposit of the thirtieth instrument of ratification or accession, this Agreement shall enter into force on the thirtieth day following the deposit of its instrument of ratification or accession.

Article 41

Provisional application

1. This Agreement shall be applied provisionally by a State or entity which consents to its provisional application by so notifying the depositary in writing. Such provisional application shall become effective from the date of receipt of the notification.

2. Provisional application by a State or entity shall terminate upon the entry into force of this Agreement for that State or entity or upon notification by that State or entity to the depositary in writing of its intention to terminate provisional application.

Article 42

Reservations and exceptions

No reservations or exceptions may be made to this Agreement.

Article 43

Declarations and statements

Article 42 does not preclude a State or entity, when signing, ratifying or acceding to this Agreement, from making declarations or statements, however phrased or named, with a view, inter alia, to the harmonization of its laws and regulations with the provisions of this Agreement, provided that such declarations or statements do not purport to exclude or to modify the legal effect of the provisions of this Agreement in their application to that State or entity.

Article 44

Relation to other agreements

1. This Agreement shall not alter the rights and obligations of States Parties which arise from other agreements compatible with this Agreement and which do not affect the enjoyment by other States Parties of their rights or the performance of their obligations under this Agreement.

2. Two or more States Parties may conclude agreements modifying or suspending the operation of provisions of this Agreement, applicable solely to the relations between them, provided that such agreements do not relate to a provision derogation from which is incompatible with the effective execution of the object and purpose of this Agreement, and provided further that such agreements shall not affect the application of the basic principles embodied herein, and that the provisions of such agreements do not affect the enjoyment by other States Parties of their rights or the performance of their obligations under this Agreement.

3. States Parties intending to conclude an agreement referred to in paragraph 2 shall notify the other States Parties through the depositary of this Agreement of their intention to conclude the agreement and of the modification or suspension for which it provides.

Article 45

Amendment

1. A State Party may, by written communication addressed to the Secretary-General of the United Nations, propose amendments to this Agreement and request the convening of a conference to consider such proposed amendments. The Secretary-General shall circulate such communication to all States Parties. If, within six months from the date of the circulation of the communication, not less than one half of the States Parties reply favourably to the request, the Secretary-General shall convene the conference.

2. The decision-making procedure applicable at the amendment conference convened pursuant to paragraph 1 shall be the same as that applicable at the United Nations Conference on Straddling Fish Stocks and Highly Migratory Fish Stocks, unless otherwise decided by the conference. The conference should make every effort to reach agreement on any amendments by way of consensus and there should be no voting on them until all efforts at consensus have been exhausted.

3. Once adopted, amendments to this Agreement shall be open for signature at United Nations Headquarters by States Parties for twelve months from the date of adoption, unless otherwise provided in the amendment itself.

4. Articles 38, 39, 47 and 50 apply to all amendments to this Agreement.

5. Amendments to this Agreement shall enter into force for the States Parties ratifying or acceding to them on the thirtieth day following the deposit of instruments of ratification or accession by two thirds of the States Parties. Thereafter, for each State Party ratifying or acceding to an amendment after the deposit of the required number of such instruments, the amendment shall enter into force on the thirtieth day following the deposit of its instrument of ratification or accession.

6. An amendment may provide that a smaller or a larger number of ratifications or accessions shall be required for its entry into force than are required by this article.

7. A State which becomes a Party to this Agreement after the entry into force of amendments in accordance with paragraph 5 shall, failing an expression of a different intention by that State:

(a) be considered as a Party to this Agreement as so amended; and

(b) be considered as a Party to the unamended Agreement in relation to any State Party not bound by the amendment.

Article 46

Denunciation

1. A State Party may, by written notification addressed to the Secretary-General of the United Nations, denounce this Agreement and may indicate its reasons. Failure to indicate reasons shall not affect the validity of the denunciation. The denunciation shall take effect one year after the date of receipt of the notification, unless the notification specifies a later date.

2. The denunciation shall not in any way affect the duty of any State Party to fulfil any obligation embodied in this Agreement to which it would be subject under international law independently of this Agreement.

Article 47

Participation by international organizations

1. In cases where an international organization referred to in Annex IX, article 1, of the Convention does not have competence over all the matters governed by this Agreement, Annex IX to the Convention shall apply mutatis mutandis to participation by such international organization in this Agreement, except that the following provisions of that Annex shall not apply:

(a) article 2, first sentence; and

(b) article 3, paragraph 1.

2. In cases where an international organization referred to in Annex IX, article 1, of the Convention has competence over all the matters governed by this Agreement, the following provisions shall apply to participation by such international organization in this Agreement:

(a) at the time of signature or accession, such international organization shall make a declaration stating:

(i) that it has competence over all the matters governed by this Agreement;

(ii) that, for this reason, its member States shall not become States Parties, except in respect of their territories for which the international organization has no responsibility; and

(iii) that it accepts the rights and obligations of States under this Agreement;

(b) participation of such an international organization shall in no case confer any rights under this Agreement on member States of the international organization;

(c) in the event of a conflict between the obligations of an international organization under this Agreement and its obligations under the agreement establishing the international organization or any acts relating to it, the obligations under this Agreement shall prevail.

Article 48

Annexes

1. The Annexes form an integral part of this Agreement and, unless expressly provided otherwise, a reference to this Agreement or to one of its Parts includes a reference to the Annexes relating thereto.

2. The Annexes may be revised from time to time by States Parties. Such revisions shall be based on scientific and technical considerations. Notwithstanding the provisions of article 45, if a revision to an Annex is adopted by consensus at a meeting of States Parties, it shall be incorporated in this Agreement and shall take effect from the date of its adoption or from such other date as may be specified in the revision. If a revision to an Annex is not adopted by consensus at such a meeting, the amendment procedures set out in article 45 shall apply.

Article 49

Depositary

The Secretary-General of the United Nations shall be the depositary of this Agreement and any amendments or revisions thereto.

Article 50

Authentic texts

The Arabic, Chinese, English, French, Russian and Spanish texts of this Agreement are equally authentic.

IN WITNESS WHEREOF, the undersigned Plenipotentiaries, being duly authorized thereto, have signed this Agreement.

OPENED FOR SIGNATURE at New York, this fourth day of December, one thousand nine hundred and ninety-five, in a single original, in the Arabic, Chinese, English, French, Russian and Spanish languages.

Annex I

STANDARD REQUIREMENTS FOR THE COLLECTION AND SHARING OF DATA

Article 1

General principles

1. The timely collection, compilation and analysis of data are fundamental to the effective conservation and management of straddling fish stocks and highly migratory fish stocks. To this end, data from fisheries for these stocks on the high seas and those in areas under national jurisdiction are required and should be collected and compiled in such a way as to enable statistically meaningful analysis for the purposes of fishery resource conservation and management. These data include catch and fishing effort statistics and other fishery-related information, such as vessel-related and other data for standardizing fishing effort. Data collected should also include information on non-target and associated or dependent species. All data should be verified to ensure accuracy. Confidentiality of non-aggregated data shall be maintained. The dissemination of such data shall be subject to the terms on which they have been provided.

2. Assistance, including training as well as financial and technical assistance, shall be provided to developing States in order to build capacity in the field of conservation and management of living marine resources. Assistance should focus on enhancing capacity to implement data collection and verification, observer programmes, data analysis and research projects supporting stock assessments. The fullest possible involvement of developing State scientists and managers in conservation and management of straddling fish stocks and highly migratory fish stocks should be promoted.

Article 2

Principles of data collection, compilation and exchange

The following general principles should be considered in defining the parameters for collection, compilation and exchange of data from fishing operations for straddling fish stocks and highly migratory fish stocks:

(a) States should ensure that data are collected from vessels flying their flag on fishing activities according to the operational characteristics of each fishing method (e.g., each individual tow for trawl, each set for long-line and purse-seine, each school fished for pole-and-line and each day fished for troll) and in sufficient detail to facilitate effective stock assessment;

(b) States should ensure that fishery data are verified through an appropriate system;

(c) States should compile fishery-related and other supporting scientific data and provide them in an agreed format and in a timely manner to the relevant subregional or regional fisheries management organization or arrangement where one exists. Otherwise, States should cooperate to exchange data either directly or through such other cooperative mechanisms as may be agreed among them;

(d) States should agree, within the framework of subregional or regional fisheries management organizations or arrangements, or otherwise, on the specification of data and the format in which they are to be provided, in accordance with this Annex and taking into account the nature of the stocks and the fisheries for those stocks in the region. Such organizations or arrangements should request non-members or non-participants to provide data concerning relevant fishing activities by vessels flying their flag;

(e) such organizations or arrangements shall compile data and make them available in a timely manner and in an agreed format to all interested States under the terms and conditions established by the organization or arrangement; and

(f) scientists of the flag State and from the relevant subregional or regional fisheries management organization or arrangement should analyse the data separately or jointly, as appropriate.

Article 3

Basic fishery data

1. States shall collect and make available to the relevant subregional or regional fisheries management organization or arrangement the following types of data in sufficient detail to facilitate effective stock assessment in accordance with agreed procedures:

(a) time series of catch and effort statistics by fishery and fleet;

(b) total catch in number, nominal weight, or both, by species (both target and non-target) as is appropriate to each fishery. [Nominal weight is defined by the Food and Agriculture Organization of the United Nations as the live-weight equivalent of the landings];

(c) discard statistics, including estimates where necessary, reported as number or nominal weight by species, as is appropriate to each fishery;

(d) effort statistics appropriate to each fishing method; and

(e) fishing location, date and time fished and other statistics on fishing operations as appropriate.

2. States shall also collect where appropriate and provide to the relevant subregional or regional fisheries management organization or arrangement information to support stock assessment, including:

(a) composition of the catch according to length, weight and sex;

(b) other biological information supporting stock assessments, such as information on age, growth, recruitment, distribution and stock identity; and

(c) other relevant research, including surveys of abundance, biomass surveys, hydro-acoustic surveys, research on environmental factors affecting stock abundance, and oceanographic and ecological studies.

Article 4

Vessel data and information

1. States should collect the following types of vessel-related data for standardizing fleet composition and vessel fishing power and for converting between different measures of effort in the analysis of catch and effort data:

(a) vessel identification, flag and port of registry;

(b) vessel type;

(c) vessel specifications (e.g., material of construction, date built, registered length, gross registered tonnage, power of main engines, hold capacity and catch storage methods); and

(d) fishing gear description (e.g., types, gear specifications and quantity).

2. The flag State will collect the following information:

(a) navigation and position fixing aids;

(b) communication equipment and international radio call sign; and

(c) crew size.

Article 5

Reporting

A State shall ensure that vessels flying its flag send to its national fisheries administration and, where agreed, to the relevant subregional or regional fisheries management organization or arrangement, logbook data on catch and effort, including data on fishing operations on the high seas, at sufficiently frequent intervals to meet national requirements and regional and international obligations. Such data shall be transmitted, where necessary, by radio, telex, facsimile or satellite transmission or by other means.

Article 6

Data verification

States or, as appropriate, subregional or regional fisheries management organizations or arrangements should establish mechanisms for verifying fishery data, such as:

(a) position verification through vessel monitoring systems;

(b) scientific observer programmes to monitor catch, effort, catch composition (target and non-target) and other details of fishing operations;

(c) vessel trip, landing and transshipment reports; and

(d) port sampling.

Article 7

Data exchange

1. Data collected by flag States must be shared with other flag States and relevant coastal States through appropriate subregional or regional fisheries management organizations or arrangements. Such organizations or arrangements shall compile data and make them available in a timely manner and in an agreed format to all interested States under the terms and conditions established by the organization or arrangement, while maintaining confidentiality of non-aggregated data, and should, to the extent feasible, develop database systems which provide efficient access to data.

2. At the global level, collection and dissemination of data should be effected through the Food and Agriculture Organization of the United Nations. Where a subregional or regional fisheries management organization or arrangement does not exist, that organization may also do the same at the subregional or regional level by arrangement with the States concerned.

Annex II

GUIDELINES FOR THE APPLICATION OF PRECAUTIONARY REFERENCE POINTS IN CONSERVATION AND MANAGEMENT OF STRADDLING FISH STOCKS AND HIGHLY MIGRATORY FISH STOCKS

1. A precautionary reference point is an estimated value derived through an agreed scientific procedure, which corresponds to the state of the resource and of the fishery, and which can be used as a guide for fisheries management.

2. Two types of precautionary reference points should be used: conservation, or limit, reference points and management, or target, reference points. Limit reference points set boundaries which are intended to constrain harvesting within safe biological limits within which the stocks can produce maximum sustainable yield. Target reference points are intended to meet management objectives.

3. Precautionary reference points should be stock-specific to account, inter alia, for the reproductive capacity, the resilience of each stock and the characteristics of fisheries exploiting the stock, as well as other sources of mortality and major sources of uncertainty.

4. Management strategies shall seek to maintain or restore populations of harvested stocks, and where necessary associated or dependent species, at levels consistent with previously agreed precautionary reference points. Such reference points shall be used to trigger pre-agreed conservation and management action. Management strategies shall include measures which can be implemented when precautionary reference points are approached.

5. Fishery management strategies shall ensure that the risk of exceeding limit reference points is very low. If a stock falls below a limit reference point or is at risk of falling below such a reference point, conservation and management action should be initiated to facilitate stock recovery. Fishery management strategies shall ensure that target reference points are not exceeded on average.

6. When information for determining reference points for a fishery is poor or absent, provisional reference points shall be set. Provisional reference points may be established by analogy to similar and better-known stocks. In such situations, the fishery shall be subject to enhanced monitoring so as to enable revision of provisional reference points as improved information becomes available.

7. The fishing mortality rate which generates maximum sustainable yield should be regarded as a minimum standard for limit reference points. For stocks which are not overfished, fishery management strategies shall ensure that fishing mortality does not exceed that which corresponds to maximum sustainable yield, and that the biomass does not fall below a predefined threshold. For overfished stocks, the biomass which would produce maximum sustainable yield can serve as a rebuilding target.

ANNEX II

Resolution I

Early and effective implementation of the Agreement for the Implementation of the Provisions of the United Nations Convention on the Law of the Sea of 10 December 1982 relating to the Conservation and Management of Straddling Fish Stocks and Highly Migratory Fish Stocks

The United Nations Conference on Straddling Fish Stocks and Highly Migratory Fish Stocks,

Having adopted the Agreement for the Implementation of the Provisions of the United Nations Convention on the Law of the Sea of 10 December 1982 relating to the Conservation and Management of Straddling Fish Stocks and Highly Migratory Fish Stocks,

Underlining the importance of early and effective implementation of the Agreement,

Recognizing, therefore, the need to provide for the provisional application of the Agreement,

Emphasizing the importance of rapid entry into force of the Agreement and early achievement of universal participation,

1. Requests the Secretary-General of the United Nations to open the Agreement for signature in New York on 4 December 1995;

2. Urges all States and other entities referred to in article 1, paragraph 2 (b), of the Agreement to sign it on 4 December 1995 or at the earliest subsequent opportunity and thereafter to ratify, or accede to it;

3. Calls upon States and other entities referred to in paragraph 2 of the present resolution to apply the Agreement provisionally.

Resolution II

Reports on developments by the Secretary-General of the United Nations

The United Nations Conference on Straddling Fish Stocks and Highly Migratory Fish Stocks,

Having adopted the Agreement for the Implementation of the Provisions of the United Nations Convention on the Law of the Sea of 10 December 1982 relating to the Conservation and Management of Straddling Fish Stocks and Highly Migratory Fish Stocks,

Recognizing the importance of periodic consideration and review of developments relating to the conservation and management of straddling fish stocks and highly migratory fish stocks,

Recalling General Assembly resolution 49/28 of 6 December 1994, in which the Assembly underlined the importance of consideration and review of the overall developments relating to the law of the sea by the Assembly, as the global institution having the competence to undertake such a review,

Recalling also the responsibility of the Secretary-General under the United Nations Convention on the Law of the Sea to report on developments pertaining to the implementation of the Convention,

Recognizing the importance of exchange of information among States, and relevant intergovernmental and non-governmental organizations concerning the implementation of the Agreement,

1. _Recommends_ to the General Assembly that it review developments relating to the conservation and management of straddling fish stocks and highly migratory fish stocks, on the basis of a report to be submitted by the Secretary-General at the second session following the adoption of the Agreement and biennially thereafter;

2. _Requests_ the Secretary-General of the United Nations, in preparing such report, to take into account information provided by States, the Food and Agriculture Organization of the United Nations and its fisheries bodies and subregional and regional organizations and arrangements for the conservation and management of straddling fish stocks and highly migratory fish stocks, as well as other relevant intergovernmental bodies and relevant non-governmental organizations;

3. _Also requests_ the Secretary-General to cooperate with the Food and Agriculture Organization of the United Nations in order to ensure that reporting on all major fisheries instruments and activities is coordinated and the required scientific and technical analysis standardized to minimize duplication and to reduce the reporting burden for national administrations.

49. UNGA RESOLUTION ON AGREEMENT FOR THE IMPLEMENTATION OF THE PROVISIONS OF THE UNITED NATIONS CONVENTION ON THE LAW OF THE SEA OF 10 DECEMBER 1982 RELATING TO THE CONSERVATION AND MANAGEMENT OF STRADDLING FISH STOCKS AND HIGHLY MIGRATORY FISH STOCKS

Doc. no.: A/Res.50/24 5 December 1995

The General Assembly,

Recalling its resolutions 47/192 of 22 December 1992, 48/194 of 21 December 1993 and 49/121 of 19 December 1994, concerning the United Nations Conference on Straddling Fish Stocks and Highly Migratory Fish Stocks,

Taking note of resolutions I and II adopted by the Conference, 69/

Recognizing the importance of the regular consideration and review of developments relating to the conservation and management of straddling fish stocks and highly migratory fish stocks,

Taking note of the report of the Secretary-General on the work of the Conference, 70/

1. Expresses its appreciation to the United Nations Conference on Straddling Fish Stocks and Highly Migratory Fish Stocks for discharging its mandate under resolution 47/192 with the adoption of the Agreement for the Implementation of the Provisions of the United Nations Convention on the Law of the Sea of 10 December 1982 relating to the Conservation and Management of Straddling Fish Stocks and Highly Migratory Fish Stocks; 71/

2. Welcomes the opening for signature of the Agreement on 4 December 1995;

3. Emphasizes the importance of the early entry into force and effective implementation of the Agreement;

4. Calls upon all States and the other entities referred to in article 1, paragraph 2 (b), of the Agreement that have not done so to sign and ratify or accede to it, and consider applying it provisionally;

5. Requests the Secretary-General to report to the General Assembly on developments relating to the conservation and management of straddling fish stocks and highly migratory fish stocks at the fifty-first session and biennially thereafter, taking into account information provided by States, relevant specialized agencies, in particular the Food and Agriculture Organization of the United Nations, and other appropriate organs, organizations and programmes of the United Nations system, regional and subregional organizations and arrangements for the conservation and management of straddling fish stocks and highly migratory fish stocks, as well as other relevant intergovernmental bodies and non-governmental organizations;

69/ A/CONF.164/38, annex.

70/ A/50/550.

71/ A/50/550, annex I; see also A/CONF.164/37.

6. Requests the Secretary-General to ensure that reporting on all major fisheries-related activities and instruments is effectively coordinated and duplication of activities and reporting minimized and that relevant scientific and technical studies are disseminated to the international community, and invites the relevant specialized agencies, including the Food and Agriculture Organization of the United Nations, as well as regional and subregional fisheries organizations and arrangements to cooperate with the Secretary-General to that end;

7. Decides to include in the provisional agenda of its fifty-first session, under the item entitled "Law of the sea", a sub-item entitled "Agreement for the Implementation of the Provisions of the United Nations Convention on the Law of the Sea of 10 December 1982 relating to the Conservation and Management of Straddling Fish Stocks and Highly Migratory Fish Stocks".

50. UNGA RESOLUTION ON LARGE-SCALE PELAGIC DRIFTNET FISHING AND ITS IMPACT ON THE LIVING MARINE RESOURCES OF THE WORLD'S OCEANS AND SEAS; UNAUTHORIZED FISHING IN ZONES OF NATIONAL JURISDICTION AND ITS IMPACT ON THE LIVING MARINE RESOURCES OF THE WORLD'S OCEANS AND SEAS; AND FISHERIES BY-CATCH AND DISCARDS AND THEIR IMPACT ON THE SUSTAINABLE USE OF THE WORLD'S LIVING MARINE RESOURCES

Doc. no.: A/Res.50/25 5 December 1995

The General Assembly,

Reaffirming its resolutions 44/225 of 22 December 1989, 45/197 of 21 December 1990 and 46/215 of 20 December 1991, as well as its decisions 47/443 of 22 December 1992, 48/445 of 21 December 1993 and 49/436 of 19 December 1994, on large-scale pelagic drift-net fishing and its impact on the living marine resources of the world's oceans and seas,

Recalling its resolution 49/116 of 19 December 1994 on unauthorized fishing in zones of national jurisdiction and its impact on the living marine resources of the world's oceans and seas,

Recalling also its resolution 49/118 of 19 December 1994 on fisheries by-catch and discards and their impact on the sustainable use of the world's living marine resources,

Recognizing the efforts that international organizations and members of the international community have made to reduce by-catch and discards in fishing operations,

Conscious of the need to promote and facilitate international cooperation, especially at the regional and subregional levels, in order to ensure the sustainable development and use of the living marine resources of the world's seas and oceans, consistent with the present resolution,

Noting that the Agreement for the Implementation of the Provisions of the United Nations Convention on the Law of the Sea of 10 December 1982 relating to the Conservation and Management of Straddling Fish Stocks and Highly Migratory Fish Stocks, 72/ adopted by the United Nations Conference on Straddling Fish Stocks and Highly Migratory Fish Stocks, provides in its general principles that States shall minimize pollution, waste, discards, catch by lost or abandoned gear, catch of non-target species, both fish and non-fish species, and impacts on associated or dependent species, in particular endangered species, through measures including, to the extent practicable, the development and use of selective, environmentally safe and cost-effective fishing gear and techniques, and further provides that States shall take measures, including the establishment of regulations, to ensure that vessels flying their flags do not conduct unauthorized fishing within areas under the national jurisdiction of other States,

Noting also that the Food and Agriculture Organization of the United Nations has adopted a Code of Conduct for Responsible Fisheries, which sets out principles and global standards of behaviour for responsible practices to conserve, manage and develop fisheries, including guidelines for fishing on the high seas and in areas under the national jurisdiction of other States, and on fishing gear selectivity and practices, with the aim of reducing by-catch and discards,

---

72/ A/CONF.164/37; see also A/50/550, annex I.

Expressing deep concern at the detrimental impact of unauthorized fishing in areas under national jurisdiction, where the overwhelming proportion of the global fish catch is harvested, on the sustainable development of the world's fishery resources and on the food security and economies of many States, particularly developing States,

Reaffirming the rights and duties of coastal States to ensure proper conservation and management measures with respect to the living resources in areas under their national jurisdiction, in accordance with international law as reflected in the United Nations Convention on the Law of the Sea,

Taking note of the reports of the Secretary-General on large-scale pelagic drift-net fishing and its impact on the living marine resources of the world's oceans and seas, 73/ and unauthorized fishing in zones of national jurisdiction and its impact on the living marine resources of the world's oceans and seas, 74/

Taking note also of the report of the Food and Agriculture Organization of the United Nations on fisheries by-catch and discards and their impact on the sustainable use of the world's living marine resources, 75/

Acknowledging with appreciation the measures taken and the progress made by members of the international community, international organizations and regional economic integration organizations to implement and support the objectives of resolution 46/215,

Expressing deep concern that there are continuing reports of activities inconsistent with the terms of resolution 46/215 and unauthorized fishing inconsistent with the terms of resolution 49/116,

1. Reaffirms the importance it attaches to compliance with its resolution 46/215, in particular to those provisions of the resolution calling for full implementation of a global moratorium on all large-scale pelagic drift-net fishing on the high seas of the world's oceans and seas, including enclosed seas and semi-enclosed seas;

2. Urges all authorities of members of the international community to take greater enforcement responsibility to ensure full compliance with resolution 46/215, and to impose appropriate sanctions, consistent with their obligations under international law, against acts contrary to the terms of that resolution;

3. Calls upon States to take the responsibility, consistent with their obligations under international law as reflected in the United Nations Convention on the Law of the Sea and resolution 49/116, to take measures to ensure that no fishing vessels entitled to fly their national flags fish in areas under the national jurisdiction of other States unless duly authorized by the competent authorities of the coastal State or States concerned; such authorized fishing operations should be carried out in accordance with the conditions set out in the authorization;

4. Urges States, relevant international organizations, and regional and subregional fisheries management organizations and arrangements to take action to adopt policies, apply measures, collect and exchange data and develop techniques to reduce by-catches, fish discards, and post-harvest losses consistent with international law and relevant international instruments, including the Code of Conduct for Responsible Fisheries;

5. Calls upon development assistance organizations to make it a high priority to support, including through financial and/or technical assistance, efforts of developing coastal States, in particular the least developed countries and the small island developing States, to improve the monitoring and control of fishing activities and the enforcement of fishing regulations;

6. Requests the Secretary-General to bring the present resolution to the attention of all members of the international community, relevant intergovernmental organizations, the organizations and bodies of the United Nations system, regional and subregional fisheries management organizations, and relevant non-governmental organizations, and invites them to provide the Secretary-General with information relevant to the implementation of the present resolution;

73/ A/50/553.

74/ A/50/549.

75/ A/50/552, annex.

7. Also requests the Secretary-General to ensure that reporting on all major fisheries-related activities and instruments is effectively coordinated and duplication of activities and reporting minimized and that relevant scientific and technical studies are disseminated to the international community, and invites the relevant specialized agencies, including the Food and Agriculture Organization of the United Nations, as well as regional and subregional fisheries organizations and arrangements, to cooperate with the Secretary-General to that end;

8. Further requests the Secretary-General to submit to the General Assembly at its fifty-first session a report on further developments relating to the implementation of resolutions 46/215, 49/116 and 49/118, taking into account the information provided by States, relevant specialized agencies, in particular the Food and Agriculture Organization of the United Nations, and other appropriate organs, organizations and programmes of the United Nations system, regional and subregional organizations and arrangements, and other relevant intergovernmental and non-governmental organizations;

9. Decides to include in the provisional agenda of its fifty-first session, under the item entitled "Law of the sea", a sub-item entitled "Large-scale pelagic drift-net fishing and its impact on the living marine resources of the world's oceans and seas; unauthorized fishing in zones of national jurisdiction and its impact on the living marine resources of the world's oceans and seas; and fisheries by-catch and discards and their impact on the sustainable use of the world's living marine resources".

51. ACTION TAKEN BY THE ORGANS, ORGANIZATIONS AND BODIES OF THE UNITED NATIONS SYSTEM TO IMPLEMENT THE PROGRAMME OF ACTION FOR THE SUSTAINABLE DEVELOPMENT OF SMALL ISLAND DEVELOPING STATES - REPORT OF THE SECRETARY-GENERAL*

Doc. no.: A/50/422

21 September 1995

CONTENTS

---

* A/50/150.

INTRODUCTION

A. Background

1. The Global Conference on the Sustainable Development of Small Island Developing States was held in Bridgetown, Barbados from 26 April to 6 May 1994. The General Assembly, at its forty-ninth session considered the Conference under agenda item 89 (e) and in its resolution 49/122 endorsed the outcomes of the Conference, including the Programme of Action for the Sustainable Development of Small Island Developing States. 1/

2. In the same resolution, the Assembly requested the Secretary-General, among other things, to report to the General Assembly at its fiftieth session on action taken by the organs, organizations and bodies of the United Nations system to implement the Programme of Action for the Sustainable Development of Small Island Developing States, and in that regard also to invite those organs, organizations and bodies of the United Nations system that had not already done so to consider the establishment of focal points and other similar mechanisms to enable them to respond effectively in the implementation of the Programme of Action. The present report has been prepared in response to that request. As requested in paragraph 128 of the Programme of Action, a similar report (A/49/425 and Add.1) was submitted to the General Assembly at its forty-ninth session; The present report represents an incremental update and does not repeat any information that is already contained in the previous report.

B. Methodology and structure of the report

3. In order to gather the information needed to prepare the report, the Secretariat invited the organizations and bodies of the United Nations system to provide information on measures taken to implement the Programme of Action, and requested those that had not already done so at the time of the preparation of the previous report to also provide information on any specific institutional arrangements they had put in place to implement the Programme of Action. A majority of the organizations that were approached responded to the Secretariat's request; they are listed in the annex. A number of organizations and bodies that were not covered in the previous report have since responded with information and are thus covered in the present report for the first time.

4. The report is divided into three chapters: chapter I provides details of the plans and programmes adopted by the organizations and bodies of the United Nations system to implement the Programme of Action; chapter II reviews the institutional arrangements either already in place or envisaged to support such implementation; and chapter III presents a few concluding observations. Information on specific projects that seem to have implications for programme development and refinement, except for pilot and other experimental projects, is contained in an addendum (A/50/422/Add.1).

I. PLANS AND PROGRAMMES

A. United Nations

1. Department for Policy Coordination and Sustainable Development

5. The Programme of Action for the Sustainable Development of Small Island Developing States, in paragraph 123, assigns the Department for Policy Coordination and Sustainable Development of the United Nations Secretariat with the primary task of providing secretariat support for facilitating its effective implementation.

6. The Department has focused its attention simultaneously on establishing the appropriate institutional mechanisms for effecting coordination, monitoring and review of the implementation process; monitoring the substantive implementation of the Programme of Action; preparing statutory reports for the General Assembly and the Commission on Sustainable Development; and organizing expert group meetings on specific issues on the sustainable development of small island developing States, as called for in General Assembly resolutions 49/122 and 49/100, and/or the Programme of Action.

7. The above-mentioned tasks are carried out by the Small Island Developing States Unit of the Department's Division for Sustainable Development. Regarding system-wide coordination, the Department has drawn the attention of the Inter-Agency Committee on Sustainable Development (IACSD) to the work arising from the Programme of Action. At its sixth meeting (Geneva, 12-14 July 1995), IACSD gave consideration to the matter, in keeping with paragraph 122 of the Programme of Action. Upon the recommendations of the Department, IACSD decided on mechanisms for such coordination. IACSD endorsed the recommendations of the Department for the inclusion of substantive aspects of the Programme of Action in the established inter-agency mechanisms for reporting to the Commission on Sustainable Development on the implementation of Agenda 21. 2/ IACSD decided to extend the existing system of task managers to include the coverage of all substantive areas of the Programme of Action that coincide with the specific themes of Agenda 21, and requested task managers to include a separate section on small island developing States in their respective reports. In addition, new task managers were designated for areas of the Programme of Action not covered by Agenda 21, namely, tourism, maritime transport, air transport, energy resources, natural and environmental disasters, and telecommunications.

8. The Department will continue in its role of liaison with IACSD task managers and focal points within organizations and bodies of the United Nations system in ensuring system-wide implementation and coordination of the Programme of Action as well as in the preparation and monitoring of all reports for submission to the General Assembly, the Commission on Sustainable Development and other relevant intergovernmental bodies.

9. The institutional modalities for coordination at the regional level have also been addressed with the involvement of the Department. Meetings to discuss the critical issues of coordination and the determination of priorities were convened by the Economic and Social Commission for Asia and the Pacific (ESCAP): Meeting of the Special Body on Pacific Island Developing Countries (20-21 April 1995), and by the Economic Commission for Latin America and the Caribbean (ECLAC): Caribbean Meeting of Experts on the Implementation of the Programme of Action for the Sustainable Development of Small Island Developing States (17-19 May 1995). At those meetings, the Department provided briefings on the issues and work arising from the Programme of Action.

10. The Department convened a meeting of member States of the Alliance of Small Island States (AOSIS) and representatives of relevant United Nations and non-United Nations organizations and bodies on 8 May 1995, at which the issues of implementation, coordination and the setting of immediate priorities were discussed.

11. The Department has undertaken the preparation of a publication entitled Selected Sources of Funding for Environmental Projects Accessible to AOSIS Member States, for use by Governments and other interested groups or organizations; Selected Sources will be issued shortly as a United Nations publication, and will be revised and updated in the future as additional information becomes available.

12. In addition to the present report, the Department, acting on a mandate contained in paragraph 120 of the Programme of Action, has initiated the preparation of a report on current donor activities in support of the sustainable development of small island developing States, for submission by the Secretary-General to the Commission on Sustainable Development at its fourth

session, when the Commission will conduct an initial review of progress achieved in the implementation of the Programme of Action, preparations for which have been initiated by the Department through IACSD. The Department will prepare that report in collaboration with the Development Assistance Committee of the Organisation for Economic Cooperation and Development (OECD) and other United Nations bodies.

13. As part of the preparation of thematic reports for the above-mentioned session, the Department has undertaken to prepare, in collaboration with UNEP, a comprehensive report on the sustainable development of tourism in small island developing States.

14. An issue of considerable importance to small island developing States and specifically requested in the Programme of Action is the development and construction of a vulnerability index. Work is currently under way in the Department to convene, in collaboration with the United Nations Conference on Trade and Development (UNCTAD), a meeting of experts from within and outside the United Nations system on approaches to the index. The conclusions and recommendations of that expert group meeting will also be submitted to the fourth session of the Commission. Actual construction of the index will begin thereafter, taking into account the recommendations of the Commission.

15. The Department plans to begin work on the compilation of an information database on small island developing States for use by task managers and other interested parties, to be linked with similar databases held by other organizations.

16. An important facet of the work of the Department in its monitoring and coordination activities concerns the involvement of a number of major non-governmental organizations in the implementation of the Programme of Action. The Department has established a dialogue with several major non-governmental organizations regarding their specific activities, which range from the convening of seminars and conferences on selective aspects of the Programme of Action to actual implementation of specific provisions of the Programme of Action.

2. United Nations Conference on Trade and Development

17. UNCTAD continues to carry out the activities reported previously (see A/49/425 and Add.1); planned activities reported therein are also currently under implementation.

18. As indicated previously (see A/49/425), UNCTAD will undertake further activities - in the areas of science and technology, human resource development, regional economic cooperation, institutional capacity-building, and measurement of the vulnerability of small island developing countries - when its capacity is strengthened, as recommended in paragraph 127 of the Programme of Action.

19. The General Assembly, in its resolution 49/100, invited the Commission on Sustainable Development to convene, during its session in 1996, a high-level panel to discuss the challenges faced by island developing countries, particularly in the area of external trade, and to assist the Commission in its review of the implementation of the Programme of Action. The panel is to be organized by UNCTAD, in cooperation with the Department for Policy Coordination and Sustainable Development.

3. United Nations Environment Programme

20. The United Nations Environment Programme (UNEP) has incorporated many of the special needs and vulnerabilities of small island developing States into its 1996-1997 work programme, which was adopted at the eighteenth session of the UNEP Governing Council, in May 1995.

21. More specifically, in its decision 18/34 on small island developing States, the Council welcomed the action already taken by the Executive Director, including the establishment of a focal point and task force within UNEP to coordinate UNEP activities relevant to the Programme of Action for the Sustainable Development of Small Island Developing States; urged the Executive Director to ensure that, in implementing the work programme agreed by the Council, appropriate attention be given to the needs and vulnerabilities of small island developing States; and encouraged an integrated approach within UNEP to addressing issues of relevance to small island developing States through the effective use and involvement of the Task Force in both programme and policy development.

22. The 1996-1997 UNEP work programme gives priority to translating the Programme of Action into mechanisms that can help small island developing States put in place policies and strategies to achieve sustainable economic and human development. While still undergoing further development and review, the work programme has identified the following programme elements in which special consideration will be given to small island developing States: (a) caring for freshwater, coastal and marine environments, and (b) caring for biological resources.

23. UNEP recognizes that the development challenges being faced by small island developing States can only be tackled through an integrated approach to the management of human activities and their supporting resource base. UNEP and the United Nations Centre for Human Settlements (Habitat) will continue to make a joint effort to promote integrated island management in small island developing States, while developing closer ties with the programmes of other United Nations bodies that have similar goals.

24. Current and planned UNEP activities and programmes are set out below within each of the priority areas of the Programme of Action. Only information additional to that contained in the previous report (A/49/425) is listed here. Previously reported UNEP activities will in general continue but at reduced funding levels, due to an overall reduction in the Environment Fund.

(a) Climate change and sealevel rise

25. UNEP co-sponsored with the World Meteorological Organization (WMO) the Intergovernmental Panel on Climate Change. It prepared a special report for the Conference of the Parties to the Framework Convention on Climate Change in 1995, and a second assessment report will become available later in 1995. The information provided through the Panel should be of considerable value to small island developing States, particularly information on the vulnerability of States to sealevel rise and its impacts. The reports provide essential information to enable the development of effective adaptive strategies.

26. A special project on climate change impacts and adaptations assessment will be initiated in Antigua and Barbuda. The following activities will be undertaken: (a) a country-wide vulnerability assessment; (b) in-depth studies in areas and sectors identified as particularly vulnerable; and (c) identification and testing of adaptation options. This activity will assist other small island developing States in formulating comprehensive strategies and measures to facilitate their adaptation to climate change and sealevel rise through the development of management tools and plans.

27. Current and planned UNEP activities within this priority area also include: (a) a number of country and site-specific case studies in the south-west Pacific, Indo-East African and Caribbean subregions on the vulnerability of selected small island developing States to the effects of climate change and sealevel rise and their socio-economic implications; and (b) the development and application of a decision-support system that will allow policy analysts to anticipate, explore and counter the risks associated with climate change and sealevel rise in small island developing States.

(b) Natural and environmental disasters

28. The joint UNEP/Habitat Task Force on the Continuum from Relief to Development will continue to address a wide range of disaster-related issues in the natural and man-made environments, including many that are of particular concern to small island developing States such as their peculiar vulnerability factors. UNEP is working with subregional bodies, such as the South Pacific Regional Environment Programme (SPREP), the South Asia Cooperative Environment Programme and the Caribbean Environment Programme, to promote improved hazard-risk mapping (landslide, flood prone areas etc.) as a means to plan and prepare for the effects of disasters.

(c) Management of wastes

29. New activities that are presently being considered within the context of the 1996-1997 UNEP work programme include: (a) preparation of a handbook on cleaner production in small island developing States aimed at raising awareness and providing information and concrete examples on cleaner production technology solutions, and (b) train the trainer workshops on environmental management systems for small island developing States. Activities under this priority area will complement similar activities under the priority areas "Coastal and marine resources" and "Freshwater resources".

(d) Coastal and marine resources

30. Building upon earlier activities and based on qualitative and quantitative assessments of the coastal and marine pollution loads from land-based sources in the eastern African subregion, including the Comoros and Seychelles, the planned development of a regional overview and strategy will lead to the implementation of various additional activities, such as monitoring programmes. A coastal profile for Grand Comoros is currently in preparation that will result in the development of an integrated coastal area strategy by the end of 1995. Within the context of the 1996-1997 UNEP work programme, it is anticipated that the Comoros will comprise demonstration or pilot projects in integrated island management. The demonstration projects will be closely linked to similar activities under the priority area entitled "Freshwater resources".

31. The environmental assessment and information management activities previously reported now include the development of a geographical analysis laboratory within the University of the South Pacific. This will support the development of data analysis and applications skills in the western Pacific. The geographical analysis skills, environmental information systems and state-of-the-environment assessment activities identified under this priority area are also relevant to the following priority areas: "Freshwater resources", "Land resources", "Tourism resources", "Biodiversity resources", "National institutions and administrative capacity" and "Regional institutions and technical cooperation".

(e) Freshwater resources

32. UNEP activities within this priority area will be expanded to include a greater number of diagnostic studies on small island developing States and action planning for the environmentally sound integrated management of freshwater resources within the context of sustainable development. Recognizing the real linkages between the fresh and marine waters of small island developing States and the integrating role of the hydrological cycle, pollution control and resource management activities associated with freshwater will complement similar activities under the priority areas "Coastal and marine resources" and "National institutions and administrative capacity".

(f) Land resources

33. UNEP, jointly with the Food and Agriculture Organization of the United Nations (FAO), the South Pacific Institute for Research, Extension and Training

in Agriculture, and SPREP, plans - subject to the availability of resources - to implement a project for providing small island developing States of the South Pacific subregion with improved knowledge for natural resources appraisal and ecosystem analysis, using the World Soil and Terrain Digital Database/ Geographical Information System. In cooperation with Habitat and the United Nations Development Programme (UNDP), UNEP is coordinating activities in the Caribbean in the area of environmental information management, specifically geographic information system development, for environmentally sustainable land use planning and settlements development.

(g) Tourism resources

34. New activities that are presently being considered within the context of the 1996-1997 UNEP work programme include: (a) training workshops on environmental management of hotels, and (b) training workshops on environmentally sound forms of tourism development. These would be based on existing programmes that will be modified to meet the special needs and vulnerabilities of small island developing States. Other activities related to tourism are included under "Coastal and marine resources" and "Freshwater resources".

(h) Regional institutions and technical cooperation

35. Ongoing UNEP activities in this area will include the control of land-based sources of pollution that degrade their waters in the programme priorities for 1995 of the International Waters Strategy of the Global Environment Facility (GEF), of which UNEP, UNDP and the World Bank are implementing agencies. This could be an important step in helping UNEP and other agencies address problems in small island developing States.

36. In the programme areas "Energy resources", "Biodiversity resources", "Science and technology", "Human resource development" and "National institutions and administrative capacity", UNEP activities will continue unchanged (see A/49/425). Additional information on specific UNEP activities in the area of national institutions and administrative capacity is included in an addendum (A/50/422/Add.1).

4. United Nations Centre for Human Settlements

37. Habitat gives the highest priority to supporting the efforts of small island developing States to elaborate strategies for the integrated management of their economic and social activities, natural resources and environment. Habitat research and development activities focus on the formulation and application of planning and management instruments in key areas of small island developing States' development, such as land use and settlements planning; infrastructure provision; waste minimization and pollution control; and natural and environmental disaster mitigation. A substantial part of Habitat capacity-building and direct support capability on settlements issues is directed to technical cooperation activities in small island developing States. Habitat is particularly active in the execution of technical support programmes in the countries of the Caribbean and Pacific subregions.

38. Issues related to sustainable settlements development in small island developing States are being considered in the preparatory process for the Second United Nations Conference on Human Settlements (Habitat II), scheduled to be held in Istanbul in June 1996. Those issues will represent an important component of the declaration of principles and global plan of action to be adopted at Habitat II.

(a) Climate change and sealevel rise

39. Habitat is collaborating with UNEP in the preparation of case studies and training materials on the impact of climate change on coastal populations and

human settlements. Selected small island developing States will participate in the initial activities of the project, which focus on the Indo-East African subregion. It is expected that the successful completion of the project could lead to the execution of a wider capacity-building programme in other regions and small island developing States.

(b) Natural and environmental disasters

40. Habitat is providing support to several Caribbean small island developing States in the application of building codes and standards especially designed for seismic and hurricane-prone areas. General codes and standards developed under an earlier Habitat programme are now being applied to specific Caribbean countries as part of a collaborative programme with the Organization of American States and the Organization of Eastern Caribbean States (OECS).

41. Following the creation of the Habitat UNEP/Task Force on the Continuum from Relief to Development, Habitat is establishing a disaster management unit to support its operational activities related to disaster prevention and rehabilitation in the area of human settlements. Particular issues related to the vulnerability of small island developing States to natural and technological disasters will be addressed by the activities of the unit.

(c) Management of wastes

42. Habitat is executing several field research activities on municipal solid-waste management in developing countries. Pilot projects take into account the specific characteristics of small island developing States in relation to waste generation and disposal, fragile ecosystems, limited resource base, geographical isolation and scarce human resources. Strategies for sustainable resource utilization and recovery, as well as for waste minimization, are integral components of such activities. In order to develop and maximize the utilization of indigenous capacities, pilot projects focus on the promotion of private-sector and community participation in waste management.

43. The regional offices of the Urban Management Programme (UMP) are actively promoting the execution of national consultations on sanitation and environmental infrastructure services in small island developing States. The UMP office for Latin America and the Caribbean has made an evaluation of solid-waste management needs in the Caribbean, and it is programming the execution of follow-up national consultations. The UMP regional office for Asia and the Pacific is supporting Pacific island States in the execution of national consultations on urban management and environmental sanitation.

44. As a result of their review of waste management conditions in small island developing States, Habitat and UNEP have initiated the formulation of a proposal for a global project on waste minimization and pollution prevention in small island developing States. The proposal emphasises, inter alia, the strengthening of regional and national capacities and institutions for waste minimization and pollution control; the introduction of monitoring and auditing techniques; technology transfer and the production of information referral instruments; and the development of management tools through field applications. It is envisaged that the final proposal will be submitted for GEF funding.

(d) Coastal and marine resources

45. Habitat is collaborating with UNEP on the formulation of integrated plans for settlements and coastal zone management in Saint Vincent and the Grenadines. The project is developing guidelines and management tools for the incorporation of marine and coastal zone considerations into settlements planning. It is expected that the management instruments to be developed by the project will be replicated in other small island developing States.

(e) Land resources

46. Habitat has a broad programme of operational activities in support of small island developing States for the formulation and application of land-use and management plans, and land development control instruments and legislation. Habitat technical cooperation programmes consider land-use planning as an integral component of overall environmental and national development management. Habitat is in the process of expanding its programme on human settlements and related environmental management issues in the Caribbean in collaboration with OECS, the Caribbean Community (CARICOM) and UNDP. The new programme puts emphasis on strengthening the linkages between natural resources and environmental management and the planning of land use and settlements for social and economic activities.

(f) Tourism resources

47. The dramatic increase of tourism in small island developing States is rapidly changing traditional development patterns and is exerting additional pressure on their resource base and the environment. Habitat operational activities support the formulation of land-use and settlement development plans in Caribbean small island States, giving special attention to the effect of tourism on land use, settlement planning and infrastructure requirements.

(g) National institutions and administrative capacity

48. Current and planned Habitat operational activities in small island developing States aim to build the capacity of national institutions in formulating land-use and settlements development plans, development control and the application of management information systems. Habitat projects are giving increasing attention to strengthening the capacity of local authorities (municipalities) to perform such functions.

49. Consultations with local stakeholders in settlement development are an integral part of Habitat technical assistance programmes. National consultations aim to increase settlements' efficiency by promoting the participation of the private sector and communities in management processes. Efforts are also being made to establish institutional coordination mechanisms for the integration of land-use and settlement planning in overall environmental and national development management.

(h) Regional institutions and technical cooperation

50. Current and planned Habitat activities include collaboration with regional institutions in the Caribbean region, namely, CARICOM and OECS, as well as research and academic institutions, through regional and subregional programmes in human settlements planning and management. Habitat is also collaborating with other regional bodies, ESCAP, ECLAC and OAS in the execution of technical cooperation activities in small island developing States.

(i) Science and technology

51. Habitat has established a significant in-house capacity to support countries in developing and applying technical instruments for land-use and settlement planning. Geographical information systems (GIS), visual information systems for settlement planning and indicators for human settlement management are some of the technologies developed by Habitat and currently being disseminated and applied in small island developing States as part of its operational activities.

(j) Human resources development

52. Habitat operational activities in this priority area cover advanced training programmes extended through fellowships and attachments, workshops, seminars and consultations on settlement planning and integrated island

development management. Given the limited human resource base of small island developing States, Habitat promotes the strengthening of regional training institutions and horizontal exchange as key elements of its human resource development activities.

5. International Research and Training Institute for the Advancement of Women

53. In 1993, the International Research and Training Institute for the Advancement of Women (INSTRAW) prepared a training module on the theme "Women and waste management". This module provides an integrated approach to water supply, sanitation and waste management, and women's role in the organization and management of waste management programmes and projects. The module contains examples of successful experiences of women's role in waste management schemes in various countries, including small island developing States.

54. In the area of "Freshwater resources", INSTRAW, in collaboration with the former Department for Technical Cooperation and Development of the United Nations Secretariat and the International Labour Organization (ILO)/Turin Centre in Italy, prepared in 1991 a multimedia training package on the theme "Women, water supply and sanitation". This training package provides a new approach to the organization and management of water supply through participation in the planning, technical operations, maintenance, assessment and implementation of water supply and sanitation projects.

55. INSTRAW has also given priority to promoting women's participation in new and renewable sources of energy, in accordance with the priority area "Energy resources". In 1990, the Institute, in cooperation with the ILO/Turin Centre, prepared a training package on the theme "Women and new and renewable sources of energy". The training package aims to promote the integration of women's needs and their participation in energy project planning and implementation, paying special attention to the development and use of new and renewable sources of energy. From 1990 to date, seven national, regional and international training seminars have been held.

56. Following the United Nations Conference on Environment and Development (UNCED), the Institute's programme has responded more directly to the guidelines and recommendations of the Conference. Environmental challenges are considered within the framework of combating poverty; hunger and disease; ensuring better access to education and health care; and productive resources, such as water, energy and environmentally sound technologies. For example, in 1994, INSTRAW prepared a comprehensive training manual on women, environmental management and sustainable development". The aim of this manual is to assist policy makers and development officials in enabling more participatory roles for women in sustainable development and environmental management, and to establish multisectoral and multidisciplinary linkages between women, sustainable development and environmental matters. The manual contains four modules on (a) women and environmental health; (b) women as agents of change in the development sector; (c) women as managers of the environment; and (d) women, environmental indicators and capacity-building programmes.

57. Although INSTRAW research and training activities under the above-mentioned areas are of world-wide scope, its main recommendations and the analyses and strategies that they propose can be applied to the environmental and developmental problems facing small island developing States. In its 1996-1998 work programme, INSTRAW will seek special funds for conducting training in small island developing States.

6. United Nations University

58. The United Nations University (UNU) has established the Small Islands Network to strengthen and link research related to small islands. The Network

involves the academic community. As an autonomous organization, UNU tackles difficult problems in close cooperation with the universities of the world, and develops research and training programmes to deal with the latest issues in sustainable small island development. The functions of the Small Islands Network are the following:

(a) To network the global academic community and link scholars so as to strengthen the academic role in the sustainable development process, by fostering increased interaction among interested scholars and organizations for the purposes of promoting research, training and the dissemination of information related to small islands;

(b) To integrate research on small islands and sustainable development under the auspices of a global network of scholars, reduce research overlap and promote collaboration in research efforts, where possible;

(c) To create a small islands information base to act as a point source directory of scholars, organizations and research findings pertaining to small islands and sustainable development;

(d) To disseminate and provide information to responsible United Nations and government bodies, as well as policy makers, official development assistance (ODA)-related donor and recipient Governments, corporations, and non-governmental organizations, for effective environmental management, risk management and government strategies for sustainable development at the global, regional and local levels;

(e) To run electronic seminars and develop a body of scholars that can act as a global think tank to test and provide scholarly input to new ideas, concepts, issues, research proposals and development projects related to small island development issues.

59. Research and training activities incorporate regional and global perspectives, with an overall focus on environmental management and governance. The objective of Network activities is to provide research methodologies and training for the purposes of developing, supporting and promoting comprehensive and integrated development policy planning and management. Impetus for the proposed set of activities to be implemented by UNU was derived from an examination of the lines of action recommended in Agenda 21 and the outcomes of the Global Conference on the Sustainable Development of Small Island Developing States. Network activities will centre on three major thematic areas:

I

Appropriate technology transfer and training

As a first step, UNU will accumulate data and technology available in Okinawa, Japan, to see what technology is available for small islands and how that technology may be transferred, including through ODA. To that end, UNU will liaise with the UNEP Environmental Technology Transfer Centre at Osaka, especially in the area of water technology.

As a second step, UNU will encourage the development and implementation of the zero emissions concept to technological transfer and development. This builds on the Zero Emissions project of UNU, and focuses primarily on beer brewing and sugar industry restructuring.

II

Sustainable management of ecosystems

UNU maintains major programmes in land management and natural disaster risk management, which will be extended to small islands. In particular, its work in responding to the needs of the International Decade for

National Disaster Reduction (IDNDR) has particular applications for small islands. The approach will focus on training the trainers and risk preparedness.

III

Environmental law and governance

Environmental governance is a major area in which UNU is undertaking work within its environmental programme. The project being developed focuses primarily on the Pacific Islands, and is concerned with designing new frameworks for regional cooperation among small islands to promote sustainable development. In particular, mechanisms for cooperation among the islands in tourism, fisheries, energy, population/migration and export/import management are of key concern. UNU will work with key institutional bodies in the region in this area.

60. The above-mentioned activities are rounded out by the inclusion of two further related areas for action by UNU:

(a) Academic capacity-building and education, which is concerned with supporting the development and capacity-building of academic institutions to effectively educate in environmental issues;

(b) A small island forums series, concerned with promoting regional economic cooperation and the effective utilization of resources for sustainable development.

61. While focusing on the academic community, the UNU Small Islands Network will include a public education function by informing local non-governmental organizations of research efforts and their results through electronic and audio-visual and other means.

7. International Decade for Natural Disaster Reduction/ Department of Humanitarian Affairs

62. The Department of Humanitarian Affairs of the United Nations Secretariat was entrusted, in General Assembly resolution 46/182, with the task of strengthening and making more effective the collective efforts of the international community, particularly those of the United Nations system, in providing humanitarian assistance. The Emergency Relief Coordinator, as Under-Secretary-General for Humanitarian Affairs, directs the Department's efforts to ensure both a rapid, integrated and effective international response to humanitarian emergencies, and the implementation of measures for disaster preparedness, prevention and mitigation.

63. In order to give particular attention to the aspects of natural disaster prevention, mitigation and preparedness related to the Programme of Action for the Sustainable Development of Small Island Developing States, the Department will serve as task manager for this issue and will prepare a report for the Commission on Sustainable Development through its focal point, the Director of the IDNDR secretariat, in close collaboration with WMO and in cooperation with other interested organizations.

64. The IDNDR secretariat within the Department of Humanitarian Affairs works with countries to reduce their vulnerability to disasters. Guided by its 25-member Scientific and Technical Committee, and promoted at the national level by national committees and focal points, the objective of IDNDR is to increase international cooperation to reduce the loss of life, economic damage and social disruption that disasters can cause. The concerted inter-agency approach of the United Nations system to IDNDR is being ensured by the Inter-Agency Committee on IDNDR and its working group.

65. The Yokohama Strategy and Plan of Action (A/CONF.172/9, chap. I, resolution 1, annex I) adopted by the World Conference on Natural Disaster Reduction in May 1994, as well as subsequent resolutions of the forty-ninth session of the General Assembly including resolution 49/22 A, and the substantive session of 1995 of the Economic and Social Council, have emphasized the particular challenge that natural disasters pose for small island developing States. They point to the specific need for international cooperation in support of the concrete reduction of vulnerability to natural hazards as an indispensable component for sustainable development.

66. The South Pacific Programme Office of the Department of Humanitarian Affairs is implementing the South Pacific Disaster Reduction Programme. This is a four-year regional programme being implemented in 15 Pacific island countries. The programme started in May 1994 and is funded by UNDP and eight bilateral donors. The programme provides training and technical assistance to Governments and non-governmental organizations; produces materials, such as guidelines and manuals; helps to develop and implement national disaster mitigation and preparedness programmes; and facilitates regional cooperation and coordination in disaster management. The Department also carries out missions to assist small island developing States in improving disaster management organizations and starting up disaster mitigation projects. Recent missions were undertaken to Cape Verde and Papua New Guinea.

B. Funds and programmes

1. United Nations Development Programme

(a) A framework for cooperation on implementation of the Programme of Action for the Sustainable Development of Small Island Developing States

67. On the basis of UNDP consultations with the small island developing States, particularly with AOSIS and relevant subregional and regional United Nations bodies, it was felt that the implementation of the Programme of Action for the Sustainable Development of Small Island Developing States could be maximized through the establishment of a clear framework for cooperation among all the development partners involved in the process. That framework will strive to promote coherence and to realign, as appropriate, relevant ongoing activities at all levels in support of the objectives of the Programme of Action, while focusing on unmet priority needs in technical cooperation, with particular emphasis on capacity-building under the 14 priority areas of the Programme of Action. While the main responsibility for the creation of such a framework should reside with small island developing States themselves since they are primarily responsible for the implementation of the Programme of Action, UNDP will none the less seek to facilitate that creation.

(b) Development of the Small Island Developing States Technical Assistance Programme Information Network

68. In paragraphs 9 (a) and 9 (b) of General Assembly resolution 49/122 of 19 December 1994, the Assembly requested the further development of the small island developing States technical assistance programme (SIDS/TAP) and the small island developing States information network (SIDS/NET), on which UNDP had prepared feasibility studies, on the basis of continuing consultations with small island developing States and other interested parties - including in regard to SIDS/NET relevant small island developing States technical experts - so as to determine the most effective means for their implementation. In paragraph 8 of the same resolution, the Assembly endorsed the request of the Global Conference that UNDP continue to carry out its lead agency mandate under Agenda 21 to organize the United Nations system in the area of capacity-building for the sustainable development of small island developing States at all levels, national, regional and interregional, particularly through its network of country offices.

Small island developing States technical assistance programme: a central element of the strategy

69. At the subregional, regional and interregional levels, the small island developing States technical assistance programme that is being developed represents an important instrument, particularly in regard to the use of technical cooperation among developing countries (TCDC) mechanisms for furthering the implementation of the Programme of Action. SIDS/TAP is designed to facilitate the exchange and transfer of experiences, knowledge, policies and practices among small island developing States intraregionally and interregionally, and between small island developing States and other countries to enhance the quality and broaden the choice of sustainable development approaches of small island developing States.

70. In the context of SIDS/TAP, UNDP has initiated activities to carry out assessment-cum-project formulation exercises in the various small island developing States subregions. These are designed to identify unmet priorities in technical cooperation, with particular emphasis on capacity-building, and to formulate TCDC-based technical cooperation activities to address those priorities. Such exercises, which should be completed before the end of the year, involve appropriate experts from within the regions and from national and regional institutions. They will follow a careful process of consultation with all stakeholders to ensure support for the priorities identified. The objective is to develop an inventory of small island developing States priorities in the various subregions for the purpose of mobilizing support and funding for their realization.

71. In keeping with the request of operative paragraph 9 (a) of the above-mentioned resolution, UNDP has been collecting, over the last several months, data relevant to the preparation of a directory of institutions and scholars with expertise on small island developing States. The collection of this information has involved the concerned UNDP country offices, which have engaged national expertise to undertake the gathering of relevant data for the purpose. The directory will be substantially completed by the end of the current calendar year. When completed, it will be made available in hard copy and will also be accessible via the Information Referral System of the UNDP Special Unit for TCDC.

Small Island Developing States Information Network: the information support mechanism

72. The Global Conference recognized as a development constraint the lack of access by small island developing States to information on a range of subject areas of importance to them; SIDS/NET was conceived against that background. It is an information system designed to provide access through the Internet to information, knowledge, experiences, policies and practices on a range of technical subject areas of importance to small island developing States, including those falling under the 14 priority areas of the Programme of Action. The system aims at providing connectivity and access to existing databases at the national, regional and global levels, such as the Small Islands Information Network organized by the Institute of Island Studies. Its main objective is to provide access rather than to create databases, many of which already exist in many specialized national and regional institutions both within and outside of small island developing States. In recognition of the disparity in the levels of computer development of the countries concerned, SIDS/NET is being structured so that individual countries can phase in connectivity to SIDS/NET on a gradual, modular basis in tandem with their overall national computer and telecommunications development.

73. In keeping with paragraph 9 (b) of General Assembly resolution 49/122, UNDP is continuing its consultations with small island developing States and relevant organizations in the further development of SIDS/NET. UNDP has widely disseminated the SIDS/NET feasibility study, as well as the related technical papers, to information specialists in small island developing States. This

distribution included a questionnaire that focuses on key issues requiring clarification and decision in regard to the development of a strategy for the implementation of SIDS/NET. Responses are expected shortly from the countries concerned on the basis of which a decision will be taken on the steps necessary for the effective implementation of the system.

(c) Elements of UNDP support

Support at the subregional, regional and interregional levels

74. Within the framework strategy and consistent with General Assembly resolution 49/122, UNDP substantive support for the implementation of the Programme of Action will be carried out at two levels. The first level of support will be at the subregional, regional and interregional levels, through its role in the operationalization of already dedicated facilities - SIDS/TAP and SIDS/NET - and also through significant UNDP-supported ongoing regional and interregional activities financed from the Indicative Planning Figure (IPF), Special Programme Resources (SPR), GEF and the Capacity 21 Fund.

Support at the country level

75. The second level of UNDP support will be at the country level in the context of its standing mandate through the UNDP resident representative/United Nations resident coordinator systems to assist Governments in coordinating the operational activities of the United Nations development system. In that connection, UNDP has mobilized its country office structure in the various small island developing States subregions to play an advocacy role for the Programme of Action at the national level; help mobilize support and funding from country-based entities, including the non-governmental organizations community, the private sector and the locally based international community; and support the formulation of small island developing States national action plans, through which countries can seek such support. Furthermore, UNDP support is also provided in the context of its country programme activities in small island developing States, in which technical cooperation takes place through national IPF funding, as well as through funding from SPR, GEF and the Capacity 21 Fund, in many cases in areas covered by some priority areas of the Programme of Action.

76. At both the supranational and country levels, UNDP will assist countries in addressing issues of coherence, coordination, focus and advocacy in the context of the Programme of Action. At both levels, it will continue to provide relevant technical assistance and, in the case of its support to SIDS/TAP and SIDS/NET, it will also act as facilitator and mobilizer of resources for the countries concerned.

Other plans and programmes

77. Climate change and sealevel rise. Through a GEF small grants programme managed by UNDP, country activities targeting indigenous non-governmental organizations and community-based organizations, such as those in the Dominican Republic on education for the protection of the ozone layer, and awareness programmes for public motorcyclists on the hazards of carbon monoxide emissions, are particularly relevant to the priority area.

78. Natural and environmental disasters. In both the Caribbean and the Pacific Island subregions, UNDP is supporting natural disaster management and reduction programmes through regional IPF funding. Those activities are intended to create national and regional capacities for dealing with natural and technological disasters as they occur, and also to address the preparation and implementation of contingency response measures and comprehensive long-term disaster management plans integrated into the national development planning process.

79. In the context of the country programmes of some small island developing States, UNDP has also supported, through the country IPF, the preparation of national disaster management plans and disaster management training of public officials, including participants from the private sector, non-governmental organizations and local community leaders.

80. Management of wastes. The UNDP Special Unit for TCDC is currently supporting, through funding from its SPR, an interregional programme that is developing a monograph on effective urban management practices, including urban waste disposal approaches, which will serve as background documentation for a series of regional workshops in which selected small island developing States will participate. The monograph as well as the results and findings of the regional meetings will be presented to (Habitat II).

2. United Nations Population Fund

81. UNFPA has reported a continuation of its activities as previously reported (see A/49/425 and Add.1). UNFPA has also reported that those activities will fall within its technical assistance programme, emphasizing in particular the needs of adolescents.

3. United Nations Children's Fund

82. Activities of the United Nations Children's Fund (UNICEF) will continue as previously reported (see A/49/425 and Add.1). In addition, UNICEF has reported that over the past 18 months it has been working closely with the Governments of 13 Pacific island countries to develop a new programme of cooperation for 1997-2000. A draft policy framework has proposed five broad strategic goals, one of which calls for strengthening capacities of Governments, non-governmental organizations, communities and families to promote the optimal survival, development and protection of their children. Environmental degradation has been identified as an underlying cause of malnutrition and health problems among children. Large-scale, high-chemical-input cash-cropping is decreasing land fertility and availability, while pollution is affecting the safety of food products, especially marine resources. Use of indigenous plants and sustainable gardening patterns with low-input technologies, such as composting, crop rotation, companion planting, and natural insecticides, will be part of the UNICEF approach to producing food while protecting the environment. A working group meeting on the formulation of priorities and strategies for the UNICEF Solomon Islands Programme of Cooperation recommended that school curricula should include environment issues and that non-formal community environmental education should be promoted.

4. World Food Programme

83. Plans and programmes of the World Food Programme (WFP) continue as previously reported (see A/49/425 and Add.1).

5. United Nations International Drug Control Programme

84. Activities of the United National International Drug Control Programme (UNDCP) continue as previously reported (see A/49/425 and Add.1). In addition, UNDCP has reported that it has been assisting the Governments of small island developing States, particularly within the Caribbean subregion, to develop and implement national, subregional and regional programmes aimed at reducing the illicit cultivation, trafficking and abuse of drugs, and also at improving the effectiveness of controls over the legal supply of drugs. In addition to a number of national projects being supported by earmarked UNDCP resources - mostly in the area of demand reduction - UNDCP is financing a number of regional projects in the areas of the coordination of police activities; customs

cooperation; the training of judicial personnel; the harmonization of legislation; the drug curriculum; the harmonization of forensic laboratories; and the training of laboratory technicians.

C. Specialized agencies

1. Food and Agriculture Organization of the United Nations

85. FAO follow-up to the Programme of Action is largely based on the conclusions and recommendations of the Inter-Regional Conference of Small Island Countries on Sustainable Development and Environment in Agriculture, Forestry and Fisheries, held in Barbados from 7 to 10 April 1992. 3/ Paragraph 34 of the Programme of Action for the Sustainable Development of Small Island Developing States notes that those conclusions and recommendations contain the consensus position of small islands in the agricultural sector. Accordingly, FAO has incorporated the recommendations into its programme of work, and the Director-General has created two subregional offices, one for the South Pacific and one for the Caribbean.

(a) Natural and environmental disasters

86. The objective of the FAO assistance is to rehabilitate the agricultural sector in case of emergencies and natural disasters.

(b) Coastal and marine resources

87. The FAO Committee on Fisheries endorsed a proposal for a programme of fisheries assistance to small island developing States in March 1995. Programme formulation has been initiated for action in the six priority areas identified by member countries: (a) institutional strengthening and national capacity-building; (b) conservation and management of exclusive economic zone fisheries; (c) improved post-harvest management and marketing; (d) safety at sea; (e) strengthening the economic role of national fisheries industries; and (f) aquaculture and inland fisheries conservation and management.

(c) Land resources

88. Sustainable agriculture and rural development has three essential goals: (a) food security through an appropriate and sustainable balance between self-sufficiency and self-reliance; (b) employment and income generation in rural areas, particularly to eradicate poverty; and (c) natural resource conservation and environmental protection. Achieving those goals implies a long process requiring a comprehensive approach and heavy investments of labour, capital, technology and research, all of which are rare in small island developing States. In order to open up avenues for improving small island developing States capacity for the sustainable development of their resources, technical cooperation is being promoted by organizing efforts more systematically, for instance with programmed subregional support from the international community (both FAO and other development agencies) with ongoing assistance in small island developing States. Two subregional programmes are being formulated for sustainable development in agriculture, forestry and fisheries in the South Pacific and Caribbean islands. Those programmes will be reviewed and endorsed at two subregional workshops, one in Samoa in March 1996, and - subject to availability of donor funding - one in Barbados, tentatively in April 1996. The programme frameworks will allow harmonizing activities in small island developing States, in particular those related to coastal and marine resources; land resources, including agriculture, nutrition and forestry; agro-biodiversity; human and institutional strengthening; and regional cooperation. Those programmes will be the basis for elaborating subregional strategies for sustainable agriculture and rural development, and for the identification of specific project proposals for subregional technical cooperation and capacity-building. The implementation of the outputs emerging

from the subregional programmes will be closely followed up by the newly created FAO subregional offices in the South Pacific and Caribbean.

(d) Tourism resources

89. Within the context of sustainable agriculture and rural development, the diversification of primary production and income generation are high on the agenda. The vital link between tourism and agriculture is being explored for promoting a regional response from the sector to meet the standards of quality, quantity and regularity of supplies of agricultural commodities to the tourism sector.

(e) Biodiversity resources

90. Within the framework of the Convention on Biological Diversity, agro-biodiversity conservation and use as well as farmer's rights are promoted.

(f) National institutions and administrative capacity

91. National institutional strengthening is promoted through the provision of policy advice, assistance in policy formulation and data collection/processing for managing the conservation and use of natural resources for sustainable agriculture, forestry and fisheries.

(g) Regional institutions and technical cooperation

92. Technical cooperation and capacity-building among island countries is promoted through regional projects in order to make the most efficient use of human resources and promote the exchange of experience and technology in agriculture, forestry and fisheries. The subregional workshops mentioned under "Land resources", planned for 1996, will offer the means to establish collaborative arrangements and networking in those sectors.

(h) Human resource development

93. National education/training and workshops are organized to build farmers and fishermen capacities to sustainably use natural resources and diversify their primary production.

2. United Nations Educational, Scientific and Cultural Organization

94. During the 1994-1995 biennium, the United Nations Educational, Scientific and Cultural Organization (UNESCO) and its Intergovernmental Oceanographic Commission (IOC) have pursued and carried out a number of initiatives in response to the Programme of Action, in particular the priority areas dealing with human resource development, science and technology, coastal and marine resources, climate change and sealevel rise, biodiversity, freshwater resources, and natural and environmental disasters. The UNESCO medium-term strategy for 1996-2001 and programme and budget for 1996-1997 both provide for the follow-up to the Global Conference.

(a) Climate change and sealevel rise/coastal and marine resources

95. IOC has been extending its programme on sealevel rise, climate change and marine and coastal pollution. IOCARIBE, an IOC programme in the Caribbean, manages the Caribbean Marine Pollution Control and Abatement Programme, which is addressing marine and coastal pollution problems of regional concern and is the lead agency for the Wider Caribbean Debris/Waste Management Programme, which is fully operational in almost every island in the Caribbean.

96. In the framework of the geological correlation studies and in cooperation with the International Lithosphere Programme of the International Council of

Scientific Unions, sealevel changes and surface vertical movements are being investigated in order to characterize the interactions of climate change, sealevel rise and natural and environmental disasters.

(b) Natural and environmental disasters

97. As a follow-up to the Yokohama Strategy and Plan of Action adopted at the World Conference on Natural Disaster Reduction, assistance is provided towards the assessment of natural hazards and the mitigation of their effects on small islands. To mark the mid-term of the International Decade for Natural Disaster Reduction, planning for risk evaluation in urban systems, including island cities was discussed at an international workshop organized by UNESCO in Jakarta. It is expected that the Pacific island countries will be the focus of enhanced activities in disaster preparedness. A programme of action is being pursued in the Caribbean in order to increase the role of the media in disaster management and preparedness, in liaison with the Caribbean Disaster Emergency Response Agency. The production of an information kit is foreseen.

(c) Coastal and marine resources

98. Central to the priority area is a new UNESCO specific interdisciplinary project on environment and development in coastal regions and small islands, which is intended to respond to both the Programme of Action and chapter 17 of Agenda 21. The overall objective of the project is to advance knowledge on the sustainable development of coastal regions and small islands, to promote the application of research results towards achieving this development, and to provide the required advanced training. UNESCO aims to assist member States in introducing integrated coastal zone planning and management so as to resolve conflicts in the utilization of natural resources and to mitigate the physical and social vulnerability of small islands. In this connection, the project builds on cooperative activities among international and intergovernmental UNESCO programmes in the environmental and social sciences, namely, IOC programmes, the Man and Biosphere Programme, the International Hydrological Programme, the International Geological Correlation Programme and the Programme on Management of Social Transformations.

99. In the framework of the Caribbean Coastal Marine Productivity network, research is being carried out on the status of the coastal ecosystems in the region, for example concerning the relation between overfishing and the degradation of coral reefs. The Coast and Beach Stability Project for the Lesser Antilles continued its support for the establishment and supervision of coastal monitoring programmes for several small islands.

(d) Freshwater resources

100. Rational use of freshwater resources has been the subject of a number of activities organized by UNESCO in the various small island developing States subregions; specific project-related information is contained in the addendum (A/50/422/Add.1).

(e) Land resources

101. Among the activities of the Man and Biosphere Programme, studies on integrated forests, agroforestry and cropland management in small islands are under way. Preservation of biological diversity in forests and coastal ecosystems is encouraged. Action plans are being developed to tackle threatened plants.

(f) Energy resources

102. In relation to energy resources, policy frameworks are promoted and information materials disseminated regarding renewable and solar energy. These activities are carried out in the context of the World Solar Summit process.

(g) Science and technology

103. The management of environmental risks is addressed by undertakings in the fields of marine, oceanographic and earth sciences. The IOC Global Programme on Global Ocean Observing System, which was recognized by UNCED as an essential environmental monitoring component, carries out activities aiming at achieving operational systems capable of covering more effectively such issues as global environmental and climate change.

(h) Human resources development

104. Capacity-building to promote sustainable development in small islands is encouraged through UNESCO educational, cultural, scientific and communication programmes. Technical cooperation is extended through international and regional cooperative projects. A new UNESCO Project on Environment, Population, Education, and Information for Human Development is expected to utilize existing interdisciplinary and inter-agency frameworks. Promotion of education is pursued at all levels, formal and non-formal. The establishment of communication structures, including for distance education aimed at producing trained communicators and building island production capacities, continues. The UNESCO-led World Decade for Cultural Development helps to address the cultural dimensions of development in small island States.

3. World Health Organization

105. Activities undertaken by the World Health Organization (WHO) in support of the Programme of Action are summarized below; they are additional to those previously reported (A/49/425 and Add.1), which continue.

(a) Natural and environmental disasters

106. The WHO Regional Office for the Western Pacific (WPRO) has been conducting a series of workshops on health support for disaster management to strengthen national capabilities to prepare for and cope with natural and environmental disasters. As a result, national action and activities were initiated in a number of countries in 1995, including Samoa, Fiji and Papua New Guinea.

(b) Management of wastes

107. WPRO has initiated a project on solid waste disposal in Pacific island countries and areas to demonstrate appropriate solid-waste disposal methods; the project will culminate in the preparation of guidelines on the subject for use by island countries and areas. The countries selected for this purpose are Papua New Guinea, Solomon Islands and Tonga.

(c) Freshwater resources

108. The new WHO guidelines for drinking water quality for the Pacific island countries/areas and their adoption were promoted with a view to setting national standards. As a result, Fiji, Tonga and Cook Islands adopted national standards of their own.

(d) Regional institutions and technical cooperation

109. WHO and the Pan-American Health Organization (PAHO) supported the Pan American Conference on Health and Environment in Sustainable Human Development (Washington, D.C., 1-3 October 1994), which addressed various questions concerning small island States. The subject of small island States was on the agenda of the Third Meeting of the Water Supply and Sanitation Collaborative Council (Barbados, October 1994) to which WHO contributed, with particular reference to the health implications, inter alia, of climate change and sealevel rise, and natural and environmental disasters.

(e) Human resource development

110. WPRO conducted a workshop on training approaches in the promotion of health through environmental health (Sydney, 17-25 July 1995). Twelve of the participants were from six Pacific island countries and areas. WPRO is also collaborating with the Samoa and Solomon Islands Governments to review the curriculum and training of assistant health inspectors. WPRO, in collaboration with the UNDP/World Bank Regional Water and Sanitation Project Team based in Jakarta, conducted an assessment of human resource development needs as well as training opportunities in the following Pacific island countries and areas: Cook Islands, Fiji, Kiribati, Niue, Papua New Guinea, Micronesia, Solomon Islands, Tonga, Tuvalu, Vanuatu and Samoa. Efforts are also under way to develop a Fiji school of medicine as a potential regional human resource to assist in tackling such challenges as health promotion, disease prevention and care of the environment, including water, sanitation and waste disposal.

4. World Bank

111. World Bank activities in the areas of human resource development, sustainable infrastructure, waste management, environmental management, natural resources management and policy reform continue as reported previously (A/49/425 and Add.1).

112. Since the adoption of the Programme of Action in 1994, the World Bank has provided financing in the amount of $186.3 million to 21 small island developing States through both World Bank and GEF projects. The focus of these projects is consonant with provisions in the Programme of Action related to climate change, energy efficiency, including renewable energy sources and related technologies, waste and watershed management, biodiversity protection, regional institutional cooperation, human resource development, technical assistance and monitoring. In addition, the Bank is actively involved in major international initiatives for coral reef protection and management and the adoption of a strategic approach to marine biodiversity conservation within the framework of protected area management. Information provided by the World Bank on project-related activities is contained in an addendum (A/50/422/Add.1).

5. International Monetary Fund

113. The substantive areas of the Programme of Action lie outside the immediate mandate of the International Monetary Fund (IMF). However, in the context of its discussions with island member countries during consultations and/or use of IMF resources discussions, IMF will continue to pay close attention to their environmental and other concerns as reflected in the Programme of Action.

6. International Civil Aviation Organization

114. ICAO activities continue as reported previously (A/49/425 and Add.1). In addition, ICAO has reported that at its eleventh session (Montreal, May 1995), the ICAO Facilitation Division, after considering the question of disinfection of aircraft, recommended limitations on aerosol spraying in aircraft cabins while passengers and crew are on board, and called for a comprehensive review of pertinent WHO regulations. The Division also sought joint ICAO/WHO guidance to minimize disruption of international air service during epidemics.

7. International Telecommunication Union

115. The activities of ITU continue as reported previously (A/49/425 and Add.1).

8. International Trade Centre

116. As the United Nations body mandated to provide assistance to developing countries in export development and import management, the International Trade Centre (ITC) of UNCTAD/the General Agreement on Tariffs and Trade (GATT), while not having a specific programme for small island developing States, can offer cooperation assistance, within its six core services, in the following technical areas: export product and market development; development of trade support services; trade information; human resource development; international purchasing and supply management; needs assessment and programme design. At present, ITC is implementing several projects of technical cooperation with a number of small island developing countries in Africa and the South Pacific, in the following areas:

(a) National institutions and administrative capacity

117. Ongoing and planned capacity-building activities for the management of export development and international purchasing and supply management in Cape Verde, Mauritius and a number of islands in the Caribbean and South Pacific, including improving knowledge and strengthening capacities of government trade strategy decision makers; upgrading knowledge and skills of both private and public sector enterprise personnel in techniques of exporting and importing; improving structures and trade support facilities and services; building permanent capacity in national institutions for trade-related human resource development.

(b) Regional institutions and technical cooperation

118. Ongoing and planned activities in small island developing States are focused on strengthening the capacity of regional and subregional institutions in the areas of trade expansion and diversification, including providing institutional support for export development and import management. These activities are carried out in collaboration with the regional commissions and regional and subregional intergovernmental bodies.

(c) Human resource development

119. Small island developing countries have benefited in the past and will continue to benefit, from ITC human resource development programmes and training materials which are focused on:

(a) Activities to strengthen the capacity of national, subregional and regional training institutions in building up a permanent capacity to design and present training courses in all aspects of export development and import management, through the training of trainers and the design of training materials, manuals, case studies and visual aids;

(b) Activities on direct training in trade-related subjects for government personnel involved in national trade promotion, and in the techniques and operations of export and import trade for the business community;

(c) Organizing short-term in-service training for trainees from developing countries in technical institutions in other countries/regions;

(d) Publication of specialized training materials, manuals, guides, case studies, training packages, videos and business games.

9. International Maritime Organization

120. Although IMO measures with respect to maritime safety and the protection of the marine environment are not generally aimed specifically at small island developing States, by virtue of their relatively long coastlines and proximity to the marine environment they stand to gain from most IMO measures such as

those aimed at the prevention of pollution from ships, routing measures, collision prevention regulations and improved radio communications.

121. As the only international body for establishing and adopting measures on an international level concerning the routing and establishment of areas to be avoided by ships, IMO is looking into the possibility of instituting measures for avoiding pollution from specialized ships through the establishment of areas to be avoided by oil, chemical or liquified gas tankers in the vicinity of certain environmentally sensitive sea areas in small island developing States.

122. Other measures of direct relevance to small island developing States are the establishment of regional pollution combating centres, direct assistance in the event of serious spills involving polluting substances, and the conduct of seminars, workshops and courses on various subjects relating to maritime safety and the protection of the marine environment. Work is under way to develop a liability insurance scheme in cases where damage is suffered through hazardous and noxious substances carried by ships. Efforts are continuing to establish regional maritime coordination networks in eastern and southern Africa and the South Pacific. Such networks, if established, would benefit a number of small island developing countries.

10. World Meteorological Organization

123. WMO has plans and programmes in nine of the priority areas of the Programme of Action: "Climate change and sealevel rise", "Natural and environmental disasters", "Freshwater resources", "Energy resources", "Tourism resources", "National institutions and administrative capacity", "Regional institutions and technical cooperation", "Science and technology", and "Human resource development". The activities of WMO continue as reported previously (A/49/425 and Add.1). New information supplied by the organization is described below and in an addendum (A/50/422/Add.1).

(a) Natural and environmental disasters

124. Under the World Weather Watch Programme (WWW), all WMO member countries and territories cooperate and share responsibilities in the generation and world wide exchange of meteorological observations, forecast products and information based on agreed upon standards, procedures and practices as well as shared infrastructure. This programme provides basic information and services for other WMO and international programmes, such as those related to tropical cyclones and other natural and environmental disasters. WWW also includes transfer of technology and other support activities to assist developing countries in acquiring at least the minimum equipment and capabilities for operating their own national meteorological services.

125. Through its Public Weather Services Programme, WMO provides guidance and assistance to its members, especially those vulnerable to natural disasters, such as the small island developing States, thus fulfilling one of its primary roles: the provision of public weather services, in particular forecasts and warnings of adverse phenomenon in support of safety of life and property and for the welfare and convenience of the people.

(b) Land resources

126. WMO implements the Agricultural Meteorology Programme which supports food and agricultural production and services by providing assistance in establishing meteorological and related services to the agricultural community. The main theme of the WMO Commission for agricultural meteorology is "operational agrometeorology for sustainable, environmentally friendly and economically viable agricultural production".

11. World Intellectual Property Organization

127. WIPO plans to assist in the implementation of the Programme of Action, as reported previously (A/49/425 and Add.1), remain unchanged.

12. United Nations Industrial Development Organization

128. UNIDO activities continue as reported previously (A/49/425 and Add.1). In addition, UNIDO has supplied the information provided below.

(a) Management of wastes

129. UNIDO has extensive experience in waste management, focusing on industrial waste reduction/prevention, treatment and control. Technical assistance is provided at the policy, institutional and enterprise levels within the frameworks of cleaner production and industrial environmental management.

(b) Coastal and marine resources

130. In promoting industrial development in small island developing States, UNIDO recognizes the importance of marine and coastal resources as a base for industrialization. Assistance is provided in the field of industrial and technology policy formulation and awareness-building, small- and medium-scale enterprise development, investment promotion, and technical assistance at a sectoral level.

(c) Freshwater resources

131. UNIDO provides technical assistance in the field of industrial water management, focusing on efficient industrial water usage, waste-water treatment and recycling. Other areas include seawater desalination technology.

(d) Energy resources

132. UNIDO work on energy-related industrial issues seek to assist developing countries in developing cost-effective energy systems and infrastructure to support industrial development, reducing the environmental impacts of energy development and meeting their commitments under the Framework Convention on Climate Change. As part of this programme, UNIDO is promoting the utilization of new and renewable energy resources, such as solar, wind, biomass and ocean wave energy and the development of related energy technologies. Specific programmes address the needs of small island developing States.

(e) Biodiversity resources

133. UNIDO is planning to increase its awareness-building and promotional activities in the field of bio-safety and the sustainable utilization of biological resources, and provides technical expertise for the establishment of national biotechnology and biodiversity development programmes.

(f) Regional institutions and technical cooperation

134. Promotion of a cluster of services for small island developing States is directed towards providing industrial information, regional cooperation mechanisms, technology management, business development, and innovation and industrial investment promotion. UNIDO is planning a feasibility study in the eastern Caribbean on remote sensing and decision support technologies for integrated coastal area management. In the Mediterranean, UNIDO is carrying out a feasibility study for the establishment of a North-South business development centre focusing on the marine industries sector. The concept is being considered for other regions, such as the Caribbean and Indian Ocean.

13. Universal Postal Union

135. The Universal Postal Union (UPU) will assist in the implementation of the Programme of Action in the area of communication within the framework of the guiding policy principles for cooperation adopted by the Universal Postal Congress (UPC) for the period 1996-2000. UPC has decided to accord priority to the least developed countries, followed by the lower-middle income countries. It has requested UPU organs (a) to take the necessary measures to enable UPU to continue providing assistance to least developed countries in the area of development of postal services; (b) to allocate the highest possible proportion of UPU resources to the least developed countries; (c) to monitor continuously the general situation of the post office in least developed countries and to report to it at its next session; and (d) to help the least developed countries to enhance their capacity for deriving further revenues from philately, international accounting and new services. All those measures will benefit small island developing States that are classified as least developed. Moreover, UPU has created a post of Regional Adviser for the Caribbean, which will become operational in January 1996. During the meeting of the postmasters-general and the Conference of Ministers responsible for postal services in the Caribbean in April 1994, it was decided to intensify efforts for the creation of a Caribbean Postal Union, in collaboration with and with the assistance of the European Union and regional organizations, notably the Caribbean Forum of the African, Caribbean and Pacific (ACP) Group of States. UPU proposes to notify regional advisers of assistance to be provided to small island developing States.

14. International Fund for Agricultural Development

136. In accordance with its lending policies and criteria, the International Fund for Agricultural Development (IFAD) has mainly provided financing for projects and programmes that are specifically designed to introduce, expand or improve food production systems and to strengthen related policies and institutions within the framework of national priorities and strategies. In allocating its resources, IFAD is guided by the need to increase food production in the poorest food-deficit countries, the potential for increasing food production in other developing countries, and the importance of increasing the nutritional levels of the poorest populations in the developing countries and improving the conditions of their lives. Since most IFAD small island developing country members are poor food-deficit countries, IFAD has devoted particular attention to the development of such countries.

137. From 1978 to July 1995, IFAD provided 25 loans to small island developing States, for a total of 44.4 million special drawing rights. Of these, 80 per cent were provided on highly concessional terms, another 16 per cent on intermediate terms and 4 per cent on ordinary terms. Such loans amount to some 1.3 per cent of a total of US$ 4,216.7 million for the 413 loans that IFAD has provided in respect of 402 projects in 104 member countries over the last 13 years.

15. International Atomic Energy Agency

138. The International Atomic Energy Agency-Marine Environment Laboratory (IAEA-MEL) is intensifying its activities in small island developing States. It is involved in pilot monitoring programmes (e.g., using corals as historical recorders of micro-pollutants) as well as in capacity-building and quality assurance activities in island States of the Caribbean and East African region. IAEA supports studies involving isotopic and nuclear techniques to study retrospective conditions (climate, sea level, pollution) and to provide time scales for small island evolution. Project-related information provided by the organization is included in an addendum (A/50/422/Add.1).

D. Regional commissions

1. Economic and Social Commission for Asia and the Pacific

139. ESCAP has undertaken specific actions in priority programme areas to facilitate the implementation of the Programme of Action for the Sustainable Development of Small Island Developing States, as described below.

(a) Transport and communication

140. The ESCAP project on inter-island shipping, as reported previously (A/49/425), continues. An additional project has just commenced to develop policy options for the replacement of the ageing ships in the Pacific island fleets.

(b) Tourism resources

141. Special efforts are being made to assist Pacific island countries in strengthening national capabilities in integrated tourism planning. A workshop on integrated tourism planning in Pacific island countries was held at Port Vila, Vanuatu, in June 1995. Guidelines on integrated tourism planning in Pacific island countries will be completed in 1995. Efforts continue to assist Pacific island countries in strengthening national capabilities to create a favourable investment climate in the tourism sector. A study entitled "Investment and economic cooperation in the tourism sector in Pacific island countries", 4/ as well as studies on foreign investment in the tourism sector in Samoa and Vanuatu, were published in 1995. A project to undertake a study on land-tenure issues related to tourism development in Pacific island countries has been prepared and is awaiting funding.

(c) Natural and environmental disasters

142. Continuing coordination with the IDNDR secretariat and the Department of Humanitarian Assistance is being maintained to improve natural disaster preparedness and response in the Pacific.

(d) Science and technology

143. Small island developing States of the Pacific are rich in natural resources, and their proper monitoring demands the use of space technology. In order to disseminate such technology, a remote sensing/GIS workshop for land and marine resources and environment management in the Pacific subregion was held in Suva, Fiji from 13 to 17 February 1995. Participants from 18 countries, including the 14 Pacific small island developing States, attended. The objectives of the workshop were to expose senior officials to new developments in remote sensing/GIS applications, formulate a subregional action plan and to promote the use of remote sensing and GIS technology for development. A project portfolio consisting of eight projects was also developed, covering various thematic applications, training and data reception, for further implementation under the regional space applications programme, with financial support from donors.

144. The Ministerial Conference on Space Applications for Development in Asia and the Pacific (Beijing, 1992) launched the regional space applications programme for sustainable development, which contains specific programme areas tailored to meet the requirements and peculiar situations of island countries.

(e) Land resources

145. Most small island countries are characterized by limited land resources and are dependent on the agricultural and fisheries sectors for livelihood. In order to make the agricultural sector more efficient, ESCAP is promoting sustainable agriculture and rural development by building the capacities of small island developing States in planning and implementing rural development

activities. Moreover, advisory services are provided in promoting the environmentally friendly use of agrochemicals. The dissemination of information on agrochemicals continues; such information includes new developments in agrochemicals, market and price situations, and the protection of land resources. Studies are planned to identify available land resources and their proper use. Recommendations emerging from the studies will assist Governments in policy formulation.

(f) National institutions and administrative capacity

146. A programme of work focusing on sustainable development issues and their integration into economic decision-making is being developed. The aim of the overall project is to provide technical assistance on the institutional setting and policy modalities for integrating environmental considerations into macroeconomic decision-making processes. The project covers Pacific island countries, as well as some other developing countries of Asia. It is proposed to conduct country studies, as well as subregional and regional workshops to share experiences. Supporting research involves a case study involving two Pacific island countries on the formulation and implementation of policies for promoting sustainable development, focusing on population growth and mobility, urbanization, international trade, agricultural production, and energy and transport costs.

147. The ESCAP/Pacific Operation Centre assists SPREP in the implementation of its Capacity 21 programme, including the design and conduct of workshops. Moreover, the Centre is working to incorporate the essence of this training into other activities, such as advisory services to small island countries on development finance and regional and national planning. It is also providing advisory services to the South Pacific Commission (SPC) and the South Pacific Forum (SPF), including recommendations for rationalizing the management of marine resources among SPF, the Forum Fisheries Agency and the South Pacific Applied Geoscience Commission (SOPAC).

(g) Human resource development

148. The ESCAP secretariat is currently implementing a programme on the theme "Reaching the poor through government/non-governmental organizations cooperation in the planning and delivery of human resource development services". As part of the activities under that programme, a national workshop is scheduled to be held in Papua New Guinea. The objective of the workshop will be to enhance the linkages between government agencies and non-governmental organizations in planning and implementing human resource development programmes. The participants in the workshop will be government officials and non-governmental organizations personnel responsible for planning and implementing human resource development programmes. Moreover, in pursuance of ESCAP resolution 51/10 of 1 May 1995, resources are also being mobilized to conduct a feasibility study on the establishment of a Pacific subregional training centre for drug demand reduction.

149. The ESCAP secretariat is involving small island countries in regional preparations for Habitat II and its follow-up, by inviting them to address their particular concerns and formulate suitable intervention at the Second Asia Pacific Urban Forum. Local authorities from small island countries are also being encouraged to join - as some have already - the Network of Local Authorities for Management of Human Settlements (CITYNET) through which ESCAP is channelling assistance in urban management.

150. In addition, a study on maritime manpower resources in the ESCAP region is being carried out, to identify the requirements for and availability of trained and qualified seafarers to meet the growing world shortage. This study will highlight the employment potential for seafarers from small island developing countries, and the economic benefits that may be derived from the training and supply of seafarers to international shipping.

2. Economic Commission for Latin America and the Caribbean

(a) Coastal and marine resources

151. ECLAC is developing a project proposal on the four essential elements and components of information - availability of information, effective means of delivery, responsiveness to user needs and effective use of information - geared towards coastal conservation. To that end, the project will establish a mechanism to provide individuals and groups of users with access to environment-related information that is integrated with indicators for economic and social policy-making in Caribbean countries. The project will also seek to enhance the ECLAC/AMBIONET system as an effective tool for delivering information and responding to the demand for the effective use of such information by the public and private sectors.

(b) Energy resources

152. In collaboration with UNESCO and the Centre for Environment and Development of the University of the West Indies (UWICED), the Caribbean Council for Science and Technology (CCST) convened a high-level regional workshop on renewable energy technologies (Saint Lucia, 5-9 December 1994), to discuss the role of renewable energy in the development process of the region in the context of sustainable development. Delegates to the meeting focused on the scope of the utilization of renewable energy as against conventional energy sources, as well as on the need to improve dialogue and awareness of the respective problems faced by the principal users of energy. The meeting adopted a model energy policy and a resolution on renewable energy. The workshop brought together participants from member countries, as well as representatives from many energy-based industries involved in the production and use of energy.

(c) Tourism resources

153. ECLAC work in this area continues as reported previously (A/49/425 and Add.1). Additional work in sustainable tourism includes the preparation of chapters of a textbook and research on economic instruments for tourism development.

(d) National institutions and administrative capacity

154. As part of its programme of work for this biennium, ECLAC is carrying out a critical examination of the availability of environmental information in the Caribbean and an assessment of implications for planning and decision-making. This environmental database is intended to increase the awareness of member states of work in the field of environment and development. It will seek to organize environmental statistics for the region and offer a directory on the sources of the information.

155. In order to focus on issues emanating from the Global Conference and to carry out its mandate to increase hemispheric cooperation, the ECLAC secretariat has included in its work programme two new subprogrammes on the promotion of cooperation among member countries of the Caribbean Development and Cooperation Council (CDCC) and between the Caribbean and Latin America and island developing countries; both subprogrammes will focus on the promotion of cooperation in functional and sectoral areas among the member countries of the Caribbean and countries of Latin America. The ECLAC programme of work will also include the needs of the non-independent Caribbean countries, which will be addressed within the broad framework of the analysis of issues related to island developing countries in the subregion and the review of initiatives taken to foster the integration of the member countries of CDCC within the wider Caribbean as well as with other countries of Latin America.

(e) Regional institutions and technical cooperation

156. In collaboration with the Department for Policy Coordination and Sustainable Development, UWICED, UNEP and UNDP, ECLAC convened a Caribbean meeting of experts on implementation of the Programme of Action in May 1995 to discuss constraints on effective implementation and to agree on priority areas for action. The meeting identified immediate sectoral priorities for the Caribbean region and for institutional arrangements for regional coordination in, inter alia, the following priority areas: "Management of wastes, "Land resources", "Coastal and marine resources", and "Natural and environmental disasters".

157. ECLAC has initiated activities that would strengthen its cooperation and collaboration with regional institutions and other United Nation agencies. To that end, there is active collaboration with UWICED, the UNEP Caribbean Environment Plan and UNDP in the implementation of work in the field of environment and development. ECLAC has signed memoranda of understanding with CARICOM, UWI, UNEP and the United Nations Institute for Training and Research (UNITAR).

(f) Science and technology

158. ECLAC is responding to the Programme of Action through activities carried out under the aegis of CCST. CCST assists member countries in their elaboration of science and technology policy and in increasing national science and technology capacities.

(g) National institutions and administrative capacity

159. ECLAC is continuing to develop its programme on information gathering and dissemination. It has put into place a communications package emphasizing the use of the UNECLAC/AMBIONET Electronic Information Exchange System. This system allows access to more than 33 libraries. It also connected to outside databases and other information systems through INTERNET.

(h) Human resource development

160. The ECLAC subregional headquarters for the Caribbean currently executes a project funded by the United Nations Population Fund (UNFPA) on the integration of population policies into development planning in the Caribbean subregion. Included in this project is a study on the migratory patterns of Caribbean peoples and a study on teenage fertility in selected Caribbean countries. A regional project on education, training and employment for teenage mothers in the Caribbean has been submitted to UNFPA for funding. CCST has presented a training workshop on project preparation and management for scientists in the region, and the Caribbean Documentation Centre has offered training workshops in the use of the CDS/ISIS and ECLAC/AMBIONET systems of operations.

161. ECLAC also undertakes activities related to the integration of women in development, focusing its attention on a range of issues of particular importance to the development of women in the Caribbean, as well as on the incorporation of population concerns and issues in the design of social and economic development plans. In addition, ECLAC continues to work in close collaboration with regional and national non-governmental organizations, and offers technical support in developing their programmes of work.

3. Economic Commission for Africa

162. The activities of the Economic Commission for Africa (ECA) continue as reported previously (A/49/425 and Add.1). In addition, consultations are under way between ECA and UNDP at the country level for possible joint activities in identifying, within the context of national workshops in the five African small island developing States, areas for building critical human and institutional

capacities, as suggested in paragraph 129 of the Programme of Action. Such activities will benefit from those of the ongoing ECA framework agenda for building and utilizing critical capacities in Africa. The focus will be on capacity-building in (a) environmental economics and resource accounting; (b) impact assessment; (c) development of the relevant legislative frameworks; (d) vulnerability assessment; and (e) resource mobilization. Consultations are also ongoing between ECA and UNDP for a joint regional workshop on unmet priorities within the Programme of Action in Africa. A regional workshop will be held during 1995 to examine the report on unmet priority assessment being prepared by UNDP and a framework for an African regional programme of action. A number of ECA programmes are already responding to elements of the global Programme of Action. Information on ECA technical assistance to the African small island developing States is included in an addendum (A/40/422/Add.1).

4. Economic Commission for Europe

163. The activities of the Economic Commission for Europe (ECE) continue as reported previously (A/49/425 and Add.1).

5. Economic and Social Commission for Western Asia

164. The Economic and Social Commission for Western Asia (ESCWA) has indicated that it is involved in the management of supply/demand of water resources in Bahrain, which depends mainly on groundwater for its water supply, supplemented by desalinated water and some treated effluent.

II. INSTITUTIONAL ARRANGEMENTS

A. United Nations

1. Department for Policy Coordination and Sustainable Development

165. The responsibilities related to the implementation of the Programme of Action and follow-up to the Global Conference are being carried out by the Division for Sustainable Development of the Department for Policy Coordination and Sustainable Development.

166. In accordance with General Assembly resolution 49/122, a small island developing States Unit has been established within the Division for Sustainable Development. Essentially, the Unit is responsible for four broad functions: (a) to provide substantive secretariat support to intergovernmental and inter-agency processes related to the monitoring, review and coordination of the implementation of the Programme of Action; (b) to act as a liaison or focal point for Governments and organs, programmes and agencies of the United Nations system on matters related to the follow-up to the Global Conference and the implementation of the Programme of Action; (c) to prepare reports for the Commission on Sustainable Development and other relevant bodies on the implementation of the Programme of Action; and (d) to provide support, as appropriate, to other activities emanating from the Programme of Action. The Unit is currently staffed by a Chief of Unit and a Sustainable Development Officer at the Professional level, supported by one General Service staff member. The Unit functions as a focal point within the Department on issues related to the Programme of Action, with the responsibilities outlined above. The Department is coordinating the implementation of the Programme of Action through the Inter-agency Committee on Sustainable Development which, at its 6th meeting (Geneva, 12-14 July 1995), took decisions on the modalities of system-wide coordination on the recommendations of the Department.

2. United Nations Conference on Trade and Development

167. UNCTAD is planning to make new institutional arrangements to carry out the aspects of the Programme of Action that fall within its mandate when its capacity is strengthened.

3. United Nations Environment Programme

168. No new institutional arrangements have been put in place since those previously reported (see A/49/425 and Add.1). UNEP designated a focal point with respect to the Global Conference and its follow-up activities, including implementation of the Programme of Action, in 1993, and immediately following the Global Conference a joint UNEP/Habitat task force was established. It is anticipated that the task force will oversee the development of a programmatic approach to the implementation of small island developing States activities within the 1996-1997 work programme of UNEP.

4. United Nations Centre for Human Settlements

169. Habitat has designated a focal point with respect to the follow-up activities for the implementation of the Programme of Action. A joint UNEP/Habitat task force is active in coordinating inter-agency policies and strategies for the execution of activities in support of the sustainable development of small island developing States.

B. Funds and programmes

1. United Nations Development Programme

170. The Special Unit for Technical Cooperation among Developing Countries has been designated to coordinate within UNDP the follow-up on the implementation of the Programme of Action. In this capacity, the Unit will work closely with the various bureaux at UNDP headquarters and the UNDP country offices responsible for small island developing States to ensure effective follow-up activities.

2. United Nations Population Fund

171. No new institutional arrangements are envisaged by UNFPA to implement the Programme of Action within those areas relevant to its mandate.

3. United Nations Children's Fund

172. UNICEF will utilize its existing institutional arrangements to support the implementation of the Programme of Action. In addition, a focal point has been established within the Environment Unit to facilitate the coordination of activities regarding small island developing States. These arrangements reflect the organization's response to Agenda 21, which has parallels with the Programme of Action.

4. United Nations International Drug Control Programme

173. UNDCP will implement the Programme of Action through its existing institutional arrangements.

C. Specialized agencies

1. Food and Agriculture Organization of the United Nations

174. The Director-General of FAO has incorporated the recommendations of the Programme of Action into the FAO programme of work, and has created two subregional offices, one for the South Pacific and one for the Caribbean.

2. United Nations Educational, Scientific and Cultural Organization

175. Prior to the Global Conference, the UNESCO Director-General established a focal point for relations with small island States within the Bureau for External Relations. The focal point will be responsible for facilitating relations with small island developing States in all matters relating to follow-up to the Global Conference. In addition, as part of his overall coordination responsibility for UNCED follow-up, the Director of the Bureau for Coordination of Environmental Programmes will also be responsible for follow-up to the Global Conference in terms of ensuring effective internal and inter-agency programme coordination.

3. World Health Organization

176. The WHO global strategy and related action plan are being implemented by WHO through its headquarters and regional offices. The American and western Pacific regional offices are the main offices dealing at an operational level with small island developing States, because of their proximity to the Caribbean and South Pacific regions, respectively. The western Pacific office recently established an environmental health unit in Fiji, which will focus on the problems faced by the Pacific island countries. WHO offices in Africa, South-East Asia and the eastern Mediterranean will also be involved in supporting those small island developing States that fall within their area of operations. Also, a new Division for Emergency and Humanitarian Action has been established, which is intended to strengthen the capabilities of WHO in the area of natural and environmental disasters. In addition, an Associate Professional Officer (APO-Environmental Engineer) was posted in Samoa to provide closer collaboration also with American Samoa, Cook Islands, Niue and Tokelau. Efforts are under way to post an APO with environmental skills and knowledge in Vanuatu and the Federated States of Micronesia to support community water and sanitation activities, as well as other environmental health activities.

4. World Bank

177. Existing World Bank institutional arrangements are supporting the implementation of the Programme of Action. An institutional focal point for small island developing States has been designated.

5. International Monetary Fund

178. IMF envisages no special institutional arrangements, because the substantive areas of the Programme of Action lie outside its immediate mandate.

6. International Civil Aviation Organization

179. ICAO will support the implementation of the Programme of Action through its existing institutional arrangements.

7. International Telecommunication Union

180. The development of technical assistance programmes for small island developing States is carried out by the Telecommunication Development Bureau, which is the development arm of ITU. The Bureau has regional and subregional offices in the Americas, Asia and the Pacific, and Africa. The Caribbean subregion will be served by the Barbados area office, while the Pacific will be served by the area office at Jakarta. Activities will be coordinated at ITU headquarters at Geneva, where a focal point on small island developing States will be established.

8. International Trade Centre

181. Activities for assistance to small island developing countries are planned and implemented by ITC utilizing, in the main, the resources of its existing institutional structure, supplemented by extrabudgetary funds, when available. No new institutional arrangements are envisaged by ITC to implement the Programme of Action within those areas relevant to its mandate.

9. International Maritime Organization

182. Efforts are continuing to establish regional maritime coordination networks in eastern and southern Africa, and in the South Pacific. These networks, if established, would benefit a number of small island developing States.

10. World Meteorological Organization

183. WMO institutional arrangements to support the implementation of the Programme of Action are included, to the extent possible, within its existing scientific and technical programmes. WMO has designated the Director of the World Weather Watch Department as the focal point for the implementation of the Programme of Action.

11. World Intellectual Property Organization

184. The World Intellectual Property Organization will utilize its existing institutional arrangements to support implementation of the Programme of Action.

12. United Nations Industrial Development Organization

185. UNIDO will implement the Programme of Action within its existing institutional arrangements.

13. International Fund for Agricultural Development

186. Existing IFAD institutional arrangements will support the implementation of the Programme of Action.

D. Regional commissions

1. Economic and Social Commission for Asia and the Pacific

187. A mechanism for the consultation and pooling of limited resources through regional cooperation between United Nations bodies and agencies, intergovernmental organizations, bilateral donors and international organizations already exists in Asia and the Pacific, through the Inter-agency Committee on Environment and Sustainable Development. In June 1994, the

Inter-agency Committee considered the outcome of the Global Conference, and decided that it would facilitate the coordination and implementation of the Programme of Action, as requested in paragraph 132 of the Programme of Action. In this connection, it was agreed that the Inter-agency Committee working group would review the priority areas of the Programme of Action and identify projects for joint implementation by the Committee members. ESCAP has also set up a special body on Pacific island States to facilitate ongoing consultations with those States.

188. In addition, ESCAP has established the ESCAP Pacific Operations Centre at Port Vila, Vanuatu, with a small complement of core staff. Its professional expertise is made available to the small island developing States in the Asia and the Pacific region through that Centre. The Centre, as well as various substantive divisions of ESCAP, also cooperate with other South Pacific regional organizations in the delivery of their programmes, including the South Pacific Forum, the South Pacific Forum Fisheries Agency, the South Pacific Commission, the South Pacific Applied Geoscience Commission, the South Pacific Regional Environment Programme, the University of the South Pacific, the Pacific Islands Development Programme and the Tourism Council of the South Pacific. Efforts are being made to further strengthen the capacity of the Pacific Operations Centre to provide technical assistance to member countries.

2. Economic Commission for Latin America and the Caribbean

189. ECLAC activities in relation to small island developing States involve its subregional headquarters for the Caribbean in Trinidad and Tobago, and the programme of work of the Natural Resources and Energy Division. The ECLAC/CDCC secretariat is responsible for guiding and promoting the economic and social development of those Caribbean countries that are members of CDCC, consisting mainly of small island developing States. An integral part of the programme is being accomplished through programme elements on environment and development of small island developing States. The secretariat has been mandated, at a regional meeting convened to consider the status of the implementation of the Programme of Action, to establish, jointly with CARICOM, a regional coordinating mechanism to promote the implementation of the Programme of Action.

3. Economic Commission for Europe

190. Existing ECE institutional arrangements can support and accommodate activities to implement the Programme of Action. ECE activities will continue as reported previously (A/49/425 and Add.1).

4. Economic Commission for Africa

191. In an effort to implement the Programme of Action with immediate effect, ECA will endeavour to implement some of its proposed actions within ongoing programmes and existing resources. However, additional resources will be needed in two areas: the provision of advisory services and data collection, and missions and training seminars and workshops. Additional resources will also be needed for coordination, including consultancies and participation by African women, and for providing increased access to resources in both the formal and informal sectors.

III. CONCLUDING OBSERVATIONS

192. The responses summarized above indicate that the relevant organizations and bodies of the United Nations system are committed to the implementation of the Programme of Action for the Sustainable Development of Small Island Developing States. They have incorporated the elements of the Programme of Action that fall within their respective mandates into their work programmes, and have begun

to implement projects to meet the priorities identified in the Programme of Action. The scope of activities undertaken varies among the different organizations and bodies depending on the extent to which the priority areas of the Programme of Action are covered by their respective mandates.

193. The information contained in the present report and an addendum (A/50/422/Add.1) on the plans and programmes of the United Nations system, which is additional to that contained in the previous report (A/49/425 and Add.1), shows that several organizations and bodies of the United Nations system have reformulated their work programmes in direct response to the provisions of the Programme of Action. It also shows that several of them have expanded their plans and programmes since their submissions for the preparation of the previous report. The present report contains information on the activities of several organizations - UPU, ITC, IDNDR/Department of Humanitarian Affairs, IFAD, UNU and INSTRAW - for the first time; many of those activities represent new initiatives under the Programme of Action.

194. The ongoing and planned activities of the organizations and bodies of the United Nations system, taken together, cover all the programme areas - sectoral and cross-sectoral - of the Programme of Action. In multisectoral areas, such as tourism, while the activities of no single organization or body cover all dimensions, their cumulative activities - if sustained and adequately funded - will go a long way towards meeting the provisions of the Programme of Action.

195. In the area of regional coordination of the implementation of the Programme of Action, four regional bodies - ECE, ESCAP, ECLAC and ECA - have reported that they have taken initiatives to fulfil their mandates. ESCAP and ECLAC have held regional meetings to identify immediate regional priorities, and have established coordination mechanisms in collaboration with regional intergovernmental organizations. ECA has reported that it is in consultation with UNDP at the country level regarding possible joint activities to identify, through national workshops in the five African small island developing States, ways to build human and institutional capacities, as well as a possible joint regional workshop on current priorities under the Programme of Action. Regarding coordination at the international level, the Department for Policy Coordination and Sustainable Development has established mechanisms for system-wide coordination through IACSD.

196. As to specific responsibilities under the Programme of Action, UNDP has reported that it is actively pursuing the refinement and operationalization of SIDS/NET and SIDS/TAP in consultation with small island developing States and other interested parties, and the Department has taken the initiative, in collaboration with UNCTAD, to organize an in-session panel discussion on trade-related issues affecting small island developing States and to explore approaches to the development of a vulnerability index.

197. It is expected that the organizations and bodies of the United Nations system will further sharpen the focus of their activities under the Programme of Action on the basis of decisions taken by the Commission on Sustainable Development at its fourth session, in 1996.

198. Of the organizations and bodies included in the present report, nine have reported that they will implement the Programme of Action through existing institutional arrangements. UNCTAD and ECA have indicated that they need additional resources to establish appropriate new institutional mechanisms. All the others have established new mechanisms, which vary among the different organizations and bodies, to oversee and coordinate the implementation of the Programme of Action.

Notes

1/ Report of the Global Conference on the Sustainable Development of Small Island Developing States, Bridgetown, Barbados, 25 April-6 May 1994 (United Nations publication, Sales No. 94.I.18), chap. I, resolution 1, annex II.

2/ Report of the United Nations Conference on Environment and Development, Rio de Janeiro, 3-14 June 1992, vol. I, Resolutions Adopted by the Conference (United Nations publication, Sales No. E.93.I.18), chap. I, resolution 1, annex II.

3/ Report of the Interregional Conference of Small Island Countries on Sustainable Development and Environment in Agriculture, Forestry and Fisheries, Christ Church, Barbados, 7-10 April 1992 (Rome, Food and Agriculture Organization of the United Nations, 1993), Part III.

4/ ESCAP Tourism Review, No. 13 (ST/ESCAP/1386).

ANNEX

List of organizations that responded to the request for inputs to the present report

1. Food and Agriculture Organization of the United Nations
2. United Nations Educational, Scientific and Cultural Organization
3. World Health Organization
4. World Bank
5. International Monetary Fund
6. International Civil Aviation Organization
7. Universal Postal Union
8. World Meterological Organization
9. International Telecommunication Union
10. International Maritime Organization
11. World Intellectual Property Organization
12. United Nations Industrial Development Organization
13. International Atomic Energy Agency
14. International Trade Centre (UNCTAD/GATT)
15. United Nations Conference on Trade and Development
16. United Nations Environment Programme
17. United Nations Children's Fund
18. United Nations Development Programme
19. World Food Programme
20. United Nations Centre for Human Settlements
21. United Nations Population Fund
22. United Nations International Drug Control Programme
23. Economic Commission for Europe
24. Economic Commission for Africa
25. Economic and Social Commission for Asia and the Pacific

26. Economic Commission for Latin America and the Caribbean

27. International Fund for Agricultural Development

28. United Nations University

29. International Research and Training Institute for the Advancement of Women

30. Department of Humanitarian Affairs of the United Nations Secretariat/ International Decade for Natural Disaster Reduction

31. Economic and Social Commission for Western Asia

52. ACTION TAKEN BY THE ORGANS, ORGANIZATIONS AND BODIES OF THE UNITED NATIONS SYSTEM TO IMPLEMENT THE PROGRAMME OF ACTION FOR THE SUSTAINABLE DEVELOPMENT OF SMALL ISLAND DEVELOPING STATES - REPORT OF THE UN SECRETARY-GENERAL*: ADDENDUM

Doc. no.: A/50/422/Add.1 20 September 1995

The following table has been prepared as an addendum to the report of the Secretary-General on action taken by the organs, organizations and bodies of the United Nations system to implement the Programme of Action for Sustainable Development of Small Island Developing States.

In preparing the table, the basic format utilized in the addendum to the previous report of the Secretary-General (A/49/425/Add.1) has been adhered to. The table contains project-related information supplied by organizations, and serves as a complement to the main report. It reflects activities reported since the preparation of the previous report; information on activities contained in the previous report that are ongoing is not repeated.

* A/50/150.

United Nations organization/ body	Description of activity	Remarks
	I. <u>Climate change and sealevel rise</u>	
UNEP	Co-sponsored with WMO the Intergovernmental Panel on Climate Change. A special report was prepared for the Conference of the Parties to the Framework Convention on Climate Change (1995) and a second report will become available in 1995.	Reference is made to UNEP activities on climate change and sealevel rise (see main report).
UNEP	A special project on climate change impacts and adaptations assessment will be initiated in Antigua and Barbuda.	The outcome will assist other small island developing States in formulating comprehensive strategies and measures for adaptation to climate change and sealevel rise.
UNDP	A GEF-funded pilot project in Maldives seeks to build national capacity to assess the impact on the country of climate change and to comply with the United Nations Framework Convention on Climate Change.	The experience and lessons learned from this pilot will be shared with the other small island developing States over the life of the project.
WHO	Collaboration with the Government of Maldives in studying the possible implications for the country of global warming, and its effects on coastal erosion and the ocean and coral ecology of the islands.	
UNESCO	In the framework of IOC Global Programme on Global Ocean Observing System, purchase, through IOCARIBE Programme, of new tide gauges, which have been installed throughout Caribbean Sea.	
UNESCO	Organization of an IOCARIBE expert group workshop on climate change in intra-Americas seas to draw up a plan of action for sealevel and climate change programmes.	
UNESCO	Provision of support to the Caribbean Community Ocean Sciences Network for the establishment of a subregional oceanographic data and information capability at the Institute of Marine Affairs in Port-of-Spain, Trinidad and Tobago.	

United Nations organization/ body	Description of activity	Remarks
WMO	Co-sponsorship, with IOC, of an IGOSS sealevel project in the Pacific to provide operational analyses of sealevel and sealevel anomalies. Co-sponsor, with IOC and UNEP, of pilot projects for coral reef monitoring and monitoring of the effects of sealevel rise in the Indian Ocean.	
World Bank a/	GEF funding of up to US$ 6.5 million approved in May 1995 for development of four-year regional programme for CARICOM member States that are parties to the United Nations Framework Convention on Climate Change to increase national and regional planning tools and skills for adapting to the effects of global climate change on coastal and marine resources. Activities include identifying policy instruments (economic, legislative and regulatory) that will help implement a long-term programme of adaptation to global climate change in vulnerable coastal areas.	Provide financing and technical assistance to assist national Governments in implementing the objectives and recommendations of the United Nations Framework Convention on Climate Change, including identification of cost-effective response and adaptation to the impacts of global climate change.
World Bank a/	GEF-financed demand-side management project in Jamaica will strengthen capabilities of public utility and implement an integrated approach to energy conservation. Mechanisms to overcome market barriers will be tested, and valuation results will be used to design full-scale sustainable long-term energy efficiency programmes. The project also implements a national cogeneration policy, which will stimulate the diversification of generation sources, including renewable services.	As above.
	II. Natural and environmental disasters	
UNICEF	Provision of oral rehydration salt packets to Mauritius, following cyclone in 1994, which resulted in increased incidence of gastro-enteritis cases.	
WHO	Preparation of guidelines on environmental health measures in emergency situations for publication in 1996.	
FAO	As of April 1995, had carried out emergency agricultural projects involving provision of tools, seedlings, stocks and locust control critical to small island developing States, mostly Haiti.	

United Nations organization/ body	Description of activity	Remarks
WMO	In collaboration with IAEA, WMO has implemented operational, worldwide arrangements for the coordinated provision of specific forecasts of the atmospheric transport of radioactive material and the deposition in case of major radiological accidents.	
WMO	WMO has implemented a globally coordinated system to provide meteorological and oceanographic advice and services to support marine pollution emergency response operations.	
IDNDR/Department of Humanitarian Affairs	Emergency cash contributions (US$ 30,000) provided to the Government of Mauritius in February 1994, following destruction by cyclone Hollanda. Disaster management team sent, comprising the Department, UNDP, WHO, UNICEF, UNFPA and WFP, including a Department team specializing in telecommunications and engineering.	
IDNDR/Department of Humanitarian Affairs	Emergency cash grant of US$ 20,000 provided to the Government of Saint Lucia, after devastation caused by tropical storm Debbie in September 1994. Donor meeting convened in Barbados, and assessment mission of Eastern Caribbean donor group organized with participation of Government, PAHO, FAO and UNICEF.	
IDNDR/Department of Humanitarian Affairs	Coordinated relief effort in Haiti (November 1994), following death and destruction caused by tropical storm Gordon. Special task force established: Department served as secretariat and as adviser to the Government. Needs assessment and evaluation conducted. Relief efforts provided over 30 metric tons of supplies; Department emergency cash (US$ 38,000) and Sasakawa emergency contribution (US$ 20,000) also provided.	
IDNDR/Department of Humanitarian Affairs	Coordinated relief activities for Cuba as a result of tropical storm Gordon (November 1994). Relief needs, priorities for action determined and donor contributions sought. Department emergency cash grant (US$ 30,000) provided, and shipment of 38 metric tons of relief goods organized. Over US$ 500,000 in donor contributions reported to Department.	

United Nations organization/ body	Description of activity	Remarks
IDNDR/Department of Humanitarian Affairs	Relief provided to Government of Cape Verde, after volcanic eruption on island of Fogo (April 1995). A United Nations Disaster Assistance Coordinator team and a Department delegate sent from Geneva to assist in relief coordination activities. Two relief flights with 35.7 metric tons of goods sent from Department's Pisa warehouse.	
IDNDR/Department of Humanitarian Affairs	The South Pacific Disaster Reduction Programme, implemented by Department's South Pacific Programme Office, began operations (May 1994) involving 15 Pacific island countries. Objective is to mitigate impact of natural disasters and improve post-disaster recovery management.	Programme objectives are to strengthen institutional capacities and develop human resources in Pacific island countries.
IDNDR/Department of Humanitarian Affairs	Various missions carried out to assist small island developing States.	
ESCAP	Contributions made to Department's training material development and training programmes.	
World Bank a/	Saint Lucia watershed and environmental management project under preparation; responds to urgent rehabilitation and protection needs resulting from severe tropical storm damage. Support for initial rehabilitation of hydraulic infrastructure of priority watersheds from damage caused by flooding and landslides. Integrated watershed management strategy and flood preparedness strategy being prepared.	Provide financing and technical assistance for natural and environmental disaster preparedness, including integrated environmental management and infrastructure rehabilitation and strengthening.
	III. Management of Wastes	
Habitat	UMP Office for Latin America and the Caribbean has made an evaluation of solid-waste management needs in the Caribbean, and is programming the execution of follow-up national consultations on urban management and environmental sanitation.	
Habitat	Habitat and UNEP have initiated the formulation of a proposal for a global project on waste minimization and pollution prevention in small island developing States.	

United Nations organization/ body	Description of activity	Remarks
WHO	WPRO has initiated an activity on solid waste disposal in Papua New Guinea, Solomon Islands and Tonga.	
UNDP	The UNDP urban management programme regional office for Asia and the Pacific has carried out, on the basis of a joint initiative with Habitat and the World Bank, consultations on urban management and environmental sanitation with a number of Pacific island countries, including Fiji, Solomon Islands, and Samoa. A second phase will include Kiribati, the Marshall Islands and the Federated States of Micronesia.	
UNDP	GEF small grants programme has supported grass-roots activities in two local communities in Barbados to construct community garbage chutes to reduce solid-waste contamination of nearby rivers, a marine reserve, and sanitary facilities to prevent contamination of a mangrove swamp.	
	IV. Coastal and marine resources	
UNEP	Preparation of a coastal profile for the Comoros, and development of an integrated coastal area strategy by the end of 1995, including demonstration projects in integrated island management.	Demonstration projects linked to similar activities under priority area "Freshwater resources".
UNEP	Support for the development of environmental information systems is being provided to Fiji and Samoa.	
Habitat	Collaboration with UNEP on the formulation of integrated plans for settlements and coastal zone management in Saint Vincent and the Grenadines. The project is developing guidelines and management tools for the incorporation of marine and coastal zone consideration into settlements planning.	It is expected that the management instruments to be developed by the project will be replicated in other small island developing States.
FAO	As of April 1995, had implemented various aspects of 7 projects essentially on fisheries development in five small island developing States.	
IAEA	Active involvement in international mussel watch project, in collaboration with IOC/UNESCO. Samples of mussels collected and analysed from throughout Central and South America.	Aim of project to assess global distribution and investigate transport of persistent organochlorine pollutants.

United Nations organization/ body	Description of activity	Remarks
IAEA	Established working group on the safe carriage of irradiated nuclear fuel by sea, in cooperation with IMO and with the participation of UNEP.	Working Group recommended adoption by the three organizations of a draft code of practice for the safe carriage of irradiated nuclear fuel, plutonium and high-level radioactive wastes on board ships.
UNDP	Supporting, through funding from the regional IPF, an off-shore fisheries development programme in the Pacific, which is executed by the South Pacific Commission.	
UNDP	IPF-funded regional fisheries development project has been designed to assist Pacific island countries in maximizing the exploitation of abundant tuna resources while at the same time assuring the sustainability of future stocks.	
	V. Freshwater resources	
UNICEF	Activities carried out in Mauritius include community protection of springs, rainwater harvesting, training of water pump operators, distribution of documentation on environmental hygiene, and advocacy on the theme "Water for life".	
UNU	UNU is working with solar corporations in ascertaining simple products for use in water purification and distillation for the islands utilizing solar energy. A series of workshops is planned on the technological options available to islands for water treatment, and defense against red tides and sealevel rise, as well as underground dams for the provision of fresh water.	This activity relates also to the priority area "Science and technology".

United Nations organization/body	Description of activity	Remarks
UNDP	Supported, through SPR resources, the establishment of the International Network on Small Hydro Power in Hangzhou, China. The Network will include selected small island developing States as participating members through their regional energy institutions, such as the South Pacific Forum, the Pacific Power Association, the African Energy Policy Research Network and the Latin American Energy Organizations.	The Network will serve as a facility for the exchange of technical information, experiences, policies and practices, as well as the exchange of technical specialists on small hydropower as an environmentally friendly and community-based source of alternative energy.
WHO	The new WHO guidelines for drinking water quality in the Pacific island countries/areas were promoted with a view to setting national standards. As a result, Fiji, Tonga and Cook Islands adopted national standards of their own.	
WHO	Hands-on training was organized in Fiji, focusing on analytical procedures (both field and laboratory) for testing water and food to ensure their safety. This resulted in establishing and strengthening laboratory capabilities in Fiji, Kiribati, Niue, Solomon Islands, Tonga, Tuvalu, Vanuatu and Samoa.	
WHO	Supported the Ministry of Health of Maldives in the formulation of a national plan of action for health and environment, and human resources development for environmental management, and in tackling problems specific to coral islands related to the provision of water and disposal of sewage.	
WMO	Organizing, in the framework of the International Hydrological Programme, and in cooperation with UNDP and the South Pacific Applied Geoscience Commission, of a workshop in Solomon Islands to set up applied research and training agenda on hydrology in the South Pacific islands, aiming at enhancing the rational use of freshwater resources; launching, as a result, a subregional project on water management in Pacific island countries; and planning similar workshops for Latin America and the Caribbean.	

United Nations organization/ body	Description of activity	Remarks
World Bank a/	Funded Seychelles Mahé integrated water supply project (US$ 20 million), financing efforts to increase freshwater supply to all areas of the country's principal city, with the goal that at least 95 per cent of the population should have access to a reliable supply of potable water.	
World Bank a/	Approved Trinidad and Tobago water sector/institutional strengthening project (US$ 25 million). Project is under Implementation and is designed to strengthen water resources management, support the transition of water-supply services to private-sector management, and prepare a programme of investment in flood control and drainage infrastructure.	Provide funding to strengthen water resources management, including the promotion of efficient private-sector delivery mechanisms.
World Bank a/	The Bank, in collaboration with other donors, is assisting small island developing States in launching the NEAP process, to address, inter alia, sustainable land use and integrated costal zone management.	Provide funding and technical assistance for the adoption of national environmental action plans (NEAPs).
	VI. Land resources	
UNEP	Implementation, jointly with FAO, SPREP and the South Pacific Institute for Research, Extension and Training in Agriculture, of a project for providing small island developing States of the South Pacific subregion with improved knowledge for natural resources appraisal and ecosystem analysis using SOTER/GIS.	
FAO	As of April 1995, had implemented 37 projects on agricultural developments, nutrition and forestry in 17 small island developing States.	
IFAD	From 1991 to 1995, provided loans to seven small island developing States, essentially to support small producers.	The total value of the seven loans is estimated at US$ 19.6 million.

United Nations organization/ body	Description of activity	Remarks
ECA	Has prepared a comprehensive report on the rationalization and improvement of cross-border food trade for the Lusaka-based MULPOC subregion that covers Comoros, Mauritius and Seychelles. Has also undertaken other project studies of benefit to all African island countries, inter alia, on the strengthening of cooperation for the exploitation and management of shared fishery resources, and subregional cooperation in the effective implementation of established exclusive economic zones, including a review of existing fishery resources in the west Indian Ocean.	
ESCAP	Advisory services provided on water resources development to Cook Islands, Vanuatu, Papua New Guinea, Samoa and Tonga. Advisory services also provided on environmentally friendly use of agrochemicals and dissemination of information on agrochemicals.	
	VII. Energy resources	
ECLAC	Regional workshop on renewable energy technologies convened by the Caribbean Council for Science and Technology in Saint Lucia in December 1994.	The workshop discussed role of renewable energy in sustainable development process in the region.
World Bank a/	GEF-financed demand-side management project in Jamaica will strengthen capabilities of public utility and implement an integrated approach to energy conservation. Mechanisms to overcome market barriers will be tested, and valuation results will be used to design full-scale sustainable long-term energy efficiency programmes. The project also implements a national cogeneration policy, which will stimulate the diversification of generation sources, including renewable sources.	Provide funding for activities promoting energy efficiency, integrated approaches to energy conservation, and diversification of generation sources, including promotion of renewable energy sources.
UNIDO	UNIDO is planning to undertake a pre-feasibility study on renewable energy options for Maldives, with a special focus on wave energy.	
UNDP	Supports a regional energy management programme in the Pacific islands, with substantial participation of the Pacific Power Association.	

United Nations organization/ body	Description of activity	Remarks
UNDP	The GEF small grants programme has supported the installation of photovoltaic systems for electric power, and the development of alternative models for production of natural gas for energy in the Dominican Republic.	
	VIII. Tourism resources	
UNU	Undertaking a study in Spain to examine indicators of sustainability with regard to tourism, which is a priority area of activities for small island developing States.	
ECLAC	Developed proposals for environmental codes of conduct for tourism sector, now being carried out by the Caribbean Tourism Association.	
UNDP	In Niue in the Pacific islands, the tourism and private-sector development programme is addressing important areas of freshwater resources, land resources, tourism development and institutional capacity-building.	Has addressed issues relating to tourism development within the overall national environmental plans of the countries concerned.
ESCAP	Workshop on integrated tourism planning in Pacific island countries held at Port Vila, Vanuatu, in June 1995. Guidelines on integrated tourism planning in Pacific island countries will be completed in 1995. ESCAP publication of ESCAP Tourism Review, No. 13 "Investment and economic cooperation in the tourism sector in Pacific island countries", and studies on foreign investment in the tourism sector in Samoa and Vanuatu completed in 1995. Project on land tenure and tourism development in Pacific island countries awaiting funding.	
UNDP	Is supporting tourism planning and management in Madagascar, as well as the creation of tourism-related job opportunities in Cape Verde.	
	IX. Biodiversity resources	
FAO	As of April 1995, had implemented four projects on the conservation and expansion of biodiversity in four small island developing States.	

United Nations organization/ body	Description of activity	Remarks
UNDP	A major undertaking in this area is the South Pacific biodiversity conservation programme, which covers 14 Pacific island countries.	This regional programme, which is funded from GEF resources at the level of US$ 10 million and from contributions of US $3.6 million from the Australian International Development Assistance Bureau, as well as contributions in kind from the South Pacific Regional Environment Programme and individual Governments, is designed to facilitate the identification, setting up and initial management of a series of in-country conservation area projects.
UNDP	Several GEF-funded activities are also being carried out at the country level, including the restoration of highly degraded and threatened native forests in Mauritius, the protection of biodiversity, and the establishment of sustainable development in the Sabana-Camaguey region in Cuba, and the conservation and management of the coastal zone in the Dominican Republic.	
World Bank a/	The Bank jointly prepared, with the Great Barrier Reef Marine Park Authority and IUCN, a global representative system of marine protected areas. The study maps - for the first time - all marine protected areas around the world, identifies major gaps in the biographic representation of marine biodiversity within this system, and prioritizes existing marine park authorities and important marine areas in urgent need of improved management and protection.	Support strategic approach to marine biodiversity conservation within a framework of protected area management.
World Bank a/	The Bank is a partner in the International Coral Reef Initiative, and as a follow-up to the recent Philippines workshop organized an international seminar focusing on revenue-generating mechanisms for both marine protected area management and the financing of conservation activities outside the protocol area framework, including eco-tourism, bio-prospecting, marine resource value-added microenterprises, and the creation of biodiversity venture-capital investment funds.	Provide financing and technical assistance for sustainable financing mechanisms for marine protected areas, including coral reef conservation and management.

United Nations organization/ body	Description of activity	Remarks
World Bank a/	A recently approved GEF biodiversity project in Mauritius will continue efforts to restore degraded habitat in Rodrigues, Isle Aux Aigrettes and Rounds Islands. It will propagate and reintroduce critically endangered flora and fauna on these three islands, and strengthen local technical and administrative skills for conservation and ecosystem restoration.	Provide funding for terrestrial biodiversity conservation and sustainable management.
	X. National institutions and administrative capacity	
UNDP	Collection over the last several months of data relevant to the preparation of a directory of institutions and scholars with expertise on small island developing States.	
UNEP	Assistance to the Government of Seychelles, in collaboration with Habitat, to formulate new land planning and development control legislation and regulations.	The objective is to establish an adequate legal and institutional framework for the management and sustainable utilization of land resources.
UNEP	Development of a project for Sao Tome and Principe, in collaboration with UNDP and IUCN, focusing on the development of national environmental legislation and related institutions within the framework of UNEP/UNDP joint project on environmental law and institutions in Africa.	The Project aims at the formulation and enactment of appropriate environmental legislation and regulations, the establishment of relevant institutions, and the training of national cadres in environmental policy, law and administration.
UNEP	Various actions, in collaboration with SPREP, aimed at the enhancement of national capacities of South Pacific small island developing States in the field of environmental law and institutions. They include formulation of a framework environmental statute for Kiribati, a needs assessment mission to Cook Islands and Samoa, and a national workshop for Cook Islands in environmental policy, law and administration.	
UNDP	Initiated the wider dissemination of the SIDS/NET feasibility study, including pertinent technical papers, to the information specialists of the small island developing States, along with a questionnaire that focuses on key issues requiring clarification and decision in regard to the development of a strategy for the implementation of SIDS/NET.	

United Nations organization/ body	Description of activity	Remarks
ECA	In 1994-1995, provided technical assistance and advisory services to the Government of Mauritius to help strengthen the capacity of the national cooperative institute and to strengthen public policy in agricultural cooperatives.	
ECA	Assisted Seychelles in elaborating a development plan for the southern Mahé, with emphasis on water resources, and provided technical assistance and advisory services to the country in the following areas: (a) the construction of input-output tables, finalization of national income and expenditure data, and holding of a training workshop on national accounts, input-output tables and econometric modelling; (b) review of the implementation of an environment management plan for Seychelles; and (c) review and advice on the development of the public-sector investment programme.	
ECA	Providing technical assistance to the African island countries for the implementation of trade liberalization and facilitation programmes within existing subregional economic groupings; establishment of subregional trade information systems and their harmonization, including systems in the IOC countries; study on policy instruments for intra-African trade finance, including facilities for investment in domestic trade; the harmonization of monetary and financial policies at the subregional level, including those of IOC countries; and assessment of the effectiveness of subregional development financial institutions with a view to strengthening them.	
ECA	Between May 1994 and February 1995, provided technical assistance and advisory services in the field of statistics to the Comoros, Mauritius, and Sao Tome and Principe.	

United Nations organization/ body	Description of activity	Remarks
UNCTAD	Preparation of a policy-oriented study, including up-to-date information of high priority to small island developing States, focusing on the formulation of proposals to assist those countries in overcoming the main obstacles to their development efforts; and provision of technical and advisory services to Governments on subjects within the responsibility of UNCTAD, including, inter alia, trade information, trade efficiency, trade negotiations, investment laws, offshore financial services and measuring economic vulnerability/development sustainability.	
UNU	In July 1995, UNU staged a global faculty training workshop on international environmental law, which produced materials that will benefit some 1500 students worldwide. Regional workshops are being developed, with one planned for the Pacific island region at the University of the South Pacific in July 1996.	
FAO	As of April 1995, had implemented 13 projects on data collection and formulation of national policies and legislation in 11 small island developing States.	
ESCAP	Development of a programme of work on sustainable development issues and their integration into economic decision-making. This project will provide technical assistance on the institutional setting and policy modalities for this purpose and will conduct studies on related issues.	
ESCAP	Workshop on remote sensing/GIS for environmental management, land and marine resources convened in Suva, Fiji in February 1995.	
ECLAC	Environmental database being examined with a view to expanding awareness of member States of work on environment and development. Will organize environmental statistics for the region and offer a directory on sources of information.	
ECLAC	Contributed to work on the feasibility studies for SIDS/NET and SIDS/TAP.	

United Nations organization/ body	Description of activity	Remarks
World Bank a/	Environmental management project in Trinidad and Tobago (US$ 6.25 million) will provide assistance in establishing necessary institutional arrangements for the regulation and management of the environment, and is defining and carrying out a priority environmental work programme based on a national environmental action plan. Includes operationalizing the environmental management agency.	Provide funding for activities in strengthening environmental management, in particular capacity-strengthening for environmental assessment, policy formulation and enforcement.
World Bank a/	Business expansion and industrial restructuring project in Trinidad and Tobago (US$27 million) designed to promote development and/or restructuring of private manufacturing of service firms, especially to enter and compete in export markets. Ancillary objective to improve technical standards used to assess the environmental impact of public and private sector projects in Trinidad and Tobago.	Provide financial and technical assistance for policies that promote a vibrant private sector, undistorted markets, efficient government structures, and taxes and prices that favour people and the environment.
UNDP	Through its Capacity 21 Fund, is supporting regional programmes in the Caribbean and the Pacific islands on capacity-building for sustainable development. The Caribbean regional programme on strengthening capacity for sustainable development in the English speaking Caribbean will assist in the establishment of sustainable development councils in the six countries covered, four of which are small island developing States. These councils are to develop national sustainable priorities and action-oriented activities in participatory process involving all sectors of the population. A sustainable development networking programme among these countries is also contemplated as a complement to SIDS/NET. The Caribbean Centre for Development Administration in Barbados is the implementing agency for the project.	
UNESCO	Analysis of the particular requirements of small island States in the areas of higher education and national scientific capacity-building; improvement of basic and applied research for human resource development.	

United Nations organization/ body	Description of activity	Remarks
UNDP	The programme of capacity-building for sustainable development in the South Pacific, which covers six small island developing States, is designed to formulate national frameworks for sustainable development in each of the three subregions of Micronesia, Melanesia and Polynesia through an integrated, cross-sectoral participatory process, and to develop legislative and enforcement mechanisms in these areas to support sound land and sea-resources management.	
WMO	WMO supports the national meteorological and hydrological services of small island developing States in programme and project planning. To facilitate this activity, WMO has three regional offices set up for Latin America and the Caribbean, Africa, and Asia and the Pacific. For small island developing States in the Mediterranean, support is provided by the WMO secretariat.	
	XI. Regional institutions and technical cooperation	
UNDP	UNDP has initiated activities in the various small island developing States subregions designed to identify unmet priorities in technical cooperation, with particular emphasis on capacity-building, and to formulate TCDC-based technical cooperation activities to address these priorities.	These activities are closely related to the priority area "Natural institutions and administrative capacity".
UNU	A project is being developed focusing on the Pacific islands, concerned with designing new frameworks for regional cooperation among and between the islands to promote sustainable development. Mechanisms for cooperation among the islands in tourism, fisheries, energy, population/migration, and export/import management are of key concern.	
FAO	As of April 1995, had implemented 19 regional projects on the development of agriculture, forestry and fisheries, including training and pest control and protection of land resources, etc. in the Pacific and Caribbean subregions.	

United Nations organization/ body	Description of activity	Remarks
World Bank a/	Caribbean environment assistance facility, under preparation, is a capacity-building project proposed to address, region-wide in the Caribbean, gaps in national technical expertise (or financial resources to acquire such) for critical interventions for environmental management. The proposed project would make available a facility through which countries can obtain a specialized expertise in various aspects of conservation and resource management. The facility's resources would be available to Governments, the private sector and community-based non-governmental organizations.	
ESCAP	Assistance to South Pacific Regional Environmental Programme in implementation of Capacity 21 programme. Advisory services to South Pacific Forum, including recommendations.	Objective is to expose senior officials to new developments in remote sensing and GIS technology for development.
UNIDO	Promotion of a cluster of services to small island developing States directed towards industrial information, regional cooperation mechanisms, technology management, business development and innovation and industrial investment promotion. UNIDO is planning a feasibility study in eastern Caribbean on remote-sensing and decision-support technologies for integrated coastal area management. In the Mediterranean, UNIDO is carrying out a feasibility study for the establishment of a north-south business development centre focusing on the marine industries sector. The concept is being considered for other regions, such as the Caribbean and the Indian Ocean.	
	XII. Transport and communications	
UNU	Staging a communication forum in October 1995, in collaboration with the University of the South Pacific, to examine the issue of information access in the Pacific islands, and ways to promote such access.	
UNESCO	Cooperation in the establishment of communication structures, including for distance education, in training of communicators; and participation in UNESCO intergovernmental programme for the development of communication.	

United Nations organization/ body	Description of activity	Remarks
UNESCO	Provision of equipment to national broadcasting systems in the Caribbean; training of news and information personnel; and mobilization of projects on community media.	
ECA	ECA has received project documents for consideration and financing under the Second United Nations Transport and Communication Decade for Africa (UNTACDA-II) as follows: (a) Sao Tome and Principe (Rehabilitation of roads network, and roads maintenance initiative); (b) Comoros (study of a medium- and long-term telecommunications master plan, and construction and purchase of equipment for international telephone transit centre); (c) Seychelles (financing of two fellowships in telecommunications, and purchase of equipment for navigation of fishing vessels); (d) Mauritius is actively benefitting from UNTACDA II activities in the implementation of the Yamoussoukro Declaration on a new African transport policy. Funding for implementation of the projects are being sought within UNTACDA II framework. In maritime transport, the African island countries will benefit from projects on establishment of coastal shipping in Africa, and also from initiatives that ECA will promote, in collaboration with the various port management associations on cooperation and development of maritime ports.	
World Bank a/	Recently approved Mauritius Port Development and environmental protection project is supporting tariff and institutional reforms to develop private-sector investment in free port area and protect surrounding environment from ship pollution and other safety hazards. Project is also supporting oil port terminal expansion with three berths to meet needs of international trade and of free-zone industry post.	Provide funding for activities in transport and telecommunications development that promote efficient sectoral management approaches, including the development of private-sector investment.
UNDP	In the Caribbean region, is supporting the establishment of an independent satellite-based regional radio and data communications network, with multilingual transmission capabilities, through the enhancement of the regional information distribution system of the Caribbean News Agency.	

United Nations organization/ body	Description of activity	Remarks
UNDP	In the Pacific islands, is supporting a telecommunications training and development programme to assist Pacific island countries in developing reliable, efficient and commercially viable telecommunications services accessible to all users. The project is partly implemented by ITU. Supports a civil aviation programme in the Pacific islands. The project, which is implemented partly by the ICAO, is assisting in the completion of the regional civil aviation manpower and training development programme, and providing technical support through consultancies and technical workshops on air transport economics, computerization, fire-fighting and rescue, and aeronautical meteorology.	
ICAO	Provision of a proposal to the Asian Development Bank for implementation of a technical assistance grant to its Pacific island developing member States. This Pacific airports facility project will provide a feasibility study for upgrading civil aviation infrastructure and air traffic management in 10 South Pacific States.	
ICAO	Proposals to European Union ACP secretariat for funding of civil aviation managerial and technical workshops in six Pacific member States of ACP.	
ICAO	Assistance with the development of aviation legislation in Fiji.	
ICAO	Assistance in identification of needs and project preparation for upgrading civil aviation training centre in Fiji, including the introduction of ICAO TRAINAIR concept and membership.	
ICAO	Proposal to Micronesia to provide assistance with licensing of aviation personnel.	
ICAO	Assistance in fellowship training to Maldives.	

United Nations organization/ body	Description of activity	Remarks
ESCAP	Project on performance improvement of inter-island shipping in the South Pacific being implemented since 1991. Phases I and II completed; phase III under way, involving extension of computerized ports and shipping management systems, and development of a database on domestic and inter-Pacific island trade. Additional project commenced to develop policy options for replacement of ageing ships in Pacific island fleets.	
WMO	Provision of regulatory material, advice and guidance on meteorological services for shipping and aviation, in collaboration with IMO and ICAO, respectively.	
IMO	Serving as task manager for maritime transport for preparation of the report of the Secretary-General to the Commission on Sustainable Development at its fourth session, and other functions, in collaboration with UNCTAD.	
	XIII. <u>Science and technology</u>	
UNU	Proposal to accumulate data on technology available in Okinawa, Japan, and determine transferability to small island developing States, including through ODA. UNU will liaise with UNEP environmental technology transfer at Osaka, especially in the area of water technology.	
UNDP	Is providing institutional support for the formulation of national science and technology plans. Also supports development of science and technology through human resource development activities in specific sectors.	
	XIV. <u>Human resource development</u>	
FAO	As of April 1995, had implemented 10 projects on national training and education, including agricultural skill development, watershed management and farm management in 7 small island developing States.	

United Nations organization/ body	Description of activity	Remarks
ECA	Carried out missions to Sao Tome and Principe to: (a) review the civil registration system and prepare a sectoral review document for the mid-term review; (b) conduct a training workshop for the analysis of the 1991 population and housing census data; and (c) follow up on census analysis. In Seychelles, technical assistance was provided in the analysis of census data.	
World Bank a/	Recently approved Bank education projects in Cape Verde, Dominica, Fiji, Maldives, Mauritius and OECS, which reflect the critical importance attached to human resource development for the sustainable development imperatives of small island developing States.	Provide funding for activities in human resource development, including education, health, nutrition and women's development.
UNDP	In the Pacific islands, UNDP regional activities focusing on sustainable human development cover areas relating to basic education and life-skills training, poverty alleviation, water and sanitation, family health and food, fruit fly control in agriculture, and small enterprise development.	
UNDP	In the Caribbean region, a project in Barbados funded through special programme resources, seeks to create sustainable livelihood and job opportunities in agriculture in selected communities of the eastern Caribbean, targeting in particular the unemployed and rural women.	
UNDP	In Trinidad and Tobago, SPR resources are to be used in a catalytic manner to supplement a larger project to support new and more effective ways to deliver social services based on non-governmental organizations and government collaboration, and to assist in the elaboration of social development strategies based on a participatory approach.	

United Nations organization/ body	Description of activity	Remarks
UNIDO	Human resource development is an integrated element in UNIDO technical assistance projects. Of particular relevance for small island developing States are the training of entrepreneurs, and training in the field of technology management and industrial policy formulation. UNIDO international centre for science and high technology is arranging training courses and is providing technical assistance in the field of geographical informations systems for integrated coastal area management.	
UNCTAD	In the framework of the TRAINFORTRADE programme of training in the field of international trade, UNCTAD contributes to developing the capacity of trade policy advisers and trade practitioners in small island developing States to enhance the external trade of those countries in a manner that is conducive to sustainable development. Ongoing projects involve the Caribbean, the Indian Ocean, the Atlantic and the Pacific.	One of the course subjects of the TRAINFORTRADE Programme is entitled "Trade and the environment in small island developing States".

a/ The World Bank has supplied project-related information by way of examples.

53. UNGA RESOLUTION ON IMPLEMENTATION OF THE OUTCOME OF THE GLOBAL CONFERENCE ON THE SUSTAINABLE DEVELOPMENT OF SMALL ISLAND DEVELOPING STATES

Doc. no.: A/Res.50/116 20 December 1995

The General Assembly,

Recalling its resolution 49/122 of 19 December 1994 on the Global Conference on the Sustainable Development of Small Island Developing States,

Recalling also its resolution 49/100 of 19 December 1994 on specific measures in favour of island developing countries,

Reaffirming that, because the development options of small island developing States are limited, there are special challenges to devising and implementing sustainable development plans, and that small island developing States will be constrained in meeting such challenges without the cooperation of the international community,

1. Notes with appreciation the report of the Secretary-General 146/ on action taken by the organs, organizations and bodies of the United Nations system to implement the Programme of Action for the Sustainable Development of Small Island Developing States, 147/ and welcomes in particular the action that has been taken by the Department for Policy Coordination and Sustainable Development of the United Nations Secretariat to support the system-wide implementation of the Programme of Action;

2. Takes note of the establishment of the Small Island Developing States Unit within the Department, and requests the Secretary-General to maintain the level of staffing and the structure and organization of the Unit in accordance with General Assembly resolution 49/122;

3. Welcomes the action that has been taken to enable the regional commissions to support activities to coordinate the outcome of the Global Conference on the Sustainable Development of Small Island Developing States;

4. Takes note of the interim measures that have been instituted to strengthen the capacity of the United Nations Conference on Trade and Development to enable it to complement the functions of the Department with respect to the implementation of the Programme of Action, and requests the Secretary-General to implement fully the relevant provisions of General Assembly resolution 49/122;

146/ A/50/422 and Add.1.

147/ Report of the Global Conference on the Sustainable Development of Small Island Developing States, Bridgetown, Barbados, 25 April-6 May 1994 (United Nations publication, Sales No. 94.I.18 and corrigenda), chap. I, resolution 1, annex II.

5. Calls upon Governments, as well as the organs, organizations and bodies of the United Nations system, other intergovernmental organizations and non-governmental organizations, to continue to implement fully all the commitments and recommendations that were made at the Conference, and to continue to take the action necessary for effective follow-up to the Programme of Action, including action to ensure the provision of the means of implementation under chapter XV thereof;

6. Welcomes, in particular, the progress made by the United Nations Development Programme in implementing General Assembly resolution 49/122, and invites the Programme to continue to implement all the provisions of both the technical assistance programme and the information network for small island developing States, as appropriate;

7. Takes note of the support that has been provided by the Commission on Sustainable Development 148/ to following up the implementation of the Programme of Action in accordance with General Assembly resolution 49/122 and the Programme of Action itself, and invites the Commission at its fourth session to consider giving due attention to small island developing States in the national presentations on coastal zone management;

8. Notes the initial action that has been taken by the United Nations Conference on Trade and Development and by the Department for Policy Coordination and Sustainable Development in preparation for the high-level panel that is being convened to discuss the challenges faced by island developing countries, particularly in the area of external trade, and invites the Conference and the Department to complete their arrangements in time for the fourth session of the Commission on Sustainable Development, and to make the report of the panel available to the Conference at its ninth session;

9. Requests the Secretary-General to ensure that the Small Island Developing States Unit of the Department include in its work programme, along with an indication of the resources of its activities and programmes, provision for the development and compilation of a vulnerability index for small island developing States, to be prepared in collaboration with the United Nations Conference on Trade and Development and other relevant organizations;

10. Requests the Secretary-General to submit to the General Assembly at its fifty-third session a report on the plans, programmes and projects for the sustainable development of small island developing States that have been implemented in response to the Programme of Action, as well as those that are under implementation and those that are envisaged for implementation within five years of the date of the report;

11. Decides to include in the provisional agenda of its fifty-first session, under the item entitled "Environment and sustainable development", the sub-item entitled "Implementation of the outcome of the Global Conference on the Sustainable Development of Small Island Developing States";

12. Requests the Secretary-General to submit to the General Assembly at its fifty-first session a report on action taken to implement the present resolution.

148/ See Official Records of the Economic and Social Council, 1995, Supplement No. 12 (E/1995/32).

54. PROJECT FOR A EUROPE-AFRICA PERMANENT LINK THROUGH THE STRAIT OF GIBRALTAR - NOTE BY THE UN SECRETARY-GENERAL* (REPORT ON STUDIES AND ACTIVITIES CARRIED OUT DURING THE PERIOD 1993-1994)

Doc. no.: E/1995/46 9 May 1995

1. The Secretary-General has the honour to transmit to the Economic and Social Council the report prepared in accordance with Council resolution 1993/60 by the Executive Secretaries of the Economic Commission for Europe and the Economic Commission for Africa on the work that has been done in connection with the project to establish a Europe-Africa permanent link through the Strait of Gibraltar.

2. The Economic and Social Council has taken an interest in this project since 1982 following a decision by the Governments of Morocco and Spain to carry out joint studies on the feasibility of the project as part of an agreement on bilateral cooperation adopted on 24 October 1980. Since then the Council has regularly requested the two regional commissions to keep track of the progress of studies relating to the project and to inform the Council of any developments.

ANNEX

Project for a Europe-Africa permanent link through the Strait of Gibraltar: report on studies and activities carried out during the period 1993-1994

CONTENTS

* E/1995/100.

INTRODUCTION

1. In its resolution 1993/60 of 30 July 1993, the Economic and Social Council, inter alia, requested the Executive Secretaries of the Economic Commission for Africa and the Economic Commission for Europe to take an active part in the follow-up to the project for a Europe-Africa permanent link through the Strait of Gibraltar and to report thereon to the Council at its substantive session of 1995.

2. This report is a response to that request. It was drawn up jointly by the two regional commissions and gives a brief overview of the main findings of the studies carried out in 1993-1994 with a view to advancing the project. It also takes account of the conclusions of the special symposium on the project which was organized under the auspices of the Economic Commission for Europe and the Economic Commission for Africa by the International Tunnelling Association (ITA) as part of its Annual General Assembly, held in Cairo on 5 April 1994.

I. GENERAL CONTEXT OF STUDIES

3. It should be recalled that studies designed to advance the project have been carried out jointly by the Governments of Morocco and Spain since 24 October 1980, the date on which the two Governments adopted a bilateral agreement on the subject. This agreement, which formally establishes both Governments' commitment to make a joint study of the feasibility of the project, stipulates the creation of a standing intergovernmental Joint Committee which was to be responsible for carrying out the agreement, and two State companies, one in Morocco and the other in Spain, which were to be responsible for conducting the studies. These companies, which have been working alongside the Joint Committee since 1981, are, on the Spanish side, Sociedad de Estudios para la Comunicación Fija a través del Estrecho de Gibraltar (SECEG), which has its head office in Madrid, and on the Moroccan side, Société Nationale d'Etudes du Détroit (SNED), whose head office is in Rabat. The studies are carried out either by the two research companies directly, or through scientific institutions from both countries or national or international firms of consultants and surveyors with whom the companies have concluded agreements or contracts for services.

4. Within the institutional framework mentioned above, which was later strengthened by a Supplementary Agreement of 27 September 1989 complementing and amplifying the previous agreement, the two companies have conducted their programmes of work in several phases. The findings of the feasibility studies currently in progress (1991-1995) will provide both Governments with information on the feasibility of the permanent link viewed in the context of the long-term development of the straits corridor while at the same time making them aware of relevant proposals concerning future programmes which have some bearing on the development of the project.

II. EVALUATION OF STUDIES CARRIED OUT BETWEEN 1982 and 1992

5. It should also be recalled that the studies carried out between 1982 and 1992 were the subject of an evaluation report in 1993 (E/1993/80) pursuant to Economic and Social Council resolution 1991/74 of 26 July 1991. This report was prepared by the two regional commissions on the basis of evaluations made by a number of international experts.

6. According to the evaluation report, the studies carried out between 1982 and 1992 enabled substantial progress to be made in coming to grips with the key aspects of this major project, touching as they did on the physical environment, engineering options and socio-economic evaluations. These studies made it possible, inter alia, to state with a reasonable degree of certainty that no major geological obstacle existed to the construction of a permanent link through the Strait of Gibraltar, regardless of whether the link was a tunnel bored under the sea or a bridge constructed on fixed supports. The studies also made it possible to identify two potential routes, the shallower or so-called "sill route" along which a tunnel or a bridge could be contemplated, and the shorter or so-called "strait route" along which only a bridge would be possible. In other respects, the studies contributed to solid progress in clarifying the respective engineering options in each case. They also highlighted the socio-economic impact of the project on countries other than Spain and Morocco, and hence the multilateral nature of the project.

7. The evaluation report on the studies carried out between 1982 and 1992 also indicated that further research was necessary in certain areas, and a number of recommendations were formulated with that in mind. With reference to the most significant of these, and considering the sheer scale of the project, it was thought indispensable to obtain greater in-depth knowledge of the geology of the submerged part of the strait, particularly in the context of the tunnel option. To achieve this goal, the evaluation report stated that the ideal solution would be to drill a narrow-bore reconnaissance gallery along the entire course decided

on for the tunnel. Without such a gallery, it was deemed necessary to conduct offshore geotechnical experimentation and drilling operations. Regarding economic studies, the evaluation report recommended, for example, that a more thorough assessment should be made of the impact of the permanent link at the local and regional level and that the technical, economic and financial feasibility of a partial implementation of the project should be studied.

III. STUDIES CONDUCTED DURING 1993-1994

8. The observations and recommendations made in the evaluation report on the studies carried out between 1982 and 1992 were noted by the companies responsible for undertaking them and adjustments were made to their work programmes as a result. The studies conducted during 1993-1994 therefore sought to expand knowledge in the areas where this had been thought necessary at the time of the evaluation process. A brief description of the most significant studies and their conclusions is given below. The studies are grouped into four general areas, namely, physical environment, engineering, socio-economic analyses and evaluation of the project.

A. Physical environment

1. Bathometry and cartography

9. The 1:5000 bathometric maps available since 1992 which cover the areas of the two possible routes were judged to be remarkable (E/1993/80, para. 17). They were considered quite adequate for the current stage of development of the project and it was therefore not thought necessary to undertake new bathometric surveys during 1993-1994.

10. Meanwhile, a new 1:25000 map of the strait which follows the sectioning and unique referencing system adopted by the Instituto Geográfico Nacional in Madrid and the Division de la Cartographie in Rabat has been completed, and the entire set of 7+7 sheets corresponding to the Spanish and Moroccan coastlines has been made available. It is planned to include bathometry in subsequent editions of the map.

2. Geotechnical studies

11. As recommended by the evaluation report (E/1993/80, paras. 21 and 31), priority was given to the galleries and shafts designed for geotechnical studies on both sides of the Mediterranean.

12. October 1993 saw the completion on the north side of the experimental shaft at Bolonia which, at 74 m deep and 3.3 m in diameter, is primarily intended to yield information about one of the most resistive rock formations in the vicinity of the strait. A number of behaviour parameters of the ground and its effect on the lining were systematically monitored until the end of 1993 using 35 measuring locations; two separate measuring surveys were conducted, one in March and the other in September 1994. The results, which were judged favourable, are being digested and extrapolated in the context of other studies relating to the project.

13. The construction of the experimental gallery at Tarifa, which had been on hold since 1992, was begun in 1994 and is currently at the tunnelling stage. The Tarifa gallery, which is also located on the north side, is a 700-metre-long blind tunnel with a diameter of 3.8 m and 70 m of average overburden; its purpose is to determine the geotechnical characteristics and observe the geomechanical behaviour of a set of geological formations which are considered extremely typical of the project zone. To this end, the gallery contains approximately 80 monitoring locations designed to measure parameters such as

convergence, the pressure exerted by the ground on the lining, and the circumferential deformation of the lining with respect to two sections of the tunnel bore.

14. The Malabata experimental shaft located on the south side has been used to conduct various geotechnical experiments and investigations for a number of years. It is a 160 m vertical shaft - the planned depth of the tunnel at this location - with an internal diameter of 2.5 m, supplemented by a system of horizontal galleries of different lengths totalling 180 m which radiate from the bottom of the shaft and have been tunnelled under the seabed. The Malabata shaft has made possible the study of the geotechnical characteristics and suitability for tunnelling of the various flysch units located in the project area which will reputedly prove resistive during the construction of the tunnel. An additional project involving the deepening of the tunnel to 313 m - equivalent to the lowest point of the tunnel crossing - and the construction at that depth of a gallery approximately 30 m long is currently under consideration.

15. These three projects have made it possible to make a highly accurate study of the geotechnical behaviour of certain formations that present special problems for the project. Although the results of the monitoring are still being interpreted, it can already be said that the ground studied is, in general, conducive to tunnelling by the tunnel-boring machine (TBM), from the stand-point of both impermeability and geomechanical behaviour.

3. Geophysics/seabed sampling

16. The Rift-Argus survey, whose purpose was the de visu exploration and video survey of the bottom of the sill of the strait from a submersible vehicle, was conducted from 5 August to 16 September 1994. The survey made it possible to view the deepest areas of the strait and confirm that at these depths the flysch units are found below the seabed and are covered almost entirely with a recent thin layer of sediment.

17. The so-called GC-94 survey was carried out from 5 to 13 November 1994 with a view to bringing the density of the sampling from the area of the path in the northern platform up to the level of the density of the representative sampling from the southern platform. The survey obtained 510 samples, including 155 flysch units and 355 recent sediments, which made it possible to increase the number of available seabed samples by 37 per cent, bringing the total to 1,866.

4. Offshore drilling

18. Offshore drilling is another activity to which the evaluation report recommended that the highest priority should be given, since such drilling is crucial to the current phase of studies. Knowledge of the thickness of recent sediments in the deep area of the sill and the study of the geological pillars with respect to depth at certain specific points of the path are decisive, indeed indispensable, factors in the final determination of the feasibility of the tunnel option. However, the specific difficulties that the strait's currents pose for offshore-drilling technologies, either by underwater drills or by drilling boats, make it necessary to undertake such surveys with considerable technological uncertainty.

19. Thus, the Short Drilling Survey 94, which was designed to carry out 50 drillings up to 5 m into the "sill route", conducted only about 30 drillings and on average penetrated to a depth of only 2.4 m, with an average net recovery of around 60 per cent. From a geological point of view, the drillings that were conducted on the platforms (at a depth of about 50 m) generally came across flysch units, while all those carried out in the deepest areas remained in Plio-Quaternary strata.

20. After long preparation, the Deep Drilling Survey 94, which was to carry out eight deep drillings in the sill of the strait, situated at points considered critical or of special interest in the path of the tunnel option, finally got under way in January 1995. These drillings total 1,120 m of penetration, approximately two thirds to be carried out by destructive drilling and one third by core drilling.

21. The partial results obtained from the short and deep borings that have been carried out so far lead one to think, pending confirmation by definitive results, that the Plio-Quaternary strata, which are recent and highly permeable formations, would be superficial and would not jeopardize the construction of the tunnel.

5. Geological and physiographical studies

22. The neotectonic study of the strait, the purpose of which was to determine the deformations in the structural orogeny (after the middle Miocene) in order to contribute to the evaluation of tectonic stability in the area of the project, was carried out between February 1993 and January 1994 on the north side. The main conclusion of the study is that the area studied (approximately between 5° 14′ and 6° 05′ meridians) has been highly stable since the Pliocene, but at the same time presenting a limited area of relative high elevation between Tarifa and Punta Canales, where the coast underwent a relative heightening since the Oudjian period (100,000 years) estimated at 20 m, which represents a relatively modest rate of elevation on the order of 0.2 mm a year. The corresponding study of the south side has been in progress since June 1993. There are plans to hold meetings between those taking part in the studies of the two sides in order to harmonize methodologies and later combine the two studies into a composite report on the strait and, in particular, the area of the project.

23. The studies of other projects involving flysch units, also recommended by the evaluation study, have resulted in two types of relatively independent activities, namely, the collection of data concerning a group of projects of interest in the Mediterranean basin (Spain, Italy, Greece, Morocco, Algeria, Tunisia) and the participation of the companies in the monitoring during the construction of the Guadiaro-Majaceite hydraulic tunnel (5 m wide, 12 km long), particularly in its section of approximately 5 km in Numidian flysch.

24. The 1988 geological map of the north side is currently being updated. The updating involves, inter alia, the revision of the structural elements (faults, folds, contacts between layers and so on), which will no doubt lead to certain changes in, and new ideas about, the tectonic interpretation of the region. This work, whose progress depends on the availability of specialized teams, is concentrated in the area of the Bolonia arc, which is of particular importance to the project. The geological map of the south side is also being updated.

25. A dating study of the coral formations found in the deepest areas of the strait was begun with a view to determining, in the initial stage, the absolute age of seven samples of coral formation covering the areas of the sill, selected from among the core samples obtained during the Short Drilling Survey 94. The carbon-14 dating of these sediments is of great interest for the project, since it contributes to the assessment of the importance of these coral deposits in which - or near which - tunnelling would not be technically viable owing to their high degree of permeability. So far, results have been obtained on four core samples taken at a depth of approximately 250 m. The results show that the oldest corals analysed are about 30,000 years old. The coral formation in question is therefore relatively recent, falling between the last glaciation (Würms) and - as the presence of living corals demonstrate - modern times. Consequently, any hypothesis attributing the presence of these formations in the deepest areas of the strait to recent tectonic phenomena should be rejected. On the other hand, although pending confirmation, the dating suggests that the

thickness of the formations in question is limited and would not affect the feasibility of the tunnel option at a depth of 400 m.

B. Engineering

26. As considered advisable in the evaluation report (E/1993/80, para. 82), the studies concerning the bridge and tunnel alternatives have been continued in parallel.

1. Bridge studies

27. The preliminary pilot project for the bridge solution has been drawn up. The bridge option, developed on the basis of an earlier descriptive study, constitutes the basic "bridge on fixed bearings" type solution favoured by the companies at the current stage of the studies. The solution proposed in the bridge pilot project follows an alignment 27.40 km long almost exactly north-south on the sill of the strait. It consists essentially of two very different parts: on the one hand, a main bridge, 13.65 km long, crossing the deep part of the sill, and on the other, two offshore access viaducts with a total length of 13.75 km linking the Moroccan and Spanish shores to the main bridge. These viaducts consist of 300 m mixed concrete-steel spans supported on piers founded in the seabed to a depth of about 55 m. The main bridge is a suspension bridge comprising three 3,550 m central spans and two 1,500 m side spans allowing 80 m headroom and placed in such a way that the two channels of the maritime traffic separation scheme in the strait would pass under the main side spans. The general characteristics of this bridge are as follows:

(a) The substructure consists of two anchorage pillars founded at a water depth of about 60 m and four gravity base concrete tetrapod piers, resistant to collisions by ships, founded at depths of 140, 315, 280 and 230 m (north-south), the design of which is based on that of large concrete petroleum platforms, as regards both structural aspects and construction methods;

(b) The superstructure, directly supported by the offshore piers, consists of:

(i) Four rigid "A"-shaped pylons - unusual in conventional suspension bridges - rising 480 m above sea level;

(ii) A conventional suspension system, in principle with two 1.07 m diameter carrying cables;

(iii) A twin-deck girder with a total width of 55 m, including 28 m air, incorporating cross bars spaced every 26 m at right angles to the suspension rods.

28. The construction cost of the "Bridge 28" solution has been estimated at about 8.7 billion European currency units (ECUs) (1994) and the construction time at about 19 years, including 4 years of additional studies. The internal rate of return would be about 5 per cent on the capital invested, for start-up in about 2015.

29. The so-called "Bridge 14" solution, crossing the canyon of the strait, has been studied briefly under the contract relating to the bridge pilot project. This "super suspension bridge" consists of: (a) a superstructure comprising two 5 km main spans, two 2.5 km side spans and three pylons rising 646 m above sealevel; (b) a substructure comprising three offshore piers founded at water depths of 95, 480 and 415 m respectively and two end anchorages, one on the Spanish side, in the vicinity of Punta Canales, and the other on the Moroccan side, near Ras Cirès. Although the study of this "superbridge" has been made only on the basis of principles extrapolating the outline and results from the calculations relating to the bridge on the sill of the strait - and therefore

without wind tunnel tests - in order for it to be technically feasible only relatively modest technological extrapolations may be needed compared to the "sill" solution.

2. Tunnel studies

30. The preliminary pilot project for the tunnel option, work on which began in early March 1994, is at the stage of the preparation of the final report, a draft of which was presented in December 1994. The structure proposed in the tunnel pilot project is of the "Channel Tunnel" type. With a length between terminals of 42.5 km, it can accommodate regular passenger and freight rail traffic and also motorway traffic, tourism and heavy cargoes, transported roll-on-roll-off on rail shuttle trains. The general characteristics of the structure are as follows:

(a) The longitudinal profile of the structure is a total length of 38.7 km including 27.7 km under the sea, with a maximum gradient of 25:1,000, which would make it possible for the alignment to go to a point 400 m below sealevel, thereby ensuring a minimum ground cover of 100 m at the deepest point where the water depth is 300 m;

(b) The transverse section consists of three galleries: two rail tunnels with a single track 7.5 m in diameter, about 60 m apart, and one service tunnel 4.8 m in diameter, situated midway between the other two tunnels and linked to them by transverse tunnels 3 m in diameter and 340 m apart.

The pilot project includes not only the basic study on the operation of the transport system which is the proposed solution, but also a description of all fixed and movable equipment.

31. One important characteristic of the "tunnel" option which is strongly emphasized in the pilot project is the possibility of building the structure in two stages. The first stage consists of the first rail tunnel and the service tunnel. The second stage supplements the first stage by adding the second rail tunnel. This possibility of carrying out the work in two stages is of great interest from the point of view of the economic feasibility of the project since it provides for a very significant staggering of costs, while ensuring, over a period estimated at 20 to 25 years, a capacity adapted to estimates of traffic requirements, with an acceptable level of service.

32. The conclusions of the preliminary pilot project call for the construction, first, of the undersea section (28 km) of the service tunnel as a reconnaissance gallery, with the dual objective of avoiding all geological and geotechnical hazards in later stages of construction and thereby reducing costs, while minimizing risks by taking advantage of the experience acquired.

33. Thus, based on these conclusions, the preliminary pilot project presents a timetable and cost estimates for three phases of the development of the project, namely, phase 0, construction of the reconnaissance gallery; phase 1, construction of the first rail tunnel and the first stage of the terminals for the operation of the single-track project; and lastly, phase 2, where two-track operations would be introduced through the construction of the second tunnel and the second stage of the terminals. According to this schedule, if all goes as currently planned, the suggested timetable is approximately as follows:

Phase 0: 1997-2002. Construction of the reconnaissance gallery.

Phase 1: 2003-2009. Construction of the first rail tunnel and the first stage of the terminals. Opening of the single-track tunnel: 2010

Phase 2: 2025-2030. Construction of the second rail tunnel and second stage of terminals. Opening of the second tunnel: 2030

34. The cost estimates proposed by the consultant are shown in the summary table below:

Summary of estimated project costs

(in millions of ECUs (MECU), tax- and customs-free, in October 1994 values)

Component	Phase 0	Phase 1	Phase 2	Total
Underground structures	347	659	547	1 553
Terminals	-	217	20	237
Equipment	-	613	414	1 027
Rolling stock (utilized in phase 1)		237	-	237
TOTAL	347	1 726 a/	981	3 054
Additional rolling stock				
purchased during single-track phase				129
purchased during dual-track phase				344
OVERALL TOTAL				3 527

a/ The cost of phase 1 assumes that phase 0 has been completed.

35. A different consultant conducted a study parallel to the preliminary pilot project for the tunnel concerning the programming and estimation of costs for the reconnaissance gallery. The study, which further analysed the costs of this project estimated earlier by the same consultant, generally confirmed the technical feasibility of the construction of the reconnaissance gallery using a tunnel boring machine, and submitted a brief analytical estimate of the costs and time required for its construction, by use of a "duration model" and a "cost model". The results obtained can be summarized as follows:

Scenario	Construction duration	Construction cost
	(months)	(MECU)
Central	42	275
Adverse 1	62	290
Adverse 2	-	320

It should be noted that these cost estimates are significantly lower than the provisional estimates currently being provided by the preliminary pilot project for the tunnel, which foresees a construction period of 56 months and a cost of 347 MECUs (1 MECU = 1 million ECUs). This represents an increase of about one third over the above estimates for the main scenario, both in terms of duration and cost of construction. In the acceptance process during that study and the preliminary pilot project, the companies intend to study the comparisons further and thus to refine the estimates as far as possible.

C. Socio-economic studies

1. Socio-economic database

36. The socio-economic and Europe-Africa traffic database established in the companies' statistical services in 1992 has been significantly expanded by the introduction of a regional component, which should be completed by May 1995. This regional component of the database covers a territorial area on both shores of approximately 27,000 sq km and a population of 4.1 million, within which an area of approximately 6,000 sq km with a population of 1.4 million, where the project's influence would be most intense, can be differentiated. There are plans to complement and refine the information available, especially on the area known as the straits region, where the project is likely to have the greatest local impact.

2. Traffic forecasting

37. In order to update and structurally and statistically improve the model, known as Model 90, for estimating traffic in passengers and goods through the permanent link, as called for in the evaluation report (E/1993/80, paras. 52 and 53), a study to develop this model further was launched in January 1993. The results of this study, which was completed at the end of 1994, represent both the fine-tuning of an updated model - the SETEC 94 model - and the application of this model to a series of multiple variations on the basic hypothesis, in order to obtain predictions of traffic through the permanent link at two baseline horizons, 2005 and 2025. The main variables studied concerned (a) two types of permanent links, the basic "bridge" and "tunnel" options, respectively, and (b) two economic development scenarios, "trend-driven" and "sustained", essentially determined by the growth of the gross domestic product (GDP) in the European and African countries of the study area. The overall results of the forecasts are as follows:

	Passengers (millions; round-trip)		Goods (millions of tons; round-trip)	
	2005	2025	2005	2025
Diverted traffic	4.25	7.58	3.69	6.59
Engendered traffic	0.59	0.97	0.18	0.34
Created traffic	1.22	2.12	0.09	0.96
TOTAL	6.07	10.67	3.97	7.98

It should be noted that, as far as passengers are concerned, these forecasts are considerably lower (by about 40 per cent) than those previously obtained with Model 90. This important fact essentially results from the use in the latest study of a more precise model of the straits corridor, with its maritime shipping lines, which took better account of the competition those lines would offer to a permanent link, particularly the Algeciras-Ceuta route. The permanent link would take over only 57 per cent of the passenger traffic in the straits corridor, although, on the other hand, it would capture 95 per cent of traffic in goods (excluding bulk shipments).

38. In addition to this study, and in order to avoid the constraints arising from the fact that the model mentioned belongs to the consultant, a separate prediction model was also developed on the same general principles and the same statistical and forecasting basis as the other, although a different approach was taken to certain sub-models. The overall results obtained by the two models (evaluated without taking into account traffic created) were found to be consistent for the most part.

D. Project feasibility studies

1. Baseline studies

39. A project evaluation model is being developed by the internal services of the SECEG company. Currently, programming of the sub-models for economic and financial evaluation is under way, the latter using formats for the financial analysis of concessionaires that are in keeping with the accounting rules generally accepted in the European Union.

40. A study of the "no project" alternative was begun in November 1994 in order to contribute to the "benchmark" scenario, the situation if the project were not built. This study is attempting in particular to explore scenarios for the long-term development of the system of maritime ferries through the straits.

41. The updating of the economic analysis known as SETEC 90 conducted in 1990 by the consultant began in July 1994, and the draft of the final report was submitted to the companies in December 1994. The study mainly consists in applying the economic and financial evaluation methodologies used in the pre-feasibility study produced by SETEC-Economics in 1990 to the current definition of the project, expressed essentially by the alternative structures defined by the preliminary pilot project, and to the traffic estimates resulting from the models recently developed.

42. The results contained in the final report, submitted in provisional form, are clearly negative for the bridge option - considered in the study exclusively for purposes of form - and clearly positive for the tunnel option, carried out in two phases, the first operating with a single tunnel. Indeed, whereas the estimated internal rate of return for start-up of the bridge in 2015 is 6.3 per cent, the estimated rate for the tunnel opening in 2010 is 14.3 per cent. The updated cash flow in 2010 of 9 per cent would be 5,400 MECUs (1993).

43. Still within the tunnel option, given a hypothetical financial arrangement such that the financial cost of the project, estimated at 4,655 MECUs, would be distributed as 33 per cent public funds, 20 per cent project capital and 47 per cent loans, the result would be an internal rate of return on its own capital of 21.6 per cent in nominal terms and 16.2 per cent in real terms, with an updated cash flow in 2010 of 9 per cent, or 10,700 MECUs (1993).

44. The above results correspond to a baseline definition of the project, which is currently undergoing minor adjustments with regard to the acceptance of the preliminary pilot project for the tunnel and models of traffic estimates. These adjustments affect, inter alia, construction costs and timetables, quite likely in the direction of greater feasibility. The final review of these elements is expected to be completed before the definitive acceptance of the studies in April 1995. Moreover, the economic study itself is undergoing final adjustments, from the point of view of both the methodology and the assumptions concerning the arrangements for the model concessionaire on which the financial analysis of the project is based. As before, it is expected that these readjustments will be finalized before the eventual acceptance of the economic study at the end of April 1995.

45. As part of the approval process for that study, the companies reviewed a series of alternatives for the financial analysis of the project, based on hypothetical institutional arrangements consisting essentially - in accordance with the technical principle of anticipating the construction of a reconnaissance gallery that would later comprise the undersea section of the service tunnel for the project - of financing the reconnaissance gallery entirely with public funds. Once it is built, it would be turned over at no charge to the concessionaire, which would then complete the construction of the project without any additional public financial assistance. The results obtained from these internal evaluations of the same hypotheses as in the

consultant's provisional report, except where the financial arrangements referred to are concerned, are indicated in the table below. All the variations correspond to a timetable envisioning the beginning of the concession period (including construction of the project) in 2003 and the beginning of project operations in 2010.

Project capital as percentage of financial cost	Concession period in years	Nominal internal rate of return, in per cent	Real internal rate of return, in per cent	Updated cash flow (2020, 9 per cent) in MECU
20	30	21.15	17.06	3 978
20	40	21.87	17.75	6 677
30	30	18.60	14.59	3 823
30	40	19.49	15.45	6 529

2. Project evaluation study

46. The work programme of the companies includes the elaboration of a general project evaluation report in accordance with generally accepted standards for the evaluation of major transport infrastructure projects, including an economic and financial analysis and a brief assessment of the regional and environmental impact on the basis of the works contemplated in the preliminary tunnel pilot project and traffic estimates resulting from the new prediction models available. The terms of reference for this study are being prepared by the companies in two parts, dealing with the economic and financial analysis of the project and its regional and environmental impact respectively. It should be noted that these terms of reference are being prepared in such a way that they can also help to guide the end-of-phase report (feasibility report), which will be prepared by the companies with the cooperation of a group of independent experts, covering the most sensitive aspects of the project's feasibility, and, as necessary, with the help of technical teams from the research offices responsible for the baseline studies.

IV. OTHER ACTIVITIES

A. Public symposium on the permanent link (Cairo, 5 April 1994)

47. At the Annual General Assembly of the International Tunnelling Association (ITA), a public symposium on the project for a permanent link through the Strait of Gibraltar was held in Cairo on 5 April 1994 under the auspices of the Economic Commission for Europe and the Economic Commission for Africa. Participants in the symposium included the two regional commissions and the companies that conducted the studies, together with many officials and experts on tunnel building from Governments and private construction firms, including experts who played an important part in the building of the Channel Tunnel.

48. At the symposium, reports were presented on the main findings of numerous and diverse studies conducted in relation to the project for a permanent link through the Strait of Gibraltar, covering such topics as geology, geotechnical aspects, marine sciences, bridge and tunnel engineering, transport questions, economic and financial analyses and legal aspects, together with the principal findings of the 1993 evaluation of these studies by independent international experts.

49. Many speakers who had participated in either the planning or the building of the Channel Tunnel reported on the lessons learned, experience gained and difficulties faced, particularly during the execution phase of the project.

50. Against the backdrop of these lessons and experiences, a discussion was held at the symposium on the aspects which needed to be carefully studied in preparing a project for a permanent link through the Strait of Gibraltar in order to avoid any problems that might arise later during the construction if these aspects were not attentively and rigorously examined.

51. The best possible understanding of the geology of the seabed of the strait and the geotechnical nature of the rocks that would have to be perforated along the way was definitely considered crucial to a project of this scope, in order to reduce to a reasonable level the risks involved. To this end, studies now in progress on the geotechnical features of the rocks by means of on-site experimental galleries and shafts were deemed to be extremely useful. Offshore drilling in the deep areas of the strait to determine and confirm the presence of continuous flysch units across the entire strait and to determine the thickness of recent sediments were considered to be extremely important, if not crucial, to the final decision on the feasibility of the tunnel.

52. Besides these fundamental aspects, logistical problems and contractual issues were identified as areas which are often regarded as peripheral, and hence are not sufficiently taken into account in infrastructure works; they may, however, create major problems in the case of such large projects as the permanent link.

B. Fourth International Colloquium on the Permanent Link (Seville, 16-18 May 1995)

53. This Colloquium, initially scheduled for autumn 1994, was postponed to 16-18 May 1995. A brief report may be presented at the substantive session of the Council.

V. PROSPECTS FOR THE DEVELOPMENT OF THE PROJECT

54. The project for a permanent link through the Strait of Gibraltar is nearing a turning-point. While the studies conducted up until 1992 had enabled substantial progress to be made in understanding the essential aspects of the project and in establishing a reasonable, relatively sound basis for elaborating a project feasibility study, research in the period 1993-1994 essentially confirmed the earlier findings and produced further, more concrete results which represent important steps in the development of the project.

55. The preliminary pilot project for the tunnel option and the economic studies done in 1994 indeed pointed up the fact that, under the assumption that the reconnaissance gallery would be financed by public funds and then turned over free of charge to the concessionaire, which would then build the rest of the tunnel - a single tunnel in the first stage - without any additional public assistance, the capital invested by the concessionaire would yield an internal rate of return comparable to that obtained in other infrastructure projects in both Spain and Morocco.

56. This tunnel option is feasible using existing, proven building techniques, will cause no harm to the marine environment, will make it possible to absorb both road and rail traffic, free of maritime navigation problems, and will meet funding imperatives; it therefore seems to be essentially the best solution in the current phase of study.

57. One fundamental aspect has yet to be addressed, i.e., consolidation of technical feasibility, which should benefit from the current off-shore drilling survey. The necessary government funds must also be found to build the undersea reconnaissance gallery; in that regard, substantial financial support from the European Union will be crucial. It is hoped that this support will be granted in the context of the European Union's Mediterranean policy, in view of the

major role this tunnel will play in the land transport infrastructure network between Europe and Africa.

58. The evaluation report to be prepared by the companies at the end of the current phase of work, with the assistance of independent consultants, should put forward some proposals as to the following phase of work. If all other conditions are met, it will perhaps be time to take the decision to choose the tunnel option as outlined above.

55. REPORT OF THE MEETING OF THE WORKING GROUP ON MARITIME COOPERATION, HELD AT VIENNA FROM 19 TO 23 SEPTEMBER 1994 AND FROM 20 TO 24 FEBRUARY 1995* (ECOSOC COMMISSION ON NARCOTIC DRUGS, 38TH SESSION, VIENNA, 14-23 MARCH 1995)

Doc. no.: E/CN.7/1995/13 6 March 1995

CONTENTS

* E/CN.7/1995/1.

RECOMMENDATIONS

The observance of the principles of international law, in particular those concerning the full respect for sovereignty and territorial integrity, and the principles of the international law of the sea regime, should govern international cooperation in the fight against illicit traffic by sea in narcotic drugs and psychotropic substances.

I. EXCHANGE OF INFORMATION

1. Each State should maintain a register containing information on vessels flying its flag and is urged to comply with the provisions of article 17, paragraph 7, of the United Nations Convention against Illicit Traffic in Narcotic Drugs and Psychotropic Substances of 1988 (E/CONF.82/15 and Corr.2), concerning the designation of an authority or authorities to receive or respond to requests made pursuant to that article. The authority or authorities designated by that State must have ready access to the information in the register.

2. Governments should improve and streamline channels for direct communication between competent authorities in order to facilitate and simplify the process of requesting and responding to requests made pursuant to article 17 of the 1988 Convention. In particular, States should:

(a) Ensure an ongoing exchange of general information about drug trafficking;
(b) Ensure the quality and accuracy of information;
(c) Ensure that information is transmitted speedily;
(d) Maintain confidentiality.

A. Standard request for boarding

3. After alternatives, including controlled delivery, have been explored and exhausted, a State requesting from the flag State authority to board a vessel may use the standard format presented below. The recommended action request should be viewed as neither exhaustive nor binding in terms of authorization. The flag State may request additional information. The flag State should make every effort to respond either affirmatively or negatively to the intervening State on the basis of the information thus provided.

Action request

1. Identification of the requesting party, including the authority issuing the request and the agency charged with taking measures
2. Vessel description, including name, flag and port of registration and any other information regarding the vessel
3. Known details concerning voyage and crew
4. Sighting information and weather report
5. Reason for request (articulation of the circumstances supporting the intervention)
6. Intended action
7. Any other relevant information
8. Action requested by the intervening State (including confirmation of vessel registry and permission to board and search, if applicable), together with any time-limits.

States may also consider using the guidelines for the exchange of general information on vessels suspected of illicit drug trafficking, which are annexed to the present recommendations.

4. In order to enhance the exchange of information through existing global channels such as the International Criminal Police Organization (ICPO/Interpol) and the World Customs Organization (also called the Customs Co-operation Council), those organizations should be requested to provide to the United Nations International Drug Control Programme (UNDCP) information on their mechanisms and networks. Based on that information UNDCP should be invited to prepare a guidebook for use by States.

5. States should make every effort to computerize a detailed set of data on vessels in their registry in order to facilitate identification of vessels flying their flag.

6. States should identify, to the extent possible, and disseminate in a timely fashion to other States directly or through ICPO/Interpol, the World Customs Organization, Mar-Info or other organizations or communication networks operating or involved in this field, those indicators that, in their judgement, may assist in the identification of vessels that are involved, or may soon become involved, in illicit drug trafficking.

II. TECHNICAL ASSISTANCE

7. More States should contribute financial and other resources to the operational activities of UNDCP to enable it to respond, in cooperation with relevant international bodies, to requests from Member States for technical assistance, including training, in order to permit those Member States to better implement article 17 of the 1988 Convention.

8. Each State may request technical assistance, including training, in accordance with articles 9 and 10 of the 1988 Convention, to upgrade, improve or install a computerized data system for vessels that are in its registry, or that fly its flag, in order to improve the accuracy and speed of information exchange. Such requests may be channelled through UNDCP, which may transmit them to States prepared to provide financial and other support.

9. UNDCP should be requested to convene, under its auspices, a meeting of experts from Governments, with due regard to the principle of equitable geographical distribution, and observers from international organizations, with expertise in the field of maritime law enforcement for the implementation of article 17 of the 1988 Convention, with a view to:

(a) Development of a training programme introducing minimum standards and safeguards in the conduct of stopping, boardings and searches at sea, in accordance with the international law of the sea;

(b) Formation of multinational mobile training teams to carry out such training programmes in States that so request;

(c) Development of training materials on techniques and methods for the inspection of vessels and establishment of timetables for their dissemination.

III. LEGAL ISSUES

A. Exercise of jurisdiction over vessels

10. States should take the necessary measures to ensure that they effectively exercise jurisdiction over ships flying their flags, in accordance with the principles of the international law of the sea.

11. States are urged to establish the jurisdictions described in article 4 of the 1988 Convention and in particular the jurisdiction contained in paragraph 1, subparagraph (b)(ii), of that article.

12. States are urged to provide information to the Secretary-General, in accordance with article 20 of the 1988 Convention, on the implementation of article 17 of that Convention and, in particular, on any assistance that may be required to facilitate such implementation.

B. Drug trafficking by vessels without nationality

13. States should take, to the fullest extent possible, the necessary measures to ensure, in accordance with international law, the exercise of jurisdiction over drug trafficking offences involving vessels without nationality or those assimilated to them in accordance with international law.

14. States should reach agreement regarding the general minimum safeguards applicable in cases involving the boarding of suspected vessels, taking into account article 17, paragraph 5, of the 1988 Convention.

15. The States concerned should reach an agreement regarding authorized measures that might be taken by the intervening State in relation to a suspicious vessel, such as stopping, boarding, inspection (including the crew, passengers and cargo) and search. Unless otherwise agreed by the States concerned, in accordance with article 17 of the 1988 Convention, the intervening State should be responsible for the procedures for the implementation of such measures and the action and should abide by the conditions and limitations posed by the flag State and established international law.

16. Where a State wishes to intervene it shall request the flag State for authority. The request may include the latest time by which the requesting State will be in a position to intervene effectively and the latest time by which a reply would permit such intervention. The flag State should immediately acknowledge the receipt of the request for authorization and should confirm its status as flag State, indicating the likely period to elapse before a reply will be sent. The request should be answered as soon as possible and wherever practicable within a few hours of receipt of the request.

17. When a request for authorization to board has been made, pursuant to article 17, paragraph 3, of the 1988 Convention, the requesting State should not intervene before receiving explicit authorization from the flag State. Absence of a response can under no circumstances be construed as tacit agreement to such a request.

C. Boarding, search and related procedures

18. In conformity with the provisions of article 17, paragraph 8, of the 1988 Convention, the intervening State should promptly inform the flag State of the results of its intervention. In the event that the

suspicion has been confirmed, the two States should agree on the appropriate measures to be taken, with due regard to the principle of the exclusive jurisdiction of the flag State as recognized in international law. The flag State may explicitly waive the exercise of its jurisdiction in favour of the intervening State, on the basis of evidence gathered during the boarding and search.

D. Costs and damages

19. Unless otherwise agreed, costs related to the boarding exercise should be borne by the intervening State. If the intervention is to be undertaken at the request of the flag State or any other State, the costs of the boarding exercise should be borne, unless otherwise agreed, by the State requesting the intervention.

20. When entering into bilateral or regional agreement or arrangements pursuant to article 17, paragraph 9, of the 1988 Convention, States should consider including relevant provisions on, inter alia, damage, loss, injury and compensation that address similar problems in existing international conventions or agreements.

21. Liability for any loss, damages or injury resulting from actions provided for under article 17 of the 1988 Convention should be agreed upon by the States concerned. Unless otherwise agreed, such loss, damages or injury arising from non-compliance with the principles of article 17, paragraph 5, of that convention should be compensated by the intervening State, if negligence or other faults are attributable to the intervening State or if the action has been conducted in a manner unjustified under international law.

IV. Procedures for implementation

22. The technique of controlled delivery usually produces better law enforcement results than does intervention in waters beyond the territorial sea. Where operational circumstances permit, preference should be given to the surveillance of vessels and the increased use of controlled delivery in order to target the crime syndicates involved, rather than to boarding operations. In this case, measures should be considered to ensure the integrity of the illicit shipment and to prevent its possible diversion or transshipment before the vessel arrives at its planned point of destination.

23. Commercial carriers, manning agencies, shipowners, port authorities, trade bodies and other professional groups active in maritime transport should be associated on the basis of voluntary cooperation in the fight against illicit drug traffic. This should be furthered by a number of means, including memoranda of understanding at the national and international levels, appropriate training of law enforcement personnel and programmes to increase the awareness of commercial carrier personnel and other professional groups active in marine transport with regard to illicit drug trafficking.

24. Regional and bilateral agreements and arrangements to enhance international cooperation against illicit drug trafficking by sea should be encouraged. To that end, UNDCP should be invited to develop a model agreement to standardize modalities of such operations and, wherever possible, to facilitate the convening of regional or subregional meetings with a view to concluding such agreements and arrangements.

Annex

GUIDELINES FOR THE EXCHANGE OF GENERAL INFORMATION ON VESSELS SUSPECTED OF ILLICIT DRUG TRAFFICKING, WHICH ARE ANNEXED TO THE PRESENT RECOMMENDATIONS

1. Name
2. Asserted nationality/flag
3. Vessel registration, document number and official number (applicable international number)
4. Type of vessel
5. Radio call-sign
6. Length overall
7. Gross tonnage
8. Owner
9. Ship-broker or agent
10. Home port
11. Purpose of voyage (if commercial, description of cargo where practicable)
12. Last port of call
13. Next port of call
14. Date and time of observation
15. Position of vessel
16. Master's name, nationality and date of birth
17. Names, nationalities and dates of birth of other persons on board, if practical
18. Reasons for suspicion and/or for requested action (if applicable, indication of circumstances that, in the view of the intervening State, support the intervention)
19. Checks already carried out
20. Identity of other authorities called in (if applicable)
21. Period of time for which authorization is requested (if applicable)
22. Alternatives considered (e.g. controlled delivery) (boarding requests only)
23. Relevant information concerning applicable liability regime

I. ORGANIZATION AND OPENING OF THE MEETING

1. The Working Group on Maritime Cooperation, convened by the Executive Director of the United Nations International Drug Control Programme (UNDCP), pursuant to paragraph 2 of Commission on Narcotic Drugs resolution 9 (XXXVII), met at Vienna from 19 to 23 September 1994 and from 20 to 24 February 1995. In that resolution the Commission entrusted the Working Group with a mandate to develop a comprehensive set of principles and specific recommendations to enhance, on a global basis, the implementation of article 17 of the United Nations Convention against Illicit Traffic in Narcotic Drugs and Psychotropic Substances of 1988 (E/CONF.82/15 and Corr.2), taking note of the recommendations of the Expert Group to Consider the Mandate, Activities and Funding of a Working Group on Maritime Cooperation (E/CN.7/1994/3), which had met at Vienna from 15 to 18 November 1993.

2. The following States were represented as members of the Working Group: Argentina, Australia, Bahamas*, Brazil, Bulgaria, Canada, Chile, China, Colombia, Ecuador, Egypt, France, Germany, Greece, India, Iran (Islamic Republic of), Italy, Japan, Kenya*, Mexico, Netherlands, Nigeria, Pakistan**, Panama, Peru, Poland, Romania, Russian Federation, Spain, Tunisia*, Ukraine, United Kingdom of Great Britain and Northern Ireland, United States of America and Venezuela. One member of the Working Group, Côte d'Ivoire, did not attend.

3. The following States were represented by observers: Indonesia, Malaysia, Morocco, Norway, Republic of Korea, South Africa, Thailand, Turkey and United Arab Emirates*.

4. The following organizations were represented by observers: Council of Europe, International Maritime Organization**, International Criminal Police Organization (ICPO/Interpol), Baltic and International Maritime Council** and World Customs Organization.

5. The Division for Ocean Affairs and the Law of the Sea of the Secretariat was represented at the first session.

6. UNDCP served as secretariat of the Working Group.

7. The Executive Director of UNDCP, in his opening address to the Working Group, drew attention to its mandate, the challenge posed by illicit drug traffic by sea and the difficulties in countering it.

8. The observer for the Council of Europe informed the Working Group that the Agreement on Illicit Traffic by Sea, Implementing Article 17 of the United Nations Convention against Illicit Traffic in Narcotic Drugs and Psychotropic Substances, had recently been concluded by States members of the Council of Europe. He described the status of adherence to the agreement.

9. The Working Group elected the following officers by acclamation:

<u>Chairman</u>:	Tadanori Inomata (Japan)
<u>Vice-Chairmen</u>:	A. Khalek Eltahawy (Egypt) Luigi Lauriola (Italy) Nilton Durán Salas (Chile)
<u>Rapporteurs</u>:	Michael Lekszycki (Poland)* Rodica Balas (Romania)**

10. At its first session, the Working Group based its discussion on the recommendations of the Expert Group to Consider the Mandate, Activities and Funding of a Working Group on Maritime Cooperation, contained in the report of the Expert Group, and a report on the status of international cooperation in implementing article 17 of the 1988 Convention based on information provided by Governments in response to a questionnaire prepared by UNDCP.

11. At the close of its first session, the Working Group agreed that the draft recommendations contained in documents UNDCP/1994/MAR.WP.3/Rev.1, UNDCP/1994/MAR.WP.4/Rev.1 and

---

* First session.
** Second session.

UNDCP/1994/MAR.WP.6, which had been redrafted following their discussion at that session, would constitute the formal basis for further discussions at its second session. Those documents could not be discussed at the first session because of time constraints. It was agreed that those documents, together with the present report, would be sent to all participants by the Secretariat. Any written comments received from Governments by 1 December 1994 would be collated by UNDCP and submitted to participants, in such form as the Secretariat deemed most appropriate, well in advance of the second session of the Working Group.

12. At its second session, the Working Group had before it a compendium of comments received from Governments on the interim report of the Working Group on maritime cooperation (UNDCP/1994/MAR.WP.5/Rev.1) and related documents (UNDCP/1995/MAR.2) and the recommendations examined at its first session, previously contained in documents UNDCP/1994/MAR.WP.3/Rev.1, UNDCP/1994/MAR.WP.4/Rev.1 and UNDCP/1994/MAR.WP.6, which had been combined into a single document (UNDCP/1995/MAR.WP.2).

II. CONSIDERATION OF SUBSTANTIVE MATTERS

A. Barriers to international cooperation

13. At its first session, the Working Group discussed barriers to international cooperation in countering illicit drug traffic by sea. It considered it necessary to endeavour to strengthen the existing international legal framework, to encourage the universal ratification of the United Nations Convention on the Law of the Sea of 1982 1/ and the 1988 Convention and to promote bilateral and multilateral agreements. The problems identified included the identification of the proper authority to consent to boarding by a foreign State; the inability to exercise jurisdiction over domestic vessels outside the territorial sea; the inability to exercise jurisdiction over stateless vessels; the concern that damage by the intervening State would not be fully compensated; and the inability to exercise jurisdiction over nationals outside the territorial sea. Another important barrier was the slow processing of requests to board vessels on the high seas owing to the absence of standard boarding procedures, to ineffective record-keeping in vessel registries and to poor communication channels. Furthermore, the maritime law enforcement capability, both within the territorial sea and on the high seas, was often weak, and domestic legal restrictions in some States regarding the use of naval vessels in drug law enforcement operations further limited the interception capabilities of several coastal States. There was a great need for training and material assistance and the establishment of effective communication channels between competent authorities.

B. Examination of specific issues by the Working Group

14. Exchanging quality information in a speedy and accurate manner was emphasized as a prerequisite for effective cooperation in countering illicit traffic by sea. Exchanging accurate information would facilitate the targeting of suspicious vessels and would avoid undue delay in rummaging vessels. With a view to ensuring the quality of information required, it was suggested that consideration should be given to the evaluation and assessment of how information was exchanged and what difficulties were encountered in that regard.

15. The Working Group was informed of the successful operation of the Mar-Info and Yacht-Info information exchange networks, in which 12 countries in western Europe were participating. The networks had led to significant seizures of cocaine, heroin and cannabis. As the networks could not be extended beyond the European region, it was suggested that parallel systems could be established worldwide through the regional intelligence liaison office network of the World Customs Organization (WCO), a network supported by UNDCP. The observer for the WCO informed the Working Group of the functioning and importance of that network in the exchange of operational information between law enforcement agencies. The observer for ICPO/Interpol referred to the protected communication network established between national police agencies for the exchange of criminal information, including illicit drug traffic by sea. The communication network, covering 174 countries, was available to assist members of ICPO/Interpol that were parties to the 1988 Convention in implementing article 17 of that Convention. Mention was also made of the existence of other regional communication networks for the exchange of information concerning illicit drug traffic by sea. It was stated that some States were bound by national and international obligations concerning data protection that might affect the scope and manner of exchange of information.

16. It was considered important for States to improve their capability for collecting and exchanging information related to traffic by sea. It was suggested that the Working Group should indicate the type of information that Governments should collect, as well as the information that should be exchanged to implement article 17. Support was expressed for the recommendation, contained in the report of the Expert Group (E/CN.7/1994/3, para.6), that Governments should improve and streamline channels for direct communication between competent authorities in order to facilitate and simplify the process of responding to requests made pursuant to article 17 of the 1988 Convention.

17. Some representatives referred to the need for assistance to be provided to their competent authorities in order to upgrade their information exchange capabilities, particularly through the computerization of the list of vessels in each of their registries, as well as particulars on those vessels. That would, in their view, enhance their ability to respond expeditiously to requests to board vessels flying their flags and would improve the exchange of information with other competent authorities. Existing expertise within the United Nations system should be utilized.

18. One speaker, referring to the practice in some States of maintaining "open registers" of vessels, stated that it was important for each of those States to establish a database to record information regarding ships flying its flag, particularly their owners and operators. That would, in her view, facilitate the identification of suspicious vessels.

19. Several representatives referred to the need for technical assistance to enhance the capabilities of their Governments to combat illicit traffic by sea. In particular there was a need for training in all fields related to the implementation of article 17 of the 1988 Convention, particularly in the surveillance of suspicious vessels, procedures for boarding, searching techniques, ship rummaging, and implementation of national legislation. It was suggested that UNDCP should initiate a maritime training programme drawing on all available expertise to meet the needs of States in that field.

20. The Working Group stressed that it was important for all States to effectively exercise jurisdiction over ships flying their flags, in line with the provisions of international law, particularly articles 91, 92 and 94 of the 1982 United Nations Convention on the Law of the Sea, concerning, respectively, the nationality of ships, the status of ships, and the duties of the flag State. It was stated that international cooperation in combating illicit traffic by sea was often hampered by the fact that several States did not exercise their jurisdiction over vessels flying their flags and, accordingly, were not in a position to reply to requests to board such vessels.

21. In order to assist States in effectively implementing article 17 of the 1988 Convention, it was suggested by some representatives that the Working Group should consider recommending the establishment of a mechanism for reporting on the implementation of the provisions of that article. Such a reporting mechanism would enable States to indicate any difficulties that they were having in complying with the provisions of the article. Other representatives felt that an information system, rather than a reporting mechanism, would suffice.

22. There was agreement that the Working Group should deal with the issue of vessels without nationality so as to preclude their operation with impunity. It was considered essential for the Working Group to consider measures to ensure the exercising of jurisdiction over drug trafficking offences by vessels without nationality. Some representatives referred to articles of the Council of Europe Agreement on Illicit Traffic by Sea concerning vessels without nationality as an example of measures that the Working Group might wish to recommend. Other speakers referred to provisions contained in the 1982 United Nations Convention on the Law of the Sea, as well as to national legislation and practice, as a basis for the elaboration of recommendations by the Working Group.

23. Some representatives stated that their national legislation on implementing article 17 of the 1988 Convention contained criteria by which vessels on the high seas were assimilated to vessels without nationality. Other representatives felt that those criteria could not be contrary to those of the international law of the sea.

24. There was support for the Working Group recommending the establishment of standard procedures and guidelines for boarding vessels suspected of drug trafficking. It was pointed out that currently there were no established procedures acceptable to all States regarding the boarding of vessels suspected of illicit traffic on the high seas. It was felt that the adoption of standardized boarding procedures, guidelines and safeguards related to the boarding of vessels suspected of being engaged in illicit maritime drug traffic would ensure predictability and allay concerns regarding liability. It was also stated, however, that due consideration should likewise be given to the examination of requests to board such vessels on a case-by-case basis, with the flag State giving its consent to board on the merit of each case.

25. With regard to the content of the request made to the flag State, there was agreement that it should cover two main issues: first, a request for confirmation by the flag State that the vessel was flying its flag; and, secondly, a request for authorization to board the suspected vessel. It was considered important for the flag State to acknowledge expeditiously requests to board one of its vessels on the high seas, as well as to confirm whether or not the vessel was flying its flag, regardless of the time required by the flag State to process the request to board one of its vessels.

26. The Working Group discussed the time-frame within which a flag State should reply to a request to board its vessels on the high seas. It was pointed out that the Council of Europe Agreement stipulated that the flag State should reply to a request to board a vessel within four hours of receipt of the request. In view of the technical limitations of several Governments and the geographical location and the circumstances of each case, the Working Group decided to take a flexible approach in considering the issue. Several representatives emphasized that it was important for the flag State to reply expeditiously, particularly where motherships were involved. It was pointed out that the time taken by a flag State to reply to a request to board a vessel flying its flag would depend on the grounds given in the request for boarding.

27. In order not to interfere with international trade and to target suspicious vessels more effectively, it was suggested that the Working Group should formulate guidelines to facilitate the identification of the types of vessels where boarding outside the territorial sea was necessary. Some representatives stated that the publication of standard procedures might alert drug traffickers to the likely scope and manner of boarding. In their view, it was also preferable not to specify which category of vessels would be boarded. In cases where vessels were boarded on the high seas, it was stressed that the elements contained in article 17, paragraph 5, of the 1988 Convention should be adhered to and that the intervening State must take special care to guarantee the safety, physical and moral integrity of persons found on board, as well as the security of the cargo.

28. The Working Group dealt with the issue of the responsibility of States at the time of boarding. It was pointed out that article 17 of the 1988 Convention did not indicate whether the law of the intervening State or of the flag State should prevail in implementing the provisions foreseen therein. There was agreement in principle that the costs of boarding should be borne by the intervening State. The Working Group, in outlining the responsibilities and liability of the various States concerned with the boarding operation, considered it important to establish the responsibility of the flag State for its vessels, particularly when a State had boarded a vessel at its request. One representative stated that the issue of state responsibility should not be considered by the Working Group.

29. The Working Group recognized the right for third parties to seek compensation for loss or damages, particularly as a result of undue delay or action taken against their vessels on unsubstantiated grounds. It was suggested that the Working Group should consider recommending the basis on which compensation should be paid to third parties as a result of unjustified boarding on the high seas or damages incurred, as well as other factors, such as the applicable law and the competent courts.

30. The Working Group considered articles 25 (concerning costs) and 26 (concerning damages) of the Council of Europe Agreement on Illicit Traffic by Sea and article 110 (concerning the right of visit), paragraph 3, of the 1982 United Nations Convention of the Law of the Sea, in drafting principles and recommendations regarding costs and damages.

31. Some representatives were of the view that the Working Group should focus its work on examining conditions that would preclude unjustified boarding on the high seas, particularly the gathering and expeditious transmission of reliable information.

32. Quality information was emphasized as a vital component in preventing unwarranted boarding. Several representatives stressed that gathering and assessing profiles and sharing information concerning vessels suspected of being engaged in illicit drug traffic were important to facilitating the detection of such vessels. On speeding the response to requests to board vessels involved in illicit drug traffic on the high seas, some speakers said that it would be useful for the Working Group to agree on the criteria for determining or the definitions of "suspicious vessels" and "reasonable grounds" for boarding. Other speakers did not share that opinion and did not believe that the Working Group needed to discuss such criteria.

33. The importance of controlled delivery as a technique to facilitate the dismantling of organized drug syndicates involved in the illicit drug traffic by sea was emphasized. The view was expressed that consideration should be given to surveillance of vessels and the increased use of controlled delivery to target the crime syndicates involved, rather than focusing on boarding operations that often resulted only in the seizure of illicit drugs. Several representatives stressed the need to improve the detection capabilities of law enforcement authorities in their countries.

34. Several representatives stated that their Governments had benefited greatly from the involvement of commercial carriers, manning agencies, shipowners and port authorities in combating illicit traffic, particularly through memoranda of understanding with commercial carriers and trading associations at the national and international levels. The Working Group was informed of the positive results achieved in countering illicit drug traffic through closer cooperation between Governments at the bilateral and regional levels. Particular reference was made to the innovative arrangements for drug law enforcement cooperation between the Governments of the Bahamas and the United States, between the Governments of Italy and Spain and between the Governments of the Netherlands and the United Kingdom. Reference was also made to ROCRAM, the operating network of maritime authorities in South American countries and in Mexico and Panama.

35. At its second session, the Working Group on maritime cooperation examined recommendations that it had elaborated in the course of its first session. The recommendations covered the exchange of information, technical assistance, legal issues and procedures for implementation. Under legal issues, the Working Group considered recommendations relating to the exercise of jurisdiction over vessels; reporting mechanisms; drug trafficking by vessels without nationality; boarding, search and related procedures; responsibility of flag States; and costs and damages. The procedures for implementation covered controlled delivery, involvement of commercial carriers and development of a network of regional and bilateral agreements.

36. Following discussions in plenary, as well as informal consultations, the Working Group adopted the recommendations contained in the present report and agreed to submit them to the Commission on Narcotic Drugs at its thirty-eighth session, in accordance with Commission resolution 9 (XXXVII). The recommendations would assist Governments in adopting laws and regulations to implement article 17 of the 1988 Convention.

37. The representative of China expressed his Government's reservations concerning recommendation 16. The representative of Malaysia withdrew his proposal concerning the exercise of jurisdiction by the coastal States over vessels in the territorial sea, a matter that the Working Group considered not to be within its mandate.

38. Because of time constraints, the Working Group was not in a position to develop, in specific terms, a comprehensive set of principles as requested by the Commission in its resolution 9 (XXXVII). There was agreement, however, that the recommendations adopted by the Working Group embodied general principles relating to the implementation of article 17 of the 1988 Convention. The Working Group considered that, should the Commission consider it essential for the general principles to be elaborated in addition to the recommendations already adopted, the Commission should examine the sequence and substance of the recommendations contained in the present report with a view to identifying such general principles. In this regard, the Commission's attention is drawn to the sequence of recommendations proposed by Spain, which the Working Group generally endorsed as a possible structure of the elements on general principles (see the annex to the present report).

Note

1/ Official Records of the Third United Nations Conference on the Law of the Sea (United Nations publication, Sales No. E.84.V.3).

Annex

POSSIBLE STRUCTURE OF THE ELEMENTS ON GENERAL PRINCIPLES RELATED TO MARITIME COOPERATION, AS PROPOSED BY SPAIN

I. GENERAL PRINCIPLES (the following paragraphs of the recommendations, to appear in the sequence indicated):

1. Paragraph 11
2. Paragraph 12
3. Paragraph 19
4. Paragraph 14
5. Paragraph 25
6. Paragraph 24
7. Paragraph 23

II. EXCHANGE OF INFORMATION

III. TECHNICAL ASSISTANCE

IV. LEGAL ISSUES

56. UN COMMISSION ON NARCOTIC DRUGS REPORT OF THE 38TH SESSION, 14-23 MARCH 1995, ECOSOC OFFICIAL RECORDS, 1995 SUPPLEMENT NO.9 (RESOLUTION 8 (XXXVIII) ON ENDORSEMENT OF THE REPORT OF THE MEETING OF THE WORKING GROUP ON MARITIME COOPERATION)

Doc. no.: E/1995/29-E/CN.7/1995/19 1995

CONTENTS

[...]

C. Other matters arising under the international drug control conventions

143. At its 1119th meeting, on 21 March 1995, the Commission considered agenda item 6 (c) entitled "Implementation of the international drug control treaties: other matters arising from the international drug control treaties". The Commission had before it a note by the Secretariat on the adequacy of existing national legislation (E/CN.7/1995/12) and the report of the Working Group on Maritime Cooperation (E/CN.7/1995/13).

1. Adequacy of existing national legislation

144. A representative of the Secretariat reviewed the legislative activities covered in the note by the Secretariat on the adequacy of existing national drug control legislation and described the legal advisory services provided by UNDCP. One representative requested advisory assistance in view of the serious drug-trafficking problems in his country.

145. At its 1122nd meeting, on 23 March 1995, the Commission adopted a draft resolution entitled "Adherence of States to the international drug control conventions" (E/CN.7/1995/L.10), sponsored by Argentina, Belarus, Croatia, Denmark, Ethiopia, Finland, France, Gabon, Germany, Greece, Hungary, Norway, Poland, Portugal, Russian Federation, Sweden, Ukraine, Uruguay, United Kingdom of Great Britain and Northern Ireland and United States of America. For the text, see chapter XII, section A, resolution 7 (XXXVIII).

146. The representative of Turkey expressed the reservations of her Government concerning the use of the term "successor States" in resolution 7 (XXXVIII) without reference to their acceptance by the United Nations or their status in international law.

2. Report of the Working Group on Maritime Cooperation

147. The Chairman of the Working Group on Maritime Cooperation, which met at Vienna from 19 to 23 September 1994 and from 20 to

24 February 1995, in introducing its report, recalled that it had been established pursuant to Commission resolution 9 (XXXVII) of 21 April 1994, and was mandated to develop a comprehensive set of principles and specific recommendations to enhance, on a global basis, the implementation of article 17 of the 1988 Convention. The report included the deliberations of the two sessions of the working group and the recommendations adopted, which also encompassed the principles required to enhance the implementation of article 17 of the 1988 Convention. The Working Group had worked in a spirit of consensus, taking into consideration the international law of the sea and article 17 of the 1988 Convention.

148. The representative of China informed the meeting that, in a spirit of cooperation, his Government was withdrawing its earlier reservation to recommendation 15 as indicated in paragraph 37 of the report of the Working Group.

149. The meeting agreed to amend recommendation 17, at the request of the representative of Spain, inserting the words "unless otherwise agreed" in front of the words "before receiving explicit authorization". In paragraph 22, the words "in waters beyond the territorial sea" would be replaced by the words "at sea".

150. The Committee of the Whole endorsed the recommendations emanating from the Working Group, as amended during the course of its deliberation. One representative indicated that his Government was initiating a resolution to further the implementation of article 17 of the 1988 Convention.

151. With reference to recommendation 23 of the report, which stated that commercial carriers, manning agencies, shipowners and port authorities should be associated in the fight against illicit drug traffic, the meeting urged Governments and authorities to ensure the safety and security of ports and cargo terminals.

152. At its 1122nd meeting, on 23 March 1995, the Commission adopted a revised draft resolution entitled "Endorsement of the report of the meeting of the Working Group on Maritime Cooperation" (E/CN.7/1995/L.18/Rev.1), sponsored by Argentina, Australia, Bahamas, Brazil, Bulgaria, Canada, Croatia, Egypt, France, Germany, Greece, Indonesia, Iran (Islamic Republic of), Italy, Japan, Madagascar, Mexico, Morocco, Netherlands, Norway, Panama, Poland, Republic of Korea, Romania, Russian Federation, Thailand, Tunisia, Turkey, United Kingdom of Great Britain and Northern Ireland, United States of America and Venezuela. For the text, see chapter XII, section A, resolution 8 (XXXVIII).

153. Following the adoption of resolution 8 (XXXVIII), the representative of Spain stated that his Government did not wish to block a consensus or enter an express reservation on the recommendations adopted by the Working Group on Maritime Cooperation. It considered, however, that recommendation 21 limited compensation for damage caused to a vessel stopped

groundlessly outside the territorial sea to cases of negligence or to other faults attributable to the intervening State, or to cases where the action was conducted in a manner unjustified under international law. In his view, the criterion of objective responsibility should have been accepted, or the relevant provisions of the United Nations Convention on the Law of the Sea of 1982 should have been followed, in order to establish the obligation of compensation in cases of unjustified stopping of a vessel in connection with the conservation of the marine environment or the exercise of hot pursuit. Stopping a vessel outside the territorial sea was a serious act, which should be resorted to in exceptional circumstances when there were well-founded grounds for believing that the vessel in question was engaged in illicit drug trafficking. The intervening State should compensate any vessel boarded recklessly or unjustifiably for damage arising from the boarding incident, independently of the liability incurred by the intervening State in the particular circumstances of fault or negligence.

154. The representative of Colombia stated that his Government would interpret resolution 8 (XXXVIII) and the recommendations deriving from it in accordance with the reservations and declarations made by Colombia at the time of ratifying the 1988 Convention.

[...]

Resolution 8 (XXXVIII)

Endorsement of the report of the meeting of the Working Group on Maritime Cooperation*

The Commission on Narcotic Drugs,

Recognizing the increasing prevalence of illicit traffic by sea related to narcotic drugs and psychotropic substances,

Reaffirming that full respect for sovereignty and territorial integrity and the principles of the international law-of-the-sea regime should govern international cooperation in the fight against illicit traffic by sea of narcotic drugs and psychotropic substances,

Bearing in mind that the unique nature of illicit trafficking by sea requires maximum cooperation by Governments in its suppression as called for in article 17 of the United Nations Convention against Illicit Traffic in Narcotic Drugs and Psychotropic Substances of 1988,1/

---

* See paragraphs 152-154 above.

<u>Noting</u> various bilateral, regional and multilateral agreements and mechanisms entered into by Governments pursuant to article 17 of the 1988 Convention,

<u>Recalling</u> its resolution 9 (XXXVII) of 21 April 1994, in which it requested the Executive Director of the United Nations International Drug Control Programme to establish and convene a working group on maritime cooperation, with the mandate to develop a comprehensive set of principles and specific recommendations to enhance, on a global basis, the implementation of article 17 of the 1988 Convention,

1. <u>Welcomes</u> and endorses the report of the meeting of the Working Group on Maritime Cooperation, held at Vienna from 19 to 23 September 1994 and from 20 to 24 February 1995, including the recommendations adopted by the Working Group, which are contained in the report;<u>2</u>/

2. <u>Commends</u> the Executive Director of the United Nations International Drug Control Programme, the Chairman of the Working Group on Maritime Cooperation and the Governments participating in the Working Group for the quality of the report;

3. <u>Urges</u> Governments to consider carefully the report, including the recommendations, of the Working Group on Maritime Cooperation as they implement the provisions of article 17 of the United Nations Convention against Illicit Traffic in Narcotic Drugs and Psychotropic Substances of 1988;

4. <u>Also urges</u> Governments, pursuant to the recommendation contained in paragraph 12 of the report, to provide information to the Secretary-General, in accordance with article 20 of the 1988 Convention, on their implementation of article 17 of that Convention;

5. <u>Recommends</u> that, pursuant to the recommendations contained in paragraph 23 of the report, Governments should encourage commercial carriers and professional groups active in maritime transport to become involved in the fight against illicit drug traffic, on the basis of voluntary cooperation and through memoranda of understanding at the national and international levels, through training to increase the awareness of maritime transport personnel with regard to illicit drug trafficking;

6. <u>Encourages</u>, as recommended in paragraph 4 of the report, the international organizations concerned to provide to the United Nations International Drug Control Programme descriptions of their information systems and mechanisms and invites the Programme, within available resources, to disseminate that information for use by States;

7. <u>Requests</u> the United Nations International Drug Control Programme to convene, within available resources, a meeting of experts to develop training and technical assistance programmes

in maritime drug law enforcement, pursuant to the recommendations contained in paragraph 9 of the report;

8. Encourages Governments to inform the United Nations International Drug Control Programme of their training and technical assistance requirements in the field of maritime drug law enforcement;

9. Also encourages Governments to consider providing voluntary contributions to enable the Programme to undertake the activities described in the present resolution;

10. Requests the Executive Director of the Programme to report on the status of the activities described in the present resolution to the Commission on Narcotic Drugs at its thirty-ninth session;

11. Requests the Secretary-General to transmit the present resolution to all Governments for consideration and implementation.

1/ Official Records of the United Nations Conference for the Adoption of a Convention against Illicit Traffic in Narcotic Drugs and Psychotropic Substances, Vienna, 25 November-20 December 1988, vol. I (United Nations publication, Sales No. E.94.XI.5).

2/ E/CN.7/1995/13.

57. ECOSOC RESOLUTION ON MEASURES TO STRENGTHEN INTERNATIONAL COOPERATION TO PREVENT DIVERSION OF SUBSTANCES LISTED IN TABLE I OF THE UN CONVENTION AGAINST ILLICIT TRAFFIC IN NARCOTIC DRUGS AND PSYCHOTROPIC SUBSTANCES OF 1988 AND USED IN THE ILLICIT MANUFACTURE OF STIMULANTS AND OTHER PSYCHOTROPIC SUBSTANCES

Doc. no.: 1995/20 24 July 1995

The Economic and Social Council,

Concerned about the recent discovery of world-wide diversion of vast quantities of ephedrine and pseudoephedrine from licit manufacture and trade to be used for the illicit manufacture of methamphetamine,

Recognizing the rapid increase in illicit trafficking and use of stimulants throughout the world, and the need for the international community to strengthen countermeasures against the illicit trafficking in stimulants and their precursors,

Taking note of the proliferation of the illicit manufacture of a variety of drugs, especially stimulants, which has occurred throughout the world, and the fact that such massive production depends upon an equally massive diversion of substances listed in table I of the United Nations Convention against Illicit Traffic in Narcotic Drugs and Psychotropic Substances of 1988, 60/

Realizing that brokers frequently serve as mediators in transactions involving substances listed in table I which are ultimately diverted,

Recognizing the need for the international community to renew its commitment to cooperation through the exchange of information and to strengthen countermeasures against the illicit traffic in and abuse of psychotropic substances, in particular stimulants, and their precursors,

Noting with appreciation the publication entitled Precursors and Chemicals Frequently Used in the Illicit Manufacture of Narcotic Drugs and Psychotropic Substances: Report of the International Narcotics Control Board for 1994 on the Implementation of Article 12 of the United Nations Convention against Illicit Traffic in Narcotic Drugs and Psychotropic Substances of 1988, 63/ and welcoming the initiative taken jointly by the International Narcotics Control Board and the Pompidou Group of the Council of Europe to hold a meeting of experts to review the issue of brokers dealing with precursors and psychotropic substances and to consider concrete measures effectively to control the operations of brokers,

---

63/ United Nations publication, Sales No. E.95.XI.1.

Recalling its resolutions 1981/7 of 6 May 1981, 1992/29 of 30 July 1992 and 1993/40 of 27 July 1993,

1. Urges Governments, where appropriate, to invoke article 12, paragraph 10 (a), of the United Nations Convention against Illicit Traffic in Narcotic Drugs and Psychotropic Substances of 1988, in order to give importing countries advance notice of any shipment of substances listed in table I of that Convention;

2. Requests the Government of an exporting country, subject to its legal provisions, to provide the following information to the competent authorities of the importing country prior to any export, even when the importing country has not yet formally requested such notification under article 12, paragraph 10 (a), of the 1988 Convention:

(a) Name and address of the exporter and importer and, when available, of the consignee;

(b) Name of the substance listed in table I of the 1988 Convention;

(c) Quantity of the substance to be exported;

(d) Expected point of entry and expected date of dispatch;

(e) Such other information as the exporting Government may deem relevant;

3. Requests, for any substance listed in table I of the 1988 Convention, the Government of an importing country, upon receipt of any form of pre-export notification from the exporting country, to undertake, through its regulatory authorities and in cooperation with the law enforcement authorities, an investigation of the legitimacy of the transaction, and, with the possible assistance of the International Narcotics Control Board, to convey information thereon to the exporting country;

4. Urges Governments of exporting countries at the same time to conduct their own investigation in questionable cases and to seek information and views from the Board, international organizations and Governments as appropriate, inasmuch as additional facts establishing suspicion may be available to them;

5. Requests Governments, where there is sufficient evidence that a substance may be diverted into illicit channels, to stop the shipments or, where circumstances warrant, to cooperate in controlled deliveries of suspicious shipments in special circumstances if the security of the shipment can be sufficiently ensured, if the quantity and nature of the chemical involved is such that it can be managed feasibly and safely by the competent authorities, and if all States whose cooperation is necessary, including transit States, agree to the controlled delivery;

6. Urges Governments to exercise, as a matter of urgency, increased vigilance over the activities of brokers handling substances listed in table I of the 1988 Convention, in view of the special role that some of them play in the diversion of such substances, and to subject them to licensing or other effective control measures as necessary;

7. Also urges Governments to ensure, as far as possible, that shipments entering or leaving free ports, free zones and bonded warehouses be subject, where permitted, to the controls necessary to safeguard against diversion;

8. Further urges Governments, subject to the provisions of national legislation on confidentiality and data protection, to inform the Board on a regular basis, upon request of the Board and in the form and manner provided for by it, of the quantities of substances listed in table I of the 1988 Convention that they have imported, exported or transshipped, and encourages them to estimate their annual licit needs;

9. Requests the Board, drawing upon the capabilities of the United Nations International Drug Control Programme, to collect information pursuant to paragraph 8 above, and to further develop and strengthen its database, in order to assist Governments in preventing diversion of substances listed in table I of the 1988 Convention and the Commission on Narcotic Drugs in discussing the control of illicit manufacture of, trafficking in and use of psychotropic substances, especially of stimulants and their precursors, and in formulating policy recommendations in this field;

10. Requests all Governments to provide the Secretary-General, subject to the provisions of national legislation on confidentiality and data protection, with names and addresses of the manufacturers, within their countries, of substances listed in table I of the 1988 Convention, and requests the Secretary-General to include that information in the publication entitled Manufacture of Narcotic Drugs and Psychotropic Substances under International Control; 64/

11. Requests the Secretary-General, with the assistance of the Executive Director of the Programme and in consultation with the Board, to convene, drawing upon voluntary contributions from Governments, expert meetings in 1995 and 1996 of regulatory and law enforcement authorities of interested Governments, in order to discuss countermeasures against the illicit manufacture of and trafficking in psychotropic substances, particularly stimulants, and the illicit use of their precursors on the basis of the study to be prepared in accordance with paragraph 12 of the present resolution;

12. Also requests the Secretary-General, with the assistance of the Executive Director of the Programme and in consultation with the Board, to undertake within existing resources a thorough study on stimulants and the use of their precursors in the illicit manufacture of and trafficking in drugs, and to prepare a report thereon for submission to the Commission, taking into account any comments that may be made on the study at the expert meetings referred to in paragraph 11 of the present resolution;

13. Encourages Governments to consider strengthening, where necessary, the working mechanisms to prevent diversion of substances listed in table II of the 1988 Convention, as described in the present resolution;

14. Requests the Secretary-General to transmit the present resolution to all Governments for consideration and implementation, and asks the Board, in cooperation with the Programme, to report on its implementation to the Commission at its thirty-ninth session.

49th plenary meeting
24 July 1995

64/ ST/NAR.4/1994/1.

58. ECOSOC RESOLUTION ON IMPLEMENTATION OF PHASE II OF THE PROGRAMME FOR THE SECOND TRANSPORT AND COMMUNICATIONS DECADE IN AFRICA

Doc. no.: 1995/23 24 July 1995

The Economic and Social Council,

Recalling resolution 710 (XXVI) of 12 May 1991 of the Conference of Ministers of the Economic Commission for Africa, 68/ in which the Conference of Ministers adopted the programme for the Second Transport and Communications Decade in Africa,

Referring to General Assembly decision 46/456 of 20 December 1991, in which the Assembly approved the programme for the Second Decade, and Assembly decision 48/455 of 21 December 1993 concerning the provision of resources for its implementation,

Recalling resolution 93/89 of 13 March 1993 of the Conference of African Ministers of Transport, Communications and Planning on the implementation of the programme for the Second Decade, 69/

Having considered the mid-term evaluation of the programme for the Second Decade and the action programme derived therefrom,

Reaffirming the continuing relevance and critical importance of the Second Decade, especially for achieving the goals of the Treaty Establishing the African Economic Community, 70/

Noting with concern the low level of programme implementation due to a lack of resources,

Recalling that new projects to be proposed for inclusion in the programme for the Second Decade should conform to the principles and criteria already adopted and be submitted to the executing agencies concerned, specifying, among other things:

68/ See Official Records of the Economic and Social Council, 1991, Supplement No. 16 (E/1991/37), chap. IV.

69/ DOC/UNTACDA/93/04.

70/ A/46/651, annex.

(a) The time-frame for implementation,

(b) Resource requirements, resource availability and prospective sources,

(c) A description of tasks to be performed and their assignment among the various partners,

1. Urges Member States to make every effort to implement the programme for the Second Transport and Communications Decade in Africa by undertaking, inter alia, the following specific activities:

(a) Facilitating and encouraging national coordinating committees to carry out activities by providing those committees with the necessary human and financial resources to enable them to accomplish their assigned tasks;

(b) According priority to national projects that contribute to the achievement of the objectives of the Second Decade;

(c) Coordinating and strengthening national efforts in fund-raising, so as to be able to gain access to regional indicative planning figures through such sources as the Fourth Lomé Convention, for the implementation of the programme for the Second Decade;

(d) Taking into account the environmental impact of all transport and communications development projects;

2. Invites Member States and intergovernmental organizations to involve the subregional and subsectoral working groups in the design of regional action programmes concerning transport and communications and to provide them with all the assistance necessary to participate effectively in the implementation of the programme for the Second Decade;

3. Requests intergovernmental organizations to take an active part in the programme for the Second Decade by carrying out, within their regular work programmes, the activities set out in that programme, giving priority to those activities that promote regional integration;

4. Invites the United Nations Development Programme to consider favourably increasing the level of its support for the Second Decade by funding part of the regional action programme for the implementation of the second phase of the programme for the Second Decade;

5. Invites all donors to contribute further to the implementation of the programme approved by the Conference of African Ministers of Transport and Communications at its tenth meeting, held at Addis Ababa on 20 and 21 March 1995;

6. Invites the General Assembly to consider providing the Economic Commission for Africa with additional resources, allocated within the regular budget, to enable it to pursue the major activities of the programme for the Second Decade;

7. Requests the African, Caribbean and Pacific Coordinating Ministers of the European Development Fund to give appropriate priority to the projects and programmes for the Second Decade in the preparation of their national and regional indicative programmes under the second financial protocol of the Fourth Lomé Convention;

8. Calls upon the development banks and participating financial institutions to continue to work with the programme machinery of the Second Decade to provide coordinated and efficient support to the development of transport and communications in Africa;

9. Appeals to the World Bank to maintain a high level of involvement in and contribution to the implementation of the programme for the Second Decade;

10. Requests African financial institutions to provide further support to the programme for the Second Decade, in particular by taking into account systematically the guidelines and priorities of the Second Decade in the preparation of the action plans for African countries;

11. Requests the subsectoral working groups to initiate such regional action as would provide a framework for intervention by those countries that plan to commercialize or privatize their transport and communications sector;

12. Decides that the Resource Mobilization Committee for the Second Transport and Communications Decade in Africa shall henceforth be known as the Advisory Committee on Programme Promotion for the Second Transport and Communications Decade in Africa, and adopts the terms of reference of that Committee, as set out in the report of the Conference of African Ministers of Transport and Communications on its tenth meeting; 71/

13. Requests the Advisory Committee to emphasize assistance for Member States in seeking, arranging and mobilizing funds for projects approved under the programme for the Second Decade;

14. Appeals to all financial institutions that are members of the Advisory Committee to play a more active role in the efforts geared to supporting the Committee's mission by providing it with the required technical expertise;

15. Requests the subsectoral working groups to assist in the evaluation of projects falling within their areas of competence, and in the coordination and integration of the Africa regional work programmes of the specialized agencies with those of the Second Decade;

16. Requests the Executive Secretary of the Economic Commission for Africa:

(a) To disseminate systematically among all partners in the Second Decade information on the implementation of the Decade through workshops, seminars, symposia, other forums and information bulletins;

(b) To play a far more active role in coordinating the programme for the Second Decade and to strengthen the capacity of the Commission to provide the necessary technical support of programme implementation;

(c) To ensure that future evaluations of the implementation of the programme for the Second Decade are based on a critical analysis of the degree to which the objectives of the Decade have been achieved;

(d) To prepare a consolidated report on the status of implementation of all the projects for the Second Decade, based on reports prepared by Member States and intergovernmental organizations on the status of their projects.

50th plenary meeting
24 July 1995

71/ E/ECA/TCD/MIN/95/100.

59. ECOSOC RESOLUTION ON EUROPE-AFRICA PERMANENT LINK THROUGH THE STRAIT OF GIBRALTAR

Doc. no.: 1995/48 24 July 1995

The Economic and Social Council,

Recalling its resolutions 1982/57 of 30 July 1982, 1983/62 of 29 July 1983, 1984/75 of 27 July 1984, 1985/70 of 26 July 1985, 1987/69 of 8 July 1987, 1989/119 of 28 July 1989, 1991/74 of 26 July 1991 and 1993/60 of 30 July 1993,

Recalling also General Assembly resolution 43/179 of 20 December 1988, by which the Assembly declared the period 1991-2000 the Second Transport and Communications Decade in Africa,

Referring to resolution 912 (1989) adopted on 1 February 1989 by the Parliamentary Assembly of the Council of Europe 126/ regarding measures to encouraged the construction of a major traffic artery in south-western Europe and to study thoroughly the possibility of a permanent link through the Strait of Gibraltar,

Also referring to the conclusions of the special meeting on the permanent link organized at Cairo on 5 April 1994 by the International Tunnelling Association on the occasion of its General Assembly, pursuant to Council resolution 1993/60,

Taking note of the recommendations and conclusions of the evaluation report on the studies relating to the project prepared in accordance with resolution 1991/74 and the follow-up report prepared in accordance with resolution 1993/60, 127/ in which substantial support for the project from the European Union is recommended,

Also taking note of the conclusions of the Fourth International Colloquium on the Permanent Link, held at Seville, Spain, from 16 to 18 May 1995 and attended by international experts and representatives of specialized international organizations,

---

126/ See Council of Europe, Parliamentary Assembly, Fortieth Ordinary Session (third part), 30 January-3 February 1989, Texts adopted by the Assembly, Strasbourg, France, 1989.

127/ E/1995/46.

Recalling the strategy adopted by the European Union at the Essen Summit in December 1994, consisting in the setting-up of a European-Mediterranean partnership through the establishment of a free-trade zone,

Recalling also the conclusions of the first meeting of the Ministers of Transport of the six western Mediterranean countries, namely, Algeria, France, Italy, Morocco, Spain and Tunisia, held in Paris on 20 January 1995, at which the Ministers undertook to identify priority projects, among them the permanent link through the Strait of Gibraltar, to be proposed to the European Union for consideration of the possibilities of financing and execution,

1. Welcomes the cooperation on the project for the link through the Strait of Gibraltar established between the Economic Commission for Africa, the Economic Commission for Europe, the Governments of Morocco and Spain and specialized international organizations;

2. Commends the Economic Commission for Europe and the Economic Commission for Africa on the work done in preparing the project follow-up report requested by the Council in its resolution 1993/60, even though necessary resources were not forthcoming from the General Assembly;

3. Thanks the International Tunnelling Association for organizing a special meeting on the project at Cairo on 5 April 1994, pursuant to Council resolution 1993/60;

4. Repeats its invitation to the competent organizations of the United Nations system to participate in the studies and work on the permanent link through the Strait of Gibraltar;

5. Invites the European Commission to consider the possibility of participating in the development of the project both institutionally and financially;

6. Requests the Executive Secretaries of the Economic Commission for Africa and the Economic Commission for Europe to take an active part in the follow-up to the project and to report to the Council at its substantive session of 1997;

7. Requests the Secretary-General to provide formal support and, to the extent that priorities permit, necessary resources, within the regular budget, to the Economic Commission for Europe and the Economic Commission for Africa in order to enable them to carry out the above-mentioned activities.

56th plenary meeting
27 July 1995

60. ECOSOC DECISION ON DOCUMENTS CONSIDERED IN CONNECTION WITH ECONOMIC AND ENVIRONMETAL QUESTIONS

Doc. no.: 1995/234 24 July 1995

At its 41st and 44th plenary meetings, on 17 and 19 July 1995, the Economic and Social Council took note of the following documents:

(a) World Economic and Social Survey, 1995; 186/

(b) Report of the Secretary-General on the methods of work of the Committee for Development Planning; 187/

(c) Note by the Secretariat containing elements of a draft programme for the International Year for the Eradication of Poverty; 188/

(d) Report of the Trade and Development Board on the second part of its forty-first session; 189/

(e) Note by the Secretary-General transmitting the report of the Director-General of the Food and Agriculture Organization of the United Nations on cooperation in fisheries in Africa; 190/

(f) Reports of the Commission on Human Settlements on its fifteenth session 191/ and on the implementation of the Global Strategy for Shelter to the Year 2000; 192/

186/ United Nations publication, Sales No. E.95.II.C.1.

187/ E/1995/82.

188/ E/1995/92.

189/ TD/B/41(2)/15 (Vol. I). For the final text, see Official Records of the General Assembly, Fiftieth Session, Supplement No. 15 (A/50/15), vol. I.

190/ E/1995/94.

191/ Official Records of the General Assembly, Fiftieth Session, Supplement No. 8 (A/50/8).

192/ Ibid., addendum (A/50/8/Add.1).

(g) Report of the Governing Council of the United Nations Environment Programme on its eighteenth session; 193/

(h) Report of the Secretary-General on products harmful to health and the environment; 194/

(i) Note by the Secretary-General transmitting the report of the Executive Director of the United Nations Environment Programme on the implementation of the Plan of Action to Combat Desertification and of the medium-term and long-term recovery and rehabilitation programme in the Sudano-Sahelian region; 195/

(j) Note by the Secretary-General transmitting the report of the Joint Inspection Unit entitled "United Nations system support for science and technology in Africa" 196/ and the comments of the Administrative Committee on Coordination thereon; 197/

(k) Report of the Secretary-General on the effective mobilization and integration of women in development: gender issues in macroeconomic policy-making and development planning; 198/

(l) Note by the Secretary-General transmitting the report of the Director-General of the World Health Organization on the progress made in the implementation of the global strategy for the prevention and control of acquired immunodeficiency syndrome; 199/

(m) Report of the Secretary-General on progress made in providing safe water supply and sanitation for all during the first half of the 1990s; 200/

(n) Oral report made by the Director of the Division for Sustainable Development on the format in which the Committee on Natural Resources and the Committee on New and Renewable Sources of Energy and on Energy for Development should present their work. 201/

193/ A/50/25. For the final text, see Official Records of the General Assembly, Fiftieth Session, Supplement No. 25 (A/50/25).

194/ A/50/182-E/1995/66 and Corr.1.

195/ A/50/227-E/1995/99.

196/ A/50/125-E/1995/19.

197/ A/50/125/Add.1-E/1995/19/Add.1.

198/ E/1995/75.

199/ A/50/175-E/1995/57.

200/ A/50/213-E/1995/87.

201/ See E/1995/SR.44.

61. ECE RESOLUTION ON ECONOMIC COOPERATION IN THE MEDITERRANEAN IN THE LIGHT OF THE FINAL ACT OF THE CONFERENCE ON SECURITY AND COOPERATION IN EUROPE

Doc. no.: E/ECE(50)/L.3 11 April 1995

The Economic Commission for Europe,

Reaffirming its decision D (49) and its prior decisions adopted by the Commission on economic cooperation in the Mediterranean,

Bearing in mind that several Commission member States in the Mediterranean are developing from an economic point of view,

Noting the growing awareness of the need for joint efforts by all Mediterranean countries to strengthen economic, social, cultural and environmental cooperation and to promote stability and peace in the Mediterranean region in the light of the Final Act of the CSCE, the Charter of Paris for a New Europe, the Helsinki Document 1992 and the Budapest Document 1994,

1. Takes note with satisfaction of the Executive Secretary's report E/ECE/1312 on Activities of the ECE to implement the pertinent provisions of the Final Act of the CSCE and other CSCE/OSCE documents, including the Charter of Paris for a New Europe, the Helsinki Document 1992 and the Budapest Document 1994, as well as economic cooperation in the Mediterranean in the light of the Final Act of the CSCE, and particularly Part II of the report pertaining to economic cooperation in the Mediterranean;

2. Takes note also of the participation of the ECE within the framework of the CSCE 1994 Budapest Summit, in the two sessions of the working group concerned with the economic dimensions that were devoted to Mediterranean questions;

3. Welcomes the activities undertaken by the secretariat addressing Mediterranean questions in the areas of environmental policy and conventions, including water management; transport questions; renewable sources of energy and use of solar energy; chemical industry and the treatment of industrial waste; harmonization of agricultural standards; forest fire prevention and control and other forestry issues; sustainable tourism; and other ongoing activities, as elaborated in Commission document E/ECE/1312, Part II;

4. Calls upon the Executive Secretary as previously requested to undertake action-oriented studies, including specific analysis of existing economic cooperation between ECE Mediterranean countries, and to identify effective means of enhancing economic cooperation in the Mediterranean in all areas of the ECE programme of work, taking into account the limits of

available resources, for consideration by the Principal Subsidiary Bodies and the Working Parties of the Commission in their programmes of work;

5. Further calls upon member States to assist the Commission in its current activities on the analysis of macroeconomic and sectoral policies with a view to taking into account the Mediterranean dimension of the ECE;

6. Requests the Executive Secretary to continue to cooperate with the Executive Secretaries of the other regional commissions concerned, as well as heads of other relevant United Nations bodies in order to secure interaction with Mediterranean countries not members of the Commission, with a view to increasing interregional cooperation on the subjects within the competence of the ECE and which are of common interest to the Mediterranean countries;

7. Takes note of the initiative of the Executive Secretary to discuss with ECE members and non-member States of the Mediterranean region, the role of the UN/ECE on cooperation in the Mediterranean and encourages further exchange of views on how to give concrete substance to the Commission decisions;

8. Takes note with satisfaction that the ECE and ECA secretariats, as requested by ECOSOC Resolution 1993/60, participated in follow-up activities to the project on the Europe-Africa permanent link through the straits of Gibraltar and are preparing jointly a report which will address the studies undertaken in the period 1994-1995 in the framework of the Project, to be submitted to ECOSOC at its substantive session in 1995;

9. Takes note with satisfaction of the recognition given by the OSCE at the Budapest Summit of December 1994 to the role played by the ECE and other relevant international organizations and institutions in support of OSCE's economic dimension priority, in particular the strengthening of security and cooperation in the Mediterranean as an important factor for stability in the OSCE region;

10. Calls upon Mediterranean countries to work closely with the OSCE to intensify the dialogue between the OSCE and non-participating Mediterranean States through seminars and high-level consultations, and invites the Executive Secretary to cooperate with the informal open-ended contact group, at the level of experts, which will be established within the framework of the OSCE Permanent Council in Vienna, pursuant to the decision on the Mediterranean adopted at the Budapest Summit 1994;

11. Requests the Executive Secretary to report to the fifty-first session on the implementation of this decision.

62. ECE RESOLUTION ON COOPERATION IN THE FIELD OF ENVIRONMENT AND SUSTAINABLE DEVELOPMENT

Doc. no.: E/ECE(50)/L.8 11 April 1995

The Economic Commission for Europe,

Recalling its decision F (49) on cooperation in the field of environment and sustainable development,

Recognizing the need to ensure that policies in all sectors are consistent with sustainable development,

Stressing the necessity to consolidate such coordination and cooperation in order to make optimal use of existing resources and to avoid duplication of work, so as to be able to respond better to the needs of the countries in the region, particularly those in transition,

1. Stresses the need for all relevant Principal Subsidiary Bodies, taking into account their respective spheres of competence, to strengthen their activities in the field of environment and sustainable development, and takes note of the report of the Committee on Environmental Policy on problems and bottlenecks in the ECE activities in the field of the environment and sustainable development and endorses the recommendations by the Committee in that respect;

2. Takes note of the clarification provided by the secretariat of the resource implications of the draft UN/ECE Action Plan to implement Agenda 21 to the Committee on Environmental Policy at its last session;

3. Invites ECE member States and the EU to continue to support the further development of the "Environment for Europe" process and the preparations for the Ministerial Conference to be held in Sofia in October 1995, and requests the Executive Secretary to continue to support, within existing resources, the Working Group of Senior Governmental Officials in coordinating this work and the Bulgarian Government in its organizational work for the Conference;

4. Welcomes the initial progress made by the OECD, increasingly in cooperation with UN/ECE, in conducting pilot Country Environmental Performance Reviews in Central and Eastern Europe, looks forward to the results of the ECE's first such Performance Review, and requests that the Committee on Environmental Policy make a decision as soon as possible concerning both the development of an ECE programme of Country Environmental Performance Reviews and the provision of necessary resources for such a work programme;

5. Takes note of the work under way in the Preparatory Committee for the Regional Conference on Transport and the Environment to take place in 1996 under the auspices of the ECE;

6. Calls upon the Inland Transport Committee and the Committee on Environmental Policy to cooperate in the promotion of sustainable development in their respective work plans and in the preparation of the Regional Conference on Transport and the Environment;

7. Calls again upon all ECE member States and the European Union to consider, if they have not already done so, the earliest possible ratification of or accession to, as appropriate, the following ECE conventions:

- the Convention on Long-range Transboundary Air Pollution,
- the Convention on Environmental Impact Assessment in a Transboundary Context,
- the Convention on the Transboundary Effects of Industrial Accidents,
- the Convention on the Protection and Use of Transboundary Watercourses and International Lakes;

8. Further calls upon all ECE member States and the European Union to consider ratification of or accession to the NOx and VOC protocols and to consider signature, ratification of or accession to, as appropriate, the 2nd Sulphur Protocol under the Convention on Long-range Transboundary Air Pollution;

9. Invites the ECE member States, intergovernmental organizations, international financial institutions and other potential donors to consider the financial and technical needs of the countries in transition in implementing the provisions of the above-mentioned Conventions and Protocols;

10. Finally requests the Executive Secretary to report to its fifty-first session on the action he will have taken to implement this decision.

63. ECE DECISION ON COOPERATION IN THE FIELD OF TRANSPORT

Doc. no.: E/ECE(50)/L.9 11 April 1995

The Economic Commission for Europe,

Recalling its decisions O (45), F (48) and G (49),

Underlining the continued high priority it assigns to the transport sector of its work which represents an important contribution to the economic development and integration in the region,

Conscious of the continuing difficulties of countries in transition to expand market economy mechanisms in all fields of transport,

Considering that one of the prerequisites for such developments is the building and the improvement of an efficient, safe and sustainable network of transport infrastructures meeting accepted and further developed environmental standards,

Confirming the need to ensure close cooperation with the European Union and organizations dealing with transport questions with a view to developing Transport Policy Concepts while avoiding duplication of work and waste of resources,

Recognizing the continuing importance of the ECE in regional transport cooperation and with a view to assisting and supporting member States, especially countries in transition, in their endeavours further to enhance their transport policies and decisions,

1. Takes note of the report and the conclusions of the fifty-seventh session of the Inland Transport Committee;

2. Commends the secretariat for its contributions to the results of the second Pan-European Transport Conference (14-16 March 1994, Crete) and the recognition received in the final declaration of the Conference namely with regard to its tasks in the field of infrastructures, road safety, vehicle construction, transport of dangerous goods, combined transport;

3. Welcomes the course and first results of the second Road Safety Week in the ECE region (27 March-2 April 1995) and thanks member States, the secretariat, participating organizations and individuals for the support and engagement, thus maintaining its continued attention to the behaviour of young drivers;

4. Takes note of the Interim report of the Preparatory Committee for the 1996 Conference on Transport and Environment;

5. Supports the findings of the Preparatory Committee on the Draft Guidelines for a Common Strategy on Transport and the Environment and requests the Preparatory Committee to continue its endeavours to elaborate draft final documents for the Conference taking into account the options contained in the Interim Report;

6. Authorizes the bureau to call the Commission for a formal session before the end of 1995, to decide on the date and venue of the Conference in the second half of 1996;

7. Emphasizes the necessity of an urgent revision of the provisions of the Customs Convention on the International Transport of Goods under Cover of TIR Carnets to provide for stable long-term solutions in this field and also to reduce the risk of possible Customs fraud and smuggling;

8. Endorses the decision of the Inland Transport Committee to set up an International Working Group for the future drafting, jointly with the other organizations concerned, of a European Agreement concerning the international carriage of dangerous goods by Inland Waterways in order to achieve prescriptions for such transport on European Inland Waterways and to provide the necessary coherence with ADNR;

9. Invites member States and the European Union to sign the Convention on Customs Treatment of Pool Containers used in International Transport possibly until 14 April 1995;

10. Takes note of the increasing number of Contracting Parties to other ECE Agreements and Conventions and invites Governments which have not yet acceded to those, especially if they are not yet in force, to examine the possibilities for doing so;

11. Takes note with satisfaction of the completion of the first step of the revision of the 1958 Agreement concerning the adoption of uniform conditions of approval and reciprocal recognition of approval for motor vehicle equipment and parts and welcomes the introduction of a second stage in the revision process concerning additional modifications of the Agreement as a global instrument;

12. Urges the Inland Transport Committee to do its utmost to complete at its next sessions regulations for combined transport on inland waterways and possibly for coastal shipping;

13. Welcomes the decisions of the fifty-seventh session of the Inland Transport Committee aimed at intensifying assistance to countries in transition and invites those countries to submit to the Inland Transport Committee respective programme proposals and their assessment of priorities;

14. Takes note of further development of TEM and TER infrastructure projects and invites ECE Governments, the European Union and relevant non-governmental institutions to cooperate closely with the Commission and TEM and TER countries in the implementation of the objectives agreed upon with a view to taking them into account in the further development of European transport networks;

15. Requests the Executive Secretary, taking into account the increase in the work load of the Transport Division with regard to the international rules on the transport of dangerous goods, to assign, within existing resources but as soon as possible an additional professional to the division for the respective work;

16. Reiterates the necessity to maintain the number and level of the professional and other staff of the Transport Division and to fill vacant posts as soon as possible;

17. Calls upon the Executive Secretary to report to the Commission at its fifty-first session on the implementation of this decision.

UNITED NATIONS ENVIRONMENT PROGRAMME
(UNEP)

DOCUMENTS REPRODUCED IN WHOLE OR IN PART:

GOVERNING COUNCIL, 18th SESSION, NAIROBI, 15-26 MAY 1996

UN GENERAL ASSEMBLY

1. MEMORANDA OF UNDERSTANDING CONCERNING COOPERATION BETWEEN THE UNEP AND OTHER ORGANIZATIONS OF THE UNITED NATIONS SYSTEM*

Doc. no.: UNEP/GC.18/Inf.1 20 February 1995

1. In its decision 17/8 of 21 May 1993, the Governing Council, conscious of the need to reduce documentation submitted to it by the Executive Director, requested the Executive Director to discontinue the practice, followed pursuant to Council decision 82 (V) of 25 May 1977, of submitting to the Council detailed information on memoranda of understanding on joint programming between UNEP and other organizations in the United Nations system but to submit a summary list of all such memoranda to future sessions of the Council.

2. In accordance with that request, the Executive Director has the honour to circulate herewith a summary list of the memoranda of understanding concluded between UNEP and other United Nations organizations since the last report on the subject to the Governing Council (UNEP/GC.17/Inf.2).

3. As requested by the Council in paragraph 2 of its decision 17/8, the full text of the memoranda of understanding have been forwarded to Governments and to the Committee of Permanent Representatives for information and record purposes.

---

* UNEP/GC.18/1.

Annex

SUMMARY LIST OF MEMORANDA OF UNDERSTANDING BETWEEN UNEP AND OTHER ORGANIZATIONS OF THE UNITED NATIONS SYSTEM

Title (date of signature by UNEP)	Subject matter	Financial implications for UNEP	Date distributed to CPR and Governments
Memorandum of Understanding between UNEP and the United Nations Secretariat of a Convention on Desertification and the amendment thereto (18 May 1993 (amended on 7 September 1993 to include new activities))	Outlines principal activities to be carried out by UNEP and the Secretariat of the Intergovernmental Committee for a Convention to Combat Desertification in cooperation, i.e. development of case-studies in Africa; preparation of subregional case-studies on combating drought and desertification; and organization of the first session of the Intergovernmental Negotiating Committee for the elaboration of an international convention on desertification (INCD). Activities added by the amendment are organization of a workshop on the relationship between migration and desertification and assistance to NGOs from selected developing countries to participate in the second session of INCD.	$360,000	February 1995
Joint statement by James Gustave Speth, Administrator, United Nations Development Programme, and Elizabeth Dowdeswell, Executive Director, United Nations Environment Programme (May 1994)	Proposes increased collaboration between UNDP and UNEP to concentrate on, inter alia, the development of national frameworks for sustainable development; assistance to Governments in the implementation of Rio and post-Rio conventions; and the dissemination of environmental information. One important aspect of the cooperation is the building of working relations between the UNDP country offices and UNEP's regional offices. The ultimate aim is to have joint programmes in support of sustainable development in a wide range of areas.	Level of resources to be detailed in project documents	February 1995

Title (date of signature by UNEP)	Subject matter	Financial implications for UNEP	Date distributed to CPR and Governments
Memorandum of Understanding between the World Health Organization European Centre for Environment and Health and the United Nations Environment Programme Environmental Assessment Programme on the Development of a Joint WHO/UNEP Environment and Health Information Network in Countries of Central and Eastern Europe (20 October 1994)	Aims at long-term objectives including: strengthening of links between information networks at the national and regional levels; establishment of international links between national networks; enabling participating Governments to access data and information from international networks, establishment of a long-term practical working relationship between the WHO and UNEP environment and health information network programmes; and a unified approach for data-collection exchange and validation, which should also facilitate data comparability.	Level of resources for implementation of activities to be detailed in project documents	February 1995
Memorandum of Understanding concerning Establishment of the Inter-Organization Programme for the Sound Management of Chemicals (31 January 1995)*	Establishes the Inter-Organization Programme for the Sound Management of Chemicals. The areas for coordination are: international assessment of chemical risks; harmonization of classification and labelling of chemicals; information exchange on chemicals and chemical risks; establishment of risk reduction programmes; strengthening of national capabilities and capacities for management of chemicals; prevention of illegal international traffic in toxic and dangerous products; and other areas as agreed by all Participating Organizations.	Level of resources for implementation of activities to be detailed in project documents	February 1995
Memorandum of Understanding on World Bank, UNEP and UNDP Collaboration: Aral Sea Basin Program - Phase I (3 February 1995)	Aims at optimizing the effectiveness of World Bank, UNEP and UNDP assistance to the Aral Sea basin States so that they are able to introduce the essential policies and institutional reforms and develop effective strategies for addressing the Aral Sea crisis. The Phase I Program annexed to the Memorandum consists of seven programme categories, including capacity-building. Donor funding is being sought. A World Bank/UNEP/UNDP Steering Committee will be responsible for overall coordination of activities.	Level of resources for implementation of activities to be detailed in project documents	February 1995

-----

* The Memorandum is open for signature by UNEP, the International Labour Organization, the Food and Agriculture Organization of the United Nations, the World Health Organization, the United Nations Industrial Development Organization, and the Organisation for Economic Cooperation and Development. Other intergovernmental organizations may also join upon the unanimous consent of the foregoing organizations that have become parties.

2. IMPROVEMENT OF THE INTERNATIONAL RESPONSE TO ENVIRONMENTAL EMERGENCIES - REPORT OF THE UNEP EXECUTIVE DIRECTOR

Doc. no.: UNEP/GC.18/2 21 February 1995

Summary

The present report reviews the implementation of Governing Council decision 17/26, which called for the development of a mechanism to improve the United Nations capacity to respond to environmental emergencies. UNEP and the United Nations Department of Humanitarian Affairs established the Joint UNEP/DHA Environment Unit following recommendations of a UNEP Governmental Advisory Meeting. The Joint Unit is facilitating the provision of international assistance, it is staffed by UNEP and is fully integrated into the existing response mechanism of the DHA Relief Coordination Branch, which has the mandate to respond to emergencies. This is a practical project which provides an independent backstop for countries facing environmental emergencies.

Suggested action by the Governing Council

The Governing Council may wish to:

1. Take note of the present report;

2. Express its satisfaction with and endorse constructive collaboration between UNEP and DHA in enhancing the ability of the United Nations to assist countries affected by environmental emergencies;

3. Welcome the establishment of the Joint UNEP/DHA Environment Unit;

4. Express its appreciation to DHA for providing the Joint Unit with emergency facilities and office space;

5. Note that the Joint Unit is rendering services in full accordance with recommendations of the UNEP Governmental Advisory Meeting, when international assistance is not otherwise provided within the framework of relevant existing conventions;

6. Welcome the establishment of the Advisory Group on Environmental Emergencies, and endorse its terms of reference;

7. Request the Joint Unit to further develop its activities and services in accordance with recommendations of the Advisory Group on Environmental Emergencies;

---

* UNEP/GC.18/1.

8. Invite Governments and relevant UN agencies, bodies and programmes to cooperate with the Joint Unit in its efforts to provide independent and unbiased assistance to countries facing environmental emergencies;

9. Request the Executive Director to allocate the necessary resources for the implementation of activities of the Joint Unit;

10. Further request the Executive Director to submit to the Governing Council at its nineteenth session a progress report on the implementation of the present decision.

I. INTRODUCTION

1. In accordance with Governing Council decision 17/26 of 21 May 1993, extensive work has been undertaken to assess the needs of developing countries in terms of response to emergencies that affect or threaten the environment, and to examine current international response mechanisms. Gaps in the existing system has been identified and proposals made to rectify the situation. Extensive consultations with Governments identified the most appropriate needs. These include the need to utilize in the most efficient manner existing facilities and resources, the need to facilitate quick direct links between affected countries and potential providers of assistance and the need for rapid initial assessment in cases of accident. Countries indicated a preference for a simple mechanism in the United Nations to expedite the delivery of such assistance, including a single entry point to the system.

2. As requested by the Governing Council, a Governmental Advisory Meeting was convened by UNEP in November 1993. It adopted a set of proposals concerning the enhancement of the international response capacity to augment the existing international response system.

3. Taking into account these recommendations, as well as consultations with countries and United Nations bodies, UNEP and the Department of Humanitarian Affairs (DHA) decided to simplify to the maximum extent possible the administrative and technical arrangements that would permit the delivery of an environmental emergency service to the international community. It was jointly recommended by the two bodies that core activities and services should be funded and provided by UNEP through the existing organizational framework of the Relief Coordination Branch of DHA.

4. Under these arrangements, UNEP retains substantive responsibility for the work to be done and functions in an effective operational association with DHA. In accordance with this joint recommendation, a small Joint UNEP/DHA Environment Unit ("the Joint Unit") was established in DHA as of 1 July 1994, to deal with environmental aspects of emergencies. The Human Health and Welfare Unit was appointed focal point for the Joint Unit within UNEP headquarters.

5. At its 45th meeting, the Committee of Permanent Representatives to UNEP at its 45th meeting, considered the report of the Executive Director on the Joint Unit, endorsed the joint recommendation of UNEP and DHA, and requested the Executive Director to implement it for an initial period of 12 months and refer the question back to the Governing Council at its eighteenth session.

II. ACTIVITIES AND SERVICES PROVIDED BY THE JOINT UNEP/DHA ENVIRONMENT UNIT

6. Taking into account rapid industrial development in different regions, it is understood that major beneficiaries of the implementation of this project are Governments of developing countries and countries with economies in transition, competent national organizations, industrial associations, as well as relevant United Nations agencies and international organizations.

7. The objective of this joint project is to deliver an environmental emergency service to Governments upon request. In full accordance with the recommendations of the UNEP Governmental Advisory Meeting, it aims to improve mobilization and coordination of the international response to environmental emergencies, by developing and implementing practical brokerage functions, and establishing an efficient information clearing-house. Other assistance tools include the provision of independent and quick initial and post-emergency assessment, utilizing resources of donating countries and partners. Since its establishment, as well as in the preceding experimental stage, the Joint Unit has assisted a number of countries in responding to a variety of environmental emergencies by using its tools and capabilities.

8. The Joint Unit is not a substitute for existing arrangements between countries but, rather, acts as a "safety net" being the "last resort" for affected countries that do not know immediately to whom to turn to in case of environmental emergencies.

9. The Unit recognizes the existence of specific international conventions of relevant organizations the International Atomic Energy Agency (IAEA), the International Maritime Organization (IMO) and others as having mechanisms for responding to emergencies in their areas of competence. There is no duplication between the activities of the Joint Unit and these bodies and conventions. Appropriate cooperation is being ensured between the Unit, other UNEP activities (including the work of the Awareness and Preparedness for Emergencies at the Local Level (APELL) programme of the Industry and Environment Programme Activity Centre; the Secretariat of the Basel Convention on the Control of Transboundary Movements of Hazardous Wastes and their Disposal; the International Register of Potentially Toxic Chemicals (IRPTC); and the International Programme on Chemical Safety (IPCS), the UNCHS (Habitat)/UNEP Task Force on the Continuum from Relief to Development, and relevant international bodies including IAEA and IMO.

10. Among major outputs in the implementation of this project will be a global network of national focal points, a roster of national capabilities as a part of the DHA Central Register of Disaster Management Capacities, a contingency plan for environmental emergencies, and a long-term strategy for the delivery of environmental emergency service to the international community.

11. In accordance with recommendations of the 1993 UNEP Governmental Advisory Meeting, an Advisory Group on Environmental Emergencies, drawn from the national focal points, has been set up jointly by UNEP and DHA to review the Unit's work and provide advice and guidance on its future activities. The draft terms of reference of the Advisory Group are annexed to the present report.

12. At its first meeting, in January 1995, the Advisory Group was informed about practical cases where the Joint Unit has assisted countries since its establishment in July 1994. In particular it was briefed on a major mission of a multinational team, organized under the auspices of DHA and UNEP, which assisted Russian authorities in assessing the consequences of a recent oil spill in the Komi Republic of the Russian Federation. The Advisory Group concluded that this mission was a good example of quick, independent and professional assessment, which highlighted the role of the United Nations in providing a backup to existing bilateral arrangements. The Group agreed that the mission demonstrated the ability of the Joint Unit to provide an unbiased assessment of environmental emergencies with a global perspective, and recognized that this approach is a valuable additional tool for the Joint Unit to use when appropriate.

13. The meeting of the Advisory Group was very positive and constructive, with the countries in full agreement as to how to improve the international capacity to respond to environmental aspects of emergencies through the Joint UNEP/DHA Environment Unit.

14. A periodic review of the implementation of the work programme and of the services provided will be carried out jointly by UNEP and DHA, with reports on the activities under this project to be submitted to their respective governing bodies, as well as to the Advisory Group on Environmental Emergencies.

Annex

DRAFT TERMS OF REFERENCE OF THE ADVISORY GROUP ON ENVIRONMENTAL EMERGENCIES

The Advisory Group on Environmental Emergencies (AGEE), established jointly by UNEP and DHA, shall:

1. Provide a forum for an exchange of views and experience, among countries, on questions related to the provision of international assistance for environmental emergencies;

2. Promote further development of international cooperation in the field of response to environmental emergencies, with special attention to specific problems in developing countries;

3. Identify and examine selected problems with regard to the provision of international assistance for environmental emergencies, which are of major concern to countries, with the aim to prepare appropriate suggestions and recommendations on possible actions at the international level;

4. Review the work of the Joint UNEP/DHA Environment Unit, and provide advice on its future activities;

5. Accept the following general provisions:

(a) Recommendations of the AGEE shall be submitted by the Joint UNEP/DHA Environment Unit to the respective heads of UNEP and DHA, for appropriate actions;

(b) The AGEE shall consist of representatives of designated national focal points; it shall be open-ended and kept as small as practicable;

(c) Individual experts and representatives of relevant international organizations may be invited to take part in meetings of the AGEE, as required;

(d) The AGEE shall meet as necessary, initially once a year;

(e) The Joint UNEP/DHA Environment Unit shall provide the secretariat to the AGEE.

-----

3. PROPOSAL FOR A FUTURE STRATEGY DOCUMENT IN THE FIELD OF THE ENVIRONMENT AS A SUCCESSOR TO THE SYSTEM-WIDE MEDIUM-TERM ENVIRONMENT PROGRAMME (SWMTEP) - REPORT OF THE UNEP EXECUTIVE DIRECTOR

Doc. no.: UNEP/GC.18/36 21 March 1995

Summary

The present document is submitted pursuant to Governing Council decision 17/16 of May 1995, on the implementation and mid-term review of the United Nations system-wide medium-term environment programme (SWMTEP) for 1995, in which the Executive Director was requested to report on the need for a United Nations system-wide strategy and planning document in the field of the environment. In consultation with the relevant United Nations organizations, the Executive Director has undertaken an assessment of the continuing need for an environmental strategy and planning document in the field of the environment on the basis of, *inter alia*, the experience gained in the implementation of SWMTEP, the emerging post United Nations Conference on Environment and Development (UNCED) institutional arrangements and the continuing need for system-wide environment coordination and consultations with executive heads, as outlined in a letter with proposals concerning the future discharge of the coordination mandate of UNEP and, specifically, the need for such a document. Proposals for a strategy and planning document were further provided for the consideration of United Nations partner organizations in a background paper (IAEG/1/2) at the first Inter-Agency Environment Coordination Group (IAEG) meeting, held from 31 October to 1 November 1994 in Geneva. On the basis of the discussions and conclusions reached at that meeting and considerations regarding the working role and responsibilities of UNEP and the Commission on Sustainable Development (CSD), the present report proposes the preparation of a *strategy* document, focusing on the major environmental challenges as contained in the proposed UNEP Fund programme, to be submitted to the Governing Council in 1997.

Suggested action by the Governing Council

The Governing Council may wish to:

(a) Take note of the report of the Executive Director concerning the need for a United Nations system-wide *strategy* document in the field of environment;

(b) Endorse the assessment of the Executive Director that there is a need for a *strategy* document and recommend that such a document be prepared as a mechanism to enable UNEP to discharge its policy guidance and coordination mandate;

(c) Endorse the recommendation that the strategy document should focus on the major environmental challenges as contained in the programme for the utilization of the resources of the Environment Fund for 1996-1997 (UNEP/GC.18/9);

(d) Stress that, in preparing the strategy, full account be taken of the role, responsibilities and work of the task managers system established for the servicing of CSD;

(e) Request the Executive Director to submit to the Governing Council at its regular session in 1997 the draft strategy document, to become operational in 1998, concurrently with the United Nations Medium-term Plan (UNMTP) for 1998-2003.

Background

1. The first system-wide medium-term environment programme (SWMTEP), as originally conceived, was a formalization of bilateral, multilateral and thematic joint programming initiated by UNEP in its early years and was endorsed by the Governing Council at its sixth session in 1978. The 1979 Administrative Committee on Coordination (ACC) report to the Governing Council focused on thematic joint programming exercises between UNEP and other United Nations agencies, and expressed the willingness of ACC to extend full cooperation in the SWMTEP endeavour and in the development of the requisite methodology during the experimental phase between 1978 and 1982. In 1979, at its nineteenth session, the Committee for Programme and Coordination (CPC) reviewed the system of United Nations medium-term planning and made several recommendations to the Economic and Social Council and the General Assembly, including that thematic joint programming should be developed into an effective programming instrument for the medium-term programme and that SWMTEP should be developed as a management tool for all organizations. The 1986 ACC report noted that SWMTEP-I was the only system-wide effort which had proved to be of great value in the planning and implementation of environmental activities. Moreover, it had offered fresh forms of dialogue and cooperation. ACC also observed that the entire United Nations system had cooperated on the development of a methodology for SWMTEP. The Governing Council subsequently invited ACC to review and further develop this methodology through the Designated Officials for Environmental Matters (DOEM).

2. SWMTEP-II covers the period 1990-1995, but has experienced difficulties in its implementation due, inter alia, to the different mandates, governance and programming cycles of the various United Nations organizations, developments in relation to the UNCED process which supersedes SWMTEP and problems in preparation and implementation. This was evidenced by the fact that SWMTEP was provided to only one governing body, apart from the UNEP Governing Council, and then only for information. As such SWMTEP-II never achieved the status of a programming document for the United Nations system in the field of environment.

3. The Governing Council at its seventeenth session had before it a report on the implementation and mid-term review of SWMTEP-II (UNEP/GC.17/6), as requested in Governing Council decision 15/21. Based on the mid-term review, which took into account self-evaluations undertaken by United Nations agencies, the Executive Director concluded that, although SWMTEP had been a useful vehicle for UNEP in environment coordination, for a number of reasons it had not served its original purpose as an instrument for planning and formulating the environment programme of the United Nations system. The Executive Director therefore recommended, inter alia, that the Governing Council should defer the decision on the future of SWMTEP, and that she would evaluate whether there was still a need for a system-wide strategy and planning document and report thereon to the Council at its eighteenth session. If it is concluded that there is a need for such a document, it would commence in 1998 to be compatible with the planning cycle of UNMTP for 1998-2003, and would take into account the lessons learned in the preparation and implementation of the current SWMTEP. In making these recommendations, the Executive Director noted that the future arrangements for system-wide coordination in the field of the environment would be of critical importance, and that a strategy and planning document would have to be compatible with and complementary to the post-UNCED institutional arrangements, especially the work of the Inter-Agency Committee on Sustainable Development (IACSD) and CSD with its multi-year thematic programme of work.

4. A background paper containing UNEP proposals for a strategy and planning document in the field of environment as a successor to SWMTEP was prepared for the consideration of the members of the IAEG, in which it was emphasized that, in view of the policy guidance and coordination mandate of UNEP, as reaffirmed in Agenda 21, and the rationale for the establishment of the IAEG, it is the assessment of the Executive Director that a strategy and planning document would provide clarity and direction to system-wide environment activities.

Furthermore, in conceptualizing the nature of such a document, the substantive priority areas for UNEP leadership, as recommended by Agenda 21, chapter 38.22, would form its core.

5. The strategy and planning document would be expected to draw on the technical and intellectual capacity of concerned United Nations organizations to develop a system-wide understanding of the evolution and strategic thrust of identified programme areas over the medium-term, which would accord with the policy guidance mandate of the UNEP Governing Council. It could also be foreseen that the parameters of the document could be defined to include areas in addition to those that have been allocated to UNEP in Agenda 21, chapter 38.22. This would enlarge the scope of the strategy to include the areas of toxic chemicals, hazardous wastes, desertification, biodiversity and, in association with the United Nations Centre for Human Settlements (Habitat), solid wastes and human settlements, in which UNEP has been designated as task manager for CSD in the United Nations system. Criteria could also be established to include additional programme areas in relation to the UNEP programme of work for 1996-1997.

6. The UNEP proposal further emphasized that it was clear from the experience of SWMTEP that a detailed and time-consuming programming exercise would be inefficient and even counter-productive. A strategy document should be perceived as providing a generally agreed policy guidance and frame of reference for individual actions or joint programming that would be influenced by the best substantive expertise available in the system. It should provide a clear picture of the relevant competence available in the system and a clear indication to the international community of the collective thrust of system-wide environmental activities.

7. The UNEP proposal noted that a strategy and planning document would also have implications with regard to the Environment Fund, which is mandated to finance wholly or partly the costs of the new environmental initiatives undertaken within the United Nations system, with the Governing Council being charged with reviewing these initiatives with a view to taking appropriate decisions as to their continued financing.

8. In terms of timing and programming cycles, the UNEP proposal also noted that the Governing Council endorsed the recommendation of the Executive Director that a strategy document, if agreed, should commence in 1998-2003, to be compatible with the planning cycle of UNMTP. An additional benefit of this timing would be that it could be brought in line with the review of the implementation of Agenda 21 and the functioning of CSD by the General Assembly in 1997. The preparatory process for the document would also greatly influence the development of the 1998-1999 UNEP biennial programme of work, which would have to be in line with the thrust of the document.

<u>System-wide views on the need for a strategy and planning document in the field of the environment, as expressed at the first IAEG meeting</u>

9. Discussion at the IAEG meeting revealed a general consensus on the value of a <u>strategic</u> as opposed to a planning document, which would help to ensure complementarity within the United Nations system, and that it should not be a SWMTEP type of document. It was noted that, even if the document were synchronized with UNMTP, it would still not be in accordance with many of the programming cycles of United Nations organizations. However, if the document were based on strategic joint goals, rather than plans which could not foresee developments in the environment field, the flexibility would make it easier to cope with the lack of synchronization. Certain IAEG members felt that it could be difficult to explain to their governing bodies, which have different mandates and priorities, the efficacy of a planning document. At the same time, they acknowledged that it would be useful to demonstrate to governing bodies how their environmental strategies fit into a system-wide approach, which would assist in justifying environmental proposals as collective views of the system, as well as serving as a day-to-day management tool.

10. Suggestions on how to develop such a document included examining the strategic elements in UNEP's biennial work programme to identify commonalities as a basis for a strategic document. It was suggested that UNEP initially collect and compile the strategies developed and approved by individual agencies in response to UNCED and other relevant material and distil from them environmental trends, synthesize and analyse interlinkages, gaps and mutually supportive goals, and determine their complementarity as a basis for further documentation. However, members cautioned that the documents collected would

be disparate in nature and noted that the term "strategy" would have to be used consistently. It was requested that, in the context of the discussion, all relevant documentation be made available to UNEP.

11. While it was noted that the Governing Council required an indication of the conceptual need for such a document and that the draft strategy would be required by 1998, it was suggested that the strategic document should be short; deal with policy and funding implications of strategies; and address, if relevant, the strategic use of the Environment Fund and the steps that would be necessary from strategy to programming. It was pointed out that strategies at the global level are often not filtering down to the country level and further work would be required on the translation of global strategies to national implementation, where relevant. It was also suggested that the document could be proactive in integrating strategic environmental relationships with United Nations conferences and conventions.

Recommendations

12. In light of the system-wide views expressed, the Governing Council may wish to decide that SWMTEP should be succeeded by a system-wide strategy document, as a common frame of reference for future work and programming of the system in the field of the environment.

13. In considering this decision, the Governing Council may take into account the fact that the mandates of the Council and the Executive Director in the field of policy guidance and coordination of the environmental activities of the United Nations system show signs of overlap with the mandates and evolving practice of CSD and IACSD, respectively, to provide for policy guidance and, through the system of task managers, coordinate the activities of the system in the field of sustainable development.

14. The Governing Council may further take into account that, partly as a consequence of the above, the Executive Director proposes to adopt a focused issue-oriented Fund programme, concentrating on major challenges in the field of the environment and taking into account the priority tasks assigned to UNEP by Agenda 21. Rather than financially supporting the activities of other parts of the United Nations system, the resources of the UNEP Fund will be used to implement and seek partnership in implementing this proposed UNEP programme of activities. In discharging her mandate to coordinate the environmental activities of the United Nations system, keep them under review and assess their effectiveness, the Executive Director will focus on UNEP's role as task manager in the implementation of Agenda 21, so as to avoid duplication of efforts.

15. Promoting and coordinating the preparation of a longer-term strategy in the field of the environment should be seen and pursued against the background of the changing role and responsibilities of UNEP and its relationship with CSD. It would follow that the strategy would principally focus on the major challenges as contained in the proposed UNEP Fund programme and that in its preparation full account would be taken of the role, responsibilities and work of the task managers, with a view to avoiding duplication of efforts and making strategy compatible with and, preferably, part of the proposals, based on the review and appraisal of Agenda 21, to be submitted to the review conference in 1997.

16. The strategy document should be presented to the Governing Council at its regular session in 1997 and would commence in 1998, to be compatible with UNMTP 1998-2003.

-----

4. PROPOSAL FOR A FUTURE STRATEGY DOCUMENT IN THE FIELD OF THE ENVIRONMENT AS A SUCCESSOR TO THE SYSTEM-WIDE MEDIUM-TERM ENVIRONMENT PROGRAMME (SWMTEP): ADDENDUM ON INTER-AGENCY ENVIRONMENT COORDINATION GROUP (IAEG) - REPORT OF THE UNEP EXECUTIVE DIRECTOR

Doc. no.: UNEP/GC.18/36/Add.1 21 March 1995

Summary

The present report outlines developments relating to the establishment of the Inter-Agency Environment Coordination Group (IAEG), pursuant to Governing Council decision 17/9, which endorsed the course of action proposed to the Governing Council at its seventeenth session by the Executive Director in document UNEP/GC.17/12/Add.1, "to enable the Executive Director to discharge effectively the coordinating role required of UNEP by various legislative authorities". Following United Nations system-wide consultations and in order to take fully into account the working of the post-United Nations Conference on Environment and Development (UNCED) arrangements at the intergovernmental and inter-agency levels, the Executive Director in August 1994 informed executive heads of United Nations agencies and organizations of her proposals concerning the future discharge of UNEP's coordination mandate. Executive heads were informed that, subject to their concurrence and as mandated by the Governing Council, she would be convening a meeting of the IAEG in the third quarter of 1994. Subsequently, the Executive Director chaired the first IAEG meeting in Geneva from 31 October to 1 November 1994. The IAEG had before it for its consideration background documents containing, *inter alia*, a proposal for the role and functioning of the IAEG. The present document outlines developments relating to the establishment of the IAEG and its role and functioning and summarizes the views of UNEP's partners as expressed at the first IAEG meeting

Suggested action by the Governing Council

The Governing Council may wish to:

(a) Take note of the report of the Executive Director on the Inter-Agency Environment Coordination Group (IAEG);

(b) Support the establishment of the IAEG as a flexible consultative and advisory body, meeting as and when required, to enable UNEP to discharge effectively its coordination mandate;

(c) Decide that the IAEG should focus on assisting the Executive Director in coordinating the activities of the United Nations system in addressing the major challenges, as contained in the programme for the utilization of the resources of the Environment Fund;

(d) Stress that, in determining the terms of reference and future activities of the IAEG, full account be taken of the role, responsibilities and work of the Inter-agency Committee on Sustainable Development (IACSD) and its task - managing system, with a view to avoiding duplication of efforts and making the coordinating role and work of UNEP compatible with and complementary to that of IACSD;

(e) Encourage the further clarification of the IAEG's terms of reference, especially with reference to the role and functioning of IACSD;

(f) Request the Executive Director to report to the Governing Council at its regular session in 1997 on progress made in the work of the IAEG.

Inter-agency Environment Coordination Group (IAEG)

1. With the establishment of the institutional arrangements following the United Nations Conference on Environment and Development (UNCED) UNEP undertook a review and refocusing of its functional coordination role. The resulting proposals for "Arrangements for system-wide cooperation and coordination in the field of the environment" (UNEP/GC.17/12/Add.1), submitted to the Governing Council at its seventeenth session, were made in the context of the reform of the Administrative Committee on Coordination (ACC) subsidiary structure and the report of the ACC Task Force on the UNCED follow-up that led to the establishment of the Inter-agency Committee on Sustainable Development (IACSD). The Task Force, *inter alia*, recommended that "the ACC invite the Executive Director of UNEP to submit specific proposal on system-wide cooperation and coordination in the field of the environment". The Executive Director proposed, *inter alia*, the establishment of the IAEG to meet when required to address policy issues, emerging issues in the field of environment and any issues of a system-wide nature emanating from coordination at the programme level that require to be addressed at the policy level.

2. The background document provided to IAEG members contained a proposal on the role and functioning of the IAEG and outlined the background to and rationale for the IAEG, in view of UNEP's reaffirmed policy guidance and coordination mandate, as provided in Agenda 21, chapter 38.21, and of the assessment that there was a continuing need for UNEP, in collaboration with partners in the United Nations system, to have an effective forum to coordinate approaches to policy matters in the field of the environment, especially the 14 priority areas for UNEP leadership outlined in Agenda 21, chapter 38.22. The proposal took into account the mandate and work of IACSD and contained an assessment of IACSD's capacity to deal with policy issues and emerging issues in the field of the environment. The following terms of reference for the IAEG's functioning were proposed:

(a) Advise the Executive Director of UNEP, in preparing reports for the Governing Council of UNEP, on the discharge of its system-wide policy guidance role, informing the Council of environmental trends and emerging policy issues;

(b) Assist the Executive Director of UNEP in the selection of topics and the substantive preparation of the ACC report to the UNEP Governing Council, for which she is responsible to the ACC;

(c) Provide a forum for the exchange of information on important new initiatives in the field of the environment and, in particular, those that may be of relevance to the programmes and mandates of UNEP and other member institutions;

(d) Provide a forum for the discussion of the policy implications of new and emerging environmental issues that would require a coordinated response by the United Nations system;

(e) Provide a forum for discussion and play an advisory role for the Executive Director of UNEP concerning the development of a system-wide policy and strategy in the field of the environment and assist in the preparation of relevant reports to the Governing Council of UNEP. This would include the follow-up to UNEP Governing Council decisions on the System-wide Medium-term Environment Programme (SWMTEP);

(f) Assist the Executive Director of UNEP in the development of biennial programmes of work for submission to the Governing Council, including the review of the impact of UNEP's work and funding on the activities of the United Nations system.

3. A new IAEG would thus have to reflect a refocusing of UNEP's functional coordination arrangements and be designed as a flexible mechanism, meeting when required, to complement and reinforce more regular coordination activities at the programme manager level. Therefore, the following criteria were proposed to guide the IAEG's functioning and enhance and maintain its relevance and utility: cost effectiveness; flexibility; value-added; complementarity;

and partnership. The first meeting of the IAEG (Geneva, 31 October - 1 November 1994) was attended by 14 concerned United Nations organizations and addressed the role and functioning of the IAEG; proposals for a future strategy and planning document in the field of the environment as a successor document to SWMTEP; the ACC report to the UNEP Governing Council; and the preparation for the 1996-1997 UNEP programme and the role of United Nations agencies and programmes therein.

4. The IAEG meeting revealed a general consensus on the potential usefulness of a flexible coordinating mechanism on environmental matters. An IAEG should form coherent positions and facilitate UNEP's catalytic and coordinating role, supplementing the coordination responsibility of UNEP programme managers at the programme level and it should, as a precondition, have distinct terms of reference which would ensure complementarity with the work and mandate of IACSD, in order to avoid duplication of effort. Such terms of reference should, therefore, initially focus explicitly on the areas of Agenda 21 designated for UNEP's leadership, which all contain significant areas for collaboration with other United Nations organizations. It was emphasized that IAEG is not an ACC subsidiary, but a consultative and advisory body, and that a functional relationship to IACSD should be established.

5. The IAEG was also viewed as an advisory body to UNEP's Executive Director, to indicate gaps and assess the effectiveness of UNEP's catalytic and coordinating role in the United Nations system and to provide access for members to UNEP's Executive Director. It was emphasized that the IAEG should be a true partnership, which should be reflected in concrete outputs. There was a general feeling that IAEG should initially operate and meet on an ad hoc basis, evolving with experience to distinguish it from IACSD and stressing the value of an informal and flexible forum, without strict institutional requirements. Hence, the agenda should be agreed on an ad hoc basis, with the meeting based on well-prepared documentation with clear points for decision. Others felt that, while a highly institutionalized body should be avoided, certain issues were of a recurrent nature and proposals for IAEG's functions should not be too broad. The proposed criteria to guide IAEG were generally agreeable.

6. The IAEG would also facilitate the flow of information on ongoing and proposed environmental programmes and the related needs of UNEP and partner organizations as a two-way communication process. UNEP could offer guidance to partner organizations in certain areas and, in turn, would be provided with feedback on new environmental thinking within United Nations organizations. Discussions on UNEP's programming were considered particularly important, in order to provide information on how UNEP views its evolving role and to define the dialogue on joint programming. The IAEG would also be used to decide collectively on topics for future ACC reports to the UNEP Governing Council, reflecting what executive heads wish to bring to Governing Council's attention. In future, the IAEG would consider how to improve coordination at the regional and country levels and possibly coordinate environmental inputs into United Nations conferences where necessary.

Recommendations

7. The system-wide views expressed at the meeting of the IAEG reveal that there may be a case for establishing an IAEG, meeting as and when required and with terms of reference which would ensure complementarity with the work and mandate of IACSD.

8. It follows that, in considering the matter, the Governing Council should take into account the fact that the mandates of the Council and of the Executive Director of UNEP in the field of policy guidance and coordination of the environmental activities of the United Nations system show signs of overlap with the mandate and evolving practice of the Commission on Sustainable Development (CSD) and IACSD, respectively, to provide for policy guidance and, through the system of task managers, coordinate the activities of the United Nations system in the field of sustainable development.

9. The Governing Council may further take into account that, partly as a consequence of the above, the Executive Director proposes that the Council adopt a focused issue-oriented Fund programme, concentrating on major challenges in the field of the environment and taking into account the priority tasks assigned to UNEP by Agenda 21. Rather than financially supporting activities of other parts of the United Nations system, the resources of the UNEP Fund will be used to implement and seek partnership in implementing the proposed UNEP programme of activities. In discharging her mandate to coordinate the environmental

activities of the United Nations system, keep them under review and assess their effectiveness, the Executive Director will focus on UNEP's role as task manager in the implementation of Agenda 21, so as to avoid duplication of efforts.

10. Coordination of the environmental activities of the United Nations system should be seen and pursued against the background of the changing role and responsibilities of UNEP and its relationship with CSD. It would follow that, in discharging her coordination mandate, the Executive Director would principally focus on the major challenges contained in the proposed UNEP Fund programme, while taking full account of the role, responsibilities and work of IACSD and its task manager system with a view to avoiding duplication of efforts and making the coordinating role and work of UNEP serve both the interests of UNEP and those of CSD and IACSD.

11. Against this background, UNEP should:

(a) Continue to clarify the IAEG's functional linkages and legal relationship to IACSD. On the basis of this clarification and opinions voiced at the first IAEG meeting, UNEP should draw up revised terms of reference for the IAEG, to be submitted to the IAEG members for their approval;

(b) Coordination and consultation at the programmatic level should be primarily the responsibility of programme managers and would be complemented by the work of the IAEG at the policy level;

(c) The IAEG should play a key role in assisting the Executive Director in preparing for the ACC's consideration of environmental matters and for the Governing Council's consideration of matters relating to system-wide environment coordination;

(d) The IAEG would function as a flexible mechanism, meeting as required.

-----

5. REPORT OF THE GOVERNING COUNCIL OF THE UNITED NATIONS ENVIRONMENT PROGRAMME* ** (18TH SESSION, NAIROBI, 15-26 MAY 1995)

Doc. no.: A/50/25 20 June 1995

CONTENTS

---

* The present document is a mimeographed version of the report of the Governing Council of the United Nation Environment Programme on its eighteenth session. The final report will be issued subsequently as *Official Records of the General Assembly, Fiftieth Session, Supplement No. 25* (A/50/25).

** The full proceedings of the Council on the work of its eighteenth session, containing, *inter alia,* chapters on the discussions in plenary meetings and the reports of the sessional committees, is being circulated to Governments under the symbol UNEP/GC.18/40.

I. INTRODUCTION

1. The eighteenth session of the Governing Council of the United Nations Environment Programme (UNEP) was held at UNEP headquarters, Nairobi, from 15 to 26 May 1995. The Council adopted the present report at the 10th meeting of the session, on 26 May 1995.

II. ORGANIZATION OF THE SESSION

A. Opening of the session

2. The eighteenth session of the UNEP Governing Council was opened on 15 May 1995 by Dr. E.O.A. Aina (Nigeria), President of the Council at its seventeenth session. Reviewing the work carried out since the seventeenth session, he said that efforts had been made to strengthen UNEP, enhance its programmes and obtain more funding commitments and pledges to contribute to the Environment Fund. Two major environmental conventions had come into force and the instrument for the restructured Global Environment Facility (GEF) had been adopted. However, there had yet to be significant progress in implementing Agenda 21 and budget reductions within the United Nations threatened to jeopardize vital UNEP programmes and the environmental activities of many developing countries.

3. At the opening meeting of the session, the Council heard a statement by the Executive Director of UNEP. The statement was subsequently circulated under the symbol UNEP/GC.18/34/Add.1.

4. At the same meeting, the Council also heard a statement by Mr. W. N'Dow, Assistant Secretary-General of the United Nations Centre for Human Settlements (UNCHS) (Habitat), delivered on his behalf by Mr. M. Hildebrand, Director of Programme Coordination, UNCHS (Habitat), who said that his organization's cooperation with UNEP had made considerable progress, particularly in the context of the Sustainable Cities Programme. While the two organizations had

different mandates, there was a solid basis for complementarity and synergy. That was of particular importance in the preparations for the Habitat II Conference, to be held at Istanbul in June 1996.

5. The representative of Kenya welcomed the participants to Nairobi.

B. Attendance

6. The following 52 States members of the Governing Council[1] were represented at the session:

Argentina
Australia
Bangladesh
Bhutan
Botswana
Brazil
Bulgaria
Burundi
Canada
Chile
China
Colombia
Congo
Costa Rica
Côte d'ivoire
Democratic People's Republic of Korea
Denmark
France
Gambia
Germany
India
Indonesia
Iran (islamic republic of)
Italy
Japan
Kenya
Malaysia
Mexico
Netherlands
Nicaragua
Nigeria
Pakistan
Poland
Portugal
Republic of Korea
Romania
Russian Federation
Rwanda
Senegal
Slovak Republic
Spain
Sri Lanka
Sudan
Sweden
Switzerland
Syrian Arab Republic
United Kingdom of Great Britain and Northern Ireland
United States of America
Venezuela
Zaire
Zambia
Zimbabwe

7. The following States not members of the Governing Council but Members of the United Nations or members of a specialized agency or of the International Atomic Energy Agency were represented by observers:

Algeria
Angola
Austria
Belgium
Benin
Burkina Faso
Comoros
Cuba
Cyprus
Czech Republic
Ecuador
Egypt
Eritrea
Ethiopia
Finland
Ghana
Greece
Grenada
Guinea
Holy See
Iceland
Iraq
Israel
Kazakhstan
Kuwait
Lebanon
Lesotho
Malawi
Mauritius
Morocco
Mozambique
New Zealand
Norway
Oman
Paraguay
Peru
Philippines
Saudi Arabia

Seychelles
South Africa
Suriname
Swaziland
Thailand
Tunisia
Turkey
Uganda
United Republic of Tanzania
Viet Nam
Yemen

8. The following United Nations bodies and Secretariat units were represented:

Department of Humanitarian Affairs
Department for Policy Coordination and Sustainable Development (UNDPCSD)
Economic Commission for Africa (ECA)
United Nations Centre for Human Settlements (Habitat)
United Nations Children's Fund (UNICEF)
United Nations Development Programme (UNDP)
United Nations Institute for Training and Research (UNITAR)
United Nations Sudano-Sahelian Office (UNSO)
International Programme on Chemical Safety (IPCS)
Intergovernmental Panel on Climate Change (IPCC)
Interim Secretariat of the Convention to Combat Desertification
Secretariat of the United Nations Framework Convention on Climate Change (UNFCC)
Secretariat of the Convention on International Trade in Endangered Species of Wild Fauna and Flora (CITES)
Multilateral Fund for the Implementation of the Montreal Protocol

9. The Commission on Sustainable Development and the Intergovernmental Negotiating Committee for a Convention to Combat Desertification (INC/CCD) were also represented.

10. The following specialized agencies were represented:

Food and Agriculture Organization of the United Nations (FAO)
International Civil Aviation Organization (ICAO)
United Nations Educational, Scientific and Cultural Organization (UNESCO)
United Nations Industrial Development Organization (UNIDO)
Universal Postal Union (UPU)
World Health Organization (WHO)
World Meteorological Organization (WMO)

The International Atomic Energy Agency (IAEA) was also represented.

11. The following other intergovernmental organizations were represented:

Asian Development Bank (ADB)
European Community
Commonwealth Secretariat
Intergovernmental Authority on Drought and Development (IGADD)
Intergovernmental Oceanographic Commission (IOC)
Inter-State Ecological Council (IEC)
League of Arab States
Organization of African Unity (OAU)
Organisation for Economic Cooperation and Development (OECD)
Permanent Commission of the South Pacific (CPPS)
Permanent Inter-State Committee for Drought Control in the Sahel (CILSS)
Preparatory Commission for the Organization for the Prohibition of Chemical Weapons (OPCW)
Red Sea and Gulf of Aden Environment Programme (PERSGA)
South Asia Cooperative Environment Programme (SACEP)

12. In addition, 37 international non-governmental organizations were represented by observers.

C. Election of officers

13. At the opening meeting of the session, the Council elected the following officers by acclamation:

President:	Mr. S. Shafqat Kakakhel (Pakistan)
Vice-Presidents:	Mr. S. Ongeri (Kenya) Mr. P. Suian (Romania) Mr. P.F. Unwin (United Kingdom)
Rapporteur:	Mr. J.M. Ovalle (Chile)

14. In his acceptance statement, the President said that the state of the global environment presented some bewildering contradictions. Growing attention was being paid to the environment at the national and international levels but there was a growing gap between what needed to be done and the measures actually adopted. Despite some progress, the overall picture was one of unabated, indeed accelerated, degradation of the environment. In the circumstances, it was necessary to enhance UNEP's standing as a politically sensitive, technically and scientifically credible and well managed organization, so that it might receive the support and resources necessary to carry out its mandates.

D. Credentials of representatives

15. In accordance with rule 17, paragraph 2, of the rules of procedure of the Council, the Bureau examined the credentials of representatives attending the session. The Bureau found the credentials in order with one exception and so reported to the Council, which approved the Bureau's report at the 8th meeting of the session, on 25 May.

E. Agenda

16. At the opening meeting of the session, the Council adopted the following agenda for the session on the basis of the provisional agenda approved by the Council at its seventeenth session, as amended at its fourth special session (UNEP/GC.18/1):

1. Opening of the session.
2. Organization of the session:
   - (a) Election of officers;
   - (b) Adoption of the agenda and organization of the work of the session.
3. Credentials of representatives.
4. Policy issues:
   - (a) State of the environment;
   - (b) Emerging policy issues;
   - (c) Coordination and cooperation within the United Nations;
   - (d) Participation of the United Nations Environment Programme in the Global Environment Facility.

5. Implementation of Agenda 21.

6. Environment and economics.

7. Administrative and budgetary matters.

8. Provisional agenda, date and place of the nineteenth session of the Council.

9. Other business.

10. Adoption of the report.

11. Closure of the session.

F. Organization of the work of the session

17. At the opening meeting of the session, the Governing Council considered and approved the organization of the work of the session in the light of the recommendations contained in the annotated provisional agenda (UNEP/GC.18/1/Add.1/Rev.1 and Corr.1) and the timetable of meetings suggested by the Executive Director (UNEP/GC.18/1/Add.1/Rev.1 and Corr.1, annex I).

18. In accordance with rule 60 of its rules of procedure and following the organizational structure for its sessions decided upon at its fifteenth session (decision 15/1, section II, paragraph 2 of 25 May 1989), the Governing Council at its opening meeting established two sessional committees of the whole, a Programme Committee to deal with programme matters and a Committee for Administrative and budgetary matters to deal with the Environment Fund and administrative and other financial matters. The Council decided that the Programme Committee should deal primarily with those parts of agenda item 4 (Policy issues) that concerned the proposed programme of work for the biennium 1996-1997, together with agenda item 5 (Implementation of Agenda 21) and agenda item 6 (Environment and economics). The Programme Committee would also take up the report of the Executive Director on review of the role and function of the regional representation of the United Nations Environment Programme, which had been issued under agenda item 7 (Administrative and Budgetary Matters). The Council also decided that the Committee for Administrative and Budgetary Matters should deal exclusively with agenda item 7 (Administrative and budgetary matters).

19. It was agreed that the two sessional committees would meet concurrently during the first week of the session to complete their work by the afternoon of Friday, 19 May. Plenary would recommence at the ministerial or equivalent level, on Monday, 22 May, in keeping with section II, paragraph 2(b), of Council decision 15/1, to discuss the policy issues raised under agenda item 4 and the remaining items of the agenda.

20. The Council also agreed that the Programme Committee and Committee for Administrative and Budgetary Matters should be chaired respectively by Mr. P. Unwin (United Kingdom) and Mr. S. Ongeri (Kenya), vice-presidents of the Council. The Council also decided that Mr. P. Suian (Romania), Vice-President of the Council, would assist the President in the performance of his functions related to plenary.

21. The Council further decided to establish an informal open-ended negotiating group under the chairmanship of the President, Mr. S.S. Kakakhel (Pakistan), with a core membership of two representatives from each regional group to consider the texts of draft decisions on policy issues before their submission to the plenary meeting of the Council for formal consideration.

G. Work of the sessional committees

22. The Programme Committee, under the chairmanship of Mr. P. Unwin (United Kingdom) held 13 meetings, from 15 to 20 May. At its 1st meeting, it approved the proposals for the organization of its work as contained in document UNEP/GC.18/PC/L.1. At its 2nd meeting, it elected Mr. W. Jasinski (Poland) as Rapporteur.

23. The Council took note of the Committee's report (UNEP/GC.18/39 and Corr.1) at its 9th plenary meeting, on 25 May.

24. The Fund Committee, under the chairmanship of Mr. S. Ongeri (Kenya), held 10 meetings, from 15 to 19 May. At its 1st meeting, on 15 May, it approved the proposals for the organization of its work as contained in document UNEP/GC.18/FC/L.1. At its 3rd meeting, on 16 May 1995, it elected Ms. D. Alopaeus-Stahl (Sweden) as Rapporteur.

25. The Council took note of the Committee's report (UNEP/GC.18/38 and Corr.1) at its 8th plenary meeting, on 25 May.

III. MATTERS REQUIRING THE SPECIAL ATTENTION OF THE GENERAL ASSEMBLY AND/OR THE ECONOMIC AND SOCIAL COUNCIL

A. Date and place of the nineteenth session of the Governing Council

26. At its 8th plenary meeting, on 25 May 1995, the Governing Council decided that its nineteenth regular session would be held at Nairobi, from 27 January to 7 February 1997.

27. It might be noted that in making its recommendation to the Council concerning the dates of the nineteenth session, the Bureau took into account "the strong desire of member States to hold the Governing Council meetings before the sessions of the Commission on Sustainable Development in order to provide the Council with the possibility to have a substantive input into the Commission's debates" (UNEP/GC.18/L.49, para. 2).

B. The role and priorities of the United Nations Environment Programme

28. By paragraph 1 of its decision 18/1 of 26 May 1995, the Governing Council appealed to Governments to accelerate the implementation of Agenda 21 on a priority basis. By paragraphs 2 and 3 of the same decision, the Council decided that the United Nations Environment Programme should concentrate on a number of major areas and that the major results of those activities should be: international arrangements to enhance environmental protection; periodic assessments and scientifically sound forecasts designed to support decision-making and the creation of an international consensus on the main environmental threats and responses; more effective coordination of environmental matters within the United Nations system; policy options and advice to Governments, multilateral organizations and others, which incoroporate the environmental dimension into the sustainable development process and strengthen environmental protection; and higher public awareness and greater capacity for environmental management and effective international responses to the threats of environmental degradation. By paragraph 5 of the same decision, the Council requested the Executive Director to bring to the attention of the Secretary-General, as a contribution to his preparations for the special session of the General Assembly in 1997 to review the follow-up of Agenda 21, the report of the Governing Council (UNEP/GC.18/40).

C. Review of the governing structures of the United Nations Environment Programme

29. By paragraph 1 of its decision 18/2 of 26 May 1995, the Governing Council, determined to strengthen the United Nations Environment Programme to enable it to fulfil its role as the central United Nations organ for the environment, decided to review at its nineteenth session the governing structures of the Programme with a view to itself taking action or, where necessary, recommending to the General Assembly to take action to modify and streamline those structures to produce in them greater efficiency, effectiveness and transparency. By paragraph 2 of the same decision, the Council requested the Executive Director to propose options to this effect to the Governing Council at its nineteenth session, after consultation with Governments.

D. In-depth evaluation of the programme on environment

30. At its thirty-fourth session, the Committee for Programme and Coordination recommended that an in-depth evaluation of the programme on environment be prepared for its consideration in 1995. Pursuant to that request, the Secretary-General transmitted to the Committee for Programme and Coordination at its thirty-fifth session, held from 15 May to 9 June 1995, a report of the Office of Internal Oversight Services of the Secretariat entitled "In-depth evaluation of the programme on environment" (E/AC.51/1995/3). The in-depth evaluation was considered by the Committee for Programme and Coordination at the 2nd and 3rd meetings of its thirty-fifth session, held on 15 and 16 May 1995. The Committee decided that the report, together with its conclusions and recommendations on it, should be transmitted to the Governing Council at its eighteenth session for consideration and appropriate action.

31. Accordingly, the Executive Director transmitted to the Governing Council at its eighteenth session, under cover of a note by the Executive Director (UNEP/GC.18/Inf.7), the report of the Office of Internal Oversight Services, as transmitted to the Committee for Programme and Coordination by the Secretary-General, together with the relevant part of the draft report of the Committee for Programme and Coordination at its thirty-fifth session (E/AC.51/1995/L.3/Add.29), which had been adopted by the Committee without amendment on 22 May 1995.

32. By its decision 18/5 of 26 May 1995, the Governing Council, having welcomed the in-depth evaluation of the programme on environment, requested the Executive Director to consider and take appropriate action on the recommendations therein and also to take due consideration of the conclusions and recommendations of the Committee for Programme and Coordination as contained in its draft report.

33. In addition, by its decision 18/4 of 26 May 1995, the Governing Council, noting, <u>inter alia</u>, the recommendations of the Office of Internal Oversight Services, requested the Executive Director to give high priority to developing a policy framework and appropriate mechanisms within the secretariat for working with appropriate non-governmental organizations involved in this field, including the assigning of the function of coordinator to an existing senior position.

E. International conventions and protocols in the field of the environment

34. In paragraph 3 of its decision 18/25 of 25 May 1995, the Governing Council authorized the Executive Director to transmit, on its behalf, her report on international conventions and protocols in the field of the environment (UNEP/GC.18/23 and Corr.1 and Add.1 and 2), together with the

comments of the Governing Council thereon, to the General Assembly at its fiftieth session, in accordance with Assembly resolution 3436 (XXX) of 9 December 1975.

F. Implementation of the Plan of Action to Combat Desertification 1993-1994

35. In response to General Assembly resolutions 35/73 of 5 December 1980 and 39/168 B of 17 December 1984, by which the Assembly requested the Governing Council to continue to report every other year to the Assembly, through the Economic and Social Council, on the overall implementation of the Plan of Action to Combat Desertification and to make the necessary arrangements at each session for submitting a report to the Assembly, through the Economic and Social Council, on the implementation in the Sudano-Sahelian region of the Plan of Action to Combat Desertification, the Governing Council, by paragraph 3 of its decision 18/26 of 26 May 1995, requested the Executive Director to submit her report on the implementation of the Plan of Action to Combat Desertification in 1993 and 1994 (UNEP/GC.18/3 and Corr.1), which included a report on the implementation of the Plan of Action in the Sudano-Sahelian region, on behalf of the Governing Council, through the Economic and Social Council, to the General Assembly at its fiftieth session.

36. By paragraph 7 of it resolution 49/234 of 23 December 1994, on elaboration of an international convention to combat desertification in those countries experiencing serious drought and/or desertification, particularly in Africa, the General Assembly requested the United Nations system, among others, to take action for the prompt implementation of the Convention and its relevant regional annexes upon its entry into force and in this regard to respond effectively to the needs in the African, Asian and Latin American and Caribbean regions. By paragraph 8 of the same resolution, the Assembly urged the United Nations system, among others, to take actions and measures for the full and effective implementation of the provisions of Intergovernmental Negotiating Committee resolution 5/1 on urgent action for Africa.

37. In response, the Governing Council, by paragraph 4 of its decision 18/26, requested the Executive Director to participate actively in assisting Governments and intergovernmental and non-governmental organizations to implement the Convention and the resolution on urgent action for Africa and to support the interim secretariat of the Convention. By paragraph 5 (b) of the same decision, the Council requested the Executive Director to contribute to the implementation of the Convention and the resolution on urgent action for Africa on the basis of the resources provided for under programme activities to implement chapter 12 of Agenda 21 in the developing countries, in particular Africa, in close collaboration with the interim secretariat of the Convention. By paragraph 6 of the decision, the Council requested the Executive Director to report to it at its nineteenth session on the activities undertaken within the framework of the decision with a view to implementing the Convention.

G. Strengthening international cooperation in the monitoring of environmental problems

38. By paragraph 2 of its resolution 48/192 of 21 December 1993, the General Assembly requested the Executive Director to prepare and to submit to the Governing Council at its eighteenth session a report on the activities of the Programme in environmental monitoring, containing proposals and recommendations within the context of Agenda 21 and a review of Earthwatch, taking into account the decisions adopted by the Governing Council at its seventeenth session, in cooperation with relevant entities within the United Nations system and, where appropriate, outside the United Nations system. By paragraph 3 of the same resolution, the Assembly invited the Governing Council to consider the above-mentioned report at its eighteenth

session and to submit its conclusions and recommendations to the Assembly at its fiftieth session, through the Economic and Social Council.

39. Accordingly, at its eighteenth session, the Governing Council had before it a report by the Executive Director on Earthwatch, environmental monitoring and assessment (UNEP/GC.18/4 and Corr.1), together with the report of the Secretary-General on chapter 40 of Agenda 21 (Information for decision-making and Earthwatch) (E/CN.17/1995/18), based on material assembled in partnership by the Department for Policy Coordination and Sustainable Development and UNEP as task managers for chapter 40 of Agenda 21 and Earthwatch, respectively, and the report of the Administrative Committee on Coordination to the Governing Council on the system-wide Earthwatch (UNEP/GC.18/33).

40. By paragraph 1 of its decision 18/27 A of 25 May 1995, the Governing Council took note of the report of the Executive Director on Earthwatch, environmental monitoring and assessment, and the associated documents. By paragraphs 2 and 3 of the same decision, it urged all partner agencies and programmes to cooperate in implementing the system-wide Earthwatch and endorsed the recommendations of the Administrative Committee on Coordination in its report regarding the development of approaches to the linking of socio-economic and environmental assessment and reporting by UNEP and the system-wide Earthwatch. By paragraph 4 of the decision, the Council endorsed the refocused strategy of UNEP to undertake, at the request of Governments or their representative bodies, policy-relevant assessment and reporting of environment and development issues of international significance through cooperating networks of appropriate national and regional agencies, organizations or institutions, and to promote the development of data and information management capacity in those bodies situated in developing countries as necessary and appropriate to ensure their full participation. By paragraphs 5 and 6 of the same decision, the Governing Council requested the Executive Director to continue providing assistance, within available resources, to developing countries to build capacity to enable them to use and benefit from the data and information acquired through the Earthwatch programme and authorized her to transmit her report and decision 18/27 A, through the Economic and Social Council, to the General Assembly at its fiftieth session.

H. <u>Issues arising from the resolutions of the General Assembly at its forty-eighth and forty-ninth sessions, specifically calling for action by UNEP</u>

41. By paragraphs 1 and 2 of its decision 18/17 of 25 May 995, the Governing Council took note of the report of the Executive Director on issues arising from the resolutions of the General Assembly at its forty-eighth and forty-ninth sessions specifically calling for action by UNEP (UNEP/GC.18/28), and the actions indicated in the report, and authorized the Executive Director to present to future sessions of the Council her report on issues arising from General Assembly resolutions as an information document.

42. In addition to the General Assembly resolutions referred to elsewhere in the present chapter, the report of the Executive Director provided information on issues arising from resolutions 48/80 of 16 December 1993 and 49/80 of 15 December 1994 on the question of Antarctica, resolutions 48/38 of 10 December 1993 and 49/32 of 9 December 1994 on effects of atomic radiation, resolution 48/175 of 21 December 1993 on drought and desertification, resolution 48/191 of 21 December 1993 on the elaboration of an international convention to combat desertification in those countries experiencing serious drought and/or desertification, especially in Africa, resolution 49/111 of 19 December 1994 on the report of the Commision on Sustainable Development on the work of its second session, resolution 49/117 of 19 December 1994 on the Convention on Biological Diversity, and resolution 49/22 B of 20 December 1994

on early warning capacities of the United Nations system with regard to natural disasters.

I. The United Nations Environment Programme and women in environment and development: message from the Governing Council to the Fourth World Conference on Women

43. By paragraph 33 of its resolution 49/161 of 23 December 1994, the General Assembly invited, inter alia, United Nations bodies to consider making concrete commitments and specifying action to meet the global priorities for the advancement of women by the year 2000 to be reflected in the Platform of Action of the Fourth World Conference on Women. In response to that invitation, the Governing Council, by paragraph 5 of its decision 18/6 of 26 May 1995, decided to send a message annexed to the decision to the Fourth World Conference on Women, to be held in Beijing from 4 to 15 September 1995. In the message, the Governing Council, inter alia, invites the Conference to give special attention to the environmental aspects of sustainable development in formulating its recommendations for the further advancement of women.

44. In addition, by paragraphs 1-3 of the same decision, the Governing Council took note of the report of the Executive Director on the role of women in environment and development (UNEP/GC.18/11) and her intention to integrate fully a gender perspective and balance into the work and activities of UNEP, welcomed the efforts of the Executive Director to achieve gender equality in UNEP, including through the setting of goals/targets, and urged Governments to assist the Executive Director in achieving those goals by proposing qualified candidates of both sexes for vacancies announced to Governments.

J. Future strategy document in the field of the environment

45. By its decision 17/16 of 21 May 1993, the Governing Council endorsed the Executive Director's recommendation, contained in her report on implementation and mid-term review of the system-wide medium-term environment programme (UNEP/GC.17/6), to assess the future arrangements for meeting the need for a strategy and planning document, in view of the new United Nations system-wide coordination arrangements being established. It further requested the Executive Director, by paragraph 3 of the same decision, to report to the Governing Council at its regular session in 1995 on the need for a United Nations system-wide strategy and planning document in the field of the environment.

46. Accordingly, at its eighteenth session, the Council had before a report by the Executive Director on the proposal for a future strategy document in the field of the environment as a successor to the system-wide medium-term environment programme (UNEP/GC.18/36 and Corr.1). Having taken note of the report, the Council, by paragraph 2 of its decision 18/13 of 26 May 1995, endorsed the assessment of the Executive Director that there is a need for a strategy document and recommended that such a document be prepared to provide for a mechanism to enable the United Nations Environment Programme to discharge its policy guidance and coordination mandate within the United Nations system. By paragraph 3 of the same decision, the Council requested the Executive Director to submit to the Council at its regular session in 1997 the draft strategy document, to become operational in 1998.

K. Inter-Agency Environment Coordination Group

47. At its eighteenth session, the Governing Council had before it a report by the Executive Director (UNEP/GC.18/36/Add.1 and Corr.1) outlining developments relating to the establishment of the Inter-Agency Environment Coordination Group pursuant to Governing Council decision 17/9 of 21 May 1993,

by which the Council had endorsed the course of action proposed by the Executive Director in her report on arrangements for system-wide coordination and cooperation in the field of the environment (UNEP/GC.17/12/Add.1) in order to enable her to discharge effectively the coordinating role required of UNEP by various legislative authorities.

48. By paragraphs 1-3 of its decision 18/14 of 26 May 1995, the Governing Council took note of the report of the Executive Director on the Inter-Agency Environment Coordination Group, welcomed the establishment of the Group as a flexible consultative and advisory body, meeting as and when required, to enable the United Nations Environment Programme to discharge effectively its coordination mandate, and decided that the Group should focus on assisting the Executive Director in coordinating the activities of the United Nations system in addressing the major challenges, as set out in the programme of work for the biennium 1996-1997. By paragraphs 4 and 5 of the same decision, the Council stressed that, in determining the terms of reference and future activities of the Group, full account should be taken of the role, responsibilities and work of the Inter-Agency Committee on Sustainable Development, and requested the Executive Director to report to the Council at its regular session in 1997 on the terms of reference and progress made in the work of the Group and proposed future activities.

L. Relationship between the United Nations Environment Programme and the Commission on Sustainable Development

49. By paragraph 2 of its resolution 48/174 of 21 December 1993, the General Assembly stressed the need for close cooperation between the United Nations Environment Programme and the Commission on Sustainable Development in implementing the recommendations of the United Nations Conference on Environment and Development, in accordance with the relevant provisions of chapter 38 of Agenda 21.

50. At its eighteenth session, the Governing Council had before it a report by the Executive Director on environment and sustainable development (UNEP/GC.18/27 and Corr.1), which, inter alia, elaborated on the mandates and practice of the Governing Council and its secretariat in relation to the mandate and practice of the Commission on Sustainable Development and the Inter-Agency Committee on Sustainable Development. Having taken note of the report of the Executive Director, the Governing Council, by paragraph 2 of its decision 18/7 of 26 May 1995, stressed the need for the United Nations Environment Programme to focus on those system-wide activities of the United Nations system for which it has been assigned a special responsibility by Agenda 21, and the major policy issues and challenges in the field of the environment, as determined by the Governing Council. By paragraph 3 of the same decision, the Council emphasized the need for the United Nations Environment Programme, in accordance with its mandate and in implementation of Agenda 21, to continue to provide effective support to the work of the Commission on Sustainable Development as the high-level policy forum for the discussions to follow up the United Nations Conference on Environment and Development, inter alia, through the provision of scientific, technical and policy information and advice on the environment. By paragraph 5 of the decision, the Council requested the Executive Director to inform the Commission on Sustainable Development of the decision.

M. Good environmental housekeeping within the United Nations system

51. By paragraph 1 of its decision 18/10 of 25 May 1995, the Governing Council, convinced, inter alia, of the need for the United Nations, its specialized agencies and its other bodies to apply and observe good environmental housekeeping standards in their building design and office systems, requested the Executive Director to consider and recommend strategies

for the promotion of best practice in environmental housekeeping for use by the United Nations Environment Programme at its headquarters and in its regional offices, and to advise and encourage the rest of the United Nations system to develop and apply similar strategies for continually improving their own environmental performance and promoting sustainable development. The Council further requested the Executive Director, by paragraph 2 of the same decision, to encourage bodies within the United Nations system in their respective regular reports, to report on the ways in which they have applied and observed the principle of good environmental housekeeping and the targets they have set themselves in this regard. By paragraph 4 of the decision, the Council requested the General Assembly to adopt a resolution calling for the application, as early as possible, of good environmental housekeeping practices by all institutions of the United Nations system on the lines indicated in the decision. Finally, by paragraph 5 of the decision, the Council requested the Executive Director to report to it at its regular sessions on the steps that have been taken and the progress achieved by the United Nations Environment Programme and other entities of the United Nations system under the decision.

N. Development of an international legally binding instrument for the application of the prior informed consent procedure for certain hazardous chemicals in international trade

52. Paragraph 19.39 (d) of Agenda 21, endorsed by the General Assembly in its resolution 47/190 of 22 December 1992, states, inter alia, that Governments and relevant international organizations with the cooperation of industry should, in the light of the experience gained in the implementation of prior informed consent (PIC) procedures, invite relevant international organizations in their respective areas of competence to consider working expeditiously towards the conclusion of legally binding instruments. More recently, the International Conference on Chemical Safety, held in Stockholm in April 1994, and the Commission on Sustainable Development at its second and third sessions, held in New York in May 1994 and April 1995, recommended that the United Nations Environment Programme, together with the Food and Agriculture Organization of the United Nations and in close consultation with other international organizations, continue to evaluate and address problems with the implementation of the voluntary prior informed consent procedure and to develop effective legally binding instruments concerning the prior informed consent procedure.

53. By paragraph 1 of its decision 18/12 of 26 May 1995, the Governing Council, having taken note with appreciation of the work of the Ad Hoc Working Group of Experts on the Implementation of the London Guidelines for the Exchange of Information on Chemicals in International Trade and of the task force established by the Group for the development of the instrument envisaged in chapter 19 of Agenda 21, authorized the Executive Director to prepare for and convene, together with the Food and Agriculture Organization of the United Nations and in consultation with Governments and other relevant international organizations, an intergovernmental negotiating committee with a mandate to prepare an international legally binding instrument for the application of the prior informed consent procedure for certain chemicals in international trade.

54. By paragraphs 5 and 7 of the same decision, the Council requested the Executive Director to invite relevant international organizations to participate in the negotiating process for the development of the instrument and to convene, together with the Director-General of the Food and Agriculture Organization of the United Nations, a diplomatic conference for the purpose of adopting and signing an international legally binding instrument for the application of the prior informed consent procedure for certain hazardous chemicals in international trade, preferably not later than early 1997.

O. Follow-up by the United Nations Environment Programme to major international events

55. By paragraph 1 of its decision 18/16 of 26 May 1995, The Governing Council took note of the report of the Executive Director (UNEP/GC.18/26) on the implications for the United Nations Environment Programme of the following major international events: the presentation by the Secretary-General of his report entitled "An Agenda for Peace" and his subsequent position paper entitled "Supplement to An Agenda for Peace"; the submission by the Secretary-General of his reports on an agenda for development (A/48/935 and A/49/665); the Global Conference on the Sustainable Development of Small Island Developing States; the International Conference on Population and Development; the entry into force of the United Nations Convention on the Law of the Sea; and the World Summit for Social Development. By paragraph 2 of the same decision, the Council endorsed the follow-up proposals of the Executive Director as contained in her report.

56. In addition, with regard to the Global Conference on the Sustainable Development of Small Island Developing States, the Governing Council, by paragraph 1 of its decision 18/34 of 26 May 1995, welcomed the action taken to date by the Executive Director in response to the Conference, including the establishment of a focal point and a task force within the United Nations Environment Programme to coordinate the Programme's activities relevant to the Barbados Programme of Action. By paragraphs 2 and 3 of the same decision, the Council urged the Executive Director to ensure that, in implementing the programme of work agreed by the Governing Council at its eighteenth session, appropriate attention is given to the needs and vulnerabilities of small island developing States, and further urged her to encourage, through the effective use and involvement of the task force in both programme activities and policy development, an integrated approach within the United Nations Environment Programme to addressing the issues of relevance to small island developing States.

P. Improvement of the international response to environmental emergencies

57. In paragraph 26 of its resolution 47/191 of 22 December 1992, reconfirmed in the fifth preambular paragraph of its resolution 48/174 of 21 December 1993, the General Assembly invited the Governing Council to report to the Assembly at its forty-eighth session on the experience gained within the United Nations Centre for Emergency Environmental Assistance, which had been established at the beginning of 1992, on an experimental basis, for a period of 18 months. In its decision 17/26 of 21 May 1993, the Governing Council decided, inter alia, to extend the experimental stage of the Centre for a further 12 months, during which time the Centre was, among other things, to develop a set of concrete proposals for the enhancement of the international response to environmental emergencies. It further decided that a governmental advisory meeting should be held in November 1993 for a first consideration of the findings of the extended experimental stage of and an initial drafting of proposals for decision.

58. Following the governmental advisory meeting, held as requested by the Governing Council in November 1993, and following a joint recommendation of the United Nations Environment Programme and the Department of Humanitarian Affairs, a Joint United Nations Environment Programme/Department of Humanitarian Affairs Unit was established in the Department of Humanitarian Affairs as of 1 July 1994.

59. At its 45th meeting, the Committee of Permanent Representatives to the United Nations Environment Programme considered the report of the Executive Director on the Joint Unit, endorsed the joint recommendation of the United Nations Environment Programme and the Department of Humanitarian

Affairs and requested the Executive Director to implement it for an initial period of 12 months and to refer the question back to the Governing Council at its eighteenth session.

60. At its eighteenth session, by paragraphs 1 and 2 of its decision 18/19 of 26 May 1995, took note of the report of the Executive Director on improvement of the international response to environmental emergencies and welcomed the establishment of the Joint Unit. By paragraph 3 of the same decision, it invited Governments and relevant United Nations agencies, bodies and programmes to cooperate with the Joint Unit in its efforts to provide assistance to countries, in particular developing countries, facing environmental emergencies. By paragraphs 5 and 6 of the decision, it urged Governments in a position to do so to provide additional resources for the operation of the Joint Unit and requested the Executive Director to prepare a detailed progress report on the activities of the Unit for an in-depth review of its activities, its resources and structure, including the involvement and contribution of the United Nations Environment Programme, and the appropriateness of the location of the Unit, by the Governing Council at its nineteenth session.

Q. Application of environmental norms by military establishments

61. In its decision 17/5 of 21 May 1995, the Governing Council, inter alia, encouraged Governments to establish a national environmental policy for the military sector and invited the Executive Director to collect information on: national preparations and activities in order to ascertain that their military establishments conform to their environmental norms in the treatment and disposal of hazardous wastes; the contribution of the military sector in the achievement of national environmental policies; and assessments of the damage as well as the need for and feasibility of the clean-up and restoration of areas where damage to the environment has been caused by military activities.

62. At its second session, held in May 1995, the Commission on Sustainable Development invited the United Nations Environment Programme to consider the feasibility of arranging regional meetings, in cooperation with the United Nations regional commissions and regional organizations, on the implementation of Governing Council decision 17/5 and on how national environmental plans for military establishments relating to hazardous waste management can be designed and implemented (E/1994/33/Rev.1-E/CN.17/1994/20/Rev.1, chap. I, paras. 186 and 187).

63. By its decision 18/29 of 25 May 1995, the Governing Council, inter alia, took note of the recommendation of the Commission on Sustainable Development and authorized the Executive Director to arrange, within available resources, regional meetings, in cooperation with the United Nations regional commissions and regional organizations, for the implementation of decision 17/5.

R. Implications for the United Nations Environment Programme of the decisions concerning forest issues adopted by the Commission on Sustainable Development at its third session

64. By paragraph 1 of its decision 18/30 of 25 May 1995, the Governing Council, having considered the decisions adopted by the Commission on Sustainable Development at its third session, whereby further actions are required to improve the conservation and sustainable management of all types of forests, and having noted with satisfaction the establishment, under the aegis of the Commission, of an Open-ended Intergovernmental Panel on Forests, requested the Executive Director of the United Nations Environment Programme to place the Programme's experience in helping nations to move forward on contentious environmental issues and arrive at consensus, as well as its

expertise in environmental issues related to forests, at the disposal of the Panel, and to further develop and strengthen this expertise through those relevant elements of its approved work programme in order to contribute effectively to the work of the Panel. By paragraph 2 of the same decision, the Council also requested the Executive Director to give full support to the implementation of the work programme of the Panel and the functioning of its secretariat.

S. Lead in gasoline

65. At its second session, the Commission on Sustainable Development noted the severe health impacts of human exposure to lead, endorsed the ongoing work on that issue in several international forums, and encouraged further efforts to reduce human exposure to lead (E/1994/33/Rev.1-E/CN.17/1994/20/Rev.1, chap. I, para. 169). At its third session, the Commission called upon all countries to consider, and all interested countries to develop, action plans with a view to phasing out or reducing the use of lead in gasoline, and invited them to inform it of their decision and progress, as appropriate, at its fourth session. By the same decision, the Commission called upon donor countries and financial institutions to assist developing countries in the financing and transfer of relevant technologies, in accordance with chapters 33 and 34 of Agenda 21.

66. In response to those decisions of the Commission on Sustainable Development, the Governing Council, by paragraph 1 of its decision 18/35 of 26 May 1995, called upon Governments to give full consideration to the costs and benefits of phasing out lead in gasoline, including the risks associated with increase aromatic components in the absence of catalytic converters. By paragraph 2 of the same decision, the Council urged countries that have not already begun to phase out the use of lead in gasoline, as well as appropriate international organizations and international financial institutions, to assist other countries in their efforts to achieve such a phase-out, in accordance with the decision of the Commission on Sustainable Development at its third session, and to promote the transfer of technology towards the overall reduction of vehicular emissions. By paragraph 3 of the decision, the Council invited the Executive Director to participate in these efforts as appropriate, within available resources and without duplication of effort, as part of her broader efforts to promote more effective approaches to emissions control.

T. Technical cooperation among African countries for the building and utilization of capacities and the mobilization of resources for sustainable development in Africa

67. In paragraph 4 of its decision 18/39 B of 26 May 1995, the Governing Council, inter alia, authorized the United Nations Development Programme to carry out a comprehensive study of the feasibility, modalities, approaches, appropriate measures and resource requirements for the successful implementation of technical cooperation among African countries and to collaborate closely with the United Nations Environment Programme on those aspects of the study relating to environmental management and sustainable development. The Council further authorized the Executive Director to request the United Nations Development Programme to present the report of the study to the Economic and Social Council at its 1996 session for policy debate.

U. Establishment of a United Nations Office at Nairobi

68. By its decision 18/43 of 25 May 1995, the Governing Council, inter alia, noted the proposal of the Secretary-General to the General Assembly on the creation of a United Nations Office in Nairobi with effect from 1 January 1996 and noted with appreciation the work done so far by both the United Nations

Environment Programme and the United Nations Centre for Human Settlements (Habitat) in the process leading to the establishment of the United Nations Office in Nairobi.

69. By paragraph 1 of the same decision, the Council approved the attachment of administrative and conference-services staff of the United Nations Environment Programme to the United Nations Office in Nairobi, as set out in the report of the Executive Director on the subject (UNEP/GC.18/32/Add.1) and the payment of the cost of their emoluments from the management and administrative support costs budget of the Environment Fund, taking into account: (a) that the separate identities and equal status of the two organizations in accordance with General Assembly resolutions 47/212 of 23 December 1992 and 48/176 of 21 December 1993 should be maintained; (b) that the Secretary-General explores the possibility of providing the subsequent budgets for the United Nations Office in Nairobi on a basis comparable to that used for other United Nations offices based in other United Nations headquarters; and (c) that, as far as possible, the reduction of staff should be through redeployment and attrition in order to realize the savings projected in the establishment of the United Nations Office in Nairobi.

V. Prevention of waste, fraud and mismanagement

70. By paragraph 1 of its decision 18/46 of 25 May 1995, the Governing Council, having welcomed the establishment of the Office of Internal Oversight Services in the United Nations Secretariat, requested the Executive Director, in consultation with the Office, to formulate and enact a specific plan of action for the United Nations Environment Programme which will heighten the awareness of all members of the staff of the United Nations Environment Programme concerning the need to combat waste, fraud and mismanagement, and will establish practical measures and procedures which will enable them to do so. By paragraph 2 of the same decision, the Council urged that the plan of action should include the following measures: formulation of a concise definition of what constitutes waste, fraud and mismanagement, and the dissemination of this statement to all levels of the organization; promotion of uniform reporting procedures so that members of the staff, at all levels, may report suspected violations to a single local authority; ensuring that briefings on waste, fraud and mismanagement are included in both staff orientation and refresher courses; ensuring also that information on the range of penalties imposed on violators, including prosecution in cases of fraud, be widely disseminated; and, local publication of offences uncovered, including the amounts of money lost and recovered, the offices in which violations occurred, and the disciplinary and follow-up actions taken by management. By paragraph 4 of the decision, the Council requested that, in the interests of transparency, Governments have access to: information on the status of all audit investigations, without prejudice to confidentiality; the results and recommendations of all audit investigations; and the response of the management of the United Nations Environment Programme. By paragraph 6 of the decision, the Council requested the Executive Director to submit to the Governing Council at its regular sessions the biennial report of the Board of Auditors to the United Nations Environment Programme as an information document.

W. Mercure satellite telecommunications system

71. By paragraph 7 of its decision 17/38 of 21 May 1993, the Governing Council approved the Executive Director's proposal to finalize an agreement with the participants in the Mercure project in full prior consultation with and with the consent of the Government of Kenya, taking into consideration the telecommunications facilities in place, so as to enable the project to be implemented expeditiously.

72. Further to that decision, and after extensive consultation within the United Nations Environment Programme and with the United Nations telecommunications services and the Government of Kenya, the Executive Director of the United Nations Environment Programme and the Director General of the European Space Agency signed an agreement on 25 November 1994 for the United Nations Environment Programme to accept the donation of a satellite-based telecommunications system.

73. By its decision 18/47 of 25 May 1995, the Governing Council, having considered the report of the Executive Director on the Mercure satellite telecommunications system (UNEP/GC.18/21 and Corr.1), expressed its gratitude to the donors and the Government of the Republic of Kenya, encouraged Governments with environmental data to provide for all countries ease of access and delivery through this initiative of the United Nations Environment Programme; encouraged the minimization of operations costs and the further expansion of the initial programme to new countries and users, requested the Executive Director to ensure that a full review and cost-benefit analysis of the system and experience gained in its initial operation be carried out and that subsequent decisions on the use and operation of the system take fully into account the results of that assessment, requested the Executive Director to present the results of the assessment, and any actions taken in response to it, to the Governing Council at its session in 1997, or to present a status report if the assessment has not been completed by that time; authorized the Executive Director to finance the costs required to implement, manage and maintain the system in 1996-1997 by charging $700,000 to the management and administrative support costs budget of the Environment Fund and the remaining costs to Environment Fund projects, requested the Executive Director to examine the possibility that, in subsequent years, such costs shall be covered by the management and administrative support costs budget and to report thereon to the Governing Council at its nineteenth session, and decided that the Mercure agreement should be submitted to the General Assembly for endorsement in accordance with relevant United Nations procedures.

[...]

18/1. The role and priorities of the United Nations Environment Programme

The Governing Council,

Recalling General Assembly resolution 2997 (XXVII) of 15 December 1972,

Noting paragraphs 38.21-23 of Agenda 21,[1] which recognize the need for an enhanced and strengthened role of the United Nations Environment Programme and its Governing Council,

Acknowledging that population, poverty, health, education, technology, patterns of production and consumption and the environment are closely interconnected within the overall framework of sustainable development,

Underlining the need for the United Nations Environment Programme to strengthen its role as the central United Nations organ for the environment, while avoiding duplication of work with other international organizations,

---

[1] Report of the United Nations Conference on Environment and Development, Rio de Janeiro, 3-14 June 1992, vol. I, Resolutions adopted by the Conference (United Nations publication, Sales No. E.93.I.8 and corrigendum), resolution 1, annex II.

1. Appeals to Governments to accelerate the implementation of Agenda 21 on a priority basis;

2. Decides that the United Nations Environment Programme should concentrate its activities in the following major areas:

(a) Assessing and addressing existing and emerging critical issues in the field of the environment;

(b) Promoting international cooperation in the field of the environment and recommending as appropriate policies to this end;

(c) Acting as a catalyst to address major threats to the environment;

(d) Monitoring the status of the global environment through gathering and dissemination of reliable environmental information;

(e) Facilitating the coordination of the activities of all United Nations bodies on matters concerned with the environment, ensuring through cooperation, liaison and expert participation, that environmental considerations are taken into account in their activities;

(f) Supporting, upon request, environment ministries and other national environmental authorities, in particular in developing countries and countries with economies in transition, in the formulation and implementation of their environmental policies, and related capacity-building activities;

(g) Furthering the development of international environmental law;

(h) Providing expert advice on the development and use of environmental economic concepts and instruments;

(i) Developing regional programmes for the environment;

3. Decides also that the major results of the activities of the United Nations Environment Programme should be:

(a) International arrangements to enhance environmental protection;

(b) Periodic assessments and scientifically sound forecasts designed to support decision-making and the creation of an international consensus on the main environmental threats and responses;

(c) More effective coordination of environmental matters within the United Nations system;

(d) Policy options and advice to Governments, multilateral organizations and others, which incorporate the environmental dimension into the sustainable development process and strengthen environmental protection;

(e) Higher public awareness and greater capacity for environmental management and effective national and international responses to the threats of environmental degradation;

4. Requests the Executive Director to take fully into account the present decision in shaping and executing the future programmes of the United Nations Environment Programme;

5. Requests the Executive Director to bring to the attention of the Secretary-General, as a contribution to his preparations for the special

session of the General Assembly in 1997 to review the follow-up of Agenda 21, the report of the Governing Council.

[...]

18/9. Further development of international environmental law aiming at sustainable development

The Governing Council,

Recalling General Assembly resolution 47/190 of 22 December 1992 endorsing Agenda 21[1] and the other documents as adopted by the United Nations Conference on Environment and Development, and, in particular the principal environmental challenges identified therein,

Desiring to achieve the implementation of tasks set out in those documents,

Recalling chapter 38 of Agenda 21 on international institutional arrangements, which reaffirms the enhanced and strengthened role of the Governing Council of the United Nations Environment Programme in providing policy guidance and coordination in the field of the environment, taking into account the development perspective, and urges the United Nations Environment Programme to concentrate, inter alia, on the implementation and further development of international environmental law,

Recognizing that chapter 38 of Agenda 21 further urges the United Nations Environment Programme to concentrate on coordinating functions arising from an increasing number of international legal agreements, inter alia, the functioning of the convention secretariats, and the provision of technical, legal and institutional advice to Governments, at their request, for developing and implementing national environmental legislation and institutions, providing training and disseminating legal information,

Recalling its decision 17/25 of 21 May 1993, by which it adopted the Programme for the Development and Periodic Review of Environmental Law for the 1990s, and decided to review the implementation of the programme not later than at its nineteenth session,

Recalling also the decision adopted by the Commission on Sustainable Development on 27 May 1994 urging the United Nations Environment Programme to study further the concept, requirements and implications of sustainable development and international law,[13]

Welcoming the progress achieved in the implementation and development of international environmental instruments and the conclusion of environmental programmes of action,

Concerned that, despite the encouraging signs, three years after the adoption of Agenda 21 only limited progress has been made in the realization of its goals and objectives and that existing and proposed legal and institutional instruments and arrangements have so far been ineffective in halting the deterioration of the global environment,

Noting the need for enhanced policy guidance with regard to the direction and coordination of United Nations system activities in the field of environment in the context of sustainable development,

---

[13] E/1994/33/Rev.1-E/CN.17/1994/20/Rev.1, chap. I, sect. A, para. 6.

Believing that in order to achieve sustainable development it is imperative to address on a priority basis the principal environmental challenges, as contained in Agenda 21, including with reference to relevant social, economic and environmental aspects which should be considered in the contest of the development of international environmental law,

Noting with appreciation the efforts being made by the United Nations Environment Programme as well as other institutions, both within and outside the United Nations system, to further the implementation and development of international environmental law aiming at sustainable development,

Believing further that innovative approaches are required in the field of the progressive development and codification of international environmental law in order to achieve sustainable development,

1. *Requests* the Executive Director to monitor the implementation of international legal instruments in the field of environment, to elaborate and recommend, where necessary, means to enhance their effectiveness and to provide support, as agreed, to the convention secretariats;

2. *Requests* the Executive Director to update, within available resources, a compilation of international environmental instruments, with a view to facilitating harmonization of international environmental law;

3. *Requests* the Executive Director, in implementing the mandate for a database on national and international environment law, to use the existing IUCN databank as the core archival system and, with view to avoiding duplication of efforts, provide the support necessary to enable it to serve the needs of the United Nations Environment Programme, in particular to assist Governments of developing countries in this field;

4. *Requests* the Executive Director to develop, in preparing the periodic review of environmental law in accordance with Council decision 17/25, a position paper for international environmental law aiming at sustainable development, containing, *inter alia*, compliance/implementation mechanisms, dispute avoidance/settlement procedures and new concepts and principles, with reference to existing international legal instruments as well as guidelines developed by institutions both within and outside the United Nations system;

5. *Requests* the Executive Director, within available resources, to prepare a study on the need for and feasibility of new international environmental instruments aiming at sustainable development, addressing, on a priority basis, the principal environmental challenges, including as they relate to the broader issues of sustainable development as set forth in Agenda 21, and, in fulfilling this task, to draw upon relevant work and activities of other United Nations agencies and international organizations;

6. *Requests* the Executive Director to keep the Committee of Permanent Representatives informed of the progress of the United Nations Environment Programme on the subject and to submit a report thereon to the Governing Council at its nineteenth session.

10th meeting
26 May 1995

18/18. Estimates of costs for the United Nations Environment Programme to implement fully those parts of Agenda 21 recommended for its attention

The Governing Council,

Recalling its decision 17/32 of 21 May 1993, by paragraph 4 of which it requested the Executive Director to present to the Council at its eighteenth session her estimates of the costs for the Programme fully to implement those parts of Agenda 21[1] specifically recommended for the United Nations Environment Programme's attention,

Takes note of the report of the Executive Director on estimates of costs for the United Nations Environment Programme to implement fully those parts of Agenda 21 recommended for its attention[31] and requests the Executive Director to present broad-based estimates to the Council at its nineteenth session.

10th meeting
26 May 1995

18/19. Improvement of the international response to environmental emergencies

The Governing Council,

Recalling its decision 16/9 of 31 May 1991, in which the Council established, on an experimental basis, the United Nations Centre for Urgent Environmental Assistance to assess and respond to man-made environmental emergencies, acting in cooperation and in coordination with other United Nations agencies,

Recalling also its decision 17/26 of 21 May 1993, in which the Council decided to extend the experimental stage of the Centre for a further twelve months, during which the Centre should restructure its activities to focus its capacities to address the mandate set out in paragraphs 4 (a) to 4 (d) of that decision,

Having considered the report of the Executive Director on improvement of the international response to environmental emergencies,[32]

Noting with appreciation the efforts of the United Nations Environment Programme and the United Nations Department of Humanitarian Affairs in successfully negotiating institutional and administrative arrangements for the establishment of a Joint United Nations Environment Programme/Department of Humanitarian Affairs Environment Unit in the Department of Humanitarian Affairs to enhance international capacity to respond to environmental emergencies,

Also noting the decision taken by the Committee of Permanent Representatives at its forty-fifth meeting, held on 8 June 1994, to accept the Executive Director's proposal for the Joint Unit and to request the Executive Director to implement her proposals for twelve months and refer the question back to the Council at its eighteenth session,[33]

---

[31] UNEP/GC.18/30.

[32] UNEP/GC.18/2.

[33] UNEP/CPR.46/2/Rev.1, annex II.

Noting further the establishment of the Advisory Group on Environmental Emergencies which will, inter alia, review the work of the Joint Unit and advise the Executive Director of the United Nations Environment Programme and the Under-Secretary-General for Humanitarian Affairs and Emergency Relief Coordinator,

Recognizing that more time is required for the Joint Unit to develop its activities and services in accordance with the recommendations of the Advisory Group on Environmental Emergencies,

1. Takes note of the report of the Executive Director on improvement of the international response to environmental emergencies;

2. Welcomes the establishment of the Joint United Nations Environment Programme/Department of Humanitarian Affairs Environment Unit;

3. Invites Governments and relevant United Nations agencies, bodies and programmes to cooperate with the Joint Unit in its efforts to provide assistance to countries, in particular developing countries, facing environmental emergencies;

4. Requests the Executive Director to allocate the necessary resources for the biennium 1996-1997 for the administration and operation of the Joint Unit with strict regard to economy;

5. Urges Governments in a position to do so to provide additional resources for the operation of the Joint Unit;

6. Requests the Executive Director to prepare a detailed progress report on the activities of the Joint Unit for an in-depth review of its activities, its resources and structure, including the involvement and contribution of the United Nations Environment Programme, and the appropriateness of the Joint Unit's location, by Governing Council at its nineteenth regular session.

10th meeting
26 May 1995

18/20. Climate

A. The Climate Agenda

The Governing Council,

Recalling its decision 17/24 C of 21 May 1993 on the Intergovernmental Meeting on the World Climate Programme,

Having considered the Executive Director's report on the Climate Agenda -- international climate-related programmes,[34]

Noting the availability of the Climate Agenda: A Proposal for an Integrating Framework for International Climate-related Programmes,[35] which encompasses all the climate-related activities of international organizations and which has been prepared jointly by the United Nations Environment Programme, the Food and Agriculture Organization of the United Nations, the International Council of Scientific Unions, the United Nations Educational,

---

[34] UNEP/GC.18/17 and Corr.1.

[35] Ibid, annex.

Scientific and Cultural Organization and its Intergovernmental Oceanographic Commission, and the World Meteorological Organization,

Noting also that the Agenda is focused upon the needs of Governments and is designed to ensure maximum synergy,

Recognizing the need to support the requirements of the United Nations Framework Convention on Climate Change,[36] the implementation of Agenda 21[1] and the work of the Intergovernmental Panel on Climate Change,

Recognizing also that the overall aims and priority areas developed along the four thrusts identified by the Intergovernmental Meeting on the World Climate Programme will only be attained through the participation of all States, which requires capacity-building in developing countries and countries with economies in transition, realized through training and development, improved institutional arrangements and technology transfer,

Aware of the concerns of the Executive Committee of the World Meteorological Organization, expressed at its forty-sixth session, in June 1994,

1. Endorses the proposal that the United Nations Environment Programme be responsible for coordinating international activities under thrust 3 of the Climate Agenda, "Studies of climate impact assessments and response strategies to reduce vulnerabilities";

2. Urges the relevant international organizations to align their climate-related activities according to the priorities of the Agenda and to implement these activities, within available resources, and to establish adequate reporting and coordinating mechanisms for the World Climate Programme towards achievement of the aims of the Agenda;

3. Requests Governments to consider the need:

(a) To undertake those parts of the programmes for which they have the required expertise and capacity;

(b) To strengthen or establish national climate programmes required by the United Nations Framework Convention on Climate Change and the Intergovernmental Meeting on the World Climate Programme;

(c) To cooperate in building the scientific and technical capacity of developing countries and countries with economies in transition in order to enable their full participation in the Agenda;

(d) To provide a modest amount of additional resources to international organizations for the targeted purpose of coordinating the implementation of the Climate Agenda and for the overall management of the programmes, through the inter-agency Coordinating Committee for the World Climate Programme, and for the management of the individual thrusts.

10th meeting
26 May 1995

---

[36] A/AC.237/18 (Part II)/Add.1 and Corr.1, annex I.

B. Intergovernmental Panel on Climate Change

The Governing Council,

Recalling its decision 17/24 A of 21 May 1993 on the report of the Chairman of the Intergovernmental Panel on Climate Change,

Having considered the report of the Executive Director on progress of work of the Intergovernmental Panel on Climate Change,[37]

Noting with satisfaction the outcome of the first meeting of the Conference of the Parties to the United Nations Framework Convention on Climate Change, held in Berlin from 28 March to 7 April 1995,

1. Takes note of the report of the Executive Director;

2. Requests the Executive Director, jointly with the Secretary-General of the World Meteorological Organization, to continue the arrangements to support the Panel and to ensure the participation of specialists with appropriate expertise in its activities;

3. Requests the Panel to continue to update the assessments of available information on the science, impacts, response options and the technical aspects of the socio-economics of climate change and related methodologies for use and application by States parties to the United Nations Framework Convention on Climate Change[36] and other interested entities, taking into account in its assessments the needs arising from the special circumstances of the developing countries and countries with economies in transition;

4. Urges Governments to continue to support the activities of the Intergovernmental Panel on Climate Change and to contribute to the trust fund for the Panel;

5. Further requests the Panel to report, through its Chairman, to the Governing Council at its nineteenth session on the progress of its activities.

9th meeting
25 May 1995

18/21. Joint International Atomic Energy Agency, International Maritime Maritime Organization, United Nations Environment Programme Working Group on the carriage of irradiated nuclear fuel by sea

The Governing Council,

Recalling its decision 17/13 of 21 May 1993 on carriage of irradiated nuclear fuel by sea,

Recalling also resolution A.748 (18), on the Code for the Safe Carriage of Irradiated Nuclear Fuel, Plutonium and High-level Radioactive Wastes in Flasks on Board Ships (INF Code), adopted by the Assembly of the International Maritime Organization at its eighteenth session, held from 25 October to 5 November 1993,

---

[37] UNEP/GC.18/12.

Having considered the report of the Executive Director on developments resulting from the work of the Joint International Atomic Energy Agency/International Maritime Organization/United Nations Environment Programme Working Group on the carriage of irradiated nuclear fuel by sea,[38]

Takes note of the report of the Executive Director and requests that the United Nations Environment Programme continue its collaboration with the relevant organizations in terms of its experience and expertise and report on progress in this regard to the Governing Council at its nineteenth session.

9th meeting
25 May 1995

[...]

18/25. International conventions and protocols in the field of the environment

The Governing Council,

Recalling its decision 24 (III) of 30 April 1975 and General Assembly resolution 3436 (XXX) of 9 December 1975,

Noting with appreciation the quality and usefulness of the Register of International Treaties and Other Agreements in the Field of Environment, which is published and distributed by the United Nations Environment Programme biennially,

1. Takes note of the report of the Executive Director on international conventions and protocols in the field of the environment;[42]

2. Requests the Executive Director to continue regular publication of the Register and invites her to consider the possibility of updating and disseminating it more frequently;

3. Authorizes the Executive Director to transmit her report, on its behalf, together with any comments made by delegations thereon, to the General Assembly at its fiftieth session, in accordance with General Assembly resolution 3436 (XXX);

4. Calls on States that have not yet done so to sign, ratify or accede to those conventions and protocols in the field of the environment to which they are eligible to become parties.

9th meeting
25 May 1995

[...]

---

[38] UNEP/GC.18/35.

[42] UNEP/GC.18/23 and Corr.1 and Add.1 and 2.

18/31. Protection of the marine environment from land-based activities

The Governing Council,

Recalling its decision 17/20 of 21 May 1993, instituting a programme of meetings leading to a global intergovernmental conference for the purpose of adopting a programme of action to protect the marine environment from degradation by land-based activities,

Welcoming the progress made at the Preliminary Meeting of Experts to Assess the Effectiveness of Regional Seas Agreements, held in Nairobi from 6 to 10 December 1993,[53] the Meeting of Government-designated Experts Focusing on the 1985 Montreal Guidelines for the Protection of the Marine Environment against Land-based Sources of Pollution, held in Montreal from 6 to 10 June 1994,[54] and the Meeting of Government-designated Experts to Review and Revise a Global Programme of Action to Protect the Marine Environment from Land-based Activities, held in Reykjavik from 6 to 10 March 1995,[55]

Having noted the draft Global Programme of Action for the Protection of the Marine Environment from Land-based Activities[56] which will be submitted to the Intergovernmental Conference to Adopt a Global Programme of Action for the Protection of the Marine Environment from Land-based Activities to be held in Washington, D.C., from 23 October to 3 November 1995,

Having noted also recent developments which are important in relation to the protection of the seas, such as the entry into force on 16 November 1994 of the United Nations Convention on the Law of the Sea,[28] the developments for enhancing the protection of the sea from the dumping of waste within the framework of the 1972 London Convention on the Prevention of Marine Pollution by Dumping of Wastes and Other Matter,[57] the strengthening at the regional level of legal instruments for the protection of the marine environment against degradation from land-based activities, in particular within the framework of the regional seas programme of the United Nations Environment Programme, the requirements of the United Nations Framework Convention on Climate Change[36] and the Convention on Biological Diversity,[58] and the ongoing implementation of the Basel Convention on the Control of Transboundary Movements of Hazardous Wastes and their Disposal,[59] the Bamako Convention on the Ban of the Import into Africa and the Control of Transboundary Movement and Management of Hazardous Wastes within Africa and other relevant

---

[53] See the report of Preliminary Meeting of Experts to Assess the Effectiveness of Regional Seas Agreements (UNEP/LBS/WG.1/1/3).

[54] See the report of the Meeting of Government-designated Experts Focusing on the 1985 Montreal Guidelines for the Protection of the Marine Environment against Land-based Sources of Pollution (UNEP/MG/IG/1/5).

[55] See the report of the Meeting of Government-designated Experts to Review and Revise a Global Programme of Action to Protect the Marine Environment from Land-based Activities (UNEP/ICL/IG/1/L.6).

[56] UNEP(OCA)/LBA/IG.2/3.

[57] United Nations, Treaty Series, vol. 1064, No. 15749.

[58] UNEP/Bio.Div/N7-INC.5/4.

[59] UNEP/WG.190/4.

conventions on transboundary movements of hazardous wastes and their disposal, with a view, inter alia, to preventing and regulating all risks and potential damage to the marine environment,

Recognizing that inadequate disposal of urban waste-water is one of the main problems affecting communities and ecosystems, stressing its implications for sustainable development in the developing world, including, inter alia, human health, infant mortality, and agricultural uses;

Noting that the use of environmentally sound technologies and facilities as well as available resources for ensuring adequate waste-water treatment in the developing world is at present limited and that therefore there is an urgent need to address the adverse socio-economic and health effects of waste-water;

1. Calls on all States, including those participating in regional conventions and programme for the protection of the marine environment, the regional seas programmes of the United Nations Environment Programme, and the relevant international and non-governmental organizations, to consider the draft Global Programme of Action for the Protection of the Marine Environment from Land-based Activities and to communicate any proposals for amendment to the Executive Director by 15 August 1995, for submission to the Intergovernmental Conference to Adopt a Global Programme of Action for the Protection of the Marine Environment from Land-based Activities to be held in Washington, D.C., from 23 October to 3 November 1995. Such suggestions could, in particular, relate to, or be derived from, new or already planned land-based activities in fields such as urban development and planning, tourism, agriculture, manufacturing industry, aquaculture, harbour operations and management of river systems, and aim at ways and means by which the Programme of Action could contribute to the development of land-based activities in a sustainable manner and support their implementation in accordance with nationally or regionally agreed environmental planning;

2. Requests the Executive Director to produce the additional information on future funding requirements and opportunities, and on clearing-house activities, as was requested by the meeting of Government-designated experts in Reykjavik, and assemble, analyse and process any proposals communicated by States or relevant organizations, in particular those resulting from further regional consultations, and distribute this information in due time before the forthcoming Intergovernmental Conference in Washington, D.C.;

3. Urges Governments to contribute additional resources to support the participation of developing countries in the Intergovernmental Conference in 1995, as well as any necessary intersessional preparatory activities;

4. Requests the Executive Director to take note of the Advisory Committee on Protection of the Sea Conference on Funding and Institutional Issues for the Washington Action Programme on Protection of the Marine Environment from Land-based Activities, due to take place in Rio de Janeiro in June 1995, and to relay any recommendations, in particular those that address the various needs of States and that may facilitate the adoption and implementation of the Global Programme of Action, in due time for information to the Intergovernmental Conference in Washington, D.C.;

5. Calls on States participating in the Intergovernmental Conference in Washington to consider how, within the Global Programme of Action, appropriate attention could be given to support action at national and regional level on urban waste-water management and treatment and persistent organic pollutants as was requested by the Reykjavik meeting of Government-designated experts, in accordance with available resources and capacities and

taking into account the relevant principles of the Rio Declaration on Environment and Development[2] and the priorities of Agenda 21[1];

6. Requests the Executive Director to initiate action to ensure appropriate linkages between the elements of the draft Global Programme of Action on persistent organic pollutants and on management and treatment of urban sewage and similar action being developed in other forums. Initial actions related to persistent organic pollutants are contained in Governing Council decision 18/32 of 25 May 1995;

7. Requests the Executive Director:

(a) To further, in cooperation with other appropriate agencies, projects aimed at the development of indigenous and basic systems for waste-water management, with focus on community-based systems and, where possible, stimulate water recycling;

(b) To provide for international know-how to assist developing countries in addressing in an efficient and effective manner the problem of adequate disposal and recycling of urban waste-water;

(c) To support activities undertaken by the United Nations Centre for Human Settlements (Habitat) in the development of operating manuals for shallow sewerage systems, and other relevant human settlement waste-water treatment and management approaches;

8. Calls on States in a position to do so, and multilateral financing institutions, to cooperate actively in new and existing regional cooperation frameworks and to support States participants in such regional frameworks, at their request, to implement the provisions of the Global Programme of Action at the appropriate national, regional and international level and to enhance the capacity to prevent degradation of the marine environment from land-based activities;

9. Requests the Executive Director to make arrangements, in the period up to the nineteenth session of the Governing Council, to promote and facilitate the implementation of the outcome of the Washington Intergovernmental Conference, in cooperation with all relevant intergovernmental organizations;

10. Requests the Executive Director to ensure immediate and high priority for these activities and to programme adequate funds and staff to facilitate implementation within the available programme resources for the relevant year for activity 7.1.4.(a);

11. Requests the Executive Director to report to the Governing Council at its nineteenth session on the outcome of the Intergovernmental Conference to Adopt a Global Programme of Action for the Protection of the Marine Environment from Land-based Activities.

9th meeting
25 May 1995

[...]

18/33. International coral reef initiative

The Governing Council,

Noting that many of the world's coral reefs are severely degraded or destroyed due to human activities,

Recalling that chapter 17 of Agenda 21 identifies coral reefs, mangroves and seagrass beds as marine ecosystems of high biological diversity and production and recommends that they be accorded high priority for identification and protection,

Noting the report of the United Nations Environment Programme-Intergovernmental Oceanographic Commission-Association of South Pacific Environmental Institutions-World Conservation Union Global Task Team on the Implications of Climate Change on Coral Reefs,[61]

Also noting that coral reefs have been designated as the coastal system chosen as the first to be developed within the coastal zone module of the Global Ocean Observing System,

Recognizing the initiative of Australia, France, Jamaica, Japan, the Philippines, Sweden, the United Kingdom and the United States to sponsor a workshop to promote an international coral reef initiative, to be held in the Philippines from 29 May to 2 June 1995,

Noting that the initiative builds upon and reflects the processes established by the Commission on Sustainable Development, which will address chapter 17 of Agenda 21 in 1996, the United Nations Convention on Biological Diversity,[58] which will address marine biological diversity in 1995, the 1995 intergovernmental meetings on protection of the marine environment from land-based activities, the United Nations Framework Convention on Climate Change,[36] the 1994 Global Conference on the Sustainable Development of Small Island Developing States, the United Nations Convention on the Law of the Sea,[28] and other relevant international programmes,

1. Welcomes the international coral reef initiative, which is a partnership of Governments, international organizations (including lending institutions), and non-governmental organizations to address capacity-building, research and monitoring and sustainable management and use of coral reefs and associated ecosystems;

2. Supports the establishment of a global coral reef monitoring network, as proposed as part of the coastal zone and shelf module of the Global Ozone Observing System by the United Nations Environment Programme, the World Conservation Union, the Intergovernmental Oceanographic Commission, the World Meteorological Organization and International Geosphere-Biosphere Programme, within existing resources, to monitor the status of reefs and enhance their management;

3. Encourages the regional programmes of United Nations Environment Programme, particularly the regional seas programmes, to incorporate recommendations of the coral reef initiative workshop, as appropriate, into relevant United Nations Environment Programme activities and, whenever appropriate, to translate them into concrete supporting measures on protection and conservation;

---

[61] C.R. Wilkinson and R.W. Buddemeier, Global Climate Change and Coral Reefs: Implications for People and Reefs. Report of the UNEP-IOC-ASPEI-IUCN Global Task Team on the Implications of Climate Change on Coral Reefs (IUCN, Gland, Switzerland, 1994).

4. Encourages continued participation of the United Nations Environment Programme in the international coral reef initiative, particularly the international coral reef initiative planning committee, regional meetings, and forthcoming session at the Commission on Sustainable Development in 1996.

10th meeting
26 May 1995

18/34. Support from the United Nations Environment Programme for small island developing States and implementation of the Programme of Action of the Global Conference on the Sustainable Development of Small Island Developing States

The Governing Council,

Recalling chapter 17 of Agenda 21,[1] which recognized the particular vulnerabilities, both ecological and economic, of small island developing States and the special challenges they face in planning for and implementing sustainable development,

Noting the outcome of the Global Conference on the Sustainable Development of Small Island Developing States, held in Barbados from 26 April to 6 May 1994,[62] in particular its Programme of Action,[63] which called for action at the international, regional and national levels,

Noting that at its fourth session, the Commission for Sustainable Development will consider chapter 17 of Agenda 21, including action taken to implement the Barbados Programme of Action,

1. Welcomes the action taken to date by the Executive Director in response to the Barbados Conference, including the establishment of a focal point and a task force within the United Nations Environment Programme to coordinate the Programme's activities relevant to the Barbados Programme of Action;

2. Urges the Executive Director to ensure that, in implementing the programme of work agreed by the Governing Council at its eighteenth session, appropriate attention is given to the needs and vulnerabilities of small island developing States;

3. Further urges the Executive Director, through the effective use and involvement of the task force in both programme activities and policy development, to encourage an integrated approach within the United Nations Environment Programme to addressing the issues of relevance to small island developing States.

10th meeting
26 May 1995

---

[62] See Report of the Global Conference on the Sustainable Development of Small Island Development States, Bridgetown, Barbados, 25 April - 6 May 1994 (United Nations publication, Sales No. E.94.I.8 and corrigendum).

[63] Ibid, chap.I, resolution I, annex II.

18/35. Lead in gasoline

The Governing Council,

Recalling the decision of the Commission on Sustainable Development at its second session, by which the Commission noted severe health impacts of human exposure to lead, endorsed the ongoing work on that issue in several international forums, and encouraged further efforts to reduce human exposure to lead,[64]

Noting with approval the efforts under way among countries to reduce exposures associated with the use of lead, in particular commitments made by a number of countries to develop action plans to phase out or reduce the use of lead in gasoline,

Noting also that, in order to maximize effectiveness and benefit to the environment, the elimination of lead in gasoline should be accompanied by the use of catalytic converters,

Further noting the decision adopted on 28 April 1995 by the Commission on Sustainable Development at its third session, calling upon all countries to consider and all interested countries to develop action plans with a view to phasing out or reducing the use of lead in gasoline, and inviting them to inform the Commission of their decision and progress as appropriate at its fourth session,

Noting also that the Commission in its decision called upon donor countries and financial institutions to assist developing countries in the financing and transfer of relevant technologies, in accordance with chapters 33 and 34 of Agenda 21,[1]

1. Calls upon Governments to give full consideration to the costs and benefits of phasing out lead in gasoline, including risks associated with increased aromatic components in the absence of catalytic converters;

2. Urges countries that have already begun to phase out the use of lead in gasoline, as well as appropriate international organizations and international financial institutions, to assist other countries in their efforts to achieve such a phase-out, in accordance with the decision of the Commission on Sustainable Development at its third session, and to promote the transfer of technology towards the overall reduction of vehicular emissions;

3. Invites the Executive Director to participate in these efforts as appropriate, within available resources and without duplication of effort, as part of her broader efforts to promote more effective approaches to emissions control.

10th meeting
26 May 1995

---

[64] E/1994/33/Rev.1-E/CN.17/1994/20/Rev.1, chap.I, para. 169.

18/36. Biological diversity

A. Support to the Secretariat of the Convention on Biological Diversity

The Governing Council,

Noting General Assembly resolution 49/117 of 19 December 1994 on the Convention on Biological Diversity,[58]

Noting decision 1/4 adopted by the first meeting of the Conference of the Parties to the Convention on Biological Diversity, held in Nassau from 28 November to 9 December 1994, on the selection of a competent international organization to carry out the functions of the Secretariat of the Convention,[65]

Welcomes the designation of the United Nations Environment Programme to carry out the functions of the Secretariat of the Convention on Biological Diversity and notes that it ensures the latter's autonomy to discharge the functions referred to in article 24 of the Convention.

10th meeting
26 May 1995

B. Biosafety

The Governing Council,

Recalling the objectives of chapter 16 of Agenda 21[1] on the promotion of environmentally sound management of biotechnology,

Further recalling the provisions of article 19 of the Convention on Biological Diversity[58] on handling of biotechnology and distribution of its benefits, in particular paragraph 3, calling on Parties to "consider the need for and modalities of a protocol setting out appropriate procedures, including, in particular, advance informed agreement, in the field of the safe transfer, handling and use of any living modified organism resulting from biotechnology that may have adverse effect on the consideration and sustainable use of biological diversity",

Noting the decision by the Conference of the Parties to the Convention on Biological Diversity at its first meeting, held in Nassau from 28 November to 9 December 1994, to consider the need for and modalities of a protocol on the safe handling and use of living modified organisms resulting from biotechnology that have adverse effects on biodiversity, and other international work on biosafety,[66]

Affirming the desirability of the United Nations Environment Programme contributing to international efforts on biosafety while avoiding duplication with other international activities currently being undertaken by other organizations, in particular the work initiated by the Conference of the Parties to the Convention on Biological Diversity,

---

[65] See the report of the first meeting of the Conference of the Parties to the Convention on Biological Diversity (UNEP/CBD/COP/1/7), annex II.

[66] Ibid, decision I/9, para. 3.

1. Welcomes the United Nations Environment Programme initiative to hold consultations on International Technical Guidelines for Safety in Biotechnology and Related Capacity-Building Requirements;

2. Notes with appreciation that three regional expert consultations on International Technical Guidelines for Safety in Biotechnology and Related Capacity-Building Requirements have so far been held and that further regional consultations are planned;

3. Supports, taking into account any relevant decision by the Conference of the Parties to the Convention on Biological Diversity at its second meeting, the holding of a global expert consultation on International Technical Guidelines for Safety in Biotechnology and Related Capacity-Building Requirements at a time after the second meeting of the Conference of the Parties to the Convention on Biological Diversity;

4. Endorses and supports United Nations Environment Programme sponsorship of regional consultations on International Technical Guidelines for Safety in Biotechnology and Related Capacity-Building Requirements, noting the need for such a programme to avoid prejudging the consideration, initiated by the Conference of the Parties to the Convention on Biological Diversity, on the need for and the modalities of a protocol on biosafety;

5. Requests the Executive Director to consult closely with the Secretariat of the Convention on Biological Diversity in the implementation of the present decision and report on progress to the Governing Council at its nineteenth session.

9th meeting
25 May 1995

[...]

18/39. Regional programmes

A. Regional programme support for Africa

The Governing Council,

Recalling General Assembly resolution 47/190 of 22 December 1992, by which the Assembly endorsed Agenda 21[1] and the emphasis it gave to regional environment and development priority activities as contained in the various regional common positions for the United Nations Conference on Environment and Development,

Reaffirming its decision 17/32 of 21 May 1993, endorsing the integrated approach to environment and sustainable development,

Appreciative of the effort made by the Executive Director in the integrated approach contained in the 1996-1997 programme of work and budget,[67]

Also appreciative of the continued inclusion of the African Ministerial Conference on the Environment among the activities of the work programme and budget,

Concerned that the key priorities in the proposed programme do not respond adequately to Africa's major environmental concerns as expressed in the African Common Position on Environment and Development submitted to the United Nations Conference on Environment and Development by Africa as addressed in the priorities of the new programme of the African Ministerial Conference on the Environment,

Believing that Africa's contribution to regional and global sustainability would be minimal if this inadequacy is not addressed,

1. Requests the Executive Director to ensure that in the implementation of the programme emphasis is placed on the following areas of major concern to Africa, which are included in the 1996-1997 programme of work of the United Nations Environment Programme:

(a) Land resources:

(i) Support for the implementation of the United Nations Convention to Combat Desertification in Those Countries Experiencing Serious Drought and/or Desertification, Particularly in Africa,[45] adopted in Paris on 17 June 1994, particularly the urgent actions for Africa; and

(ii) Conservation and rehabilitation strategies in conflict areas;

(b) Water resources:

(i) Strengthening African inland water management groups and regional technical cooperation networks;

(ii) Reclamation and rehabilitation of African lakes and wetland areas;

(c) Biological resources: promotion of the implementation of the Convention on Biological Diversity[58] and related programmes in Africa;

(d) Coastal and marine resources:

(i) Updated inventory of coastal and marine resources of four African regional seas programmes;

(ii) Ratified and implemented African regional seas conventions and protocols;

(e) Major groups: support to the African preparations for the follow-up to the Fourth World Conference on Women;

(f) Global and regional servicing and support:

(i) Support to the programmes of the African Ministerial Conference on the Environment and capacity-building of its secretariat;

(ii) Strengthening of the Regional Office for Africa;

(iii) Focus on capacity-building, especially greater support and training for implementing post-Rio national plans, environmental management systems, policies, programmes, international environmental conventions, regional agreements, protocols, treaties and conventions, and new national laws/frameworks for environmental protection;

(iv) Public awareness, information and participation programmes, including those aimed at providing tangible opportunities for working with major groups, especially women, youth, and local communities in the implementation of decisions of the Governing Council;

2. Also requests the Executive Director to implement the above activities within available resources;

3. Further requests the Executive Director to report to the Governing Council at its nineteenth session on the implementation of the present decision.

10th meeting
26 May 1995

B. Technical cooperation among African countries for the building and utilization of capacities and for mobilization of resources for sustainable development in Africa

The Governing Council,

Cognizant of the urgent need to promote environmental management and sustainable development in the African region,

Recognizing that African countries need to develop and fully utilize internal capacities and fully mobilize resources available in the region as the driving force in attaining desirable levels of environmental management and sustainable development,

Conscious of the central position that internal capacity-building and utilization and resource mobilization would play in environmental management and sustainable development, especially when supplemented by external capacities, where necessary,

Aware of the successes made in capacity-building and resource mobilization through the technical cooperation among developing countries mechanism and desirous to bring similar benefits closer home to Africa in the field of environmental management and sustainable development,

Convinced of the need for support for technical cooperation among African countries to contribute to the implementation of Agenda 21[1] in the region through capacity-building and utilization measures,

Considering the position of the Conference of Ministers of the United Nations Economic Commission for Africa on the subject of technical cooperation among African countries during its twenty-first session, held in Addis Ababa in May 1995,

Cognizant of Africa's disadvantaged role in the global political economy and hence the need for such initiatives and mechanisms to help lift Africa and place her on the path towards full participation in the global human development endeavour,

1. Urges the Executive Director:

(a) To work closely in partnership with the United Nations Development Programme to increase and focus support for technical cooperation among African countries in the field of environmental management and sustainable development through appropriate capacity-building and utilization measures and mechanisms, and, within available resources, to urge the United Nations Development Programme to explore the possibility of opening a special window for technical cooperation among African countries within the framework of the technical cooperation among developing countries mechanism as a starting point;

(b) To facilitate measures for promoting technical cooperation among African countries and capacity-building and utilization in the field of environmental management and sustainable development for the African region;

(c) To collaborate with the United Nations Development Programme in seeking support for the mobilization of resources from within the United Nations system, bilateral and multilateral agencies, non-governmental organizations and the private sector to facilitate the development and implementation of further measures for technical cooperation among African countries;

2. Further urges:

(a) Other members of the United Nations system, multilateral and bilateral agencies, international non-governmental organizations and the private sector to render concrete support to measures to promote technical cooperation among African countries in the field of environmental management and sustainable development;

(b) African Governments, local non-governmental organizations, universities and foundations and the local private sector also to support technical cooperation among African countries;

3. Requests the Executive Director to urge:

(a) The Economic Commission for Africa to incorporate environmental management and sustainable development into its capacity-building and utilization initiative for Africa;

(b) The Organization of African Unity and the subregional organizations (Common Market for Eastern and Southern Africa, Economic Community of West African States, Economic Community of Central African States, Arab Maghreb Union, Southern African Development Community, Intergovernmental Authority on Drought and Development, Permanent Inter-State Committee for Drought Control in the Sahel) to incorporate measures and mechanisms for technical cooperation among African countries and capacity-building and utilization for Africa into the programming of their resource mobilization and policy design strategies;

4. Authorizes the Executive Director:

(a) To request the United Nations Development Programme to carry out a comprehensive study of the feasibility, modalities, approaches, appropriate measures and resource requirements for the successful implementation of technical cooperation among African countries and to collaborate closely with the United Nations Environment Programme on those aspects of the study relating to environmental management and sustainable development;

(b) To request the United Nations Development Programme to present the report of the study to the Economic and Social Council at its 1996 session for policy debate;

(c) To report to the Governing Council at its nineteenth session on the results of these efforts as they relate to the field of environmental management and sustainable development.

10th meeting
26 May 1995

C. Programmes of the Council of Arab Ministers Responsible for the Environment and the regional programme for West Asia

The Governing Council,

Recalling its decision 17/28 of 21 May 1993 in which it requested the Executive Director, inter alia, to continue her efforts to link the implementation of the regional programmes undertaken by the United Nations Environment Programme with other international organizations, particularly the United Nations Development Programme and the regional economic commissions, in a coordinated manner,

Recalling also its decision 16/33 of 31 May 1991, in which it requested the Executive Director, inter alia, to encourage ways and means of facilitating the transfer and acquisition of technology by the developing countries in respect of cleaner production and its techniques,

Recalling further Agenda 21[1] adopted by the United Nations Conference on Environment and Development, particularly chapter 34 on the transfer of environmentally sound technology, cooperation and capacity-building, and chapter 38 on international institutional arrangements, as well as its chapter 1, which calls for cooperation and implementation at the regional and subregional levels,

Noting the possibilities of improving and activating environmental activities in the Arab region, in general, and in West Asia, in particular, especially in the areas of capacity-building, provision and exchange of information, improving public awareness and education and combating desertification and pollution,

Expressing its appreciation of the results achieved by the cooperation between the United Nations Environment Programme and the Council of Arab Ministers Responsible for the Environment,

Recognizing the role of the Arab League Liaison Office in Cairo, in support of the cooperation between the Council of Arab Ministers Responsible for the Environment, and the United Nations Environment Programme and its regional offices,

Requests the Executive Director to support, within available resources, the goals and aims of the Council of Arab Ministers Responsible for the Environment and the Regional Office for West Asia, with particular reference to support for Arab priority project proposals within the framework of Arab programmes for sustainable development approved for implementation by the Council of Arab Ministers Responsible for the Environment and Regional Office for West Asia.

10th meeting
26 May 1995

D. North-East Asia Regional Environment Programme

The Governing Council,

Recalling its decision 17/28 of 21 May 1993, in which it, inter alia, requested the Executive Director to continue making efforts to link the implementation of the regional programmes of the United Nations Environment Programme in a coordinated manner with other international organizations, particularly the United Nations Development Programme and the regional economic commissions,

Recalling also its decision 16/33 of 31 May 1991, in which it, inter alia, called upon the Executive Director to promote the identification of ways and means to facilitate access by and transfer of technology to developing countries in respect of cleaner production methods, techniques and technologies,

Further recalling the Agenda 21 programme of action[1] as adopted by the United Nations Conference on Environment and Development, particularly its chapter 34 (Transfer of environmentally sound technology, cooperation and capacity-building), and chapter 38 (International institutional arrangements), section I, on regional and subregional cooperation and implementation,

Noting with appreciation the collaborating work of six Governments of the North-East Asian subregion, namely, China, Democratic People's Republic of Korea, Japan, Mongolia, Republic of Korea and Russian Federation, through senior officials' meetings on environmental cooperation in North-East Asia, organized by the Economic and Social Commission for Asia and the Pacific, substantively supported by the Asian Development Bank and the United Nations Development Programme, and supported technically by the United Nations Environment Programme and the World Bank,

Taking into account the deliberations of the Economic and Social Commission for Asia and the Pacific at its fifty-first session, held from 24 April to 1 May 1995 on, inter alia, the subject of the North-East Asia Regional Environment Programme,

Requests the Executive Director to support fully, within available resources, the aims and objectives of the North-East Asia Regional Environment Programme so as to carry out the catalytic and coordinating role of the United Nations Environment Programme through its strengthened regional office in Thailand and also its International Environmental Technology Centre in Japan, particularly in its work programme of the biennium 1996-1997, inter alia, by:

(a) Technical and financial support to the third meeting on environmental cooperation in North-East Asia, scheduled to be held in early 1996 in Mongolia; and

(b) Technical support to the priority project proposals unanimously adopted by the second meeting on environmental cooperation in North-East Asia for implementation.

9th meeting
25 May 1995

E. Action Plan for the Protection and Management of the Marine and Coastal Environment of the South Asian Seas Region

The Governing Council,

Noting the provisions of Agenda 21,[1] in particular its chapter 17, the United Nations Convention on the Law of the Sea,[28] and the international efforts towards a Global Programme of Action for the Protection of the Marine Environment from Land-based Activities,

Recognizing the importance of these provisions for the large coastal populations in the South Asian Seas region,

Taking into account the needs of the peoples in the region, particularly in the marine and coastal areas of the five maritime States of the region, namely, Bangladesh, India, Maldives, Pakistan and Sri Lanka,

<u>Also noting</u> that the five above-mentioned States have agreed on an Action Plan and have made financial commitments for its implementation,

<u>Calls upon</u> the Executive Director:

(a) To give due attention, within the context of the regional seas programme of the United Nations Environment Programme, to the further development and implementation of the Action Plan for the Protection and Management of the Marine and Coastal Environment of the South Asian Seas Region;

(b) To provide, within available resources, adequate finances and staff time for the implementation of the Action Plan for the Protection and Management of the Marine and Coastal Environment of the South Asian Seas Region.

<u>10th meeting</u>
<u>26 May 1995</u>

[...]

6. STRENGTHENING OF THE UNITED NATIONS ENVIRONMENT PROGRAMME* - REPORT OF THE UN SECRETARY-GENERAL

Doc. no.: A/50/171 21 July 1995

1. The present report was prepared pursuant to General Assembly resolution 48/174 of 21 December 1993 on the strengthening of the United Nations Environment Programme. In that resolution, the Assembly, inter alia, reaffirmed the central role of the United Nations Environment Programme (UNEP) as the principal body to catalyse, coordinate and stimulate action in the field of the environment within the United Nations system, invited the Secretary-General to strengthen further the liaison function at Nairobi for the Commission on Sustainable Development, urged Member States to make their contributions to the Environment Fund in accordance with UNEP Governing Council decision 17/32 of 21 May 1993 and requested the Secretary-General to ensure that the conference facilities in UNEP headquarters at Nairobi were utilized to the maximum and in a cost-effective manner and to report to the Assembly at its fiftieth session on the implementation of the resolution. Progress in that regard is outlined below.

2. Since its assumption of responsibility for the liaison function of the Commission on Sustainable Development, a number of further steps have been taken by UNEP to strengthen this, on the basis of arrangements made at the United Nations Conference on Environment and Development and taking into account the relevant provisions of General Assembly resolution 47/191 of 22 December 1992.

3. Prior to the adoption of resolution 48/174 and following the conclusion of the first substantive session of the Commission on Sustainable Development (New York, 14 to 25 June 1993), the Executive Director of UNEP offered to the Under-Secretary-General for Policy Coordination and Sustainable Development of the Secretariat the services of UNEP in providing for the discharge of the liaison function. The offer was accepted and, in February 1994, following agreement on terms of reference, a staff member of UNEP was appointed on a full-time basis as Liaison Officer in Nairobi for the secretariat of the Commission, with associated logistical, travel and communications expenses being borne by UNEP. That arrangement has proved extremely useful for UNEP in playing a major role in preparing for Commission on Sustainable Development sessions, as well as for the permanent missions, non-governmental organizations and global and regional organizations headquartered at Nairobi.

---

* A/50/150.

4. In order to strengthen further the liaison function and to enhance its relevance to increased cooperation between UNEP and the secretariat of the Commission on Sustainable Development, the liaison function has, since early 1995, been placed with the Division of Environmental Policy in UNEP. That move is expected to facilitate liaison with the Commission leading to enhanced cooperation between UNEP and the Commission, since the Division of Environmental Policy also handles inter-agency affairs within UNEP and is the principal focal point for all matters relating to the General Assembly.

5. In its decision 17/32, the Governing Council reaffirmed that UNEP would require access to adequate financial resources, particularly in accordance with chapters 33 and 38 of Agenda 21, to enable it to exercise all the functions assigned to it by Agenda 21.

6. Despite the provisions of decision 17/32, however, there has been little change in contribution patterns. Pledges and contributions for 1995 have not only fallen short of the target established by the Governing Council, but may be insufficient to finance the Fund programme of activities for the biennium 1994-1995. The problem is further compounded by late payments. Governments should make their pledges in advance of the year in which they intend to pay their contributions and do so early in the year in order for the secretariat to plan and execute the programme more effectively. Late payment leads to the need to carry over cash balances from biennium to biennium, which not only disrupts proper planning and effective implementation of the programme of work, but also provides an inaccurate portrayal of the level of resources.

7. In the same decision the Governing Council also recognized the need to broaden the base of contributions to the Environment Fund and called upon all Governments to contribute to the Environment Fund and, where they were already contributing, to increase their contributions.

8. Despite the enhanced mandate given to UNEP by Agenda 21 and the increased number of assignments given to the secretariat by the Governing Council at every succeeding session, contributions to the Environment Fund are declining in real terms. The secretariat has undertaken measures to increase productivity and effectiveness, but this anomaly can only be corrected by increased and timely contributions by Governments and by broadening the base of contributions. In order to enable UNEP to respond effectively to the challenges it faces, Governments would have to respond to their own decisions to increase their contributions to the Fund.

9. As requested in paragraph 7 of resolution 48/174, the Executive Director of UNEP has actively pursued the possibilities of holding major meetings related to the environment programme in the conference facilities at Nairobi. More meetings of the convention secretariats were held at Nairobi in 1994 than in earlier years. The Fourth Conference of the Parties to the Convention on the Conservation of Migratory Species of Wild Animals and other related meetings took place from 4 to 14 June, the second meeting of the Intergovernmental Committee on the Convention on Biological Diversity was held from 17 June to 1 July and the tenth meeting of the expanded working group on the Montreal Protocol on Substances that Deplete the Ozone Layer and related meetings followed from 4 to 8 July. Conference-servicing staff recruited on a temporary basis serviced all these meetings in sequence, thus entailing savings on travel costs for each of the three entities involved. Several other meetings under the Montreal Protocol were held at Nairobi in September and October.

10. Several meetings under the Intergovernmental Panel on Climate Change were held in November 1994 and the seventh session of the Intergovernmental Negotiating Committee for the Elaboration of an International Convention to Combat Desertification in those Countries Experiencing Serious Drought and/or Desertification, particularly in Africa will be held at Nairobi from 7 to 18 August 1995.

11. Continuous efforts are being made to programme meetings back to back in order to maximize the opportunities for savings on conference-servicing costs. In April and May 1995, the fifteenth session of the Commission on Human Settlements was held simultaneously with the Preparatory Committee for the United Nations Conference on Human Settlements (Habitat II), followed by the meeting of the Ad Hoc Expert Group of the Montreal Protocol from 8 to 12 May and the eighteenth session of the UNEP Governing Council from 15 to 26 May 1995. All these meetings were serviced to the extent possible by the same interpreters, again saving considerably on travel costs (one round-trip instead of three).

12. In addition, UNEP has made a special effort to provide remote translation services via electronic means to meetings held away from Nairobi. This has meant that UNEP no longer has to send teams of translators and typists to the venues of meetings, thereby cutting down considerably on travel costs.

-----

7. UNEP CONVENTION ON BIOLOGICAL DIVERSITY* - REPORT OF THE EXECUTIVE SECRETARY

Doc. no.: A/50/218 20 June 1995

I. INTRODUCTION

1. In its resolution 47/190 of 22 December 1992, the General Assembly noted with satisfaction that the Convention on Biological Diversity had been opened for signature and signed by a large number of States at the United Nations Conference on Environment and Development, held at Rio de Janeiro, Brazil, from 3 to 14 June 1992, and stressed the need for the Convention to come into force as soon as possible.

2. In its resolution 49/117 of 19 December 1994, the General Assembly, deeply concerned by the continuing loss of the world's biological diversity and reiterating the commitment to the conservation of biological diversity and the sustainable use of its components, as well as the fair and equitable sharing of benefits arising from the use of genetic resources, welcomed the early entry into force of the Convention, and the convening of the first meeting of its Conference of Parties, held at Nassau from 28 November to 9 December 1994; and called upon those States which had not yet ratified the Convention to expedite their internal procedures of ratification, acceptance or approval.

3. In the same resolution, the General Assembly also decided to consider the progress achieved in the implementation of the Convention at its fiftieth session and invited the Executive Secretary of the Convention on Biological Diversity to report, through the Commission on Sustainable Development and the Economic and Social Council, on the results of the first meeting of the Conference of the Parties to the Convention. The present report is submitted by the Executive Secretary of the Convention on Biological Diversity in response to that request.

II. THE FIRST MEETING OF THE CONFERENCE OF THE PARTIES

4. Convened in accordance with article 23, paragraph 1, of the Convention, the first meeting of the Conference of the Parties was opened by the Executive Director of the United Nations Environment Programme (UNEP). It was preceded by informal consultations held on 27 November 1994. Messages to the meeting from

* A/50/50/Rev.1.

the Secretary-General of the United Nations and the President of the forty-ninth session of the General Assembly were presented. Mr. Hubert A. Ingraham, Prime Minister of the Bahamas, addressed the meeting. The meeting also witnessed the inauguration of a Biodiversity Technology Fair organized under the aegis of UNEP and the Government of the Bahamas with the support of the Government of Canada.

5. All States were invited to participate in the meeting. Ninety-six parties were represented. The Committee on Credentials established in accordance with rule 19 of the rules of procedure of the Conference of the Parties found all credentials of parties to be in order. Thirty-four States were represented by observers. Twenty-two intergovernmental organizations and 120 non-governmental organizations were also represented.

6. The Ministerial Segment of the first meeting of the Conference of the Parties was held from 7 to 9 December 1994. At its opening ceremony statements were made by the President of the meeting, Ms. I. Dumont; the Executive Director of UNEP, Ms. E. Dowdeswell; the Chairman of the Commission on Sustainable Development, Mr. K. Töpfer; the Minister of Foreign Affairs of the Bahamas, Mrs. Janet Bostwick. Forty-eight States were represented at ministerial level. At the closure of the meeting, the Ministers adopted the Bahamas Ministerial Declaration on the Convention on Biological Diversity.

7. The Conference of the Parties adopted its rules of procedure with the exception of paragraph 1 of rule 40. It also adopted decisions related to financial resources and mechanism, technical and scientific matters, the Commission on Sustainable Development, a medium-term programme of work and administrative and budgetary issues, and established its Subsidiary Body on Scientific, Technical and Technological Advice.

A. Financial resources and mechanism

8. In its decision 1/2, the Conference of the Parties decided to adopt the policy, strategy, programme priorities and eligibility criteria for access to and utilization of financial resources as well as the list of developed country parties and other parties that voluntarily assume the obligations of developed country parties; decided also that the restructured Global Environment Facility (GEF) should continue to serve as the institutional structure to operate the financial mechanism under the Convention on an interim basis, in accordance with article 39 of the Convention, authorized the Secretariat to consult with the restructured GEF on the content of a memorandum of understanding that should be formally considered at the second meeting of the Conference of the Parties. Pending the adoption of such a memorandum, the Conference of the Parties adopted interim guidelines for monitoring and evaluation of the utilization of financial resources by the restructured GEF; requested the Secretariat to present at its second meeting a report on the financial mechanism as well as a study on the availability of financial resources additional to those provided through the restructured GEF, and on the ways and means for mobilizing and channelling those resources in support of the objectives of the Convention; and also requested the Secretariat to include items on the agenda of the Conference of the Parties at its second meeting that would enable the latter to review the financial resources and to take a decision at that meeting on which institutional structure should be designated in accordance with article 21 of the Convention.

B. Technical and scientific matters

9. In its decision 1/3, the Conference of the Parties decided to implement the provisions of article 18, paragraph 3, of the Convention on the establishment of a clearing-house mechanism to promote and facilitate technical and scientific cooperation, operating under the authority of the Conference of the Parties; requested the Secretariat to prepare, and report back to the Conference of the Parties at its second meeting on, a comprehensive study containing concrete costed recommendations to assist the Conference of the Parties in the

establishment of the clearing-house mechanism; and decided to include the issue on the agenda of its second meeting.

10. In its decision 1/7, the Conference of the Parties requested the Subsidiary Body to consider its modus operandi and to prepare a proposal for its medium-term programme of work based on the priorities set in the programme of work of the Conference of the Parties and on article 25 of the Convention.

C. Statement to the Commission on Sustainable Development

11. In its decision 1/8, the Conference of the Parties invited its President to transmit the statement to the high-level segment of the third session of the Commission on Sustainable Development. The statement of a political character contained eight action-oriented recommendations addressed to the third session of the Commission on Sustainable Development.

D. Medium-term programme of work

12. In its decision 1/9, the Conference of the Parties decided to adopt the medium-term programme of work for the period 1995-1997; also decided to establish an open-ended ad hoc group of experts nominated by Governments to consider the need for and modalities of a protocol setting out appropriate procedures, including, in particular, advance informed agreement, in the field of the safe transfer, handling and use of any living modified organism resulting from biotechnology that might have an adverse effect on the conservation and sustainable use of biological diversity; decided further that the open-ended group of experts would consider, as appropriate, existing knowledge, experience and legislation in the field of biosafety, including the views of the parties, subregional, regional and international organizations, with a view to presenting a report for the consideration of the second meeting of the Conference of the Parties, so as to enable the Conference to reach an informed decision on the need for and modalities of a protocol; and requested the Secretariat to establish a panel of 15 experts nominated by Governments, with an equitable geographical representation, in consultation with the Bureau of the Conference of the Parties, assisted by the United Nations Industrial Development Organization (UNIDO), UNEP, the Food and Agriculture Organization of the United Nations (FAO) and the World Health Organization (WHO), to prepare a background document to be submitted to the open-ended ad hoc group of experts.

E. Administrative and budgetary issues

13. In its decision 1/4, the Conference of the Parties designated UNEP to carry out the functions of the Secretariat of the Convention while ensuring its autonomy to discharge the functions referred to in article 24. It requested the Executive Director of UNEP to select the Executive Secretary of the Convention in consultation with the Bureau of the Conference of the Parties.

14. In its decision 1/5, the Conference of the Parties welcomed the willingness demonstrated by international organizations to support and cooperate with the Secretariat of the Convention for the effective discharge of its functions, and in particular the concrete offers made by FAO and the United Nations Educational, Scientific and Cultural Organization (UNESCO), including by secondment of staff; invited other competent organizations that wished to do so to make further proposals to the Secretariat in that regard; and requested the Executive Secretary to establish contact with the secretariats of the conventions dealing with matters covered by the Convention with a view to establishing appropriate forms of cooperation between the Convention and those conventions and to report to the Conference of the Parties on the issue, as provided for in article 23.4 (h) of the Convention.

15. In part I of its decision 1/6, the Conference of the Parties adopted the Financial Rules for the Administration of the Trust Fund for the Convention on Biological Diversity; designated UNEP as the Trustee of the Trust Fund; decided that the Trust Fund should be established for an initial period of two years, beginning on 1 January 1995 and ending on 31 December 1996; adopted the budget for 1995 and urged all the Parties to pay promptly their contributions to the Trust Fund; requested the parties and States not parties to the Convention, as well as governmental, intergovernmental and non-governmental organizations and other sources, to contribute to the Trust Fund; and requested the Executive Director of UNEP to ensure, by advances, that the 1995 budget of the Convention was financed until such time as sufficient contributions had been paid in 1995 to allow for the functioning of the Secretariat.

16. In part II of its decision 1/6, the Conference of the Parties adopted the scale of contributions for 1995 and requested the Secretariat to make available the comprehensive review of all aspects of scale methodology to be presented to the General Assembly at its fiftieth session, as well as information related to scale methodology in other international organizations and information provided by Governments to assist the second meeting of the Conference of the Parties in its consideration of the matter; and decided to transfer to its next meeting, for further consideration, paragraphs 4 and 16 of the Financial Rules.

F. Other matters

17. In its decision 1/11, the Conference of the Parties requested the Secretariat to assist in the organization of regional and subregional meetings for the preparation of the second meeting of the Conference of the Parties, which will take place at Jakarta from 6 to 17 November 1995; and invited the developed countries and international organizations to make voluntary contributions to fund such regional and subregional meetings and to facilitate the participation of the developing countries, and in particular the least developed amongst them, in such meetings as well as in the meetings convened under the Convention.

18. In its decision 1/12, the Conference of the Parties recommended to the General Assembly at its forty-ninth session that it consider 29 December, the date of entry into force of the Convention on Biological Diversity, International Day for Biological Diversity.

19. In its decision 1/13, the Conference of the Parties expressed its sincere gratitude to the Government of the Bahamas and to its people for the cordial welcome they had accorded to the Conference and to those associated with its work, and for their contribution to the success of the Conference.

III. RELATIONSHIP WITH THE GENERAL ASSEMBLY AND ITS ORGANS

20. At its first meeting, the Conference of the Parties in adopting the statement addressed to the third session of the Commission on Sustainable Development, stressed the need to establish links with other bodies and processes relevant to biodiversity issues with a view to promoting coherent and urgent attention to those issues. In that context, the Conference of the Parties attached importance to the development of a substantive relationship with the Commission on Sustainable Development, given the Commission's responsibilities in respect of Agenda 21 and the complementarity of its mandate with that of the Conference of the Parties to the Convention on Biological Diversity. It appealed to the Commission on Sustainable Development to make all efforts in its own right to advance the concerns of the Convention on Biological Diversity.

21. The Conference of the Parties invited the Commission on Sustainable Development:

(a) To urge States that had not yet done so to become parties to the Convention;

(b) To consider the biodiversity issue in the light of the three interrelated objectives of the Convention;

(c) To approach the subject of biodiversity as a multisectoral issue that is relevant to virtually all of its concerns;

(d) To urge Governments to recognize the mutually supportive relationship between biodiversity and sustainable development;

(e) To encourage Governments to improve coordination among departments at the national level in order more effectively to implement measures for the conservation of biological diversity and the sustainable use of its components, given the cross-cutting nature of these issues;

(f) To consider the sectoral issues to be addressed at its 1995 session in the context of their close interrelationship with biodiversity;

(g) To urge States to work cooperatively to address the subject of poverty in the context of its close interrelationship with biodiversity;

(h) To stress to Governments the advantages deriving from coordination between its work, that of the Convention on Biological Diversity, and that of other conventions, intergovernmental bodies and for forums concerned with the conservation of biological diversity and the sustainable use of its components.

22. The General Assembly, as the supreme organ of the United Nations, in considering the report of the first meeting of the Conference of the Parties to the Convention on Biological Diversity as well as the outcome of the work of the third session of the Commission on Sustainable Development regarding the implementation of chapter 15 of Agenda 21 and other chapters related to biological diversity, can make a significant contribution to advancing the goals and objectives of the Convention.

23. In the light of the importance attached to the implementation of the goals and objectives of the Convention, the General Assembly decided, in adopting its resolution 49/119 of 19 December 1994, to proclaim 29 December, the date of the entry into force of the Convention on Biological Diversity, International Day for Biological Diversity. The Assembly may wish at its fiftieth session to give direction to Member States on the ways and means to make such an international event a success.

IV. CONCLUSION

24. The second meeting of the Conference of the Parties will take place at Jakarta from 6 to 17 November 1995. It will be preceded by the first meeting of the Subsidiary Body on Scientific, Technical and Technological Advice to be held at UNESCO, Paris, from 4 to 8 September 1995. The second meeting of the Conference of the Parties will also examine the report of the open-ended ad hoc group of experts on biosafety on the implementation of article 19, paragraph 3, of the Convention to be held at Madrid from 24 to 28 July 1995. Preparations for the Madrid meeting were made at a meeting of a panel of 15 experts nominated by Governments held at Cairo from 1 to 5 May 1995.

-----

8. ACTIVITIES OF THE UNITED NATIONS ENVIRONMENT PROGRAMME IN ENVIRONMENTAL MONITORING* - NOTE BY THE UN SECRETARY-GENERAL

Doc. no.: A/50/371 24 August 1995

The Secretary-General has the honour to transmit to the General Assembly, pursuant to its resolution 48/192 of 21 December 1993, the report of the Governing Council of the United Nations Environment Programme (UNEP).

ANNEX

Earthwatch, environment monitoring and assessment

Report of the Governing Council

I. INTRODUCTION

1. The present report has been prepared in response to the request contained in General Assembly resolution 48/192 of 21 December 1993 for "a report on the activities of the Programme in environmental monitoring, containing proposals and recommendations within the context of Agenda 21 and a review of Earthwatch". a/ The General Assembly in that resolution also invited the Governing Council of the United Nations Environment Programme (UNEP) to consider the report at its eighteenth session and submit its conclusions and recommendations to the General Assembly at its fiftieth session, through the Economic and Social Council.

2. In its decision 18/27 A, adopted on 25 May 1995, the Governing Council authorized the Executive Director of UNEP to transmit the present report to the General Assembly at its fiftieth session, through the Economic and Social Council.

II. THE UNITED NATIONS SYSTEM-WIDE EARTHWATCH

3. In response to General Assembly resolutions 44/224 of 22 December 1989 and 48/192, to UNEP Governing Council decision 16/37 and to Agenda 21 (Report of the United Nations Conference on Environment and Development, Rio de Janeiro,

* A/50/150.

3-14 June 1992) (paras. 38.22 (d), 40.8 and 40.13), the United Nations system-wide Earthwatch is being revitalized as a closely linked collaborative set of international efforts to coordinate, harmonize and integrate observing, assessment and reporting activities. This requires timely information on the status and trends of key global resources, the pressures on them, the variables and processes in both natural and human systems and the range of possible responses to problems in these areas. It also requires a more rapid flow of information through the system and the more direct targeting of decision-making processes, so that policy makers can receive more timely and appropriate information.

4. The United Nations system-wide Earthwatch cannot be content to assess each problem in isolation, but must examine them in combination and draw out the key policy issues to be addressed by the international community. In this regard, the Administrative Committee on Coordination report to the Governing Council (UNEP/GC.18/37) recommended that UNEP and the system-wide Earthwatch should continue to develop approaches to the linking of socio-economic and environmental assessment and reporting, and requested the Earthwatch Working Party to give further attention to the conceptual issues involved. Each participating agency should, within the limitations of available resources, strengthen its contributions to information for decision-making and improve its linkages with cooperating partners. UNEP, in its coordinating role for the environment, should focus on how all of the parts fit together into an integrated whole.

5. The Earthwatch Working Party of all the concerned United Nations organizations was set up to facilitate the taking of decisions in common, in order to develop concrete plans and increase efficiency and effectiveness by reducing redundancy. UNEP has established a small Earthwatch secretariat to maintain continuous liaison between the partners and to assist in implementing common activities. It is envisaged that many functions of Earthwatch can be carried out by ad hoc groups of experts drawn from all of the agencies. Some of the first initiatives being developed are described in the report to the third session of the Commission on Sustainable Development b/ of the Secretary-General on chapter 40: Information for decision-making and Earthwatch, developed jointly by UNEP and the Department for Policy Coordination and Sustainable Development, which contains annexes elaborating on the principal agency and inter-agency elements supporting Earthwatch and which highlights the need for all States to support the Earthwatch process, including through the provision of expertise and data.

6. On the basis of an in-depth study of Earthwatch c/ and the increased collaboration now established, as well as the results of the review of chapter 40 of Agenda 21 by the Commission on Sustainable Development and the review of Earthwatch [by the UNEP Governing Council, the critical needs to implement] Earthwatch across the United Nations system in close cooperation with Governments are being defined (reports of the Earthwatch Working Party, 1-2 June 1994 and 22-23 March 1995). A major task will be to conceive an internationally accepted policy and coordination framework for Earthwatch. The requirements will be assembled into a coherent package of specific, well-targeted activities, together with proposals for long-term funding strategies for interested Governments and other donors as a further step towards the effective implementation of this important dimension of Agenda 21.

III. ENVIRONMENT MONITORING

7. Building on the experience of the Global Environment Monitoring System (GEMS) and other efforts, major international scientific planning and inter-agency cooperative efforts are under way to advance a set of complementary global observing systems - the Global Climate Observing System, the Global Ocean Observing System, and the Global Terrestrial Observing System - covering the major environmental compartments. These systems intend to go beyond inherently time-limited research programmes towards the operational data collection and

assessment necessary to identify and respond to the long-term and widespread changes which may affect the human condition. UNEP is a co-sponsor of all these systems and, logically, their close interrelation and complementarity should be ensured as part of Earthwatch. A realistic and long-term funding strategy must be developed.

8. UNEP sees a particular role for itself in trying to minimize, to the extent possible, the data disparities between countries. In this regard, Earthwatch is exploring the potential to use schools, non-governmental organizations (NGOs), the media and other groups in building a more complete picture of the status of species, land uses, development activities, pollution problems and other characteristics of the human and natural environment as inputs for state-of-the-environment reporting and as a basis for selective continued monitoring of national and global trends and for filling data gaps.

IV. ENVIRONMENT ASSESSMENT WITHIN THE UNITED NATIONS ENVIRONMENT PROGRAMME

9. In response to the mandates in Agenda 21 and to the growing demands for environmental information that take development aspects into consideration, UNEP has reviewed its monitoring, assessment and reporting functions. The refocused environment assessment programme of UNEP, to be coordinated by the Division of Environment Assessment, includes the assessment and reporting functions of GEMS, incorporating the former State of the Environment Unit, the data management functions of the Global Resource Information Database (GRID), the capacity-building and regional networking of the environment and natural resources information networks, and United Nations system-wide Earthwatch coordination.

10. The programme has been reshaped to attend more explicitly to the needs of policy makers and to the data and information-handling capabilities of countries. It is geared towards making the best use of UNEP's own areas of comparative advantage: global and regional assessment and reporting; data and information management, harmonization and dissemination; regional environment and natural resources information network servicing. The proposed programme structure addresses the needs for policy-relevant information products supported by a scientifically valid, user-friendly information base developed through regional networks of capable information providers, integrators and users. This approach has received broad acceptance in several areas: by Governments in regional users' consultations; by the United Nations Development Programme (UNDP) in defining joint activities, especially in the Asia and Pacific region; by the science community and NGO partners; and by the agencies involved in the Earthwatch Working Party.

11. The programme has developed a strategic plan to weave sectoral and regional assessments and the biennial Global Environment Outlook series into a process which will culminate in the 2002 decadal state-of-the-environment report. The framework on which the process will be based is currently being developed through international consultations. It provides for linking socio-economic driving forces with observed impacts on the environment and human welfare. United Nations system-wide efforts to develop indicators for sustainable development (see para. 14) are also based on this framework.

12. The assessment process will give priority attention to analysis of the interactions between environment and development, identification of current and potential emerging issues of international importance and possible effective strategies in response to the major pressures exerted on the environment and on human welfare. UNEP assessments and reports are being produced through participatory processes, drawing on the best available expertise and knowledge existing at national, regional and global institutes, steered by a growing global network of collaborating institutes and relevant United Nations agencies. They rely on regional policy consultations throughout the production process to reflect priority issues and concerns and ensure that the assessment findings have operational relevance. Associated benefits are a better scientific

understanding of the relationships between environment and the socio-economic fabric of life and better tools to analyse and quantify these relationships as well as their projected impacts in the future.

13. In full cooperation with United Nations partners, particularly DPCSD and the United Nations Statistical Division, and with scientific groups, such as the Scientific Council on Problems of the Environment, the environment assessment programme is contributing to the internationally harmonized development of sustainable development indicators for measuring progress in their particular sectors on priority issues, and to provide countries with a range of choice of indicators suitable to specific environmental, social and economic settings. In addition, UNEP is planning an indicators network to facilitate information flow among those working in the field. The organizations cooperating in the United Nations system-wide Earthwatch (see paras. 3-6) should be able to help the Department for Policy Coordination and Sustainable Development to support national efforts to use indicators for policy-making and as guides to sustainability, as well as in reporting to the Commission on Sustainable Development.

14. UNEP's environment assessment programme is building on the success of activities such as GRID for information management, data harmonization and dissemination. Thus, the data and information management component of the Division of Environment Assessment is operating a computerized catalogue ("meta-database") on environmental data and information, developing critical datasets for assessments and assisting and supporting national Governments, regional data networks and other programmes in their efforts to improve access to and management of relevant and meaningful data and information on the environment.

15. The regionally focused institutional capacity-enhancement and servicing component of the programme aims to build a sustainable information base for both national and international assessment and reporting. The Environment and Natural Resource Information Networks provide an enabling environment for acquiring, handling, sharing and analysing environmental data and generating policy-relevant information. Predicated on partnerships with donors and other United Nations agencies, particularly UNDP, this programme component is linking regional and national institutions in a cooperative network to address issues of particular regional significance.

16. A realistic funding strategy for UNEP's environment assessment programme needs to include the following elements: ensuring adequate and sufficient core funding within UNEP to maintain a basic assessment functionality and to provide the forum for regional or global cooperation; ensuring partnership with national agencies through the decentralized national networks of UNEP's environment assessment programme; developing close working partnerships with multilateral and bilateral donors active in the field of environment and sustainable development to coordinate and implement priority activities and programmes; identifying agency national focal points to guide in harnessing existing national capacities, with capacity-building assistance as necessary, to ensure that programmes address national needs as well as issues of international significance within cooperating international environment assessment networks.

Notes

a/ The term "Earthwatch" has been used since the United Nations Conference on the Human Environment, held at Stockholm in 1972, often ambiguously, to refer both to UNEP's programme in the area of environment assessment and to the United Nations system-wide environment assessment activities. Although attempts have been made in the past few years to confine its use to the United Nations system-wide context, as in "United Nations system-wide Earthwatch", conventional usage persists in applying "Earthwatch" to UNEP's environment assessment activities, to the relevant system-wide activities, or to both. In the present report, the term "Earthwatch" is confined to the United Nations system-wide context.

b/ E/CN.17/1995/18 and Add.1.

c/ "The United Nations system-wide Earthwatch programme", 10 March 1995.

-----

9. UNGA RESOLUTION ON REPORT OF THE GOVERNING COUNCIL OF THE UNITED NATIONS ENVIRONMENT PROGRAMME

Doc. no.: A/Res.50/110 20 December 1995

The General Assembly,

Recalling its resolution 2997 (XXVII) of 15 December 1972, in which it decided to establish the Governing Council of the United Nations Environment Programme,

Recalling its resolution 47/191 of 22 December 1992, in which it endorsed the recommendations on international institutional arrangements to follow up the United Nations Conference on Environment and Development, as contained in chapter 38 of Agenda 21, 106/ in which, inter alia, the need for a strengthened role for the United Nations Environment Programme and its Governing Council was stressed and priority areas on which the Programme should concentrate were elaborated,

Having considered the report of the Governing Council of the United Nations Environment Programme on its eighteenth session, 107/ the report of the Secretary-General on the strengthening of the Programme, 108/ the note by the Secretary-General on the activities of the Programme in environmental monitoring, 109/ and the note by the Secretary-General on international conventions and protocols in the field of the environment, 110/

1. Endorses the report of the Governing Council of the United Nations Environment Programme on its eighteenth session and the decisions contained therein; 111/

2. Recognizes, in particular, Governing Council decisions 18/1 on the role and priorities of the United Nations Environment Programme, 18/5 on the in-depth evaluation of the programme on environment, 18/7 on environment and sustainable development and 18/10 on good environmental housekeeping within the United Nations system; 112/

106/ Report of the United Nations Conference on Environment and Development, Rio de Janeiro, 3-14 June 1992, vol. I, Resolutions Adopted by the Conference (United Nations publication, Sales No. E.93.I.8 and corrigendum), resolution 1, annex II.

107/ Official Records of the General Assembly, Fiftieth Session, Supplement No. 25 (A/50/25).

108/ A/50/171.

109/ A/50/371.

110/ A/C.2/50/2.

111/ Official Records of the General Assembly, Fiftieth Session, Supplement No. 25 (A/50/25), annex.

112/ Ibid.

3. Requests the Governing Council to prepare a report on the role and activities of the Programme in the implementation of Agenda 21, in accordance with its mandate, and to submit that report to the General Assembly at its special session on the overall review and appraisal of the implementation of Agenda 21;

4. Notes the importance of sufficient and timely contributions to the Environment Fund, and calls upon Governments to make contributions in a timely fashion in order to allow for the full and effective implementation of the work programmes;

5. Welcomes the efforts of the United Nations Environment Programme to promote maximum and cost-effective utilization of the conference facilities at its headquarters at Nairobi, and calls upon Governments and relevant intergovernmental bodies to support such efforts to ensure optimum utilization of the capacity of all United Nations conference facilities;

6. Requests the Secretary-General to inform the General Assembly at its fifty-second session on the implementation of the present resolution.

UNITED NATIONS CONFERENCE ON TRADE AND DEVELOPMENT
(UNCTAD)

DOCUMENTS REPRODUCED IN WHOLE OR IN PART:

REPORTS BY THE UNCTAD SECRETARIAT

STANDING COMMITTEE ON DEVELOPING SERVICES SECTORS: FOSTERING COMPETITIVE SERVICES SECTORS IN DEVELOPING COUNTRIES: SHIPPING, 3RD SESSION, GENEVA, 6-9 JUNE 1995

JOINT UNCTAD/IMO INTERGOVERNMENTAL GROUP OF EXPERTS ON MARITIME LIENS AND MORTGAGES AND RELATED SUBJECTS

DOCUMENTS NOT REPRODUCED:

REPORTS BY THE UNCTAD SECRETARIAT

10.	Doc. no.:	UNCTAD/SDD/SHIP/2
	Date:	24 March 1995
	Title:	Changes in Shipper Representation - Note by the UNCTAD Secretariat
11.	Doc. no.:	UNCTAD/SDD/SHIP/3
	Date:	8 May 1995
	Title:	Ship Finance for Developing Countries - Report by the UNCTAD Secretariat

STANDING COMMITTEE ON DEVELOPING SERVICES SECTORS: FOSTERING COMPETITIVE SERVICES SECTORS IN DEVELOPING COUNTRIES: SHIPPING, 3RD SESSION, GENEVA, 6-9 JUNE 1995

12.	Doc. no.:	TD/B/CN.4/46
	Date:	28 March 1995
	Title:	Competitive Services in Multimodal Transport - Report by the UNCTAD Secretariat
13.	Doc. no.:	TD/B/CN.4/47
	Date:	28 March 1995
	Title:	Technical Cooperation and Human Resource Development in Shipping, Ports and Multimodal Transport - Report by the UNCTAD Secretariat

1. REVIEW OF MARITIME TRANSPORT 1994* - REPORT BY THE UNCTAD SECRETARIAT

Doc. no.: TD/B/CN.4/49 1995

CONTENTS

* Only Introduction and Chapters I and II are reproduced here.

LIST OF TABLES

LIST OF BOXES

LIST OF GRAPHS

ABBREVIATIONS

cif	cost, insurance and freight
CIS	Commonwealth of Independent States
DMEC	developed market-economy country
dwt	deadweight tons
EEC	European Economic Community
EU	European Union
FEU	forty-foot equivalent unit
fob	free on board
GDP	gross domestic product
grt	gross registered tons
ldt	light displacement tons
LNG	liquefied natural gas
Mgt	million gross tons
MTO	multimodal transport operator
NIC	newly industrializing countries
NVO-MTO	non-vessel-operating multimodal transport operator
OECD	Organisation for Economic Cooperation and Development
TEU	twenty-foot equivalent unit
ULCC	ultra-large crude carrier
VLCC	very large crude carrier
VO-MTO	vessel-operating multimodal transport operator
WS	Worldscale

EXPLANATORY NOTES

Tons refer to metric tons, unless otherwise stated.

Details and percentages presented in tables, due to rounding, do not necessarily add up to the totals.

Two dots (..) indicate that data are not available or are not separately reported.

A dash (-) signifies that the amount is nil, or less than half the unit used.

In some tables, the data shown for earlier years have been revised and updated. and may therefore differ from those shown in previous issues of this *Review*.

In the tables and the text, the use of the term "countries" refers to countries, territories or areas.

INTRODUCTION

The *Review of Maritime Transport* is an annual publication prepared by the secretariat of UNCTAD, in accordance with section B of the programme of work of the Committee on Developing Services Sectors: Fostering Competitive Services Sectors in Developing Countries: Shipping. */ The purpose of the *Review* is to identify the main developments in world maritime transport and to provide relevant statistical data. Emphasis is given to the development of the merchant marines in developing countries as compared with other groups of countries.

To maintain historical continuity and special characteristics on shipping practices, the overall structure of the *Review of Maritime Transport* is similar to previous editions, i.e. classification of countries and territories which has been detailed in annex I for statistical purposes only. The current issue, however, includes several new features such as a review of regional development - South America.

SUMMARY OF MAIN DEVELOPMENTS

Development of the world economy and seaborne trade

- The world real GDP increased in 1994 by 3.1 per cent over 1993. The industrial countries experienced a growth of 2.7 per cent over the previous year, while developing countries registered an average increase of 5.6 per cent.

- The volume of world merchandise exports grew in 1994 by 9 per cent, more than double the rate of 1993. This higher growth was attributed partially to a substantial recovery of trade in Western Europe.

- The total OECD industrial production index in 1994 soared by 4.4 per cent to 103.4 from 99.0 in 1993 (1990=100).

- World seaborne trade reached a new record at 4.46 billion tons. The annual growth rate increased to 3.0 per cent in 1994, as compared to 2.6 per cent in the previous year.

- The total services in ton-miles in global trade rose in 1994 by 2.8 per cent over 1993 to 19,500 billion.

Development of the world fleet

- The world merchant fleet continuously expanded to 719.8 million dwt by the end of 1994. This fleet expansion was mainly due to a net gain of newbuildings deliveries (29.3 million dwt) over scrapping (20.8 million dwt).

- The combined share of the world fleet of developed market-economy countries and the major open-registry countries maintained almost the same share as the previous year (67.5 per cent). The developing countries' share of the 1994 world total marginally increased to 22.6 per cent.

Productivity of the world fleet and supply and demand in world shipping

- The main operational productivity indicators of the world fleet constantly rose to a relatively high level in 1994. In 1994, 6.19 tons of cargo carried per dwt was a record high. Ton-miles performed per dwt also continued on an upward trend to reach a new record of 27,135.

- The world total surplus tonnage decreased by 11.9 per cent over the previous year to 63.4 million dwt. The surplus capacity in the oil tanker sector and the dry bulk sector declined by 10.3 per cent and 14.0 per cent respectively over 1993 to 39.0 million dwt and 20.3 million dwt, respectively.

Shipbuilding, second-hand market and demolition

- The 1994 overall newbuilding contracts for main types of vessels were less than those in 1993, registering 42 million dwt. Shipbuilding activities

---

*/ *Report of the Standing Committee on Developing Services Sectors: Fostering Competitive Services Sectors in Developing Countries: Shipping, first session*, TD/B/39(2)/5-TD/B/CN.4/13, annex I.

in terms of deadweight were mainly concentrated on tankers and dry bulk carriers, accounting for 32.9 per cent and 47.3 per cent respectively of the total tonnage of the main types.

- The world total deliveries of newbuildings decreased in 1994 by 5.6 per cent in gross-registered tons over 1993, registering 18.8 million grt. Shipyards of developed market-economy countries maintained their predominant share of 63.7 per cent.

- In the five-year-old second-hand market for tankers, prices were somewhat static in most segments as compared to 1993. For dry bulk carriers, a moderate increase in values for modern tonnages was observed. The total dry bulk and tanker tonnages traded decreased by 31.8 per cent to 29.1 million dwt as compared to 42.6 million dwt in 1993.

Port development

- World total container traffic broke the 110 million TEU barrier, reaching 112,400,000 TEU in 1993, of which 43,400,000 TEU were handled at the ports of developing countries (38.6 per cent).

Freight markets

- The overall 1994 liner freight index continued to fall to the average level of 74, which was a two-point decline from the average of 1993 and the lowest since 1988 (1985=100).

- The overall increase in dry bulk charter markets in 1994 was attributed to an estimated increase of 2.2 per cent in the seaborne trade of main dry bulk commodities.

- Increasing demand for crude oil tanker tonnages, during the second half of 1994, pushed the average rate levels up substantially higher than the corresponding period of the previous year.

- World total freight payments as a proportion of total import value climbed to 5.59 per cent in 1993 from 5.37 per cent in 1992. While the proportion of developed market-economy countries increased in 1993 to 4.54 per cent from 4.33 in 1992, that of developing countries decreased to 8.33 per cent as compared to 8.52 per cent in 1992.

Multimodal transport and technological developments

- In 1994, 1.06 million TEUs were produced throughout the world, up 9.3 per cent over 0.97 million TEUs in 1993.

- By size, 40-foot-long containers significantly increased in 1994 to 4.55 million TEUs, accounting for 54.6 per cent of the world total container fleet. Eight-foot-6-inch-high and 9-foot-6-inch-high containers increased to 7.16 million TEUs and 1.04 million TEUs respectively, representing 85.8 per cent and 12.5 per cent respectively of the world total container fleet, whilst 8-foot-high containers continued to be phased out.

Other developments

- The Joint UNCTAD/IMO Intergovernmental Group of Experts met in Geneva in December 1994, preparing a set of "Draft Articles for a Convention on the Arrest of Ships".

- Ministers and decision makers from the world attended the United Nations International Symposium on Trade Efficiency in Columbus (Ohio, United States) in October 1994, proposing innovative ways to improve efficiency in international trade, which could result in a reduction of transaction costs of up to US$ 100 billion annually by the year 2000.

Box 1

Vessel and registry groupings used in the Review of Maritime Transport

As in the previous year's *Review*, five vessel groupings have been used throughout most shipping tables in this report. The cut-off point for all tables based on data from Lloyd's Maritime Information Services Ltd. is 100 grt, except those tables dealing with ownership where the cut-off level is 1,000 grt. The groups aggregate 20 principal types of vessel categories, as noted below.

Review group	Constituent ship types
Oil tankers	Oil tankers
Bulk carriers	Ore and bulk carriers, ore/bulk/oil carriers
General cargo	Refrigerated cargo, specialized cargo, ro-ro cargo, general cargo (single- and multi-deck), general cargo/passenger
Containerships	Fully cellular
Other ships	Oil/chemical tankers, chemical tankers, other tankers, liquefied gas carriers, passenger ro-ro, passenger, tank barges, general cargo barges, fishing, offshore supply, and all other types
Total all ships	Summation of all the above-mentioned vessel types

With the formation of new States in Eastern Europe, the registry situation as at 31 December 1993 had changed. Lloyd's Register advises that vessels are only allocated to a new register after confirmation that a new registry has been created and ships entered into a registry. The following guidelines are offered by Lloyd's Maritime Information Services Ltd. for the Review of Maritime Transport, 1994 tables relating to fleet development.

Former USSR

(i)Confirmation has been received from the Latvian (LAV), Lithuanian (LTH) and Estonian (ETN) registries, and these flag codes have been created and maintained.
(ii)The Russian (RUS), Ukrainian (UKE), Azerbaijani (AZE) and Georgian (GEO) republics have by this time started their own registries and these have also been allocated accordingly.
(iii)The other republics, Armenia (ARM), Belarus (BEL), Kazakhstan (KAZ), Kyrgyzstan (KYR), Moldova (MOL), Tajikistan (TAJ), Turkmenistan (TUR) and Uzbekistan (UZB), have not confirmed the establishment of registries. Lloyd's Register has however, received information from the Russian Registry as flag arrangements are still coordinated through this body. In consequence, ships have been coded where appropriate. Only a handful of ships are still held under the USSR flag (USR) where no confirmation has been received.

Former Yugoslavia

Ships have been allocated to either Croatia (CRT) or Slovenia (SLO). Any as yet unallocated have been left under Yugoslavia (YUG).

Source: Lloyd's Maritime Information Services Ltd. (London).

Chapter I

DEVELOPMENT OF INTERNATIONAL SEABORNE TRADE

The initial chapter of the Review of Maritime Transport provides an overview of the demand for global shipping services, together with background information on the world economic situation and a review of developments in world seaborne trade.

A. World economic background

1. Developments in the world economy directly affect demand for shipping services. In 1994, the world real GDP increased by 3.1 per cent over 1993, reflecting a continuous economic growth in North America, and clearer signs of recovery across the European Union and in Japan. The GDP of industrial countries grew by 2.7 per cent, while continuing strong performance of developing countries as a whole yielded an average increase of 5.6 per cent over the previous year, although in the latter countries, discrepancies between individual countries continue to be large. Among the regional groups of countries, Asia including China (11.0 per cent) was particularly strong with an average rate of growth of 8.0 per cent over the previous year. Conversely, the countries in transition experienced a fourth consecutive decline of 8.3 per cent in 1994, with Russia even suffering a more dramatic decline of 12.0 per cent compared with 1993.[1/]

2. The volume of world merchandise exports grew by 9.0 per cent in 1994, which was the strongest annual increase since 1976, and more than double the rate of 1993. This higher growth of world merchandise trade was primarily attributable to a sharp recovery of trade in Western Europe, and the continuation and strengthening of the trade expansions in Asia, North America and Latin America. Western Europe's higher import demand (8.0 per cent in 1994 as compared to -1.5 per cent in 1993) spilled over onto its export growth (9.0 per cent in 1994 and 1.5 per cent in 1993), mainly due to the intraregional trade. Higher export volume growth was reported by Germany which benefited from the strength of demand for capital goods. North America's merchandise imports in 1994, which were boosted by the United States' high growth of domestic demand, increased by 12.5 per cent, the largest volume gain since 1984. North America's exports were up 9.5 per cent, twice the rate of the preceding year, but remained below the level of import growth for the third consecutive year. For Latin America, the strength of import demand in North America and from within the region brought about a rise in exports off 10.5 per cent, the largest annual rise in volume since 1983. The region's export growth was however lower than the import growth (13.5 per cent in 1994). This reflects the trend of recent years. Asia's merchandise import volume growth was further accelerated in 1994 to 13.5 per cent, exceeding for the fourth consecutive year its export growth. Factors on the region's import expansion include the remarkably higher imports of Japan (up 13.5 per cent) and the Republic of Korea (up 21 per cent), which offset the slowdown in China. Asia's export growth nearly doubled from the previous year primarily due to sharp increases in export volumes of China, Singapore and the Republic of Korea. In contrast, the rise (2.0 per cent) in the volume of Japan's merchandise exports was the smallest among the world's ten leading merchandise exporters.[2/]

3. Industrial production, particularly of the OECD countries is another fundamental indicator for the global maritime sector. Graph 1 shows the relationship between the annual change in OECD industrial production and world seaborne trade. In 1994 the total OECD industrial production index substantially soared by 4.4 per cent to 103.4 from 99.0 in 1993 (1990=100) when they had experienced a set-back of 0.4 per cent. This climb primarily reflects a 5.4 per cent increase in the United States (4.1 per cent increase in 1993) and another favourable 4.9 per cent rise in the OECD European countries (3.0 per cent decrease in 1993). Japan marginally increased industrial production by 1.2 per cent during 1994 (a 4.2 per cent decrease in 1993).[3/] In parallel the world seaborne trade also increased in 1994 at a steady rate of 3.0 per cent over the previous year. The trade of manufactured goods was up nearly 4 per cent in 1994, while tanker cargoes and main dry bulk commodities increased in 1994 by 2.8 per cent and 1.8 per cent, respectively (see table 1).

B. World seaborne trade

4. World seaborne trade continued to expand in 1994, as indicated in table 1 and graph 2. Total cargo tonnage reached a new record at 4.46 billion tons, marking the ninth consecutive annual increase. The annual growth rate again turned upwards, reaching 3.0 per cent, which was the highest since 1990, but remained slightly below the average annual rate of growth of 3.1 per cent over the period 1986-1993. By broad segments of maritime trade, tanker cargoes represented 44.6 per cent of the total 1994 seaborne trade, increasing by 2.3 per cent to 1,990 million tons, as compared to the 1993 growth of 4.6 per cent (reaching 1,945 million tons). The volume of total dry bulk commodities registered an increase of 3.5 per cent to 2,468 million tons in 1994, while main bulk commodities marginally increased by 2.2 per cent to

Graph 1

Annual change in OECD industrial production and world seaborne trade, 1985-1994

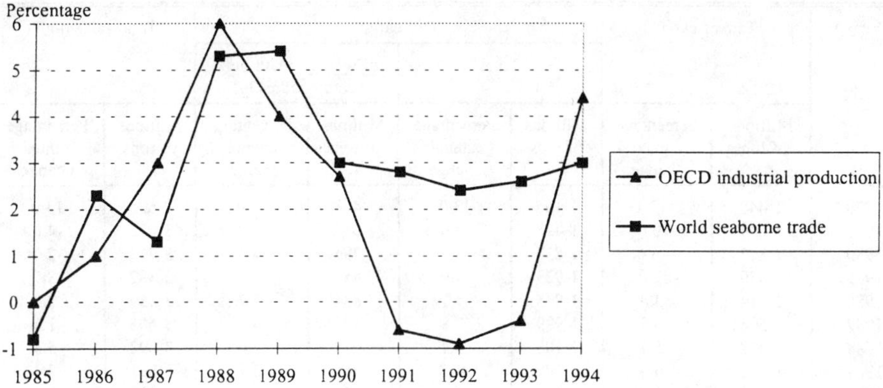

Source: OECD, *Main Economic Indicators*, March 1995.

Graph 2

International seaborne trade for selected years

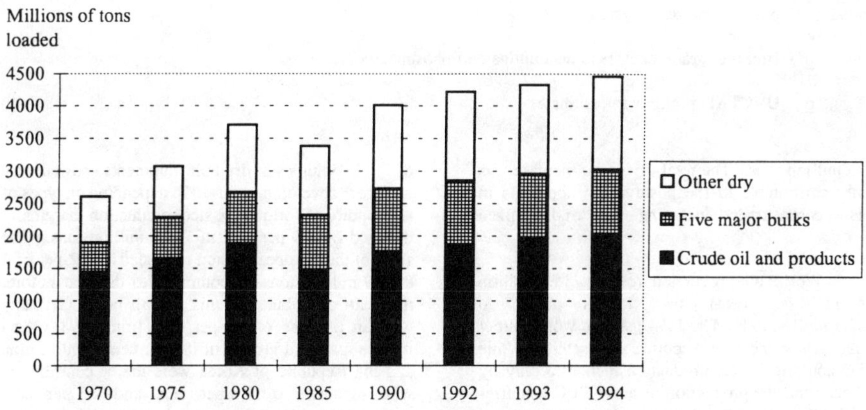

Source: *Review of Maritime Transport*, various issues.

Table 1

Development of international seaborne trade, a/ 1970, 1975, 1980 and 1985-1994
(Estimates of goods loaded)

Year	Tanker cargo		Dry cargo				Total (all goods)	
			Total		of which: main bulk commodities b/			
	Millions of tons	Percentage annual change	Millions of tons	Percentage annual change	Millions of tons	Percentage annual change	Millions of tons	Percentage annual change
1970	1 440	13.1	1 165	13.0	448	16.0	2 605	13.0
1975	1 644	-10.0	1 428	-3.0	635	-5.0	3 072	-4.0
1980	1 871	-6.6	1 833	3.3	796	4.5	3 704	-2.0
1985	1 459	-22.0	1 923	4.9	857	7.7	3 382	-8.7
1986	1 514	3.8	1 945	1.1	834	-2.7	3 459	2.3
1987	1 506	-0.5	1 999	2.8	875	4.9	3 505	1.3
1988	1 587	5.4	2 105	5.3	940	7.4	3 692	5.3
1989	1 692	6.6	2 199	4.5	965	2.7	3 891	5.4
1990	1 755	3.7	2 253	2.5	968	0.3	4 008	3.0
1991	1 790	2.0	2 330	3.4	1 005	3.8	4 120	2.8
1992	1 860	3.9	2 360	1.3	990	-1.5	4 220	2.4
1993	1 945	4.6	2 385	1.1	993	0.3	4 330	2.6
1994 c/	1 990	2.3	2 468	3.5	1 015	2.2	4 458	3.0

Sources: Based on data from the United Nations Statistical Office; Fearnleys (Oslo), *World Bulk Trades 1993* and *Review 1994*, UNCTAD data bank and other specialized sources.

a/ Including international cargoes loaded at ports of the Great Lakes and St. Lawrence system for unloading at ports of the same system.

b/ Iron ore, grain, coal, bauxite/alumina and phosphate.

c/ UNCTAD preliminary estimates.

1,015 million tons. The total dry cargo increase was mainly attributable to the positive developments in general cargo trades including steel and unitized cargo.

5. World oil production rose by 36.2 million tons (1.14 per cent) over 1993's output to 3,202.5 million tons. The 1994 gains in world output are the largest increases reported since 1990. While OPEC countries' total production increased only by 0.88 per cent, the production of non-OPEC countries gained 1.33 per cent, of which Western European countries, primarily Norway and the United Kingdom showed the remarkable increase of 14.08 per cent and 26.78 per cent, respectively).[4/] Crude oil shipments increased moderately by 1.8 per cent in 1994, with all growth from areas outside the Persian Gulf. Oil product shipments substantially increased by 4.7 per cent from 358 million tons to 375 million tons with continuing large increases in imports of countries in South-East Asia and the Far East, and growing imports of the United States[5/] (see also table 1).

6. Volumes of dry bulk shipments showed very divergent developments in 1994 depending on types of commodity. World crude steel production marginally declined by 0.9 per cent to 723.3 million tons. The share of the European Union expanded by 5.2 per cent to 139 million tons, as compared to the year before, the main contributor to this growth being Germany with an increase of 8.5 per cent from 1993. Asia made a marginal growth of 0.5 per cent, while China and the Republic of Korea were major contributors with increases of 3.2 per cent and 2.3 per cent respectively, whereas Japan reduced by 1.3 per cent. The Commonwealth of Independent States, including Russia, registered a remarkable decline of nearly 21 per cent from 1993.[6/] Notwithstanding the slight decline of the world crude steel production in 1994, seaborne iron ore volumes increased by over 7 per cent from 354 million tons in 1993 to 380 million tons in 1994, as the European steel industry improved its performance and the increase in production in China was sufficient to compensate for the reduction in ore-based steel output in Japan.[7/] Coal shipments

showed a modest increase of about 1 per cent to 370 million tons. This increase applied both to coking coal as the steel industry recovered specifically in Western Europe, and to thermal coal, which gained some market shares from oil. China's exports rose over 20 per cent, supplying thermal coal to South-East Asian markets. South Africa and Canada also improved their volumes substantially.[8/] Grain shipments again fell considerably in 1994 (-4.6 per cent) from 194 million tons in 1993 to 185 million tons. The most dramatic decline could be observed in imports of the former Soviet Union, which were about halved from 1993 levels.[9/] This affected primarily the exports of the United States and Argentina. These countries' overall exports declined in 1994 by 11.4 per cent and 10.4 per cent, respectively.[10/] The trades of primary aluminium products slightly improved as the world production increased in 1994 by 1.7 per cent to 15.2 million tons as compared to those in 1993, primarily due to a substantial increase of 22.4 per cent in Western Europe, despite a decline of 7.4 per cent in North America.[11/]

7. Shipments of "other dry cargo", mainly general cargo including steel and unitized cargo increased by 4.4 per cent over 1993 (see table 1). The 1994 global steel consumption reached almost 610 million tons.[12/] China, the largest importer in 1993 reduced its import from 30 million tons to 20 million tons in 1994. On the other hand the United States' imports rose about 60 per cent in the first 10 months to 24.7 million tons, primarily from the former Soviet Union and Eastern Europe.[13/] The total global liner trade in 1994 was estimated to have reached about 31.8 million TEUs, an increase of 8.1 per cent over 1993. The United States was very active in 1994, with a 9 per cent increase in exports, bolstered by strong advances to the Far East, and with imports from most sources totalling a near 13 per cent increase. Europe's exports registered a sustainable expansion of 6.5 per cent over 1993 with a tremendous growth at 14 per cent in the trades with the Far East. The high yen was the cause of Japan's strong import growth in 1994 (over 9 per cent) from nearly all supplying countries.[14]

8. Graph 3 illustrates the export structure and direction of trade of developing countries. The direction of the developing countries' exports by value is indicated, with 60.5 per cent of the total destined to developed market-economy countries and 26.0 per cent within the developing countries for 1994, as compared to 61.5 per cent and 23.4 per cent respectively for the previous year. The structure of exports by value comprises five broad categories. Manufactured goods, fuels and all food items are the dominant cargoes, accounting for 92.0 per cent of the total (92.6 per cent for 1993). Conversely, in terms of weight, developing countries' exports compose dominantly bulk cargoes with fuels, grains and ores sharing almost 80 per cent of the total.

Graph 3

Export structure and direction of trade for developing countries
(1991 percentage distribution by value)

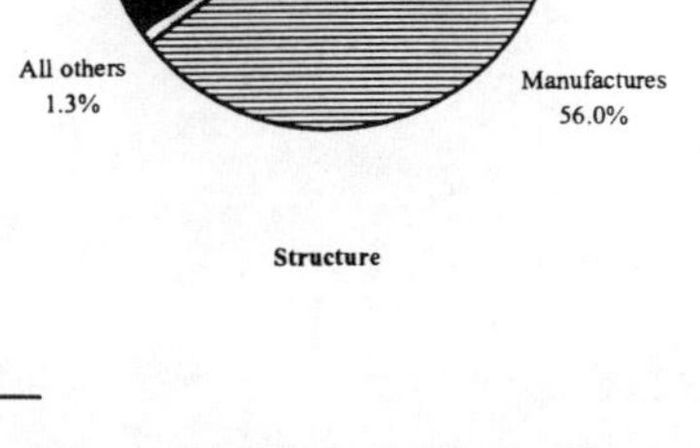

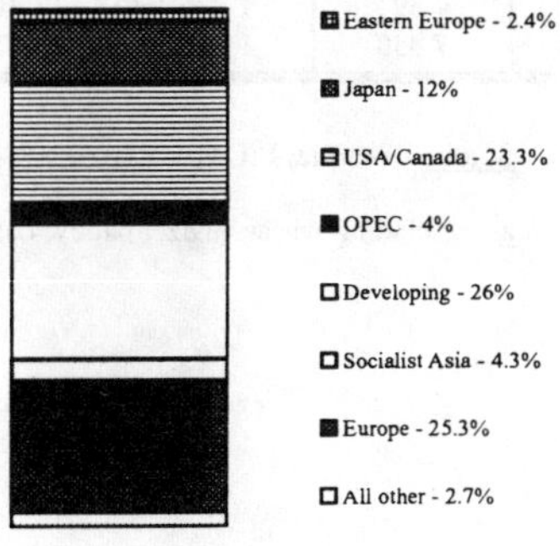

Source: UNCTAD, *Handbook of International Trade and Development Statistics, 1993* (United Nations publication, Sales No. E/F.94.II.D.24) table 3.2, p. 76.

9. Total demand for shipping services expressed in ton-miles is reflected in table 2. Total services provided in global trades rose by 2.8 per cent in 1994. This was lower than the 1993 growth rate of 4.2 per cent, also far below the 10-year average annual growth-rate of 4.2 per cent. Performance in different market segments, however, varied significantly. Developments in crude oil trades marginally increased by 0.5 per cent in 1994, reflecting a small increase (1.8 per cent) in world crude oil shipments, with all growth from areas outside the Persian Gulf. Conversely in oil product trades, the ton-miles registered a substantial increase of 5.9 per cent from 1993, resulting from a continuous surge of oil-product imports to countries in South-East Asia and the Far East, and the United States, with the global growth of oil products at 4.7 per cent. The most notable development in ton-miles could be observed in iron ore shipments, which expanded by 8.3 per cent in 1994 due to increasing long-haul movements of iron ore, mainly to Europe and China. Grain transport services marked a considerable reduction of 3.7 per cent in 1994 from the year before and were the second lowest since 1981. This could be attributed mainly to the dramatic reduction in world grain trade (4.6 per cent down from 1993), specifically the reduction in imports to the former Soviet Union from the United States and Argentina. In the "other cargo" segment, improvements in steel shipments and liner trades in 1994 substantially contributed to the growth rate of 5.4 per cent in ton-miles.

Table 2

World seaborne trade by types of cargo, 1970, 1980 and 1985-1994
(Billions of ton-miles)

Year	Oil		Iron ore	Coal	Grain a/	Other cargo	Total trade
	Crude	Products					
1970	5 597	890	1 093	481	475	2 118	10 654
1980	8 385	1 020	1 613	952	1 087	3 720	16 777
1985	4 007	1 150	1 675	1 479	1 004	3 750	13 065
1986	4 640	1 265	1 671	1 586	914	3 780	13 856
1987	4 671	1 320	1 728	1 653	1 061	3 840	14 273
1988	5 065	1 445	1 919	1 719	1 117	4 040	15 305
1989	5 736	1 540	1 983	1 798	1 095	4 250	16 402
1990	6 261	1 560	1 978	1 849	1 073	4 440	17 161
1991	6 757	1 530	2 008	1 999	1 069	4 510	17 873
1992	6 970	1 620	1 896	2 001	1 091	4 650	18 228
1993	7 391	1 775	2 001	1 949	1 038	4 840	18 994
1994	7 430	1 880	2 167	1 955	1 000	5 100	19 532

Source: Fearnleys (Oslo), *Review 1994*.

a/ Including wheat, maize, barley, oats, rye, sorghum and soya beans.

Box 2

Possible expansion of the world natural gas and LNG markets

The world natural gas consumption was in 1993 about 2,158 billion m^3 (2,125 in 1992). International natural gas trade accounted for only 347 billion m^3. Over 76 per cent or 264 billion m^3 was piped and only 24 per cent, i.e. 83 billion m^3 or 61.3 million tons was transported as LNG (in 1992: 81 billion m^3 or 60 million tons).

Prudent estimation is putting the world gas consumption by 2010 at 3,100 billion m^3, an increase of over 40 per cent. It is based on a steady world economic growth and on the necessity of environment and atmosphere protection where natural gas is definitely the challenger to oil, coal and nuclear and has become more and more efficient and economical in power generation.

In Europe (EEC only), production by 2010 is estimated to develop to 225/245 billion m^3 whilst demand should reach 440/470 billion m^3. Imports in 1993 was about 170 billion m^3. At current level of imports, the deficit by 2010 would reach 45/55 billion m^3, already partially covered by agreed piped gas and LNG contracts under development.

The Far East (Japan, Republic of Korea and Taiwan Province of China), although a much smaller market, is depending almost entirely on LNG imports which reached in 1993: 61.35 billion m^3 or 45 million tons (60 billion m^3 and 44 million tons in 1992).

In that part of the world, estimates are putting demand already by the year 2000 at between 92/95 billion m^3 or 68/70 million tons. By the year 2010, demand could reach 109/117 billion m^3 or 81 to 86 million tons. Current supply commitments are amounting to about 92.5 billion m^3 or 73 million tons to be reached before 2000.

Shell's conservative estimates of world LNG demand of a minimum of 80 million tons (108 billion m^3) by 2000 will be met easily.

Shell's estimates of demand by 2010 of 100 million tons (135 billion m^3) could also be met when considering the numerous proposed expansions and grass root projects. However, the question awaiting a favourable reply is whether the world economy will recover enough to push oil prices up, allowing better project economics and financing but also higher LNG price ...

The steady increase, although at a slower pace of 2.5 per cent of the LNG trade to 61.3 million tons in 1993 has resulted in the contracting of 15 ships in 1993 bringing the total since 1989 to 33 newbuildings. Within the balance of 1994 or in 1995, at least 6 to 7 ships should be ordered, all for delivery between 1997 and 2000.

Beyond 1995, about 20 to 30 vessels of all sizes could be ordered for delivery between 1999 and 2004.

To conclude, proposed grassroots supply projects are plenty and could meet demand but the dramatic increase of costs to develop most of them (not to mention some presenting very difficult and expensive technical challenges), the scarcity of reasonable cost financing, the LNG pricing and indexation, the relatively limited number of specialized shipyards, the cost of new ships (although the unreasonable upward trend seems to have recently slowed down), the availability of skilled officers and trained crews, remain the other problems and obstacles which will have to be solved and overcome before the LNG industry legitimate expectations become reality.

Moreover and not to be ignored, several new proposed projects of gas pipelines are being studied linking the Middle East to Europe and India, Eurasia to Western, Central Europe, China and even Japan, another from Russia to Korea and Japan. Although distances, borders, depth of seas could make such proposals unrealistic, it is believed that some will materialize in the future.

Source: Barry Rogliano Salles, *Survey of the World LNG Fleet*, August 1994.

10. Summarized data on seaborne trade by major cargo segments and country groups are provided in table 3 and graph 4. In terms of regional distribution, developing countries in 1994 registered a small increase in their share of both oil and dry cargoes for the fourth consecutive year to a combined share of 50.8 per cent in world trade for loading, whilst their share for unloading slightly declined to 26.8 per cent after a constant increase over the previous years. Within the group, Asian countries continuously expanded their share in world trade in 1993 to 26.9 per cent (26.2 per cent in 1992) for loading and 17.6 per cent (17.3 per cent in 1992) for unloading. In 1993, American countries maintained their share at almost the same level as in 1992 for both directions of trade. Conversely, the share of African economies continued to diminish in 1993 to 10.2 per cent for loading and 4.2 per cent for unloading, as compared to 10.5 and 4.3 per cent respectively in 1992. Developed market-economy countries experienced a marginal increase in 1994 to 43.2 per cent and 67.9 per cent in world trade for loading and unloading, respectively. Countries of Central and Eastern Europe suffered a decrease to 3.8 per cent for loading and 3.2 per cent for unloading in 1994. It is notable that the share of the socialist countries of Asia turned upward in 1994 to 2.2 per cent for loading and 2.1 per cent for unloading after remaining at 2.1 and 2.0 per cent respectively since 1991.

Table 3

World seaborne trade a/ in 1970, 1992, 1993 and 1994 (est.) by types of cargo and country groups b/

Country group	Year	Goods loaded				Goods unloaded			
		Oil		Dry cargo	Total all goods	Oil		Dry cargo	Total all goods
		Crude	Products			Crude	Products		
		(Trade in millions of tons)							
World total	1970	1 110	330	1 165	2 605	1 101	302	1 127	2 530
	1992	1 394	466	2 360	4 220	1 414	451	2 480	4 345
	1993	1 443	502	2 385	4 330	1 465	480	2 477	4 422
	1994	1 483	507	2 468	4 458	1 486	486	2 574	4 546
		(Percentage share of each category of goods in total)							
World total	1970	42.6	12.7	44.7	100.0	43.5	11.9	44.6	100.0
	1992	33.0	11.1	55.9	100.0	32.5	10.4	57.1	100.0
	1993	33.3	11.6	55.1	100.0	33.1	10.9	56.0	100.0
	1994	33.3	11.4	55.3	100.0	32.7	10.7	56.6	100.0
		(Percentage share of trade by groups of countries)							
Developed market-economy countries	1970	2.0	27.1	60.0	31.1	80.4	79.6	79.1	79.9
	1992	13.3	33.5	63.1	43.4	72.9	82.3	61.9	67.6
	1993	13.9	33.7	62.7	43.0	73.0	81.9	61.8	67.7
	1994	13.3	33.6	63.2	43.2	73.3	82.2	62.1	67.9
Countries of Central and Eastern Europe (including the former USSR)	1970	3.4	8.0	6.9	5.6	1.2	1.0	3.8	2.3
	1992	3.6	9.8	3.5	4.2	2.0	0.2	5.3	3.7
	1993	3.9	10.1	3.3	4.3	1.7	0.2	5.0	3.4
	1994	3.0	9.0	3.2	3.8	1.5	0.2	4.8	3.2
Socialist countries of Asia	1970	-	-	1.2	0.5	0.5	0.1	2.0	1.2
	1992	2.5	0.9	2.1	2.1	0.3	0.3	3.3	2.0
	1993	2.4	0.9	2.2	2.1	0.3	0.4	3.4	2.0
	1994	2.5	0.9	2.2	2.2	0.3	0.4	3.5	2.1

Table 3 (continued)

Country group	Year	Goods loaded				Goods unloaded			
		Oil		Dry cargo	Total all goods	Oil		Dry cargo	Total all goods
		Crude	Products			Crude	Products		
Developing countries	1970	94.6	64.9	31.9	62.8	17.9	19.4	15.1	16.6
	1992	80.6	55.9	31.4	50.3	24.8	17.3	29.5	26.7
	1993	79.8	55.3	31.8	50.6	25.0	17.5	29.8	26.9
	1994	81.2	56.5	31.4	50.8	24.9	17.2	29.6	26.8
of which in:									
Africa	1970	25.5	2.4	9.1	15.2	1.7	4.7	3.6	2.9
	1992	22.6	7.4	4.1	10.5	5.4	2.0	4.0	4.3
	1993	21.4	7.1	4.0	10.2	5.3	2.1	4.0	4.2
America	1970	12.2	35.4	13.8	16.0	10.5	5.6	4.4	7.2
	1992	13.5	12.0	13.2	13.2	5.5	3.5	4.0	4.4
	1993	13.4	11.8	13.1	13.1	5.4	3.4	4.0	4.4
Asia	1970	56.9	27.0	8.1	31.3	5.5	8.5	6.7	6.4
	1992	44.5	36.2	13.4	26.2	13.3	11.1	20.0	16.7
	1993	45.0	36.1	14.0	26.9	13.7	11.4	21.0	17.6
Europe	1970	-	-	-	-	-	0.1	0.1	-
	1992	-	0.2	0.3	0.2	0.7	0.4	0.8	0.7
	1993	-	0.2	0.3	0.2	0.6	0.3	0.7	0.6
Oceania	1970	-	0.1	0.8	0.4	-	0.5	0.3	0.2
	1992	-	0.1	0.4	0.2	-	0.5	0.1	0.2
	1993	-	0.1	0.4	0.2	-	0.3	0.1	0.1

Sources: Based on statistics provided by the United Nations Statistical Office, the UNCTAD data bank, and other specialized sources.

a/ Including international cargoes loaded at ports of the Great Lakes and St. Lawrence system for unloading at ports of the same system, but excluding such traffic in main bulk commodities.

b/ See annex I for the composition of these groups, and note 4 thereto regarding the recording of trade of land-locked countries.

11. A forecast of world seaborne trade by main cargo sectors from 1995 to 2005 is provided in graph 5. The World Sea Trade Service (WSTS) forecasts that the trade, estimated at 3.870 billion tons for 1994, will increase by an average of 4.1 per cent per year, reaching 5.456 billion tons by 2005. Containerized and other general cargoes are projected to increased at a high rate of 6.3 per cent per year to 1.601 billion tons. Dry bulk cargo and oil tanker cargo, estimated at the average growth rate of 4.5 per cent and 2.6 per cent per year, are forecasted to reach 1.685 billion tons and 2.170 billion tons respectively by 2005.

Graph 4

World seaborne trade by country groups
(Percentage distribution of tonnage, 1994)

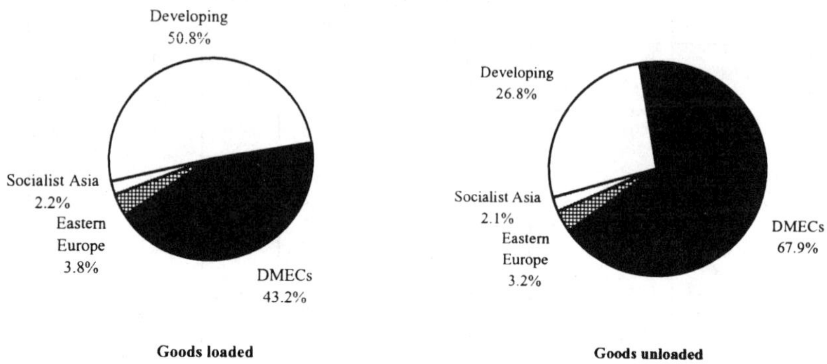

Source: UNCTAD data bank.

Graph 5

Forecast of world seaborne trade, 1995-2005

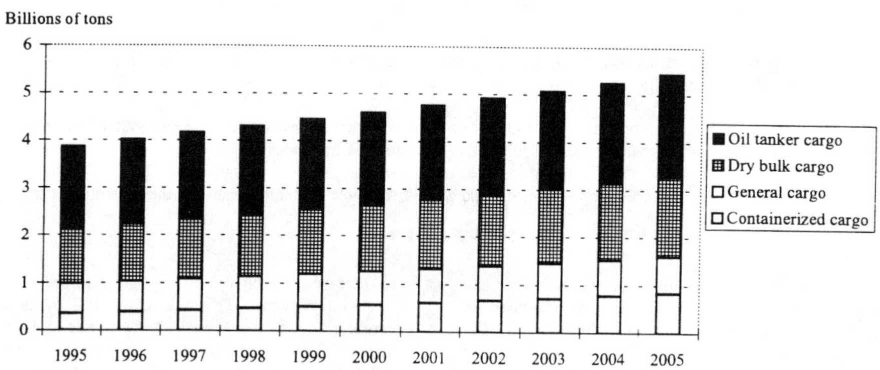

Source: DRI/McGraw-Hill, World Sea Trade Service.

Chapter II

DEVELOPMENT OF THE WORLD FLEET

This chapter reviews the supply of the world maritime industry. The information and data comprehensively cover structure and ownership of the world fleet, the comparison of cargo generation and fleet ownership, and a forecast for fleet development.

A. Structure of the world fleet

12. Comparative time series data for 1992, 1993 and 1994 are presented in table 4. The world merchant fleet aggregated 719.8 million dwt by the end of 1994. This represents a 1.3 per cent increase over 1993, which is noticeably less than the 2.3 per cent increase of 1993, but largely exceeds the 0.36 per cent yearly average growth of the 1983-1993 period. The 1994 fleet expansion occurred mainly because newbuilding deliveries (29.3 million dwt) increased more than scrapping (20.8 million dwt), leaving a net gain of 8.5 million dwt.[15/]

13. By vessel type, oil tankers and dry bulk carriers continued to dominate the world fleet. The former represented 37.7 per cent of the 1994 world total tonnage and the latter 34.8 per cent. The shares of general cargo ships and containerships were 14.4 per cent and 5.4 per cent, respectively. Comparative data on tonnage structures reveal that the shares of ore/bulk carriers and containerships are continuously increasing, whilst the relative growth of oil tankers halted after increasing for four consecutive years, and the share of general cargo ships and ore/bulk/oil carriers are on the decline. Graph 6 illustrates world fleet size trends by principal types of vessel for the 1980-1994 period.

14. The world fleet of fully cellular containerships continued to expand both in terms of TEU capacity and number of ships, reaching 1,603 ships of 2,367,000 TEU by the end of 1994. Developments since 1992 show an 11.5 per cent annual average increase in the world total TEU capacity and a 2.6 per cent increase in carrying capacity per ship. Table 5 indicates developments in detail for the 1992-1994 period.

15. The 1994 world containership fleet continued to expand in open-registry countries to 31.2 per cent of the world TEU capacity as compared to 28.7 per cent in 1993. Conversely, the share of developed market-economy countries fell for three consecutive years to 33.7 per cent in 1994 from 36.6 per cent in 1992. The combined share of the two groups, however, increased to 65.0 per cent from 62.8 per cent in 1993 (62.6 per cent in 1992).

16. The share of developing countries in TEU capacity of the world fleet continued to decrease to 15.7 per cent in 1994, the lowest level since 1990. This trend is attributed mainly to the decreasing share of the developing countries of Asia which represents the major proportion (82 per cent) of the containership fleet registered in developing countries. In 1994, Asia's share fell to 12.1 per cent of the world containership fleet, the lowest since 1990. Conversely, the share of developing countries of America slightly increased to 2.5 per cent. The share of other developing regions remained stagnant or practically non-existent.

17. Table 6 provides data on the age distribution of the world merchant fleet by types of vessel and by groups of countries and territories. It can be observed that the problematic ageing of the world fleet has not continued further in 1994. The average age of the total world fleet decreased marginally to 15.00 years, representing a decrease of 3.2 per cent over 1993. By types of vessel, the average age of tankers fell by 9.0 per cent to 15.35 years in 1994 from the previous year's age (16.86 years). The share of tanker tonnage aged 15 years and more decreased to 58.8 per cent in 1994 from 63.3 per cent in 1993, due to increasing scrapping of older tankers (13.1 million tons in 1994 versus 10.7 million tons in 1993). Conversely, ageing of the bulk carriers fleet continued with the average age up by 7.1 per cent (14.58 years in 1994 versus 13.61 years in 1993), reflecting a low level of scrapping activities in 1994 as a result of the surge in dry bulk freight markets, specifically in the second half of 1994. Containerships still represented the youngest fleet with an improved average age of 12.03 years (12.82 years in 1993).

18 By country grouping, developing countries showed the lowest average age of all ships (14.31 years) followed by developed market-economy countries (14.75 years), major open-registry countries (15.81 years) and countries of Central and Eastern Europe (16.76 years). Socialist countries of Asia have the oldest fleet, with vessels built 15 and more years ago representing 66.1 per cent of their total fleet (60.5 per cent in 1993).

Table 4

World fleet size by principal types of vessel, 1992-1994 a/
(Thousands of dwt)
(End-year figures)

Principal types	1992	1993	1994	Percentage change 1993/1994
1. Oil tankers	263 334 *37.9*	271 222 *38.2*	270 997 *37.7*	-0.1
2. Bulk carriers	239 973 *34.5*	242 134 *34.1*	250 294 *34.8*	3.4
Ore/bulk/oil	36 460 *5.3*	34 207 *4.8*	27 445 *3.8*	-19.8
Ore/bulk	203 513 *29.3*	207 927 *29.3*	222 849 *31.0*	7.2
3. General cargo ships	104 933 *15.1*	106 866 *15.0*	103 731 *14.4*	-2.9
4. Containerships	32 408 *4.7*	34 848 *4.9*	39 005 *5.4*	11.9
5. Other types of ships	54 043 *7.8*	55 552 *7.8*	55 778 *7.8*	0.4
Liquefied gas carriers	12 721 *1.8*	13 388 *1.9*	14 044 *2.0*	4.9
Chemical tankers	7 113 *1.0*	7 381 *1.0*	7 616 *1.1*	3.2
Miscellaneous tankers	627 *0.1*	539 *0.1*	592 *0.1*	9.8
Ferries and passenger ships	3 673 *0.5*	3 811 *0.5*	3 951 *0.6*	3.7
Others	29 909 *4.3*	30 433 *4.3*	29 575 *4.1*	-2.8
World total	694 691 *100.0*	710 622 *100.0*	719 805 *100.0*	1.3

Source: Lloyd's Maritime Information Services Ltd. (London).

a/ Percentage shares are shown in italics.

Graph 6

World fleet size by principal types of vessel: selected years 1980-1994

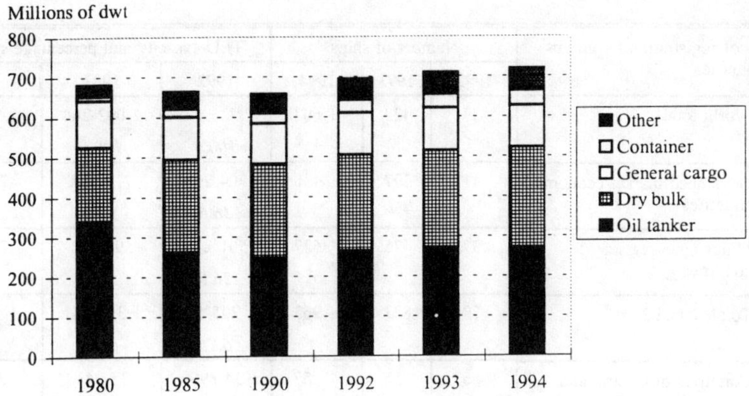

Source: Lloyd's Maritime Information Services Ltd. (London).

B. Ownership of the world fleet

19. Table 7 and graph 7 provide information on the distribution of the world merchant fleet by groups of countries for the years 1980, 1993 and 1994. Developed market-economy countries and major open-registry countries owned 67.5 per cent of the 1994 total. This represents almost the same level as 1993, but a significant decline from 82.4 per cent in 1980. The developing countries' share of the total 1994 dwt marginally increased to 22.6 per cent, as compared to 22.2 per cent in 1993. This is a tremendous increase over 1980, with an average annual increase of 6.7 million dwt, which is the largest increase in dwt among the country groups. The fleet tonnage of developing countries in Asia in 1994 increased by 3.1 per cent from the previous year to 97.5 million dwt, which accounted for 60.1 per cent of the developing countries' total. The share of socialist countries in Asia remained almost the same as the previous year (3.6 per cent). On the other hand, the shares of the countries of Central and Eastern Europe slightly declined to 5.1 per cent in 1994 (5.4 per cent in 1993).

20. Table 8 provides more detailed data on fleet distribution by vessel types and country groups for the years 1980, 1993 and 1994. In the oil tanker sector, the share of developed market-economy countries in the world total tonnage decreased to 33.0 per cent in 1994. On the other hand, the share of major open-registry countries increased to 44.2 per cent, resulting in a combined share of 77.2 per cent of the two groups, which remained almost unchanged from the previous year, but tremendously decreased from 88.7 per cent in 1980. The developing countries in Asia very marginally decreased to 10.5 per cent in 1994, which represented the lowest share in their principal types of vessel.

21. In the dry bulk carrier sector, the tonnage share of developed market-economy countries in the world total continued to decrease to 24.6 per cent in 1994. Conversely, major open-registry countries expanded their share to 38.2 per cent. The combined tonnage accounts for 62.8 per cent, which remained unchanged from 1993. Developing countries' share in 1994 slightly expanded to 26.8 per cent from the 26.4 per cent share in 1993. The share of developing countries in Asia slightly increased in 1994 to 17.7 per cent, which however was the highest in their principal types of vessel.

Table 5

Distribution of the world fleet and TEU capacity of fully cellular containerships by groups of countries, 1992, 1993 and 1994
(End-year figures)

Flags of registration by groups of countries	Number of ships			TEU capacity and percentage shares a/		
	1992	1993	1994	1992	1993	1994
1. World total	1 371	1 423	1 603	1 925 177 *100.0*	2 092 204 *100.0*	2 366 720 *100.0*
2. Developed market-economy countries	417	397	436	704 258 *36.6*	714 088 *34.1*	797 994 *33.7*
3. Major open-registry countries b/	377	426	527	501 281 *26.0*	599 753 *28.7*	739 454 *31.2*
Total, 2 and 3	794	823	963	1 205 539 *62.6*	1 313 841 *62.8*	1 537 448 *65.0*
4. Countries of Central and Eastern Europe (including the former USSR)	67	55	57	34 899 *1.8*	35 343 *1.7*	37 698 *1.6*
5. Socialist countries of Asia	69	73	83	65 592 *3.4*	70 297 *3.4*	94 487 *4.0*
6. Developing countries	289	292	322	320 127 *16.6*	329 200 *15.7*	351 664 *14.9*
of which in: Africa	3	3	3	585 -	585 -	585 -
America	55	66	90	36 075 *1.9*	41 282 *2.0*	59 736 *2.5*
Asia	225	218	224	279 867 *14.5*	285 495 *13.7*	287 370 *12.1*
Europe	2	1	2	2 336 *0.1*	574 -	2 833 *0.1*
Oceania	4	4	3	1 264 *0.1*	1 264 *0.1*	1 140 *0.1*
7. Other, unallocated	152	180	178	299 020 *15.5*	343 523 *16.4*	345 423 *14.6*

Source: Lloyd's Maritime Information Services Ltd. (London).

a/ Percentage shares are shown in italics.

b/ Including Malta and Vanuatu.

Table 6

Age distribution of the world merchant fleet by types of vessel, as at 31 December 1994
(Percentage of total in terms of dwt)

Country grouping	Types of vessel	Total	0-4 years	5-9 years	10-14 years	15 years and over	Average age (years) a/	Average age (years) 1993 a/
World total	All ships	100	15.2	14.7	17.6	52.5	15.00	15.05
	Tankers	100	19.7	11.2	10.3	58.8	15.35	16.86
	Bulk carriers	100	12.1	17.7	23.5	46.7	14.58	13.61
	General cargo	100	7.5	13.0	19.4	60.1	16.61	15.03
	Containerships	100	24.7	21.3	18.4	35.6	12.03	12.82
	All others	100	14.7	16.6	21.6	47.1	14.41	14.14
Developed market-economy countries	All ships	100	14.7	16.3	18.7	50.3	14.75	14.44
	Tankers	100	15.2	10.3	11.3	63.2	16.29	16.65
	Bulk carriers	100	11.4	20.5	26.1	42.0	14.04	12.70
	General cargo	100	12.5	19.6	21.4	46.5	14.42	13.26
	Containerships	100	28.0	19.9	17.1	35.0	11.71	13.07
	All others	100	16.5	20.8	22.0	40.7	13.38	13.17
Major open-registry countries b/	All ships	100	16.1	10.4	14.1	59.4	15.81	15.88
	Tankers	100	23.5	8.5	7.5	60.5	15.28	17.26
	Bulk carriers	100	8.7	10.1	19.9	61.3	16.76	15.22
	General cargo	100	6.0	13.1	20.0	60.9	16.84	14.34
	Containerships	100	26.9	21.5	16.2	35.4	11.78	13.73
	All others	100	16.5	17.1	16.8	49.6	14.46	14.11
Subtotal	All ships	100	15.3	13.8	16.8	54.1	15.19	15.23
	Tankers	100	18.9	9.5	9.6	62.0	15.84	16.99
	Bulk carriers	100	10.2	15.8	23.3	50.7	15.26	14.13
	General cargo	100	9.8	16.9	20.8	52.5	15.43	13.91
	Containerships	100	27.7	20.3	16.9	35.1	11.73	13.32
	All others	100	16.5	19.8	20.6	43.1	13.67	13.55
Countries of Central and Eastern Europe	All ships	100	4.9	15.6	19.2	60.3	16.76	14.87
	Tankers	100	1.0	14.7	23.6	60.7	17.24	14.13
	Bulk carriers	100	5.4	17.1	21.4	56.1	16.22	13.58
	General cargo	100	5.7	14.0	16.0	64.2	17.14	16.20
	Containerships	100	0.0	28.0	33.6	38.4	14.44	11.29
	All others	100	7.0	16.1	15.6	61.3	16.63	15.56
Socialist countries of Asia	All ships	100	7.8	11.5	14.6	66.1	17.26	16.66
	Tankers	100	14.6	10.5	14.5	60.4	16.06	17.38
	Bulk carriers	100	8.7	12.8	15.6	62.9	16.78	16.23
	General cargo	100	3.5	8.8	12.9	74.8	18.69	17.40
	Containerships	100	11.4	25.0	20.5	43.1	13.92	10.54
	All others	100	3.4	4.7	11.4	80.5	19.48	19.04
Developing countries (excluding open-registry countries)	All ships	100	13.5	20.1	19.8	46.6	14.31	14.35
	Tankers	100	16.3	14.2	11.1	58.4	15.50	16.61
	Bulk carriers	100	13.7	31.8	27.1	27.4	11.78	11.12
	General cargo	100	3.4	9.1	17.6	69.9	18.20	16.34
	Containerships	100	31.1	19.7	16.5	32.7	11.18	12.78
	All others	100	13.2	10.3	27.6	48.9	15.06	15.09

Source: Compiled on the basis of data supplied by Lloyd's Maritime Information Services Ltd. (London).

a/ To calculate average age, it has been assumed that the ages of vessels are distributed evenly between the lower and upper limit of each age group. For the 15-years-and-over age group, the mid-point has been assumed to be 22 years.

b/ Including Malta and Vanuatu.

Table 7

Distribution of world tonnage (grt and dwt) by groups of countries of registration, 1980, 1993 and 1994 a/
(End-year figures)

Flags of registration by groups of countries	Tonnage and percentage shares b/						Increase in tonnage (millions of dwt) d/	
	In grt (millions)			In dwt (millions)				
	1980 c/	1993	1994	1980 c/	1993	1994	1980-1994	1993-1994
1. World total	414.5	457.4	476.2	682.8	710.6	719.8	2.6	9.2
	100.0	*100.0*	*100.0*	*100.0*	*100.0*	*100.0*		
2. Developed market-economy countries	214.3	142.7	144.5	350.1	216.6	211.9	-9.9	-4.7
	51.7	*31.2*	*30.3*	*51.3*	*30.5*	*29.4*		
3. Major open-registry countries	114.2	158.8	171.6	212.6	263.4	273.6	4.4	10.2
	27.6	*34.7*	*36.0*	*31.1*	*37.1*	*38.0*		
Total 2 and 3	328.5	301.5	316.1	562.7	480.0	485.5	-5.5	5.5
	79.3	*65.9*	*66.4*	*82.4*	*67.6*	*67.5*		
4. Countries of Central and Eastern Europe (including the former USSR)	32.0	33.2	32.3	37.8	38.2	36.8	-0.1	-1.4
	7.7	*7.3*	*6.8*	*5.5*	*5.4*	*5.1*		
5. Socialist countries of Asia	7.3	16.5	17.3	10.9	24.7	25.6	1.1	0.9
	1.8	*3.6*	*3.6*	*1.6*	*3.5*	*3.6*		
6. Developing countries	44.7	99.6	104.1	68.4	157.9	162.3	6.7	4.4
	10.8	*21.8*	*21.9*	*10.0*	*22.2*	*22.6*		
of which in:								
Africa	4.9	5.1	5.0	7.2	6.9	6.6	-0.0	-0.3
America	14.5	18.7	19.3	21.8	28.8	28.8	0.5	0.0
Asia	25.0	59.3	62.0	39.1	94.6	97.5	4.2	2.9
Europe	0.1	14.4	15.7	0.2	24.6	26.6	1.9	2.0
Oceania	0.1	2.1	2.1	0.1	3.0	2.8	0.2	-0.2
7. Other, unallocated	2.0	6.6	6.4	3.0	9.8	9.6	0.5	-0.2
	0.5	*1.4*	*1.3*	*0.4*	*1.4*	*1.3*		

Source: Lloyd's Maritime Information Services Ltd. (London).

a/ Excluding the United States Reserve Fleet and the United States and Canadian Great Lakes fleets, which in 1994 amounted respectively to 2.9, 1.1 and 1.5 million grt (3.8, 2.0 and 2.1 million dwt).

b/ Percentage shares are shown in italics.

c/ Mid-year figure.

d/ Average.

Graph 7

World tonnage by country groups, 1994
(Percentage distribution of dwt)

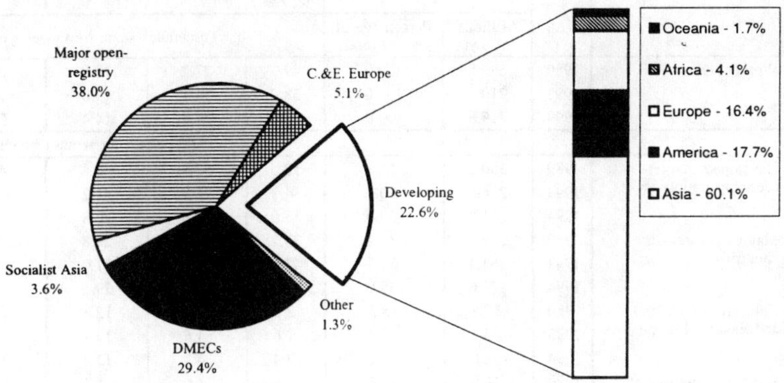

Source: Lloyd's Maritime Information Services Ltd. (London).

22. In the sector of general cargo ships, the combined share of developed market-economy countries and major open-registry countries was on the downward trend, recording 50.2 per cent in 1994, as compared to 64.2 per cent in 1980. Developing countries continuously expanded to 27.8 per cent in 1994 (17.6 per cent in 1980), which represented the highest percentage proportion in their principal types of vessel.

23. The containership sector expanded to 5.4 per cent of the world deadweight in 1994, representing a constant expansion from 1.6 per cent in 1980. Developed market-economy countries decreased their share of the containership deadweight tons further to 39.5 per cent in 1994. On the other hand, the open-registry countries' share constantly expanded to 30.9 per cent in 1994. The 1994 combined share of the two country groups (70.4 per cent) exceeded their 1993 share (68.6 per cent). The share of developing countries in the world containership fleet further declined to 16.9 per cent in 1994, of which 12.5 per cent was registered by the developing countries in Asia.

24. The 1994 structure of the merchant fleet of the main country groups is provided in table 9. Developed market-economy countries' tonnage in oil tankers and dry bulk carriers reached 71.3 per cent of the group's total fleet, which is a small decrease from 71.9 per cent in 1993. Their general cargo ships amounted to 10.2 per cent (10.4 per cent in 1993), while containerships accounted for 7.3 per cent, as compared to 6.6 per cent in 1993. Major open-registry countries have a greater proportion of their fleets in the oil tanker and dry bulk carrier sector, accounting for a combined 78.8 per cent in 1994, which is the same share as in 1992 (78.2 per cent in 1993). Their share of general cargo ships (11.2 per cent) is higher than in developed market-economy countries (10.2 per cent); however containerships (4.4 per cent) account for less than the developed market-economy countries (7.3 per cent).

Table 8

Percentage shares of world tonnage by types of vessel and country groups
1980 (as at 1 July), 1993 and 1994 (as at 31 December) a/
(In terms of dwt)

Country group	Year	Total dwt		Oil tankers	Bulk carriers b/	General cargo ships	Container ships	Other ships
		Millions of dwt	Percentage of world total	Percentage share by vessel type				
World total	1980	682.8	100.0	49.7	27.2	17.0	1.6	4.5
	1993	710.6	100.0	38.2	34.1	15.0	4.9	7.8
	1994	719.8	100.0	37.6	34.8	14.4	5.4	7.8
				Percentage share by group of countries				
Developed market-economy countries	1980	350.1	51.3	52.5	52.7	43.4	74.3	50.4
	1993	216.6	30.5	34.3	25.9	21.2	40.8	43.3
	1994	211.8	29.4	33.0	24.6	20.8	39.5	42.6
Major open-registry countries	1980	212.5	31.1	36.2	31.7	20.8	13.5	17.0
	1993	263.4	37.1	43.0	37.0	31.0	27.8	26.3
	1994	273.6	38.0	44.2	38.2	29.5	30.9	27.7
Countries of Central and Eastern Europe	1980	37.8	5.5	2.8	4.2	12.3	2.9	19.2
	1993	38.2	5.4	2.6	4.6	13.1	1.9	9.5
	1994	36.8	5.1	2.4	4.3	13.4	1.8	8.8
Socialist countries of Asia	1980	10.9	1.6	0.6	1.6	4.7	0.1	1.3
	1993	24.6	3.5	1.5	4.1	7.5	3.8	2.6
	1994	25.7	3.6	1.5	4.1	8.0	4.2	2.4
Developing countries	1980	68.4	10.0	7.7	9.2	17.6	7.6	12.0
	1993	158.0	22.2	18.1	26.4	26.7	17.7	18.2
	1994	162.2	22.5	18.2	26.8	27.8	16.9	18.3
of which in: Africa	1980	7.1	1.0	1.1	0.1	2.3	..	2.1
	1993	6.9	1.0	0.7	0.5	2.1	..	2.6
	1994	6.6	0.9	0.8	0.5	1.9	..	2.1
America	1980	21.8	3.2	2.3	3.3	5.6	0.1	3.7
	1993	28.8	4.1	3.1	3.7	7.3	2.4	5.1
	1994	28.8	4.0	3.0	3.5	7.7	3.0	4.9
Asia	1980	39.1	5.7	4.3	5.7	9.8	2.7	5.7
	1993	94.6	13.3	10.7	17.1	13.4	14.0	8.9
	1994	97.5	13.5	10.5	17.7	14.0	12.5	9.4
Europe	1980	1.2	..	..	..	0.1	-	-
	1993	24.6	3.5	3.6	4.3	3.3	1.2	0.9
	1994	26.5	3.7	3.9	4.4	3.7	1.3	1.1
Oceania	1980	0.2	..	..	..	0.1	-	-
	1993	3.1	0.4	..	0.8	0.6	0.1	0.7
	1994	2.8	0.4	..	0.7	0.6	0.1	0.8
Other, unallocated	1980	3.0	0.4	0.2	0.6	0.9	1.6	0.1
	1993	9.8	1.4	0.5	2.0	0.5	8.0	0.1
	1994	9.6	1.3	0.6	1.9	0.4	6.6	0.2

Source: Compiled on the basis of data supplied by Lloyd's Maritime Information Services Ltd. (London).

a/ Excluding the United States Reserve Fleet and the United States and Canadian Great Lakes fleets.

b/ Ore and bulk carriers, including combined ore/oil and ore/bulk/oil carriers.

Table 9

Structure of the merchant fleets of the main country groups, as at 31 December 1994 a/
(Million dwt and percentage shares)

	World		Developed market-economy countries		Major open-registry countries		Developing countries		Countries of Central and Eastern Europe		Socialist countries of Asia	
	Million dwt	%	Million dwt	%	Million dwt	%	Million dwt	%	Million dwt	%	Million dwt	%
Total fleet	719.8	100.0	211.9	100.0	273.6	100.0	162.2	100.0	36.8	100.0	25.6	100.0
of which: Oil tankers	271.0	37.7	89.5	42.2	119.8	43.8	49.4	30.5	6.5	17.7	4.1	16.0
Bulk carriers	250.3	34.8	61.6	29.1	95.7	35.0	67.2	41.4	10.7	29.1	10.2	39.8
General cargo	103.7	14.4	21.6	10.2	30.6	11.2	28.8	17.8	14.0	38.0	8.3	32.4
Containerships	39.0	5.4	15.4	7.3	12.0	4.4	6.6	4.1	0.7	1.9	1.7	6.6
Other ships	55.8	7.8	23.8	11.2	15.5	5.7	10.2	6.3	4.9	13.3	1.3	5.1

Source: Compiled on the basis of data supplied by Lloyd's Maritime Information Services Ltd. (London).

a/ Ships of 100 grt and over, excluding the United States Reserve Fleet and the United States and Canadian Great Lakes fleets.

25. Tonnage distribution in developing countries is characterized by a comparatively high proportion of dry bulk carriers (41.4 per cent) and general cargo ships (17.8 per cent), while containerships represent only 4.1 per cent, which however slightly increased from 3.9 per cent in 1993. The low share of technically advanced containerships reflects ongoing structural deficiencies which characterize the liner fleet of developing countries. In the countries of Central and Eastern Europe, general cargo fleets were most concentrated, accounting for 38.0 per cent, while containerships made up only 1.9 per cent (1.8 per cent in 1993). The socialist countries of Asia continued to have a predominant share of both dry bulk carriers (39.8 per cent) and general cargo ships (32.4 per cent) in their merchant fleets.

C. The 35 most important maritime countries and territories

26. The 35 most important maritime countries in dwt terms are ranked in table 10. This table comprises merchant vessels registered under the national flag or a foreign flag when the controlling interest of the vessels is located in the maritime country or territory. These 35 countries control 93.1 per cent of the world merchant fleet. The five largest countries or territories control 51.5 per cent of the world fleet and the top ten control 67.7 per cent.

27. The trend for increasing foreign flag registry continued in 1994. Total tonnage registered under foreign flags in 1994 reached 319.6 million dwt, representing 51.9 per cent of the 35 countries' total fleet, as compared to 50.7 per cent in 1993. This means that more than half of the tonnage beneficially owned by the 35 countries was not registered in the countries of domicile of the parent companies. While registry under foreign flags has been a long-standing practice by owners from developed market-economy countries, it is gradually becoming a common practice in other country groups, including developing countries.

D. Major open registries

28. Foreign registers continue to expand their share in the world merchant fleet, as reviewed in the preceding paragraphs. Table 11 summarizes the tonnage distribution of the five major open-registry countries by principal types of vessels. The total tonnage registered in 1994 rose by 3.3 per cent to 250.2 million dwt from 242.2 million dwt in the previous year. Panama continuously increased to 86.5 million dwt, following Liberia whose fleet increased by 3.4 million dwt to 91.8 million dwt, thus regaining the level of 1992. While the Bahamas and Cyprus also increased their tonnage, Bermuda decreased to 4.5 million dwt from 5.1 million dwt in 1993. By vessel type, oil tankers represent 45.0 per cent of the total dwt (45.3 per cent in 1993), followed by dry bulk carriers with 33.9 per cent (33.1 per cent in 1993), general cargo ships with 10.8 per cent (12.3 per cent in 1993) and containerships with 4.6 per cent (3.8 per cent in 1993), thus clearly revealing the trend to also flag out container tonnage.

29. The participation of nationals in the registry of the most important open or international registers is provided in table 12. The information compares the total tonnage registered in the selected countries of registry with the tonnage owned by the nationals of, and registered in, the countries of registry. For most open-registry countries, except Cyprus, the share owned by the nationals is minimal or zero. However, with international registry, ownership remained unchanged from the 1993 level at over 90 per cent.

30. The true nationality of the five major open-registry fleets is surveyed in table 13. In 1994 total tonnage of the 20 countries or territories account for 92.0 per cent of the total five major open-registry fleets (92.4 per cent in 1993). Ownership is concentrated in 10 countries or territories which control 79.9 per cent of the dwt and 74.7 per cent of the number of vessels of the total five major open-registry fleets. These percentage figures compare with 81.2 per cent and 74.7 per cent respectively in 1993. Japan was again placed at the top in 1994 with the largest share (18.5 per cent) of the five major open-registry fleets, although Greece became the largest foreign-flag-fleet owner with 65.9 million dwt over Japan with 58.5 million dwt.

E. Comparison of cargo turnover and fleet ownership

31. The correlation between cargo volume handled in different country groups and their fleet ownership in 1980, 1993 and 1994 is summarized in table 14. In 1994, developed market-economy countries, either directly or through open or international ship registers, controlled 67.5 per cent (67.6 per cent in 1993) of the world fleet, while they handled 55.8 per cent of the world seaborne trade (55.5 per cent in 1993). On the other hand, the share of developing countries in the world cargo turnover stood at 38.5 per cent (38.6 per cent in 1993), while their merchant fleet constituted 22.5 per cent (22.2 per cent in 1993) of the total world fleet in deadweight tons.

Table 10

The 35 most important maritime countries, as at 31 December 1994 a/

Country of domicile b/	Number of vessels			Deadweight tonnage				
	National flag c/	Foreign flag	Total	National flag	Foreign flag	Total	Foreign flag as percentage of total	Total as percentage of world total
Greece	1 048	1 889	2 937	52 457 838	65 941 146	118 398 984	55.69	17.89
Japan	1 018	1 853	2 871	27 009 824	58 545 022	85 554 846	68.43	12.93
United States	543	669	1 212	15 053 345	37 328 292	52 381 637	71.26	7.92
Norway	922	510	1 432	31 933 615	18 121 570	50 055 185	36.20	7.56
China	1 518	308	1 826	22 197 888	12 069 687	34 267 575	35.22	5.18
Hong Kong	98	514	612	5 545 416	24 097 041	29 642 457	81.29	4.48
United Kingdom	391	490	881	5 776 437	15 767 968	21 544 405	73.19	3.26
Russian Federation	2 755	236	2 991	15 491 549	4 892 433	20 383 982	24.00	3.08
Republic of Korea	450	234	684	9 829 152	9 657 492	19 486 644	49.56	2.95
Germany	561	823	1 384	6 373 965	9 865 754	16 239 719	60.75	2.45
Taiwan Province of China	179	239	418	7 446 166	5 564 354	13 010 520	42.77	1.97
Italy	502	112	614	8 738 013	3 137 302	11 875 315	26.42	1.79
Sweden	178	143	321	2 110 872	9 636 860	11 747 732	82.03	1.78
Denmark	449	211	660	6 240 644	5 487 214	11 727 858	46.79	1.77
India	372	53	425	10 292 034	1 352 923	11 644 957	11.62	1.76
Singapore	345	202	547	6 972 882	3 262 870	10 235 752	31.88	1.55
Brazil	233	16	249	8 724 415	1 499 900	10 224 315	14.67	1.55
Saudi Arabia	61	49	110	891 704	7 309 085	8 200 789	89.13	1.24
Turkey	384	10	394	8 005 759	44 587	8 050 346	0.55	1.22
France	177	101	278	3 865 777	3 318 301	7 184 078	46.19	1.09
Iran, Islamic Rep. of	145	1	146	6 708 775	1 600	6 710 375	0.02	1.01
Ukraine	611	38	649	5 530 957	296 649	5 827 606	5.09	0.88
Netherlands	449	195	644	3 367 475	2 108 753	5 476 228	38.51	0.83
Philippines	307	17	324	4 826 953	165 407	4 992 360	3.31	0.75
Romania	267	30	297	3 807 881	998 868	4 806 749	20.78	0.73
Switzerland	14	160	174	626 475	3 728 973	4 355 448	85.62	0.66
Indonesia	440	95	535	2 636 599	1 497 282	4 133 881	36.22	0.62
Belgium	37	125	162	178 296	3 600 098	3 778 394	95.28	0.57
Spain	203	119	322	1 056 087	2 715 548	3 771 635	72.00	0.57
Finland	108	60	168	1 115 346	2 597 791	3 713 137	69.96	0.56
Cyprus	43	32	75	2 856 083	745 541	3 601 624	20.70	0.54
Australia	83	21	104	3 170 397	275 497	3 445 894	7.99	0.52
Kuwait	33	5	38	2 891 849	509 760	3 401 609	14.99	0.51
Croatia	36	132	168	194 429	3 093 567	3 287 996	94.09	0.50
Malaysia	150	17	167	2 707 528	399 827	3 107 355	12.87	0.47
Total (35 countries)	15 110	9 709	24 819	296 632 425	319 634 962	616 267 387	51.87	93.14
Percentage	60.9	39.1	100	48.1	51.9	100		
World total	17 955	10 493	28 448	326 938 555	334 733 824	661 672 379	50.59	100.00
Percentage	63.1	36.9	100	49.4	50.6	100		

Source: Lloyd's Maritime Information Services Ltd. (London).

a/ Vessels of 1,000 grt and above, excluding the United States Reserve Fleet and the United States and Canada Great Lakes fleets.

b/ The country of domicile indicates where the controlling interest of the fleet is located, in terms of the parent company. In several cases, this has required certain judgements to be made. Thus, for instance, Greece is shown as the country of domicile with respect to vessels owned by a Greek owner with representative offices in New York, London and Piraeus, although the owner may be domiciled in the United States.

c/ Including vessels flying the national flag but registered in territorial dependencies or associated self-governing territories. For the United Kingdom, British flag vessels are included under the national flag, except for Bermuda (listed in table 11 as an open-registry country) and Hong Kong (shown separately in the present table).

Table 11

Tonnage distribution of major open-registry fleets, a/ as at 31 December 1994

Country	Oil tankers		Dry bulk carriers		General cargo		Containerships		Others		1994 Total		1993 Total	
	Ships	Thousand dwt	Ships	Thousand dwt	Ships	Thousand dwt	Ships	Thousand dwt	Ships	Thousand dwt	Ships	Thousand dwt	Ships	Thousand dwt
Liberia	404	51 933	415	26 172	245	3 786	122	3 399	307	6 473	1 493	91 763	1 461	88 354
Panama	358	32 262	693	32 052	1 389	11 779	222	5 863	560	4 505	3 222	86 461	3 151	82 992
Cyprus	88	6 081	493	19 226	583	5 748	78	1 250	70	623	1 312	32 928	1 230	32 669
Bahamas	167	19 192	124	7 190	434	5 581	39	847	209	1 699	973	34 509	921	33 062
Bermuda	15	3 210	7	209	9	79	7	149	29	845	67	4 492	78	5 098
Total	1 032	112 678	1 732	84 849	2 660	26 973	468	11 508	1 175	14 145	7 067	250 153	6 841	242 175

Source: Based on data supplied by Lloyd's Maritime Information Services Ltd. (London).

a/ Ships of 1,000 grt and above. This table is not fully comparable with tables 7 and 9, which list ships of 100 grt and above as the base.

Table 12

Tonnage owned by the nationals of, and registered in, the country of registry in the total fleet of the most important open and international registers, as at 31 December 1994 a/
(Thousand dwt)

Country of registry or register	Total tonnage registered in the country of register	Tonnage owned by nationals of, and registered in, the country of registry	Share of tonnage owned by nationals in the total registered fleet (%)
Liberia	91 764	0	0.0
Panama	86 460	0	0.0
Cyprus	35 785	2 856	8.0
Bahamas	34 697	187	0.5
Norwegian International Ship Registry	31 533	29 676	94.1
Danish International Ship Registry	6 170	6 039	97.9
Bermuda	4 493	0	0.0

Source: Based on data supplied by Lloyd's Maritime Information Services Ltd. (London).

a/ Ships of 1,000 grt and above. This table is not fully comparable with tables 7 and 9, which list ships of 100 grt and above as the base.

32. In long-term comparisons, the gap between cargo turnover and fleet ownership narrowed significantly in both developed market-economy countries and developing countries. The ratio of goods loaded and unloaded in 1994 was almost unchanged from that in 1980 for both groups. In the meantime, the fleet ownership of developed market-economy countries fell considerably from as high as 82.4 per cent of the world fleet in 1980 to 67.5 per cent in 1994. At the same time, developing countries substantially raised their share to 22.5 per cent in 1994 from the 10.0 per cent registered in 1980.

F. Forecast for world fleet development

33. Forecasts for world fleet development by vessel type (four main types) are shown in graph 8. The World Fleet Forecast Service (WFFS) projects that the total world fleet will increase from 649.2 million dwt in 1995 to 883.9 million dwt by the year 2005. The combined tonnage of container and general cargo ships is expected to increase at the average annual growth rate of 5.4 per cent over the decade. Dry bulk carriers and oil tankers will increase by an annual average of 4.3 per cent and 2.1 per cent, respectively, by the year 2005.

Table 13

True nationality of major open-registry fleets, as at 31 December 1994

Flag country / Country or territory of domicile	Liberia			Panama			Cyprus			Bahamas			Bermuda			Subtotal			Total foreign-flag fleet	
	Thousand dwt	No. of vessels	%	Thousand dwt	No. of vessels	%	Thousand dwt	No. of vessels	%	Thousand dwt	No. of vessels	%	Thousand dwt	No. of vessels	%	Thousand dwt	No. of vessels	%	Thousand dwt	No. of vessels
Greece	10 662	128	11.6	7 909	340	9.2	22 148	737	67.3	5 000	128	14.5	-	-	0.0	45 719	1 333	18.3	65 941	1 889
Japan	9 176	217	10.0	35 884	1 261	41.5	156	20	0.5	1 058	36	3.1	-	-	0.0	46 274	1 534	18.5	58 545	1 853
United States	18 952	225	20.7	2 220	125	2.6	104	8	0.3	8 100	119	23.5	737	5	16.4	30 113	482	12.0	37 328	669
Hong Kong	6 647	109	7.2	12 288	263	14.2	338	1	1.0	370	8	1.1	-	-	0.0	19 643	381	7.9	24 097	514
Norway	7 150	148	7.8	1 662	65	1.9	1 956	16	5.9	5 402	146	15.7	214	8	4.8	16 384	383	6.6	18 122	510
United Kingdom	4 008	88	4.4	519	56	0.6	215	15	0.7	2 242	116	6.5	1 710	20	38.1	8 694	295	3.5	15 768	490
Germany	3 216	123	3.5	1 389	30	1.6	2 218	223	6.7	40	7	0.1	54	1	1.2	6 917	384	2.8	9 866	823
Republic of Korea	1 527	16	1.7	7 325	182	8.5	275	1	0.8	-	-	0.0	-	-	0.0	9 127	199	3.7	9 657	234
Sweden	5 050	31	5.5	80	4	0.1	-	-	0.0	1 615	34	4.7	916	2	20.4	7 661	71	3.1	9 637	143
China	4 735	72	5.2	4 202	122	4.9	315	20	1.0	-	-	0.0	-	-	0.0	9 252	214	3.7	12 070	308
Russian Federation	2 595	42	2.8	179	21	0.2	1 144	43	3.5	111	8	0.3	-	-	0.0	4 029	114	1.6	4 892	236
Taiwan Province of China	813	25	0.9	3 930	187	4.6	274	2	0.8	-	-	0.0	-	-	0.0	5 017	214	2.0	5 564	239
Saudi Arabia	6 323	21	6.9	212	12	0.3	-	-	0.0	510	2	1.5	-	-	0.0	7 045	35	2.8	7 309	49
France	368	2	0.4	740	17	0.9	21	3	0.1	1 495	44	4.3	-	-	0.0	2 624	66	1.1	3 318	101
Finland	-	-	0.0	22	5	0.0	254	1	0.8	2 169	39	6.3	-	-	0.0	2 445	45	1.0	2 598	60
Switzerland	298	9	0.3	1 104	62	1.3	201	11	0.6	684	16	2.0	-	-	0.0	2 287	98	0.9	3 729	160
Denmark	1 367	19	1.5	200	18	0.2	151	1	0.5	843	78	2.4	-	-	0.0	2 561	116	1.0	5 487	211
Italy	767	21	0.8	136	10	0.2	283	8	0.9	473	14	1.4	-	-	0.0	1 659	53	0.7	3 137	112
Singapore	319	14	0.4	703	77	0.8	339	3	1.0	566	12	1.6	-	-	0.0	1 927	106	0.8	3 263	202
Belgium	473	14	0.5	63	8	0.1	120	19	0.4	187	8	0.5	-	-	0.0	843	49	0.3	3 600	125
Subtotal	84 446	1 324	92.0	80 767	2 865	93.4	30 512	1 132	92.7	30 865	815	89.4	3 631	36	80.8	230 221	6 172	92.0	303 928	8 928
Others	7 317	169	8.0	5 694	357	6.6	2 416	180	7.3	3 644	158	10.6	861	31	19.2	19 932	895	8.0	30 806	1 565
TOTAL	91 763	1 493	100.0	86 461	3 222	100.0	32 928	1 312	100.0	34 509	973	100.0	4 492	67	100.0	250 153	7 067	100.0	334 734	10 493

Source: Based on data supplied by Lloyd's Maritime Information Services Ltd. (London).

Table 14

Comparison between total cargo turnover and fleet ownership by groups of countries, 1980, 1993 and 1994

Country grouping	Year	Goods loaded and unloaded (millions of tons)		Total of goods loaded and unloaded (millions of tons)	Merchant fleet (millions of dwt)	Percentage of world total of	
		Loaded	Unloaded			Goods loaded and unloaded	Merchant fleet owned (dwt)
Developed market-economy and major open-registry countries	1980	1 424	2 626	4 050	562.7	54.9	82.4
	1993	1 864	2 994	4 858	480.0	55.5	67.6
	1994	1 935	3 091	5 026	485.6	55.8	67.5
Developing countries	1980	2 033	808	2 841	68.4	38.5	10.0
	1993	2 189	1 188	3 377	158.0	38.6	22.2
	1994	2 258	1 212	3 470	162.2	38.5	22.5
Countries of Central and Eastern Europe (including the former USSR)	1980	201	145	346	37.8	4.7	5.5
	1993	186	150	336	38.2	3.8	5.4
	1994	169	147	316	36.8	3.5	5.1
Socialist countries of Asia	1980	46	100	146	10.9	2.0	1.6
	1993	91	90	181	24.6	2.1	3.5
	1994	96	96	192	25.6	2.1	3.6
World total a/	1980	3 704	3 679	7 383	682.8		
	1993	4 330	4 422	8 752	710.6		
	1994	4 458	4 546	9 004	719.8		

Source: As per tables 3 and 8.

a/ Including unallocated tonnage indicated in annex III.

Graph 8

Forecast of world fleet by principal types of vessel, 1995-2005

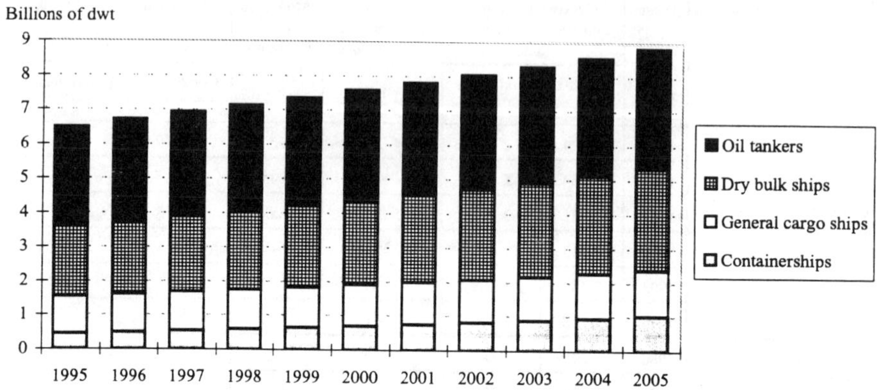

Source: DRI/McGraw-Hill, World Fleet Forecast Service.

[...]

2. LEGAL ASPECTS OF FINANCIAL SHIP LEASING IN DEVELOPING COUNTRIES: PRELIMINARY STUDY - REPORT BY THE UNCTAD SECRETARIAT

Doc. no.: UNCTAD/SDD/LEG/4 4 May 1995

CONTENTS

INTRODUCTION

1. The Standing Committee on Developing Services Sectors: Fostering Competitive Services Sectors in Developing Countries - Shipping, at its first period of sessions in November 1992, requested the UNCTAD secretariat to "analyse legal aspects of ship leasing in developing countries, including problems faced by these countries" (TD/B/CN.4/13, p. 16, para. 13).

2. This report has been prepared in response to that request. In order to obtain the necessary information, questionnaires were sent to the Governments of developing countries and through them to the commercial parties involved,

requesting information concerning the viability of the system and existing legislation. Information was also requested of financial bodies and lawyers' firms specialized in ship finance. At a regional meeting held in Santiago de Chile (19-27 October 1994), jointly organized by the UNCTAD secretariat and BIMCO (Baltic and International Maritime Council) on ship financing and chartering policies, additional information was obtained from the speakers' papers and ensuing discussions.

3. The report prepared in 1991 by the UNCTAD secretariat on "Container Ship Leasing" (TD/B/C.4/339) stated in one of its conclusions 1/ that utilization of the leasing concept in developing countries was not common and had been inhibited by a number of factors including:

(a) Legal factors (e.g. the legal system of the developing country may not recognize the special nature of the modern equipment lease and may treat the lease as a traditional rental of property, thus placing inappropriate responsibility on the lessor);

(b) Tax or revenue factors (e.g. the tax system of either the lessee's or the lessor's home country may not allow the lessor to take sufficient advantage of the tax benefits of equipment ownership);

(c) Practical factors (e.g. the lessor may perceive a high risk in terms of his ability to inspect or repossess the leased property in a developing country);

(d) Contractual factors (e.g. the terms of the typical financial lease provide that the user or lessee may not cancel the lease and thus all risk as to the suitability of the leased property is borne by the lessee).

4. To these factors the report added the fact that in many developing countries this method of financing did not yet appear to be well known or understood.

5. Similarly, the UNCTAD secretariat's 1992 report on "Ship Finance for Developing Countries" (UNCTAD/SHIP/642), after mentioning the convenience of this type of finance for developing countries due to the fact that it required practically no initial financial outlay, concluded by saying that it was perhaps not used in developing countries owing to the absence there of a suitable legal framework to facilitate this type of finance. The report suggests that it might be advisable to introduce suitable changes in the legislation of developing countries in order to facilitate ship leasing. 2/ This preliminary report is complementary to those earlier reports and therefore does not go into the genesis or operation of financial ship leasing, or into the advantages and drawbacks of the system, risk problems, or any other themes already dealt with.

6. The UNCTAD secretariat would like to thank all the financial entities and specialized lawyers who supplied valuable information for the preparation of this report.

SUMMARY AND CONCLUSIONS

7. While the financial leasing contract as such is not regulated in most legal systems, its fiscal effects have been regulated in most of the developed countries. This lack of positive regulation is offset by the wide distribution of standard leases. 3/ These standard leases cannot, however, make up in practice for the absence of legislation with respect to taxation, registration or bankruptcy, to mention but a few examples.

8. It appears from the replies received to the questionnaire prepared by the UNCTAD secretariat that many developing countries have not planned any form of financial leasing legislation, and have no experience in the leasing of ships. One group of developing countries 4/ recently adopted ministerial resolutions specifically recognizing that it would be useful for those countries to adopt common legislation to facilitate financial ship leasing. Another group of countries have only fragmented leasing legislation, difficult to apply to ship leasing and of doubtful effect.

9. On the basis of these replies, and the information obtained through other channels, especially the comments made by financial institutions in developed countries, the UNCTAD secretariat suggests that a series of legislative measures should be adopted in order to promote financial ship leasing in developing countries. The proposed measures would tend to make it more attractive from the economic point of view through favourable tax legislation. It is also important that national legislations should ensure the legal security of the ship lessor - usually established in a developed country - who is interested not in operating the ship for its own account, but in allowing a third party to do so. In this respect it is suggested: (i) that a modern and efficient ship registration system be established, which, amongst others, would allow the lessor the option of registering the leasing contract in a public registry, so as to be able to make it effective against third parties; (ii) that the lessor, in the event of a suspension of payments, insolvency or bankruptcy on the part of the lessee, should be allowed to recover possession of the ship, with the effect that the latter would not be considered part of the bankruptcy assets; and lastly, (iii) that in cases of financial leasing, the exemption from liability of the lessor should be recognized for hidden defects of the ship, with a very few limited exceptions.

10. Lastly, it is suggested that the UNCTAD secretariat should continue its study of the problems of financial ship leasing in developing countries in two ways: (i) by disseminating or promoting the concept, (ii) by preparing model legislation for consideration by developing countries wishing to introduce that type of leasing.

Chapter I

CONCEPT AND DEFINITION OF FINANCIAL LEASING

11. The leasing contract generally comes in two forms:

(a) Financial leasing, which is a form of lease with an option to purchase and where lease payments may be considered as payment for the cost of the ship, and

(b) Operating leasing, which is usually used on a relatively short-term basis and where the lessee acts as if the ship were his own. In this case, the lease payments do not entail amortization of the leased equipment.

12. Many legislations of developing countries do not have any special regulation for financial leasing contracts and they include such cases in general leasing rules, without considering that type of contract as a separate case. There are also different descriptive definitions of financial leasing, which vary according to the legal system to which they refer. Thus, while in some countries the financial leasing contract must necessarily include a purchase option on expiry, in favour of the user or lessee, in other countries this purchase option implies that the contract will be considered as an instalment sale rather than a financial lease. 5/

13. Financial leasing is normally long-term leasing, where the lessee is not entitled to cancel the contract. Moreover, a financial lease is usually fully

amortized ("full-payout lease"), since the lease hire is calculated to cover the cost of the purchase of the leased equipment, any additional expenses incurred by the lessor, and part of his profit. 6/ Financial leasing transactions usually have the following characteristics: 7/

(a) The equipment is for business or professional purposes;

(b) The specifications and choice of the equipment lie with the lessee;

(c) The supplier of the equipment purchased by the lessor is selected by the user or lessee;

(d) The lessor remains the owner of the equipment;

(e) The risks usually borne by an owner of equipment are transferred to the user (employment, destruction, impairment, etc.);

(f) Any remedies of the lessor arising out of imperfect performance of the supply contract are assigned to the user or lessee; and

(g) In return for this assignment, claims by the user or lessee against the owner (lessor) resulting from defects of the equipment are contractually excluded.

14. Sometimes parties agree upon:

(a) A purchase option for the lessee at the end of the lease;

(b) A sharing of the proceeds of a sale of the leased equipment after the lease has expired; or

(c) An extension of the lease on more favourable terms after expiry of the original lease.

15. From a legal point of view, the right of either party to cancel the lease is normally considered as a characteristic of an operating lease, as opposed to a financial lease. Another characteristic which distinguishes the former from the financial lease is that usually the property concerned in the operating lease is not purchased by the lessor according to the lessee's specifications.

16. Since in practice any ship leasing usually implies a "bareboat charter", whether or not a lease is "financial" or "operational" will depend on whether the contract includes non-cancellation clauses, generally known as "hell or high water clauses". 8/ If such clauses are included, it may be assumed that the lease contract is financial, while the absence of such a clause would indicate that it is an ordinary operating lease. 9/

Chapter II

USE OF FINANCIAL SHIP LEASING IN DEVELOPING COUNTRIES

17. The replies received by the UNCTAD secretariat indicate that financial ship leasing is rarely used in most developing countries. A few of these, however, especially those of the Andean Group (Bolivia, Colombia, Ecuador, Peru and Venezuela), have recognized its usefulness as a valid alternative for acquiring ships for shipping companies in the subregion. The Andean Group, through the mechanisms of the Cartagena Agreement Council, is preparing draft regulations to cover leasing with purchase option for ships used by shipping companies in the subregion. 10/

18. According to leasing companies, which are usually established in the developed countries, the more significant drawbacks of ship leasing include the risks inherent in the registered ownership of the ship. They are particularly concerned regarding their joint liability for environmental risks due to maritime pollution. 11/ United States legislation on maritime pollution, known as OPA 1990 (1990 Oil Pollution Act), is frequently referred to in the replies received by the secretariat. This act establishes joint liability of a ship's lessor and lessee for damage due to oil pollution. 12/ This liability, assumed by the lessor against his will, may be offset by appropriate insurance cover 13/ during the leasing period, as appears to be always required under ship leasing contracts. 14/ In some cases, however, the risk coverage is either difficult to obtain or extremely costly, since the liability established under that act is practically unlimited. It is also worth bearing in mind that insurance cover usually does not cover all the risks inherent in leasing. One important example of exclusion is claims arising from the contractual liability of the lessee, which are normally not covered by Protection and Indemnity insurance.

19. The replies received also indicate other factors which inhibit ship leasing in developing countries. Reasons include the absence of any rules governing the register of ships, as well as the lack of any protection for the lessor in bankruptcy proceedings, and with regard to dispossession for defects of the ship or hidden defects.

Chapter III

LEGAL MEASURES TO FACILITATE FINANCIAL SHIP LEASING IN DEVELOPING COUNTRIES

1. Tax measures

20. Both those authors who have dealt with the concept of financial leasing and the replies received to the questionnaire from UNCTAD's Secretariat concurred as to the importance of extending favourable tax treatment to this type of financing. A number of the replies received, and at least one author, 15/ even doubted whether financial leasing could continue to exist if tax benefits disappeared. Leasing has evolved in developing countries thanks to the direct relationship between the use of this type of financing and the tax benefits it enjoys. In principle, the law may regulate the manner in which the lessee shipping company - which is based in a developing country - treats the periodic rentals it has agreed to pay to the lessor and owner of the vessel in three ways:

(a) It may treat the payments as expenditure, in which case the lessee may charge the rentals against the earnings of the financial year in which they are due (operating lease), thereby reducing its annual profit and consequently the income tax due.

(b) It may debit the periodic rentals due each financial year from an asset account (financial leasing). This avoids having to reduce the lessee's profits by the amount of the rentals it has to pay, thereby also improving the lessee's creditworthiness when it comes to obtaining fresh financing for other purposes, taking on new liabilities or entering into new contracts. In this variant, when the lessee takes up his purchase option, and the option comes into effect, making the lessee the owner of the property, the residual amount it would have to pay will also be debited from the same asset account.

(c) A third possibility, and probably the most advisable, is to permit the lessee to choose the most suitable of the above alternatives. The law may also introduce a number of variants based on any of the above options.

21. Since virtually all ship-leasing contracts in the developing countries are with foreign lessors, it is important that the tax treatment given to value added tax and income tax, 16/ which will finally be borne by the lessee shipping company, does not cancel out the benefits of this type of financing. 17/

22. Another important consideration is the tax treatment of the transfer of ownership of ships in a financial leasing arrangement. Although some countries exempt the transfer of ships and aircraft from any form of tax, many countries levy property transfer tax on the transfer of property. It is important for countries that wish to levy some form of tax to adopt as the tax base the residual value agreed upon, rather than the value of the newly-built vessel or the amount of the periodic rentals paid in the course of the financial leasing contract plus the residual amount agreed upon. 18/ In this case, the tax benefit is enjoyed directly by the lessee of the vessel, and indirectly by the lessor, the leasing company, a factor which encourages this type of financing.

2. Establishment of suitable legal norms to regulate the shipping register

23. Since the fundamental characteristic of ship leasing is the fact that the lessor retains ownership of the vessel until such time as the lessee takes up the purchase option, it is important for the lessor duly to secure its ownership. Consequently, a proper shipping register must be kept to permit those States that wish to do so to offer the possibility of registering bareboat charter or a temporary change of flag. In this connection, it may be pointed out that many financial leasing operations involve a temporary change of the vessel's flag. This practice is provided for under the Standard Bareboat Charter "BARECON 89", drawn up by the Baltic and International Maritime Conference (BIMCO), paragraph V (optional).

24. Articles 11 and 12 of the 1986 United Nations Convention on Conditions for Registration of Ships specifically provides for the possibility of a vessel temporarily flying another flag, and article 16 of the International Convention on Maritime Liens and Mortgages, 1993 lays down rules for the increasingly common practice of authorizing the temporary suspension of the flag of ships registered in the national registers, when they are bareboat-leased to a foreign lessee. The Convention stipulates that in this case it is the legislation of the State of registration that is determinative for the purpose of recognition of registered mortgages, "hypothèques" and charges, and also provides for a system of cross references and information between the State of registration and the flag State.

25. A striking example of the importance of a proper shipping register for developing countries that wish to foster the financial leasing of ships as a means of financing is to be found in the draft decision on the Andean shipping register, proposed to the Cartagena Agreement Commission. 19/ The draft, which is intended to encourage the purchase of vessels and the development of the merchant marine of the member countries in the subregion provides, inter alia, for the registration of ships on bareboat charter.

3. Public notice of the leasing contract

26. The characteristic of the leasing contract is that it transfers to the lessee full possession and use of the ship (its commercial and nautical management), thereby making the lessee the ship operator (the person who operates the ship and assumes the risks and results of its operation), completely and totally disassociating the owner from its operation. The leasing contract will be effective with regard to third parties, as the owner will be held harmless for claims arising out of the ship's operation, from the moment he ceases to be the ship's operator by virtue of the contract. 20/

There are a number of exceptions to this general principle, which indirectly engage the responsibility of the owner towards third parties, even though the claims in question arise from the ship's operation, and are consequently the sole responsibility of the lessee:

(a) First, the so-called "maritime claims" whether preferred or not. These are claims that may be enforced against the ship, regardless of against whom they are made. 21/ In some cases, certain maritime claims that were entered into by the lessee are also secured by a "maritime lien" enforceable in rem on the ship, 22/ which will not be extinguished by a change of ownership, registration or flag.

(b) Under a number of international conventions and national laws, the registered owner of the ship is responsible for some types of claims, regardless of any lease. Most of the answers to the questionnaire received concur that it is precisely this responsibility - which is absolute in the case of damage caused by pollution - which is the major concern of shipowners leasing out vessels, 23/ and which in many cases reduces the attractiveness of leasing as a commercial activity.

(c) Claims against the lessor of the ship arising out of its operation, other than those described in subparagraphs (a) and (b).

27. It is precisely this third category of claims that offers some room for manoeuvre to States that wish to allow the much sought-after legal protection of the lessor of the ship against third parties. It would thus seem advisable to offer the possibility of registering the ship-leasing contract in a public register - possibly the ordinary shipping register - thereby formally publicizing it to third parties. This is in line with the clauses of the standard bareboat charters which require material publicity by the lessee. 24/

28. In this respect, French law, whose Act of 3 January 1967 relating to the "legal status of vessels" requires leasing contracts of over one year to be put down in writing, sets an interesting precedent. Under article 91 of the Decree of 27 October 1967, such contracts must subsequently be recorded under the entry for the vessel kept by the customs office, thereby fully publicizing the contract, which is necessary to make it effective against third parties. 25/

29. Until this possibility of formal registration and public notice has been accepted, the shipowner will run the risk of being held responsible for claims resulting from the operation of the vessel, for which the lessee is in principle alone responsible. 26/ This accounts for the contractual provision in standard bareboat charter, giving a right of recovery or compensation for the owner against the lessee, either if the vessel is seized or arrested (actions in rem), or if the owner has been compelled to assume responsibilities pertaining to the lessee operator. 27/

4. Protective measures in bankruptcy proceedings

30. Several replies to the UNCTAD secretariat's questionnaire point to the practical difficulty facing a mortgagee who wishes to foreclose a mortgage against an encumbered ship. This difficulty is seen as a major hurdle, particularly when the ship's State of registration is not a party to the 1926 International Convention for the Unification of Certain Rules Relating to Maritime Liens and Mortgages. 28/ It is felt that one of the advantages deriving from the financial leasing of ships is precisely that the ownership of the ship is not transferred during the duration of the ship-leasing contract, as a result of which in the case of default by the lessee, the lessor is in principle able to recover the ship without the need for lengthy and costly legal proceedings. 29/

31. In order to protect the lessor from the possibility of the lessee's bankruptcy, it is important for national legislation to permit the lessor to recover possession of the ship if the bankrupt debtor (the lessee) is unable to provide adequate security for the lessor's interests. This implies that in the case of bankruptcy the lessor will be able to exercise "separatio ex iure dominio" in order to remove the ship from the bankrupt estate. 30/

32. It is worth mentioning at this point that although article 7 of the 1988 UNIDROIT Convention on International Financial Leasing 31/ expressly recognizes the lessor's rights against the lessee's creditors and determines that the applicable law shall be that of the State in which the ship is registered - the State of registration - paragraph 5 of the article voids the protection, in so far as it stipulates that the latter is subordinate to any right of arrest, detention or disposition, which has been conferred specifically in relation to the ship, under the law applicable by virtue of the rules of private international law.

33. Although clearly the lessor will be unable to protect himself if the bankrupt's creditors also hold a maritime lien or claim authorizing the arrest and compulsory sale of the ship - regardless of the fact that the lessor as shipowner is not personally their debtor - in all other cases there is a need for a rule permitting the withdrawal of the ship from the bankruptcy assets. 32/

5. Responsibility of the lessor with regard to a dispossession action

34. Financial ship leasing operations generally involve three parties: the lessor, the lessee and the builder or seller of ships, who is generally chosen by the lessee. Consequently, the legal aspect of financial ship leasing involves two distinct contracts: the contract for the building or sale agreed upon by the lessor and the shipyard or seller, and the leasing contract between the lessor and the lessee. From the legal angle, although each contract is independent of the other, this does not preclude a connection between them, particularly as regards the technical characteristics of the vessel, which enter into both contracts. 33/ Thus, as a general rule, all financial ship leasing contracts stipulate that the lessor is in no way responsible for any defects or for function or fitness for any particular purpose of the vessel. This is so because although the lessor orders and purchases the ship, it is chosen by the lessee, who also approves the plans and supervises the construction if it is a new ship. The lessee chooses the shipyard in which the ship is to be built and the lessor merely finances its construction. 34/

35. Although most European countries' legislation holds financial-leasing companies harmless, 35/ the absence of legislation on financial leasing in many developing countries means that this is not necessarily the case there. 36/

36. Article 8 of the 1988 UNIDROIT Convention on International Financial Leasing also absolves the lessor from any liability. This principle is mitigated by a number of exceptions designed to protect on the one hand the lessee and on the other the supplier. Thus, in its article 8 (i) (a) the Convention stipulates that the lessor is liable to the extent that the lessee has suffered loss as the result of its reliance on the lessor's skill and judgement and of the lessor's intervention in the selection of the supplier or the specifications of the equipment. In addition, although article 12 (i) (a) recognizes the right of the lessee as against the lessor to reject the equipment or to terminate the leasing agreement - in conformity with the terms of paragraph 4 of the article - he is only able to take such action if the failure to deliver, late delivery or delivery of equipment that fails to conform to the supply agreement are attributable to an act or omission on the part of the lessor. Article 10 (i) of the Convention stipulates that the

duties of the supplier under the supply agreement 37/ shall also be owed to the lessee as if it were a party to that agreement and as if the equipment were to be supplied directly to the lessee. The same article also specifies that the supplier shall not be liable to both the lessor and the lessee in respect of the same damage.

37. The provisions of the Convention regarding the exemption from liability of the lessor for defects in the leased equipment, and direct action by the lessee against the supplier in cases of financial leasing provide an alternative solution to the problem that no doubt merits more careful thought, and their adaption to the specific business of ship leasing.

Notes

1/ TD/B/C.4/339, p. 8.

2/ UNCTAD/SHIP/642, pp. 21 and 22.

3/ BARECON 89; "HADAKA" policy (Japan Shipping Exchange Inc.); SHELLDEMISE; ITALSCAFO.

4/ Andean Group: Bolivia, Colombia, Ecuador, Peru and Venezuela.

5/ See article 1 of the 1988 UNIDROIT Convention on International Financial Leasing, which describes the characteristics of this type of leasing.

6/ Arroyo considers a financial lease as a contract by virtue of which one party temporarily (normally for a period between 10 and 20 years) grants the other party the right to peaceful use of a property (ship) with an option to purchase in return for a rental. It is a mixed contract for the lease of property (ship in bareboat condition, neither commissioned nor equipped) plus an option to purchase. The lessor is a leasing company or financier, which is interested not in exploiting the ship on its own account, but in granting that right to a third party, namely the ship operating company. "Shipbuilding and Financial Leasing", UNCTAD/BIMCO Symposium on Ship Financing and Charter Policies, Santiago de Chile, 19-27 October 1994.

7/ Analysis of Equipment Leasing Contracts, op. cit., p. 6, and Report by the UNCTAD secretariat of Financial Ship Leasing, p. 16.

8/ Such clauses imply that the bareboat hire will continue to be paid and may be waived only in two cases: if the lessor is compensated by its insurance in the case of total loss of the ship and at the time the established lease period expires. G.V. Ryan, comments on C.P. Barrington, "Leasing for European Shipowners: Shipowners and Bankers in Leasing", Seatrade publication, 1973, p. 65.

9/ On the differences between financial leasing and operating leasing of ships, see Roger Heward, "Seminar on Bareboat Charter Parties: Bareboat Charter for Trading Vessels", CMI, Knokke-Zoute, April 1989, p. 85 et seq.

10/ Resolution V-50 of the Andean Committee of Water Transport Authorities, "Fomento a las marinas mercantes del Grupo Andino", of 4 November 1994.

11/ The International Convention on Civil Liability for Oil Pollution Damage (art. 3 (1)), as amended by the 1984 Protocol (art. 4 (2)), expressly attributes liability for oil pollution damage to the registered shipowner, regardless of who the ship operator may be.

12/ Under OPA rules, any tanker entering the United States after 28 December 1994 must maintain evidence of financial responsibility for the ship in the fleet with the highest tonnage multiplied by $1,500 per gross ton. Ships failing to meet this requirement may not enter the United States, or if they do so will be subject to embargo or seizure of the ship. Under this law, the party defined as "responsible" for an oil spillage is jointly and severally liable for all damage caused by the spillage, regardless of whether it is to blame or not. The law defines the "responsible party" as the owner, operator or "demise charterer" of a ship or facility. Neither the wording of the act nor its legal precedents throw any further light on the meaning of these terms, nor have they been interpreted by any case law. It is considered, nevertheless, that the term "owner" refers to the ship-registry owner and that the term "demise charterer" refers to the bareboat charterer, who has absolute control over the crew and ship. See Juan Anduiza: "Responsabilidad del Fletador Ante la Ley Ambiental Estadounidense OPA 1990 - Certificado de Responsabilidad Financiera", UNCTAD/BIMCO Symposium on Ship Financing and Charter Party, Santiago de Chile, 19-27 October 1994.

13/ The registered owner of an oil tanker - transporting oil or bulk shipments - even though he is not operating the vessel, requires liability insurance for any pollution the ship might produce. The need to insure also arises for the lessee of the vessel, in so far as the owner may pass on a claim against him, if the damage is due to the lessee's fault or negligence, once the owner has settled the damage caused by the pollution. Furthermore, the insurance company may exercise its right of subrogation once it has compensated the insured party or the third party affected (art. 3 (5) of the 1969 Convention). In practice, the owner normally requires the lessee of the vessel to take out liability insurance for oil pollution protecting the interests of both parties, thus avoiding both the need for two insurances with separate premiums for the same risk, and especially the effects of subrogation and recourse against the ship's lessee. M. Clavero, "Clubs de P & I", European Institute of Maritime Studies, Madrid 1992, p. 202.

14/ Clause 12 of the BARECON 89 policy stipulates that during the leasing period, the Lessee shall maintain the ship insured at its expense against marine, war and Protection and Indemnity risks in a form approved by the owner in writing. Clause 14 of the SHELLDEMISE policy, expressly drafted for the leasing of oil tankers, establishes that during the period of lease, the ship shall remain insured by the lessees and at their expense against marine, war and Protection and Indemnity risks ... such insurance shall be taken out by the lessee to protect the interests of both owners and lessees.

15/ Arroyo. "Construcciones navales y arrendamiento financiero", UNCTAD/BIMCO Symposium on Ship Financing and Charter Party, Santiago, Chile, 19-27 October 1994.

16/ Peruvian legislation has maintained - in principle until 31 December 2000 - income tax exemption for rentals. However, exemption from value added tax on rentals, initially included in legislative decree 299, has been abolished.

17/ Hernández Berenguel: "Arrendamiento Financiero de Buques", UNCTAD/BIMCO Symposium on Ship Financing and Charter Party, Santiago, Chile, 19-27 October 1994.

18/ Article 4 of Ecuador's Commercial Leasing Act (Decree 3121 of 22 December 1978 - R O No. 645, 5 January 1979) stipulates that if the lessee takes up his option to purchase for the residual cost, this will be taken as the tax base for calculating any government or municipal taxes due on the transfer of ownership.

19/ Final Act of the Fifth Extraordinary Meeting of the Andean Committee of Water Transport Authorities. Document JUN/R CAATA/V-E/Final Act of 3 June 1993, pp. 13 et seq.

20/ Carlon: "Naturaleza y disciplina del contrato de arrendamiento de buque", RDM 1969, p. 27.

21/ Under the 1952 International Convention relating to the Arrest of Seagoing Ships, the ship from which the "maritime claim" arises may always be arrested by the claimant regardless of whether its owner is the debtor.

22/ See article 2 of the 1926 International Convention for the Unification of Certain Rules relating to Maritime Liens and Mortgages.

23/ See article 3 (1) of the International Convention of 29 November 1969 on Civil Liability for Oil Pollution Damage. See, also, David W. Abecassis: Oil Pollution from Ships: Persons Liable and Exempt from Liability (Butterworths, London, 1978), pp. 176-178.

24/ See clause 15 of BIMCO's "Standard Bareboat Charter: 'BARECON 89'".

25/ René Rodière: "Droit Maritime: Le navire", (Dalloz, Paris, 1980), Chapter VII, pp. 211 et seq. See, too, article 60 of the General Regulations of the Bolivian Merchant Navy, chapter VI, "Contracts relating to the use of vessels", which stipulates that contracts for the hire of vessels must be set down in writing and, in order for them to be invoked by third parties, be registered with the National Ship Registry and entered in the ship's certificate of registration. Turkish legislation also requires ship leasing contracts to be registered with the Register of Shipping (Act No. 3226 on Financial Leasing of June 1985). Article 93 of the Act on Maritime Navigation under the Swiss flag, of 23 September 1953, stipulates that if the ship-leasing contract has not been registered in the Swiss shipping register, the owner is responsible, as shipowner, in relation to any third party who has not been informed of the leasing arrangement.

26/ See Rodríguez Carrion: "Contrato de Arrendamiento de Buques: Efectos del contrato frente a terceros; Problemática de la publicidad del contrato". This author emphasizes the need for the leasing contract to be duly registered in order for it to be invoked against third parties, thereby protecting the owner-lessor of the ship. Anuario de Derecho Marítimo, Vol. III, Government of the Basque Autonomous Region, 1981. Lefebvre-Pescatore: "Manuale di Diritto della Navigazione", 1953, takes the view that where contractual responsibility is concerned, there is no need for the ship to be really encumbered in respect of a maritime claim, once it is known, through a system of legal publicity, at the time of entering into the contract that the contract is with a ship operator who is not the owner.

27/ J.M. Ruiz Soroa: "Manual de Derecho del Transporte Marítimo: el arrendamiento y los terceros", Government of the Basque Autonomous Region, 1986, pp. 41-43.

28/ The following developing countries are parties to the Convention: Argentina, Cuba, Brazil, Algeria, Uruguay, Lebanon, Zaire, Iran, Syria and Madagascar. "Conventions de Droit Maritime", Ministère des Affaires étrangères, du commerce extérieur et de la coopération au développement of Belgium, 24 May 1994.

29/ Regarding the practice of financial leasing companies that have taken out a first mortgage on the ship, in order to secure their interest therein to the exclusion of claims secured by a maritime lien, see Richard B. Barnett: "Protection of Lessors: Problems for the lessor arising out of financial difficulties of user". Colloquium on Protection Against Insolvency in Maritime Law, CMI Preliminary Papers, Tulane, 1987, pp. 79 and 80.

30/ See, María-José Morillas Jarillo: "Algunos aspectos del leasing de aeronaves en España", RDM No. 208, Madrid, 1993, p. 505.

31/ This Convention will come into force on 1 May 1995, when the three instruments of ratification, acceptance, approval or accession required by its article 16, have been deposited. As of 13 February 1995, the following States were parties to the Convention: France, Italy and Nigeria.

32/ Article 9 of the Ecuador's Act on Commercial Leasing, op. cit., stipulates that in case of suspension of payments, insolvency or bankruptcy on the part of anyone possessing goods under commercial leasing, the lessor may recover them in conformity with the procedure laid down by the relevant Decree (No. 3121, of 22 December 1978). Consequently, the assets will not form part of the bankrupt estate, nor may they be included in a settlement. Similarly, article 11 of Peru's Legislative Decree No. 299 of 26 July 1984 stipulates as follows: "property that is leased may not be arrested, encumbered or charged by an administrative or judicial order against the lessee. The judge must annul any precautionary measure over such assets subject to the sole requirement of presentation of the proof of the public instrument relating to the financial leasing. No appeal may be made until the asset has been released and handed over to the lessor".

33/ See, Ignacio Arroyo: "Construcciones Navales y Arrendamiento Financiero", UNCTAD/BIMCO Symposium on Ship Financing and Charter Party, Santiago, Chile, 19-27 October 1994.

34/ See, "Container Ship Leasing: lessor's obligation to deliver the vessel", TD/B/C.4/339, pp. 18 and 19.

35/ See, María-José Morillas Jarillo, op. cit., p. 537.

36/ The legislation on commercial leasing of a number of developing countries, such as Ecuador (Decree No. 31212 of 22 December 1978; R O No. 745 of 5 January 1979), stipulates that "unless otherwise agreed, the commercial lessor shall not be liable to the lessee for dispossession or for hidden defects of the object of the lease. In this case, the right of the lessee to claim possession with respect to third parties, particularly manufacturers and suppliers, is recognized" (art. 6). Similarly, article 5 of Peru's Legislative Decree No. 299 of 26 July 1984 on financial leasing stipulates that "the lessor is not responsible for defects and damage to the goods, responsibility for taking the appropriate actions against the supplier lying with the lessee".

37/ Arroyo, op. cit., p. 5, describes the contract for the construction of the ship as "a contract of work by an enterprise", as the shipyard undertakes to produce a result involving the performance of a work in compliance with the principal's orders.

-----

3. REVIEW OF THE WORK PROGRAMME OF THE STANDING COMMITTEE WITH SPECIAL EMPHASIS ON THE PREPARATIONS FOR UNCTAD IX - PROGRESS REPORT BY THE UNCTAD SECRETARIAT

Doc. no.: TD/B/CN.4/48 29 March 1995

CONTENTS

INTRODUCTION

(i) The Standing Committee on Developing Services Sectors: Fostering Competitive Services Sectors in Developing Countries/Shipping was established in accordance with paragraph 70 of the Cartagena Commitment. At its first session, held in Geneva from 2 to 6 November 1992, it adopted its work programme covering the period between UNCTAD VIII and UNCTAD IX.

(ii) This progress report is not dealing with substantive issues covered by the agenda items 3 and 4, for which reference should be made to the documents TD/B/CN.4/46 (on multimodal transport) and TD/B/CN.4/47 (on technical assistance activities and human resource development). Nevertheless, to comply with the structure of the work programme these issues are briefly referred to in chapters III and V. The Committee may wish to take into account that this report has a complementary function to the other sessional documents and an impression of an imbalance might be created which arises from an effort to avoid repetitions and overlapping of issues which are presented in full length elsewhere. However, as this report is aiming at an overall assessment by the Standing Committee with regard to the work accomplished under the work programme, cross references have been made particularly in the part related to summary and conclusions deriving from the work as a whole in which multimodal transport and technical cooperation and human resource development have also played a major role.

(iii) Paragraph 68 of the Cartagena Commitment requests the Trade and Development Board to "conduct, midway between Conferences, a review and evaluation of the work programme of the intergovernmental machinery .... so as to ensure full integration of all work undertaken by UNCTAD and to establish or adjust priorities for the period up to the following Conference". In order to meet these requirements the Trade and Development Board, at its forthieth session, decided to make provision for the holding of a resumed session of the Trade and Development Board (25-27 May 1994) for the Mid-term Review.

(iv) In preparation of the resumed session of the Trade and Development Board, a Mid-term Review Informal Working Group composed of representatives of States members of UNCTAD was established. The Mid-term Review Informal Working Group held nine meetings. A report of the proceedings of these meetings is contained in TD/40(2)/L.7 and Add.1.

(v) With regard to the working of the Standing Committees, the following conclusion was recommended: "The Standing Committees have not been able to carry out enough of their work programmes to allow for an in-depth review of their performance at this stage". In any case as the Cartagena Commitment calls for such a review to be carried out immediately before UNCTAD IX it is for this session of the Committee to undertake a review of the work accomplished.

(vi) On the basis of the work programme the secretariat was requested to produce a list of specific outputs and activities to be submitted to the Trade and Development Board through its President. The list of outputs for sessional documents, background documents, recurrent publications and technical material (TD/B/EX(2)/3 - TD/B/CN.4/16), which was subsequently endorsed by the Trade and Development Board, was amended in the light of new developments and requirements by the second session of the Standing Committee. The annex to this report provides an overview of the outputs and activities carried out by the secretariat within the period under consideration. In addition, and as recommended by the second session of the Standing Committee, the secretariat has produced and distributed a semi-annual review (TD/B/CN.4/Misc.10) listing outputs which have been accomplished during the period from July 1994 to June 1995. This informal document of the secretariat is intended to provide delegates with further information pertaining to the work programme.

(vii) In chapter VI the secretariat attempts to draw conclusions from the in-depth analysis of the various issues with the aim to facilitate the discussions with regard to the assessment of the work of this Standing Committee and possible recommendations to the Trade and Development Board.

(viii) The secretariat would also like to draw attention to the increasing number of requests for assistance in the area of improved transport efficiency and logistics. The secretariat has so far responded to these requests within the framework of its technical cooperation programmes. Delegations may wish to link their deliberations with considerations resulting from the United Nations International Symposium on Trade Efficiency (cf. TD/SYMP.TE/6).

(ix) As this third session is the last session before UNCTAD IX, delegations are invited to comment on the performance of the working of the Standing Committee. Any recommendation or conclusion in this regard could possibly form the basis for an assessment of the working of the Standing Committee.

Chapter I

SHIPPING

1. The work of the secretariat in the field of shipping has been based on the work programme as adopted by the Standing Committee on Developing Services Sectors: Shipping on its first session (TD/B/CN.4/13) and the recommendations adopted by the Standing Committee on its second session (TD/B/CN.4/39, Annex I).

A. <u>Impact of progressive liberalization on the development of shipping services</u>

2. At its second session the Standing Committee extensively discussed measures of progressive liberalization and their impact on the development of competitive shipping services. It emerged from these discussions that a wide diversity existed with regard to the stage of formulation and implementation of policy reform measures, depending *inter alia* on levels of development and the degree of involvement by the countries concerned in the supply of shipping services. Given this diversity and the limited experience so far accumulated, the Standing Committee requested the secretariat to continue to undertake comparative analyses of national shipping sectors and policy reform measures and to continue monitoring and reporting on measures taken aimed at fostering fair and competitive shipping services through progressive liberalization and associated policies.

3. In response to these requests the secretariat has prepared two reports which are available to the Standing Committee as background documents. These are:

- Progressive liberalization and the development of shipping services in developing countries - country experience (UNCTAD/SDD/SHIP/5); and

- Maritime policy reforms in the New Independent States of the former Soviet Union (NIS) (UNCTAD/SDD/SHIP/4).

4. Examples of experience with policy reform measures given in document UNCTAD/SDD/SHIP/5, support the observations made in the earlier report entitled "Progressive liberalization and the development of shipping services in developing countries" (TD/B/CN.4/34) that liberalization may have a substantial impact on the ability of developing country and country in transition shipping companies to participate in the supply of services. Many companies which had previously operated under the protection of stringent cargo reservation measures have suffered severe financial losses and some have gone out of business. While this can partly be considered a direct result of the implementation of liberalization policies, it certainly also reflects a lack of technological and organizational adaptation, which has become particularly visible and crucial with the advent of liberalized market access. Yet at the same time liberalization has opened opportunities for private sector companies in many developing countries and countries in transition, even though in general their participation in trade has often remained limited in the face of increasing competition from mainline global operators from developed countries.

5. Shipping companies of developing countries which have operated successfully in newly liberalized environments have been those which have introduced radical changes in operations, particularly by changing from break-bulk to containerised operations, in certain cases relying on chartered tonnage or slots and entering into consortia or other forms of cooperation with other shipping companies especially from developed countries.

6. Examples of developed countries demonstrate the important role being given to support measures designed to manage liberalization processes, in particular to competition rules as a vital element in safeguarding functioning maritime transport markets. In designing and implementing liberalized maritime transport policies, developing countries and countries in transition may wish to consider a variety of support policies which need to be taken to ensure not only a desirable level of competition, but also of participation in trade by national carriers.

7. Given the importance attached by the Standing Committee at its second session to the extension of the scope of its activities to include countries in transition, the secretariat has prepared a "country study" on the experiences of the new independent States (NIS) of the former Soviet Union in the formulation and implementation of policy reform programmes in maritime transport.

8. The reform programmes of NIS are largely based on two equally important pillars, i.e. privatization of former State-owned shipping companies and liberalizing access to shipping markets. The speed and extent of privatization and liberalization programmes, however, differ considerably among the countries concerned. In order to improve the competitiveness of national merchant marines, the Russian Federation has most vigorously pursued

privatization as a policy option even though practical results have been limited up to now. Other countries, such as the Baltic States and Ukraine, have embarked on commercialization programmes without initiating ownership transfer to the private sector.

9. Liberalization of shipping markets is part of the on-going process of economic restructuring that is presently taking place in the NIS. It provides the framework for a reduction in government involvement in shipping and the establishment of commercially viable enterprises. At present, however, the situation of most of the shipping industries of NIS is rather difficult. Companies that had enjoyed monopolistic positions in the former USSR trades today have to face competition without being necessarily prepared for it. The commercialization programmes have forced companies to compete for cargo, yet have neither made sufficient provisions for the adaptation of management structures, nor for improved access to finance necessary for the modernization of existing fleets.

10. The results of this study show a large degree of similarity with developing countries in all regions. Economies of developing countries and countries in transition are undergoing a process of progressive liberalization of market access, and privatization of former State-owned enterprises. This development affects the shipping and transport sectors more than other domestic economic activities because of the inherent international nature of the industry. In other words, the countries concerned, even if they so wish, can hardly escape the process of liberalization including the adverse short-term effects that this might have on their local shipping industry.

11. Experience gained so far clearly indicates that an adequate framework and regulatory mechanisms are required to back up the process of liberalization and privatization avoiding some of the major pitfalls, such as the inability to compete on commercial terms, or, in the case of privatization, the transfer from State to private monopolies. Such frameworks and mechanisms can include competition rules, incentives to national investors, promotional policies to the benefit of the local maritime industry, etc.

12. Even though the need for a proper management of the liberalization process is apparent, it is, at this stage, too early to judge the impact of the new policies. Available information indicates that a number of developing countries and countries in transition have embarked on policies of progressive liberalization of shipping markets backed by selective support measures without, however, necessarily formulating a comprehensive support policy. Furthermore, none of the countries concerned have up to now undertaken a thorough analysis of the impact of policy programmes and action. Further experience will have to be accumulated to clearly establish the causal relationship between policy reform and specific market and fleet developments. Furthermore it should be equally clear that a certain time-frame is required for shipping companies to undertake the necessary management reform programmes thus enabling them to commercially compete for cargoes both in national trades as well as cross trades.

13. In order to avoid the proliferation of national measures which in one way or another will be taken, it would be desirable to discuss and establish the appropriateness of a harmonized approach to the problem of managing liberalization processes within the Standing Committee or, possibly, within a wider context at UNCTAD IX. The analysis of policy management methods and measures is particularly important given the fact that

- a number of developing countries and countries in transition have been able to seize the opportunities arising from economic globalization and liberalization in the field of shipping, while others continue to lag behind thus accentuating their economic marginalization;

- globalization and liberalization tend to create interlinkages and thus to reduce the autonomy of governments in economic management. This is particularly true in the field of shipping, an inherently international industry.

B. <u>Changes in national practices covering shipper/ocean carrier relations</u>

14. The world economy is characterized by the perceptible process of globalization of economic activities affecting both commercial and intergovernmental relations. At the macro level it leads to structural transformation of nations reflected in a large scale withdrawal of the public

sector from economic activities, in increasing tendencies to enter into regional integration agreements and in parallel moves towards multilateral arrangements aimed at progressive liberalization of trade in goods and services. At the micro level, globalization is resulting in more flexible approaches to production and marketing as well as strengthening of links between companies in the production process.

15. While these phenomena have accelerated the integration of a number of developing countries and their industries in the global economy, they have also resulted in the marginalization of others, particularly the least developed among them. Many developing countries have up to now not been able to adapt existing institutional infrastructure and mechanisms to these new developments. Furthermore they often lack the know-how to keep pace with changes and to upgrade their management capabilities particularly in newly-emerging fields of activities, such as services. These countries see their competitive situation steadily deteriorating, as previous advantages based on preferential treatment are gradually losing in importance.

16. The implementation of globalized production processes and marketing arrangements has been made possible by policy reforms and, most important, by improvements in transport and communications. New production patterns have greatly benefitted from the responsiveness of the shipping industry to changing transport requirements of shippers. However, new opportunities offered by the shipping and transport industry have primarily benefitted large shippers. Small- and medium-sized shippers, particularly from developing countries, are often confronted with a wide choice of shipping opportunities which, however, they cannot effectively exercise due to lack of expertise and information.

17. Small- and medium-sized shippers will only be able to take advantage of the opportunities offered by developments in the liberalized transport sector, if a certain level of assistance is rendered. Such assistance will have to be permanently available and will have to be provided on a cooperative basis by the trading community itself. Shippers' councils would constitute the obvious institutional framework for such assistance, if they overcome the public service approach still prevailing in many countries and are transformed into professional, service-oriented organizations.

18. A number of shippers' councils have already adapted to the changing needs of the trading community. Depending on the stage of development, two different directions can be discerned. Thus, some councils have developed into industry associations who see their primary role as shippers' lobbies *vis-à-vis* governments and intergovernmental organizations. Other councils, particularly in developing countries, continue to focus their activities on the relationship between buyers and sellers of transport services, with a reorientation towards the direct assistance mentioned above.

19. Many shippers' councils are still struggling to adapt to the necessary changes, both with regard to new functions as well as corresponding organizational structures. In order to successfully transform existing councils, a process of professionalization has to be set in motion, which would include extensive human resource development programmes to enable council staff to provide the assistance needed by shippers. The document entitled "Changes in national practices covering shipper/ocean carrier relations" (UNCTAD/SDD/SHIP/2) makes a number of recommendations with regard to the necessary restructuring process. These recommendations are based on information provided by the shippers' councils as well as assistance activities that the secretariat has undertaken with councils wishing to engage in the process of transformation.

20. As most developing countries are primarily users of shipping services, questions relating to shipper/carrier relations in general and to the protection of shippers' interest and its institutional framework in particular, continue to be of special interest to them. The formulation and implementation of appropriate consumer policies with regard to shipping services, remain of particular importance to developing countries as a whole to ensure the expansion of their trade through the provision of quality low-price shipping services.

C. Ship finance for developing countries

21. Shipping continues to be a very capital-intensive industry and adequate access to capital markets be it as equity or loan capital is crucial for the

success of any shipping venture. In view thereof, the Standing Committee has attached considerable importance to the analysis of prevailing ship financing arrangements and their adequacy for developing countries' operators. In doing so, the Standing Committee has revitalized an activity which had also figured prominently in the work programme of the suspended Committee on Shipping. Thus, in response to resolution 65 (XIV), the secretariat issued document UNCTAD/SHIP/642 in September 1992, which was widely disseminated among governments and industry circles, but not considered by the Standing Committee itself. Consequently, the report entitled "Ship finance for developing countries" (UNCTAD/SDD/SHIP/3) submitted to the Standing Committee, is based on the previous one and mainly covers new developments which have occurred since 1992, and that have an impact on the availability of ship finance for developing countries.

22. The report indicates that the demand for ship financing is increasing. Total ship financing for newbuilding is now estimated to be in excess of $30.0 billion per annum, largely due to increasing capacity requirements to meet the expansion in world seaborne trade, to the continuing ageing of the global fleet and to the resulting need to replace technical obsolete tonnage.

23. For developing countries and countries in transition financing requirements for newbuildings and second-hand tonnage are estimated to exceed 93.3 billion over the 1993-1997 period. These capital requirements will be more difficult to finance because second-hand tonnage usually requires more equity participation than newbuildings and because the fleet profile for these two country groups consists of many technically obsolete vessels. In addition, the shipping industry of developing countries, just as much as of other countries, has to compete for scarce capital with other industries that often provide for better short-term return on capital and reduced risks.

24. The difficulties faced by the industry to attract capital are not due to deficient capital market mechanisms. On the contrary financial institutions have been innovative in structuring loans and tailoring the main variables (term, balloon payments, moratoria, down payments etc.) to meet the cash flows of borrowers. Thus, the essential issue is the inability of the shipping industry to compete for the limited pool of global capital that can obtain higher yields from more profitable projects. These conditions can only be redressed by reducing the tonnage imbalance and eliminating promotional policies that distort markets by artificial prices or protectionism.

D. Review of Maritime Transport

25. The promotion of transparency was identified as one of the main sections of the work programme of the Standing Committee. In response thereto the secretariat continues to prepare and disseminate the annual Review of Maritime Transport, which provides, on a continuous basis, information on global developments in the field of shipping services, shipping markets and the evolution of national fleets, particularly of developing countries. Apart from global issues, the Review is increasingly dealing with developments in specific market segments and of particular geographic regions. Thus, the 1993 issue contains a special chapter on shipping and seaborne trade in Asia, while the 1994 edition will deal with particular aspects of the maritime sector of Latin American countries.

E. Other developments

26. In this context the Standing Committee may wish to recall the latest developments with regard to the United Nations Convention on a Code of Conduct for Liner Conferences. As of 31 December 1994, there were 78 countries Contracting parties to the Code and five signatories subject to ratification. In the course of 1994, two countries became Contracting parties, i.e. Spain (3 February 1994) and Qatar (31 October 1994).

27. It may furthermore be recalled that resolution 2 adopted at the resumed session of the first Review Conference: (1) requests the Registrar to provide guidance and assistance to Governments towards a better understanding and effective implementation of the Convention, (2) requests the Secretary-General of the United Nations to convene the next Review Conference in accordance with article 52 of the Convention, and (3) instructs the depositary to seek the views of all States entitled to attend the next Review Conference in preparing the relevant documentation for the Conference. Based on these requests, work continues to advise governments on code implementation through correspondence and, in exceptional cases, missions.

The secretariat also continues to contribute to meetings/seminars organized by industry or governments aiming at a better understanding and effective implementation of the Code.

28. Pursuant to article 52 of the Code and the corresponding request contained in resolution 2 of the Review Conference, the secretariat is presently undertaking preliminary work towards the organization of the second Review Conference. The secretariat will orally inform the Standing Committee of the state of preparations and of any decisions which might need to be taken by governments entitled to attend the Review Conference. Given the time-frame for the next Review Conference provided for in article 52 of the Convention, the secretariat will commence late 1995/early 1996 seeking the views of governments in preparing the relevant documentation for the Conference.

Chapter II

PORTS AND PORT SERVICES

29. Modern and efficient ports are necessary and powerful tools for facilitating trade and development. In addition to the traditional role of bringing goods to the consumer, ports are now serving international manufacturing which requires an efficient transportation network in which ports act as a node for maritime and land transport. Nowadays, ports must offer efficient and reliable services to ships and cargo, including documentation and customs procedures, to allow the timely flow of goods through the transport chain, which has, in fact, become a production chain. To assist in this flow, some countries have developed distribution or logistic centers in the port area which are used for the storage, preparation and transformation of cargo. Therefore, ports are no longer simply a place for cargo exchange but are a functional element in a logistics system. Thus a port can be a crucial element in developing a competitive advantage of a country and therefore Governments and port authorities need to adopt port policies to allow the nation to reap this potential benefit.

30. Since world trade, and the subsequent transport costs, are part of a highly competitive market, all ports are directly involved in this international competition. To survive and prosper in such circumstances, port management needs to be given autonomy and be made accountable for its operational and financial performance. Ports are often a place in which international market forces become evident in the national economies. Governments have to steer a careful course to meet these challenges in order to take advantage of opportunities open by international trade and technological development and do so taking into consideration the level of social and economic development of the country. In a few countries in which the national fabric has collapsed ports are a vital sector to revitalize in order to rebuild the national administration and economy of these countries. Further, the United Nations International Symposium on Trade Efficiency recently held in Colombus, recognised the importance of transport for trade facilitation and recommended that governments encourage commercial practices and private investment, which is of particular significance for their port sector.

31. The progress accomplished in this programme (as indicated in TD/B/CN.4/13) to July 1994, was reported on in the progress report (TD/B/CN.4/36) prepared for the Committee. The main points are the convening, in 1993 in Geneva, of an Intergovernmental Group of Experts on Ports to assist the Standing Committee in its work because of the specialized nature of the subjects. The Group reviewed the four technical reports 1/ completed in 1992 and another two 2/ finalized in 1993. The Group carried out a

---

1/ *The principles of modern port management and organization*, TD/BC.4/AC.7/13; *Port marketing and the challenge of the third generation ports*, TD/BC.4/AC.7/14; *Legal aspects of port management*, UNCTAD/SHIP/639; and *The management and development of human resources in ports*, UNCTAD/SHIP/644.

2/ *Strategic planning for port authorities*, UNCTAD/SHIP/646; and *Sustainable development for ports*, UNCTAD/SDD/PORT/1.

comprehensive examination of the work so far carried out, indicated priorities for the approved work programme and prepared a report (TD/B/CN.4/28) on their findings and recommendations. This report was submitted to the last session of the Standing Committee. The Group considered there was a need for wider dissemination of the work done by the United Nations in the field of port organization and management which it considered of particular interest for developing countries and countries in transition. The Group considered training one of the most important domains where assistance by UNCTAD could be provided and recommended that the training programmes should be maintained and reinforced. .

32. The Standing Committee expressed its appreciation for the report of the Intergovernmental Group of Experts on Ports and believed that the group has made an important contribution to the implementation of the approved work programme. The Committee requested the secretariat to convene a second session of the Intergovernmental Group of Experts of Ports in early 1996 to assess the progress made in implementing the work programme, to review any new or outstanding issues in the fields of port efficiency, modernization and development and to make recommendations to the Standing Committee. A tentative date for this meeting would be 15-19 April 1996, a decision on the final date would be determined through the consultation mechanism of the Secretary General and endorsed by the Trade and Development Board.

33. As done for the first session of the Group, a policy seminar would be held before the meeting which would provide the opportunity for delegates from developing countries and countries in transition to receive information and raise questions on current developments in ports. This meeting for officials from governments, industry and regional bodies provides a global forum for discussion on policy and economic issues of port development. The provisional agenda for the second session will focus on factors affecting port performance (restructuring, financing, pricing techniques, cooperation, information technology) and human resource development. While focusing on these two issues, the Group will also review the reports prepared by the secretariat and comment on their applicability and dissemination and provide guidance on key issues to be considered in any future work programme.

34. At the time of writing, the study on *Strategic port pricing* (UNCTAD/SDD/PORT/2) has been completed and work is almost completed on the study on *A Comparative analysis of privatization, commercialization and decentralization* (UNCTAD/SDD/PORT/3). The first report provides a framework for ministries responsible for transport, port authorities and port managers on how pricing techniques can be used to improve the competitiveness of ports while keeping them financially viable. The second report analyses the objectives of institutional restructuring, the major methods of institutional reform, the conditions for their implementation and the control, adjustment and evolution of restructuring methods. These two reports will provide information to developing countries and countries in transition on how to make their port services more market oriented.

35. Work on sustainable development has required a joint approach with IMO. In fact, the subject is related to the adopted chapter 17 of Agenda 21 of the United Nations Conference on Environment and Development which calls on States to take necessary measures to prevent further degradation of the marine environment. In particular it requested that the necessary measures be taken to facilitate the establishment of port reception facilities for the collection of oil and chemical residues and garbage from ships as defined by the annexes of MARPOL 73/78. Therefore, cooperation has been initiated between UNCTAD and IMO aimed at designing a financial instrument that would ensure the funding of investments and operations of waste reception facilities in ports. A jointly prepared document entitled "Reception Facilities" (SPI 3/4) was submitted to the 3rd meeting of the Ship/Port Interface Working Group held at IMO, 24-28 October 1994. The document proposed the establishment of a fund for reception facilities, structured and organized on the principle that the "polluter pays" and to give an incentive to ships to use facilities. The Working group noted the requirements that need to be met and established a correspondence group to further develop the scheme in line with these requirements. The UNCTAD secretariat is a member of the correspondence group.

36. Another report on the subject of the relationship between cities and ports is being prepared in collaboration with the International Association of Cities and Ports. The subject is now important as a result of obsolescence of port facilities due to technological changes and includes inland

environmental features. Work has started on a study of *Financing port development* and on a study on *Regional cooperation in the ports field.*

37. To complement the publication of technical reports, two issues of the *Ports Newsletter* were prepared since the last meeting of the Committee, one in November 1994 and another in May 1995, which in addition to a review of UNCTAD's work in the ports field, included technical information on the most recent developments of direct interest to ports. The *Newsletter* is distributed to an informal network of 350 correspondents in over 160 countries and thirteen issues have been prepared. In addition, the secretariat has continued to cooperate with the International Association of Ports and Harbors (IAPH) to publish the UNCTAD Monographs on Port Management. These monographs, which are prepared by experts on a no-charge basis and are edited and published by the secretariat in English, French, Spanish and Arabic, provide information to managers on current port issues. They are distributed via the informal network and sold to interested parties through the official channels. The latest Monograph issued deals with *Marketing promotion tools for ports* (UNCTAD/SHIP/494(12)). Also, on a routine basis the secretariat continues to reply to frequent requests for port publication and training materials from both developing and developed countries.

38. UNCTAD's work in assisting port development in developing countries began in the late 60's and has made effective and practical inputs to the international port community, particularly in developing countries. Its reports, studies and monographs are regarded by practitioners as major references in the port field, continue to provided guidelines for governments and port authorities for port policy and development, and have often been the core for human resource development programmes. The steady demand for these documents and requests for training courses are an indication of the effectiveness of the UNCTAD work in the port field in general and of the current programme in particular. This demand also comes from the private sector, notably from consulting companies providing managerial inputs and training on a commercial basis or bilateral assistance packages, often using material produced by UNCTAD. Another likely reasons is that there are numerous countries whose port organizations lack the ability to study the latest developments in ports and to train their staff in the modern techniques of port management and therefore rely on the recognized UNCTAD expertise in the ports field.

39. Further, the UNCTAD's contribution to the ports sector is probably the only one UN inter-regional approach targeted to the technical and economic issues faced by managers and Government officials responsible for ports. In this it follows the port industry characterized by the coexistence, and successfully functioning, of worldwide and regional port associations which retain both the global features of international trade and maritime transport as well as the peculiarities of each trading region. Other UN organizations are providing inputs on partial basis to this important sector, often in collaboration with UNCTAD. The IMO through the WMU is providing training on navigational aspects in ports, handling of dangerous goods and related security. This is being complemented by UNCTAD which also provides inputs on management and economic aspects of ports. The ILO, through its technical cooperation programme, is providing training for dock workers. The Economic Commissions are also making inputs at the regional level. Some of UNCTAD's large technical assistance programmes can use ports to develop trade points and to monitor transport chains as port authorities are often strong organization with good communication links and foreign exchange resources and would be a strong partner for important undertaking in the transport domain.

40. Preliminary conclusions are that this port development programme, benefiting from the available in-house experience, has been successful and made a positive contribution to the development of ports in developing countries. It has adapted to the widely different needs of countries which span from port development for serving a modern and global international trade to managing ports to support humanitarian and peace-keeping operations undertaken by the UN. The programme has prepared and disseminated port studies that provide information to improve the competitiveness of port and port related services. It has substantially contributed to strengthen human resource development and has provided advice and assistance in the management of ports. The future orientation of this program should concentrate on helping international ports reach a minimum standard of performance and to better integrate the national economy with international trade. In particular the effects of institutional restructuring on performance should be studied as well as on the financing of infrastructure. This information should continue to be disseminated via the Ports Newsletter. Finally the

secretariat's activities in port management training should be continued with new port management policy seminars being developed and where possible strengthened through extra-budgetary funds.

Chapter III

MULTIMODAL TRANSPORT

41. Since agenda item 3 of the third session deals specifically with multimodal transport, containerization and technological developments, the secretariat prepared a report entitled "Competitive services in multimodal transport" (TD/B/CN.4/46) which is making a number of suggestions for action which the Standing Committee may wish to consider. To assist delegates in their deliberations,, this sessional document is also complemented by two background studies entitled "Facing the challenge of integrated transport services" (UNCTAD/SDD/MT/7) and "Multimodal Transport Handbook" (UNCTAD/SDD/MT/8).

42. Door-to-door transport is probably one of the most important transport subjects for developing countries and countries in transition to consider. At present there are very few multimodal transport operators in these countries, partly because door-to-door traffic is limited there, partly because of a lack of know-how. The consequence is that while this technology is developing and is being perfected in developed countries, transport providers elsewhere are not following this evolution and are thus not capable of providing their local traders with competitive multimodal transport services. The on-going process of liberalization and market access is, at the same time, sharpening competition. The result of this will be a marginalization of transport providers from developing countries and countries in transition that will be relegated to the status of subcontractors.

Chapter IV

MARITIME AND TRANSPORT LEGISLATION

A. Joint UNCTAD/IMO Intergovernmental Group of Experts - Seventh Session: Review of the 1952 Convention on Arrest of Sea-going Ships

43. The seventh session of the Joint UNCTAD/IMO Intergovernmental Group of Experts was held in Geneva from 5 to 9 December 1994. The session had been convened following the resolution adopted by the UN/IMO Conference of Plenipotentiaries on a Convention on Maritime Liens and Mortgages, which, having adopted the International Convention on Maritime Liens and Mortgages, 1993, recommended that "the relevant bodies of UNCTAD and IMO, in the light of the outcome of the Conference, reconvene the Joint Intergovernmental Group with a view to examining the possible review of the International Convention for the Unification of Certain Rules Relating to the Arrest of Sea-going Ships, 1952.": See report of the Conference, A/CONF.162/8, annex I. The recommendations contained in the resolution were endorsed by the UNCTAD Trade and Development Board at its fourth (Pre-Sessional) Executive Session and by the IMO Assembly at its eighteenth session.

44. The Joint Group, having completed preliminary consideration of the subject, prepared a set of "Draft Articles for a Convention on Arrest of Ships": See report of the Joint UNCTAD/IMO Intergovernmental Group of Experts on its seventh session, TD/B/CN.4/GE.2/3, annex II. The draft articles were based on the Draft Revision of the 1952 Convention on Arrest of Ships prepared by the Comité Maritime International (CMI), the changes required as a result of the adoption of the International Convention on Maritime Liens and Mortgages, 1993 and the views expressed by delegations during the session.

45. The Joint Group, having held a preliminary exchange of views on the draft articles, agreed to continue the examination of the subject at its next session, which is to be held at IMO headquarters in London in October 1995.

B. General average

46. The Standing Committee on Developing Services Sectors/Shipping, at its second session, requested the secretariat "to inform the Committee, wherever

appropriate, about developments concerning general average taking place within the relevant international organizations and industry, including CMI and IUMI": Para 14 of the recommendations adopted by the Standing Committee, TD/B/CN.4/39. Following this request a report entitled "General Average - Reform of the system" (UNCTAD/SDD/LEG/3) has been prepared and will be before the Committee.

47. It may be recalled that two reports had already been prepared by the secretariat on general average containing, inter alia, data and statistics concerning the extent and impact of general average, highlighting some of the problems which arise in the operation of the system, including problems encountered by developing countries: "The Place of General Average in Marine Insurance Today" (UNCTAD/SDD/LEG/1); "General Average - a preliminary analysis" (TD/B/C.4/ISL/58). The documents had also reported on the work within the Comité Maritime International (CMI) on the revision of the York-Antwerp Rules 1974, as amended 1990, namely that the CMI International Sub-Committee (ISC), charged with the task of studying the law of general average and the York-Antwerp Rules, met twice and prepared recommendations for the revision of the Rules. The recommendations of the ISC were submitted to the CMI Conference which was held in Sydney in October 1994.

48. The Conference adopted a new set of Rules, known as the York-Antwerp Rules 1994, and recommended that they should be applied in the adjustment of general average as soon as practicable after 31 December 1994.

49. The report prepared by the UNCTAD secretariat, "The Place of General Average in Marine Insurance Today", had been circulated to delegations of the CMI Conference. Close co-operation had been maintained between the secretariats of UNCTAD, CMI, and indeed with other interested organizations, including the International Union of Marine Insurance (IUMI) and the International Association of European General Average Adjusters (AIDE).

50. The document, "General Average - Reform of the system", reports on the work carried out within the CMI, including a brief commentary on the changes introduced into the York-Antwerp Rules 1994.

51. It also reports on the activities of the IUMI on general average; namely that the General Average Working Party set up by IUMI produced a document containing a detailed statistical study of the general average system. The study highlights a number of unsatisfactory aspects of general average. It focuses on issues such as number, size and costs of general average incidents, the causes of general average by number and value of claims, type of ships involved, age of ships at time of general average, allocation of costs between hull and cargo, costs of administering general average, time taken to prepare general average adjustments and absorption clauses and their impact in reducing the number of incidents currently treated as general average. The findings of the IUMI report confirmed those of the UNCTAD secretariat study. The IUMI study was circulated to delegations attending the CMI Sydney Conference and to IUMI member associations. It was also submitted to the IUMI annual Conference, held in Toronto in September 1994. The subject was debated within the IUMI Conference and it was firmly stated that under no circumstances could IUMI accept expansion of the scope of general average.

52. IUMI is presently continuing its research concerning the impact of the new York-Antwerp Rules and on the shortcomings of the general average system, with a view to finding a commercial solution to the problems involved. It has, therefore, placed general average on the agenda for its next annual Conference.

53. The document further reports on the development within the London insurance market. The London market played an active part in the work carried out by IUMI prior to the Sydney Conferemce, including the preparation of the IUMI study. To address shortcomings identified by the IUMI study would have required far more fundamental reforms than those achieved at the CMI Conference. The London market has therefore decided to continue research and analysis into general average and sees this as independent of the outcome of the CMI Conference.

54. The purpose of its work will be to: (a) examine the potential for reform of various aspects of general average which appear unsatisfactory; (b) estimate the costs of the different constitutent elements in the system; and (c) develop workable proposals for change. Some reforms, such as increased use of absorption clauses in hull policies, will be possible to implement

through action by the insurance industry alone, others would require more general agreement among the maritime community.

55. As seen from the above, the insurance industry is continuing work towards an appropriate reform of the general average system. It should be noted, however, that the move towards reform of general average began following the commencement of work within UNCTAD on the subject, including recommendations for investigations by insurance interests into finding insurance solutions to the problems involved. It is therefore important that developments are kept under review and the Committee is informed of further developments and, indeed, of the final outcome.

C. Legal aspects of ship leasing in developing countries - A preliminary review

56. Pursuant to the work programme adopted by the Standing Committee on Developing Services Sectors at its first session, a report entitled "Legal aspects of ship leasing in developing countries - A preliminary review" (UNCTAD/SDD/LEG/4) has been prepared and will be before the Committee for consideration. The report attempts to provide information concerning the legal framework regulating ship leasing in developing countries. Information required for the preparation of the report was obtained, inter alia, by sending questionnaires to Governments of developing countries and to law firms and financial institutions involved in ship leasing operations. The findings of the secretariat confirm that utilization of ship leasing in developing countries is not very common and is inhibited by a number of factors. This is the case in spite of the fact that leasing provides a shipping company the entire possession and use of a vessel without capital outlay. (See "Container ship leasing", TD/B/C.4/339).

57. The preliminary report outlines the legal factors that might deter potential lessors from entering into ship leasing operations in developing countries - such as, inter alia, lack of tax incentives, outdated legislation on ship registration, liability of the lessor as registered owner of the vessel, risks in case of insolvency by the lessee and for latent defects of the vessel - and suggests some reforms to facilitate its use in those countries. The suggested reforms focus on:

(i) Providing lessor and lessee with tax incentives.

58. In the absence of tax benefits it seems that few financial institutions/lessors, if any, would be willing to enter into a leasing transaction. Thus it is suggested that legislation may be enacted in order to provide the lessor with capital allowances or other forms of tax depreciation and that these tax benefits to the lessor be reflected at a rate lower than the amount of interest and principal that might be required to be paid under a conventional ship mortgage loan. Furthermore, it is suggested that for those States wishing to tax the final acquisition of the ship by the lessee at the end of the contract, only the residual value of same should be considered for tax purposes.

(ii) Modern and comprehensive legislation on ship registration.

59. Taking into account that the lessor remains the registered owner of the ship during the contract, it is of paramount importance that his rights are fully protected. This protection could be achieved through a proper ship registration mechanism. Furthermore, and for those States wishing to enact legislation permitting bareboat registration, it is suggested that careful consideration should be given to relevant provisions of the UN Convention on Conditions for Registration of Ships, 1986 and to the International Convention on Maritime Liens and Mortgages, 1993. It is in the interest of mortgagees, lessors and lessees to ensure that there is uniformity and certainty in this area of international law.

(iii) Publicity of the ship leasing contract.

60. Having complete control and entire possession of the ship, the lessee is solely responsible for the operation of the vessel. The lessor has legal title to the property and as owner of the vessel can incur liabilities and obligations, many imposed by statute and many of which cannot be contracted out of. In order to protect the lessor against the risk of contractual liability, it seems advisable to provide the lessor with the possibility of

registering (entering) the contract of leasing in a public register. This approach has been adopted by several countries in order to protect the lessor as the "formal" owner of the vessel against third party claims. The protection afforded would not however prevent a maritime lien holder in enforcing his maritime lien by arresting the vessel and applying for a forced sale of the ship, irrespective of the fact that the lessor as her owner does not personally owe anything to the claimant. It is however assumed that publicity of the contract would improve the protection of the lessor vis-à-vis third party claimants.

(iv) Protection of lessors against insolvency.

61. The interests of a lessor are considerably affected if the lessee's insolvency results in the commencement of bankruptcy proceedings against the lessee. The legal consequences of this are determined by the applicable national bankruptcy law. The report reviews some examples of existing legislation in developing countries aiming to secure that the lessor's real rights in the vessel are valid against the lessee's trustee in bankruptcy and creditors, including creditors who have obtained an attachment or execution. Reference is as well made to article 7 of the UNIDROIT Convention on International Financial Leasing, 1988. It is suggested that developing countries may wish to introduce legislation giving the lessor the right to terminate the ship leasing contract and to repossess the vessel upon commencement of bankruptcy proceedings against the lessee.

(v) Lessor's responsibility for latent defects of the vessel.

62. In most cases, although the vessel is ordered and purchased by the lessor, it is the lessee who selects the vessel and if it is to be a newbuilding, approves the building plans and supervises the construction process. It is for this very reason that contractual stipulations - such as those used in BARECON 89 (Part III) - always disclaim the responsibility of the lessor regarding the condition of the ship. The report reviews samples of existing legislation in developing countries and articles 8 and 12 of the UNIDROIT Convention on International Financial Leasing governing this important issue.

63. In order to ensure that the lessor should not incur any liability to the lessee in respect of the condition of the vessel, save in a few limited cases (e g, when the lessor intervenes in the selection of the shipyard), assigning in the meantime any remedies granted under the building contract in case of unsatisfactory performance to the lessee, it is suggested that developing States may introduce appropriate legislative reforms.

64. The report finally suggests that as a follow-up to this preliminary review, based on information received by the secretariat, further work should be undertaken in order to: (i) prepare model legislation as guidelines for developing countries who wish to promote ship leasing, (ii) promote awareness as to the operation and functioning of ship leasing and its potential advantage for developing countries.

Chapter V

HUMAN RESOURCES DEVELOPMENT AND TECHNICAL COOPERATION

65. Since agenda item 4 of the third session of the Standing Committee deals specifically with strengthening technical cooperation and human resource development, the secretariat prepared a report entitled "Technical Cooperation and Human Resource Development in Shipping, Ports and Multimodal Transport" (TD/B/CN.4/47). This comprehensive document describes all the activities conducted by the various sections and programmes and presents a number of suggestions for action which the Standing Committee may wish to consider.

66. The report also presents the findings of independent evaluations of three major programmes, Advance Cargo Information System (ACIS), TRAINMAR and Improving Port Performance (IPP) and confirm that, not only are these programmes making an important contribution to the development objectives, but they are doing so in a cost-effective manner.

Chapter VI

SUMMARY AND CONCLUSIONS

67. On the basis of the adopted work programme, the Committee has addressed a number of main issues in its work which emerged from the overall development changes in the world economy in the area of shipping, ports, multimodal transport and maritime and transport legislation.

68. In order to cope with the growing interdependence of the world economy and increasing globalization of production processes, as well as the trend towards progressive liberalization, international transport, particularly maritime transport, has to pass through a process of structural and organizational adjustments leading to an integration of shipping, ports and land-transport services. As far as developing countries and countries in transition to market economies are concerned, these developments affect their position both as consumers and as suppliers of shipping services. While a number of countries have seized the opportunities afforded by extended shipping opportunities, others, owing to a lack of expertise and information on the part of the trading communities, have not been able to take advantage of it and consequently continue to lag behind, thus aggravating the risk of further economic marginalization.

69. Progressive liberalization of shipping markets is part of the ongoing general process of economic restructuring and calls for the formulation of related policies at both the national and international levels. UNCTAD has monitored and analysed the success of, and problems encountered by, developing countries and countries in transition with regard to policy reform programmes aimed at fostering the development of commercially viable, competitive shipping services.

70. The strategy of fostering competitive shipping services is an ongoing one and it is too early to establish clearly a causal relationship between policy reform measures and specific market and fleet developments. The continuing process of progressive liberalization of shipping markets requires further analysis and, beyond that, the elaboration and development of tools enabling a proper management of liberalization and privatization. The resulting measures should ensure that all countries are put in a position to reap the benefits of new shipping opportunities, while at the same time enabling their service suppliers to undertake the necessary restructuring as smoothly as possible.

71. Ports can no longer be considered as terminal points of a transport mode but as an essential link in a transport chain. In the light of this, many ports have developed into service centres. The underlying concept of these services centres is to upgrade port activities from pure cargo handling at terminal points to offering a comprehensive transport service package. One of the means used by more and more countries to improve the efficiency of ports is the revision of the role of the public sector in ports. Many ports are actively pursuing programmes of privatization and commercialization. The various aspects of the changing role of ports in a transport chain are reflected in a number of studies prepared by the secretariat for submission to the second session of the Intergovernmental Group of Experts on Ports to be held early 1996 which in turn will submit its recommendations to the relevant governing body.

72. The slow expansion of multimodal transport towards developing countries is essentially due to a number of intersectoral problems involving governmental and commercial parties. Many developing countries have not yet realized that the implementation of multimodal transport based on appropriate coordination between parties can contribute to the development of national transport capabilities and economies. The secretariat will analyse the various processes and provide advice and assistance to governments as well as to commercial parties to enable them to set up the necessary institutional, legal and operational environment for a better use of the multimodal transport concept linked to modern transport technology. To achieve transport efficiency governments are urged to implement coordinated intersectoral policies based on a progressive liberalization of the sector.

73. In the field of maritime and transport legislation, the activities of UNCTAD should, in a cooperative spirit with other organizations, aim at facilitating international trade and transport by promoting and establishing a framework of modern commercial, economic and administrative norms and standards within which the industry can operate efficiently. It is

recognized that in a process of globalization, economic norms and standards as well as delineation of responsibilities gain a new momentum.

74. Technical cooperation has always been viewed by UNCTAD as an important complement to its research and policy analysis and it has been a prominent feature of UNCTAD's work on maritime and related transport services. These activities concentrate on assisting developing countries and countries in transition in the economic, commercial and legal aspects of maritime and multimodal transport. As such, they are complementary to the assistance available from other organizations. UNCTAD collaborates closely with these other organizations and a number of projects are conducted jointly.

75. Most of the projects are interconnected to the overall development approach of regions or subregions in order to respond to the increasing complexity of development issues. In the light of scarce resources UNCTAD should continue in its future work of technical cooperation and human resource development to focus on projects which have a major impact in the context of development dimensions in the sector under consideration.

Annex

As referred to in paragraph (vi) of the introduction of this progress report, the list of specific outputs and activities submitted to the Trade and Development Board and subsequently endorsed at its second (pre-sessional) executive session, is reproduced below in its original format for ease of reference. Document symbols/identification for these outputs have been shown in square brackets against each item.

1. Substantive services/meetings

1993
- United Nations Conference of Plenipotentiaries on a draft Convention on Maritime Liens and Mortgages; [A/CONF.162/8]
- Intergovernmental Group of Experts on Ports; [TD/B/CN.4/28]

1994
- Standing Committee on Developing Services Sectors: Shipping, second session; [TD/B/CN.4/39]
- Joint UNCTAD/IMO Intergovernmental Group of Experts for amending the 1952 Convention on Arrest of Ships; [TD/B/CN.4/GE.2/3]
- Intergovernmental Group of experts on Multimodal Transport; [Not mandated]

1995
- Shipping Policy Forum on Privatization/Commercialization of Shipping; [Not mandated]
- Intergovernmental Group of Experts on Ports; [postponed to early 1996]
- Standing Committee on Developing Services Sectors: Shipping, third session; [Report of 3rd session]

2. Outputs: Reports/studies on:

(a) Sessional documents

1993
- Rules of procedure for the United Nations Plenipotentiaries Conference; [A/CONF.162/5]
- Compilation of comments and proposals by governments, IGO and NGOs on the draft Convention; [A/CONF.162/3/Add.1-3]
- Review of activities in the field of ports; [TD/B/CN.4/GE.1/2]

1994
- Liberalization of trade in shipping services - impact on developing countries; [TD/B/CN.4/34]
- Report of the IGE on ports; [TD/B/CN.4/35] (+)
- Review of the activities of the secretariat in the fields of multimodal transport, maritime legislation, technical assistance and human resources development; [TD/B/CN.4/36]
- Review of the activities in the field of multimodal transport; [Terminated]

1995
- Review of activities in the field of ports; [Under preparation]
- Comparative analysis of national shipping policies, including policies on privatization of shipping services; [UNCTAD/SDD/SHIP/4]
- Review of activities in the fields of maritime legislation, technical assistance and human resources development; [TD/B/CN.4/48]

(b) Background documents

1993 - Development of human resources in the field of ports; [UNCTAD/SHIP/644]
- Legal and regulatory aspects of port activities; [UNCTAD/SHIP/639]
- Strategic port planning; [UNCTAD/SHIP/646]
- Impact of mega multimodal transport operators; [UNCTAD/SDD/MT/4]
- Ship acquisition pre-feasibility study; [Coastal shipping - RAF/89/061]
- ECDC in Shipping; [UNCTAD/SDD/SHIP/1]
- Sustainable development of ports; [UNCTAD/SDD/PORT/1]
- Developments in containerization; [UNCTAD/SDD/MT/2]
- Completion on the work on general average; [UNCTAD/SDD/LEG/1]
- Implementation of the TRAINMAR Action Plan; [UNCTAD/SDD/TRN/1]

1994 - The impact of commercialization/privatization programmes on the development of shipping services; [UNCTAD/SDD/SHIP/5]
- Multimodal transport and trading opportunities; [UNCTAD/SDD/MT/5]
- Comparative analysis of privatization, commercialization and deregulation in the ports field; [UNCTAD/SDD/PORT/3]
- Strategic port pricing; [UNCTAD/SDD/PORT/2]
- Implementation of the 1978 United Nations Convention on the Carriage of Goods by Sea (Hamburg Rules); [Part of TD/B/CN.4/36]
- Ship acquisition pre-feasibility study; [Coir fibre study with FAO]

1995 - Developments in shipper/ocean carrier relations; [UNCTAD/SDD/SHIP/2]
- Potentialities for increased regional co-operation in the field of ports; [Under preparation]
- Financial aspects of ports management; [Under preparation]
- New developments in ship financing; [UNCTAD/SDD/SHIP/3]
- ECDC: Institutional and policy changes and their results; [Under preparation]
- Legal aspects of ship leasing in developing countries; [UNCTAD/SDD/LEG/4]
- Ship acquisition pre-feasibility study; [No request yet]
- Facing the challenge of integrated transport services; [UNCTAD/SDD/MT/7] (+)
- MT Handbook; [UNCTAD/SDD/MT/8]
- General average - Reform of the system; [UNCTAD/SDD/LEG/3] (+)

(c) Recurrent publications

Annual Review of Maritime Transport; [TD/B/CN.4/27 (1993), TD/B/CN.4/37 (1994) and under preparation for 1995]

(d) Technical material

- The UNCTAD Ports Newsletter; [Issues No. 9 and 10 for 1993, 11 and 12 for 1994, and 13 for 1995]
- The UNCTAD Multimodal Transport Newsletter; [Issues No. 5 and 6: UNCTAD/SDD/MT/1 for 1993 and UNCTAD/SDD/MT/6 for 1994]
- The TRAINMAR Newsletter, quarterly; [Issue No. 17 in Dec. 1993, none in 1994]
- The TRAINMAR Catalogue; [1 each year]
- The TRAINMAR network report; [1 each year]

1993 - 2 monographs on computerized container terminal management [UNCTAD/SHIP/494(10)] and on EDI in ports [UNCTAD/SHIP/494(11)]
- 2 sets of Improving Port Performance (IPP) courses; [IPP 4 on port pricing and IPP 5 on commercialization under preparation]

1994 - Course material for a workshop for potential multimodal transport operators; [TRAINMAR module 5.4]
- Educational programme on charter parties; [UNCTAD/SDD/LEG/2]
- 2 sets of Improving Port Performance (IPP) courses on human resources development and strategic planning; [Not yet started]
- 2 Monographs; [UNCTAD/SHIP/494(12) on marketing tools for ports and issue No 13 under preparation]

1995
- 2 sets of IPP courses on port computerization/EDI and marketing; [Not started]
- 2 Monographs; [Pending contributions]
- Multiship Model II, Version 7 (Computer Software); [Outside expertise required]

4. REPORT OF THE STANDING COMMITTEE ON DEVELOPING SERVICES SECTORS: FOSTERING COMPETITIVE SERVICES SECTORS IN DEVELOPING COUNTRIES - SHIPPING ON ITS 3RD SESSION, GENEVA, 6-9 JUNE 1995

Doc. no.: TD/B/42(1)/5-TD/B/CN.4/50 1995

CONTENTS

INTRODUCTION

1. The Standing Committee on Developing Services Sectors: Fostering Competitive Services Sectors in Developing Countries - Shipping, established in accordance with paragraphs 70 and 72 of the Cartagena Commitment, held its third session at the Palais des Nations, Geneva, from 6 to 9 June 1995. In the course of the session, the Standing Committee held six plenary meetings.*

Introductory statements

2. The **Deputy to the Secretary-General of UNCTAD** noted the importance of the Standing Committee's third session at a time when stock was being taken of the implementation of the recommendations agreed at Cartagena and preparations were being made for UNCTAD IX. He stressed the importance of international maritime transport services in enabling the developing countries, particularly the least developed ones, to participate more effectively in the globalization and liberalization processes, emphasizing also that transport efficiency was a prerequisite for trade efficiency.

3. Some coordination and harmonization of policy reform programmes for maritime transport services was called for to avoid a proliferation of policies which could hamper rather than promote development. To assist suppliers of shipping services from developing countries and countries in transition, mechanisms should be developed to manage the process of liberalizing trade in shipping services. A gradual and phased policy of liberalization would enable those countries with national fleets to develop competitive services and thus benefit from trade in shipping services.

4. Multimodal transport operations offered significant benefits to international trade, even though mega carriers could threaten national transport industries. However, the lack of a harmonized international legal environment and of national multimodal transport regulations often impeded the development of this form of transport. Modern commercial and technical practices used in multimodal transport could allow transport operators from developing countries and countries in transition to improve rapidly the quality and price of services offered and at the same time make greater use of rail, inland waterways and short-sea shipping.

5. With the globalization of manufacturing, ports were now playing a key role in the production and distribution process. Inefficient ports and port services could render exporters' goods less competitive in the international market place, and Governments and port authorities thus needed to adopt policies that would contribute to efficient management and sustainable development of ports and related port services.

6. In the field of maritime legislation, work had been carried out with the various sectors of the shipping and insurance industries to reform and simplify certain rules and practices. Presently work was ongoing, via the Joint UNCTAD/IMO Intergovernmental Group of Experts, to review the 1952 International Convention on the Arrest of Sea-going Ships.

7. Technical cooperation had allowed UNCTAD to implement the results of its research work for the benefit of developing countries. In particular he thanked the Governments of Belgium, France and Germany and the European

---

* For the terms of reference of the Standing Committee, see Trade and Development Board decision 398 (XXXVIII), annex B.

Commission for the support they had given to the Advance Cargo Information System project for logistics management. Emphasis continued to be placed on human resource development to allow developing countries to become self-sufficient. With this objective in view, the TRAINMAR programme was playing a leading role in the development of training capability in developing countries, and he thanked those donors who had made this work possible.

8. The **Officer-in-charge of the Services Development Division** recalled the discussions which had taken place at the second session of the Standing Committee and noted that it had been the general view that, because of its importance, shipping policy reform should be further discussed at the Committee's third session. To assist the deliberations, the secretariat had prepared two background documents, namely "Progressive liberalization and the development of shipping services in developing countries" (UNCTAD/SDD/SHIP/5) and "Maritime policy reform in the NIS of the former Soviet Union" (UNCTAD/SDD/SHIP/4). In the view of the secretariat, any specific recommendations in the field of shipping should centre around the formulation and implementation of policy reform programmes. The secretariat did not consider it necessary to have a general discussion on the merits or otherwise of the concept of liberalization, although it was useful to have discussions on specific issues such as the management of the liberalization process and the definition of the future role which UNCTAD in general and the Committee in particular could play in the process of liberalization.

9. Liberalization and globalization would be the underlying themes of UNCTAD IX. In his opinion globalization could only take place if there was an effective transport system to support it. The secretariat strongly believed that the formulation of national and international measures to promote growth and sustainable development required the support of maritime transport.

10. Human resources development had been given prominence in the work of the secretariat, since for developing countries to achieve economic development, it was indispensable to enhance the skills and knowledge of the workforce. To this end, the Division had established various programmes, the most prominent of which was TRAINMAR, which had been in existence for more than a decade and from which many employees in the maritime industry in developing countries had benefited.

11. The Division had been working on the medium-term budget for the biennium 1996-1997. This had required anticipating the results of the current session of the Committee and of UNCTAD IX. He assured the Committee that the secretariat would be prepared to fulfil the work programme established for it within the resources allocated to it.

12. Referring to suggestions made at the Committee's second session concerning transparency, he pointed out that the secretariat had produced a review of the Division's activities (TD/B/CN.4/Misc.10), and he hoped that the Committee would examine the contents of the document and make suggestions as appropriate. He informed the Committee on the collaboration with the International Maritime Organization, and in this connection he said that, as a result of the adoption by the United Nations Conference on Environment and Development of Agenda 21 and its Chapter 17 dealing with ocean affairs, the Secretary-General of the United Nations was required to report on the implementation of that particular aspect of the Programme to the General Assembly in 1997. To assist the Secretary-General in that respect, UNCTAD was expected by the other agencies to assist in the development of ideas and possibly mechanisms through which some of the costs of environmental actions could be recovered for the providers of certain specific services. One of the practical issues that UNCTAD and IMO were dealing with jointly was the development of a system by which costs for providing reception facilities for oily waters to tankers in their loading ports could be recovered. He believed that a progress report on this issue would be discussed in the

forthcoming IMO Council. There were other issues under discussion in the area of coastal management, which was linked to the Barbados Plan of Action and for which UNCTAD had responsibility.

Chapter I

GENERAL DEBATE

13. The representative of the **Czech Republic** informed the Committee about the situation of the transport sector in his country, the location of which meant that it had an important role to play in the trade of Europe. The transport reforms that were taking place in his country went hand in hand with the economic reforms being undertaken since 1990; the Czech Parliament had already enacted new legislation on road traffic, railways and inland navigation, and new legislation on civil aviation and ocean navigation was being prepared. The Czech transport infrastructure was important for the integration of European transport networks. He also informed the Committee about the programme for the construction of a network of motorways, railways and airports.

14. Referring to multimodal transport, he noted that in the short history of multimodal transport in the Czech Republic, conditions had not been right for the development of this system, which was now applied all over the world. However, due to pressure from its trading partners, the Czech Republic had been forced to containerize, and many lines from the territory of the Czech Republic to sea ports were now in operation. The main problems hindering multimodal transport operations continued to be poor infrastructure and border-crossing operations and regulations. In his opinion, it was important to solve some of these problems, and to that end efforts would have to be made in respect of coordination of border-crossing procedures, liberalization of initial and terminal road haulage, government support in the provision of terminal infrastructure and operations and the development of multimodal transport operators. Such efforts were currently being made within the framework of a programme established by the Ministry of Transport.

15. The representative of the **Russian Federation** said that UNCTAD and its Standing Committee on Developing Services Sectors had an important role to play in establishing sustainable and equitable cooperation in the field of maritime transport, excluding all forms of discrimination and economic sanctions. The UNCTAD secretariat had prepared high-quality documentation for the Committee's session, but in that connection he suggested that, in its future activities, the secretariat should make recommendations on the improvement of maritime transport taking into account the needs of countries in transition. The recent developments in the shipping policies of his country were closely linked with the profound changes in the economic environment, for example privatization, conversion of State enterprises into shareholding companies and free pricing, which were directed towards the creation of a competitive environment. A licensing system had been introduced in the maritime sector and for related activities, and work was being carried out on a new maritime code, on adherence to the Paris Memorandum on Ports, and on signing maritime agreements with the other Republics of the former Soviet Union. He considered that, with the creation of the World Trade Organization, UNCTAD and its Standing Committee on Developing Services Sectors should take an innovative approach to the problems of world maritime transport and develop effective cooperation with other international organizations.

16. The representative of **France**, speaking on behalf of the **European Union**, said that maritime transport played an important role in world transport. It carried a substantial part of international trade, and at the same time contributed to economic development. The European Union had welcomed the adoption of the Cartagena Commitment in 1992, which permitted UNCTAD to

address concrete issues of maritime transport with a view to the promotion of market-oriented policies. The advantages of open markets were now more accepted as allowing efficient and competitive maritime transport services. The European Union was convinced that economic development was ill-served by protectionist maritime policies, since they distorted markets and increased costs.

17. The third session of the Standing Committee was taking place at an important time in the life of UNCTAD. For example, with regard to its work on liberalization, consideration had to be given to the work of the World Trade Organization. The Committee also had to consider the future of UNCTAD in the context of the work of UNCTAD IX. He emphasized that UNCTAD remained an unequalled forum for negotiations between developed and developing countries, and within the United Nations it was one of the bodies with competence in maritime matters.

18. The work of UNCTAD in maritime transport would succeed if a number of conditions were met, namely universal participation by as many parties as possible, particularly developing countries, the setting of realistic goals and the completion of programmes before embarking on new initiatives. He suggested that, in this connection, the programmes on training and human resources development must be encouraged so as to meet the needs of developing countries.

19. The representative of the **European Community**, referring to document TD/B/CN.4/48, said that, with regard to the impact of progressive liberalization on the development of shipping services, he had serious doubts that the Committee could embark on the harmonization of liberalization policies, or establish a regulatory mechanism for liberalization and privatization. He pointed out that each country found itself in a situation where it had to take measures suited to its particular circumstances. He also pointed out that there was a risk of interfering with the GATS negotiations at the WTO, where the approach taken was one of negotiating commitments of individual countries rather than trying to determine a harmonized approach to liberalization. In his view, a harmonized approach should be avoided both as a matter of principle and on practical grounds.

20. With regard to changes in national practices covering shipper/ocean-carrier relations and specifically the suggestion to formulate and implement consumer policies with regard to shipping services, he said that, as long as there existed effective competition, he saw no reason why government intervention would be necessary to ensure high-quality, low-price shipping services. Furthermore, in the view of the European Community, a redefinition of the role of shippers' councils in developing countries should not be the task of governmental or intergovernmental bodies, since it was precisely that approach which had led to the current unsatisfactory situation in some of the developing countries. The redefinition should be left to professional organizations, although during the discussions in the Committee the possible role to be played by UNCTAD could be considered.

21. With regard to ship financing, the report of the secretariat confirmed the view of the European Community that it was the commercial soundness of a project that counted rather than whether a company was from a developed or a developing country. On the issue of ports and port services, he noted that useful work had been carried out, and the Community was prepared to look in detail at the initiatives which the UNCTAD secretariat was suggesting.

22. Concerning multimodal transport (TD/B/CN.4/46), with regard to the recommendations made concerning the impact of multimodal transport systems and tariffs on trading opportunities in the context of liberalization and privatization, the European Community would give close consideration to any views that might be expressed by representatives of the industry before

considering requests arising from the deliberations of the Committee. As regards developments in containerization and related transport technology, specifically the impact of MT systems and tariffs on trading opportunities in the context of liberalization and privatization, he agreed on the usefulness of continuing to monitor developments. However, he doubted the need for the proposed seminar on the basis of the mandate given to the Committee. Referring to chapter 2 of document TD/B/CN.4/46 on future work on multimodal transport, he appreciated the effort made in undertaking a wide-ranging survey of issues, but considered that the programme was too ambitious and that the need for it had not been demonstrated in relation to the mandate given to the Committee. He also recalled that, in adopting its programme of work, the Committee had not wished to approve the activities which were being proposed, and in particular he cast particular doubt on some of the "general policy issues" on the list, although some of them would appear to be useful. Specifically, the European Community believed that there was no particular interest in global harmonization of multimodal transport legislation. As regards the development of telematics and software tools, he believed that, without the application of such technologies, shipping companies and multimodal operators of developing countries would be at a competitive disadvantage, and he therefore welcomed the suggestion to monitor and to distribute information on technological developments in the industry in developing countries, in close collaboration with other international organizations.

23. On maritime and transport legislation, he said that he would like to see UNCTAD concentrate its activities on monitoring legal problems encountered by developing countries in the field of shipping. Document TD/B/CN.4/48 envisaged the undertaking of substantive work relating to legal aspects of ship leasing in developing countries in order to prepare model legislation as guidelines for developing countries and promote awareness on the operation and functioning of ship leasing. Concerning the first issue, namely model legislation, only experts in the area of ship leasing could give proper opinions and, in any case, such work, if needed, would be within the competence of international organizations dealing with legal work. On the other hand, the promotion of awareness on the operation and functioning of ship leasing was appropriate.

24. Finally, with regard to strengthening technical cooperation and human resource development (TD/B/CN.4/47), he noted that this type of activity was potentially very helpful to developing countries, and the Community took a generally positive view of the work of the UNCTAD secretariat in this area. The Community continued to attach importance to technical cooperation, which had also been endorsed by UNCTAD VIII. He underlined that such technical cooperation was meant to support and assist developing countries in identifying their weaknesses and capabilities in the services sector and making it more competitive.

25. The spokesman for the **African Group** (Ghana) acknowledged the important role played by UNCTAD in the development of the maritime transport sector. He noted that the World Trade Organization provided a framework for opening world markets, while UNCTAD provided a framework for the orderly development of economies and the transport sector. The principles established in WTO, for example national treatment, required studies and guidance. He suggested that competition rules should be looked at in order to assist operators in developing countries. He thanked UNCTAD for developing and installing the Advance Cargo Information System (ACIS) in a number of developing countries, especially in Africa. He regarded ACIS as an instrument for providing an on-line system capable of generating relevant statistics for decision-making. He noted that RailTracker and the Harbour Master module of PortTracker had started to have an impact in his country, since they were producing useful data for the managements of the railway and ports authorities. While liberalization might promote efficiency, it must be carried out in a manner

that would not lead to the marginalization of economic operators in the developing countries. Training was therefore a critical requirement. He called attention to the undue generalization of statistics (for example in sub-Saharan Africa) and to the fact that decisions taken by multilateral organizations based on these aggregated statistics tended to obscure the needs of individual countries. It was therefore necessary to pay due attention to the differences that existed among developing countries. Finally, he referred to proposals being made by developed countries to do away with shippers' councils in developing countries. In this connection he noted that developing countries required special arrangements to support competition, and further review of this question was therefore required.

26. The representative of the **International Federation of Freight Forwarders Associations** (FIATA) stressed that freight forwarders acted as carriers accepting overall responsibility for the transport chain and, by issuing a single transport document, for instance the FIATA Multimodal Transport Bill of Lading, backed up by a liability insurance cover, were becoming MTOs. He supported UNCTAD's view that privatization of State-owned transport enterprises would increase their efficiency. He stressed that any inland price-fixing cartel operated by maritime carriers would eliminate free competition in multimodal transport to the detriment of shippers and would be harmful to multimodal transport providers, especially in developing countries. FIATA viewed the formation of joint ventures between freight forwarders from developing and developed countries as a useful tool to overcome structural weaknesses. However, joint ventures should also promote training as a means of increasing freight forwarders' professional status in developing countries, if necessary. Regarding the creation of national trade and transport facilitation committees, FIATA felt that such a consultation mechanism could contribute to the removal of obstacles and promote multimodal transport. However, it should not impede the flexibility of freight forwarders and transport operators. He felt that the establishment of voluntary minimum standards for MTOs would constitute an inflexible frame and would not prevent fraudulent actions. FIATA was of the opinion that it would be necessary to harmonize the introduction of multimodal transport legislation in the different parts of the world on a contractual basis within the freight forwarding industry itself. He suggested that harmonization of multimodal transport legislation at the global level could be undertaken by UNCTAD with the assistance of FIATA. Regarding container standards, he felt that the freight-forwarding industry was interested in as few internationally accepted dimensions as possible. To reduce the negative effects of transport on the environment, he offered FIATA's cooperation in the development of appropriate strategies. Finally, he noted that FIATA did not consider quality assurance as the main thrust for improved competitiveness of multimodal transport providers, but suggested that training should play a major role in the improvement of the professional status of transport providers.

27. The representative of **Mexico** noted the importance of multimodal transport in international goods trade because it represented an important part of final transaction costs. Although Mexico had ratified the Multimodal Transport Convention in 1982, by 1989 it had felt it necessary to develop a more competitive market and to enact national regulations on multimodal transport. Through these regulations, users had the freedom to use either a multimodal or a segmented transport contract in international trade, to choose any carrier on the basis of operational conditions and tariffs, and to use temporarily imported containers in domestic trade. As a result, several new transport operators had registered as MTOs. To improve operations through the use of technology and the streamlining of Customs documentation, coordination had been organized between the public and private sectors. He felt that training of human resources was crucial in developing an efficient multimodal transport sector and therefore suggested that UNCTAD should continue its programme for developing human resources. Finally, he indicated that Mexico wanted to rejoin the TRAINMAR network in the near future.

28. The representative of **Australia** said that the work programme of the secretariat should be manageable and attainable. With regard to multimodal transport and other issues, discussions should emphasize the interests of shippers as well as the interests of suppliers of shipping services, and restrictions on multimodal transport operators should be avoided.

29. The representative of **Colombia**, speaking on behalf of the **Andean Group**, said that the elimination of cargo reservation in the member States of the Andean Group since 1993 had been of great significance for maritime transport services and the shipping industry of the subregion. As a result of the lifting of cargo reservation, the competitive edge of the shipowners in the region had been severely affected, and it was to be regretted that the liberalization measures that had taken place in the region had not been reciprocated by other countries that required bilateral agreements in order to allow access to cargo. The Andean Group, in consultation with the Andean Association of Shipowners, had therefore considered it necessary to establish community criteria in order to secure effective commercial reciprocity, without affecting fair competition, and thus to rationalize the services and to allow economic recovery of the merchant fleets in the subregion. Other community norms intended to improve the competitiveness of the merchant marines in the subregion were also under consideration. The principal mechanisms being considered were the establishment of an Andean ship registry, the preparation of legislation to facilitate ship leasing, and the establishment of rules on competition to avoid unfair commercial practices.

30. UNCTAD should continue to treat maritime transport issues. She strongly believed that the experience accumulated by UNCTAD was of great value for the establishment and dissemination of principles aimed at rationalizing competition in this important field of services. She emphasized the role of UNCTAD in the field of human resource development and stressed its importance in the field of shipping, ports and maritime legislation. She praised the legal assistance provided by UNCTAD and the support given to the Andean Group in order to increase the competitiveness of their national merchant fleets. She especially referred to the establishment of the Andean ship registry and the legal measures to facilitate ship leasing. In all these subjects and in the field of multimodal transport legislation, the UNCTAD secretariat had the necessary legal expertise. Concerning multimodal transport, she informed the Committee that the Andean Group had recently enacted community legislation applicable to all contracting States. She insisted that training should be among institutional priorities. Technical assistance was important for the improvement of transport services, particularly with regard to the introduction of mechanisms for improving competitiveness such as multimodal transport. Countries should support UNCTAD in seeking funds for technical assistance.

31. The representative of the **Central American Integration System** (SICA) expressed the appreciation of countries of Central America both to UNCTAD and to donors for the technical assistance provided, notably through the TRAINMAR and LEGISMAR programmes. Both programmes had benefited trade by facilitating adjustment to recent changes in the maritime field. He stressed that projects could never lead to complete adjustment within a fixed time-span; it was up to recipient countries to respond positively to the assistance provided, which was a gradual process, and he hoped that ways could be found by UNCTAD and the international community to provide follow-up for the projects.

32. Concerning the conclusion of the LEGISMAR project, which consisted in updating and harmonizing the maritime legislation of the Central American countries, he said that the Draft Maritime Treaty for Central America was being studied by the Central American International Court of Justice to enable a final draft to be submitted to the meeting of Presidents. The Draft Treaty contained a chapter on multimodal transport. It was important that the region continue to receive assistance in the field of maritime legislation.

33. The representative of the **International Labour Organization** (ILO) outlined the work of his Organization in the field of training and the development of human resources in the ports field. This work was carried out in close collaboration with UNCTAD, as shown by the two regional meetings in Latin America and the most recent one in October 1994 in Asia. More specifically, ILO was near to completing the PDP series of courses (Port Development Programme), with the first 30 courses amounting to more than 500 hours of teaching for training supervisors of container terminals. These courses, which had been developed thanks to funds provided by the Government of the Netherlands, had been tested in Kenya and in the United Republic of Tanzania. An agreement with the Government of India to implement them in 11 ports from 1996 using the same source of financing had already been reached. Finally, work on the impact of technological changes on ports would be reviewed at the next International Maritime Conference, which was convened every 10 years and which would take place in November 1995 to review the implementation of the four ILO conventions in this field.

34. The representative of **Tunisia** said that transport policies should be designed to promote reliable transport, and liberalization should give priority to the observance of quality standards. Procedures and legislation had to be harmonized and adapted to international standards. With regard to privatization, there should be properly organized programmes involving all sectors of shipping.

35. The representative of **Lithuania** said that this was the first time that the Lithuanian delegation had participated in a session of the Standing Committee, and he found the documents and discussion very useful and instructive from the point of view of the transport situation in Lithuania. From the re-establishment of its independence in 1990, the country had pursued a policy of liberalization and integration of its economy into the European and world markets. In view of its geographic situation, its main goal in the sphere of transport was to serve as a bridge between the East and the West of Europe, and the development of multimodal transport corridors was therefore one of the main priorities.

36. Two of the nine priority transport corridors declared at the Crete Conference in 1994 passed through Lithuanian territory, and the East-West corridor passing through the port of Klaipeda was especially important. The port of Klaipeda was the fifth port in the Baltic in terms of volume of cargo handled (15-16 million tons a year), and it had regular ferry links with many European ports. The further development of its container and ro-ro handling facilities and the reconstruction of the passenger terminal, as well as the development of adjacent transport infrastructure in the transport corridor, were the main priorities at present, and the international financial institutions were assisting in these developments.

37. In order to facilitate the establishment of national and joint-venture transport operators, the country's transport legislation was in the process of being harmonized with that of the European Union. All road freight transport companies had already been privatized, and the commercial entities in the port of Klaipeda would be privatized in the near future. This was therefore in contradiction with the statement made in documents TD/B/CN.4/48 and UNCTAD/SDD/SHIP/4, according to which the port of Klaipeda and the shipping company would not be privatized. His delegation would study the documents of the Standing Committee attentively and intended to participate actively in the future work of the Standing Committee.

Chapter II

FOSTERING COMPETITIVE MULTIMODAL TRANSPORT SERVICES

(Agenda item 3)

38. The **Officer-in-charge of the Services Development Division**, introducing the documentation on agenda item 3, referred to chapter I of the document entitled "Fostering competitive multimodal transport services" (TD/B/CN.4/46) and indicated that the three items of the work programme of the Committee relating to multimodal transport, containerization, logistics and technological developments which the secretariat had been requested to prepare before UNCTAD IX would be completed in time.

39. With regard to the three background documents on "Multimodal transport and trading opportunities" (UNCTAD/SDD/MT/5), "Containerization and standards" (UNCTAD/SDD/MT/2), and "Mega multimodal transport operators and mega carriers" (UNCTAD/SDD/MT/4), the first report showed that multimodal transport and logistics could have an impact on trading opportunities by providing an efficient transport system serving a country's international trade, as well as a means to increase the domestic activity of the national transport sector. The second report showed that there was no global alternative to the present International Organization for Standardization (ISO) standard ISO 668 on container dimensions, and that the apparent decline in the introduction of oversized containers might solve the problem. The third report stressed that, while the overall effect of mega carriers on world trade might be beneficial, their impact on other transport operators would be significant and might relegate many smaller carriers to the role of feeder operators or subcontractors for the mega carriers.

40. He then referred to the background document "Draft Multimodal Transport Handbook" (UNCTAD/SDD/MT/8 and UNCTAD/SDD/MT/Misc.1), prepared in connection with the second item on the Committee's work programme, and asked the Standing Committee for its views on the draft, so that the handbook could be completed in as useful a form as possible. Turning to the background document "Facing the challenge of integrated transport services" (UNCTAD/SDD/MT/7), he said that the document attempted to address some of the trends regarding technological and operational developments in modern multimodal transport and that it suggested that the experience of national trade and transport facilitation committees (NTTFCs) be presented at a global forum with a view to enabling countries to avoid repeating mistakes made by others, thereby leapfrogging onto a higher level of development. He also reminded delegates that there was no legally binding international legal regime that dealt with multimodal transport and that incompatible national multimodal transport legislation was only making matters worse.

41. He stressed that there were other aspects which required the attention of the Standing Committee, since the multimodal transport industry continued to develop rapidly. These aspects, dealt with in chapter II of document TD/B/CN.4/46, were the effects of liberalization of services and increased competitiveness, the evolution of multimodal transport operations into physical distribution, multimodal logistics and total transport service providers, as well as issues such as the environment, safety and the quality of services. Their promotion would have an impact on the fostering of competitive multimodal transport services in deep-sea shipping, as well as in other modes of transport such as feeder services and coastal or short-sea trades. Suggestions for further work to be considered by the Committee were presented in three main areas: (i) general policy issues; (ii) technical issues; and (iii) operational issues.

42. He concluded by suggesting that the Standing Committee might recommend to the Trade and Development Board that the services sector be given due attention at UNCTAD IX as a key component in fostering the development of trade.

43. The representative of **Poland** presented his country's experience in the development of multimodal transport and the service sector. Rules for the establishment of companies had been liberalized, commercialization and privatization in the services sector had advanced rapidly, joint ventures with foreign partners had been facilitated, and free access for international cargo existed on the basis of reciprocity. However, the expansion of multimodal transport had been slow, as there had been a certain amount of inertia and only limited capital was available for the development of essential infrastructure and equipment. Existing and new national freight-forwarding companies, many of which were private, were developing as MTOs. To accelerate further the development of this sector, the Government had ratified the "European Agreement on Important International Combined Transport Lines and Related Installations" (AGTC) to integrate the Polish transport system with that of other European countries. Secondly, the Government, in conjunction with the national ports and railways, had established an MTO (POLCOMBI), made up of both private and public firms, to develop multimodal transport from and to Polish ports. Block trains for containers had been set up between the container terminal in the port of Gdynia and inland centres, and the infrastructure required for containerization and multimodal transport was being partially financed by the Government. Multimodal transport should be promoted further, and in that connection he noted that, in Poland's experience, the deficiencies in the international legal framework had not been a barrier to its development. Finally, he felt that the development of minimum standards for MTOs would be useful.

44. The spokesman for the **African Group** (Ghana) expressed his concern that developments in containerization and multimodal transport were widening the gap between developed and developing countries, which could lead to the domination of the transport chain by developed-country operators. Inadequate infrastructure, limited transport equipment and demurrage charges due to long stays of empty containers had restricted the growth of multimodal transport in Africa. Mega carriers had reduced freight rates to and from feeder ports, and while that was beneficial to shippers, it had made it extremely difficult for local transport operators to compete commercially. In addition to their special equipment requirements, oversized and overweight containers could cause great damage to roads and were thus restricted to the port area. The promotion of environmentally friendly transport services, the use of new INCOTERMS, the creation of national trade and transport facilitation committees and the setting of minimum standards would assist in the orderly development of multimodal transport. Liberalization might not stimulate competition or increase the choice available to traders, but could lead to the marginalization of national operators and generate considerable unemployment. Liberalization should be used to assist in developing domestic transport providers through such activities as the establishment of joint ventures and alliances. Multimodal transport markets should be open on a reciprocal basis, thus enabling developing countries to compete globally. He believed that antitrust regulations might be required to control the activities of large transport providers. Finally, he noted that seminars and workshops on multimodal transport laws and regulations were required for the successful implementation of multimodal transport, and that seminars on environmentally sound methods of production of containers should be supported.

45. The representative of the **Russian Federation** agreed with the conclusion reached in document TD/B/CN.4/46 that the use of the multimodal transport concept would not only contribute to the efficiency of the transport system but also serve as a means to help safeguard the environment through the use of less environmentally intrusive modes of transport such as inland waterways,

railways and combined and coastal shipping. Regarding the document on "Containerization and standards" (UNCTAD/SDD/MT/2), he felt that at present there was no acceptable alternative to the existing international Series I container standards. He suggested that the future activity of the secretariat in the field of multimodal transport should involve practical assistance to Governments, operators and transport users, with particular emphasis on the maritime leg of the multimodal transport chain.

46. With regard to the situation in the Russian Federation, multimodal transport was extremely important for the development of the Russian transport system. The Ministry of Transport of the Russian Federation was implementing a number of programmes in that connection, including the programme "Terminal" covering the creation of a legislative basis for multimodal transport, the modernization of infrastructure and specialized rolling stock, the introduction of informatics and EDI on the basis of EDIFACT, and the integration of the Russian transport system with the transport systems of other States. The Government, as well as many private financial institutions and transport users in Russia, had expressed interest in the programme and were participating in its financing along the Black Sea-Moscow-Baltics corridor. UNCTAD's technical assistance in the field of multimodal transport had an important role to play, in particular through the organization of workshops, consultancies and the provision of technical expertise. The UNCTAD secretariat had in fact agreed to hold a workshop in October 1995 in which other former Soviet republics were invited to participate.

47. The representative of **India** said that a series of economic reforms, including deregulation of the economy and stimulation of foreign investment, had been introduced in his country. Regarding multimodal transport, the Multimodal Transportation of Goods Act had been enacted in 1993 and provided a legal regime to govern, on a uniform basis, MTOs' liabilities and responsibilities for services covered under a single document. Containerized traffic was growing at a rapid pace, and private parties were allowed to set up inland clearance depots (ICDs) and container freight stations (CFSs). His Government was also interested in linking the various public and private commercial parties through the use of EDI and possibly replacing multimodal transport documents by EDI messages. To stimulate competition among MTOs and ensure quality services, foreign companies were also allowed to register as MTOs, as long as they complied with the regulations in force and obtained insurance cover. He welcomed the UNCTAD/ESCAP initiatives for developing multimodal transport systems in the Asian region and for providing the latest technologies and information on modern transport systems. He also supported the idea of recommending that the question of "fostering competitive multimodal transport services" be part of UNCTAD IX. Regarding technical cooperation and human resource development, UNCTAD training activities should be aimed at upgrading the skills of port personnel, as well as those of MTOs and ICD and CFS operators, with a view to developing an efficient and coherent multimodal transport system. He offered Indian technical cooperation to assist UNCTAD in its work in less developed countries. Finally, he suggested that UNCTAD could prescribe some acceptable guidelines regarding the reduction of accidents in the movements of goods, the maintenance of ecological balance, and the conservation of fuel.

Chapter III

STRENGTHENING TECHNICAL COOPERATION AND HUMAN RESOURCE DEVELOPMENT

(Agenda item 4)

48. The **Officer-in-charge of the Services Development Division**, introducing the item, said that document TD/B/CN.4/47 described secretariat activities organized as a complement to its regular activities. Technical cooperation

was generally funded from extrabudgetary sources, but there had in recent years been a move away from UNDP as the principal donor to new donors such as the European Commission and certain European Governments. Bringing about this change had required an energetic reappraisal of its activities by the secretariat. He drew attention in particular to one of the major technical cooperation programmes, the Advance Cargo Information System (ACIS), of which a demonstration would be provided for Committee members.

49. Human resource development involved a variety of training activities which were made available to countries on request, as was the TRAINMAR programme which strengthened local training capacity. There had been a General Meeting of the TRAINMAR network the previous week.

50. Finally, he expressed appreciation to the donors that had made so many activities possible and invited those beneficiaries attending the Committee's session to give some insights into how they had been able to benefit and ensure sustainability of the results.

51. The spokesman for the **African Group** (Ghana) expressed appreciation to UNCTAD and to donors for the training programmes provided. However, he also expressed concern that most of the training currently offered in his country was directed towards the public sector, and he therefore feared that private sector needs were not being met and that this would be detrimental to further development. He asked that UNCTAD give particular attention to training for the private sector and to ways of attracting capable staff into the private sector.

Chapter IV

REVIEW OF THE WORK PROGRAMME OF THE STANDING COMMITTEE, WITH SPECIAL EMPHASIS ON THE PREPARATIONS FOR UNCTAD IX

(Agenda item 5)

52. The **Officer-in-charge of the Services Development Division**, introducing the item, said that, on the question of shipping (TD/B/CN.4/48, chap. I), the secretariat had prepared two background documents, "Progressive liberalization and the development of shipping services in developing countries - country experiences" (UNCTAD/SDD/SHIP/5) and "Maritime policy reforms in the Newly Independent States of the former Soviet Union" (UNCTAD/SDD/SHIP/4). The preliminary conclusions of these reports indicated that there was insufficient experience to clearly establish a causal relationship between policy reform and specific market and fleet developments.

53. In addition, he noted the changes that had occurred in national practices covering shipper/ocean-carrier relations. To date, the process of globalization of economic activities and progressive liberalization in the shipping and transport industry had benefited large shippers, while small and medium-sized shippers, particularly from developing countries, had often been unable to benefit effectively due to a lack of expertise and information. The document entitled "Changes in national practices covering shipper/ocean-carrier relations" (UNCTAD/SDD/SHIP/2) contained a number of recommendations for dealing with this restructuring process. Finally, in the area of ship finance, he drew the Committee's attention to the report "Ship finance for developing countries" (UNCTAD/SDD/SHIP/3), which concluded that the difficulty faced by the shipping industry in attracting capital was the result of the inability of many shipping investments to achieve financial yields that were competitive with more profitable projects. Regarding the United Nations Convention on a Code of Conduct for Liner Conferences, under its article 52, Review Conferences were to be convened every five years, and the next Conference was due in 1996 or 1997. In this

connection, States entitled to attend the Review Conference would be contacted in order to obtain their views.

54. The work on ports was being carried out in line with the new competitive environment that prevailed in many routes and was guided by the Intergovernmental Group of Experts on Ports, which had met in 1993 in Geneva. The studies and reports that had been prepared recognized the role of ports as logistical centres and the need to have a proactive attitude towards traffic changes, and they promoted the idea of port marketing.

55. The spokesman for the **African Group** (Ghana) said that his Group attached great importance to the work carried out in the area of maritime and transport legislation, dealt with in document TD/B/CN.4/48, chapter IV. He congratulated the Joint UNCTAD/IMO Intergovernmental Group of Experts for the remarkable progress achieved during its seventh session, held in Geneva from 5 to 9 December 1994 to review the 1952 International Convention on the Arrest of Sea-Going Ships. He noted that the Joint Group had succeeded in preparing a set of draft articles for a Convention on Arrest of Ships and had agreed to continue examination of the subject at its next session, to be held at IMO headquarters in London in October 1995. The subject of arrest of ships was of crucial importance to the shipping community.

56. Regarding the work carried out on general average, he said that the three studies produced by the secretariat on the subject identified the shortcomings of the system and made proposals with a view to identifying a commercial solution to the problems encountered. The current move towards reform of general average by the London insurance market and others had begun after commencement of work within UNCTAD on the subject, and he hoped that reform in the area in question would be pursued with a view to facilitating the operation of the system for the benefit of international trade. He requested the UNCTAD secretariat to keep developments under review and to inform the Committee accordingly.

57. Concerning the preliminary review prepared by the secretariat on "Legal aspects of ship leasing in developing countries" (UNCTAD/SDD/LEG/4), he regretted that the document had not yet been translated into all the United Nations official languages. The subject of ship leasing was of the utmost importance to developing countries, since it provided a shipping company with the entire possession and use of a vessel without capital outlay. The permanent shortage of capital in most developing countries made ship leasing an attractive alternative to acquiring new ships or replacing ageing fleets. In view of its practical importance, he recommended that the secretariat continue its research on the subject in order to prepare model legislation to serve as guidelines for developing countries that wished to promote ship leasing and to promote awareness as to the operation and functioning of ship leasing and its potential advantages for developing countries.

58. Finally, he pointed out that the process of liberalization and privatization of maritime transport services currently under way in many African countries would require as a matter of priority the adoption of an adequate legal framework and regulatory mechanism to promote competitiveness and minimize any negative consequences involved in the process.

59. The representative of the **Russian Federation** said that in general he agreed with the conclusions of the secretariat's report "Progressive liberalization and the development of shipping services in developing countries - country experiences" (UNCTAD/SDD/SHIP/5). However, he suggested that the effect of liberalization on maritime transport should be evaluated taking into account the impact of many different and important factors of State policy such as taxation, free ship registration, reservation of State

cargo, use of foreign crews, etc., as well as the economic situation of the country and of its foreign trade.

60. With regard to the report on "Maritime policy reforms in the NIS of the former Soviet Union" (UNCTAD/SDD/SHIP/4), he noted that the report on the whole gave a realistic picture of the process of reform in the countries in question, as well as of the goals of the maritime policy of these countries, namely enabling national fleets to participate effectively in international shipping on the basis of the principle of free access to transport markets, equality and fair competition. Liberalization had to be considered as part of economic restructuring and as a framework for limiting the participation of the State in shipping and for the establishment of conditions for the functioning of economically viable enterprises.

61. At present the maritime industry of the countries concerned was facing difficulties, and it was too early to evaluate the impact of the process of reform, which was still unfinished.

62. With regard to the Review of Maritime Transport, he underlined the importance of the work of the secretariat as a basis for solving the problems of imbalance in the maritime transport market. He suggested that the Review should not only reflect the problems of countries in transition, but also give an analysis and recommendations for their resolution. It was also desirable to publish the next issue of the Review in the first half of 1996.

63. The representative of **China**, referring to the subject of liberalization, concurred with paragraph 11 of the secretariat's report contained in document TD/B/CN.4/48, namely that regulatory mechanisms must be established to back up liberalization in order to avoid the pitfalls of competition. Such mechanisms could include competition rules and incentives for enterprises, and he suggested that the secretariat should pursue this subject further. He also concurred with paragraph 70 of the secretariat's report and suggested that there should be further analysis on how to improve management and commercialization. With regard to the Review of Maritime Transport, he noted that it provided useful information and recommended that the secretariat should continue with its publication.

64. He noted the beneficial work accomplished in the field of ports and port services and agreed with the arrangement to convene a second session of the Intergovernmental Group of Experts on Ports in early 1996 to assess progress and to review any new or outstanding issues in port efficiency, modernization and development.

65. On the work programme on maritime and transport legislation, he endorsed and praised the work achieved by the Joint UNCTAD/IMO Intergovernmental Group of Experts on the review of the 1952 International Convention on Arrest of Sea-going Ships. Concerning the work carried out on reform of general average and the newly adopted York-Antwerp Rules 1994, he requested the secretariat to monitor developments closely and to keep the Committee duly informed. As to the preliminary review prepared by the secretariat on "Legal aspects of ship leasing in developing countries" (UNCTAD/SDD/LEG/4), he endorsed the recommendations of paragraph 64 and requested that the secretariat undertake further work in this area to prepare model legislation as guidelines for developing countries wishing to promote ship leasing and to promote awareness as to the operation and functioning of ship leasing and its potential advantages for developing countries.

Action by the Standing Committee

66. Under agenda item 5 and at the end of its deliberations, the Standing Committee reviewed its work since UNCTAD VIII and reported to

the Trade and Development Board as set out in the following paragraphs (paras. 67-72).

1. **Report on work accomplished so far** 1/

A. Transparency

67. The following activities were undertaken:

In the field of shipping: publication of the Review of Maritime Transport 1992, 1993 and 1994 issues;

In the field of ports: publication of five regular newsletters (Nos. 9-13 in E/F/S) which monitored technological and structural changes in ports and disseminated information on port-related activities within the secretariat; contributions made to the annual Review of Maritime Transport; responded to multiple requests for information and studies on ports;

In the field of multimodal transport: publication of three issues of the MT Newsletter (5, 6 and 7) to disseminate technological and institutional aspects; contributions also made to the annual Review of Maritime Transport; participation in various technical meetings on multimodal transport organized by the private sector; ad hoc contributions to professional and academic forums;

In the field of maritime legislation: ad hoc contributions made through academic and professional institutions on disseminating legal issues and/or instruments in the maritime sector which have been adopted (e.g. charter parties, marine insurance, general average, etc.); contributions to the annual Review of Maritime Transport;

In the field of training and human resource development: publication by the TRAINMAR programme of newsletters (4), the annual course catalogue, and a report on the implementation of the TRAINMAR Action Plan.

B. Fostering competitive services

68. The following activities were undertaken:

In the field of shipping: research and preparation of reports on the impact of progressive liberalization on the development of shipping services in developing countries and maritime policy reforms in the Newly Independent States of the former Soviet Union (NIS), changes in national practices covering shipper/ocean carrier relations, prevailing ship financing arrangements and consideration of their adequacy in meeting the requirements of developing countries, and cooperation between developing countries in the field of shipping, ports and multimodal transport;

In the field of ports: completion of research studies on the development of human resources, on legal and regulatory aspects, on strategic port planning and on sustainable development in ports; preparation of overall documentation for, and servicing of, the Intergovernmental Group of Experts on Ports which reviewed work and recommended continuation on port policy issues, organization and management. Completion of studies for second session of the Intergovernmental Group of Experts on Ports (initially scheduled for first part of 1995) on strategic port pricing, comparative analysis of deregulation,

---

1/ Outputs for all activities described in section 1 are listed in the annex of TD/B/CN.4/48.

commercialization and privatization. Publication of three monographs (computerized container terminal management, EDI and marketing tools);

<u>In the field of multimodal transport and technological development</u>: preparation of documentation for and servicing of Standing Committee sessions (containerization and standards, mega multimodal transport operators and mega carriers, multimodal transport and trading opportunities, facing the challenge of integrated transport services, multimodal transport handbook for officials and practitioners (draft), fostering competitive multimodal transport services); preparation of documentation for, and servicing of, Group of Experts on Multimodal Transport (review of work programme, proposals for future work; participation in elaboration of the UNCTAD/ICC Rules for Multimodal Transport Documents; participation in meetings of intergovernmental and non-governmental organizations;

<u>In the field of maritime legislation</u>: preparation of documentation for and servicing of: the UN/IMO Conference of Plenipotentiaries, which resulted in the adoption of the International Convention on Maritime Liens and Mortgages, 1993; the Joint UNCTAD/IMO Intergovernmental Group of Experts (seventh session), which is considering the review of the 1952 Convention on Arrest of Ships (draft articles for a Convention on Arrest of Ships); preparation of documentation on general average (identification of problems and proposals for simplification by the industry) for the Standing Committee (second and third sessions); preparation of a preliminary report on legal aspects of ship leasing in developing countries for the Standing Committee (third session); advice to developing countries on implementation of international shipping instruments.

C. <u>Technical cooperation and human resource development</u>

69. The following activities were undertaken:

<u>In the field of shipping</u>: assistance to improve commercial shipping management: 9 workshops (STRATSHIP), 10 JOBMAR placements and 2 feasibility studies. In addition, work on seaborne trade statistics was revived in cooperation with UNSTAT and private sector information management companies;

<u>In the field of ports</u>: assistance provided to Somali ports after the civil strife (under UNOSOM); two Container Terminal Management seminars and three Port Marketing seminars, all funded by the Government of Belgium, were delivered; three courses on Container Terminal Planning, three courses on Equipment Management and a Strategic Planning seminar were delivered at the World Maritime University; two ad hoc seminars were organized (Challenge of Third Generation Ports and Port Liability and Insurance);

<u>In the field of multimodal transport</u>: regular deliveries of various multimodal transport workshops financed from the regular budget (two per year); as well as deliveries of similar workshops from extrabudgetary resources (4); development of Workshop for Multimodal Operators; contribution to the elaboration of new workshop material (Strategic Workshop on Short-Sea Shipping); technical assistance (Pakistan, Mozambique, Colombia, Central Asian Republics, India, Viet Nam, Ethiopia and Democratic People's Republic of Korea).

<u>In the field of maritime legislation</u>: updating and harmonizing of maritime legislation at both national and subregional levels, e.g. draft Maritime Treaty for five Central American States (LEGISMAR/IMO); preparation of guidelines and recommendations on maritime legislation (West and Central African countries); assistance to Andean Group on Community ship registry; contribution to a draft Community act on multimodal transport legislation; in the area of training: subregional seminars on marine cargo insurance (Central America) and on the Hamburg Rules and multimodal transport

(West Africa), on charter parties and ship financing (South America), national seminar on general average (Nigeria), assistance in setting up an association of port lawyers (LEGIPORT), lecturing at the World Maritime University (WMU) on charter parties and international trade and transport.

TRAINMAR programme: expansion of the TRAINMAR network (35 to 50 centres); development of techniques and pedagogical support material; preparation and delivery of courses for general use (7); quality control regarding the pedagogical and technical content of courses (annual catalogue); dissemination of information and coordination of interregional activities (annual regional training meetings in Latin America, Caribbean, Asia, North Africa, West and Central Africa, southern Africa, Europe); tri-annual interregional meeting for network; advice to centres and contacts in the maritime sector and training needs identification (missions to the field on training needs analysis);

ACIS programme: software development pursued on the basic and optional tracking modules for ports (PortTracker), railways (RailTracker) and lakes (LakeTracker); technical specifications prepared for the Backbone Information System; PortTracker installed in 2 African ports, RailTracker installed on 13 African networks and LakeTracker on 3 lakes; funding obtained (European Union) for launching of multi-country multi-modular project to install ACIS in Eastern Africa, in association with COMESA - first phase;

Advisory services: provision of services, upon request, to developing countries and countries in transition, and in cooperation with other international organizations (World Bank and ILO) both to Governments and the private sector.

2. Remaining work for the period up to the next Conference

70. The following activities are envisaged during the period leading up to UNCTAD IX:

In the field of shipping: production of the Review of Maritime Transport; continuation of monitoring of the impact of progressive liberalization and privatization and of changes in national practices in shipper/carrier relations; continuation of activities and policies aimed at enhancing cooperation in the area of shipping; preparation of training material for strategic planning for bulk shipping companies and continuation of STRATSHIP and JOBMAR programmes;

In the field of ports: Ports Newsletters (2), studies on financial aspects of port management; and potentialities for increased regional cooperation; preparation and servicing of the second session of the Intergovernmental Group of Experts on Ports dealing with organization and management; seminars on container terminal management and port marketing; training programme on port pricing; development of a certificate course in port management (in collaboration with the TRAINMAR programme); ongoing backstopping of port management rehabilitation project for Somalia; contribution to annual Review of Maritime Transport;

In the field of multimodal transport: MT Newsletter (1); contribution to annual Review of Maritime Transport; final draft of Multimodal Transport Handbook; development of course material for a diploma course in logistics (in collaboration with the TRAINMAR programme); deliveries of workshops; technical assistance in operational, institutional and facilitation aspects of multimodal transport in Central Asian Republics, Latin America, Asia;

In the field of maritime legislation: preparation for and servicing of the Joint UNCTAD/IMO Intergovernmental Group on reviewing the 1952 Convention on Arrest of Sea-going Ships (eighth session), monitoring current developments and reforms of the general average system by insurance industry, completion of the work on legal aspects of ship leasing in developing countries, finalization of draft maritime codes (Côte d'Ivoire and Ethiopia), preparation and servicing of subregional UNCTAD/ESCAP colloquium on charter parties and ship financing (South-East Asia); contribution to annual Review of Maritime Transport;

TRAINMAR programme: extension of support to new centres and networks (developing countries and countries in transition); preparation of training materials for, and organization of, a seminar on port human resources (support for Asia and francophone countries); training of trainers for the seminar on logistics in short-sea shipping; and development of a certificate course in port management (in collaboration with the Ports Section) and of a diploma course in logistics (in collaboration with the Multimodal Transport Section);

ACIS programme: pursuit of development of basic versions and options of port, railway and lake-tracking modules and of Backbone Information System; pursuit ACIS installation in Africa (COMESA and West/Central Africa), extension to Central Asia (Turkmenistan, Uzbekistan), Asia (Bangladesh, Viet Nam) and Latin America (Bolivia, Chile, Cuba); preparation of project document and prospecting for funds in response to requests from potential beneficiaries.

3. Suggestions for possible future activities that might be considered by the Trade and Development Board for its deliberations of subjects to be considered at UNCTAD IX

71. On the basis of the work carried out so far, and without prejudicing the decisions to be taken by UNCTAD IX, the following items might warrant consideration for future work by UNCTAD without duplicating work in other global intergovernmental organizations:

(a) Technical cooperation and human resource development;

(b) Shipping aimed at fostering progressive liberalization and facilitating the provision of free and fair competitive shipping services;

(c) Ports;

(d) Multimodal transport involving a sea-leg; and

(e) Maritime and transport legislation aimed at fostering international trade and transport of developing counties.

72. In respect of the issue "maritime and transport legislation", the Chairman noted two different positions:

(a) Some countries would like future work in the area of maritime and transport legislation to be limited to monitoring legal problems in maritime legislation affecting developing countries and offering assistance upon request;

(b) Other countries considered that the above issue was important for the development process of developing countries and countries in transition, as this enabled these countries to participate actively in the decision-making process of the global scenario of maritime and transport legislation on an equitable basis.

Closing statements

73. The representative of **Brazil** said that the role of UNCTAD in the development of shipping in developing countries and countries in transition

was of the utmost importance. The documentation prepared for the Standing Committee provided up-to-date reference material for policy formulation, and UNCTAD meetings provided a universal forum for exchanges of experience. However, UNCTAD was not the only international body dealing with shipping, and IMO and WTO also had important roles to play. The specificities of the work programme of each organization must be taken into account in order to avoid duplication.

74. UNCTAD had an important role to play in capacity-building, and in that connection his country was restudying the question of its eventual adhesion to the TRAINMAR programmes. On the question of multimodal transport, too ambitious an agenda would not facilitate an in-depth analysis by the Standing Committee. For its part, the Handbook on Multimodal Transport was useful and should be published. Generally speaking, the multimodal documentation prepared by UNCTAD was extremely helpful and had, for example, been used as a basis for discussion in MERCOSUR negotiations.

75. UNCTAD must continue to play an important role in the analysis of the liberalization of the maritime sector to help developing countries and countries in transition to participate in decision-making on an equitable basis. Liberalization, deregulation and privatization reflected a world trend, but the progressive reduction of protection for maritime activities should be counterbalanced by the creation of operational conditions that enabled shipping companies to become competitive. Companies must be given time to adapt. Brazil favoured the gradual liberalization of maritime transport within the framework of an overall economic policy that encouraged free and fair competition and promoted the beneficial aspects of liberalization.

76. The spokesman for the **African Group** (Ghana) emphasized the importance that developing countries attached to UNCTAD. Although these countries had not developed as rapidly as might have been hoped, the situation would have been much worse without the efforts of UNCTAD. He therefore appealed to the developing countries' partners to show understanding and to maintain a forum that was of importance for development. Liberalization was fashionable, but it was important to liberalize and deregulate where possible and where necessary. It was now taboo to talk of protectionism, but protection from mega operators and from marginalization would continue to be necessary for some time to come, and UNCTAD should help in that connection. It was therefore important that UNCTAD should be strengthened after UNCTAD IX.

77. The representative of **France**, speaking on behalf of the **European Union**, said that the European Union was genuinely committed to development, while at the same time attaching importance to the effective use of resources. Development was a long-term and difficult task that required great patience on everyone's part, and the European Union, for its part, would continue to demonstrate patience, perseverance and tolerance and would remain an attentive partner of the developing countries. Finally, with regard to UNCTAD IX, the participants at UNCTAD VIII had worked well, and it was only to be hoped that the participants at UNCTAD IX would work just as well.

78. The spokesman for the **Latin American and Caribbean Group** (Argentina) said that the documentation prepared for the Standing Committee's third session had been very useful, and in fact UNCTAD was the only forum where such material could be obtained. The technical assistance being provided by UNCTAD to Latin American countries was also proving very useful.

79. The representative of **China** said that China was a maritime country and therefore attached great importance to maritime questions. There were many international organizations involved in such questions, and UNCTAD was one of them. UNCTAD had done a great deal of work on maritime issues in the past,

and it would continue to play an important role in the future, particularly with regard to helping developing countries participate in maritime transport.

Chapter V

ORGANIZATIONAL MATTERS

A. Opening of the session

80. The third session of the Standing Committee on Developing Services Sectors (Shipping) was opened on 6 June 1995 by Mr. M. Meynet (France).

B. Election of officers

(Agenda item 1)

81. In accordance with the rules of procedure of the main Committees of the Trade and Development Board and the decision taken by the Board at the first part of its thirty-ninth session, the Standing Committee on Developing Services Sectors (Shipping), at its 10th (opening) meeting on 6 June 1995, elected the officers to serve on the Bureau of the third session as follows:

Chairman:	Mr. Sergio García Torres	(Colombia)
Vice-Chairmen:	Mr. Paolo Octavio de Paiva Almeida	(Brazil)
	Mr. Krzysztof Dabrowski	(Poland)
	Mr. Andrew Togba Davies	(Liberia)
	Mr. Douglas Pelkola	(Canada)
	Mr. Stefan Schimming	(Germany)
Rapporteur:	Mr. A. Wahab Arsad	(Malaysia)

C. Adoption of the agenda and organization of work

(Agenda item 2)

82. Also at its opening meeting, the Standing Committee adopted the provisional agenda circulated in TD/B/CN.4/45 and endorsed the suggestions therein for the organization of work. The agenda for the third session therefore read as follows:

1. Election of officers
2. Adoption of the agenda and organization of work
3. Fostering competitive multinational transport services
4. Strengthening technical cooperation and human resource development
5. Review of the work programme of the Standing Committee, with special emphasis on the preparations for UNCTAD IX
6. Other business
7. Adoption of the report of the Standing Committee (Shipping) to the Trade and Development Board.

D. Adoption of the report of the Standing Committee (Shipping) to the Trade and Development Board

(Agenda item 7)

83. At its 15th (closing) plenary meeting, on 9 June 1995, the Standing Committee adopted its draft report (TD/B/CN.4/L.15 and Add.1), subject to any amendments made by delegations to country statements, and authorized the Rapporteur to finalize the text in the light of the proceedings of the closing plenary.

Annex I

ATTENDANCE 1/

1. The following States members of UNCTAD, members of the Standing Committee, were represented at the session:

Algeria
Argentina
Australia
Benin
Bolivia
Brazil
Bulgaria
Cameroon
Canada
China
Colombia
Congo
Côte d'Ivoire
Czech Republic
Democratic People's Republic of Korea
Ecuador
Egypt
El Salvador
Finland
France
Gabon
Germany
Ghana
Greece
Honduras
India
Indonesia
Iran (Islamic Republic of)
Iraq
Israel
Jamaica
Japan
Liberia
Libyan Arab Jamahiriya
Madagascar
Malaysia
Mexico
Mongolia
Morocco
Netherlands
Norway
Pakistan
Paraguay
Peru
Poland
Republic of Korea
Romania
Russian Federation
Spain
Sudan
Sweden
Switzerland
Thailand
Trinidad and Tobago
Tunisia
United Kingdom of Great Britain and Northern Ireland
United States of America
Uruguay
Venezuela

2. The following other States members of UNCTAD, not members of the Standing Committee, were represented as observers at the session:

Barbados
Lithuania
Nicaragua
Portugal
South Africa

1/ For the list of participants, see TD/B/CN.4/INF.8.

3. The following specialized and related agency was represented at the session:

International Labour Organization

The World Trade Organization was also represented at the session.

4. The following intergovernmental organizations were represented at the session:

European Community
League of Arab States
Organisation for Economic Cooperation and Development
Organization of African Unity
Central American Integration System

5. The following non-governmental organizations were represented at the session:

General Category

International Chamber of Commerce
World Federation of United Nations Associations

Special Category

Council of European and Japanese National Shipowners
International Federation of Freight Forwarders Associations

Annex II

CHECK-LIST OF DOCUMENTS

Symbol	Title	Agenda item
	Sessional documentation	
TD/B/CN.4/45	Provisional agenda, annotations to the provisional agenda and suggestions for the organization of the work of the Committee: Note by the UNCTAD secretariat	2
TD/B/CN.4/46	Competitive services in multimodal transport: Report by the UNCTAD secretariat	3
TD/B/CN.4/47	Technical cooperation and human resource development in shipping, ports and multimodal transport: Report by the UNCTAD secretariat	4
TD/B/CN.4/48	Review of the work programme of the Standing Committee with special emphasis on the preparations for UNCTAD IX: Report by the UNCTAD secretariat	5
TD/B/CN.4/Misc.10	Review of activities: Note by the secretariat	
TD/B/CN.4/L.15 and Add.1	Draft report of the Standing Committee on its third session	7

Symbol	Title	Agenda item
	Background documentation	
TD/B/CN.4/37	Review of Maritime Transport, 1993	5
TD/B/CN.4/GE.2/3	Report of the Joint UNCTAD/IMO Intergovernmental Group of Experts on its seventh session	5
UNCTAD/SDD/MT/2	Containerization and standards	3
UNCTAD/SDD/MT/4	Mega multimodal transport operators and mega carriers	3
UNCTAD/SDD/MT/5	Multimodal transport and trading opportunities	3
UNCTAD/SDD/MT/7	Facing the challenge of integrated transport services: Report by the UNCTAD secretariat	3
UNCTAD/SDD/MT/8	Multimodal Transport Handbook for Officials and Practitioners: Note by the UNCTAD secretariat	3
UNCTAD/SDD/MT/Misc.1	Multimodal Transport Handbook for Officials and Practitioners	3
UNCTAD/SDD/SHIP/2	Changes in national practices covering shipper/ ocean carriers relations - Changes in shipper representation: Note by the UNCTAD secretariat	5
UNCTAD/SDD/SHIP/3	Ship finance for developing countries: Report by the UNCTAD secretariat	5
UNCTAD/SDD/SHIP/4	Maritime policy reforms in the New Independent States of the former Soviet Union - Experiences and proposals: Report by the UNCTAD secretariat	5
UNCTAD/SDD/SHIP/5	Progressive liberalization and the development of shipping services in developing countries - country experiences: Report by the UNCTAD secretariat	5
UNCTAD/SDD/PORT/2	Strategic port pricing: Report by the UNCTAD secretariat	5
UNCTAD/SDD/PORT/3	Comparative analysis of privatization, commercialization and decentralization	5
UNCTAD/SDD/LEG/1	The place of general average in marine insurance today: Report by the UNCTAD secretariat	5
UNCTAD/SDD/LEG/3	General average - Reform of the system: Report by the UNCTAD secretariat	5
UNCTAD/SDD/LEG/4	Legal aspects of ship leasing in developing countries - A preliminary review	5

-----

5. CONSIDERATION OF THE POSSIBLE REVIEW OF THE INTERNATIONAL CONVENTION FOR THE UNIFICATION OF CERTAIN RULES RELATING TO THE ARREST OF SEA-GOING SHIPS, 1952, 8TH SESSION, LONDON, 9-10 OCTOBER 1995 - NOTE BY THE UNCTAD SECRETARIAT

Doc. no.: TD/B/CN.4/GE.2/5 15 June 1995

The attached document */ has been prepared for the eighth session of the Joint Intergovernmental Group of Experts.

Introduction

To facilitate the work of the Joint Intergovernmental Group of Experts, a revised set of draft articles for a convention on arrest of ships has been prepared by the two Secretariats, taking account of the discussions at the seventh session of the Joint Group.

REVISED DRAFT ARTICLES FOR A CONVENTION ON ARREST OF SHIPS

Article 1
Definitions

(1) "Maritime claim" means any claim concerning or arising out of the ownership, construction, possession, management, operation or trading of any ship, or out of a mortgage or an "hypothèque" or a registrable charge of the same nature on any ship, or out of salvage operations relating to any ship, such as any claim in respect of:

(a) physical loss or damage caused by the operation of the ship other than loss of or damage to cargo, containers and passengers' effects carried on the ship; (1993 MLM Convention, article 4 (1) (e));

(b) loss of life or personal injury occurring, whether on land or on water, in direct connection with the operation of the ship; (1993 MLM Convention, article 4 (1) (b));

(c) salvage operations or any salvage agreement;

---

*/ Also circulated under the symbol LEG/MLM/32.

(d) liability to pay compensation or other remuneration in respect of the removal or attempted removal of a threat of damage, or of preventive measures or similar operations, whether or not arising under any international convention, or any enactment or agreement;

(e) costs or expenses relating to the raising, removal, recovery or destruction of the wreck of the ship or its cargo;

(f) any agreement relating to the use or hire of the ship, whether contained in a charter party or otherwise;

(g) any agreement relating to the carriage of goods or passengers in the ship, whether contained in a charter party or otherwise;

(h) loss of or damage to or in connection with goods (including luggage) carried in the ship;

(i) general average;

(j) towage;

(k) pilotage;[1]

(l) goods, materials, provisions, bunkers, equipment (including containers) or services supplied to the ship for its operation or maintenance;

(m) construction, repair, converting or equipping of the ship;

(n) port, canal, and other waterway dues and pilotage dues; (1993 MLM Convention, article 4 (1) (d));

(o) wages and other sums due to the master, officers and other members of the ship's complement in respect of their employment on the ship, including costs of repatriation and social insurance contributions payable on their behalf; (1993 MLM Convention, article 4 (1) (a));

(p) disbursements made in respect of the ship, by or on behalf of the master, owner, demise or other charterer or agent;

(q) insurance premiums (including mutual insurance calls) in respect of the ship, payable by or on behalf of the shipowner or demise charterer,

(r) any commissions, brokerages or agency fees payable in respect of the ship by or on behalf of the shipowner or demise charterer;

(s) any dispute as to ownership or possession of the ship;

(t) any dispute between co-owners of the ship as to the employment or earnings of the ship;

(u) a mortgage or an "hypothèque" or a registrable charge of the same nature on the ship;

(v) any dispute arising out of a contract for the sale of the ship.

---

[1] It was suggested that in view of the inclusion of "pilotage dues" in subparagraph (n) of this article, this subparagraph could be repetitive.

(2) "Arrest" means any detention, or restriction on removal, of a ship by order of a Court to secure a maritime claim when at the time of such detention or restriction that ship is physically within the jurisdiction of the State where the order has been made.

"Arrest" includes "attachment" or other conservatory measures, but does not include measures taken in execution or satisfaction of an enforceable judgement or arbitral award.

(3) "Person" includes individuals, partnerships, unincorporated associations and bodies corporate, governments, their departments and public authorities.

(4) "Claimant" means any person asserting a maritime claim.

(5) "Court" means any competent judicial authority of a State.

Article 2
Powers of arrest

(1) A ship may be arrested or released from arrest only by or under the authority of a Court of the State in which the arrest is demanded or has been effected.

(2) A ship may be arrested in respect of a maritime claim but in respect of no other claim.

(3) A ship may be arrested even though it is ready to sail or is sailing.

(4) A ship may be arrested for the purpose of obtaining security notwithstanding that by virtue of a jurisdiction clause, arbitration clause or choice of law clause in any relevant contract the maritime claim in respect of which the arrest is effected is to be adjudicated in a State other than the State where the arrest is effected, or is to be arbitrated, or is to be adjudicated subject to the law of another State.

(5) Subject to the provisions of this Convention, the procedure relating to the arrest of a ship or its release shall be governed by the law of the State in which the arrest is demanded or has been effected.

Article 3
Exercise of right of arrest

(1) Arrest is permissible of any ship in respect of which a maritime claim is asserted if:

Alternative 1:

[(a) the claim is secured by a maritime lien and is within any of the following categories (1993 MLM Convention, article 4 (1)):

(i) wages and other sums due to the master, officers and other members of the ship's complement in respect of their employment on the ship, including costs of repatriation and social insurance contributions payable on their behalf,

(ii) loss of life or personal injury occurring, whether on land or on water, in direct connection with the operation of the ship,

(iii) reward for the salvage of the ship,

(iv) port, canal, and other waterway dues and pilotage dues,

(v) physical loss or damage caused by the operation of the ship other than loss of or damage to cargo, containers and passengers' effects carried on the ship;] or

Alternative 2:

[(a) the claim is secured by a maritime lien;][2]

Alternative 3:

This alternative requires keeping the text of the paragraph 1(a) of alternative 1 together with a new sub-paragraph (b) which would read as follows:

[(b) the claim is secured by a maritime lien granted by the law of the State where the arrest is requested pursuant to the provisions of article 6 of the International Convention on Maritime Liens and Mortgages, 1993;][3]

If this alternative is adopted the following subparagraphs (b), (c) and (d) will accordingly be re-ordered as (c), (d) and (e):

(b) the claim is based upon a registered mortgage or a registered "hypothèque" or a registered charge of the same nature; or

(c) the claim is related to ownership or possession of the ship; or

(d) the claim is not covered by (a), (b) or (c) above and if:

(i) the person who owned the ship at the time when the maritime claim arose is personally liable for the claim and is owner of the ship when the arrest is effected, or

(ii) the demise charterer of the ship is personally liable for the claim and is demise charterer or owner of the ship when the arrest is effected.

(2) Arrest is also permissible of any other ship or ships which, when the arrest is effected, is or are owned by the person who is personally liable for the maritime claim and who was, when the claim arose:

(a) owner of the ship in respect of which the maritime claim arose; or

(b) demise charterer, time charterer or voyage charterer of that ship.

This provision does not apply to claims in respect of ownership or possession of a ship.

(3) Notwithstanding the provisions of paragraphs (1) and (2) of this article, the arrest of a ship which is not owned by the person allegedly liable for the claim shall be permissible only if, under the law of the State where the arrest is demanded, a judgement in respect of that claim can be enforced against that ship by judicial or forced sale of that ship.

---

[2] Proposal by the delegation of the United States of America. For discussion on the three alternatives see the report on the work of the Sessional Group, document JIGE (VII)/3 (TD/B/CN.4/GE.2/3-LEG/MLM/30), para. 42.

[3] Proposal by the Chairman of the Informal Group on consideration of national maritime liens.

Article 4
Release from arrest

(1) A ship which has been arrested shall be released when sufficient security has been furnished in a satisfactory form.

(2) In the absence of agreement between the parties as to the sufficiency and form of the security, the Court shall determine its nature and the amount thereof, not exceeding the value of the ship.

(3) Any request for the ship to be released upon security being provided shall not be construed as an acknowledgement of liability nor as a waiver of any defence or any right to limit liability.

(4) (a) If a ship has been arrested in a non-party State and is not released although security has been given in a State Party, that security shall be ordered released on application to the Court in the State Party save in exceptional cases where it would be unjust to do so.

(b) If in a non-party State the ship is released upon satisfactory security being provided, any security given in a State Party shall be ordered released to the extent that the total amount of security given in the two States exceeds:

(i) the claim for which the ship has been arrested, or

(ii) the value of the ship,

whichever is the lower.

Such release shall, however, not be ordered unless the security given in the non-party State will actually be available to the claimant and will be freely transferable.

(5) Where pursuant to paragraph (1) of this article security has been provided, the person providing such security may at any time apply to the Court to have that security reduced, modified or cancelled.

Article 5
Right of rearrest and multiple arrest

Alternative 1:

(1) Where in any State a ship has already been arrested and released or security in respect of that ship has already been given to secure a maritime claim, that ship shall not thereafter be rearrested or arrested in respect of the same maritime claim unless:

(a) the nature or amount of the security already obtained in respect of the same claim is inadequate, provided that the aggregate amount of security may not exceed the value of the ship; or

(b) the person who has already given the security is not, or is unlikely to be, able to fulfil some or all of his obligations[; or

(c) the ship arrested or the security previously given was released either:

(i) upon the application or with the consent of the claimant acting on reasonable grounds, or

(ii) because the claimant could not by taking reasonable steps prevent the release].

(2) Any other ship which would otherwise be subject to arrest in respect of the same maritime claim shall not be arrested unless:

(a) the nature or amount of the security already obtained in respect of the same claim is inadequate; or

(b) the provisions of paragraph (1) (b) or (c) of this article are applicable.

(3) "Release" for the purpose of this article shall not include any unlawful release or escape from arrest.

Alternative 2:

[(1) Where in any State a ship has already been arrested and released or security in respect of that ship has already been given to secure a maritime claim, that ship shall not thereafter be rearrested or arrested in respect of the same maritime claim, unless there has been fraud or material misrepresentation in connection with the release or the posting of the security.

(2) Any other ship which would otherwise be subject to arrest in respect of the same maritime claim shall not be arrested unless the nature or the amount of the security already obtained in respect of the same claim is inadequate.

(3) "Release" for the purpose of this article shall not include any unlawful release or escape from arrest.][4]

Article 6
Protection of owners and demise charterers of arrested ships

(1) The court may as a condition of the arrest of a ship, or of permitting an arrest already effected to be maintained, impose upon the claimant who seeks to arrest or who has procured the arrest of the ship the obligation to provide security of a kind and for an amount, and upon such terms, as may be determined by that Court for any loss which may be incurred by the defendant as a result of the arrest, and for which the claimant may be found liable, including but not restricted to such loss or damage as may be incurred by that defendant in consequence of:

(a) the arrest having been wrongful or unjustified; or

(b) excessive security having been demanded and obtained.

(2) The Courts of the State in which an arrest has been effected shall have jurisdiction to determine the extent of the liability, if any, of the claimant for loss or damage caused by the arrest of a ship, including but not restricted to such loss or damage as may be caused in consequence of:

(a) the arrest having been wrongful or unjustified, or

(b) excessive security having been demanded and obtained.

(3) The liability, if any, of the claimant in accordance with paragraph (2) of this article shall be determined by application of the law of the State where the arrest was effected.

---

[4] Proposal by delegations of the United States of America, Liberia and the Republic of Korea.

(4) If a Court in another State or an arbitral tribunal is to determine the merits of the case in accordance with the provisions of article 7, then proceedings relating to the liability of the claimant in accordance with paragraph (2) of this article may be stayed pending that decision.

(5) Where pursuant to paragraph (1) of this article security has been provided, the person providing such security may at any time apply to the Court to have that security reduced, modified or cancelled.

Article 7
Jurisdiction on the merits of the case

(1) The Courts of the State in which an arrest has been effected or security given to prevent arrest or obtain the release of the ship shall have jurisdiction to determine the case upon its merits, unless the Parties validly agree or have agreed to submit the dispute to a Court of another State which accepts jurisdiction, or to arbitration.

(2) Notwithstanding the provisions of paragraph (1) of this article, the Courts of the State in which an arrest has been effected, or security given to prevent arrest or obtain the release of the ship, may refuse to exercise that jurisdiction where that refusal is permitted by the law of that State and a Court of another State accepts jurisdiction.

(3) In cases where a Court of the State where an arrest has been effected or security given to prevent arrest or obtain the release of the ship:

(a) does not have jurisdiction to determine the case upon its merits; or

(b) has refused to exercise jurisdiction in accordance with the provisions of paragraph (2) of this article,

such Court may, and upon request shall, order a period of time within which the claimant shall bring proceedings before a competent Court or arbitral tribunal.

(4) If proceedings are not brought within the period of time ordered in accordance with paragraph (3) of this article then the ship arrested or the security given shall, upon request, be ordered released.

(5) If proceedings are brought within the period of time ordered in accordance with paragraph (3) of this article, or if proceedings before a competent Court in another State are brought in the absence of any such order, then unless such proceedings do not satisfy general requirements in respect of due process of law, any final decision resulting therefrom shall be recognized and given effect with respect to the arrested ship or to the security given in order to prevent its arrest or obtain its release.

(6) Nothing contained in the provisions of paragraph (5) of this article shall restrict any further effect given to a foreign judgement or arbitral award under the law of the State where the arrest of the ship was made or security given to prevent its arrest or obtain its release.

Article 8
Application

(1) This Convention shall apply to any seagoing ship, whether or not that ship is flying the flag of a State Party.

(2) The Convention shall not apply to ships owned or operated by a State and used only on Government non-commercial service. (See 1993 MLM Convention, article 13 (2)).

(3) Nothing in this Convention shall be construed as creating a maritime lien.

(4) This Convention does not affect any rights or powers vested in any Government or its departments, or in any public authority, or in any dock or harbour authority, under any international convention or under any domestic law or regulation, to detain or otherwise prevent from sailing any ship within their jurisdiction.

(5) This Convention shall not affect the power of any State or Court to make orders affecting the totality of a debtor's assets.

(6) Nothing in this Convention shall affect the application of international conventions providing for limitation of liability, or domestic law giving effect thereto, in the State where an arrest is effected.

(7) Nothing in this Convention shall modify or affect the rules of law in force in the States Parties relating to the arrest of any ship physically within the jurisdiction of the State of its flag procured by a person who has his habitual residence or principal place of business in that State, or by any other person who has acquired a claim from such person by subrogation, assignment or otherwise.

Article 9
Reservations

A State may, when signing, ratifying, accepting or acceding to this Convention, reserve the right to refrain from applying the Convention to ships not flying the flag of a State Party.

6. REPORT OF THE JOINT UNCTAD/IMO INTERGOVERNMENTAL GROUP OF EXPERTS ON MARITIME LIENS AND MORTGAGES AND RELATED SUBJECTS ON ITS 8TH SESSION, LONDON, 9-10 OCTOBER 1995

Doc. no.: TD/B/CN.4/GE.2/10 5 December 1995

The attached report (JIGE(VIII)/7) */ has been prepared on the eighth session of the Joint UNCTAD/IMO Intergovernmental Group of Experts on Maritime Liens and Mortgages and Related Subjects.

CONTENTS

Annexes

---

*/ Also circulated by IMO under the symbol LEG/MLM/37.

INTRODUCTION

1 The Joint Intergovernmental Group of Experts on Maritime Liens and Mortgages and Related Subjects (JIGE), established by the International Maritime Organization (IMO) and the United Nations Conference on Trade and Development (UNCTAD) held its eighth session at the International Maritime Organization, London, from 9 to 10 October 1995.

2 During the session, 2 plenary meetings and 4 informal meetings of the Sessional Group of the Whole were held. The present report reflects the proceedings at those meetings.

Opening statements

3 The Secretary-General of IMO, speaking on behalf of IMO and the Secretary-General of UNCTAD, welcomed the participants to the meeting and commended as a remarkable achievement the fact that at its last session in Geneva the JIGE had been able to agree to work on a basic text of a new Arrest Convention.

4 He also highlighted the importance of the co-operation between IMO and UNCTAD reflected in the field of maritime liens and mortgages. He stated that this co-operation should be seen as a demonstration of the strong commitment of both UN bodies towards the achievement of unification of international maritime law with regard to matters of paramount importance for the shipping community. This commitment would be truly successful if the treaties prepared by the JIGE became widely accepted.

5 In this regard, the Secretary-General stated that the conditions for the entry into force of the 1993 International Convention on Maritime Liens and Mortgages should be met as soon as possible. Governmental action in this regard would decisively complement work by the JIGE of a new Arrest Convention.

Chapter I

CONSIDERATION OF THE POSSIBLE REVIEW OF THE INTERNATIONAL CONVENTION FOR THE UNIFICATION OF CERTAIN RULES RELATING TO THE ARREST OF SEA-GOING SHIPS, 1952

(Agenda item 3)

6 For its consideration of this item, the Joint Intergovernmental Group of Experts had before it the following documentation:

"Consideration of the possible review of the International Convention for the Unification of Certain Rules Relating to the Arrest of Sea-going Ships, 1952" - Note by the Secretariats of IMO and UNCTAD (LEG/MLM/32-JIGE(VIII)/2-TD/B/CN.4/GE.2/5);

Submission by the International Association of Ports and Harbors (IAPH) (LEG/MLM/33-JIGE(VIII)/3-TD/B/CN.4/GE.2/6);

Submission by the International Chamber of Shipping (ICS) (LEG/MLM/34-JIGE(VIII)/4-TD/B/CN.4/GE.2/7);

Submission by the International Ship Suppliers Association (ISSA) (LEG/MLM/35-JIGE(VIII)/5-TD/B/CN.4/GE.2/8);

Submission by the Institute of International Container Lessors (IICL) (LEG/MLM/36-JIGE(VIII)/6-TD/B/CN.4/GE.2/9).

Consideration of agenda item 3 in the Sessional Group of the Whole

7 At its opening plenary, the Joint Intergovernmental Group decided to establish an informal Sessional Group of the Whole to consider agenda item 3.

8 The Sessional Group decided to adopt as a basic text for its deliberations a revised set of draft articles for a convention on arrest of ships prepared by the Secretariats of IMO and UNCTAD (JIGE VIII/2). The Group introduced several amendments to the draft and decided to revert to its consideration at its next session. A small working group was set up with the task of ensuring that all claims with maritime liens status under the 1993 MLM Convention are included in the list of maritime claims.

9 At its last meeting, on 12 October 1995, the Sessional Group of the Whole adopted its draft report to the plenary (JIGE (VIII)/WP.1).

Action by the Joint Intergovernmental Group of Experts

10 At its closing plenary, on 12 October 1995, the Joint Intergovernmental Group of Experts approved the report of the Sessional Group of the Whole and decided to annex the Sessional Group's report to its own report (see annex I below).

Chapter II

ORGANIZATIONAL MATTERS

A. Opening of the session

11 The eighth session of the Joint Intergovernmental Group of Experts was opened on 9 October 1995 by Mr. G.G. Ivanov (Russian Federation), Chairman of the Group at its seventh session.

B. Election of officers

(Agenda item 1)

12 At its opening plenary meeting, on 9 October 1995, the Joint Intergovernmental Group of Experts agreed that the officers for its eighth session would be the same as for its seventh session. The officers for the eighth session were thus as follows:

Chairman	Mr. G.G. Ivanov	(Russian Federation)
Vice-Chairmen:	Mr. I. Melo Ruiz	(Mexico)
	Mr. K.-J. Gombrii	(Norway)
Vice-Chairman cum-Rapporteur:	Mr. Zengjie Zhu	(China)

C. Adoption of the agenda and organization of work

(Agenda item 2)

13 At its opening plenary meeting, on 9 October 1995, the Joint Intergovernmental Group of Experts adopted its provisional agenda, as contained in document JIGE(VIII)/1-TD/B/CN.4/GE.2/4-LEG/MLM/31. The agenda for its eighth session was thus as follows:

1. Election of officers

2. Adoption of the agenda and organization of work

3. Consideration of the possible review of the International Convention for the Unification of Certain Rules Relating to the Arrest of Sea-going Ships, 1952

4. Provisional agenda and date of the ninth session of the Joint Intergovernmental Group of Experts

5. Other business

6. Adoption of the report of the Joint Intergovernmental Group on its eighth session.

14 Also at its opening plenary, the Joint Intergovernmental Group decided to establish an informal Sessional Group of the Whole to consider agenda item 3.

D. Membership and attendance

15 The following States Members of IMO and UNCTAD participated in the session: Argentina, Australia, Brazil, Canada, Chile, China, Cuba, Cyprus, the Democratic People's Republic of Korea, Denmark, Ecuador, Egypt, Finland, France, Gabon, Germany, Greece, Indonesia, Israel, Italy, Japan, Latvia, Liberia, Madagascar, Malaysia, Mauritius, Mexico, Morocco, Namibia, the Netherlands, Nigeria, Norway, Panama, Peru, Poland, the Republic of Korea, the Russian Federation, Saudi Arabia, Singapore, Solomon Islands, South Africa, Spain, Sweden, the Syrian Arab Republic, Tunisia, Ukraine, the United Kingdom of Great Britain and Northern Ireland, the United States of America, Vanuatu and Venezuela.

16 An Associate Member of IMO, Hong Kong, participated in the session.

17 A representative of the INTERNATIONAL LABOUR ORGANIZATION participated in the session.

18 Observers from the following intergovernmental organizations participated in the session:

COMMISSION OF THE EUROPEAN COMMUNITY
LEAGUE OF ARAB STATES

19 The following non-governmental organizations were represented at the session:

INTERNATIONAL CHAMBER OF SHIPPING
INTERNATIONAL CONFEDERATION OF FREE TRADE UNIONS
INTERNATIONAL MARITIME COMMITTEE
INTERNATIONAL ASSOCIATION OF PORTS AND HARBORS
INTERNATIONAL ASSOCIATION OF CLASSIFICATION SOCIETIES
INTERNATIONAL CARGO HANDLING CO-ORDINATION ASSOCIATION
OIL COMPANIES INTERNATIONAL MARINE FORUM
INSTITUTE OF INTERNATIONAL CONTAINER LESSORS
INTERNATIONAL ASSOCIATION OF DRY CARGO SHIPOWNERS
INTERNATIONAL UNION FOR CONSERVATION OF NATURE AND NATURAL RESOURCES
INTERNATIONAL SHIP SUPPLIERS ASSOCIATION
IBEROAMERICAN INSTITUTE OF MARITIME LAW
THE FEDERATION OF NATIONAL ASSOCIATIONS OF SHIP BROKERS AND AGENTS

E. Provisional agenda and date of the ninth session of the Joint Intergovernmental Group of Experts

(Agenda item 4)

20 At its closing plenary, on 12 October 1995, the Joint Intergovernmental Group of Experts was informed that its ninth session, which would take place in Geneva, would be held from 2 to 6 December 1996. The provisional agenda will be submitted for its consideration and approval at the ninth session.

F. Adoption of the report of the Joint Intergovernmental Group on its eighth session

(Agenda item 6)

21 At its closing session, on 12 October 1995, the Joint Intergovernmental Group of Experts adopted its draft report (JIGE (VIII)/WP.1) and authorized the Secretariat to complete the final text in order to reflect the proceedings of the closing plenary.

Annex I

REPORT ON THE WORK OF THE SESSIONAL GROUP OF THE JOINT UNCTAD/IMO INTERGOVERNMENTAL GROUP OF EXPERTS ON MARITIME LIENS AND MORTGAGES AND RELATED SUBJECTS AT ITS EIGHTH SESSION

Item 3 Consideration of the possible review of the International Convention for the Unification of Certain Rules Relating to the Arrest of Sea-going Ships, 1952

1 The Sessional Group discussed extensively whether the 1952 Convention or the draft articles for a new convention for arrest of ships prepared by the Secretariat should be considered as the basic text for its deliberations.

2 Some delegations favoured using the 1952 Arrest Convention as the basic text. In their opinion it provided legal certainty regarding the conditions for arrest of ships. This was particularly important in connection with the definition of maritime claims to be secured by arrest. In their view the closed list system regulated in the 1952 Convention ensured that procedures of arrest were limited to claims properly defined. The alternative of an open list, such as the one established by the draft articles prepared by the Secretariat on the basis of the CMI Lisbon text, would introduce uncertainty and could become the source of disputes as to whether a specific maritime claim could be subject to arrest. Moreover, it was stated that the reference to national law in article 3, paragraph 3, and article 6 of the draft, would not contribute to any further unification. The view was also expressed that in establishing a list of claims giving right to arrest, an equitable balance between the interest of the major and the small creditors should be maintained.

3 These delegations were of the view that in principle, the scope of revision of the 1952 Convention should be restricted to the introduction of amendments consequential upon the adoption of the 1993 International Convention on Maritime Liens and Mortgages and minor adjustments to take account of other developments since the adoption of the 1952 Convention. The view was expressed that, in the light of the 1993 MLM Convention, no changes to the 1952 Arrest Convention were necessary. If, however, other changes were to be considered necessary, they should be kept to a minimum. Bearing in mind the wide international acceptance of the 1952 Convention, it was essential not to go too far in its revision so as to avoid undermining the unification achieved through the Convention.

4 The vast majority of delegations, however, were in favour of using the draft articles prepared by the Secretariat at the request by the Group at its VIIth session as the basis for its further deliberations.

In their opinion, the considerations in connection with the possible up-dating of the 1952 Arrest Convention in the light of the 1993 Convention on Maritime Liens and Mortgages provided an excellent opportunity to undertake a general review of the 1952 Convention. This had been the background for the request by the 1993 Diplomatic Conference to reconvene the JIGE. A general review would enable the Group to take stock of many years of international experience of application of the 1952 Convention to repair some deficiencies in the present system and to consider some further amendments which had prevented certain countries from becoming parties to the Convention. This could be done without deviating from the basic principles established by the 1952 Convention.

5 In response to those advocating a closed list it was suggested that an open list was to be preferred; it allowed claims to be secured which, while not specifically addressed in the open list, were beyond doubt of a maritime nature such as claims for unpaid insurance premiums, agency fees and stevedoring charges. An open list would furthermore provide flexibility for future developments in this regard.

6 In the view of one delegation an open list would provide uncertainty rather than flexibility for future developments.

7 After further discussions the Group decided to use the draft articles prepared by the Secretariat as the basis for its deliberations.

8 Several comments were made in connection with the format of the instrument to be finally agreed upon by the Group. The alternative for a new convention rather than a protocol amending the present 1952 Convention was considered advisable, bearing in mind the comprehensive character of the review and the procedures to be accomplished for adoption of the new treaty by a Conference convened by the United Nations and IMO. The draft articles prepared by the Secretariat would provide the substantive contents of the new treaty and the Preamble and Final Clauses would be prepared as appropriate, bearing in mind the usual procedures involved in treaty making preparatory work.

9 Several delegations made reference to discrepancies between the English text of the draft articles and texts in other languages. These delegations were invited to submit their comments or proposals in writing to the Secretariat, in order to ensure that the texts in all languages reflected the same substantive meaning.

10 Bearing in mind its preliminary discussions and the decisions adopted at its last session, the Group started to consider the revised set of draft articles contained in document JIGE(VIII)/2.

Article 1 Definitions

Paragraph 1

11 The Sessional Group considered the proposal put forward by the International Chamber of Shipping (ICS) to delete the words **"such as"** in the chapeau of article I in order to avoid creating an open-ended list of maritime claims so as to keep arrest as an exceptional measure to be used only as a last resort to secure a maritime claim. Some delegations which favoured the approach adopted by the 1952 Convention supported this proposal. It was argued that having a closed list of maritime claims provided certainty as to the exercise of right of arrest. In that connection concern was expressed that the words **"such as"** would be interpreted differently in various jurisdictions. Most delegations, however, preferred an open-ended list of maritime claims so as to retain flexibility and avoid excluding genuine maritime claims from having right of arrest. It was at the same time noted that the present draft text, although open-ended, restricted the power of arrest to types of claims similar to those listed within article 1(1). In response, the observer for the ICS pointed out that although in common law countries the principle of ***ejusdem generis*** would probably apply, this would possibly not be the case in all civil law countries.

12 The observer for the International Union for Conservation of Nature and Natural Resources (IUCN) drew attention to the fact that environmental claims, such as costs for the restoration of the environment, did not fit in the categories of listed maritime claims. His delegation would therefore prefer to retain the open-ended approach in the present draft.

13 In view of the above, the Sessional Committee decided to retain the words **"such as"** in the chapeau.

14 One delegation questioned the purpose of using the words **"concerning or arising out of"** and **"out of"** in the chapeau. The observer for the CMI explained that the wording was mistakenly abbreviated and the intention was to express the same thing in the second and third lines of the chapeau by repeating **"concerning or arising out of"**. The question was considered to be a matter of drafting. Some delegations questioned whether the use of the words **"salvage operations"** in the chapeau and **"salvage operations and any salvage agreement"** in sub-paragraph (c) was repetitive.

15 The majority of delegations agreed that the claims giving rise to a maritime lien under the 1993 Convention on Maritime Liens and Mortgages should be included among the claims listed in article 1(1). It was, however, pointed out that merely aligning terminology with the 1993 MLM Convention could result in creating contradiction between various sub-paragraphs of article 1(1), as was the case with sub-paragraphs (a) and (h). It was therefore suggested that the words **"other than loss of or damage to cargo"** in sub-paragraph (a) be deleted. Other delegations proposed the deletion of the word **"physical"** at the beginning of sub-paragraph (a) so as to include also economic and consequential loss. Some delegations, however, preferred to retain the word **"physical"**. One delegation doubted whether it was necessary to have any link at all between the MLM and Arrest Conventions. In response it was explained that linkage between the two Conventions was necessary to the extent that all maritime liens covered in the MLM Convention needed to be included in the list of maritime claims in the Arrest Convention. In other words, linkage referred to the wording and not to the Conventions. The two Conventions should remain entirely independent.

16 One delegation proposed the inclusion of a reference to **"in direct connection with the operation of the ship"** in sub-paragraph (d) in the same way as in sub-paragraph (b), so as to exclude claims not related to the operation of the vessel.

17 The observer for the Institute of International Container Lessors (IICL) favoured the present text of sub-paragraph (1) provided that it was not taken to mean that containers had to be supplied to a particular ship.

18 Some delegations proposed the establishment of a small informal working group entrusted with the task of ensuring that all claims with maritime liens status under the 1993 MLM Convention are included in the list of maritime claims without creating duplication or contradiction and also to ensure that there was no conflict between various sub-paragraphs of article 1(1). One delegation stated that while sub-paragraphs (b) and (o) could be retained as they are presently drafted, other subparagraphs such as (a) and (h), as well as (k) and (n), need to be adjusted.

19 The Sessional Group agreed to set up an informal working group with the task of carrying out the work.

20 At the end of the session the Chairman of the working group reported to the Sessional Group that the working group had met twice and considered various proposals. The group had prepared new wording for sub-paragraphs (a), (b) and (d) which will be submitted to the plenary session. The working group could not conclude its work and would be prepared to continue consideration of the matter at the next session of the JIGE. The report of the Chairman is attached to the report of the Joint Intergovernmental Group at annex II.

Paragraph 2

21 Several comments and proposals were made in connection with the definition of arrest. It was noted that the definition in the basic text substantially differed from the one contained in the 1952 Convention in that the latter did not include the requirement that the ship is physically within the jurisdiction of the State where the order of arrest has been made. In this regard, it was explained that the purpose of the inclusion of this requirement was to distinguish physical arrest from the so-called documentary arrest, which refers to the registration of arrest in the ships' registry. Some delegations were

of the opinion that this restriction should be considered in connection with the recognition of judicial orders; other delegations suggested that this provision should be placed in article 8; otherwise the requirement of the physical presence of the ship in the definition of arrest would affect the implementation of several articles of the Convention. These delegations favoured the inclusion of the definition of the 1952 Convention instead of the one in the basic text.

22 One delegation suggested that if the definition in the 1952 Convention were to attract thepreference of the Sessional Group, the second part contained in the present text should be retained. This delegation proposed that new language should be added securing that arrest can be ordered in cases where there is a real risk for the alleged claim not to be satisfied.

23 Other delegations were of the view that the physical presence of the ship in the jurisdiction of the State where the arrest order has been made should be considered as an enforcement requirement inherent in the concept of arrest. Accordingly, it should be included within the definition.

24 It was suggested that the expression **"where the order has been made"** could be replaced by **"where the arrest is effected"**. In this way, if the ship was not physically under the jurisdiction of a Court issuing an arrest order, it would nevertheless be clear that the arrest would be enforced only under the authority of the Court in the jurisdiction where the ship is physically present.

25 One delegation suggested that the term **"judgement"** be preferred to that of **"order"**, so as to make clear that the defendant would have the benefit of appearing in Court to contest the request for arrest. This view was opposed by several delegations on the grounds that circumstances of arrest frequently do not permit the delay caused by the procedures leading to a judgement. It was stated that judicial guarantees were implied by the fact that the order should be issued by a Court. Some delegations favoured the use of the expression **"judicial process"** as used in the 1952 Convention.

26 In response to comments by several delegations it was noted that the preventative character of arrest, as opposed to the seizure for the execution of a judgement, was clearly reflected in the definition of arrest. It was also noted that any reference to this preventative character specifically attached to the expression of **"arrest"** in languages other than English was a question of terminology only to be considered in connection with the texts in those languages.

27 The Group decided to revert to the definition of arrest contained in article 1, paragraph 2 of the 1952 Convention.

Paragraph 3

28 In response to a question from one delegation, it was indicated that the expression **"unincorporated associations"** intended to cover cases of companies which, although not incorporated, were considered legal entities in accordance with the national law in some countries.

Paragraph 5

29 It was noted that the main purpose of the introduction of the definition of "Court" was to indicate that arrest could only be ordered by a competent judicial authority.

30 The Group decided to revert to the consideration of this article at a later stage of its discussions.

Article 2 Powers of arrest

Paragraph 1

31 It was noted that the expression **"by or under"** the authority of a Court had been introduced to cover arrest effected by Court Officers as well as by other authorities in charge of executing a Court order of arrest. The opinion was also expressed that an arrested vessel should be released following an agreement of the parties involved, to that effect.

32 Some delegations were in favour of the formulation contained in article 4 of the 1952 Convention, which avoided the expression **"is demanded"** contained in this paragraph. It was noted that this expression reappeared in article 2 paragraph 5 but was omitted in article 6, paragraph 2 and article 7, paragraph 1, 2, and 3 of the basic draft. It was suggested that this expression might have been used to refer to situations where an application for arrest was made but not granted because security was deposited before the arrest took place.

Paragraph 2

33 A proposal was made to include the expression **"only"** after the word **"may"** (as in article 4 of the 1952 Convention). It was also suggested that the expression **"but in respect of no other claim"** could be deleted. The latter proposal was objected to by several delegations. In this connection, reference was made to the English version of article 2 of the 1952 Convention that contained the same words.

Paragraph 3

34 The Observer delegation of ICS introduced its submission that it might be impractical or dangerous to arrest a ship which **"is sailing"** and accordingly this expression should be deleted.

35 This proposal was supported by some delegations. The majority of delegations, however, were against this proposal on grounds that their national legislation as well as International Law, specifically the United Nations Convention on the Law of the Sea, enabled States to arrest a ship in connection with civil law cases as long as the ship was in their territorial jurisdiction, including the right of hot pursuit, and a valid order for the arrest could be produced.

36 One delegation cautioned against mixing private law issues such as arrest with situations clearly under the scope of public law. In this regard it was stated that the limits to the power of a Court to arrest ships were clearly established in paragraph 2 and related to the nature of the claims rather than the situation of the ship. The view was also expressed that claimants should not be encouraged to apply for an arrest at the last moment, thus creating extreme difficulties and unnecessary expense.

37 A number of comments were made regarding the proper meaning of the expression **"is sailing"**. It could be seen as offering a rather wide scope of application in that it could cover situations as different as that of a ship already unmoored and ready to sail or taken in tow inside the harbour or a ship already sailing.

Paragraph 4

38 Although the Group found that this provision was in principle acceptable, proposals were made to clarify the meaning of the expression **"for the purpose of obtaining security"** or to delete those words, since that expression was already used in article 1, paragraph 2.

Paragraph 5

39 One delegation suggested that although procedures leading to arrest should be regulated by national law, it was important that a new convention established an obligation for the claimant to notify the shipowner of the nature and amount of the claim. This proposal was not supported.

40 The observer delegation of IAPH referred to the observations made in its submission. The delegation stated that since the effective arrest of a ship could only take place in a port, the implications for ports of the arrest should be clearly addressed. Port authorities could be unable to exploit for months the space of berth in which the arrested ship is moored. They were also compelled to take measures to ensure safety and the protection of the marine environment. In order to ensure that port interests were adequately protected, a new paragraph under article 2 could be included, which would stipulate that port authorities should be involved in the proceedings leading to arrest. The new provision could also provide that the claimant would have to deposit a financial guarantee to cover for port costs.

41 Several delegations expressed their support to the need of protecting legitimate interests of ports vis-a-vis the enforcement of arrest procedures. In this regard, it was suggested that the interests of port authorities be safeguarded, particularly when the period between the arrest and judgement phases is long. It was also proposed that suitable provisions be included in article 2(5) on the procedures to be effected during the period of arrest.

42 However, most delegations stated their opposition to the proposed new paragraph. In their view reasons of expediency in the pursuance of maritime claims made unpractical the involvement of port authorities in arrest procedures. The deposit of a guarantee with the port authorities to cover for costs incurred by port authorities would mean a financial burden for the claimant in addition to any eventual advance payment required in some jurisdictions as a precondition for the enforcement of the arrest.

43 The Group decided to revert to the consideration of this article at a later stage of its discussions.

Article 3 Exercise of right of arrest

44 The Sessional Group had before it three alternative texts related to the exercise of the right of arrest irrespective of the personal liability of the owner. Alternative one permitted such an arrest for claims secured by maritime liens listed in article 4 of the MLM Convention. Alternative 2, which had been proposed by the delegation of the United States of America, also covered national liens granted under article 6 of the MLM Convention. Alternative 3, which had been proposed by the Chairman of the Informal Group on consideration of national maritime liens set up during the VIIth session, in addition to maritime liens set out in article 4 of the MLM Convention, also permitted arrest in respect of a claim secured by a maritime lien granted by the law of the state where the arrest is requested in accordance with article 6 of the MLM Convention.

45 The delegation of the United States of America emphasized that the success of both the MLM Convention and the Revised Arrest Convention depended to a large extent on resolution of this matter. In its view the difficulty arose because the MLM Convention did not specifically address the choice of law rule to be applied in deciding the effect to be given to national maritime liens. In the view of this delegation alternative 2 was the only alternative which fully implemented the compromise adopted regarding article 6 of the MLM Convention which provided shorter life spans for national maritime liens especially following the sale of a vessel. If such liens were not recognised internationally by State Parties to the Arrest Convention, then article 6 of the MLM Convention would be rendered meaningless.

46 Its delegation offered as a possible compromise another alternative based on alternative 3 to read as follows:

> **"Article 3(1)**
>
> **(a) ... (no change from Alternative 1);**
> **(b) the claim is secured by a maritime lien recognized by the law of the State where the arrest is requested;**
> **(b) - (d) ... (reordered as (c) - (e) with no change)".**

47 It was stated that the proposal did not impose any obligation on States to recognize maritime liens beyond what was permitted by their domestic law. It was left to the applicable law in the jurisdiction where the arrest is requested to determine if a maritime lien existed. Furthermore, reference to article 6 of the MLM Convention had been removed, because it was felt that the prospective arrest convention should stand on its own.

48 Some delegations considered that the proposal contained positive elements but needed further examination at the next session. Some other delegations felt that alternative 2 as referred to by the delegation of the United States of America was contrary to the compromise adopted by article 6 of the MLM Convention. As compared to alternative 2, the proposal now introduced by the United States of

America was considered to be a step in the right direction. In keeping with the said compromise, the proposal did not imply an obligation on a State Party to the MLM Convention to recognise national maritime liens and would not place an obligation to do so on a State Party to the Revised Arrest Convention. However, a choice of law rule in the proposed form would lead to forum shopping and thus defy the object of the MLM Convention.

49 Many delegations favoured the text of alternative 1, but expressed their readiness to consider the other alternatives to see if they could form the basis for a compromise. One delegation which felt that the problem was caused by having an open-ended list of maritime claims in article 1 preferred to have a closed list of maritime claims in article 1 and keep flexibility in article 3. In the view of this delegation there were problems also with regard to the structure of article 3, and noted, for instance, that the key provision was given only in paragraph (1)(d)(i).

50 One delegation stated that the sole purpose of article 3 should be to supplement other provisions by allowing arrest of any ship for claims secured by a maritime lien if it was not owned by the person liable. This delegation proposed the following text for article 3: **"Arrest is also permissible of any ship for the purpose of enforcing a lien securing a maritime claim indicated in article 1(1)."**

51 The observer for the International Ship Suppliers Association (ISSA) expressed a view that the present text of article 3, even if accepted on the basis of any of the three alternatives in the present draft, may deprive a ship supplier of the right to arrest a ship which has not paid for supplies. Where there was no maritime lien and the supply was not to the shipowner or to the demise charterer but, for example, to a time charterer who did not own a ship, the ship supplier could not effect an arrest under article 3 of either the ship to which the supply was furnished or a sister ship. Nor did this article assist a ship supplier when the owner at the time of the supply was not the same as at the time of the arrest. This was considered a lacunae and a radical departure from the 1952 Convention.

52 The observer for the Federation of National Associations of Ship Brokers and Agents (FONASBA) stated that it would support the proposal of the ISSA if the proposal of the United States of America is not adopted.

53 The Sessional Group agreed to continue its examination of article 3 at the next session.

Article 4 Release from arrest

Paragraph (1)

54 A proposal was made to include, in paragraph 1 of article 4, other cases where the vessel can be released as in case of extinction of claim or lapse of time for commencing substantive proceeding, etc. While the proposal received some support, most delegations were cautious in establishing an exhaustive list to that effect. It was pointed out that paragraph (1) was not restrictive and covered other cases of possible release. Furthermore it would be difficult to provide an exhaustive list of cases where the vessel can be released. However, one delegation favoured adopting language which would permit release only upon payment also of custody costs.

55 The observer for the International Chamber of Shipping (ICS) expressed concern regarding the use of the term **"satisfactory form"** which did not exist in the 1952 Arrest Convention. It was explained that the words had been added so as to permit the court which decides on release to decide also on the satisfactory form of security.

56 In view of the above the Sessional Group agreed to retain the text of article 4(1) as presently drafted.

Paragraph (2)

57 One delegation proposed to delete the words **"not exceeding the value of the ship"** from paragraph (2). It was argued that, as the security was fixed on the basis of the amount of the claim, arrest could not be limited to the value of the ship. Furthermore, the words did not exist in the 1952 Convention. Alternatively, this delegation proposed to add after **"thereof"** a semicolon and to replace the words in question by the words **"if the arrest is limited to the ship, the security shall not exceed the value of the ship."**

58 The proposal received some support, but the majority of delegations were in favour of retaining the text as drafted. It was pointed out that since the security was a substitute for the ship, it could not exceed the value of the ship. It was further explained that the arrest under the Convention was for a maritime claim on the ship, therefore security had to be limited to the value of the ship.

59 The Sessional Group, therefore, agreed to keep the present text of article 4(2).

60 The observer for the Iberoamerican Institute of Maritime Law (IIDM) questioned whether the term **"In the absence of agreement between the parties"** was intended as a pre-condition for a recourse to the court. It was explained that there was no such intention and the paragraph could be reworded so as to avoid any ambiguity, for example by using the words **"unless parties have agreed."**

Paragraph 3

61 Two delegations questioned whether the text of this paragraph could not be misinterpreted as implying acknowledgment of the shipowner's liability. In response, it was noted that the deposit of a security was clearly related to the characterization of arrest as a conservatory measure. This conservatory character meant that the deposit of a security to obtain release from arrest could not be interpreted as an acknowledgment of liability or as prejudicing any consideration related to the shipowner's liability in connection with the claim which led to the arrest of the ship.

Paragraph 4

62 It was noted that the expression **"unjust"** in sub-paragraph (a) was not appropriate treaty language due to its imprecise meaning. It was also suggested that the whole reference to **"exceptional cases"** in which it would be unjust to release the security should be deleted.

63 One delegation suggested that an additional provision should be added to the effect of relating the upper limits of the limitation fund established to cover for the liability of the shipowner to the limits of the security to be requested to release the ship.

Paragraph 5

64 No comments were made in connection with this paragraph.

65 The Group decided to revert to this article at a later stage.

Closure

66 The Group decided to continue with the consideration of the draft articles at its next session.

67 The Chairman urged delegations wishing to introduce amendments to the draft articles to submit their written proposals well in advance of the next session of the Group and not later than 1 June 1996 to enable these proposals to be circulated to other delegations prior to that session.

***

ANNEX II

REPORT OF THE CHAIRMAN OF THE INFORMAL WORKING GROUP ON ARTICLE 1

Pursuant to the direction of the Joint Intergovernmental Group of Experts, an informal Working Group convened to consider issues relating to the definition of "maritime claim" under article 1, definitions of the revised draft articles for a Convention on Arrest of Ships (LEG/MLM/32). The Committee directed the Group to consider the draft of paragraph 1 of article 1 and to take into account the necessity of being compatible with the provisions of the 1993 MLM Convention, bearing in mind that repetitions should be avoided.

The Working Group met from 9 to 10 October 1995. Mr. P. Calmon Filho (Brazil) was unanimously elected as Chairman. Delegations from Brazil, Canada, China, France, Germany, Greece, Italy, Liberia, Mexico, Netherlands, Norway, Poland, the Russian Federation and Spain were represented.

1 The Group considered whether to add a sub-paragraph or paragraph under article 1, containing a precise reference to the Maritime Liens and Mortgages Convention 1993, in order to make it clear that maritime claims secured by a lien under the 1993 MLM Convention would fall within the scope of article 1.

2 The Group did not reach a decision and concluded that the matter should be further discussed particularly in connection with article 3.

3 As to the wording of clause 1, the Group took into consideration the various proposals presented in the plenary and agreed, in principle, with the following:

4 Chapeau: To add "concerning or arising" after "any ship, or", at the 2nd line, and to delete what comes after "on any ship" in the 3rd line. So the text reads as follows:

> "Maritime claim" means any claim concerning or arising out of the ownership, construction, possession, management, operation or trading of any ship, or concerning or arising out of a mortgage or an "hypotheque" or a registrable charge of the same nature on any ship, such as any claim in respect of:

5 Item (a): Delete "physical" from the beginning of the sentence, and what comes after "operation of the ship" in the first line, so the text reads as follows:

> "loss or damage caused by the operation of the ship;"

The question had been raised as to whether it would be sufficient to follow the 1952 Arrest Convention text, and to delete the word "loss or". It was felt that this has to be decided by the plenary.

6 Item (b): Delete "direct" in the first line. So it reads as follows:

> "loss of life or personal injury occurring, whether on land or on water, in connection with the operation of the ship;"

The Group considered that in this way the text of the sub-paragraph would be consistent with the chapeau and with the 1952 Convention, which does not have the restrictive word "direct".

7 Item (d): There was no time to conclude the discussions. At the time the meeting was adjourned it was agreed in principle (except for the final phrase) that the following wording replace the present (d) on the draft:

> "Preventive measures, the removal or attempted removal of a threat of damage or similar operations **if the aim was to mitigate a maritime claim**:

As to the last words (underlined) there was no agreement. One delegation proposed to replace "to mitigate a maritime claim", with "similar operations **in connection with the operation of the ship**."

8 The Group further agreed that this issue should be discussed further.

9 Some delegates had reservations on issues of substance and it was agreed that the participation in and the result of the work of the Working Group is without prejudice to the positions sustained by these delegations in the plenary.

FOOD AND AGRICULTURE ORGANIZATION (FAO)

DOCUMENTS REPRODUCED IN WHOLE OR IN PART:

GENERAL

COMMITTEE ON FISHERIES

DOCUMENTS NOT REPRODUCED

10.	Doc. no.:	COFI/95/1
	Date:	January 1995
	Title:	Provisional Annotated Agenda and Timetable.
11.	Doc. no.:	COFI/95/2
	Date:	November 1994
	Title:	Draft Code of Conduct for Responsible Fisheries.
12.	Doc. no.:	COFI/95/3
	Date:	January 1995
	Title:	World Fisheries: Problems and Prospects.

13. Doc. no.: COFI/95/5
Date: December 1994
Title: Fisheries Needs of Small Island Developing States.

14. Doc. no.: COFI/95/6
Date: January 1995
Title: Implementation Report 1992-94.

15. Doc. no.: COFI/95/7
Date: January 1995
Title: Priorities for Major Programme 2.2: Fisheries over the Long and Medium Term and for the 1996-97 Biennium.

16. Doc. no.: COFI/95/8
Date: December 1994
Title: FAO Follow-up to UNCED Recommendations Relevant to Fisheries and Aquaculture.

17. Doc. no.: COFI/95/10
Date: February 1995
Title: Broadening the Mandate of the FAO Commission on Plant Genetic Resources to Include Other Categories of Organisms Used for Food and Agriculture.

18. Doc. no.: COFI/95/Inf.3
Date: March 1995
Title: Statement by Dr. Jacques Diouf, Director-General of FAO to the Ministerial Session of the Twenty-First Session of the Committee on Fisheries.

19. Doc. no.: COFI/95/Inf.7
Date: January 1995
Title: Report on the United Nations Conference on Straddling Fish Stocks and Highly Migratory Fish Stocks.

20. Doc. no.: COFI/95/Inf.9
Date: January 1995
Title: Fish Utilization and Trade.

21. Doc. no.: COFI/95/Inf.10
Date: January 1995
Title: The Role of Fisheries in Food Security.

22. Doc. no.: COFI/95/Inf.11
Date: January 1995
Title: Technical Assistance Projects in Fisheries Executed by FAO During 1992-93.

24. Doc. no.: COFI/95/Inf.12
Date: February 1995
Title: Report on the Progress in Implementing the 1984 FAO World Fisheries Conference Strategy for Fisheries Management and Development.

25. Doc. no.: COFI/95/Inf.13
Date: January 1995
Title: Report of the Twentieth Session of the Committee on Fisheries (Rome, 15-19 March 1993).

26. Doc. no.: COFI/95/Inf.14
Date: January 1995
Title: Report of the Fourth Session of the COFI Sub-Committee on Fish Trade (Rome, 5-8 October 1993).

27.	Doc. no.:	COFI/95/Inf.15
	Date:	January 1995
	Title:	FAO Assistance to Small-Scale Fisheries (Extract from the Programme Evaluation Report 1992-93).

FISHERIES DEPARTMENT

29.	Doc. no.:	Fisheries Technical Paper 347
	Date:	1995
	Title:	Reference Points for Fisheries Management by J.F. Caddy and R. Mahon.
30.	Doc. no.:	Fisheries Circular No. 898, FID/C898
	Date:	December 1995
	Title:	Structure and Process of the 1993-95 United Nations Conference on Straddling Fish Stocks and Highly Migratory Fish Stocks.

1. CODE OF CONDUCT FOR RESPONSIBLE FISHERIES

1995

INTRODUCTION

Fisheries, including aquaculture, provide a vital source of food, employment, recreation, trade and economic well-being for people throughout the world, both for present and future generations and should therefore be conducted in a responsible manner. This Code sets out principles and international standards of behaviour for responsible practices with a view to ensuring the effective conservation, management and development of living aquatic resources, with due respect for the ecosystem and biodiversity. The Code recognizes the nutritional, economic, social, environmental and cultural importance of fisheries and the interests of all those concerned with the fishery sector. The Code takes into account the biological characteristics of the resources and their environment and the interests of consumers and other users. States and all those involved in fisheries are encouraged to apply the Code and give effect to it.

ARTICLE 1 - NATURE AND SCOPE OF THE CODE

1.1 This Code is voluntary. However, certain parts of it are based on relevant rules of international law, including those reflected in the United Nations Convention on the Law of the Sea of 10 December 1982[1]. The Code also contains provisions that may be or have already been given binding effect by means of other

---

1 References in this Code to the United Nations Convention on the Law of the Sea, 1982, or to other international agreements do not prejudice the position of any State with respect to signature, ratification or accession to the Convention or with respect to such other agreements.

obligatory legal instruments amongst the Parties, such as the Agreement to Promote Compliance with International Conservation and Management Measures by Fishing Vessels on the High Seas, 1993, which, according to FAO Conference resolution 15/93, paragraph 3, forms an integral part of the Code.

1.2 The Code is global in scope, and is directed toward members and non-members of FAO, fishing entities, subregional, regional and global organizations, whether governmental or non-governmental, and all persons concerned with the conservation of fishery resources and management and development of fisheries, such as fishers, those engaged in processing and marketing of fish and fishery products and other users of the aquatic environment in relation to fisheries.

1.3 The Code provides principles and standards applicable to the conservation, management and development of all fisheries. It also covers the capture, processing and trade of fish and fishery products, fishing operations, aquaculture, fisheries research and the integration of fisheries into coastal area management.

1.4 In this Code, the reference to States includes the European Community in matters within its competence, and the term fisheries applies equally to capture fisheries and aquaculture.

ARTICLE 2 - OBJECTIVES OF THE CODE

The objectives of the Code are to:

a) establish principles, in accordance with the relevant rules of international law, for responsible fishing and fisheries activities, taking into account all their relevant biological, technological, economic, social, environmental and commercial aspects;

b) establish principles and criteria for the elaboration and implementation of national policies for responsible conservation of fisheries resources and fisheries management and development;

c) serve as an instrument of reference to help States to establish or to improve the legal and institutional framework required for the exercise of responsible fisheries and in the formulation and implementation of appropriate measures;

d) provide guidance which may be used where appropriate in the formulation and implementation of international agreements and other legal instruments, both binding and voluntary;

e) facilitate and promote technical, financial and other cooperation in conservation of fisheries resources and fisheries management and development;

f) promote the contribution of fisheries to food security and food quality, giving priority to the nutritional needs of local communities;

g) promote protection of living aquatic resources and their environments and coastal areas;

h) promote the trade of fish and fishery products in conformity with relevant international rules and avoid the use of measures that constitute hidden barriers to such trade;

i) promote research on fisheries as well as on associated ecosystems and relevant environmental factors; and

j) provide standards of conduct for all persons involved in the fisheries sector.

ARTICLE 3 - RELATIONSHIP WITH OTHER INTERNATIONAL INSTRUMENTS

3.1 The Code is to be interpreted and applied in conformity with the relevant rules of international law, as reflected in the United Nations Convention on the Law of the Sea, 1982. Nothing in this Code prejudices the rights, jurisdiction and duties of States under international law as reflected in the Convention.

3.2 The Code is also to be interpreted and applied:

a) in a manner consistent with the relevant provisions of the Agreement for the Implementation of the Provisions of the United Nations Convention on the Law of the Sea of 10 December 1982 Relating to the Conservation and Management of Straddling Fish Stocks and Highly Migratory Fish Stocks;

b) in accordance with other applicable rules of international law, including the respective obligations of States pursuant to international agreements to which they are party; and

c) in the light of the 1992 Declaration of Cancun, the 1992 Rio Declaration on Environment and Development, and Agenda 21 adopted by the United Nations Conference on Environment and Development (UNCED), in particular Chapter 17 of Agenda 21, and other relevant declarations and international instruments.

ARTICLE 4 - IMPLEMENTATION, MONITORING AND UPDATING

4.1 All members and non-members of FAO, fishing entities and relevant sub-regional, regional and global organizations, whether governmental or non-governmental, and all persons concerned with the conservation, management and utilization of fisheries resources and trade in fish and fishery products should collaborate in the fulfilment and implementation of the objectives and principles contained in this Code.

4.2 FAO, in accordance with its role within the United Nations system, will monitor the application and implementation of the Code and its effects on fisheries and the Secretariat will report accordingly to the Committee on Fisheries (COFI). All States, whether members or non-members of FAO, as well as relevant international organizations, whether governmental or non-governmental should actively cooperate with FAO in this work.

4.3 FAO, through its competent bodies, may revise the Code, taking into account developments in fisheries as well as reports to COFI on the implementation of the Code.

4.4 States and international organizations, whether governmental or non-governmental, should promote the understanding of the Code among those involved in fisheries, including, where practicable, by the introduction of schemes which would promote voluntary acceptance of the Code and its effective application.

ARTICLE 5 - SPECIAL REQUIREMENTS OF DEVELOPING COUNTRIES

5.1 The capacity of developing countries to implement the recommendations of this Code should be duly taken into account.

5.2 In order to achieve the objectives of this Code and to support its effective implementation, countries, relevant international organizations, whether governmental or non-governmental, and financial institutions should give full recognition to the special circumstances and requirements of developing countries, including in particular the least-developed among them, and small island developing countries. States, relevant intergovernmental and non-governmental organizations and financial institutions should work for the adoption of measures to address the needs of developing countries, especially in the areas of financial and technical assistance, technology transfer, training and scientific cooperation and in enhancing their ability to develop their own fisheries as well as to participate in high seas fisheries, including access to such fisheries.

ARTICLE 6 - GENERAL PRINCIPLES

6.1 States and users of living aquatic resources should conserve aquatic ecosystems. The right to fish carries with it the obligation to do so in a responsible manner so as to ensure effective conservation and management of the living aquatic resources.

6.2 Fisheries management should promote the maintenance of the quality, diversity and availability of fishery resources in sufficient quantities for present and future generations in the context of food security, poverty alleviation and sustainable development. Management measures should not only ensure the conservation of target species but also of species belonging to the same ecosystem or associated with or dependent upon the target species.

6.3 States should prevent overfishing and excess fishing capacity and should implement management measures to ensure that fishing effort is commensurate with the productive capacity of the fishery resources and their sustainable utilization. States should take measures to rehabilitate populations as far as possible and when appropriate.

6.4 Conservation and management decisions for fisheries should be based on the best scientific evidence available, also taking into account traditional knowledge of the resources and their habitat, as well as relevant environmental, economic and social factors. States should assign priority to undertake research and data collection in order to improve scientific and technical knowledge of fisheries including their interaction with the ecosystem. In recognizing the transboundary nature of many aquatic ecosystems, States should encourage bilateral and multilateral cooperation in research, as appropriate.

6.5 States and subregional and regional fisheries management organizations should apply a precautionary approach widely to conservation, management and exploitation of living aquatic resources in order to protect them and preserve the aquatic environment, taking account of the best scientific evidence available. The absence of adequate scientific information should not be used as a reason for postponing or failing to take measures to conserve target species, associated or dependent species and non-target species and their environment.

6.6 Selective and environmentally safe fishing gear and practices should be further developed and applied, to the extent practicable, in order to maintain biodiversity and to conserve the population structure and aquatic ecosystems and protect fish quality. Where proper selective and environmentally safe fishing gear and practices exist, they should be recognized and accorded a priority in establishing conservation and management measures for fisheries. States and users of aquatic ecosystems should minimize waste, catch of non-target species, both fish and non-fish species, and impacts on associated or dependent species.

6.7 The harvesting, handling, processing and distribution of fish and fishery products should be carried out in a manner which will maintain the nutritional value, quality and safety of the products, reduce waste and minimize negative impacts on the environment.

6.8 All critical fisheries habitats in marine and fresh water ecosystems, such as wetlands, mangroves, reefs, lagoons, nursery and spawning areas, should be protected and rehabilitated as far as possible and where necessary. Particular effort should be made to protect such habitats from destruction, degradation, pollution and other significant impacts resulting from human activities that threaten the health and viability of the fishery resources.

6.9 States should ensure that their fisheries interests, including the need for conservation of the resources, are taken into account in the multiple uses of the coastal zone and are integrated into coastal area management, planning and development.

6.10 Within their respective competences and in accordance with international law, including within the framework of subregional or regional fisheries conservation and management organizations or arrangements, States should ensure compliance with and enforcement of conservation and management measures and establish effective mechanisms, as appropriate, to monitor and control the activities of fishing vessels and fishing support vessels.

6.11 States authorizing fishing and fishing support vessels to fly their flags should exercise effective control over those vessels so as to ensure the proper application of this Code. They should ensure that the activities of such vessels do not undermine the effectiveness of conservation and management measures taken in accordance with international law and adopted at the national, subregional, regional or global levels. States should also ensure that vessels flying their flags fulfil their obligations concerning the collection and provision of data relating to their fishing activities.

6.12 States should, within their respective competences and in accordance with international law, cooperate at subregional, regional and global levels through fisheries management organizations, other international agreements or other arrangements to promote conservation and management, ensure responsible fishing and ensure effective conservation and protection of living aquatic resources throughout their range of distribution, taking into account the need for compatible measures in areas within and beyond national jurisdiction.

6.13 States should, to the extent permitted by national laws and regulations, ensure that decision making processes are transparent and achieve timely solutions to urgent matters. States, in accordance with appropriate procedures, should facilitate consultation and the effective participation of industry, fishworkers, environmental and other interested organizations in decision-making with respect to the development of laws and policies related to fisheries management, development, international lending and aid.

6.14 International trade in fish and fishery products should be conducted in accordance with the principles, rights and obligations established in the World Trade Organization (WTO) Agreement and other relevant international agreements. States should ensure that their policies, programmes and practices related to trade in fish and fishery products do not result in obstacles to this trade, environmental degradation or negative social, including nutritional, impacts.

6.15 States should cooperate in order to prevent disputes. All disputes relating to fishing activities and practices should be resolved in a timely, peaceful and cooperative manner, in accordance with applicable international agreements or as may otherwise be agreed between the parties. Pending settlement of a dispute, the States concerned should make every effort to enter into provisional arrangements of a practical nature which should be without prejudice to the final outcome of any dispute settlement procedure.

6.16 States, recognising the paramount importance to fishers and fishfarmers of understanding the conservation and management of the fishery resources on which they depend, should promote awareness of responsible fisheries through education and training. They should ensure that fishers and fishfarmers are involved in the policy formulation and implementation process, also with a view to facilitating the implementation of the Code.

6.17 States should ensure that fishing facilities and equipment as well as all fisheries activities allow for safe, healthy and fair working and living conditions and meet internationally agreed standards adopted by relevant international organizations.

6.18 Recognizing the important contributions of artisanal and small-scale fisheries to employment, income and food security, States should appropriately protect the rights of fishers and fishworkers, particularly those engaged in subsistence, small-scale and artisanal fisheries, to a secure and just livelihood, as well as preferential access, where appropriate, to traditional fishing grounds and resources in the waters under their national jurisdiction.

6.19 States should consider aquaculture, including culture-based fisheries, as a means to promote diversification of income and diet. In so doing, States should ensure that resources are used responsibly and adverse impacts on the environment and on local communities are minimized.

ARTICLE 7 - FISHERIES MANAGEMENT

7.1 General

7.1.1 States and all those engaged in fisheries management should, through an appropriate policy, legal and institutional framework, adopt measures for the long-term conservation and sustainable use of fisheries resources. Conservation and management measures, whether at local, national, subregional or regional levels, should be based on the best scientific evidence available and be designed to ensure the long-term sustainability of fishery resources at levels which promote the objective of their optimum utilization and maintain their availability for present and future generations; short-term considerations should not compromise these objectives.

7.1.2 Within areas under national jurisdiction, States should seek to identify relevant domestic parties having a legitimate interest in the use and management of fisheries resources and establish arrangements for consulting them to gain their collaboration in achieving responsible fisheries.

7.1.3 For transboundary fish stocks, straddling fish stocks, highly migratory fish stocks and high seas fish stocks, where these are exploited by two or more States, the States concerned, including the relevant coastal States in the case of straddling and highly migratory stocks, should cooperate to ensure effective conservation and management of the resources. This should be achieved, where appropriate, through the establishment of a bilateral, subregional or regional fisheries organization or arrangement.

7.1.4 A subregional or regional fisheries management organization or arrangement should include representatives of States in whose jurisdictions the resources occur, as well as representatives from States which have a real interest in the fisheries or the resources outside national jurisdictions. Where a subregional or regional fisheries management organization or arrangement exists and has the competence to establish conservation and management measures, those States should cooperate by becoming a member of such organization or a participant in such arrangement, and actively participate in its work.

7.1.5 A State which is not a member of a subregional or regional fisheries management organization or is not a participant in a subregional or regional fisheries management arrangement should nevertheless cooperate, in accordance with relevant international agreements and international law, in the conservation and management of the relevant fisheries resources by giving effect to any conservation and management measures adopted by such organization or arrangement.

7.1.6 Representatives from relevant organizations, both governmental and non-governmental, concerned with fisheries should be afforded the opportunity to take part in meetings of subregional and regional fisheries management organizations and arrangements as observers or otherwise, as appropriate, in accordance with the procedures of the organization or arrangement concerned. Such representatives should be given timely access to the records and reports of such meetings, subject to the procedural rules on access to them.

7.1.7 States should establish, within their respective competences and capacities, effective mechanisms for fisheries monitoring, surveillance, control and enforcement to ensure compliance with their conservation and management measures, as well as those adopted by subregional or regional organizations or arrangements.

7.1.8 States should take measures to prevent or eliminate excess fishing capacity and should ensure that levels of fishing effort are commensurate with the sustainable use of fishery resources as a means of ensuring the effectiveness of conservation and management measures.

7.1.9 States and subregional or regional fisheries management organizations and arrangements should ensure transparency in the mechanisms for fisheries management and in the related decision-making process.

7.1.10 States and subregional or regional fisheries management organizations and arrangements should give due publicity to conservation and management measures and ensure that laws, regulations and other legal rules governing their implementation are effectively disseminated. The bases and purposes of such measures should be explained to users of the resource in order to facilitate their application and thus gain increased support in the implementation of such measures.

7.2 Management objectives

7.2.1 Recognizing that long-term sustainable use of fisheries resources is the overriding objective of conservation and management, States and subregional or regional fisheries management organizations and arrangements should, *inter alia*, adopt appropriate measures, based on the best scientific evidence available, which are designed to maintain or restore stocks at levels capable of producing maximum sustainable yield, as qualified by relevant environmental and economic factors, including the special requirements of developing countries.

7.2.2 Such measures should provide *inter alia* that:

a) excess fishing capacity is avoided and exploitation of the stocks remains economically viable;

b) the economic conditions under which fishing industries operate promote responsible fisheries;

c) the interests of fishers, including those engaged in subsistence, small-scale and artisanal fisheries, are taken into account;

d) biodiversity of aquatic habitats and ecosystems is conserved and endangered species are protected;

e) depleted stocks are allowed to recover or, where appropriate, are actively restored;

f) adverse environmental impacts on the resources from human activities are assessed and, where appropriate, corrected; and

g) pollution, waste, discards, catch by lost or abandoned gear, catch of non-target species, both fish and non-fish species, and impacts on associated or dependent species are minimized, through measures including, to the extent practicable, the development and use of selective, environmentally safe and cost-effective fishing gear and techniques.

7.2.3 States should assess the impacts of environmental factors on target stocks and species belonging to the same ecosystem or associated with or dependent upon the target stocks, and assess the relationship among the populations in the ecosystem.

7.3 Management framework and procedures

7.3.1 To be effective, fisheries management should be concerned with the whole stock unit over its entire area of distribution and take into account previously agreed management measures established and applied in the same region, all removals and the biological unity and other biological characteristics of the stock. The best scientific evidence available should be used to determine, *inter alia*, the area of distribution of the resource and the area through which it migrates during its life cycle.

7.3.2 In order to conserve and manage transboundary fish stocks, straddling fish stocks, highly migratory fish stocks and high seas fish stocks throughout their range, conservation and management measures established for such stocks in accordance with the respective competences of relevant States or, where appropriate, through subregional and regional fisheries management organizations and arrangements, should be compatible. Compatibility should be achieved in a manner consistent with the rights, competences and interests of the States concerned.

7.3.3 Long-term management objectives should be translated into management actions, formulated as a fishery management plan or other management framework.

7.3.4 States and, where appropriate, subregional or regional fisheries management organizations and arrangements should foster and promote international cooperation and coordination in all matters related to fisheries, including information gathering and exchange, fisheries research, management and development.

7.3.5 States seeking to take any action through a non-fishery organization which may affect the conservation and management measures taken by a competent subregional or regional fisheries management organization or arrangement should consult with the latter, in advance to the extent practicable, and take its views into account.

7.4 Data gathering and management advice

7.4.1 When considering the adoption of conservation and management measures, the best scientific evidence available should be taken into account in order to evaluate the current state of the fishery resources and the possible impact of the proposed measures on the resources.

7.4.2 Research in support of fishery conservation and management should be promoted, including research on the resources and on the effects of climatic, environmental and socio-economic factors. The results of such research should be disseminated to interested parties.

7.4.3 Studies should be promoted which provide an understanding of the costs, benefits and effects of alternative management options designed to rationalize fishing, in particular, options relating to excess fishing capacity and excessive levels of fishing effort.

7.4.4 States should ensure that timely, complete and reliable statistics on catch and fishing effort are collected and maintained in accordance with applicable international standards and practices and in sufficient detail to allow sound statistical analysis. Such data should be updated regularly and verified through an appropriate system. States should compile and disseminate such data in a manner consistent with any applicable confidentiality requirements.

7.4.5 In order to ensure sustainable management of fisheries and to enable social and economic objectives to be achieved, sufficient knowledge of social, economic and institutional factors should be developed through data gathering, analysis and research.

7.4.6 States should compile fishery-related and other supporting scientific data relating to fish stocks covered by subregional or regional fisheries management organizations or arrangements in an internationally agreed format and provide them in a timely manner to the organization or arrangement. In cases of stocks which occur in the jurisdiction of more than one State and for which there is no such organization or arrangement, the States concerned should agree on a mechanism for cooperation to compile and exchange such data.

7.4.7 Subregional or regional fisheries management organizations or arrangements should compile data and make them available, in a manner consistent with any applicable confidentiality requirements, in a timely manner and in an agreed format to all members of these organizations and other interested parties in accordance with agreed procedures.

7.5 Precautionary approach

7.5.1 States should apply the precautionary approach widely to conservation, manage-ment and exploitation of living aquatic resources in order to protect them and preserve the aquatic environment. The absence of adequate scientific information should not be used as a reason for postponing or failing to take conservation and management measures.

7.5.2 In implementing the precautionary approach, States should take into account, *inter alia*, uncertainties relating to the size and productivity of the stocks, reference points, stock condition in relation to such reference points, levels and distribution of fishing mortality and the impact of fishing activities, including discards, on non-target and associated or dependent species as well as environmental and socio-economic conditions.

7.5.3 States and subregional or regional fisheries management organizations and arrangements should, on the basis of the best scientific evidence available, *inter alia*, determine:

a) stock specific target reference points, and, at the same time, the action to be taken if they are exceeded; and

b) stock specific limit reference points and, at the same time, the action to be taken if they are exceeded; when a limit reference point is approached, measures should be taken to ensure that it will not be exceeded.

7.5.4 In the case of new or exploratory fisheries, States should adopt as soon as possible cautious conservation and management measures, including, *inter alia*, catch limits and effort limits. Such measures should remain in force until there are sufficient data to allow assessment of the impact of the fisheries on the long-term sustainability of the stocks, whereupon conservation and management measures based on that assessment should be implemented. The latter measures should, if appropriate, allow for the gradual development of the fisheries.

7.5.5 If a natural phenomenon has a significant adverse impact on the status of living aquatic resources, States should adopt conservation and management measures on an emergency basis to ensure that fishing activity does not exacerbate such adverse impact. States should also adopt such measures on an emergency basis where fishing activity presents a serious threat to the sustainability of such resources. Measures taken on an emergency basis should be temporary and should be based on the best scientific evidence available.

7.6 Management measures

7.6.1 States should ensure that the level of fishing permitted is commensurate with the state of fisheries resources.

7.6.2 States should adopt measures to ensure that no vessel be allowed to fish unless so authorized, in a manner consistent with international law for the high seas or in conformity with national legislation within areas of national jurisdiction.

7.6.3 Where excess fishing capacity exists, mechanisms should be established to reduce capacity to levels commensurate with the sustainable use of fisheries resources so as to ensure that fishers operate under economic conditions that promote responsible fisheries. Such mechanisms should include monitoring the capacity of fishing fleets.

7.6.4 The performance of all existing fishing gear, methods and practices should be examined and measures taken to ensure that fishing gear, methods and practices which are not consistent with responsible fishing are phased out and replaced with more acceptable alternatives. In this process, particular attention should be given to the impact of such measures on fishing communities, including their ability to exploit the resource.

7.6.5 States and fisheries management organizations and arrangements should regulate fishing in such a way as to avoid the risk of conflict among fishers using different vessels, gear and fishing methods.

7.6.6 When deciding on the use, conservation and management of fisheries resources, due recognition should be given, as appropriate, in accordance with national laws and regulations, to the traditional practices, needs and interests of indigenous people and local fishing communities which are highly dependent on fishery resources for their livelihood.

7.6.7 In the evaluation of alternative conservation and management measures, their cost-effectiveness and social impact should be considered.

7.6.8 The efficacy of conservation and management measures and their possible interactions should be kept under continuous review. Such measures should, as appropriate, be revised or abolished in the light of new information.

7.6.9 States should take appropriate measures to minimize waste, discards, catch by lost or abandoned gear, catch of non-target species, both fish and non-fish species, and negative impacts on associated or dependent species, in particular endangered species. Where appropriate, such measures may include technical measures related to fish size, mesh size or gear, discards, closed seasons and areas and zones reserved for selected fisheries, particularly artisanal fisheries. Such measures should be applied, where appropriate, to protect juveniles and spawners. States and subregional or regional fisheries management organizations and arrangements should promote, to the extent practicable, the development and use of selective, environmentally safe and cost effective gear and techniques.

7.6.10 States and subregional and regional fisheries management organizations and arrangements, in the framework of their respective competences, should introduce measures for depleted resources and those resources threatened with depletion that facilitate the sustained recovery of such stocks. They should make every effort to ensure that resources and habitats critical to the well-being of such resources which have been adversely affected by fishing or other human activities are restored.

7.7 Implementation

7.7.1 States should ensure that an effective legal and administrative framework at the local and national level, as appropriate, is established for fisheries resource conservation and fisheries management.

7.7.2 States should ensure that laws and regulations provide for sanctions applicable in respect of violations which are adequate in severity to be effective, including sanctions which allow for the refusal, withdrawal or suspension of authorizations to fish in the event of non-compliance with conservation and management measures in force.

7.7.3 States, in conformity with their national laws, should implement effective fisheries monitoring, control, surveillance and law enforcement measures including, where appropriate, observer programmes, inspection schemes and vessel monitoring systems. Such measures should be promoted and, where appropriate, implemented by subregional or regional fisheries management organizations and arrangements in accordance with procedures agreed by such organizations or arrangements.

7.7.4 States and subregional or regional fisheries management organizations and arrangements, as appropriate, should agree on the means by which the activities of such organizations and arrangements will be financed, bearing in mind, *inter alia*, the relative benefits derived from the fishery and the differing capacities of countries to provide financial and other contributions. Where appropriate, and when possible, such organizations and arrangements should aim to recover the costs of fisheries conservation, management and research.

7.7.5 States which are members of or participants in subregional or regional fisheries management organizations or arrangements should implement internationally agreed measures adopted in the framework of such organizations or arrangements and consistent with international law to deter the activities of vessels flying the flag of non-members or non-participants which engage in activities which undermine the effectiveness of conservation and management measures established by such organizations or arrangements.

7.8 Financial institutions

7.8.1 Without prejudice to relevant international agreements, States should encourage banks and financial institutions not to require, as a condition of a loan or mortgage, fishing vessels or fishing support vessels to be flagged in a jurisdiction other than that of the State of beneficial ownership where such a requirement would have the effect of increasing the likelihood of non-compliance with international conservation and management measures.

ARTICLE 8 - FISHING OPERATIONS

8.1 Duties of all States

8.1.1 States should ensure that only fishing operations allowed by them are conducted within waters under their jurisdiction and that these operations are carried out in a responsible manner.

8.1.2 States should maintain a record, updated at regular intervals, on all authorizations to fish issued by them.

8.1.3 States should maintain, in accordance with recognized international standards and practices, statistical data, updated at regular intervals, on all fishing operations allowed by them.

8.1.4 States should, in accordance with international law, within the framework of subregional or regional fisheries management organizations or arrangements, cooperate to establish systems for monitoring, control, surveillance and enforcement of applicable measures with respect to fishing operations and related activities in waters outside their national jurisdiction.

8.1.5 States should ensure that health and safety standards are adopted for everyone employed in fishing operations. Such standards should be not less than the minimum requirements of relevant international agreements on conditions of work and service.

8.1.6 States should make arrangements individually, together with other States or with the appropriate international organization to integrate fishing operations into maritime search and rescue systems.

8.1.7 States should enhance through education and training programmes the education and skills of fishers and, where appropriate, their professional qualifications. Such programmes should take into account agreed international standards and guidelines.

8.1.8 States should, as appropriate, maintain records of fishers which should, whenever possible, contain information on their service and qualifications, including certificates of competency, in accordance with their national laws.

8.1.9 States should ensure that measures applicable in respect of masters and other officers charged with an offence relating to the operation of fishing vessels should include provisions which may permit, *inter alia*, refusal, withdrawal or suspension of authorizations to serve as masters or officers of a fishing vessel.

8.1.10 States, with the assistance of relevant international organizations, should endeavour to ensure through education and training that all those engaged in fishing operations be given information on the most important provisions of this Code, as well as provisions of relevant international conventions and applicable environmental and other standards that are essential to ensure responsible fishing operations.

8.2 Flag State duties

8.2.1 Flag States should maintain records of fishing vessels entitled to fly their flag and authorized to be used for fishing and should indicate in such records details of the vessels, their ownership and authorization to fish.

8.2.2 Flag States should ensure that no fishing vessels entitled to fly their flag fish on the high seas or in waters under the jurisdiction of other States unless such vessels have been issued with a Certificate of Registry and have been authorized to fish by the competent authorities. Such vessels should carry on board the Certificate of Registry and their authorization to fish.

8.2.3 Fishing vessels authorized to fish on the high seas or in waters under the jurisdiction of a State other than the flag State, should be marked in accordance with uniform and internationally recognizable vessel marking systems such as the FAO Standard Specifications and Guidelines for Marking and Identification of Fishing Vessels.

8.2.4 Fishing gear should be marked in accordance with national legislation in order that the owner of the gear can be identified. Gear marking requirements should take into account uniform and internationally recognizable gear marking systems.

8.2.5 Flag States should ensure compliance with appropriate safety requirements for fishing vessels and fishers in accordance with international conventions, internationally agreed codes of practice and voluntary guidelines. States should adopt appropriate safety requirements for all small vessels not covered by such international conventions, codes of practice or voluntary guidelines.

8.2.6 States not party to the Agreement to Promote Compliance with International Conservation and Management Measures by Vessels Fishing in the High Seas should be encouraged to accept the Agreement and to adopt laws and regulations consistent with the provisions of the Agreement.

8.2.7 Flag States should take enforcement measures in respect of fishing vessels entitled to fly their flag which have been found by them to have contravened applicable conservation and management measures, including, where appropriate, making the contravention of such measures an offence under national legislation. Sanctions applicable in respect of violations should be adequate in severity to be effective in securing compliance and to discourage violations wherever they occur and should deprive offenders of the benefits accruing from their illegal activities. Such sanctions may, for serious violations, include provisions for the refusal, withdrawal or suspension of the authorization to fish.

8.2.8 Flag States should promote access to insurance coverage by owners and charterers of fishing vessels. Owners or charterers of fishing vessels should carry sufficient insurance cover to protect the crew of such vessels and their interests, to indemnify third parties against loss or damage and to protect their own interests.

8.2.9 Flag States should ensure that crew members are entitled to repatriation, taking account of the principles laid down in the "Repatriation of Seafarers Convention (Revised), 1987, (No.166)".

8.2.10 In the event of an accident to a fishing vessel or persons on board a fishing vessel, the flag State of the fishing vessel concerned should provide details of the accident to the State of any foreign national on board the vessel involved in the accident. Such information should also, where practicable, be communicated to the International Maritime Organization.

8.3 Port State duties

8.3.1 Port States should take, through procedures established in their national legislation, in accordance with international law, including applicable international agreements or arrangements, such measures as are necessary to achieve and to assist other States in achieving the objectives of this Code, and should make known to other States details of regulations and measures they have established for this purpose. When taking such measures a port State should not discriminate in form or in fact against the vessels of any other State.

8.3.2 Port States should provide such assistance to flag States as is appropriate, in accordance with the national laws of the port State and international law, when a fishing vessel is voluntarily in a port or at an offshore terminal of the port State and the flag State of the vessel requests the port State for assistance in respect of non-compliance with subregional, regional or global conservation and management measures or with internationally agreed minimum standards for the prevention of pollution and for safety, health and conditions of work on board fishing vessels.

8.4 Fishing operations

8.4.1 States should ensure that fishing is conducted with due regard to the safety of human life and the International Maritime Organization International Regulations for Preventing Collisions at Sea, as well as International Maritime Organization requirements relating to the organization of marine traffic, protection of the marine environment and the prevention of damage to or loss of fishing gear.

8.4.2 States should prohibit dynamiting, poisoning and other comparable destructive fishing practices.

8.4.3 States should make every effort to ensure that documentation with regard to fishing operations, retained catch of fish and non-fish species and, as regards discards, the information required for stock assessment as decided by relevant management bodies, is collected and forwarded systematically to those bodies. States should, as far as possible, establish programmes, such as observer and inspection schemes, in order to promote compliance with applicable measures.

8.4.4 States should promote the adoption of appropriate technology, taking into account economic conditions, for the best use and care of the retained catch.

8.4.5 States, with relevant groups from industry, should encourage the development and implementation of technologies and operational methods that reduce discards. The use of fishing gear and practices that lead to the discarding of catch should be discouraged and the use of fishing gear and practices that increase survival rates of escaping fish should be promoted.

8.4.6 States should cooperate to develop and apply technologies, materials and operational methods that minimize the loss of fishing gear and the ghost fishing effects of lost or abandoned fishing gear.

8.4.7 States should ensure that assessments of the implications of habitat disturbance are carried out prior to the introduction on a commercial scale of new fishing gear, methods and operations to an area.

8.4.8 Research on the environmental and social impacts of fishing gear and, in particular, on the impact of such gear on biodiversity and coastal fishing communities should be promoted.

8.5 Fishing gear selectivity

8.5.1 States should require that fishing gear, methods and practices, to the extent practicable, are sufficiently selective so as to minimize waste, discards, catch of non-target species, both fish and non-fish species, and impacts on associated or dependent species and that the intent of related regulations is not circumvented by technical devices. In this regard, fishers should cooperate in the development of selective fishing gear and methods. States should ensure that information on new developments and requirements is made available to all fishers.

8.5.2 In order to improve selectivity, States should, when drawing up their laws and regulations, take into account the range of selective fishing gear, methods and strategies available to the industry.

8.5.3 States and relevant institutions should collaborate in developing standard methodologies for research into fishing gear selectivity, fishing methods and strategies.

8.5.4 International cooperation should be encouraged with respect to research programmes for fishing gear selectivity, and fishing methods and strategies, dissemination of the results of such research programmes and the transfer of technology.

8.6 Energy optimization

8.6.1 States should promote the development of appropriate standards and guidelines which would lead to the more efficient use of energy in harvesting and post-harvest activities within the fisheries sector.

8.6.2 States should promote the development and transfer of technology in relation to energy optimization within the fisheries sector and, in particular, encourage owners, charterers and managers of fishing vessels to fit energy optimization devices to their vessels.

8.7 Protection of the aquatic environment

8.7.1 States should introduce and enforce laws and regulations based on the International Convention for the Prevention of Pollution from Ships, 1973, as modified by the Protocol of 1978 relating thereto (MARPOL 73/78).

8.7.2 Owners, charterers and managers of fishing vessels should ensure that their vessels are fitted with appropriate equipment as required by MARPOL 73/78 and should consider fitting a shipboard compactor or incinerator to relevant classes of vessels in order to treat garbage and other shipboard wastes generated during the vessel's normal service.

8.7.3 Owners, charterers and managers of fishing vessels should minimize the taking aboard of potential garbage through proper provisioning practices.

8.7.4 The crew of fishing vessels should be conversant with proper shipboard procedures in order to ensure discharges do not exceed the levels set by MARPOL 73/78. Such procedures should, as a minimum, include the disposal of oily waste and the handling and storage of shipboard garbage.

8.8 Protection of the atmosphere

8.8.1 States should adopt relevant standards and guidelines which would include provisions for the reduction of dangerous substances in exhaust gas emissions.

8.8.2 Owners, charterers and managers of fishing vessels should ensure that their vessels are fitted with equipment to reduce emissions of ozone depleting substances. The responsible crew members of fishing vessels should be conversant with the proper running and maintenance of machinery on board.

8.8.3 Competent authorities should make provision for the phasing out of the use of chlorofluorocarbons (CFCs) and transitional substances such as hydrochlorofluorocarbons (HCFCs) in the refrigeration systems of fishing vessels and should ensure that the shipbuilding industry and those engaged in the fishing industry are informed of and comply with such provisions.

8.8.4 Owners or managers of fishing vessels should take appropriate action to refit existing vessels with alternative refrigerants to CFCs and HCFCs and alternatives to Halons in fire fighting installations. Such alternatives should be used in specifications for all new fishing vessels.

8.8.5 States and owners, charterers and managers of fishing vessels as well as fishers should follow international guidelines for the disposal of CFCs, HCFCs and Halons.

8.9 Harbours and landing places for fishing vessels

8.9.1 States should take into account, *inter alia*, the following in the design and construction of harbours and landing places:

a) safe havens for fishing vessels and adequate servicing facilities for vessels, vendors and buyers are provided;

b) adequate freshwater supplies and sanitation arrangements should be provided;

c) waste disposal systems should be introduced, including for the disposal of oil, oily water and fishing gear;

d) pollution from fisheries activities and external sources should be minimized; and

e) arrangements should be made to combat the effects of erosion and siltation.

8.9.2 States should establish an institutional framework for the selection or improvement of sites for harbours for fishing vessels which allows for consultation among the authorities responsible for coastal area management.

8.10 Abandonment of structures and other materials

8.10.1 States should ensure that the standards and guidelines for the removal of redundant offshore structures issued by the International Maritime Organization are followed. States should also ensure that the competent fisheries authorities are consulted prior to decisions being made on the abandonment of structures and other materials by the relevant authorities.

8.11 Artificial reefs and fish aggregation devices

8.11.1 States, where appropriate, should develop policies for increasing stock populations and enhancing fishing opportunities through the use of artificial structures, placed with due regard to the safety of navigation, on or above the seabed or at the surface. Research into the use of such structures, including the impacts on living marine resources and the environment, should be promoted.

8.11.2 States should ensure that, when selecting the materials to be used in the creation of artificial reefs as well as when selecting the geographical location of such artificial reefs, the provisions of relevant international conventions concerning the environment and safety of navigation are observed.

8.11.3 States should, within the framework of coastal area management plans, establish management systems for artificial reefs and fish aggregation devices. Such management systems should require approval for the construction and deployment of such reefs and devices and should take into account the interests of fishers, including artisanal and subsistence fishers.

8.11.4 States should ensure that the authorities responsible for maintaining cartographic records and charts for the purpose of navigation, as well as relevant environmental authorities, are informed prior to the placement or removal of artificial reefs or fish aggregation devices.

ARTICLE 9 - AQUACULTURE DEVELOPMENT

9.1 Responsible development of aquaculture, including culture-based fisheries, in areas under national jurisdiction

9.1.1 States should establish, maintain and develop an appropriate legal and administrative framework which facilitates the development of responsible aquaculture.

9.1.2 States should promote responsible development and management of aquaculture, including an advance evaluation of the effects of aquaculture development on genetic diversity and ecosystem integrity, based on the best available scientific information.

9.1.3 States should produce and regularly update aquaculture development strategies and plans, as required, to ensure that aquaculture development is ecologically sustainable and to allow the rational use of resources shared by aquaculture and other activities.

9.1.4 States should ensure that the livelihoods of local communities, and their access to fishing grounds, are not negatively affected by aquaculture developments.

9.1.5 States should establish effective procedures specific to aquaculture to undertake appropriate environmental assessment and monitoring with the aim of minimizing adverse ecological changes and related economic and social consequences resulting from water extraction, land use, discharge of effluents, use of drugs and chemicals, and other aquaculture activities.

9.2 Responsible development of aquaculture including culture-based fisheries within transboundary aquatic ecosystems

9.2.1 States should protect transboundary aquatic ecosystems by supporting responsible aquaculture practices within their national jurisdiction and by cooperation in the promotion of sustainable aquaculture practices.

9.2.2 States should, with due respect to their neighbouring States and in accordance with international law, ensure responsible choice of species, siting and management of aquaculture activities which could affect transboundary aquatic ecosystems.

9.2.3 States should consult with their neighbouring States, as appropriate, before introducing non-indigenous species into transboundary aquatic ecosystems.

9.2.4 States should establish appropriate mechanisms, such as databases and information networks to collect, share and disseminate data related to their aquaculture activities to facilitate cooperation on planning for aquaculture development at the national, subregional, regional and global level.

9.2.5 States should cooperate in the development of appropriate mechanisms, when required, to monitor the impacts of inputs used in aquaculture.

9.3 Use of aquatic genetic resources for the purposes of aquaculture including culture-based fisheries

9.3.1 States should conserve genetic diversity and maintain integrity of aquatic communities and ecosystems by appropriate management. In particular, efforts should be undertaken to minimize the harmful effects of introducing non-native species or genetically altered stocks used for aquaculture including culture-based fisheries into waters, especially where there is a significant potential for the spread of such non-native species or genetically altered stocks into waters under the jurisdiction of other States as well as waters under the jurisdiction of the State of origin. States should, whenever possible, promote steps to minimize adverse genetic, disease and other effects of escaped farmed fish on wild stocks.

9.3.2 States should cooperate in the elaboration, adoption and implementation of international codes of practice and procedures for introductions and transfers of aquatic organisms.

9.3.3 States should, in order to minimize risks of disease transfer and other adverse effects on wild and cultured stocks, encourage adoption of appropriate practices in the genetic improvement of broodstocks, the introduction of non-native species, and in the production, sale and transport of eggs, larvae or fry, broodstock or other live materials. States should facilitate the preparation and implementation of appropriate national codes of practice and procedures to this effect.

9.3.4 States should promote the use of appropriate procedures for the selection of broodstock and the production of eggs, larvae and fry.

9.3.5 States should, where appropriate, promote research and, when feasible, the development of culture techniques for endangered species to protect, rehabilitate and enhance their stocks, taking into account the critical need to conserve genetic diversity of endangered species.

9.4 Responsible aquaculture at the production level

9.4.1 States should promote responsible aquaculture practices in support of rural communities, producer organizations and fish farmers.

9.4.2 States should promote active participation of fishfarmers and their communities in the development of responsible aquaculture management practices.

9.4.3 States should promote efforts which improve selection and use of appropriate feeds, feed additives and fertilizers, including manures.

9.4.4 States should promote effective farm and fish health management practices favouring hygienic measures and vaccines. Safe, effective and minimal use of therapeutants, hormones and drugs, antibiotics and other disease control chemicals should be ensured.

9.4.5 States should regulate the use of chemical inputs in aquaculture which are hazardous to human health and the environment.

9.4.6 States should require that the disposal of wastes such as offal, sludge, dead or diseased fish, excess veterinary drugs and other hazardous chemical inputs does not constitute a hazard to human health and the environment.

9.4.7 States should ensure the food safety of aquaculture products and promote efforts which maintain product quality and improve their value through particular care before and during harvesting and on-site processing and in storage and transport of the products.

ARTICLE 10 - INTEGRATION OF FISHERIES INTO COASTAL AREA MANAGEMENT

10.1 Institutional framework

10.1.1 States should ensure that an appropriate policy, legal and institutional framework is adopted to achieve the sustainable and integrated use of the resources, taking into account the fragility of coastal ecosystems and the finite nature of their natural resources and the needs of coastal communities.

10.1.2 In view of the multiple uses of the coastal area, States should ensure that representatives of the fisheries sector and fishing communities are consulted in the decision-making processes and involved in other activities related to coastal area management planning and development.

10.1.3 States should develop, as appropriate, institutional and legal frameworks in order to determine the possible uses of coastal resources and to govern access to them taking into account the rights of coastal fishing communities and their customary practices to the extent compatible with sustainable development.

10.1.4 States should facilitate the adoption of fisheries practices that avoid conflict among fisheries resources users and between them and other users of the coastal area.

10.1.5 States should promote the establishment of procedures and mechanisms at the appropriate administrative level to settle conflicts which arise within the fisheries sector and between fisheries resource users and other users of the coastal area.

10.2 Policy measures

10.2.1 States should promote the creation of public awareness of the need for the protection and management of coastal resources and the participation in the management process by those affected.

10.2.2 In order to assist decision-making on the allocation and use of coastal resources, States should promote the assessment of their respective value taking into account economic, social and cultural factors.

10.2.3 In setting policies for the management of coastal areas, States should take due account of the risks and uncertainties involved.

10.2.4 States, in accordance with their capacities, should establish or promote the establishment of systems to monitor the coastal environment as part of the coastal management process using physical, chemical, biological, economic and social parameters.

10.2.5 States should promote multidisciplinary research in support of coastal area management, in particular on its environmental, biological, economic, social, legal and institutional aspects.

10.3 Regional cooperation

10.3.1 States with neighbouring coastal areas should cooperate with one another to facilitate the sustainable use of coastal resources and the conservation of the environment.

10.3.2 In the case of activities that may have an adverse transboundary environmental effect on coastal areas, States should:

a) provide timely information and, if possible, prior notification to potentially affected States;

b) consult with those States as early as possible.

10.3.3 States should cooperate at the subregional and regional level in order to improve coastal area management.

10.4 Implementation

10.4.1 States should establish mechanisms for cooperation and coordination among national authorities involved in planning, development, conservation and management of coastal areas.

10.4.2 States should ensure that the authority or authorities representing the fisheries sector in the coastal management process have the appropriate technical capacities and financial resources.

ARTICLE 11 - POST-HARVEST PRACTICES AND TRADE

11.1 Responsible fish utilization

11.1.1 States should adopt appropriate measures to ensure the right of consumers to safe, wholesome and unadulterated fish and fishery products.

11.1.2 States should establish and maintain effective national safety and quality assurance systems to protect consumer health and prevent commercial fraud.

11.1.3 States should set minimum standards for safety and quality assurance and make sure that these standards are effectively applied throughout the industry. They should promote the implementation of quality standards agreed within the context of the FAO/WHO Codex Alimentarius Commission and other relevant organizations or arrangements.

11.1.4 States should cooperate to achieve harmonization, or mutual recognition, or both, of national sanitary measures and certification programmes as appropriate and explore possibilities for the establishment of mutually recognized control and certification agencies.

11.1.5 States should give due consideration to the economic and social role of the post-harvest fisheries sector when formulating national policies for the sustainable development and utilization of fishery resources.

11.1.6 States and relevant organizations should sponsor research in fish technology and quality assurance and support projects to improve post-harvest handling of fish, taking into account the economic, social, environmental and nutritional impact of such projects.

11.1.7 States, noting the existence of different production methods, should through cooperation and by facilitating the development and transfer of appropriate technologies, ensure that processing, transporting and storage methods are environmentally sound.

11.1.8 States should encourage those involved in fish processing, distribution and marketing to:

a) reduce post-harvest losses and waste;

b) improve the use of by-catch to the extent that this is consistent with responsible fisheries management practices; and

c) use the resources, especially water and energy, in particular wood, in an environmentally sound manner.

11.1.9 States should encourage the use of fish for human consumption and promote consumption of fish whenever appropriate.

11.1.10 States should cooperate in order to facilitate the production of value-added products by developing countries.

11.1.11 States should ensure that international and domestic trade in fish and fishery products accords with sound conservation and management practices through improving the identification of the origin of fish and fishery products traded.

11.1.12 States should ensure that environmental effects of post-harvest activities are considered in the development of related laws, regulations and policies without creating any market distortions.

11.2 Responsible international trade

11.2.1 The provisions of this Code should be interpreted and applied in accordance with the principles, rights and obligations established in **the World Trade Organization** (WTO) Agreement.

11.2.2 International trade in fish and fishery products should not compromise the sustainable development of fisheries and responsible utilization of living aquatic resources.

11.2.3 States should ensure that measures affecting international trade in fish and fishery products are transparent, based, when applicable, on scientific evidence, and are in accordance with internationally agreed rules.

11.2.4 Fish trade measures adopted by States to protect human or animal life or health, the interests of consumers or the environment, should not be discriminatory and should be in accordance with internationally agreed trade rules, in particular the principles, rights and obligations established in the Agreement on the Application of Sanitary and Phytosanitary Measures and the Agreement on Technical Barriers to Trade of the WTO.

11.2.5 States should further liberalize trade in fish and fishery products and eliminate barriers and distortions to trade such as duties, quotas and non-tariff barriers in accordance with the principles, rights and obligations of the WTO Agreement.

11.2.6 States should not directly or indirectly create unnecessary or hidden barriers to trade which limit the consumer's freedom of choice of supplier or that restrict market access.

11.2.7 States should not condition access to markets to access to resources. This principle does not preclude the possibility of fishing agreements between States which include provisions referring to access to resources, trade and access to markets, transfer of technology, scientific research, training and other relevant elements.

11.2.8 States should not link access to markets to the purchase of specific technology or sale of other products.

11.2.9 States should cooperate in complying with relevant international agreements regulating trade in endangered species.

11.2.10 States should develop international agreements for trade in live speci-mens where there is a risk of environmental damage in importing or exporting States.

11.2.11 States should cooperate to promote adherence to, and effective implementation of relevant international standards for trade in fish and fishery products and living aquatic resource conservation.

11.2.12 States should not undermine conservation measures for living aquatic resources in order to gain trade or investment benefits.

11.2.13 States should cooperate to develop internationally acceptable rules or standards for trade in fish and fishery products in accordance with the principles, rights, and obligations established in the WTO Agreement.

11.2.14 States should cooperate with each other and actively participate in relevant regional and multilateral fora, such as the WTO, in order to ensure equitable, non-discriminatory trade in fish and fishery products as well as wide adherence to multilaterally agreed fishery conservation measures.

11.2.15 States, aid agencies, multilateral development banks and other relevant international organizations should ensure that their policies and practices related to the promotion of international fish trade and export production do not result in environmental degradation or adversely impact the nutritional rights and needs of people for whom fish is critical to their health and well-being and for whom other comparable sources of food are not readily available or affordable.

11.3 Laws and regulations relating to fish trade

11.3.1 Laws, regulations and administrative procedures applicable to international trade in fish and fishery products should be transparent, as simple as possible, comprehensible and, when appropriate, based on scientific evidence.

11.3.2 States, in accordance with their national laws, should facilitate appropriate consultation with and participation of industry as well as environmental and consumer groups in the development and implementation of laws and regulations related to trade in fish and fishery products.

11.3.3 States should simplify their laws, regulations and administrative procedures applicable to trade in fish and fishery products without jeopardizing their effectiveness.

11.3.4 When a State introduces changes to its legal requirements affecting trade in fish and fishery products with other States, sufficient information and time should be given to allow the States and producers affected to introduce, as appropriate, the changes needed in their processes and procedures. In this connection, consultation with affected States on the time frame for implementation of the changes would be desirable. Due consideration should be given to requests from developing countries for temporary derogations from obligations.

11.3.5 States should periodically review laws and regulations applicable to international trade in fish and fishery products in order to determine whether the conditions which gave rise to their introduction continue to exist.

11.3.6 States should harmonize as far as possible the standards applicable to international trade in fish and fishery products in accordance with relevant internationally recognized provisions.

11.3.7 States should collect, disseminate and exchange timely, accurate and pertinent statistical information on international trade in fish and fishery products through relevant national institutions and international organizations.

11.3.8 States should promptly notify interested States, WTO and other appropriate international organizations on the development of and changes to laws, regulations and administrative procedures applicable to international trade in fish and fishery products.

ARTICLE 12 - FISHERIES RESEARCH

12.1 States should recognize that responsible fisheries requires the availability of a sound scientific basis to assist fisheries managers and other interested parties in making decisions. Therefore, States should ensure that appropriate research is conducted into all aspects of fisheries including biology, ecology, technology, environmental science, economics, social science, aquaculture and nutritional science. States should ensure the availability of research facilities and provide appropriate training, staffing and institution building to conduct the research, taking into account the special needs of developing countries.

12.2 States should establish an appropriate institutional framework to determine the applied research which is required and its proper use.

12.3 States should ensure that data generated by research are analyzed, that the results of such analyses are published, respecting confidentiality where appropriate, and distributed in a timely and readily understood fashion, in order that the best scientific evidence is made available as a contribution to fisheries conservation, management and development. In the absence of adequate scientific information, appropriate research should be initiated as soon as possible.

12.4 States should collect reliable and accurate data which are required to assess the status of fisheries and ecosystems, including data on bycatch, discards and waste. Where appropriate, this data should be provided, at an appropriate time and level of aggre-gation, to relevant States and subregional, regional and global fisheries organizations.

12.5 States should be able to monitor and assess the state of the stocks under their jurisdiction, including the impacts of ecosystem changes resulting from fishing pressure, pollution or habitat alteration. They should also establish the research capacity necessary to assess the effects of climate or environment change on fish stocks and aquatic ecosystems.

12.6 States should support and strengthen national research capabilities to meet acknowledged scientific standards.

12.7 States, as appropriate in cooperation with relevant international organizations, should encourage research to ensure optimum utilization of fishery resources and stimulate the research required to support national policies related to fish as food.

12.8 States should conduct research into, and monitor, human food supplies from aquatic sources and the environment from which they are taken and ensure that there is no adverse health impact on consumers. The results of such research should be made publicly available.

12.9 States should ensure that the economic, social, marketing and institutional aspects of fisheries are adequately researched and that comparable data are generated for ongoing monitoring, analysis and policy formulation.

12.10 States should carry out studies on the selectivity of fishing gear, the environmental impact of fishing gear on target species and on the behaviour of target and non-target species in relation to such fishing gear as an aid for management decisions and with a view to minimizing non-utilized catches as well as safeguarding the biodiversity of ecosystems and the aquatic habitat.

12.11 States should ensure that before the commercial introduction of new types of gear, a scientific evaluation of their impact on the fisheries and ecosystems where they will be used should be undertaken. The effects of such gear introductions should be monitored.

12.12 States should investigate and document traditional fisheries knowledge and technologies, in particular those applied to small-scale fisheries, in order to assess their application to sustainable fisheries conservation, management and development.

12.13 States should promote the use of research results as a basis for the setting of management objectives, reference points and performance criteria, as well as for ensuring adequate linkages between applied research and fisheries management.

12.14 States conducting scientific research activities in waters under the jurisdiction of another State should ensure that their vessels comply with the laws and regulations of that State and international law.

12.15 States should promote the adoption of uniform guidelines governing fisheries research conducted on the high seas.

12.16 States should, where appropriate, support the establishment of mechanisms, including, *inter alia*, the adoption of uniform guidelines, to facilitate research at the subregional or regional level and should encourage the sharing of the results of such research with other regions.

12.17 States, either directly or with the support of relevant international organizations, should develop collaborative technical and research programmes to improve understanding of the biology, environment and status of transboundary aquatic stocks.

12.18 States and relevant international organizations should promote and enhance the research capacities of developing countries, *inter alia*, in the areas of data collection and analysis, information, science and technology, human resource development and provision of research facilities, in order for them to participate effectively in the conservation, management and sustainable use of living aquatic resources.

12.19 Competent international organizations should, where appropriate, render technical and financial support to States upon request and when engaged in research investigations aimed at evaluating stocks which have been previously unfished or very lightly fished.

12.20 Relevant technical and financial international organizations should, upon request, support States in their research efforts, devoting special attention to developing countries, in particular the least developed among them and small island developing countries.

Annex 1

BACKGROUND TO THE ORIGIN AND ELABORATION OF THE CODE

1. This annex describes the process of elaboration and negotiation of the Code, which led to its submission for adoption to the Twenty-eighth Session of the FAO Conference. It has been felt useful to annex this section as a reference to the origin and the development of the Code and thus reflect the interest generated and the spirit of compromise of all the parties involved in its elaboration. It is hoped that this will contribute to the promotion of the commitment necessary for its implementation.

2. At various international fora, concern had long been expressed regarding the clear signs of over-exploitation of important fish stocks, damage to ecosystems, economic losses, and issues affecting fish trade - all of which threatened the long-term sustainability of fisheries and, in turn, harmed the contribution of fisheries to food supply. In discussing the current state and

prospects of world fisheries, the Nineteenth Session of the FAO Committee on Fisheries (COFI), held in March 1991, recommended that FAO should develop the concept of responsible fisheries and elaborate a Code of Conduct to this end.

3. Subsequently, the Government of Mexico, in collaboration wiht FAO, organized an International Conference on Responsible Fishing in Cancùn, in May 1992. The Declaration of Cancún endorsed at that Conference further developed the concept of responsible fisheries, stating that "this concept encompasses the sustainable utilization of fisheries resources in harmony with the environment; the use of capture and aquaculture practices which are not harmful to ecosystems, resources or their quality; the incorporation of added value to such products through transformation processes meeting the required sanitary standards; the conduct of commercial practices so as to provide consumers access to good quality products".

4. The Cancún Declaration was brought to the attention of the UNCED Rio Summit in June 1992, which supported the preparation of a Code of Conduct for Responsible Fisheries. The FAO Technical Consultation on High Seas Fishing, held in September 1992, further recommended the elaboration of a Code to address the issues regarding high seas fisheries.

5. The One Hundred and Second Session of the FAO Council, held in November 1992, discussed the elaboration of the Code, recommending that priority be given to high seas issues and requested that proposals for the Code be presented to the 1993 session of the Committee on Fisheries.

6. The Twentieth Session of COFI, held in March 1993, examined general principles for such a Code, including the elaboration of guidelines and endorsed a timeframe for the further elaboration of the Code. It also requested FAO to prepare, on a "fast track" basis, as part of the Code, proposals to prevent reflagging of fishing vessels which affect conservation and management measures on the high seas.

7. The further development of the Code of Conduct for Responsible Fisheries was accordingly carried out in consultation and collaboration with relevant United Nations Agencies and other international organizations including non-governmental organizations.

8. In pursuance of the instructions of the FAO Governing Bodies, the draft Code was formulated in such a way as to be consistent with the 1982 United Nations Convention on the Law of the Sea, taking into account the 1992 Declaration of Cancún, the 1992 Rio Declaration and the provisions of Agenda 21 of UNCED, the conclusions and recommendations of the 1992 FAO Technical Consultation on High Seas Fishing, the Strategy endorsed by the 1984 FAO World Conference on Fisheries Management and Development, and other relevant instruments including the outcome of the then ongoing United Nations Conference on Straddling Fish Stocks and Highly Migratory Fish Stocks which,

in August 1995, adopted an Agreement for the Implementation of the Provisions of the United Nations Convention on the Law of the Sea of 10 December 1982 Concerning Straddling Fish Stocks and Highly Migratory Fish Stocks.

9. The FAO Conference, at its Twenty-seventh Session in November 1993, adopted the Agreement to Promote Compliance with International Conservationa and Management Measures by Fishing Vessels on the High Seas and recommended that the General Principles of the Code of Conduct for Responsaible Fisheries be prepared on a "fast track" in order to orientate formulation of thematic articles. Accordingly, a draft text of the General Principles was reviewed by an informal Working Group of Government-nominated experts, which met in Rome in February 1994. A revised draft was widely circulated to all FAO Members and Associate Members as well as intergovernmental and non-governmental organizations. Comments received on the second version of the General Principles were incorporated in the draft Code together with proposals for an alternative text. This document was also the subject of informal consultation with non-governmental organizations on the occasion of the Fourth Session of the United Nations Conference on Straddling Fish Stocks and Highly Migratory Fish Stocks, held in August 1994 in New York.

10. In order to facilitate consideration of the full text of the draft Code, the Director-General proposed to the Council at its Hundred and Sixth Session in June 1994, that a Technical Consultation on the Code of Conduct for Responsible Fishing be organized, open to all FAO Members, interested non-members, intergovernmental and non-govermental organizations, in order to provide an opportunity for the widest involvement of all concerned parties at an early stage of its elaboration.

11. This Technical Consultation took place in Rome from 26 September to 5 October 1994 and a draft for the entire Code and a first draft of technical guidelines to support most of the Thematic Articles of the Code were presented. Following a thorough review of all the Articles of the complete draft Code of Conduct, an Alternative Secretariat Draft was then prepared on the basis of comments made during the discussions in plenary and specific drafting changes submitted in writing during the Consultation.

12. The Consultation was able to review also in detail an alternative draft for three of the six Thematic Articles of the Code, i.e., Article 9 "Integration of Fisheries into Coastal Area Management", Article 6 "Fisheries Management", Article 7 "Fishing Operations", except for those principles which were likely to be affected by the outcome of the ongoing UN Conference on Straddling Fish Stocks and Highly Migratory Fish Stocks. A short Administrative Report was prepared and presented to the FAO Council and to COFI.

13. The Technical Consultation proposed to the Council at its Hundred and Seventh Session, 15-24 November 1994, that the final wording of those principles dealing mainly with high seas issues be left in abeyance pending the outcome of

the UN Conference. The Council generally endorsed the proposed procedure, noting that following discussions at the next session of COFI, a final draft of the Code would be submitted to the FAO Council in June 1995 which would then decide upon the necessity for a Technical Committee to meet in parallel to that Session of the Council in order to elaborate further the detailed provisions of the Code if required.

14. Based upon the substantial comments and detailed suggestions received at the Technical Consultation, the Secretariat elaborated a revised draft of the Code of Conduct for Responsible Fisheries, which was submitted to the Twenty-first Session of the Committee on Fisheries, held from 10 to 15 March 1995.

15. The Committee on Fisheries was also informed that the UN Conference was expected to conclude its work in August 1995. It was proposed that principles left in abeyance in the draft text of the Code could then be reconciled with the language agreed upon at the UN Conference in accordance with a mechanism to be decided upon by the Committee and the Council, before submission of the complete Code for its adoptiton at the Twenty-eighth Session of the FAO Conference in October 1995.

16. The Committee was informed of the various steps the Secretariat had undertaken in preparing the draft Code of Conduct. The Committee established an open-ended Working Group in order to review the draft text of the Code. The Working Group, which met from 10 to 14 March 1995, undertook a detailed revision of the draft Code in continuation of the work carried out by the Technical Consultation. It completed and approved the text of Articles 8 to 11. In view of the time constraints, the Working Group provided directives to the Secretariat to redraft Articles 1 to 5. It was also recommended that the elements of research and cooperation as well as aquaculture be included in Article 5, General Principles, to reflect issues developed in the Thematic Articles of the Code.

17. The Committee supported the proposal endorsed by the Hundred and Seventh Session of the Council on mechanisms to finalize the Code. The final wording of those principles dealing mainly with issues concerning straddling fish stocks and highly migratory fish stocks, which formed only a small part of the Code, should be re-examined in the light of the outcome of the UN Conference. The Group also recommended that once agreement was reached on the substance, it would be necessary to harmonize legal, technical and idiomatic aspects of the Code, in order to facilitate its final approval.

18. The Report of the open-ended Working Group was presented to a Ministerial Meeting on Fisheries, held on 14 and 15 March 1995, in conjunction with the COFI Session. The Rome Consensus on World Fisheries emanating from this meeting urged that "Governments and international organizations take prompt action to complete the International Code of Conduct for Responsible

Fisheries with a view to submitting the final text to the FAO Conference in October 1995".

19. The Hundred and Eighth Session of the Council was presented with a revised version of the Code of Conduct. The Council established an open-ended Technical Committee, which held its First Session from 5 to 9 June 1995, with a broad regional representation of members and observers. A number of intergovernmental and non-governmental organizations also participated.

20. The Council was informed by the Technical Committee that it had undertaken a thorough review of Articles 1 to 5 including the Introduction. It had also examined, amended and approved Aticles 8 to 11. The Council was also informed that the Committee had started the revision of Article 6.

21. The Council approved the work carried out by the Technical Committee and endorsed its recommendation for a Second Session to be held from 25 to 29 September 1995 to complete the revision of the Code once the Secretariat had harmonized the text linguistically and juridically, taking into account the outcome of the UN Conference on Straddling Fish Stocks and Highly Migratory Fish Stocks.

22. A revised version of the Code as approved by the Open-ended Technical Committee at its First Session (5-9 June 1995) and endorsed by the One Hundred and Eighth Session of the Council was issued, both as a Conference document (C 95/20) and as a working paper for the Second Session of the Technical Committee. Elements pending agreement were clearly identified.

23. In order to facilitate the finalization of the entire Code, the Secretariat prepared the document "Secretariat Proposals for Article 6, Fisheries Management, and Article 7, Fishing Operations, of the Code of Conduct for Responsible Fisheries", taking into account the Agreement relating to the Conservation and Management of Straddling Fish Stocks and Highly Migratory Fish Stocks, adopted by the UN Conference in August 1995. The Secretariat also completed proposals for the harmonization of the text on legal and linguistic aspects and made this available to the Committee in three languages for the session (English, French and Spanish).

24. A Second Session of the Open-ended Technical Committee of the Council met from 25 to 29 September 1995, with a wide representation of regions and interested organizations. The Committee, working in a full spirit of collaboration, successfully concluded its mandate, finalizing and endorsing all Articles and the Code as a whole. The Technical Committee agreed that the negotiations of the text of the Code were finalized. An Open-ended Informal Group on Language Harmonization held an additional session and, together with the Secretariat, completed the harmonization on the basis of the text as adopted at the closing session. The Technical Committee instructed the Secretariat to already submit the finalized version as a revised Conference document to the Hundred and

Ninth Session of the Council and to the Twenty-eighth Session of the Conference for its adoption. The Council endorsed the Code of Conduct as finalized by the Technical Committee. The Secretariat was requested to prepare the required draft resolution for the Conference, including also a call on countries to ratify, as a matter of urgency, the Compliance Agreement adopted at the last session of the Conference. The Twenty-eighth Session of the Conference adopted on 31 October 1995, by consensus, the Code of Conduct for Responsible Fisheries and the respective Resolution shown in Annex 2.

2. THE ROLE OF REGIONAL FISHERY ORGANIZATIONS AND ARRANGEMENTS IN FISHERIES MANAGEMENT

Doc. no.: COFI/95/4 December 1994

I. INTRODUCTION

1. At its Eighteenth Session, the Committee on Fisheries (April 1989) discussed the functions and achievements of the FAO regional fishery bodies and their role in Technical Cooperation among Developing Countries (TCDC) and Economic Cooperation between Developing Countries (ECDC). In reviewing the terms of reference of these bodies, four groups of activities were identified as common to all of them: i.e., data collection, research and training, management and development. Evaluation of the achievements of these regional fishery bodies was recognized as a difficult task since, in spite of their basic common activities, there were many differences as regards the state of development of member countries, the importance of fisheries in the regions concerned and the length of time the bodies had been in existence.

2. The Committee expressed unanimous support for the work of these bodies which had assisted technical and economic cooperation among developing countries in many ways. It noted that most of them had held symposia and workshops at which there had been valuable exchanges of information and experience. It also noted that several bodies had also established working parties in which a wide range of technological and scientific topics had been discussed and which had helped to guide research and to promote technological improvements in many countries. The Committee recommended that the outcome of these meetings be appropriately followed up[1].

3. The present document reviews the overall achievements of the FAO regional fishery bodies and their subsidiary bodies. It gives a brief account of the recent developments in high seas fisheries and discusses the need for improved fisheries conservation and management, stressing the regional approach. It makes proposals concerning the strengthening and the future of the Commissions/Committees and their subsidiary bodies and analyzes the financial implications to the Organization and to members of these bodies arising from the proposed restructuring.

---

[1] Report of the Eighteenth Session of COFI, Rome, April 1989 (FIPL/R.416) paras. 29-44

4. The document endeavours to stimulate and assist the Committee's discussions by examining some of the major issues common to all the regional fishery bodies, the Committee's views upon which would be of value to the various regional bodies and to the Organization as they seek jointly to ensure the efficient functioning of these mechanisms for technical and economic collaboration in fisheries.

II. AN OVERVIEW OF THE FUNCTIONS AND ACHIEVEMENTS OF THE FAO REGIONAL FISHERY BODIES

5. Nine regional fishery bodies have been established by FAO with responsibilities for the conservation and management of fish resources and for fishery development (see Annex 2). These bodies cover about 50 percent of the total area of the world's oceans and all of the inland waters of Africa, Latin America, Asia and Europe. One hundred and forty Members of FAO participate in at least one of these bodies.

6. The first bodies were created over 40 years ago: IPFC (now APFIC) in 1948 and GFCM in 1949. Other bodies were gradually established: EIFAC in 1957; CARPAS (which has been inactive for a number of years) in 1961; CECAF and IOFC in 1967; CIFA in 1971; WECAFC in 1973 and COPESCAL in 1976. Most of these bodies have also established sub-regional bodies or technical committees[2].

7. As stated earlier, the groups of activities given prominence by all FAO regional fishery bodies are data collection, research and training, development and management. In reviewing the activities and assessing the achievements of these bodies, consideration must be given to several other aspects. The first is the set of problems resulting from the changes that have occurred, and are occurring, in both the internal and external conditions in which the bodies operate. A second issue arises from the disparities among the different regions, which make generalizations difficult.

8. One of the changes that has occurred has been the extension of maritime jurisdiction. While this has increased the importance of fisheries to many countries, it has had a significant effect on only one of the FAO regional bodies, i.e. CECAF. The other FAO bodies cover areas of inland waters, areas where jurisdiction has not yet been extended (GFCM), or areas where foreign fishing has had only limited significance.

9. A second type of change arises from the shift in relative importance of the different issues facing regional fishery bodies. To some extent, the shift may be a partial indicator of success on the part of the bodies. For example, most of the bodies focused a large part of their early discussions on improvements in the collection of data. This issue, though still important in some cases, is receiving relatively less attention than it did in the past and greater priority is being given to fisheries conservation and management. This change has two elements. First, there is an increasing awareness of the scarcity of fishery resources, the significance of overfishing and over-investment in fleets, and increasing severity of conflicts among different groups of fishermen. This is accompanied by a growing realization that the development of under-exploited stocks has not always been successful and does not generally provide a solution to the problems associated with the over-exploitation of inshore resources. The second element is the greater perception of the complexities and difficulties of adopting and implementing fisheries conservation and management measures. Earlier conservation and management approaches are now recognized as being over-simplified and ineffective.

---

[2] A list of acronyms used in this document is given in Annex 1.

10. Since most of the FAO regional fishery bodies were established many years ago, it is not surprising that there have been changes in the relative importance of the different issues confronting the work of these bodies. What is significant for the purposes of evaluation is whether these regional bodies have been sufficiently flexible to adjust to the changes and respond effectively to new perceptions and needs. The Fishery Committee for the Eastern Central Atlantic (CECAF) has recently revised its terms of reference. Both the Indo-Pacific Fishery Commission (IPFC), now the Asia-Pacific Fisheries Commission (APFIC) and the Indian Ocean Fishery Commission (IOFC) have embarked on a restructuring exercise which will have far reaching implications on their future and views have been expressed at several fora on the need to further strengthen the General Fisheries Council for the Mediterranean (GFCM).

11. Change has also occurred in the increased emphasis being given to the social and economic aspects of fisheries, e.g. the Committee for Inland Fisheries of Africa (CIFA), the Fishery Committee for the Eastern Central Atlantic (CECAF), the General Fisheries Council for the Mediterranean (GFCM) and the IOFC Committee for the Development and Management of Fisheries in the Southwest Indian Ocean (IOFC/SWIO). This has occurred as a result of the growing awareness that the development of the large-scale, industrial fisheries has not always resulted in net benefits to countries. Indeed, in some cases, the welfare of artisanal fishermen has been damaged by the increase in competition for scarce resources and by conflicts in gear between the large and small-scale operations.

12. Finally, in evaluating the achievements of the regional fishery bodies, it must also be recognized that their functions and the relative importance of the issues they address may differ significantly because of differences in situations and circumstances. For example, in Asian coastal States, fisheries are generally more important as sources of income, employment and nutrition than in African coastal states. In Asia, therefore, greater attention has generally been given to the sector and fishery administrations tend to be more fully developed and experienced. Differences also exist in the presence or absence of non-FAO regional fishery bodies, in the rate of economic growth and, of course, in the status of the fish stocks.

13. Optimally, the achievements of regional fishery bodies should be measured in accordance with their individual mandate and by the extent to which such bodies have contributed to an increase in the net benefits (economic, social or nutritional) received by the Members from the fishery resources. This, however, is extremely difficult to do. Although most countries have indicators of changes in gross benefits (such as increases in total catch), only a few have measures of these benefits in value terms. Even fewer countries have measures of the costs to their economies of achieving the benefits. There is, therefore, very little information on how net benefits have changed over time and even less information on the extent to which these changes have occurred in response to government actions and policies whether formulated independently or in response to advice or recommendations of regional fishery bodies.

14. The FAO regional fishery bodies have undoubtedly been of great value as mechanisms for the coordination of the Organization's activities and programmes with those of other, non-FAO bodies concerned with fisheries. Because FAO is part of the UN System and there has always been a high degree of impartiality, which allows for discussions of problems and issues that might be difficult to raise in other contexts.

15. Impediments to the work of regional fishery bodies include problems associated with insufficient attendance at meetings or attendance by persons with disparate interests who are not briefed on subject matters being discussed. This may be the result of governments not perceiving the meetings as being sufficiently relevant to their needs and interests. Experience has also shown that difficulties arise when the membership in the bodies is so broad that some members have divergent interests (e.g. Coastal States and foreign fishers) and thus the basis for cooperation is not always strong.

16. Another critical issue is that of financial resources to support, both administratively and technically, the functioning of the network of FAO regional fishery bodies and the operations of associated inter-regional and regional technical assistance programmes or projects. Increasing difficulties have been encountered in obtaining the extra-budgetary funding needed to implement the work of these technical support units, whose interactions with the relevant regional bodies have proven so effective. The reduction of available financial resources for assistance and the expressed preference by donors inter alia for discipline-orientated projects, rather than those of geographical criteria, have combined to deprive the regional bodies of this very valuable support.

III. RECENT DEVELOPMENTS IN THE MANAGEMENT OF HIGH SEAS FISHERIES

17. A number of events have recently taken place which have contributed to the strengthening of opinion on the need for more collaborative action to ensure the conservation and management of fishery resources:

(i) The Declaration of Cancún

18. The concept of responsible fisheries emerged during the Nineteenth Session of the Committee on Fisheries in 1991. The idea was taken up by the international community and in May 1992 the Government of Mexico, in close collaboration with FAO, organized the International Conference on Responsible Fishing, whose conclusions are embodied in the Declaration of Cancún. The declaration further developed the concept of responsible fisheries and called upon FAO to prepare a Code of Conduct for Responsible Fisheries.

(ii) The Rio Conference

19. The United Nations Conference on Environment and Development (UNCED), held in Rio de Janeiro, Brazil in June 1992, adopted the Rio Declaration and Agenda 21. Chapter 17 of Agenda 21 sets out a Programme of Action for Sustainable Development for the Protection of the Oceans and Coastal Areas. It points out that the management of high seas fisheries, including the adoption, monitoring and enforcement of effective conservation measures, is inadequate in many areas and some resources are over-utilized. It further notes that "there are problems of unregulated fishing, overcapitalization, excessive fleet size, vessels reflagging to escape controls, insufficiently selective gear, unreliable databases and lack of sufficient cooperation between States." States are required to "take effective action, including bilateral and multilateral cooperation, where appropriate at the sub-regional, regional and global levels, to ensure that high seas fisheries are managed in accordance with the provisions of the United Nations Convention on the Law of the Sea."[3]

(iii) The FAO Technical Consultation on High Seas Fishing

20. The FAO Technical Consultation on High Seas Fishing, which was held in Rome in September 1992, concluded that (a) management of high seas fisheries was necessary, (b) FAO should prepare a Code of Conduct for Responsible Fisheries, (c) reflagging of fishing vessels to "flag of convenience" was a matter of critical concern and one which should be addressed urgently, (d) high seas fisheries management should be, wherever possible, undertaken on a regional basis through regional and sub-regional organizations, and (e) effective monitoring, control and surveillance was an essential requirement for high seas fisheries management.

---

[3] Programme Areas of UNCED Chapter 17, Agenda 21.

(iv) The Compliance Agreement

21. The Agreement to Promote Compliance with International Conservation and Management Measures by Fishing Vessels on the High Seas, which was developed in the course of 1993, was approved unanimously by the FAO Conference at its Twenty-Seventh Session in November 1993 and circulated for acceptance on 14 February 1994. This Compliance Agreement provides for the responsibility of flag States to take measures including the authorization of fishing operations on the high seas to ensure that their flag vessels do not undermine the effectiveness of international conservation and management measures. The Agreement further provides for the establishment of a data base on fishing vessels authorized to fish on the high seas and the exchange of information on such vessels.

(v) Preparation of the International Code of Conduct for Responsible Fisheries

22. Following the call by the Declaration of Cancún for the preparation of an International Code of Conduct on Responsible Fisheries and its subsequent endorsement by the Technical Consultation on High Seas Fishing, the FAO Council in November 1992 formally authorized the preparation of the Code. Proposals regarding the content of the Code and a time-frame for its adoption and implementation were submitted to and agreed upon by the FAO Committee on Fisheries (COFI) in March 1993. The Committee recommended that the Code should have an encompassing umbrella of general principles which would provide the framework for detailed guidelines on the issues to be covered. The Code in its draft Article 5.12 states that:

> "States should, within their respective competencies and in accordance with international law, cooperate at sub-regional, regional, and global levels through fisheries management organizations, other international agreements or other arrangements to promote conservation and management and to ensure responsible fishing and effective conservation and protection of living aquatic resources throughout their range of distribution, taking into account the need for compatible and coordinated measures within and beyond national jurisdiction. Decision-making processes should be transparent and achieve timely solutions to urgent problems."

(vi) The UN Conference on Straddling Fish Stocks and Highly Migratory Fish Stocks

23. Following the Preparatory Session of the Conference in New York in April 1993, the Second Session was held in New York in July 1993. At the conclusion of this session a Negotiating Text, prepared by the Chairman, was the principal document that would form the basis for discussion and negotiation in subsequent sessions.

24. The Third Session of the Conference was convened in New York in March 1994, and the Fourth Session of the Conference in August 1994. At the end of the Third Session the Chairman issued a Revised Negotiating Text, and at the completion of the Fourth Session, although the issue of the form of the outcome of the Conference had not been agreed formally, the Chairman issued a Draft Agreement for the Implementation of the Provisions of the United Nations Convention on the Law of the Sea of 10 December 1982 Relating to the Conservation and Management of Straddling Fish Stocks and Highly Migratory Fish Stocks. The Draft Agreement is based principally on text contained in the Revised Negotiating Text and the outcome of negotiations in the early part of the Fourth Session.

25. Following the introductory clauses, the Chairman's Draft Agreement is divided into 13 parts and three annexes. These are as follows:

Part I	General Provisions
Part II	Conservation and Management of Straddling Fish Stocks and Highly Migratory Fish Stocks
Part III	Mechanisms for International Cooperation Concerning Straddling Fish Stocks and Highly Migratory Fish Stocks
Part IV	Responsibilities of the Flag State
Part V	Compliance and Enforcement
Part VI	Port State Enforcement
Part VII	Requirements of Developing States
Part VIII	Peaceful Settlement of Disputes
Part IX	Non-participants
Part X	Abuse of Rights
Part XI	Non-parties to this Agreement
Part XII	Reports on Implementation and Review Conference
Part XIII	Final Provisions
Annex 1	Minimum Standard for Collection and Sharing of Data
Annex 2	Suggested Guidelines for Application of Precautionary Reference Points in Conservation and Management of Straddling Fish Stocks and Highly Migratory Fish Stocks
Annex 3	Arbitration Procedures

26. The Objective of the Chairman's Draft Agreement, as stated in Article 2, is "...to ensure the long-term conservation and sustainable use of straddling fish stocks and highly migratory fish stocks". The mechanisms for international cooperation are specified in Part III including, in particular the role, functions and activities of regional fishery management organizations and arrangements.

27. Part III is composed of nine articles (Articles 8 to 16). Article 8 addresses cooperation for conservation and management; Article 9, regional fisheries management organizations or arrangements; Article 10, functions of regional fisheries management organizations and arrangements; Article 11, strengthening existing organizations or arrangements; Article 12 Collection and provision of information; Article 13, enclosed and semi-enclosed seas; Article 14, areas of high seas forming an enclave surrounded entirely by areas under the national jurisdiction of one State; Article 15, transparency, and Article 16, new participants.

28. Part III of the Chairman's Draft Agreement, inter alia, calls for international cooperation in the conservation and management of straddling fish stocks and highly migratory fish stocks through regional fisheries management organizations or arrangements. In general, coastal States and States fishing on the high seas are to cooperate bilaterally or multilaterally in relation to straddling fish stocks and highly migratory fish stocks through regional fisheries organizations or arrangements. The purpose of such cooperation is to agree on conservation and management measures with respect to particular fish stock(s). Where a regional or sub-regional fisheries body exists and has the mandate and competence to establish conservation and management measures for straddling and highly migratory fish stocks, States fishing for the stock(s) on the high seas and coastal States with an interest in the stock(s) are to give effect to their duty to cooperate by participating in the work of that body. States with an interest in the stock(s) which are not parties to an existing fishery organization or arrangements are encouraged to participate in the work of the organization. In the absence of such participation, exclusion from access to the regulated fishery is envisaged. States are also required to cooperate to strengthen existing regional and sub-regional fisheries management organizations and arrangements in order to improve their effectiveness in establishing and implementing conservation and management measures.

29. Of particular relevance to any discussion on the role of regional fishery bodies in the management of transboundary stocks, including highly migratory and straddling fish stocks, are the

provisions of Article 9 of the Chairman's Draft Agreement which give the main characteristics of such bodies, as follows:

Article 9
Regional fisheries management organizations or arrangements

In establishing sub-regional or regional fisheries management organizations or arrangements for the conservation and management of straddling fish stocks and highly migratory fish stocks, States shall agree, inter alia on:

(a) the stock(s) to which conservation and management measures shall apply, taking in to account the biological characteristics of the stock(s) concerned and the nature of the fisheries involved;

(b) the area of application, taking into account the relevant provisions of the Convention and the characteristics of the region, including socio-economic, geographical and environmental factors;

(c) the relationship between the work of the new organization or arrangement and the role, objectives and operations of any existing fisheries organizations or arrangements; and

(d) the mechanisms by which the organization or arrangement will obtain scientific advice and review the status of the stock(s) including, where appropriate, the establishment of a scientific advisory body.

30. Also of relevance are the provisions of Article 10 of the Draft Agreement which list the functions that States must ensure are carried out through such bodies.

Article 10
Functions of regional fisheries management organizations
and arrangements

In fulfilling their obligation to cooperate through sub-regional or regional fisheries management organizations or arrangements, States shall:

(a) agree on and comply with conservation and management measures to ensure long-term sustainability of the stock(s);

(b) agree, as appropriate, on allocation of participatory rights such as allocations of allowable catch or levels of fishing effort;

(c) adopt and apply generally recommended international minimum standards for the responsible conduct of fishing operations;

(d) adopt mechanisms by which the organization or arrangement will obtain scientific advice and review the status of the stock(s) and assess the impact of fishing on non target and ecologically related species;

(e) agree on standards for collection, reporting, verification and exchange of data on fisheries for the stock(s);

(f) compile and disseminate accurate and complete statistical data, as described in Annex 1, to ensure that the best scientific evidence is available, while maintaining confidentiality where appropriate;

(g) promote and conduct scientific assessments of the stocks and relevant research and disseminate the results thereof;

h) establish appropriate cooperative mechanisms for effective monitoring, control, surveillance and enforcement;

(i) agree on means by which the fishing interests of new members of, or participants in, the organization or arrangement will be accommodated;

(j) agree on decision-making procedures which facilitate the adoption of conservation and management measures in a timely and effective manner;

(k) *agree on procedures for the peaceful settlement of disputes by means of compulsory procedures leading up to binding decisions without undue delay, in accordance with Part VIII of this Agreement; and*

(l) *ensure the full cooperation of their relevant national agencies and industries in the work of the sub-regional or regional fisheries management organization or arrangement.*

31. While the Chairman's Draft Agreement must still be considered an informal document at the present time, the final instrument eventually adopted by the UN Conference will inevitably have significant implications for the restructuring of the FAO regional fishery bodies, which will need to be considered and taken into account by the Members of the Commissions/Committees.

32. Pending the concurrence of the Forty-eighth Session of the United Nations General Assembly, it is proposed that the Fifth session of the UN Conference will be held in New York in March 1995 and the concluding session in July 1995.

IV. NEED FOR FISHERIES MANAGEMENT

33. The need for more effective fisheries conservation and management has been stressed at several international fora. The conservation and management of highly migratory fish stocks (such as tuna and tuna-like species) has been catered for in almost all the oceans: the Inter-American Tropical Tuna Commission (IATTC) for the Eastern Pacific Ocean, the International Commission for the Conservation of Atlantic Tunas (ICCAT) for Atlantic and adjacent seas, the South Pacific Forum Fisheries Agency (SPFFA) for the Central and West Pacific Ocean. The establishment of the Indian Ocean Tuna Commission responds to this perceived need of the Indian Ocean.

34. The management of other stocks in other waters is also provided for, e.g. The General Fisheries Council for the Mediterranean (GFCM), the International Baltic Sea Fisheries Commission (IBSFC), the North Atlantic Salmon Conservation Organization (NASCO), the North East Atlantic Fisheries Commission (NEASC), the Pacific Salmon Commission (PSC), etc. While many high sea resources are considered to be primarily oceanic when they are distributed and caught beyond the outer (continental) shelf and/or migrate extensively across the open ocean, it should be noted that many may have a key stage of their life cycle close inshore and yield large catches inside EEZs.

V. REGIONAL APPROACH TO FISHERIES MANAGEMENT

35. The changes in the legal regime of the sea do not, on the face of it, alter greatly the conditions under which the fisheries beyond the limits of national jurisdiction are carried out. The role of regional fishery bodies is widely recognized in the 1982 United Nations Convention on the Law of the Sea. Within this Convention the term "regional" and/or "sub-regional" with reference to organizations appears many times. Regional or sub-regional arrangements may also be implied in the frequent references in the 1982 Convention to "competent (or appropriate) international organizations". Various sections of the 1982 Convention call upon countries concerned to collaborate with a view to achieving rational management. This has been further stressed, as explained above, by the UN Conference on Straddling Fish Stocks and Highly Migratory Fish Stocks.

36. It is now widely recognized that the effective conservation and management of high seas resources calls for action at the regional and sub-regional levels. The essential functions of regional fishery bodies in promoting collaboration, harmonizing policies and in providing for meaningful cooperative research activities, can also be more effectively carried out in a smaller region. An ocean wide body dealing with resources that are of a rather low value or importance in a limited area only might find it difficult to generate the necessary interest and support from all its members.

37. In order to function effectively, a regional or sub-regional fishery organization needs a clear mandate to manage the resources, the active participation by States concerned in the work of the organization, and compliance by these states with conservation and management measures adopted by the organization. Mechanisms for reaching agreement on management measures including allocation of quotas, effort control and surveillance and enforcement, are essential to an effective conservation and management structure. This requirement has two immediate implications for the existing FAO regional and sub-regional fishery bodies and for a number of non-FAO bodies. One is that the mandate of existing bodies dealing with high seas fisheries will have to be modified to include such mechanisms. The second implication is that for such mechanisms to operate effectively, existing bodies will need substantially increased budgets. This second consideration is of particular relevance to FAO regional fishery bodies, whose mandates in the conservation and management of the high seas fisheries are limited and which operate on very limited budgets.

38. In this context, it should be noted that there are a number of regional economic and other organizations that have intensified their activities in the field of fisheries. This has been the case particularly with the Asia Pacific Economic Cooperation (APEC), the Association of Southeast Asian Nations (ASEAN), the European Community (EC), the Cooperation Council for the Arab States of the Gulf (GCC), the Organization of Eastern Caribbean States (OECS), the Pacific Economic Cooperation Conference (PECC), the Preferential Trade Area for Eastern and Southern African States (PTA), the Southern Africa Development Community (SADC). Regional economic groupings, however, are in most cases based upon linguistic, economic interests or political affinities and might not always coincide with fisheries natural conservation and management areas, and thus do not always provide an adequate geographical framework for cooperation in the conservation and management of fish stocks. However, given the strong links among their members, such organizations play a very important role in facilitating the development and management process. Regional fishery bodies should thus be encouraged to increase further their cooperation with these groupings which could in turn provide the necessary political will for implementing management measures.

VI. PROPOSED OPTIONS FOR INCREASING EFFECTIVENESS OF REGIONAL FISHERY BODIES IN FISHERIES CONSERVATION AND MANAGEMENT

39. The means of strengthening or restructuring specific bodies are primarily the concern of those FAO Members that participate in regional bodies. Similarly, the recommendations of these bodies are also subject to the ultimate review of the governing bodies of the Organization. Recent developments and the wide recognition of the shortcomings of the present international fishery management arrangements have prompted the need for the current review.

40. The Draft Agreement formulated by the Chairman of the UN Conference on Straddling Fish Stocks and Highly Migratory Fish Stocks, while still an informal document, provides an excellent basis for analyzing the capacity of fishery bodies to execute conservation and management functions in respect of high seas and/or transboundary stocks. Measured against the requirements proposed in that document, it is clear that the FAO regional fishery bodies are lacking, both in management achievements and in the structure and type of their mandates. While the bodies have undertaken a number of important functions, the Commissions/Committees have rarely been able to implement fisheries conservation and management measures such as effort and catch controls, apart from the establishment of closed seasons for shrimp fishing in the Gulfs region and some ad hoc advice in some other regions. Nor, as noted above, are their mandates in the area of fisheries conservation and management adequate.

41. In this connection, however, it must be recognized that management decision-making is not simply a technical process but involves the taking of decisions that are essentially political such as the allocation of fishing effort and catches and the monitoring, control and surveillance of transboundary stocks or those stocks outside national jurisdictions. Given the nature of the decision-making process required for these policy decisions, the first question to be answered is whether

fisheries conservation and management can be more effectively carried out by bodies established within the framework of FAO or by bodies established outside the framework of FAO.

(i) Advantages and disadvantages of establishing a Fisheries Management body within the framework of FAO

42. A number of regional fisheries management bodies have been established within the framework of FAO, either by separate agreements adopted under Article XIV of the FAO Constitution[4], or directly by Resolutions of the FAO Conference or Council under Article VI of the FAO Constitution[5]. Other regional fisheries management bodies have been established as a result of initiatives promoted by FAO, but under agreements adopted outside the framework of the FAO Constitution[6] or as the result of processes entirely separate and independent from FAO[7].

43. The main advantages of establishing a regional fisheries management body within the framework of FAO are that the body and its members are thereby assured of the technical and financial support of FAO in both management and development functions, and can rely on the impartiality and competence of scientific work carried out as part of those functions.

44. The disadvantages are that bodies established within the framework of FAO are sometimes perceived as being too closely linked to FAO and therefore as not "belonging" to the region concerned or being responsive enough to the wishes of that region. This is particularly so with respect to regional bodies established under Article VI of the FAO Constitution which are in effect an integral part of the Organization, wholly financed by FAO and ultimately responsible to FAO, its Director-General and its Governing Bodies. Commissions established by agreements adopted under Article XIV of the Constitution have a greater degree of autonomy, including the possibility of having their own independent budgets financed by contributions by their own members.

45, During the Twenty-sixth Session of the FAO Conference in November 1991, amendments were adopted to Part R of the Basic Texts[8], which were intended to devolve more independence and

---

[4] e.g. the Indo-Pacific Fishery Commission (IPFC) (now the Asia-Pacific Fishery Commission) (APFIC), the General Fisheries Council for the Mediterranean (GFCM) and the new Indian Ocean Tuna Commission

[5] e.g. the Indian Ocean Fishery Commission (IOFC), the Western Central Atlantic Fishery Commission (WECAFC), the Fishery Committee for the Eastern Central Atlantic (CECAF) and the Regional Fisheries Advisory Commission for the South West Atlantic (CARPAS)

[6] e.g. the International Commission for the Conservation of Atlantic Tunas (ICCAT), and the now defunct International Commission for the Southeast Atlantic Fisheries (ICSEAF)

[7] e.g. the Northwest Atlantic Fisheries Organization (NAFO); the North East Atlantic Fisheries Commission (NEAFC); the International Baltic Sea Fishery Commission; the North Atlantic Salmon Conservation Organization (NASCO), the Inter-American Tropical Tuna Commission (IATTC) and the new Western Indian Ocean Tuna Organization (WIOTO)

[8] Principles and Procedures which should govern Conventions and Agreements concluded under Articles XIV and XV of the Constitution and Commissions and Committees established under Article VI of the Constitution

autonomy on commissions established under agreements adopted under Article XIV of the Constitution, and in particular those with autonomous budgets. The amendments were intended, in particular, to allow for more independent decision-making by such bodies in such matters as the adoption of management measures, the approval of autonomous budgets, amendments to the constitutive agreements, adoption of financial regulations and rules of procedure, and the selection and appointment of the secretary of the commission concerned.

46. While the modifications to Part R of the Basic Texts will certainly increase the autonomy of regional fishery bodies in important respects, the fact remains that such bodies by definition continue to exist within the constitutional framework of FAO and are therefore subject, by necessity of that fact, to the overall authority of FAO Governing Bodies. One consequence of this fact is that members, perhaps more for psychological than for legal or constitutional reasons, may find it more difficult to commit themselves to taking the important policy decisions in such matters as the restriction of fishing effort, or the setting/allocation of quotas, and the enforcement of such measures within the framework of a body, however autonomous in its management, that is legally dependent on FAO.

47. In practice, the nature of the comparative advantages and disadvantages of locating regional fisheries bodies within FAO, and in particular those of a financial and technical character, have led to the increased use of FAO bodies in developing areas of the world not yet having adequate financial and technical resources to support bodies independent of FAO.

48. While a decision will need to be taken on this issue by Member Nations in the light of all relevant factors, one possible approach consistent with the present resources available to coastal States in the region, might be to retain the location of the fisheries management mechanism within FAO for the present, albeit with the maximum autonomy and most appropriate mandate and powers, while envisaging a movement away to fully independent mechanisms to be set up by the region itself with FAO's assistance, at a planned date in the future. Depending on different circumstances and countries wishes, the time schedule for implementing such mechanisms could vary between different regions.

(ii) Establishing a fishery management body within the framework of FAO.

49. As noted above, fisheries bodies established within the framework of FAO can be of two types, either: (i) bodies established under Article VI of the Constitution, and (ii) bodies established by agreements adopted under Article XIV.

50. In broad terms, bodies established under Article VI are more closely tied into the internal structure of FAO and are in principle only advisory to the Director-General or the Governing Bodies of FAO, without independent decision-making powers of their own. They also cannot have their own autonomous budgets. Article XIV bodies, on the other hand, being established by separate agreements with a legal life of their own, can have a great deal more independence and flexibility and can in practice have decision-making powers of their own. Article XIV bodies fall into one of the following three categories:

(a) bodies entirely financed by the Organization;

(b) bodies that, in addition to being financed by the Organization, may undertake cooperative projects financed by members of the body; and

(c) bodies that, in addition to being financed by the Organization, have autonomous budgets.

51. Bodies belonging to the third category also have the power to circulate recommendations relating to fisheries management matters directly to their members for consideration and action rather

than passing such recommendations through the Director-General. Membership of Article XIV bodies is governed by the constitutive agreement itself, and can include States that are members of the United Nations, specialized agencies or the International Atomic Energy Agency (IAEA) that are not Members of FAO. Article XIV agreements of a regional nature are normally approved by the FAO Council and then opened for signature and ratification or circulated for acceptance. A brief comparison of Article VI and Article XIV bodies is given in Annex 3 to this document.

52. From the above brief comparison, it is readily apparent that, if an effective fisheries conservation and management body to meet the criteria being established by the UN Conference, is to be established within the constitutional framework of FAO, then only agreements adopted under Article XIV setting up bodies with autonomous budgets can provide for an appropriate structure and adequate decision-making powers.

VII FINANCIAL IMPLICATIONS TO THE MEMBERS AND THE ORGANIZATION

53. It should be pointed out that the restructuring proposed does not merely represent modifications of the mandates or in some cases extensions of the areas of competence of the existing FAO institutions in the region, but would also entail increased intersessional activities by the Members and the Secretariats of these bodies. The present frequency of the sessions of these bodies will have to be augmented from e.g. one session per statutory body in a biennium to at least annual sessions. There will thus be additional budgetary implications to both the Organization and the Members. It has also been stressed throughout this document that for these bodies to function more effectively, extra-budgetary contributions from members will be required.

54. The members will have to increasingly shoulder the additional responsibility of organizing meetings of ad hoc scientific and technical working groups, to gather information, assess stocks, set standards, harmonize practices or policies, to train manpower etc. Member countries would also be expected in future to take the lead in implementing priority activities identified by the Commissions/Committees. Greater collaboration with other organizations concerned with fisheries affairs and the marine environment will need to be encouraged. Such close contacts are essential in order to promote joint activities so as to reduce or avoid duplication of effort and to ensure optimal use of the scarce human and financial resources of the region.

55. It should be noted that while the urgency for establishing management schemes varies between regions and even between different stocks in the same region, the call to strengthen FAO regional fishery bodies seems applicable to almost all of them. A selective approach in introducing all the necessary changes in the structure and functions of these will be required. These proposals will require further consideration by the bodies themselves.

VIII. SUGGESTED ACTION BY THE COMMITTEE

56. The Committee is invited to examine the various issues raised in the document and may wish to consider the above proposals with respect to the restructuring of the FAO fisheries bodies, bearing in mind the possible outcome of the UN Conference on Straddling Fish Stocks and Highly Migratory Fish Stocks. In particular, the Committee is invited to offer guidance and advice on the proposed strengthening of FAO bodies under Article XIV of the FAO Constitution and to make recommendations, especially as regards the objectives and functions of the FAO regional fishery bodies, in order to enable them to acquire more powers and greater flexibility in their operations.

3. REPORT OF THE HIGH-LEVEL PANEL OF EXTERNAL EXPERTS IN FISHERIES

Doc. no.: COFI/95/9 January 1995

Summary

A High-level Panel of External Experts met in Rome from 17 to 20 January 1995. The Panel was invited by the Director-General to advise on FAO's priorities and programmes affecting the sustainability of fisheries and aquaculture and the contribution of this sector to world food supplies and food security. The Panel was to look at ways in which FAO could most effectively promote action to ensure continued growth in fish supplies and the contribution of fisheries to economic growth. The main findings and conclusions of the Panel, including key recommendations to the Director-General, are summarized in the attached report. The Ministerial Session of the Committee on Fisheries is invited to review these findings and provide the Director-General with any further guidance on the issues discussed.

SUMMARY AND KEY RECOMMENDATIONS TO THE DIRECTOR-GENERAL OF FAO

1. Living aquatic resources are vital for the food security and economic livelihood of a major portion of the human population. Their productivity and renewability is dependent on both a good management and a good natural environment. Fish contribute substantially to human nutrition, not only in terms of quantity but also in quality. The contribution of aquatic living resources to human health (eg: essential dietary lipid) is firmly acknowledged. Unfortunately, the current yields from living aquatic resources, both fisheries and aquaculture, are being threatened by marked declines in fishing operations and management as well as human impacts on the coastal and inland habitats.

2. At current levels of harvesting, fish is theoretically capable of meeting the minimum daily requirements of animal protein of the world's human population. However, to meet these requirements it will require changes in how fish is utilized and in patterns of distribution.

3. It is expected that through proper management, product use and distribution, currently harvested aquatic resources and production from aquaculture can continue to meet the minimum

daily protein requirement of humankind through the year 2010 when human population is expected to reach 8 billion.

4. It is estimated that by the year 2050 the human population will reach 10 billion. Unless an unforeseen development in the harvest of presently unutilized species of aquatic animals or major breakthrough in aquaculture occurs growth in production of protein from aquatic resources will not keep pace with demand.

5. It is important to note that in comparison to forestry and agriculture, the ocean is the remaining area of the globe where in the main the harvest of resources is dependent on natural systems. It is important, indeed critical, to maintain the oceans as a natural system.

6. The Panel recommends that:

The Director-General of FAO

* convey to the member governments, and to the international community, the urgency of bringing about a more rational exploitation of the world's fish resources. This is essential in order to cope with increasing food demands, ensuring greater stability and sustainability of supply, and enhanced economic and social returns from fishing;

* undertake a campaign to widely disseminate and promote the principles and guidelines laid out in the Code of Conduct for Responsible Fisheries once adopted. All sectors associated with fishing activities should be targeted;

The Organization

* encourage technical consultations on by-catch and discards in fisheries to elucidate the multiple issues involved and propose means of improving resource utilization;

* seek the collaboration of the ACC/Sub-Committee on Oceans and Coastal Areas in organizing international and regional conferences on integrated coastal area management, stressing the importance of coastal areas for sustainable fisheries and aquaculture;

* provide further information and advice to member states on all aspects of fishery management and related environmental issues so as to allow these states to meet their national and international obligations and responsibilities;

* discourage current and future fisheries subsidies that lead to over-fishing and over-capitalization;

* investigate means to improve access to capital by the private sector in states unable to make use of their aquatic resources because of inadequate financial resources, particularly in respect of small-scale operators;

* encourage states which are initiating harvesting of underutilized stocks to adopt a precautionary approach as emphasized in the Code of Conduct for Responsible Fisheries;

* assist governments which have developing aquaculture and fishery sectors to assess their manpower requirements and provide appropriate training opportunities to meet the wide variety of expertise required to ensure success;

* increase assistance to developing countries in formulating strategies for sustainable fisheries, especially in connection with negotiations on bilateral agreements;

* promote collaboration in interdisciplinary research on multiple stock and ecosystem responses to fishing. Collaboration with universities and national and other research institutions should be sought;

* promote research on new technologies for sustainable aquaculture, including especially use of feeds which do not require fish meal, control of diseases, and genetic improvement of the stocks. Such research should be collaboratively shared among governmental, university and other research institutions, including the private sector.

PREAMBLE

7. The Panel met at FAO Headquarters in Rome from 17-20 January 1995. The Members, drawn from all regions, participated in their personal capacities. The Terms of Reference (Appendix 1) presented for the Panel's consideration were dealt with following the Agenda in Appendix 2.

8. The Panel, which was chaired by Mr Nasser O. Alsaleh (Saudi Arabia), presented its recommendations to the Director-General on Friday 20 January, 1995. The rapporteur was Mr H. Francis Henderson (United States) and the meeting was attended by the Assistant Director-General Fisheries, a.i., Mr Wolfgang Krone, as the FAO resource person. The list of members is given in Appendix 3.

4. REPORT OF THE FOURTH SESSION OF THE COFI SUB-COMMITTEE ON FISH TRADE

Doc. no.: COFI/95/11 January 1995

Summary

This document contains a brief overview of the topics discussed at the Fourth Session of the Sub-Committee on Fish Trade and summarizes its main recommendations. The full report of the Fourth Session is available as document COFI/95/Inf.14. The Committee is invited to note the outcome of the Sub-Committee.

INTRODUCTION

1. The Fourth Session of the Sub-Committee on Fish Trade of the Committee on Fisheries was held in Rome from 5 to 8 October 1993. It reviewed recent developments in world fish trade, the prospects of the availability of fish supplies for international trade, possibilities for promoting joint ventures and investment in fisheries, and product and market opportunities for fish trade among developing countries. It considered fish trade impediments and criteria for fair trade and provided guidance with regard to the desirable contents of the Code of Conduct for Responsible Fisheries, specifically its chapter on post-harvest practices and trade. Issues of international trade, environment and sustainable fisheries development were discussed and the status of cooperation with the Common Fund for Commodities was examined. The report of the Session is available as document COFI/95/Inf.14.

MAJOR ITEMS OF DISCUSSIONS AND SUMMARY OF RECOMMENDATIONS

2. The Sub-Committee requested FAO to expand the coverage and analysis of impediments to trade due to certain commercial practices and to expand its advice and technical assistance in this regard. It acknowledged the work accomplished in the preparation of the chapter on trade in the Code of Conduct for Responsible Fisheries at the time and provided guidance for the outstanding work. The currently valid version is Article 10 in document COFI/95/2 which is subject of discussion under agenda item 4. The Sub-Committee recognized the specialized knowledge and expertise of FAO in the fisheries sector and stressed that this should be put at the disposal of other

institutions involved in trade matters, including the World Trade Organization (WTO) and the Convention on International Trade in Endangered Species of Wild Fauna and Flora (CITES).

3. During the discussion of the report on recent developments in world fish trade the Sub-Committee identified the need for harmonization of sanitary regulations. FAO should continue its successful training programme in the field of quality control and quality assurance as a way to achieve this objective and in order to achieve an optimum multiplier effect it should collaborate with local institutes and available expertise. The pertinent DANIDA funded project has in the meantime been extended for a third phase (1995-1999). FAO was encouraged to continue providing information on changes in the conditions of international fish trade on a regular basis. A study on the implications of the results of the Uruguay Round of trade negotiations (Marrakesh Agreement leading to the Establishment of WTO) for international fish trade has been initiated and should be available by mid-1995. It was suggested that FAO should provide advice to CITES and FAO was requested to get in contact with and collaborate with other existing and new regional organizations involved in the international trade of fishery products in order to avoid duplication of effort and to achieve optimum quality in assistance provided.

4. With regard to the prospects of the availability of fish supplies for international trade the Sub-Committee noted that in view of current trends and possible developments in resource exploitation and related market implications it has to be assumed that fishery product supplies grow much slower than demand. It was suggested that a more in-depth analysis should be made of issues such as the impact of trade restrictions on supply and availability of resources. Future analysis should be done by product form, as well as by species groups. The importance of developing aquaculture as a means of assuring future supplies of fish, and the priority that should be given to the use of fish for human consumption were stressed. Provisions have been made in the work programme of the Fish Utilization and Marketing Service for the analyses requested, for discussions by the Sub-Committee at its Fifth Session.

5. The Sub-Committee asked FAO to continue to play a stimulating role in the promotion of joint ventures and investment in fisheries. The intention of establishing a regional marketing information service for Central and Eastern Europe covering joint venture and financing assistance was supported and was mentioned as a positive move and an opportunity for greater cooperation. A Workshop on Privatization in Fisheries (Bremen, Germany, June 1994), in which FAO and the World Bank participated, strongly supported the idea of creating INFORYBA/EASTFISH and the Danish Ministry of Fisheries has informed FAO about its readiness to consider support for such a project.

6. FAO was requested to provide studies on factors influencing the trade of fishery products among developing countries, and their interaction and the Organization was encouraged to continue its activities related to the upgrading of handling, storage and packaging of fishery products. Special studies by FAO and other agencies regarding fishery products produced in developing countries were identified as an important tool for improving trade in such commodities among developing countries.

7. While the ultimate resolution of issues concerning international trade, environment and sustainable fisheries development would take place in WTO, the Sub-Committee underlined that FAO could play an important and useful role especially with respect to the need for effective implementation of international fishery conservation and management agreements, e.g., FAO could initiate action including the reduction of by-catch through selective fishing gear and the use of discards for human food. It was suggested that the regional fish marketing information services established by FAO should promote the linkage between environment, trade and sustainability, in particular to obtain exchanges of views between industry and governments.

8. In view of the global nature of the issues related to trade, environment and sustainability and the complexity of the matter and noting the need for the world community to arrive at solutions to them, Japan proposed to hold a conference on the theme "Sustainable contribution of fisheries to food security". The Sub-Committee welcomed the proposal and in endorsing this initiative reiterated its basic desire to find solutions to the various issues raised.

9. The Sub-Committee noted with concern the delay experienced in the approval of fisheries projects for funding by the Common Fund for Commodities and urged for renewed efforts by FAO to prepare fisheries projects for CFC financing, meeting the established criteria. In the meantime, one project has been approved for execution by INFOPECHE. Projects prepared by INFOFISH and INFOSAMAK are under consideration by the Fund's authorities.

10. The invitation of the City of Bremen, Germany, to hold the Fifth Session in this city in June 1994 or 1996 was noted with appreciation. Since due to lack of funds no meeting of the Sub-Committee could be organized in the current biennium, preparations have begun for holding the Fifth Session from 3 to 6 June 1996 in Bremen, Germany.

SUGGESTED ACTION BY THE COMMITTEE

11. The Committee is invited to note the outcome of the Fourth Session of its Sub-Committee on Fish Trade.

5. PROVISIONAL LIST OF DOCUMENTS

Doc. no.: COFI/95/Inf.1.Rev.1 March 1995

PROVISIONAL LIST OF DOCUMENTS

		Distribution
COFI/95/1	Provisional annotated agenda and timetable	(1)
2	Draft Code of Conduct for Responsible Fisheries	(2)
3	World fisheries: Problems and prospects	(2)
4	The role of regional fishery organizations and arrangements in fisheries management	(2)
5	Fisheries needs of small island developing States	(2)
6	Programme Implementation Report 1992-94	(2)
7	Priorities for Major Programme 2.2: Fisheries over the long- and medium-term and for the 1996-97 biennium	(2)
8	FAO follow-up to UNCED recommendations relevant to fisheries and aquaculture	(2)
9	Report of the High-level Panel of External Experts in Fisheries (Rome, 17-20 January 1995)	(2)
10	Broadening the Mandate of the FAO Commission on Plant Genetic Resources to Include other Categories of Organisms used for Food and Agriculture	(2)

---

(1) With the invitation
(2) Before the Session
(3) At the Session

		Distribution
COFI/95/11	Report on the Fourth Session of the COFI Sub-Committee on Fish Trade (Rome, 5-8 October 1993)	(2)
COFI/95/Inf.1	Provisional list of documents	(2)
Inf.2	Provisional list of delegates	(3)
Inf.3	Statement by the Director-General at the Ministerial Session	(3)
Inf.4	Report on the Technical Consultation on the Code of Conduct for Responsible Fishing (Rome, 26 September - 5 October 1994)	(2)
Inf.5	Written comments received by the FAO Secretariat on those aspects of the draft Code of Conduct for Responsible Fishing dealing with high seas issues	(2)
Inf.6	Recommendations for the marking of fishing gear (FAO Fisheries Report No. 485 and FAO Fisheries Report No. 485, Supplement)	(3)
Inf.7	Report on the UN Conference on Straddling Fish Stocks and Highly Migratory Fish Stocks	(2)
Inf.8	Not issued	
Inf.9	Fish utilization and trade	(2)
Inf.10	The role of fisheries in food security	(2)
Inf.11	Technical Assistance Projects in fisheries executed by FAO during 1992-94	(2)
Inf.12	Report on the progress in implementing the 1984 FAO World Fisheries Conference Strategy for Fisheries Management and Development	(2)
Inf.13	Report of the Twentieth Session of the Committee on Fisheries (Rome, 15-19 March 1993)	(3)
Inf.14	Report of the Fourth Session of the COFI Sub-Committee on Fish Trade (Rome, 5-8 October 1993)	(3)
Inf.15	FAO Assistance to Small-scale Fisheries (Extract from the Programme Evaluation Report 1992-93 (C 93/4))	(3)
Inf.16	European Community and Member States: Declaration of competence and the right to vote	(3)
Inf.17	Report of the Pre-COFI Meeting of Non-Governmental Organizations	(3)

6. WRITTEN COMMENTS ON PRINCIPLES OF THE CODE OF CONDUCT FOR RESPONSIBLE FISHERIES DEALING WITH HIGH SEAS ISSUES

Doc. no.: COFI/95/Inf.5 December 1994

(Draft Covering Note)

Following agreement at the Technical Consultation on the Code of Conduct for Responsible Fishing, this document presents written comments received by the Secretariat on those principles of the code of Conduct dealing mainly with high seas fisheries issues. These principles were identified at the Technical Consultation as shown in page 3; they pertain to Article 6 "Fisheries Management" and Article 7 "Fishing Operations" and are identified with an asterisk in the Draft Code of Conduct submitted to this Committee in Document COFI/95/2.

According to decisions endorsed by the Council at its Hundred and Seventh Session, final wording of these principles would be left pending the outcome of the United Nations Conference on Straddling Fish Stocks and Highly Migratory Fish Stocks which is scheduled to end in July 1995. The Committee on Fisheries and the Council at the Hundred and Eighth Session of the Council in June 1995 will provide guidance on the mechanism to harmonize and finalize the text of the Code for submission to the Twenty-eight Session of the Conference for its final adoption.

CONTENTS

TECHNICAL CONSULTATION ON THE
CODE OF CONDUCT FOR RESPONSIBLE FISHING

CONSULTATION TECHNIQUE SUR LA CODE DE
CONDUITE POUR UNE PECHE RESPONSABLE

CONSULTA TECNICA SOBRE EL CODIGO DE CONDUCTA
PARA LA PESCA RESPONSABLE

Rome/Roma, Italy/Italie/Italia
26 September/septembre/de septiembre-5 October/octobre/de octubre de 1994

- Principles pending outcome of UN Conference on Straddling Fish Stocks and Highly Migratory Fish Stocks

- Principes sous réserve des conclusions de la Conférence des Nations Unies sur les stocks chevauchants et les stocks de poissons grands migrateurs.

- Principios pendientes de los resultados de la Conferencia de las Naciones Unidas sobre poblaciones de peces cuyos territorios se encuentran dentro y fuera de las zonas económicas exclusivas y las poblaciones de peces altamente migratorias.

Article/Article/Articulo 6 - Fisheries Management/Aménagement des pêches/Ordenación pesquera

6.1.6, 6.1.7, 6.1.8, 6.1.9,

6.3.2, 6.3.3, 6.3.6,

6.4.1, 6.4.4, 6.4.5

6.5 (6.5.1, 6.5.2, 6.5.3, 6.5.4, 6.5.5)

6.6.1.1, 6.6.1.2, 6.6.1.3, 6.6.1.4, 6.6.1.5

6.6.5

6.7.2, 6.7.4, 6.7.5, 6.7.6

Article/Article/Articulo 7 - Fishing Operations/Opérations de pêche/Operaciones pesqueras

7.2.1, 7.2.2, 7.2.4, 7.2.5

7.3.1

ARTICLE 6 - FISHERIES MANAGEMENT

6.1 Rights and obligations

6.1.6 Where no appropriate subregional or regional fisheries management authorities exist to establish conservation and management measures for fisheries resources in high seas or in other international waters, States should cooperate to establish effective conservation and management of the resources.

<u>Comments</u>:

P.R. CHINA

6.1.6 3rd line, add "concerned" before "States".

JAPAN

6.1.6 Where no appropriate subregional ......, States should cooperate to establish such authority or otherwise enter into appropriate arrangement to ensure conservation and management of fisheries resources and participate in the work of such authority or arrangement.

EUROPEAN COMMUNITY

6.1.6 Delete "effective conservation and management of the resources" and insert "cooperate to establish such authority or otherwise enter into appropriate agreements to ensure conservation and management of fisheries resource and participate in the work of such authority or agreement".

6.1.7 Where a subregional or regional fisheries management authority exists and has the mandate to establish conservation and management measures, coastal States and States fishing for the resources on the high seas should give effect to their duty to cooperate by participating in the work of the fisheries management authority.

Comments:

EUROPEAN COMMUNITY

6.1.7 delete "coastal States and" and "fishing for the resources of the high seas"

Insert after participating in "the terms and seeking to ensure the effectiveness of"

U.S.A.

6.1.7 Revise as follows: "Where a subregional or regional fisheries management authority exists and has the mandate to establish conservation and management measures, coastal States and States fishing for the resources on the high seas should give effect to their duty to cooperate by participating in **and seeking to ensure the effectiveness of** the work of the regional fisheries management authority."

6.1.8 Where a State is not a member of a subregional or regional fisheries management authority and does not participate in its work, that State is still under the obligation to give effect to the measures concerning the conservation and management of the regulated stock or stocks adopted by that authority.

Comments:

ARGENTINA

6.1.8 Where a State is a not a member of a sub-regional or regional fisheries management authority, this sub-regional or regional authority will ask it to participate in the relevant work of fisheries management and conservation and it should, in all events, cooperate in the conservation and management of the regulated stock or stocks.

EUROPEAN COMMUNITY

6.1.8 delete "is not" and insert "does not want to be"
delete last part of the paragraph from "is still under" on and insert "is thereby not discharged from the obligation to cooperate in the conservation and management of the resources concerned"

JAPAN

6.1.8 Where a State is not a member ...., that State is not discharged from the obligation to cooperate in the conservation and management of relevant stock.

KOREA

6.1.8 add the following sentence: In case of new entry of a state who is not a member of a subregional or regional fisheries management authority, non-discriminatory principle should be applied for its rights and duties

MEXICO

6.1.8 This obligation is incongruous with international law.

PERU

6.1.8 (Replace the entire phrase by: Paragraph 1 of Art. 32 of Draft Agreement on Straddling Stocks and Highly Migratory Stocks (New York))..

U.S.A.

6.1.8 The United States supports the obligation of States not members of subregional or regional fisheries management authorities to abide by the management competence of these organizations.

6.1.9 As a precondition to ensuring the effectiveness of conservation and management measures, States should give priority to reduce over-harvest and over-capacity to a level of fishing effort commensurate with the sustainable utilization of fisheries resources.

Comments:

EUROPEAN COMMUNITY

6.1.9 delete "over-capacity" and insert "excess fishing capacity"

MEXICO

6.1.9 New text: "The States should consider, inter alia, the following conservation and management measure: reduction in over-harvesting to a level of fishing effort commensurate with the sustainable utilization of resources."

The fact that some States depend heavily on fishing should also be taken into account, hence the obvious advantage of appropriately training fishermen from these areas in species capture and protection techniques. It would also be desirable to include aspects on the processing and marketing both of the species themselves and of by-products.

U.S.A.

6.1.9 The United States strongly supports the need for governments, including the United States, to address the problem of gross overcapitalization of word fishing fleets.

6.3 Management framework and procedures

6.3.2 States or fisheries management authorities should use the best evidence in order to determine, *inter alia*, the geographical extent of the resource and the jurisdictions within which it lies or through which it migrates during its life cycle.

Comments:

EUROPEAN COMMUNITY

6.3.2 Delete "States or"
delete "evidenced" and insert "scientific evidence available"

JAPAN

6.3.2 Delete "the jurisdictions within which it lies or through which .... cycle".

NEW ZEALAND

6.3.2, 6.3.3 and 6.4.4 should be left open pending finalization of the UN Conference on Straddling Stocks and Highly Migratory Fish Stocks

6.3.3 A subregional or regional fisheries management authority should be constituted to include representatives of all States through whose jurisdictions the resources move or are located as well as representatives from States whose nationals have habitually fished the resources.

Comments:

EUROPEAN COMMUNITY

6.3.3 delete last part of the sentence "whose nationals ..." and insert "that have a fishing interest in the resources concerned"

PERU

6.3.3.bis "The decisions of the sub-regional or regional authority regarding measures relating to resources lying within zones under the jurisdiction of a State or which migrate through these zones, can only be adopted with the consent of the State concerned."

VENEZUELA

6.3.3 " ... the resources move or are located as well as, in the case of stocks situated partially or totally on the high seas, representatives from States whose nationals ..."

6.3.6 Fisheries management authorities should foster and promote international cooperation and coordination in all matters related to fisheries, including information gathering and exchange, fisheries research, management and development in order to promote responsible fishing.

Comments:

U.S.A.

6.3.6 revise as follows" "Fisheries management authorities should foster and promote international cooperation and coordination in all matters related to fisheries, including information gathering and exchange, fisheries research, management, development, **and compliance** in order to promote responsible fishing."

EUROPEAN COMMUNITY

6.3.6 Delete "international"

6.36(bis) Alternative Secretariat Draft but delete "arrangement, shall" and insert "agreement, should" add at the end: "and have due regard to its view"

6.4 Management advice and data gathering

6.4.1 When considering the introduction of conservation and management measures, fisheries management authorities should take account of the best scientific evidence available to evaluate the likely impacts of the measures on the resources and consider the resources and the interests of participants.

Comments:

PERU

6.4.1 ..... to evaluate the [likely] impacts ....

MEXICO

6.4.1 Delete "likely".

6.4.1 to 6.4.6 The subject and source of the advice are unclear.

EUROPEAN COMMUNITY

6.4.1 Delete "likely" and insert "possible"
Delete "consider" and insert "with due consideration for"

6.4.4 States should compile fishery-related and other supporting scientific data relating to transboundary, straddling and highly migratory stocks or other high seas stocks in an internationally agreed format and provide them in a timely manner to the relevant fisheries management authority.

Comments:

EUROPEAN COMMUNITY

6.4.4 Delete

6.4.5 Fisheries management authorities should compile data and make them available in a timely manner and in an agreed format to all interested States and interested parties.

Comments:

JAPAN

6.4.5 Add "under the terms and conditions established by the multilateral and bilateral agreement" at the end.

MEXICO

6.4.5 Add "Guaranteeing that the information will remain confidential and not be used to the detriment of the States".

ICSF

6.4.5 Fisheries management authorities should develop systems for compiling data which are comparable nationally and internationally.

VENEZUELA

6.4.5 (fisheries management authorities) should compile the necessary data for the conservation and use of fisheries resources and make them available in a timely manner ..."

6.5 Precautionary approach

6.5.1 In order to reduce the risk of damage to the marine environment and living aquatic resources, the precautionary approach should be widely applied.

Comments:

KOREA

6.5.1 delete "widely"

MEXICO

6.5.1 Delete "living" and "widely".

U.S.A.

The United States suggests that the draft be revised to reflect more current UN language and prefers the follows:

6.5.1 In order to reduce the risk of damage to the marine environment and living aquatic resources a precautionary approach to fishery exploitation and management should be designed to ensure long-term resource conservation, and exploitation should be cautious.

EUROPEAN COMMUNITY

6.5.1 Delete and replace by following text:

"In order to protect living marine resources and their environment, the precautinary approach should be applied by States, directly or through regional fisheries management organizations, to the management, conservation and exploitation of all stocks, regarded as biological units, throughout their range of distribution."

6.5.2 In applying precautionary approach, fisheries management authorities should take into account, *inter alia*, uncertainties with respect to the size, productivity and state of the stocks, management reference points, levels and distributions of fishing mortality and the impact of fishing activities on associated and dependent species including discard mortality, as well as climatic, environmental, social and economic conditions.

Comments:

U.S.A.

6.5.2 In applying a precautionary approach, fisheries management authorities should take into account, inter alia, uncertainties with respect to the size, productivity, state of the marine resources and the impact of fishing activities on target, associated and dependent species. Fishery management authorities should be more cautious when information is poor. Lack of information should not be used as a reason for deferring management action to protect the resources.

EUROPEAN COMMUNITY

6.5.2 Delete and replace by following text:

"The precautionary approach should be based on the best scientific evidence available, including all appropriate techniques and be aimed at setting stock-specific minimum standards for conservation and management, taking into due consideration impacts on the ecosystems. States should be more cautious when the scientific information is poor.

6.5.3 The precautionary approach should be based on the best scientific evidence available, include all appropriate techniques and be aimed at setting stock-specific minimum standards for conservation and management. Fishery management authorities should be more cautious when information is poor. They should determine precautionary management reference points and apply precautionary measures consistent with management objectives.

Comments:

EUROPEAN COMMUNITY

6.5.3 Delete and replace by following text:

"The lack of adequate scientific information should not justify postponing or not taking apppropriate measures based on the best scientific evidence available, especially where there are threats of serious or irreversible damage.

MEXICO

6.5.3 The phrase "setting stock-specific minimum standards" may cause problems since the differing weather, geographical and technological conditions of each State require that measures be adopted on a case-by-case basis.

6.5.3 and 6.5.4 Include "the best scientific evidence".

U.S.A.

6.5.3 Fishery managers should set clear management goals and develop management strategies to attain these goals using the best scientific information available. Management reference points should be defined (as described in Annex 2 of the Guidelines for Responsible Management of Fisheries to this Code) to indicate when an objective is being approached (a target reference point) and also to indicate when the conservation of the resource is under threat (a limit reference point). When a limit reference point is approached, measures should be taken to ensure that it will not be exceeded. These measures should be negotiated in advance, wherever possible. If a limit reference point is exceeded, a recovery plan should be implemented immediately to restore the resource."

6.5.4 When precautionary or limit reference points are approached, measures should be taken to ensure that they will not be exceeded. These measures should where possible be pre-negotiated. If such reference points are exceeded, recovery plans should be implemented immediately to restore the stocks.

Comments:

JAPAN

6.5.4 Precautionary reference points consist of two types: 1) Limit reference points; 2) Target reference points. We found some technical confusion in the FAO draft and elaboration is needed.

PERU

6.5.4 2nd line: correct as follows: **"these measures should, where appropriate, by previously agreed upon.** Logically, in zones under national jurisdiction, it is not appropriate for the so-called competent authorities to negotiate the measures as this is the sole responsibility of the coastal state. In point 6.5.5, first line in Spanish, second line in English, where it reads "should be established", insert "by the competent authorities" so that it is understood that these are the authorities of the State in the zones under national jurisdiction and the so-called "fisheries management authority" on the high seas.

U.S.A.

6.5.4 In the case of new and exploratory fisheries, conservation measures including precautionary catch or effort limits and exploratory harvest regimes, should be established as soon as possible in cooperation with those initiating the fishery and should remain in force until there are sufficient data to allow assessment of the impact of any increase in fishing intensity on long-term sustainability of the stocks and associated ecosystems.

EUROPEAN COMMUNITY

6.5.4 Delete and replace by following text:

The precautionary approach should set stock specific management limit reference points and apply precautionary measures consistent with management objectives. In aplying precautionary approach, States should take into account inter alia, uncertainties with respect to the size, productivity and state of the stocks, management limit reference points, the levels and distributions of fishing mortality and the impact of fishing activities on associated and dependent species, as well as other relevant factors, including climatic, oceanic and environmental changes and socio-economic conditions."

6.5.5 In the case of new or exploratory fisheries, conservation measures including precautionary catch or effort limits should be established as soon as possible in cooperation with those initiating the fishery and should remain in force until there are sufficient data to allow assessment of the impact of any increase in fishing intensity on the long-term sustainability of stocks and associated ecosystems.

Comments:

JAPAN

6.5.5 Delete "and associated ecosystem".

MEXICO

6.5.5 After "precautionary catch or effort limits" add, "if and when scientific information exists in cooperation ...... since it is not advisable that management methods be applied without at least some knowledge of the species or its fishery".

EUROPEAN COMMUNITY

6.5.5 Delete and replace by following text:

"Where management limit reference points are approached, measures should be taken to ensure that they will not be exceeded. These measures should where possible be pre-negotiated. If such minimum reference points are exceeded, recovery plans should be implemented immediately to restore the stock(s)."

6.6 Management measures

6.6.1.1 that no vessel be allowed to fish unless so authorized;

Comments:

EUROPEAN COMMUNITY

6.6.1.1 Add at the end: "and that such authorization be carried on board".

6.6.1.2 that all vessels authorized to fish be properly marked in accordance with international law and the FAO Standard Specifications for the Marking and Identification of Fishing Vessels;

Comments:

EUROPEAN COMMUNITY

6.6.1.2 Delete (overlaps with 7.2.4)

6.6.1.3 that the authorization to fish be carried on board vessels at all times;

Comments:

EUROPEAN COMMUNITY

6.6.1.3 delete

6.6.1.3.bis Delete "require" and insert "ensure"
Insert after "vessels in" the term "maintained"

6.6.1.4 that a record of authorized fishing vessels be maintained containing relevant details for every vessel authorized, including type and size of vessel;

Comments:

EUROPEAN COMMUNITY

6.6.1.4 Delete

PERU

6.6.1.4 1st line (Not applicable to English?)

6.6.1.5 that data maintained in the record be used to monitor the capacity of the fleets in terms of catch requirements, capital invested and cost of operation;

Comments:

EUROPEAN COMMUNITY

6.6.1.5 Insert after "that" the term "available"
Delete "maintained in the record"
Delete "capital invested ... operation"

MEXICO

6.6.1.5 to 6.6.1.9 One may ask what role and what measures adopted by the State to guarantee that the fisheries are profitable. The introduction of subsidies runs counter to other international agreements and the measures recommended imply that the States follow certain fiscal policies which may not necessarily be compatible with their needs and current practices. This may adversely affect fisheries management and conservation measures.

6.6.5 In order to protect juveniles or spawners, avoid wastage and reduce the catch which is not sought or retained by the fishers, fisheries management authorities should implement technical measures such as minimum landing size limits, mesh or gear regulations, closed areas, including marine reserves, or closed seasons where necessary. Regulations governing multispecies fisheries should be designed to minimize discarding.

Comments:

EUROPEAN COMMUNITY

6.6.5 delete ", including marine reserves"

ICSF

6.6.5 In order to protect ... mesh or gear regulations, zoning of the sea (to protect the rights of artisanal fishers) .... discarding, and should consider the phasing out of non-selective and destructive fishing practices.

NEW ZEALAND

6.6.5 delete ", including marine resources"

PERU

6.6.5 1st line (No change in English)
2nd line: before "authorities" add "the States and"
3rd line: delete the word "landing"

U.S.A.

6.6.5 The United States supports the importance of protecting juveniles or spawners, avoiding bycatch and wastage as expressed in this article.

The United States also recommends that a section 6.6.5 is added to read: "To the extent feasible, States should management fisheries to limit bycatch of non-target species. Substantial bycatch problems can have an impact on the health of an ecosystem, limit availability of fishery products for other fisheries, and threaten the maintenance of biological diversity. Technologies to reduce bycatch, e.g., TED's should be utilized. Indiscriminate technologies with high bycatch, such as drift gillnets should not be utilized. In instances where a fishery has a major impact on vulnerable species, management measures, such as time and area closures should be used to reduce the impact on such species."

6.7 Implementation

6.7.2 Fisheries management authorities should promote the implementation of fisheries monitoring, control, surveillance and law enforcement measures. Where appropriate, such measures should be conducted on a subregional or regional basis and in accordance with regionally-agreed procedures. Within subregions or regions, States should cooperate in the enforcement of their respective fisheries laws and regulations having regard to any specific agreements for that purpose.

Comments:

P.R. CHINA

6.7.2 add the following sentence at the end of the paragraph:
In order to implement the fisheries management measures, the developing countries should be encouraged to actively adopt measures as consistent as possible with the Code of Conduct. At the same time, the concerned international organizations should be encouraged to establish training bases on a regional basis, in order to help developing countries train high quality management personnel.

PERU

6.7.2 begin the paragraph with "**The States**" and in the first line after "fisheries management" insert "within the scope of their respective competency"

U.S.A.

6.7.2 Add a final sentence: "States should cooperate in exploring, through regional fishery management authorities additional options to ensure comprehensive adherence to multilaterally agreed conservation measures."

6.7.4 States should establish a transparent mechanism by which the effectiveness of a fisheries management authority is regularly reviewed in order to ensure that conservation and management objectives are achieved.

Comments:

EUROPEAN COMMUNITY

6.7.4 insert after "the effectiveness of a" the term "subregional or regional"

GREENPEACE INTERNATIONAL

6.7.4 after "States" insert "regional and subregional organizations at the local, national and international level ..."

MEXICO

6.7.4 Replace "transparent" by "appropriate" and "an authority" by "their authority".

PERU

6.7.4 if the term "fisheries management authority" is maintained (in the second line) this should be proceeded by "regional or subregional".

6.7.5 States should adopt procedures for compulsory and binding settlement of disputes, consistent with relevant international agreements, to ensure the expeditious resolution of disputes. A State or States opposing a conservation and management measure should continue to observe the measure until the dispute is settled.

Comments:

EUROPEAN COMMUNITY

6.7.5 Delete last sentence

JAPAN

6.7.5 Delete 2nd sentence: "A state or .... the dispute is settled".

KOREA

6.7.5 "opposing" should read "engaged in"
"continue to observe the measure" should read "seek interim measure"

MEXICO

6.7.5 Since the Code, if voluntary, we should ask if the disputes will have a legal nature and in which forum they will be settled. The alternative to a compulsory Code requires the development or specification of a mechanism for dispute settlement and choice of forum.

PERU

6.7.5 begin as follows: "Without prejudice to the procedures to be adopted under the relevant provisions of the United Nations Convention on the Law of the Sea".

U.S.A.

6.7.5 Does the United States agree that in the case of an international dispute we should abide by the decision of another entity "until the dispute is settled"?

VENEZUELA

6.7.5 Without prejudice to the procedures to adopt as provided for by the United Nations Convention on the Law of the Sea and consistent with relevant international agreements, the States should adopt procedures for the prevention and prompt, effective and definitive settlement of disputes, including procedures for compulsory and binding settlement.

JAPAN

6.7.6 bis [NEW PROPOSAL]

Trade Measures

(a) States which are members of or participate in a subregional or regional fisheries management organization or arrangement shall, with a view to ensuring effectiveness of conservation and management measures established by that organization or arrangement, jointly request non-participants whose vessels engage in activities that undermine the effectiveness of the measures, to participate in that organization or arrangement, or to otherwise cooperate in the measures.

(b) Notwithstanding the above request, where the activities by fishing vessels of such non-participants are not rectified, States may, within a framework of that organization or arrangement and consistent with the international law, restrict the introduction into their domestic markets of fish and fish products originated by vessels of such non-participants in waters where the conservation and management measures are applied.

Such restriction shall be withdrawn as soon as the non-participant has ceased to undermine the effectiveness of the measures concerned.

Article 7 - FISHING OPERATIONS

7.2 Flag State Responsibility

7.2.1 The Flag State should maintain a record of fishing vessels entitled to fly its flag and indicate in that record details of the vessels, their ownership and authorization(s) to fish.

Comments:

KOREA

7.2.1 insert "if possible" between "and" and "authorization to fish".

INTERNATIONAL COLLECTIVE IN SUPPORT OF FISHWORKERS (ICSF)

7.2.2 The Flag should... by the competent authority(ies), and should comply with international regulations regarding health, safety, and social security and human rights.

JAPAN

Propose to add at end of paragraph

7.2.1 ... in accordance with international agreements.

EUROPEAN COMMUNITY

7.2.1 Initial Secretariat Draft add at the end: "in accordance with international agreements".

7.2.2 The Flag State should ensure that no fishing vessels entitled to fly its flag should fish on the high seas or in the EEZ of another State unless authorized to do so and that such fishing operations are carried out in accordance with the conditions set out by the authority(ies). Such vessels should carry on board the authorization(s) to fish issued by the competent authority(ies).

Comments:

KOREA

7.2.2 combine both articles or delete 7.2.2
7.2.3 "

7.2.4 All fishing vessels authorized to fish on the high seas or in the EEZ of another State should be properly marked in accordance with international law and the FAO Standard Specification and Guidelines for Marking and Identification of Fishing Vessels.

Comments:

KOREA

7.2.4 Include exceptions in applying this article like Art. V.3 of Flagging Agreement.

7.2.5 All fishing gear should be marked, as appropriate, by such standards and guidelines as may be agreed, so the owner of the gear can be identified.*

Comments:

JAPAN

7.2.5 We appreciate the wording here with regard to marking of fishing gear because we, Government of Japan, still reserve our position on the Standard Specification and Guidelines for the Marking of Fishing Gear drafted at FAO mostly because of practical and technical reasons. We are now preparing comments on the Guidelines and would like to submit them to the Secretariat as soon as possible.

KOREA

7.2.5 Reserve our position

MEXICO

7.2.5 Add after "standards and guidelines" the phrase "relevant at the international and regional level" and at the end of the paragraph "in accordance with the national laws of the country in which said national is resident".

7.3 Port State Responsibility

7.3.1 Port States should take, in accordance with international law, such measures as are necessary to assist other States in achieving the objectives of this Code and other relevant international agreements or arrangements (including those resulting from the UN Conference on Straddling Stocks and Highly Migratory Species). *

Comments:

KOREA

7.3.1 Change sentence as follows: "Port State may, with the consent of Flag State take, and in accordance with international law, such measures as are necessary to assist Flag State in achieving the objective of this Code and other relevant interntional agreements or arrangements".

INTERNATIONAL COLLECTIVE IN SUPPORT OF FISHWORKERS (ICSF)

7.3.2 Port States should have the authority to inspect vessels in port, and to see that they comply with international standards of health and safety, and general living and working conditions.

7.3.3 Port States should be vested with the powers to take action against vessels which have violated the fishing regulations of other countries, particularly those that do not have adequate monitoring, control and surveillance systems.

EUROPEAN COMMUNITY

7.3.1 Alternative Secretariat Draft, insert after "international law" the terms: "and in cooperation with other States concerned"
Delete "other" and insert "those"

JAPAN

7.3.1 We appreciate the wording with regard to the Port State Responsibility in this paragraph because it well reflects our discussion in Canada and takes appropriate consideration to the UN Conference. However, we could not stand without saying the Guidelines distributed as Inf. 6 include a lot of problems mostly because the wording in the Guidelines seem to prejudge the outcome of the discussion on this particular issue at UN Conference or inconsistent with what discussed in New York. Therefore, we would like to reserve our position on the details of the details of this issue for the time being.

7. REPORT OF THE EXPERT CONSULTATION ON THE MARKING OF FISHING GEAR AND RECOMMENDATIONS FOR THE MARKING OF FISHING GEAR

Doc. no.: COFI/95/Inf.6 February 1995

1. INTRODUCTION

These guidelines have been developed with regard to the format followed by the Food and Agriculture Organization for the Standard System for the Marking of Fishing Vessels. The guidelines are in two parts. The first outlines an approach to developing a standard system for the marking of fishing gear; the second provides actual technical specifications for the marks and where they should be placed on various types of gear. These guidelines are also designed to provide a basis for drafting appropriate legislation. They will provide administrators, owners and users of fishing gear with a reference and a means of providing information and guidance to the fishing community.

As with the marking of fishing vessels, it is likely, in the first instance, that the standard system and specifications for the marking of fishing gear recommended would be used on a voluntary basis.

The two main purposes of the guidelines are to:

i) identify ownership of the fishing gear, and

ii) identify its position.

The first requirement is more easily met since the methods of identification are technically simple and internationally approved marking systems can be readily applied. The identification of the position of the fishing gear is more complicated because of the possible conflict with other forms of position identifiers employed by other users of the seas, rivers and lakes. In some cases, International Conventions are in force regulating the use of such marks. For these reasons, some guidance is given on how conflict with other systems can be avoided.

2. GENERAL PROVISIONS

2.1 Purpose and Scope

2.1.1 Fishing gear should be marked for identification of ownership and its position as an aid to fisheries management, safety of navigation and the protection of the maritime environment.

2.1.2 For the purpose of the standard system, fishing gear to be marked refers to any type of fishing gear or fishing implement used in any fishery.[1]

---

[1] This does not imply that <u>all</u> fishing gear need necessarily be marked but only that which is considered practical and necessary.

2.2 Definitions

Fisheries Administration: The government body or any designated authority responsible for the management and control of fisheries and empowered to impose fishing regulations.

Owner: An owner is the person, persons or entity holding title to the fishing gear. This term may include skippers and any other persons for the time being responsible for the operation of the fishing gear in question.

2.3 Standard Marking System Objectives

The objectives of the standard system are to:

i) provide a simple, workable, and enforceable means of identifying the ownership and position of fishing gear

ii) provide a system which can be universally adopted

iii) aid resource management systems and meet obligations of international conventions

3. THE MARKING SYSTEM

3.1 General

3.1.1 Fisheries Administrations should ensure that suitable marks indicating ownership are attached to all fishing gear carried on or deployed from any vessel, or used for the purpose of fishing from beaches, lakes or river banks, etc. Such a requirement should apply only where an Fisheries Administration considers it practical and necessary to the proper management of its fisheries. It may also assist in meeting its obligations under appropriate international conventions. Initially, their introduction should be without prejudice to any existing national marking system which falls within the ambit of these guidelines.

3.1.2 So that the marks can identify the owner of the gear, a unique identifier (marker distinguishing symbol, etc.) should be issued by the Fisheries Administration to the owner of the gear. This will be capable of being cross-referenced to the Register of Gear referred to in 3.2.3. Applications for gear marks are referred to under 4.1.

3.1.3 Appendix 1 (in a Supplement) describes tags and other means for the identification of ownership.

3.1.4 Appendix 2 (in a Supplement) indicates where the tag or mark should be fixed to the fishing gear.

3.2 Register of Marks

3.2.1 Marks should be of a type and design approved by the Fisheries Administration and fitted in accordance with technical specifications provided below.

3.2.2 The marks should be:

- simple
- inexpensive
- easily manufactured having regard to locally available materials
- easily read or deciphered
- easily attached or bonded to the fishing gear
- able to stay attached
- durable
- designed not to interfere with the operation and performance of the fishing gear and, in the case of tags, capable of accepting a variety of printed or embossed data.

3.2.3 Such marking may be a condition of any fishing licence and should be recorded in the form of a fishing gear register. The register should also contain details of fishing gear which is not subject to a licensing regime but is nevertheless considered by the Fisheries Administration to require marking.

3.2.4 The register should record as a minimum the following information:

- type of mark
- serial number
- date issued

- name and address of owner
- type of gear (FAO Code)
- material
- general area of use; and
- principal target species

3.3 Record of Gear Lost or Found

3.3.1 A record/register of fishing gear reported as being found, lost, abandoned, or otherwise disposed of[2] should be maintained by the Fisheries Administration. This record/register should include details of:

- type of gear
- any fishing gear marks
- the markings on the gear
- date, time, position of loss, depth of water etc.
- reason for loss (if known)
- weather conditions
- any other relevant information.

4. RESPONSIBILITIES OF OWNERS OF GEAR AND FISHERIES AUTHORITIES

4.1 Any owner wishing to use fishing gear should make application to the Fisheries Administration for the issue of an approved gear mark or for approval of the owner's own mark. In doing so, the applicant should provide the following details:

- name, address, name of boat (if relevant)
- gear type
- material
- expected area of use[3]
- principal target species[3]

4.2 Where gear is lost from a vessel, the owner of the gear concerned should immediately warn other mariners giving details of the lost gear. Skippers of foreign vessels which have lost gear while fishing in the waters of a Coastal State should be required to report to the Fisheries Administration of the Coastal State concerned. The Fisheries Administration should promulgate the details and last known position of any gear lost by the most effective local means such as navigation warnings broadcast as marine safety information eg. Coastguard as information services.

4.3 Where gear is not used from a vessel and it is lost or abandoned, details of the gear should be reported to the Fisheries Administration by the owner of the gear.

4.4 In the event that the skipper of the vessel concerned is not the owner of the lost or abandoned fishing gear, the skipper will:

i) have the report endorsed by the owner or agent of the gear;

ii) be considered by the administration concerned as a representative of the owner if it is impractical to meet the conditions of (i) above.

5. GEAR MANUFACTURERS

5.1 Manufacturers could be encouraged to keep registers of the type of gear or parts thereof, the materials of construction and the name and address of the customer[4].

5.2 Retailers, if different from the manufacturer, could also be encouraged to keep customer records in the form required by the owner to report to the Fisheries Administration for the allocation of the mark.

---

[2] Includes fishing gear sold or put ashore and destroyed.

[3] Gear which is not subject to a licensing regime as described in para 3.2.3 may be exempt from this requirement.

[4] A standard form may suffice which could also be used by the owner in support of his application for the allocation of a "mark".

6. **RECOVERY OF LOST OR ABANDONED FISHING GEAR**

6.1 **The Fisheries Administration should ensure that owners of fishing gear have adequate equipment for the recovery of gear.**

6.2 **In the event of the failure of the owner to recover any lost or abandoned gear, particularly if it:**

- **presents a hazard to navigation or surface and sub-surface vessels**
- **fouls reefs**
- **fouls spawning beds**
- **becomes an impediment to fishing, or**
- **continues to ghost fish**

the Fisheries Administration should take appropriate action to recover the gear.

6.3 **Fisheries Administrations should encourage the re-use of recovered gear.**

7. **SALVAGE OF LOST OR ABANDONED FISHING GEAR**

7.1 **Notwithstanding national legislation covering salvage, the following rules should apply:**

i) **Fishing gear found or picked up at sea whether marked or unmarked should be delivered as soon as possible to the competent authority responsible for dealing with wrecks, including fishing gear. In some cases this may not be the Fisheries Administration, but an authority responsible for materials found at sea, for example.**

ii) **The competent authority shall inform owners, national or foreign, of the gear found (if adequately marked) and arrange to restore the gear to them or their representative after the interests of the salvor have been guaranteed.**

iii) **In addition to the rights of the salvor, the Fisheries Administration, in cooperation with the competent authority, may levy a fee for each piece of gear retrieved. This income may be used to offset the costs of recovery by the Fisheries Administration as set out in paragraph 6.2 above.**

8. **LIABILITIES**

8.1 **It should be an offence under national law for any person to deliberately discard or dump any gear or piece of fishing gear, whether marked or not, into the aquatic environment, except in those cases which involve force majeure or other circumstances involving the safety of the fishing vessel or its crew.**

8.2 **Nothing in these guidelines shall be seen as a waiver of an owner's obligations under Civil and Criminal Law in respect of claims for damage or injury to third parties resulting from gear lost or discharged.**

9. **PENALTIES**

9.1 **A Fisheries Administration may impose appropriate penalties and fines on an owner, in particular, for the following actions:**

i) **deploying fishing gear for which the owner has failed to obtain a mark;**

ii) **deploying fishing gear without displaying the allocated mark;**

iii) **deliberate removal of a mark prior to abandoning gear[6].**

iv) **use of marks allocated to another owner or to other gear**

v) **providing false declarations to Fisheries Administrations on the use or disposal of fishing gear.**

10. **CONTROL**

10.1 **The owners of all fishing gear placed in the sea should be responsible for marking it with appropriate devices as illustrated in Appendix 1 (presented in a Supplement). Fisheries Administrations shall carry out inspection on a regular basis to ensure that owners mark their fishing gear in the approved manner.**

---

[6] **The onus of proof of ownership would lie with the Fisheries Administration.**

10.2 Fisheries Administrations may allocate a mark to a company, fishermen's organization or similar entity if it can be demonstrated that the individual unit of fishing gear can be used by more than one group of users or vessels on a rotational or common pool basis. Such identification marks should be followed by an individual gear identifier and the owner shall keep a log of the location of the gear.

10.3 For fishing gear which is to be deployed in waters of a State for which the administration allocating the mark has no jurisdiction, the administration of the country in whose waters the gear is to be deployed may require the owners to:

i) supply details of the mark[6]; or
ii) apply for a new mark.

10.4 In the case of motherships, the fishing gear used by catcher vessels may carry the mark of the mothership.

10.5 In the advent of a tag being lost, the owner should provide to the Fisheries Administration a declaration detailing the circumstances of the loss.

11. MARKING POSITION OF GEAR

11.1 Care should be taken that lights and shapes which indicate the position of fishing gear do not conflict with navigation marks or systems. Furthermore, due account should be taken of:

i) the international regulations for preventing collision at sea;

ii) any local rules governing river, lake or coastal navigation;

iii) any regulations pertaining to offshore structures.

11.2 Pots and traps, fyke nets, stake nets, and other similar gear, should be marked with a buoy or other device at the surface to indicate its position.

11.3 Where practicable, all position indicators attached to fishing gear shall:

i) be as conspicuous as possible in a clear daytime atmosphere from a distance of at least two miles at sea level;

ii) carry radar and light reflectors

iii) carry lights with characteristics which do not conflict with those of navigational marks and visible on a clear night at a distance of not less than two miles;

iv) fitted with fluorescent coloured flag or flags as an aid to daytime visibility.

11.4 Extremities of fishing gear set below the level of the sea and extending from an anchor or parent vessel, shall be marked both at its extremities and at intermediate positions. The distance between intermediate marks, and between the intermediate markers closest to the extremities and the extremity markers shall not exceed one mile. In the case of fishing gear attached to a vessel, the extremity of the gear nearer to the vessel need not carry a marker.

11.5 For fishing gear set within the upper two metres of the water column, and therefore a hazard to small transitting vessels shall be marked at its extremities by marker buoys carrying top marks which shall consist of two spherical marks, one above the other no more than one metre apart. The diameter of the upper of these two marks shall be be smaller but no less than half that of the lower one. The lights attached to the buoys at the extremity of the gear shall be of a different characteristic to those fitted to intermediate buoys. (See Appendix 3)(In a Supplement)

11.6 Suitable electronic devices such as transponders which automatically and continuously indicate their position by means of signals relayed through satellites or radio systems may be employed with the approval of Fisheries Administrations in addition to marks. However, due regard should be paid to the need and obligation of Fisheries Administrations to ensure that such devices do not conflict with other similar devices employed for navigation and search and rescue purposes.

11.7 In a similar manner, Fisheries Administrations must ensure that signals emitted by homing devices fitted to fishing gear do not interfere with internationally allocated radio frequencies.

---

[6] Such conditions could be expected in the case of joint venture or access agreements.

11.8 **With respect to active gear such as used in anchor seining, fly dragging and purse seining, the dahn-buoy employed shall meet the minimum specifications for buoy set out in 11.3.**

11.9 **Fisheries Administrations may permit the use of retro-reflective material to enhance visibility in poor light conditions but not to replace the need for a light.**

12. FISH AGGREGATING DEVICES

12.1 **Fisheries Administrations shall establish a system of approval for the deployment of Fish Aggregating Devices (FADs) and a register of owners. This register shall record as a minimum requirement:**

- **mark assigned for the identification of ownership**
- **name and address of owners**
- **type of FAD**
- **location of allocated datum geographical position**

12.2 **Fish aggregating devices, whether drifting or anchored, are to be treated in the same way as fishing gear and carry means to identify their position by day and by night and as a minimum requirement, they shall also comply with the specifications set out in paragraph 11.3.**

12.3 **The responsibility to recover drifting FADs lies with its owner and, in the case of such FADs being constructed of bio-degradable materials, the owner retains the responsibility to recover the marker once the FAD has ceased to be a possible danger to other vessels.**

12.4 **The loss of FADs (drifting or anchored) is to be reported by the owner to the Fisheries Administration in the same manner as lost or abandoned fishing gear.**

12.4 **The Fisheries Administrations shall take appropriate action in accordance with paragraph 3.3 and 6.2 above, in the event of a lost or abandoned FAD being considered a hazard to navigation.**

13. ARTIFICIAL REEFS

13.1 **For the purpose of these guidelines, artificial reefs shall be treated in the same way as any other underwater obstruction or offshore structure in respect of safety of navigation.**

8. COMMUNITY DECLARATION ON BEHALF OF THE COMMUNITY AND ITS MEMBER STATES ON COMPETENCES AND VOTING RIGHTS[1]

Doc. no.: COFI/95/Inf.16

March 1995

Technical Session:

1. Opening of the Technical Session	
2. Adoption of the agenda and arrangements for the Session	Competence: mixed Vote: Member States
3. Election of Officers	Competence: Member States Vote: Member States
4. Draft Code of Conduct for Responsible Fishing	Competence: see Annex Vote: see Annex
5. Present status of world fisheries: problems and prospects	Competence: EC Vote: EC
6. The role of regional fishery organizations and arrangements in fisheries management	Competence: mixed Vote: EC
7. Fisheries needs of small island developing States	Competence: mixed Vote: Member States
8. FAO's Programmes in Fisheries	Competence: mixed Vote: Member States
9. Any other matters[2]	

---

[1] The present statement applies within the limits specified in the general statement of competences made at the occasion of the accession of the Community to the FAO, in particular with regard to the territories of Member States where the Treaty is not applicable.

[2] The nature of the competences and voting rights are to be decided on an ad hoc basis in light of the issues discussed.

ANNEX

1. "Introduction" and "General principles"	Competence: mixed Vote: EC
2. "Fisheries management"	Competence: EC Vote: EC
3. "Fishing operations"	Competence: mixed Vote: EC
4. "Aquaculture development"	Competence: mixed Vote: EC
5. "Integration of fisheries into coastal area management"	Competence: mixed Vote: Member States
6. "Post-harvest practices and trade"	Competence: mixed Vote: EC
7. "Fisheries research"	Competence: mixed Vote: Member States

Ministerial Session:

1. Opening of the Ministerial Session	
2. Designation of Chairperson and Vice-Chairpersons	Competence: Member States Vote: Member States
3. FAO follow-up to the United Nations Conference on Environment and Development (UNCED) recommendations relevant to fisheries and aquaculture	Competence: mixed Vote: EC
4. Sustainable Contribution of Fisheries and Aquaculture to Food Supplies	Competence: mixed Vote: Member States
5. Concluding Session	

9. FAO MEETING WITH NON-GOVERNMENTAL ORGANIZATIONS ON FISHERIES (SUMMARY REPORT)

Doc. no.: COFI/95/Inf.17 March 1995

1. The FAO meeting with the Non-Governmental Organizations in Fisheries was attended by some 20 individuals representing national and international NGOs, which represented a variety of interests and constituencies including environmental, developmental, cooperatives, workers, fishing industry, women's rights etc. A list of NGOs who participated is attached.

2. The meeting elected Ms Gracie Fong, **Women and Fisheries Network** (Fiji), as chairperson. Mr Sebastian Mathew, **International Collective in Support of Fishworkers (ICSF)** and Mr Lee Weddig, **International Coalition of Fisheries Associations (ICFA)**, were elected as rapporteurs.

3. The draft agenda of the meeting proposed by FAO was adopted with a modification in the sequence of the agenda items.

Collaboration Between FAO and NGOs in the Area of Fisheries

4. The meeting considered the modalities and procedure for NGO participation in the meetings and work of FAO. It agreed that more precise guidelines for NGO participation in meetings and work of FAO were needed, particularly with regard to NGO participation in statutory bodies such as FAO's Committee on Fisheries (COFI).

5. A view expressed by several NGOs was that FAO should not solicit or expect consensus from NGOs, maintaining that their very divergence precluded either consensus input or the ability of NGOs to express their specific views.

6. In order to set guidelines for NGO interaction with FAO, to maximise NGO usefulness, and to provide procedures that permit FAO proceedings to go forward in an orderly fashion, it was suggested for consideration that NGO input be restricted to written statements; that oral input at meetings be prohibited; that a single representative of each NGO be allowed in the meeting at one time, that international NGOs be singular and not representative of many NGOs; and that fees be charged to cover the FAO costs.

7. Several other NGOs, however, disagreed with the imposition of any kinds of restrictive measures which would impede comprehensive and constructive collaboration between NGOs and FAO. NGO participation in FAO's work was considered essential to give voice to the various interest groups in the fisheries sector which could not be assumed to be always well represented through governmental interactions. In particular, the proximity of many NGOs to the grass roots will ensure that there is a reciprocal flow of information which will help both policy making and implementation. The NGOs with these views recommended that FAO consider adopting the procedures of International Maritime Organization (IMO) which provided for comprehensive NGO participation.

8. In response to the presentation by the FAO Secretariat of the long term and medium term priorities for fisheries, some NGOs observed that no specific reference was made to areas of FAO/NGO collaboration. They encouraged FAO to delineate in future areas for collaboration in greater detail.

Issues of Concern to NGOs in the Context of Follow-up to UNCED

9. Some NGOs expressed concern that fishery resources and technical issues appeared to be the main focus, rather than people (including both fishworkers and consumers), of the UNCED implementation process. The importance of fishworkers and establishing guidelines and indicators on the status of fishworkers were stressed. It was proposed by some NGOs that FAO undertake to document the status of fishworkers, in the same way that they document the status of fish resources and fishing effort.

10. Attention was drawn to high seas fisheries and Flags of Convenience (FoCs), and how FoCs are used to flout international regulations. Concern was expressed by some NGOs about the lack of political will of several Flag States in implementing internationally agreed regulations.

11. It was also noted by an NGO that shore based activities can have a negative impact on fisheries resources. The longer term impact of such activities, and methods for estimating the full economic, social and environmental costs need greater attention.

12. The importance of technology considerations in the conservation and sustainable development of marine resources was stressed by one participant. It was pointed out that technical efficiency and short term economic gain were afforded higher priority over longer term sustainable development of resources, livelihood and food security. This NGO asked for guidelines and recommendations for restricting the use of non-selective and environmentally damaging techniques.

13. Another NGO observed that while there may be examples of implementing Agenda 21 at the country level, at the international level implementation has been weak. As an example there is no inclusion of small-scale fisheries issues in the text of the UN Conference on Straddling Fish Stocks and Highly Migratory Fish Stocks. The need for international lending institutions to pay heed to Agenda 21 was also stressed.

14. Some NGOs noted that although the role of women in fisheries is recognised by FAO and UNCED, nothing has really been achieved. Citing the case of the South Pacific, it was observed that women are vital to conservation and management of coastal areas and that recognition of women's role should not stay at the rhetorical level.

15. The meeting noted that many government representatives appear to be unaware of the content of the Rio Declaration and Agenda 21. There is a need to raise awareness about Agenda 21 and its implications among governments and NGOs.

16. Some NGOs observed that the importance of the artisanal sector is not adequately recognised. Concern was expressed about the transgression of long distance fleets into artisanal fishing zones. The role of artisanal sector in producing food for domestic consumption was highlighted, particularly when drought conditions curtail agricultural production.

Code of Conduct for Responsible Fisheries

17. After a briefing by the FAO Secretariat on the status of the Code of Conduct, many NGOs expressed concern over actual implementation of the code, questioning if and how countries would adopt it and put its provisions into practice. The draft document does not say how implementation is to occur.

18. The need for COFI to recommend strongly to governments that they respect the Code of Conduct and support coastal and worker organizations as a means of implementing the Code was expressed by some NGOs. Good information flow to organizations of fishers is deemed essential to successful implementation of the Code.

19. A view was expressed by an NGO that a nation could be considered 'responsible' in its fishery policies even if it did not conform to all precise details of the Code, provided that its decisions on how to manage and utilize resources of its economic zone were made in a manner that best served its citizens and economy.

20. Some NGOs observed that the Code of Conduct is a very positive step towards sustainable fisheries practices. However, the importance of ensuring the real participation of fishworkers, and their organizations (including cooperatives) at all levels of decision making was stressed. It was further observed that the fishworkers are the people who live in close contact with the marine environment, and their participation in the implementation of the Code is essential to ensure its success.

21. A view expressed by an NGO was that the Code needs stronger emphasis on elements other than the technical provisions of management, such as social, environmental and nutritional concerns. The Code also should apply to such organizations as development banks, and it should reflect the impact of international trade in fishery products on the environment and food security.

22. Several NGOs stated that responsible fishing should encompass social and employment aspects. In respect to health and safety at sea, it was observed that a precautionary approach to the safety of workers on-board vessels is needed, and that responsibilities to strengthen safety and health of workers be added.

23. One NGO raised the problem of abandoned fishermen, and suggested that where the company was bankrupt the responsibility for their repatriation should devolve onto the flag state. It was also suggested that there was a need to collate, on an international basis, the data on accidents to fishermen.

FAO's Work Programme

24. Several NGOs offered comments on the FAO work programme. Included were suggestions that research be conducted on the effects of pollution, and global warming, stock enhancement and the impact of marine mammal populations on fish stocks, and that education and public awareness development is a very important need.

Appreciation

25. NGO representatives thanked FAO for organising the meeting, and for providing opportunity for participating in COFI. Some NGOs welcomed such new and constructive initiatives made by FAO to ensure participation of NGOs in important FAO Meetings. NGOs would like this spirit of cooperation to continue, and observed that this NGO/FAO Conference is the first step in a process of getting to know how FAO and NGOs can work together.

List of Non-Governmental Organizations which participated in the meeting

International

Earth Council
European Bureau for Conservation and Development
Greenpeace International
Intermediate Technology Development Group
International Coalition of Fisheries Associations
International Collective in Support of Fishworkers (ICSF)
International Cooperative Alliance (ICA)
International Council of Women
International Transport Workers' Federation (ITF)
International Wildlife Management Consortium (IWMC)
Women and Fisheries Network

National

BIKIS-LAKAS
Collectif national des pêcheurs artisanaux du Sénégal (CNPS)
Comitato Internazionale per lo Sviluppo dei Popoli (CISP) - Movimondo
Comité catholique contre la faim et pour le développement (CCFD)
Confederación de Pescadores Artesanales de Chile (CONAPACH)
Global Guardian Trust
SOLAGRAL

INTERNATIONAL ATOMIC ENERGY AGENCY
(IAEA)

DOCUMENTS REPRODUCED IN WHOLE OR IN PART:

IAEA GENERAL CONFERENCE

IAEA PRESS RELEASES

DOCUMENTS NOT REPRODUCED:

1. IAEA ANNUAL REPORT FOR 1994

Doc. no.: GC(39)/3 July 1995

Member States of the International Atomic Energy Agency

AFGHANISTAN
ALBANIA
ALGERIA
ARGENTINA
ARMENIA
AUSTRALIA
AUSTRIA
BANGLADESH
BELARUS
BELGIUM
BOLIVIA
BRAZIL
BULGARIA
CAMBODIA
CAMEROON
CANADA
CHILE
CHINA
COLOMBIA
COSTA RICA
COTE D'IVOIRE
CROATIA
CUBA
CYPRUS
CZECH REPUBLIC
DENMARK
DOMINICAN REPUBLIC
ECUADOR
EGYPT
EL SALVADOR
ESTONIA
ETHIOPIA
FINLAND
FRANCE
GABON
GERMANY
GHANA
GREECE
GUATEMALA
HAITI
HOLY SEE
HUNGARY
ICELAND
INDIA
INDONESIA
IRAN,
ISLAMIC REPUBLIC OF
IRAQ
IRELAND
ISRAEL
ITALY
JAMAICA
JAPAN
JORDAN
KAZAKHSTAN
KENYA
KOREA, REPUBLIC OF
KUWAIT
LEBANON
LIBERIA
LIBYAN ARAB JAMAHIRIYA
LIECHTENSTEIN
LITHUANIA
LUXEMBOURG
MADAGASCAR
MALAYSIA
MALI
MARSHALL ISLANDS
MAURITIUS
MEXICO
MONACO
MONGOLIA
MOROCCO
MYANMAR
NAMIBIA
NETHERLANDS
NEW ZEALAND
NICARAGUA
NIGER
NIGERIA
NORWAY
PAKISTAN
PANAMA
PARAGUAY
PERU
PHILIPPINES
POLAND
PORTUGAL
QATAR
ROMANIA
RUSSIAN FEDERATION
SAUDI ARABIA
SENEGAL
SIERRA LEONE
SINGAPORE
SLOVAKIA
SLOVENIA
SOUTH AFRICA
SPAIN
SRI LANKA
SUDAN
SWEDEN
SWITZERLAND
SYRIAN ARAB REPUBLIC
THAILAND
THE FORMER YUGOSLAV
REPUBLIC OF MACEDONIA
TUNISIA
TURKEY
UGANDA
UKRAINE

UNITED ARAB EMIRATES
UNITED KINGDOM OF
GREAT BRITAIN AND
NORTHERN IRELAND
UNITED REPUBLIC OF TANZANIA
UNITED STATES OF AMERICA
URUGUAY
UZBEKISTAN
VENEZUELA
VIET NAM
YEMEN
YUGOSLAVIA
ZAIRE
ZAMBIA
ZIMBABWE

The Agency's Statute was approved on 23 October 1956 by the Conference on the Statute of the IAEA held at United Nations Headquarters, New York; it entered into force on 29 July 1957. The Headquarters of the Agency are situated in Vienna. Its principal objective is "to accelerate and enlarge the contribution of atomic energy to peace, health and prosperity throughout the world".

Printed by the IAEA in Austria
July 1995

CONTENTS

CONTENTS

INTRODUCTION

During 1994, the Agency continued its wide ranging programme of work aimed at a balanced delivery to all Member States. This programme encompasses: nuclear power and its fuel cycle, waste management, the safety of nuclear installations and radiation safety, international safeguards and the use of nuclear techniques to help improve human health, the supply of food and environmental protection within the context of sustainable development. In particular, the Agency's contributions to international security through its verification activities and to the transfer of nuclear technology continued to be major focal points of its work.

The Agency's activities during 1994 continued to be conducted within the framework of a zero real growth Regular Budget — the tenth year of operation under such conditions. Furthermore, the Regular Budget appropriation for Agency programmes of some $214 million was reduced by $20 million in anticipation of shortfalls in contributions. On the other hand, activities with a value of $17.3 million deferred from previous years were implemented. Total new resources amounting to $52 million were available for the technical co-operation programme in 1994. Pledges to the Technical Assistance and Co-operation Fund stood at 72.5% of the target of $58.5 million. Extrabudgetary funds, apart from those directed to technical co-operation and the ICTP, and those received from other United Nations organizations, rose by 11% to $16.4 million and remained vital to some programmes, notably safeguards and nuclear safety.

This introduction highlights the overall activities of the Agency. The main achievements within individual programmes are recorded in the overviews at the beginning of each chapter.

The credibility of commitments made by States not to acquire nuclear weapons has become increasingly important, particularly as States which do possess nuclear weapons move to reduce their arsenals. The Agency's system of safeguards for verifying that nuclear energy is used exclusively for peaceful purposes has a vital role to play in enhancing this credibility because it enables States to demonstrate compliance with their international undertakings.

In recent years the Agency has introduced a number of measures to improve the safeguards system and further steps in this direction were taken in 1994. With the extensive co-operation and support of Member States, work progressed on Programme "93+2" — a comprehensive set of measures to improve the cost effectiveness of safeguards on declared nuclear material and increase the assurance of the completeness of information on nuclear activities in States with comprehensive safeguards agreements. The work undertaken in this area was reviewed by the Agency's Standing Advisory Group on Safeguards Implementation (SAGSI) and by the Board of Governors.

SAFEGUARDS IN THE NEWLY INDEPENDENT STATES OF THE FORMER USSR

By the end of 1994, 12 of the newly independent States had acceded to the Treaty on the Non-Proliferation of Nuclear Weapons (NPT). Three of these (Armenia, Lithuania and Latvia) had concluded safeguards agreements with the Agency and inspections to verify the initial inventories were carried out. In other States with substantial nuclear programmes:

- Preparations were made for the implementation of safeguards, with 18 technical visits made to States, including visits to major facilities, particularly in Belarus, Kazakhstan and Ukraine;
- Preliminary information was obtained regarding nuclear installations, nuclear materials and nuclear material accountancy and control systems;
- Safeguards requirements and the need for support by donor States, co-ordinated by the Agency, were identified.

An important part of the Agency's support in 1994 was in the form of training in nuclear material accountancy organized for personnel from national control bodies as well as facilities. In all, there were training events for 218 participants.

Once initial inspection activities have been completed, the total safeguards effort in the newly independent States is expected to amount to about 6% of the Agency's current total inspection effort.

Overall, the effort to improve the safeguards system has been successful. One example is the so-called "New Partnership Approach", which began replacing the previous "observation" and "joint team" arrangements between the Agency and EURATOM in 1994, allowing the two organizations to meet their respective safeguards responsibilities more effectively and efficiently. The result of the implementation of the new approach has been a substantial decrease in the cost of the Agency's inspection effort in the ten non-nuclear-weapon States of the European Union. These savings have permitted redirection of resources to new requirements in other regions.

However, some specific measures that were introduced have yet to generate their full benefits. For example, in February 1993 the Board of Governors endorsed a proposal for the establishment of a reporting scheme for the export and import of nuclear material as well as the export of specified equipment and non-nuclear material. By the end of 1994, only 43 Member States and the European Union had subscribed to the scheme and only 22 States had actually submitted reports.

The negotiation during the year of comprehensive safeguards agreements with the newly independent States (NIS) of the former USSR which have significant nuclear facilities marked an important step towards the full implementation of safeguards in those countries.

To date, safeguards agreements in connection with the Treaty on the Non-Proliferation of Nuclear Weapons (NPT) have been concluded with eight NIS States. Also, a comprehensive safeguards agreement was concluded with Ukraine covering all nuclear material in peaceful use. In preparing for the full implementation of safeguards in the NIS, the Agency provided advice on the legal framework for control of nuclear activities and, in collaboration with a number of Member States, provided assistance in establishing State systems of accounting and control of nuclear material, and advice on physical protection and on mechanisms for the reporting of imports and exports relevant to safeguards.

Developments in other regions have led to, or have opened the way to, Agency safeguards being applied to additional nuclear activities. Argentina, Brazil and Chile ratified the Treaty of Tlatelolco and the Quadripartite Safeguards Agreement between Argentina, Brazil, the Brazilian-Argentine Agency for Accounting and Control of Nuclear Materials (ABACC) and the Agency entered into force in March. With the announcement by Cuba that it had signed the Tlatelolco Treaty, it can be expected that this Treaty will soon enter into force, thus formalizing the nuclear weapon free status of the Latin American and Caribbean region.

At the request of the General Conference, the Director General continued consultations with countries in the Middle East to facilitate the early application of Agency safeguards to all nuclear activities in the region. Furthermore, in the context of promoting mutual confidence and security in the Middle East, the Agency provided expert assistance to the participants in the Multilateral Working Group on Arms Control and Regional Security.

The implementation of safeguards in the Democratic People's Republic of Korea remained a matter of great concern during the year. Following an understanding with the Democratic People's Republic of Korea in February on the inspection activities required to provide continuity of safeguards knowledge at declared facilities, an inspection was carried out in March. However, refuelling of the 5 MW experimental reactor at Nyongbyon started without the presence of Agency inspectors and despite the subsequent arrival of an inspection team, no Agency verification of selected discharged fuel was permitted. In June, the Board of Governors decided to suspend non-medical assistance to the Democratic People's Republic of Korea. On 15 June, the Agency was informed that the Democratic People's Republic of Korea had decided to withdraw from the Agency with effect from 13 June. This withdrawal did not affect the validity of the safeguards agreement, which remains in force.

Bilateral talks between the Democratic People's Republic of Korea and the USA resulted in an "Agreed Framework", signed in Geneva on 21 October. On 4 November, the President of the United Nations Security Council issued a statement requesting the Agency to take all steps it might deem necessary, as a consequence of the Agreed Framework, to monitor the freeze on the graphite moderated reactors and related facilities in the Democratic People's Republic of Korea. An Agency technical team visited the country in November to discuss the implementation of safeguards and arrangements were made to enable the Agency to meet most of its objectives. The Agency team visited the facilities subject to the freeze and was able to confirm that they were not in operation and that construction work had stopped.

During 1994, the Agency carried out 5 inspections in Iraq, bringing the total number of inspections to 27. It continued to carry out activities related to the destruction, removal and rendering harmless of items requiring such action pursuant to United Nations Security Council Resolution 687. The remaining action in that regard, the removal of a further 100 spent fuel assemblies from Iraq, was completed under a contract between the Russian Federation and the Agency in February. The fuel assemblies will be processed and stored, under Agency safeguards, in the Russian Federation. The Agency continued to phase in elements of the plan, approved by the Security Council in Resolution 715, for the ongoing monitoring and verification of Iraq's compliance with Security Council Resolutions 687 and 707.

As a result of the dismantling of nuclear weapons by the USA and the Russian Federation and the ongoing reprocessing of spent nuclear fuel, substantial quantities of plutonium and high enriched uranium are being recovered. President Clinton and President Yeltsin agreed in January 1994 to establish a joint working group to consider "steps to ensure the transparency and irreversibility of the process of reduction of nuclear weapons, including the possibility of putting a portion of the fissionable material under Agency safeguards". The USA submitted to Agency safeguards a portion of its fissile material no longer needed for defence purposes and Agency inspections commenced at two locations.

In December 1993, the United Nations General Assembly adopted a resolution which recommended the negotiation of a verifiable treaty banning the production of fissile material for nuclear weapons or other explosive devices. The Assembly requested the Agency "to provide assistance for examination of verification arrangements for such a treaty as required". In compliance with this request the Agency began examining the verification issues involved and preparing background papers.

During the year the Agency was invited by the Ad Hoc Committee on a Nuclear Test Ban of the Conference on Disarmament to provide information about its infrastructure and technical expertise in connection with the discussion on the verification arrangements for a Comprehensive Test Ban Treaty (CTBT). Although the scope of the treaty and the modalities for its verification are not yet agreed, the draft text of a CTBT being considered by the negotiating States, noting the need for cost effective arrangements and for effective use of relevant experience and expertise, foresees a role for the Agency in the verification of compliance with a future treaty.

An increase in reports of illicit trafficking in nuclear materials caused the Agency's General Conference in September to call upon Member States "to take all necessary measures to prevent illicit trafficking in nuclear material" and to invite the Secretariat to prepare proposals for Agency activities, in consultation with experts designated by Member States and competent international organizations. The consultations took place in November and in December the Board gave initial consideration to a set of proposals to increase the Agency's support to Member States in strengthening their systems to ensure security of nuclear materials and other radioactive sources.

The Conference on the Nuclear Power Option, convened by the Agency in September, showed that while it is relatively easy to describe the current status of nuclear power, it is hard to predict the timing of its future growth. Some Member States continue expanding their nuclear power capacity, while others expect to expand their supply when current surplus capacity has been utilized and a few are decided opponents of nuclear power. However, even with ambitious conservation efforts the world must increase its use of electricity in the coming decades in order to secure economic development, environmental benefits and improvements in standards of living. The consensus of the conference was that nuclear power will continue to provide about the same proportion of electricity as at present. A mix of nuclear and other fuels is beneficial in achieving stability in supply and the price of electricity. At the same time global concern with the production of so-called greenhouse gases and the prospect of climate change was reflected by the entry into force in March 1994 of the United Nations Framework Convention on Climate Change. Underpinning international efforts in this area are the scientific assessments being conducted by the Intergovernmental Panel on Climate Change (IPCC). The Agency has contributed to some elements of that work. The latest IPCC assessments prepared in 1994 will be circulated to participating governments for comment before finalization in 1995. In the Agency's view the draft assessments do not adequately reflect the potential contribution that nuclear energy could make to meeting energy demands while reducing carbon dioxide emissions.

To assist Member States in assessing and comparing the costs and benefits of nuclear and other sources of energy for electricity generation, the Agency, together with a number of other international organizations, has been developing tools for the comparative assessment of different electricity generation options taking into account economic, environmental and health considerations. This inter-agency joint project, known as DECADES, has now evolved from its development phase to a point where the Agency has begun responding to Member State requests to utilize the tools for assessment purposes.

A major accomplishment in the area of nuclear safety was the adoption in June of the Convention on Nuclear Safety — the culmination of three years of preparation and negotiation. In addition, the new Basic Safety Standards sponsored by six international organizations, including the Agency, were approved by the Board of Governors in September. They contain guidelines on responsibilities for the control and safety of radiation sources as well as for the protection of workers, the general public and medical patients, together with guidelines for intervention levels in emergency situations. Both the Convention and the new Basic Safety Standards supplement the existing extensive framework of safety guidelines and standards and the Conventions on Early Warning and Assistance in the Event of a Nuclear Accident. Negotiations continued on a more widely accepted international regime for liability for nuclear damage. The importance of an early conclusion of a new convention on liability has been heightened by the practical requirement for an acceptable liability framework for upgrading safety at nuclear power plants of older designs.

The Agency's activities on the safety of nuclear power plants in eastern Europe and countries of the former USSR resulted in a consensus between the operators and the countries engaged in safety assistance programmes on the safety issues to be addressed, and on their significance, in relation to the different models of WWER and RBMK reactors. This consensus provided guidance for both national programmes to improve safety and the international assistance co-ordinated through the G-24 mechanism. It also offered information of relevance for the work being performed by the World Association of Nuclear Operators (WANO). Special attention was given to the nuclear power plant at Chernobyl after the decision of Ukraine in 1993 to continue its operation. Following examination of the plant by an Agency team of safety experts, a meeting was convened in April to consider possible measures to deal with the safety situation which had been identified. A clear majority of the participants expressed the view that operation of the Chernobyl plant should be discontinued as soon as conditions allow. At the end of the year the matter was still under discussion between Ukraine and countries which might offer assistance.

The preparation for the joint project with UNDP for assistance to the newly independent States of the former USSR in strengthening nuclear and radiation safety infrastructures has resulted in the identification of needs and the preparation of plans for remedial action. Implementation of the plans will depend on the availability of funding. Since no resources have yet been raised by UNDP, other channels will now have to be pursued.

The management of spent fuel from research reactors was the subject of increased international discussion. The life of a large number of research reactors is being extended and this is leading to a need to expand interim spent fuel storage capacities pending decisions on longer term solutions. The Agency has established a database on research reactor spent fuel inventories and has registered the problems of individual facilities.

International normative work regarding radioactive wastes continued to progress under the Agency's Radioactive Waste Safety Standards (RADWASS) programme. Two documents, the Safety Fundamentals on the principles of radioactive waste management and a Safety Standard on establishing a national system for radioactive waste management, were prepared for consideration by the Board of Governors. The preparation of the documents involved an extensive process of consultations amongst Member States with a view to obtaining international consensus. As a further step towards codifying good waste management practices, the General Conference in September invited the Board and the Director General to commence preparations for a convention on the safe management of radioactive wastes.

CONVENTION ON NUCLEAR SAFETY AND THE NEW BASIC SAFETY STANDARDS

There were two important developments in the areas of radiation and nuclear safety.

- On 17 June 1994, at a Diplomatic Conference in Vienna, representatives from 84 countries adopted the text of the Convention on Nuclear Safety. The Convention applies to "nuclear installations", defined as land based civil nuclear power plants. It stipulates that the Agency shall provide the Secretariat for the meetings of the Contracting Parties. The Convention was opened for signature on 20 September 1994 in conjunction with the thirty-eighth regular session of the General Conference. It will enter into force after the deposit with the Director General of "the twenty-second instrument of ratification, including the instruments of seventeen States, each having at least one nuclear installation which has achieved criticality in a reactor core" (Article 31). As of 1 February 1995, 54 States had signed the convention and 1 State (Norway) had ratified it. The Convention provides that not later than six months after its entry into force, a "preparatory meeting" of Contracting Parties is to be held. At that meeting the Contracting Parties shall adopt Rules of Procedure and Financial Rules and shall establish, inter alia, guidelines regarding the form and structure of the reports to be submitted to the "review meetings" of the Contracting Parties, as well as the process for reviewing such reports.

- In September, the Board of Governors gave approval for the publication of the International Basic Safety Standards for Protection Against Ionizing Radiation and for the Safety of Radiation Sources. This new edition, jointly sponsored by the FAO, IAEA, ILO, OECD/NEA, PAHO and WHO, is based on the latest assessments of the biological effects of radiation made by the United Nations Scientific Committee on the Effects of Atomic Radiation and on recommendations from the International Commission on Radiological Protection and the International Nuclear Safety Advisory Group. The Standards reflect the achievement of international consensus on requirements for radiation protection and safety for the following:

  - Planned practices such as nuclear power generation and the use of radiation and radioactive materials in medicine and industry;
  - Intervention in existing situations such as chronic exposure to natural sources of radiation or exposure following an accident;
  - Control of radiation sources, including notification and authorization and criteria for exemption.

  Consensus guidance is also given on:

  - Occupational radiation protection;
  - Protection of patients in radiography, fluoroscopy, computer tomography, mammography and nuclear medicine;
  - Protection of members of the public from exposure to radioactive materials released to the environment;
  - Prevention of incidents giving rise to potential exposures;
  - Intervention in a radiological emergency.

The Agency's Safety Standards as approved by the Board of Governors must be applied to all Agency technical co-operation projects. In this connection, a systematic approach to help strengthen radiation protection and waste management infrastructures in Member States has been introduced in the technical co-operation programme, where specific activities are being implemented within the framework of a model project initiative. The proposed activities will help Member States to reach the required level of expertise for their particular circumstances. In its first year, this new approach has already resulted in considerable improvements in terms of legislation, codes of practice, licensing and personnel monitoring.

At the meeting of Contracting Parties to the Convention on Prevention of Marine Pollution by Dumping of Wastes and Other Matter (London Convention 1972) in November 1993, the dumping of radioactive wastes at sea was banned by international agreement. When the ban became operative on 20 February 1994 for all Contracting Parties except those which had made a declaration of non-acceptance before that date, the Russian Federation declared that it was not able to comply with it. However, it is presently working together with other countries to find technical solutions which would remove its need to dispose of low level wastes at sea. During 1994, the IAEA-MEL participated in scientific missions to examine the environment surrounding the sites of past dumping of radioactive wastes and equipment in the Kara Sea in the Arctic and in seas further to the east (i.e. the Sea of Japan, Sea of Okhotsk, Yellow Sea), and of the nuclear submarine which sank in the North Atlantic containing two nuclear warheads and a nuclear reactor. While it appears that there are no effects at present from the dumped wastes, the gradual deterioration of the waste packages and containments could lead to impacts in the future.

The lack of adequate waste management facilities for low and intermediate level radioactive wastes sometimes raises problems for small and developing nuclear programmes where nuclear techniques are applied only in research, medicine, agriculture and industry. Waste management strategies are required if there is to be confidence in the use of such applications. In this connection, the Agency began to assess the feasibility of applying a regional approach to the management of spent radium sources in Africa.

The Agency's technical co-operation programme continued to be redirected by the development of the model project approach. Of the 12 model projects approved for 1994, 11 have been successfully started. One, however, has been delayed by the failure to attract adequate extrabudgetary funding. Building on the ideas behind the original initiative, the Agency prepared proposals for a further set of model projects which were approved by the Board of Governors for implementation starting in 1995–1996. Unlike the first set, which were based mainly on initiatives of the Secretariat, the new projects stem from proposals made by Member States and reflect the extent to which the reorientation to an emphasis on demonstrable benefit for end users has been embraced. It is expected that the characteristics of model projects will in time be observable across the spectrum of the technical co-operation programme and indeed the work of other areas of the Agency which are contributing to technology transfer.

Simultaneously with the introduction of the model project approach, the Agency has sought to collaborate more closely with other international organizations such as FAO, WHO and UNIDO. It has also sought to tap new and additional sources of multilateral and bilateral funding by demonstrating how effectively nuclear techniques can contribute to the development process. In this way the Agency aims to become an effective "partner in development".

In accordance with global priorities, the focus of the Agency's technical co-operation activities continues to be on the transfer of technology that will help to increase food supplies, improve human health and contribute to sustainable development and protection of the environment. A fourth focus of emphasis — and one which emerges from the Agency's own work — is to ensure adequate radiation protection.

In September the Agency convened the Third Technical Co-operation Policy Review Seminar at which Member States: agreed that high priority be assigned to radiation protection and waste management; accepted a proposal for introducing medium term country plans to provide a framework for future co-operation programmes; and considered the extent to which the Agency should reorient its technical co-operation activities towards maximizing direct socio-economic impacts.

While there was widespread support for these new directions in the technical co-operation programme, contributions to the Technical Assistance and Co-operation Fund (TACF) dropped to 72.5% of the target compared with 76.5% in 1993. The downward trend in pledges and payments in relation to the agreed targets for the TACF is a major obstacle to meeting the priority needs of Member States.

Within the area of the Agency's work on the use of nuclear techniques to help increase the supply of food, the programme related to the control of rinderpest in Africa has attained an important turning point. The programme, which uses regular budget, extrabudgetary and TACF resources, has involved the use of a nuclear based technique for testing the effectiveness of the vaccination campaign, and a programme of quality control amongst the regional institutes which carried out the actual testing. The campaign has now reached the stage where the cumulative impact of vaccinations, as confirmed by the Agency's testing programme, is leading to a reduced need for intervention. Additional extrabudgetary resources have now been offered to enable the Agency to continue monitoring progress in the coming years.

ERADICATION OF INSECT PESTS

Significant achievements were made in the Agency's programme on the use of the sterile insect technique (SIT) for the eradication of insect pests:

- Major progress was made in the eradication of the Mediterranean fruit fly in the Province of Mendoza in Argentina. In collaboration with the provincial and federal governments, all activities in the SIT programme were scaled up and by the end of 1994 two hundred million sterile flies were being released each week over the half a million hectares of orchards and urban areas of the province. Commercial fruit crops are already free of the pest and eradication in urban areas will be attempted in the 1995–1996 season.

- The SIT programme on Zanzibar, United Republic of Tanzania, to eradicate the tsetse fly made rapid progress. Sterile tsetse flies were released for the first time by air and the whole southern part of the island, including the Jozani and Muyuni forests where the highest tsetse populations are located, is now under aerial releases. The first phase of the refurbishment of the Tanga facility was completed, thereby increasing significantly the sterile fly production capacity. Monitoring indicates that already one fourth to one third of all wild tsetse females captured in the southern part of the island show signs of induced sterility. With increasing fly production, the aerial release of sterile flies will be extended progressively to the northern half of the island.

- Important advances were made in the improvement and field evaluation of Mediterranean fruit fly genetic sexing strains developed by the Agency's Laboratory at Seibersdorf. As part of the assessment, weekly shipments of sterile males of two genetic sexing strains were made in support of a technical co-operation project in Tozeur, Tunisia. On the basis of these field results, as well as previous evaluations in Greece and ongoing tests in Guatemala, there is now confidence that these advanced sexing strains possess the necessary robustness to play an important role in large scale SIT programmes. As an example of this confidence, the United States Department of Agriculture in Hawaii recently requested one of these sexing strains for production at one of its mass rearing facilities.

- The Mediterranean fruit fly mass rearing facility in Arica, Chile, initiated operations. Joint Chile–Peru preventive releases of sterile flies are now replacing insecticide sprays along the border of these two countries to deal with wild flies moving south to fly free areas. A programme was initiated in Madeira, Portugal, with the objective of using the SIT against the Mediterranean fruit fly, the only fruit fly pest on the island. A sterile fly mass rearing facility has been designed and construction will be initiated in 1995.

Other highlights in the area of food and agriculture include the following. Genetically improved varieties of sorghum and African rice developed through an Agency CRP are now ready to be released in Mali for testing in the field under the auspices of a model technical co-operation project. Bulk reagents for a new and inexpensive radioimmunoassay technique for monitoring fertility in animals, developed by the Agency's Laboratory at Seibersdorf and tested through co-operation with Member States, are now being made generally available, leading to greater reliance on and more sustained use of this aid to livestock production. A number of advances were made in the use of the sterile insect technique (SIT) for pest control.

In the work on human health, preparations were made to commence a CRP and initiate a model project to foster the use of nuclear technologies to monitor applied nutritional intervention programmes. In response to approaches by the Agency, some commercial manufacturers have begun producing simple, low cost, updated gamma cameras and brachytherapy machines and discussions are continuing with companies to produce simple, low cost SPECT (single photon emission tomography) systems and teletherapy units. These developments are leading to lower costs for the supply of these items under technical co-operation projects and wider commercial availability in developing countries. Agency sponsored research activities received commendation at the 1994 World Congress of Nuclear Medicine for their novel approach to randomized, multicentre, clinical trials for the validation of new treatment strategies in cancer patients.

The analytical capabilities of the Agency's Laboratory at Seibersdorf in the field of environmental monitoring have been strengthened through the acquisition of additional equipment and technologies. Examples include the following. The Agency has acquired access to a beam line facility which will be used for the measurement of low levels of contamination in environmental samples. An inductively coupled plasma mass spectrometer will provide state-of-the-art elemental analysis in environmental and biological samples. Newly acquired molecular based technology will complement a battery of techniques already available for research and diagnostic purposes in the agricultural area.

The Laboratory continued to provide direct support to field projects. For example, fellowship training in 1994 reached a total of over one hundred fellows from more than fifty countries. More than 1.8 million tsetse fly pupae were shipped to the eradication project on Zanzibar, United Republic of Tanzania. A major reduction in the tsetse fly population on the island has already been achieved. In the area of verification, the Safeguards Analytical Laboratory participated in field trials of environmental sampling for safeguards under Programme "93+2".

As noted above, the IAEA-MEL made a particular contribution to the monitoring of radioactive contamination in the marine environment. The laboratory was awarded the Philip Morris Scientific Prize for Biogeochemistry for its pioneering work, along with French scientists, on the use of isotopic techniques and direct particulate sampling to quantify the carbon flux in the oceans — a matter of major relevance to the understanding of climate change. This important work is continuing with extrabudgetary support.

By the end of the year, the Agency had taken major steps to simplify and standardize its programme, budget and accounting systems in order to provide managers with more timely and relevant information and make the Agency's operations more transparent. A revision of the financial rules and regulations had been completed and a framework for systematic programme monitoring and evaluation had been introduced.

PROGRAMME PERFORMANCE ASSESSMENT SYSTEM

In 1994 the Agency expanded the introduction of the systematic application of the Programme Performance Assessment System (PPAS). Under the PPAS, it is the responsibility of Agency managers to:

- Assess the merits of proposed projects in terms of their potential benefits to Member States;
- Develop clear project objectives, set completion dates and establish performance indicators for reviews at predetermined intervals;
- Examine completed projects and evaluate their actual success and benefits to Member States.

During the year, approximately thirty Agency projects were selected for performance review on the basis of their importance to the overall programme of work. Each of the selected projects received a performance review at mid-year to:

- Verify its continued relevance;
- Determine the status of the tasks planned;
- Compare the estimated expenditures against budgeted amounts;
- Clarify deviations from the work plan and/or budget;
- Identify potential problems or planned improvements.

In order to assist programme and project managers, training seminars and briefings on the principles and procedures of PPAS were held. Over one hundred staff members received this training.

The Agency has continued to work closely with other elements in the international system. In matters relating to verification, the Agency continued to interact with the United Nations Security Council as the body politically responsible for ensuring implementation of nuclear arms control measures. The Agency continued to play its part in system wide efforts to promote sustainable development through the many programmes and technical assistance projects which directly or indirectly support the objectives of Agenda 21. Its co-operation with other organizations in the United Nations system continued to be extensive. In this regard, special mention may be made of the thirtieth anniversary of the establishment of the Joint FAO/IAEA Division set up to pursue the use of nuclear techniques for food production and preservation.

In 1995 the fiftieth anniversary of the United Nations and the Review and Extension Conference of the NPT will provide focal points for thinking about future directions of Agency activity. However, the immediate priorities are clear: the financing of safeguards and of technical co-operation; the implementation of the recommendations of Programme "93+2" for strengthening the effectiveness and improving the efficiency of safeguards; preparations for the entry into force of the Convention on Nuclear Safety and for the negotiation of a convention on the safe management of radioactive wastes; the implementation of the various initiatives relating to the technical co-operation programme, including the outcomes of the policy review seminar in 1994; the introduction of a new programme for enhancing the security of nuclear and radioactive materials; and the continued effort to introduce improved management practices and systems which will provide a better basis for decisions about resource allocation.

Member States have an interest in the effective pursuit of all the functions and activities foreseen in the Statute of the Agency and in ensuring that none of them are neglected. The various activities are mutually supportive and to make a distinction between promotional and regulatory functions does not do justice to the full range of the Agency's endeavours. The real constraint to the strengthening of various parts of its mandate lies not in any statutory limitation, but in the zero real growth policy that has been followed for over ten years.

[...]

ACTIVITIES IN 1994

RADIOACTIVE WASTE MANAGEMENT

Programme overview

In response to a request by Member States for more international guidance and co-ordination in the field of radioactive waste management and in recognition of the need to assist some Member States in improving their waste management programme infrastructures, the Agency in 1994 focused on: the continued implementation of the Radioactive Waste Safety Standards (RADWASS) programme; the development of radiological and safety criteria for waste disposal and the co-ordination of international radiological and environmental assessment projects; and the implementation of programmes for improving national infrastructures and the development of mechanisms for better and more effective technology transfer. Other areas receiving emphasis included direct advisory and review services, guidance on the safety, technical and planning aspects of decommissioning, quality assurance management for waste packaging and disposal systems, safety assessment of near surface disposal facilities and the environmental restoration of contaminated land masses.

The RADWASS programme continued to be one of the core efforts of the Agency's waste management programme. In addition, RADWASS became a basic foundation for many of the tasks and projects within other subprogrammes. The importance of RADWASS to Member States was again reaffirmed during the 1994 regular session of the General Conference by a resolution which requested the Agency to maintain emphasis in the field of radioactive waste management. In addition, to better co-ordinate, harmonize and facilitate consensus for key RADWASS documents, a subgroup of the International Radioactive Waste Management Advisory Committee (INWAC) was created to review all documents requiring approval of the Board of Governors.

In a resolution adopted at the regular session of the General Conference in September 1994, Member States "invited the Board of Governors and the Director General to commence preparation for a convention on the safety of waste management and begin the process of collecting relevant background information (including appropriate RADWASS documents) that would be useful in drafting the convention".

With the changes in eastern Europe and the countries of the former USSR, information has become available revealing the existence of environmental problems. Workshops were organized in 1994 to focus on detailed planning methods and technologies available for the restoration of contaminated sites.

The Agency is the competent international body on matters related to radioactivity to the Convention on the Prevention of Marine Pollution by Dumping of Wastes and Other Matter (London Convention 1972). In 1994, the Agency was requested to develop guidance on exemption in the context of disposal of materials at sea. The disposal of radioactive wastes by dumping at sea was banned by international agreement in February 1994. The purpose of the Agency's work is to provide guidance on how to define 'radioactive' in the context of the London Convention.

A CRP on the validation of environmental model predictions (VAMP) was completed. The objective of the VAMP studies, started in 1988, was to provide a mechanism for the validation of assessment models by using the environmental data on radionuclide transfer which have resulted from the Chernobyl release. The project has resulted in both technical and administrative achievements in the field of model validation.

Efforts are under way to upgrade waste management programme infrastructures in Member States which generate wastes primarily from nuclear applications. In addition, development began of 'Minimum Acceptable Waste Infrastructure' criteria to be used for evaluating waste management programmes and needs in developing Member States. Activities are co-ordinated under an Agency model project on waste management and through advisory missions.

The development of a report on in situ solidification processes aimed at converting contaminated soil and sludges, currently stored in underground tanks, into a durable leach resistant product which will meet current requirements for near surface waste disposal, was restarted in 1994 after temporary deferment in 1993 due to budgetary constraints.

The first draft of a technical manual on the application of the Sealed Radiation Sources (SRS) Registry as a tool for record keeping and information management was prepared in late 1994, after deferred funds from 1992 were released.

IAEA-MEL contributed to the International Arctic Seas Assessment Project (IASAP) by offering assistance in analytical quality assurance, radioactivity monitoring, computer based dispersion modelling, radiological assessment and database provision. It participated in the 1994 Russian–Norwegian expedition to the Arctic dump sites to sample and subsequently analyse water, sediment and biota in the region. The first set of analyses of sea water and sediment samples from a joint expedition to the Sea of Japan was completed. The IAEA-MEL also continued its involvement in the Agency's Emergency Response System and in an expanded environmental monitoring programme in which waste effluents provide useful isotopic signals in the marine and aquatic environment.

IAEA-MEL's contribution to marine carbon flux studies was acknowledged by its winning, along with collaborators in France, of the 1994 Philip Morris Scientific Prize for Biogeochemistry.

HANDLING, TREATMENT, CONDITIONING AND STORAGE OF RADIOACTIVE WASTES

Minimizing volumes of radioactive wastes generated from nuclear fuel cycle facilities

Two reports were in preparation covering the technical, administrative and procedural options which can be applied at the front and back ends of the nuclear fuel cycle to minimize the generation of radioactive wastes. This is one of the vital aims of radioactive waste management which must be taken into account during the design stage and through the entire operational phase of all nuclear facilities. The report on the back end of the cycle was completed.

Quality assurance and quality control requirements for radioactive waste packages

Work continued on providing technical guidance on quality assurance (QA) requirements for all types of waste packages. A report specifying QA requirements to be met during container fabrication, waste immobilization and packaging, interim storage and waste emplacement operations was completed and approved for publication. A second report, being developed in parallel, will provide guidance on the QA arrangements and process controls for low and intermediate level wastes which need to be established to ensure that the waste packages produced will meet waste acceptance criteria for disposal.

Support for the safe management of spent radiation sources in developing countries

A report on the methods to identify and locate spent radiation sources was completed and approved for publication. A report was prepared providing practical guidance on conditioning and interim storage methods for spent radium sources. Two expert missions, in which actual conditioning of spent radium and other spent sealed sources was carried out, were completed in 1994.

Technical manuals for the handling and processing of radioactive wastes generated from nuclear applications

A series of technical manuals was completed with the publication of the last two documents. This series was undertaken to meet the needs of Member States that generate small volumes of radioactive wastes, providing straightforward and low cost solutions to waste handling and processing problems. A second phase of the programme was initiated during the year to determine areas of applications not covered in the initial programme development. A supplementary document on the handling and disposal of radioisotopes used for agricultural studies is in preparation.

CRPs in progress

Year of start	Subject	Year of completion	Participating institutions
1991	Performance of high level waste forms and packages under repository conditions	1995	14
1992	Treatment technologies for low and intermediate level wastes generated from nuclear applications	1995	15
1992	Waste treatment and immobilization technologies involving inorganic sorbents	1996	14

Training courses and seminars held

Course name	Location	No. of participants	Duration
Seminar on radioactive waste management practices and issues in developing countries	China	About 100	1 week

Publications

Series and No.	Title
Technical Reports Series No. 360	Status of technology for volume reduction and treatment of low and intermediate level solid radioactive waste
Technical Reports Series No. 366	Assessment and comparison of waste management system costs for nuclear and other energy sources
Technical Reports Series No. 370	Advances in technologies for the treatment of low and intermediate level radioactive liquid wastes
IAEA-TECDOC-775	Handling, treatment, conditioning and storage of biological radioactive wastes
IAEA-TECDOC-776	Reference design for a centralized waste processing and storage facility

RADIOACTIVE WASTE DISPOSAL

Technologies for near surface disposal systems for low and intermediate level radioactive wastes

A report on the design of near surface disposal facilities was completed. The document identifies technical principles and requirements, phases of implementation and design considerations. The requirements cover detailed items to be considered with respect to waste and site characteristics, engineered barriers, operational considerations and post-closure performance assessment. Conceptual, basic and detailed design phases are defined, as well as specific technical objectives and the scope of design activities for each phase. The document also includes a summary of Member State experience and a checklist of design requirements.

Technologies for deep geological disposal systems for high level radioactive wastes

A document on the methodology for selecting, siting and characterizing a geological repository for high level wastes was completed. This report presents the general processes and factors to be considered in selecting geological repository sites. The report also reviews Member State experience in selecting and characterizing sites for geological repositories, including the knowledge and data gained in siting underground research laboratories.

CRPs in progress

Year of start	Subject	Year of completion	Participating institutions
1991	Performance of engineered barrier materials in near surface disposal facilities	1995	14

Publications

Series and No.	Title
IAEA-TECDOC-764	Interfaces between transport and geological disposal systems for high level radioactive waste and spent nuclear fuel

DECONTAMINATION AND DECOMMISSIONING OF NUCLEAR INSTALLATIONS

Project planning and management for decommissioning operations

A report describing and assessing safe enclosure as a precursor to dismantling a nuclear installation was finalized and approved for publication. The report reviews the relevant safety, technical and economic factors for this possible decommissioning strategy.

During 1994, the focus of a project on environmental restoration in the countries of eastern Europe and the former USSR was the identification and characterization of radioactively contaminated sites. Before any action in regard to environmental restoration could be taken, it was necessary to obtain an overview of the environmental state in each of the countries. The Agency therefore requested selected Member State experts to survey and categorize the sites according to location, volume, radioactive concentration, proximity to populous areas and potential spreading of contamination. An IAEA-TECDOC collecting the results of the project will be published in 1995.

Publications

Series and No.	Title
Technical Reports Series No. 362	Decommissioning of facilities for mining and milling of radioactive ores and closeout of residues
Technical Reports Series No. 373	Decommissioning techniques for research reactors

RADIOLOGICAL AND ENVIRONMENTAL ASPECTS OF WASTE MANAGEMENT

Application of exemption principles to radioactive waste management

Since the international consensus was reached on principles for the exemption of radiation sources and practices from regulatory control in 1988, published as Safety Series No. 89, the principles have been used as a basis for developing practical guidance for use in relation to radioactive waste management. Various national and international studies concerned with deriving clearance levels for very low level wastes and for the recycle and reuse of materials from the nuclear fuel cycle have been published since 1988. On the basis of all of these studies, international guidance has been developed on clearance levels for radionuclides in solid materials. These levels, termed 'unconditional clearance levels', can be used as a basis for decision making when it is desired to release materials containing very small amounts of radionuclides from regulatory control. It is expected that the levels will find use in relation to transboundary movements of materials. For use in this application, there should be no further need for concern after release no matter what the use or destination of the materials might be and, therefore, the values have been derived taking into account amounts of exposure in a wide range of possible circumstances. After extensive review by expert groups, a document on this subject, containing values derived taking into account exposures in a wide range of possible circumstances, has been approved for publication as RADWASS Safety Guide No. 111-G-1.5.

Development of safety criteria for radioactive waste repositories

The discussions of the INWAC Subgroup on Principles and Criteria for Radioactive Waste Disposal on the subject of appropriate indicators of safety for waste repositories and of the nature of safety assessments at long time-scales, which have taken place over the last three years, culminated in the publication of a report (IAEA-TECDOC-767). It is expected that the concepts and ideas contained in the report will be used in the future development of RADWASS documents on the subject of geological disposal. The Subgroup is continuing to discuss other issues related to the safety of waste repositories, notably the problem of complying with regulatory criteria at long times in the future when predictive uncertainties become large.

Safety assessment in radioactive waste management and disposal facilities

The first test case of a CRP on the safety assessment of near surface disposal facilities was completed and evaluated. A report on the test case, in which the results of participants are presented, analysed and discussed, has been prepared and approved for publication as an IAEA-TECDOC.

Validation and assessment of radionuclide transfer models (cont.)

In 1988, the Agency started a CRP on the validation of environmental model predictions (VAMP) with the following objectives: to provide a mechanism for the validation of assessment models by using the environmental data on radionuclide transfer which resulted from the Chernobyl release; to acquire data from affected countries for that purpose; and to produce reports on the current status of environmental modelling and the improvements achieved as a result of post-Chernobyl validation efforts. In October 1994, the last meeting of the VAMP programme was held in Vienna. At this meeting, the progress made and the achievements of the programme were reviewed. The results of the VAMP study are in the process of being documented in the IAEA-TECDOC series.

Environmental studies in relation to marine disposal

The Agency is committed to presenting a report in 1996 on the potential impact of the high level radioactive wastes dumped in the shallow waters of the Kara Sea, and on the feasibility of possible remedial measures, to the London Convention 1972. Progress was made on this project in 1994, especially in obtaining a more detailed understanding of the nature of the wastes and of the form of their containment. It has been possible to postulate release rates of radionuclides from the wastes into the surrounding water as a function of time. The national modelling groups taking part in the project are improving their ability to represent radionuclide movement in the Kara and surrounding seas. The third joint Norwegian–Russian cruise to the area in 1994 obtained useful data on the wastes dumped in two of the bays. The measurements made during the cruise confirmed that very little radioactivity has been released to date from the dumped wastes. IAEA-MEL participated in the third joint Russian–Norwegian exploratory cruise to the Kara Sea to sample and subsequently analyse seawater and sediment samples. It also organized analytical laboratory control exercises for the participating Norwegian and Russian laboratories. Analyses of samples from the 1993 cruise have shown that leakage from dumped objects in the Stepovovo and Tsivolky Bays of Novaya Zemlya has occurred, leading to contamination with ^{137}Cs and ^{60}Co of locally restricted areas, but at radiologically insignificant levels.

A set of analyses was completed of seawater and sediment samples from the first joint expedition (Japan, Republic of Korea and the Russian Federation) to the Sea of Japan. The measured levels of typical anthropogenic radionuclides in the marine environment ($^{239+240}$Pu for alpha emitters, ^{90}Sr for beta emitters and ^{137}Cs for gamma emitters) represent the expected global fallout concentrations.

Environmental studies in relation to marine disposal (cont.)

IAEA-MEL also participated in the cruise to sample sea water and sediment around the sunken nuclear submarine 'Komsomolets' in the Norwegian Sea. The samples are presently under investigation.

Support for marine radioactivity monitoring

During 1994, two reports on intercomparison exercises were completed. Sea water and fish were collected in the Irish Sea for large scale intercomparison exercises. A specific exercise was organized at the request of the French Commissariat à l'energie atomique to analyse biological samples collected around the Mururoa atoll. The Laboratory also continued its association with the Helsinki Commission's Group of Experts on Monitoring of Radioactive Substances in the Baltic Sea and three specific intercomparison exercises on sediment samples were completed.

A new technique based on liquid scintillation counting was established for the analysis of soft beta emitters of ^{3}H, ^{129}I and ^{241}Pu in the marine environment, while collaboration with the Japan Atomic Energy Research Institute has allowed renovation and upgrading of the inductively coupled plasma mass spectrometer used for multi-element and radionuclide assays.

IAEA-MEL analysed several samples in the framework of the programme on environmental monitoring for safeguards purposes and participated in the intercomparison exercise for the analysis of safeguards samples.

A final report of a CRP on sources of radioactivity in the marine environment and their relative contributions to overall dose assessment from marine radioactivity was completed and for the first time dose rates based on ^{137}Cs and ^{210}Po in sea water and fish have been estimated for the world population. It has been shown that the doses to humans from anthropogenic radionuclides (^{137}Cs) in the marine environment are generally two to three orders of magnitude less than the doses from natural radionuclides (^{210}Po).

In-service training in radionuclide measurements and radiotracer applications in environmental studies continued to be a major focus in IAEA-MEL's activities. As a means of 'hands-on' training, IAEA Fellows from Colombia and Turkey directly participated in laboratory experiments aimed at assessing the behaviour of natural and artificial radionuclides in corals and other benthic organisms. In addition, Fellows from Mexico, France and Belgium, funded by external sources, participated in similar research projects dealing with laboratory radiotracer applications.

Research radionuclides in the marine environment

As part of the International Joint Global Ocean Flux Studies (JGOFS), particle flux samples from 200 and 1000 m depths covering a period of 323 days were obtained in the northwestern Mediterranean using sediment traps moored in the deep sea. These long term, time-series samples were essential for quantifying variations in carbon removal to the deep sea.

In the Adriatic, four cruises were undertaken to examine the flux of carbon and radionuclides in contrasting areas of high and low sedimentation rates. Emphasis was placed on the use of radioactive disequilibrium between particle reactive ^{234}Th and its soluble parent ^{238}U to evaluate the downward flux of particulate organic carbon produced in the surface layers. Through the EC sponsored ELNA programme, three stations in the northern Adriatic were profiled for these natural radionuclides. Additional sampling to test the ^{234}Th scavenging model for carbon export and the seasonal scavenging behaviour of ^{210}Po and ^{210}Pb by particles was carried out in the northwestern Mediterranean under the French JGOFS programme DYFAMED.

Research radionuclides in the marine environment (cont.)

Techniques were developed in the application of multitracer gamma spectrometry for simultaneously measuring the transfer of radionuclides and heavy metals through key marine food chains. Laboratory experiments utilizing these techniques have demonstrated that certain bottom dwellers such as starfish and sea urchins accumulate and strongly retain the key radionuclides ^{137}Cs, ^{241}Am and ^{60}Co as well as several heavy metals. These results are essential for developing radionuclide food chain transfer models in the Arctic and other seas.

In collaboration with the European Oceanological Observatory in Monaco, methodologies were developed to culture coral in small microcosms in which multitracer techniques were used to quantify the uptake and release rates of radionuclides and trace elements in different tropical coral colonies. Results showed a marked preferential uptake and strong binding of certain artificial radionuclides (such as ^{241}Am) into coral skeleton rather than in the living tissues, an observation which suggests that dead corals may serve as a sink for certain long lived radionuclides.

To better evaluate the intake of the key natural radionuclide ^{210}Po by humans living in the Mediterranean basin, fresh seafood samples of fish, shrimp, oysters, clams, mussels and squid were collected and analysed for ^{210}Po and its parent ^{210}Pb. The effect of cooking procedures on ^{210}Po and ^{210}Pb concentrations in seafood was also examined, as well as the natural radioactivity ingested with complete meals of similar seafoods which were obtained commercially.

Laboratory research continued on the interaction and behaviour of ^{210}Po and ^{210}Pb in marine biota and particulates. Work focused on measuring rates of ^{210}Po and ^{210}Pb sorption by sedimenting particles and on the influence of organic matter on the sorption processes. In addition to various classes of non-living detrital particles, the role of marine bacteria in ^{210}Po and ^{210}Pb cycling was investigated.

CRPs in progress

Year of start	Subject	Year of completion	Participating institutions
1988	Sources of radioactivity in the marine environment and their relative contributions to overall dose assessment from marine radioactivity	1994	17
1990	Safety assessment of near surface radioactive waste disposal facilities (NSARS)	1996	17
1993	Application of tracer techniques in the study of the Black Sea	1996	13
1993	Modelling of the radiological impact of waste dumping in the Arctic seas	1996	7

Training courses and seminars held

Course name	Location	No. of participants	Duration
Regional course on strategies and methodologies for applied marine radioactivity studies	Australia Turkey	29 12	2 weeks 2 weeks
Safety assessment methodology for near surface disposal facilities	USA	28	3 weeks

Publications

Series and No.	Title
Technical Reports Series No. 364	Handbook of parameter values for the prediction of radionuclide transfer in temperate environments
IAEA TECDOC-755	Assessing the radiological impact of past nuclear activities and events
IAEA TECDOC-767	Safety indicators in different time frames for the safety assessment of underground radioactive waste repositories

WASTE MANAGEMENT PLANNING AND INFRASTRUCTURE

Assessment of waste management status and trends

The second edition of the *Radioactive Waste Management Profiles*, which contains data provided by Member States during the 1991–1992 biennial update, was published. The Profiles contain data about national programme plans and activities, including data on waste management authorities and organizations, waste type and volume, treatment and conditioning methods, storage and disposal plans, and site information.

Radioactive Waste Safety Standards (RADWASS)

The RADWASS programme, which seeks to provide a series of documents in the fields of radioactive waste management, decontamination and decommissioning, and environmental restoration, is periodically reviewed by INWAC. In 1994, an Extended INWAC was formed to review all RADWASS documents prior to approval by the Board of Governors. This Committee reviewed two high category documents, the Safety Fundamentals and a Safety Standard on establishing a national system for radioactive waste management. Although broad consensus on these documents was reached, some Member States requested further harmonization with other Agency Safety Series publications before submission to the Board of Governors.

Radioactive Waste Safety Standards (RADWASS) (cont.)

In a resolution adopted at the regular session of the General Conference in September, Member States "invited the Board of Governors and the Director General to commence preparation for a convention on the safety of waste management and continue the process of collecting relevant background information (including appropriate RADWASS documents) that would be useful in drafting the convention". Preparations for such a convention have been initiated.

Direct assistance and support for national waste management programmes

In December 1993, the Nuclear Regulatory Authority of Slovakia requested the Agency to review the pre-operational safety report for the Mochovce waste disposal facility. This facility is a near surface repository for the disposal of low and intermediate level short lived radioactive wastes generated by the Bohunice and the proposed Mochovce nuclear power plants. The Agency convened a team of experts from Canada, Finland, France, Germany and Spain under the Waste Management Assessment and Technical Review Programme (WATRP). The expert team reviewed the source material provided by the Nuclear Regulatory Authority and met with Slovak experts during a meeting held in May.

Four Waste Management Advisory Programme (WAMAP) missions were conducted to: Lebanon, Saudi Arabia, the United Arab Emirates and Uruguay. The mission to Saudi Arabia was a joint RAPAT–WAMAP mission.

Training courses and seminars held

Course name	Location	No. of participants	Duration
Management of low level radioactive wastes	Argentina	24	3 weeks
Radioactive waste management techniques	Egypt	25	3 weeks

Publications

Series and No.	Title
Safety Series No. 111-G-1.1	Classification of radioactive waste
Safety Series No. 111-G-3.1	Siting of near surface disposal facilities
Safety Series No. 111-G-4.1	Siting of geological disposal facilities
Miscellaneous	Radioactive waste management glossary: Third edition
Technical document	Radioactive waste management profiles, No. 2
Miscellaneous	Waste Management Assessment and Technical Review Programme (WATRP)

[...]

SAFE TRANSPORT OF RADIOACTIVE MATERIAL

Maintenance and implementation of the Agency's Transport Regulations

The Standing Advisory Group for the Safe Transport of Radioactive Material (SAGSTRAM) met in March to advise on the priority of work for the transport safety programme, focusing on the task of comprehensively revising, through a Revision Panel, the Agency's Transport Regulations in 1996. At the meeting endorsement was given to the incorporation of a system of radiological protection that is consistent with the new Basic Safety Standards. The Revision Panel met in October to discuss the preparation of a second draft of the Regulations for distribution to Member States for formal comment in January 1995. The Panel considered the input from two Technical Committee meetings: on radiation protection matters, held in June, and on the air mode, held in August, as well as six meetings utilizing consultants services held during 1994. As a result of this major effort, the revision process is almost complete. The second draft will include the more stringent regulatory requirements for packaging used to carry large amounts of radioactive material by air.

Several tasks associated with the implementation of the Regulations were completed in 1994. A training manual was translated into Russian and Spanish with publication scheduled for early 1995. A training video on the safe transport of radioactive material which complements the policy document published in 1993 was produced. Also, an electronic version of Safety Series Nos 6, 7, 37 and 80, called HYPERTRANS!, was released by the Agency. This tool provides users of these publications with an easy method to search for text and follow the extensive cross-referencing within the documents.

A CRP on the development of probabilistic safety assessment techniques related to the safe transport of radioactive materials was completed. A computer program, called INTERTRAN-2, was prepared to assess the safety of transporting radioactive material. The program can be run on a PC, and a supporting manual will be published. To improve the underlying data set of INTERTRAN-2, a follow-up CRP was established to analyse relevant accident data.

The maritime transport of radioactive material continues to be the subject of debate within bodies such as the IMO. A newly established CRP on accident severity at sea with particular reference to fires on board ships will contribute to the review of the joint IAEA/IMO Code of Practice for the Safe Carriage of Irradiated Nuclear Fuel, Plutonium and High Level Waste on Board Ships.

CRPs in progress

Year of start	Subject	Year of completion	Participating institutions
1989	Development of probabilistic safety assessment techniques related to the safe transport of radioactive materials	1994	12
1992	Assessment of the safety of UF_6 transport packages in fires	1995	6

CRPs established in the current year

Subject	No. of years	Participating institutions
Development of relevant accident data for quantifying risks associated with transporting radioactive material	3	7
Accident severity at sea during the transport of radioactive material	3	4

Training courses and seminars held

Course name	Location	No. of participants	Duration
Regional course on the safe transport of radioactive material	Germany	24	3 weeks
Seminar on developments in radioactive waste transport	Head-quarters	86	1 week

Publications

Series and No.	Title
Safety Series No. 112	Compliance assurance for the safe transport of radioactive material
Safety Series No. 113	Quality assurance for the safe transport of radioactive material
Electronic guide	HYPERTRANS!
IAEA-NCAL-25	National competent authorities responsible for approvals and authorization in respect of the transport of radioactive material. List No. 25
IAEA-TECDOC-750	Interim guidance for the safe transport of reprocessed uranium
IAEA-TECDOC-758	Directory of national competent authorities' approval certificates for package design, special form material and shipment of radioactive material: 1994 edition
IAEA/TSRA/2	Transport safety research abstracts, No. 2

EMERGENCY PLANNING AND PREPAREDNESS

Emergency assistance services

Work continued on maintaining and improving the capabilities of the Emergency Response Unit and the overall effectiveness of the Agency to respond to a nuclear accident or radiological emergency. These activities included:

— Drills and training to maintain a basic response capability; monthly internal communications exercises to test the ability to contact Agency staff and quickly form a team to respond to the initial notification of a nuclear accident or radiological emergency; periodic external communication exercises involving Member States and other international organizations; periodic Agency staff training, and participation in emergency exercises with Finland, the Nordic Countries, the Russian Federation and the EC.
— Upgrading and modernizing communication with emergency Duty Officers during off-duty hours.

At the request of the Estonian Government, the Agency provided medical and radiological assistance for an emergency situation involving the overexposure of several individuals resulting from the theft and mishandling of a radioactive source. One individual died and several others received very high exposures.

There was continued effort to sustain and upgrade co-ordination and co-operation with other United Nations organizations which would have a role to play in responding to a nuclear accident or radiological emergency. These activities included:

— Participation in the development of the WMO's Environmental Emergency Response programme, which has been developed primarily to support State meteorological services. In the event of a nuclear accident, specialized meteorological centres will provide atmospheric transport products to the Agency for quick identification of those States most likely to feel the impact of a nuclear accident. Specific operating procedures for this arrangement were adapted. The Agency can request these services whenever there is a need.
— Agency participation in workshops in eastern and central Europe to discuss the Agency's Emergency Response System, as a result of recent interest expressed by the United Nations for the inclusion of military and civil defence assets in disaster relief operations. The United Nations has, as a consequence, established an on-line 'Register of Emergency Stockpiles' which can be used in the event of a major accident.
— Development of operating procedures for the interface between the United Nations Department of Humanitarian Affairs and the Agency's Emergency Response Unit.
— Start of work with UNEP's Global Resources Information Database (GRID) programme for the development of requirements for local site and regional maps of nuclear power plants.

The Agency was invited by various Member States to observe and evaluate comprehensive nuclear power plant exercises in the USA, South Africa, Slovenia and the Russian Federation.

Training courses and seminars held

Course name	Location	No. of participants	Duration
Regional workshop on off-site planning and countermeasures for radiological emergencies	Australia	26	2 weeks

Publications

Series and No.	Title
Safety Series No. 109	Intervention criteria in a nuclear or radiation emergency
IAEA-TECDOC-733	The utilization of real time models as a decision aid following a large release of radionuclides into the atmosphere

SAFETY OF RADIATION SOURCES

Design, control and safe use of radiation sources

A project proposal was approved at the regular session of the General Conference in September to direct efforts to assist Member States in the prevention of further accidents involving radiation sources. This will initially focus on large industrial irradiators with the compilation of an inventory of such irradiators, the collection of design and safety information and the provision of safety assessment services. Work has started on the implementation of this project.

A major collaborative project with WHO to produce a series of five training manuals on aspects of the medical uses of radiation has been essentially completed. The manuals are being reviewed prior to publication by WHO. Work has also continued on the production of Practical Radiation Safety Manuals and the development of computer based training assessment modules to accompany them.

Provision of information on radiation sources

An international reporting system, including a database, on unusual events involving radiation sources was designed in 1994. The reporting system will collect global information in order to learn from incidents and events relevant to radiation safety. The system will be implemented in 1995.

The Sealed Source Registry was finalized; this provides computer software for compiling the inventory of radiation sources in Member States.

Training courses and seminars held

Course name	Location	No. of participants	Duration
National workshop on radiation protection and quality assurance in diagnostic radiology	Lebanon	20	2 weeks
National workshop on radiation protection in industrial radiology	Viet Nam	15	1 week
Regional course on a system of notification, registration and control of radiation sources and installations	United Republic of Tanzania	15	3 weeks
Regional course on radiation protection in medical practice: Occupational protection of medical staff and protection of patients in diagnostic radiology and radiotherapy	Tunisia	9	3 weeks

RADIATION SAFETY SERVICES

Radiation Protection Advisory Team (RAPAT) services

The only specific RAPAT mission carried out during the year was made in conjunction with a WAMAP mission to Saudi Arabia. However, a number of missions of a similar type were mounted under a joint IAEA/UNDP programme for the improvement of radiation protection, nuclear safety and waste management infrastructures for countries of the former USSR.

A major field evaluation of the effectiveness of RAPAT and WAMAP missions was carried out for four countries in the Asia and Pacific region. One of the conclusions was that a more systematic procedure was required for monitoring and providing assistance in the implementation of recommendations. Accordingly, a system was set up involving 'country officers' who would be responsible for assembling and maintaining current information on the radiological protection infrastructure of a country and using it to provide the most appropriate assistance.

Laboratory services

The Agency continued to routinely monitor more than 400 of its staff categorized as radiation workers (external dose exposure and internal contamination monitoring). There were no cases of internal or external overexposure. As in the previous year, all individual doses were maintained far below the annual dose limits.

Individual monitoring services continued to be provided to Member States and co-operation with WHO continued. Approximately 9000 dosimeters were distributed and 1000 finger dosimeters were sent to Member States.

RADIOLOGICAL CONSEQUENCES OF THE CHERNOBYL ACCIDENT

Promoting research and development on Chernobyl related issues

Support was continued for the United Nations International Co-operation on Chernobyl. In particular, a major effort was undertaken to collect precise information on the increased incidence of thyroid cancers among children in Belarus, Ukraine and the Russian Federation.

[...]

DIRECTION AND SUPPORT

ADMINISTRATION

Regular Budget

The General Conference appropriated an amount of $200 103 000 for the Agency's Regular Budget on the basis of an exchange rate of 12.70 Austrian Schillings to one United States dollar, of which $195 018 000 was related to Agency programmes. The latter amount was adjusted to $213 946 000 in accordance with the adjustment formula presented in the attachment to Resolution GC(XXXVII)/RES/610 in order to account for the average United Nations exchange rate of 11.41 Austrian Schillings to one US dollar which was actually experienced during the year. However, because of a shortfall in expected contributions, steps were taken to reduce the budget by 9.3% to $194 048 700.

The Regular Budget for 1994, at an exchange rate of 11.41 Austrian Schillings to one US dollar, amounted to $219 536 000, of which $210 863 000 was to be financed from contributions by Member States on the basis of the 1994 scale of assessment, $5 590 000 from income from reimbursable work for others and $3 083 000 from other miscellaneous income.

Expenditures

The actual expenditures for the Agency's Regular Budget in 1994 amounted to $197 252 145, of which $190 839 587 was related to the Agency's programmes. In addition, the authority to spend an amount of $13 468 800 was reserved for Deferred Programme Activities to be carried out in 1995 if arrears of contributions would be received in time. The unused budget from Agency programmes amounted to $9 637 613, whereas the total unused budget was $8 815 055 after taking into account reimbursable work for others.

Total 1993 and 1994 expenditures amounted to $13 967 199 from a total of $16 254 297 for the 1992 Deferred Programme Activities related to the Agency's budget. Total expenditures incurred in 1994 amounted to $13 216 058 from a total of $16 662 248 for the 1993 Deferred Programme Activities related to the Agency's budget.

Voluntary contributions

The target for voluntary contributions to the Technical Assistance and Co-operation Fund in 1994 was established at $58.5 million, of which $42.4 million was pledged by Member States.

Extrabudgetary contributions

A total of $55 888 877 in extrabudgetary funds was provided by Member States, the United Nations, other international organizations and other sources during 1994. Of this amount, $6 844 713 was in support of safeguards, $5 244 093 was for technical co-operation projects, $2 886 550 for projects in the field of food and agriculture, $2 584 103 for nuclear safety and $10 768 125 for the implementation of United Nations Security Council Resolution 687 on Iraq. In addition to $1 846 154 set aside for accrued end of service allowances, an amount of $19 088 727 (supplemented by the Agency's contribution of $1 486 828) was available for the ICTP, and $2 137 646 (supplemented by the Agency's contribution of $2 626 332) for IAEA-MEL. The remaining $6 334 920 was in support of various other projects implemented by the Agency.

Trust funds

In 1994, a total of $126 202 was provided by Member States for technical assistance and co-operation activities as funds-in-trust. Furthermore, a total of $1 247 559 was administered on behalf of research institutions and $2 400 000 for ITER.

Financial Regulations and Financial Rules

The Agency's Financial Regulations, which have governed the financial administration of the Agency's activities, included a number of provisions reflecting neither the practices of the Agency's organs nor the Agency's budget and financing structure. A comprehensive review of the Regulations and Rules was thus initiated in mid-1993, in accordance with an action plan and timetable determined by the Board of Governors. Following extensive consultations with the Board and Member States, the revised Financial Regulations, which represent a complete overhaul of the previous Regulations, were adopted by the Board in September 1994 and became operative on 1 January 1995. The Interim Financial Rules have also been reviewed in the light of the newly adopted Financial Regulations; the new Rules came into effect on the same date.

Personnel

At the end of 1994 the number of members of the Secretariat was 2248 — 861 in the Professional and higher categories and 1387 in the General Service category. These figures represent: regular staff (1671), temporary assistance staff (148), extrabudgetary (326), cost-free experts (76) and consultants (27). Among the 622 staff members in posts subject to geographical distribution, 87 nationalities were represented.

The General Conference adopted resolutions GC(XXXVIII)/RES/12 and GC(XXXVIII)/RES/13 which request the Director General to intensify his efforts and take specific measures to increase the staff drawn from developing countries and the number of women in the Secretariat. A number of steps were taken internally as well as in respect of Member States to facilitate the implementation of these resolutions. In particular, the services of a consultant were used to carry out a qualitative assessment of a representative sample of applications received from people in developing countries. The report indicated that no cases of discrimination against an applicant from a developing country or a female applicant had been found. Also, a cost-free expert was provided by a Member State for a period of six months to develop an action plan to improve the representation of women in the Agency. A report was submitted in November.

Personnel (cont.)

At the end of 1994 the percentage of women among the Professional staff was 16.7%; at the same time developing countries provided 31.8% of the staff subject to geographical distribution.

With funds from the deferred programmes, training continued through 1994 with the delivery of further courses on the essentials of management in which 60 middle level managers participated. Training in the analysis of programme performance (Programme Performance Assessment System) was completed for 97 project managers. Skills training in interviewing, presentation and non-technical writing was introduced and 165 staff members benefitted from these courses. In addition, approval was granted for external training in programme specific areas to 20 staff members. Induction Courses and Insight Series for orientation purposes were held for 217 staff members. Training provided in the above areas reached 22.2% of staff during 1994. In addition, more than 200 staff members participated in language training in the official languages as well as in German.

The personnel part of the new payroll/personnel system, developed by an outside company with financial support from Germany, became available.

Management services

A total of 12 projects aimed at promoting good management and cost effective working practices were completed during the year. In addition to management and efficiency reviews in various areas of the Secretariat, project support was provided for the introduction of new administrative systems and procedures, notably in the areas of procurement, home leave entitlement and information technology management.

Liability for nuclear damage

The Standing Committee on Liability for Nuclear Damage concentrated on the proposals for the revision of the Vienna Convention of 21 May 1963 on Civil Liability for Nuclear Damage and the establishment of a supplementary compensation system. The consideration of the two issues continued, for the time being, in an integrated manner with a view to finalizing the preparatory work in time to submit them to the same diplomatic conference. The proposals on international State liability and its relationship to the civil liability regime were not directly addressed but remained before the Committee for consideration in the context of the Vienna Convention revision.

In the absence of agreement on the basis of the initial proposals regarding a supplementary funding convention, i.e. the "levy" and "pool" drafts, the Standing Committee, in order to expedite negotiations, considered new approaches to the structure of compensation under both the revised Vienna Convention and a supplementary funding system. In particular, it was agreed to insert the installation State tier in the revised Vienna Convention, and on the basis of this, a new single draft convention on supplementary funding was prepared for further discussion. It is linked to the Vienna and Paris conventions and envisages an additional level of compensation provided by all States Parties collectively in accordance with an agreed formula (the "collective State contributions" draft). As the draft contains alternative formulations on some fundamental issues such as geographical scope, and a system of and criteria for contributions, including the status of States without nuclear installations in this regard, it was agreed to take decisions, within the mandate of the Committee, at its forthcoming session.

The Standing Committee also considered a new proposal for a convention on supplementary compensation for transboundary nuclear damage from a nuclear

Liability for nuclear damage (cont.)

incident at a civil nuclear power plant (the "umbrella" draft). This draft convention sets out basic principles of nuclear liability in a manner allowing adherence to it regardless of participation in other international agreements on nuclear liability. The Standing Committee agreed to continue in-depth discussion of the "umbrella" draft, including its relationship to existing conventions.

Several Member States from Latin America stated that they were studying the creation of a regional mechanism for nuclear liability taking into account the characteristics of their nuclear sectors. In their opinion the formula for a world-wide supplementary funding system should be compatible with the regional approach.

During the consideration of the question of nuclear liability by the Board of Governors in June and the thirty-eighth regular session of the General Conference, the Standing Committee was urged to expedite general agreement and completion of the preparatory work so that the diplomatic conference could be convened at an early date. In the meantime, further adherences to the existing instruments on nuclear liability were welcomed.

Convention on Nuclear Safety

The Group of Experts on a Nuclear Safety Convention, set up by the Board of Governors in 1992, completed the task of finalizing a draft text of a convention in January 1994. The Board of Governors at its February session requested the Director General to convene a diplomatic conference in June 1994 for the purpose of adopting the Convention on Nuclear Safety. The four day Diplomatic Conference adopted the Convention on 17 June 1994 without a vote. The Convention was then opened for signature on 20 September 1994, in conjunction with the thirty eighth regular session of the General Conference. By the end of 1994, 54 States had signed the Convention and one had ratified it. It will enter into force on the 90th day after deposit of the 22nd instrument of ratification, acceptance or approval, including the instruments of 17 States each having at least one nuclear installation which has achieved criticality in a reactor core.

The Convention provides that it shall apply to "nuclear installations", defined as "land-based civil nuclear power plants". The obligations of the Contracting Parties are based to a large extent on the principles contained in the Safety Fundamentals document *The Safety of Nuclear Installations*. They include, in particular, the obligation to establish and maintain a legislative and regulatory framework for nuclear installations and the obligation to implement a number of measures, based on general safety considerations, regarding, for example, the availability of financial and human resources, the assessment and verification of safety, quality assurance and emergency preparedness. Other obligations concern technical aspects of the safety of nuclear installations, including siting, design, construction and operation.

For the Agency, the most relevant feature is that the Convention provides for an obligation of the Contracting Parties to submit reports on the implementation of the Convention for review at meetings of the Contracting Parties: the Convention provides that after its entry into force the Contracting Parties shall hold, at regular intervals, meetings for the purpose of reviewing national reports to be submitted by each Contracting Party on the measures taken by it in fulfilling its obligations under the Convention. The Agency will provide the secretariat for these meetings. The Convention also provides that the Director General of the Agency shall be the Depositary of the Convention.

Status of conventions and agreements

During 1994, there was no change in the number of Parties to the Agreement on the Privileges and Immunities of the IAEA (reproduced in document INFCIRC/9/Rev.1). The number of Member States who have accepted the Agreement remains at 65.

The Vienna Convention on Civil Liability for Nuclear Damage, which entered into force on 12 November 1977, now has 24 Parties as a result of accession or succession by four States.

In 1994, two States acceded to the Convention on the Physical Protection of Nuclear Material (reproduced in document INFCIRC/274/Rev.1), which entered into force on 8 February 1987. Thus, by the end of the year there were 52 Parties.

The Convention on Early Notification of a Nuclear Accident (reproduced in document INFCIRC/335), which entered into force on 27 October 1986, was ratified or acceded to by three States. The total number of Parties by the end of 1994 was 74.

The Convention on Assistance in the Case of a Nuclear Accident or Radiological Emergency (reproduced in document INFCIRC/336), which entered into force on 26 February 1987, was ratified or acceded to by two States. There were 70 Parties by the end of the year.

The Joint Protocol Relating to the Application of the Vienna Convention and the Paris Convention (reproduced in document INFCIRC/402) entered into force on 27 April 1992. During 1994, 5 States acceded to or accepted the Protocol, bringing the number of States Party to 17.

The African Regional Co-operative Agreement for Research, Development and Training Related to Nuclear Energy (AFRA) (reproduced in document INFCIRC/377), which entered into force on 4 April 1990, was accepted by two States during 1994. By the end of the year 19 States had accepted the Agreement.

The Agreement to Extend the Regional Co-operative Agreement for Research, Development and Training Related to Nuclear Science and Technology, 1987 (RCA) (reproduced in document INFCIRC/167/Add. 15), entered into force on 11 June 1992. By the end of the year 3 States had accepted the Agreement, bringing to 17 the total number of acceptances.

The Convention on Nuclear Safety (reproduced in document INFCIRC/449) was signed by 54 States and ratified by 1.

Publications

Series and No.	Title
Legal Series No. 3	Agreements registered with the International Atomic Energy Agency (11th edition)
Legal Series No. 7-S1	The law and practices of the International Atomic Energy Agency 1970–1980. Supplement 1 to the 1970 edition of Legal Series No. 7
Legal Series No. 16	Convention on nuclear safety

[...]

ABBREVIATIONS

ADBF	Division of Budget and Finance (IAEA)
ADEX	Division of External Relations (IAEA)
ADGS	Division of General Services (IAEA)
ADLG	Legal Division (IAEA)
ADMS	Office of Management Services (IAEA)
ADPI	Division of Public Information (IAEA)
ADPR	Division of Personnel (IAEA)
ADPU	Division of Publications (IAEA)
ARCAL	Regional Co-operative Arrangements for the Promotion of Nuclear Science and Technology in Latin America
BWR	Boiling water reactor
CANDU	Canadian deuterium-uranium (reactor)
CRP	Co-ordinated research programme
DDG	Deputy Director General (IAEA)
EC	European Commission
ESCAP	United Nations Economic and Social Commission for Asia and the Pacific
EURATOM	European Atomic Energy Community
FAO	Food and Agriculture Organization of the United Nations
FORATOM	Forum atomique européen
HTGR	High temperature gas cooled reactor
HWR	Heavy water reactor
IA	Office of Internal Audit and Evaluation Support (IAEA)
IAEA-MEL	IAEA Marine Environment Laboratory
ICRP	International Commission on Radiological Protection
ICRU	International Commission on Radiation Units and Measurements
ICTP	International Centre for Theoretical Physics
IEA	International Energy Agency (OECD)
IIASA	International Institute for Applied Systems Analysis
ILO	International Labour Organisation
IMO	International Maritime Organization
INDC	International Nuclear Data Committee
INIS	International Nuclear Information System
IOC	Intergovernmental Oceanographic Commission of UNESCO
ISO	International Organization for Standardization
LMFR	Liquid metal fast reactor
LWR	Light water reactor
MAED	Model for Analysis of Energy Demand
NDA	Non-destructive assay
NEA	Nuclear Energy Agency of the OECD
NENF	Division of Nuclear Fuel Cycle and Waste Management (IAEA)
NENP	Division of Nuclear Power (IAEA)
NENS	Division of Nuclear Safety (IAEA)
NESI	Division of Scientific and Technical Information (IAEA)
NUSS	The Agency's programme on nuclear safety standards for nuclear power plants
OAU	Organization for African Unity
OECD	Organisation for Economic Co-operation and Development
OLADE	Organización Latinoamericana de Energía

OPANAL	Organismo para la Proscripción de las Armas Nucleares en América Latina y el Caribe
OPEC	Organization of Petroleum Exporting Countries
PAHO	Pan American Health Organization/WHO
PHWR	Pressurized heavy water reactor
PWR	Pressurized water reactor
RCA	Regional Co-operative Agreement for Research, Development and Training Related to Nuclear Science and Technology
RI	Department of Research and Isotopes (IAEA)
RIAL	Agency's Laboratory, Seibersdorf
RIFA	Joint FAO/IAEA Division of Nuclear Techniques in Food and Agriculture
RIHU	Division of Human Health (IAEA)
RIML	See IAEA-MEL
RIPC	Division of Physical and Chemical Sciences (IAEA)
RITP	See ICTP
SEC	Secretariat, Policy-making Organs (of the Agency)
SGCP	Division of Concepts and Planning (Department of Safeguards) (IAEA)
SGDE	Division of Development and Technical Support (Department of Safeguards) (IAEA)
SGEE	Effectiveness Evaluation (Department of Safeguards) (IAEA)
SGIT	Division of Safeguards Information Treatment (IAEA)
SGOP	Division of Operations (Department of Safeguards) (IAEA)
SGPR	Programme and Resources (Department of Safeguards) (IAEA)
SQ	Significant quantity
TCIM	Division of Technical Co-operation Implementation (IAEA)
TCPM	Division of Technical Co-operation Programmes (IAEA)
TCSEV	Technical Co-operation Servicing, Evaluation
TCSPC	Technical Co-operation Servicing, Programme Co-ordination
UNCED	United Nations Conference on Environment and Development (1992)
UNCTAD	United Nations Conference on Trade and Development
UNDP	United Nations Development Programme
UNECE	United Nations Economic Commission for Europe
UNEP	United Nations Environment Programme
UNESCO	United Nations Educational, Scientific and Cultural Organization
UNIDO	United Nations Industrial Development Organization
UNIPEDE	International Union of Producers and Distributors of Electrical Energy
UNSCEAR	United Nations Scientific Committee on the Effects of Atomic Radiation
UNU	United Nations University
VIC	Vienna International Centre
WANO	World Association of Nuclear Operators
WASP	Wien Automatic System Planning Package
WEC	World Energy Council
WHO	World Health Organization
WISE	World Information Service on Energy
WMO	World Meteorological Organization
WOCA	World outside centrally planned economies area
WTO	World Trade Organization
WWER	Water cooled and moderated reactor (former USSR)

ORGANIZATIONAL CHART
(as of 31 December 1994)

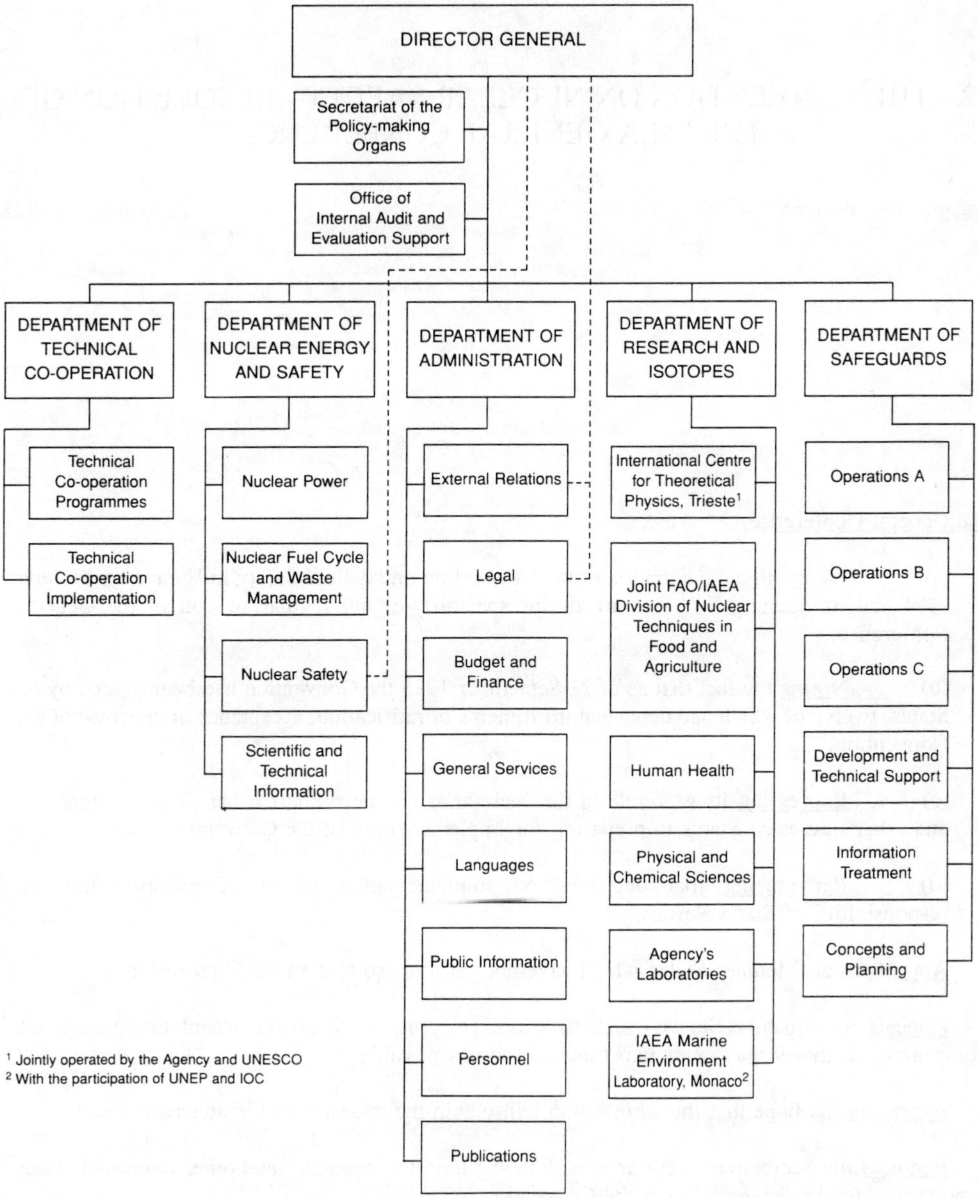

[1] Jointly operated by the Agency and UNESCO
[2] With the participation of UNEP and IOC

2. THE CONVENTION ON NUCLEAR SAFETY - RESOLUTION OF THE IAEA GENERAL CONFERENCE

Doc. no.: GC(39)/RES/13 22 September 1995

The General Conference,

(a) Welcoming the adoption of the Convention on Nuclear Safety in Vienna on 17 June 1994 and its opening for signature during the thirty-eighth regular session of the General Conference,

(b) Noting the fact that as of 21 September 1995 the Convention had been signed by 61 States, twelve of which had deposited instruments of ratification, acceptance or approval of the Convention,

(c) Expressing its gratitude to the Secretariat for the support it has given to signatory and other interested States in preparing for implementation of the Convention, and

(d) Recognizing that decisions on implementation of the Convention are the responsibility of States Parties,

1. Appeals to all Member States which have not yet done so to sign the Convention;

2. Appeals to signatory States which have not yet done so to ratify, accept or approve the Convention, so that it may enter into force as soon as possible;

3. Expresses the hope that the Convention will obtain the widest possible adherence; and

4. Requests the Secretariat to continue with their support to signatory and other interested States in preparing for implementation of the Convention.

22 September 1995
Agenda item 15
GC(39)/OR.9, paras 100 and 101

3. STRENGTHENING OF THE AGENCY'S TECHNICAL COOPERATION ACTIVITIES - RESOLUTION OF THE IAEA GENERAL CONFERENCE

Doc. no.: GC(39)/RES/14 22 September 1995

The General Conference,

(a) Recalling resolution GC(XXXVIII)/RES/8 on "Strengthening of the Agency's technical co-operation activities",

(b) Noting that the objectives of the Agency as stated in Article II of the Statute are "to accelerate and enlarge the contribution of atomic energy to peace, health and prosperity throughout the world" and to ensure that the assistance provided is not used to further any military purpose,

(c) Noting also that one of the statutory functions of the Agency is to "encourage and assist research on, and development and practical application of, atomic energy for peaceful uses throughout the world",

(d) Considering that an expansion of technical co-operation activities relating to the peaceful uses of nuclear energy will contribute to the well-being of the peoples of the world, and particularly those of developing Member States of the Agency,

(e) Stressing the importance of the transfer of nuclear technology to the developing countries for enhancing their scientific and technological capabilities and thereby generating rapid economic development,

(f) Conscious of the great potential of nuclear power for meeting energy requirements in many countries and the need to protect the environment,

(g) Desiring that the Agency's resources for technical co-operation activities be assured and sufficient,

(h) Taking note of the report by the Director General contained in document GOV/2821-GC(39)/13, and

(i) Welcoming the decision to establish the Standing Advisory Group on Technical Assistance and Co-operation (SAGTAC),

1. Stresses the need, in conformity with the Statute, to strengthen technical co-operation activities and also their effectiveness and efficiency;

2. Requests the Director General to pursue, in consultation with Member States, efforts to strengthen the technical co-operation activities of the Agency through the development of effective programmes aimed at improving the scientific and technological capabilities of developing countries, account being taken of the infrastructure and the level of technology of the countries concerned, in the fields of peaceful applications of nuclear energy, including both the applications of nuclear methods and techniques and the production of electricity, and achieving sustainable development;

3. Further requests the Director General to follow-up actions on initiatives mentioned in his report;

4. Requests the Director General to continue to take account of the view of the General Conference on this question when requesting Member States to pledge their respective shares of the Technical Co-operation Fund targets and to make timely payments to the Fund; and

5. Requests the Director General and the Board of Governors to remain seized of this matter and further requests the Director General to report to the Board of Governors periodically and to the General Conference at its fortieth regular session on the implementation of this resolution under an agenda item entitled "Strengthening of the Agency's technical co-operation activities".

22 September 1995
Agenda item 16
GC(39)/OR.9, para. 102

4. PLAN FOR PRODUCING POTABLE WATER ECONOMICALLY - RESOLUTION OF THE IAEA GENERAL CONFERENCE

Doc. no.: GC(39)/RES/15 22 September 1995

The General Conference,

(a) Recalling resolutions GC(XXXIII)/RES/515, GC(XXXIV)/RES/540, GC(XXXV)/RES/563, GC(XXXVI)/RES/592, GC(XXXVII)/RES/617 and GC(XXXVIII)/RES/7,

(b) Noting the study on the "Technical and economic evaluation of potable water production through the desalination of sea water by using nuclear energy or other means" attached to document GC(XXXVI)/1013, which concludes that the use of nuclear energy as an alternative option to the use of fossil fuelled plants for supplying energy for sea water desalination is technically feasible and in general economically competitive, and document GOV/INF/708,

(c) Noting the main conclusion of the Advisory Group on Demonstration Facilities, attached to document GC(XXXVIII)/8, which includes the conclusion that there is a need to establish a programme for identifying a practical set of options from which one or more demonstration facilities with well-defined objectives might be chosen,

(d) Noting also the interest of a number of Member States in activities relating to sea water desalination using nuclear energy as reflected in document GC(XXXVII)/INF/323,

(e) Aware that the acute shortage of potable water in some Member States remains a major problem, and

(f) Underlining the vital importance of sufficient potable water supplies for mankind and of regional and international co-operation in solving the problem of potable water shortages in Member States and the interest of potential beneficiaries and technology holders in the provision of low-cost potable water,

1. Welcomes the progress made in this regard, and especially the initiation of a two-phase Options Identification Programme (described in document GC(39)/12) which aims at evaluating data relevant to a demonstration programme and analysing the most practical options for demonstration;

2. Urges the Secretariat to secure sufficient funding, through appeals to international organizations and prospective donor countries, so that the second phase of the Options Identification Programme will be completed in 1996 and a final report presented to the General Conference for consideration at its fortieth session;

3. Requests the Director General to continue consultations with interested States, the competent organizations of the United Nations system and other relevant intergovernmental organizations concerning the main conclusions of the "Technical and economic evaluation of potable water production through the desalination of sea water by using nuclear energy or other means"

4. Invites the Director General to undertake similar consultations for the implementation of the main recommendations of the Advisory Group on Demonstration Facilities;

5. Stresses the vital importance of producing potable water and further requests the Director General to include the nuclear desalination of sea water in future programmes of the Agency, with appropriate priority, in the process of preparing the Agency's programme and budget;

6. Calls upon Member States in a position to provide expert services and extrabudgetary resources in support of the activities relating to sea water desalination using nuclear energy to make such services and resources available; and

7. Requests the Director General to report on the progress made in the implementation of this resolution to the Board of Governors and to the General Conference at its fortieth session under an appropriate agenda item.

22 September 1995
Agenda item 17
GC(39)/OR.9, para. 103

5. MEASURES AGAINST ILLICIT TRAFFICKING IN NUCLEAR MATERIALS AND OTHER RADIOACTIVE SOURCES - RESOLUTION OF THE IAEA GENERAL CONFERENCE

Doc. no.: GC(39)/RES/18 22 September 1995

The General Conference,

Recalling its resolution GC(XXXVIII)/RES/15 regarding measures against illicit trafficking in nuclear material,

1. Takes note of the progress report by the Secretariat in document GC(39)/19;

2. Welcomes the measures taken by the Secretariat in support of efforts to prevent illicit trafficking;

3. Invites the Director General during the coming year to continue working in accordance with the conclusions of the Board of Governors; and

4. Requests the Director General to submit a report to the General Conference at its next regular session on activities undertaken by the Agency in the intervening period.

22 September 1995
Agenda item 20
GC(39)/OR.9, para.106

6. NUCLEAR POWER STATUS IN 1994

Doc. no.: PR 95/9 26 April 1995

A total of 480 nuclear power plants were operating or being built around the world in 1994, based on data reported to the International Atomic Energy Agency (IAEA) Power Reactor Information System (PRIS). During 1994, four nuclear power plants with altogether 3356 MW(e) were newly connected to electricity grids in China, Japan, Republic of Korea and Mexico, bringing the world's total number of operating reactors to 432 in 29 countries and Taiwan, China. Additionally, a total of 48 reactors were reported as being constructed in 15 countries.

Nuclear power's share of electricity production remained high in 1994, in seven countries – Lithuania, 76.4; France 75.3; Belgium, 55.8; Sweden, 51.1; Slovak Republic, 49.1; Bulgaria, 45.6, and Hungary, 43.7 – representing close to half or more of their total electricity use. All in all, 18 countries (including Taiwan, China) relied upon nuclear power plants to supply at least a quarter of their total electricity needs.

Worldwide in 1994, total nuclear power generation amounted to 2130.13 terawatt-hours of electricity. This is more than the world's total electricity generation – 1912 terawatt-hours – from all sources in 1958. Overall nuclear power plants provided approximately 17 percent of the world's electricity production in 1994. Cumulative worldwide operating experience from civil nuclear reactors at the end of 1994 was over 7200 years.

A table showing the electricity supplied by nuclear power reactors in 1994 and the respective percentages of electricity produced by nuclear energy is attached.

Nuclear Power Reactors in operation and under construction at the end of 1994

Country Name	Reactors in operation: No. of units	Reactors in operation: Total MW(e)	Reactors under construction: No. of units	Reactors under construction: Total MW(e)	Electricity supplied by nuclear power reactors in 1994: TW(e).h	Electricity supplied by nuclear power reactors in 1994: % of total	Total operating Experience to end 1994: Years	Total operating Experience to end 1994: Months
Argentina	2	935	1	692	7.68	13.77	32	7
Belgium	7	5527			38.20	55.77	128	7
Brazil	1	626	1	1245	0.04	0.01	12	9
Bulgaria	6	3538			15.33	45.63	77	1
Canada	22	15755			101.73	19.07	326	11
China	3	2100			13.50*	1.49*	5	4
Czech R.	4	1648	2	1824	12.13*	28.22*	34	8
Finland	4	2310			18.33	29.51	63	4
France	56	58493	4	5810	341.80	75.29	822	10
Germany	21	22657			143.00	29.33	490	1
Hungary	4	1729			13.23	43.73	38	2
India	9	1493	5	1010	4.32	1.37	119	3
Iran			2	2146				
Japan	49	38875	5	4799	258.3	30.70	652	2
Kazakh.	1	70			0.38	0.58	21	6
Korea RP	10	8170	6	4820	55.92	35.48	90	4
Lithuania	2	2370			6.63	76.37	18	6
Mexico	2	1308			4.28	3.22	5	11
Nethlnds	2	504			3.70	4.86	47	9
Pakistan	1	125	1	300	0.52	1.01	23	3
Romania			5	3250				
Russia	29	19843	4	3375	97.83	11.39	497	6
S. Africa	2	1842			9.69	5.69	20	3
Slovak R.	4	1632	4	1552	12.13	49.05	57	5
Slovenia	1	632			4.39	38.01	13	3
Spain	9	7105			52.80	34.97	138	2
Sweden	12	10002			70.20	51.13	207	2
Switzrld	5	2985			22.98	36.84	98	10
UK	34	11720	1	1188	79.40	25.79	1028	5
Ukraine	15	12679	6	5700	68.85	34.20	158	11
USA	109	98784	1	1165	639.36	21.98	1919	8
Total	**432**	**340347**	**48**	**38876**	**2130.13**		**7230**	**8**

Note: The total includes the following data in Taiwan, China:
- 6 units, 4890 MW(e) in operation;
- 33.48 TW(e).h of nuclear electricity generation, representing 31.72% of the total electricity generated there;
- 80 years 1 month of total operating experience.

Construction at 3 reactors was suspended:2 in Cuba (Juragua 1&2) and 1 in the USA(Watts Bar 2).
Two reactors were shut down: one in France (Bugey 1) and one in the UK (PFR Dounrey).
This table shows operating experience of countries which have reactors in operation and under construction.
* Not officially confirmed

<u>Connection to the grid during 1994</u>

China	CN-3, Guangdong-2	PWR
Japan	JP-47, Ikata-3,	PWR
Korea RP	KR-11, Yonggwang Unit3(KNU-),	PWR
Mexico	MX-2, Laguna Verde-2,	BWR

(Source IAEA PRIS)

7. HIGHLIGHTS OF STATEMENT OF THE IAEA DIRECTOR GENERAL DR. HANS BLIX TO THE 39TH SESSION OF THE IAEA GENERAL CONFERENCE

Doc. no.: PR 95/13 18 September 1995

Global nuclear developments are accelerating the evolution of IAEA roles and responsibilities to meet new needs of States in areas of nuclear verification, safety, and technology transfer, IAEA Director General Hans Blix said today in an opening statement to the Agency's General Conference. The Conference of the IAEA's 122 Member States, which sets the Agency's programmes and policies, is meeting this week in Vienna, Austria.

"Credible IAEA verification that nuclear materials and related items remain in peaceful activities is an increasingly important factor in nuclear disarmament and global security planning," Dr. Blix said. "At the same time, the magnitude and complexity of the safeguards task continues to increase." In addition, he pointed out, "large increases in the verification effort may result if nuclear materials removed from the military sphere of nuclear-weapon States are placed under safeguards." The Agency started verifying such material last year, he noted.

In reviewing the Agency's programmes and plans, Dr. Blix highlighted developments in a number of specific areas. They included the IAEA's consideration of a request by France to conduct a radiological assessment of its current series of nuclear tests; the Agency's ongoing verification in the Democratic People's Republic of Korea; IAEA nuclear inspections in Iraq under the mandate of the UN Security Council; measures to strengthen IAEA nuclear safeguards; possible new verification roles for the Agency; actions against the illicit trafficking in nuclear materials; steps for greater global cooperation in nuclear safety and radioactive waste management; nuclear energy and the environment; and initiatives to strengthen technical cooperation activities.

In many cases, he pointed out, measures being taken at the IAEA are moving forward in spite of continuing budget constraints, and he attributed progress to extrabudgetary resources provided by some Member States, ongoing improvements in programme management and implementation, and the efficiency and skills of IAEA

staff. "The machinery of the IAEA has been working at full steam, even with some overpressure," he said, "and we can register considerable movement forward in many areas."

Selected highlights of the Director General's address follow.

French nuclear tests. **The Director General noted a recent letter he received from the French Foreign Minister, making reference to the irreversible commitment of France to conclude a comprehensive nuclear test ban in 1996 and its intention to undertake a final series of nuclear tests before that time, and inviting the Agency to conduct a radiological assessment of its series of nuclear tests, Dr. Blix said that the IAEA is considering the request. Agency officials are now consulting French authorities, he said, on matters pertaining to the objectives, scope, modalities, and required expertise for such a scientific mission. He pointed out that the Agency has some "first hand experience" in this field, in light of scientific studies it has previously done at the French Pacific test sites, as well as at sites connected with the former Soviet Union's military nuclear programme at Semipalatinsk in Kazakhstan.**

Safeguards in the DPRK. **The IAEA recently held technical discussions with authorities in the DPRK as part of its ongoing verification efforts, he said. "To come into full compliance with the safeguards agreement," Dr. Blix said, "the DPRK will have to do something it has not yet been willing to do, namely enable the Agency effectively to verify the accuracy and completeness of the DPRK's initial report of nuclear material subject to the agreement." The recent discussions resulted in limited progress on some issues, Dr. Blix said. A substantial paper of technical proposals transmitted by the Agency was accepted "only for study, not for discussion" he said.**

Nuclear inspections in Iraq. **The Agency is verifying new information and data it has received concerning Iraq's thwarted plans in 1990-91 to develop a nuclear weapon, Dr. Blix said. He said that so far in its review of the new information, "nothing suggests that a change is warranted" in the Agency's conclusion that the essential components of Iraq's clandestine nuclear weapons programme have been identified and destroyed, removed, or rendered harmless. He noted that the new Iraqi statements, and all the documents and materials that the Agency has received, will have to be carefully examined for new data. "That they have been withheld for so long is clearly a breach of Iraq's obligations under Security Council resolutions," he said.**

Strengthening IAEA safeguards. **Dr. Blix reviewed key components of Agency measures -- some already being implemented and others remaining under consideration -- to develop and implement a strengthened and more cost-effective safeguards system. He noted in particular steps to ensure increased access to information about nuclear programmes and broader inspector access to sites within a State. "By making their nuclear activities as transparent as possible to the Agency," he said, "States can help provide the basis for more effective and efficient safeguards." Regarding the costs of strengthening measures, he said they may be offset by efficiencies elsewhere in the safeguards systems. However, he added, "any significant increase in the number of countries accepting full-scope safeguards, or in**

the number of facilities and amount of material under safeguards, will inevitably involve additional costs."

New and emerging verification roles. **Citing developments in areas of nuclear non-prolferation, arms control, and disarmament, Dr. Blix said that some possible new verification roles for the Agency are in sight. "Far-reaching implications" for the IAEA's future work, he said, emanate from the outcome of the Review and Extension Conference of Parties to the Treaty on the Non-Proliferation of Nuclear Weapons (NPT) in May 1995. Among other things, he noted that the Conference expressly recognized the IAEA as the competent authority responsible for verifying and assuring compliance with safeguards agreements; recommended that nuclear material released from military use should be placed under IAEA safeguards; envisaged the universal application of safeguards once the elimination of nuclear weapons had been achieved; set 1996 as the target date for the conclusion of a Comprehensive Test Ban Treaty; called for the early conclusion of a "cut-off" agreement to end the production of nuclear material for use in weapons; and endorsed the creation of additional nuclear-weapon-free zones (NWFZs). Dr. Blix pointed out that IAEA safeguards are being considered as an "essential element" of the verification mechanism for a cut-off agreement; that the Agency would have a verification role in any new NWFZ, given existing models; and that the IAEA already carries out safeguards tasks of relevance to verification of a test ban treaty, though its possible roles under a specific test ban treaty remain to be determined.**

Illicit trafficking in nuclear materials. **In reviewing key elements of the Agency's action programme against problems of illicit nuclear trafficking, Dr. Blix noted that the work is part of efforts by nuclear, customs, and enforcement authorities of many countries and a number of international organizations to strengthen and coordinate controls on radioactive materials. "It is clear that more efforts are needed and that States must exercise greater prudence in the use and storage of all radioactive materials," he said. He noted that the Agency's programme is largely directed to assisting States in areas related to the accounting and control of nuclear materials; physical protection methods and technology; and the establishment of a database to provide factual information about reported incidents of trafficking.**

Nuclear safety and radioactive waste management. **The Director General cited a number of developments. He said that the Convention on Nuclear Safety, adopted in June 1994, could enter into force as early as next year, and that preparations for a Convention on Radioactive Waste Safety have been "encouraging", with a final draft possible by next year. Work also is continuing, he noted, for a Diplomatic Conference in 1996 to revise the Vienna Convention on liability for nuclear damage. Regarding the Agency's work on the safety assessment of nuclear power plants in Eastern Europe and the former Soviet Union, he said that an international consensus now exists that identifies the major safety issues and their significance for each of the various reactor types. He further noted that Agency experts have been working closely with authorities in Armenia and Russia regarding safety issues at the Medzamor nuclear plant, which the Government of Armenia plans to restart. Separately, he noted, the Agency is working with Russian authorities on possible cooperative activities between Russia and other States in areas of radioactive waste management. The Director General also pointed towards a major international conference being organized for April 1996 by the IAEA, World Health Organization,**

and European Union to sum up the accumulated knowledge about the nature and magnitude of the consequences of the Chernobyl accident.

Nuclear energy and the environment. **The Director General reviewed the Agency's programme on the comparative assessment of energy sources, which is providing documented data, methodologies, and analyses on the comparative economic social, health, and environmental aspects of different energy sources for electricity generation. "Detailed studies on the emissions and residuals from nuclear, fossil, and renewable energy chains show that nuclear power in normal operation is one of the most environmentally friendly ways of generating electricity," he said. He noted that the IAEA is convening an international symposium next month to review recent progress in the Agency's programme.**

Technical cooperation. **The IAEA's technical cooperation programme delivery is the highest ever in the history of the Agency, the Director General noted. He attributed the increase to improved management practices, better design and support of projects and other iniatives. He further emphasized that the success of programmes depends on the availability of predictable resources, and appealed for full contributions to the Technical Cooperation Fund. In reviewing specific projects, Dr. Blix referred to special reports before the General Conference on isotope hydrology and the use of nuclear energy for potable water production.**

The full text of the Director General's statement is available from the IAEA Division of Public Information. The statement -- as well as other background information and documents from the IAEA General Conference -- is globally on-line through the IAEA's *World Atom* Internet services, which can be accessed at the World Wide Web address http://www.iaea.or.at.

8. IAEA DIRECTOR GENERAL DR. HANS BLIX ADDRESSES THE 50TH UN GENERAL ASSEMBLY

Doc. no.: PR 95/18 | 1 November 1995

Addressing the 50th session of the United Nations General Assembly today in New York, Director General Hans Blix of the International Atomic Energy Agency (IAEA) emphasized the importance of international efforts to secure the safe and peaceful development of nuclear energy. He specifically reviewed developments in areas of IAEA nuclear safeguards and verification; nuclear safety; nuclear power development; and technical co-operation.

Long a key component of the world's nuclear non-proliferation regime, the IAEA's safeguards system is being strengthened as part of international steps against the further spread of nuclear weapons, he noted. "Governments and the public now demand that the system should have the capacity to detect any secret, undeclared nuclear material and installations," Dr. Blix said, citing lessons from the Agency's ongoing nuclear inspections in Iraq under mandate of the UN Security Council. The stronger safeguards system now being developed, he said, focuses on a number of essential elements: increased access to information about a State's nuclear activities; broader access to sites and locations within a State; short-notice inspections; and the maximum use of new and available technologies to increase detection capacity.

He further pointed out that IAEA verification of States' compliance with their nuclear arms-control pledges is becoming an increasingly important factor in global security and nuclear disarmament. He noted the Agency's verification of nuclear material released from the military programmes of nuclear-weapon States. "These expanded efforts could require new arrangements to ensure that the released material would permanently remain under safeguards and that the financing of such verification is assured," he said. Possible new verification roles for the Agency additionally are emerging from other arms-control and disarmament initiatives, Dr. Blix said, including the Comprehensive Test Ban Treaty which States seek to conclude

in 1996. Of relevance to note, he said, is that the IAEA already verifies such a ban in more than 170 States which have accepted comprehensive Agency safeguards on all their nuclear activities.

The Director General also addressed Agency efforts against illicit trafficking in nuclear materials. "It is clear that greater efforts are needed and that States must pay increased attention to the physical protection of all radioactive material, and especially weapons useable nuclear material, whether in use, transport, or storage," he said. While the States concerned carry the primary responsibility in combatting illegal trafficking, Dr. Blix said that steps are being taken to improve international co-ordination of efforts. The Agency's actions, he noted, include establishing a database of trafficking incidents in support of factual analyses and technically assisting States in areas of nuclear material accountancy and control, and in physical protection methods and technology.

Also commanding greater attention are issues of nuclear and radiation safety, Dr. Blix said. Building on the IAEA's long-standing work in the field, States have developed binding international safety standards, he noted, notably in adopting the Convention on Nuclear Safety that is nearing entry into force, and in moving to finalize preparation of a Convention on Radioactive Waste Safety. "There is a clear manifestation of the increased interest of the international community that nuclear safety be at a high level everywhere," Dr. Blix said.

The Director General further called for an expansion of nuclear power for electricity generation as part of steps to meet the world's growing needs for environmentally clean and economically proven energy sources. He noted the Agency's co-operative work with seven international organizations for comparatively assessing the benefits and risks of different options for electricity production. "All sources and uses of energy have their risks," he said, "as indeed an absence of energy carries risks. Only an analysis of different options side by side can tell us which energy policy is economically and ecologically least burdensome."

In underlining the high interest of States, particularly developing countries, in peaceful nuclear applications, Dr. Blix reviewed initiatives the Agency is taking to strengthen its technical co-operation programme. Emphasis is being placed on nuclear techniques and targeted projects that will contribute to sustainable development, food production and preservation, the harnessing of fresh water resources, industrial applications, and the promotion of human health, he said.

Dr. Blix concluded by commending efforts to improve the effectiveness of global co-operation and the efficiency of intergovernmental organizations. "Effective action by organizations in the UN family is in many cases directly dependent on the degree of co-operation that can be achieved between States," he said. "There is also much action, however, that is undertaken mainly by the Secretariats. Here, effectiveness depends largely upon the availability of adequate and predictable resources, co-operation of States that may be affected, and last, but not least, the competence and skill of management and staff in the Secretariats. We stand or fall on the quality of our management and staff."

Copies of the Director General's address may be obtained from the IAEA Division of Public Information, or through the IAEA's *World Atom* on-line information services on the Internet/World Wide Web at the following address: http://www.iaea.or.at/worldatom.

INTERNATIONAL MARITIME ORGANIZATION
(IMO)

DOCUMENTS REPRODUCED IN WHOLE OR IN PART:

DOCUMENTS NOT REPRODUCED:

ASSEMBLY 19th Session 13-24 November 1995

8.	Doc. no.:	A 19/7
	Date:	1 August 1995
	Title:	Report on the Status of the Convention and Membership of the Organization

9. Doc. no.: A 19/8 + Add. 1
Date: 1 August 1995
Title: Report on the Status of Conventions and Other Multilateral Instruments in respect of which the Organization Performs Functions

10. Doc. no.: A 19/Res.784
Date: 6 December 1995
Title: Resolution A.784(19). Adopted on 23 November 1995. Amendments to the International Convention on Load Lines, 1966

11. Doc. no.: A 19/Res.786
Date: 12 December 1995
Title: Resolution A.786(19). Adopted on 23 November 1995. Strategy of Ship/Port Interface

12. Doc. no.: A 19/Res.787
Date: 29 November 1995
Title: Resolution A.787(19). Adopted on 23 November 1995. Procedures for Port State Control

13. Doc. no.: A 19/Res.788
Date: 8 December 1995
Title: Resolution A.788(19). Adopted on 23 November 1995. Guidelines on Implementation of the International Safety Management (ISM) Code by Administrations

14. Doc. no.: A 19/Res.789
Date: 8 December 1995
Title: Resolution A.787(19). Adopted on 23 November 1995. Specifications on the Survey and Certification Functions of Recognized Organizations Acting on Behalf of the Administration

15. Doc. no.: A 19/Res.790
Date: 12 December 1995
Title: Resolution A.790(19). Adopted on 23 November 1995. Review of the Code for the Safe Carriage of Irradiated Nuclear Fuel, Plutonium and High-Level Radioactive Wastes in Flasks on Board Ships

16. Doc. no.: A 19/Res.791
Date: 6 December 1995
Title: Resolution A.791(19). Adopted on 23 November 1995. Application of the International Convention on Tonnage Measurement of Ships, 1969, to Existing Ships

17. Doc. no.: A 19/Res.794
Date: 5 December 1995
Title: Resolution A.794(19). Adopted on 23 November 1995. Surveys and Inspections of Ro-Ro Passenger Ships

18. Doc. no.: A 19/Res.826
Date: 15 December 1995
Title: Resolution A.826(19). Adopted on 23 November 1995. Procedure for Adoption and Amendment of Traffic Separation Schemes, Routeing Measures other than Traffic Separation Schemes, and Ship Reporting Systems

19. Doc. no.: A 19/Res.832
Date: 8 December 1995
Title: Resolution A.832(19). Adopted on 23 November 1995. Follow-up Action to the United Nations Conference on Environment and Development, 1992

COUNCIL 74th Session 12-16 June 1995; 18th Extraordinary Session 10 November 1995; 75th Session 24 November 1995

20. Doc. no.: C 74/22(a) + Add. 1
Date: 24 February 1995
Title: Relations with the United Nations and the Specialized Agencies, (a) Report on the Decisions of the General Assembly of the United Nations on Matters of Relevance to IMO. Note by the Secretary General

21. Doc. no.: C 74/D
Date: 21 June 1995
Title: Summary of Decisions

22. Doc. no.: C/ES.18/D
Date: 16 November 1995
Title: Summary of Decisions

23. Doc. no.: C 75/D
Date: 21 December 1995
Title: Summary of Decisions

LEGAL COMMITTEE 72nd Session 3-7 April 1995; 73rd Session 9-13 October 1995

24. Doc. no.: LEG 72/4 + Corr. 1 + Add. 1
Date: 20 January 1995
Title: Consideration of a Draft International Convention on Liability and Compensation for Damage in Connection with the Carriage of Hazardous and Noxious Substances by Sea (HNS). Note by the Secretariat

25. Doc. no.: LEG 72/5
Date: 27 January 1995
Title: Consideration of Revision of the Convention on Limitation of Liability for Maritime Claims, 1976. Note by the Secretariat

26. Doc. no.: LEG 72/8/1
Date: 27 January 1995
Title: Any Other Business. Code for the Safe Carriage of Irradiated Nuclear Fuel, Plutonium and High Level Radioactive Wastes in Flasks on Board Ships (INF Code). Note by the Secretariat

27. Doc. no.: LEG 72/8/4
Date: 2 March 1995
Title: Any Other Business. UNCED Agenda 21. Issues Relating to the Work Programme of the Legal Committee. Note by the Secretariat

28. Doc. no.: LEG 72/9
Date: 10 April 1995
Title: Report of the Legal Committee on the Work of its Seventy-Second Session

29. Doc. no.: LEG 73/5
Date: 21 July 1995
Title: Consideration of Possible Work on the Draft Convention on Offshore Mobile Craft. "The Sydney Draft" Revised by the CMI. Note by the Secretariat

30. Doc. no.: LEG 73/11
Date: 8 August 1995
Title: Consideration of a Draft Convention on Wreck Removal. Submitted by Germany, the Netherlands and the United Kingdom

31. Doc. no.: LEG 73/14
Date: 16 october 1995
Title: Report of the Legal Committee on the Work of its Seventy-Third Session.

MARINE ENVIRONMENT PROTECTION COMMITTEE 37th Session 11-15 September 1995

32. Doc. no.: MEPC 37/2
Date: 26 July 1995
Title: Status of International Conventions Relating to Marine Pollution of which IMO is Depositary or Responsible for Secretariat Duties. Note by the Secretariat

33. Doc. no.: MEPC 37/5/1
Date: 16 June 1995
Title: Flag State Implementation. Report of the Correspondence Group on the Review of the Definition of "Severe Pollution". Submitted by Greenpeace International

34. Doc. no.: MEPC 37/5/2
Date: 16 June 1995
Title: Flag State Implementation. Amalgamation of Port State Control Resolutions. Submitted by France, Germany, the Netherlands, Sweden, the United Kingdom and the Commission of the European Communities

35. Doc. no.: MEPC 37/5/3
Date: 16 June 1995
Title: Flag State Implementation. Amalgamation of Port State Control Resolutions. Report of the Correspondence Group. Submitted by the United States

36. Doc. no.: MEPC 37/10/5
Date: 16 June 1995
Title: Follow-up Action to UNCED. Report of the Correspondence Group on the Application of the Precautionary Approach. Submitted by the Netherlands

37. Doc. no.: MEPC 37/10/6
Date: 16 June 1995
Title: Follow-up Action to UNCED. Guidelines and Framework for Application of the Precautionary Approach to the Work of the International Maritime Organization. Submitted by Greenpeace International

38. Doc. no.: MEPC 37/10/7
Date: 16 June 1995
Title: Follow-up Action to UNCED. Precautionary Approach in the IMO: TBT Case Study. Submitted by the WWF

39. Doc. no.: MEPC 37/11/Rev.1
Date: 30 March 1995
Title: Consideration and Adoption of Amendments to Annex V of MARPOL 73/78. Note by the Secretariat

40. Doc. no.: MEPC 37/11/2
Date: 16 June 1995
Title: Consideration and Adoption of Amendments to Annex V of MARPOL 73/78. Interpretation and Amendments of MARPOL 73/78 and Related Codes. Report of the Correspondence Group on Development of "Guidelines on Developing Shipboard Waste Management Plans" and Review of the Layout of the Whole of Annex V in Line with the New Layout of Annexes I and II of MARPOL 73/78. Submitted by the United States

41. Doc. no.: MEPC 37/12/3
Date: 14 March 1995
Title: Interpretation and Amendments of MARPOL 73/78 and Related Codes. Definition of "Nearest Land". Submitted by Australia

42. Doc. no.: MEPC 37/12/13
Date: 20 July 1995
Title: Interpretation and Amendments of MARPOL 73/78. Boundary of the Antarctic Special Area. Note by the Secretariat

43. Doc. no.: MEPC 37/13
Date: 1 December 1994
Title: Prevention of Air Pollution from Ships. Legal Framework Options for Making the Air Pollution Annex Mandatory under MARPOL 73/78. Note by the Secretariat

44. Doc. no.: MEPC 37/13/6/Add. 1
Date: 29 June 1995
Title: Prevention of Air Pollution from Ships. The North Sea as a Special Area. Submitted by Norway

45. Doc. no.: MEPC 37/13/7
Date: 8 June 1995
Title: Prevention of Air Pollution from Ships. Recognition of the Baltic Sea Area as a "Special Area" under the New Annex to MARPOL 73/78 on Prevention of Air Pollution from Ships. Submitted by Denmark, Estonia, Finland, Germany, Latvia, Lithuania, Poland, Russia and Sweden

46. Doc. no.: MEPC 37/13/10
Date: 16 June 1995
Title: Prevention of Air Pollution from Ships. New Annex to MARPOL 73/78 on Air Pollution. Criteria and Procedures for Designation of Special Areas. Submitted by the United Kingdom

47. Doc. no.: MEPC 37/13/12
Date: 16 June 1995
Title: Prevention of Air Pollution from Ships. Report of the Correspondence Group on Revising the Annex. Submitted by the United States

48. Doc. no.: MEPC 37/14
Date: 23 December 1994
Title: Finalization of the Interim Guidelines under Regulation 13F of Annex I of MARPOL 73/78. Note by the Secretariat

49. Doc. no.: MEPC 37/15
Date: 27 January 1995
Title: Implementation of the OPRC Convention and the OPRC Conference Resolutions. Report of the OPRC Working Group

50. Doc. no.: MEPC 37/18
Date: 12 December 1994
Title: Unwanted Aquatic Organisms in Ballast Water. Report of the Ballast Water Working Group convened during MEPC 36

51. Doc. no.: MEPC 37/21/7
Date: 21 July 1995
Title: Any Other Business. Ship Reporting System for the Torres Strait Region and the Inner Route of the Great Barrier Reef. Submitted by Australia

MARITIME SAFETY COMMITTEE 65th Session 9-17 May 1995

52. Doc. no.: MSC 65/4/Rev.1
Date: 21 April 1995
Title: Ro-Ro Ferry Safety. Report of the Panel of Experts on Ro-Ro Ferry Safety to the Steering Committee on Ro-Ro Ferry Safety. Note by the Chairman of the Panel of Experts

53. Doc. no.: MSC 65/4/7
Date: 26 April 1995
Title: Ro-Ro Ferry Safety. Report of the Steering Committee on Ro-Ro Ferry Safety to the Maritime Safety Committee

54. Doc. no.: MSC 65/16 + Add. 1, 2
Date: 10 February 1995
Title: Piracy and Armed Robbery Against Ships. Note by the Secretariat

55. Doc. no.: MSC 65/19/3
Date: 10 February 1995
Title: Implementation of Instruments and Related Matters. Turkish Instruction concerning the Basis, Principles, Rules and Modalities in Implementing their Rules for Ships Navigating in the Black Sea Straits and the Marmara Sea. Submitted by the Russian Federation

56. Doc. no.: MSC 65/19/4
Date: 10 February 1995
Title: Implementation of Instruments and Related Matters. Navigation through the Strait of Istanbul, the Strait of Canakkale and the Marmara Sea. Submitted by Greece

57. Doc. no.: MSC 65/21
Date: 10 February 1995
Title: Existing Ships' Safety Standards. Report of the Correspondence Group on the Application of Grandfather Clauses. Submitted by the Netherlands

58. Doc. no.: MSC 65/24
Date: 10 February 1995
Title: Any Other Business. Draft Progress Report on the Review of the Code for the Safe Carriage of Irradiated Nuclear Fuel, Plutonium and High-Level Radioactive Wastes in Flasks on Board Ships (INF Code). Note by the Secretariat

SUB-COMMITTEE ON FLAG STATE IMPLEMENTATION 3rd Session 20-24 February 1995

59. Doc. no.: FSI 3/3/5 + Corr. 1
Date: 30 December 1994
Title: Responsibilities of Governments under Safety and Pollution Prevention Conventions. Flag State Responsibility. Submitted by the United Kingdom

60. Doc. no.: FSI 3/6
Date: 29 July 1994
Title: Role of the Human Element in Maritime Casualties. ISM Code Implementation Guidelines. Submitted by IACS

61. Doc. no.: FSI 3/7/2
Date: 23 December 1994
Title: Port State Control. Regional Co-operation. Progress Report on Regional Port State Control Agreements. Note by the Secretariat

62. Doc. no.: FSI 3/12
Date: 8 December 1994
Title: Pseudo-Certificates of Non-Party States (MARPOL 73/78 and SOLAS 74). Information on Why States Have not Ratified MARPOL. Note by the Secretariat

63. Doc. no.: FSI 3/17
Date: 23 March 1995
Title: Report to the Maritime Safety Committee and the Marine Environment Protection Committee

SUB-COMMITTEE ON SAFETY OF NAVIGATION 41st Session 18-22 September 1995

64. Doc. no.: NAV 41/5/1
Date: 16 June 1995
Title: Vessel Traffic Services (VTS) and Ship Reporting. Review of Resolution A.578(14). Note by the Government of the Netherlands

65. Doc. no.: NAV 41/6/21
Date: 21 July 1995
Title: Navigational Aids and Related Matters. Automatic Ship Identification Transponder Systems. Use of a Transponder System for Ship-to-Ship and Ship-to-Shore Identification and the Enhancement of the Safety of Navigation. Note by the Friends of the Earth International

66. Doc. no.: NAV 41/6/27
Date: 20 July 1995
Title: Navigation Aids and Related Matters. Automatic System for Ship Identification. Submitted by INTERTANKO

67. Doc. no.: NAV 41/6/32
Date: 21 July 1995
Title: Navigation Aids and Related Matters. Carriage of Automatic Ship Identification Systems. Note by the United Kingdom

68. Doc. no.: NAV 41/23
Date: 19 October 1995
Title: Report to the Maritime Safety Committee

SUB-COMMITTEE ON STANDARDS OF TRAINING AND WATCHKEEPING 27th Session 6-10 February 1995

69. Doc. no.: STW 27/3/25
Date: 22 December 1994
Title: Comprehensive Review of the 1978 STCW Convention and Preparation of Related Conference Resolutions. Control Procedures. Submitted by the Governments of the Netherlands and the United Kingdom

70. Doc. no.: STW 27/16
Date: 28 February 1995
Title: Report to the Maritime Safety Committee

TECHNICAL CO-OPERATION COMMITTEE 41st Session 15 June 1995

71. Doc. no.: TC 41/13
Date: 22 June 1995
Title: Report of the Technical Co-operation Committee on its Forty-First Session

LONDON CONVENTION 1972 18th Meeting 4-8 December 1995

72. Doc. no.: LC 18/2
Date: 6 September 1995
Title: Status of the London Convention 1972. Report of the Secretary-General on the Status of the London Convention 1972

73. Doc. no.: LC 18/8
Date: 14 August 1995
Title: Matters Related to the Disposal at Sea of Radioactive Wastes. Statement by the OECD/NEA Executive Group for Research on Sea Disposal of Radioactive Waste (CRESP). Note by the Secretariat

74. Doc. no.: LC 18/8/1
Date: 5 October 1995
Title: Matters Related to the Disposal at Sea of Radioactive Wastes. The Concept of "De Minimis". Submitted by the IAEA

LONDON CONVENTION 1972 AMENDMENT GROUP 3rd Meeting 24-28 April 1995

75. Doc. no.: LC/AM 3/2/5
Date: 20 January 1995
Title: Proposed Amendments to the Convention and/or its Annexes. The "Polluter-Pays-Principle". Submitted by Sweden

76. Doc. no.: LC/AM 3/2/6
Date: 6 February 1995
Title: Proposed Amendments to the Convention and/or its Annexes. Comments and Views on the Issue of "Reverse Listing" and the London Convention 1972. Submitted by the United States

77. Doc. no.: LC/AM 3/7 + Corr. 1
Date: 17 May 1995
Title: Report of the Third Meeting of the London Convention 1972 Amendment Group

SCIENTIFIC GROUP ON DUMPING 18th Meeting 10-14 July 1995

78. Doc. no.: LC/SG 18/4
Date: 16 May 1995
Title: Global Waste Survey: Consideration of Final Report. Global Waste Survey Final Report

79. Doc. no.: LC/SG 18/13
Date: 1 August 1995
Title: Report of the Eighteenth Meeting of the Scientific Group

INTERNATIONAL OIL POLLUTION COMPENSATION FUND ASSEMBLY 18th Session 17-20 October 1995

80. Doc. no.: FUND/A.18/12 + Add. 1
Date: 31 July 1995
Title: Entry Into Force of the 1992 Protocols Amending the 1969 Civil Liability Convention and the 1971 Fund Convention. Note by the Director

81. Doc. no.: FUND/A.18/12/1
Date: 25 July 1995
Title: Entry Into Force of the 1992 Protocols Amending the 1969 Civil Liability Convention and the 1971 Fund Convention. Compulsory Denunciation of the 1969 Civil Liability Convention and the 1971 Fund Convention. Note by the Director

82. Doc. no.: FUND/A.18/26
Date: 20 October 1995
Title: Record of Decisions of the Eighteenth Session of the Assembly

IMO/UNCTAD JOINT INTERGOVERNMENTAL GROUP OF EXPERTS ON MARITIME LIENS AND MORTGAGES AND RELATED SUBJECTS 8th Session 9-10 October 1995

83. Doc. no.: LEG/MLM/32
Date: 15 June 1995
Title: Consideration of the Possible Review of the International Convention for the Unification of Certain Rules Relating to the Arrest of Sea-Going Ships, 1952. Note by the IMO Secretariat

84. Doc. no.: LEG/MLM/37
Date: 8 November 1995
Title: Report of the Joint Intergovernmental Group of Experts on Maritime Liens and Mortgages and Related Subjects on its Eighth Session

INTERNATIONAL CONFERENCE OF PARTIES TO STCW 78 and INTERNATIONAL CONFERENCE ON STANDARDS OF TRAINING, CERTIFICATION AND WATCHKEEPING FOR FISHING VESSEL PERSONNEL held from 26 June - 7 July 1995

85. Doc. no.: STCW/CONF/10
Date: 7 July 1995
Title: Adoption of the Final Act and Any Instruments, Resolutions and Recommendations Resulting from the Work of the Conference. Final Act of the Conference of Parties to the International Convention on Standards of Training, Certification and Watchkeeping for Seafarers, 1978. Text adopted by the Conference

86. Doc. no.: STCW/CONF/DC/1 + Corr. 1
Date: 5 July 1995
Title: Consideration of the Draft Amendments to the International Convention on Standards of Training, Certification and Watchkeeping for Seafarers, 1978. Draft Attachment 1 to the Final Act of the Conference - Draft Conference Resolution 1 and Proposed Draft Regulations of the STCW 1978 Convention. Submitted by the Drafting Committee

87. Doc. no.: STCW/CONF/DC/2 + Corr. 1
Date: 5 July 1995
Title: Consideration of the Draft Seafarers' Training, Certification and Watchkeeping (STCW) Code. Draft Conference Resolution 2 - Draft Attachment 2 to the Final Act of the Conference - Adoption of the Seafarers' Training, Certification and Watchkeeping Code. Submitted by the Drafting Committee

88. Doc. no.: STCW/CONF/DC/3 + Corr. 1
Date: 5 July 1995
Title: Consideration of Draft Resolutions and Recommendations and Related Matters. Draft Attachment 3 to the Final Act of the Conference - Draft Conference Resolutions 3 to 14. Submitted by the Drafting Committee

INTERNATIONAL CONFERENCE TO SOLAS 74, held on 20, 27, 28 and 29 November 1995

89. Doc. no.: SOLAS/CONF.3/45/Rev.1
Date: 29 November 1995
Title: Adoption of the Final Act of the Conference. Final Act of the Conference of Contracting Governments to the International Convention for the Safety of Life at Sea, 1974. Text Adopted by the Conference

1. RESOLUTION A.827(19). ADOPTED ON 23 NOVEMBER 1995. SHIPS' ROUTEING*

Doc. no.: A 19/Res.827 15 December 1995

THE ASSEMBLY,

RECALLING Article 15(j) of the Convention on the International Maritime Organization concerning the functions of the Assembly in relation to regulations and guidelines concerning maritime safety and the prevention and control of marine pollution from ships,

RECALLING FURTHER resolution A.377(X) by which it established procedures for the adoption and amendment of routeing systems other than traffic separation schemes,

HAVING CONSIDERED the reports of the Maritime Safety Committee at its sixty-third, sixty-fourth and sixty-fifth sessions,

1. CONFIRMS the adoption by the Organization of the new and amended routeing measures other than traffic separation schemes set out in Annex 1 to the present resolution;

2. CONFIRMS ALSO the adoption by the Organization of the Rules and Recommendations on Navigation through the Strait of Istanbul, the Strait of Canakkale and the Marmara Sea set out in Annex 2 to the present resolution;

3. CONFIRMS FURTHER that the Rules and Recommendations on Navigation through the Strait of Istanbul, the Strait of Canakkale and the Marmara Sea are established purely for the purpose of safety of navigation and environmental protection and are not intended in any way to affect or prejudice the rights of any ship using the Straits under international law, including the United Nations Convention on the Law of the Sea, 1982 and the 1936 Montreux Convention, and that national regulations promulgated by the coastal State should be in total conformity with the said rules and recommendations;

4. INVITES Governments to bring the Rules and Recommendations, set out in Annex 2, to the attention of shipowners, shipmasters and seafarers of ships which use the Strait of Istanbul, the Strait of Canakkale and the Marmara Sea and to ensure that these Rules and Recommendations are available on board such ships for information and compliance;

---

* Only Annexes 2 and 3 are reproduced.

5. REQUESTS the Maritime Safety Committee to review, on the basis of submissions from Governments, the operation of the Rules and Recommendations set out in Annex 2 and the conditions in the Strait of Istanbul, the Strait of Canakkale and the Marmara Sea, to consider, as appropriate, any suggestions for changes in the said Rules and Recommendations and to report on these matters to the next session of the Assembly;

6. CONFIRMS FURTHER the adoption of amendments to the General Provisions on Ships' Routeing consequential to the adoption of new SOLAS regulation V/8 set out in Annex 3 to the present resolution.

[...]

ANNEX 2

ROUTEING MEASURES OTHER THAN TRAFFIC SEPARATION SCHEMES

RULES AND RECOMMENDATIONS ON NAVIGATION THROUGH THE STRAIT OF ISTANBUL, THE STRAIT OF CANAKKALE AND THE MARMARA SEA*

1 USE OF SHIPS' ROUTEING

1.1 Vessels navigating in the Straits shall exercise full diligence and regard for the requirements of the traffic separation schemes (TSSs).

1.2 A vessel that is not able to comply with the requirements of the TSS shall inform the traffic control station well in advance. In such circumstances, the competent authority may temporarily suspend the particular TSS, or section[s] of it, and inform the vessels sailing in the area and advise them to comply with rule 9 of the International Regulations for Preventing Collisions at Sea, 1972.

1.3 In order to ensure safe transit of vessels which cannot comply with the TSS, the competent authority may temporarily suspend two-way traffic and regulate one-way traffic to maintain a safe distance between vessels.

2 SHIP REPORTING AND NAVIGATION INFORMATION

2.1 All vessels entering the Straits are strongly recommended to participate in the reporting system (TUBRAP) established by the competent authority and concerning which the appropriate information has been promulgated by notices to mariners and other means.

2.2 For the purpose of efficient and expeditious traffic management, in the interest of safety of navigation and protection of the marine environment, vessels intending to pass through the Straits are strongly advised to give prior information on the size of the vessel, whether in ballast or loaded condition and whether carrying any hazardous and noxious cargo, as defined in relevant international conventions.

*(Hereinafter referred to as the Straits)

2.3 All vessels navigating in the Straits are recommended to make use of the information broadcasts made by the information services operated by the competent authority, and to keep watch on VHF as appropriate, in accordance with the TUBRAP scheme.

3 PILOTAGE

3.1 Masters of vessels passing through the Straits are strongly recommended to avail themselves of the services of a qualified pilot in order to comply with the requirements of safe navigation.

4 DAYLIGHT TRANSIT

Vessels having a maximum draught of 15 m or more and vessels over 200 m in overall length are advised to navigate the Straits in daylight.

5 TOWING

Passage of a vessel under tow may only be carried out when using tugboat[s] or vessel[s] suitably equipped for the operation in order to ensure safe navigation.

6 ANCHORAGE

When required, vessels may use the anchorages designated for this purpose.

ANNEX 3

AMENDMENTS TO THE GENERAL PROVISIONS ON SHIPS' ROUTEING

INTRODUCTION

The General Provisions of Ships' Routeing are established pursuant to regulation V(8) of the SOLAS Convention

1 OBJECTIVES

.1 Insert new subparagraph 1.2.6, as follows:

".6 the organization of safe traffic flow in or around or at a safe distance from environmentally sensitive areas;"

.2 Renumber existing subparagraphs 1.2.6 and 1.2.7 as subparagraphs 1.2.7 and 1.2.8.

2 DEFINITIONS

.1 Insert after subparagraph 2.1.1 on the definition of Routeing system a new definition for "Mandatory routeing system" as follows:

".2 Mandatory routeing system

A routeing system adopted by the Organization, in accordance with the requirements of regulation V/8 of the International Convention for the Safety of Life at Sea 1974, for mandatory use by all ships, certain categories of ships or ships carrying certain cargoes."

.2 Renumber existing subparagraphs 2.1.2 to 2.1.14 as subparagraphs 2.1.3 to 2.1.15.

3 PROCEDURES AND RESPONSIBILITIES

Procedures and functions of IMO

.1 Amend paragraph 3.1 to conform with paragraphs (a) and (b) of SOLAS regulationV/8 as amended. The text should read as follows:

"3.1 IMO is recognized as the only international body responsible for establishing and adopting measures on an international level concerning ships' routeing systems for use by all ships, certain categories of ships or ships carrying certain cargoes."

.2 Insert a new paragraph 3.5 to deal with the procedures for adopting mandatory routeing systems, as follows:

"3.5 In deciding whether or not to adopt or amend a mandatory routeing system, IMO will, in addition to the provisions of paragraphs 3.2, 3.3, as appropriate, and 3.4, consider whether:

.1 proper and sufficient justification for the establishment of a mandatory routeing system has been provided by the sponsoring Government or Governments;

.2 ports or harbours of littoral States would be adversely affected."

.3 Insert new paragraphs 3.6 and 3.7 to deal with the procedures for adopting a routeing system which is intended to protect an environmentally sensitive area, as follows:

"3.6 In deciding whether or not to adopt or amend a routeing system which is intended to protect the marine environment, IMO will consider whether:

.1 the proposed routeing system can reasonably be expected to prevent or significantly reduce the risk of pollution or other damage to the marine environment of the area concerned;

.2 given the overall size of the area to be protected, or the aggregate number of environmentally sensitive areas established or identified in the geographical region concerned, the use of routeing systems - particularly areas to be avoided - could have the effect of unreasonably limiting the sea area available for navigation; and

.3 the proposed routeing system meets the requirements of these General Provisions.

3.7 IMO will not adopt a proposed routeing system until it is satisfied that the proposed system will not impose unnecessary constraints on shipping and is completely in accordance with the requirements of regulation V/8, paragraph (j) of the SOLAS Convention. In particular, an area to be avoided will not be adopted if it would impede the passage of ships through an international strait."

Responsibilities of Governments and recommended and compulsory practices

.4 Renumber existing paragraphs 3.5 and 3.6 as paragraphs 3.8 and 3.9. No amendments to these paragraphs are proposed.

.5 Delete existing paragraph 3.7.

.6 Insert a new paragraph 3.10 to read as follows:

"3.10 When establishing or amending a routeing system in a particular area where two or more Governments have a common interest, they should formulate joint proposals for adoption by IMO in accordance with SOLAS chapter V, regulation 8(f)."

.7 Renumber existing paragraph 3.8 as paragraph 3.11 and amend this paragraph to read as follows:

"3.11 A Government, or Governments jointly, proposing a new routeing system or an amendment to an adopted system, any part which lies beyond its or their territorial sea or seas or in straits used for international navigation, should consult IMO so that such system may be adopted or amended by IMO for international use. Such Government or Governments should furnish all relevant information, in particular with regard to:

.1 the objectives of the proposed routeing system and a demonstrated need for its establishment, including the consideration of alternative routeing measures and the reasons why the proposed routeing system is preferred;

.2 the traffic pattern, hazards to navigation, aids to navigation and the state of hydrographic surveys;

.3 marine environmental considerations;

.4 the application to all ships, certain categories of ships or ships carrying certain cargoes of a routeing system or any part thereof;

.5 any alternative routeing measure, if necessary, for all ships, certain categories of ships or ships carrying certain cargoes which may be excluded from using a routeing system or any part thereof; and

.6 the number, edition and, where possible, the geodetic datum of the reference chart used for the delineation of the routeing system, together with copies of the reference charts listed in the description of the routeing system showing the new system or the amendments to existing systems."

.8 Delete present paragraph 3.9.

.9 Renumber existing paragraph 3.10 as 3.12 and amend this paragraph to read as follows:

"3.12 Governments are recommended to ensure, as far as practicable, that drilling rigs (MODUs), exploration platforms and other similar structures are not established within the traffic lanes of routeing systems adopted by IMO or near their terminations. When the temporary positioning of a drilling rig or similar structure in a traffic lane of an adopted traffic separation scheme cannot be avoided, the system should, if necessary, be amended temporarily in accordance with the guidelines given in section 7.

In the case of mandatory routeing systems, Governments should ensure that drilling rigs (MODUs), exploration platforms and other structures obstructing navigation and not being an aid to navigation will not be established within the traffic lanes of a traffic separation scheme being part of a mandatory routeing system."

.10 Renumber existing paragraph 3.11 as paragraph 3.13.

.11 Renumber existing paragraph 3.12 as paragraph 3.14 and amend this paragraph to read as follows:

"3.14 Governments establishing routeing systems, no part of which lie beyond their territorial seas or in straits used for international navigation, are requested to design them in accordance with IMO guidelines and criteria for such systems and submit them to IMO for adoption."

.12 Renumber present paragraph 3.13 as paragraph 3.15 and amend in the first and second line "traffic separation scheme" to read "routeing system" and amend in the third and fifth lines the word "scheme" to read "system".

.13 Renumber present paragraph 3.14 as paragraph 3.16 and amend the references to present paragraph 3.12 and 3.13 as 3.14 and 3.15.

.14 Insert a new paragraph 3.17 to cover the last two amended sentences of existing paragraph 3.8, as follows:

"3.17 A routeing system, when adopted by IMO, shall not be amended or suspended before consultation with and agreement by IMO, unless local conditions or the urgency of the case as described in paragraph 3.19, require that earlier action be taken. In considering the proposal, IMO shall take account of the objectives, procedures, responsibilities, methods and criteria for routeing systems as set out in these General Provisions. A mandatory routeing system, when adopted by IMO, shall not be temporarily amended or suspended except in urgent cases as described in paragraph 3.19."

.15 Insert a new paragraph 3.18 to deal with reviews of mandatory routeing systems, as follows:

"3.18 Mandatory routeing systems should be reviewed, as necessary, by the Government or Governments concerned taking into account pertinent comments, reports and observations on the routeing system. Elements under review might include variations to traffic patterns, offshore exploration and exploitation, hydrographical changes, effectiveness of aids to navigation and other developments."

.16 Insert a new paragraph 3.19 to replace existing paragraph 3.9 as follows:

"3.19 In an emergency such as might result from the unexpected blocking or obstruction of a traffic lane or any other part of a routeing system by a wreck or other hazard, immediate temporary changes in the use of the affected traffic separation scheme or other routeing system may be made by the responsible and sponsoring Government or Governments, with the objective of directing traffic flow clear of the new hazard. In such cases, every possible measure shall be taken by the Government or Governments concerned to immediately inform shipping of the hazard and of the temporary changes which have been made.

The responsible and sponsoring Government or Governments should inform IMO as soon as possible of any such changes and their justification."

.17 Renumber existing paragraph 3.15 as paragraph 3.20 and in the second line amend the second word "her" to read "its".

.18 Delete existing paragraph 3.16.

4 METHODS

.1 No amendment to this section is proposed.

Include in figure 3 symbols for inshore traffic zone in the eastern ITZ.

5 PLANNING

Delete present paragraph 5.1 and renumber the remaining paragraphs accordingly.

5.4 Delete present paragraph 5.4 and insert a new paragraph 5.3 as follows:

"5.3 A Government or Governments planning, implementing and maintaining mandatory routeing systems should consider whether, because of the particular circumstances in the area or parts of the area concerned, an associated monitoring service, a reporting service or VTS should be established in accordance with the guidelines adopted by IMO for such services*, as appropriate."

6 DESIGN CRITERIA

.1 Amend paragraph 6.11 as follows:

"6.11 Position fixing

6.11.1 It should be possible for ships to fix their position anywhere within the limits of and in the immediate approaches to a traffic separation scheme by one or more of the following means, both by day and by night:

---

*Refer to resolution MSC.43(64) - Guidelines and criteria for ship reporting systems and resolution A.578(14) - Guidelines for Vessel Traffic Sevices.

.1 visual bearing of readily identifiable objects;

.2 radar bearings and ranges of readily identifiable objects;

.3 D/F bearings;

.4 other radionavigation equipment suitable for use throughout the intended voyage.

6.11.2 The position fixing of ships may be supplemented or substituted by shore-based radar and radio direction finder systems to assist ships which have difficulty to establish their position accurately with the means prescribed under 6.11.1. Such shore-based systems should be approved by IMO before they are recognized as a position fixing system for supporting the safety of navigation in or near traffic separation schemes."

.2 Insert after paragraph 6.15 new paragraphs 6.16 and 6.17 as follows:

"Mandatory routeing systems

6.16 The extent of a mandatory routeing system should be limited to what is essential in the interest of safety of navigation and the protection of the marine environment.

6.17 It shall be possible for ships to fix their positions in relation to a mandatory routeing system by one or more of the means mentioned in paragraph 6.11 of this section."

.3 Renumber existing paragraphs 6.16 to 6.18 as 6.18 to 6.20. No amendments to these paragraphs are proposed.

7 TEMPORARY ADJUSTMENTS TO TRAFFIC SEPARATION SCHEMES

.1 Amend the title of this section to read as follows:

"7 TEMPORARY ADJUSTMENTS AND SUSPENSIONS"

.2 After the title of this section insert the subtitle:

"Traffic separation schemes"

.3 Insert after paragraph 7.5 a new subtitle and paragraph as follows:

"Mandatory routeing systems

7.6 Mandatory routeing systems should not be temporarily adjusted. If necessary for the safety of navigation in the area concerned, a mandatory routeing system may be entirely or partly suspended by the Contracting Government or Governments which have implemented such systems. The responsible Government or Governments should inform IMO of such a suspension and promulgate details of the suspension by all appropriate means."

8 THE USE OF ROUTEING SYSTEMS

.1 Insert a new paragraph 8.1.

"8.1 Unless stated otherwise, routeing systems are recommended for use by all ships and may be made mandatory for all ships, certain categories of ships or ships carrying certain cargoes."

.2 Renumber paragraph 8.1 as 8.2. No amendment to this paragraph is proposed.

.3 Renumber paragraph 8.2 and amend to read:

"8.3 Bearing in mind the need for adequate under-keel clearance, a decision to use a routeing system must take into account the charted depth, the possibility of changes in the sea-bed since the time of the last survey, and the effects of meteorological and tidal conditions on water depths."

.5 Renumber existing paragraphs 8.3 to 8.9 as 8.4 to 8.10. No amendments to these paragraphs are proposed.

9 REPRESENTATION ON CHARTS

A new legend for mandatory routeing systems is added to paragraph 9.2 "Use of legend on charts and notes" as follows:

"

LEGEND	USE OF LEGEND
Mandatory Routeing	Not usually shown on charts but referred to in notes

"

2. REPORT ON THE STATUS OF THE CONVENTION AND MEMBERSHIP OF THE ORGANIZATION - NOTE BY THE SECRETARIAT

Doc. no.: C 74/3/1 13 March 1995

1 In considering the prospects for the entry into force of the amendments to the IMO Convention adopted in November 1993, the Council at is seventy-third session in November 1994 requested the Secretariat to undertake a study on whether, on the basis of the provisions in the Vienna Convention on the Law of Treaties, 1969, these amendments could be applied provisionally.

A BACKGROUND

The 1993 amendments

2 The Assembly at is eighteenth session (25 October - 5 November 1993) adopted by resolution A.735(18) amendments to Articles 16, 17 and 19 of the IMO Convention. When in force, these amendments will increase the number of Council Members from 32 to 40.

Entry into force requirements

3 In accordance with Article 66 of the IMO Convention, each amendment shall come into force for all Members twelve months after its acceptance by two-thirds of the Members of the Organization, other than Associate Members.

4 A declaration of acceptance under Article 66 shall be made by the communication of an instrument to the Secretary-General for deposit with the Secretary-General of the United Nations. The Secretary-General will notify Members of the receipt of any such instrument and of the date when the amendment enters into force (Article 68).

5 At present IMO has 151 Members. In accordance with Article 66, therefore, amendments will enter into force for all Members twelve months after having been accepted by 101 Members.

6 To date only 18 acceptances have been received. With a similar development one cannot realistically expect the present amendments to enter into force in time for the new rules to be applied before the twentieth Assembly in 1997.

B RETROSPECTIVE AND PROVISIONAL APPLICATION: VIENNA CONVENTION ON THE LAW OF TREATIES

7 The issue under study is whether the 1993 amendments to the IMO Convention can be applied provisionally before their entry into force on the basis of the Vienna Convention on the Law of Treaties . With regard to the retrospective application of the Vienna Convention, Article 4 of the Convention provides that:

> "Without prejudice to the application of any rules set forth in the present Convention to which treaties would be subject under international law independently of the Convention, the Convention applies only to treaties which are concluded by States after the entry into force of the present Convention with regard to such States."

The Convention entered into force in 1980 and therefore could not technically apply to the IMO Convention which entered into force in 1958. However, as Article 4 is without prejudice to the application of any rules to which a treaty would be subject under international law, the Vienna Convention, regarded as applicable customary international law, has been extensively applied in relation to treaties between States which were adopted before its entry into force.

8 This seems to provide the legal basis for the application of the Vienna Convention also in respect of the IMO Convention.

9 Regarding the issue of provisional application, Article 25, paragraph 1, of the Vienna Convention provides that:

> "A treaty or a part of a treaty is applied provisionally pending its entry into force if:
> (a) the treaty itself so provides; or
> (b) the negotiating States have in some other manner so agreed."

The IMO Convention does not explicitly provide for provisional application. Nor was such a decision taken in connection with the adoption of the amendments to the IMO Convention. However, as the IMO Assembly is the organ empowered to adopt amendments to the IMO Convention, it follows that the Assembly also has the authority to decide upon provisional application. Such a decision would, for the purpose of Article 25 of the Vienna Convention, be regarded as one of the ways in which the "negotiating States have in some other manner so agreed".

10 A number of other organizations have in the past applied provisionally amendments to treaty instruments on the basis of agreements between the negotiating States. Some examples of this practice can be found in the International Telecommunication Union (ITU) and the United Nations.

11 The Member States of the ITU have, for many years, approved the concept of provisional application in their revision of the International Telecommunication Convention. In December 1992 the ITU Additional Plenipotentiary Conference, Geneva, adopted a new Constitution and Convention for ITU, and at the same time adopted a resolution providing that the provisions of the Constitution and the Convention relating to the new structure and working methods of the ITU should be applied provisionally as from 1 March 1993.

12 In the case of the United Nations, the General Assembly, recognizing the need to provide for provisional application of the Agreement relating to the implementation of Part XI of the United Nations Convention on the Law of the Sea of 10 December 1982, adopted General Assembly Resolution 48/263 which provided *inter alia* in Article 7(1) that "if on 16 November 1994 this Agreement has not entered into force, it shall be applied provisionally pending its entry into force".

C CAN THE APPLICATION BE MANDATORY?

13 It is obvious that, just like an amendment to the IMO Convention becomes binding on all IMO Members once it enters into force, a decision to apply such an amendment provisionally will also have to be

binding in respect of all Members. Another issue to be considered is therefore whether a decision of the Assembly to apply provisionally the 1993 amendments can be applied to those Members who voted against the decision. It could be said that a fundamental premise of treaty law is that a party is not compelled to apply a treaty or treaty amendments until the treaty or its amendments enter into force for that party. However, it could also be argued that the "mandatory" character of provisional application is a necessary element in applying a provision of this procedural nature. The study undertaken indicates that provisional application is usually applied only in respect of those parties who explicitly agree thereto but also provides examples where provisional application has been binding on all parties, irrespective of whether they have voted against or even participated in the decision.

D MAJORITY REQUIRED?

14 Finally, the question arises what majority should be required for a decision on provisional application. There is no specific provision in the IMO Convention regarding this.

15 Article 57 (b) of the IMO Convention indicates that decisions shall normally be taken by a majority vote of the Members present and voting, unless a two-thirds majority vote is required. One example where this qualified majority is stipulated is the adoption of amendments to the IMO Convention (Article 66). It could be argued on the one hand that a decision on provisional application is not an amendment to the Convention but a decision on procedure, in which case a simple majority would be required. However, it could also be equally argued that as the decision brings into effect the amendments, the same requirement of two-thirds majority should be applicable. In view of the fact that the votes may provide an indication whether the requisite acceptances for entry into force would eventually be received, the latter argument may be worth considering.

E CONCLUSIONS

16 From the above, the following conclusions can be drawn:

- Article 25 of the Vienna Convention on the Law of Treaties on provisional application can be applied in respect of amendments to the IMO Convention.

- The IMO Assembly has the power to decide on provisional application. In that connection the Assembly would have to agree:

  (a) on the majority required for a decision on provisional application; and
  (b) that provisional application of the 1993 amendments is binding on all IMO Members.

Action to be taken by the Council

17 The Council is invited to consider the information contained in this document and to comment and decide as it may deem appropriate.

3. FOLLOW-UP ACTION TO UNCED. REPORT OF THE UNCED WORKING GROUP*

Doc. no.: MEPC 37/10 18 January 1995

1 Introduction

[...]

1.1 The UNCED Working Group met from 31 October to 4 November 1994 under the chairmanship of Mr. Jens H. Koefoed (Norway).

1.2 The session was attended by delegations from:

AUSTRALIA
CANADA
FINLAND
JAPAN
MALAYSIA
NETHERLANDS
NORWAY
REPUBLIC OF KOREA
SINGAPORE
SOLOMON ISLANDS
SWEDEN
UNITED KINGDOM
UNITED STATES

by a representative from the following Associate Member of IMO:

HONG KONG

and by observers from the following non-governmental organizations:

OIL COMPANIES INTERNATIONAL MARINE FORUM (OCIMF)
OIL INDUSTRY INTERNATIONAL EXPLORATION AND PRODUCTION FORUM (E & P FORUM)
GREENPEACE INTERNATIONAL
WORLD WIDE FUND FOR NATURE (WWF)

1.3 The Working Group had before it the following documents:

MEPC 36/8/Add.1	-	Secretariat
MEPC 36/8/1	-	Netherlands
MEPC 36/8/2	-	Secretariat
MEPC 36/8/3	-	International Hydrographic Bureau

* Only Annex 3 is reproduced.

1.4 The Working Group was requested to consider the following issues:

.1 finalization of IMO's report to the Commission on Sustainable Development (CSD) with a view to adoption of the report by the Committee at its 36th session;

ANNEX 3

DOCUMENTATION ISSUED BY IMO SUBSEQUENT TO THE RIO CONFERENCE

Chapter 17 reference:	***17.30(a)(i),(ii): Ratification & implementation of shipping conventions & protocols***	***17.30(a)(iii): Monitoring of marine pollution from ships (illegal discharges)***	***17.30(a)(iv), (v): Protection of particularly sensitive areas and preservation of rare or fragile ecosystems***	***17.30(a)(vi): Non-indigenous organisms in ballast water***
Council	C 69/INF.2; C 69/15(d); C 72/8/Add.2	C 69/INF.2; C 69/15(d); C 72/8/Add.2	C 69/INF.2; C 69/15(d); C 72/8/Add.2	C 69/INF.2; C 69/15(d); C 72/8/Add.2
MSC				
MEPC	MEPC 34/INF.6; MEPC 35/7/1, annex, section 1; MEPC 35/7/3, appendix 1; MEPC 36/8, annexes 1 & 2; MEPC 36/8/Add.1, section 3	MEPC 34/INF.6; MEPC 35/7/1, annex, section 2; MEPC 35/7/3, appendix 1; MEPC 36/8, annex 2; MEPC 36/8/Add.1, section 4	MEPC 34/INF.6; MEPC 35/7/1, annex, section 3; MEPC 35/7/3, appendix 1; MEPC 36/8, annex 2; MEPC 36/8/Add.1, section 5	MEPC 34/INF.6; MEPC 35/7/1, annex, section 4; MEPC 35/7/3, appendix 1; MEPC 36/8, annexes 1 & 2; MEPC 36/8/Add.1, section 6
FAL				
Legal				
TCC	TC 40/6	TC 40/6	TC 40/6	TC 40/6
Sub-Committee				
Other Secretariat				
Non-UN Agency				
Product	IMO report to CSD adopted by MEPC 36 (31/10/94-4/11/94)	IMO report to CSD adopted by MEPC 36 (31/10/94-4/11/94)	IMO report to CSD adopted by MEPC 36 (31/10/94-4/11/94)	IMO report to CSD adopted by MEPC 36 (31/10/94-4/11/94)
Comments				

Chapter 17 reference:	***17.30(a)(vii): Navigational safety***	***17.30(a)(viii): Stricter regulations to reduce risk of accidents and pollution from cargo ships***	***17.30(a)(ix): Carriage of irradiated nuclear fuel on board ships***	***17.30(a)(x): Revision, update and implementation of the IMO Code of Safety for Nuclear Merchant Ships***
Council	C 69/INF.2; C 69/15(d); C 72/8/Add.2	C 69/INF.2; C 69/15(d); C 72/8/Add.2	C 69/INF.2; C 69/15(d); C 72/8/Add.2	C 69/INF.2; C 69/15(d); C 72/8/Add.2
MSC	MSC 63/19/2			
MEPC	MEPC 34/INF.6; MEPC 35/7/1, annex. section 5; MEPC 35/7/3, appendix 1; MEPC 36/8, annexes 1 & 2; MEPC 36/8/Add.1, section 7; MEPC 36/8/3	MEPC 34/INF.6; MEPC 35/7/1, annex, section 6; MEPC 35/7/3, appendix 1; MEPC 36/8, annexes 1 & 2; MEPC 36/8/Add.1, section 8	MEPC 34/INF.6; MEPC 35/7/1, annex, section 7; MEPC 35/7/3, appendix 1; MEPC 36/8, annexes 1 & 2; MEPC 36/8/Add.1, section 9	MEPC 34/INF.6; MEPC 35/7/1, annex, section 8; MEPC 35/7/3, appendix 1; MEPC 36/8, annex 1; MEPC 36/8/Add.1, section 10
FAL				
Legal				
TCC	TC 40/6	TC 40/6	TC 40/6	TC 40/6
Sub-Committee				
Other Secretariat				
Non-UN Agency				
Product	IMO report to CSD adopted by MEPC 36 (31/10/94-4/11/94)	IMO report to CSD adopted by MEPC 36 (31/10/94-4/11/94)	IMO report to CSD adopted by MEPC 36 (31/10/94-4/11/94)	IMO report to CSD adopted by MEPC 36 (31/10/94-4/11/94)
Comments				

Chapter 17 reference:	***17.30(a)(xi): Air pollution from ships***	***17.30(a)(xii): Transportation of hazardous & noxious substances, including liability and compensation for pollution damage***	***17.30(b)(i): London Convention, 1972***	***17.30(b)(ii): Cessation of ocean dumping and incineration of hazardous substances***
Council	C 69/INF.2; C 69/15(d); C 72/8/Add.2	C 69/INF.2; C 69/15(d); C 72/8/Add.2	C 69/INF.2; C 69/15(d); C 72/8/Add.2	C 69/INF.2; C 69/15(d); C 72/8/Add.2
MSC				
MEPC	MEPC 34/INF.6; MEPC 35/7/1, annex, section 9; MEPC 35/7/3, appendix 1; MEPC 36/8, annex 2; MEPC 36/8/Add.1. section 11	MEPC 34/INF.6; MEPC 35/7/1, annex, section 10; MEPC 35/7/3, appendix 1; MEPC 36/8, annexes 1 & 2; MEPC 36/8/Add.1, section 12		
FAL				
Legal				
TCC	TC 40/6	TC 40/6		
Sub-Committee	BCH draft air pollution annex for MEPC 36			
Other Secretariat			London Convention, 1972	London Convention, 1972
Non-UN Agency				
Product	IMO report to CSD adopted by MEPC 36 (31/10/94-4/11/94)	IMO report to CSD adopted by MEPC 36 (31/10/94-4/11/94)		
Comments				

Chapter 17 reference:	*17.30(c): Offshore oil and gas platforms*	*17.30(d): Port reception facilities*	*17.31: Marine pollution in areas of congested shipping*	*17.32: Organotin compounds in anti-fouling paints*
Council	C 69/INF.2; C 69/15(d); C 72/8/Add.2	C 69/INF.2; C 69/15(d); C 72/8/Add.2	C 69/INF.2; C 69/15(d); C 72/8/Add.2	C 69/INF.2; C 69/15(d); C 72/8/Add.2
MSC				
MEPC	MEPC 34/6, annex 2; MEPC 34/23, paras. 6.6, 6.9; MEPC 35/INF.3; MEPC 35/7/3, appendix 1; MEPC 36/8, paras. 5.2-5.7; MEPC 36/8, annex 2; MEPC 36/8/Add.1, section 1	MEPC 34/6, annex 3; MEPC 34/23, para.6; MEPC 35/7; MEPC 35/7/3, appendix 1; MEPC 35/21, paras. 7.12-7.14; MEPC 36/8, paras. 5.8-5.14; MEPC 36/8, annex 2; MEPC 36/8/Add.1, section 2	MEPC 34/INF.6; MEPC 35/7/1, annex, section 11; MEPC 35/7/3, appendix 1; MEPC 36/8/Add.1, section 13	MEPC 34/INF.6; MEPC 35/7/1, annex, section 12; MEPC 35/7/3, appendix 1; MEPC 36/8, annex 2; MEPC 36/8/Add.1, section 14
FAL				
Legal				
TCC	TC 40/6	TC 40/6	TC 40/6	TC 40/6
Sub-Committee				
Other Secretariat	London Convention, 1972		UNCLOS	
Non-UN Agency	Cartagena Convention (Land-based sources); Montreal Guidelines (Land-based sources)			
Product	IMO report to CSD adopted by MEPC 36 (31/10/94-4/11/94)	IMO Manual on Port Reception Facilities; IMO report to CSD adopted by MEPC 36 (31/10/94-4/11/94)	IMO report to CSD adopted by MEPC 36 (31/10/94-4/11/94)	IMO report to CSD adopted by MEPC 36 (31/10/94-4/11/94)
Comments	Further action to be mandated by CSD	SPI Working Group will report to MEPC 37		

Chapter 17 reference:	***17.33; 17.34: Oil and chemical spill response***
Council	C 69/INF.2; C 69/15(d); C 72/8/Add.2
MSC	
MEPC	MEPC 34/INF.6; MEPC 35/7/1, annex, section 13; MEPC 35/7/3, appendix 1; MEPC 36/8, annex 2; MEPC 36/8/Add.1, section 15
FAL	
Legal	
TCC	TC 40/6
Sub-Commmittee	
Other Secretariat	
Non-UN Agency	
Product	IMO report to CSD adopted by MEPC 36 (31/10/94-4/11/94)
Comments	

4. REPORT OF THE MARINE ENVIRONMENT PROTECTION COMMITTEE ON ITS THIRTY-SEVENTH SESSION, 11-15 SEPTEMBER 1995*

Doc. no.: MEPC 37/22 + Add. 1(+ Corr. 1), 2, 3 — 11 October 1995

Table of contents

* Only paras 5.1, 5.7-5.19, 11.1-11.11 and 15.15-15.21 and Annexes 10 and 13 are reproduced.

ANNEXES

ANNEX 6 DRAFT ASSEMBLY RESOLUTION ON PROCEDURES FOR PORT STATE CONTROL

ANNEX 7 DRAFT ASSEMBLY RESOLUTION ON GUIDELINES ON IMPLEMENTATION OF THE INTERNATIONAL SAFETY MANAGEMENT (ISM) CODE BY ADMINISTRATIONS

ANNEX 8 DRAFT ASSEMBLY RESOLUTION ON STRATEGY FOR SHIP/PORT INTERFACE

ANNEX 9 AMENDMENTS TO GUIDELINES ON THE ENHANCED PROGRAMME OF INSPECTION DURING SURVEYS OF BULK CARRIERS AND OIL TANKERS (A.744(18))

ANNEX 10 RESOLUTION MEPC.67(37) ON GUIDELINES ON APPLICATION OF THE PRECAUTIONARY APPROACH

ANNEX 11 STRATEGY OF EXTRA-BUDGETARY ACTIVITIES RELATING TO ENVIRONMENTALLY SUSTAINABLE DEVELOPMENT

ANNEX 12 DRAFT ASSEMBLY RESOLUTION ON FOLLOW-UP ACTION TO THE UNITED NATIONS CONFERENCE ON ENVIRONMENT AND DEVELOPMENT, 1992

ANNEX 13 RESOLUTION MEPC.65(37) ON AMENDMENTS TO THE ANNEX OF THE PROTOCOL OF 1978 RELATING TO THE INTERNATIONAL CONVENTION FOR THE PREVENTION OF POLLUTION FROM SHIPS, 1973 (AMENDMENTS TO REGULATION 2 AND NEW REGULATION 9 OF ANNEX V)

ANNEX 14 DRAFT TEXT OF AMENDMENTS TO PROTOCOL I OF MARPOL 73/78

ANNEX 15 STATEMENTS BY THE DELEGATIONS OF ARGENTINA, THE BAHAMAS, BAHRAIN, GERMANY, NORWAY, SWEDEN, THE UNITED KINGDOM, THE UNITED STATES, VENEZUELA AND OF ICS, IAPH, FOEI, IADC AND INTERTANKO ON PROPOSALS ON THE REGULATIONS OF ANNEX VI OF MARPOL 73/78 OR ON THE ISSUE OF AIR POLLUTION BY SHIPS AS SUCH

ANNEX 16 RESOLUTION MEPC.66(37) - INTERIM GUIDELINES FOR THE APPROVAL OF ALTERNATIVE METHODS OF DESIGN AND CONSTRUCTION OF OIL TANKERS UNDER REGULATION 13F(5) OF ANNEX I OF MARPOL 73/78

ANNEX 17 AGENDA FOR OPRC SPECIALIZED SEMINAR WORKSHOP

ANNEX 18 LIST OF SUBSTANTIVE ITEMS TO BE INCLUDED IN THE AGENDA OF MEPC 38

ANNEX 19 FUTURE WORK PROGRAMME OF THE MARINE ENVIRONMENT PROTECTION COMMITTEE

ANNEX 20 LONG-TERM WORK PLAN (UP TO 2002) OF THE MARINE ENVIRONMENT PROTECTION COMMITTEE

ANNEX 21 WORK PROGRAMMES OF THE BLG SUB-COMMITTEE, THE SPI WORKING GROUP AND THE OPRC WORKING GROUP

ANNEX 22 STATEMENTS OF ARGENTINA AND THE UNITED KINGDOM

5 FLAG STATE IMPLEMENTATION

5.1 The Committee had the following documents under this agenda item: MEPC 37/5, MEPC 37/5/4 (Secretariat), MEPC 37/5/1 (Greenpeace International), MEPC 37/5/2 (France, Germany, the Netherlands, Sweden, United Kingdom and the Commission of the European Communities), MEPC 37/5/3 (United States), MEPC 37/5/5 (Vanuatu) and MEPC 37/5/6 (International Association of Classification Societies (IACS)).

[...]

Consideration of the Correspondence Group report on the definition of "severe pollution"

5.7 The Committee had before it the report of the Correspondence Group (MEPC 37/5/1) which was submitted by Greenpeace International, acting as Co-ordinator, and with terms of reference as set out in paragraph 6.6 of MEPC 36/22.

5.8 After discussion, the Committee agreed that the definition of "severe pollution" as decided by the FSI Sub-Committee at its second session (FSI 2/22, paragraph 6.15) would suffice for the purposes of selection of casualties for which a casualty investigation report would be requested of the flag States.

Consideration of the amalgamation of port State control resolutions

5.9 The Committee had before it: the report of the intersessional work of the Correspondence Group, chaired by the United States (MEPC 37/5/3); the outcome of the STCW Conference 1995 regarding control procedures for manning and certification (MEPC 37/5/4); the comments of the European Union countries (MEPC 37/5/2); the comments of Vanuatu (MEPC 37/5/5); and, a proposal by IACS (MEPC 37/5/6). There was extensive discussion in the plenary on the various issues raised by the Vanuatu submission relating to onus on proof in claims of undue delay, clear grounds for detailed inspection, port State reporting, code of conduct for port State control officers and guidelines for detention of ships of all sizes.

5.10 The Committee noted that the MSC, at its sixty-fifth session (paragraphs 10.6-10.9), invited the Committee to finalize the work of the Correspondence Group on the amalgamation of PSC resolutions and forward the draft resolution for consideration and adoption by the nineteenth Assembly.

5.11 In considering MEPC 37/5/6 (IACS) on referencing Guidelines on Statistics of deficiencies in the draft Assembly resolution, views were divided on whether to accept the proposal. Therefore, the Committee decided to defer the proposal pending experience gained with the new PSC Procedures.

5.12 The delegation of Canada, supported by some delegations, proposed that the reference to the 1969 Tonnage Convention should be deleted from the revised PSC procedures. Several delegations, noting that guidelines on port State control procedures under the Tonnage Convention do not exist at present, considered that such procedures should be included to ensure the uniform application of that Convention. The Committee agreed that all reference to that Convention should be placed in square brackets for further consideration.

5.13 The Committee noted that the MSC approved (paragraph 10.10 of MSC 65/25) to append the draft MSC Circulars on interim procedural guidelines and training and certification requirements for port State control officers, subject to concurrence by MEPC, to the amalgamated Assembly resolution when, after adoption, the texts are published. With support from Panama and Liberia, Vanuatu proposed that the guidelines be appended as an appendix to the PSC procedures as decided by the MSC. Following an exchange of views, the Committee agreed with the proposal by Japan that the revised PSC procedures should include an additional paragraph in Section 2.6 on general procedural guidelines for PSCOs to the effect that an extract from the section should be carried by PSCOs when carrying out inspections.

5.14 Within plenary, concern was raised on whether to retain the existing paragraph 2.1.4 of the PSC procedures addressing 'onus of proof of undue delay'. Opinions were evenly divided between those concerned that this principle contravenes with their national legislation and others which pointed out that the principle had been accepted without dissent by the Assembly and included in resolutions A.681(17) and A.742(18). The Committee, taking into account all views expressed, agreed that the issue could not be resolved within this forum and decided to keep the existing text of paragraph 2.1.4 in square brackets for consideration by the nineteenth Assembly.

5.15 The United Kingdom drew attention to the difficulties that adoption of the final sentence of paragraph 2.1.4 on 'onus of proof of undue delay', as drafted, would raise. The principle put forward in the 'onus of proof' clause is contradictory to underlying procedures in UK law. It understood that this was the position in some other States and proposed that the clause should be deleted from the amalgamated resolution. This view was supported by Australia, Belgium, Canada, Denmark, Finland, France, Germany, Netherlands, Norway, Spain, Sweden and the EC Commission.

5.16 In order to finalize drafting of an Assembly resolution, including final drafting of the extensive annex on port State control procedures, the Committee agreed to establish a Drafting Group under the chairmanship of Mr. Norman Lemley (United States). The Committee instructed the Drafting Group to: finalize the port State control procedures contained in MEPC 37/5/3; consider issues in square brackets from a purely drafting perspective; and, prepare an Assembly resolution.

5.17 The Committee noted the report of the Drafting Group (MEPC 37/WP.8) which offered explanation to, and proposed solutions for, the contentious issues within the draft PSC procedures. Owing to the time constraints, however, the revised draft PSC procedures could not be finalized for printing and translation for submission to the Committee.

5.18 The Committee requested that the Secretariat issue a complete text of the draft Assembly resolution with its annexed revised PSC procedures as soon as possible after the session. Subject to the above, the Committee approved the forwarding of the draft Assembly resolution, as set out in annex 6 to this report, to the nineteenth Assembly for consideration and adoption.

5.19 The Committee considered that it is highly desirable for the revised PSC procedures to be adopted by the nineteenth Assembly and, recognizing that the draft procedures involve a number of unresolved issues, urged delegations to be prepared to discuss the substantive issues in Committee II of the Assembly.

[...]

10 FOLLOW-UP ACTION TO UNCED

10.1 The Committee had before it documents MEPC 37/10 (report of the UNCED Working Group), MEPC 37/10/1 and MEPC 37/10/4/Rev.1 (Secretariat), MEPC 37/10/2 (Denmark, Norway, Russian Federation, United Kingdom), MEPC 37/10/3 (Norway), MEPC 37/10/5 (Netherlands), MEPC 37/10/6 (Greenpeace International), MEPC 37/10/7 (World Wide Fund for Nature (WWF)), MEPC 37/10//8 (International Union for the Conservation of Nature and Natural Resources (IUCN) and WWF), and MEPC 37/INF.2, MEPC 37/INF.17 and MEPC 37/INF.18 (Secretariat).

10.2 The Committee approved in general the report of the UNCED Working Group held from 31 October to 4 November 1994 under the chairmanship of Mr. Jens H. Koefoed (Norway) (MEPC 37/10).

10.3 The Committee noted that the full text of IMO's report to the Commission on Sustainable Development (CSD), as agreed at its 36th session, had been circulated in the English, French and Spanish languages under cover of MEPC 37/INF.2. It also noted the summary of actions taken by other IMO Committees on UNCED issues, referred to them by MEPC 36 (document MEPC 37/10/4/Rev.1). In this connection, the Committee expressed appreciation for the steps taken by the Technical Co-operation Committee to initiate the mobilization of resources for IMO's UNCED Strategy for Extra-budgetary Activities (see paragraphs 10.14 to 10.18 below).

10.4 The Committee dealt with the following issues on the basis of the UNCED Working Group's report and documents submitted subsequently:

- Guidelines for the Application of the Precautionary Approach (documents MEPC 37/10/5 (report of the Correspondence Group led by the Netherlands), MEPC 37/10/6 (Greenpeace), MEPC 36/10/7 (WWF) and MEPC 37/10/9 (INTERTANKO));

- IMO-UNCED Strategy for Extra-Budgetary Activities (MEPC 37/10/1 (Secretariat));

- financing scheme for reception facilities (documents MEPC 37/10/3 (report of the Correspondence Group led by Norway));

- draft Assembly resolution on UNCED follow-up (document MEPC 37/10/2 (Denmark, Norway, Russian Federation and the United Kingdom); and

- draft Assembly resolution on the protection of particularly sensitive sea areas and areas designated by coastal States to protect and preserve rare or fragile ecosystems (document MEPC 37/10/8 (IUCN and WWF)).

The outcome of the Committee's deliberations is recorded in the following paragraphs.

Application of the Precautionary Approach

10.5 The Committee recalled that a Correspondence Group under the leadership of the Netherlands had been established by MEPC 35 to develop guidelines on this subject. Progress of the Correspondence Group was reviewed by the UNCED Working Group during MEPC 36 as reported in document MEPC 37/10, paragraphs 2.1 and 2.2 and annex 1. The Correspondence Group continued to work during the intersessional period and its report, submitted to this session (MEPC 37/10/5), invites the Committee to accept the draft Guidelines on the Application of the Precautionary Approach annexed thereto.

10.6 The Committee decided to apply the Guidelines to its own work in the first instance. Based upon experience gained, steps could be taken to extend their application to the work of other Committees.

10.7 Having received the text of the draft Guidelines from the drafting group (MEPC 37/WP.12, annex 1), the Committee adopted the Guidelines under cover of resolution MEPC.67(37) as shown at annex 10.

10.8 Greenpeace International expressed its continued concern that the Guidelines do not provide sufficient detail to ensure that the precautionary approach can be easily and effectively applied to the work of IMO. Greenpeace International believed that the Guidelines would require substantial improvement and refinement over time.

[...]

11 CONSIDERATION AND ADOPTION OF AMENDMENTS TO ANNEX V OF MARPOL 73/78

11.1 The Committee had before it the following documents: MEPC 37/11/Rev.1 (Secretariat), MEPC 37/11/Rev.1/Corr.1 (Secretariat - Spanish only), MEPC 37/11/1 (IADC), MEPC 37/11/2 (United States), MEPC 37/11/3 (Japan), MEPC 37/11/4 (Greece), MEPC 37/INF.3 (Australia) and MEPC 36/INF.8 (Australia).

11.2 The Committee took note of document MEPC 37/INF.3 (Australia) and MEPC 36/INF.8 (Australia).

11.3 The Committee did not agree to the proposal made by Greece (MEPC 37/11/4) to amend regulation 7 by requesting Parties to provide the Organization with information on reception facilities for transmission to Parties concerned, since such requirement is already incorporated in article 11 of the Convention. The Committee reaffirmed its earlier decision to provide the required information on an annual basis.

11.4 The Committee recalled that, at its thirty-sixth session, it considered the report of the Correspondence Group on "Placards, Waste Management Plans and Refuse Record-keeping for Ships under Annex V" (MEPC 36/9/5) and approved, in principle, the amended regulation 2 and the new regulation 9 of Annex V of MARPOL 73/78, and that the proposed amendment to Annex V was circulated to IMO Members under cover of Circular letter No.1789 of 23 December 1994. The proposed amendment was also issued as document MEPC 37/11/Rev.1 (Secretariat).

11.5 After considering the proposed amendments and the comments made thereto, the Committee established a Drafting Group to carry out an editorial review using document MEPC 37/11/Rev.1 as a base document, taking into account the comments made in Plenary.

11.6 The report of the Drafting Group (MEPC 37/WP.7) containing the editorially revised texts of regulation 2 and regulation 9 to Annex V of MARPOL, as well as the appendix to the Annex (Garbage Record Book), and a draft resolution, was approved by the Committee.

11.7 The Committee decided also that a waiver could be provided to fixed and floating platforms for maintaining a Garbage Record Book and amended regulation 9(4)(ii) accordingly. The waiver could be given by the "Host State" rather than the "Flag State".

11.8 The Netherlands brought to the attention of the Committee that during discussions it was not clear that the "Record of Garbage Discharges" would also become mandatory as it had only been intended as an example during previous correspondence. It therefore proposed that the text of regulation 9(3) be amended to reflect this. This view was supported by the United States.

11.9 On the other hand, the Japanese delegation, supported by other delegations, was of the opinion that the "Record of Garbage Discharges" should remain mandatory, otherwise there is uncertaintity on how garbage discharged is assigned into which group or category, and this would create difficulties in carrying out port State control.

11.10 After discussion the Committee decided that the draft text prepared by the Drafting Group should remain unchanged.

11.11 After the above-mentioned decisions and observations had been made, the Parties to Annex V of MARPOL 73/78 adopted by resolution MEPC.65(37), regulation 2 as amended, regulation 9 and the appendix to Annex V (Garbage Record Book) in accordance with article 16 of MARPOL 73/78. The resolution and the text of amendments to Annex V are set out at annex 13.

[...]

15 IMPLEMENTATION OF THE OPRC CONVENTION AND THE OPPR CONFERENCE RESOLUTIONS

[...]

Matters concerning INF Code

15.15 The Committee agreed that the INF Code be augmented and improved to include provisions for emergency planning. The Committee envisaged that such provisions will assist in the preparation of a voyage plan that outlines procedures for preventing and responding to various incidents, and facilitates, in the event of an accident, prompt notification of all relevant Parties. It further agreed that other aspects of emergency preparedness and response not strictly related to shipboard emergency plans be considered.

15.16 The Committee endorsed the proposal of the Secretary-General to convene a special consultative meeting of entities involved with carriage of material subject to the INF Code and the coastal States involved for the purpose of sharing information, concerns, and ideas, and to gain a better understanding of the safety and environmental aspects involved. It agreed that the objectives of the meeting should be to identify and disseminate information regarding all issues involved in the maritime transport of materials covered by the INF Code, and, in co-operation with the LEG, MSC and relevant subcommittees, to encourage a thorough examination of issues complementary to the INF Code, taking into account the recommendations of the Joint IAEA/IMO/UNEP Working Group and other pertinent information. It was also agreed that subjects to be considered in the meeting should include, but not be limited to, items recommended by the desk study (MEPC 37/15/6), voyage planning, consequences of an accident, and hazard evaluation to determine the measures to be taken, including recovery and means to implement such measures.

15.17 The Committee recommended that the Secretary-General, in consultation with IAEA and UNEP, organize and convene this meeting as a matter of high priority. It noted that it would be essential to the success of this meeting that all entities concerned with the transportation of material subject to the INF Code participate in full.

15.18 The United Kingdom welcomed the proposal of the Secretary-General to convene a special consultative meeting of entities involved in the carriage of material subject to the INF Code and the coastal States involved, and offered to participate in the funding of such a venture. The Committee also welcomed the offer of UNEP to contribute, both in funding and in kind.

15.19 At the request of the United States delegation regarding the timing for the Secretary-General's special consultative meeting, the Secretary indicated that, although the date and duration still needed to be determined, he felt it would probably be held in the first quarter of 1996.

15.20 The Japanese delegation noted that, during discussion of the special consultative meeting within the OPRC Working Group, various opinions were expressed concerning the purpose of the meeting, and the expected output. By exchanging information at such a meeting, Japan believes that all participants will be able to gain better understanding of the safety and environmental aspects involved and eventually their concerns will be addressed. The goal is to make such a meeting successful for all entities attending and, to achieve this, Japan is of the opinion that discussions should be carried out on the basis of purely scientific and technical viewpoints. Japan will communicate frequently with the Secretariat to ensure the views, positions and desires of all countries concerned are presented.

15.21 The Committee instructed the Secretariat to prepare the progress report to the Assembly regarding progress made by the MEPC in the implementation of its resolution A.748(18) on the basis of annex 1 to MEPC 37/WP.4, as amended.

[...]

ANNEX 10

RESOLUTION MEPC.67(37)
adopted on 15 September 1995

GUIDELINES ON INCORPORATION OF THE PRECAUTIONARY APPROACH IN THE CONTEXT OF SPECIFIC IMO ACTIVITIES

THE MARINE ENVIRONMENT PROTECTION COMMITTEE

RECALLING Article 38(c) of the Convention on the International Maritime Organisation concerning the functions of the Marine Environment Protection Committee,

NOTING that General Assembly resolution 47/191 requests the United Nations Specialized agencies to report on steps taken to strengthen and adjust their activities in line with Agenda 21,

NOTING ALSO that the Marine Environment Protection Committee, as IMO's focal point for UNCED follow-up actions, approved in November 1994 a report to the Commission on Sustainable Development in fulfilment of General Assembly Resolution 47/191,

AWARE that principle 15 of the Rio Declaration calls for the application of the Precautionary Approach,

ADOPTS these guidelines on incorporation of the Precautionary Approach in the context of specific IMO activities,on an interim basis until further experience with their application has been gained,

REQUESTS all relevant IMO bodies to review the guidelines and provide comments to the Committee with a view to their eventual submission to the Assembly for adoption as guidance for all relevant IMO activities.

ANNEX

GUIDELINES ON INCORPORATION OF THE PRECAUTIONARY APPROACH IN THE CONTEXT OF SPECIFIC IMO ACTIVITIES

1 The precautionary approach referred to IMO as set out in Principle 15 of the Rio Declaration states:

> "In order to protect the environment, the precautionary approach shall be widely applied by States according to their capabilities. Where there are threats of serious or irreversible damage, lack of full scientific certainty shall not be used as a reason for postponing cost-effective measures to prevent environmental degradation."

and in Agenda 21, chapter 17:

> "17.21 A precautionary and anticipatory rather than a reactive approach is necessary to prevent the degradation of the marine environment. This requires, *inter alia*, the adoption of precautionary measures, environmental impact assessments, clean production techniques, recycling, waste audits and minimization, construction and/or improvement of sewage treatment facilities, quality management criteria for the proper handling of hazardous substances, and a comprehensive approach to damaging impacts from air, land and water. Any management framework must include the improvement of coastal human settlements and the integrated management and development of coastal areas.
>
> 17.22 States, in accordance with the provisions of the United Nations Convention on the Law of the Sea on protection and preservation of the marine environment, commit themselves, in accordance with their policies, priorities and resources, to prevent, reduce and control degradation of the marine environment so as to maintain and improve its life-support and productive capacities. To this end, it is necessary to:
>
> (a) Apply preventive, precautionary and anticipatory approaches so as to avoid degradation of the marine environment, as well as to reduce the risk of long-term or irreversible adverse effects upon it;
>
> (b) Ensure prior assessment of activities that may have significant adverse impacts upon the marine environment;
>
> (c) Integrate protection of the marine environment into relevant general environmental, social and economic development policies;
>
> (d) Develop economic incentives, where appropriate, to apply clean technologies and other means consistent with the internalization of environmental costs, such as the polluter pays principle, so as to avoid degradation of the marine environment;

(e) Improve the living standards of coastal populations, particularly in developing countries, so as to contribute to reducing the degradation of the coastal and marine environment."

Incorporation of the precautionary approach in the work of IMO

2 Many accidents and incidents giving rise to damage to the environment are due to failure to comply with existing standards and procedures, rather than to inadequacies in the instruments concerned. Damage to the environment may also be caused by operational pollution, human error, system failures or *force majeure*.

3 Many of the current IMO activities are directed at achieving improved compliance, viz. flag State implementation, port State control and the International Ship Management (ISM) Code. The underlying philosophy of the precautionary approach as set out in Principle 15 of the Rio Declaration and particularly the section on "lack of full scientific certainty shall not be used as a reason for postpoing cost-effective measures to prevent environmental degradation" could usefully be applied.

Decision-making and management processes

4 The following elements for decision-making and management processes, which would seem desirable if a precautionary approach is to be routinely incorporated into the work of IMO should ensure:

.1 anticipation and prevention of environmental problems arising from any regulatory activities of IMO and striving for continual improvement in all facets of those activities;

.2 that solutions to problems and consideration of new and existing policies, programmes, guidelines and regulations are developed in accordance with the precautionary approach;

.3 that; where action is necessary and options may involve uncertainty, all options are evaluated consistent with the precautionary approach;

.4 adoption of cost effective practices and practical solutions to problems and promotion of their continued development;

.5 where appropriate, that decision-making is preceded by environmental assessment and risk analysis to identify the environmental impacts of the proposed or alternative courses of action, whether these impacts can be prevented or minimized and how this might be done;

.6 improvement of decision-making and management by obtaining and providing baseline and other data, identifying and explaining environmental changes;

.7 promotion of national and international research, analysis and information programmes to identify, understand and disseminate information about threats to the environment from maritime operations, to contribute to defining problems, including analysis of the degree of risk involved, by which uncertainties are reduced, and developing and testing solutions to problems;

.8 consideration and adoption of economic incentives to encourage environmental responsibility so as to conserve the marine environment and avoid its further degradation;

.9 support for development of new and existing policies, programmes, guidelines or regulations, where appropriate, which contribute to the protection and enhancement of the marine and coastal environment consistent with IMO's mandate;

.10 that, as necessary and appropriate, IMO should, through programmes such as its Integrated Technical Co-operation Programme, assist countries to improve their capabilities in order to comply with IMO standards in the shortest possible time;

.11 where existing practices fail to provide adequate environmental protection, encouragement of the development and use of cost-effective interim protective measures within feasible time-frames, which include best environmental practice and best available technology;

.12 promotion of clean technologies and waste minimization techniques for maritime activities, including use of best environmental practice and best available technology to ensure improving environmental performance.

The precautionary approach should not be considered in isolation of other IMO practices, procedures and resolutions, including resolutions A.500 and A.777 and principles such as the "polluter pays" principle as reflected in Rio Declaration principle 16.

Framework for incorporation of the precautionary approach into the programmes and activities of IMO

5 In order to promote incorporation of preventive, precautionary and anticipatory approaches as identified above in the programmes and activities of IMO that might impact the environment, the decision-making and management framework outlined below should be followed.

	(1)
Consistent with resources and worload demands, the review and consideration should include environmental assessments and a systematic review of IMO's work.	Review and consider environmental risks when prioritizing IMO's work
	(2)
In developing measures to prevent or reduce pollution, priority should be given to the use of cost-effective pollution prevention measures such as clean production, product substitution, and waste minimization. Not engaging in polluting activities should be considered as an option when there are imminent threats of serious or irreversible damage.	Evaluate feasibility of pollution prevention measures
	(3)
Where pollution prevention measures are not available, discharge standards or other cost-effective measures to protect the marine environment should be established, based upon the best available scientific information. This should include consideration of the results of any environmental assessments used in step (1).	Where measures under (2) are not available, use best available information and science to set standards

In developing environmental measures, consideration should also be given to the steps needed for their effective implementation. This might include enforcement provisions, verification procedures and techniques, achievable schedules and deadlines, and capacity-building and technical co-operation programmes for developing countries.	(4)	Identify implementation steps and procedures
Where scientific uncertainties arise as to the sufficiency of standards, targets or the availability of appropriate technology, these uncertainties should be identified. The results should be used to incorporated into an action plan used to encourage and promote, within IMO and the Member States, research to reduce or eliminate the uncertainties. The outcome of such research should then be used to review and improve the measures adopted and to establish, where appropriate, phase-in dates for improved technology.	(5)	Promote research or gather more data to reduce uncertainties or improve technology
Following development of measures, their effectiveness in protecting the environment and the extent to which they are actually implemented must be reviewed. If the measures do not prove effective or are not being successfully implemented, then appropriate corrective measures should be undertaken	(6)	Assess effectiveness of implementation

***

ANNEX 13

RESOLUTION MEPC.65(37) adopted on 14 September 1995

AMENDMENTS TO THE ANNEX OF THE PROTOCOL OF 1978 RELATING TO THE INTERNATIONAL CONVENTION FOR THE PREVENTION OF POLLUTION FROM SHIPS, 1973
(Amendments to Regulation 2 and new Regulation 9 of Annex V)

THE MARINE ENVIRONMENT PROTECTION COMMITTEE,

RECALLING Article 38(a) of the Convention on the International Maritime Organization concerning the function of the Committee conferred upon it by international conventions for the prevention and control of marine pollution,

NOTING article 16 of the International Convention for the Prevention of Pollution from Ships, 1973 (hereinafter referred to as the "1973 Convention") and article VI of the Protocol of 1978 relating to the 1973 Convention (hereinafter referred to as the "1978 Protocol") which together specify the amendment procedure of the 1978 Protocol and confers upon the appropriate body of the Organization the function of considering and adopting amendments to the 1973 Convention, as modified by the 1978 Protocol (MARPOL 73/78),

NOTING ALSO that there is a need to provide for a more effective implementation of Annex V of MARPOL 73/78,

REQUIRING a more systematic approach to the enforcement and control of the requirements of Annex V, MARPOL 73/78

HAVING CONSIDERED the amendments to Annex V of MARPOL 73/78, agreed at its thirty-sixth session and circulated in accordance with article 16(2)(a) of the 1973 Convention,

1. ADOPTS, in accordance with article 16(2)(b) of the 1973 Convention, amendments to Annex V of MARPOL 73/78, the text of which is set out in the annex to the present resolution;

2. DETERMINES, in accordance with article 16(2)(f)(iii) of the 1973 Convention, that the amendments shall be deemed to have been accepted on 1 January 1997, unless prior to the date, not less than one-third of the Parties or the Parties, the combined merchant fleets of which constitute not less than fifty per cent of the gross tonnage of the world's merchant fleet, have communicated to the Organization their objections to the amendments;

3. INVITES the Parties to note that in accordance with article 16(2)(g)(ii) of the 1973 Convention the amendments shall enter into force on 1 July 1997 in accordance with paragraph 2 above,

4. REQUESTS the Secretary-General, in conformity with article 16(2)(e) of the 1973 Convention, to transmit to all Parties to Annex V of the 1978 Protocol certified copies of the present resolution and the text of the amendments contained in the annex;

5. REQUESTS FURTHER the Secretary-General to transmit to the Members of the Organization which are not Parties to Annex V of the 1978 Protocol copies of the resolution and its annex.

ANNEX

TEXTS OF AMENDMENTS TO ANNEX V OF MARPOL 73/78

Regulation 2

Application

The existing text of regulation 2 is replaced by the following:

"Unless expressly provided otherwise, the provisions of this Annex shall apply to all ships."

New regulation 9 is added as follows:

Regulation 9

Placards, garbage management plans and garbage record-keeping

(1) (a) Every ship of 12 metres or more in length overall shall display placards which notify the crew and passengers of the disposal requirements of regulations 3 and 5 of this Annex, as applicable.

(b) The placards shall be written in the official language of the State whose flag the ship is entitled to fly and, for ships engaged in voyages to ports or offshore terminals under the jurisdiction of other Parties to the Convention, in English or French.

(2) Every ship of 400 tons gross tonnage and above, and every ship which is certified to carry 15 persons or more, shall carry a garbage management plan which the crew shall follow. This plan shall provide written procedures for collecting, storing, processing and disposing of garbage, including the use of the equipment on board. It shall also designate the person in charge of carrying out the plan. Such a plan shall be in accordance with the guidelines developed by the Organization and written in the working language of the crew.

(3) Every ship of 400 tons gross tonnage and above and every ship which is certified to carry 15 persons or more engaged in voyages to ports or offshore terminals under the jurisdiction of other Parties to the Convention and every fixed and floating platform engaged in exploration and exploitation of the sea-bed, shall be provided with a Garbage Record Book. The Garbage Record Book, whether as a part of the ship's official logbook or otherwise, shall be in the form specified in the Appendix to this Annex;

(a) each discharge operation, or completed incineration, shall be recorded in the Garbage Record Book and signed for on the date of the incineration or discharge by the officer in charge. Each completed page of the Garbage Record Book shall be signed by the master of the ship. The entries in the Garbage Record Book shall be both in an official language of the State whose flag the ship is entitled to fly, and in English or French. The entries in an official national language of the State whose flag the ship is entitled to fly shall prevail in case of a dispute or discrepancy;

(b) the entry for each incineration or discharge shall include date and time, position of the ship, description of the garbage and the estimated amount incinerated or discharged;

(c) the Garbage Record Book shall be kept on board the ship and in such a place as to be available for inspection in a reasonable time. This document shall be preserved for a period of two years after the last entry is made on the record;

(d) in the event of discharge, escape or accidental loss referred to in regulation 6 of this Annex an entry shall be made in the Garbage Record Book of the circumstances of, and the reasons for, the loss.

(4) The Administration may waive the requirements for Garbage Record Books for:

(i) any ship engaged on voyages of 1 hour or less in duration which is certified to carry 15 persons or more; or

(ii) fixed or floating platforms while engaged in exploration and exploitation of the sea-bed.

(5) The competent authority of the Government of a Party to the Convention may inspect the Garbage Record Book on board any ship to which this regulation applies while the ship is in its ports or offshore terminals and may make a copy of any entry in that book, and may require the master of the ship to certify that the copy is a true copy of such an entry. Any copy so made, which has been certified by the master of the ship as a true copy of an entry in the ship's Garbage Record Book, shall be admissible in any judicial proceedings as evidence of the facts stated in the entry. The inspection of a Garbage Record Book and the taking of a certified copy by the

competent authority under this paragraph shall be performed as expeditiously as possible without causing the ship to be unduly delayed.

(6) In the case of ships built before 1 July 1997, this regulation shall apply as from 1 July 1998.

[...]

5. REPORT OF THE MARITIME SAFETY COMMITTEE ON ITS SIXTY-FIFTH SESSION, 9-17 MAY 1995*

Doc. no.: MSC 65/25 + Corr. 1 + Add. 1, 2(+ Corr. 1) 30 May 1995

* Only paras 19.5-19.17 and 24.1-24.8 and Annex 2 are reproduced.

LIST OF ANNEXES

ANNEX 4	DRAFT AMENDMENTS TO THE 1974 SOLAS CONVENTION
ANNEX 5	PROPOSED AMENDMENTS TO THE DRAFT TEXTS OF THE REVISED 1978 STCW CONVENTION AND THE ASSOCIATED PARTS OF THE STCW CODE
ANNEX 6	DRAFT ASSEMBLY RESOLUTION - SAFETY CULTURE IN AND AROUND PASSENGER SHIPS
ANNEX 7	DRAFT ASSEMBLY RESOLUTION - STRENGTH AND SECURING AND LOCKING ARRANGEMENTS OF BOW DOORS ON RO-RO PASSENGER SHIPS
ANNEX 8	DRAFT ASSEMBLY RESOLUTION - SURVEYS AND INSPECTIONS OF RO-RO PASSENGER SHIPS
ANNEX 9	DRAFT ASSEMBLY RESOLUTION - RECOMMENDATIONS ON A DECISION SUPPORT SYSTEM FOR MASTERS ON PASSENGER SHIPS
ANNEX 10	DRAFT ASSEMBLY RESOLUTION - SAFETY OF SHIPS CARRYING SOLID BULK CARGOES
ANNEX 11	DRAFT ASSEMBLY RESOLUTION - GUIDELINES FOR THE EVALUATION OF THE ADEQUACY OF TYPE C TANK VENT SYSTEMS
ANNEX 12	DRAFT ASSEMBLY RESOLUTION - PERFORMANCE STANDARDS FOR SHIPBORNE VHF RADIO INSTALLATIONS CAPABLE OF VOICE COMMUNICATION AND DIGITAL SELECTIVE CALLING
ANNEX 13	DRAFT ASSEMBLY RESOLUTION - PERFORMANCE STANDARDS FOR SHIPBORNE MF RADIO INSTALLATIONS CAPABLE OF VOICE COMMUNICATION AND DIGITAL SELECTIVE CALLING
ANNEX 14	DRAFT ASSEMBLY RESOLUTION - PERFORMANCE STANDARDS FOR FLOAT-FREE VHF EMERGENCY POSITION-INDICATING RADIO BEACONS
ANNEX 15	DRAFT ASSEMBLY RESOLUTION - PERFORMANCE STANDARDS FOR SHIPBORNE MF/HF RADIO INSTALLATIONS CAPABLE OF VOICE COMMUNICATION, NARROW-BAND DIRECT PRINTING AND DIGITAL SELECTIVE CALLING
ANNEX 16	DRAFT ASSEMBLY RESOLUTION - PERFORMANCE STANDARDS FOR INMARSAT-C SHIP EARTH STATIONS CAPABLE OF TRANSMITTING AND RECEIVING DIRECT-PRINTING COMMUNICATIONS
ANNEX 17	DRAFT ASSEMBLY RESOLUTION - PERFORMANCE STANDARDS FOR SHIP EARTH STATIONS CAPABLE OF TWO-WAY COMMUNICATIONS
ANNEX 18	DRAFT ASSEMBLY RESOLUTION - PERFORMANCE STANDARDS FOR SURVIVAL CRAFT TWO-WAY VHF RADIOTELEPHONE APPARATUS

ANNEX 19 DRAFT ASSEMBLY RESOLUTION - PERFORMANCE STANDARDS FOR FLOAT-FREE SATELLITE EMERGENCY POSITION-INDICATING RADIO BEACONS (EPIRBs) OPERATING ON 406 MHz

ANNEX 20 DRAFT ASSEMBLY RESOLUTION - PERFORMANCE STANDARDS FOR A SHIPBORNE INTEGRATED RADIOCOMMUNICATION SYSTEM (IRCS) WHEN USED IN THE GMDSS

ANNEX 21 DRAFT ASSEMBLY RESOLUTION - PERFORMANCE STANDARDS FOR FLOAT-FREE SATELLITE EMERGENCY POSITION-INDICATING RADIO BEACONS (EPIRBs) OPERATING THROUGH THE GEOSTATIONARY INMARSAT SATELLITE SYSTEM ON 1.6 GHz

ANNEX 22 DRAFT ASSEMBLY RESOLUTION - GENERAL REQUIREMENTS FOR ELECTROMAGNETIC COMPATIBILITY (EMC) FOR ALL ELECTRICAL AND ELECTRONIC SHIP'S EQUIPMENT

ANNEX 23 DRAFT ASSEMBLY RESOLUTION - GUIDELINES FOR AVOIDING FALSE DISTRESS ALERTS

ANNEX 24 DOCUMENT ON OBLIGATIONS OF INMARSAT TO CONTINUE TO PROVIDE MARITIME DISTRESS, SAFETY AND GENERAL COMMUNICATION SERVICES

ANNEX 25 DRAFT ASSEMBLY RESOLUTION - [1995] CODE ON ALARMS AND INDICATORS

ANNEX 26 DRAFT ASSEMBLY RESOLUTION - [1995] CODE OF SAFETY FOR DIVING SYSTEMS

ANNEX 27 RESOLUTION MSC.44 (65) - STANDARDS FOR FIXED SPRINKLER SYSTEMS FOR HIGH SPEED CRAFT

ANNEX 28 RESOLUTION MSC.45 (65) - TEST PROCEDURES FOR FIRE-RESISTING DIVISIONS OF HIGH SPEED CRAFT

ANNEX 29 INSTRUCTIONS TO SUB-COMMITTEES ON THE HUMAN ELEMENT

ANNEX 30 WORK PROGRAMMES OF THE SUB-COMMITTEES

ANNEX 31 LONG-TERM WORK PLAN OF THE COMMITTEE FOR THE PERIOD 1998 TO 2002

ANNEX 32 STATEMENT BY THE DELEGATION OF TUNISIA

ANNEX 33 STATEMENT BY THE DELEGATION OF MOROCCO

ANNEX 34 STATEMENT AND SUBSEQUENT INTERVENTION BY THE DELEGATION OF THE RUSSIAN FEDERATION

ANNEX 35 STATEMENT BY THE DELEGATION OF GREECE

ANNEX 36 STATEMENT BY THE DELEGATION OF CYPRUS

ANNEX 37 STATEMENT BY THE DELEGATION OF BULGARIA

ANNEX 38 STATEMENT BY THE DELEGATION OF TURKEY

ANNEX 39 STATEMENT BY THE DELEGATION OF ROMANIA

ANNEX 40 STATEMENT BY THE DELEGATION OF THE UNITED STATES

ANNEX 41 STATEMENT BY THE DELEGATION OF LEBANON

ANNEX 42 STATEMENT BY THE DELEGATION OF ISRAEL

ANNEX 43 STATEMENT BY THE DELEGATION OF THE SYRIAN ARAB REPUBLIC

ANNEX 44 STATEMENT BY THE DELEGATION OF MOROCCO

ANNEX 45 STATEMENT BY THE DELEGATION OF THE LEAGUE OF ARAB STATES

ANNEX 46 STATEMENT BY THE DELEGATION OF SPAIN

ANNEX 47 STATEMENT BY THE DELEGATION OF CANADA

ANNEX 48 STATEMENT BY THE DELEGATION OF THE UNITED STATES

[...]

19 IMPLEMENTATION OF INSTRUMENTS AND RELATED MATTERS

Acceptance of conventions

19.1 The Committee noted information on the status of acceptance, as of 28 February 1995, of safety-related conventions, protocols and amendments thereto (MSC 65/19 and MSC 65/INF.7) and was advised orally by the Secretariat of additional acceptances notified after the above date.

Implementation of codes, recommendations, guidelines, etc.

19.2 The Committee also noted information on the status of implementation, as of 10 March 1995, of safety-related codes, recommendations, guidelines and other non-mandatory instruments presented in a consolidated tabulation based on information provided by Member Governments (MSC 65/19/1).

19.3 The Committee reiterated its request to the sub-committees to review the list of codes, recommendations, guidelines and other non-mandatory instruments annexed to MSC 65/19/1, so that it would, in the future, contain information provided by maritime Administrations only on those instruments for which there is a need to record their status of implementation.

19.4 The delegation of Croatia, referring to documents MSC 65/19/1 and MSC 65/INF.7, expressed surprise that Yugoslavia, which dissolved itself a few years ago into five States, four of which are currently Members of IMO, still appeared as such in the above documents and in other IMO instruments.

Implementation of rules of navigation

19.5 The Committee, recalling that at its sixty-third session it adopted, subject to confirmation by the nineteenth Assembly, Rules and Recommendations on navigation through the Strait of Istanbul, Strait of Canakkale and the Marmara Sea (MSC 63/23, paragraph 7.22 and SN/Circ.166), which were implemented on 24 November 1994, noted comments by the Russian Federation (MSC 65/19/2 and MSC 65/19/3) and Greece (MSC 65/19/4) in relation to the conformity of relevant Turkish national Rules and Regulations to the aforementioned IMO Rules and Recommendations.

19.6 The Committee further recalled the position of the Legal Committee (LEG 71/13, paragraphs 142 and 143) that any remaining difficulty regarding the conformity of the Turkish national Rules and Regulations with the IMO Rules and Recommendations should be dealt within the Organization.

19.7 The Russian Federation (MSC 65/19/2 and MSC 65/19/3) considered that the Turkish national Regulations were still not in conformity with the IMO Rules and Recommendations or with international law and the 1936 Montreux Convention, particularly in the matters of freedom of transit, authorization procedures and pilotage, in spite of the introduction by Turkey, on 28 November 1994, of instructions to its relevant authorities on how to apply the national regulations complementary to the IMO Rules and Recommendations. The Russian Federation was of the opinion that:

.1 the matter of implementation of the IMO decision on alignment of the Turkish Regulations with the IMO Rules and Recommendations and generally recognized norms of international law has become a question of principle. In the case that Turkey did not change their position, they considered it expedient for the Organization to recommend seafarers to use only the IMO Rules and Recommendations, applicable norms of international law and generally recognized practice of transit passage through international straits when navigating in the area (MSC 65/19/2); and

.2 according to the decision of the Legal Committee, remaining difficulties regarding the conformity of the Turkish Regulations with the IMO Rules and Recommendations, the Montreux Convention and other generally recognized norms of international law should be considered within the Organization until necessary conformity has been achieved (MSC 65/19/3).

(The full statement and a subsequent intervention made by the delegation of the Russian Federation in the context of the above two documents are reproduced in annex 34).

19.8 Greece (MSC 65/19/4) stated that it was the responsibility of Turkey to properly implement the IMO Rules and Recommendations to ensure safety in the Straits, that the Turkish national Regulations did not conform to the IMO Rules and Recommendations and that Turkey had an obligation to state and IMO a responsibility to clarify which regulations are legally binding for ships using the Straits. (The full statement of the delegation of Greece is reproduced in annex 35.)

19.9 The delegation of the Ukraine stated that the IMO Rules and Recommendations were to be implemented by all Governments concerned. They were of the view that instead of Turkey complying with the Rules and Recommendations, they imposed economic sanctions in the Straits.

19.10 The delegation of Cyprus expressed, once again, grave concern over the new rules adopted by Turkey which, despite the further instructions they issued in November 1994, contravene international law. That delegation reiterated that they strenuously opposed the new rules, since they violate international law, and that they were strongly opposed to any unilateral attempts to change the regime of the Straits as this is governed by the Montreux Convention of 1936 and other international instruments. (The full statement of the delegation of Cyprus is reproduced in annex 36.)

19.11 The delegation of Bulgaria stated that their position on the issue was well known and duly reflected in previous reports of the Committee and the Legal Committee. They noted some positive solutions from the Turkish instructions on the implementation of the relevant national regulations but still had some legitimate concerns in regard to the legal status of the instructions and the practical problems of safe and expeditious navigation in the Straits. They reiterated the view that, due to the geographical nature of the Bosphorus, a traffic separation scheme under rule 10 of the International Regulations for Preventing Collisions at Sea (COLREGs), 1972 is not suitable and that the scheme should be governed by rule 9 (Narrow channels). (The full statement of the delegation of Bulgaria is reproduced in annex 37.)

19.12 The delegation of Turkey stated that the decision of MSC 64 was explicitly clear as to on what basis and in which context this issue would be dealt with at this session. The subject solely concerned IMO Rules and Recommendations on navigation in the Turkish Straits and the merits of three papers submitted would necessarily be judged in the light of the criteria. None of the papers were related to this subject. They have not addressed this issue, nor put forward any suggestion on the need to re-evaluate IMO Rules and Recommendations in the interest of improvement of maritime safety.

The papers represented a repetition of the unfounded assertions and misrepresentation of traffic regulations in the Straits. Turkey has already expressed its views in this respect and they would not go into these points at this time.

The Turkish delegation underlined that since the three papers did not concern the issue under consideration and Turkey on its part did not see reason to further improve the IMO Rules and Recommendations at this stage, there existed no grounds for any action by the MSC on this issue at present.

The artificial confusion created in IMO over this issue and repeated attempts by some delegations to keep the matter artificially alive is bound to bring about serious consequences in undermining safety of navigation in the Straits. The Turkish delegation urged the Committee to consider this potential danger.

IMO should play a more constructive and useful role in enhancing safety in the Straits. Continuation of this confrontation pattern pursued by some States would serve no useful purpose.

Turkey would not be a party to such an exercise in futility. Everyone should squarely face its responsibilities. If there would be a demonstrated need for further improvement of the IMO Rules and Recommendations, then IMO practices and procedures should be followed as Turkey had done in initiating action in IMO in this respect as the sole responsible country on issues concerning navigation in the Turkish Straits. (The full statement of the delegation of Turkey is reproduced in annex 38.)

19.13 The delegation of Romania reiterated their sympathy for any country aiming to higher safety standards. They stated that their position was based on unanimously recognized provisions of international law, specifically the 1936 Montreux Convention, which recognizes the freedom of navigation through the Straits in terms of safe passage. That delegation was of the opinion that national regulations relating to passage through the Straits should be in accordance with the Rules and Recommendations adopted by the Committee in May 1994. (The full statement of the delegation of Romania is reproduced in annex 39.)

19.14 The delegation of the United States stated that they disagreed with many of the assertions and conclusions contained in the three papers submitted on the item, particularly the assertion that the regime of transit passage applies in the Black Sea Straits, notwithstanding the words of article 35(c) of the 1982 Law of the Sea Convention, which are to the contrary. They considered that there is still insufficient information that there have been any major difficulties in the implementation of the IMO Rules and Recommendations since their coming into force only five months ago. The delegation of the United States, in view of the number and size of ships seeking to pass through the Straits is continuing to rise, called upon the user States and Strait States to put aside their differences and to work together to ensure the safety of navigation of ships transiting the Straits. (The full statement of the delegation of the United States is reproduced in annex 40.)

19.15 In summing up the discussion, the Chairman referred to the adoption by MSC 63, subject to confirmation by the nineteenth Assembly, of Rules and Recommendations on Navigation through the Strait of Istanbul, the Strait of Canakkale and the Marmara Sea to ensure safety of navigation for all ships using the Straits and the associated traffic separation schemes adopted by the Organization and established therein. These Rules and Recommendations were subsequently disseminated by SN/Circ.166 and implemented on 24 November 1994.

The Chairman recalled (paragraph 2 of SN/Circ.166) that:

.1 the Rules and Recommendations were established purely for the purpose of safety of navigation and environmental protection and were not intended in any way to affect or prejudice the rights of any ship using the Straits under international law, including the United Nations Convention on the Law of the Sea, 1982 and the 1936 Montreux Convention; and

.2 national regulations promulgated by the coastal State should be in total conformity with the IMO Rules and Recommendations.

19.16 The Chairman then suggested that if, in the light of experience gained in the implementation of the IMO Rules and Recommendations, the need emerges, on the basis of submissions by Governments and international organizations concerned, for action to be taken on technical issues related to the navigation through the areas covered by the Rules and Recommendations, the Organization is the right forum to take such action and the mechanism exists in the NAV Sub-Committee's Working Group on Ships' Routeing to do so.

19.17 He added that ships sailing through the areas covered by the IMO Rules and Recommendations should observe them as well as applicable rules of international law.

[...]

24 ANY OTHER BUSINESS

Review of the INF Code

24.1 The Committee, at its sixty-fourth session (MSC 64/22, paragraph 19.27), recalling the need to report to the nineteenth Assembly (resolution A.748(18), part B, operative paragraph 3) on the progress made on the review of the INF Code in the interim, instructed the Secretariat to prepare a draft progress report for approval by MSC 65 and submission, subject to concurrence by MEPC 37, to the nineteenth Assembly for consideration, taking into account the outcome of consideration of the matter by the various sub-committees concerned (MSC 65/24). NAV 41 was authorized to submit any additional comments on matters relating to the INF Code directly to the nineteenth Assembly.

24.2 Greenpeace International submitted a report on Safety Issues in the Sea Transport of Vitrified High-Level Radioactive Wastes to Japan (MSC 65/24/1 and MSC 65/INF.2) concluding that there were enough serious questions regarding the safety of the sea transport of such materials to justify postponement of these shipments, pending the results of further investigation.

24.3 The Committee noted the outcome of the consideration of the matter by BC 34 on packaging issues (MSC 65/12, paragraph 28) and LEG 72 on legal concerns with regard to routeing restrictions (MSC 65/2). It further noted that:

.1 in accordance with an MEPC 36 decision a consultant had been contracted to prepare a desk study on emergency response issues for submission to MEPC 37;

.2 IAEA had agreed to expedite the revision of their emergency response planning provisions (SS87) to start in the fall of 1996; and

.3 IAEA had started work in a Consultant Research Programme on the severity of accidents at sea studying all relevant accident scenarios, in particular fire accidents *vis-à-vis* packaging performance standards.

24.4 The delegation of the Solomon Islands, supported by the delegations of Argentina, Brazil, Chile, Cuba, Democratic People's Republic of Korea, Iceland, Indonesia, Ireland, Peru and Venezuela, expressed disappointment at the limited progress made since the eighteenth Assembly. These delegations pointed out that, although the transport of irradiated nuclear fuel, plutonium and high-level radioactive waste was currently in operation, the work aimed at the transport of these cargoes appeared to be losing focus. In their opinion, although through the complexity of the issue it was difficult to formulate specific proposals, there were some clear steps of action that could be taken, including the setting of criteria for restrictions to enter or the exclusion of certain sea areas; exploring compulsory salvage; or preparing the mechanism of consultation between exporting/importing States and coastal States involved.

24.5 There was some support expressed on BC 34's proposal to reconvene the joint IMO/IAEA/UNEP Working Group to continue its deliberations on how to establish measures to complement resolution A.748(18). However, a number of delegations considered this premature, pointing out that the working group had completed its work with respect to the INF Code and that, as yet, there was no apparent need for them to reconvene.

24.6 The United States delegation, supported by many delegations, proposed that NAV 41 should make decisions on routeing. Considering the different substances involved, IAEA should be invited to contribute to, and participate in, that meeting to assist with its expert advice.

24.7 Following discussion, the Committee:

.1 reiterated its decision (MSC 65/24, annex, paragraph 8) that the question of routeing measures should be considered by the NAV Sub-Committee;

.2 agreed that work on matters complementary to the INF Code needed to be expedited and instructed the sub-committees involved to act accordingly; and

.3 agreed to invite Member Governments and international organizations concerned to submit substantive proposals for that work to the next session of the Committee and its relevant sub-committees.

24.8 The Committee approved the progress report for submission, following endorsement, updating and finalization by MEPC 37 and NAV 41, to the nineteenth Assembly.

[...]

ANNEX 2

RESOLUTION MSC.46(65)

adopted on 16 May 1995

ADOPTION OF AMENDMENTS TO THE INTERNATIONAL CONVENTION FOR THE SAFETY OF LIFE AT SEA, 1974

THE MARITIME SAFETY COMMITTEE,

RECALLING Article 28(b) of the Convention on the International Maritime Organization concerning the functions of the Committee,

RECALLING FURTHER article VIII(b) of the International Convention for the Safety of Life at Sea (SOLAS), 1974, hereinafter referred to as "the Convention", concerning the procedures for amending the Annex to the Convention,

HAVING APPROVED, at its sixty-fourth session, amendments to the Convention proposed and circulated in accordance with article VIII(b)(i) thereof,

1. ADOPTS, in accordance with article VIII(b)(iv) of the Convention, the amendments to the Convention the text of which is set out in the Annex to the present resolution;

2. DETERMINES, in accordance with article VIII(b)(vi)(2)(bb) of the Convention, that the amendments set out in the Annex shall be deemed to have been accepted on 1 July 1996 unless, prior to that date, more than one third of the Contracting Governments to the Convention or Contracting Governments the combined merchant fleets of which constitute not less than fifty per cent of the gross tonnage of the world's merchant fleet, have notified their objections to the amendments;

3. INVITES Contracting Governments to note that, in accordance with article VIII(b)(vii)(2) of the Convention, the amendments set out in the Annex shall enter into force on 1 January 1997 upon their acceptance in accordance with paragraph 2 above;

4. REQUESTS the Secretary-General, in conformity with article VIII(b)(v) of the Convention, to transmit certified copies of the present resolution and the text of the amendments contained in the Annex to all Contracting Governments to the Convention;

5. FURTHER REQUESTS the Secretary-General to transmit copies of the resolution and its Annex to Members of the Organization which are not Contracting Governments to the Convention.

ANNEX

AMENDMENTS TO THE INTERNATIONAL CONVENTION FOR THE SAFETY OF LIFE AT SEA, 1974

Regulation V/8 - Routeing

The existing heading and text of the regulation are replaced by the following:

"Ship's routeing

(a) Ships' routeing systems contribute to safety of life at sea, safety and efficiency of navigation, and/or protection of the marine environment. Ships' routeing systems are recommended for use by, and may be made mandatory for, all ships, certain categories of ships or ships carrying certain cargoes, when adopted and implemented in accordance with the guidelines and criteria developed by the Organization.[1]

(b) The Organization is recognized as the only international body for developing guidelines, criteria and regulations on an international level for ships' routeing systems. Contracting Governments shall refer proposals for the adoption of ships' routeing systems to the Organization. The Organization will collate and disseminate to Contracting Governments all relevant information with regard to any adopted ships' routeing systems.

(c) This regulation, and its associated guidelines and criteria, does not apply to warships, naval auxiliary or other vessels owned or operated by a Contracting Government and used, for the time being, only on government non-commercial service; however, such ships are encouraged to participate in ships' routeing systems adopted in accordance with this regulation.

(d) The initiation of action for establishing a ships' routeing system is the responsibility of the Government or Governments concerned. In developing such systems for adoption by the Organization, the guidelines and criteria developed by the Organization* shall be taken into account.

(e) Ships' routeing systems should be submitted to the Organization for adoption. However, a Government or Governments implementing ships' routeing systems not intended to be submitted to the Organization for adoption or which have not been adopted by the Organization are encouraged to follow, wherever possible, the guidelines and criteria developed by the Organization[1].

(f) Where two or more Governments have a common interest in a particular area, they should formulate joint proposals for the delineation and use of a routeing system therein on the basis of an agreement between them. Upon receipt of such proposal and before proceeding with the consideration of it for adoption, the Organization shall ensure details of the proposal are disseminated to the Governments which have a common interest in the area, including countries in the vicinity of the proposed ships' routeing system.

(g) Contracting Governments shall adhere to the measures adopted by the Organization concerning ships' routeing. They shall promulgate all information necessary for the safe and effective use of adopted ships' routeing systems. A Government or Governments concerned may monitor traffic in those systems. Contracting Governments will do everything in their power to secure the appropriate use of ships' routeing systems adopted by the Organization.

(h) A ship shall use a mandatory ships' routeing system adopted by the Organization as required for its category or cargo carried and in accordance with the relevant provisions in force unless there are compelling reasons not to use a particular ships' routeing system. Any such reason shall be recorded in the ship's log.

(i) Mandatory ships' routeing systems shall be reviewed by the Contracting Government or Governments concerned in accordance with the guidelines and criteria developed by the Organization.[1]

(j) All adopted ships' routeing systems and actions taken to enforce compliance with those systems shall be consistent with international law, including the relevant provisions of the 1982 United Nations Convention on the Law of the Sea.

(k) Nothing in this regulation nor its associated guidelines and criteria[1] shall prejudice the rights and duties of Governments under international law or the legal regime of international straits."

Note

1. Refer to the General Provisions on Ships' Routeing adopted by the Organization by resolution A.572(14), as amended.

***

6. REPORT OF THE EIGHTEENTH CONSULTATIVE MEETING, 4-8 DECEMBER 1995*

Doc. no.: LC 18/11 16 January 1996

Table of Contents

* Only paras 3.1-3.7, 8.1-8.6 and 8.9-8.13 are reproduced.

[...]

3 DISPOSAL OF OFFSHORE INSTALLATIONS

3.1 The delegation of Denmark introduced a draft resolution on sea disposal of offshore installations (LC 18/3), requesting the Meeting "to adopt a moratorium on the disposal at sea of decommissioned offshore installations until the London Convention 1972 has been amended with a view to banning the disposal of offshore installations at sea". This was inspired by the outcome of the Fourth International Conference on the Protection of the North Sea, 8 and 9 June 1995, at which the majority of countries bordering the North Sea had agreed that decommissioned offshore installations shall either be reused or be disposed of on land. Denmark further informed the Meeting that, accordingly, the majority of Parties to the Convention for the Prevention of Marine Pollution by Dumping from Ships and Aircraft (Oslo, 1972) had agreed on a moratorium on sea disposal of decommissioned offshore installations which entered into force on 4 August 1995.

3.2 The delegation of Norway expressed its concern that the proposed moratorium would exclude one of several options for disposal, without any scientific basis. Norway was pursuing a case-by-case approach, taking into account all relevant factors. There was no scientific evidence that land-based disposal is the preferable alternative in all cases. Norway favoured multilateral, scientific-based rules to ensure that disposal of decommissioned offshore installations meets commonly agreed environmental objectives. A similar position was expressed by the delegation of the United Kingdom which also had adopted a case-by-case approach and emphasized that in a number of cases land-based disposal may be the preferred option, based on sound science and on high environmental standards.

3.3 Other Parties to the Oslo Convention supported the Danish proposal for a moratorium within the London Convention 1972. Iceland would also support such a moratorium. However, that delegation underlined the need that specific guidance be developed within the framework of the London Convention 1972 concerning disposal of offshore installations and structures. Several delegations felt that the text of the draft resolution proposed by Denmark could be improved. The delegation of New Zealand agreed that the matter deserved further scientific study, although the outcome should not be prejudged. That delegation expressed the view that a moratorium, perhaps for a limited time, could be consistent with such an approach.

3.4 A clear majority of Contracting Parties did not support the proposal submitted by Denmark, indicating that this was not based on any scientific evidence and that flexible approaches should be used in reaching decisions particularly in different geographical areas. It was further noted that an open-ended moratorium was not acceptable and that adoption of the Danish proposal would prejudge the outcome of ongoing negotiations in relation to the review of the London Convention 1972.

3.5 The Consultative Meeting further recalled that the Scientific Group in 1989, requested by the Consultative Meeting for advice in regard to the then proposed IMO Guidelines and Standards for the Removal of Offshore Installations and Structures on the Continental Shelf and in the Exclusive Economic Zone, concluded that the existing provisions of the London Convention's Annex III and the guidelines thereto were sufficient to address environmental aspects in relation to disposal at sea (LDC/SG 12/13, paragraph 7.11). In 1992 the Scientific Group reaffirmed this view (LDC/SG 15/17, paragraph 8.3).

3.6 The Meeting also noted that the IMO Guidelines and Standards provide for specific determination of the potential effect on the marine environment of the removal of offshore installations and structures and that these Standards provide that: "on or after 1 January 1998, no installation or structure should be placed on any continental shelf or in any EEZ unless the design and construction of the installation or structure is such that entire removal upon abandonment or permanent disuse would be feasible" (IMO resolution A.672(16), paragraph 3.13).

3.7 The Consultative Meeting concluded that, pending further development, Contracting Parties should apply the London Convention 1972 and the IMO Guidelines and Standards of A.672(16) in their national practice on a case-by-case basis and requested the Scientific Group to again review status of the disposal at sea of offshore installations, taking into account:

.1 the introduction of the Waste Assessment Framework in the London Convention;

.2 current notification and consultation procedures; and

.3 existing technical international guidelines and standards

in order to assess their adequacy and to report back to the Consultative Meeting in 1997.

[...]

8 MATTERS RELATED TO DISPOSAL AT SEA OF RADIOACTIVE WASTES

The concept of *de minimis*

8.1 The Consultative Meeting noted the response of the International Atomic Energy Agency (IAEA) to its request that IAEA should define *de minimis* (exempt) levels of radioactivity in relation to "radioactive wastes or other radioactive matter" listed in paragraph 6 of Annex I to the Convention. Wastes or other materials (e.g. sewage sludge and dredged material) containing such levels of radioactivity would not fall under the radioactive waste prohibition of Annex I but be subject to provisions of Annexes II and III, as appropriate (LC 18/8/1).

8.2 The representative of the IAEA informed the Meeting that the *de minimis* concept as used by her Agency included two separate elements, corresponding to:

.1 situations where radiation sources and practices were not amenable to control through regulation, called **exclusion** in the context of radioprotection; and

.2 situations where radiation sources and practices have only trivial consequences and, therefore, are **exempted** from regulation.

In addition, for those radiation sources and practices which have been under regulatory control but do present only a trivial risk due to radioactive decay or some form of processing, regulatory control may also be removed, i.e. they are **cleared**.

8.3 After these introductory notes, the Consultative Meeting was informed that the IAEA in 1994, in response to the request from the Consultative Meeting, convened a Technical Committee Meeting to consider a draft document containing generic exempt levels expressed as activity concentrations. The Technical Committee, however, expressed its view that generic values for exempt concentrations were no longer needed, taking into account recent amendments of the London Convention 1972. The Technical Committee emphasized that in most cases the exemption or exclusion in the context of radioprotection was automatic and that in the cases where numerical guidance was needed, these should be based on assessments carried out by the national regulatory authorities of Contracting Parties. The Technical Committee prepared a new document which provides guidance for making judgments on whether materials can be automatically excluded or exempted, or whether a specific assessment is needed. In light of these conclusions, the IAEA was now in the position of having two draft documents expressing conflicting views, and therefore requested guidance from the Consultative Meeting on which approach it should follow. The three options, which IAEA could further develop, were as follows:

.1 a document which gives guidance on which materials can be automatically excluded or exempted and leaves the site specific case-by-case assessment to be carried out by national radiological protection authorities on the basis of internationally accepted principles and criteria;

.2 a document which gives the guidance above, but which also gives numerical exempt values, derived using generic models, for sea disposal of bulk amounts of material;

.3 a document which gives the same guidance as the first alternative, but which also contains practical advice on how the national authority should carry out the site specific assessment.

8.4 In the subsequent discussion, different views were expressed by Contracting Parties on which of the above options should be further developed by IAEA and applied within the framework of the London

Convention 1972; however, there was no clear majority on either of the options offered by the IAEA. Several Contracting Parties preferred a combination of the second and third options outlined above. Other Contracting Parties expressed their view that no further efforts in integrating the *de minimis* concept into the London Convention 1972 were necessary, as such concept is being included in the currently developed IAEA Waste Management Safety Convention; this was strongly supported by France. The United States delegation reiterated its view that the option listed under paragraph 8.3.3 above was the only technically feasible approach.

8.5 The Consultative Meeting requested the IAEA to continue its work on the *de minimis* exemption levels of radioactivity and either work out both the second and third options listed above, or seek a solution in a combination of these two options. The Meeting further requested Contracting Parties involved in IAEA work concerning the definition of *de minimis* exemption levels of radioactivity to ensure that their participating experts are familiar with the requirements of the London Convention 1972, and the views expressed on the *de minimis* concept at meetings held within the framework of that Convention.

8.6 The representative from the IAEA expressed her disappointment that this Consultative Meeting had not been able to provide clear advice to her Agency on what direction the work related to the development of the application of exclusion and exemption principles to disposal at sea of wastes and other matter should proceed. The IAEA would consider whether continuation of the work was useful or not, taking into account the above requests and their financial implications.

[...]

Russian-Norwegian investigations in the Arctic

8.9 The Norwegian delegation introduced paper LC 18/INF.2 summarizing the result of the 1993 Russian-Norwegian expedition to the Kara Sea. This document, which is directed at a general audience, discusses the sources and effects of radioactivity, summarizes the extent of radioactive waste dumping in the Kara and Barents Seas and briefly describes the nature and results of surveys that have been conducted under Russian-Norwegian auspices.

8.10 The Norwegian delegation then introduced paper LC 18/INF.9 comprising an extended summary of the results of joint Russian-Norwegian investigations of radioactive contamination of the Kara Sea during the period 1992-1994. This document outlines the basis and nature of investigations of radioactivity in the Arctic, especially in connection with radioactive waste objects dumped in the Kara Sea. It concludes that enhanced levels of artificial radionuclides can be found in sediments in the immediate vicinity of most dumped objects; however, the associated radiological consequences of such contamination are negligible.

Disposal of High-level Radioactive Wastes at Sea

8.11 The Meeting took note of information submitted by Greenpeace International (LC 18/INF.7) concerning plans by a private company to carry out disposal of radioactive wastes into the seabed and the subsoil thereof, starting from 1996. The company concerned had made contacts in, among others, Italy and South Africa, to offer its services.

8.12 The Meeting expressed its concerns on these plans, as sub-seabed disposal of radioactive wastes would not be in compliance with resolution LC.51(16) concerning sea disposal of radioactive wastes and other matter. The delegations of Italy and South Africa undertook to contact their capitals to validate any involvement in this matter within their countries. They were determined to stop any further involvement if such plans were to be confirmed, to contact the involved company, and to inform the Secretariat of the results.

8.13 The Consultative Meeting agreed to request Contracting Parties to inform the Secretariat of any known contacts or involvement concerning disposal in the sea-bed or the subsoil thereof of any radioactive waste or other highly toxic material. The Meeting requested the Chairman to inform the involved company that the planned disposal activities are not sanctioned under the London Convention 1972. It also requested the IAEA to contact the involved company, and expressed its appreciation to Greenpeace International for informing the Meeting of this matter..

[...]

7. CONSIDERATION AND ADOPTION OF AMENDMENTS TO THE INTERNATIONAL CONVENTION FOR THE SAFETY OF LIFE AT SEA, 1974. CONSIDERATION AND ADOPTION OF RESOLUTIONS AND RECOMMENDATIONS AND RELATED MATTERS. CONFERENCE RESOLUTION 1 AND AMENDMENTS TO THE 1974 SOLAS CONVENTION ANNEXED THERETO AND CONFERENCE RESOLUTIONS 2 TO 14 - AS ADOPTED BY THE CONFERENCE*

Doc. no.: SOLAS/CONF.3/46 6 December 1995

Attached in the annex are the texts of:

.1 Conference resolution 1 and amendments to the International Convention for the Safety of Life at Sea, 1974 annexed thereto, as set out in attachment 1 to the Final Act of the Conference ; and

.2 Conference resolutions 2 to 14, as set out in attachment 2 to the Final Act of the Conference.

***

[...]

RESOLUTION 14

REGIONAL AGREEMENTS ON SPECIFIC STABILITY REQUIREMENTS FOR RO-RO PASSENGER SHIPS

THE CONFERENCE,

HAVING ADOPTED amendments to the International Convention for the Safety of Life at Sea (SOLAS), 1974, concerning the safety of ro-ro passenger ships,

---

* Only Resolution 14 is reproduced.

CONSIDERING new SOLAS regulation II-1/8-1 by which every ro-ro passenger ship shall comply with regulation II-1/8, as amended by resolution MSC.12(56), in the future,

RECALLING the provisions of article VII of the SOLAS Convention,

ACKNOWLEDGING the desire of certain Contracting Governments that, having regard to the prevailing sea conditions and other local conditions, specific stability requirements should apply to all ro-ro passenger ships undertaking regular scheduled voyages between designated ports of those Contracting Governments,

1. **AGREES** that two or more Contracting Governments may conclude agreements modifying the requirements of regulation II-1/8-1 in respect of every ro-ro passenger ship carrying passengers on regular scheduled voyages between designated ports in their territory, provided that these ships comply with safety requirements which are adequate in the opinion of these Governments for the voyages to be undertaken;

2. **AGREES ALSO** that, if these safety requirements include specific stability requirements, they should not exceed those specified in the Annex to the present resolution;

3. **DECIDES** that Contracting Governments proposing an agreement shall notify the Secretary-General of the International Maritime Organization of their intention to negotiate an agreement and shall make appropriate arrangements for other interested Contracting Governments to be involved in the negotiations. When notifying the Secretary-General of their intention to negotiate an agreement, and on the concluding of an agreement, the Contracting Governments involved shall communicate to the Secretary-General all relevant particulars relating to it for circulation to all Contracting Governments. An agreement shall not enter into force until 12 months after its conclusion has been notified to the Secretary-General;

4. **URGES** all Contracting Governments to apply the provisions of such agreements on ro-ro passenger ships entitled to fly their flags when engaged on regular scheduled voyages between designated ports covered by such agreements.

[...]

UNITED NATIONS EDUCATIONAL, SCIENTIFIC AND CULTURAL ORGANIZATION (UNESCO)

DOCUMENTS REPRODUCED IN WHOLE OR IN PART:

INTERGOVERNMENTAL OCEANOGRAPHIC COMMISSION

REPORTS OF GOVERNING AND MAJOR SUBSIDIARY BODIES

DOCUMENTS NOT REPRODUCED:

INTERGOVERNMENTAL OCEANOGRAPHIC COMMISSION

REPORTS OF GOVERNING AND MAJOR SUBSIDIARY BODIES

2.	Doc. no.:	UNESCO SC-95/CONF.214/LD.5;IOC/EC-XXVIII/3
	Date:	1 August 1995
	Title:	Report No. 58: Twenty-eighth Session of the Executive Council. Paris, 12 June 1995.
3.	Doc. no.:	UNESCO SC-95/CONF.217/LD.7;IOC-WMO-UNEP/I-GOOS-II/3
	Date:	20 September 1995
	Title:	Report No. 60: Second Session of the IOC-WMO-UNEP Committee for the Global Ocean Observing System (I-GOOS-II). Paris, 6-9 June 1995.
4.	Doc. no.:	UNESCO SC-95/CONF.223/LD.1;IOC/ITSU-XV/3
	Date:	29 November 1995
	Title:	Report No. 62: Fifteenth Session of the International Co-ordination Group for the Tsunami Warning System in the Pacific. Papeete, Tahiti, French Polynesia, 24-28 July 1995.
5.	Doc. no.:	UNESCO SC-95/CONF.220/LD.3;IOC-FAO/IPHAB-III/3
	Date:	20 February 1996
	Title:	Report No. 63: Third Session of the IOC-FAO Intergovernmental Panel on the Harmful Algal Blooms. Paris, 6-9 June 1995.

1. REPORT NO. 59: EIGHTEENTH SESSION OF THE ASSEMBLY, PARIS, 13-26 JUNE 1995

Doc. no.: SC/MD/106 25 August 1995

TABLE OF CONTENTS

SUMMARY REPORT

D. CO-OPERATION

1. OPENING

1 The Chairman, Dr. Manuel Murillo, opened the Eighteenth Session of the IOC Assembly at 10.15 on 13 June 1995.

2 **The Assembly received and noted** with great appreciation statements by the Chairman and by the Director-General of UNESCO, Dr. Federico Mayor, on the occasion of the opening of the Assembly. Their statements are given in Annex III, Parts A and B. The Chairman expressed great satisfaction for the strong and continued support given by the Director-General to the IOC, as evidenced throughout the biennium and through the proposals of the Director-General to the 28th General Conference of UNESCO.

3 The Chairman called on participants to stand in silence for one minute as a mark of respect for distinguished oceanographers who have passed away since the Seventeenth Session of the Assembly. Special reference was made to Klaus Voigt (Germany), Oleg Mamayev (Russian Federation), Erdugan Akyüz (Turkey) and Lee Byung-Don (Republic of Korea).

4 In particular, the Chairman and the Director-General remembered Dr. Klaus Voigt who had served the Commission with great dedication for many years.

5 On 20 June 1995 **the Assembly received** the information that South Africa had been reinstated in the IOC. This news was received with great appreciation and strongly welcomed by the Assembly who then listened to the statement of the Ambassador of South Africa (see Annex III-C). On behalf of all the Member States, the Chairman warmly welcomed this reinstatement.

2. BRUUN MEMORIAL LECTURES

6 **The Assembly noted** that the theme of the Bruun Memorial Lectures, to be given on 16 and 21 June, would be "Results and applications, including the socio-economic ones, of the TOGA Programme". These would be presented by Dr. Pablo Lagos and Dr. James O'Brien (the abstracts are given in Annex V). The texts will be published in the IOC Technical Series.

7 **The Assembly noted** the exhibition and demonstration of ocean observation products arranged in the conference hall, and **expressed** its appreciation to those involved in organizing these.

3. ADMINISTRATIVE ARRANGEMENTS

3.1 ADOPTION OF THE AGENDA

8 **The Assembly adopted** the Agenda as given in Annex I.

3.2 DESIGNATION OF THE RAPPORTEUR

9 **The Assembly accepted** the proposal by Bulgaria to designate Dr. V. Jivago, Russian Federation, to serve together with Dr. B. Smirnov as Rapporteurs for the Session.

3.3 CONDUCT OF THE SESSION, TIMETABLE AND DOCUMENTATION

10 **The Assembly noted** that under Rule of Procedure No. 12(2), the Executive Council, acting as the Steering Committee for the Assembly, had appointed a Nominations' Committee for the Assembly with the following composition: Poland (Chairman), Chile, China, Greece, Indonesia, Islamic Republic of Iran, Kenya, Russian Federation and the United States of America.

11 As proposed by the Executive Council, **the Assembly accepted** the establishment of a Technical Review Committee for Resolutions with the following composition: Russian Federation (Chairman), Brazil, Colombia, China, France, Nigeria, Thailand, Turkey and the United States of America.

12 **The Assembly adopted** the Provisional Timetable (Document IOC-XVIII/1 Add. prov. rev. 2). The List of Working Documents is given in Annex VIII; the List of Participants in Annex IX; and the List of Acronyms in Annex X.

A. PROGRAMME IMPLEMENTATION

4. REPORT ON ACTIVITIES

4.1 SECRETARY'S REPORT ON INTERSESSIONAL ACTIVITIES; REPORT ON THE COMMISSION'S ACTIVITIES, 1993-1994, AND FINANCIAL STATEMENT, FOLLOWED BY DEBATE

13 In presenting his report on activities since the Seventeenth Session of the Assembly and the Twenty-seventh Session of the Executive Council (1994) together with the Biennial Report 1993-1994, (Annual Report 1994 and Document IOC-XVIII/6), the Executive Secretary provided an overview of the major activities and implementation of the Resolutions adopted by the sessions of the Assembly in 1993 and the Executive Council in 1994. The main body of the Annual Report 1994 presents the actions in three sub-sections:

A. Implementation of resolutions;
B. Programme activities; and
C. Co-operation and development.

14 In summary: of 27 adopted resolutions, 17 have been fully implemented and 10 partially so. Implementation rates of several programmes need strengthening in order to achieve the desired results and impacts.

15 In the Science part of the programme, activities with respect to ocean and climate research, to living and non-living marine resources studies, to ocean mapping, to global and regional research and monitoring of marine pollution and to coastal zone, public awareness and related training actions, are presented.

16 Ocean services actions include data management and information exchange, observing system developments, in particular GOOS, Tsunami warning system actions and developments. Several practical results have been obtained resulting in the publication of CD-ROMs with data, including the NOAA World Ocean Atlas 1994, software systems and specific global temperature and salinity data sets. The close linkage of the development of the ocean observing system to the scientific results and programmes is maintained, as seen, for instance, in the report of the Ocean Observing System Development Panel (OOSDP). The results of IGOSS and the Data Buoy Co-operation Panel highlight how international agreements in relation to systematic observations can ensure cost-efficiency and sustained observations. The development of GOOS shows the increasing importance of ocean services in IOC programmes.

17 TEMA activities span practically all IOC actions, and some specific training activities are presented in a separate section on TEMA. This, however, does not reflect all TEMA-related actions. The development of a new TEMA strategy adjusted to the needs of UNCED follow-up and implementation of the UN Convention on the Law of the Sea are particularly emphasized.

18 In a separate section, activities in twelve different coastal and ocean regions or regimes are presented. Many of these are co-operative efforts involving partners from the United Nations system as well as others, including NGO's, in particular ICSU and SCOR. As regards the IOC they are mostly based on regional subsidiary bodies composed of national institutions.

19 The last section of the Annual Report provides information concerning growing co-operation between IOC and other bodies, including co-operation through joint programmes such as GIPME, GOOS, GCOS and Ocean Mapping. This co-operation helps ensure that communities outside the ocean science and observation sectors are involved with the IOC. In particular, this concerns the Conventions adopted by UNCED (FCCC and Biological Diversity).

20 Public awareness and policy-oriented actions in relation to the Second Conference on Oceanography (Lisbon, 1994) and others, including the Third WESTPAC Symposium (Bali, 1994) and Global Coastal Change Conference (Bordeaux, 1995) were also highlighted.

21 The Executive Secretary reviewed how programme actions relate to and fit the programme and budget adopted by the Assembly (1993) for 1994-1995. He informed the Assembly of the status of the IOC budget, and the overall use of available funds. He also briefly presented the Biennial Report 1993-94 (Document IOC-XVIII/6). He emphasized that the wide range of activities is spreading IOC thin, that the follow-up is insufficient, and that the impact could be much higher if some concentration of effort was achieved in the programming. In this context, he also recalled the significant role of the IOC in the ACC Sub-Committee on Oceans and Coastal Areas, and with respect to ICSPRO. His statement is given in Annex III-D.

22 In the debate which followed, about thirty delegations made statements of a very substantive nature. All delegations praised the Annual Report 1994, welcomed the activities and report as very useful. Specific suggestions were made as regards the balance and text of the Biennial Report, which will be taken into account in the final version to be submitted to the Twenty-eighth Session of the General Conference. The Assembly congratulated the Executive Secretary IOC on his recent appointment to the level of Assistant Director General.

23 Many delegations supported the Director General's proposal for provision of a 'grant-in-aid' relationship between IOC and UNESCO, and stated that such a change would be of great value. Some delegations, however, expressed concern, and stressed that IOC must continue to function with appropriate oversight and financial accountability within UNESCO. Most delegations stressed that IOC needs greater managerial control to set its priorities and to have flexibility in allocating people and funds in a timely manner and to respond to new opportunities. Many delegations expressed their view that GOOS should be a primary focus for IOC, but closely linked to science. In responding to the Executive Secretary's assessment of IOC's principal challenges: (i) insufficient ability to create adequate awareness about IOC and its results at relevant decision-making levels; (ii) inadequate budgetary resources; delegations expressed the view that if IOC can better sell what it does and why it is important, the inadequate budget will be taken care of. An example involves the coastal zone: linking what IOC does with human activities on land, e.g., the associated run-off, degradation of water quality and habitat loss, and with associated economic impacts on fisheries, tourism, and ultimately on the quality of life. IOC cannot afford to simply focus on doing good ocean science. IOC should institutionalize its data collection and translate data into useful information - that is the task for GOOS. The IOC should also help interpret the results into a form people understand, value and get excited about.

24 The IOC should change to a more interdisciplinary approach. The future of coastal oceanography depends on this. Some delegations expressed concern with the proposal to separate the MRI - part of IOC/MRI - from IOC, along with its budget to provide for the new interdisciplinary and intersectoral project focused on coastal zones and small islands. Changes in organizational structures need to enhance prospects for integration, not separate them as it appears in this instance.

25 Many delegations stressed the need for greater emphasis on regional programme development and implementation, and the strengthening of the IOC Regional Secretariats for the Sub-Commissions. Some of the delegations cautioned against regionalization and emphasized the need to maintain a global IOC with global programmes.

26 Most delegations emphasized the need for a strong TEMA and an adjustment of the TEMA strategy to meet the new challenges, focusing on a regional approach. The importance of sustainable management of ocean resources and the marine environment was highlighted, together with the role of IOC to provide scientific input and systematic ocean observations to this end.

27 Several points were raised as to the significance of a financial allocation (grant-in-aid) arrangement with UNESCO, and how this would affect IOC. Many delegations emphasized that IOC must improve its impact and ability to deliver the message of the importance of oceans for the conditions on earth, the role of ocean resources for society, and the significance of the coastal zone. It is important that scientific uncertainties continue to be addressed.

28 The importance of co-operation was brought out, as well as the fact that IOC must be sufficiently strong to be an adequate partner. The representative of WMO, in reviewing the wide range of co-operation between IOC and WMO, pointed out that his Organization wants the IOC to be as strong a partner as possible, with stable and dependable resources, in particular for joint activities.

29 The Representative of the Secretariat for the Convention on Biological Diversity expressed a strong interest in co-operating with IOC in the relevant fields of marine biological diversity.

30 The Executive Secretary responded to the questions raised and reviewed the current programmatic problems of the IOC. His response is given in summary in Annex III-E.

31 **The Assembly adopted** the Annual Report for 1994 and the Biennial Report 1993-1994 for submission to the Twenty-eighth General Conference of UNESCO, subject to some revisions which had been specifically suggested by delegations.

B. STATUS AND EVOLUTION OF THE IOC

5. DEVELOPMENTS WITHIN UNESCO, FOLLOW-UP TO DOSS, AND REVISED RULES OF PROCEDURE

32 The Executive Secretary IOC, in introducing this agenda item, made reference to the following points that were tabled for discussion and their related documentation, as set out in the Annotated Provisional Agenda (Document IOC-XVII/2, paras 16 to 20):

(i) Revised IOC Rules of Procedure (Document IOC-XVIII/2 Annex 2); and
(ii) Further Implementation of IOC Resolution XVII-20: Part II of its Annex (Document IOC-XVIII/2 Annex 8).

33 In regard to (i), he informed the Assembly that the analysis had been prepared in accordance with instructions provided by the governing bodies. Particular reference was made to the Twenty-seventh Session of the Executive Council which had reviewed an initial draft (Document IOC/EC-XXVII/Inf.1) and requested (Document IOC/EC-XXVII/3, para. 152) that:

> *'the revised draft rules of procedure should be polished in light of these comments and delivered to the Assembly'.*

34 In regard to (ii), he reminded the Assembly that, in adopting IOC Resolution XVII-20, the majority of proposals made by the *ad hoc* Study Group on IOC Development, Operations, Structure and Statutes (DOSS) as found in Part I of the Annex to the Resolution had been agreed upon. On the other hand, five topics, including revised draft rules of procedure, were deferred for further study, the state of which and suggestions for future elaboration are reported upon in Document IOC-XVIII/2 Annex 8.

35 The Assembly was also informed of recent developments concerning proposals made by the Director-General, as set forth in the UNESCO Draft Programme and Budget for 1996-1997 (Draft 28 C/5: paras 2364-2379), to the effect that the support provided by UNESCO to the IOC be made in the form of a financial allocation. In this respect, reference was made to the Annex to IOC Resolution XVII-20, in particular para. 10 of Part I through which the Assembly:

*"**Decides** that one means of achieving greater dependability in IOC resources, within the principle that the Commission is a body with functional autonomy established within UNESCO, would be to seek a "subvention" or "grant-in-aid" relationship with its parent body".*

It was noted that the term 'grant-in-aide' was subsequently replaced by the term 'financial allocation' by the 27th UNESCO General Conference when deciding on similar arrangements for the IIEP.

36 The Chairman provided information regarding discussions that had taken place at the 146th UNESCO Executive Board in regard to the establishment of a Special Account for the IOC and related financial regulations. Having received the proposals of the Director-General on New Arrangements for the IOC, as found in Document 146 EX/20, the Executive Board, through its Decision 5.3.1, deferred the matter to its 147th Session, pending further clarification. The two referenced documents were distributed to the Assembly for its information.

37 The ensuing debate generated a wide range of comments from Member States, with the majority of speakers expressing their support of the proposal found in the UNESCO Draft 28 C/5 to provide support to the IOC in the form of a financial allocation. A few speakers, however, emphasized the concerns that their representatives to the UNESCO Executive Board had expressed, particularly in regard to the fact that the IOC Assembly had not yet expressed its final views.

38 In order to discuss these matters in more depth, an *ad hoc* sessional working group on Agenda Item 5 was established under the Chairmanship of U. Lie, Past Chairman IOC and Delegate of Norway. The group, open to all Member States, held two meetings and, through its Chairman, reported to plenary with proposals for: (i) a draft resolution containing revised terms of reference and composition for continuation of the work of the ad hoc Study Group on DOSS; (ii) the structure and elements of response that IOC would provide to the Director-General for his use in preparing a report to the 147th UNESCO Executive Board to facilitate their consideration of the new arrangements for IOC; (iii) a draft resolution by which the IOC Assembly provides its final views in reaction to Decision 5.3.1 of the 146th UNESCO Executive Board.

39 In regard to the revival of the *ad hoc* Study Group on DOSS, now called DOSS 2, **the Assembly emphasized** the importance of ensuring that the expertise associated with the work of the Study Group would indeed reflect the interests and concerns of IOC Member States. To this end, **the Assembly encouraged** all Member States to provide proposals to the secretariat of those individuals who could contribute to the studies at hand, with an indication of the particular fields of expertise.

40 **The Assembly adopted** Resolution XVIII-1.

41 In considering Decision 5.3.1 of the 146th UNESCO Executive Board, **the Assembly agreed** that two aspects should be addressed.

42 The first concerns para. 5 of Decision 5.3.1 which requested that the Director-General submit a report to the Executive Board at its 147th session.

43 **The Assembly took note** of Decision 5.3.1 of the 146th UNESCO Executive Board and, in particular, para. 5 by which the Director-General is requested to submit a report to the Board at its 147th session.

44 **The Assembly instructed** the Executive Secretary IOC to provide such information, based upon the following background material as the contribution of the IOC to the requested report:

(i) Statement of the Executive Secretary IOC as presented to the Eighteenth Session of the IOC, following debate under Agenda Item 4.

(ii) Brief statement on the principles under which the IOC has been established as a body with functional autonomy within UNESCO.

(iii) Administrative modalities to improve the effective response of IOC to the wishes of its Member States.

(iv) Bibliography of related documentation to provide adequate information to the Executive Board, facilitate its work and increase awareness of the role of the IOC as the marine science arm of UNESCO.

45 The second concerns para. 4 of Decision 5.3.1 by which it was observed that the IOC Assembly had not provided its "final views".

46 Discussion regarding para. 4 of Decision 5.3.1 stimulated a great deal of debate, during which Member States expressed their views and requested clarification of the basic principles at hand.

47 **The Assembly reiterated** the position taken in IOC Resolution XVII-20 (Part I of the Annex: para. 10) to the effect that the Commission seeks as *"one means of achieving greater dependability in IOC resources ... a 'subvention' or 'grant-in-aid' relationship with its parent body"*. It was duly noted that 'financial allocation' is the appropriate term as subsequently decided upon by the 27th UNESCO General Conference (when deciding on similar arrangements for IOC).

48 **The Assembly expressed** its deep gratitude to the Director-General for his positive response to this Resolution, as demonstrated by the inclusion within the Draft UNESCO 28 C/5 of provisions for a financial allocation to the IOC.

49 Some Delegations stressed the need for the IOC Secretariat to clarify the supervisory mechanisms and ways and means that it proposes for financial and administrative autonomy within UNESCO, as soon as possible.

50 **The Assembly noted** that the administrative practice of UNESCO requires that a Special Account be established before such a financial allocation drawn from the UNESCO regular budget can be received by the Commission, should the 28th UNESCO General Conference approve the proposal.

51 In order to ensure that the required internal administrative practice of UNESCO is operational by 1 January 1996 (the first day of the coming UNESCO biennium), **the Assembly underlined** that all due regulations and rules applicable to the Special Account should be transmitted to the governing bodies of UNESCO.

52 **The Assembly expressed** its appreciation to the UNESCO Executive Board for the interest in IOC that had been demonstrated by the request for further information and for the proposed amendments to the financial regulations which would provide an opportunity for the IOC to make periodic reports, with due accountability, to the governing bodies of both the UNESCO Executive Board and the General Conference.

53 **The Assembly noted** that it was desirable to foster exchanges of information between the national action addresses and committees of the IOC and the national commissions and permanent delegations of UNESCO.

54 The Assembly adopted Resolution XVIII-2.

55 In conclusion, **the Assembly expressed** its appreciation to the Executive Secretary IOC and to those in the UNESCO secretariat responsible for administrative and financial matters, for the work undertaken in a spirit of collaboration and with a common view to providing the practical conditions for the improved functioning of the IOC.

6. SECOND INTERNATIONAL CONFERENCE ON OCEANOGRAPHY - FOLLOW-UP

56 The Chairman of the Conference, Prof. Mario Ruivo (Portugal), introduced the item recalling the objectives of the Conference together with the results and identified needs for follow-up actions. He referred to Resolution XVII-16 which specified the actions which had been undertaken. He recalled that the Conference was a joint venture of the Government of Portugal and IOC.

57 He also referred to the IOC Annual Report 1994 where the Conference objectives and structure were presented, together with the texts of the Declaration and Shared Vision resulting from the Conference. Finally he presented the Draft Report of the Conference (Document IOC-XVIII/Inf.3) in which a summary of presentations and debates is given. The Conference took place in Lisbon, Portugal, from 14-19 November 1994 and was attended by over 150 participants from about 60 countries covering all geographical regions. It was a truly global conference, with about 40 developing countries represented.

58 The Conference identified the scientific needs and required capabilities, as well as the institutional requirements for research, development and protection of the marine environment and its resources at the approach of the Third Millennium. The Conference defined global challenges to society presented by the concepts of sustainable development and bio-diversity protection, identified the scientific and technical elements for a rational response to these challenges, including the limits to the carrying and productive capacity of the ocean, as well as the need for a special effort aimed at developing public awareness.

59 Prof. Ruivo emphasized the importance of the Declaration and Shared Vision approved by the Conference which contains a call upon Member States to take urgent action to ensure that a cohesive and co-operative approach to ocean science, ocean services and related capacity building, is applied within the UN System, using the IOC as an appropriate institution for facilitating this. The draft Summary Report of the Second International Conference on Oceanography was prepared by the General Rapporteur of the Conference (Dr. Sidney Holt) and made available to the Assembly (Document IOC-XVIII/Inf.3). The proceedings of the Conference are in preparation.

60 **The Assembly acknowledged with appreciation** the results of the Conference and paid tribute to the government of Portugal and to Prof. Ruivo, personally, for the excellent work in the preparation and implementation of the Conference and for the provided hospitality.

61 **The Assembly agreed** that the Conference signifies an important achievement in bringing together scientists and decision and policy-makers and in establishing a dialogue between these groups, in sensitizing them to the importance of the ocean for sustainable development, required capacity building as regards the key role of scientific research and knowledge in such a process.

62 **The Assembly supported the view** of the Conference concerning the important role IOC can play to ensure the reinforcement of the ocean partnership for integrated management of oceans and coastal areas, and all types of seas that would help to ensure sustainability of the global ecosystem.

63 **The Assembly strongly endorsed** the invitation of the Conference to the Director-General of UNESCO to consider appropriate measures to further reinforce IOC, so as to enable it to respond fully to its mandate and role in ocean and coastal affairs within the UN System. It also **expressed** its appreciation of the willingness of the Government of Portugal to bring the outcome of the Conference to the attention of the Commission on Sustainable Development (CSD), as a contribution to the agenda item on the Oceans, and **strongly endorsed** such an action.

64 The importance of increasing the dialogue with management-oriented, economic and socio-economic sectors of society in order to achieve the full benefits of the results of the ocean and coastal area research and observations, which had been brought out at the Conference, was also emphasized.

65 A few countries stressed the need to find the best way to ensure a more active participation of Member States in IOC activities through TEMA, as well as to strengthen national capacities in marine science and applications.

66 The Delegate of Malta drew special attention to the need to strengthen the IOC National Committees, and called on Member States to improve the links between national institutions and IOC, and to make the IOC National Committees more responsive to the IOC needs.

67 **The Assembly called upon** the Chairman of the Conference to convey the invitation of the Assembly to the Portuguese Government to bring the findings and decisions of the Conference to the UN General Assembly and to give wide publicity to the scientific conclusions of the Conference.

7. MEDIUM-TERM PLAN 1996-2001 AND PRELIMINARY CONSIDERATION OF PROGRAMME AND BUDGET FOR 1996-1997

68 The Chairman recalled the decision of the Assembly in 1993 that early consideration should be given to the Programme and Budget for the coming biennium at each Assembly. He referred to the Expanded Annotated Agenda (Document IOC-XVIII/2) and its Annex 7 which presents the proposal on the Draft Programme and Budget for 1996-1997. He invited the First Vice-Chairman to introduce the proposal.

69 The First Vice-Chairman, in his introduction, emphasized several points to be considered in the programming and budget specifications, including the need to set priorities, concentration, and ensure a time limit to projects. He emphasized the role of the IOC in the UN system to deal with ocean science and services to help resolve global and regional ocean issues. He analyzed three points related to the budget: its size; dependability of resources; and presentation of related resources.

70 With respect to the programme, he emphasized the need for increased concentration, efficiency, effectiveness, evaluations and completion of projects. He concluded by stressing the need for the proposed *ad hoc* sessional group on the further development of the Draft Programme and Budget to concentrate its attention on the presentation of information regarding the budget, and the process of focusing the programme on urgent issues and how Member States could contribute to this process. His statement is given in Annex III-F.

71 The Chairman proposed, and the **Assembly decided** to establish an open-ended *ad hoc* sessional group to further develop and complete the draft proposal for the Programme and Budget for 1996-1997, taking into account the concerned debates and instructions of the Assembly in its work. Some delegations made preliminary comments on the proposed Draft Programme and Budget, and pointed out that the Executive Board had decided on a three percent lapse factor, instead of two percent, which should be taken into account.

72 The Chairman drew the attention of the Assembly to the Draft IOC Medium-Term Strategy (Document IOC-XVIII/2 Annex 3). The Executive Secretary, in introducing this document, recalled the debate of the Twenty-seventh Session of the Executive Council and that the suggestions made then were fully taken into account in the revised IOC Draft Medium-Term Strategy. He emphasized that the proposed strategy takes an issue-oriented approach, and endeavors to relate the IOC programmes to major current issues of society regarding the oceans and the marine environment conditions. He presented the basic elements, recalling in this context the IOC Strategy for the Future adopted at the Sixteenth Session of the Assembly (Document SC/MD/97, Annex VII). He emphasized the objectives, mechanisms, evaluation processes, and indicated expected results over the medium-term period (1996-2001).

73 He again emphasized the need for concentration of effort and limitation of programme extensions.

74 Finally, in referring to Document IOC-XVIII/2 Annex 7, he suggested a strengthening and focusing of the IOC Secretariat through relating its structure to the major programme elements. This would result in three major units on: sciences; services (including GOOS); TEMA and regional activities. Each would be headed by a senior UNESCO staff member.

75 In the ensuing debate, the statements of the delegations showed overall support to, and concurrence with, the proposed Draft Medium-Term Strategy, welcomed the approach and agreed on the value of an overall path for future programming and directions. Several proposals were made for additional programme elements and focusing, e.g., inclusion of deep-sea floor ecology studies; biodiversity; emphasis on GOOS and services; establishment of regional research programmes, driven by regional interests from within the regions, but attracting the participation of scientists from outside the regions associated with leading scientific institutions.

76 The overall great significance of the TEMA Programme and need for its re-structuring and strengthening were re-emphasized by several delegations, by putting special emphasis on the regional approach.

77 Some delegations pointed out that in areas where no regional IOC subsidiary bodies exist, regional co-operative programmes are nevertheless carried out, e.g., in the western Atlantic through ASOS. Some adjustments to the text of Document IOC-XVIII/2 Annex 3, were requested, which have been taken up in the final version.

78 Several delegations referred to the mechanism of decentralization as a possibility to re-enforce the Secretariat, e.g., through carefully decentralizing well defined tasks to competent national or international laboratories.

79 Delegates emphasized the need to: (i) strengthen the links to the scientific community and also to attract young scientists; (ii) improve the links with users and application sectors; (iii) strengthen the role of IOC in integrated coastal area management; (iv) strengthen the IOC contribution to the follow-up to the Small Islands Developing States Conference and the related action plan; and (v) raise public awareness and strengthen the role and capacity of relevant national bodies.

80 The Medium-Term Strategy should also bear in mind the 1998 International Year of the Ocean.

81 Finally, it was pointed out that proper evaluations must be ensured and also the results of the programmes with reference to the identified major issues must be presented. The assessment process should be a continuous one, and should also be used to help obtain budget reinforcement, and obtain further support from co-operating partners.

82 **The Assembly decided** that the Medium-Term Strategy document should be revised taking into account the comments and proposals made and be attached to the Assembly Report as Annex VI.

C. PROGRAMME DEVELOPMENT

8. FOLLOW-UP OF THE 1992 UNITED NATIONS CONFERENCE ON ENVIRONMENT AND DEVELOPMENT

8.1 AGENDA 21 AND ACC SUB-COMMITTEE ON OCEANS AND COASTAL AREAS

83 In introducing this agenda item, the IOC Senior Assistant Secretary for Information and Co-ordination, Ms. N. Philippon-Tulloch, spoke also in her capacity as Secretary of the ACC Sub-Committee on Oceans and Coastal Areas. Following reference to the Annotated Provisional Agenda (Document IOC-XVIII/2: paras 29-33) and the Report of the Second Session of the Sub-Committee (issued as an information document as IOC/INF-989), she provided an overview of progress made to date by the Sub-Committee in fulfilling its responsibilities for monitoring, reporting upon and proposing ideas for implementation of Chapter 17 of Agenda 21.

84 Ms. Philippon-Tulloch made particular reference to the agreements reached by Members of the Sub-Committee at its first two sessions (FAO Headquarters, Rome, 19-21 April 1994 and WMO Headquarters, 23-27 January 1995) in regard to timely completion of its report which will be submitted through the Inter-Agency Committee on Sustainable Development (IACSD) to the Commission on Sustainable Development (CSD) in 1996 as concerns:

(i) distribution of responsibilities among the participating agencies for each of the Programme Areas contained in Chapter 17, and

(ii) progress made at the Second Session towards improving ways and means by which the UN System collaborates in implementation of Chapter 17 as a whole, including cross-sectoral issues, especially within the perspective of agreeing upon co-operative programme frameworks.

85 The Assembly was also informed of the consultations with Member States and concerned non-governmental organizations which would be undertaken by the CSD Secretariat in New York in the form of a questionnaire. The purpose of this questionnaire is to seek information from Member States as well as their views on relevant matters so that they can be taken into account in completion of the report.

Noting that the diversity of sectoral subjects in Chapter 17 seen in the composition of the Sub-Committee is also reflected at the national level, Ms. Philippon-Tulloch encouraged IOC national contacts to make every effort to ensure that a full response was provided to the CSD Secretariat.

86 The Chairman of the Sub-Committee, Dr. S. Garcia, who also represented FAO, reiterated that collaboration between agencies will only be truly effective when based upon effective co-ordination at the national level, and also emphasized the importance of a concerted approach in mobilizing funding.

87 In the ensuing debate, a number of Member States provided information regarding national initiatives that were being stimulated as a result of UNCED and the stimulation provided through Agenda 21 as a framework for activities at the national, regional and global levels.

88 The Representative of the United Kingdom informed the Assembly of a UK Workshop on Environmental Science, Comprehensiveness and Consistency in Global Decisions on Ocean Issues, to be held 29 November-1 December 1995. In referring to the long-established need to raise awareness amongst high-level decision makers of ocean and coastal area concerns, he noted that the workshop was being organized following the initiative of the Secretary of State for the Environment who is also a member of the CSD.

89 Other representatives, including those of Canada, India and Indonesia, provided information on the development of specific national policy statements and guidelines as examples of how the UNCED process is beginning to bear fruit in regard to development of strategies on ocean and coastal area issues. All speakers emphasized the importance of accelerating efforts that would lead to integrated coastal area management and its related human and infrastructure aspects, the ocean component of which is an integral and vital element.

90 The Representative of the United Nations made special reference to the Train-Sea-Coast Programme which was being undertaken in collaboration with and several other UN bodies, including the IOC, and which would serve as a joint contribution to the human resource component of the co-operative programme frameworks being developed by the Sub-Committee.

91 **The Assembly emphasized** that a concerted approach within the UN System, together with appropriate national mechanisms, was an essential factor to successful implementation of Agenda 21 as a whole and Chapter 17 in particular.

92 **The Assembly conveyed** to the ACC Sub-Committee on Oceans and Coastal Areas its appreciation of the complexity of the tasks at hand and **suggested** the following observations as a contribution to its work:

(i) the importance of a concerted approach within the UN System to human and institutional resource development at the national level;

(ii) the need to encourage the establishment, or strengthening, of appropriate national coordination mechanisms for ocean and coastal area concerns;

(iii) the need to take into account the socio-economic dimension, especially in regard to the priority that should be accorded to integrated coastal area management and, in particular, to "vulnerable" areas - whether influenced by critical dwelling, environmental degradation or natural disaster factors.

93 **The Assembly requested** the Secretary of the Sub-Committee to keep IOC Member States informed of action taken by the CSD Secretariat in regard to soliciting national input to the process of preparing a comprehensive report in 1996.

8.2 UN YEAR OF THE OCEAN 1998

94 The Chairman referred to Document IOC-XVIII/2, paragraphs 34-39, providing the necessary background for the item, and recalled Resolution XVII-17, which had initiated the process.

95 The Executive Secretary briefly introduced Document IOC-XVIII/2 Annex 4, explaining the proposed approach in using existing and planned IOC programme actions to support the Year of the Ocean, emphasizing public awareness creation and additional educational actions, as well as the proposal for an IOC preparatory task team for the IOC contribution to 1998 International Year of the Ocean. He also explained that, in view of the need for IOC to prepare public information and educational material, some financial resources for these preparations had been included in the proposed programme and budget 1996-97 (Document IOC-XVIII/2 Annex 7). He invited the *ad hoc* sessional group on the draft programme and budget to consider this matter.

96 In the ensuing debate, all delegations expressed strong support for IOC's participation and leading role within UNESCO, in the 1998 International Year of the Ocean, and in association with the United Nations System through the ICSPRO mechanism, as well as in seeking co-operation with non-governmental organizations in this matter. The great importance of public awareness creation and general educational activities was stressed by most delegations.

97 The Delegations generally concurred with the approach adopted in Document IOC-XVIII/2 Annex 4, and endorsed the creation of a time-limited preparatory task team, with regional participation. Several additional regions to those mentioned, e.g. Southeast Pacific through CPPS, and Western Atlantic through ASOS, expressed interest in also being involved in the task team.

98 This event in 1998 was considered by many delegations as a unique opportunity for IOC to create much more awareness about itself, at national and international levels.

99 The Year of the Ocean should be seen as a charter for public education as regards the role of oceans for society. Appropriate media mechanisms should be used; the IOC could possibly make an inventory of the TV material on ocean science-related actions and, if possible, create a special educational production. Posters should also be prepared for this purpose by IOC.

100 The Canadian Delegate proposed an Ocean Charter that could be developed further by the Executive Council and Assembly and possibly open for signature by governments during the Year of the Ocean in 1998. The draft text is included (Annex VII-A). This initiative was welcomed by several delegates. The Delegate also emphasized the promotion of 8 June as Ocean Day. He mentioned the "Summit of the Sea Conference", scheduled for 1997 in Newfoundland, and the hosting by Canada of the WOCE Conference in 1998.

101 The Delegate of Portugal provided additional information on the on-going planning of 1998 International Year of the Ocean and EXPO.98. The latter mechanism will also provide many opportunities for public awareness creation of the IOC. It is possible that aspects of EXPO.98 will be under the UN umbrella with UNESCO and IOC as the lead agency for that particular part. He referred to several planned conferences, including "Ocean and Society on the Threshold of the Third Millennium" and a Conference on satellite remote sensing on ocean applications in new technology. He invited IOC to consider association with these events, and to perhaps arrange some of its planned meetings in Lisbon at EXPO.98. This was seconded by some other delegations.

102 Several delegates furthermore informed the Assembly of national plans with respect to public awareness creation, education, policy formulation and the strengthening of the research link with users and applications.

103 The Delegate of Cuba referred to the organization in 1997 of the Fourth International Marine Science Conference in Cuba, and invited IOC to plan an associated regional activity.

104 All delegations confirmed the interest of their countries in participating in activities within the 1998 Year of the Ocean, in partnership with IOC. Many expressed interest in being associated with the preparatory task team. Specific proposals for actions were made, including the restoration of historical marks, and commemoration of historical voyages.

105 **The Assembly confirmed** IOC's association with 1998 Year of the Ocean and EXPO.98; **emphasized** that as far as possible the activities should be part of the planned or on-going IOC programmes and in conformity with present provisions; **stressed** the focus on public awareness creation and education; and **instructed** the Executive Secretary to follow-up the proposals made, using the basic approach presented in Document IOC-XVIII/2 Annex 4 (Annex VII-B), including the servicing of the task team, which, however, would work mainly through correspondence.

106 **The Assembly adopted Resolution XVIII-3.**

9. IOC AND UNCLOS

107 The Chairman introduced the agenda item, referring to documents IOC/INF-990 (Report of the *ad hoc* Working Group on IOC Responsibilities and Actions in Relation to UNCLOS), and IOC/INF-1007 (Summary Report of the IOC/OSNLR *ad hoc* Expert Consultation on UNCLOS).

108 He referred to the Twenty-seventh Session of the IOC Executive Council, Paris, 5-12 July 1994, when the item "IOC In Relation to the UN Convention on the Law of the Sea" was considered, in view of the imminent coming into force of the Convention. The Executive Council discussed at some length document IOC/EC-XXVII/15 (IOC and UNCLOS: Responsibilities and Actions) prepared by Prof. Yankov in co-operation with the Secretariat, and decided to establish an *ad hoc* Intersessional Working Group on IOC Responsibilities and Actions in Relation to UNCLOS with clearly defined terms of reference, to further study the implications of UNCLOS on IOC and suggest actions to be taken.

109 He briefed the Assembly on follow-up actions taken by the Secretariat in accordance with the decisions of the Executive Council in terms of IOC short-term responsibilities, including the compilation of a list of experts for use by the Special Arbitral Tribunal together with activities to assist the work of the Commission on the Limits of the Continental Shelf (CLCS), both actions taken at the request of UN-DAOLOS. He also informed the Assembly of actions taken in relation to the *ad hoc* working group on UNCLOS, which had been established as an open-ended group of the Executive Council. He stressed the need for the IOC to carry out its long-term duties in relation to UNCLOS, especially in the promotion of marine scientific research, training and capacity building, the transfer of marine technology, in addition to IOC short-term responsibilities in relation to the Special Arbitral Tribunal and the CLCS. He pointed out that the Assembly might wish to move towards a clear definition of specific role and responsibilities for the IOC based upon which IOC could take the appropriate further actions.

110 At the invitation of the Chairman, Prof. Yankov, the author of Document IOC/EC-XXVII/15 and former Chairman of Committee III (on marine scientific research and protection and preservation of the marine environment) of the Third UN Conference on the Law of the Sea (1973-1982), gave some additional background information on the subject. He noted that the responses from the *ad hoc* working group on UNCLOS concurred with the proposed new and evolving responsibilities of the IOC and the logical expansion of IOC's existing functions and actions as a result of UNCLOS, as well as the classification of IOC's new role and responsibilities into three categories as mentioned in Annex II of Document IOC/EC-XXVII/15. He pointed out that the revised version of the role and responsibilities presented in Annex II of IOC/INF-990, with proposed adjustments, still need further elaboration so as to more fully reflect the possible role and responsibilities of IOC. He suggested that IOC should co-operate with the International Sea-Bed Authority whose present work is mainly to conduct research, studies and assessment in relation to the exploitation and exploration of deep sea resources. He drew the attention of the Assembly to the special role of international organizations, in accordance with Article 247 of the Convention, to possibly facilitate marine scientific research through the formulation of more detailed and practical guidelines, criteria and procedures in addition to the efforts made by the United Nations in this regard.

111 The Executive Secretary IOC also drew the attention of the Assembly to the UN General Assembly's resolution on the Law of the Sea at its Forty-ninth Session, December 1994, which *inter alia*, called upon the designated, competent international organizations to take specific actions to ensure the effective implementation of the Convention. He informed the Assembly that IOC has been invited by the UN to contribute to the Annual Report of the UN Secretary-General on the Law of the Sea at the Fiftieth Session of UN General Assembly.

112 To facilitate discussion on the subject, the Assembly decided to establish an open-ended sessional working group led by the Second Vice-Chairman, Dr. Metalnikov, to first exchange views on the subject.

113 The sessional Working Group held three meetings on 16, 19 and 20 June, with the participation of about twenty delegations. The following main concerns were expressed:

(i) Document IOC/INF-990 is based on a very limited number of responses from Member States to the IOC Circular Letter No. 1436 in the light of the decisions of the Twenty-seventh Session of the Executive Council, and includes little and insufficient adjustments to Document IOC/EC-XXVII/15, particularly its Annex II (List of Articles of UNCLOS Relevant to the Role and Functions of IOC), which is considered not to have correctly reflected the IOC role under UNCLOS and requires reconsideration and redrafting (see statements of Argentina and Brazil in Annex III-G);

(ii) There are questions on the juridical basis of IOC holding consultations on issues in relation to the Commission on the Limits of the Continental Shelf (CLCS) since Document IOC/EC-XXVII/15 was strongly questioned during the last Executive Council. Some wording in IOC/INF-1007 does not truly reflect the provisions of UNCLOS (see statements of Argentina and Brazil in Annex III-G);

(iii) More time is needed to examine IOC/INF-990 and IOC/INF-1007 before substantial comment could be made;

(iv) The decision of the Twenty-seventh Session of the Executive Council has not been fully implemented regarding the establishment of an intersessional working group on IOC responsibilities and activities related to UNCLOS. For this reason, there is a need to establish such a special group to study the matter.

114 Many Delegations expressed their general support for IOC to take positive and effective action to respond to UNCLOS as a competent international organization in the field of marine scientific research.

115 The Delegate of Greece proposed that a meeting of the open-ended intersessional Working Group on IOC in Relation to UNCLOS be hosted in Greece. This proposal is subject to official confirmation from the Greek Government to the Executive Secretary IOC. The Assembly thanked the Delegate of Greece for this offer.

116 The Delegate of Pakistan suggested that IOC publish a handbook on IOC and UNCLOS highlighting those provisions of UNCLOS that fall within this area of competence of IOC, which will help increase the visibility of IOC in governments in the context of UNCLOS.

117 The Delegate of the Russian Federation noted that UNCLOS presents a satisfactory balance with regard to the inter-relation between the rights of coastal and researching States concerning marine scientific research on the continental shelf and in the Exclusive Economic Zone. This is why B.2 of the Annex to IOC Resolution XVIII-4 does not reflect this balance, has no direct connection with the role of IOC, and has a more political than legal nature.

118 The Delegation of Turkey sees the ultimate objective of the work to be carried out by the Working Group as the achievement of technical and scientific co-operation to which the Turkish Government is fully and enthusiastically dedicated. It sees great merit in this ultimate goal and has pursued it long before its signature of the UN Convention on the Law of the Sea.

119 The Delegation of Turkey understands that issues pertaining to general legal aspects of UNCLOS and their political implications, are strictly outside the scope of the task of the Working Group and the results of the work of the Working Group will in no way prejudice the positions of the Government with regard to UNCLOS.

120 **The Assembly took note** with satisfaction of the consensus achieved in the *ad hoc* sessional working group on UNCLOS concerning the ways to proceed with the work in relation to UNCLOS through an *ad hoc* intersessional working group with its terms of reference. **The Assembly expressed** its appreciation to Dr. Metalnikov for successfully chairing the sessional working group as well as to all participants for their spirit of co-operation and willingness to find a solution.

121 **The Assembly noted** that the study on the implications of UNCLOS on IOC has been carried out since the early 1980s and thus should be completed as soon as possible, so that IOC could concentrate on the actual implementation of relevant activities.

122 **The Assembly adopted** Resolution XVIII-4.

10. OCEANS SCIENCES

10.1 OCEANS AND CLIMATE

123 The Chairman made a brief overall introduction referring to previous decisions and resolutions of the Assembly at its Seventeenth Session (1993) and the Executive Council at its Twenty-seventh Session (1994). These demonstrate the importance that the Commission attaches to the issue of oceans and climate. In particular, he recalled the decision of the IOC to formally co-sponsor WCRP, and to become associated with the Interagency Co-ordinating Committee on the World Climate Programme. He recalled the participation of the IOC in the Second World Climate Conference in 1990 and the Intergovernmental Meeting on the World Climate Programme in 1993. He also referred to the participation of the IOC in the Intergovernmental Negotiating Committee on a Framework Convention on Climate Change and the First Conference of the Parties to that Convention in 1995.

124 The Chairman then suggested that, in view of the inter-relationship of the sub-items of this Agenda item, the introductions be made in sequence, and that in the subsequent debate Delegations should identify which sub-items they are addressing. He drew the attention of the Assembly to the relevant pages in the Expanded Annotated Agenda (Document IOC-XVIII/2), and the actions requested of the Assembly.

10.1.1 WCRP-JSC, including TOGA and CLIVAR

125 Dr. Hartmut Grassl, Director of the WCRP, began his introduction of this agenda item by reviewing the successes of the completed TOGA programme and the remarkable degree of international participation in the current intensive observational phase of WOCE that will result in some 90% of the WOCE Hydrographic Programme (WHP) sections being occupied. The increasingly skillful forecasts of El Niño, up to a year in advance in some cases, are already being used to advantage by a few nations in crop planning, water resource management, etc. The post-TOGA emphasis is now to spread the benefits being realized by these few nations to all the nations affected by the ENSO by enhancing their capability to exploit climate forecasts. In the case of WOCE, the focus is to lay the groundwork for the development of longer range climate predictability. The new WCRP initiative, the Climate Variability and Predictability (CLIVAR) Programme aims to advance the understanding of natural climate variability as well as the influence of human activities on this variability and to determine climate predictability on both the interannual and interdecadal timescales. Dr. Grassl stressed that he was very pleased with the way the WMO-IOC-ICSU were co-operating and that the WMO Congress had just approved the continuation of this co-sponsorship arrangement for the WCRP. He emphasized that the co-sponsorship by the IOC of the WCRP had ensured the full involvement of the oceanographic community in that Programme, which is of utmost importance for its success.

126 **The Assembly expressed** its appreciation to Dr. Grassl for his introduction and its satisfaction with IOC's participation in and contribution to the WCRP. **The Assembly decided** that the IOC should continue this co-sponsorship.

10.1.2 WOCE

127 Dr. John Church informed the Assembly of the excellent progress in WOCE and reminded the Member States that the important next phase, the analysis, interpretation modelling and synthesis phase, was scheduled to continue through 2002. He described the functioning network of data centres and analysis centres set up to facilitate this phase and illustrated some of the early impressive results of the WOCE program derived from preliminary analyses of few of the first sections completed in the WHP. A North Atlantic section at 24°N shows long-term warming consistent with model predictions of global warming, while another section at 58°N shows unexpected long-term cooling. Some of the early tracer observations of high latitude deep convection revealed defects in the parameterization of the processes in models. The TOPEX-POSEIDON observations underscore the value of high quality altimeter observations for measuring long-term ocean circulation variability. He called on nations to enlarge the community of scientists involved in data assimilation, to assure the continuation of high quality satellite altimeter observations and to give high priority to a gravity mission to extract the most value from the altimeter data. He concluded his presentation by noting that the real payoff from WOCE depended on completion of the WHP sections from shore to shore and the analysis and synthesis phase. The former depends on access to EEZ waters of Member States in order to obtain measures of heat and other transports across the sections. The latter depends on strengthening the international data assembly and special analysis centres and safeguarding funding for WOCE through its scheduled completion in 2002.

128 Dr. Leonard Otto reported on the outcome of the meeting of the Intergovernmental WOCE Panel held the week prior to the IOC Assembly. He drew the attention of the Assembly the Executive Summary (Document IOC-WMO/IWP-III/3S) which contained a number of recommendations the Panel believed were fundamental to the realization of the full benefit of the enormous resources already invested in WOCE. These recommendations were incorporated in Resolution XVIII-5 which was **adopted** by the Assembly. He emphasized several points in relation to these recommendations where action by Member States is called for:

(i) Access to certain areas under national jurisdiction where close-to-shore boundary currents exist is crucial to completing the WHP sections necessary for calculating heat, fresh water and other transports.

(ii) Secondments by Member States for even short periods of 3-6 months to the DACs and SACs will help the staffs of these centers to acquire and process WOCE data. This assistance would be of direct benefit to the Member State as well, in that it would enhance the capability of the seconding nation to utilize data and realize the full benefit of the entire WOCE system of data centres, a network which is destined to be taken over by CLIVAR after WOCE.

(iii) The International WOCE Conference to be hosted by Canada in 1998 merits the full support of all Member States.

129 Several delegations informed the Assembly of national activities in relation to WOCE. They all emphasized the need to ensure the completion of WOCE, welcomed the recommendations and, in particular, the proposed WOCE Conference planned for 1998.

130 **The Assembly reconfirmed** the strong commitment of IOC to the completion of WOCE and **endorsed** the results and recommendations of the Third Session of the IWP.

10.1.3 Relations with UN-FCCC, including the First Conference of the Parties (COP), and IPCC

131 Referring to the request of the Executive Council at its Twenty-seventh Session (Document IOC/EC-XXVII/3, para 30), the second Vice-Chairman presented the in-depth Report on Climate-related Issues with an attached draft resolution for consideration by the Assembly (Document IOC-XVIII/2 Annex 5). He referred to the specific provisions of Chapter 17 of Agenda 21 of UNCED which requested IOC and other relevant competent United Nations bodies, with the support of countries having the resources and expertise, to carry out analysis, assessments and systematic observations of the role of oceans as a carbon sink. The report has three main sections devoted to, respectively, IOC activities in the World Climate Programme, in the UN-FCCC and COP process, and in the IPCC, as well as an additional part concerning IOC's interaction with the GCOS.

132 Attention was drawn to some results of a number of specific events:

(i) Conclusion and recommendations of two meetings of Scientific and Technical Experts organized in Malta in 1991 and 1994, by the IOC with the support of the Foundation of International Studies of the University of Malta;

(ii) A special paper "CO_2 and Ocean: A review of the State of Knowledge", edited by Arthur G. Alexiou;

(iii) The briefing on sea-level rise for AOSIS States, provided by the GLOSS Chairman Dr. David Pugh at INC-X;

(iv) The transfer of related IOC publications to the UN-FCCC Secretariat.

133 Among the actions proposed for the future were:

(i) Strengthening the co-operative links between IOC and IPCC, and IOC and SBSTA of the UN-FCCC/COP;

(ii) Preparation of the GLOSS Sea-Level information data base on floppy disks for demonstration and distribution among AOSIS States during the COP-2 of UN-FCCC (1996);

(iii) Organization of the third meeting of Scientific and Technical Experts in Malta for consideration of the problem of greenhouse gases (besides CO_2) interactions with World Ocean;

(iv) Initiation of the Coral Reefs Study from the carbon accumulation viewpoint;

(v) Preparation and transfer to the IPCC of the list of the IOC experts.

134 Many delegations expressed support to IOC's association with the development and implementation of relevant aspects of the UN-FCCC and related bodies.

135 The representative of the UN-FCCC Secretariat, Mr. Sálvano Briceño, made a statement in which he informed the Assembly as to how the UN-FCCC was created, developed and signed in 1992 in Rio. He pointed out that the Convention came into force in March 1994, and is now ratified by 136 states. He also informed the Assembly that in April 1995 the COP-1 was held in Berlin and important decisions were made such as the adoption of the "Berlin mandate" for negotiation of the next step in the reduction of anthropogenic carbon dioxide emissions by developed states. He noted that two subsidiary bodies were established by the Convention - for Science and Technical Advice and for Implementation (SBSTA and SBI) and they would be meeting soon. He recommended the Assembly to strengthen links with the IPCC and participate in the SBSTA. He also noted the importance of the ocean-atmosphere interaction and underlined the significance of systematic observations for UN-FCCC. He set much store by the IOC's efforts to present the best available knowledge related to oceans and climate. He also thanked the IOC for the support provided thus far to the UN-FCCC Secretariat. His statement is given in Annex III-H to this report.

136 The Assembly decided that IOC should maintain its links and co-operation with bodies and mechanisms of the UN-FCCC, in particular with the Climate Change Secretariat and the SBSTA.

10.1.4 OOSDP and the Second Meeting of Scientific and Technical Experts on Oceans and Climate (Malta, 1994)

137 Dr. Arthur Alexiou introduced this item by bringing to the attention of the Assembly the complete set of publications produced by the OOSDP which includes a comprehensive Final Report and seven scientific background reports. He noted that the final document had gone through several stages of review before being published. The report has been endorsed by the JSC of the WCRP, the JSTC, and J-GOOS, which forwarded it to I-GOOS. I-GOOS has agreed to form a Panel to consider the Report from a Member State's implementation perspective. J-GOOS, JSTC and the JSC have taken steps to establish a follow-on Ocean Observations Panel for Climate (OOPC). J-GOOS is also planning to open the OOSDP report to a wider audience via a 3-4 day workshop in order to generate more public debate among implementation agencies and managers of user groups of ocean climate observations.

138 Dr. Alexiou also introduced the separate item concerning the second meeting of Scientific and Technical Experts on Oceans and Climate hosted by the Government of Malta. As a direct consequence of international agreements embodied in Chapter 17 of Agenda 21, this meeting was oriented to the problem of the oceans and CO_2, with particular consideration of the ocean capacity as a CO_2 sink. The magnitude of uncertainties in ocean carbon fluxes is still too large to reliably partition between the land and the ocean, the fate of that fraction of the anthropogenic CO_2 that is known to have been injected into the atmosphere that is not there now. The Malta 1994 meeting provided a basis for developing a strategy for further analyses, assessments and observations called for in Agenda 21. It is important for IOC to maintain this activity and assure a response to the Commission on Sustainable Development with respect to Chapter 17 of Agenda 21.

139 Many delegations made interventions on the these items that included descriptions of their contributions to climate studies as well as comments regarding IOC's climate-related activities. All comments were in the same vein, recognizing IOC's support of developing countries' participation in ocean climate science activities such as IAPSO, as well as congratulating IOC for the Malta document and voicing continued support for WOCE, CLIVAR and other programmes of the WCRP with particular mention of the WOCE International Conference and encouraging continued joint efforts with ICSU and WMO and the continued joint efforts with SCOR and JGOFS with regard to ocean CO_2. They also reacted favourably to the OOSDP Report and the establishment of a joint follow-on OOPC. The importance of moving forward with the climate module of GOOS was noted by referring to the success of TOGA and the benefits already being accrued by some countries and that efforts should be accelerated to spread these benefits to all nations impacted by ENSO. Strengthening of links with other intergovernmental climate activities, such as the IPCC, by assigning a specific individual within the IOC secretariat to serve as liaison and co-ordinator for all its climate-related activities was encouraged. It was agreed that the IOC should also invite Professor Bert Bolin, Chairman of the IPCC, to address the next Assembly as a means of enhancing further the IOC's contribution.

The Assembly adopted Resolution XVIII-6.

10.1.5 World Climate Programme (WCP) Joint Proposal

140 The Executive Secretary of the IOC presented "The Climate Agenda" (Document IOC-XVIII/Inf.1), which contains the Extensive Policy Makers' Summary and the Executive Summary of the "Climate Agenda". The proposal for this Integrating Framework was prepared by FAO, ICSU, UNEP, UNESCO and its IOC, and WMO, through the Co-ordinating Committee for the World Climate Programme. He explained that it had been agreed that this would be presented to the governing bodies of the co-sponsors. The Assembly was then invited to provide its comments. The requirements and needs of systematic observations as regards climate change are important justifications of this serious development of the WCP initiated by the intergovernmental meeting on WCP held in Geneva, April 1993. The implementation of this significant, wide-ranging programme needs to properly develop the mechanism of co-ordination on international and national levels. In this connection, the IOC participation in this process is extremely important, including membership in the Inter-Agency Co-ordination Committee.

141 Seventeen delegations took part in the discussions on this item. All of them recognized the IOC participation in climate-related programmes as successful and important. Many delegations stressed the need to continue the IOC contribution in this direction.

142 **The Assembly decided** that IOC should continue and expand its association with the WCP, and **endorsed** the Climate Agenda.

10.2 OCEANS AND GLOBAL CHANGE: LOICZ; JGOFS, INCLUDING CO_2 PANEL; COASTAL ZONES (COASTS)

143 The Executive Secretary introduced the item referring to Document IOC-XVIII/2, item 10.2 and Documents IOC/INF-987 and IOC/INF-987 Add. He recalled Resolution XVII-1 "Coastal Zone Activities" through which the Assembly had set up an *ad hoc* IOC Group of Experts on Coastal Zone Activities including representatives from Member States and the Commission's regional and global programmes. This group was requested to prepare a report for this Assembly. Since the Working Group had completed its mandate through the presentation of Document IOC/INF-987, he proposed that the *ad hoc* IOC Group of Experts had completed its work and could be terminated.

144 With respect to training matters he recalled that IOC is a partner in the UN (DOALOS)-UNDP Train-Sea Coast Programme, at present, as regards IOC, with emphasis on Africa.

145 The Executive Secretary also recalled several activities of the IOC related to ICAM at regional level, and the association of these activities with the Coastal Change Conference (Bordeaux 1995) through regional preparation of related cases on coastal zone studies and management aspects, which can provide input for a series of manuals.

146 He recalled the instruction to the Secretary IOC during the Twenty-seventh Session of the Executive Council to develop a training programme on integrated coastal zone management for the benefit of managers, decision-makers and technicians who are actually involved in coastal zone management and to submit a draft programme to this Assembly. This proposed draft programme is presented in Document IOC/INF-987 Add.

147 He briefed the Assembly on the development of the Coastal Ocean Advanced Science and Technology Study (COASTS), the Workshop in Liege, May 1994, and the continued development of the programme at regional level in WESTPAC through modelling and observation of the coastal zone circulation.

148 He informed the Assembly on IOC's involvement in coral reef monitoring and research activities through the pilot monitoring experiment (see item 11.1.1), and the co-ordination of this activity with the International Coral Reef Initiative (ICRI) and the support provided from the United States of America to this end, as well as offers of support from several other Member States.

149 The Executive Secretary informed the Assembly that IOC has a Memorandum of Understanding on co-operation with IGBP-LOICZ, and that co-operation with LOICZ is proceeding well. The IOC was a co-sponsor of the recent open science meeting of LOICZ (The Philippines, 24-28 April 1995) where agreement had been reached on cooperation between LOICZ and the IOC regional subsidiary bodies in Africa (IOCEA and IOCINCWIO) in the implementation of the LOICZ regional activities in those parts of Africa.

150 He noted that the CO_2 question and JGOFS had been partially considered under item 10.1.

151 Finally, the Executive Secretary mentioned the IGBP/START initiative, which is now also sponsored by WCRP and SHS. Through WCRP, the IOC is thus also associated with START. He suggested that the need for co-ordination and harmonization of related training activities be discussed under TEMA (Agenda item 12).

152 **The Assembly endorsed** the Report on Coastal Zone Studies and Co-ordination of Coastal Zone Activities with its Addendum and agreed that the *ad hoc* Intersessional Working Group on Coastal Zone Activities, having fulfilled its mandate, was hereby terminated.

153 **The Assembly noted** with satisfaction the various activities carried out by the IOC on both a regional and global basis and IOC's role in the co-ordination of system-wide coastal zone activities, as reflected in Document IOC/INF-987.

154 Some delegations put questions on the IOC contribution to and role in the newly proposed UNESCO Project on Environment and Development in Coastal Regions and in Small Islands, which is based on the joint statement of the chairpersons of IOC, IHP, MAB, IGCP to Commission III of the 27th General Conference of UNESCO. It aims at ensuring co-ordination among the relevant UNESCO programme activities in IOC, MAB, IHP and IGCP and MOST. These delegations expressed their concern on the possibility of losing unity for IOC/MRI in this proposed Project. Some argued that since this Project is more concerned with the coastal zone and IOC/MRI contributes a greater part of the fund, IOC/MRI should take the leading role in this project. **The Assembly established** a small *ad hoc* sessional working group chaired by the Fourth Vice-Chairman, to define the possible activities of IOC during the intersessional period, in particular, with respect to the proposed intersectorial project.

155 **The Assembly emphasized** that coastal zone activities represent a new development for IOC, as well as a major trend in the development of future IOC activities. **The Assembly realized** that integrated coastal area management (ICAM) is a very complicated process and involves efforts both in terms of the interdisciplinary study of natural and social sciences and well co-ordinated administration at various levels. **The Assembly encouraged** more interaction between IOC scientific programmes and socio-economic aspects in the further implementation of coastal zone activities. **The Assembly decided** that a co-ordinator should be designated in the IOC Secretariat to ensure the effective linkage between scientific programmes and coastal zone management needs.

156 **The Assembly realized** the need to streamline the existing IOC coastal zone-related activities, define a co-ordinator, and possibly develop a harmonized and focussed coastal zone programme which will be distinct from existing IOC activities and with separate funding. This could be the dedicated training programme outlined in IOC-INF/987 Add. **The Assembly urged** the strengthening of the present subject-oriented programmes, e.g. OSLR, OSNLR, GIPME, and others, so as to produce more products from these programmes for users.

157 **The Assembly also realized** the importance of developing common methodologies to be used by marine scientists in coastal zone management, and agreed that IOC should take initiatives in this respect. **The Assembly acknowledged** the importance of a regional approach in coastal zone management and flexibility in adopting top-down or bottom-up approaches in different cases.

158 Many delegations briefed the Assembly on their national activities, experience and plans in the coastal zone. The Delegate of the Netherlands informed the Assembly on their initiative to attract donors to various aspects of integrated coastal zone management and invited IOC to become involved in this activity. **The Assembly took note** of this information with appreciation.

159 **The Assembly attached** much value to IOC/INF-987 Add. as an excellent framework on the IOC coastal zone training programme, particularly to the classification of three categories of training courses, to serve the needs of different target groups of managers. **The Assembly emphasized** the importance of data collection using GIS in coastal zone management and suggested that the use of GIS be included in all categories of proposed IOC training courses. The Delegates of Turkey and China made offers to organize such proposed international coastal zone management training courses in co-operation with IOC in their countries, possibly in 1996. **The Assembly expressed** its thanks for these offers.

160 With regard to IOC co-operation with IGBP, **the Assembly took note** with satisfaction of the progress, particularly in terms of the conclusion of a Memorandum of Understanding with LOICZ, the IOC co-sponsorship of IGBP/START and the continued interaction with SCOR-JGOFS mainly through the CO_2 Panel, and urged the Executive Secretary IOC to ensure that this co-operation be further maintained and broadened, particularly in its co-operation with START, using extrabudgetary resources.

161 Several Delegations expressed their thanks to IOC for sponsoring their scientists' participation in the LOICZ meeting in the Philippines.

162 Considering the Memorandum of Understanding between LOICZ and IOC, the Delegation of Nigeria supported the recommendations of the African group at that meeting and urged IOC to co-operate with LOICZ in the implementation of the recommendations.

163 **The Assembly adopted** Resolution XVII-7 on "Coastal Regions and Small Islands", and **invited** the IOC Action Addressees to bring this Resolution to the attention of the UNESCO National Commissions.

10.3 OCEAN SCIENCE IN RELATION TO LIVING RESOURCES (OSLR); IPHAB; GLOBEC; CONVENTION ON BIOLOGICAL DIVERSITY

164 The presentation and discussion of the OSLR Programme focussed on Harmful Algal Blooms, Marine Biodiversity, and the SCOR-IOC-ICES-PICES International Global Ocean Ecosystems Dynamics (GLOBEC) Programme.

165 The Executive Secretary IOC recalled Resolution XVII-2, adopted by the Seventeenth Session of the Assembly, on the refocussing of the OSLR Programme. In the intersessional period the OSLR Programme has developed with respect to Harmful Algal Blooms and marine biological diversity. Other components of the Programme have been maintained, but their development has been impeded by lack of a permanent Technical Secretary for OSLR, as well as lack of funds.

166 The Representative of FAO informed the Assembly that due to resource problems and the need to focus on selected actions, FAO has decided to withdraw as formal co-sponsor of OSLR. He noted that the present activities of OSLR no longer corresponded to the priorities of FAO. Nevertheless he stressed that FAO continues to have an interest in the science needed to understand oscillations of marine living resources and in drawing on the scientific advice of, e.g., IPHAB. FAO will also co-operate in the Living Resource Module of GOOS, and GLOBEC.

167 The out-going Chairman of the IOC-FAO Intergovernmental Panel on Harmful Algal Blooms (IPHAB), Dr. Bernt I. Dybern (Sweden), introduced the problems associated with harmful algae, and informed the Assembly of the developments of the HAB Programme as well as the decisions and Recommendations of the Third Session of the Panel. The occurrence of harmful algae was presented as a global problem which has serious economical and health impacts in many Member States. The HAB Programme Office needs additional staff to ensure continuity of Programme development and implementation. The HAB Training and Capacity Building Programme is proceeding well, but requires the persistent support of Member States. The formation of working groups on marine biotoxins, transfer of phytoplankton by ballast water of ships, and a regional HAB working group for South America, are recommended to facilitate scientific progress. The incorporation of HAB monitoring into national, regional and inter-regional GOOS activities is considered a priority.

168 The Chairman of the IOC-NOAA *ad hoc* Consultation on Marine Biodiversity, Prof. Ulf Lie (Norway), referred to Document IOC-XVIII/2 Annex 9, and presented the results and Recommendations of the Consultation (Paris, 3-5 May 1995), with respect to: (i) the requirement for a fundamentally different approach to studies of biological diversity in the marine environment than in the terrestrial one; (ii) the need to provide education at the community level on the value of marine biodiversity in sustainable utilization of marine resources; (iii) the importance of monitoring changes in marine biodiversity and ecosystem conditions; (iv) the need for advice on proper and relevant data management along with training programmes for development of national inventories; (v) the effects of possible exploitation of sea-bed resources on deep-sea biodiversity; (vi) the reduction of collections within museums and scientific institutions due to budgetary and staff shortages; (vii) the scarcity of experts on the taxonomy of marine organisms, particularly in developing countries, the necessity to upgrade taxonomic expertise and the need for para-taxonomists for the rapid assessment of biodiversity; (viii) the importance of the protection of species and habitats including an integrative perspective.

169 The Deputy-Secretary of the Secretariat to the Convention on Biological Diversity, Mr. Ahmed Djoghlaf, recalled the history of the Convention and its objectives, and referred to the medium-term programme of work for 1995-97 adopted by the Conference of the Parties to the Convention on Biological Diversity at its First Session (Nassau, Bahamas, 28 November-9 December 1994), which, *inter alia*, concerns the conservation and sustainable use of coastal and marine biological diversity. Reference was made to the First Meeting of the Subsidiary Body on Scientific, Technical and Technological Advice (SBSTTA) to the Conference of the Parties to the Convention, the Agenda of which includes an item dealing with scientific, technical and technological aspects of the conservation and sustainable use of coastal and marine biological diversity. He informed the Assembly that the meeting would take place at UNESCO Headquarters, 3-7 September 1995, and remarked that this has to be seen as a sign of co-operation between the Convention, UNESCO, and IOC. He referred to the IOC-NOAA *ad hoc* Consultation on Marine Biodiversity as a very important contribution of IOC to the activities of the Convention on Biological Diversity, and pointed out the existing basis for co-operation between the IOC and the Convention.

170 The Executive Secretary IOC introduced the GLOBEC item and referred to Resolution IOC-XVII-2, which endorsed IOC co-sponsorship of the GLOBEC Programme. He pointed out that IOC's role is to ensure intergovernmental linkages and that GLOBEC should be associated with other international research programmes.

171 **The Assembly responded strongly** to the issues with twenty-two Delegations providing comments regarding their interest and participation in OSLR activities.

172 **The Assembly noted** the need for a permanent Technical Secretary for OSLR, and the need for staff for the HAB Programme Office, and expressed its grave concern about the present situation as regards staffing.

173 **The Assembly noted with appreciation** the secondment by Denmark and Italy of Associate Experts for OSLR.

174 **The Assembly welcomed** the indication from the United States at the Seventeenth Session of the Assembly, that it would consider the partial financing of a permanent post as Technical Secretary for OSLR, and expressed its great appreciation that this had been fulfilled, and that funds had been made available to the IOC, but **noted with concern** that matching funds had not yet been identified.

175 **The Assembly noted** with regret the withdrawal of FAO as co-sponsor of OSLR, and stressed the importance of proper linkage between relevant IOC activities and the fisheries community, e.g. with respect to the further development of the Living Resource Module of GOOS.

176 **The Assembly urged** that negotiations be taken up at the appropriate level of UNESCO-IOC and FAO so as to ensure the basis for continued joint activity and co-operation.

177 **The Assembly commended** the IPHAB on its achievements, and the Secretariat on its fast development and co-ordinated implementation of the Programme with relatively few resources. The HAB Programme was referred to as a model for an inter-disciplinary programme combining research, monitoring, training, and policy aspects of a problem. Several Member States referred to their serious problems with harmful algae, and the establishment of national HAB groups.

178 **The Assembly stressed** the need to develop existing and new regional components of the HAB Programme.

179 **The Assembly noted with satisfaction** the opening of the IOC Science and Communication Centre on Harmful Algae at the University of Copenhagen, Denmark on 5 May 1995. The Centre is established for a five-year period, and has been made possible through a major contribution to the IOC Trust Fund by Denmark (DANIDA).

180 The Delegate of Spain informed the Assembly on the progress in establishing an IOC Science and Communication Centre on Harmful Algae at the Instituto Español de Oceanografía, Vigo, Spain, as offered by Spain at the Seventeenth Session of the Assembly. The Centre is expected to be established for the period 1996-2000 through a contribution to the IOC Trust Fund or another appropriate arrangement with IOC.

181 **The Assembly noted with satisfaction** the planned opening of the Centre in Vigo in 1996.

182 **The Assembly thanked** the United States for its offer to let the National HAB Office at the Woods Hole Oceanographic Institution serve the Programme.

183 **The Assembly took note** of the information that the Science and Communication Centres will, in particular, focus on the implementation of the HAB Training and Capacity Building Programme, and communication and information networks, and that activities of the Centres will be complementary and co-ordinated by IPHAB and the IOC Secretariat.

184 **The Assembly welcomed** the indication by Japan that it will provide additional resources to the IOC Trust Fund for HAB training activities in WESTPAC.

185 **The Assembly also welcomed** the indication from Italy that it will strengthen the activities of the IPHAB through the new Chairman of IPHAB, Dr. Adriana Zingone (Italy).

186 **The Assembly welcomed** the offer from Sweden and Chile to support the preparation and publication respectively of information leaflets on the HAB Programme.

187 **The Assembly stressed** the need to ensure appropriate co-ordination between HAB Programme activities on marine biotoxins, monitoring, and transfer by ballast water of ships, and the already identified activities on the same topics by the GIPME Groups of Experts and the Health of the Ocean Panel for GOOS.

188 The Representative of ICES confirmed the continued co-operation with IOC on addressing the important and urgent problems related to HAB, including the already existing ICES-IOC Working Group on the Dynamics of Harmful Algal Blooms. ICES appreciated the opportunity to participate in IPHAB-III. ICES welcomed the support of IOC and IMO in helping to ensure the success of a theme session on "Ballast water: ecological and fisheries implication" at the ICES 1995 Annual Science Conference, Aalborg, Denmark, September 1995. This event has attracted cutting-edge papers from all over the world. In this context the proposals contained in Recommendation IPHAB-III.3 on the formation of a new working group on ballast water with ICES and IMO co-sponsorship is both timely and appropriate. ICES will give this matter urgent consideration, should the working group be established.

189 **The Assembly adopted** Resolution XVIII-8.

190 **The Assembly noted** the importance for IOC to be associated with the Convention on Biological Diversity, in view of the scientific advice which IOC can provide to the Conference of the Parties to the Convention, through its SBSTTA.

191 **The Assembly took note** of the recommendations of the IOC-NOAA *ad hoc* Consultation on Marine Biodiversity, including the proposed establishment of a two years IOC Pilot Programme on Marine Biodiversity.

192 **The Assembly agreed** on the urgent need to identify parameters and development of methodologies for monitoring changes in marine biodiversity.

193 **The Assembly took note** of the information on the activities of the Expert-center for Taxonomic Identification (ETI) in Amsterdam, which was set-up by the Government of the Netherlands and the University of Amsterdam, with the assistance of UNESCO. ETI serves as a mechanism for compilation of taxonomy-oriented products as well as training activities, and is presently contributing to the IUBS-ICSU-IUMS Species 2000 Programme.

194 **The Assembly stressed** the importance of co-operation with UNEP and FAO for marine biodiversity, as well as the UNESCO Man and Biosphere Programme.

195 Several Delegations referred to national activities in the field of marine biodiversity and the importance of addressing marine biodiversity also from a deep-sea perspective. **The Assembly welcomed** the suggestion from the Russian Federation to establish a long-term deep-ocean international programme on the study of marine biodiversity in hydrothermal vents.

196 The Delegate of the Islamic Republic of Iran urged IOC to closely co-operate with the Convention on International Trade in Endangered Species of Wild Fauna and Flora (CITES), bearing in mind the Terms of Reference of CITES and the immense experience gained by this relevant body with regard to the protection of endangered species/creations, including marine biological resources. Such co-operation would enable IOC to fulfill its commitment more appropriately in this regard.

197 **The Assembly adopted** Resolution XVIII-9.

198 **The Assembly reiterated** the importance of GLOBEC and expressed strong support for continued IOC participation in its further development.

199 Several Delegations noted that GLOBEC is essential to supplement information gathered by other international research programmes, e.g. WOCE.

200 The Representative of ICES informed the Assembly that an ICES Project Office for the co-ordination of activities within the GLOBEC Cod and Climate Programme will be opened by the end of 1995. The Office will be sponsored by USA and Norway.

10.4 OCEAN SCIENCE IN RELATION TO NON-LIVING RESOURCES (OSNLR) INCLUDING THE CONFERENCE ON COASTAL CHANGE (BORDEAUX, 1995)

201 Dr. Claude Latouche, IOC Consultant for the programme Ocean Science in Relation to Non-Living Resources (OSNLR), introduced the agenda item, referring to IOC Workshop Report No. 105 and

Document IOC/INF-987. He presented the most important actions in OSNLR during the intersessional period. The Coastal Change Conference (Bordeaux, France, 6-10 February 1995) was organized following Resolution XVII-3 of the Assembly relative to the development of OSNLR. One of the major aims of the Conference within the framework of, and as a follow-up to UNCED, was to examine the nature, origin and impact - including socio-economic effects - of physical coastal changes and to facilitate effective communication between scientists and the user community. The Conference was jointly organized and supported by IOC and the Aquitaine Region (France) with additional support from SCOR and the EC. Support was given to a substantial number of participants from developing countries and Eastern European Member States. Over three hundred scientists and coastal zone managers from fifty countries and non-governmental organizations (NGOs) participated. Through ninety oral presentations, sixty posters and two days pre- and post conference field trips, the following questions were addressed: (i) what are the phenomena responsible for physical coastal changes? (ii) what are the socio-economic implications of changes? and (iii) how can science be used for integrated coastal zone management? Many papers documenting the threats currently facing the coastal zone highlighted the need to take an holistic approach when addressing problems of the coastal zone, with scientists working together with managers.

202 Proceedings for the Conference will be published very soon. One significant output is the agreement to use some of the selected case studies presented to produce a set of practical manuals that will facilitate the assessment of coastal changes and provide guidelines to coastal scientists on the ways in which they can effectively contribute to coastal zone management.

203 Referring to Document IOC/INF-991, Dr. Latouche explained that an *ad hoc* Consultation on OSNLR was organized during the Coastal Change Conference, 8 February 1995. The objective was to obtain ideas and advice on the future development of OSNLR, particularly in the context of the IOC follow-up to UNCED and a possible role in relation to UNCLOS. The *ad hoc* Consultation considered that OSNLR, particularly its coastal components, has a major role to play in this follow-up and, to this end, proposed various actions to be further developed.

204 Referring to Document IOC/INF-1007, Dr. Latouche recalled the IOC-OSNLR *ad hoc* Expert Consultation on UNCLOS (Paris, 20-21 March 1995), as part of IOC's short-term responsibilities in relation to UNCLOS, as well as to the request of the UN-DOALOS concerning IOC assistance to determine the limits of the continental shelf.

205 The Delegate of Canada recalled the International Conference "Coastal Zone Canada 94", held in Halifax, 20-23 September 1994. He informed the Assembly that a draft Conference Statement and Call for Action has now been prepared and a limited number of copies were available to delegates.

206 At the regional level, a great deal of action had been implemented within the framework of OSNLR, particularly its coastal components. Workshops on coastal erosion related to sea-level rise have been convened by IOCARIBE Sub-Commission, Martinique (November 1993), devoted to Small Islands (IOC Workshop Report No. 97); at Isla Margarita, Venezuela (May 1994) dedicated to the cartography of critical coastal areas. The WESTPAC Sub-Commission organized a workshop on Palaeogeographic Maps in Kuta, Bali, Indonesia, 20-21 November 1994 (IOC Workshop Report No.106). A workshop jointly supported by IOC, UNEP, WMO and SAREC was convened in Zanzibar, Tanzania, 17-21 January 1994 (IOC Workshop Report No. 96). A Symposium on Sedimentary Budgets along the coast of West Africa was held in Lagos, Nigeria, 17-20 May 1994 and a plan of action for the implementation of OSNLR was adopted at the Fourth IOCEA Session (Document IOCEA-IV/3S). In the south west Atlantic, the following OSNLR regional group activities have taken place: the organization of an oceanographic cruise, a training course and regional group meetings; development of co-operative studies on beach evolution; presentation of papers.

207 **The Assembly expressed** its appreciation of the development, and **stressed** the importance of the OSNLR Programme, particularly the follow-up to the Coastal Change Conference.

208 **The Assembly stressed** that the coastal zone is one of the major resources of the human environment. Its morphological characteristics have to be monitored and then protected taking into account the human factor and natural relationships of the coastal zone both with the open ocean and adjacent basins.

209 **The Assembly acknowledged** that, in the framework of IOC's follow-up to UNCED, the OSNLR Programme and relevant recent activities can provide the most appropriate scientific basis for research relative to coastal zone management.

210 **The Assembly adopted** the suggestions for improving the OSNLR Programme presented by the *ad hoc* consultation on OSNLR and **recommended** that, without neglecting the other components of the programme, a plan for a specific development of OSNLR in the framework of the global IOC Strategy relative to the Coastal Zone, be prepared by a small group of experts.

211 **The Assembly emphasized** that the necessary multidisciplinary approach requires the adoption of a precise methodology, as well as co-ordination between all the organizations and programmes participating in coastal zone management.

212 **The Assembly recommended** that, based on appropriate case studies, such as those presented at the Coastal Change Conference, guidelines and manuals on regional coastal zone management should be prepared within the framework of OSNLR. As a first attempt to this objective, a volume relative to the temperate zone will be made available by France at the end of 1995.

213 The delegate of Nigeria offered the use of the Nigerian research vessel for a second IOCEA cruise in the Gulf of Guinea to use acoustic methods to study sediment fluxes, and urged the Executive Secretary to ensure that the cruise be organized in 1996.

214 **The Assembly noted** that the Delegates of Argentina and Brazil specially requested a revision of the juridical basis of some parts of Document IOC/INF-1007 relative to UNCLOS. Their statements are included in Annex III-G.

10.5 OCEAN MAPPING

215 The item was introduced by Mr. Desmond P. D. Scott referring to document IOC/INF-899, Report of the Consultative Group on Ocean Mapping to the Eighteenth Session of the Assembly. He reviewed the state of development of the General Bathymetric Chart of the Ocean (GEBCO), the International Geological-Geophysical Atlases of the Atlantic and Pacific Oceans (GAPA) and the regional international bathymetric chart series. He informed the Assembly about the results of the Fifth Meeting of the Consultative Group on Ocean Mapping (CGOM), Bremerhaven, 24-25 April 1995 and the Joint IOC-IHO Guiding Committee for GEBCO, Monaco, 15-17 May 1995. He also drew attention to the close and mutually beneficial co-operation which obtained between IHO and IOC relevant to the Ocean Mapping Programme and related activities.

216 The Delegate of Italy expressed his thanks to Commander Desmond Scott for his enthusiastic and very efficient work for the oceanographic community. As a consequence, IOC regards IBCM as a model project whose importance is paramount to the earth's sciences. It was therefore decided to complete the information contained in the geological-geophysical data which constitutes the series, and to include the information of near or under-bottom characteristics, all together reducing the uncertainties inherent in one single parameter. Thanks is also expressed to Russian colleagues for the perfect technical presentations.

217 Sixteen delegations stressed the importance of the Ocean Mapping Programme and expressed gratitude to Mr. Scott, Chairman of the Consultative Group on Ocean Mapping, and Permanent Secretary GEBCO, for his input to the advancement of the Ocean Mapping Programme.

218 Mr. Scott thanked the delegates for the high appraisal of his activities and informed the Assembly of his intention to resign from the post of Permanent Secretary GEBCO at the end of this year. His replacement in this post, Mr. Brian Harper, formerly of the British Hydrographic Office, had already been nominated.

219 **The Assembly expressed** its strong satisfaction that the global programme of Ocean Mapping is developing very well and emphasized that it is the basis for many IOC projects and would be relevant to UNCLOS. **The Assembly welcomed** the digitization programme, and in particular, the issue of the GEBCO Digital Atlas on CD-ROM, and noted that it is indeed a revolution in bathymetry. The application of modern observational and analytical techniques was considered to be of great importance as these techniques can provide additional very valuable information to the scientific community.

220 **The Assembly decided** on the need to pursue the preparation of the regional bathymetric chart series and also noted the considerable progress made, particularly with regard to the International Bathymetric Chart of the Mediterranean and its Geological-Geophysical series, the International Bathymetric Charts of the Caribbean Sea and the Gulf of Mexico, and of the Central Eastern Atlantic.

221 Certain delegations emphasized that priority should be given to the work on the International Bathymetric Chart of the Western Pacific and requested the IOC Executive Secretary to find the necessary funds in order to organize the next Editorial Board Meeting for the above-mentioned project by 1996.

222 Several delegations informed the Assembly of their on-going national programmes contributing to Ocean Mapping.

223 Mr. Scott mentioned the centenary of the GEBCO project at the turn of the century (1999-2004) and reported on plans to publish a scientific report on the history of GEBCO, followed by a popular book to celebrate this event.

224 The Delegate of the Russian Federation confirmed financial support for a seconded staff member to the IOC Secretariat and, at the same time, requested the IOC Executive Secretary to ask the Director-General of UNESCO to establish a permanent professional post for Ocean Mapping. **The Assembly strongly endorsed** this proposal.

225 **The Assembly decided** that the Ocean Mapping Programme was one of the most successful projects of IOC and should be provided with the necessary support.

226 **The Assembly thanked** the Governments of Canada, the Russian Federation, UK, USA, and other countries for their permanent efforts to support ocean mapping activities.

227 **The Assembly took note** of the information provided in IOC Document IOC-XVIII/2 Appendix 1, on the financial requirements for a satisfactory implementation of the Ocean Mapping Programme, including the coverage of the IOC Consultative Group on Ocean Mapping activities and meetings of the Regional Editorial Board.

228 **The Assembly adopted** Resolution XVIII-10.

10.6 MARINE POLLUTION RESEARCH AND MONITORING (GIPME/MARPOLMON) AND RELATED PROGRAMMES

229 This agenda item was introduced by Dr. Neil Andersen, Chairman of the Committee for GIPME. He noted that the IOC Annual Report for 1994 described many of the recent accomplishments in this Programme. He made particular reference to the recently completed review of the Marine Environmental Studies Laboratory (MESL) of the Marine Environmental Laboratory (MEL) of the International Atomic Energy Agency (IAEA) in Monaco which was conducted in April of this year. This laboratory plays an integral part in the implementation of GIPME, particularly with regard to the preparation of manuals, standard reference materials and intercalibration activities. It was pointed out that the results of the review indicated that the quality of the work being conducted at the laboratory continues to be of a high-level and the importance to the GIPME Programme remains undiminished. However, this is not to say that there are no problems. Because of increasing budgetary restrictions being faced by just about every organization at this time, the IAEA has been forced to curtail resources at the Monaco facility that are identified with non-nuclear work. Additionally, there is a strong possibility that due to cutbacks in UNEP budgets in general, there will be a reduction in resources being provided to MESL. The review noted that if IOC could become a full partner in the umbrella project between the laboratory and UNEP, this would ease the problems considerably. The decentralization issue discussed under Agenda Item 7, which received no dissenting comments during the related debate, can also be expected to contribute to a solution of the problem.

230 Developments in the next phase of the Open Ocean Baseline Project, publications of JGOFS Protocols, implementation of the Time Series Programme in the Cariaco Trench jointly between Venezuela and the US, development of two brochures for the GIPME Programme, plans for the next steps to be taken with regard to finalizing the Strategic Plan for the Health of the Ocean Module for GOOS, and contributions to the ACOPS Conference on land-based sources of marine pollution, were all referred to as just completed or on-going activities. In concluding his introduction, Dr. Andersen referred to several on-going regional activities as examples of aspects of the Programme that, when taken together, comprise a portion of the global perspective on marine pollution being provided by GIPME.

231 Dr. Manfred Nauke of the IMO then added several comments from the perspective of his organization as to the importance of co-sponsoring the GIPME Programme. He referred to the important aspects of using the available GIPME mechanisms in implementing the conventions which are IMO's responsibility, namely, the London, MARPOL, and Oil Pollution Prevention and Preparedness Conventions. He further noted the important contributions being provided by GIPME to implementing UNDP-IMO-GEF Projects in the East Asian Seas Region concerned with baseline and monitoring studies and data management, as well as to GESAMP's work in generating the next version of the State of the Marine Environment. He pointed out that all IMO delegations were not totally informed of the important benefit to the IMO of the collaboration with IOC through GIPME. He expressed hope that the brochure that will be printed by IMO will help to resolve this issue but encouraged delegations present to bring the message home.

232 In noting that he had made an identical intervention at EC-XXVII, Dr. Mario Ruivo, Chairman of the IOC-UNEP Intergovernmental Panel, made an intervention for the specific purpose of pointing out that the Panel was not functioning. He strongly recommended that a substantive evaluation was needed and a decision made to either continue it, if it could function, or, if not, disband it.

233 Twelve delegations then made interventions. Strong support was given to continuation of the GIPME Programme. Many delegations described national activities which were viewed as contributions to GIPME and MARPOLMON. The work being conducted on developing the Health of the Ocean Module through GIPME was recognized as a very important development. In particular, the United Kingdom referred to the oil spill that occurred in their coastal waters several years ago, noting that two reports were available concerning a study and a legal investigation. The Ukraine Delegation considered GIPME to be one of the most important programmes of the IOC. The Delegation of Malaysia felt that GIPME was vital to the health of their maritime area. The Delegation of the Russian Federation pointed out the importance of the Programme in the context of its upcoming increasing oil and gas prospecting in the Barents and Black Seas. The Delegation of Japan took note, along with that of the Islamic Republic of Iran, of the work done in the Persian Gulf on the oil spill following the recent hostilities. The Delegate of Portugal noted its support for the Programme in general, and the annual work plan and, in particular, for collaboration with the Marine Environment Studies Laboratory (MESL), noting the importance of maintaining the state of the health of coastal areas and its management based on integrated studies. The Delegate of Portugal offered to host a GEEP Workshop in 1997. The Delegation of Canada, in stressing its support, in particular for the MESL contribution, voiced its agreement with Dr. Ruivo concerning the GIPME Panel to either have it function or disband it. The Delegations of Bulgaria, Greece, Pakistan, Thailand and the United States voiced their support for the Programme.

234 The Delegate of the Islamic Republic of Iran referred to the environmental problems of the Persian Gulf area, and noted that monitoring had been done some years ago and suggested that further investigations be made under the auspices of UNESCO and IOC, to study long-term aspects. He also pointed out the overlap of conferences on these matters in the Islamic Republic of Iran and Japan, and suggested that this should be avoided.

235 The Representative of the United Nations Industrial Development Organization (UNIDO), Dr. Chidi Ibe, informed the Assembly that UNIDO is the executing agency for a new UNDP-GEF initiative on Marine Environmental Management in the Gulf of Guinea on the Western African coast. It is a programme that has, as its foci, the prevention of coastal water pollution and conservation of biodiversity. The Programme receives technical backstopping and other in-kind contribution from the US Department of Commerce National Oceanic and Atmospheric Administration (NOAA) and has UNEP as an associated agency. The approaches used are based on the Large Marine Ecosystem concept of marine pollution and living resources management and are predicated on the conviction that the agents of marine pollution and living marine resources respect no jurisdictional boundaries and few geographic ones and so necessarily require large scale, concerted and holistic approaches for assessment and management. However, it was noted that to be successful, the concept of LME management must be coupled with the Management of Marine Catchment Basins (MCBs) which are defined as the areas adjacent to the LMEs from where much of the human impacts derive. This approach is analogous to the current global emphasis on understanding and controlling Land Based Sources (LBS) of marine pollution as a key to preventing the continued deterioration of the marine environment from pollution effects.

236 Given the limitations of the individual countries in the Gulf of Guinea and the magnitude of the problems of water pollution and biodiversity conservation, a regional approach is imperative and consists of five major elements:

(i) Strengthening of regional institutional capacities to prevent and remedy pollution;

(ii) Development of an integrated information management and decision-making support system;

(iii) Establishment of a national and regional, sustainable programme for co-ordinated monitoring and assessment of the changing state of health of the region's coastal ecosystem;

(iv) Prevention and control of land-based sources of marine pollution;

(v) Development of national and regional strategies and policies for the long-term management and protection of the Gulf of Guinea LME.

237 It is obvious that the IOC would be a natural partner in this project. As a result, and as the Co-ordinator of the programme and the Director of the Regional Co-ordination Centre based in Abidjan, Côte d'Ivoire, Dr. Ibe informed the meeting that he has initiated and would, while here in Paris continue discussions with the Executive Secretary IOC on ways and means of taking advantage of the expertise inherent in the programmes and activities of the IOC with a view to bringing to fruition the immediate and long-term objectives of the Gulf of Guinea LME Programme. Areas of envisaged co-operation would cut across programmes such as IODE, OSLR, TEMA but it was his expectation that the GIPME Programme, with its current emphasis on the development of a Health of the Ocean module of GOOS, would provide the umbrella for the envisaged co-operation. Through this association with the HOTO module of GOOS, the linkages between the LME approaches and the measurements of global scale ocean-wide processes to be collected under GOOS operations would be self-evident.

238 Dr. Ibe expressed the hope that the IOC Assembly would endorse the principle of co-operation that UNIDO seeks with the IOC, and emphasized that UNIDO does not seek in the context of this co-operation, to impose additional strain on the financial resources of the IOC but would, in fact, be willing and able to make available to IOC financial allocations for the tasks to be assigned to it, as UNIDO believes that this would be a most cost-effective approach to attaining the programme objectives.

239 Finally, Dr. James Readman of the MESL of the IAEA, took the floor and amplified on previous comments concerning data quality and compatibility. He pointed out that the assessment of environmental contamination invariably requires measurement (or monitoring) of the contaminants. It is upon these data that environmental managers base their decisions. If the analytical data is wrong then, in turn, the management actions will also be wrong. Hence it is critical that the analytical data is correct, and to ensure that this is the case, requires considerable effort. To produce good quality data the following are needed: well trained analysts; appropriate laboratory facilities and well maintained instruments; the use of proven analytical methods; calibration of instruments with high purity standards; testing of methodologies with "reference materials" containing known concentrations of pollutants; and, external testing of laboratory performance (through intercomparison exercises). He indicated that a system which incorporates all these components has been developed during the past decade at IAEA-MEL, the only marine laboratory within the UN system, which is generously hosted by the Government of the Principality of Monaco. Through a tripartite Memorandum of Understanding between IOC, IAEA and UNEP, these services are already incorporated within some IOC programmes. In addition, these agencies co-operate substantially within the GIPME Programme and the International Mussel Watch. However, to continue and to extend these non-nuclear activities which are outside the mandate of the IAEA, additional financial support is now needed.

240 In response to these interventions, the Executive Secretary of IOC noted that a GIPME Officers' Meeting, scheduled to meet right after the Assembly, would be able to take up many of the items referred to by the delegations. Dr. Andersen expressed his appreciation from both a programmatic as well as a personal view of the comments from the delegations. He noted that he looked forward to discussing the various points raised in more detail with the representatives over the next few days, for further preparation of the GIPME Officers' Meeting.

241 **The Assembly decided** that the GIPME Programme should continue to be strengthened at global level, that the co-operation with UNEP, IMO and IAEA should also be strengthened, that relevant use be made of the IAEA-MESL, and that the programme should monitor its regional presence through co-operation with relevant regional programmes, including with UNIDO in relation to the UNDP-GEF project on the Gulf of Guinea referred to above.

242 **The Assembly decided** that the IOC and UNEP Secretariats should consult together on the further existence of the Intergovernmental Panel and report to the GIPME Officers and the IOC Executive Council, at its next session.

243 **The Assembly expressed** its great appreciation to Dr. Andersen for his extensive efforts to develop GIPME.

11. OCEAN SERVICES

11.1 GLOBAL OCEAN OBSERVING SYSTEM AND RELATED ACTIVITIES

11.1.1 Second Session of the IOC-WMO-UNEP Committee for GOOS

244 Prof. M. Glass, Chairman of I-GOOS, first welcomed the re-instalment of South Africa in IOC and stressed the importance of the future role of this country for GOOS. He then described the evolution of GOOS during the intersessional period and stressed the fact that GOOS is now a well accepted concept and that countries now have a clearer view of its content. Some key committees are installed and working hard. Several national committees for GOOS were, or are in the process of being created.

245 He noticed however that much work remains to be done in order to achieve successful implementation. GOOS must ultimately provide relevant ocean products to wide categories of users. This means that the user market must be both identified and developed, to ensure that user needs are correctly met. Highly specialized studies on socio-economic benefits arising from GOOS can provide such assessments. Moreover GOOS must be treated as a complete system, including all the elements from observing systems, through data management to delivery of products. GOOS is such a large programme that immediate implementation is unrealistic, for financial, as well as for human resources reasons. Priorities must be set in its development. In this, context, he highlighted the fact that the regional development of GOOS such as EuroGOOS or NEAR-GOOS seemed most appropriate.

246 Prof. Glass described the internal structure of the GOOS organization as confirmed at the first Planning Session in Melbourne (1994), based on two Committees, the IOC-WMO-UNEP Committee for GOOS (I-GOOS) and the Joint Scientific and Technical Committee (J-GOOS) sponsored by IOC, WMO and ICSU. I-GOOS is assisted in its work by the Strategy Sub-Committee (SSC) whose composition includes experts, as well as representatives of important economic categories of users. The Implementation Panels of I-GOOS, have not yet been established due to the scarcity of funds. Most of the J-GOOS scientific panels are meeting at regular intervals, but are at different stages of scientific design of their respective observing systems. J-GOOS at its second session provided some recommendations endorsed by I-GOOS, in order to foster a balanced development of the system. The SSC held its First Session in Geneva in March 1995 and provided the outline of a strategic plan for GOOS implementation that was approved at the Second Session of I-GOOS held in Paris just prior to this Assembly.

247 Referring to the Executive Summary of I-GOOS-II, Document IOC-WMO-UNEP/I-GOOS-II/3S, Prof. Glass reported on the major issues addressed by the Committee and the Resolutions that it adopted:

(i) establishment of an *ad hoc* panel for the coastal module and an *ad hoc* working group for the marine and meteorological services;

(ii) establishment of a task team in order to define a GOOS Space Plan;

(iii) maintaining close co-operation with GCOS and nominate a rapporteur in order to strengthen the relationship with the Global Terrestrial Observing System (GTOS);

(iv) establishment of a steering group for identification of funding of a series of regional workshops, the regional approach being considered as the most appropriate for effective capacity building;

(v) use these regional workshops to conduct economical surveys on the applications of GOOS data products in developing countries and promote the conduct of more detailed case studies. An international workshop on methodologies co-sponsored by OECD is proposed. Take advantage of such studies undertaken by GCOS;

(vi) establishment of an *ad hoc* working group to identify priorities for GOOS, and organize a GOOS Priority Agreement meeting where commitments will be sought based on the initial Implementation Plan prepared by this group.

248 The Committee further recognized that a clear data policy is required, in the light of the decisions of the WMO Congress with regard to data exchange. A GOOS Handbook will be prepared. In conclusion, Prof. Glass stressed the crucial role played by the GOOS Support Office and the importance of permanent staffing and appropriate funding.

249 **The Assembly unanimously recognized and stressed** the importance of GOOS for all countries and the central role played by IOC, including through the GOOS Support Office. The views expressed by the participants reflected a wide variety of concerns among the Member States. The elements to implement and strengthen the development of GOOS are still in the initiation period. A general agreement on the importance of the coastal module was noticeable. Most of the countries have already implemented elements of observations on a local scale and are looking for clear guidance provided by GOOS on the ways to upgrade, standardize and integrate on-going programmes into a sustainable system. It is indeed the task of J-GOOS bodies to continuously evaluate the scientific adequacy of elements of existing programmes to be incorporated into GOOS, and to provide standards and methodology.

250 **The Assembly took note** with satisfaction of the secondment by France of an expert as Director a.i. for the GOOS support office, and **stressed** the need to strengthen the GOOS support office staffing.

251 **The Assembly also welcomed** the offer of Brazil to second an expert to the GOOS support office and the offer of the USA to support Dr. Neil Andersen, of the University of Maryland, following his retirement from the National Science Foundation, to assist IOC in the development and implementation of the Health of the Ocean module and related marine pollution research and monitoring activities.

252 **The Assembly stressed** the importance of capacity building in order to allow all developing countries to effectively participate in, and take advantage of GOOS. The use of regional workshops and socio-economic studies was highly supported, and the help of specialized experts in this domain highlighted. Malta proposed to host one of these workshops. **The Assembly emphasized** the importance of local and regional scales to address the implementation issues and the role of pilot projects to foster the interest of bordering countries. Several countries stated that some elements of operational systems should be implemented quickly to demonstrate the usefulness of GOOS. Prof. Glass mentioned that such initiatives may result from agreements of countries to co-operate on a specific regional project, or they can be conducted and co-ordinated through IOC regional bodies. In particular, China, Japan and the Republic of Korea asked the Assembly to support the NEAR-GOOS project. The IOC Executive Secretary mentioned that the related map included in Document IOC/INF-992 is incorrect and should be deleted. **The Assembly emphasized** that, at the national level, close co-ordination between different agencies or organizations is a prerequisite for the success of GOOS operations. This co-ordination can be achieved in various ways, including the establishment of GOOS National Committees, or by the creation of a GOOS Secretariat, such as in Germany, or through the National Committee for IOC, such as in Japan.

253 The Delegates of Greece, Israel and Italy pointed out that regional sub-programmes such as MedGOOS (Mediterranean GOOS) can provide good opportunities to carry out case studies, as well as to develop co-operation between developed and developing countries.

254 The Delegate of the United Kingdom stated that the three national agencies which are members of EuroGOOS are collaborating with fourteen other agencies from twelve different European countries to promote operational oceanographic projects within GOOS, and to perform pilot studies and test cases.

255 **The Assembly agreed** on the fact that in order to increase the interest of governments and facilitate funding of GOOS, some early and concrete results must be ensured and made rapidly available. The principle of organizing a priority identification meeting was therefore warmly welcomed.

256 The WMO representative expressed the same opinion and reported that the Twelfth Meteorological Congress had recognized the potential importance of GOOS and had therefore strongly supported the continued WMO co-sponsorship of, and contribution to GOOS implementation. He emphasized the importance of the finalization of the GOOS Strategic Plan. He noted further that the free and unrestricted exchange of required oceanographic data and products will be essential to GOOS and recommended that IOC consider mechanisms to address this question.

257 **The Assembly adopted** Resolution IOC-XVIII-11.

258 **The Assembly also adopted** Resolution XVIII-12 on the "International Coral Reef Initiative", regarding the development of the Global Coral Reef Monitoring Network.

11.1.2 Global Climate Observing System (GCOS)

259 Dr. T. Spence, Director of the GCOS Joint Planning Office, reported on the progress in the development of GCOS.

260 GCOS was one of the principal topics of the Intergovernmental Meeting on the World Climate Programme (Geneva, April 1993) and it is one of the four main thrusts of the WCP recommended by the IGM-WCP.

261 The Joint Scientific and Technical Committee for GCOS, jointly sponsored by WMO, IOC, UNEP and ICSU, has identified scientific priorities regarding the observations of GCOS in particular: (i) observations needed for seasonal and inter-annual prediction; (ii) observations required for detection of climate change and the attribution of the causes of such changes at the earliest possible time. GCOS would provide essential information in support of the IPCC, elements of Agenda 21, and requirements of the United Nations Framework Convention on Climate Change. The Joint Scientific and Technical Committee established several scientific design panels to address atmospheric, oceanic, terrestrial observations, and cross-cutting panels to address data and information management and space-based observations to develop specific plans for action.

262 The Joint Scientific and Technical Committee has prepared and published an overall plan for GCOS as well as plans for data and information management and space-based observations.

263 The Twelfth WMO Congress decided that the GCOS should be continued as an essential activity in support of the WCP and other climate-related intergovernmental activities. The Congress also recognized with appreciation the inter-agency co-operation in the process of planning and developing GCOS and, in particular, in developing a close partnership between GCOS, GOOS and GTOS.

264 Many countries have established GCOS national committees which, in several cases, deal both with GCOS and GOOS.

265 GOOS and GCOS share a common ocean climate module. The Joint Scientific and Technical Committee for GCOS received the draft OOSDP report and endorsed its publication as the scientific design for the ocean climate requirement. He emphasized the need for continued support from the sponsoring agencies, which is particularly required for the common module.

266 The Assembly recognized the role of the IOC in the development of a comprehensive climate observing system by supporting the implementation of the GOOS climate module. The delegates expressed their strong support for GOOS and, in particular, its close interaction with GCOS.

267 The Assembly decided that IOC should continue its co-sponsorship of the development of GCOS.

268 Many delegations pointed to the need for an integrated approach to the observing systems, linking in particular GOOS and GCOS.

269 The Assembly wished to encourage the Executive Secretary IOC and the GOOS bodies to continue close collaboration with the Joint Scientific and Technical Committee for GCOS, and the GCOS Planning Office, particularly in planning and developing a common climate module of GOOS as well as other common interest needs, including data policy and management; socio-economic studies; preparation of useful products and satellite-related issues.

270 The Assembly instructed the Executive Secretary IOC to continue providing support for GCOS development in accordance with the Memorandum of Understanding (MOU) on GCOS.

11.1.3 Global Sea-Level Observing System (GLOSS)

271 Dr. D. Pugh, Chairman of the IOC Group of Experts on GLOSS, presented a report on progress on the implementation of GLOSS and the outcome of the Fourth session of the Group, Bordeaux, 31 January-3 February 1995. The report of the Fourth Session of the IOC Group of Experts on GLOSS was available to the participants.

272 As an example of the operation of GLOSS, he noted that Georgia had supplied more than 200 years of previously unavailable data at this Session of the Assembly. Dr. Pugh highlighted the scientific aspects of the GLOSS network strategy and application of GLOSS data.

273 The meeting of the GLOSS Group of Experts had been preceded by the IOC/GLOSS-IAPSO Scientific Workshop on Sea-Level Variability and Southern Ocean Dynamics, which provided a stimulating scientific introduction to the GLOSS session. A special scientific session on sea-level changes and coastal impacts was held during the BORDOMER Conference after GLOSS-IV (6-10 February 1995) with the participation of GLOSS experts; GLOSS maintains contacts with IAPSO and the IPCC. The Chairman of the Group of Experts had also provided a briefing on sea-level observations at the Twelfth Session of the INC-FCCC.

274 The GLOSS strategy, as proposed by the Group of Experts includes the integration of GLOSS tide gauges and satellite altimetry for monitoring global and regional sea-level variability, and connection of selected GLOSS Tide-Gauge Bench Marks to a global geodetic reference system, with the use of the Global Positioning System (GPS). Close contacts have been established and maintained with the scientific operational communities dealing with GPS, particularly with the International GPS Service (IGS). Information dissemination on GLOSS through the World Wide Web started in 1995.

275 Applications of GLOSS data include preparation and wide distribution of sea-level products and data/information services as shown in the annex to the report of the Fourth Session of the GLOSS Group of Experts. Regional co-operation in establishing sea-level networks and producing sea-level products is strongly encouraged. In this connection the attention of the Assembly was brought to the Afro-American GLOSS News produced by Brazil, as a good example of promoting GLOSS co-operation.

276 The Group of Experts gave special consideration to TEMA-related activities, and encouraged real partnership among countries, as well as the use of extra-budgetary funds, particularly from GEF, to cover demands for training and technical assistance, to augment the limited resources available at IOC.

277 Dr. Pugh invited the Assembly to endorse the recommendations of the Group and the Plan of Action for 1995-1997 proposed by the Group (as shown in Annex VI of the report).

278 Dr. A. Tolkatchev informed the participants of the development of the Pilot Activity on Sea-Level Changes and Associated Coastal Impacts in the Indian Ocean with the active participation of India, Kenya,

Tanzania, Mozambique, Madagascar, Seychelles, Maldives, Bangladesh and Malaysia and recently jointed by Sri Lanka. Within the framework of this project a Training Workshop on Sea- Level Analysis is being organized by IOC in collaboration with India to be held in Dehra Dun, India, from 21 November to 1 December 1995.

279 **The Assembly expressed** strong support for the development of GLOSS, and emphasized the need for the continued and strengthened support of this IOC activity.

280 **The Assembly noted** that I-GOOS at its Second Session received the report of the Chairman of the IOC Group of Experts on GLOSS and **requested** the J-GOOS to study those GLOSS elements and activities which are relevant to GOOS.

281 Many delegates noted that GLOSS can be considered as an important building block of GOOS. **The Assembly invited** the IOC Group of Experts on GLOSS to work together with I-GOOS and J-GOOS in identifying those elements of GLOSS that will be part of GOOS, particularly in developing GOOS Climate and Coastal Modules.

282 In discussing GLOSS **the Assembly emphasized** the following points:

(i) the importance of GLOSS for regional and national research, and practical applications;

(ii) the readiness of countries to provide sea-level data for international exchange;

(iii) the importance of integration of *in situ* data with satellite altimetry data for monitoring and assessment of global and regional sea-level variability and changes;

(iv) the importance of the development of regional components of GLOSS such as the Mediterranean Sea-level Regional Network (MED-GLOSS) and EuroGLOSS;

(v) the need for training in the field of sea-level analysis with the use of GLOSS station data and satellite altimetry information for regional and local sea-level studies and the need for free access to the satellite altimetry data;

283 **The Assembly endorsed** the GLOSS strategy as proposed by the IOC Group of Experts on GLOSS aimed at integrating *in situ* measurements at GLOSS stations with satellite altimetry and geodesy, and preparing the global and regional sea-level products required for monitoring and assessment of global changes, as well as for regional research and practical applications.

284 **The Assembly urged** Member States to consider their possible support and assistance (either through IOC or bilateral agreements) in the provision and installation of tide-gauges in the GLOSS sites of Sierra Leone and Côte D'Ivoire (available in Germany and donated by Sweden), and the Pacific Coast of Russia which has been destroyed during the recent tsunami events, and which is of great importance to the tsunami warning system for the country and the Pacific Ocean region.

285 The Delegate of Nigeria thanked the Governments of the United States of America and Sweden for providing sea-level equipment and training. He offered the assistance of Nigerian experts in the installation of three other analogue tide-gauges in other countries of the region.

286 **The Assembly urged** Member States to work together with assistance from the IOC Secretariat and the Group of Experts in preparing and submitting proposals to the Global Environmental Facility (GEF) and other potential funding agencies for assistance in establishing and up-grading GLOSS stations and related training activities.

287 **The Assembly adopted** Resolution XVIII-13.

11.1.4 Integrated Global Ocean Services System (IGOSS)

288 The Chairman of the IOC-WMO Joint Committee for IGOSS, Dr. D. Kohnke, presented recent activities of the IGOSS programme. The Chairman introduced and explained the structure of the proposed

Ship-of-Opportunity Programme (SOOP), and the proposal for IGOSS to assume co-ordination of that programme (SOOP) as it evolves into an operational component of the Global Ocean Observing System (GOOS).

289 The goal of the end-to-end management proposal is to provide operational measurements of temperature and salinity, to be performed with Expendable Bathythermographs (XBT), thermo-salinographs, and hull-mounted thermistors. The OOSDP report emphasized the value for global climatic studies to measure the upper ocean thermal heat content using ship-of-opportunities and maintaining the existing programme.

290 An IGOSS Operations Management Committee (IOMC) will have the responsibility of overseeing resource allocation and determining operational sampling strategies, with guidance from the research community. The SOOP Implementation Panel (SOOPIP) will include the IGOSS Operations Co-ordinator and national SOOP managers. SOOPIP will execute decisions and directions given by the IOMC.

291 I-GOOS-II, June 1995, endorsed the IGOSS proposal and requested IGOSS to begin its implementation.

292 The Chairman reported on other intersessional IGOSS activities, including:

(i) The publishing of the full scientific paper on revised fall-rate equations by members of the Task Team on Quality Control of Automated Systems (TT/QCAS) in IOC Technical Series. A short form of the paper will be published in the Journal of Deep-Sea Research.

(ii) The implementation of the new BATHY Code in November 1995.

(iii) The continued support of the IGOSS Products Bulletin (IPB) by Canada, Germany and the USA, and the creation of an electronic version of the IPB on the World Wide Web (WWW).

(iv) The preparation of the IGOSS Plan and Implementation Programme (PIP) for the period 1996-2003. The PIP will be reviewed at IGOSS-VII in November 1995 and the results presented to the IOC Executive Council in 1996.

293 **The Assembly expressed** its thanks to the Chairman for his presentation and the continued support for IGOSS. IGOSS is one of several foundations for GOOS and continued close interaction is needed between IGOSS and GOOS. Members noted with appreciation that IGOSS and the other Ocean Services discussed under item 11 have been very responsive to GOOS. It was suggested that IGOSS consider ways to synthesize more products to be used in promoting the programme.

294 **The Assembly expressed** its thanks for continued publication of the IGOSS Products Bulletin, and **stressed** that the IPB is a useful resource for many countries in soliciting funding for national observing programmes.

295 The Representative of WMO reminded the Assembly of the joint sponsorship of IGOSS by WMO and IOC, and considered IGOSS essential to the acquisition of upper ocean thermal data for use in climate prediction and analyses. The IGOSS-IODE Data Management Plan may well serve as a model for data management within GOOS. Likewise, GTSPP is another jointly-sponsored programme that ensures high quality data and timely delivery of thermal and salinity observations.

296 The Representative stressed that IGOSS and other ocean services and GOOS are seen to be forming working relationships naturally and should not be forced or hurried. WMO will continue to support operational oceanography for climate and weather prediction.

297 **The Assembly took note** of these points.

11.1.5 Data Buoy Co-operation Panel (DBCP)

298 This agenda item was presented by the Secretariat on behalf of the Panel's chairman, Mr. D. Painting, the United Kingdom Meteorological Office, who was unable to attend the session. **The Assembly**

recalled that the Panel, established jointly by WMO and IOC in 1985, had been in existence for more than ten years, and had benefitted from the services of a Technical Co-ordinator funded through voluntary contributions from its Member States for more than seven years. **The Assembly noted** the following main achievements of the Panel:

(i) the improvement and final definition of a code form for transmission of buoy data over the WMO Global Telecommunication System (GTS), as well as various improvements in telecommunication procedures;

(ii) the definition, partial funding and running of a new Argos processing sub-system to allow flexibility in transmitting buoy data over the GTS;

(iii) the definition and implementation of a set of procedures for controlling the quality of buoy data forwarded over the GTS;

(iv) collaboration with the WOCE Surface Velocity Programme (SVP) in designing, on the basis of the SVP drifter, and testing a low-cost lagrangian drifter equipped with a barometer (SVP-B drifter);

(v) the support and/or establishment of various "action groups", such as: the European Group on Ocean Stations (EGOS); the International Arctic Buoy Programme (IABP); the International Programme for Antarctic Buoys (IPAB); and the International South Atlantic Buoy Programme (ISABP). The latter was established by the Panel at the request, and with the assistance of GCOS within two years time and is being made up of more than 70 drifting buoys in an ocean area previously considered as "data-sparse".

299 The Panel is now focusing on specific tasks which come out of present international activities regarding the study and monitoring of the marine environment. These tasks include: (i) the establishment of a closer connection with the scientific community, through, *inter alia*, the incorporation of scientific and/or technical presentations at future Panel sessions; (ii) collaboration with existing groups involved in data buoy technical development; (iii) developing mechanisms for collaboration in planning buoy deployment strategies; (iv) initiating the establishment of new action groups to deal with data-sparse areas of the ocean (e.g. the Indian Ocean).

300 **The Assembly decided** that the Panel was playing an important role in the development of operational oceanography, as part of those existing systems and/or bodies that work well and are ready to contribute to the setting up of GOOS. **It commended** the Panel upon its achievements so far **and agreed** that they depended very much on the availability of a Technical Co-ordinator. **It therefore urged** as many Member States as possible to contribute to the funding of the Panel, on the rationale that, whereas only a handful of countries are contributing to the Panel fund, all countries benefit from the global effect of obtaining and exchanging more and better data from the world ocean.

301 **The Assembly specifically highlighted** the Panel's actions with regard to data quality control, to co-operation between the scientific and the "operational" communities and to the establishment of action groups. In so doing, it **recognized** within several interventions a request for an action group for the Indian Ocean **and expressed satisfaction** to the fact the Panel was already aware of the problem and trying to solve it.

11.1.6 Satellite Remote Sensing and Relation to CEOS

302 The Executive Secretary IOC introduced the agenda item noting that remote sensing activities were umbrella activities of the IOC covering GOOS as well as other IOC programmes. It included aircraft and land based radars in addition to remote sensing from space and data management is an integral component. The objectives of the programme are to provide for the widest possible access to and exchange of satellite data within the ocean community including in developing countries and to bring those needs to the attention of the satellite agencies through the Committee on Earth Observing Satellites (CEOS) as well as other organizations. To meet these objectives IOC addressed the areas of sensor requirements, data requirements and capacity building toward sustainable development. CEOS provided a vehicle to address all of these requirements in co-operation with the space agencies. CMM, IGOSS and IODE had joined together to form the sub-group on Oceanic Satellites and Remote Sensing to provide a focal point within their organizations as well as GOOS to address remote sensing issues. Data Management was seen as a key area of activity for IOC and GOOS within the context of CEOS. IOC is working in co-operation with the space agencies as well as other IOC programmes to develop pilot projects leading to satellite products of interest to the ocean community. Capacity building and access to satellite data for developing countries is a key IOC remote sensing activity.

303 **The Assembly welcomed** the report and expressed strong support for the remote sensing activities of the IOC.

304 **The Assembly emphasized** the need to implement remote sensing projects in conjunction with and through the IOC regional bodies. High priority was given to continued co-operation with CEOS as well as WMO and GCOS especially in the development and promotion of ocean remote sensing requirements.

305 **The Assembly endorsed** the development of pilot projects to improve access to and exchange of satellite as well as other remotely sensed data.

306 **The Assembly stressed** that the role of IOC should also include the establishment of a dialogue with developing countries on these matters so the needs of these countries can be addressed with the full participation of these Member States. The IOC regional subsidiary bodies are relevant mechanisms.

11.1.7 Global Terrestrial Observing System (GTOS)

307 Dr. J. Withrow, the IOC Senior Assistant Secretary charged with GTOS co-ordination, introduced the agenda item, noting that GTOS is in the early stages of development and the relations with other global observing systems are just starting. One of the main objectives of GTOS of interest to the ocean community is the detection and understanding of natural and anthropogenic impacts on terrestrial, freshwater and estuarine ecosystems; the quantification and mapping of such changes at all scales; and the assessment of the consequences of such changes for land use, biodiversity, biogeochemistry and climate change. IOC has ongoing work in these areas and has already made progress in the context of marine pollution research and monitoring, providing inputs for management in co-operation with UNEP and IAEA and in biodiversity. Proposals are now being studied on how GTOS and GOOS could interface in the coastal zone and how the freshwater, estuarine and terrestrial strategies of GTOS could be integrated. IOC also has linkages with WMO is this area.

308 The IOC places great importance on the harmonization of environmental data especially at the land-ocean interface. IOC's International Oceanographic Data and Information Exchange (IODE) programme is addressing the related issues in the context of IGBP and the coastal module of the Global Ocean Observing System (GOOS). The recent meeting of the I-GOOS noted the importance of the development of LOICZ of IGBP in coastal zone activities. IOC has established formal co-operation with IGBP of LOICZ and see this as an essential first step. I-GOOS decided to nominate a rapporteur to maintain close ties with GTOS and respond as necessary to co-operation requirements.

309 **The Assembly emphasized** the importance of the coastal zone module of GOOS. The coastal zone is also of great interest to GTOS and represents an interface between GOOS and GTOS. In the light of the limited resources available for work in the coastal zone, **the Assembly directed** the Secretariat to co-ordinate closely with GTOS to avoid duplication and make the best use of the limited resources.

11.2 INTERNATIONAL OCEANOGRAPHIC DATA AND INFORMATION EXCHANGE (IODE) AND RELATED ACTIVITIES

11.2.1 Data Management

310 Dr. J.R. Wilson, Chairman of the Committee on IODE, introduced this agenda item. He referred to the very active programme carried out by IODE over the past two and a half years. In particular, progress has been made in the implementation of GTSPP and GODAR projects, and in Marine Information Management and capacity building activities.

311 In evaluating how the IODE programme might be made more effective, a "Think Tank" meeting was held in Paris in March 1995. The meeting was attended by 20 participants primarily from international organizations and programmes dealing with ocean data and information, and the client programmes of IODE. This meeting concluded:

(i) that IODE should broaden its expertise and services by working directly with the scientists and programmes that collect data types that are not now handled routinely by IODE;

(ii) that IODE data centres should enter into partnerships with marine agencies, universities, and other organizations collecting marine data in order to counteract diminishing resources available for managing data in many member states;

(iii) IODE should take full advantages of the CD-ROM and Internet technologies to increase the range of products and services provided to client programmes;

(iv) IODE should use the opportunity that has been presented by the new electronic publishing technology to improve its capacity building programme based on Ocean-PC, CD-ROM publication, Internet and a comprehensive training programme.

312 A few delegates informed the Assembly on national activities, and of the assistance provided by IOC in programme implementation; such as Malta - Training Course on the Use of Personal Computers in Data and Information Management for Countries in the Mediterranean Region and the GODAR-IV workshop; UK UK-EDMED development and CD-ROMs with JGOFS and North Sea project data; Iran - IOC feasibility mission and national training course; Japan - annual training courses in data management; China - regional training course on ASFA and MIM.

313 The Delegate of the Islamic Republic of Iran requested that, pursuant to training courses and other actions of IOC to support the establishment of the Iranian NODC, which is also vital for IOCINDIO, IOC-UNESCO should provide further help to the center to complete previous actions.

314 **The Assembly expressed** its gratitude to the Chairman of the IOC Committee on IODE and Members of the Secretariat for their efforts in making the programme successful and **requested** the Executive Secretary to secure the necessary funds for programme implementation and developing country assistance in hardware and software acquisition for oceanographic data and information management, and also **urged** Member States to provide further contributions to IODE.

315 **The Assembly expressed** its appreciation for the development of the GODAR project, noting the publication of the World Ocean Atlas '94 set of CD-ROMs, **thanked** the US Government, CEC, ICSU, ICES and IOC Member States for providing support to the project, and **requested** the Executive Secretary and IODE Chairman to continue their support to the project and to enhance co-operation with other international organizations in implementing this important activity.

316 **The Assembly commended** the programme for the achievements in TEMA and capacity building as well as for the results of the Think Tank meeting which marked a very special landmark in the history of programme development by identifying new challenges in oceanographic data and information handling in the next century. **The Assembly encouraged** continued efforts in arranging training courses and workshops, especially on Ocean-PC, GODAR and general issues related to oceanographic data and information management.

317 **The Assembly noted** with satisfaction that, during the intersessional period, the IODE programme had been active and progressive, especially in adopting new technologies for oceanographic data and information management and exchange, including multimedia technology, electronic mail arrangements, CD-ROM.

318 **The Assembly expressed** satisfaction with the efforts of some Member States in the declassification of their naval data for international exchange. In this regard, information on the plans of the Russian Navy to transfer, to the international domain, not less than 100,000 BT observations and 4,000 hydrological stations in 1995/96 was especially acknowledged.

319 **The Assembly**, in spite of a certain positive trend, **expressed** its concern with regard to the long delays in acquiring data from scientists. **The Assembly called** for increased partnerships with scientific institutions and users. It was also noted with regret that a significant number of countries still does not actively participate in data exchange and **the Assembly requested** the IODE National Coordinators to more actively promote the IODE programme.

320 **The Assembly underscored** the importance of IODE as a partner in the implementation of GOOS, **called** on IODE to assist GOOS in the development of a data and information plan, and **advised** the IODE Chairman to prepare a report for the coming session of IODE on the coordinated IODE-GOOS data policy issue.

321 **The Assembly expressed** satisfaction with the production and beneficial co-operation between IOC and ICES under the IODE programme. A few joint activities have been noted such as Ocean-PC, GODAR, RNODC-Formats. The establishment by ICES of a WWW server to promote the objectives of IODE **was acknowledged by the Assembly. The Assembly directed** more attention to standardization of methods of data exchange and to Quality Control procedures.

322 The Delegate of the WMO informed the Assembly of the status of data policy discussion taking place at the WMO Congress. **The Assembly noted** with interest the information presented and directed the IODE Chairman and IOC Executive Secretary to monitor development.

323 **The Assembly expressed** its appreciation for the report provided by Greece on the preparations being made for the Fifteenth Session of the IOC Committee on IODE, which will be held in Athens, Greece, 23-31 January 1996, co-sponsored by CEC-MAST and the Government of Greece in addition to IOC.

11.2.2 Global Temperature-Salinity Pilot Project (GTSPP)

324 The GTSPP has continued to develop its programme. The real time data flow is working very well with data being distributed to client programmes on the Internet three times per week. It is now accepted that GTSPP has resulted in a 30% increase in the capture of real-time data. Scientific quality control is being standardized with the participation of the WOCE Upper Ocean Thermal Programme Centres. This will provide a more complete and effective quality control for all temperature-salinity data once these procedures have been fully implemented.

325 The flow of delayed mode data into the GTSPP data base needs to be improved however. Only 50% of the 1990 data has been submitted and 25% of the 1993 data. This is a general problem in other areas of the IODE programme as well. Member States are requested to encourage and assist their scientists to submit their data in a more timely manner.

326 The GODAR project has been so successful that it will most likely increase the amount of temperature and salinity data in the global databases by a factor of three. A major task for GTSPP in the future will be to pass all of these data through GTSPP quality control procedures and enter it into the GTSPP continuously managed database.

327 Marine information aspects of the GTSPP programme include the publication of the GTSPP CD-ROM and the GTSPP Home Page on the World Wide Web. These projects have been carried out in co-operation with the IODE GE-MIM. The GTSPP CD-ROM includes both data and information. For example, the CD-ROM includes every document, publications and data product prepared by GTSPP. This provides a very effective method to deliver the information component of GTSPP along with the data. This will improve the availability of information and therefore the capacity building aspect of the IODE programme. In working with WOCE and other global programmes, IODE is strongly encouraging and assisting with similar merging of information and data to provide for the wide circulation of information, as well as data in developed and developing countries.

328 **The Assembly expressed** its satisfaction with the efforts made by IGOSS and IODE in the development of the GTSPP CD-ROM. MEDS of Canada was especially **commended** for its contribution to and its leading role in this project.

329 **The Assembly recommended** that training courses and workshops should include GTSPP material.

11.2.3 Marine Information Management

330 The Chairman of the IOC Committee on IODE, Dr. R. Wilson, introduced the agenda item.

331 Despite a chronic shortage of funds and lack of staff, thanks to great efforts made by the Group of Experts on MIM, the programme was able to achieve a good implementation rate of its Action Plan, agreed upon during its Fourth Session in October 1993. The Chairman highlighted the development of the "MIM Publication Series" which was very well received by information managers worldwide, as well as the publication of the "IOC Titles and Acronyms", the revitalization of the MEDI catalogue, the development of a Global Directory of Institutions and Scientists, and the development of standards for directories and bibliographies, the latter in co-operation with the ASFA Advisory Board.

332 An IOC FTP file server has been installed on the UNESCO Internet server in order to provide Member States with direct and immediate access to IOC Publications and other relevant documents. The server is intended to complement the IOC Publication services providing a tool to better reach the marine science community. Software developed within the framework of IOC programme activities will also be available through this server, as well as the MEDI catalogue.

333 In response to Resolution XVII-7, the IOC Secretariat participated in inter-Secretariat consultations on the future of ASFA. This resulted in the negotiation of a new publishing contract with the publisher of ASFA and of a new partnership agreement with the ASFA partners. The role of the UN co-sponsoring partners has effectively been redefined to focus on capacity building to enable developing countries to actively participate in ASFA as input centres. As a follow-up to the GE-MIM action plan and as an ASFA activity supported by the ASFA Trust Fund, a user-friendly input and output interface was developed for the use and preparation of ASFA input by ASFA partners, and also by marine information centres for the management of libraries and information centres.

334 At the regional level reference was made to the RECOSCIX-WIO Project (Regional Co-operation in Scientific Information Exchange in the Western Indian Ocean) which has now come to maturity.

335 **The Assembly stressed** the importance of documentation and information as essential tools in scientific research and **expressed** strong concern about its continuing unavailability in developing countries. Libraries and information centres in developing countries are unable to expand or maintain their collections and have no access to on-line or other information servers. This undermines efforts in TEMA and capacity building and **the Assembly urged** the IODE Committee to discuss this issue during its upcoming session and identify appropriate solutions at the regional and global levels.

336 **The Assembly noted** that, unless developing countries have access to advanced electronic communication technology, there is little chance that they can actively and effectively participate in global scientific programmes. **The Assembly recommended** that concerted actions be taken to overcome this problem.

337 Thanks to support from the United States in 1994, it was made possible to provide electronic mailboxes to several institutions in the IOCINCWIO region. The support has been extended to 1995.

91 **The Assembly commended** the Government of Belgium for its support of the RECOSCIX-WIO project between 1992 and 1995 and **expressed** the hope that the support would be continued as the project provides a unique opportunity to ensure efficient links between data and information. During IOCINCWIO-III, the Member States in the region decided to expand the terms of reference of the project to include data management.

338 **The Assembly noted** with satisfaction the development of the RECOSCIX-CEA project for the IOCEA region, requested the Executive Secretary IOC to support the project, and invited Member States to contribute towards its development.

339 The Delegate from Kenya, referring to the success of the RECOSCIX-WIO project, welcomed the development of similar networks in other regions and volunteered the know-how gained during the development of RECOSCIX-WIO.

340 The Delegate from Portugal stressed the need for information and documentation as essential tools in the furthering of scientific research. Noting their continuing lack in developing countries, he called on Member States to assist in providing these tools. In this respect, he repeated the offer made by Portugal during IOCEA-III to assist in the production and publication of a regional IOCEA newsletter. **The Assembly took note** of the offer with appreciation.

341 **The Assembly noted** with appreciation the announced development of the IOC WWW Home Page which will function as a central information point for users interested in IOC's activities and will include jumps to Member States Home Pages if available, thereby emphasizing the partnership philosophy of the IOC programmes. The plan to release a CD-ROM complementary to the WWW Home Page for those who do not have access to the Internet at this time was **supported** and **endorsed**.

342 **The Assembly expressed** thanks to the Director-General of UNESCO for the creation and recruitment in May 1995 of the professional post for Marine Information Management, announced during the Twenty-seventh Session of the IOC Executive Council.

343 **The Assembly noted** with satisfaction the readiness of China to provide facilities for future training courses on ASFA and Marine Information Management.

344 **The Assembly took note** of language problems faced by some Member States in the effective use of IODE products and **urged** the Committee on IODE to discuss this issue and to consider assistance for the translation of documents in order to provide effective services to the local community.

11.3 INTERNATIONAL TSUNAMI WARNING SYSTEM IN THE PACIFIC AND RELATED ACTIVITIES

345 Mr. H. Gorziglia, Chairman of ICG/ITSU, introduced this item. He referred to the objectives and functions of the Group and summarized the results of activities undertaken by the Member States of the Pacific in the implementation of the decisions of the Fourteenth Session of the ICG/ITSU which took place in the fall of 1993 in Tokyo, Japan.

346 He highlighted the increasing tsunami generating seismic activity which have been experienced during the last two years by the Pacific countries which cost thousands of lives and caused great damage to property in the coastal tsunami-prone areas. He informed the Assembly of the progress made by the ICG/ITSU in mitigating natural disasters: the TIME Project is being successfully implemented due to support provided by Japan and the USA; the Earthquake and Tsunami Risk Evaluation System TREMORS was developed by France and the Group recommended that it should be widely used; an Expert Tsunami Database for the Pacific was developed by Russia; textbooks on earthquakes and tsunamis for kindergartens, schools and colleges have been prepared, published and widely distributed in Spanish by Chile. An English version in camera-ready form is also available for publication thanks to the support from Canada. Mr. Gorziglia pointed out that all these and many other activities fully correspond to the main principle of the Yokohama (1994) Conference Strategy to give the highest priority to natural disaster prevention measures.

347 He then drew the attention of the Assembly to the financial problems, noting that in spite of a decision of the Session of the IOC Governing Bodies which gave the highest priority to the Programme, the funds available to implement the Programme are very limited and support is provided by only a few countries from the Pacific region. He identified two ways to increase support to the Programme: (i) Member States should increase direct and in-kind support to the Programme by providing more economic, scientific and human resources; (ii) the Executive Secretary IOC should convey to the Director-General of UNESCO the unique status of the Tsunami Programme as the only operational natural disaster warning system fully meeting the objectives of IDNDR. Mr. Gorziglia appealed to Member States to take the opportunity of the coming session of the UNESCO General Conference to be held in the fall of this year, to emphasize the importance of this Programme and to request the Conference to secure the necessary funds in order to make the Programme successful.

348 Finally, Mr. Gorziglia thanked the Government of France for the facilities provided for the Fifteen Session of the ICG/ITSU which will take place in Tahiti, French Polynesia, 25-28 July of this year and invited all Member States to participate in the Session.

349 **The Assembly congratulated** the Chairman of the ICG/ITSU for the successful management of the Programme and **noted** that Tsunami presents a real and increasing danger because of the dramatic increase of the population in the coastal areas.

350 **The Assembly considered** the Programme as one of the most effective activities of the IOC providing practical results, and **expressed** satisfaction of its successful implementation.

351 **The Assembly noted** the progress in increasing awareness of the population of the danger of tsunamis through drilling exercises, video films, publication of brochures, posters and textbooks. **The Assembly requested** the continuation and intensification of ICG/ITSU.

352 The achievements of the programme in real-time operational work and tsunami data collection and exchange have been specially noted and it was **recommended** to consider wider usage of high technology for communicating warning messages to remote tsunami-prone areas.

353 **The Assembly expressed** its appreciation to the USA for hosting PTWC and ITIC which showed its effectiveness during the devastating earthquakes and tsunami which struck Japan, Russia, and Indonesia during the past few years, and to Mexico for responding favourably to numerous requests of the IOC Governing Bodies to provide staff for the post of Associate Director of ITIC.

354 **The Assembly considered** it important that more action be taken by national authorities responsible for tsunami services to meet new and increasing requirements for a reliable and effective warning system. The activities of Canada, Chile, Colombia, Japan, Peru, in this regard were noted with satisfaction. **The Assembly was concerned** with the information provided by the Delegate of the Russian Federation on the destruction of the tide gauges on Kuril Islands caused by the tsunami of October 1994. **The Assembly agreed** that this may have a negative consequence on the effectiveness of the tsunami warning regional system in the north Pacific and **invited** the Executive Secretary IOC and Member States to consider ways to support Russia in reconstructing the warning system in the tsunami affected area. Taking into account the importance of keeping the international community informed of the effects of the 1994 tsunami, **the Assembly requested** the Executive Secretary IOC to consider support for the publication of the Report of the International Group which visited the affected area immediately after the tsunami occurred.

355 **The Assembly noted** that an intersectorial project on natural disaster reduction was not included in the UNESCO Fourth Medium-Term Plan and **requested** the Executive Secretary IOC and the Chairman IOC to confirm efforts to make the tsunami programme the basis for future UNESCO interdisciplinary co-operation of UNESCO environment programmes in response to IDNDR.

356 **The Assembly took note** of the problems in the development of the Tsunami Warning System for the South-west Pacific and **recommended** that the project proposal should be redefined and implemented. Member States were requested to support the project through the UNDP National Representatives.

357 **The Assembly expressed** its thanks to the Government of France for hosting the Fifteenth Session of the ICG/ITSU and to the Government of Peru for offering facilities for the Sixteenth Session in 1997.

358 Dr. Oliounine, Senior Assistant Secretary IOC, informed the Assembly of recent developments in establishing a co-operative project on storm surge mitigation jointly with WMO and UNESCO-IOC. The WMO Workshop on Storm Surges for the Bay of Bengal, was held in Bangkok, Thailand, 14-19 November 1994, with the participation of IOC, and the common interest of hydrologists, meteorologists and oceanographers in this natural disasters phenomena were noted. A strong request was expressed to bring the knowledge and resources of different international agencies together in order to develop a joint project. Dr. Oliounine emphasized that in order to develop reliable forecasting systems for tropical cyclone storm surges there is a need for both atmospheric and oceanographic data. He then referred to the decision of the WMO Congress taken at its Twelfth Session (30 May - 21 June 1995, Geneva, Switzerland) to support "*the establishment of a storm surge project particularly for the Bay of Bengal and the Northern*

part of the Indian Ocean, with the joint co-operation of WMO, IOC, UNESCO and UNEP". He stressed that if this position of WMO is supported it will fully correspond to the recommendations of UNCED on the sustainable development and co-operation between the international organizations and to the principles of the Yokohama Strategy documents and objectives of IDNDR.

359 Several Delegates (Australia, China, India, Philippines, Thailand) expressed strong support to the actions taken by the Executive Secretary IOC in bringing the storm surges mitigation issue in the frontline of IOC activities, noting that coastal floods associated with storms surges constitutes the world's foremost natural disaster, surpassing many others for loss of life and property damage. Although in some countries there is a notable progress in the development of models for storm surges predictions, there is a need for data to verify these models.

360 **The Assembly emphasized** that this project, if implemented, will meet the needs and desires of the Member States in saving life and property.

361 **The Assembly instructed** the Executive Secretary IOC to convey to other agencies the readiness of IOC to co-operate in the development of the project and to take the necessary actions to establish operational mechanisms of co-operation with WMO, UNESCO, and UNEP in developing a storm surges project.

362 **The Assembly recalled** the plans under the GLOSS programme to have a training workshop on Sea-Level Analysis in India in November this year. **The Assembly recommended** the study of the possibilities to use this opportunity to hold a meeting of the joint IOC-WMO-UNESCO-UNEP Group of Experts which will start the development of the project.

363 **The Assembly noted and reiterated** support to the decisions of the IOC Executive Council taken at its Twenty-fifth Session (para.156) that "*projects related to storm-surge mitigation... should not be initiated within the framework of the IOC tsunami programme*".

364 **The Assembly requested** the Executive Secretary IOC to identify resources to support the project.

12. CAPACITY BUILDING IN MARINE SCIENCES, SERVICES AND OBSERVATIONS - TEMA

365 The Chairman of the TEMA Committee, Professor Michel Vigneaux, introduced the agenda item referring to the Summary Report of the TEMA Strategy *ad hoc* Meeting (Document IOC/INF-999), as well as the Draft TEMA Strategy in Response to UNCLOS and UNCED (Document IOC-XVIII/2 Annex 6). The Chairman developed the concept of a new strategy for capacity building/TEMA emphasizing the need for a pragmatic approach: multidisciplinarity, co-ordination, continuity of efforts, awareness, close North-South and South-South partnership, and a continued and close relationship with political and socio-economic spheres would be essential. The most productive way to apply this approach is through regional and sub-regional networks. In this context, integrated coastal area management and environmental risks constitute priority issues. The same considerations should be applied, in developing close co-operation with relevant UNESCO programmes, particularly the Coastal and Small Islands Multidisciplinary Project.

366 During the discussion that followed, twenty-five Member States and one Organization (CPPS), participated.

367 **The Assembly considered** and **appreciated** the report submitted by Dr. S. M. Haq, "Observations and Experiences of Selected TEMA Activities During 1984-94" (IOC-XVIII/Inf.2), as a valuable input for future analysis of capacity building/TEMA.

368 **The Assembly concurred** with the importance of incorporating aspects related to public awareness, and **encouraged** teaching of marine sciences starting at the primary and secondary levels. The Delegation of Chile gave a copy of an atlas to the Secretariat.

369 **The Assembly supported** the fact that training activities should keep continuity and increase regionalization and decentralization, the latter to permit closer association with Member States' priorities and therefore harmonize national and regional interests.

370 **The Assembly acknowledged** with satisfaction the increased co-operation between developing countries in marine science. **The Assembly**, to reinforce this tendency, **emphasized** the need to further strengthen human resources, also at the technical level, in order to ensure correct maintenance and running of equipment, sampling and laboratory procedures. The delegation of Kenya recommended, in the framework of biodiversity studies, the need of para-taxonomists as a crucial matter calling for training.

371 **The Assembly recalled** the need for easy access to new pedagogic materials, as well as new means of disseminating information. It **emphasized** the use of networks as a special mechanism to perform this.

372 **The Assembly decided** to submit selected TEMA topics related to the Convention, to the Intersessional Working Group on the Possible IOC Role in Relation to UNCLOS.

373 **The Assembly accepted** the Recommendation to incorporate the Floating University project as a TEMA component of IOC through co-ordinated efforts with the TREDMAR Programme.

374 **The Assembly adopted** Resolution XVIII-14.

375 **The Assembly concurred** with the fact that integrated coastal area management is a priority issue for developing Member States as regards TEMA.

376 Germany offered the possibility of high level courses using the services of German professors, as well as grants for students and researchers in developing countries in need of specific training requirements, to be combined with possibilities through bilateral arrangements. Germany actually has developed a co-operative project for the Red Sea in which Egypt, Israel and Palestine participate. IOC was called to play a catalytic role, to facilitate co-ordination and interaction among the partners concerned. The TEMA Group of Experts for Capacity Building can play a significant role in this co-ordination. Germany also proposed that at each IOC Assembly a "Dr. Panikkar Lecture" be established honoring the former Chairman of IOC, to address capacity building in marine science issues at regional and/or national levels. India gratefully acknowledged the initiative of Germany, and offered the facilities of the National Institute of Oceanography and the newly established National Institute of Marine Technology, Madras, for training activities particularly in the IOCINDIO region.

377 Iran offered facilities for training in the framework of the Caspian Sea activities, should IOC-UNESCO agree to allocate sufficient resources to implement the programme decided upon by the IAEA-IOC-UNESCO Workshop in May 1995.

378 The Delegate of Nigeria made a renewed pledge to accommodate two scientists from the IOCEA region for two months, for training on coastal and marine dynamics.

379 **The Assembly endorsed** the new strategy proposed for Capacity Building/TEMA to be further developed by the TEMA Group of Experts for Capacity Building, its first session to be scheduled for the first half of 1996. Portugal and the Netherlands kindly offered to host this meeting.

380 **The Assembly also endorsed** the plan to hold the Dr. Panikkar Lecture at each Assembly.

381 In order to properly plan and organize all these activities, the **Assembly emphasized** the urgent need to strengthen in a sizeable manner the Capacity Building/TEMA Programme in the IOC Secretariat.

382 **The Assembly endorsed** the Summary Report of the TEMA Strategy *ad hoc* Meeting (Document IOC/INF-999), as well as the Draft TEMA Strategy in Response to UNCLOS and UNCED (Document IOC-XVIII/2 Annex 6).

383 **The Assembly adopted** Resolution XVIII-15.

13. REGIONAL SUBSIDIARY BODIES

384 The Executive Secretary IOC made an overall introduction referring to Document IOC-XVIII/2.

13.1 IOCARIBE, INCLUDING EVALUATION

385 This agenda item was introduced by the Vice-Chairman of IOCARIBE, Dr. Guillermo Garcia Montero, who apologized for the absence of the Chairman, Dr. Hernan Perez-Nieto. His report referred to the Annotated Agenda (IOC-XVIII/2 para. 165-169, pages 36-37), IOC Annual Report for 1994 (pages 44-46) and Document IOC/INF-993: Interim Report on IOCARIBE Evaluation, and briefly summarized recent IOCARIBE activities.

386 He also announced the coming events in the region, in particular the next IOCARIBE Session in Barbados, 11-15 December 1995, and the Seminar on Small Island Developing States to take place immediately before (8-9 December 1995). It is intended that related results obtained in the region will be discussed with a view to formulating a regional Integrated Coastal Zone Management Programme. He also mentioned the Fourth Workshop on Marine Debris to be held in the Dominican Republic, 21-24 August 1995.

387 After the return of Dr. Fernando Robles to Paris, Dr. Fred Berry was seconded by the USA to work as Acting Secretary for IOCARIBE. He carried out most of the 1994 work reported in the annual report. Among relevant activities there is the Workshop on Small Island Oceanography, Martinique, of which the Proceedings will be published as soon as they are edited by Dr. G. Maul. Despite the constraints in the Secretariat after return of F. Robles and F. Berry, many projects are still being carried out, as clearly shown in the Annual Report for 1994.

388 IOC Consultant and Acting Secretary for IOCARIBE, Mr. Rafael Steer-Ruiz, presented the Interim Progress Report on the IOCARIBE evaluation, (Document IOC/INF-993). He recalled that this evaluation was being carried out following the decision of the Twenty-seventh Session of the Executive Council. It provides Member States in the region with the information required to take decisions as to the future strategies of the Sub-Commission as well as regional co-operation. This is also a positive and constructive evaluation, which seeks to learn from past errors so as not to repeat them. Mr. Steer-Ruiz described how IOCARIBE had passed through two evolutions since its inception with the approval of the IOC Assembly in 1975, demonstrating its adaptability to changing circumstances. Feed-back and advice are expected from this Assembly on the Evaluation report.

389 The IOC Consultant explained that the methodological approach for the evaluation consists of five main components:

(i) regional programmes and their impact in the region;
(ii) Member States' participation and commitment;
(iii) Secretariat, including the Cartagena-Paris relationship;
(iv) management structure and interactions among these elements within the Sub-Commission;
(v) regional scenario and IOCARIBE's relations with other organizations.

390 He presented the preliminary results as described in document IOC/INF-993 and explained that it refers to the first three components mentioned above. The next phase in the upcoming months will enlarge them and incorporate others.

391 The Delegate from Colombia congratulated the Secretariat on Document IOC/INF-993, noting that it would benefit the region. He stressed the fact that IOCARIBE had served the region in providing a forum for training, research and exchange of information. He informed the Assembly that negotiations had been initiated to increase the Colombian contribution to the Secretariat headquarters.

392 The Delegate from Canada stressed the importance of the evaluation and advised the Secretariat to focus on programme activities when preparing for SC-IOCARIBE-V. Member States must feel that they are not only a part of IOCARIBE but a partner and owner as well. He declared that Canada was aware of the growth in institutional building and horizontal networking taking place in the region (13 UN family programmes and nine regional programmes), and suggested that IOCARIBE should take care of

vertical networking. IOCARIBE should work towards greater political and management visibility/structure within these countries and to participate in decision-making. He also stressed the need for a greater involvement of the private sector, to stimulate the contribution of financial resources. Concern was expressed over the lack of accounting expertise in the Secretariat. This should be resolved in order to attract donor support. He informed the Assembly of the upcoming Workshop of donor agencies interested in marine affairs, being organized by Canada/CIDA and IOC.

393 The Delegate of the USA recalled his country's secondment of Dr. Fred Berry to the IOCARIBE Secretariat. He informed the Assembly that Southeast Fisheries Centre (SEFC) funded the Highly Migratory & Straddling Species Workshop in Miami, March 1995. SC-IOCARIBE-V will be crucial to demonstrate the need for a permanent IOCARIBE and presence of a staffed secretariat in the region, which the USA fully supports. He also urged Member States to take responsibility for securing funds for IOCARIBE activities.

394 The Delegate of Cuba stressed the need for a critical review, aimed at learning from past experiences, in the evaluation of the Sub-Commission.

395 **The Assembly approved** the progress report, **decided** that the evaluation should be reported to the Twenty-ninth Session of the Executive Council after having been reviewed by IOCARIBE-V and **thanked** Colombia, France, Sweden, the USA, and donor agencies for contributing to the IOCARIBE Secretariat and its activities.

The Assembly adopted Resolution XVIII-16.

13.2 WESTPAC

396 Prof. Su Jilan, Chairman of the IOC Sub-Commission for WESTPAC, introduced the agenda item referring to Document IOC/EC-XXVII/6 and the IOC Annual Report 1994, emphasizing the implementation of WESTPAC programmes during the last intersessional period. The successful organization of the Third IOC/WESTPAC Scientific Symposium, 22-26 November 1994 attracted more that 200 scientists from both inside and outside the WESTPAC region. Special attention was given to integrated coastal zone management, which aimed at increasing interaction between marine scientists and coastal zone managers.

397 He informed the Assembly that the office of the IOC Regional Secretariat for WESTPAC had been officially inaugurated on 29 November 1994, at the facilities provided by the National Research Council of Thailand (NRCT). The Chairman also informed the Assembly briefly on the development of a regional GOOS component in the region, the NEAR-GOOS, as a model project to give effect to operational oceanography and contribute to daily mapping of the ocean condition of the region, which would be expanded eventually to the whole WESTPAC region.

398 **The Assembly expressed** sincere thanks to the Government of Thailand for hosting the IOC/WESTPAC Regional Secretariat in Bangkok, and for providing support to the office.

399 **The Assembly also expressed** its appreciation to the Government of Indonesia for its generous support to host the Third IOC/WESTPAC Scientific Symposium.

400 **The Assembly expressed** satisfaction on the establishment of the Regional Secretariat for WESTPAC, and stressed that the office should play an important role in co-ordinating the implementation of the WESTPAC programmes and projects, in ocean sciences and services, through increasing co-operation with other organizations in the region.

401 With regard to the staff situation in the Regional Secretariat, many delegates indicated the urgent need to establish a senior professional post for the Director of the Regional Secretariat for WESTPAC, either by UNESCO or through secondment by Member States, to ensure effective operation of the office.

402 **The Assembly noted** that most activities identified by the last WESTPAC Session as the intersessional work programme, had been satisfactorily carried out. However, it was also recognized that a review of existing projects is urgently needed for WESTPAC Member States in order to evaluate the need for continuation of the existing projects and the initiation and concentration on certain priority projects, such as NEAR-GOOS.

403 The Delegate of Japan informed the Assembly that his government will make further efforts to second a Japanese expert to the office of the Regional Secretariat and increase the extra-budgetary contribution to WESTPAC in the form of UNESCO Funds-in-Trust, with emphasis on supporting training activity on HAB, and relevant activities in NEAR-GOOS.

404 The Delegate of the United States of America informed the Assembly that his government will continue to provide staffing support for the Regional Secretariat. However, he indicated the need for UNESCO to create a post, so that the contribution from his government could be used for project implementation.

405 The Delegate of France confirmed the intention of France to second one staff member to the Regional Secretariat, taking into account the appropriate actions that have been taken by the IOC in strengthening the regional approaches.

406 The Delegate of Canada informed the Assembly that his country intended to work towards co-ordinating more of its bilateral regional activities with the WESTPAC-related programmes and liaise more closely with WESTPAC.

407 **The Assembly expressed** appreciation to the Governments of Japan, the United States of America and France for their contribution to WESTPAC activities through the secondment of professional staff to the Regional Secretariat and the increase in financial contributions.

408 **The Assembly urged** the Executive Secretary IOC to negotiate with the Director-General to establish a UNESCO post in the IOC Regional Secretariat for WESTPAC as soon as possible.

409 **The Assembly welcomed** the generous offer of the Government of Japan, and **decided** that the Third Session of the IOC Sub-Commission for the Western Pacific will be organized in Tokyo, Japan, 26 February-1 March 1996.

13.3 IOCINCWIO

410 Dr. E. Okemwa, Vice-Chairman of the IOC Regional Committee for the Co-operative Investigation in the North and Central Western Indian Ocean (IOCINCWIO) introduced this item.

411 During the Third Session of IOCINCWIO in 1992, an extensive Implementation Plan of 29 actions to be completed between 1993 and 1995 was agreed upon. Thanks to funding from several donors including Belgium, Germany, Sweden, the United States of America and others, more than 20 actions have been implemented so far.

412 Referring to the Annual Report 1994, Dr. Okemwa proceeded to sum up the activities undertaken in which 84 scientists from the region participated. An additional twelve individual travel grants were provided to enable scientists to participate in international conferences and workshops.

413 Special attention was drawn to the further strengthening of the Western Indian Ocean Marine Sciences Association (WIOMSA). A total of twelve Marine Research Grants were allocated for 1995 of which six have been attributed already.

414 Attention was further drawn to the active role played by the RECOSCIX-WIO project in exchange and dissemination of information, the recent addition of data in RECOSCIX-WIO scope, and the development of a regional e-mail network. The Vice-Chairman concluded by welcoming South Africa as a new member of IOCINCWIO, expressing the hope that their participation would strengthen marine science capabilities in the region.

415 **The Assembly expressed** great satisfaction with these developments **and called** on Member States to actively support the further development and maintenance of the RECOSCIX-WIO network.

416 The Delegate of Pakistan expressed his satisfaction with the extensive achievements in the IOCINCWIO region in terms of human capacity building, but pointed out that national infrastructure was still poorly developed. He called on donors to assist Member States in the region in this respect and highlighted equipment, equipment maintenance and literature as priorities. He also pointed out that capacities available in the neighboring IOCINDIO region might be available for collaboration with IOCINCWIO.

417 The Delegate of the Russian Federation stressed the importance of the northern part of the IOCINCWIO region in relation to ocean-atmosphere interactions and climate investigations. The Delegate regretted that his country has scaled down its activities with countries of the region for economic reasons, but nevertheless expressed his country's intention to co-operate as much as possible.

418 The Delegate of the United States of America announced the planned organization of a Workshop on Marine Mammals, Coral Reefs and Sea Turtles, to be organized jointly between the New England Aquarium and IOMAC, and of a workshop to be organized by the International Coral Reef Initiative, both of which will be hosted by Kenya. The Executive Secretary IOC informed the Assembly that IOC had been invited to be associated with the former workshop.

419 The Delegate of Madagascar informed the Assembly that in the past, Madagascar had serious difficulties in terms of communication which had hampered its participation in IOCINCWIO activities, but reported that measures were now being taken to solve these problems. The Delegate submitted Madagascar's invitation to host the Fourth Session of IOCINCWIO. **The Assembly thanked** the Government of Madagascar and **accepted** its kind offer to host the Fourth Session of IOCINCWIO, which will be held in September 1996.

13.4 IOCINDIO

420 The Executive Secretary IOC introduced this Agenda Item, referring to documents IOC-XVIII/2 and the IOC Annual Report 1994.

421 He briefed the Assembly on several activities that are going on in the region related to JGOFS, WOCE, coral reef and marine conservation programmes. He pointed out that these activities need to be considered in the context of IOCINDIO and should be carried out in co-operation and co-ordination with IOCINCWIO. He also recalled several activities undertaken by IOC in the region (see Annual Report 1994).

422 He referred to the offer made by the Government of India, to host the Second Session of the IOCINDIO Regional Committee, in Madras, India, in the first quarter of 1996, and stated that the necessary financial arrangement were being made for this purpose.

423 He recalled that the First Session of the Regional Committee was held in 1988, and that it was high time to set the programme in focus and identify priority activities, so as to give impetus to the development of the Committee.

424 **The Assembly was glad to note** the progress made during the intersessional period, particularly the news of the Second Session of the Committee, as a sign of revival of this Regional Committee. **The Assembly hoped** that more actions would be taken to further accelerate the development of the Committee.

425 The Delegate of India confirmed his Government's offer to host the Second Session of the Regional Committee for IOCINDIO in early 1996, and expressed his welcome to countries wishing to participate in the meeting. **The Assembly welcomed** this offer with appreciation.

426 At the Sixteenth Session of the IOC Assembly, Dr. Quraishee, Chairman of IOCINDIO, pointed to a matter in connection with IOCINDIO's activities, and stated that, for different reasons and difficulties, IOCINDIO had been unable to fulfil its duties and to be active as was expected. The Delegation of the Islamic Republic of Iran confirmed this statement based upon their experience gained within the past four years. It would seem that the situation remains unchanged and the problems unsolved. Despite the interest of the IOC Secretariat as well as the willingness of the region's related oceanographic institutes, there has been no success in revitalizing IOCINDIO. The Delegation of the Islamic Republic of Iran requested the IOC Secretariat to take the necessary measures to activate IOCINDIO. Should any major obstacles arise, the Delegation recommended that the IOC Secretariat resolve the problems with the assistance of the governments of the region and UNESCO, and that the IOC Secretariat would keep the governments of the region informed of its actions.

13.5 IOCEA

427 The Chairman of the IOC Regional Committee for the Central Eastern Atlantic (IOCEA), Dr. N'diaga Gueye, informed the Assembly of the main results and decisions of the Regional Committee's Fourth Session and its Recommendation (Documents IOCEA-IV/3S and IOCEA-IV/3S Add.). He expressed his appreciation of the efforts made by IOC to ensure good participation of the countries of the region, and drew the attention of the Assembly to the limited participation of IOCEA countries in the present Session, which is certainly not the result of weak interest on their part, but due to their limited financial resources. He emphasized the need for a particular effort in training and capacity building, mentioning in particular the need for the development of university level courses in marine research in the region.

428 He thanked France for its offer to make available the expertise of ORSTOM for the development of a regional electronic network of communication.

429 The Delegate of Portugal reiterated the offer made by his country to hold a workshop for the development of a regional cephalopodes project, and to contribute to the development of the regional network for exchange of information. In particular, this would be by publishing, on an experimental basis, a regional newsletter as a complement to the IMS Newsletter, and by facilitating information transfer and resource-sharing with the support of the Division of Information and Documentation of the Portuguese Institute of Marine Research (IPMAR-DID).

430 The Delegate of France confirmed the availability of the facilities and expertise of ORSTOM for the development of the regional electronic network of communication, and recommended that the FAO should be associated with the regional project on cephalopodes and the workshop to be held in Portugal.

431 The Delegate of Germany drew the attention of the Assembly to the initiative for co-operation in the Southeastern Atlantic, particularly in the Benguela upwelling ecosystem, which has many similarities with the Northwest African upwelling system. There are good reasons to apply similar methods and approaches to the study of both regions. He added that in a recent workshop held in Namibia, and co-sponsored by IOC, a proposal was elaborated which called for major co-operation in the study of the Benguela current system, focussing especially on fisheries resources in relation to the environment, and to involve Angola, Namibia and South Africa, together with support from European countries.

The Delegate of Nigeria recalled the First Workshop on Marine Debris/Waste Management for the Gulf of Guinea, held at the Nigerian Institute for Oceanography and Marine Research, Lagos, December 1994, and expressed support for the implementation of the resulting Marine Debris/Waste Management Action Plan for the Gulf of Guinea.

432 The Delegate of Morocco strongly supported the recommendation of the Session of the Regional Committee, at which his country could not officially be represented. He informed the Assembly of the organization of the international workshop, to be held in October in Rabat, entitled "Space Oceanography, Climate and Marine Resources in Northwest Africa". Regarding the budget project for the region, he stressed the inadequacy of the allocation proposed (US $100,000), in view of the importance of the IOCEA region.

433 The Delegate of Ukraine expressed the strong interest of Ukrainian scientists in IOCEA activities, mentioning the realization of a geophysical atlas covering part of region, and hoped that co-operation would continue with the COMARAF projects.

434 **The Assembly agreed** with the proposal made by several delegations for the broadening of the geographical area of IOCEA in order to encompass Namibia and South Africa.

435 **The Assembly accepted** the Summary of Proceedings and Recommendation IOCEA-IV/3S.

13.6 COLLABORATION WITH ROPME AND PERSGA

436 The Executive Secretary IOC introduced the item, referring to the Annual Report 1994 and Document IOC-XVIII/2. He recalled extensive co-operation with ROPME in relation to marine pollution research and monitoring, including the organization of several cruises and the planning of an international conference to review the results, in the Islamic Republic of Iran towards the end of 1995.

437 He informed the Assembly of the planned workshop on the Red Sea and the Gulf of Aden region on the establishment of a regional research and monitoring programme related to problems associated with coastal zones and land-based activities influencing the marine environment, rescheduled now for October 1995. This workshop is a co-operative effort with UNEP, PERSGA, IUCN and ACOPS. The results will be presented to the Sea-to-Sea Conference in Saudi Arabia, October 1995.

438 The Delegate of Israel expressed interest in, and support for the development of an IOC programme for the Red Sea, without any institutional developments and open to participation of all interested parties.

439 The Delegate of Japan informed the Assembly of several oceanographic cruises which his country had carried out in co-operation with ROPME and IOC, and the convening of an international symposium to evaluate the results in Tokyo, 8-11 December 1995.

440 The Delegate of Canada recalled the R/V MOUNT MITCHELL cruise and its follow-up, and considered these actions as very good examples of what the IOC could do. He wished to see their fruitful continuation.

441 **The Assembly expressed** satisfaction with the development and **requested** the Executive Secretary IOC to continue efforts to develop co-operative oceanographic work in these regions in coordination with the relevant regional and other organizations.

13.7 MEDITERRANEAN

442 Mr. Gualter Soares, IOC Senior Assistant Secretary, introduced this item. He informed the Assembly of the progress achieved on the major activities supported by IOC and developed in co-operation with ICSEM, and on important initiatives of a regional character which IOC is following with great interest.

443 With regard to PRIMO (The International Research Programme in the Western Mediterranean), following the strategic lines established in the preparatory meetings at the end of the sixties, PRIMO focused its attention on straits and passages of the Western Mediterranean Sea. Straits and passages are to be considered as crucial places where it is possible to observe the time-scales of the circulation and those where experimental results can be directly compared with the response of numerical models.

444 In the last two years, 1993 to 1995, the activities of PRIMO mostly concerned the Central Mediterranean region, between Sicily, Sardinia and Tunisia. The Sicily Strait and the Sardinia Channel and the Sicily-Sardinia sections were monitored by current-meters and specific oceanographic campaigns carried out in close collaboration with Italian, French, Spanish and Tunisian teams. The results were exciting, mostly because they concern an area which, despite its importance for the understanding of the dynamics of the whole Mediterranean Sea, is one of the least known of the basin.

445 Within the framework of POEM-BC (Physical, Chemical and Biological Oceanography of the Eastern Mediterranean) work continued in 1993-1995 on intercalibration and analysis of the data collected during the multi-ship multidisciplinary survey of the eastern Mediterranean which was carried out in 1991, as well as on planning of the Levantine Intermediate Water Experiment. In addition, in the winter and spring of 1995, POEM-BC conducted a multiship study on the formation and dispersion of the Levantine Intermediate Waters. The experiment involved research vessels from Germany, Turkey, Greece, Italy and Israel and also US AXBT flights. In July 1995, a POEM-BC Steering Committee will take place to review the results of this study and to plan the final phase of the programme.

446 Regarding the programme on insular coastal dynamics (a regional OSNLR component) which, to some degree, is being implemented in Malta through the Euro-Mediterranean Centre on Insular Dynamics), consultations were held with the Chairman of the Group of Experts, Prof. Busuttil, who accepted to continue to make the necessary efforts for its effective regional development.

447 Co-operation with ICSEM has been pursued and the possibility of increasing co-operation was examined during consultations held with the ICSEM Executive Director. IOC participated in the last Congress of ICSEM held in Malta, March 1995.

448 ICSEM and IOC are interested in a proposal for developing an automated marine information system, using remote sensing data coupled with *in situ* data.

449 Co-operation with the UNEP Mediterranean Action Plan is continuing on marine pollution research and monitoring, with particular emphasis on modelling, and biogeochemical cycles studies. The recent Contracting Parties meeting in Barcelona, 5-8 June 1995, recommended to the coastal states of the Mediterranean to endeavour to participate in GOOS regional programmes. It also included, in the priorities of their action plans for the next decade, the assessment and control of marine and coastal litter which is an activity also co-ordinated by IOC.

450 Regarding GLOSS activities, the establishment of a regional operational sea-level network as a regional Mediterranean component of GLOSS was proposed at an informal meeting during the present Session.

451 IOC is considering and carefully following the development of the three following regional initiatives: (i) The "UNESCO Mediterranean Programme"; (ii) the Conference MED 21 held in Tunis in November 1994; and (iii) the new European Union initiative for Multilateral Science, Technology and Co-operation between the European Union and Southern and Eastern Mediterranean nations. The Conference MED 21 adopted the creation under MAP, of a Mediterranean Commission for Sustainable Development, and the European initiative is focusing on a European-Mediterranean Network (EUROMEDNET) in Marine Science and Technology.

452 The Delegate of Israel highlighted the need for continued scientific research in the Mediterranean and the growing interest in operational oceanography in the region, and proposed that IOC develop a new coherent and unified Mediterranean Programme which would build on the results of the existing separate programmes in the eastern and western basins (POEM and PRIMO). This new programme should be designed to improve the understanding of the oceanographic processes in the Mediterranean as well as to serve relevant needs in operational oceanography in the region. He further proposed that the 1996/97 biennium should be considered as a period of transition from the existing IOC programmes in the Mediterranean to the new unified Mediterranean programme, and that during this period IOC should continue to support the existing programmes by appropriate credits to be sought in the budget. The Delegates of Greece, Italy, Lebanon, Morocco and Turkey strongly supported these proposals. The Delegate of Turkey added that the new unified Mediterranean programme should include elements of permanency as well as a TEMA component. The Delegates of Israel, Italy and Malta requested that the IOC budget for 1996-97 should include an allocation of a minimum of US$100,000 to support the existing Mediterranean programmes (mainly workshops and planning meetings of the Steering Committees). **The Assembly recognized** this need and **instructed** the Executive Secretary of IOC to take appropriate action. **The Assembly endorsed** this strategy for further development of IOC activities in the Mediterranean.

453 The Delegate of the Russian Federation expressed great interest in studies being pursued, and indicated the availability of Russian research and hydrographic vessels for participation in such studies.

454 The Delegate of Croatia informed the Assembly on the oceanographic activities in her country from 1993 to 1995, during an extremely difficult period, and mentioned the development of an electronic network to link up with other Internet systems worldwide. She expressed the willingness of her country's scientific institutions to participate in many IOC programmes, such as GOOS, IODE and TEMA. She told the Assembly that on the occasion of its sixty-fifth anniversary, the Institute of Oceanography and Fisheries, Split, is organizing a symposium entitled "Croatian Marine Fisheries on the Threshold of the 21st Century" to be held from 16-18 October 1995 in Split.

455 The Delegate of Malta informed the Assembly that the importance which Malta attaches to IODE activities, especially with regard to its data management component, is shown by the contribution which Malta has made to the this programme during the intersessional period (hosting the GODAR Mediterranean Workshop last April, as well as a training course for Mediterranean countries on the use of computers for the processing, management, exchange and dissemination of marine information and data. This contribution was also made in consideration of the great need in the Mediterranean, to bring together the mosaic of communities and cultures bordering this Sea, in order to address the pressing issue of persistent stress and the state of degradation faced by the marine environment. No comprehensive, basin-wide initiatives so essential to the sustainable use of marine resources in this region, can be effectively undertaken before the South and Eastern Mediterranean (SEM) countries receive the necessary boost that allows them to reach a level of capability in the marine sphere, thus enabling them to participate as partners in such an initiative.

456 He stressed that his country, due to its geographical position, its historical background, and its solid political relations with both northern- and southern-shore countries, is obliged to play a significant role in this process. They believe that one of the most important steps towards this direction is Malta's initiative to establish a Marine Research Centre which, besides meeting national needs, would also aim at providing a functional mechanism whereby benefits of research, training, capacity building and oceanographic data and information management could be equally shared by all the Mediterranean countries. The IODE network will, of course, be reinforced by such a Centre, and will, moreover, favour the operation of GOOS in the Mediterranean.

13.8 OTHER REGIONS, INCLUDING THE SOUTHWEST ATLANTIC, SOUTHEAST PACIFIC, SOUTHERN OCEAN, ARCTIC BASIN AND THE CASPIAN SEA

457 The Executive Secretary IOC introduced the item referring to the Annual Report 1994 and the Annotated Expanded Agenda (Document IOC-XVII!/2).

458 He recalled the establishment of ASOS as a co-operative mechanism of Argentina, Brazil and Uruguay, following their joint statement at the Seventeenth Session of the Assembly, and the several activities carried out in that framework.

459 He emphasized the co-operation between CPPS and IOC in the Southeast Pacific on studies of El Niño, aspects of marine pollution research and monitoring and development of training. He informed the Assembly of several missions organized by UNESCO-IOC to the region.

460 The Executive Secretary IOC provided further updated information on actions of IOC in relation to the Southern Ocean, the Caspian Sea, and invited advice of the Assembly as regards IOC role with respect to the Arctic Basin.

461 Several Delegations informed the Assembly of actions of their countries in the different regions. The Canadian Delegate advised that it was not necessary to initiate IOC actions in the Arctic Basin in view of several other regional on-going programmes there (see also section 15.3). However, IOC should ensure that information of developments and results of these programmes is provided. This could perhaps be ensured by the identification of a rapporteur. The Delegate of Poland supported this view. The Delegates of Argentina and Brazil confirmed that ASOS is working well and that IOC's association and support is important.

462 The Delegates of Chile, Peru and the Representative of CPPS confirmed the interest of CPPS to continue and expand the co-operation between CPPS and IOC in scientific matters.

463 The Australian Delegation advised the Assembly that the Australian Government has decided to convene a special meeting of South Pacific environment ministers to discuss the environmental impact of nuclear testing and the possible establishment of a monitoring programme in the Pacific.

464 The Delegation of France made the following statement:

"France has taken note of the statement made by the head of the Australian Delegation concerning the French decision to proceed with a final series of nuclear tests of a limited number and

duration, prior to the signature by France in 1996, at the latest, of the Comprehensive Test-Ban Treaty (CTBT).

It respects all the different opinions expressed about this decision. It observes, however, that the Assembly of the Intergovernmental Oceanographic Commission is not at all the appropriate forum for voicing political opposition to a decision that is ultimately a matter of French national sovereignty. France regrets the risk that has thus been taken of giving to the Assembly's debates a polemic character not in keeping with the nature of its work. It notes that the French authorities have amply informed its main partners, especially the countries of the South Pacific, of the reasons that have led them to take the decision to proceed with a final series of tests and to reaffirm France's commitment to be a party to the conclusion of the CTBT at the time set by the international community. It stresses that it would not have been able to take that second decision without the first.

France considers that it would be inappropriate to hold a special meeting of Environment Ministers of the South Pacific to discuss the consequences of the nuclear tests that it is preparing to conduct in Mururoa. It considers unfounded the idea of establishing a monitoring programme for that purpose. With reference to these two points, it points out that it has been demonstrated on many occasions in the past by scientific experts of undisputed international standing that French nuclear tests at Mururoa have no impact whatever on the environment and on ecological balance. It confirms that its forthcoming tests will be conducted under conditions of total safety and absolute respect for the environment. It reaffirms its readiness to again invite high-level expert missions to note at the end of its next and final series of tests the absence of any effects on the environment caused by the last tests that it will be carrying out".

Southern Ocean

465 **The Assembly noted** that, upon the initiative of Germany, the Executive Secretary IOC took actions to organize the First Southern Ocean Forum, scheduled to be held in Bremerhaven, Germany, in spring 1996. The purpose of the Forum will be to review on-going and planned ocean research and observational programmes in the Southern Ocean and to prepare proposals on future IOC activities in the region, taking into account programmes and activities of other international organizations as well as proposals on the IOC links with, and contributions to, international conventions and treaties related to this oceanic area. The following countries have already responded positively to the IOC letter on this matter: Australia, Argentina, Brazil, Chile, France, Germany, Peru, Russia, the United Kingdom and the United States of America. IOC has also invited other international organizations concerned: CCAMLR, IHO, IWC, SCAR, SCOR, UNEP and WMO. Positive replies have been received from CCAMLR and WMO. In response to the request of the Seventeenth Session of the Assembly, the following countries have designated their official national contacts for SOC: Argentina, Australia, Brazil, Chile, China, Ecuador, France, Germany, Peru, Russia and the United Kingdom.

466 The Delegate of Argentina noted that the Forum should not constitute a formal, independent structure, but should be seen as an integral part of IOCSOC. Participants could include scientists, legal experts and government representatives. In addition, he observed that the activities of SCOR, in the framework of the Forum, should be carried out in close co-operation with SCAR.

467 **The Assembly welcomed** the initiative of Germany and **instructed** the Executive Secretary IOC to continue preparations for the Forum.

Caspian Sea

468 **The Assembly noted** that, upon the request of the 27th Session of the UNESCO General Conference (1993), the Joint Workshop on Sea-Level Rise and the Multidisciplinary Studies of Environmental Processes in the Caspian Sea region was organized by IOC, jointly with IAEA and IHP of UNESCO, in Paris, 9-12 May 1995. The Workshop was attended by specialists of all the riparian countries of the Caspian Sea as well as of France and representatives of IAEA, IHP and WMO. The Workshop reviewed the present knowledge of the causes of the rapid sea-level rise (2.25m since 1978); formulated a plan of action to initiate in 1995-1996 the Caspian Sea Regional Project, proposed and supported by IAEA, which includes the use of isotope techniques for the study of marine environmental processes; and, made proposals for further regional co-operation.

469 In view of the multidisciplinary and the multisectorial nature of the environmental problem in the Caspian Sea the Workshop urged international organizations, such as IMO, UNDP, UNEP, UNESCO, WHO, WMO and the World Bank, to work together in tackling the Caspian Sea problem.

470 The Delegate of the Islamic Republic of Iran, in emphasizing the importance of the research programme in the Caspian Sea, and the recommendations made at the Workshop, supported the establishment of an oceanographic data centre for this region as a priority and confirmed his country's readiness to help.

471 The Delegate of the Islamic Republic of Iran also emphasized the problem of the sea-level rise in the Caspian Sea and supported the proposal that IOC-UNESCO allocate required funds to implement research programmes, in order to determine the causes of sea-level rise and of pollution in the Caspian Sea.

472 **The Assembly also noted** that a second workshop was being planned to be held in Tehran, Iran, at a later date, to further consider and formulate regional co-operation of the Caspian Sea countries related to the study of the Caspian Sea.

473 **The Assembly realized** that the rapid rise of the sea level had caused great concern for all of the riparian countries of the Caspian Sea. **The Assembly recognized** that a solution for the problem in the Caspian Sea would require a multidisciplinary approach and the involvement of many of the international organizations mentioned above.

474 **The Assembly noted** the IOC activities which relate to the problems of the Caspian Sea, and which were initiated as a follow-up to decisions of the Twenty-Seventh General Conference of UNESCO in view of the importance of this region. **It stressed** the need to continue these efforts within the mandate of the IOC and available resources.

13.9 BLACK SEA

475 The Executive Secretary IOC introduced the item, referring to the Annotated Expanded Agenda (Document IOC-XVIII/2), the Annual Report 1994, and the Executive Summary of the Intergovernmental Meeting on Co-operation in Marine Sciences and Services in the Black Sea (Paris, 7-9 June 1995; Document IOC/IGM-BS/3S) together with the related draft resolution.

476 He recalled Resolution XVII-15 on Regional Black Sea Co-operation, and the subsequent related decision of the 27th General Conference of UNESCO (Document 27 C/5 1.2.1 and DR.190 of 1993). He informed the Assembly of the outcome of the Black Sea Workshop held in Varna, Bulgaria (September 1994). This resulted in a proposal for an IOC Black Sea regional programme in marine sciences and services.

477 In accordance with subsequent consultations with all the Black Sea coastal states, an intergovernmental meeting in which all the Black Sea coastal states took part, was organized in Paris, 7-9 June 1995, to discuss further tasks identified in Resolution XVII-15.

478 This resulted in an agreement to approve an IOC Black Sea Regional Programme in Marine Sciences and Services, with an associated IOC regional co-ordinating mechanism (Document IOC/IGM-BS/3S). Finally, the Executive Secretary IOC recalled the participation of IOC in on-going programmes in the Black Sea, including COMSBLACK and the GEF Black Sea Environmental Programme.

479 The Delegates of Ukraine, Bulgaria, Turkey and the Russian Federation expressed their strong support to approve an IOC Black Sea regional programme in marine sciences and services, with an IOC regional committee as the management body. They recalled the uniqueness of the Black Sea in its oceanographic characteristics, the influence exerted on it through river runoffs, the serious degradation of parts of its ecosystem, and the strong need for sustained research, together with a region-wide systematic monitoring system addressing priorities. They stressed the timeliness of this initiative in the light of present on-going activities in the Black Sea so as to ensure that the IOC mechanism is now established on a long-term basis to generate coherent and sustained co-operation in the region with the participation of other interested international organizations.

480 The Delegations recalled the wider interest of many Member States in the unique Black Sea, and pointed out the demonstrated interest of countries outside the region to participate in Black Sea programmes, e.g., through COMSBLACK, EROS 2000, NATO, the GEF Black Sea Environmental Programme, and the UNEP Regional Seas Programme activities there.

481 Through this initiative IOC will become more involved with the Black Sea, and will also gain an identity in the region, so as to be able to act as a catalyzer in marine research as well as regional GOOS-related developments.

482 The potential economic benefits were also indicated, e.g., in the field of living resources and recreation resources. The influence on the Black Sea ecosystem from land-based human activities outside the Black Sea coastal states e.g., from the River Danube, was also stressed.

483 The Representative of UNEP welcomed this initiative and expressed the interest of UNEP to co-operate with IOC in this matter. He also recalled the considerable efforts of UNEP in the region and the tasks which have been given UNEP by the Black Sea States as regards environmental management.

484 The Chairman concluded that the debate had clearly shown the support of the Assembly to the proposals made in Document IOC/IGM-BS/3S.

485 **The Assembly adopted** Resolution XVIII-17 on the IOC Black Sea Regional Programme in Marine Sciences and Services.

14. PROGRAMME AND BUDGET

14.1 DRAFT PROGRAMME AND BUDGET FOR 1996-1997

486 The Chairman presented the background documentation as found in the: (i) Annotated Provisional Agenda (Document IOC-XVIII/2: paras 219-222); (ii) Proposal on the Draft Programme and Budget 1996-1997 and the Related General Conference Draft Resolution (Document IOC-XVIII/2 Annex 7); and, (iii) Status Report on the IOC Programme and Budget (Document IOC-XVIII/7). Attention was also drawn to the IOC Comprehensive Action Plan (Document IOC-XVIII/2 Annex 1) and the Draft IOC Medium-term Strategy (Document IOC-XVIII/2 Annex 3).

487 In introducing this agenda item, the First Vice-Chairman provided a general review of the financial and staffing situation and made reference to the way in which the programme and budget is being developed and presented, following relevant recommendations from the *ad hoc* Study Group on DOSS. He also recalled that for a considerable period of time the IOC had recognized the desirability of balancing needs and resources, but that the decision process leading to programme concentration was indeed a difficult one, taking into account the wide range of Member States interests.

488 The First Vice-Chairman concluded his remarks by recalling previous statements that emphasized the importance of all of the programmes of the Commission. In this respect, it was clear that priorities will change from region to region and from country to country and that choices made by the Assembly would need to take the above into account. His introductory statement is found as Annex III-F.

489 The Chairman proposed that, following a general exchange of views in plenary, an *ad hoc* sessional working group on the programme and budget be established - open to all Member States - to facilitate discussion on specific financial matters, including the draft resolution proposed in Document IOC-XVIII/2 Annex 7.

490 Following the meetings of the *ad hoc* sessional working group, the First Vice-Chairman presented the conclusions of those Member States who had participated as summarized below.

491 Full and in-depth discussion of programme and budget matters requires a process to facilitate provision of advice by the Assembly to the Executive Secretary IOC on programme priorities, as well as a process of oversight and evaluation. An essential element to this process is clear and understandable presentation of programme and budget information.

492 To this end, **the Assembly agreed** that the budget structure and that of the programme need to be similar, with clear functions and sufficient detail, so that Member States can understand the relationship between expenditure and results, and their implications for future programme planning.

493 **The Assembly was of the view** that a more detailed presentation of programme elements would assist Member States in their endeavours to monitor programme implementation, and to mobilize direct and in-kind support for activities of special interest to their country.

494 In expressing its satisfaction with the improvements made in the presentation of programme and budget matters, especially in regard to a multi-year period, **the Assembly instructed** the Executive Secretary IOC to take further action in this direction and to present a model to be used for the 1998-99 biennium to the Twenty-ninth Session of the Executive Council for its comment.

495 **The Assembly agreed** that, in order to adjust to day-to-day uncertainties and opportunities, the Executive Secretary IOC needs to exercise some flexibility in programme management and its associated financing.

496 Recalling the recommendations of the *ad hoc* Study Group on DOSS, **the Assembly requested** that the Officers of the Commission play an active role during the intersessional period in providing advice and guidance to the Executive Secretary IOC on matters requiring immediate attention.

497 To enhance the process of monitoring and evaluation, **the Assembly instructed** the Executive Secretary IOC to amalgamate information found in the status report on the programme and budget with the Annual Report, providing wherever possible, greater detail in regard to linkages between activities and expenditure.

498 **The Assembly recognized** that financial auditing is needed, but that the responsibility of Member States should focus on ensuring that such auditing had been carried out under the UNESCO administration, and the satisfaction of the auditor as reported to the Commission.

499 **The Assembly adopted** Resolution XVIII-18.

500 **The Assembly reviewed** the Status Report on the IOC Programme and Budget (1994-1995) as presented in Document IOC-XVIII/7, and also **took into account** considerations raised during relevant agenda items, together with their financial implications.

501 **The Assembly requested** that the Director-General continue to accord priority to the IOC as the marine science arm of UNESCO should any further adjustments to the programme of work and budget be required, within the perspective of protecting remaining funding and, if possible, responding to new opportunities.

502 **The Assembly noted** with appreciation the special allocation of $300,000 provided by the Director-General in 1994, especially in light of the financial constraints being faced by UNESCO, and **viewed** this as an indication of the priority accorded to the IOC by its parent body.

503 **The Assembly also noted** the positive response of IOC Member States to the need to mobilize increased contributions to the IOC Trust Fund which had reinforced implementation of IOC Programmes and, in some measure, reduced the potentially negative impact of the reduction of 20% in resources provided by UNESCO during the current biennium.

504 **The Assembly invited** the 28th UNESCO General Conference to consider, within the UNESCO Participation Programme, the possibility of giving priority to requests from Member States and non-governmental organizations in support of the 1998 International Year of the Ocean, eventually through a specific allocation within the overall funding identified for the Participation Programme.

14.2 OTHER ASPECTS OF THE UNESCO ENVIRONMENT AND NATURAL RESOURCES MANAGEMENT PROGRAMME

505 The Executive Secretary IOC introduced the item referring to the Expanded Annotated Agenda (Document IOC-XVIII/2) and the Draft 28 C/5. In particular, he referred to the joint statement provided to the 27th General Conference from the meeting of the chairs of IOC, MAB, IHP, IGCP. This had been very well received in view of its emphasizing the need for increased co-operation and specific joint actions between them.

506 He recalled the discussion under Agenda Item 10.2. In this discussion, the Assembly had considered the proposed UNESCO Project on Environment and Development in Coastal Regions and in Small Islands, which is based on the joint statement referred to. He noted that the Assembly had established a small *ad hoc* sessional working group to consider IOC activities in this context. This had resulted in a Draft Resolution welcoming this initiative, proposing the IOC action in this regard and providing advice accordingly to Member States and UNESCO (Resolution XVIII-7).

507 He also noted that in the Draft Programme and Budget proposed for IOC, 1996-1997, reference was made to this project, and certain financial resources were suggested so as to ensure the appropriate participation of the IOC in the project.

508 **The Assembly noted** this information, **concurred** with proposed IOC participation in the project, **and stressed** that IOC's leadership role should be commensurate with its resource allocations to the project.

509 **The Assembly encouraged** IOC Action Addresses to bring Resolution XVIII-7 to the attention of their respective UNESCO National Commissions.

D. CO-OPERATION

15. CO-OPERATION WITH OTHER ORGANIZATIONS OF THE UNITED NATIONS SYSTEM AND OTHER BODIES

15.1 THE INTER-SECRETARIAT COMMITTEE ON SCIENTIFIC PROGRAMMES RELATING TO OCEANOGRAPHY (ICSPRO); CO-OPERATION WITH MEMBER ORGANIZATIONS (UN, FAO, UNESCO, WMO, IMO, IAEA, UNEP)

510 The Executive Secretary IOC introduced the item, referring to the Annotated Expanded Agenda (Document IOC-XVIII/2) and recalling that two consultations had been held with ICSPRO. These had identified the role of ICSPRO in relation to the ACC Sub-Committee on Oceans and Coastal Areas, and had also noted that ICSPRO was established through an entirely different mechanism under an agreement between Heads of Agencies. In particular, it was noted that ICSPRO could serve as an interagency mechanism for matters related to the various conventions, the United Nations Convention on the Law of the Sea, the United Nations Framework Convention on Climate Change, and joint activities with respect to the 1998 Year of the Ocean, as well as in the context of new scientific developments and emerging issues and concerns where scientific advice and data are required.

511 Several delegations expressed support for ICSPRO as a reliable co-ordination mechanism and welcomed its expanded membership.

512 The Delegate of Argentina suggested that a representative of ICSPRO be invited to the intersessional working group on IOC's possible role in relation to UNCLOS.

513 The Delegate of Canada emphasized the use of ICSPRO in several important matters, including UNCLOS. He also proposed that consultations should be held with the Director-General of UNESCO with respect to IOC's membership of ICSPRO.

514 The Delegate of Pakistan drew attention to the need for a counterpart mechanism of co-ordination to ICSPRO at the national level, for instance in relation to ICAM, and invited the preparation of an information document on how the ICSPRO mechanism works, which could be communicated to Member States.

515 The Chairman concluded that the Assembly concurs with the use of ICSPRO as suggested and that the membership status of the IOC should be discussed.

516 The Representative of UNEP expressed the full satisfaction of UNEP with the extent and level of co-operation between IOC and UNEP at all levels - global, regional and national.

517 Specifically he (i) welcomed IOC to become a full, co-operating and contributing partner in the umbrella project between IAEA and UNEP in order to further strengthen the Marine Environmental Studies Laboratory; (ii) concurred that the Intergovernmental Panel for GIPME should be activated and revitalized in order to play its intended role in forging the consolidation and integration of our joint marine pollution monitoring programmes. He recalled that decisions 17/20 and 18/3 of the Governing Council of UNEP request the Executive Director of UNEP to co-operate closely, *inter alia,* with the Intergovernmental Oceanographic Commission of UNESCO in preparation for the Intergovernmental Conference on Land-based Activities, Washington DC, 23 October-3 November 1995, and expressed his wish to co-operate with IOC on this important activity. He furthermore invited IOC to co-operate with UNEP in questions relating to the role of the oceans as a carbon sink. He informed the Assembly that UNEP intends to co-sponsor OSLR and to work closely with IOC on matters related to the protection of marine biodiversity, and the management and sustainable utilization of living marine and coastal resources under the UNEP Marine Living Resources Sub-Programme within the framework of the newly integrated programme of UNEP. He stressed the wish of UNEP to work and co-ordinate more closely with IOC in areas such as the South-west Atlantic, with Argentina, Brazil and Uruguay, as well as in the Red Sea, the Black Sea and the Caspian Sea regions with their respective riparian states, using the successful model of CEPPOL. He welcomed UNESCO's initiative to launch the interdisciplinary project on coastal zones and small islands, and stated that this fits well with the new integrated approach adopted by the UNEP Governing Council at its 18th Session, concerning the management of marine and coastal areas, and the associated watershed and river basins. He also stated that UNEP looks forward to establishing effective co-operation between this project and its work on Integrated Coastal Area Management in the context of the Barbados Plan of Action for Small Islands Developing States (SIDS).

518 The Chairman thanked the Representative of UNEP for his very positive statement (see full text in Annex III-H). **The Assembly welcomed** the statement and **strongly endorsed** the existing and expanding co-operation between IOC and UNEP.

519 The WMO representative noted that WMO had been a long-time member of ICSPRO, and continued to provide both professional and secretarial staff support to IOC under the terms of the ICSPRO agreement. He indicated the concurrence of WMO with the conclusions of both the recent ICSPRO consultations, and stressed that ICSPRO had a continuing and important role to play as an interagency co-ordination and information exchange mechanism in marine science, which WMO fully supported. The full statement of the WMO representative is given in Annex III-H.

520 The Chairman thanked the Representative of WMO for his very positive statement. **The Assembly welcomed** the statement and **strongly endorsed** the existing and expanding co-operation between IOC and WMO.

15.2 CO-OPERATION WITH ICSU AND SCOR

521 The Executive Secretary IOC recalled that extensive co-operation exists between IOC, ICSU and SCOR which is reflected in the substantive programmes, and under those agenda items. This is also reflected in several existing agreements on co-operation and in joint working groups and committees.

522 **The Assembly took note** of the information and in particular **noted** the references to ICSU and SCOR in the context of several programmes, and fully endorsed this co-operation.

15.3 CO-OPERATION WITH OTHER BODIES INCLUDING UNU, ICES, ECOR, CPPS, IOMAC, CCOP AND SOPAC

523 This agenda item was introduced by the Executive Secretary IOC, with reference to Document IOC-XVIII/2, and to progress made during the last intersessional period with regard to co-operation with other organizations. Through co-operation and co-ordination via the IOC scientific and services programmes, e.g. GIPME, HAB and regional activities, IOC has provided scientific inputs to various partners which are dealing with prevention of marine pollution, rational uses of living marine resources and integrated coastal zone management.

524 The Delegate of Canada, speaking on behalf of the Arctic Ocean Science Board (AOSB) made the following statement to the Assembly:

> *"The AOSB had its fourteenth meeting at the Alfred Wegener Institute in Bremerhaven in March this year. The Board functions as a co-ordinating body of about twelve Arctic and sub-Arctic countries in promoting and implementing programmes of mutual interest in Arctic ocean science.*
>
> *The Greenland Sea Project represents an international multi-year study of the oceanography of the Greenland Sea involving all types of measurements from satellites to acoustic arrays over several years. It has recently been concluded with a symposium in Hamburg with many new and controversial results being presented. Its proceedings will be published later this year with up to 25 refereed papers. The GSP data set is being maintained at ICES. An on-going programme of the AOSB is the International Arctic Polynia Programme (IAPP). This programme is looking at the processes and ecology of Arctic polynia and to date has concentrated on the polynia to the North-East of Greenland and the second significant effort in this area will be an over-wintering Expedition late in 1995. The R/V POLARSTERN of Germany will be used to land the party.*
>
> *The Board is co-operating with the IOC/IODE Committee to study the subject of an Arctic Ocean Data Centre. A future thrust is considering a programme of study for physical, chemical, biological and geological processes of major Arctic river systems and their changes through the last 15,000 years. This should prove a useful contribution to the WCRP-ACSYS programme and will offer another possible area of co-operation with the IOC".*

525 The Delegate of Canada confirmed that he will continue to keep the IOC Assembly informed of the new development of this organization. He agreed to act as the IOC Rapporteur for Arctic research and observations.

526 The Delegate of India informed the Assembly of the training programme in Madras, India, in co-operation with IOI and, encouraged IOC to strengthen links with IOI in this regard.

527 **The Assembly noted** with satisfaction the progress made in co-operation with other organizations. **The Assembly stressed** that further efforts in this regard should be carried out in a co-ordinated and harmonized way, in order to avoid duplication of effort.

E. CONCLUDING MATTERS

16. ELECTIONS

528 **The Assembly noted** the report by the Chairman of the Nominations Committee, following which:

(i) some improvements were to be made by the Secretariat during the next intersessional period upon the French version of document IOC/INF-620 rev. 3 "Technical Arrangements for the Elections of Officers of the Commission and Other Members of the Executive Council";

(ii) a note appearing in an earlier version of Document IOC-XVIII/NOM-WP.1 (posted only just before the last meeting of the Nominations Committee), stating that the proposal of Germany to nominate Mr. L. Laubier for the IOC chairmanship made "*on behalf of the European Union*", was not to be considered by the Nominations Committee, but rather by the Assembly, due consideration being taken of the nomination form itself;

(iii) all the nomination forms before it were valid and should therefore be forwarded to the Assembly, as document IOC-XVIII/NOM-WP.1.

529 **The Assembly further noted** that an in-depth study should be undertaken to make sure that all "*electoral groups*" as defined by UNESCO be duly represented amongst the IOC Officers in future, whilst recognizing that this would imply an amendment to the IOC Statutes and Rules of Procedure.

16.1 ELECTION OF THE OFFICERS OF THE COMMISSION

530 **The Assembly noted** that there were two nominees for the position of Chairman of the Commission. Mr. G. L. Holland, nominated by Canada, proposed by Thailand and seconded by Norway, was introduced by the Delegate of Norway, and Mr. L. Laubier, nominated by France, proposed by Germany and seconded by Egypt, was introduced by the Delegate of Italy. The ensuing vote showed an exact balance between the two candidates. The following ballot was decisive. There was then only one candidate for each of the positions of Vice-chairmen of the Commission, who were elected by acclamation.

531 The newly elected Officers of the Commission are:

Chairman:	Mr. G. L. Holland	(Canada)
1st Vice-chairman:	Lic. G. Garcia Montero	(Cuba)
2nd Vice-chairman:	Prof. M. Ravindran	(India)
3rd Vice-chairman:	Prof. V. G. Neiman	(Russian Federation)
4th Vice-chairman:	Dr. E. Okemwa	(Kenya)

16.2 ELECTION OF THE MEMBERS OF THE EXECUTIVE COUNCIL

532 **The Assembly noted** that, including the addition of the failed candidate for the chairmanship of the Commission, there were 31 candidates to Member State seats on the Executive Council, viz the exact maximum number of those seats. The Members of the Executive Council were therefore elected by acclamation:

533 The Member States represented on the Executive Council as a result of the elections, as well as the list of Member States of the Commission, are given in Annex IV hereto.

17. DATES AND PLACES OF THE NINETEENTH SESSION OF THE ASSEMBLY AND THE TWENTY-EIGHTH AND TWENTY-NINTH SESSIONS OF THE EXECUTIVE COUNCIL

534 The Executive Secretary IOC reminded the Assembly of the dates for the Twenty-ninth Session of the Executive Council, 7-18 October 1996. He informed the Assembly that possible dates for the Nineteenth Session of the Assembly were 17 June-4 July 1997, and for the Thirtieth Session of the Executive Council, 16 June 1997.

535 **The Assembly took note** of these dates. The Delegates of France and Italy pointed out the potential conflict between the period for the Twenty-ninth Executive Council and the session of the UNESCO Executive Board or its related meetings. The Secretariat will look into this so as to avoid conflicting dates.

536 **The Assembly decided** that the dates for the Twenty-ninth Session of the Executive Council should be decided when the dates for the UNESCO Executive Board are decided so as to avoid any clash of dates.[1]

---

[1] Following consultations with UNESCO and in the light of the Executive Board Meeting, the dates for IOC/EC-XXIX are 30 September-10 October 1996.

537 The Executive Secretary IOC also drew the attention to the preliminary consideration of themes for the Bruun Memorial Lectures and indicated as a possible theme "Aspects of Coastal Area Management including Socio-economic Ones".

538 **The Assembly took note** of this proposal and **agreed** that further analysis should be carried out and reported on to the Twenty-ninth Session of the Executive Council for its decision.

539 The elected First Vice-Chairman agreed to be responsible for this matter.

18. ADOPTION OF THE SUMMARY REPORT

540 **The Assembly adopted** the Summary Report of the Session together with eighteen Resolutions (Annex II hereto).

19. CLOSURE

541 The Chairman thanked all concerned, including the Vice-Chairmen, the Delegations, the Secretariat, support staff and interpreters for their active participation in the Assembly, and their support towards a productive and fruitful session. He particularly expressed his appreciation to the Executive Secretary and the IOC Conference Officer/Documentalist, for their untiring support and professionalism. He also congratulated the incoming Chair and Vice-Chairs and wished them all success. The incoming Chair expressed his great appreciation of the Chairman and thanked him for his firm leadership and guidance of IOC throughout his period of office. He presented the Chairman with a book of signatures.

542 The Delegate of Brazil, on behalf of all the Delegations, thanked the Chairman for his outstanding management of the Session and his great contribution to IOC. The Delegate also confirmed his great satisfaction with the results of the Session, and also the manner of using mechanisms of *ad hoc* meetings and consultations during the Sessions, so as to find the most constructive approach.

543 The Chairman warmly thanked the Delegate of Brazil, and all the other Delegations, and again expressed his appreciation for such close co-operation.

544 The Chairman then closed the Eighteenth Session of the IOC Assembly at 20.30 on 26 June 1995.

ANNEX I

AGENDA

1. OPENING

2. BRUUN MEMORIAL LECTURES

3. ADMINISTRATIVE ARRANGEMENTS

3.1 ADOPTION OF THE AGENDA

3.2 DESIGNATION OF THE RAPPORTEUR

3.3 CONDUCT OF THE SESSION, TIMETABLE AND DOCUMENTATION

A. PROGRAMME IMPLEMENTATION

4. REPORT ON ACTIVITIES

4.1 SECRETARY'S REPORT ON INTERSESSIONAL ACTIVITIES; REPORT ON THE COMMISSION'S ACTIVITIES, 1993-1994, AND FINANCIAL STATEMENT, FOLLOWED BY DEBATE

B. STATUS AND EVOLUTION OF THE IOC

5. DEVELOPMENTS WITHIN UNESCO, FOLLOW-UP TO DOSS, AND REVISED RULES OF PROCEDURE

6. SECOND INTERNATIONAL CONFERENCE ON OCEANOGRAPHY - FOLLOW-UP

7. MEDIUM-TERM PLAN 1996-2001 AND PRELIMINARY CONSIDERATION OF PROGRAMME AND BUDGET FOR 1996-1997

C. PROGRAMME DEVELOPMENT

8. FOLLOW-UP OF THE 1992 UNITED NATIONS CONFERENCE ON ENVIRONMENT AND DEVELOPMENT

8.1 AGENDA 21 AND ACC SUB-COMMITTEE ON OCEANS AND COASTAL AREAS

8.2 UN YEAR OF THE OCEAN 1998

9. IOC AND UNCLOS

10. OCEAN SCIENCES

10.1 OCEANS AND CLIMATE

10.1.1 WCRP-JSC, including TOGA and CLIVAR
10.1.2 WOCE
10.1.3 Relations with FCCC, including First Conference of the Parties (COP), and IPCC
10.1.4 OOSDP; Second Meeting of Scientific and Technical Experts on Oceans and Climate (Malta, 1994)
10.1.5 WCP Joint Proposal

10.2 OCEANS AND GLOBAL CHANGE: LOICZ; JGOFS, INCLUDING CO_2 PANEL; COASTAL ZONES (COASTS)

10.3 OCEAN SCIENCE IN RELATION TO LIVING RESOURCES (OSLR); IPHAB; GLOBEC; CONVENTION ON BIOLOGICAL DIVERSITY

10.4 OCEAN SCIENCE IN RELATION TO NON-LIVING RESOURCES (OSNLR), INCLUDING CONFERENCE ON COASTAL CHANGE (BORDEAUX, 1995)

10.5 OCEAN MAPPING

10.6 MARINE POLLUTION RESEARCH AND MONITORING (GIPME/MARPOLMON) AND RELATED PROGRAMMES

11. OCEAN SERVICES

11.1 GLOBAL OCEAN OBSERVING SYSTEM AND RELATED. ACTIVITIES

11.1.1 Second Session of the IOC-WMO-UNEP Committee for GOOS
11.1.2 Global Climate Observing System (GCOS)
11.1.3 Global Sea-Level Observing System (GLOSS)
11.1.4 Integrated Global Ocean Services System (IGOSS)
11.1.5 Data Buoy Co-operation Panel (DBCP)
11.1.6 Satellite Remote Sensing and Relation to CEOS
11.1.7 Global Terrestrial Observing System (GTOS)

11.2 INTERNATIONAL OCEANOGRAPHIC DATA AND INFORMATION EXCHANGE (IODE) AND RELATED ACTIVITIES

11.2.1 Data Management
11.2.2 Global Temperature-Salinity Pilot Project (GTSPP)
11.2.3 Marine Information Management

11.3 INTERNATIONAL TSUNAMI WARNING SYSTEM IN THE PACIFIC AND RELATED ACTIVITIES

12. CAPACITY BUILDING IN MARINE SCIENCES, SERVICES AND OBSERVATIONS - TEMA

13. REGIONAL SUBSIDIARY BODIES

13.1 IOCARIBE, INCLUDING EVALUATION

13.2 WESTPAC

13.3 IOCINCWIO

13.4 IOCINDIO

13.5 IOCEA

13.6 COLLABORATION WITH ROPME AND PERSGA

13.7 MEDITERRANEAN

13.8 OTHER REGIONS, INCLUDING SOUTH-WEST ATLANTIC, SOUTHEAST PACIFIC, SOUTHERN OCEAN, ARCTIC BASIN, AND CASPIAN SEA

13.9 BLACK SEA

14. PROGRAMME AND BUDGET

14.1 DRAFT PROGRAMME AND BUDGET FOR 1996-1997
14.2 OTHER ASPECTS OF THE UNESCO ENVIRONMENT AND NATURAL RESOURCES MANAGEMENT PROGRAMME

D. CO-OPERATION

15. CO-OPERATION WITH OTHER ORGANIZATIONS OF THE UNITED NATIONS SYSTEM AND OTHER BODIES

15.1 THE INTER-SECRETARIAT COMMITTEE ON SCIENTIFIC PROGRAMMES RELATING TO OCEANOGRAPHY (ICSPRO); CO-OPERATION WITH MEMBER ORGANIZATIONS (UN, FAO, UNESCO, WMO, IMO, IAEA, UNEP)

15.2 CO-OPERATION WITH ICSU AND SCOR

15.3 CO-OPERATION WITH OTHER BODIES INCLUDING UNU, ICES, ECOR, CPPS, IOMAC, CCOP AND SOPAC

E. CONCLUDING MATTERS

16. ELECTIONS

16.1 ELECTION OF THE OFFICERS OF THE COMMISSION

16.2 ELECTION OF THE MEMBERS OF THE EXECUTIVE COUNCIL

17. DATES AND PLACES OF THE NINETEENTH SESSION OF THE ASSEMBLY AND THE TWENTY-EIGHTH (INCLUDING PROPOSALS ON AGENDA ITEMS) AND THE TWENTY-NINTH SESSIONS OF THE EXECUTIVE COUNCIL

18. ADOPTION OF THE SUMMARY REPORT

19. CLOSURE

ANNEX II

ADOPTED RESOLUTIONS

No.	Agenda Item	Title	Page
1	5	*Ad hoc* Study Group on IOC Development, Operations, Structure and Statutes (DOSS)	2
2	5	Financial Regulations Applicable to the Special Account of the IOC	3
3	8.2	UN Year of the Ocean 1998	7
4	9	IOC and UNCLOS	7
5	10.1.2	Intergovernmental WOCE Panel	8
6	10.1.3	Climate Related Issues	10
7	10.2	Coastal Regions and Small Islands	11
8	10.3	Third Session of the Joint IOC-FAO Intergovernmental Panel on Harmful Algal Blooms (IPHAB)	12
9	10.3	Marine Biodiversity	15
10	10.5	Support to the Joint IOC-IHO Ocean Mapping Programme	16
11	11.1.1	Second Session of the IOC-WMO-UNEP Committee for the Global Ocean Observing System (I-GOOS)	17
12	11.1.1	International Coral Reef Initiative	19
13	11.1.3	Global Sea-Level Observing System (GLOSS) Activities 1996-1997	20
14	12	The Floating University Project	21
15	12	Capacity Building in Marine Sciences, Services and Observations - TEMA	22
16	13.1	IOC Sub-Commission for the Caribbean and Adjacent Regions (IOCARIBE)	23
17	13.9	IOC Black Sea Regional Programme in Marine Sciences and Services	24
18	14.1	Programme and Budget 1996-97	26

Resolution XVIII-1

AD HOC STUDY GROUP ON IOC DEVELOPMENT, OPERATIONS, STRUCTURE AND STATUTES (DOSS)

The Intergovernmental Oceanographic Commission,

Having considered the Revised Rules of Procedure as found in Document IOC-XVIII/2 Annex 2 and the Report on Implementation of Points 1-3 and 5 of Part II of the Annex to Resolution XVII-20 as found in Document IOC-XVIII/2 Annex 8,

Recalling IOC Resolution XVII-20 and, in particular, the subjects that require further study, as listed in Part II of its Annex,

Decides to continue the work of the *ad hoc* Study Group on IOC Development, Operations, Structure and Statutes (DOSS) with the revised composition and terms of reference as found in the Annex;

Invites Member States to participate as observers in sessions of the *ad hoc* study group if they so wish;

Instructs the Executive Secretary IOC to circulate to all Member States the provisional agenda and timetable for the sessions of the *ad hoc* study group no less than two months before the session;

Requests the *ad hoc* Study Group to provide a progress report to the Executive Council at its Twenty-ninth Session in 1996, an interim report to the Nineteenth Session of the Assembly in 1997 with specific recommendations for possible adoption by that session of the Assembly, and a final report to the Twentieth Session of the Assembly in 1999.

Financial implications: to be defined in function of the composition of the *ad hoc* Study Group and required secretariat support.

Annex to Resolution XVIII-1

Ad hoc Study Group on IOC Development, Operations, Structure and Statutes (DOSS)

(Revised Composition and Terms of Reference)

I. Composition

The revived *ad hoc* Study Group on IOC Development, Operations, Structure and Statutes (DOSS 2) shall be composed of 8 individuals who will bring to this matter their expertise on missions and programmes of the IOC, as well as on financial, legal and administrative aspects.

The previous Chairman of the Commission, Professor Manuel M. Murillo, Costa Rica, shall serve as Chairman of the study group and the new Chairman of IOC will be *ex officio* member of the group.

II. Terms of Reference

The revived *ad hoc* Study Group on IOC Development, Operations, Structure and Statutes (DOSS), taking into account the previous work undertaken by the Study Group and views expressed at the Eighteenth Session of the Assembly, shall undertake further study on the following subjects:

(i) The Statutes and Rules of Procedures of the IOC, taking into account the previous studies and the need for adjustments to better reflect IOC practice in accordance with the functional autonomy of IOC within UNESCO;

(ii) The feasibility, in the longer term, of an IOC Pledging System;

(iii) All aspects having a bearing on geographical distribution;

(iv) Administrative and management matters, including:

- The adequacy of the financial contributions to IOC in the light of its present responsibilities and those with which it may be intrusted in the future;
- Methods and mechanisms to ensure continuing budgetary responsibility and administrative efficiency of the Commission;
- The need for an objective methodology for regular evaluation of the IOC programmes, structures and procedures;
- The frequency of meetings for the IOC Assembly and Executive Council on the basis of the roles and responsibilities of these bodies;
- The role of the elected officers of the IOC, individually and as a group, and the need for a Bureau, together with its composition and role;
- Evaluation and advice on staffing requirements, including making the best use of all available resources for the IOC.

Resolution XVIII-2

FINANCIAL REGULATIONS APPLICABLE TO THE SPECIAL ACCOUNT OF THE IOC

The Intergovernmental Oceanographic Commission,

Recalling Resolution 10.4 adopted by the UNESCO General Conference at its 24th session and, in particular, Article 1 of the IOC Statutes which provides the legal and political framework for the Commission,

Having received Decision 5.3.1 on "New Arrangements for the Intergovernmental Oceanographic Commission" of the 146th UNESCO Executive Board,

Noting that the UNESCO Executive Board, on a recommendation of its Group of Experts on Financial and Administrative Matters, has proposed three amendments to the proposed text, as reflected in the Annex to this Resolution,

Confirms its agreement to the proposed financial regulations, as amended by the Group of Experts on Administrative and Financial Matters of the UNESCO Executive Board;

Instructs the Executive Secretary IOC to prepare detailed financial rules applicable to the Special Account for initial consideration by the Twenty-ninth Session of the IOC Executive Council and subsequent submission to the Nineteenth Session of the Assembly.

Annex to Resolution XVIII-2

Financial Regulations Applicable to the Special Account of the Intergovernmental Oceanographic Commission

Article 1 - Creation of a Special Account

1.1 In accordance with Article 6, paragraph 6, of the Financial Regulations of UNESCO, there is hereby created a Special Account for the Intergovernmental Oceanographic Commission, hereafter referred to as IOC. The following Regulations shall govern the operation of this account.

Article 2 - Financial period

2.1 The biennial financial period shall follow that of UNESCO.

Article 3 - Income

3.1 The income of the Special Account shall be divided into four sub-classifications, as follows: (a) the financial allocations voted by the General Conference of UNESCO; (b) voluntary contributions, endowments, gifts and bequests allocated or offered by institutions of the United Nations, governments, public and private bodies, associations, foundations and individuals, provided that the purposes for which they are made are consistent with the policies, aims and activities of IOC; (c) fees collected for special purposes; (d) miscellaneous revenue.

3.2 The Secretary of IOC, hereafter referred to as the Secretary, acting under the authority of the Director-General of UNESCO, may accept on behalf of IOC the income defined in Article 3.1, subject to the prior approval of the IOC Assembly, hereafter referred to as the Assembly, in any case which would entail additional obligations for IOC.

3.3 The Secretary shall report to the Assembly on the subventions, voluntary contributions, endowments, gifts and bequests accepted.

Article 4 - Budget

4.1 The Secretary shall prepare, in a form to be determined by the Assembly, a biennial budget and shall submit it to the Assembly for approval.

4.2 The budget appropriations voted shall constitute an authorization to incur obligations and make expenditures for the purposes for which the appropriations were voted and up to the amounts available for each source of financing.

4.3 The appropriations shall remain available for obligation during the financial period to which they relate.

4.4 The appropriations shall remain available for one year following the end of the financial period to which they relate to the extent that they are required to discharge obligations in respect of goods supplied and services rendered in the financial period and to liquidate any other outstanding legal obligations of the financial period.

4.5 The balance of the appropriations remaining unobligated at the close of a financial period shall be credited to the General Account of IOC.

4.6 At the end of the one-year period provided for in Article 4, paragraph 4, the then remaining unspent balance of appropriations shall be credited to the General Account of IOC.

Article 5 - General Account

5.1 There shall be established a General Account, as part of the Special Account, to which shall be credited the income of IOC as described in Article 3 of these Regulations, and which shall be used to finance the approved budget of IOC.

5.2 The balance remaining of this General Account shall be carried forward from one financial period to the next.

5.3 The use to which the funds in this General Account may be put shall be determined by the Assembly.

Article 6 - Custody and investment of funds

6.1 All the funds of IOC shall be deposited without delay with banks or other depositories selected by the Secretary or by another officer of UNESCO to whom such power is delegated by the Secretary.

6.2 The Secretary may make such investments of moneys not needed for immediate requirements as he or she considers necessary, within the framework of the policy implemented by the Comptroller with respect to the investments of UNESCO.

6.3 The income earned on such investments shall be credited under the miscellaneous revenue of IOC.

Article 7 - Trust Funds, Reserves and Special Accounts

7.1 The Secretary shall establish Reserves to finance the Working Capital Fund, end-of-service indemnities and other obligations of IOC. A review of these Reserves shall be conducted biennially at the time when the budget is approved.

7.2 Trust Funds, Reserves and Special Accounts may be established by the Secretary and shall be reported to the Assembly.

7.3 The Secretary may when necessary in connection with the purpose of a Trust Fund, Reserve or Special Account prepare special financial regulations to govern the operations of these funds or accounts and shall report thereon to the Assembly. Unless otherwise provided these funds and accounts shall be administered in accordance with these Regulations.

Article 8 - Internal control

8.1 The Secretary shall:

(i) Establish, for approval by the Assembly, detailed financial rules and procedures in order to ensure effective financial administration and economy.

(ii) Cause all payments to be made on the basis of supporting vouchers and other documents which ensure that the services or goods have been received, and that payment has not previously been made.

(iii) Designate the officers who may receive moneys, incur obligations and make payments on behalf of IOC.

(iv) Maintain an internal financial control which shall provide for an effective current examination and for review of financial transactions in order to ensure:

(a) the regularity of the receipt, custody and disposal of all funds and other financial resources of IOC;

(b) the conformity of obligations and expenditures which may be determined by the Assembly, or with the purposes and rules relating to Trust Funds and Special Accounts;

(c) the economic use of the resources of IOC.

(v) Ensure that the obligations incurred do not exceed the moneys actually received and available to cover those obligations.

8.2 No obligations shall be incurred until allotments or other appropriate authorizations have been made in writing under the authority of the Secretary.

8.3 The Secretary may, after full investigation, authorize the writing-off of losses of cash, stores and other assets, provided that a statement of all such amounts written-off shall be submitted to the External Auditor for examination with the accounts.

Article 9 - The accounts

9.1 The Secretary shall maintain such accounting records as are necessary and shall submit annual accounts to the IOC Executive Council for the first year of the biennial financial period and to the Assembly, and to the UNESCO Executive Board and General Conference, for the full biennial period, showing, for the financial period to which they relate:

(i) the income and expenditure of all funds;

(ii) the budgetary situation including:

(a) original appropriations;

(b) the appropriations as modified by any transfers or additional appropriations as approved by IOC Executive Council;

(c) the amounts charged against these appropriations;

(iii) the assets and liabilities of IOC.

He or she shall also give such other information as may be appropriate to indicate the current financial position of IOC.

9.2 The biennial accounts of IOC shall be presented in US dollars. Accounting records may, however, be kept in such currency or currencies as the Secretary may deem necessary.

9.3 Appropriate separate accounts shall be maintained for all Trust Funds, Reserves and Special Accounts.

Article 10 - External audit

10.1 The accounts of IOC as approved by its Secretary will form an integral part of the overall financial statements of UNESCO that are submitted to the External Auditor of UNESCO for audit and shall be presented to the IOC Executive Council and Assembly, as well as to the UNESCO Executive Board and General Conference for their approval.

Resolution XVIII-3

UN YEAR OF THE OCEAN 1998

The Intergovernmental Oceanographic Commission,

Recalling its Resolution XVII-17, "1998 - The International Year of the Ocean",

Noting that the 27th General Conference by its Resolution 2.5 adopted the proposal of the IOC to declare 1998 "International Year of the Ocean",

Noting further that the General Assembly of the United Nations at its forty-ninth session adopted Resolution 49/131, proclaiming 1998 as the "International Year of the Ocean",

Being informed that the UNESCO Executive Board at its 146th Session instructed the Director-General to take all necessary measures likely to ensure the success of this activity,

Having considered the proposals for the IOC to be associated with the 1998 International Year of the Ocean as stated in Document IOC-XVIII/2 Annex 3,

Decides that the IOC shall participate through its different programmes in activities organized in the framework of "1998 - The International Year of the Ocean" and in activities initiated within the framework of EXPO 98;

Instructs the Executive Secretary IOC to organize the work of an IOC preparatory task team for "1998 - The International Year of the Ocean", in close consultation with the Chairman;

Instructs further the Executive Secretary IOC to report on the progress and proposals at the Twenty-ninth Session of the Executive Council and the Nineteenth Session of the Assembly.

Financial implications: in accordance with agreements in force there should be no or very limited costs to existing IOC sources for this activity; additional funds can, however, be sought.

Resolution XVIII-4

IOC AND UNCLOS

The Intergovernmental Oceanographic Commission,

Taking note of the entry into force, on 16 November 1994, of the United Nations Convention on the Law of the Sea (UNCLOS),

Recognizing that it is necessary to identify the IOC role with respect to the relevant provisions of the Convention,

Expresses its thanks to Prof. Alexander Yankov for the considerable work that he has undertaken on this matter;

Decides to establish an open-ended Intersessional Working Group on the IOC Role in Relation to UNCLOS (IOC-LOS), to work in accordance with the terms of reference contained in Annex I of this resolution;

Instructs the Executive Secretary IOC to:

(i) distribute to Member States the views and any proposals made by the Working Group at least three months prior to the Twenty-ninth Session of the Executive Council;

(ii) arrange, depending on the progress of work, a preparatory meeting open to all Member States of the Commission, prior to the Twenty-ninth Session of the Executive Council, in order to examine the Working Group's proposals;

(iii) make available the Final Report of the Group with sufficient time to allow for its circulation in advance of the Nineteenth Session of the Assembly.

Financial implications: Participation in possible open-ended working group meeting at national expense; service of potential meeting, including relevant interpretations if required at IOC expense.

Annex to Resolution XVIII-4

Terms of Reference for the Intersessional Working Group on IOC's Possible Role in Relation to UNCLOS

A. PROCEDURE

1. The bulk of the Group's work shall be done by correspondence, with the co-ordination of the Executive Secretary IOC.

2. An appropriate balance shall be encouraged in the membership of the Working Group between experts with training in the law of the sea and experts with training in marine sciences.

B. SUBSTANCE

1. The Working Group shall review all provisions of UNCLOS that may have explicit or implicit relevance to the role of the IOC.

2. The Working Group shall take into account:

   (a) the purpose and functions established by the IOC Statutes and the Rules of Procedure;

   (b) the competence of the bodies established under UNCLOS and that of other existing bodies in the United Nations system;

   (c) the rights and duties of the Coastal States as stipulated in UNCLOS, particularly those relating to the general principles of prior consent for the implementation of activities in the Exclusive Economic Zone (EEZ) and on the continental shelf.

Resolution XVIII.5

INTERGOVERNMENTAL WOCE PANEL

The Intergovernmental Oceanographic Commission,

Noting with satisfaction that the field phase of the World Ocean Circulation Experiment (WOCE) will conclude by 1998, but that in order to realize the maximum benefit, analysis, interpretation, modelling and synthesis must continue until 2002,

Recognizing that access to areas under national jurisdiction is fundamental to deriving the full scientific value of WOCE hydrographic sections, since continuous sections from the deep ocean into shallow water are essential for the accurate determination of transports in the boundary currents,

Recognizing further that to accomplish its mission, WOCE infrastructure must be maintained throughout WOCE and beyond,

Being aware that WOCE has put forward a strategy that includes major workshops and conferences and that present commitments exist for a major WOCE Conference hosted by Canada in mid-1998, and a Southern Ocean Workshop to be hosted by Australia in 1997; and that additional workshops on the South Atlantic, Pacific, Indian, and North Atlantic Oceans are needed,

Noting with appreciation the contributions of Member States to continue their efforts through the observational period of WOCE, and in particular the offer of continued support for the WOCE International Project Office (IPO) in the UK,

Recognizing the request for a carefully considered transition of WOCE-like activities to the new WCRP Programme on Climate Variability and Predictability (CLIVAR),

Noting the very successful demonstration of satellite altimetry to provide unprecedented and extremely accurate global data sets of the ocean circulation and its changes,

Considering the unique importance of the few existing open ocean time series observations in confirming long-time scale ocean variability,

Decides:

(i) to support WOCE activities into the analysis, interpretation, modelling and synthesis phase that will continue beyond the completion of the observational phase;

(ii) to continue to foster the concept of the rapid free and open exchange of data, to support for the WOCE Data Assembly and Special Analysis Centres and to assist the process by encouraging Member States to second scientists to WOCE Data Assembly Centres (DACs) and Special Analysis Centres (SACs) for periods of 2-6 months;

(iii) to endorse and support the planned WOCE International Conference to be hosted by Canada in 1998 (the International Year of the Ocean);

(iv) to endorse the planned series of regional and subject-related workshops, including the Southern Ocean Workshop in 1997 to be hosted by Australia;

Invites Member States to consider the need for WOCE observational programmes to acquire data in areas under national jurisdiction in order to complete planned WOCE observations;

Urges Member States to continue existing oceanic time series measurements and to initiate new ones as important elements in the transition from WOCE to those follow-on programmes that will investigate long-term climate variability and will represent an important part of the climate module of GOOS;

Instructs the Secretary IOC to convey to the relevant space agencies the need for continuing satellite altimeter observations of the highest quality possible, for a dedicated gravity mission to make possible the extraction of the highest accuracy from the altimeter data, and for global scatterometer coverage in support of other climate-related programmes.

Estimated financial implications for the IOC: US$20,000 in support of WOCE International Conference and related matters.

Resolution XVIII-6

CLIMATE RELATED ISSUES

The Intergovernmental Oceanographic Commission,

Acknowledging the central importance of the ocean in the global climate system, and the necessity to obtaining comprehensive and accurate observations of the ocean for incorporation into numerical predictions of climate,

Emphasizing the central importance of climate-related activities to the work of the Commission, and the necessity of effective IOC participation in the World Climate Programme, particularly in its integrated Climate Agenda,

Recalling that Chapter 17 of Agenda 21 of UNCED calls on relevant competent United Nations bodies to carry out analysis, assessment and systematic observations in the role of the oceans in the global climate,

Taking into account that successful implementation of the UN Framework Convention on Climate Change will address the needs of sustainable development,

Noting that the First Conference of Parties to the Framework Convention on Climate Change (FCCC) has established a Subsidiary Body for Scientific and Technological Advice (SBSTA) with the principal task of linking the scientific, technical and technological assessments to the policy-oriented needs of the Parties,

Recognizing that the IOC has a substantial role to play in informing the SBSTA of investigations into the role of the ocean in global climate change, and of the IOC's programme contributions in this regard,

Recognizing also that IOC needs to collaborate with other governmental and non-governmental scientific bodies in an integrated way to develop and present new knowledge with respect to the role of the ocean in global climate change,

Takes note of the Executive Summary and Policy Makers Summary of the Climate Agenda as prepared by the Co-ordinating Committee for the World Climate Programme;

Instructs the Executive Secretary IOC to:

(i) continue to participate in the further development of the Climate Agenda, and in the UN FCCC process;

(ii) consult with the Chairman of the SBSTA regarding the specific needs and requirements of this body for scientific data and assessments which can be provided through IOC;

(iii) undertake the appropriate arrangements to establish close working links with the IPCC and maintain established co-operation with the Climate Change Secretariat;

(iv) adjust the resources of the Secretariat so as to reflect the importance of climate-related activities to the work of the Commission;

Invites the Chairman of the IPCC to make a presentation to the next IOC Assembly;

Urges Member States to support related climate activities in their own national programmes and ensure proper international co-ordination through the IOC and other appropriate bodies.

Financial implications for IOC budget: US$ 100,000 for a reasonable implementation, in addition to WCRP, GOOS and GCOS.

Resolution XVIII-7

COASTAL REGIONS AND SMALL ISLANDS

The Intergovernmental Oceanographic Commission,

Recalling:

(i) Agenda 21, Chapter 17 of UNCED, which emphasized the important role of integrated coastal area management for sustainable use of the coastal zone for national development and the need for scientifically valid information, as well as related capacity building,

(ii) IOC Resolution XVII-1: "Coastal Zone Activities", which calls for more effective mechanisms to co-ordinate IOC programmes with those of other organizations, as proposed in IOC/INF-987,

(iii) the UN Conference on Small Island Developing States (Barbados, April-May 1994) whose outcome stressed the important role IOC has to play in providing scientific input and data for addressing such issues as sea-level rise, natural environmental disasters, management of marine resources, marine biodiversity, as well as development of marine science and technology, and related human resources, and

(iv) the United Nations Convention on the Law of the Sea,

Taking note of the proposed UNESCO Project on Environment and Development in Coastal Regions and in Small Islands (hereafter, the Project), based on the joint statement by the Chairpersons of IOC, IGCP, IHP and MAB to the 27th session of the UNESCO General Conference,

Welcomes this constructive initiative which aims at providing a framework for co-operative and co-ordinated activities on Coastal Regions and Small Islands among UNESCO's international and intergovernmental programmes in the environmental and social sciences: MAB, IGCP, IHP, MOST (hereafter referred to as "the programmes concerned") and the IOC;

Decides:

(i) to review its coastal activities in general, to optimize the way its ocean science and services programmes contribute to actual integrated management of coastal regions, specifically promoting the development of methodologies, institutional infrastructure, and associated training and education, making use of regional subsidiary bodies and building on local efforts;

(ii) to invite the UNESCO programmes concerned, together with the IOC, to jointly undertake an improved and refined definition of the scope and context of the Project, outlining how it can add value over and above what individual programmes and countries could accomplish; the Project should make full use of the scientific potential offered by programmes of the UN and ICSU, as appropriate, and the capacity building mechanisms of START;

Recommends that:

(i) a small, representative group of experts designated by the UNESCO programmes concerned and the IOC be convened in order to produce the improved and refined definition;

(ii) the approach for implementation be based on pilot projects/case studies;

Invites the UNESCO programmes concerned together with the IOC to:

(i) assess their respective roles addressing the interdisciplinary requirements of the Project; and

(ii) recommend the interdisciplinary composition and head of the management unit required to implement the project;

Requests that the Chairman of the Commission convey to the Director-General of UNESCO the interest and willingness of IOC to collaborate in the interdisciplinary and intersectoral Project, as well as the suggestion that the management arrangements should reflect the complementary interests of, and contributions made to the Project by the UNESCO programmes concerned and the IOC.

Resolution XVIII-8

THIRD SESSION OF THE JOINT IOC-FAO INTERGOVERNMENTAL PANEL ON HARMFUL ALGAL BLOOMS (IPHAB)

The Intergovernmental Oceanographic Commission,

Recalling that the IOC, at the Twenty-seventh Session of its Executive Council, through Resolution EC-XXVII.3 approved the continuation of the Joint IOC-FAO Intergovernmental Panel on Harmful Algal Blooms (IPHAB),

Considering the Executive Summary of the Third Session of the Panel together with the three Resolutions and seven Recommendations adopted at the Session;

Takes note of the "Action Plan and Implementation Schedule" and the "Summary of Financial and Staff Requirements for the Biennium 1996-1997" attached to the Executive Summary;

Decides to take the following action on the Recommendations:

Recommendation 1 - Staffing of the HAB Programme Office

(i) **Approves** the Recommendation and **invites** UNESCO and other Member States to provide matching funds to those provided by the USA partially supporting a Technical Secretary for OSLR of which the HAB programme is one component;

(ii) **Urges** Denmark and the USA to maintain their support to OSLR/HAB and also **urges** other Member States to consider pooling resources for additional posts specifically for HAB;

Recommendation 2 - HAB Training and Capacity Building Programme

(i) **Approves** the Recommendation subject to availability of resources;

(ii) **Urges** Member States to co-sponsor training activities both in cash and in kind;

Recommendation 3 - Working Group on Transfer of Phytoplankton by Ballast Water of Ships

Approves the Recommendation;

Recommendation 4 - Working Group on Aquatic Biotoxins Related to Harmful Algae

Approves the Recommendation subject to availability of resources;

Recommendation 5 - Working Group on Harmful Algal Blooms in South America

Approves the Recommendation subject to availability of resources;

Recommendation 6 - Linkage between the HAB Programme and GOOS

(i) **Approves** the Recommendation;

(ii) **Urges** Member States to incorporate national or regional HAB monitoring into national, regional and international GOOS activities;

<u>Recommendation 7 - Operation of the IOC Intergovernmental Panel on Harmful Algal Blooms</u>

(i) **Approves** the Recommendation;

(ii) **Invites** the Panel to provide an Executive Summary of its Report, with a proposed Resolution for possible adoption, including an estimate of financial implications, to the Nineteenth Session of the Assembly;

(iii) **Instructs** the Executive Secretary IOC to convene the Fourth Session of the joint IOC-FAO Panel prior to the Nineteenth Session of the Assembly.

Annex 1 to Resolution XVIII-8

Action Plan and Implementation Schedule

Main Activities	1996	1997
PROGRAMME SUPPORT		
Fourth Session of the IOC Intergovernmental Panel on Harmful Algal Blooms (IPHAB-IV)		(Paris)
Establishment of IOC HAB Science and Communication Centres	Vigo, Spain	US, WESTPAC Member States
Second Report of the IPHAB Task Team on Programme Development		IPHAB-IV
Inf. brochure on the Programme	X	
EDUCATIONAL ELEMENTS		
INFORMATION NETWORK:		
IOC newsletter: Harmful Algae News	4 issues	4 issues
IOC Manual on Harmful Marine Microplankton	1.ed.	
TRAINING:		
Taxonomy		
Toxin Chemistry	Copenhagen, Denmark; Vigo Spain; Aberdeen, UK; Tokyo, Japan, and regional	Copenhagen, Denmark; Vigo Spain; Aberdeen, UK; Tokyo, Japan, and regional
Monitoring & Management		
SCIENTIFIC ELEMENTS		
Final Report of IPHAB Task Team on Aquatic Biotoxins	X X	X X
Regional HAB Science Planning Workshops		IPHAB-IV S-America
ICES-IOC Working Group on the Dynamics of Harmful Algal Blooms	Brest, France	
ICES-IOC Working Group Workshop	Kristineberg, Sweden	
SCOR-IOC/NATO Advanced Study Institute (SCOR-IOC WG 97)	Bermuda	
(Working Group on dessimination of phytoplankton by ballast water)	X	
(Working group on Aquatic Biotoxins related to Harmful Algae)	X	
OPERATIONAL ELEMENTS		
Final Report of IPHAB Task Team on Design and Implementation of HAB Monitoring Programmes	X	
International Conference/Training Workshop on Design and Implementation of HAB Monitoring and Management Programmes	X	

Annex 2 to Resolution XVIII-8

Summary of Financial and Staff Requirements for the Biennium 1996-97 (in US $)

Activity (see Action Plan)	A. Total financial implication of IPHABIII decisions and Recommendations	B. Estimated available funds (RP and TF)	C. Additional potential extra-budgetary contributions	D. Required extra-budgetary contributions for full programme implementation (A-(B+C)
PROGRAMME SUPPORT General (excl. Centres)	15.000	8.000	-	7.000
Staff	2 seconded	-	1 seconded	1 seconded
EDUCATIONAL ELEMENTS NETWORK (excl. publication)	10.000	2.000	-	8.000
TRAINING (incl. Centres)	350.000	190.000		160.000
SCIENTIFIC ELEMENTS	40.000	10.000		30.000
OPERATIONAL ELEMENTS	70.000	20.000	20.000	30.000
TOTAL	485.000	230.000	20.000	235.000

Resolution XVIII-9

MARINE BIODIVERSITY

The Intergovernmental Oceanographic Commission,

Recognizing the great importance of conserving marine biodiversity, including the need for research in the subject area,

Taking into account that successful implementation of the Convention on Biological Diversity will address the conservation of biological diversity, the sustainable use of its components, and the fair and equitable sharing of the benefits arising out of the utilization of genetic resources,

Taking into account the United Nations Convention on the Law of the Sea,

Noting that the Convention on Biological Diversity calls on the assistance, where appropriate, of competent international organizations to the Contracting Parties to the Convention, for its implementation,

Noting also that the First Meeting of the Conference of the Parties to the Convention on Biological Diversity adopted decision I/7 pertaining to the Subsidiary Body on Scientific, Technical and Technological Advice (SBSTTA), which, *inter alia,* states that at its first ordinary meeting, SBSTTA shall consider its *modus operandi* as well as the need to draw on relevant existing institutional structures; and, that the provisional agenda for SBSTTA's first ordinary meeting, as reported in decision I/7, will *inter alia* deal with provision of advice on the scientific, technical and technological aspects of the conservation and sustainable use of coastal and marine biological diversity (priority item),

Emphasizing the importance of re-evaluating the IOC existing programmes and activities to review the scope for enhancing marine biodiversity study as an IOC activity,

Recognizing that IOC has a substantial role to play in providing the Conference of the Parties to the Convention on Biological Diversity, through its Subsidiary Body on Scientific, Technical and Technological Advice, with advice on scientific issues concerning marine biodiversity,

Decides to continue the *ad hoc* Consultation of Experts on Marine Biodiversity as needed, drawing on other relevant programme activities of the IOC for implementation of its recommendations;

Instructs the Executive Secretary IOC to communicate with the Chair of SBSTTA on: the submission on behalf of IOC to the First meeting of SBSTTA of the report of the IOC-NOAA *ad hoc* Consultation on Marine Biodiversity; and, the identification of specific needs and requirements of SBSTTA for scientific input which can be provided by IOC;

Instructs the Executive Secretary IOC to interact with the International Sea-Bed Authority on matters of the effects of possible future exploitation of sea-bed resources and dumping on marine biodiversity, as well as to discuss the possibility for IOC to provide scientific input to the International Sea Bed Authority in this respect;

Instructs also the Executive Secretary IOC to strengthen links with the Man and Biosphere Programme in order to develop joint activities in the field of sustainable use and conservation of marine biodiversity;

Urges Member States to undertake efforts at the national and regional levels to compile inventories of their marine flora and fauna, building on existing data bases, containing *inter alia* species description and figures, ecological information and distribution and economical importance;

Takes note of activities listed in Annex 1 attached to the Executive Summary of the *ad hoc* Consultation (Document IOC-XVIII/2 Annex 9), and particularly **encourages** the pursuit of those activities which can be conducted at no cost to the IOC.

Financial implications: US$ 55,000

Resolution XVIII-10

SUPPORT TO THE JOINT IOC-IHO OCEAN MAPPING PROGRAMME

The Intergovernmental Oceanographic Commission,

Noting that the Assembly at its Seventeenth Session (March 1993) stressed that the Ocean Mapping Programme is a priority action of the IOC and should be provided with necessary support,

Recognizing that the demand for an improved authoritative and global description of the bathymetry of the world's oceans from physical and biological oceanographers who are involved in modelling the ocean environment and predicting changes in global circulation, is steadily becoming more insistent, in addition to the increasingly fine resolution requirements of marine geologists and geophysicists,

Recognizing also that on a global scale, existing bathymetric data are widely scattered and of very variable quality in depth and position, but that there are now available high quality multi beam swath-sounding techniques and accurate position control systems,

Emphasizing that repeated routine ocean observations, as anticipated in the IOC's Global Ocean Observing System (GOOS), will be required to monitor oceanic change, and that this will require a secure framework of global bathymetry,

Acknowledging that the entry into force of the UN Convention on the Law of the Sea (UNCLOS) in November 1994 brings into focus the needs of coastal states to define and possibly exploit resources within national jurisdiction, and hence the requirement for detailed and accurate bathymetry of the margins,

Thanks the Russian Federation for seconding staff to support the Ocean Mapping Programme;

Instructs the Executive Secretary IOC:

(i) to initiate discussions on how to establish scientific priorities for bathymetric surveys of the world's oceans and then, in collaboration with the International Hydrographic Organization, to establish a well co-ordinated and comprehensive plan for the coming decade;

(ii) in the interim, to investigate the possibility of improving the level of funding in the regular programme for Ocean Mapping, with a view to ensuring that the biennial cycle of meetings of the Consultative Group on Ocean Mapping (CGOM) and the Regional Ocean Mapping projects is maintained, in order to retain the necessary impetus in the various activities of these bodies, with, in particular, the paramount requirement for a meeting of the Editorial Board for the International Bathymetric Chart of the Central Eastern Atlantic (IBCEA) (possibly in Lisbon or Brest) in 1996, of the Editorial Board for the International Bathymetric Chart of the Western Pacific by 1996, and of CGOM early in 1997;

Invites the Director-General of UNESCO to establish one professional post for the Ocean Mapping Programme as of 1996;

Invites the International Hydrographic Organization to consider the above proposal, and assist with the development of a plan for the proposed co-ordinated bathymetric surveys.

Financial implications for the 1996-1997 period:

- Participation of Ocean Mapping Officers, staff and experts in the relevant activities of Ocean Mapping and other programmes and organizations in 1996-1997 - US$ 15,000;

- The biennial cycle of the meeting of the Consultative Group on Ocean Mapping in 1997 - US$ 10,000;

- The meetings of the Editorial Boards for the biennial cycle: IBCM, IBCWIO, IBCCA, IBCEA and IBCWP in 1996-1997 - US$ 95,000;

- Contracts with the Chairman of CGOM and participants of the Ocean Mapping Programme in 1996-1997 - US$ 20,000;

- Professional staff at P-4 level for Ocean Mapping Programme - annual cost US$ 100,000.

Total required: US$ 240,000.

Resolution XVIII-11

SECOND SESSION OF THE IOC-WMO-UNEP COMMITTEE FOR THE GLOBAL OCEAN OBSERVING SYSTEM (I-GOOS)

The Intergovernmental Oceanographic Commission,

Having considered the Executive Summary of the Second Session of the IOC-WMO-UNEP Committee for GOOS (Document IOC-WMO-UNEP/I-GOOS-II/3S),

Recalling Resolutions XVII.5 and EC-XXVII.6 on GOOS,

Noting:

(i) Resolutions I-GOOS-II.1 to I-GOOS-II.5,

[...]

Invites UNEP, IUCN, UNESCO, WMO and ICSU (IGBP/LOICZ) to join IOC in the participation and co-sponsorship of proposed Global Coral Reef Network, subject to available resources, and **urges** Member States to make direct and in-kind contributions to the IOC to support this endeavour.

Financial implications: Implementation of the actions proposed has been funded to some extent by extra-budgetary funds from Member States; additional contributions from Member States and International Organizations will be required in order to ensure the implementation of the GCRMN. About US$ 40,000 will be required from IOC to support participation of the experts from the Indian and Pacific Oceans in the Eighth International Coral Reef Symposium in 1996.

Resolution XVIII-13

GLOBAL SEA-LEVEL OBSERVING SYSTEM (GLOSS) ACTIVITIES 1996-1997

The Intergovernmental Oceanographic Commission,

Having reviewed the report of the Fourth Session of the IOC Group of Experts on GLOSS (Bordeaux, 31 January - 3 February 1995),

Taking into account the views expressed by the Second Session of the IOC-WMO-UNEP Committee on GOOS regarding GLOSS-GOOS interaction,

Noting with satisfaction:

(i) the development of data/information sea-level products and services based on satellite and GLOSS stations measurements;

(ii) the co-operation with the International Global Positioning System Service (IGS) in connecting some GLOSS TGBM to a Global Geodetic Reference System aimed at monitoring changes in the absolute global sea-level;

(iii) the development of the Pilot Activity on Sea-Level Changes and Associated Coastal Impacts in the Indian Ocean;

(iv) the production of "Afro-America GLOSS News" by Brazil;

(v) the preparation and dissemination of the GLOSS Bulletin via the World Wide Web;

(vi) the continued support to international GLOSS activities provided by Australia, Brazil, India, UK, USA and many other countries; and,

(vii) the close interaction of the GE/GLOSS with the IAPSO Commission on Mean Sea-Level,

Noting with concern the decrease in the financial support of GLOSS international activities, particularly needed for training activities,

Endorses the report of the Fourth Session of the IOC Group of Experts on GLOSS, including the GLOSS Strategy and Plan of Action for 1995-1997;

Requests the IOC Group of Experts on GLOSS to:

(i) pursue the strategy aimed at integrating *in situ* measurements from GLOSS stations with satellite altimetry and geodesy and producing global and regional sea-level products;

(ii) continue collaborating with I-GOOS and J-GOOS on matters related to sea-level network design, data and information exchange, and sea-level products preparation and dissemination;

(iii) continue providing scientific and technical advice on the implementation of the Pilot Activity on Sea-Level Changes and Associated Coastal Impacts in the Indian Ocean;

(iv) continue to submit its reports directly to the IOC Governing Bodies;

Instructs the Executive Secretary IOC to:

(i) make a separately identified allocation of funds for GLOSS in the IOC Draft Programme and Budget for 1996-1997;

(ii) consider increasing support for GLOSS through the IOC regional and TEMA activities to enable implementation of the Plan of Action for 1995-1997;

(iii) continue investigating the establishment of a dedicated post in the Secretariat to develop GLOSS and related sea-level studies and applications;

Urges Member States to continue their support of GLOSS implementation by:

(i) maintaining and up-grading national GLOSS stations;

(ii) developing GLOSS regional components, including EuroGLOSS and the Mediterranean regional network;

(iii) providing data to PSMSL and other international and regional sea-level centres; and,

(iv) providing contributions to the IOC Trust Fund to ensure the implementation of the GLOSS training and assistance programme;

Calls upon IOC Regional Subsidiary Bodies to support the activities of the GLOSS Regional Co-ordinators, particularly in organizing GLOSS training and technical assistance activities in their respective regions.

Financial implications for the 1996-1997 period:

- Training courses (2: 1 in 1996 and 1 in 1997) - US$ 60,000
- Support for the activities on sea-level data collection and dissemination; preparation of sea-level products; sea-level information exchange (GLOSS Handbook, GLOSS Bulletins, GLOSS CD ROM, etc.), (1996-1997) - US$ 50,000
- Advice and assistance to countries on installation and operation of tide-gauges (1996-1997) - US$ 20,000
- Participation of GLOSS officers, staff and experts in the relevant activities of GOOS and other programmes and organizations (1996-1997) -US$ 15,000
- Fifth Session of the IOC Group of Experts on GLOSS (1997) - US$ 25,000

Total required: US$ 170,000.

Resolution XVIII-14

THE FLOATING UNIVERSITY PROJECT

The Intergovernmental Oceanographic Commission,

Being informed on the productive 5-year operation of the UNESCO(IOC/MRI) (TREDMAR) "Floating University" Project in the Mediterranean, Black and Baltic Seas, involving co-operative "training-through-research" planning, participation, data reduction, networking, and use of the UNESCO (IOC/MRI) (TREDMAR) computer-based modules in remote sensing and seismic tasks,

Having considered the Summary Report and recommendations of the TEMA Strategy *ad hoc* Meeting (March 1995) recommending a strengthened relationship with, among others, TREDMAR, and the need to enhance complementarity between UNESCO and IOC programmes, especially with respect to coastal regions and small islands,

Calling attention to the necessity of quick and adequate sharing and transfer of knowledge among the Member States, and of developing and supporting existing, and new, forms of "training-through-research" and advanced education in regions,

Notes with appreciation the offer of the Russian Federation to continue its support to the UNESCO (TREDMAR) "Floating University" Project, in particular through the Mediterranean, Black and Baltic Seas facilities, and **accepts** its invitation to IOC for co-sponsorship of the project;

Decides to co-sponsor through TEMA the "Floating University" Project in the Mediterranean, Black and Baltic Seas, as well as the computer-based learning module project, in view of enhancing the continuation of these initiatives;

Financial implications to the IOC: US$ 20,000.

Invites Member States to put forward proposals and support leading to the establishment of the "Floating University" Project in other regions.

Resolution XVIII-15

CAPACITY BUILDING IN MARINE SCIENCES, SERVICES AND OBSERVATIONS - TEMA

The Intergovernmental Oceanographic Commission,

Having considered the request of the Twenty-seventh Session of the Executive Council regarding a "Draft TEMA Strategy to respond to UNCED Agenda 21, Chapter 17, Part E",

Acknowledging with appreciation the information provided by the document "Observations and Experiences of Selected TEMA Activities During 1984-94" (Doc. IOC-XVIII/Inf.2 by Dr. S.M. Haq),

Emphasizing the importance of the IOC TEMA Programme for Capacity Building in marine science and services, as well as to stimulate national, regional and global co-operation in marine science; the latter being main components of the IOC Comprehensive Action Plan (Doc. IOC-XVIII/2 Annex 1),

Takes note of recommendations submitted by the TEMA Strategy *ad hoc* Meeting (IOC/INF-999) including the proposed "Draft TEMA Strategy in response to UNCLOS and UNCED" (Doc. IOC-XVIII/2 Annex 6);

Decides to establish a TEMA Group of Experts for Capacity Building composed of six to eight qualified experts in the field of training, education and mutual assistance, as proposed by Member States with representation from the regions, to interact with the relevant TEMA focal points of IOC Subsidiary Bodies. The Group of Experts, will perform the following tasks:

(i) further develop a strategy for TEMA activities and a revised TEMA Action Plan for Capacity Building (to include evaluation techniques as a permanent managerial tool), for consideration during the forthcoming Session of the IOC Executive Council;

(ii) establish closer partnerships with other relevant Capacity Building programmes such as UN-DOALOS-UNDP Train-Sea-Coast, and others in the framework of ICSPRO (the Coast and Small Islands Project of UNESCO, in particular), and the ACC Sub-Committee on Ocean and Coastal Areas;

(iii) foster as a main mechanism for the Programme, the development of regional and sub-regional co-ordination and thematic networking;

(iv) assist Member States of the regions in the preparation of proposals to GEF and other potential funding agencies, programmes and donors, and thereby, formulate elements of a strategy for mobilizing financial and other forms of support;

(v) undertake a feasibility study to develop a Clearing House Reference System on training opportunities in the framework of UN Agencies of ICSPRO and ACC Sub-Committee on Ocean and Coastal Areas;

Instructs the Executive Secretary IOC to:

(i) organize, in consultation with the Co-chairmen of the TEMA Strategy *Ad hoc* Meeting, an intersessional meeting of the TEMA Group of Experts for Capacity Building, not later than the first half of 1996, taking all necessary provisions to assure the successful accomplishment of the tasks assigned to the Group;

(ii) assure effective co-ordination for this meeting with relevant activities of ICSPRO and ACC Sub-Committee on Ocean and Coastal Areas programmes, as well as with those of scientific advisory bodies of the Commission;

(iii) provide proper support for implementation of the Capacity Building TEMA activities in the Secretariat of the Commission;

Invites Member States to consider a substantial increase in support of Capacity Building through the TEMA Programme, through staff secondments, and contributions to the IOC/TEMA Trust Fund.

Financial implications: US$ 30,000.

Resolution XVIII-16

IOC SUB-COMMISSION FOR THE CARIBBEAN AND ADJACENT REGIONS (IOCARIBE)

The Intergovernmental Oceanographic Commission,

Recalling Recommendation SC-IOCARIBE-IV.8 (Strengthening of the IOCARIBE Secretariat), approved by Resolution XVII-11 of the IOC Assembly, which called for appointing necessary staff to the Secretariat in Cartagena,

Having considered the Interim Report on IOCARIBE Evaluation (Document IOC/INF-993) provided to the Assembly to facilitate discussion of Agenda Item 13.1,

Acknowledging benefits which could derive from the IOCARIBE evaluation and the methodology developed, in order to provide Member States with appropriate information for decision-making, especially in the coming IOCARIBE Session in Barbados, December 1995,

Recognizing that a strong and efficient regional Secretariat, adequate to present and future requirements of the region, is needed for the future in order to:

(i) implement strategies applicable to a regional comprehensive plan,

(ii) to enhance the representativity of the Sub-Commission in the region,

(iii) to effectively mobilize and manage funds, and

(iv) to provide timely appropriate support for Programmes, Experts and Member States,

Invites the Director General of UNESCO and **instructs** the Executive Secretary IOC to continue supporting the evaluation until it is completed and presented to the Fifth Session of IOCARIBE, December 1995;

Notes with concern the interim situation of staffing in the regional Secretariat since the Assistant Secretary for IOCARIBE post was transferred to Paris without replacement, and the secondment of experts from France and Sweden was discontinued;

Further invites the Director General of UNESCO to implement Resolution XVII-11 of the IOC Assembly, particularly Recommendation SC-IOCARIBE-IV.8 (Strengthening of the IOCARIBE Secretariat) and provide, the post of Assistant Secretary for IOCARIBE;

Urges Member States to provide seconded or associate experts for the Regional Secretariat;

Invites IOC Member States to actively participate in the IOCARIBE evaluation at the Fifth Session of the IOCARIBE Sub-Commission, Barbados, 11-15 December 1995.

Resolution XVIII-17

IOC BLACK SEA REGIONAL PROGRAMME IN MARINE SCIENCES AND SERVICES

The Intergovernmental Oceanographic Commission,

Recalling Resolution of the 27th General Conference of UNESCO (Doc. 27 C/5 1.211 and DR 190),

Recalling also Resolutions XVI-7 "Black Sea Project" and XVII-15 "Regional Black Sea Co-operation Programme",

Recalling further the implementation of decision of the IOC Executive Council (Document IOC/EC-XXV/3, paras. 84 and 85) to take action towards sponsorship of the "Co-operative Marine Science Programme for the Black Sea (COMSBLACK)" (document IOC/INF-924) and the support provided by IOC,

Recognizing the urgency of the international effort aimed at the implementation of the regional programme in support of the effective integrated management of the Black Sea,

Recognizing also that special attention had already been given to specific regional requirements of the Back Sea region, e.g., within the International Oceanographic Data and Information Exchange (IODE) and the Global Investigation of Pollution in the Marine Environment (GIPME) programmes, and especially through the GEF Black Sea Environmental Programme,

Noting the UNESCO support to various intersectorial co-operative initiatives within the Black Sea region, in particular the "UNESCO-Chernobyl" and the "Blue Danube" projects,

Noting also the significance of the Convention for the Protection of the Black Sea against Pollution (Bucharest, Romania, 22 April 1992), and the Ministerial Declaration on the Protection of the Black Sea (Odessa, 7 April 1993),

Taking into account the relevant provisions of the UN Convention on the Law of the Sea,

Being aware of the efforts being undertaken by the United Nations Environment Programme within its Regional Seas Programme in response to the requests made to UNEP by the riparian states of the Black Sea, and in the framework of the Bucharest Convention and the Odessa Declaration, to set up a Regional Seas Programme for the Black Sea,

Noting further the results of the Regional Black Sea Workshop, Varna, September 1994, in the form of a regional programme, with initiation through two pilot projects in the framework of this programme;

Expresses its appreciation to the countries from the region and several countries and donors from outside the region for the support provided to the COMSBLACK initiative;

Takes note of the proposals and recommendations of the Black Sea Intergovernmental Meeting, UNESCO Headquarters, 7-9 June 1995, in which all Black Sea states participated;

Reaffirms the decision taken by the EC-XXV to continue actions for IOC to support and sponsor COMSBLACK within the context of GIPME;

Notes with satisfaction the establishment of the IOC Black Sea Regional Programme in Marine Sciences and Services for an initial period of four years;

Establishes an IOC Black Sea Regional Committee as the management body for the IOC Black Sea Regional Programme, with the Terms of Reference given in Annex 1 to this Resolution, together with the initial work plan;

Instructs the Executive Secretary IOC to make available the support required to facilitate the initial activities of the Regional Committee and to seek additional funding and technical support from governments and donors in order to undertake pilot projects already agreed upon and others to be further elaborated; possible initial activities and related financial implications are given in Annex 2 to this Resolution;

Further instructs the Executive Secretary IOC, in consultation with the appropriate authorities, to elaborate a Memorandum of Understanding regarding scientific co-operation and inputs to the Black Sea Environmental Programme, currently sponsored by the GEF and other donors in order to promote a coherent region-wide approach to environmental management in the spirit of UNCED Agenda 21;

Invites the Regional Committee to report on progress of the implementation of the programme at the next session of the Assembly.

Financial implications: It is estimated that to facilitate expert meetings, exchange and participation of experts in scientific activities, gradual establishment of a communications network and data bases, an annual support from IOC of a minimum of US$50,000 will be required, to be supplemented by other UNESCO funding resources, as well as national in-kind and other resources.

Annex 1 to Resolution XVIII-17

Terms of Reference for the IOC Black Sea Regional Committee

In accordance with the IOC Manual, Section 5: Guidelines for the Structure and Responsibilities of the Subsidiary Bodies of the Commission (Doc. IOC/INF-785, 1989, page 37, in English version):

(i) The IOC Regional Committee shall promote, develop and co-ordinate the regional joint marine sciences and services programmes, identify the requirements for resources, prepare the overview budgets and report to the Governments and the IOC Assembly; in its work it should draw as appropriate upon IOC programmes.

(ii) The IOC Regional Committee shall plan and co-ordinate the marine sciences and services activities of the IOC Black Sea Regional Programme, taking into account the relevant provisions of the Convention for Protection of the Black Sea against Pollution, the UN Convention on the Law of the Sea, the Black Sea Fisheries Convention, and international programmes carried out by international institutions and organizations (UNESCO, UNEP, WMO, WHO, IMO, IAEA, FAO, UNDP, NATO, the World Bank, PHARE, the European Union, etc.), so as to avoid overlap and duplication of efforts and ensure co-ordination with other relevant activities.

(iii) The IOC Regional Committee shall establish close connection with all existing relevant regional programmes, so as to avoid duplications and also help the linkage between science and management aspects.

(iv) The IOC Regional Committee shall report on programme implementation, proposals and budget requirements to the IOC Assembly.

Annex 2 to Resolution XVIII-17

IOC Black Sea Regional Committee -
Initial Tasks for the period 1996-1997

(i) Elaborate and start phased implementation of two proposed pilot projects, and possibly others within the framework of regional programmes, using proposals and specifications already provided by Black Sea Member States; and adjust implementation in accordance with available resources.

(ii) Identify products and possible economical benefits expected to result from the pilot projects and the programme as a whole.

(iii) Establish in a phased manner a regional communication network adequate for and adjusted to the data exchange needs.

(iv) Prepare project proposals for donor applications, using the identified expected products and their relationship or input to the management of the Black Sea Marine Environment.

(v) Establish dialogue and co-operation as required with other IOC programmes and on-going relevant regional programmes and projects.

(vi) Gradually establish verified scientific data bases for applications, e.g., in relation to emergencies, coastal zone pollution, disturbances, erosion and other management-related problems.

(vii) Gradually establish a combined modelling and observation capacity which can be used in forecasting environmental conditions in the Black Sea.

(viii) Develop and implement TEMA components aimed at establishing modern capacity-building facilities for the successful implementation of the Regional Programme.

Resolution XVIII-18

PROGRAMME AND BUDGET 1996-1997

The Intergovernmental Oceanographic Commission,

Recalling the advice provided by IOC *ad hoc* study groups and ensuing decisions of IOC Governing Bodies, notably through IOC Resolution XVII-20, in regard to the evolution of the IOC within UNESCO and its role therein as an intergovernmental body with functional autonomy,

Having considered the Proposal on the Draft Programme and Budget 1996-97 as contained in Document IOC-XVIII/2 Annex 7,

Having taken note of IOC entry contained in paras 02364-02379 of the Draft UNESCO Programme and Budget 1996-97 (Draft 28 C/5),

Recognizing the responsibilities that devolve on the IOC, through the arrangements proposed in the Draft 28 C/5, by which UNESCO will provide its support to the IOC through a financial allocation,

Expressing its satisfaction regarding the positive reaction of the United Nations (through Resolution A/RES/49/131), to the IOC proposal that 1998 be declared the UN International Year of the Ocean,

Approves, as a basis for future planning, the IOC Draft Programme and Budget 1996-97, based upon anticipated resources emanating from the UNESCO financial allocation and from other sources;

Urges Member States to continue and increase their support to the IOC through direct and in-kind contributions;

Expresses its appreciation to the Director-General for the initiatives taken to clarify the role of the IOC within UNESCO and to create favourable conditions within which the IOC can respond properly to its mandate and its role in relation to UNCLOS and UNCED in accordance with the expressed needs of its Member States;

Submits to the 28th UNESCO General Conference the Programme Resolution contained in the Annex;

Authorizes the IOC Executive Council at its Twenty-ninth Session to approve any adjustments to the Programme and Budget that may be required in light of resources and expenditure.

Annex to Resolution IOC-XVIII-18

PROPOSED RESOLUTION

THE INTERGOVERNMENTAL OCEANOGRAPHIC COMMISSION

The General Conference,

Recalling that, by amendment of the Statutes of the Intergovernmental Oceanographic Commission (IOC) in 1987, the 24th General Conference confirmed that the IOC "is established as a body with functional autonomy within UNESCO",

Having taken note of the report on the activities of the Intergovernmental Oceanographic Commission (IOC) during the biennium 1993-1994 and matters brought to its attention by the Eighteenth Session of the IOC Assembly,

1. **Requests** the IOC, in accordance with its statutes, to pursue the programme of work for 1996-1997, as approved by the IOC Assembly at its Eighteenth Session, and in particular:

   (a) Objective 1. To reduce the scientific uncertainties on oceans and coastal areas related to Agenda 21;

   (b) Objective 2. To strengthen data exchange and ocean services;

   (c) Objective 3. To foster capacity building in developing countries for marine research and systematic ocean observations;

   (d) Objective 4. To stimulate international and regional co-operation in marine science and systematic ocean observations;

2. **Authorizes** the Director-General to support the IOC by providing a financial allocation in the amount of $ 6,430,100 under the regular programme, Major Programme II;

3. **Expresses** its appreciation to the Member States and organizations that have supported the IOC programmes through voluntary and in-kind contributions, including staff, and invites them to continue their support for the 1996-1997 biennium;

4. **Further requests** the IOC to make recommendations and provide technical guidance on interdisciplinary aspects of relevance to UNCED follow-up, and in regard to preparation of the 1998 United Nations International Year of the Ocean and as to the formulation and execution of the marine science aspects of the project on environment and development of coastal regions and the small islands.

[...]

G. Statements by the Delegations of Argentina and Brazil on Agenda Item 9

(i) Delegation of Argentina

Mr Chairman,

The Delegation of Argentina wishes to congratulate the IOC Secretariat, and more particularly Dr. Latouche, for the information provided on the scientific part of Document IOC/INF-1007, presented in a very serious and detailed way. On the other hand, we regret that we are unable to say the same regarding the legal aspect of this document.

In this regard, Argentina apologizes to the other Delegations attending the Session for having altered the serenity of a scientific discussion, undoubtedly interesting, with legal questions which, together with policy matters, should be alien to the major part of the work of this Commission. Nevertheless, several questions arise from the legal basis of the above mentioned Document IOC/INF-1007, for example:

a) It would be interesting to know whether the IOC Secretariat explained to the experts who participated in the meeting referred to in Document IOC/INF-1007, that Document IOC/EC-XXVII/15 had been seriously questioned during the last Session of the Executive Council, to the extent that it was decided to establish an intersessional group to study this matter in depth. This is very important; therefore, it would be regrettable that the limited financial resources of the Commission be used to carry out study and evaluation activities, which Member States, also members of the Law of the Sea Convention, could consider *a posteriori* not to be within the IOC's sphere of competence.

b) It would also be advisable that a copy of Dr. Yankov's presentation to the meeting, which is described in Document IOC/INF-1007, be distributed, since some of his remarks do not seem to have been taken into account. For example, Item 3.2, page 2; it is asserted - and I am quoting in English since there has been no other language version of this document - that Dr. Yankov *"emphasized that the Commission [regarding limits of the continental shelf] is not an arbitration mechanism and its recommendation is advisory in nature but will become final and legally binding if a country accepts the recommendation"*. Strictly speaking, the IOC resolutions are never mandatory; according to Article 67, para. 8 of the Convention, only the limits defined by a State taking as a basis such recommendations, are final and compulsory; this is not the same.

c) Third, Item 3.3, page 2; and Item 4.5.3, page 6 of the referred document: a report requested by UN-DOALOS to IOC is mentioned, on scientific and technical matters regarding the limit of the outer limit of the continental shelf. It would undoubtedly be more beneficial to know the legal basis and scope of the UN-DOALOS request, with a view to discussing them during this Assembly, when the corresponding item of the agenda is dealt with.

d) Fourth, Item 4.1, page 3 of the document refers to the delimitation of the *"foot of the continental shelf"*. Furthermore, in Document IOC/INF-1007 reference is made to *"precise delimitation"* of this foot. However, it is necessary that the present Assembly discuss whether the Law of the Sea Convention is really giving authority to IOC to decide about this *"precise delimitation"*.

e) Finally, in Item 8.3, page 9 - still referring to Document IOC/INF-1007 - it is stated that Member States which claim a continental shelf to be over 200 nautical miles, should do so within ten years from their ratification of the Law of the Sea Convention. Even without considering whether the deadline taken into consideration should be the date of ratification by each State, or the date when the Convention entered into force - and we shall refer to the latter when speaking about discussions on the corresponding item - this affirmation, again, is inaccurate for the following reason: according to Item 4 of Annex II, of the Law of the Sea Convention, the correct way for a coastal state which desires to establish the outer limit of its continental shelf beyond 200 nautical miles, is to submit to Commission on the Limits of the Continental Shelf (CLCS) - in the defined deadline - the characteristics of this limit together with the scientific and technical supporting data.

Mr. Chairman,

Argentina wishes that the above-mentioned remarks be recorded in the report of the Assembly, taking into account that this question will be discussed in due time by this Assembly. The legal basis of the competence of IOC regarding the delimitation of the continental shelf may not be pre-defined by Document IOC/INF-1007. This has to be carefully and thoroughly discussed in the light of Item 3, para. 2 , Annex II of Law of the Sea Convention, according to which *"the Commission [speaking of the limits of continental shelf] will be allowed to co-operate, as far as it is considered useful and necessary, with the Intergovernmental Oceanographic Commission of UNESCO, the International Hydrographic Commission and other qualified international organizations, in order to exchange scientific and technical information which could be of benefit to the fulfilment of the Commission's functions"*. This seems to have been clearly understood by several of the Delegations, for instance the Delegation of Canada which, as a result of Annex II to Document IOC/INF-990, expressed - and I have again to quote in English - *"while Canada supports the Role of GEBCO on the provision of scientific advice, it feels that it should be the responsibility of coastal states to acquire the data and information necessary for the delineation of limits of their continental shelves as defined under Article 76 of the Convention"*.

Thank you, Mr. Chairman.

(ii) Delegation of Brazil

With reference to the report stated above, the Brazilian Delegation wishes to point out the following aspects:

1. The report itself is of reasonably good quality, and we agree with most of its considerations, but ask the Assembly to rectify the last sentence on page 11, as it is not correctly stated:

> *"In view of the 10-year timeframe starting from ratification for a country to submit the application for a continental shelf beyond 200 miles, and taking into account the fact that for some countries, due to an early ratification of the Convention, may have much less than 10 years before the deadline, the experts urged IOC to bring to the attention of IOC Member States the urgent issue of the delimitation of outer edge of the continental shelf under UNCLOS, and strengthen co-operation with UN-DOALOS, CLCS and IHO in discharging its responsibilities"*

This statement clashes with Article 4 of Annex II of UNCLOS, that reads as follows:

> *"Where a Coastal State intends to establish, in accordance with Article 76, the outer limits of its continental shelf beyond 200 nautical miles, it shall submit particulars of such limits to the Commission along with supporting scientific and technical data as soon as possible,* ***but in any case within 10 years of the entry into force of this Convention*** *for that State. The Coastal State shall, at the same time, give the names of any Commission members who have provided it with scientific and technical advice".*

More proof of evidence that the statement in document IOC/INF-990 is not appropriate can be found in Article 308 of UNCLOS that reads:

> *"1. This Convention shall enter into force 12 months after the date of deposit of the sixtieth instrument of ratification of accession.*
>
> *2. For each State ratifying or acceding to this Convention after the deposit of the sixtieth instrument of ratification or accession, the Convention shall enter into force on the thirtieth day following the deposit of its instrument of ratification or accession, subject to paragraph 1".*

It is therefore absolutely clear that the 10 year timeframe will start counting from 16 November 1994 for all countries that:

(i) ratified the Convention before 16 November 1993 (Article 308, item 1); or
(ii) ratified the Convention until 16 November 1994 (Article 308, item 2).

For those countries that have deposited their instrument of ratification or accession after 16 November 1994, the Convention will enter into force on the thirtieth day following the deposit of the instrument of ratification or accession.

For different countries, the Convention may enter into force in different dates, but never before the date clearly defined in Article 308, item 1.

No committment will bind the State Party before the Law of the Sea enters into force.

The scientific and technical data that support the intent of a Coastal State to extend the outer limit of its continental shelf beyond 100 nautical miles, shall be submitted to the Commission on the Limits of the Continental Shelf (CLCS). This Commission will come into life only within 18 months after the date of entry into force of the Convention.

2. The Brazilian Delegation disagrees vividly with most of the statements contained in Annex II of the same IOC/INF-990 document and understands that it should be entirely rewritten. A few examples can be drawn:

(i) Article 76(8) and Annex II, items 3.1 and 3.2 of UNCLOS:

The transcription of the content of those articles is partial, giving a wrong idea of the meaning and spirit of UNCLOS.

Annex II, Article 2, Item 2, not reproduced in this document, reads:

"The Secretary-General of the United Nations shall address a letter to the State Parties, inviting the submission of nominations, after appropriate regional consultations, within three months. The Secretary-General shall prepare a list in alphabetical order, of all persons thus nominated and shall submit it to all the State Parties".

From what is states above, it seems quite clear that IOC has no mandate to draw up, in parallel, a list of experts that may potentially limit the sovereign right of a State Party to nominate its experts and see them elected by a meeting convened by the Secretary-General at the UN Headquarters.

So, in our point of view, at least Item 2 of the IOC Secretariat Action related to Article 76, should be dropped out from this document. In fact, Item 2 of Member States Action, as the Canadian Delegation has already pointed out, is also incorrect. According to Article 76 of UNCLOS, Items 8 and 9, as well as Annex II, Article 4, is the Coastal State's responsibility, intending to establish the outer limits of its continental shelf beyond 200 nautical miles, to submit the particulars of such limits and the scientific and technical data that support the plea.

(ii) Article 287 - 1(d) and Annex VIII, Article 2 (2) and 5 of UNCLOS:

The quotation omits Annex VIII, Article 2, Item 3, that states:

"Every State Party shall be entitled to nominate two experts in each field whose competence in the legal, scientific or technical aspects of such field is established and generally recognized and who enjoy the highest reputation for fairness and integrity. The names of the persons so nominated in each field shall constitute the appropriate list"

In respect of this consideration, I wish to congratulate the Executive Secretary IOC, Dr. Gunnar Kullenberg, who expressed very clearly and precisely this question in IOC Circular Letter No.1424, dated 14 August 1994. Brazil has not yet answered this letter because of the misunderstandings that document IOC-XVII/15 has introduced within our Government, bringing the idea that IOC is limiting the rights of Coastal States in drawing up the list in consultation with other scientific organizations. We realize the importance of this list of scientific experts, to be at the disposal of the State Parties (Annex III, Articles 3(b) and (c)), the Secretary-General of the UN (Annex III, Article 3(e)) and courts and tribunals related to the Law of the Sea (Article 289).

(iii) Article 289:

The quotation is incomplete; we ask to quote Article 289 of UNCLOS in full.

(iv) Article 247:

The quotation is also incomplete. It is omitted that one condition to the simplified authorization of marine scientific research to be granted, is that the Coastal State concerned be notified, indicating the competent organization of IOC that took the decision to approve the scientific project, the date and the place of the meeting. Only if the Coastal State has not expressed any objection within four months, the authorization is deemed as granted.

In the form that the item is presented, it may bring the idea that the provisions of prior consent of research projects within the Coastal States Exclusive Economic Zone or Continental Shelf, as stated in UNCLOS, is derrogated.

In summary, many other articles in Document IOC/INF-990 are quoted only partially and we propose a complete revision of its Annex II, before any consideration of it may be taken in Plenary.

3. With respect to Document IOC/INF-1007, entitled Summary Report of the IOC/OSNLR *ad hoc* Expert Consultation on UNCLOS, Paris, 20-21 March 1995, the Brazilian Delegation wishes to express the view that the document presents very good scientific information, but that it also presents some juridical difficulties with respect to what is stated in UNCLOS. For instance, in Item 3.2 and Item 8.3 of IOC/INF-1007 it is stated incorrectly:

> *"The claims of countries on continental shelves beyond 200 nautical miles should be submitted to the Commission within 10 years after their ratification of the Convention".*
>
> With respect to Item 7.2, we also disagree with the following recommendation:
>
> *"The experts recommended that IOC develop two lists of experts. One should be of a general nature, composed of expertise in various disciplines of marine science, including geologists and geophysicists, for possible use in providing advice to states and other organizations. The other should be composed solely of marine geologists and geophysicists, for the purpose of advising the Commission on the Limits of the Continental Shelf".* In this line of thought, Brazil objects to *"the preparation of a list of geologists, geophysicists and hydrographers to assist in the work of the Commission on the Limits of the Continental Shelf"*, as the proposal formulated in item 9 (iii) of the above-mentioned document, for the reasons already exposed in item 2 (i) of this document.

4. Finally, I would like to bring to your attention, Mr. Chairman, that the views of the Brazilian expert invited to participate in the IOC/OSNLR *ad hoc* Experts Consultation Group on UNCLOS with special reference to the implementation of Article 76, held in Paris, last March, do not necessarily reflect the views of the Brazilian Government. His participation had not been previously co-ordinated with the IOC national focal point.

Thank you, Chairman.

[...]

ANNEX IV

MEMBER STATES OF THE COMMISSION AND ITS OFFICERS

A. List of Member States of the Commission (124)
(as of 28 June 1995)

AFGHANISTAN
ALBANIA
ALGERIA
ANGOLA
*ARGENTINA
*AUSTRALIA
AUSTRIA
BAHAMAS
BANGLADESH
BARBADOS
BELGIUM
BENIN
*BRAZIL
BULGARIA
CAMEROON
*CANADA
CAPE VERDE
*CHILE
*CHINA
*COLOMBIA
CONGO
*COSTA RICA
COTE D'IVOIRE
CROATIA
*CUBA
CYPRUS
DEMOCRATIC PEOPLE'S REPUBLIC OF KOREA
DENMARK
DOMINICAN REPUBLIC
ECUADOR
*EGYPT
EL SALVADOR
ERITREA
ESTONIA
ETHIOPIA
FIJI
FINLAND
*FRANCE
GABON
GAMBIA
GEORGIA
*GERMANY
GHANA
*GREECE
GUATEMALA
*GUINEA
GUINEA-BISSAU
GUYANA
HAITI
ICELAND
*INDIA
*INDONESIA
*IRAN, ISLAMIC REPUBLIC OF
IRAQ
IRELAND
ISRAEL
*ITALY
JAMAICA
*JAPAN
JORDAN
*KENYA
KUWAIT
*LEBANON
LIBYAN ARAB JAMAHIRIYA
MADAGASCAR
MALAYSIA
MALDIVES
MALTA
MAURITANIA
MAURITIUS
*MEXICO
MONACO
MOROCCO
MOZAMBIQUE
MYANMAR
NETHERLANDS
NEW ZEALAND
NICARAGUA
*NIGERIA
*NORWAY
OMAN
PAKISTAN
PANAMA
*PERU
*PHILIPPINES
POLAND
*PORTUGAL
QATAR
*REPUBLIC OF KOREA
REPUBLIC OF YEMEN
ROMANIA
*RUSSIAN FEDERATION
SAMOA
SAINT LUCIA
SAUDI ARABIA
SENEGAL
SEYCHELLES
SIERRA LEONE
SINGAPORE
SLOVENIA
SOLOMON ISLANDS
SOMALIA
*SOUTH AFRICA
*SPAIN
SRI LANKA
SUDAN
SURINAM
SWEDEN
SWITZERLAND
SYRIAN ARAB REPUBLIC
*THAILAND
TOGO
TONGA
TRINIDAD & TOBAGO
TUNISIA
*TURKEY
*UKRAINE
UNITED ARAB EMIRATES
*UNITED KINGDOM OF GREAT BRITAIN & NORTHERN IRELAND
UNITED REPUBLIC OF TANZANIA
*UNITED STATES OF AMERICA
URUGUAY
VENEZUELA
VIETNAM

MEMBERS OF THE EXECUTIVE COUNCIL ARE INDICATED WITH AN ASTERISK *

[...]

ANNEX X

LIST OF ACRONYMS

ACC	Administrative Committee on Co-ordination
ACOPS	Advisory Committee on the Protection of the Sea
ACSYS	Arctic Climate System Study
AOSB	Arctic Ocean Science Board
AOSIS	Association of Small Island States
ASFA	Aquatic Sciences and Fisheries Abstracts
ASOS	Automated Seismological Observation System
BATHY	Bathythermograph Report
BT	Bathythermograph
CCAMLR	Commission for the Conservation of Antarctic Marine Living Resources
CCOP	Committee for Co-ordination of Joint Prospecting for Mineral Resources in Asian Offshore Areas
CD-ROM	Compact Disc with a Read-Only Memory
CEA	Central Eastern Atlantic
CEC	Commission of the European Communities
CEOS	Committee on Earth Observing Satellites
CEPPOL	Joint IOC-UNEP Marine Pollution Assessment and Control Programme for the Wider Caribbean Region
CIDA	Canadian International Development Agency
CITES	Convention on International Trade in Endangered Species of Wild Fauna and Flora
CLCS	Commission on the Limits of the Continental Shelf
CLIVAR	Climate Variability and Predictability
CMM	Centre météorologique mondial
COASTS	Programme on Coastal Ocean Advanced Science and Technology Study
COMARAF	Regional Project for Research and Training on Coastal Marine Systems in Africa
COMSBLACK	Co-operative Marine Science Programme for the Black Sea
COP	Conference of Parties
CPPS	Permanent Commission for the South Pacific
CSD	Commission on Sustainable Development
CTBT	Comprehensive Test-Ban Treaty
CZSI	Coastal Zones and Small Islands
DAC	Data Assembly Centre
DANIDA	Danish Agency for International Development
DBCP	Data Buoy Co-operation Panel
DOALOS	Division for Ocean Affairs and the Law of the Sea (UN)
DOSS	*Ad hoc* Study Group on IOC Development, Operations, Structure and Statutes
ECOR	Engineering Committee on Oceanic Resources
EEZ	Exclusive Economic Zone
EGOS	European Group on Ocean Stations
EL NIÑO	Meteorological and Ocenaographic Phenomenon off the West Coast of South America
ENSO	El Niño and the Southern Oscillation (An Ocean/Atmosphere Inteaction Study) (USA)
EROS-2000	European River-Ocean Systems Programme
ETI	Expert-center for Taxonomic Identification (The Netherlands)
EuroGLOSS	European Programme for the Global Sea-Level Observing System
EuroGOOS	European Programme for the Global Ocean Observing System
EUROMED.NET	European-Mediterranean Network
FAO	Food and Agriculture Organization of the United Nations
FCCC	Framework Convention on Climate Change
FTP	(see Peter P)
GAPA	International Geological/Geophysical Atlases of the Atlantic and Pacific Oceans

GCOS	Global Climate Observing System
GEBCO	General Bathymetric Chart of the Oceans
GEEP	Group of Experts on Effects of Pollution
GEF	Global Environment Facility
GE-MIM	Group of Experts on Marine Information Management
GESAMP	IMO-FAO-UNESCO-WMO-WHO-IAEA-UN-UNEP Joint Group of Experts on the Scientific Aspects of Marine Environmental Protection
GIPME	Global Investigation of Pollution in the Marine Environment
GIS	Geographic Information System
GLOBEC	Global Ocean Ecosystem Dynamics
GLOSS	Global Sea Level Observing System
GODAR	Global Oceanographic Data Archaeology and Rescue Project
GOOS	Global Ocean Observing System
GPS	Global Positioning System
GTOS	Global Terrestrial Observing System
GTS	Guinean Trawling Survey
GTSPP	Global Temperature-Salinity Pilot Project
HAB	Harmful Algal Blooms
HOTO	Health of the Oceans
IABP	International Arctic Buoy Programme
IACSD	Inter-Agency Committee on Sustainable Development
IAEA	International Atomic Energy Agency
IAPSO	International Association for the Physical Sciences of the Ocean
IAPP	International Arctic Polynia Programme
IAPSO	International Association for the Physical Sciences of the Ocean
IBCM	International Bathymetric Chart of the Mediterranean and its Geological/Geophysical Series
ICAM	Integrated Coastal Areas Management (IOC/GIPME)
ICG	International Co-ordination Group
ICES	International Council for the Exploration of the Sea
ICRI	International Coral Reef Initiative
ICSEM	International Commission for the Scientific Exploration of the Mediterranean Sea
ICSPRO	Intersecretariat Committee on Scientific Programmes Related to Oceanography
ICSU	International Council of Scientific Unions
IDNDR	International Decade for Natural Disaster Reduction (1990-1999)
IGBP	International Geosphere-Biosphere Programme - A Study of Global Change
IGCP	International Correlation Programme
I-GOOS	IOC-WMO-UNEP Committee for the Global Ocean Observing System
IGOSS	Integrated Global Ocean Services System
IGS	International GPS Service
IHO	International Hydrographic Organization
IHP	International Hydrological Programme
IIEP	International Institute of Educational Planning
IMO	International Maritime Organization
IMS	International Marine Science Newsletter
IOC	Intergovernmental Oceanographic Commission (of UNESCO)
IOCARIBE	IOC Sub-Commission for the Caribbean and Adjacent Regions
IOCEA	IOC Regional Committee for the Central Eastern Atlantic
IOCINCWIO	IOC Regional Committee for the Co-operative Investigation in the North and Central Western Indian Ocean
IOCINDIO	IOC Regional Committee for the Central Indian Ocean
IOCSOC	IOC Regional Committee for the Southern Ocean
IODE	International Oceanographic Data and Information Exchange
IOI	International Ocean Institute
IOMAC	Organization for Indian Ocean Marine Affairs Co-operation
IOMC	IGOSS Operations Management Committee
IPAB	International Programme for Antarctic Buoys
IPB	IGOSS Products Bulletin

IPCC	Intergovernmental Panel on Climate Change
IPHAB	Intergovernmental Panel on Harmful Algal Blooms
IPMAR-DID	Portuguese Institute of Marine Research - Division of Information and Documentation
ISABP	International South Atlantic Buoy Programme
ITIC	International Tsunami Information Centre
ITSU	*See*: International Co-ordination Group for the Tsunami Warning System in the Pacific
IUBS	International Union of Biological Sciences
IUMS	International Union of Microbiological Societies
IWC	International Whaling Commission
IWP	IOC-WMO Intergovernmental WOCE Panel
JGOFS	Joint Global Ocean Flux Study
J-GOOS	Joint Scientific and Technical Committee for the Global Ocean Observing System
JSTC	Joint Scientific and Technical Committee
LBS	Land Based Sources
LME	Large Marine Ecosystems
LOICZ	Land-Ocean Interaction in the Coastal Zone
MAB	Programme on Man and the Biosphere
MAP	Mediterranean Action Plan
MARPOL73/78	International Convention for the Prevention of Pollution from Ships, 1973 as modified by the Protocol of 1978 relating thereto
MARPOLMON	Marine Pollution Monitoring System
MAST	Specific Research and Technological Development Programme in the field of Marine Science and Technology
MCBs	Marine Catchment Basins
MedGLOSS	Mediterranean Programme for the Global Sea-Level Sea-Level Observing System
MedGOOS	Mediterranean Programme for the Global Ocean Observing System
MEDS	Marine Environmental Data Service (Canada)
MEDI	Marine Environmental Data Information Referral System
MEL	Marine Environmental Laboratory
MESL	Marine Environmental Studies Laboratory
MIM	Group of Experts on Marine Information Management
MOST	Management of Social Transformations
MOU	Memorandum of Understanding
MRI	Marine Science Related Issues (UNESCO)
NATO	North Atlantic Treaty Organization
NearGOOS	North-East Asian Regional GOOS
NGO	Non Governmental Organization
NOAA	National Oceanic and Atmospheric Administration (USA)
NODC	National Ocean Data Centre
NRCT	National Research Council of Thailand
OECD	Organization for Economic Co-operation and Development
OM	Ocean Mapping
OOPC	Oceans Observations Panel for Climate
OOSDP	Ocean Observing System Development Panel
ORSTOM	Institut français de recherche scientifique pour le développement en coopération
OSLR	Ocean Science and Living Resources
OSNLR	Ocean Science and Non-Living Resources
QCAS	Quality Control of Autmomated Systems
PERSGA	Red Sea and Gulf of Aden Environment Programme
PICES	North Pacific Marine Science Organization
PIPICO	Panel on International Programs and International Co-operation in Ocean Affairs (USA)
POEM-BC	Physical Oceanography of the Eastern Mediterranean
PRIMO	International Research Programme in the Western Mediterranean (France)
PTWC	Pacific Tsunami Warning Center (USA)
RECOSCIX-WIO	Regional Co-operation in Scientific Information Exchange in the Western Indian Ocean

ROPME	Regional Organization for the Protection of the Marine Environment
RNODC	Responsible National Oceanographic Data Centre
SAREC	Swedish Agency for Research Co-operation with Developing Countries
SBSTA	Subsidiary Body for Science and Technical Advice
SBSTTA	Subsidiary Body on Scientific, Technical and Technological Advice
SCAR	Scientific Committee on Antarctic Research
SCOR	Scientific Committee on Oceanic Research
SEFC	Southeast Fisheries Centre
SEM	South and Eastern Mediterranean
SIDS	Small Island Developing States
SOC	Specialized Oceanographic Centre
SOOP	Ship-of-Opportunity Programme
SOOPIP	Ship-of-Opportunity Programme Implementation Programme
SOPAC	South Pacific Applied Geoscience Commission
SSC	Strategy Sub-Committee
START	Global Change System for Analysis, Research and Training
SVP	WOCE Surface Velocity Programme
TEMA	Training, Education and Mutual Assistance programme
TIME	Tsunami Inundation Modelling Exchange Project
TOGA	Tropical Atmosphere and Global Atmosphere
TREDMAR	Marine Science Training and Education Programme
TREMORS	Tsunami Risk Evaluation through Seismic Movement from Real-time System
TT/QCAS	Task Team on Quality Control of Automated Systems
UNCED	United Nations Conference on Environment and Development
UNCLOS	United Nations Convention on the Law of the Sea
UN/DOALOS	United Nations Division for Ocean Affairs and the Law of the Sea
UNDP	United Nations Development Programme
UNEP	United Nations Environment Programme
UNESCO	United Nations Educational, Scientific and Cultural Organization
UK-EDMED	United Kingdom contribution to the European Directory of Marine Environmental Data
UNIDO	United Nations Industrial Development Organization
UNU	United Nations University
WCP	World Climate Programme
WCRP	World Climate Research Programme
WESTPAC	IOC Sub-Commission for the Western Pacific
WHP	WOCE Hydrographic Programme
WIO	Western Indian Ocean
WIOMSA	Western Indian Ocean Marine Science Association
WMO	World Meteorological Organization
WOCE	World Ocean Circulation Experiment
WWW	World-Wide Web
XBT	Expendable Bathythermographs

INDEX OF KEYWORDS

B

F

G

H

I

K

L

M

O

P/Q

V

W

Z